# Lecture Notes in Computer Science 10677

Commenced Publication in 1973
Founding and Former Series Editors:
Gerhard Goos, Juris Hartmanis, and Jan van Leeuwen

More information about this series at http://www.springer.com/series/7410

Yael Kalai · Leonid Reyzin (Eds.)

# Theory
# of Cryptography

15th International Conference, TCC 2017
Baltimore, MD, USA, November 12–15, 2017
Proceedings, Part I

 Springer

*Editors*
Yael Kalai
Microsoft Research New England
Cambridge, MA
USA

Leonid Reyzin
Boston University
Boston, MA
USA

ISSN 0302-9743          ISSN 1611-3349  (electronic)
Lecture Notes in Computer Science
ISBN 978-3-319-70499-9          ISBN 978-3-319-70500-2  (eBook)
https://doi.org/10.1007/978-3-319-70500-2

Library of Congress Control Number: 2017957860

LNCS Sublibrary: SL4 – Security and Cryptology

Printed on acid-free paper

This Springer imprint is published by Springer Nature
The registered company is Springer International Publishing AG
The registered company address is: Gewerbestrasse 11, 6330 Cham, Switzerland

# Preface

The 15th Theory of Cryptography Conference (TCC 2017) was held during November 12–15, 2017, at Johns Hopkins University in Baltimore, Maryland. It was sponsored by the International Association for Cryptographic Research (IACR). The general chair of the conference was Abhishek Jain. We would like to thank him for his great work in organizing the conference.

The conference received 150 submissions, of which the Program Committee (PC) selected 51 for presentation (with three pairs of papers sharing a single presentation slot per pair). Each submission was reviewed by at least three PC members, often more. The 33 PC members (including PC chairs) were helped by 170 external reviewers, who were consulted when appropriate. These proceedings consist of the revised version of the 51 accepted papers. The revisions were not reviewed, and the authors bear full responsibility for the content of their papers.

As in previous years, we used Shai Halevi's excellent web-review software, and are extremely grateful to him for writing, maintaining, and adding features to it, and for providing fast and reliable technical support whenever we had any questions. Based on the experience from previous years, we made extensive use of the interaction feature supported by the review software, where PC members may directly and anonymously interact with authors. This was used to clarify specific technical issues that arose during reviews and discussions, such as suspected bugs or suggested simplifications. We felt this approach helped us prevent potential misunderstandings and improved the quality of the review process.

This was the fourth time TCC presented the Test of Time Award to an outstanding paper that was published at TCC at least eight years ago, making a significant contribution to the theory of cryptography, preferably with influence also in other areas of cryptography, theory, and beyond. This year the Test of Time Award Committee selected the following paper, presented at TCC 2006: "Efficient Collision-Resistant Hashing from Worst-Case Assumptions on Cyclic Lattices," by Chris Peikert and Alon Rosen, "for advancing the use of hard algebraic lattice problems in cryptography, paving the way for major theoretical and practical advances." The authors delivered an invited talk at TCC 2017.

The conference also featured an invited talk by Cynthia Dwork.

We are greatly indebted to many people and organizations who were involved in making TCC 2017 a success. First of all, a big thanks to the most important contributors: all the authors who submitted fantastic papers to the conference. Next, we would like to thank the PC members for their hard work, dedication, and diligence in reviewing and selecting the papers. We are also thankful to the external reviewers for their volunteered hard work and investment in reviewing papers and answering questions, often under time pressure. We thank Stefano Tessaro for organizing the Program Committee meeting. For running the conference itself, we are very grateful to the general chair, Abhishek Jain, and the people who helped him, including Anton

Dahbura, Revelie Niles, Jessica Finkelstein, Arka Rai Choudhuri, Nils Fleishhacker, Aarushi Goel, and Zhengzhong Jin. For help with these proceedings, we thank Anna Kramer, Alfred Hofmann, Abier El-Saeidi, Reegin Jeeba Dhason, and their staff at Springer. We appreciate the sponsorship from the IACR, the Department of Computer Science and the Information Security Institute at Johns Hopkins University, Microsoft Research, IBM, and Google. Finally, we are thankful to the TCC Steering Committee as well as the entire thriving and vibrant TCC community.

November 2017                                                    Yael Kalai
                                                              Leonid Reyzin

# TCC 2017

# Theory of Cryptography Conference

Baltimore, Maryland, USA
November 12–15, 2017

Sponsored by the *International Association for Cryptologic Research.*

## General Chair

Abhishek Jain                    Johns Hopkins University, USA

## Program Committee

| | |
|---|---|
| Benny Applebaum | Tel Aviv University, Israel |
| Elette Boyle | IDC Herzliya, Israel |
| Nir Bitansky | MIT, USA and Tel Aviv University, Israel |
| Zvika Brakerski | Weizmann Institute of Science, Israel |
| Ran Canetti | Boston University, USA and Tel Aviv University, Israel |
| Alessandro Chiesa | University of California, Berkeley, USA |
| Kai-Min Chung | Academia Sinica, Taiwan |
| Dana Dachman-Soled | University of Maryland, USA |
| Stefan Dziembowski | University of Warsaw, Poland |
| Serge Fehr | CWI Amsterdam, The Netherlands |
| Ben Fuller | University of Connecticut, USA |
| Divya Gupta | Microsoft Research India, USA |
| Carmit Hazay | Bar-Ilan University, Israel |
| Yael Kalai (Co-chair) | Microsoft Research New England, USA |
| Anja Lehmann | IBM Research Zurich, Switzerland |
| Benoît Libert | CNRS and ENS de Lyon, France |
| Pratyay Mukherjee | Visa Research, USA |
| Omer Paneth | MIT, USA |
| Rafael Pass | Cornell University, USA |
| Krzysztof Pietrzak | IST Austria |
| Mariana Raykova | Yale University, USA |
| Leonid Reyzin (Co-chair) | Boston University, USA |
| Guy Rothblum | Weizmann Institute of Science, Israel |
| Ron Rothblum | MIT, USA |
| Amit Sahai | University of California, Los Angeles, USA |
| Elaine Shi | Cornell University, USA |
| Stefano Tessaro | University of California, Santa Barbara, USA |
| Salil Vadhan | Harvard University, USA |

Venkata Koppula
Pravesh Kothari
Luke Kowalczyk
Mukul Kulkarni
Ashutosh Kumar
Alptekin Küpçü
Eyal Kushilevitz
Kim Laine
Tancrède Lepoint
Zengpeng Li
Jyun-Jie Liao
Han-Hsuan Lin
Huijia Rachel Lin
Wei-Kai Lin
Feng-Hao Liu
Qipeng Liu
Yamin Liu
Xianhui Lu
Lin Lyu
Vadim Lyubashevsky
Fermi Ma
Mohammad Mahmoody
Hemanta K. Maji
Daniel Malinowski
Alex Malozemoff
Antonio Marcedone
Daniel Masny
Peihan Miao
Daniele Micciancio
Pratyush Mishra
Payman Mohassel
Tal Moran

Andrew Morgan
Kirill Morozov
Fabrice Mouhartem
Tamalika Mukherjee
Gregory Neven
Hai H. Nguyen
Adam O'Neill
Claudio Orlandi
Alain Passelègue
Valerio Pastro
Alice Pellet-Mary
Thomas Peters
Benny Pinkas
Oxana Poburinnaya
Antigoni Polychroniadou
Manoj Prabhakaran
Baodong Qin
Willy Quach
Somindu C. Ramanna
Peter Rasmussen
Ling Ren
Silas Richelson
Peter Byerley Rindal
Aviad Rubinstein
Alexander Russell
Alessandra Scafuro
Christian Schaffner
Peter Scholl
Adam Sealfon
Maciej Skórski
Pratik Soni
Akshayaram Srinivasan

Damien Stehlé
Ron Steinfeld
Noah
Stephens-Davidowitz
Björn Tackmann
Qiang Tang
Aishwarya
Thiruvengadam
Eran Tromer
Dominique Unruh
Vinod Vaikuntanathan
Margarita Vald
Eduardo Soria Vazquez
Muthuramakrishnan
    Venkitasubramaniam
Daniele Venturi
Frederik Vercauteren
Damien Vergnaud
Emanuele Viola
Satyanarayana Vusirikala
Wen Weiqiang
Mor Weiss
David Wu
Keita Xagawa
Haiyang Xue
Sophia Yakoubov
Avishay Yanay
Arkady Yerukhimovich
Karol Żebrowski
Bingsheng Zhang
Cong Zhang
Giorgos Zirdelis

## Sponsors

Platinum Sponsors:

- Department of Computer Science, Johns Hopkins University
- Johns Hopkins University Information Security Institute

Gold Sponsors:

- Microsoft Research
- IBM

Silver Sponsor:

- Google

# Contents – Part I

## Encryption

## Moderately Hard Functions

## Blockchains

## Multiparty Computation

# Contents – Part II

## Non-Malleable Codes

## Secret Sharing

## OT Combiners

## Signatures

## Verifiable Random Functions

## Fully Homomorphic Encryption

# Database Privacy

# Assumptions

# Impossibilities and Barriers

# Barriers to Black-Box Constructions
# of Traitor Tracing Systems

Bo Tang[1] and Jiapeng Zhang[2]($\boxtimes$)

[1] University of Oxford, Oxford, UK
tangbonk1@gmail.com
[2] University of California, San Diego, USA
jpeng.zhang@gmail.com

**Abstract.** Reducibility between different cryptographic primitives is a fundamental problem in modern cryptography. As one of the primitives, traitor tracing systems help content distributors recover the identities of users that collaborated in the pirate construction by tracing pirate decryption boxes. We present the first negative result on designing efficient traitor tracing systems via black-box constructions from symmetric cryptographic primitives, e.g. one-way functions. More specifically, we show that there is no secure traitor tracing scheme in the random oracle model, such that $\ell_k \cdot \ell_c^2 < \widetilde{\Omega}(n)$, where $\ell_k$ is the length of user key, $\ell_c$ is the length of ciphertext and $n$ is the number of users, under the assumption that the scheme does not access the oracle to generate private user keys. To our best knowledge, all the existing cryptographic schemes (not limited to traitor tracing systems) via black-box constructions from one-way functions satisfy this assumption. Thus, our negative results indicate that most of the standard black-box reductions in cryptography cannot help construct a more efficient traitor tracing system.

We prove our results by extending the connection between traitor tracing systems and differentially private database sanitizers to the setting with random oracle access. After that, we prove the lower bound for traitor tracing schemes by constructing a differentially private sanitizer that only queries the random oracle polynomially many times. In order to reduce the query complexity of the sanitizer, we prove a large deviation bound for decision forests, which might be of independent interest.

## 1 Introduction

*Traitor tracing* systems, introduced by Chor et al. [11], are *broadcast encryption* schemes that are capable of tracing malicious "traitor" coalitions aiming at building pirate decryption devices. Such schemes are widely applicable to the distribution of digital commercial content (e.g. Pay-TV, news websites subscription, online stock quotes broadcast) for fighting against copyright infringement. In particular, consider a scenario where a distributor would like to send digital contents to $n$ authorized users via a broadcast channel while users possess different secret keys that allow them to decrypt the broadcasts in a non-ambiguous

J. Zhang—Research supported by NSF CAREER award 1350481.

Y. Kalai and L. Reyzin (Eds.): TCC 2017, Part I, LNCS 10677, pp. 3–30, 2017.
https://doi.org/10.1007/978-3-319-70500-2_1

fashion. Clearly, a pirate decoder, built upon a set of leaked secret keys, could also extract the cleartext content illegally. To discourage such piracy in a traitor tracing system, once a pirate decoder is found, the distributor can run a *tracing* algorithm to recover the identity of at least one user that collaborated in the pirate construction.

As a cryptographic primitive, traitor tracing system, together with its various generalizations, has been studied extensively in the literature (e.g., [6,15,24,28, 31]). Considerable efforts have been made on the construction of more efficient traitor tracing scheme from other primitives, in terms of improving two decisive performance parameters – the length of user key and the length of ciphertext. To illustrate, we exhibit in Table 1 the relation between cryptographic assumptions and the performance of the *fully collusion resistant* traitor tracing systems where tracing succeeds no matter how many users keys the pirate has at his disposal.

**Table 1.** Some previous results on fully collusion resistant traitor tracing systems.

| Hardness assumption | User key length | Ciphertext length | Reference |
|---|---|---|---|
| Existence of one-way functions | $\widetilde{O}(n^2)$ | $O(1)^{a}$ | [7] |
| Existence of one-way functions | $O(1)$ | $\widetilde{O}(n)$ | [11,32] |
| Bilinear group assumptions[b] | $O(1)$ | $\widetilde{O}(\sqrt{n})$ | [8] |
| Indistinguishability obfuscation | $O(1)$ | $(\log n)^{O(1)}$ | [9,16] |

[a]All terms in the table including $O(1)$ terms should depend on the security parameters.
[b]Specifically, they need to assume the Decision 3-party Diffie-Hellman Assumption, the Subgroup Decision Assumption and the Bilinear Subgroup Decision Assumption.

Obviously, as we illustrate in Table 1, more efficient traitor tracing schemes can be constructed based on stronger assumptions. Nonetheless, it is natural to ask whether the known constructions can be made more efficient if we only rely on the most fundamental cryptographic assumption – the existence of one-way functions. Impagliazzo and Rudich [21] first studied this type of questions in the context of key agreement. They observed that for most constructions in cryptography, the starting primitive is treated as an oracle, or a "black-box" and the security of the constructed scheme is derived from the security of the primitive in a black-box sense. Based on this observation, they showed that a black-box construction of key agreement built upon one-way functions implies a proof that $P \neq NP$. This approach has been subsequently adopted in investigating the reducibility between other cryptographic primitives, such as one-way permutations [23], public-key encryption [18,19], universal one-way hash functions [25]. In particular, in the context of traitor tracing, the question is whether there exists a more efficient traitor tracing scheme via black-box constructions based on one-way functions. In this paper, we focus on this problem and provide a partial answer to it.

## 1.1   Our Results

We consider traitor tracing systems in the *random oracle model* [4], which is an ideal model using one way functions in the strongest sense. In this model, the constructed cryptographic scheme can access a random oracle $O$ which can be viewed as a fully random function. In spite of the criticism on its unjustified idealization in practical implementations [10], the random oracle model seems to be an appropriate model and a clean way to establish lower bounds in cryptography (e.g. [1, 21]). As there is no security measure defined on the oracle, one common way to prove security for oracle based constructions is to rely on the fully randomness of the oracle and the restriction on the number of queries the adversary (even computationally unbounded) can ask.

Our main result is a lower bound on the performance of traitor tracing systems satisfying a property we call INDKEYS. Roughly speaking, a cryptographic scheme is said to be INDKEYS if the scheme does not use the black-box hardness of the starting primitive to generate private keys. Here we give an informal definition of the INDKEYS property for any cryptographic systems and defer the formal definition tailored for traitor tracing systems to Sect. 2.

**Definition 1 (informal).** *Let $\Pi^{(\cdot)}$ be a cryptographic scheme that takes other cryptographic primitives or ideal random functions as oracles. We say that $\Pi^{(\cdot)}$ is* INDKEYS *if $\Pi^{(\cdot)}$ does not access the oracles while generating private keys.*

*Remark 1.* Considering all cryptographic primitives (not restriced in the private-key traitor tracing systems we study here), it should be mentioned that the IND-KEYS property does not require any independence between the public keys and the oracles. Indeed, some of the known black-box constructions of cryptographic primitives use the black-box hardness to generate public keys, (e.g. one time signature [26]), but the private keys are still generated independent of the oracles as requested in INDKEYS. To our best knowledge, all the exisiting cryptographic schemes via black-box reductions from one-way functions are INDKEYS. Thus, our negative result for INDKEYS systems shows that most of the standard black-box reductions in cryptography cannot help to construct a more efficient traitor tracing system. At last, as the INDKEYS property is defined on all cryptographic schemes, it might be helpful to investigate the technical limitations of known black-box reductions and derive more lower bounds for other primitives.

In this paper, we show a lower bound on the performance (or efficiency) of the INDKEYS traitor tracing systems in terms of the lengths of user keys and ciphertexts. We summarize the main theorem informally as follows and defer the rigorous statement to Sect. 2.

**Theorem 1 (informal).** *Let $\Pi_{\mathrm{TT}}^{(\cdot)}$ be a secure traitor tracing system that is* INDKEYS, *then*

$$\ell_k \cdot \ell_c^{\,2} \geq \widetilde{\Omega}(n)$$

*where $\ell_k$ is the length of user key, $\ell_c$ is the length of ciphertext and $n$ is the number of users.*

## 1.2   Our Approach

We prove our results by building on the connection between traitor tracing systems and *differentially private sanitizers* for counting queries discovered by Dwork et al. [13]. Informally, a database sanitizer is differentially private if its outputs on any two databases that only differ in one row, are almost the same. Dwork, Naor, Reingold, et al. showed that any differentially private and accurate sanitizer (with carefully calibrated parameters) can be used as a valid pirate decoder to break the security of traitor tracing systems. Intuitively, a pirate decoder can be viewed as a sanitizer of databases consist of leaked user keys.

Built upon this connection, we show the lower bound on traitor tracing systems by constructing a sanitizer in the random oracle model. We first build a natural extension of sanitizers and differential privacy in presence of random oracles in Sect. 3. The main difference from standard definitions is that we relax the accuracy requirement by asking sanitizer to be accurate with high probability w.r.t. the random oracle. That is, an accurate sanitizer under our definition might be (probabilistic) inaccurate for some oracle but must be accurate for most oracles. This relaxation allows us to derive a query-efficient sanitizer.

Our sanitizer is developed upon the *median mechanism* designed by Roth and Roughgarden [30], which maintains a set $\mathcal{D}$ of databases and for each counting query: (1) compute the results of the query for all databases in $\mathcal{D}$; (2) Use the median *med* of these results to answer the query if *med* is close to the answer $a^*$ of the true database; (3) If not, output $a^*$ added with a Laplacian noise and remove the databases in $\mathcal{D}$ whose result of the query is not close to $a^*$. Note that when computing *med*, the median mechanism need to query the oracle for all databases in $\mathcal{D}$ whose size might be exponential in $\ell_k$. Thus, it will make exponentially many queries to the oracle.

We design a query-efficient implementation of the median mechanism by using the expectations of query results (taken over all oracles) to compute *med* without querying the real oracle. Our mechanism would be accurate if the answers are concentrated around their expectations taken over all random oracles. Unfortunately, such concentration property does not hold for arbitrary queries and databases. But fortunately, we can show that it holds if there is no "significant" variables in the decryption (or query answering). More specifically, we generalize the deviation bound proved in [2] where they required the size of the database (decision forest) to be relatively larger than the "significance" of the variable (see formal definitions in Sect. 6). Our bound does not make this requirement and is much more applicable. We prove this bound by generalizing two previous deviation bounds proved by Beck et al. [2] and Gavinsky et al. [17]. Note that the INDKEYS property is essential in our proof since the deviation bound only holds for uniformly distributed oracles.

To put it together, our mechanism maintains a set of databases $\mathcal{D}$ and for each counting query: ($a$) remove the variables which are significant for most databases in $\mathcal{D}$; ($b$) privately check whether the decryption process corresponding to the true database has a significant variable; ($c$) if there is a significant variable $x^*$, output the noisy true answer and remove the databases that do not view $x^*$ as a significant variable; ($d$) otherwise, compute the median $med$ among all expected answers of databases in $\mathcal{D}$; ($e$) if $med$ is close to true answer, use it to answer the query; ($f$) otherwise, output the noisy answer and remove databases in $\mathcal{D}$ whose expected answer is not close to the true answer.

## 1.3   Related Work

Starting with the seminal paper by Impagliazzo and Rudich [21], black-box reducibility between primitives has attracted a lot of attention in modern cryptography. Reingold et al. [29] revisited existing negative results and gave a more formal treatment of the notions of black-box reductions. In their notions, our results can be viewed as a refutation of the *fully black-box reduction* of INDKEYS traitor tracing systems to one-way functions. Our usage of the random oracle model also follows the work by Barak and Mahmoody-Ghidary [1], where they proved lower bounds on the query complexity of every black-box construction of one-time signature schemes from symmetric cryptographic primitives as modeled by random oracles. To our best knowledge, there is no lower bound results on the performance of traitor tracing systems prior to our work.

Differential privacy, as a well studied notion of privacy tailored to private data analysis was first formalized by Dwork et al. [12]. They also gave an efficient sanitizer called *Laplace Mechanism* that is able to answer $n^2$ counting queries. A remarkable following result of Blum et al. [5] shows that the number of counting queries can be increased to sub-exponential in $n$ by using the *exponential mechanism* of McSherry and Talwar [27]. Subsequently, interactive mechanisms, with running time in polynomial of $n$ and universe size, are developed to answer sub-exponentially many queries adaptively by Roth and Roughgarden [30] (*median mechanism*) and Hardt and Rothblum [20] (*multiplicative weights mechanism*). On the other hand, based on the connection between traitor tracing systems and sanitizers, Ullman [32] proved that no differentially private sanitizer with running time in polynomial of $n$ and the logarithm of the universe size can answer $\widetilde{\Theta}(n^2)$ queries accurately assuming one-way functions exist. Our sanitizer constructions are inspired by the above mechanisms and also rely on the composition theorem of differentially private mechanisms by Dwork et al. [14]. Thus, our results can be viewed as an application of advanced techniques of designing differentially private sanitizer in proving cryptographic lower bounds.

This paper is also technically related to previous deviation bounds on Boolean decision forests. Gavinsky et al. [17] showed that for any decision forest such that every input variable appears in few trees, the average of the decision trees' outputs should concentrate around its expectation when the input variables are distributed independently and uniformly. Similar bounds have also been proved by Beck et al. [2] for low depth decision tress but with a weaker "average" condition (see Sect. 6). As an application, they used this deviation bound to show that $AC^0$ circuits can not sample good codes uniformly. By a finer treatment on the conditions stated in the above two works, we are able to prove a more general deviation bounds for decision forests, which we believe should have other applications.

## 1.4   Organization

The rest of the paper is organized as follows. In Sect. 2, we review the formal definition of traitor tracing systems in the random oracle model and state our main theorem. Then we review the connection between traitor tracing systems and differentially private sanitizers in Sect. 3. In Sect. 4, we prove a weaker lower bound which is $\widetilde{\Omega}(n^{1/3})$ to illustrate the main ideas via using a general large deviation bound for decision forests. Then we improve the bound to $\widetilde{\Omega}(n)$ as stated in our main theorem in Sect. 5 by more elaborate arguments. Then, in Sect. 6, we exhibit the proof the large deviation bound for decision forests which is omitted in the proof in Sect. 2. Due to space limit, some proofs are deferred in Appendix A. Furthermore, in Appendix B, we show an oralce separation result between one-way functions and secure traitor tracing systems as a straight-forward implication of our main theorem.

## 2   Traitor Tracing Systems

In this section, we give a formal definition of traitor tracing systems in the random oracle model and state our main theorem. For any security parameter $\kappa \in \mathbb{N}$, an oracle can be viewed as a Boolean function $O : \{0,1\}^{\ell_o(\kappa)} :\longrightarrow \{0,1\}$, where $\ell_o$ is a function from $\mathbb{N}$ to $\mathbb{N}$.

**Definition 2.** *Let $n$, $m$, $\ell_k$, $\ell_c$, and $\ell_o$ be functions : $\mathbb{N} \to \mathbb{N}$, a traitor tracing system in the random oracle model denoted by $\Pi_{\mathrm{TT}}$ with $n$ users, user-key length $\ell_k$, ciphertext length $\ell_c$, $m$ tracing rounds and access to an oracle with input length $\ell_o$, also contains the following four algorithms. We allow all the algorithms to be randomized except* Dec.

- Gen$^O(1^\kappa)$, *the setup algorithm, takes a security parameter $\kappa$ as input and a Boolean function $O : \{0,1\}^{\ell_o(\kappa)} \to \{0,1\}$ as an oracle, and outputs $n = n(\kappa)$ user-keys $k_1, \ldots, k_n \in \{0,1\}^{l_k(\kappa)}$. Formally, $\mathbf{k} = (k_1, \ldots, k_n) \leftarrow_R$ Gen$^O(1^\kappa)$.*
- Enc$^O(\mathbf{k}, b)$, *the encrypt algorithm, takes $n$ user-keys $\mathbf{k}$ and a message $b \in \{0,1\}$ as input, and outputs a ciphertext $c \in \{0,1\}^{l_c(\kappa)}$ via querying an oracle $O$. Formally, $c \leftarrow_R$ Enc$^O(\mathbf{k}, b)$.*
- Dec$^O(k_i, c)$, *the decrypt algorithm takes a user-key $k_i$ and a ciphertext $c$ as input, and outputs a message $b \in \{0,1\}$ via querying an oracle $O$. Formally, $b =$ Dec$^O(k_i, c)$.*
- Trace$^{O,\mathcal{P}^O}(\mathbf{k})$, *the tracing algorithm, takes $n$ user-keys $\mathbf{k}$ as input, an oracle $O$ and a pirate decoder $\mathcal{P}^O$ as oracles, and makes $m(\kappa)$ queries to $\mathcal{P}^O$, and outputs the name of a user $i \in [n]$. Formally, $i \leftarrow_R$ Trace$^{O,\mathcal{P}^O}(\mathbf{k})$.*

*Formally, $\Pi_{\mathrm{TT}} = (n, m, \ell_k, \ell_c, \ell_o, \mathrm{Gen}^{(\cdot)}, \mathrm{Enc}^{(\cdot)}, \mathrm{Dec}^{(\cdot)}, \mathrm{Trace}^{(\cdot,\cdot)})$.*

For simplicity, when we use the notation $\Pi_{\mathrm{TT}}$ without any specification, we also mean all these functions and algorithms are defined correspondingly. We also abuse the notations of functions of $\kappa$ to denote the values of functions when $\kappa$ is clear from the context, (e.g., $n$ denotes $n(\kappa)$).

Intuitively, the pirate decoder $\mathcal{P}$ can be viewed as a randomized algorithm that holds a set of user-keys $\mathbf{k}_S = (k_i)_{i \in S}$ with $S \subseteq [n]$. The tracing algorithm Trace is attempting to identify a user $i \in S$ by making queries to $\mathcal{P}$ interactively. In particular, in each round $j \in [m]$, Trace submits a ciphertext $c_j$ to $\mathcal{P}$ and then $\mathcal{P}$ answers a message $\widehat{b}_j \in \{0, 1\}$ based on all the previous ciphertexts $c_1, \ldots, c_j$. Formally, $\widehat{b}_j \leftarrow_R \mathcal{P}^O(\mathbf{k}_S, c_1, \ldots, c_j)$. Note that we allow the tracing algorithm to be *stateful*. That our lower bounds apply to stateful Traitor Tracing Systems makes our results stronger. Given a function $\ell_o$ and a security parameter $\kappa$, let $\mathcal{O}_{\mathrm{unif}}$ denote the uniform distribution over all oracles with size $\ell_o(\kappa)$, i.e. the uniform distribution for all Boolean functions with input $\{0, 1\}^{\ell_o(\kappa)}$. We also abuse $\mathcal{O}_{\mathrm{unif}}$ to denote the support of this distribution. As a pirate decoder, $\mathcal{P}$ should be capable of decrypting ciphertext with high probability as defined formally as follows.

**Definition 3.** *Let $\Pi_{\mathrm{TT}}$ be a traitor tracing system and $\mathcal{P}^{(\cdot)}$ be a pirate decoder, we say that $\mathcal{P}$ is $m$-available if for every $S \subseteq [n]$ s.t. $|S| \geq n - 1$,*

$$\Pr_{\substack{O \sim \mathcal{O}_{\mathrm{unif}}, \mathbf{k} \leftarrow_R \mathrm{Gen}^O(1^\kappa) \\ c_j \leftarrow_R \mathrm{Trace}^{O, \mathcal{P}}(\mathbf{k}, \widehat{b}_1, \ldots, \widehat{b}_{j-1}) \\ \widehat{b}_j \leftarrow_R \mathcal{P}^O(\mathbf{k}_S, c_1, \ldots, c_j)}} \left[ \begin{array}{c} \exists j \in [m], b \in \{0, 1\} \\ (\forall i \in S, \mathrm{Dec}^O(k_i, c_j) = b) \wedge (\widehat{b}_j \neq b) \end{array} \right] \leq neg(n(\kappa))$$

Similarly, a traitor tracing system should decrypt the ciphertext correctly.

**Definition 4.** *A traitor tracing system $\Pi_{\mathrm{TT}}$ is said to be correct if for all oracle $O$, user $i \in [n]$ and message $b \in \{0, 1\}$,*

$$\Pr_{\substack{\mathbf{k} \leftarrow_R \mathrm{Gen}^O(1^\kappa) \\ c \leftarrow_R \mathrm{Enc}^O(\mathbf{k}, b)}} [\mathrm{Dec}^O(k_i, c) = b] = 1$$

In addition, we require the traitor tracing system to be efficient in terms of the number of queries it makes. In particular, we use $\mathrm{QC}(\mathcal{A}^O)$ to denote the query complexity of $\mathcal{A}^O$, i.e. the number of queries $\mathcal{A}^O$ makes to $O$.

**Definition 5.** *A traitor tracing system $\Pi_{\mathrm{TT}}$ is said to be efficient if for any oracle $O$ with input size $\ell_o(\kappa)$ and for any pirate decoder $\mathcal{P}$, the query complexity of $\mathrm{Gen}^O, \mathrm{Enc}^O, \mathrm{Dec}^O, \mathrm{Trace}^O$ are in polynomial of their input size respectively. Formally, $\mathrm{QC}(\mathrm{Gen}^O) = \mathrm{poly}(\kappa)$, $\mathrm{QC}(\mathrm{Enc}^O) = \mathrm{poly}(n, \ell_k)$, $\mathrm{QC}(\mathrm{Dec}^O) = \mathrm{poly}(\ell_k, \ell_c)$ and $\mathrm{QC}(\mathrm{Trace}^{O, \mathcal{P}}) = \mathrm{poly}(n, m, \ell_k)$.*

Note that we do not make any restriction on the computational power of the traitor tracing systems. Obviously, any computationally efficient $\Pi_{\mathrm{TT}}$ is also query efficient but the other direction does not hold. That our lower bounds apply to efficient $\Pi_{\mathrm{TT}}$ in the above definition makes our results apply to computational efficient $\Pi_{\mathrm{TT}}$ directly. Similarly, we say a pirate decoder $\mathcal{P}$ is *efficient* if $\mathrm{QC}(\mathcal{P}^O) = \mathrm{poly}(n, \ell_k, \ell_c)$ in each round of its interaction with Trace.

**Definition 6.** *A traitor tracing system* $\Pi_{TT}$ *is said to be* secure *if for any efficient* $m(\kappa)$-*available pirate decoder* $\mathcal{P}$ *and* $S \subseteq [n(\kappa)]$,

$$\Pr_{\substack{O \sim \mathcal{O}_{\text{unif}} \\ \mathbf{k} \leftarrow_R \text{Gen}^O}} [\text{Trace}^{O, \mathcal{P}^O}(\mathbf{k}_S)(\mathbf{k}) \notin S] \leq o\left(\frac{1}{n(\kappa)}\right)$$

**Definition 7 (IndKeys).** *A traitor tracing system* $\Pi_{TT}$ *is said to be* INDKEYS *if for all a security parameter* $\kappa \in \mathbb{N}$ *and any two oracles* $O$ *and* $O'$, *the distribution of* $\mathbf{k}$ *generated by* $\text{Gen}^O(1^\kappa)$ *and* $\text{Gen}^{O'}(1^\kappa)$ *are the same distribution. Equivalently, conditioned on any particular user-keys* $\mathbf{k}$, *the oracle* $O$ *can still be viewed as a random variable drawn from* $\mathcal{O}_{\text{unif}}$.

*Remark 2.* Note that all known traitor tracing systems via black-box hardness are INDKEYS. The scheme designed by with $\ell_k = O(n^2\kappa)$ and $\ell_c = O(\kappa)$ does not require oracles and the one designed by Chor et al. [11] and modified by Ullman [32] with $\ell_k = O(\kappa)$ and $\ell_c = O(n\kappa)$ does not need the oracle to generate private keys.

The following theorem is our main theorem whose proof is deferred to Sects. 4 and 5.

**Theorem 2.** *In the random oracle model, for any* $\theta > 0$, *there is no query-efficient, correct and secure traitor tracing system* $\Pi_{TT}^{(\cdot)}$ *which is* INDKEYS, *such that for any security parameter* $\kappa \in \mathbb{N}$,

$$\ell_k(\kappa) \cdot \ell_c(\kappa)^2 \leq n(\kappa)^{1-\theta}.$$

# 3  Differentially Private Sanitizers in Random Oracle Model

In this section, we formally define differentially private sanitizers for counting queries in the random oracle model by extending the standard definitions. After that we show its connection with traitor tracing systems by slightly modifying the proofs in [13, 32]. For ease of presentation, we reuse the notations used in Sect. 2, (e.g. $n, m, \ell_k, \ell_c, \ell_o$) to denote their counterparts in the context of private data analysis.

A counting query on $\{0,1\}^{\ell_k}$ is defined by a deterministic algorithm $q^{(\cdot)}$ where given any oracle $O : \{0,1\}^{\ell_o} \to \{0,1\}$, $q^O$ is a Boolean function $\{0,1\}^{\ell_k} \to \{0,1\}$. Abusing notation, we define the evaluation of the query $q^{(\cdot)}$ on a database $D = (x_1, \ldots, x_n) \in (\{0,1\}^{\ell_k})^n$ with access to $O$ to be $q^O(D) = \frac{1}{n} \sum_{i \in [n]} q^O(x_i)$. Let $\mathcal{Q}$ be a set of counting queries. A sanitizer $\mathcal{M}^{(\cdot)}$ for $\mathcal{Q}$ can be viewed as a randomized algorithm takes a database $D \in (\{0,1\}^{\ell_k})^n$ and a sequence of counting queries $\mathbf{q}^{(\cdot)} = (q_1^{(\cdot)}, \ldots, q_m^{(\cdot)}) \in \mathcal{Q}^m$ as input and outputs a sequence of answers $(a_1, \ldots, a_m) \in \mathbb{R}^m$ by accessing an oracle $O$. We consider interactive mechanisms, that means $\mathcal{M}^{(\cdot)}$ should answer each query without knowing subsequent queries. More specifically, the computation of $a_i$ can only depends on the first $i$ queries, i.e. $(q_1^{(\cdot)}, \ldots, q_i^{(\cdot)})$. One might note that our definition differs from the traditional definition of sanitizers by allowing both sanitizers and queries to access oracles. Actually, this kind of sanitizers are defined in such a specific way which makes them useful in proving the hardness for the traitor tracing systems defined in Sect. 2. It is also not clear for us if it has any real application in the context of privately data analysis. Here we use the term "query" in two ways, one referring to the query answered by the santizer and the other one meaning the query sent by algorithms to oracles. Without specification, only when we say "query complexity" or "query efficient", we are referring the oracle queries.

We say that two databases $D, D' \in (\{0,1\}^{\ell_k})^n$ are *adjacent* if they differ only on a single row. We use $\mathbf{q}^{(\cdot)} = (q_1^{(\cdot)}, \ldots, q_m^{(\cdot)})$ to denote a sequence of $m$ queries. Next, we give a natural extension of *differential privacy* to the setting with oracle access.

**Definition 8.** *A sanitizer $\mathcal{M}^{(\cdot)}$ for a set of counting queries $\mathcal{Q}$ is said to be $(\varepsilon, \delta)$-differentially private if for any two adjacent databases $D$ and $D'$, oracle $O$, query sequence $\mathbf{q}^{(\cdot)} \in \mathcal{Q}^m$ and any subset $S \subseteq \mathbb{R}^m$,*

$$\Pr[\mathcal{M}^O(D, \mathbf{q}^O) \in S] \leq e^\varepsilon \Pr[\mathcal{M}^O(D', \mathbf{q}^O) \in S] + \delta$$

*If $\mathcal{M}^{(\cdot)}$ is $(\varepsilon, \delta)$-differentially private for some constant $\varepsilon = O(1)$ and $\delta = o(1/n)$, we will drop the parameters $\varepsilon$ and $\delta$ and just say that $\mathcal{M}^{(\cdot)}$ is differentially private.*

**Proposition 1 (Lemma 3.7 from [20]).** *The following condition implies $(\varepsilon, \delta)$-differential privacy. For any two adjacent databases $D$ and $D'$, oracle $O$ and any query sequence $\mathbf{q}^{(\cdot)} \in \mathcal{Q}^m$,*

$$\Pr_{a \leftarrow_R \mathcal{M}^O(D, \mathbf{q}^O)} \left[ \left| \log \left( \frac{\Pr[\mathcal{M}^O(D, \mathbf{q}^O) = a]}{\Pr[\mathcal{M}^O(D', \mathbf{q}^O) = a]} \right) \right| > \varepsilon \right] \leq \delta$$

Moreover, a sanitizer should answer any sequence of queries accurately with high probability.

**Definition 9.** *A sanitizer $\mathcal{M}^{(\cdot)}$ is said to be $(\alpha, \beta)$-accurate for a set of counting queries $\mathcal{Q}$ if for any database $D$*

$$\Pr_{O \sim \mathcal{O}_{\text{unif}}} \left[ \forall \mathbf{q}^{(\cdot)} \in \mathcal{Q}^m, \left\| \mathcal{M}^O(D, \mathbf{q}^O) - \mathbf{q}^O(D) \right\|_\infty \leq \alpha \right] \geq 1 - \beta$$

*If $\mathcal{M}^{(\cdot)}$ is $(\alpha, \beta)$-accurate for some constant $\alpha < 1/2$ and $\beta = o(1/n^{10})$, we will drop parameters $\alpha$ and $\beta$ and just say that $\mathcal{M}^{(\cdot)}$ is accurate.*

Finally, we consider the query complexity of sanitizers. Clearly, a sanitizer cannot be query efficient if the evaluation of some counting query $q^{(\cdot)}$ is not query efficient. Let $\mathcal{Q}_{\text{Enf}}$ be the set of all *efficient* queries, i.e. for any database $D = (\{0,1\}^{\ell_k})^n$ and any oracle $O$, any $q^O(D) \in \mathcal{Q}_{\text{Enf}}$ can be evaluated in $\texttt{poly}(n, \ell_k, \ell_c)$ number of queries to $O$. A sanitizer is said to be *efficient* if for any oracle $O$, database $D$ and any query sequence $\mathbf{q}^{(\cdot)} \in \mathcal{Q}_{\text{Enf}}^m$, $\mathcal{M}^O(D, \mathbf{q}^O)$ can be computed in $\texttt{poly}(n, m, \ell_k)$ number of queries to $O$.

**Theorem 3.** *Given functions* $n, m, \ell_k, \ell_c$ *and* $\ell_o : \mathbb{N} \to \mathbb{N}$, *if for any query set* $\mathcal{Q} \subseteq \mathcal{Q}_{\mathrm{Enf}}$ *with size* $|\mathcal{Q}| \leq 2^{\ell_c(\kappa)}$, *there exists an* efficient, differentially private *and* accurate *sanitizer for any database* $D \in (\{0,1\}^{\ell_k(\kappa)})^{n(\kappa)}$ *and any* $m$-*query sequence in* $\mathcal{Q}^m$, *then there exists no* efficient, correct *and* secure *traitor tracing system* $\Pi_{\mathrm{TT}} = (n, m, \ell_k, \ell_c, \ell_o, \mathsf{Gen}, \mathsf{Enc}, \mathsf{Dec}, \mathsf{Trace})$.

*Remark 3.* The proof idea is similar to [13,32], that is if there exist such a sanitizer and a traitor tracing system, we can slightly modify the sanitizer to be an available pirate decoder for the traitor tracing system. The only technical difference is that the traitor tracing system and the sanitizer defined here have access to a random oracle $O$. So we need to modify the proof in [32] to accommodate these oracle accesses and the definitions in Sects. 2 and 3.

# 4   Lower Bounds on Traitor Tracing Systems

In this section, we exhibit the proof of a weaker version of Theorem 2. That is, there is no efficient, correct and secure traitor tracing system such that $\ell_k(\kappa) \cdot \ell_c(\kappa)^2 \leq n(\kappa)^{\frac{1}{3}-\theta}$ for any $\theta > 0$. Assume to the contrary that there exists such a system $\Pi_{\mathrm{TT}}$, let $q_\pi$ denote the maximum query complexity of $\mathsf{Dec}^O(\mathbf{k}, c)$ over all database $\mathbf{k}$, ciphertext $c$ and oracle $O$. We will construct an efficient, differentially private and accurate sanitizer $\mathcal{M}$ for any $m$ queries from the query set $\{\mathsf{Dec}^{(\cdot)}(\cdot, c) \,|\, c \in \{0,1\}^{\ell_c}\}$ and any database $D \in (\{0,1\}^{\ell_k})^n$ (inspired by [20,30]). In this section, we abuse the notation $\mathsf{Dec}^{(\cdot)}(\mathbf{k}, c)$ to denote the function $\frac{1}{n} \cdot \sum_{i \in [n]} \mathsf{Dec}^{(\cdot)}(k_i, c)$. Before describing the santizer, we first define significant variable for decryption.

**Definition 10.** *Given a database* $\mathbf{k} \in (\{0,1\}^{\ell_k})^n$, *a decrypt algorithm* $\mathsf{Dec}^{(\cdot)}$ *and a ciphertext* $c$, *we say a variable* $x \in \{0,1\}^{\ell_o}$ *is* $\beta$-*significant for* $\mathsf{Dec}^{(\cdot)}(k_i, c)$ *if*

$$\Pr_{O \sim \mathcal{O}_{\mathrm{unif}}} \left[ \mathsf{Dec}^O(k_i, c) \text{ queries } x \right] \geq \beta$$

*We say* $x$ *is* $\beta$-*significant for* $\mathsf{Dec}^{(\cdot)}(\mathbf{k}, c)$, *if* $x$ *is* $\beta$-*significant for at least one* $k_i \in \mathbf{k}$. *We say* $x$ *is* $(\alpha, \beta)$-*significant for* $\mathsf{Dec}^{(\cdot)}(\mathbf{k}, c)$, *if* $x$ *is* $\beta$-*significant for at least* $\alpha n$ *entries of* $\mathbf{k}$.

Our sanitizer is described as Algorithm 1 by setting the parameters $\sigma, \alpha, \beta$ to be

$$\sigma = n^{\theta/3}\sqrt{\frac{\ell_k}{n}}, \qquad \alpha = \frac{1}{\ell_c n^\theta}, \qquad \beta = \frac{1}{54 n^4 q_\pi^3}$$

The intuition behind the calibration of parameters is that we need the condition that $\alpha$ dominates $\sigma \ell_k$ which will be used in the later analysis. Since $\ell_k \cdot \ell_c^2 \leq n^{\frac{1}{3}-\theta}$, by simple calculation, we have $\alpha/(\sigma \ell_k) \geq n^{\theta/6}$.

The main idea is to maintain a set of potential databases denoted by $\mathcal{D}_j$ for each round $j$. Note that the INDKEYS property of the system guarantees that conditioned on any particular database, the oracles are always distributed uniformly. This allows us to focus on the available databases not the database and oracle pairs. For each ciphertext $c_j$, the sanitizer consists of three phases. In phase 1, we examine all $x \in \{0,1\}^{\ell_o}$ and determine a set (denoted by $W_j$) of significant variables which is queried with probability at least $\beta/2$ over randomness over all $O \in \mathcal{O}_{\text{unif}}$ and $\mathbf{k} \in \mathcal{D}_{j-1}$. Roughly speaking, we pick all variables which are significant for most databases. It should be emphasized that even though some variables are not picked in this phase, they might be significant for some database. Then for each variable in $W_j$, we query $O^*$ on it and simplify the decrypt algorithm by fixing the value of this specific variable. Note that, this phase does not depend on the true database $\mathbf{k}^*$ so it is clear that there is no privacy loss here. On the other hand, as we will show in Lemma 1, the total number of queries we ask to the oracle $O^*$ in this phase is polynomial in $n$.

In phase 2, we check if the $\text{Dec}^{(\cdot)}(\mathbf{k}^*, c_j)$ has $(\alpha, \beta)$-significant variables by using a variant of the exponential mechanism. If there is a significant variable, the santizer outputs $\widehat{a}_j$ the true answer with a noise and modifies $\mathcal{D}_j$. If there are no $(\alpha, \beta)$-significant variables, the sanitizer runs phase 3, where it "guesses" the answer by using the median of database set $\mathcal{D}'_{j-1}$ which is the set of all databases in $\mathcal{D}_{j-1}$ which has no $(\alpha, \beta)$-significant variables. The sanitizer outputs the guess $med_j$ if it is close to the true answer. Otherwise, the sanitizer outputs $\widehat{a}_j$ and modify $\mathcal{D}_j$.

## 4.1 Efficiency Analysis

**Lemma 1.** *The query complexity of Algorithm 1 is $O(n\ell_k q_\pi/\beta)$ which is polynomial in $n$.*

*Proof.* Let $\mathbf{x} = (x_1, \ldots, x_{q_\pi})$ be a sequence of $q_\pi$ oracle variables where $x_i \in \{0,1\}^{\ell_o}$ and $\mathbf{b} = (b_1, \ldots, b_{q_\pi})$ be a sequence of $q_\pi$ bits where $b_i \in \{0,1\}$. We define an indicator function of $\mathbf{x}, \mathbf{b}, O$ and $\mathbf{k}$ as follows.

$$\mathbf{1}_{\mathbf{x},\mathbf{b}}(O, \mathbf{k}) = \begin{cases} 1 & \text{if } \text{Dec}^O(\mathbf{k}, c_j) \text{ queries } x_1, \ldots, x_{q_\pi} \text{ sequentially and } \mathbf{b} = O(\mathbf{x}) \\ 0 & \text{otherwise.} \end{cases}$$

Then we define a potential function $\Phi = \sum_{\mathbf{x},\mathbf{b}} \sum_{O \in \mathcal{O}_{\text{unif}}, \mathbf{k} \in \mathcal{D}_{j-1}} \mathbf{1}_{\mathbf{x},\mathbf{b}}(O, \mathbf{k})$. Clearly, the value of $\Phi$ at the beginning of Phase 1 is at most $2^{n\ell_k q_\pi}$ since $|\mathcal{D}_{j-1}| \leq 2^{n\ell_k}$ and for any particular $\mathbf{k}$ and $c_j$, the number of all possible query histogram of $\text{Dec}^{(\cdot)}(\mathbf{k}, c_j)$ is at most $2^{q_\pi}$.

We will show that when fixing a variable $x \in W_j$ such that

$$\Pr_{\mathbf{k} \sim \text{Unif}(\mathcal{D}_{j-1}), O \sim \mathcal{O}_{\text{unif}}} [\text{Dec}^O(k_i, c_j) \text{ queries } x \text{ for some } k_i \in \mathbf{k}] \geq \beta/2$$

the value of $\Phi$ will decrease by a factor $(1 - \beta/4)$. This is because fixing the value of $x$ will kill all pair of $O$ and $\mathbf{k}$ such that $\text{Dec}^O(\mathbf{k}, c_j)$ queries $x$ but $O$ is not consistent to $O^*$ on $x$. Since $\Phi$ can be less than 1, there are at most $O(n\ell_k q_\pi/\beta)$ elements in $W_j$. $\qquad\square$

---

**Algorithm 1.** Sanitizer for Traitor Tracing Lower Bound

---

**Input**: $n, m$, an oracle $O^* : \{0,1\}^{\ell_o} \to \{0,1\}$, a database $k^* = \{k_1^*, \ldots, k_n^*\}$ with $k_i^* \in \{0,1\}^{\ell_k}$, a sequence of queries $\left(\mathtt{Dec}^{(\cdot)}(\cdot, c_1), \ldots, \mathtt{Dec}^{(\cdot)}(\cdot, c_m)\right)$ with $c_j \in \{0,1\}^{\ell_c}$

**Output**: A sequence of answers $ans_1, \ldots, ans_m$ with $a_j \in \mathbb{R}$ or a fail symbol FAIL

1   Initialize $\mathcal{D}_0 \leftarrow$ the set of all databases of size $n$ over $\{0,1\}^{\ell_k}$;

2   **for** *each query* $\mathtt{Dec}^{(\cdot)}(\cdot, c_j)$ *where* $j = 1, \ldots, m$ **do**

3      Sample a noise $\Delta a_j \sim \mathtt{Lap}(\sigma)$;

4      Compute the true answer $a_j \leftarrow \mathtt{Dec}^{O^*}(\mathbf{k}^*, c_j)$ and the noisy answer $\widehat{a}_j \leftarrow a_j + \Delta a_j$;

     /* Phase 1: Fix significant variables by querying $O^*$            */

5      Initialize the set of significant variables $W_j \leftarrow \emptyset$;

6      **repeat foreach** $x \in \{0,1\}^{\ell_o} \setminus W_j$ **do**

7         **if** $\mathrm{Pr}_{\mathbf{k} \sim \mathrm{Unif}(\mathcal{D}_{j-1}), O \sim \mathcal{O}_{\mathrm{unif}}}[\mathtt{Dec}^O(k_i, c_j)$ *queries* $x$ *for some* $k_i \in \mathbf{k}] \geq \beta/2$ **then**

8            Query $O^*$ on $x$ and fix $x$ to be $O^*(x)$ in $\mathtt{Dec}^{(\cdot)}(\cdot, c_j)$;

9            $W_j \leftarrow W_j \cup \{x\}$;

10     **until** $W_j$ *is not changed in the last iteration*;

     /* Phase 2: Examine whether $k^*$ has $(\alpha, \beta)$-significant variables. */

11     $\mathcal{U}_j \leftarrow \{x \notin W_j \mid \exists \mathbf{k} \in \mathcal{D}_{j-1}$ s.t. $x$ is $\beta$-significant for $\mathtt{Dec}^{(\cdot)}(\mathbf{k}, c_j)\}$;

12     **foreach** $x \in \mathcal{U}_j$ **do**

13        $S_j(x) \leftarrow \{k_i^* \mid x$ is $\beta$-significant for $\mathtt{Dec}^{(\cdot)}(k_i^*, c_j)\}$;

14        Sample $\Delta I_j(x) \sim \mathtt{Lap}(\sigma)$;

15        $I_j(x) \leftarrow |S_j(x)|/n$;

16        $\widehat{I}_j(x) \leftarrow I_j(x) + \Delta I_j(x)$;

17     $x_j^* \leftarrow \mathrm{argmax}\{\widehat{I}_j(x)\}$;

18     **if** $\widehat{I}_j(x_j^*) \geq \alpha/2$ **then**

19        $u_j \leftarrow 1$; **if** $\sum_{t=1}^{j} u_t > n\ell_k$ **then** abort and output FAIL;

20        $\mathcal{D}_j \leftarrow \mathcal{D}_{j-1} \setminus \{\mathbf{k} \mid x_j^*$ is not $\beta$-significant for $\mathtt{Dec}^{(\cdot)}(\mathbf{k}, c_j)\}$;

21        Output $ans_j \leftarrow \widehat{a}_j$;

22     **else** /* Phase 3: Check whether the median is a good estimation. */

23        $\mathcal{D}'_{j-1} \leftarrow \mathcal{D}_{j-1} \setminus \{\mathbf{k} \mid \exists x \in \{0,1\}^{\ell_o} \setminus W_j, x$ is $(\alpha, \beta)$-significant for $\mathtt{Dec}^{(\cdot)}(\mathbf{k}, c_j)\}$;

24        $med_j \leftarrow$ the median value of $\mathbb{E}_{O \sim \mathcal{O}_{\mathrm{unif}}}[\mathtt{Dec}^O(\mathbf{k}, c_j)]$ among all $\mathbf{k} \in \mathcal{D}'_{j-1}$;

25        **if** $|med_j - \widehat{a}_j| > 0.2$ **then**

26           $u_j \leftarrow 1$; **if** $\sum_{t=1}^{j} u_t > n\ell_k$ **then** abort and output FAIL;

27           $\mathcal{D}_j \leftarrow \mathcal{D}'_{j-1} \setminus \{\mathbf{k} \mid |\widehat{a}_j - \mathbb{E}_{O \sim \mathcal{O}_{\mathrm{unif}}}[\mathtt{Dec}^O(\mathbf{k}, c_j)]| > 0.2\}$;

28           Output $ans_j \leftarrow \widehat{a}_j$;

29        **else** $u_j \leftarrow 0$; $\mathcal{D}_j \leftarrow \mathcal{D}_{j-1}$; Output $ans_j \leftarrow med_j$;

---

## 4.2  Utility Analysis

In this section, we show that the sanitizer is $(1/3, neg(n))$-accurate. We use $\mathbf{c} = (c_1, \ldots, c_m)$ to denote a sequence of $m$ ciphertexts. Let $\mathcal{M}^O(\mathbf{k}, \mathbf{c})$ be the sanitizer described as Algorithm 1 running on database $\mathbf{k}$ and ciphertext sequence $\mathbf{c}$. We first show that with high probability, $\widehat{a}_j$ is close to $a_j$ for all round $j$.

**Lemma 2.** *For any $O^* \in \mathcal{O}_{unif}$, any database $\mathbf{k}^* \in (\{0,1\}^{\ell_k})^n$ and any sequence of $m$ ciphertexts $\mathbf{c} \in (\{0,1\}^{\ell_c})^m$,*

$$\Pr_{\widehat{\mathbf{a}} \leftarrow_R \mathcal{M}^{O^*}(\mathbf{k}^*, \mathbf{c})} \left[ \exists j \in [m], |\widehat{a}_j - a_j| > 0.1 \right] \leq neg(n)$$

*Proof.* Since $\Delta a_j$ is drawn from $\mathsf{Lap}(\sigma)$, $\Pr[|\Delta a_j| > 0.1] \leq e^{-0.1/\sigma} = neg(n)$. The lemmas follows by using union bound on all $j \in [m]$.  □

Then we show that with high probability, the phase 2 can successfully detect the significant variable in $\mathsf{Dec}^{(\cdot)}(\mathbf{k}^*, c_j)$ for all round $j$.

**Lemma 3.** *In the execution of Algorithm 1, for any round $j$ where $\mathsf{Dec}^{(\cdot)}(\mathbf{k}^*, c_j)$ has a $(\alpha, \beta)$-significant variable after Phase 1,*

$$\Pr\left[ \widehat{I}_j(x_j^*) < \alpha/2 \right] < neg(n)$$

*Proof.* Let $\tau$ be $\max_x\{I_j(x)\}$. Note that $\tau \geq \alpha$ since $\mathsf{Dec}^{(\cdot)}(\mathbf{k}^*, c_j)$ has a $(\alpha, \beta)$-significant variable. So we have

$$\Pr[\tau + \mathsf{Lap}(\sigma) < \alpha/2] < \frac{1}{2} \cdot e^{-\frac{\alpha}{2\sigma}} = neg(n)$$

The lemma follows the fact that $\widehat{I}_j(x_j^*) < \alpha/2$ implies $\tau + \mathsf{Lap}(\sigma) < \alpha/2$.  □

Before bounding the failure probability of the sanitizer, we first exhibit a large deviation bound for decision forest whose proof is deferred to Sect. 6.

**Proposition 2.** *For any $c_j \in \{0,1\}^{\ell_c}$ and $\mathbf{k} \in (\{0,1\}^{\ell_k})^n$, if there is no $(\alpha, \beta)$-significant variable in $\mathsf{Dec}^{(\cdot)}(\mathbf{k}, c_j)$ then for any $\delta_1 > 0$ and $\delta_2 > 0$,*

$$\Pr_{O^* \sim \mathcal{O}_{unif}} \left[ \left| \mathsf{Dec}^{O^*}(\mathbf{k}, c_j) - \mathop{\mathbb{E}}_{O \sim \mathcal{O}_{unif}} \left[ \mathsf{Dec}^{O^*}(\mathbf{k}, c_j) \right] \right| > \delta_1 + h\delta_2 + n^2 h\sqrt{\beta} \right] \leq e^{-2\delta_1^2/\alpha} + h^8 e^{-\delta_2^2/\beta}$$

*where $h$ is the query complexity of $\mathsf{Dec}^{(\cdot)}(\mathbf{k}, c_j)$.*

**Lemma 4.** *For any database $\mathbf{k}^* \in (\{0,1\}^{\ell_k})^n$, if there is no $(\alpha, \beta)$-significant variables in $\mathsf{Dec}^O(\mathbf{k}^*, c)$, then*

$$\Pr_{O^* \sim \mathcal{O}_{unif}} \left[ \exists c \in \{0,1\}^{\ell_c}, \left| \mathsf{Dec}^{O^*}(\mathbf{k}^*, c) - \mathop{\mathbb{E}}_{O \sim \mathcal{O}_{unif}} \left[ \mathsf{Dec}^O(\mathbf{k}^*, c) \right] \right| > 0.1 \right] \leq neg(n)$$

*Proof.* Let $T = 0.1$, by Proposition 2 (setting $\delta_1 = T/3$, $\delta_2 = T/(3q_\pi)$, $h = q_\pi$) and noting that $\beta = T/(3n^4 q_\pi^3)$,

$$\Pr_{O^* \sim \mathcal{O}_{\text{unif}}} \left[ \left| \text{Dec}^{O^*}(\mathbf{k}^*, c) - \mathbb{E}_{O \sim \mathcal{O}_{\text{unif}}} \left[ \text{Dec}^O(\mathbf{k}^*, c) \right] \right| > T \right] \leq 2e^{-T^2/(9\alpha)} + 2q_\pi^8 e^{-2Tn^4 q_\pi/3}$$

By taking union bound over all $c \in \{0,1\}^{\ell_c}$, the lemma follows that $\alpha = 1/(\ell_c n^\theta)$.     $\square$

*Remark 4.* Note that the statement of Lemma 4 requires that, with high probability, for all ciphertext $c \in \{0,1\}^{\ell_c}$, $\text{Dec}^{O^*}(k^*, c)$ should concentrate around the expectation. One might wonder whether this requirement is too stringent as the sanitizer only answers $m$ (which may be far less than $2^{\ell_c}$) queries. Unfortunately, it seems that this condition cannot be relaxed because the $m$ queries asked by the adversary might depend on the oracle $O^*$. So when considering all $O^*$, the number of possible queries can be much greater than $m$.

In order to bound the failure probability of the sanitizer, we divide all the query rounds $1, \ldots, m$ into three types.

- **Type 1:** $\text{Dec}^{(\cdot)}(\mathbf{k}^*, c_j)$ has a $(\alpha, \beta)$-significant variable. So $\widehat{a}_j$ is used to answer the query.
- **Type 2:** The median $med_j$ is not close to $\widehat{a}_j$. So $\widehat{a}_j$ is used to answer the query.
- **Type 3:** The mechanism use $med_j$ to answer the query.

We say a round is *bad* if it is in Type 1 or 2 otherwise it is said to be *good*.

**Lemma 5.** *For any database* $\mathbf{k} \in (\{0,1\}^{\ell_k})^n$,

$$\Pr_{O^* \sim \mathcal{O}_{\text{unif}}} \left[ \forall \mathbf{c} \in (\{0,1\}^{\ell_c})^m, \text{ the number of bad rounds in } \mathcal{M}^{O^*}(\mathbf{k}, \mathbf{c}) > n\ell_k \right] \leq neg(n)$$

*Proof.* We first show that, in any bad round $j$, the size of $\mathcal{D}_j$ will shrink by at least a factor of 2, i.e. $|\mathcal{D}_j| \leq |\mathcal{D}_{j-1}|/2$. Consider any Type 1 round $j$. Let $x_j^*$ be the significant variable picked at this round. Since $x_j^* \notin W_j$,

$$\sum_{O \in \mathcal{O}_{\text{unif}}, k \in \mathcal{D}_{j-1}} \mathbf{1}_{\text{Dec}^O(\mathbf{k}, c_j) \text{ queries } x_j^*} \leq |\mathcal{D}_{j-1}| \cdot |\mathcal{O}_{\text{unif}}| \cdot \beta/2$$

On the other hand, since $\mathcal{D}_j$ is obtained by removing all database $\mathbf{k}$ where $x_j^*$ is not $\beta$-significant for $\text{Dec}(\mathbf{k}, c_j)$, we have

$$\sum_{O \in \mathcal{O}_{\text{unif}}, k \in \mathcal{D}_{j-1}} \mathbf{1}_{\text{Dec}^O(\mathbf{k}, c_j) \text{ queries } x_j^*} \geq |\mathcal{D}_j| \cdot |\mathcal{O}_{\text{unif}}| \cdot \beta$$

Combine above two inequalities, we have $|\mathcal{D}_j| \leq |\mathcal{D}_{j-1}|/2$. Consider any Type 2 round $j$. Suppose $|\mathcal{D}_j| > |\mathcal{D}_{j-1}|/2 \geq |\mathcal{D}'_{j-1}|/2$. By the definition of $\mathcal{D}_j$ and $med_j$, we have $|med_j - \widehat{a}_j| \leq T$ which contradicts the fact that $j$ is a Type 2 round.

Next we show that $\mathbf{k}^* \in \mathcal{D}_m$ with probability $1 - neg(n)$ by induction on $j$. Clearly, $\mathbf{k}^* \in \mathcal{D}_0$. If $j$ is Type 1, in order to show $\mathbf{k}^* \notin \mathcal{D}_{j-1} \setminus \mathcal{D}_j$, it suffices to show that $x_j^*$ is $\beta$-significant for $\text{Dec}^{(\cdot)}(\mathbf{k}^*, c_j)$ with probability $1 - neg(n)$. For any $x$ which is not $\beta$-significant for $\text{Dec}^{(\cdot)}(\mathbf{k}^*, c_j)$n, we have $I_j(x) = 0$. Thus, a

$$\Pr[\widehat{I}_j(x) \geq \alpha/2] \leq \frac{1}{2}e^{-\alpha/2\sigma}$$

On the other hand, $|\mathcal{U}_j|$ is at most $2^{\ell_k}\beta/q_\pi$ since

$$|\mathcal{U}_j| \cdot |\mathcal{O}_{\text{unif}}| \cdot \beta \leq \sum_{O \in \mathcal{O}_{\text{unif}}, k \in \mathcal{D}_{j-1}, x \notin W_j} \mathbf{1}_{\text{Dec}^O(k, c_j) \text{ queries } x} \leq |\mathcal{D}_{j-1}| \cdot |\mathcal{O}_{\text{unif}}| \cdot q_\pi$$

By taking union bound over all $x \in \mathcal{U}_j$, we have the probability that $x_j^*$ is not $\beta$-significant for $\text{Dec}^{(\cdot)}(\mathbf{k}^*, c_j)$ is at most $|\mathcal{U}_j| \cdot e^{-\alpha/2\sigma} \leq 2^{\ell_k}\beta/q_\pi \cdot e^{-\alpha/2\sigma}$. Since $\alpha/(\sigma\ell_k) \geq n^{\theta/6}$, this probability is negligible.

If $j$ is Type 2, by Lemma 3, $\mathbf{k}^* \in \mathcal{D}'_{j-1}$ with probability at least $1 - neg(n)$. Then by Lemmas 2 and 4, with probability at least $1 - neg(n)$, $|\widehat{a}_j - a_j| \leq 0.1$ and $|a_j - \mathbb{E}_{O \sim \mathcal{O}_{\text{unif}}}[\text{Dec}^O(\mathbf{k}^*, c_j)]| \leq 0.1$. Thus, $\mathbf{k}^* \notin \mathcal{D}'_{j-1} \setminus \mathcal{D}_j$ by triangle inequality. If $j$ is Type 3, it is obvious since $\mathcal{D}_{j-1} = \mathcal{D}_j$.

Putting it all together, the lemma follows the facts that $|\mathcal{D}_0| = 2^{n\ell_k}$, $|\mathcal{D}_m| \geq 1$ with probability $1 - neg(n)$ and $|\mathcal{D}_j| \leq |\mathcal{D}_{j-1}|/2$ for all bad rounds.   $\square$

**Lemma 6** *(Utility). Algorithm 1 is $(0.3, neg(n))$-accurate, i.e., for any database $\mathbf{k}^* \in (\{0,1\}^{\ell_k})^n$,*

$$\Pr_{O^* \sim \mathcal{O}_{\text{unif}}} [\forall \mathbf{c} \in (\{0,1\}^{\ell_c})^m, \forall j \in [m], |ans_j - a_j| < 0.3] \geq 1 - neg(n)$$

*where $ans_j$ is the answer output by $\mathcal{M}^{O^*}(\mathbf{k}^*, \mathbf{c})$ at round $j$ and $a_j$ is the true answer $\text{Dec}^{O^*}(\mathbf{k}^*, c_j)$.*

*Remark 5.* Actually, the outermost probability should also be taken over the random coins in $\mathcal{M}$, i.e. the randomness of the Laplace noises. We omit this for the ease of presentation since these random coins are independent from the choice of $O^*$ and $\mathbf{c}$.

*Proof.* By the description of Algorithm 1, if the sanitizer succeeds, $|ans_j - \widehat{a}_j| \leq 0.2$ for all round $j$. Thus the lemma follows from Lemmas 2 and 5.   $\square$

## 4.3   Privacy Analysis

Our goal in this section is to demonstrate that, Algorithm 1 is $(\varepsilon, neg(n))$-differentially private. We first simplify the output of our sanitizer as a vector $\mathbf{v}$, which will be shown to determine the output transcript of the sanitizer.

$$v_j = \begin{cases} \widehat{a}_j, x_j^* & \text{if round } j \text{ is Type 1} \\ \widehat{a}_j, \bot & \text{if round } j \text{ is Type 2} \\ \bot, \bot & \text{if round } j \text{ is Type 3} \end{cases}$$

**Lemma 7.** *Given the oracle $O^*$ and $\mathbf{v}$, the output of Algorithm 1 can be determined.*

Fix an oracle $O^*$ and two adjacent databases $\mathbf{k}, \mathbf{k}' \in (\{0,1\}^{\ell_k})^n$. Let $A$ and $B$ denote the output distributions of our sanitizer when run on the input database $\mathbf{k}$ and $\mathbf{k}'$ respectively. We also use $A$ and $B$ to denote their probability density function $dA$ and $dB$. The support of both distributions is denoted by $\mathcal{V} = (\{\perp\} \cup \mathbb{R}, \{\perp\} \cup \{0,1\}^{\ell_o})^n$. For any $\mathbf{v} \in \mathcal{V}$, we define the *loss* function $L : \mathcal{V} \to \mathbb{R}$ as

$$L(\mathbf{v}) = \log\left(\frac{A(\mathbf{v})}{B(\mathbf{v})}\right)$$

By Proposition 1, it suffices to show that

$$\Pr_{\mathbf{v} \sim A}[L(\mathbf{v}) > \varepsilon] < neg(n)$$

Given a transcript $\mathbf{v}$, by chain rule,

$$L(\mathbf{v}) = \log\left(\frac{A(\mathbf{v})}{B(\mathbf{v})}\right) = \sum_{j \in [m]} \log\left(\frac{A_j(v_j \mid \mathbf{v}_{<j})}{B_j(v_j \mid \mathbf{v}_{<j})}\right)$$

where $A_j(v_j \mid \mathbf{v}_{<j})$ is the probability density function of the conditional distribution of Algorithm 1 outputting $v_j$, conditioned on $\mathbf{v}_{<j} = (v_1, \ldots, v_{j-1})$.

Now fix a round $j \in [m]$ and $\mathbf{v}_{<j}$. We define two borderline events on the noise values $\Delta I_j(x)$ and $\Delta a_j$. Let $\mathcal{E}_1$ be the event that $\widehat{I}_j(x_j^*) > \alpha/2 - \sigma$ and $\mathcal{E}_2$ be the event that $|\widehat{a}_j - med_j| > T - \sigma$. It should be emphasized that given $\mathbf{v}_{<j}$, both $\mathcal{E}_1$ and $\mathcal{E}_2$ events only depends on the Laplacian noises $\{\Delta I_j(x)\}_{x \in \mathcal{U}_j}$ and $\Delta a_j$. Equivalently, $\mathcal{E}_1$ is the event that $\{\Delta I_j(x)\}_{x \in \mathcal{U}_j}$ is in the set of noises such that $\widehat{I}_j(x_j^*) > \alpha/2 - \sigma$ and $\mathcal{E}_2$ is the event that $\Delta a_j > T - \sigma + med_j - a_j$ or $\Delta a_j < med_j - a_j - T + \sigma$. In the following lemma, we show that conditioned on $\mathcal{E}_1 \vee \mathcal{E}_2$, with probability at least $1/e$, a round $j$ is a bad round.

**Lemma 8.** $\Pr[j \text{ is of Type 1} \mid \mathcal{E}_1] \geq 1/e$ and $\Pr[j \text{ is of Type 2} \mid \overline{\mathcal{E}}_1, \mathcal{E}_2] \geq 1/e$.

Then we show upper bounds on the privacy loss for three cases $\overline{\mathcal{E}}_1 \wedge \overline{\mathcal{E}}_2$, $\overline{\mathcal{E}}_1 \wedge \mathcal{E}_2$ and $\mathcal{E}_1$. By combining all these three cases, we are able to show the following lemma. Due to space limit, we defer all the proofs in Appendix A.

**Lemma 9.** *Algorithm 1 is $(\varepsilon, neg(n))$-differently private.*

## 5    Improved Lower Bound

In this section, we show how to improve the bound proved in Sect. 4 to $\widetilde{\Omega}(n)$ by modifying the sanitizer and the proof a bit. Suppose $\ell_k \cdot \ell_c^2 \leq n^{1-\theta}$. Set parameters $\sigma, \alpha, \beta$ to be

$$\sigma = n^{\theta/3} \sqrt{\frac{\ell_k}{n}}, \qquad \alpha = \frac{1}{\ell_c n^\theta}, \qquad \beta = \frac{1}{54 n^4 q_\pi^3}$$

Since $\ell_k \cdot \ell_c{}^2 \leq n^{1-\theta}$, by simple calculation, we have $\alpha/\sigma \geq n^{\theta/6}$.

We modify the definition of $\mathcal{U}_j$ in the line 10 of Algorithm 1 as follows.

Algorithm 1 :   $\mathcal{U}_j \leftarrow \{x \notin W_j \mid \exists \mathbf{k} \in \mathcal{D}_{j-1} \text{ s.t. } x \text{ is } \beta\text{-significant for } \mathtt{Dec}^{(\cdot)}(\mathbf{k}, c_j)\}$

New Algorithm :   $\mathcal{U}_j \leftarrow \{x \notin W_j \mid x \text{ is } \beta\text{-significant for } \mathtt{Dec}^{(\cdot)}(\mathbf{k}^*, c_j)\}$

The efficiency of the new sanitizer follows Lemma 1. The only difference in the utility analysis is in the proof of Lemma 5 where we show $k^* \in \mathcal{D}_m$ if $j$ is Type 1. In the new algorithm, this is straight forward since $x_j^* \in \mathcal{U}_j$ must be a $\beta$-significant variable for $\mathtt{Dec}^{(\cdot)}(\mathbf{k}^*, c_j)$.

In the privacy analysis, the only difference is that the new definition of $\mathcal{U}_j$ does depend on the true database. Given any adjacent databases $\mathbf{k}, \mathbf{k}'$, we fix a round $j$ and $\mathbf{v}_{<j}$. Let $\mathcal{U}$ and $\mathcal{U}'$ denote the set $\mathcal{U}_j$ when the sanitizer running on $\mathbf{k}$ and $\mathbf{k}'$ respectively. We also use $x^*$ and $x^{*\prime}$ to denote the variable $x_j^* = \mathrm{argmax}_x\{\widehat{I}_j(x)\}$ for $\mathbf{k}$ and $\mathbf{k}'$ respectively. Let $\mathcal{H}_j$ be the event that there exists $x \in \mathcal{U} \setminus \mathcal{U}'$ such that $\Delta I_j(x) \geq \alpha/2 - \sigma - 1/n$ or there exists $x \in \mathcal{U}' \setminus \mathcal{U}$ such that $\Delta I'_j(x) \geq \alpha/2 - \sigma - 1/n$.

**Lemma 10.** $\Pr[\mathcal{H}_j | \mathbf{v}_{<j}] \leq neg(n)$.

*Proof.* First, note that $|\mathcal{U}| \leq q_\pi/\beta$ since

$$|\mathcal{U}| \cdot |\mathcal{O}_{\mathrm{unif}}| \cdot \beta \leq \sum_{O \in \mathcal{O}_{\mathrm{unif}}, x \notin W_j} \mathbf{1}_{\mathtt{Dec}^O(\mathbf{k}, c_j) \text{ queries } x} \leq |\mathcal{O}_{\mathrm{unif}}| \cdot q_\pi$$

On the other hand, since $\Delta I_j(x)$ is drawn from $\mathtt{Lap}(\sigma)$ and $\alpha/\sigma \geq n^{\theta/6}$,

$$\Pr[\Delta I_j(x) \geq \alpha/2 - \sigma - 1/n] \leq \frac{1}{2} \cdot e^{-(\alpha/2-\sigma)/\sigma} = neg(n)$$

The lemma follows by taking union bound over all $x \in \mathcal{U} \setminus \mathcal{U}'$ and applying similar arguments for $x \in \mathcal{U}' \setminus \mathcal{U}$.  □

We define another random variable $A'_j$ such that $d_{tv}(A_j, A'_j) \leq neg(n)$ and $\mathcal{H}_j$ never occurs with respect to $A'_j$ (similar ideas has been also used in proving Theorem 3.5 of [14]). Observe that, conditioned on $\overline{\mathcal{H}}_j$, $\mathcal{E}_1$ implies $x^*, x^{*\prime} \in \mathcal{U} \cap \mathcal{U}'$ and $\overline{\mathcal{E}}_1$ implies the round $j$ is not Type 1 for both $\mathbf{k}$ and $\mathbf{k}'$. Let $L'(\mathbf{v})$ be the analogues of $L(\mathbf{v})$ by replacing $A_j$ by $A'_j$ for all $j \in [m]$. Clearly $d_{tv}(L, L') \leq m \cdot neg(n) = neg(n)$. Following the proof of Lemma 9, we can show $\Pr[L'(\mathbf{v}) \geq \varepsilon] \leq neg(n)$ for any $\varepsilon = \Omega(1)$. Thus $\Pr[L(\mathbf{v}) \geq \varepsilon] \leq neg(n)$ follows.

## 6   Large Deviation Bound for Decision Forests

In this section, we show the large deviation bound for $\mathtt{Dec}^{(\cdot)}(\mathbf{k}, c_j)$ for any given $\mathbf{k} \in (\{0,1\}^{\ell_k})^n$ and $c_j \in \{0,1\}^{\ell_c}$. Intuitively, a decrypt algorithm $\mathtt{Dec}^{(\cdot)}(k_i, c_j)$ can be viewed as a decision tree and similarly, $\mathtt{Dec}^{(\cdot)}(\mathbf{k}, c_j)$ represents a decision forest (see formal definition below). So throughout this section, we will use the terms like decision trees/forest instead of decrypt algorithms to present our result on large deviation bound for decision forest.

A *decision tree* $D$ is a binary tree whose internal nodes are labeled with Boolean variables while leaves labeled with 0 or 1. Given an input assignment $\mathbf{a} = (a_1, \ldots, a_m) \in \{0,1\}^n$ to the variables $x_1, \ldots, x_m$, the value computed by $D$ on this input $\mathbf{a}$ is denoted by $D(\mathbf{a})$. This value $D(\mathbf{a})$ is the value of the leaf at a path on $D$ determined in the following way. The path starts from the root of $D$ and then moves to the left child if the current internal node is assigned 0 and to right otherwise. A variable $x_i$ is said to be queried by $D(\mathbf{a})$ if the corresponding path passes through a node labeled $x_i$. Clearly, every $x_i$ can only be queried by $D(\mathbf{a})$ at most once.

A *decision forest* $\mathcal{F}$ is a collection of $|\mathcal{F}|$ decision trees. For any assignment $\mathbf{a}$ of $\mathbf{x}$, $\mathcal{F}(\mathbf{a})$ denotes the $|\mathcal{F}|$-dimensional vector computed by $\mathcal{F}$ on $\mathbf{a}$, whose $i$th component is the value computed by the $i$th tree. We use $w(\mathcal{F}(\mathbf{a}))$ to denote the fractional hamming weight of $\mathcal{F}(\mathbf{a})$, i.e.,

$$w(\mathcal{F}(\mathbf{a})) = \frac{\sum_{D_j \in \mathcal{F}} D_j(\mathbf{a})}{|\mathcal{F}|}.$$

In most cases, we assume the assignment $\mathbf{a}$ are drawn from the uniform distribution on $\{0,1\}^m$. We also use the shorthand notations $\mathrm{Pr}_\mathbf{a}$ and $\mathbb{E}_\mathbf{a}$ to denote the probability and expectation when $\mathbf{a}$ are uniformly distributed when it is clear from the context. We may also abuse the $\mathrm{Pr}_\mathbf{a}$ or $\mathbb{E}_\mathbf{a}$ inside another $\mathrm{Pr}_\mathbf{a}$ or $\mathbb{E}_\mathbf{a}$ to denote the probability or expectation corresponding to another random variable when it is not ambiguous, e.g. $\mathrm{Pr}_\mathbf{a}\left[w(\mathcal{F}(\mathbf{a})) > \mathbb{E}_\mathbf{a}[w(\mathcal{F}(\mathbf{a}))]\right]$.

**Definition 11 ($(\alpha, \beta)$-significant).** *For a decision forest $\mathcal{F}$ and an input $\mathbf{x}$, a Boolean variable $x_i$ is said to be $(\alpha, \beta)$-significant if at least $\alpha$ fraction of trees $D$ in $\mathcal{F}$ satisfy $\mathrm{Pr}_\mathbf{a}\left[D(\mathbf{a}) \text{ queries } x_i\right] \geq \beta$.*

For comparison, we discuss the difference between the above definition and the notion called "average significance" used in [2]. Recall that the average significance of $x_i$ on $\mathcal{F}$ is defined as

$$\frac{1}{|\mathcal{F}|} \cdot \sum_{D \in \mathcal{F}} \mathrm{Pr}_\mathbf{a}\left[D(\mathbf{a}) \text{ queries } x_i\right].$$

Obviously, if $x_i$ is $(\alpha, \beta)$-significant, the average significance of $x_i$ is at least $\alpha \cdot \beta$. On the other hand, if $x_i$ is not $(\alpha, \beta)$-significant, it can be shown that the average significance of $x_i$ is at most $\alpha + \beta$. To see this, let $\mathcal{F}_1 \subseteq \mathcal{F}$ be the set of trees $D$ such that $\mathrm{Pr}_\mathbf{a}[D(\mathbf{a}) \text{ queries } x_i] \geq \beta$.

$$\frac{1}{|\mathcal{F}|} \cdot \sum_{D \in \mathcal{F}} \Pr_{\mathbf{a}}[D(\mathbf{a}) \text{ queries } x_i]$$

$$\leq \frac{1}{|\mathcal{F}|} \left( \sum_{D \in \mathcal{F}_1} \Pr_{\mathbf{a}}[D(\mathbf{a}) \text{ queries } x_i] + \sum_{D \in \mathcal{F} \setminus \mathcal{F}_1} \Pr_{\mathbf{a}}[D(\mathbf{a}) \text{ queries } x_i] \right)$$

$$\leq \frac{1}{|\mathcal{F}|} \left( |\mathcal{F}_1| + \sum_{D \in \mathcal{F} \setminus \mathcal{F}_1} \beta \right) \leq \alpha + \beta$$

We restate two theorems from [2, 17] in our terms.

**Theorem 4 (Theorem 1.1. in [17]).** *Let $\mathcal{F}$ be a decision forest that has no $(\alpha, 0)$-significant variable and $n$ be $|\mathcal{F}|$. Then for any $\delta > 0$,*

$$\Pr_{\mathbf{a}} \left[ \left| w(\mathcal{F}(\mathbf{a})) - \mathbb{E}_{\mathbf{a}}[w(\mathcal{F}(\mathbf{a}))] \right| \geq \delta \right] \leq e^{-2\delta^2/\alpha}$$

**Theorem 5 ([2]).** *Let $\mathcal{F}$ be a decision forest of height at most $h$ that has no $(\beta, \beta)$-significant variable. Then for any $\delta > 0$,*

$$\Pr_{\mathbf{a}} \left[ \left| w(\mathcal{F}(\mathbf{a})) - \mathbb{E}_{\mathbf{a}}[w(\mathcal{F}(\mathbf{a}))] \right| \geq h\delta \right] \leq h^8 e^{-\delta^2/\beta}$$

We state the main theorem that we will prove in this section.

**Theorem 6.** *Let $\mathcal{F}$ be a decision forest of height at most $h$ that has no $(\alpha, \beta)$-significant variable. Then for any $\delta_1 > 0$ and $\delta_2 > 0$,*

$$\Pr_{\mathbf{a}} \left[ \left| w(\mathcal{F}(\mathbf{a})) - \mathbb{E}_{\mathbf{a}}[w(\mathcal{F}(\mathbf{a}))] \right| > \delta_1 + h\delta_2 + n^2 h\sqrt{\beta} \right] \leq e^{-2\delta_1^2/\alpha} + h^8 e^{-\delta_2^2/\beta}$$

For the rest of this section, we fix $\mathcal{F}$ to be a decision forest of size $n$ and height $h$, which has no $(\alpha, \beta)$-significant variables. Let $S$ denote the set of all variables $x_i$ such that there exists $D \in \mathcal{F}$, $\Pr_{\mathbf{a}}[D(\mathbf{a}) \text{ queries } x_i] \geq \sqrt{\beta}$. Clearly, $|S| \leq nh/\sqrt{\beta}$. We use $\bar{S}$ to denote the complement set of $S$ and $\mathbf{a}_S$ to denote the partial assignment truncated on $S$.

**Definition 12 (pruning).** *Let $\mathcal{F}_\mathcal{P}$ be the pruned forest of $\mathcal{F}$ defined as follows. For each variable $x_i \in S$ and $D \in \mathcal{F}$, if $\Pr_{\mathbf{a}}[D(\mathbf{a}) \text{ queries } x] \leq \beta$, we deleted $x_i$ from the corresponding tree in $\mathcal{F}_\mathcal{P}$ and instead replaced with leaves assigning the value 0.*

We only show one side of the Theorem 6, i.e.

$$\Pr_{\mathbf{a}} \left[ w(\mathcal{F}(\mathbf{a})) < \mathbb{E}_{\mathbf{a}}[w(\mathcal{F}(\mathbf{a}))] - \delta_1 - h\delta_2 - n^2 h\sqrt{\beta} \right] \leq e^{-2\delta_1^2/\alpha} + h^8 e^{-\delta_2^2/\beta}$$

The proof of the other side is symmetric by changing the definition of pruning to replacing $x_i$ by 1.

The proof sketch of Theorem 6 can be described as follows. Note that for any assignment $\mathbf{a}$, $w(\mathcal{F}(\mathbf{a})) \geq w(\mathcal{F_P}(\mathbf{a}))$. On the other hand, $\mathbb{E}_{\mathbf{a}}[w(\mathcal{F_P}(\mathbf{a}))] \geq \mathbb{E}_{\mathbf{a}}[w(\mathcal{F}(\mathbf{a}))] - n\beta \cdot nh/\sqrt{\beta}$ since pruning each variable in $|S|$ decreases the expectation value at most $\beta n$ and $|S| \leq nh/\sqrt{\beta}$. Hence, to prove Theorem 6, it suffices to prove that $w(\mathcal{F_P}(\mathbf{a}))$ is close to $\mathbb{E}_{\mathbf{a}}[w(\mathcal{F_P}(\mathbf{a}))]$ with high probability, which can be established in two steps. We first show that, in Lemma 11, for any partial assignment $\mathbf{a}_{\bar{S}}$, $w(\mathcal{F_P}(\mathbf{a}_S, \mathbf{a}_{\bar{S}}))$ is close to $\mathbb{E}_{\mathbf{a}_S}[w(\mathcal{F_P}(\mathbf{a}_S, \mathbf{a}_{\bar{S}}))]$ with high probability (w.r.t. the randomness of $\mathbf{a}_S$). Then in Lemma 12, we prove that with respect to the randomness of $\mathbf{a}_{\bar{S}}$, $\mathbb{E}_{\mathbf{a}_S}[w(\mathcal{F_P}(\mathbf{a}_S, \mathbf{a}_{\bar{S}}))]$ is close to $\mathbb{E}_{\mathbf{a}}[w(\mathcal{F_P}(\mathbf{a}))]$ with high probability. Therefore, Theorem 6 follows union bound.

**Lemma 11.** *For any partial assignment $\mathbf{a}_{\bar{S}}$ and $\delta > 0$,*

$$\Pr_{\mathbf{a}_S}\left[\left|w(\mathcal{F_P}(\mathbf{a}_S, \mathbf{a}_{\bar{S}})) - \mathbb{E}_{\mathbf{a}_S}[w(\mathcal{F_P}(\mathbf{a}_S, \mathbf{a}_{\bar{S}}))]\right| \geq \delta\right] \leq e^{-2\delta_1^2/\alpha}$$

*Proof.* Given an assignment $\mathbf{a}_{\bar{S}}$, it is not hard to see that the decision forest $\mathcal{F_P}(\mathbf{x}_S, \mathbf{a}_{\bar{S}})$, which only takes $\mathbf{x}_S$ as input, has no $(\alpha, 0)$-significant variable. Otherwise, such variable must be $(\alpha, \beta)$-significant in $\mathcal{F}$. Hence the lemma follows Theorem 4. $\qquad\square$

**Lemma 12.** *For any $\delta > 0$,*

$$\Pr_{\mathbf{a}_{\bar{S}}}\left[\left|\mathbb{E}_{\mathbf{a}_S}\left[w(\mathcal{F_P}(\mathbf{a}_S, \mathbf{a}_{\bar{S}}))\right] - \mathbb{E}_{\mathbf{a}}[w(\mathcal{F_P}(\mathbf{a}))]\right| \geq h\delta\right] \leq h^8 e^{-\delta^2/\beta}$$

Before proving Lemma 12, we define an operation on $\mathcal{F_P}$.

**Definition 13 (truncating).** *Let $\mathcal{F_T}$ be a truncated forest of $\mathcal{F_P}$ with size $2^{|S|} \cdot |\mathcal{F_P}|$. For each tree $D \in \mathcal{F_P}$, there are $2^{|S|}$ trees in $\mathcal{F_T}$ that corresponds to all possible assignments of $\mathbf{x}_S$.*

*Proof.* We first show that there is no $(\sqrt{\beta}, \sqrt{\beta})$-significant variables in $\mathcal{F_T}$. Note that all the variables in $\mathcal{F_T}$ are in $\bar{S}$. Assume to the contrary that there exists $x_i \in \bar{S}$ that is $(\sqrt{\beta}, \sqrt{\beta})$-significant. Then

$$\sum_{D \in \mathcal{F_P}} \Pr_{\mathbf{a}}[D(\mathbf{a}) \text{ queries } x_i]/n = \sum_{D_T \in \mathcal{F_T}} \Pr_{\mathbf{a}_{\bar{S}}}[D_T(\mathbf{a}_{\bar{S}}) \text{ queries } x_i]/(n \cdot 2^{|S|}) \geq \sqrt{\beta} \cdot \sqrt{\beta} = \beta$$

which implies there is a $D \in \mathcal{F_P}$ such that $\Pr_{\mathbf{a}}[D(\mathbf{a}) \text{ queries } x_i] \geq \beta$. This is a contradiction with the definition of $\bar{S}$.

Thus, by Theorem 5,

$$\Pr_{\mathbf{a}_{\bar{S}}}\left[\left|w(\mathcal{F_T}(\mathbf{a}_{\bar{S}})) - \mathbb{E}_{\mathbf{a}_{\bar{S}}}[w(\mathcal{F_T}(\mathbf{a}_{\bar{S}}))]\right| \leq h\delta\right] \leq h^8 e^{-\delta^2/\beta}$$

Therefore, the lemma follows the fact that $w(\mathcal{F_T}(\mathbf{a}_{\bar{S}})) = \mathbb{E}_{\mathbf{a}_S}[w(\mathcal{F_P}(\mathbf{a}_S, \mathbf{a}_{\bar{S}}))]$. $\quad\square$

*Proof (Proof of Theorem 6).* Combining Lemmas 11 and 12, with probability at least $1 - e^{-2\delta_1^2/\alpha} - h^8 e^{-\delta_2^2/\beta}$, we have $w(\mathcal{F_P}(\mathbf{a})) \geq \mathbb{E}_{\mathbf{a}}[w(\mathcal{F_P}(\mathbf{a}))] - \delta_1 - h\delta_2$. Then the theorem follows that $w(\mathcal{F}(\mathbf{a})) \geq w(\mathcal{F_P}(\mathbf{a}))$ and $\mathbb{E}_{\mathbf{a}}[w(\mathcal{F_P}(\mathbf{a}))] \geq \mathbb{E}_{\mathbf{a}}[w(\mathcal{F}(\mathbf{a}))] - n^2 h\sqrt{\beta}$. $\qquad\square$

**Acknowledgement.** We would like to thank Shachar Lovett, Jon Ullman and Salil Vadhan for helpful discussion. Jiapeng Zhang would also like to thank his wife, Yingcong Li.

# A  Missing Proofs

*Proof (of Theorem 3).* Assume there exist such a traitor tracing system $\Pi_{\mathsf{TT}}$ and a sanitizer $\mathcal{M}$. We define the pirate decoder $\mathcal{P}$ as follows. The database of $\mathcal{M}$ is the set of user keys hold by the pirate decoder. For each ciphertext sent from Trace to $\mathcal{P}$, we use $\mathcal{M}$ to answer it and then return 1 is the answer is at least $1/2$ and return 0 otherwise.

Clearly, the $\mathcal{P}$ is efficient and available since $\mathcal{M}$ is efficient and accurate. Let $S = \{k_i\}_{i \in [n]}$. Now consider two experiments: in the first one, we run Trace on $\mathcal{P}^{(\cdot)}(S, \cdot)$. Since Trace is secure, there must exist a user $i^*$ such that

$$\Pr_{\substack{O \sim \mathcal{O}_{\mathrm{unif}} \\ \mathbf{k} \leftarrow_R \mathsf{Gen}^O}} [\mathsf{Trace}^{O, \mathcal{P}^O(S)}(\mathbf{k}) = i^*] \geq \frac{1}{n(\kappa)} - o\left(\frac{1}{n(\kappa)}\right)$$

Let $S' = S \setminus \{i^*\}$. We run the second experiments on Trace and $\mathcal{P}^{(\cdot)}([n] \setminus \{i^*\}, \cdot)$. Since $\mathcal{M}$ is differentially private for any $O \in \mathcal{O}_{\mathrm{unif}}$, we have

$$\Pr_{\substack{O \sim \mathcal{O}_{\mathrm{unif}} \\ \mathbf{k} \leftarrow_R \mathsf{Gen}^O}} [\mathsf{Trace}^{O, \mathcal{P}^O(S')}(\mathbf{k}) = i^*] \geq \Omega\left(\frac{1}{n(\kappa)}\right)$$

To complete the proof, notice that since $i^* \notin S'$, a secure $\Pi_{\mathsf{TT}}$ can only output $i^*$ with probability $o(1/n(\kappa))$, a contradiction. $\qquad\square$

*Proof of Lemma 7).* By the description of Algorithm 1, the only variable (or information) passed from round $j - 1$ to round $j$ is $\mathcal{D}_{j-1}$. So it suffices to show that given $\mathbf{v}$, the adversary can recover $\mathcal{D}_j$ for all $j \in [m]$. We prove this by induction on $j$. Clearly, it holds when $j = 0$. Given $\mathcal{D}_{j-1}$, $\mathcal{D}_j$ can be construct as follows. Since Phase 1 does not use any information about $\mathbf{k}*$, the adversary first simulate it by querying $O^*$ on significant variables and simplifying $\mathsf{Dec}^O(; c_j)$. Next, if $\mathbf{v} = (\hat{a}_j, x_j^*)$, $\mathcal{D}_j \leftarrow \mathcal{D}_{j-1} \setminus \{\mathbf{k} \mid x_j^* \text{ is not } \beta\text{-significant for } \mathsf{Dec}^{(\cdot)}(\mathbf{k}, c_j)\}$. If $\mathbf{v} = (\hat{a}_j, \perp)$, $\mathcal{D}_j \leftarrow \mathcal{D}'_{j-1} \setminus \{\mathbf{k} \mid |\hat{a}_j - \mathbb{E}_{O \sim \mathcal{O}_{\mathrm{unif}}}[\mathsf{Dec}^O(\mathbf{k}, c_j)]| > 0.2\}$. If $\mathbf{v} = (\perp, \perp)$, $\mathcal{D}_j \leftarrow \mathcal{D}_{j-1}$. Obviously, this $\mathcal{D}_j$ is exactly the same one used in Algorithm 1. Finally, we need to argue the case where the sanitizer outputs FAIL. It is not hard to see, the sanitizer fails only if $v_j \neq (\perp, \perp)$ for more than $n\ell_k$ number of rounds. So the adversary can recognize the failure of the sanitizer. $\qquad\square$

Before proceeding, we first state two obvious probability facts.

**Lemma 13.** *For any $\mu \in \mathbb{R}$ and $\sigma > 0$, $\Pr[\mathsf{Lap}(\sigma) > \mu \mid \mathsf{Lap}(\sigma) > \mu - \sigma] \geq 1/e$ and $\Pr[\mathsf{Lap}(\sigma) < \mu \mid \mathsf{Lap}(\sigma) < \mu + \sigma] \geq 1/e$.*

*Proof.* We only prove the first inequality. The second follows similar arguments. If $\mu \geq \sigma$, the probability is

$$\frac{\frac{1}{2}e^{-\mu/\sigma}}{\frac{1}{2}e^{-(\mu-\sigma)/\sigma}} = 1/e$$

If $\mu \in (0, \sigma)$, the probability is

$$\frac{\frac{1}{2}e^{-\mu/\sigma}}{1 - \frac{1}{2}e^{-(\mu-\sigma)/\sigma}} \geq \frac{\frac{1}{2e}}{\frac{1}{2}} = 1/e$$

If $\mu \leq 0$, the probability is

$$\frac{1 - \frac{1}{2}e^{\mu/\sigma}}{1 - \frac{1}{2}e^{(\mu-\sigma)/\sigma}} \geq \frac{1}{2}$$

$\square$

**Lemma 14.** *Let $A, B, C, D$ be four random events such that $\Pr[A \wedge B] = 0$. Then*

$$\Pr[A \vee B \mid C \vee D] \geq \min\{\Pr[A \mid C], \Pr[B \mid D]\}$$

*Proof.*

$$\begin{aligned}
\Pr[A \vee B \mid C \vee D] &= \Pr[A \mid C \vee D] + \Pr[B \mid C \vee D] \\
&\geq \Pr[A \mid C]\Pr[C \mid C \vee D] + \Pr[B \mid D]\Pr[D \mid C \vee D] \\
&\geq \min\{\Pr[A \mid C], \Pr[B \mid D]\} \cdot (\Pr[C \mid C \vee D] + \Pr[D \mid C \vee D]) \\
&\geq \min\{\Pr[A \mid C], \Pr[B \mid D]\}
\end{aligned}$$

$\square$

*Proof (of Lemma 8).* Note that $j$ is of Type 1 iff $\widehat{I}_j(x_j^*) \geq \alpha/2$. So by Lemma 13,

$$\begin{aligned}
&\Pr\left[\widehat{I}_j(x_j^*) \geq \alpha/2 \mid \widehat{I}_j(x_j^*) \geq \alpha/2 - \sigma\right] \\
&= \Pr[\mathsf{Lap}(\sigma) \geq \alpha/2 - S_j(x_j^*)/n \mid \mathsf{Lap}(\sigma) \geq \alpha/2 - S_j(x_j^*)/n - \sigma] \geq 1/e
\end{aligned}$$

Similarly, conditioned on $\overline{\mathcal{E}}_1$, $j$ is of Type 2 iff $\widehat{a}_j - med_j > T$ or $\widehat{a}_j - med_j < -T$. By Lemma 13,

$$\Pr\left[\widehat{a}_j - med_j \leq -T \mid \widehat{a}_j - med_j \leq -(T - \sigma)\right] \geq 1/e$$
$$\Pr\left[\widehat{a}_j - med_j \geq T \mid \widehat{a}_j - med_j \geq T - \sigma\right] \geq 1/e$$

Since $T \geq \sigma$, the second part of the lemma follows by combining the above two inequalities. $\square$

Then in the following three lemmas, we show upper bounds on the privacy loss for three cases $\overline{\mathcal{E}}_1 \wedge \overline{\mathcal{E}}_2$, $\overline{\mathcal{E}}_1 \wedge \mathcal{E}_2$ and $\mathcal{E}_1$.

**Lemma 15.** *For every $v_j \in \mathcal{V}$,*

$$\log\left(\frac{A_j(v_j \mid \overline{\mathcal{E}}_1, \overline{\mathcal{E}}_2, \mathbf{v}_{<j})}{B_j(v_j \mid \overline{\mathcal{E}}_1, \overline{\mathcal{E}}_2, \mathbf{v}_{<j})}\right) = 0$$

*Proof.* Conditioned on $\overline{\mathcal{E}}_1$ and $\overline{\mathcal{E}}_2$, we have $\widehat{I}_j(x_j^*) \leq \alpha/2 - \sigma$ and $|\widehat{a}_j - med_j| \leq T - \sigma$. Then the round $j$ must be of Type 3 for both $\mathbf{k}$ and $\mathbf{k}'$ since $|a_j - a_j'| \leq 1/n$ and $|I_j(x) - I_j'(x)| \leq 1/n$. □

**Lemma 16.** *For every $v_j \in \mathcal{V}$,*

$$\log\left(\frac{A_j(v_j \mid \overline{\mathcal{E}}_1, \mathcal{E}_2, \mathbf{v}_{<j})}{B_j(v_j \mid \overline{\mathcal{E}}_1, \mathcal{E}_2, \mathbf{v}_{<j})}\right) \leq \frac{1}{\sigma n}$$

*Proof.* Following similar argument in Lemma 15, the round $j$ cannot be Type 1 for $\mathbf{k}$ and $\mathbf{k}'$. For any $v_j \in (\mathbb{R}, \perp)$, the sanitizer outputs $v_j$ is either with probability 0 for both $\mathbf{k}, \mathbf{k}'$ or with probabilities differing by an $e^{1/\sigma n}$ ratio. Similarly, for $v_j = (\perp, \perp)$, the probabilities by $\mathbf{k}$ and $\mathbf{k}'$ differ by an $e^{1/\sigma n}$ ratio since $|a_j - a_j'| \leq 1/n$. □

**Lemma 17.** *For every $v_j \in \mathcal{V}$,*

$$\log\left(\frac{A_j(v_j \mid \mathcal{E}_1, \mathbf{v}_{<j})}{B_j(v_j \mid \mathcal{E}_1, \mathbf{v}_{<j})}\right) \leq \frac{3}{\sigma n}$$

*Proof.* If $v_j \in (\mathbb{R}, \{0,1\}^{\ell_o})$, let $v_j = (a^*, z)$. We couple the random noise $\Delta I_j(x)$ and $\Delta I_j'(x)$ for all $x \in \mathcal{U}_j \setminus \{z\}$. Let $h$ and $h'$ denote $\max_{x \in \mathcal{U}_j \setminus \{z\}}\{\widehat{I}_j(x_j)\}$ and $\max_{x \in \mathcal{U}_j \setminus \{z\}}\{\widehat{I}_j'(x_j)\}$ respectively. Then we have,

$$A_j(v_j \mid \mathcal{E}_1, \mathbf{v}_{<j}) = \Pr[a_j + \Delta a_j = a^* \wedge \Delta I_j(z) \geq \max\{\alpha/2, h\} - I_j(z) \mid \mathcal{E}_1, \mathbf{v}_{<j}]$$
$$B_j(v_j \mid \mathcal{E}_1, \mathbf{v}_{<j}) = \Pr[a_j' + \Delta a_j' = a^* \wedge \Delta I_j'(z) \geq \max\{\alpha/2, h'\} - I_j'(z) \mid \mathcal{E}_1, \mathbf{v}_{<j}]$$

Thus the ratio between the above two probabilities is at most $e^{\frac{3}{\sigma n}}$ since $|a_j - a_j'| \leq 1/n$, $|I_j(z) - I_j'(z)| \leq 1/n$ and $|h - h'| \leq 1/n$.

If $v_j \in (\perp \cup \mathbb{R}, \perp)$, the santizer outputs $v_j$ only if the round $j$ is not of Type 1. Similarly to the above argument, it is not hard to see that the probabilities that the round $j$ is not of Type 1 for $\mathbf{k}$ and $\mathbf{k}'$ differ at a $e^{2/\sigma n}$ ratio. Then the lemma follows the similar arguments in Lemmas 15 and 16. □

Combining all the above three cases, we are able to bound the expected privacy loss for each round $j$ by using the following two propositions.

**Proposition 3 (Lemma 3.2 in [14]).** *For any two distributions $A, B$ on a common support $\mathcal{V}$, if*

$$\sup_{v \in \mathcal{V}} \left|\log\left(\frac{A(v)}{B(v)}\right)\right| \leq \varepsilon$$

*then*

$$\mathbb{E}_{v \sim A}\left[\log\left(\frac{A(v)}{B(v)}\right)\right] \leq 2\varepsilon^2$$

**Proposition 4 (Convexity of KL Divergence).** *Let $A, B, A_1, B_1, A_2, B_2$ be distributions over a common probability space such that for some $\lambda \in [0,1]$, $A = \lambda A_1 + (1 - \lambda)A_2$ and $B = \lambda B_1 + (1 - \lambda)B_2$. Then*

$$\mathop{\mathbb{E}}_{v \sim A} \left[ \log \left( \frac{A(v)}{B(v)} \right) \right] \leq \lambda \mathop{\mathbb{E}}_{v \sim A_1} \left[ \log \left( \frac{A_1(v)}{B_1(v)} \right) \right] + (1 - \lambda) \mathop{\mathbb{E}}_{v \sim A_2} \left[ \log \left( \frac{A_2(v)}{B_2(v)} \right) \right]$$

**Lemma 18.** *For all $j \in [m]$,*

$$\mathbb{E} \left[ \log \left( \frac{A_j(v_j \mid \mathbf{v}_{<j})}{B_j(v_j \mid \mathbf{v}_{<j})} \right) \right] \leq \frac{9}{(\sigma n)^2}$$

*Proof.* Applying Proposition 3 to Lemmas 15, 16 and 17, we have

$$\mathbb{E} \left[ \log \left( \frac{A_j(v_j \mid \overline{\mathcal{E}}_1, \overline{\mathcal{E}}_2, \mathbf{v}_{<j})}{B_j(v_j \mid \overline{\mathcal{E}}_1, \overline{\mathcal{E}}_2, \mathbf{v}_{<j})} \right) \right] = 0$$

$$\text{and } \mathbb{E} \left[ \log \left( \frac{A_j(v_j \mid \overline{\mathcal{E}}_1, \mathcal{E}_2, \mathbf{v}_{<j})}{B_j(v_j \mid \overline{\mathcal{E}}_1, \mathcal{E}_2, \mathbf{v}_{<j})} \right) \right] \leq \frac{1}{(\sigma n)^2}$$

$$\text{and } \mathbb{E} \left[ \log \left( \frac{A_j(v_j \mid \mathcal{E}_1, \mathcal{E}_2, \mathbf{v}_{<j})}{B_j(v_j \mid \mathcal{E}_1, \mathcal{E}_2, \mathbf{v}_{<j})} \right) \right] \leq \frac{9}{(\sigma n)^2}$$

Then we can express $A_j(v_j \mid \mathbf{v}_{<j})$ as a convex combination in the form

$$\Pr[\overline{\mathcal{E}}_1, \overline{\mathcal{E}}_2 \mid \mathbf{v}_{<j}]A_j(v_j \mid \overline{\mathcal{E}}_1, \overline{\mathcal{E}}_2, \mathbf{v}_{<j}) + \Pr[\overline{\mathcal{E}}_1, \mathcal{E}_2 \mid \mathbf{v}_{<j}]A_j(v_j \mid \overline{\mathcal{E}}_1, \mathcal{E}_2, \mathbf{v}_{<j})$$
$$+ \Pr[\mathcal{E}_1 \mid \mathbf{v}_{<j}]A_j(v_j \mid \mathcal{E}_1, \mathbf{v}_{<j})$$

and express $B_j(v_j \mid \mathbf{v}_{<j})$ similarly. By Proposition 4,

$$\mathbb{E} \left[ \log \left( \frac{A_j(v_j \mid \mathbf{v}_{<j})}{B_j(v_j \mid \mathbf{v}_{<j})} \right) \right] \leq \frac{9}{(\sigma n)^2} \cdot \Pr[\mathcal{E}_1 \vee \mathcal{E}_2 \mid \mathbf{v}_{<j}]$$

The lemma follows the fact that any probability is at most 1.     □

We say a round $j$ is a borderline round if in this round, either $\mathcal{E}_1$ or $\mathcal{E}_2$ occurs. The following lemma gives a bound on the number of borderline round.

**Lemma 19.** *Let $m'$ be the number of borderline rounds in Algorithm 1.*

$$\Pr[m' > n^{1+\theta/3}\ell_k] \leq neg(n)$$

*Proof.* By Lemmas 8 and 14,

$$\Pr\left[j \text{ is a borderline round} \mid j \text{ is Type 1 or Type 2}\right] \geq 1/e$$

Thus, $\mathbb{E}[m'] \leq e \cdot n\ell_k$. Note that the noises added in each round are independent from other rounds. Hence, by Hoeffding's bound, the lemma follows.     □

**Proposition 5 (Azuma's Inequality).** *Let $A_1, \ldots, A_m$ be real-valued random variables such that for every $i \in [m]$,*

1. $\Pr[|A_1| \le \alpha] = 1$, and
2. for every $(a_1, \ldots, a_n) \in \text{Supp}(A_1, \ldots, A_m)$,

$$\mathbb{E}[A_i | A_1 = a_1, \ldots, A_{i-1} = a_{i-1}] \le \beta.$$

Then for any $z > 0$, we have

$$\Pr\left[\sum_{i=1}^{m} A_i > m\beta + z\sqrt{m} \cdot \alpha\right] \le e^{-z^2/2}$$

*Proof (of Lemma 9).* We apply Proposition 5 the set of $m'$ borderline rounds. Let $J \subset [m]$ be the set of borderline rounds. For each $j \in J$, let

$$X_j = \log\left(\frac{A_j(v_j \mid \mathbf{v}_{<j})}{B_j(v_j \mid \mathbf{v}_{<j})}\right).$$

Note that $\mathbb{E}[X_j | \mathbf{v}_{<j}] \le 9/(\sigma n)^2$, $|X_j| \le 3/(\sigma n)$ and $L(\mathbf{v}) = \sum_{j \in J} X_j$. By Proposition 5 (setting $\alpha = 3/(\sigma n)$, $\beta = 9/(\sigma n)^2$ and $z = n^{\theta/7}n$),

$$\Pr[L(\mathbf{v}) > 9m'/(\sigma n)^2 + 3n^{\theta/7}\sqrt{m'}/(\sigma n)] < neg(n)$$

Since $m' \le n^{1+\theta/6}\ell_k$ with probability $1 - neg(n)$, we have

$$9m'/(\sigma n)^2 + 3n^{\theta/7}\sqrt{m'}/(\sigma n) \le \frac{9\ell_k n^{1+\theta/3}}{\ell_k n^{1+2\theta/3}} + \frac{3n^{\theta/7+\theta/6}\sqrt{n\ell_k}}{n^{\theta/3}\sqrt{n\ell_k}} = o(1) \qquad \square$$

# B   Oracle Separation

In this section, we prove that there exists an oracle such that relative to this oracle, there exist one-way functions but no secure traitor tracing systems. Indeed, we show that given an NP-oracle and a random oracle, one can implement the sanitizer designed in Sects. 4 and 5 computationally efficiently (instead of query efficiently as required before). Recall that the sanitizer in Sect. 4 (with modification described in Sect. 5) need to take exponential time to compute the median value. To make it run in polynomial time, we use the NP-oracle to uniformly sample an NP-set by adopting the algorithms in [3,22].

**Proposition 6 ([3]).** *Let $R$ be an NP-relation. Then there is a uniform generator for $R$ which is implementable in probabilistic polynomial time with an NP-oracle.*

By using the above proposition we can prove the following theorem.

**Theorem 7.** *Given an NP-oracle and a random oracle, there is a computationally efficient, accurate and differentially private sanitizer.*

*Proof.* We prove this theorem by implementing the sanitizer designed in Sect. 4 (with modification described in Sect. 5) efficiently. We first show that given an uniform generator for all $\mathcal{D}_j$, one can implement the sanitizer in polynomial time. Then we show how to construct the desired uniform generator by using Proposition 6.

First, we modify the Phase 3 of the sanitizer such that the estimation can be computed in polynomial time. The idea is that, instead of recording all the $\mathcal{D}_j$ and $\mathcal{D}'_j$, we use the uniform generator to sample databases from them uniformly. Indeed, we sample $n$ times from the uniform generator of $\mathcal{D}_j$ and compute $\mathbb{E}_{O \sim \mathcal{O}_{\text{unif}}}[\text{Dec}^O(\mathbf{k}, c_j)]$ where $\mathbf{k}$ is sampled from generator. Note that $\mathbb{E}_{O \sim \mathcal{O}_{\text{unif}}}[\text{Dec}^O(\mathbf{k}, c_j)]$ can be approximately computed efficiently by sampling $O \sim \mathcal{O}_{\text{unif}}$. Let $avg_j$ be the average value of these samples. By Chernoff bound, we have

$$\Pr\left[\left|avg_j - \underset{\mathbf{k} \sim \mathcal{D}_j, O \sim \mathcal{O}_{\text{unif}}}{\mathbb{E}}[\text{Dec}^O(\mathbf{k}, c_j)]\right| > 0.01\right] \leq neg(n)$$

Then we replace $med_j$ by $avg_j$ in the sanitizer. To prove the correctness of the sanitizer, it suffices to show that if $|avg_j - \hat{a}_j| > 0.2$, the size of $\mathcal{D}_j$ is at most $0.9 \cdot |\mathcal{D}_{j-1}|$. Suppose not. We have

$$\left|\underset{\mathbf{k} \sim \mathcal{D}_j, O \sim \mathcal{O}_{\text{unif}}}{\mathbb{E}}[\text{Dec}^O(\mathbf{k}, c_j)] - \hat{a}_j\right| \leq \frac{|\mathcal{D}_{j-1} \setminus \mathcal{D}_j|}{|\mathcal{D}_{j-1}|} \cdot 1 + \frac{|\mathcal{D}_j|}{|\mathcal{D}_{j-1}|} \cdot 0.2 = 0.19$$

that contradicts the triangle inequality. Similar modifications can be made in other phases of the sanitizer to remove the explicit use of $\mathcal{D}_j$.

Finally, we show how to construct such uniform generators for $\mathcal{D}_j$ and $\mathcal{D}'_j$. By Proposition 6, it suffices to define the corresponding NP-relations. We prove this by induction on the round number $j$. For the base case where $j = 1$, we have $\mathcal{D}_{j-1} = \mathcal{D}_0$ is the uniform distribution over all databases. Clearly, this can be sampled without using the NP-oracle. For the inductive step, we define the NP-relation between the databases and the algorithm running histories (including the first $j$ queries and all the random coins used). A database is in the NP-relation if and only if it is in the set $\mathcal{D}_{j-1}$ that is consistent with algorithm running history. In other words, the databases are the witness of histories in the relation. It is easy to see that this relation can be verified in polynomial time. Therefore we get uniform generators for them by Proposition 6.    □

# References

1. Barak, B., Mahmoody-Ghidary, M.: Lower bounds on signatures from symmetric primitives. In: FOCS 2007, pp. 680–688. IEEE (2007)
2. Beck, C., Impagliazzo, R., Lovett, S.: Large deviation bounds for decision trees and sampling lower bounds for $AC_0$-circuits. In: FOCS 2012, pp. 101–110. IEEE (2012)
3. Bellare, M., Goldreich, O., Petrank, E.: Uniform generation of NP-witnesses using an NP-oracle. Inf. Comput. **163**(2), 510–526 (2000)

4. Bellare, M., Rogaway, P.: Random oracles are practical: a paradigm for designing efficient protocols. In: CCS 1993. ACM Request Permissions, December 1993
5. Blum, A., Ligett, K., Roth, A.: A learning theory approach to non-interactive database privacy. In: STOC 2008, New York, USA, p. 609. ACM Request Permissions, New York, May 2008
6. Boneh, D., Franklin, M.: An efficient public key traitor tracing scheme. In: Wiener, M. (ed.) CRYPTO 1999. LNCS, vol. 1666, pp. 338–353. Springer, Heidelberg (1999). doi:10.1007/3-540-48405-1_22
7. Boneh, D., Naor, M.: Traitor tracing with constant size ciphertext. In: CCS 2008, pp. 501–510. ACM (2008)
8. Boneh, D., Sahai, A., Waters, B.: Fully collusion resistant traitor tracing with short ciphertexts and private keys. In: Vaudenay, S. (ed.) EUROCRYPT 2006. LNCS, vol. 4004, pp. 573–592. Springer, Heidelberg (2006). doi:10.1007/11761679_34
9. Boneh, D., Zhandry, M.: Multiparty key exchange, efficient traitor tracing, and more from indistinguishability obfuscation. In: Garay, J.A., Gennaro, R. (eds.) CRYPTO 2014. LNCS, vol. 8616, pp. 480–499. Springer, Heidelberg (2014). doi:10.1007/978-3-662-44371-2_27
10. Canetti, R., Goldreich, O., Halevi, S.: The random oracle methodology, revisited. In: STOC 1998, pp. 209–218. ACM (1998)
11. Chor, B., Fiat, A., Naor, M.: Tracing traitors. In: Desmedt, Y.G. (ed.) CRYPTO 1994. LNCS, vol. 839, pp. 257–270. Springer, Heidelberg (1994). doi:10.1007/3-540-48658-5_25
12. Dwork, C., McSherry, F., Nissim, K., Smith, A.: Calibrating noise to sensitivity in private data analysis. In: Halevi, S., Rabin, T. (eds.) TCC 2006. LNCS, vol. 3876, pp. 265–284. Springer, Heidelberg (2006). doi:10.1007/11681878_14
13. Dwork, C., Naor, M., Reingold, O., Rothblum, G.N., Vadhan, S.: On the complexity of differentially private data release. In: STOC 2009, pp. 381–390. ACM Press, New York (2009)
14. Dwork, C., Rothblum, G.N., Vadhan, S.: Boosting and differential privacy. In: FOCS 2010, pp. 51–60. IEEE (2010)
15. Fiat, A., Tassa, T.: Dynamic traitor tracing. In: Wiener, M. (ed.) CRYPTO 1999. LNCS, vol. 1666, pp. 354–371. Springer, Heidelberg (1999). doi:10.1007/3-540-48405-1_23
16. Garg, S., Gentry, C., Halevi, S., Raykova, M., Sahai, A., Waters, B.: Candidate indistinguishability obfuscation and functional encryption for all circuits. In: FOCS 2013, pp. 40–49. IEEE (2013)
17. Gavinsky, D., Lovett, S., Saks, M., Srinivasan, S.: A tail bound for read-k families of functions. Random Struct. Algorithms 47(1), 99–108 (2015)
18. Gennaro, R., Gertner, Y., Katz, J., Trevisan, L.: Bounds on the efficiency of generic cryptographic constructions. SIAM J. Comput. 35(1), 217–246 (2005)
19. Gertner, Y., Kannan, S., Malkin, T., Reingold, O., Viswanathan, M.: The relationship between public key encryption and oblivious transfer. In: FOCS 2000, pp. 325–335. IEEE (2000)
20. Hardt, M., Rothblum, G.N.: A multiplicative weights mechanism for privacy-preserving data analysis. In: FOCS 2010, pp. 61–70. IEEE (2010)
21. Impagliazzo, R., Rudich, S.: Limits on the provable consequences of one-way permutations. In: STOC 1989, pp. 44–61. ACM Request Permissions, New York, February 1989
22. Jerrum, M.R., Valiant, L.G., Vazirani, V.V.: Random generation of combinatorial structures from a uniform distribution. Theor. Comput. Sci. 43, 169–188 (1986)

23. Kahn, J., Saks, M., Smyth, C.: A dual version of Reimer's inequality and a proof of Rudich's conjecture. In: CCC 2000, pp. 98–103. IEEE (2000)
24. Kiayias, A., Yung, M.: On crafty pirates and foxy tracers. In: Sander, T. (ed.) DRM 2001. LNCS, vol. 2320, pp. 22–39. Springer, Heidelberg (2002). doi:10.1007/3-540-47870-1_3
25. Kim, J.H., Simon, D.R., Tetali, P.: Limits on the efficiency of one-way permutation-based hash functions. In: FOCS 1999, p. 535. IEEE Computer Society, Washington, D.C. (1999)
26. Lamport, L.: Constructing digital signatures from a one-way function. Technical report, October 1979
27. McSherry, F., Talwar, K.: Mechanism design via differential privacy. In: FOCS 2007, pp. 94–103. IEEE (2007)
28. Naor, D., Naor, M., Lotspiech, J.: Revocation and tracing schemes for stateless receivers. In: Kilian, J. (ed.) CRYPTO 2001. LNCS, vol. 2139, pp. 41–62. Springer, Heidelberg (2001). doi:10.1007/3-540-44647-8_3
29. Reingold, O., Trevisan, L., Vadhan, S.: Notions of reducibility between cryptographic primitives. In: Naor, M. (ed.) TCC 2004. LNCS, vol. 2951, pp. 1–20. Springer, Heidelberg (2004). doi:10.1007/978-3-540-24638-1_1
30. Roth, A., Roughgarden, T.: Interactive privacy via the median mechanism. In: STOC 2010, pp. 765–774. ACM Request Permissions, New York, June 2010
31. Safavi-Naini, R., Wang, Y.: Sequential traitor tracing. In: Bellare, M. (ed.) CRYPTO 2000. LNCS, vol. 1880, pp. 316–332. Springer, Heidelberg (2000). doi:10.1007/3-540-44598-6_20
32. Ullman, J.: Answering $n^{2+o(1)}$ counting queries with differential privacy is hard. In: STOC 2013. ACM Request Permissions, June 2013

# On the Impossibility of Entropy Reversal, and Its Application to Zero-Knowledge Proofs

Shachar Lovett$^{(\boxtimes)}$ and Jiapeng Zhang

University of California, San Diego, USA
slovett@cs.ucsd.edu, jpeng.zhang@gmail.com

**Abstract.** Zero knowledge proof systems have been widely studied in cryptography. In the statistical setting, two classes of proof systems studied are Statistical Zero Knowledge (SZK) and Non-Interactive Statistical Zero Knowledge (NISZK), where the difference is that in NISZK only very limited communication is allowed between the verifier and the prover. It is an open problem whether these two classes are in fact equal. In this paper, we rule out efficient black box reductions between SZK and NISZK.

We achieve this by studying algorithms which can reverse the entropy of a function. The problem of estimating the entropy of a circuit is complete for NISZK. Hence, reversing the entropy of a function is equivalent to a black box reduction of NISZK to its complement, which is known to be equivalent to a black box reduction of SZK to NISZK [Goldreich et al. CRYPTO 1999]. We show that any such black box algorithm incurs an exponential loss of parameters, and hence cannot be implemented efficiently.

**Keywords:** Entropy reversal · Statistical zero-knowledge proofs · Black-box reductions

## 1 Introduction

The notion of *Zero-Knowledge Proof Systems* was introduced in the seminal paper of Goldwasser et al. [11]. Informally, an interactive proof system is a protocol that involves a computational unbounded prover $P$ and a polynomial time verifier $V$. The prover attempts to convince the verifier that an assertion is a YES instance $x$ of some promise problem.

A promise problem $\Pi$ consists of two disjoint sets $\Pi_Y$ and $\Pi_N$, e.g., yes instances and no instances. A zero-knowledge proof system for the problem $\Pi$ requires the following three conditions:

- *Completeness:* If $x \in \Pi_Y$, then $\Pr[(P, V)(x)$ accepts$] \geq 2/3$.
- *Soundness:* If $x \in \Pi_N$, then for every adversary $P^*$, $\Pr[(P^*, V)(x)$ accepts$] \leq 1/3$.

S. Lovett and J. Zhang—Research supported by NSF CAREER award 1350481.

Y. Kalai and L. Reyzin (Eds.): TCC 2017, Part I, LNCS 10677, pp. 31–55, 2017.
https://doi.org/10.1007/978-3-319-70500-2_2

– *Zero-knowledge:* There is a polynomial time simulator $S$ such that $S(x)$ and $(P, V)(x)$ are "indistinguishable", for every $x \in \Pi_Y$.

Different zero knowledge proof systems differ in the allowed communication protocol, and in the notion of indistinguishability applied to the simulator. In this paper, we restrict our attention to statistical proof systems (SZK and NISZK), where the corresponding notion is that of statistical indistinguishability.

*Statistical zero knowledge (SZK).* The complexity class SZK consists of the problems that have a statistical zero-knowledge proof, where any efficient interactive communication is allowed between the verifier and the prover. Surprisingly, there are complete problems for SZK which have nothing to do with interaction. This was first discovered by Sahai and Vadhan [17].

A distribution $D$ over $\{0,1\}^m$ is said to be *efficiently sampleable* if there exists a polynomial size boolean circuit $C : \{0,1\}^n \to \{0,1\}^m$, such that the distribution $D$ can be obtained by applying $C$ to uniformly sampled input bits. By an abuse of notation, we identify $C$ with this distribution. Given two distributions $C_1, C_2$ over $\{0,1\}^m$, we denote by $\mathrm{dist}(C_1, C_2)$ their statistical distance. The following problem, called *Statistical Difference*, was shown by Sahai and Vadhan [17] to be complete for SZK.

**Definition 1 (Statistical Difference [17]).** *The promise problem* Statistical Difference, *denoted by* $\mathrm{SD} = (\mathrm{SD}_Y, \mathrm{SD}_N)$, *consists of*

– $\mathrm{SD}_Y = \{(C_1, C_2) : \mathrm{dist}(C_1, C_2) \leq 1/3\}$
– $\mathrm{SD}_N = \{(C_1, C_2) : \mathrm{dist}(C_1, C_2) \geq 2/3\}$

*Here* $C_1, C_2$ *denote polynomial size circuits with the same output length.*

**Theorem 1 [17].** SD *is* SZK-*complete.*

In a follow up work, Goldreich and Vadhan [10] gave another SZK-complete problem, called *Entropy Difference*. Below, $\mathrm{H}(C)$ denotes the Shannon entropy of the distribution induced by $C$.

**Definition 2 (Entropy Difference [10]).** *The promise problem* Entropy Difference, *denoted by* $\mathrm{ED} = (\mathrm{ED}_Y, \mathrm{ED}_N)$, *consists of*

– $\mathrm{ED}_Y = \{(C_1, C_2) : \mathrm{H}(C_1) \geq \mathrm{H}(C_2) + 1\}$
– $\mathrm{ED}_N = \{(C_1, C_2) : \mathrm{H}(C_2) \geq \mathrm{H}(C_1) + 1\}$

*Here* $C_1, C_2$ *denote polynomial size circuits with the same output length.*

**Theorem 2 [10].** *The problem* ED *is* SZK-*complete.*

This in particular gives a slick proof to the fact that SZK is closed under complement, which might be hard to guess from the original definition. Given an input $(C_1, C_2)$ to ED, one can simply reverse their order.

*Non-interactive statistical zero knowledge (NISZK).* The notion of *Non-Interactive Zero-Knowledge Proof Systems*, or NISZK was introduced by Blum et al. [2], allows for very restricted communication between the verifier and the prover. Both parties share a common uniformly random string (a random challenge), and the prover sends a single message to the verifier based on this random challenge.

Since the model has been introduced, several problems have been shown to be in NISZK. Originally these were problems arising in number theory, such as Quadratic Nonresiduosity and its variants [1,2,4,6,7]. More recently, this was extended to several natural problems in lattices [16].

The problem of finding complete problems for NISZK arose naturally. De Santis et al. [5], introduced a problem called *Image Density*, and proved that is complete for NISZK. Subsequently, Goldreich et al. [9] studied the following two problems and showed that they too are complete for NISZK.

**Definition 3 (Statistical Difference from Uniform [9]).** *The promise problem* Statistical Difference from Uniform, *denoted by* $\mathrm{SDU} = (\mathrm{SDU}_Y, \mathrm{SDU}_N)$, *consists of*

- $\mathrm{SDU}_Y = \{C : \mathrm{dist}(C, \mathcal{U}) \leq 1/n\}$
- $\mathrm{SDU}_N = \{C : \mathrm{dist}(C, \mathcal{U}) \geq 1 - 1/n\}$

*Here $C$ denotes a polynomial size circuit which outputs $n$ bits, and $\mathcal{U}$ denotes the uniform distribution on $\{0,1\}^n$.*

**Definition 4 (Entropy Approximation [9]).** *The promise problem* Entropy Approximation, *denoted by* $\mathrm{EA} = (\mathrm{EA}_Y, \mathrm{EA}_N)$, *consists of*

- $\mathrm{EA}_Y = \{(C, k) : \mathrm{H}(C) \geq k + 1\}$
- $\mathrm{EA}_N = \{(C, k) : \mathrm{H}(C) \leq k - 1\}$

*Here $C$ denotes a polynomial size circuit and $k \geq 1$ is an integer parameter.*

**Theorem 3 [9].** SDU *and* EA *are NISZK-complete.*

The main open problem that motivated the current paper is *what is the relationship between* NISZK *and* SZK. Goldreich et al. [9] made a significant progress towards resolving this problem.

**Theorem 4 [9].** *The following statements are equivalent:*

(1). SZK = NISZK.
(2). NISZK *is closed under complement.*
(3). NISZK *is closed under* $NC^1$ *truth-table reductions.*
(4). ED, *or* SD *Karp-reduces to* EA, *or* SDU *respectively.*
(5). EA *or* SDU *Karp-reduces to its complement.*

The main goal of the current paper is to show that these statements are all false, at least in a limited model of computation. Concretely, our goal is to rule out *black box reductions* between NISZK and its complement. When we consider black box reductions, the notion of efficient computation disappears, and we replace the study of circuits with the study of arbitrary functions (which can be seen as oracle functions).

## 1.1   Black-Box Reductions

We describe the notion of black box reductions of functions in this section.

Let $\mathcal{F}_{n,m}$ denote the family of functions $f : \{0,1\}^n \to \{0,1\}^m$. A promise problem $\Pi$ over $\mathcal{F}_{n,m}$ consists of a family of yes instances $\Pi_Y$ and a family of no instances $\Pi_N$, where $\Pi_Y, \Pi_N \subset \mathcal{F}_{n,m}$ and $\Pi_Y \cap \Pi_N = \emptyset$.

**Definition 5 (Black-Box Reduction).** *Let $\Pi = (\Pi_Y, \Pi_N)$ and $\Pi' = (\Pi'_Y, \Pi'_N)$ be promise problems over functions $\mathcal{F}_{n,m}$ and $\mathcal{F}_{n',m'}$, respectively. a black-box reduction from $\Pi$ to $\Pi'$ is an algorithm $A^{(\cdot)} : \{0,1\}^{n'} \to \{0,1\}^{m'}$ with oracle access to a function $f \in \mathcal{F}_{n,m}$, such that the following holds:*

- *If $f \in \Pi_Y$ then $A^f \in \Pi'_Y$.*
- *If $f \in \Pi_N$ then $A^f \in \Pi'_N$.*

*Given an input $w \in \{0,1\}^{n'}$, the algorithm makes a number of queries to $f$ (the query locations may depend on $w$ and be adaptive), and outputs a value $z \in \{0,1\}^{m'}$. We define $A^f(w) = z$. The query complexity of $A$, denoted $QC(A)$, is the maximal number of queries to $f$ performed over an input.*

Our definition of black-box reduction does not relate to decidability, and instead relates to functionality. This type of black-box reduction is well studied in cryptography. Many reductions in the literature are in fact black-box reductions. Examples include the the flatting lemma of [9], the polarization lemma of [17], the reduction from Statistical Difference to its complement [17], constructions of pseudorandom generators from one-way functions [12,13], constructions of pseudorandom functions from pseudorandom generators [8], and many more.

## 1.2   Our Results

We define the function version of the Entropy Approximation (EA) problem.

**Definition 6 (Function Entropy Approximation).** *The promise problem Function Entropy Approximation, denoted by $\text{FEA} = (\text{FEA}_Y, \text{FEA}_N)$, consists of*

- $\text{FEA}_Y = \{(f,k) : \text{H}(f) \geq k+1\}$
- $\text{FEA}_N = \{(f,k) : \text{H}(f) \leq k-1\}$

*Here $n, m, k \geq 1$ and $f \in \mathcal{F}_{n,m}$. Note that the interesting regime of parameters (where the problem is not trivial) is when $1 \leq k \leq n-1$.*

A black box reduction from NISZK to its complement needs to map FEA to its complement. In particular, an efficient reduction would stay efficient even if we fix $n, m, k$ to favourable values (we will later set $m = 3n$, $k = n-3$). We call such a reduction an *Entropy Reverser*.

**Definition 7 (Entropy Reverser).** *Let $n, m, k, n', m', k' \geq 1$. An $(n, m, k; n', m', k')$ entropy reverser is a black box reduction $A$ from $\mathcal{F}_{n,m}$ to $\mathcal{F}_{n',m'}$ such that*

- *If $H(f) \geq k + 1$ then $H(A^f) \leq k' - 1$.*
- *If $H(f) \leq k - 1$ then $H(A^f) \geq k' + 1$.*

Our main result is that entropy reversers require either exponential output length $n', m'$ or exponential query complexity. In particular, when they are applied to a function $f$ computed by a polynomial size circuit, their output $A^f$ is computed by an exponential size circuit. We state and prove our result for a concrete setting of parameters $m = 3n$, $k = n - 3$. We note that our work can be extended to a much wider set of parameters. However, we did not see any applications of pursuing this.

**Theorem 5 (Main theorem).** *Let $A$ be an $(n, m, k; n', m', k')$ Entropy Reverser for $m = 3n, k = n - 3$. Then $QC(A) \geq 2^{n/5}/poly(n', m')$.*

### 1.3 Related Works

Relations between zero knowledge proofs have been previously studied [14,18], where certain black box reductions were ruled out. However, previous works only ruled out restricted forms of black box reductions, where the only access to a function $f$ is via independent and uniform samples. In particular, these reductions are non adaptive. We note that this is a much weaker notion of black box reductions, and indeed some of the black box reductions we already mentioned (e.g. the reduction from Statistical Difference to its complement [17]) require the ability to correlate inputs. As far as we know, ours is the first work in this context which rules out general black box reductions without any restriction on the access pattern or adaptivity.

### 1.4 Proof Overview

Let $n \geq 1$ and fix $m = 3n, k = n - 3$.

The first step in our proof is to apply a black box reduction of Goldreich et al. [9], which converts high/low entropy distributions to distributions which are close to uniform, or supported on a small set, respectively (Lemma 1). This allows us to assume stronger properties of the functions generated by the supposed Entropy Reverser. Concretely, that we are given a black box reduction $A$ from $\mathcal{F}_{n,m}$ to $\mathcal{F}_{n',m'}$ such that:

- If $H(f) \geq k + 1$ then $A^f$ is distributed close to uniform (concretely, $\mathrm{dist}(A^f, \mathcal{U}) \leq 0.1$).
- If $H(f) \leq k - 1$ then the distribution of $A^f$ is supported on a small set (concretely, of size $\leq 0.1 \cdot 2^{m'}$).

As this black box reduction is efficient, it incurs a blowup of only $poly(n', m')$ in the query complexity. See Sect. 3.1 for the details. From now on, we focus on this stronger notion of an Entropy Reverser, and show that for it it holds that $QC(A) \geq \Omega(2^{n/5})$.

Next, we consider several distributions over functions $\mathcal{F}_{n,m}$. Fix $b = 256$. We denote by $\mathbf{B} = (B_1, \ldots, B_s)$ a partition of the input space $\{0,1\}^n$ into $s$ blocks, each of size $b$. For $0 \le j \le s$ we define a distribution $\mathcal{D}_j$ over $\mathcal{F}_{n,m}$ as follows:

- Sample a random partition $\mathbf{B} = (B_1, \ldots, B_s)$ of $\{0,1\}^n$.
- Sample $y_1, \ldots, y_j \in \{0,1\}^m$ uniformly and independently.
- If $x \in B_i$, $i \le j$ then set $f_j(x) = y_i$.
- If $x \in B_i$, $i > j$ then sample $f_j(x) \in \{0,1\}^m$ uniformly and independently.

It is not hard to show that as $j$ increases, the entropy of $f_j \sim \mathcal{D}_j$ decreases. Concretely, we show (Claim 3.2) that with very high probability it holds that

$$\mathrm{H}(f_{s/4}) = n - 2, \qquad \mathrm{H}(f_{s/2}) = n - 4.$$

Thus, by the assumptions of our Entropy Reverser (as we set $k = n-3$), it should hold that $A^{f_{s/4}}$ is supported on a small set, while $A^{f_{s/2}}$ is distributed close to uniform. We show that this requires exponential query complexity. From now onwards, let $q = \mathrm{QC}(A)$ denote this query complexity.

Let $z \in \{0,1\}^{m'}$ be chosen uniformly, and let $p_j$ for $0 \le j \le s$ denote the probability that $z$ belongs to the support of $A^{f_j}$:

$$p_j = \Pr[\exists w \in \{0,1\}^{n'}, \; z = A^{f_j}(w)].$$

By our assumptions, $p_{s/2} \ge 0.9$ while $p_{s/4} \le 0.1$. Our goal is to apply a hybrid argument and show that if $q$ is small then $p_{j-1} \approx p_j$ for all $s/4 \le j \le s/2$.

We can couple the choice of $f_{j-1}, f_j$, so that we jointly sample $\mathbf{B}, y_1, \ldots, y_j$, and the only difference between $f_{j-1}$ and $f_j$ is that they differ on the block $B_j$ ($f_{j-1}$ maps each point in $B_j$ to a uniformly chosen point in $\{0,1\}^{m'}$, while $f_j$ maps all the points in $B_j$ to a single point). As the partition to blocks is random, the probability that a specific query belongs to the block $B_j$ is $1/s$. As the algorithm makes $q$ queries, this should "intuitively" give the bound

$$p_j - p_{j-1} \le \frac{q}{s}.$$

(we say "intuitively" as the black box reduction is an adaptive algorithm, while the above analysis works straightforwardly only for non-adaptive algorithms). However, such a bound is useless for us, as we need to apply it $\Omega(s)$ times. Thus, we need a more refined analysis.

In order to do so, let $f \in \{f_{j-1}, f_j\}$. We say that an input $w$ to $A^f$ respects the block structure of $\mathbf{B}$ if any block $B_i$ in $\mathbf{B}$ is queried at most once by $A^f(w)$. Intuitively, such an input should not be able to "distinguish" between $f_{j-1}$ and $f_j$. On the other hand, the probability over a random partition that any two fixed points belong to $B_j$ is $\approx 1/s^2$, and hence as there are $q$ queries, this should "intuitively" give an improved bound of

$$p_j - p_{j-1} \le \frac{q^2}{s^2}.$$

If such a bound is indeed true, then applying it $(s/2) - (s/4) = s/4$ times would give that $|p_{s/4} - p_{s/2}| \leq O(q^2/s)$, which would imply that $q^2 \geq \Omega(s) = \Omega(2^n)$, and hence we obtain an exponential lower bound on $q$.

Formalizing this intuition turns out to be quite delicate, as the algorithm $A^f$ is an adaptive algorithm, and hence various choices are dependent on each other. Our main technical Lemma (Lemma 3) show that, if we restrict our attention to inputs which respect the block structure and define

$$p'_j = \Pr[\exists w \in \{0,1\}^{n'}, z = A^{f_j}(w), w \text{ respects the block structure of } \mathbf{B}]$$

then $p'_j$ is a good proxy for $p_j$ (Lemma 2), for which a better bound can be obtained:

$$p'_j - p'_{j-1} \leq O\left(\frac{q^{5/3}}{s^{4/3}}\right).$$

While this bound is worse than the "intuitive" bound of $q^2/s^2$, it still suffices for our purposes, as when we apply it $\Theta(s)$ times we obtain that $p'_{s/2} - p'_{s/4} \leq O(q^{5/3}/s^{1/3})$ and hence we still get an exponential lower bound on $q$, namely $q \geq \Omega(2^{n/5})$.

*Paper organization.* We give some preliminary definitions in Sect. 2. In Sect. 3 we formalize the above proof overview, and give the proof of our main theorem, Theorem 5, assuming our main technical lemma, Lemma 3. The proof of Lemma 3 is given in Sect. 4. We conclude with some open problems in Sect. 5.

## 2   Preliminaries

Let $\mathcal{F}_{n,m}$ denote the family of functions $f : \{0,1\}^n \rightarrow \{0,1\}^m$. A *black box reduction* from $\mathcal{F}_{n,m}$ to $\mathcal{F}_{n',m'}$ with is an algorithm which, given query access to $f \in \mathcal{F}_{n,m}$, computes a function $A^f \in \mathcal{F}_{n',m'}$ as follows. Given an input $w \in \{0,1\}^{n'}$, the algorithm makes a number of queries to $f$ (the query locations can depend on $w$ and be adaptive), and outputs a value $z \in \{0,1\}^{m'}$. We define $A^f(w) = z$. The query complexity of $A$ is the maximum number of queries to $f$ performed over an input, which we denote by $\mathrm{QC}(A)$.

Let $X$ be a random variable taking values in $\{0,1\}^m$. We recall some basic definitions. The support of $X$ is $\mathrm{supp}(X) = \{x : \Pr[X = x] > 0\}$. The Shannon entropy of $X$ is

$$\mathrm{H}(X) = \sum_x \Pr[X = x] \cdot \log_2(1/\Pr[X = x]).$$

The statistical distance of two random variables $X, Y$ is

$$\mathrm{dist}(X, Y) = \tfrac{1}{2} \sum_x |\Pr[X = x] - \Pr[Y = x]|.$$

We denote by $\mathcal{U}_m$ the uniform distribution over $\{0,1\}^m$.

We will identify $f \in \mathcal{F}_{n,m}$ with the random variable of its output distribution in $\{0,1\}^m$, given a uniformly sampled input in $\{0,1\}^n$. As such, we extend the definition of support, Shannon entropy and statistical distance to functions. In the special case where $f$ is computable by a circuit $C : \{0,1\}^n \to \{0,1\}^m$ of size poly($m$), we say that this distribution is an *efficiently sampleable distribution*.

## 3  Proof of Main Theorem: Theorem 5

### 3.1  A Useful Reduction

As a first step towards proving Theorem 5, we make use of a black box reduction of Goldreich et al. [9]. It allows us to strengthen the assumptions in Theorem 5.

**Lemma 1** [9]. *Let $n', m', k' \geq 1$. There exists a black box reduction $A_1$ from $\mathcal{F}_{n',m'}$ to $\mathcal{F}_{n'',m''}$, where $n'', m'', QC(A_1) \leq poly(n', m')$, such that the following holds for any $f \in \mathcal{F}_{n',m'}$:*

- *If $H(f) \geq k' + 1$ then $\mathrm{dist}(A_1^f, \mathcal{U}_{m''}) \leq 0.1$.*
- *If $H(f) \leq k' - 1$ then $|\mathrm{supp}(A_1^f)| \leq 0.1 \cdot 2^{m''}$.*

Let $A_5$ denote the black box reduction from $\mathcal{F}_{n,m}$ to $\mathcal{F}_{n',m'}$ assumed in Theorem 5. Let $A_1$ denote the black box from $\mathcal{F}_{n',m'}$ to $\mathcal{F}_{n'',m''}$ given in Lemma 1. Let $A$ be their composition. Namely, $A$ is a black box reduction from $\mathcal{F}_{n,m}$ to $\mathcal{F}_{n'',m''}$, obtained by first applying $A_5$ and then $A_1$. That is,

$$A^f = A_1^{A_5^f}.$$

Observe that $QC(A) \leq QC(A_5)QC(A_1) \leq QC(A_5)poly(n', m')$, that $n'', m'' \leq poly(n', m')$, and that $A$ satisfies the following:

- If $H(f) \geq k + 1$ then $|\mathrm{supp}(A^f)| \leq 0.1 \cdot 2^{m''}$.
- If $H(f) \leq k - 1$ then $\mathrm{dist}(A^f, \mathcal{U}_{m''}) \leq 0.1$.

We will prove a lower bound on the query complexity of $A$, which would then imply a lower bound on the query complexity of $A_5$.

### 3.2  Preparations

In order to prove Theorem 5, we will exhibit two distributions over functions, one of high entropy functions, the other of low entropy functions, and show that black box reductions with low query complexity cannot "reverse" the entropy relation between them.

**Definition 8 (Sample distribution).** *Let $n, m \geq 1$ and let $b \geq 2$ be a parameter (block size) to be determined later, and set $s = 2^n/b$. We denote by $\mathbf{B} = (B_1, \ldots, B_s)$ a partition of $\{0,1\}^n$ into $s$ blocks of equal size $2^n/s = b$. For any $0 \leq j \leq s$ we define a distribution over partitions $\mathbf{B}$ and functions $f_j \in \mathcal{F}_{n,m}$ as follows:*

- *Sample a random partition $\mathbf{B} = (B_1, \ldots, B_s)$ of $\{0,1\}^n$.*
- *Sample $y_1, \ldots, y_j \in \{0,1\}^m$ uniformly and independently.*
- *If $x \in B_i$, $i \leq j$ then set $f_j(x) = y_i$.*
- *If $x \in B_i$, $i > j$ then sample $f_j(x) \in \{0,1\}^m$ uniformly and independently.*

We denote the joint distribution of $(\mathbf{B}, f_j)$ as $\mathcal{D}_j$. With an abuse of notation, when we write $f_j \sim \mathcal{D}_j$, we simply omit the block structure from the sample. Note that $f_0 \sim \mathcal{D}_0$ is uniformly distributed over $\mathcal{F}_{n,m}$. The following simple claim argues that as we increase $j$, the entropy of $f_j \sim \mathcal{D}_j$ decreases. It is specialized to our desired application.

*Claim.* Let $m = 3n$. Sample $f_j \sim \mathcal{D}_j$. Then with probability $1 - 2^{-n}$ over the choice of $f_j$, it holds that

$$\mathrm{H}(f_j) = n - (j/s) \log b.$$

In particular, if we set $b = 256$ then

$$\mathrm{H}(f_{s/4}) = n - 2, \qquad \mathrm{H}(f_{s/2}) = n - 4.$$

*Proof.* Let $0 \leq j \leq s$ and sample $f_j \sim \mathcal{D}_j$. Let $y_1, \ldots, y_j$ be the single value that $f_j$ obtains on blocks $B_1, \ldots, B_j$. Consider $y_1, \ldots, y_j, (f_j(x) : x \in B_i, i > j)$. Lets denote by $E_0$ the event that no two values in this list collide. The probability that any two of these values are equal is $2^{-m}$. As there are $\leq 2^n$ values, the probability that any two intersect is bounded by $2^{2n-m} \leq 2^{-n}$. Thus $\Pr[E_0] \geq 1 - 2^{-n}$.

Lets assume that $E_0$ holds. Then, the distribution of $f_j$ is as follows: there are $j$ values (namely, $y_1, \ldots, y_j$) that each is obtained with probability $1/s = b/2^n$. All other $2^n - bj$ values are each obtained with probability $2^{-n}$. Thus

$$\mathrm{H}(f_j | E_0) = j \cdot (b/2^n) \cdot \log(2^n/b) + (2^n - bj) \cdot 2^{-n} \cdot \log(2^n) = n - (j/s) \log b.$$

We treat $\mathcal{D}_{s/4}$ as a distribution over (mostly) high entropy functions, and $\mathcal{D}_{s/2}$ as a distribution over (mostly) lower entropy functions.

### 3.3   Block Compatible Inputs

Given $w \in \{0,1\}^{n''}$ and $f \in \mathcal{F}_{n,m}$, we denote by $\mathrm{Query}(A^f(w)) \subset \{0,1\}^n$ the set of inputs of $f$ queried by $A^f$ on input $w$. To recall, the functions that we focus attention on are defined together with a block structure $\mathbf{B} = (B_1, \ldots, B_s)$. Below, we specialize our attention to inputs and their corresponding outputs, for which at most one value in each block is queried.

**Definition 9 (Block compatible inputs).** *Let* $\mathbf{B} = (B_1, \ldots, B_s)$ *be a partition of* $\{0,1\}^n$, $f : \{0,1\}^n \to \{0,1\}^m$. *We say that* $w \in \{0,1\}^{n''}$ *is a block compatible input with respect to* $(f, \mathbf{B})$ *if, when computing* $A^f(w)$, *each block of* $\mathbf{B}$ *is queried at most once. We denote by* $I(f, \mathbf{B})$ *the set of all block compatible inputs:*

$$I(f, \mathbf{B}) = \{w \in \{0,1\}^{n''} : |Query(A^f(w)) \cap B_i| \leq 1 \quad \forall i = 1, \ldots, s\}$$

**Definition 10 (Block compatible outputs).** *Let* $\mathbf{B}$ *be a partition of* $\{0,1\}^n$, $f : \{0,1\}^n \to \{0,1\}^m$. *We say that* $z \in \{0,1\}^{m''}$ *is a block compatible output with respect to* $(f, \mathbf{B})$ *if* $A^f(w) = z$ *for a block compatible input* $w$. *We denote by* $O(f, \mathbf{B})$ *the set of all block compatible inputs:*

$$O(f, \mathbf{B}) = \{z \in \{0,1\}^{m''} : \exists w \in I(f, \mathbf{B}), A^f(w) = z\}.$$

Observe that the definition of $I(f, \mathbf{B}), O(f, \mathbf{B})$ does not depend on the order of the blocks in $\mathbf{B}$. This will turn out to be crucial later on in the analysis. Thus, for $\mathbf{B} = (B_1, \ldots, B_s)$ define $\{\mathbf{B}\} = \{B_1, \ldots, B_s\}$ (that is, forgetting the order of the blocks) and note that

$$I(f, \mathbf{B}) = I(f, \{\mathbf{B}\}) \qquad O(f, \mathbf{B}) = O(f, \{\mathbf{B}\}).$$

It is obvious that $O(f, \mathbf{B}) \subset \text{supp}(A^f)$. Next, we argue that if the distribution of $A^{f_j}$ is close to uniform, then $O(f_j, \mathbf{B})$ is large.

**Lemma 2.** *Sample* $(\mathbf{B}, f_j) \sim \mathcal{D}_j$, *and assume that*

$$\Pr_{f_j} \left[ \text{dist}(A^{f_j}, \mathcal{U}_{m''}) \leq \varepsilon \right] \geq 1 - \delta.$$

*Then*

$$\mathbb{E}[|O(f_j, \mathbf{B})|] \geq \left(1 - \frac{q^2}{s} - \varepsilon - 3\delta\right) 2^{m''}.$$

*Proof.* We first argue that for each fixed $w$,

$$\Pr_{(\mathbf{B}, f_j) \sim \mathcal{D}_j} [w \in I(f_j, \mathbf{B})] \geq 1 - \frac{q^2}{s}.$$

To see that, let $Q = \{(x_1, y_1, \ldots, x_q, y_q)\} \subset \{0,1\}^{q(n+m)}$ be all possible queries and answers made by $A^f(w)$. That is, $x_1 = x_1(w)$ is the first query made. If $f(x_1) = y_1$ then $x_2$ is the second query made, and so on. Note that each $x_i$ is determined by $w, x_1, y_1, \ldots, x_{i-1}, y_{i-1}$, while $y_i$ can take any value in $\{0,1\}^m$. In particular, $|Q| = 2^{mq}$.

Next, fix $x_1, \ldots, x_q$ and let $\mathbf{B}$ be a randomly chosen partition. Then

$$\Pr_{\mathbf{B}}[x_1, \ldots, x_q \text{ in distinct blocks}] \geq 1 - \sum_{i \neq j} \Pr_{\mathbf{B}}[x_i, x_j \text{ in the same block}] \geq 1 - \frac{q^2}{s}.$$

Note that if $x_1, \ldots, x_q$ are in distinct blocks, then $f_j(x_1), \ldots, f_j(x_q)$ are independently and uniformly chosen in $\{0,1\}^m$. Thus

$$\Pr_{(\mathbf{B}, f_j) \sim \mathcal{D}_j} [w \in I(f_j, \mathbf{B})]$$

$$= \sum_{(x_1, y_1, \ldots, x_q, y_q) \in Q} \Pr[w \in I(f_j, \mathbf{B}) \wedge f_j(x_1) = y_1 \wedge \ldots \wedge f_j(x_q) = y_q]$$

$$= \sum_{(x_1, y_1, \ldots, x_q, y_q) \in Q} \Pr[x_1, \ldots, x_q \text{ in distinct blocks} \wedge f_j(x_1) = y_1 \wedge \ldots \wedge f_j(x_q) = y_q]$$

$$= \sum_{(x_1, y_1, \ldots, x_q, y_q) \in Q} \Pr[x_1, \ldots, x_q \text{ in distinct blocks}] \cdot$$

$$\Pr[f_j(x_1) = y_1 \wedge \ldots \wedge f_j(x_q) = y_q | x_1, \ldots, x_q \text{ in distinct blocks}]$$

$$\geq \sum_{(x_1, y_1, \ldots, x_q, y_q) \in Q} \left(1 - \frac{q^2}{s}\right) 2^{-mq}$$

$$= 1 - \frac{q^2}{s}.$$

We next consider $O(f_j, \mathbf{B})$. Recall that we assume that the distribution of $A^{f_j}$ is $\varepsilon$-close in statistical distance to the uniform distribution $\mathcal{U}_{m''}$. Let $w \in \{0,1\}^{n''}$ be chosen uniformly and consider the random variable $z = A^{f_j}(w)$. We have

$$\Pr_{(\mathbf{B}, f_j) \sim \mathcal{D}_j, w \in \{0,1\}^{n''}} [z \in O(f_j, \mathbf{B})] \geq \Pr[w \in I(f_j, \mathbf{B})] \geq 1 - \frac{q^2}{s}.$$

On the other hand, let $u \in \{0,1\}^{m''}$ be chosen uniformly and independently of all other random variables. Let $E = E(f_j)$ denote the event

$$E := \left[\mathrm{dist}(A^{f_j}, \mathcal{U}_{m''}) \leq \varepsilon\right].$$

If we condition that $E$ holds then $\mathrm{dist}(z, u) = \mathrm{dist}(A^{f_j}, \mathcal{U}_{m''}) \leq \varepsilon$. Thus for every fixing of $\mathbf{B}, f_j$ for which $E$ holds we get

$$\Pr[u \in O(f_j, \mathbf{B}) | \mathbf{B}, f_j, E] \geq \Pr[z \in O(f_j, \mathbf{B}) | \mathbf{B}, f_j, E] - \varepsilon.$$

Averaging over the choices of $\mathbf{B}, f_j$ we obtain that

$$\Pr[u \in O(f_j, \mathbf{B}) | E] \geq \Pr[z \in O(f_j, \mathbf{B}) | E] - \varepsilon.$$

We next remove the conditioning on $E$. As $\Pr[E] \geq 1 - \delta$, we can bound

$$\Pr[u \in O(f_j, \mathbf{B})] \geq \Pr[u \in O(f_j, \mathbf{B}) | E] \Pr[E] \geq \Pr[u \in O(f_j, \mathbf{B}) | E] - \delta$$

and

$$\Pr[z \in O(f_j, \mathbf{B})] \leq \frac{\Pr[z \in O(f_j, \mathbf{B})]}{\Pr[E]}$$

$$\leq \Pr[z \in O(f_j, \mathbf{B}) | E] + \Pr[\neg E] / \Pr[E]$$

$$\leq \Pr[z \in O(f_j, \mathbf{B}) | E] + 2\delta.$$

Thus

$$\Pr[u \in O(f_j, \mathbf{B})] \geq \Pr[z \in O(f_j, \mathbf{B})] - 3\delta \geq 1 - \frac{q^2}{s} - \varepsilon - 3\delta.$$

This concludes the proof as

$$\mathbb{E}[|O(f_j, \mathbf{B})|] = 2^{m''} \Pr[u \in O(f_j, \mathbf{B})] \geq \left(1 - \frac{q^2}{s} - \varepsilon - 4\delta\right) 2^{m''}.$$

### 3.4   Main Technical Lemma

The main step in proving Theorem 5 is showing that $O(f_{j-1}, \mathbf{B})$ is not much smaller than $O(f_j, \mathbf{B})$.

**Definition 11.** *Let us jointly sample* $\mathbf{B}, f_{j-1}, f_j$ *as follows:*

- *Sample* $(\mathbf{B}, f_{j-1}) \sim \mathcal{D}_{j-1}$.
- *Sample* $y_j \in \{0,1\}^m$ *independently and uniformly, and set*

$$f_j(x) = \begin{cases} f_{j-1}(x) & x \notin B_j \\ y_j & x \in B_j. \end{cases}$$

We denote this joint distribution over $\mathbf{B}, f_{j-1}, f_j$ by $\mathcal{D}_{j-1,j}$. Observe that if we omit $f_{j-1}$, then the marginal distribution over $(\mathbf{B}, f_j)$ is indeed $\mathcal{D}_j$.

**Lemma 3 (Main lemma).** *Assume that* $\delta s \leq j \leq (1-\delta)s$ *and sample* $(\mathbf{B}, f_{j-1}, f_j) \sim \mathcal{D}_j$. *Then for any* $z \in \{0,1\}^{m''}$ *it holds that*

$$\Pr\left[z \in O(f_{j-1}, \mathbf{B})\right] \geq \Pr\left[z \in O(f_j, \mathbf{B})\right] - \varepsilon,$$

*where* $\varepsilon = \frac{4q^{5/3}b^{2/3}}{\delta^{4/3}s^{4/3}}$. *In particular, if we set* $b = 256$ *and* $\delta = 1/4$ *then* $\varepsilon = O(q^{5/3}/s^{4/3})$. *Averaging over a uniform choice of* $z$ *gives that*

$$\mathbb{E}\left[|O(f_{j-1}, \mathbf{B})|\right] \geq \mathbb{E}\left[|O(f_j, \mathbf{B})|\right] - \varepsilon 2^{m''}.$$

We note that it is crucial in Lemma 3 that $\varepsilon \ll 1/s$, as we will apply it to relate $O(f_{s/4}, \mathbf{B})$ to $O(f_{s/2}, \mathbf{B})$, which will incur an additional factor of $s$. Most of the technical challenge in proving Lemma 3 is achieving that, as achieving weaker bounds of the form $\varepsilon = \text{poly}(q)/s$ is much easier. We defer the proof of Lemma 3 to Sect. 4, and next show how it implies Theorem 5.

### 3.5   Deducing Theorem 5

Let $A_5$ be the assumed black box reduction given in Theorem 5, specialized for $m = 3n, k = n - 3$. Let $n', m'$ denote the input and output size of $A_5^f$ in this case and let $k' = k'(n, m, k)$. Let $A$ be the black box reduction obtained by first applying $A_5$ to $f \in \mathcal{F}_{n,m}$, then applying $A_1$ to $A_5^f$. Thus $A^f \leq \mathcal{F}_{n'',m''}$ where $n'', m'' \leq \text{poly}(n', m')$. We have $\text{QC}(A) \leq \text{QC}(A_5)\text{QC}(A_1) \leq \text{QC}(A_5)\text{poly}(n', m')$.

**Definition 12 (Hybrid distribution).** *Sample $(f_j : j = 0, \ldots, s)$ jointly as follows:*

- *Sample a random partition $\mathbf{B} = (B_1, \ldots, B_s)$ of $\{0,1\}^n$.*
- *Sample $y_1, \ldots, y_s \in \{0,1\}^m$ uniformly and independently.*
- *Sample a uniform function $g : \{0,1\}^n \to \{0,1\}^m$.*
- *If $x \in B_i$, $i \leq j$ then set $f_j(x) = y_i$.*
- *If $x \in B_i$, $i > j$ then sample $f_j(x) = g(x)$.*

Observe that the marginal distribution of $(\mathbf{B}, f_j)$ is $\mathcal{D}_j$, and moreover, the marginal distribution of $(\mathbf{B}, f_{j-1}, f_j)$ is $\mathcal{D}_{j-1,j}$. According to Claim 3.2, we have the following statements by setting $b = 256$,

- $\Pr_{f_{s/4} \sim \mathcal{D}_{s/4}}[\mathrm{H}(f_{s/4}) = n - 2] \geq 1 - 2^{-n}$.
- $\Pr_{f_{s/2} \sim \mathcal{D}_{s/2}}[\mathrm{H}(f_{s/2}) = n - 4] \geq 1 - 2^{-n}$.

By the guarantees of $A$ we have that

- If $\mathrm{H}(f_{s/4}) \geq (n - 3) + 1$ then $|\mathrm{supp}(A^{f_{s/4}})| \leq 0.1 \cdot 2^{m''}$.
- If $\mathrm{H}(f_{s/2}) \leq (n - 3) - 1$ then $\mathrm{dist}(A^{f_{s/2}}, U_{m''}) \leq 0.1$.

Let $q = \mathrm{QC}(A)$. Applying Lemma 2 to $f_{s/2}$, and assuming that $q^2/s \leq 0.1$ gives that

$$\mathbb{E}\left[|O(A^{f_{s/2}}, \mathbf{B})|\right] \geq 0.8 \cdot 2^{m''}.$$

On the other hand,

$$\mathbb{E}\left[|O(A^{f_{s/4}}, \mathbf{B})|\right] \leq |\mathrm{supp}(A^{f_{s/4}})| \leq 0.1 \cdot 2^{m''}.$$

Lemma 3, applied for $s/4 \leq j \leq s/2$, gives that

$$\mathbb{E}\left[|O(A^{f_{j-1}}, \mathbf{B})|\right] \geq \left[|O(A^{f_j}, \mathbf{B})|\right] - \varepsilon 2^{m''},$$

where $\varepsilon = O(q^{5/3}/s^{4/3})$. For all these to hold we need to have

$$\varepsilon(s/2 - s/4) \geq 0.7$$

which gives the required bound

$$\mathrm{QC}(A) = q \geq \Omega(s^{1/5}).$$

This then gives us the bound

$$\mathrm{QC}(A_5^f) \geq \Omega(2^{n/5}/\mathrm{poly}(n', m')).$$

## 4  Proof of Main Technical Lemma: Lemma 3

We prove Lemma 3 in this section. To recall, $A$ is a black box reduction from $\mathcal{F}_{n,m}$ to $\mathcal{F}_{n'',m''}$. We fix $1 \le j \le s$ and $z \in \{0,1\}^{m''}$ from here onwards. We sample $(\mathbf{B}, f_{j-1}, f_j) \sim \mathcal{D}_{j-1,j}$ and wish to compare $\Pr[z \in O(f_{j-1}, \mathbf{B})]$ and $\Pr[z \in O(f_j, \mathbf{B})]$. To simplify notations define

$$O(f_{j-1}) = O(f_{j-1}, \mathbf{B}) \qquad I(f_{j-1}) = I(f_{j-1}, \mathbf{B}).$$

Define the events

$$X := [z \in O(f_{j-1})] \qquad Y := [z \in O(f_j)].$$

Our goal is to show that if $Y$ holds, then with high probability also $X$ holds. The "common information" between $X, Y$ is captured by the random variable

$$\mathcal{C} := (\{(B_i, f_j|_{B_i})\}_{1 \le i \le j-1}, B_j, \{(B_i, f_j|_{B_i})\}_{j+1 \le i \le s}).$$

Observe that $\{\mathbf{B}\}$ can be computed from $\mathcal{C}$, which we denote as $\{\mathbf{B}\} = \{\mathbf{B}\}(\mathcal{C})$, and that furthermore

$$f_{j-1} = f_{j-1}(\mathcal{C}, f_{j-1}|_{B_j}) \quad f_j = f_j(\mathcal{C}, f_j|_{B_j}).$$

Thus

$$X = X(\mathcal{C}, f_{j-1}|_{B_j}) \quad Y = Y(\mathcal{C}, f_j|_{B_j}).$$

In particular, given any fixing of $\mathcal{C}$, we have that $f_{j-1}|_{B_j}$ is a uniform function from $B_j$ to $\{0,1\}^m$, that $f_j|_{B_j}$ is a random constant function, and that the two are independent of each other. We obtain the following claim:

*Claim.* For any fixing of $\mathcal{C}$, the random variables $X|\mathcal{C}$ and $Y|\mathcal{C}$ are independent.

Recall that $f_{j-1}$ and $f_j$ differ only in their evaluation on the block $B_j$. We define a partial function $\hat{f}$ to be the set of inputs where $f_{j-1}$ and $f_j$ agree, namely all inputs outside $B_j$, and outputs "?" otherwise. Formally, we define the function $\hat{f} : \{0,1\}^n \to (\{0,1\}^m \cup \{?\})$ as follows:

$$\hat{f}(x) = \begin{cases} f_{j-1}(x) & \text{if } x \notin B_j \\ ? & \text{if } x \in B_j \end{cases}$$

if $x \notin B_j$ then $\hat{f}(x) = f_{j-1}(x) = f_j(x)$. As we now allow for partial functions, we will also need to allow running the black box reduction $A$ on partial functions. We do so by outputing a "?" if the black box reduction queries a point where the partial function is not defined. Observe that $\hat{f}$ can be computed given $\mathcal{C}$:

$$\hat{f} = \hat{f}(\mathcal{C}).$$

**Definition 13 (Black box reduction of a partial function).** *Let $A$ be a black box reduction from $\mathcal{F}_{n,m}$ to $\mathcal{F}_{n'',m''}$. Let $f : \{0,1\}^n \to (\{0,1\}^m \cup \{?\})$ be a partial function. We define $A^f : \{0,1\}^{n''} \to (\{0,1\}^{m''} \cup \{?\})$ to be the following partial function. When computing $A^f(w)$, follows the queries made by $A$ as if $f$ was a total function. However, if at any point we query a point $x$ where $f(x) =?$ then we abort and output $?$.*

We also extend the definition of block compatible inputs and outputs to partial functions in the obvious manner. Define $O(\hat{f}) := O(\hat{f}, \{\mathbf{B}\})$ and define the event $E_1$ as
$$E_1 = E_1(\mathcal{C}) := [z \in O(\hat{f})].$$

*Claim.* If $E_1$ holds then both $X$ and $Y$ also hold: $E_1 \Rightarrow X \wedge Y$.

*Proof.* If $E_1$ holds then by definition, there exists $w \in I(\hat{f})$ for which $A^{\hat{f}}(w) = z$. This implies that $A^{f_{j-1}}(w) = A^{f_j}(w) = z$, as since $A^{\hat{f}}(w)$ didn't return a "?", it only queried locations outside $B_j$, where $f_{j-1}, f_j$ agree. Also, as $w \in I(\hat{f})$ this means that $A^{\hat{f}}(w)$ queries each block $B_i$ at most once, while block $B_j$ is never queried. Thus also $w \in I(f_{j-1}), w \in I(f_j)$. This implies that $z \in O(f_{j-1}), z \in O(f_j)$ which means that $X, Y$ hold.

According to Claim 4 we have,
$$\Pr[X \wedge E_1] = \Pr[Y \wedge E_1] = \Pr[E_1]$$

and hence
$$\begin{aligned}
&\Pr[X] - \Pr[Y] \\
&= \Pr[X \wedge E_1] + \Pr[X \wedge \neg E_1] - \Pr[Y \wedge E_1] - \Pr[Y \wedge \neg E_1] \\
&= \Pr[X \wedge \neg E_1] - \Pr[Y \wedge \neg E_1]
\end{aligned}$$

Thus, from now on we focus on the case that $\neg E_1$ holds.

## 4.1   Analyzing the Case that $E_1$ Doesn't Hold

For each $x \in B_j, y \in \{0,1\}^m$ we define the following extension of $\hat{f}$. Define a partial function $\hat{f}_{x,y} : \{0,1\}^n \to (\{0,1\}^m \cup \{?\})$ as follows:

$$\hat{f}_{x,y}(x') := \begin{cases} \hat{f}(x') & \text{if } x' \notin B_j \\ y & \text{if } x' = x \\ ? & \text{if } x' \in B_j \text{ and } x' \neq x \end{cases}$$

For each $x \in B_j$ define
$$R(x) = R_{\hat{f}}(x) := \{y \in \{0,1\}^m : z \in O(f_{x,y})\}.$$

Namely, $R(x)$ is the set of values $y$ for which, if we allow the algorithm to make a single query to $B_j$ at point $x$ which returns $y$, then $z$ becomes a block compatible output. Observe that the definition of $R(x)$ depends only on $\hat{f}$, and hence on $\mathcal{C}$. Crucially, it does not depend on the values of either $f_{j-1}$ or $f_j$ on $B_j$. We further define

$$r(x) := \Pr_{y \in \{0,1\}^m} [y \in R(x)] = \frac{|R(x)|}{2^m}.$$

As $R(x), r(x)$ depend only on $\mathcal{C}$, we may consider the following experimant: first sample $\mathcal{C}$ and then sample $f_{j-1}, f_j$ conditioned on $\mathcal{C}$. That is, $f_{j-1}, f_j$ are equal to $\hat{f} = \hat{f}(\mathcal{C})$ outside $B_j = B_j(\mathcal{C})$, and on $B_j$ we sample $f_{j-1}$ as a random function, while $f_j(x) = y_j$ for all $x \in B_j$, where $y_j$ is randomly chosen. Recall that $E_1 = E_1(\mathcal{C})$.

*Claim.* For any fixing of $\mathcal{C}$ sample $f_{j-1}, f_j | \mathcal{C}$. Then

$$\Pr[X | \mathcal{C}, \neg E_1] = 1 - \prod_{x \in B_j} (1 - r(x))$$

and

$$\Pr[Y | \mathcal{C}, \neg E_1] \leq \sum_{x \in B_j} r(x).$$

*Proof.* Consider any fixing of $\mathcal{C}$ and sample $f_{j-1}, f_j$ conditioned on it. Recall that $r(x)$ is a function of $\mathcal{C}$.

Let $f : \{0,1\}^n \to \{0,1\}^m$ be any function which agrees with $\hat{f}$ on all $x \notin B_j$. If $z \in O(f)$ then there exists $w \in I(f)$ for which $A^f(w) = z$. As we assume that $\neg E_1$ holds, for any such $w$, $A^f(w)$ must query the block $B_j$ at least once, and since $w \in I(f)$ it is exactly once, say at point $x_w \in B_j$. But then also $z \in O(\hat{f}_{x_w, f(x_w)})$, which means that $f(x_w) \in R(x_w)$. The converse direction also holds: if $f(x) \in R(x)$ for any $x \in B_j$ then by definition of $R(x)$, there exists $w_x$ such that $w_x \in I(f)$ and $A^f(w_x) = z$ (and moreover $A^f(w_x)$ queries the block $B_j$ exactly at $x$) and in particular $z \in O(f)$. Thus

$$z \in O(f) \quad \Longleftrightarrow \quad \bigvee_{x \in B_j} [f(x) \in R(x)].$$

Next, we apply this logic to both $f_{j-1}$ and $f_j$. For $f_{j-1}$, each point $f_{j-1}(x)$ for $x \in B_j$ is uniformly and independently chosen, hence

$$\begin{aligned}
\Pr[X | \mathcal{C}, \neg E_1] &= \Pr[z \in O(f_{j-1}) | \mathcal{C}, \neg E_1] \\
&= 1 - \Pr[f_{j-1}(x) \notin R(x) \; \forall x \in B_j] \\
&= 1 - \prod_{x \in B_j} (1 - r(x)).
\end{aligned}$$

For $f_j$, all the evaluations $\{f_j(x) : x \in B_j\}$ are equal to a uniformly chosen point $y_j$. Hence by the union bound

$$\Pr[Y|\mathcal{C}, \neg E_1] = \Pr[z \in O(f_j)|\mathcal{C}, \neg E_1]$$
$$\leq \sum_{x \in B_j} \Pr[y_j \in R(x)]$$
$$\leq \sum_{x \in B_j} r(x).$$

The following definition allow us to compare the two bounds appearing in Claim 4.1.

**Definition 14.** *Let $\gamma > 0$. A sequence of numbers $r_1, \ldots, r_b \in [0,1]$ is said to be $\gamma$-balanced if*

$$(1 - \gamma) \sum r_i \leq 1 - \prod (1 - r_i).$$

Let $\gamma > 0$ to be determined later, and define the event $E_2$ as

$$E_2 = E_2(\mathcal{C}) := [(r(x) : x \in B_j) \text{ is } \gamma\text{-balanced}].$$

The following is a corollary of Claim 4.1 and the definition of $X, Y$.

*Claim.* For any fixing of $\mathcal{C}$ for which $\neg E_1, E_2$ hold, it holds that

$$\Pr[X|\mathcal{C}, \neg E_1, E_2] \geq (1 - \gamma) \Pr[Y|\mathcal{C}, \neg E_1, E_2].$$

*Proof.* Fix $\mathcal{C}$ such that $\neg E_1, E_2$ hold. This fixes in particular $B_j$ and $(r(x) : x \in B_j)$. As $E_2$ holds, we obtain by Claim 4.1 that

$$\Pr[X|\mathcal{C}] = 1 - \prod_{x \in B_j} (1 - r(x)) \geq (1 - \gamma) \sum_{x \in B_j} r(x) \geq (1 - \gamma) \Pr[Y|\mathcal{C}].$$

Following up on (1), we have

$$\Pr[X] - \Pr[Y] = (\Pr[X \wedge \neg E_1 \wedge E_2] - \Pr[Y \wedge \neg E_1 \wedge E_2])$$
$$+ (\Pr[X \wedge \neg E_1 \wedge \neg E_2] - \Pr[Y \wedge \neg E_1 \wedge \neg E_2])$$

The second term can simply be bounded by $\Pr[\neg E_1 \wedge \neg E_2]$, which we bound in the next section. For now, lets focus on the first term. Consider any fixing of $\mathcal{C}$ for which $\neg E_1, E_2$ hold. By Claim 4.1 we have that $\Pr[X|\mathcal{C}] \geq (1 - \gamma) \Pr[Y|\mathcal{C}]$. By averaging over such $\mathcal{C}$, we obtain that

$$\Pr[X \wedge \neg E_1 \wedge E_2] - \Pr[Y \wedge \neg E_1 \wedge E_2] \geq -\gamma \Pr[Y \wedge \neg E_1 \wedge E_2].$$

We can bound the right hand side by

$$\Pr[Y \wedge \neg E_1 \wedge E_2] \leq \Pr[Y \wedge \neg E_1] = \Pr[Y] \Pr[\neg E_1|Y].$$

*Claim.* $\Pr[\neg E_1|Y] \leq q/j$.

*Proof.* Sample $(\mathbf{B}, f_{j-1}, f_j) \sim \mathcal{D}_{j-1,j}$. In addition, sample $t \in \{1, \ldots, j\}$ uniformly. We will define a "proxy" $f_{j-1}$ obtained from $f_j$ by changing the value on $B_t$ to a random function. We will then argue that with high probability, this misses any specific set of queries. To that end, define the following random variables:

- $f'_{j-1} : \{0,1\}^n \rightarrow \{0,1\}^m$ is a random function defined as follows: if $x \notin B_t$ then $f'_{j-1}(x) = f_j(x)$; and if $x \in B_t$ then $f'_{j-1}(x)$ is a uniformly random element in $\{0,1\}^m$.
- $\hat{f}' : \{0,1\}^n \rightarrow (\{0,1\}^m \cup \{?\})$ is a partial function defined as follows: $\hat{f}'(x) = f'_{j-1}(x) = f_j(x)$ if $x \notin B_t$, and $\hat{f}'(x) =?$ if $x \in B_t$.
- $\mathbf{B}'$ is equal to $\mathbf{B}$ with blocks $B_t, B_j$ swapped. Namely,

$$\mathbf{B}' = (B_1, \ldots, B_{t-1}, B_j, B_{t+1}, \ldots, B_{j-1}, B_t, B_{j+1}, \ldots, B_s).$$

Observe that the joint distributions of $(\mathbf{B}, f_j, f_{j-1}, \hat{f})$ and $(\mathbf{B}', f_j, f'_{j-1}, \hat{f}')$ are identical. Next, define the following events:

- $Y' := [z \in O(f_j, \{\mathbf{B}'\})]$.
- $E'_1 := [z \in O(\hat{f}', \{\mathbf{B}'\})]$.

Observe that $Y' = Y$ since $\{\mathbf{B}'\} = \{\mathbf{B}\}$, and that the joint distributions of $(E_1, Y)$ and $(E'_1, Y) = (E'_1, Y')$ are identical. Next, fix $\mathbf{B}, f_j$ such that $Y$ holds. This means that there exists $w \in I(f_j, \{\mathbf{B}\}) = I(f_j, \{\mathbf{B}'\})$ such that $A^{f_j}(w) = z$. Let $Q = \text{Query}(A^{f_j}(w))$ be the set of queries made by the algorithm, where $|Q| \leq q$. Observe that if $B_t \cap Q = \emptyset$ then $E'_1$ holds, and that $Q, t$ are independent random variables. Let $T = T(\mathbf{B}, f_j) = \{i \in \{1, \ldots, j\} : B_i \cap Q \neq \emptyset\}$, where $|T| \leq |Q| \leq q$. Thus

$$\Pr[\neg E'_1|\mathbf{B}, f_j, Y] \leq \Pr[B_t \cap Q \neq \emptyset | \mathbf{B}, f_j, Y] = \Pr[t \in T | \mathbf{B}, f_j, Y] \leq \frac{|T|}{j} \leq \frac{q}{j}.$$

By averaging over $\mathbf{B}, f_j$, we obtain that $\Pr[\neg E'_1|Y] \leq q/j$. Thus also

$$\Pr[\neg E_1|Y] = \Pr[\neg E'_1|Y] \leq \frac{q}{j}.$$

We thus have

$$\Pr[X \wedge \neg E_1 \wedge E_2] - \Pr[Y \wedge \neg E_1 \wedge E_2] \geq -\gamma(q/j)\Pr[Y]$$

which implies that

$$\Pr[X] - \Pr[Y] \geq -\gamma(q/j)\Pr[Y] - \Pr[\neg E_1 \wedge \neg E_2]$$

which in turn gives the bound

$$\Pr[X] \geq (1 - \gamma(q/j))\Pr[Y] - \Pr[\neg E_1 \wedge \neg E_2]. \tag{1}$$

To conclude, we need to upper bound $\Pr[\neg E_1 \wedge \neg E_2]$, which is what we do in the next section.

### 4.2   Bounding the Probability that both $E_1, E_2$ Don't Hold

We first need a simple corollary of the definition of $\gamma$-balanced.

*Claim.* Let $r_1, \ldots, r_b \in [0, 1]$ be a sequence which is not $\gamma$-balanced. Then there exist distinct $1 \leq i, j \leq b$ such that $r_i, r_j \geq \gamma/b$.

*Proof.* Assume not. Then without loss of generality, $r_2, \ldots, r_b \leq \gamma/b$. By the inclusion-exclusion principle

$$1 - \prod (1 - r_i) \geq \sum r_i - \sum_{i<j} r_i r_j$$

and by our assumption

$$\sum_{i<j} r_i r_j \leq \left( \sum_{j \geq 2} r_j \right) \left( \sum_{i \geq 1} r_i \right) \leq \gamma \sum r_i.$$

Thus

$$1 - \prod (1 - r_i) \geq (1 - \gamma) \sum r_i,$$

which means that the sequence $r_1, \ldots, r_b$ is $\gamma$-balanced.

We next define the notion of critical blocks. Informally, a block $B_j$ is critical if all block compatible input $w$ for which $A^f(w) = z$, $A^f(w)$ queries exactly one point in $B_j$.

**Definition 15 (Critical block).** *Given $f : \{0,1\}^n \to \{0,1\}^m$ and a partition $\mathbf{B} = (B_1, \ldots, B_s)$ of $\{0,1\}^n$, we say that the block $B_j$ is critical for $f$ if*

$$(A^f(w) = z) \wedge (w \in I(f, \mathbf{B})) \quad \Rightarrow \quad |Query(A^f(w)) \cap B_j| = 1.$$

A double critical block is a critical block where the output $z$ can be obtained by two block compatible inputs $w_1, w_2$ which query different points $x_1, x_2$ in the block.

**Definition 16 (Double critical block).** *Given $f : \{0,1\}^n \to \{0,1\}^m$ and a partition $\mathbf{B} = (B_1, \ldots, B_s)$ of $\{0,1\}^n$, we say that the block $B_j$ is double critical for $f$ if*

*(i) $B_j$ is a critical block for $f$.*
*(ii) There exist distinct $w_1, w_2 \in I(f, \mathbf{B})$ and distinct $x_1, x_2 \in B_j$ such that*

$$(A^f(w_i) = z) \wedge (Query(A^f(w_i)) \cap B_j = \{x_i\}) \qquad i = 1, 2.$$

**Lemma 4.** *Sample $(\mathbf{B}, f_{j-1}) \sim \mathcal{D}_{j-1}$. Then*

$$\Pr[B_j \text{ is double critical for } f_{j-1}] \leq \frac{2q^3}{(s - j + 1)^2}.$$

*Proof.* We can jointly sample $\mathbf{B}, f_{j-1}$ as follows:

(1) Sample disjoint blocks $B_1, \ldots, B_{j-1}$ and $y_1, \ldots, y_{j-1} \in \{0,1\}^m$, and set $f_{j-1}(x) = y_i$ if $x \in B_i$, $i < j$.
(2) Let $U := \{0,1\}^m \setminus (B_1 \cup \ldots \cup B_{j-1})$. Sample $f_{j-1}(x) \in \{0,1\}^m$ uniformly and independently for all $x \in U$.
(3) Sample $B_j, \ldots, B_s$ a random partition of $U$ to $s - j + 1$ blocks of size $b$.

From now on, we fix $f_{j-1}, U$ and consider only the randomness in step (3), namely the random partition of $U$. For simplicity of notation we say that $B_j$ is critical, or double critical, where in both cases we refer with respect to $f_{j-1}$. Define

$$W := \{w \in \{0,1\}^{n''} : A^{f_{j-1}}(w) = z, |\mathrm{Query}(A^{f_{j-1}}(w)) \cap B_i| \leq 1 \ \forall i = 1, \ldots, j-1\}.$$

The set $W$ is the set of *potential* elements in $I(f_{j-1}, \mathbf{B})$, in the sense that they satisfy the requirement $|\mathrm{Query}(A^{f_{j-1}}(w)) \cap B_i| \leq 1$ for the blocks defined so far, namely $B_1, \ldots, B_{j-1}$. If $W$ is empty then no block can be critical, and the lemma follows. So, we assume that $W$ is nonempty. For simplicity of notation define $Q(w) := \mathrm{Query}(A^{f_{j-1}}(w)) \cap U$. Note that so far these definitions do not depend on the choice of the partition of $U$ to $B_j, \ldots, B_s$.

Next, sample a random partition $(B_j, \ldots, B_s)$ of $U$. We say that an input $w$ is *legal* if $A^{f_{j-1}}(w)$ queries each block at most once:

$$W_{\mathrm{legal}} := \{w \in W : |Q(w) \cap B_i| \leq 1 \ \forall i = j, \ldots, s\}.$$

Equivalently, $W_{\mathrm{legal}} = \{w \in I(f, \mathbf{B}) : A^{f_{j-1}}(w) = z\}$. The definitions of critical and double critical can then be cast as

$$B_j \text{ is critical} \Leftrightarrow |B_j \cap Q(w)| = 1, \ \forall w \in W_{\mathrm{legal}} \ ;$$
$$B_j \text{ is double critical} \Leftrightarrow B_j \text{ is critical and } |B_j \cap (\cup_{w \in W_{\mathrm{legal}}} Q(w))| \geq 2.$$

Fix $w_1 \in W$ and assume for now that $w_1 \in W_{\mathrm{legal}}$. We will handle the case that $w_1 \notin W_{\mathrm{legal}}$ later.

If $B_j$ is critical then $|B_j \cap Q(w_1)| = 1$. Say $B_j \cap Q(w_1) = \{x_1\}$. If $B_j$ is double critical then there must be another legal $w_2 \in W_{\mathrm{legal}}$ such that $B_j \cap Q(w_2) = \{x_2\}$ where $x_2 \neq x_1$. In particular, $x_1 \notin Q(w_2)$. Thus, for each $x_1 \in Q(w_1)$ define

$$W_{x_1} := \{w \in W : x_1 \notin Q(w)\}.$$

Note that if $W_{x_1}$ is empty then it is impossible that $B_j$ is double critical, $w_1$ is legal and $B_j \cap Q(w_1) = \{x_1\}$. Thus let

$$Q'(w_1) := \{x_1 \in Q(w_1) : |W_{x_1}| \geq 1\}.$$

For each $x_1 \in Q'(w_1)$ fix an arbitrary $w_{x_1} \in W_{x_1}$. By definition, $x_1 \notin Q(w_{x_1})$. We can bound the probability that $B_j$ is double critical and $w_1$ is legal by requiring that $B_j \cap Q(w_1) = \{x_1\}$ and $B_j \cap Q(w_{x_1}) = \{x_2\}$, where by definition $x_1 \neq x_2$, and summing over all choices for $x_1, x_2$:

$$\Pr[B_j \text{ is double critical} \wedge w_1 \in W_{\text{legal}}]$$

$$\leq \sum_{x_1 \in Q'(w_1)} \sum_{x_2 \in Q(w_{x_1})} \Pr[x_1, x_2 \in B_j]$$

$$\leq \frac{q^2}{(s-j+1)^2}$$

where the bound follows from the union bound and the fact that as $B_j, \ldots, B_s$ is a random partition of $U$, for any fixed distinct $x_1, x_2 \in U$ it holds that $\Pr[x_1, x_2 \in B_j] \leq 1/(s-j+1)^2$.

To conclude the proof, we need to handle the event that $w_1$ is not legal. First, note that

$$\Pr[w_1 \notin W_{\text{legal}}] \leq \sum_{x_1, x_2 \in Q(w_1), x_1 \neq x_2} \Pr[x_1, x_2 \text{ in the same block}] \leq \frac{q^2}{s-j+1}.$$

We will bound $\Pr[B_j \text{ is double critical}|w_1 \notin W_{\text{legal}}]$. To do that, lets condition on which block does every element of $Q(w_1)$ belong to. Let $H_1$ denote the family of all functions $h : Q(w_1) \to \{j, \ldots, s\}$. Let $F_h$ denote the event

$$F_h := [x \in B_{h(x)} \quad \forall x \in Q(w_1)].$$

Note that the events $F_h$ are disjoint, and that the event $w_1 \notin W_{\text{legal}}$ is equivalent to $F_h$ holding where $h$ has at least one collision. Thus let

$$H_2 := \{h \in H_1 : \exists x_1, x_2 \in Q(w_1), h(x_1) = h(x_2)\}.$$

We have $w_1 \notin W_l \iff \cup_{h \in H_2} F_h$.

For each $h \in H_2$ let $W_h$ denote the set of $w \in W$ for which $Q(w)$ is not already illegal given $h$, namely

$$W_h := \{w \in W : \neg \exists x_1, x_2 \in Q_w \cap Q_{w_1}, h(x_1) = h(x_2)\}.$$

If $W_h$ is empty then it is impossible that $B_j$ is double critical and that $F_h$ holds, as there are no legal inputs. Thus let

$$H_3 := \{h \in H_2 : |W_h| \geq 1\}.$$

For each $h \in H_3$ fix an arbitrary $w_h \in W_h$. By definition, if $B_j$ is double critical then we must have $|B_j \cap Q(w_h)| = 1$. We can thus bound

$$\Pr[B_j \text{ is double critical}|w_1 \notin W_{\text{legal}}] = \sum_{h \in H_3} \Pr[B_j \text{ is double critical}|F_h] \Pr[F_h|w_1 \notin W_{\text{legal}}]$$

$$\leq \sum_{h \in H_3} \sum_{x \in Q(w_h)} \Pr[x \in B_j|F_h] \Pr[F_h|w_1 \notin W_{\text{legal}}].$$

In order to help bound this expression, note that both $h \in H_3$ and $\Pr[F_h|w_1 \notin W_{\text{legal}}]$ are invariant to permutations of the output of $h$. That is, if we replace $h(x)$ with $\pi(h)(x) = \pi(h(x))$ for any permutation $\pi$ on $\{j, \ldots, s\}$, then $h \in H_3 \iff \pi(h) \in H_3$ and $\Pr[F_h|w_1 \notin W_{\text{legal}}] = \Pr[F_{\pi(h)}|w_1 \notin W_{\text{legal}}]$. Thus

$$\Pr[B_j \text{ is double critical}|w_1 \notin W_{\text{legal}}]$$
$$\leq \mathbb{E}_\pi \sum_{h \in H_3} \sum_{x \in Q(w_h)} \Pr[x \in B_j|F_{\pi(h)}] \Pr[F_{\pi(h)}|w_1 \notin W_{\text{legal}}]$$
$$= \mathbb{E}_\pi \sum_{h \in H_3} \sum_{x \in Q(w_h)} \Pr[x \in B_{\pi^{-1}(j)}|F_h] \Pr[F_h|w_1 \notin W_{\text{legal}}].$$

When we average over $\pi$ we get that $\Pr[x \in B_{\pi^{-1}(j)}|F_h] = \frac{1}{s-j+1}$, and hence

$$\Pr[B_j \text{ is double critical}|w_1 \notin W_{\text{legal}}] \leq \frac{1}{s-j+1} \sum_{h \in H_3} \sum_{x \in Q(w_h)} \Pr[F_h|w_1 \notin W_{\text{legal}}] = \frac{q}{s-j+1}.$$

We obtained the bound

$$\Pr[B_j \text{ is double critical} \wedge w_1 \notin W_{\text{legal}}]$$
$$= \Pr[B_j \text{ is double critical}|w_1 \notin W_{\text{legal}}] \Pr[w_1 \notin W_{\text{legal}}]$$
$$\leq \frac{q}{s-j+1} \cdot \frac{q^2}{s-j+1} = \frac{q^3}{(s-j+1)^2}.$$

Combining the two bounds we obtained, we conclude that

$$\Pr[B_j \text{ is double critical}]$$
$$= \Pr[B_j \text{ is double critical} \wedge w_1 \in W_{\text{legal}}] + \Pr[B_j \text{ is double critical} \wedge w_1 \notin W_{\text{legal}}]$$
$$\leq \frac{q^2}{(s-j+1)^2} + \frac{q^3}{(s-j+1)^2} \leq \frac{2q^3}{(s-j+1)^2}.$$

*Claim.* Let $\mathcal{C}$ be such that $\neg E_1, \neg E_2$ hold. Sample $f_{j-1}|\mathcal{C}$. Then

$$\Pr[B_j \text{ is double critical for } f_{j-1}|\mathcal{C}] \geq (\gamma/b)^2.$$

In particular,

$$\Pr[B_j \text{ is double critical for } f_{j-1}|\neg E_1, \neg E_2] \geq (\gamma/b)^2.$$

*Proof.* Fix any $\mathcal{C}$ such that $\neg E_1, \neg E_2$ hold. By Claim 4.2 there are distinct $x_1, x_2 \in B_j$ such that $r(x_i) \geq \gamma/b$. Note that if $f_{j-1}(x_i) \in R(x_i)$ for both $i = 1, 2$, then $B_j$ is double critical for $f_{j-1}$. As $f_{j-1}(x_i)$ are sampled independently, we have

$$\Pr[B_j \text{ is double critical for } f_{j-1}|\mathcal{C}] \geq \Pr[f_{j-1}(x_i) \in R(x_i), i = 1, 2|\mathcal{C}] \geq (\gamma/b)^2.$$

Combining Lemma 4 and Claim 4.2 gives a bound on the probability that both $E_1, E_2$ don't hold.

**Corollary 1.** $\Pr[\neg E_1 \wedge \neg E_2] \leq \frac{2q^3 b^2}{\gamma^2(s-j+1)^2}$.

*Proof.* Let $F := [B_j$ is double critical for $f_{j-1}]$. We have

$$\Pr[\neg E_1 \wedge \neg E_2] = \frac{\Pr[\neg E_1 \wedge \neg E_2 \wedge F]}{\Pr[F | \neg E_1 \wedge \neg E_2]} \leq \frac{\Pr[F]}{\Pr[F | \neg E_1, \neg E_2]} \leq \frac{2q^3 b^2}{\gamma^2(s-j+1)^2}.$$

The claim then follows.

We can finally prove Lemma 3. Appealing to (1) we have that

$$\Pr[X] \geq \left(1 - \frac{\gamma q}{j}\right) \Pr[Y] - \frac{2q^3 b^2}{\gamma^2(s-j+1)^2} \geq \Pr[Y] - \left(\frac{\gamma q}{j} + \frac{2q^3 b^2}{\gamma^2(s-j+1)^2}\right). \tag{2}$$

Let us denote

$$\varepsilon = \frac{\gamma q}{j} + \frac{2q^3 b^2}{\gamma^2(s-j+1)^2}.$$

We now choose $\gamma$ to minimize $\varepsilon$. Let us assume (as we have) that $\delta s \leq j \leq (1-\delta)s$ for some absolute constant $\delta > 0$. Then

$$\varepsilon \leq \frac{\gamma q}{\delta s} + \frac{2q^3 b^2}{\gamma^2 \delta^2 s^2}.$$

We choose $\gamma = (2q^2 b^2 / \delta s)^{1/3}$ to equate the two terms, so that

$$\varepsilon \leq \frac{4q^{5/3} b^{2/3}}{\delta^{4/3} s^{4/3}}.$$

In particular, as we choose $b, \delta$ to be absolute constants, we have $\varepsilon \leq O(q^{5/3}/s^{4/3})$.

## 5  Conclusions and Open Problems

In this paper, we studied impossibility of reversing entropy in black-box constructions. An obvious question that remains open is whether our result can be extended to the computational setting, given some complexity assumptions. Note that if we assume that $P = NP$ then P = NISZK = SZK = NP.

Besides considering the relationship between NISZK and SZK, it is also interesting to explore relationships between other non-computational zero-knowledge proof systems. Concretely, what are the relationships between NIPZK and PZK, the perfect statistical analogs of NISZK and SZK, and the statistical versions. In particular, Malka [15] gave a complete problem for NIPZK, which can be a good starting point to apply the techniques developed in this paper and separate NISZK and NIPZK. In a recent work of Bouland et al. [3] gave an oracle to separate NISZK and NIPZK, however we are still interested in whether we can separate them in random oracle model.

**Acknowledgement.** We would like to thank Iftach Haitner and Salil Vadhan for helpful discussion, and we would also like to thank anonymous TCC reviewers for their comments. Jiapeng Zhang would also like to thank his wife, Yingcong Li.

# References

1. Blum, M., De Santis, A., Micali, S., Persiano, G.: Noninteractive zero-knowledge. SIAM J. Comput. **20**(6), 1084–1118 (1991)
2. Blum, M., Feldman, P., Micali, S.: Non-interactive zero-knowledge and its applications. In: Proceedings of the Twentieth Annual ACM Symposium on Theory of Computing, pp. 103–112. ACM (1988)
3. Bouland, A., Chen, L., Holden, D., Thaler, J., Vasudevan, P.N.: On SZK and PP. arXiv preprint arXiv:1609.02888 (2016)
4. De Santis, A., Di Crescenzo, G., Persiano, G.: The knowledge complexity of quadratic residuosity languages. Theoret. Comput. Sci. **132**(1–2), 291–317 (1994)
5. De Santis, A., Di Crescenzo, G., Persiano, G., Yung, M.: Image density is complete for non-interactive-SZK. In: Larsen, K.G., Skyum, S., Winskel, G. (eds.) ICALP 1998. LNCS, vol. 1443, pp. 784–795. Springer, Heidelberg (1998). doi:10.1007/BFb0055102
6. De Santis, A., Di Crescenzo, G., Persiano, P.: Randomness-efficient non-interactive zero knowledge. In: Degano, P., Gorrieri, R., Marchetti-Spaccamela, A. (eds.) ICALP 1997. LNCS, vol. 1256, pp. 716–726. Springer, Heidelberg (1997). doi:10.1007/3-540-63165-8_225
7. Gennaro, R., Micciancio, D., Rabin, T.: An efficient non-interactive statistical zero-knowledge proof system for quasi-safe prime products. In: Proceedings of the 5th ACM Conference on Computer and Communications Security, pp. 67–72. ACM (1998)
8. Goldreich, O., Goldwasser, S., Micali, S.: How to construct random functions. J. ACM (JACM) **33**(4), 792–807 (1986)
9. Goldreich, O., Sahai, A., Vadhan, S.: Can statistical zero knowledge be made non-interactive? or on the relationship of SZK and *NISZK*. In: Wiener, M. (ed.) CRYPTO 1999. LNCS, vol. 1666, pp. 467–484. Springer, Heidelberg (1999). doi:10.1007/3-540-48405-1_30
10. Goldreich, O., Vadhan, S.: Comparing entropies in statistical zero knowledge with applications to the structure of SZK. In: Proceedings of the Fourteenth Annual IEEE Conference on Computational Complexity, pp. 54–73. IEEE (1999)
11. Goldwasser, S., Micali, S., Rackoff, C.: The knowledge complexity of interactive proof systems. SIAM J. Comput. **18**(1), 186–208 (1989)
12. Haitner, I., Harnik, D., Reingold, O.: On the power of the randomized iterate. In: Dwork, C. (ed.) CRYPTO 2006. LNCS, vol. 4117, pp. 22–40. Springer, Heidelberg (2006). doi:10.1007/11818175_2
13. Håstad, J., Impagliazzo, R., Levin, L.A., Luby, M.: A pseudorandom generator from any one-way function. SIAM J. Comput. **28**(4), 1364–1396 (1999)
14. Holenstein, T., Renner, R.: One-way secret-key agreement and applications to circuit polarization and immunization of public-key encryption. In: Shoup, V. (ed.) CRYPTO 2005. LNCS, vol. 3621, pp. 478–493. Springer, Heidelberg (2005). doi:10.1007/11535218_29
15. Malka, L.: How to achieve perfect simulation and a complete problem for non-interactive perfect zero-knowledge. In: Canetti, R. (ed.) TCC 2008. LNCS, vol. 4948, pp. 89–106. Springer, Heidelberg (2008). doi:10.1007/978-3-540-78524-8_6

16. Peikert, C., Vaikuntanathan, V.: Noninteractive statistical zero-knowledge proofs for lattice problems. In: Wagner, D. (ed.) CRYPTO 2008. LNCS, vol. 5157, pp. 536–553. Springer, Heidelberg (2008). doi:10.1007/978-3-540-85174-5_30
17. Sahai, A., Vadhan, S.: A complete problem for statistical zero knowledge. J. ACM (JACM) **50**(2), 196–249 (2003)
18. Vadhan, S.: Personal Communication (2016)

# Position-Based Cryptography and Multiparty Communication Complexity

Joshua Brody[1], Stefan Dziembowski[2(✉)], Sebastian Faust[3,4], and Krzysztof Pietrzak[5]

[1] Swarthmore College, Swarthmore, USA
brody@cs.swarthmore.edu
[2] University of Warsaw, Warsaw, Poland
s.dziembowski@crypto.edu.pl
[3] Ruhr University Bochum, Bochum, Germany
sebastian.faust@rub.de
[4] TU Darmstadt, Darmstadt, Germany
[5] IST Austria, Klosterneuburg, Austria
pietrzak@ist.ac.at

**Abstract.** *Position based cryptography (PBC)*, proposed in the seminal work of Chandran, Goyal, Moriarty, and Ostrovsky (SIAM J. Computing, 2014), aims at constructing cryptographic schemes in which the identity of the user is his geographic position. Chandran et al. construct PBC schemes for *secure positioning* and *position-based key agreement* in the *bounded-storage model* (Maurer, J. Cryptology, 1992). Apart from bounded memory, their security proofs need a strong additional restriction on the power of the adversary: he cannot compute *joint* functions of his inputs. Removing this assumption is left as an open problem.

We show that an answer to this question would resolve a long standing open problem in multiparty communication complexity: finding a function that is hard to compute with low communication complexity in the simultaneous message model, but easy to compute in the fully adaptive model.

On a more positive side: we also show some implications in the other direction, i.e.: we prove that lower bounds on the communication complexity of certain multiparty problems imply existence of PBC primitives. Using this result we then show two attractive ways to "bypass" our hardness result: the first uses the random oracle model, the second weakens the *locality* requirement in the bounded-storage model to *online computability*. The random oracle construction is arguably one of the simplest proposed so far in this area. Our results indicate that constructing improved provably secure protocols for PBC requires a better understanding of multiparty communication complexity. This is yet another

S. Dziembowski—Supported by the ERC starting grant CNTM-207908 and by the FNP *Team* grant 2016/1/4.

S. Faust—Supported by the Emmy Noether Program FA 1320/1-1 of the German Research Foundation (DFG).

K. Pietrzak—Supported by the European Research Council, ERC consolidator grant (682815 - TOCNeT).

Y. Kalai and L. Reyzin (Eds.): TCC 2017, Part I, LNCS 10677, pp. 56–81, 2017.
https://doi.org/10.1007/978-3-319-70500-2_3

example where *negative* results in one area (in our case: lower bounds in multiparty communication complexity) can be used to construct secure cryptographic schemes.

# 1    Introduction

The standard way to identify participants in cryptographic protocols is to check their knowledge of some secret data (like a password or a key), to verify some biometric information, or the possession of some hardware tokens. A new intriguing idea, known under the name of *position-based cryptography (PBC)* [16] is to construct algorithms in which the participating parties are identified by *their geographic position.* For example, consider the setting where we want to grant access to a server only to the personnel within some military base. A position-based system could be used to give access to every user that is physically located within the base, but deny it to everybody outside. There are many other examples one can think of where position-based authentication would be useful. Say, a protocol for sending confidential documents to everyone who is present in some conference room, granting WiFi access to people within some building, or checking if a food delivery was indeed ordered from some physical address. Of course, such protocols can be combined with other means of authentication, and hence they can also serve for providing an additional layer of security. See [16] for more on potential applications of this concept.

PBC protocols are typically based on the physical characteristics of wireless communication channels; concretely, they are based on the fact that electronic signals are traveling at the speed of light, denoted $c$ (and hence traveling from point $\widehat{\mathcal{A}}$ to $\widehat{\mathcal{B}}$ takes time $\|\widehat{\mathcal{A}\mathcal{B}}\|/c$, where $\|\cdot\|$ denotes the length of the segment $\widehat{\mathcal{A}\mathcal{B}}$). Thus, if a *verifier* $\mathcal{V}$ sends a message at time $T$ and receives a reply from a *prover* $\mathcal{P}$ within time $T'$, the verifier can be sure that this reply was sent by a machine that is positioned at distance no more than $c \cdot (T' - T)/2$. A natural idea would be to exploit this fact, and use some standard trilateration techniques (like the one used in the GPS system) by having a group of verifiers $\mathcal{V}_1, \ldots, \mathcal{V}_n$ positioned in space and letting them jointly verify the distance from the prover. Unfortunately, as shown by Chandran et al. [16], the problem of designing PBC protocols is harder than it may seem at the first sight. In fact, they show that in the so-called *vanilla model* (i.e. without any additional assumptions), PBC is impossible: There exists an adversarial strategy which places devices around some point $\widehat{\mathcal{A}}$, and these devices can jointly convince the verifiers in any PBC protocol that they are at point $\widehat{\mathcal{A}}$, thus breaking the scheme. One way to get around this would be to restrict the number of adversary's devices (as the number of devices required in their attack is as large as the number of the verifiers used in the protocol). This however is not very realistic, as deploying several adversarial devices is usually easy in practice, since modern wireless devices are cheap and small.

Chandran et al. is use Maurer's bounded-storage model (BSM) [26], studied in a number of papers, including [3, 11, 19, 25, 27, 36], the bounded-*retrieval* model

(BRM) is a closely related variant of the BSM [13,17,20]. In this model, it is assumed that the users of cryptographic protocols have short time access to a long random string $X$ that is so large that it cannot be stored by the adversary in its entirety. The only thing that the adversary can do is to compute and store some function adv on $X$ (where $|\mathsf{adv}(X)| \leq \xi|X|$, for a constant $0 \leq \xi \ll 1$). On the other hand, the honest parties of a protocol should be only required to access small parts of $X$ in order to complete the protocol. The way this model is used in [16] is as follows: it is assumed that there is a group of *verifiers* $\mathcal{V}_i$ positioned in space. Suppose that a *prover* $\mathcal{P}$ claims to be at some position $\widehat{\mathcal{P}}$. Each of the verifiers broadcasts a long string $X_i$ in such a way that all the $X_i$'s arrive at $\widehat{\mathcal{P}}$ at the same time $T$. When this happens, the prover computes some function $f$ on the $X_i$'s, and takes some actions that depend on the computed value (e.g. sends the computed value back to the verifiers in order to prove that he is in point $\widehat{\mathcal{P}}$). The function $f$ should be very efficiently computable. In particular, to compute it one should only have to access a small fraction of the $X_i$'s [16].

In this model Chandran et al. construct a *positioning protocol*, where a prover convinces the verifiers that he is physically at some point $\widehat{\mathcal{P}}$. In practice a protocol like this is not very useful as a standalone primitive, since it comes with no guarantee that any future communication will be happening with the machine that is indeed in $\widehat{\mathcal{P}}$ (due to man-in-the-middle attacks). Chandran et al. also construct a more advanced primitive, called a *position-based key-agreement protocol*. Here the final output of the honest parties is a key $K$ which is not known to a potential adversary. Both the positioning and the position-based key agreement protocols have a very simple structure (see Sect. 2.3). Namely, in case of the positioning protocol the prover just sends back $f(X_1, \ldots, X_n)$ to the verifiers (who check if this value is correct and was received at the right time). For the position-based key agreement the prover simply lets the agreed key $K$ be equal to $f(X_1, \ldots, X_n)$. Such protocols are called *one-round*, and are very attractive because of their simplicity. They will also be the focus of this paper.

The proof in [16] requires one additional restriction on the power of the adversary, namely, it is assumed (see [16], p. 1294, Sect. 1.2) that whenever an adversarial device receives strings $X_{i_1}, \ldots, X_{i_a}$ at the same time, it cannot compute an arbitrary joint function adv on $X_{i_1}, \ldots, X_{i_a}$ (with short output). Instead, it can only compute several (adaptively chosen) functions on each $X_{i_j}$ independently (the same restriction applies to the honest parties). Removing this assumption is left as an "important open problem" in [16] and studying this open question is the main topic of this work. We show deep connections between the problem of constructing positioning and position-based key agreement protocols in the *unrestricted BSM* model (i.e. without restrictions on the adv function except of a bound on its output size), and the area of *multiparty communication complexity*. Before describing our contribution in more detail (in Sect. 1.2) let us provide a short introduction to this area (more formal definitions are given in Sect. 2.2, and for a more comprehensive introduction see [24]).

## 1.1 Multiparty Communication Complexity

In a typical communication complexity problem, there are $k$ players, denoted $\text{PLR}_1, \ldots, \text{PLR}_k$. There are also $k$ inputs $x_1, \ldots, x_k \in \{0,1\}^n$, and the players must communicate to compute some function $f(x_1, \ldots, x_k)$ of the inputs. The *communication cost* of a protocol is measured as the worst-case maximal number of bits communicated, taken over all possible inputs and all choices for the random string.

In the multiplayer setting (when $k > 2$) there are two different models for how the input is shared. In the number-in-hand (NIH) model, each player $\text{PLR}_i$ sees the $i$th input $x_i$. In the number-on-the-forehead (NOF) model, each $\text{PLR}_i$ sees all inputs *except* $x_i$. One can imagine in an NOF protocol that all players meet in a room, and $\text{PLR}_i$ has $x_i$ written on her forehead. In this way, players can see all inputs *except* what is written on their foreheads. When $k = 2$, the NIH and NOF models are one and the same, but for $k > 2$, they are quite different. In particular, communication in the NOF model becomes intuitively very easy, because so much information is shared. This makes proving NOF communication lower bounds *harder*. In this paper, we focus on NOF communication complexity.

It is particularly interesting to understand what role *interaction* plays in communication complexity. In an arbitrary ("fully adaptive") protocol, players are allowed to speak back and forth, and messages are broadcast. It is also interesting to consider a more restrictive model, where each player sends a single message to a referee, who does not see the inputs, and must compute $f(x_1, \ldots, x_k)$ only from the messages sent by the players. This restricted model of communication is called the Simultaneous Messages (SM) model. Occasionally, the communication complexity of problems can be the same in the SM and interactive model, but for other problems, allowing interactive communication can even lead to an exponential decrease in the communication complexity. The NOF communication model was invented thirty years ago in [15], who also gave as an application lower bounds for branching programs.

Position based cryptography was partly inspired by the area called *secure positioning* [8,12,33,37]. More recently there was work towards constructing PBC protocols based on other "physical" assumptions, such as quantum channels [10,14,35][1] (see also [9] and the webpage [34]) or noisy channels [21].

## 1.2 Our Contribution

We show that constructing a one-round positioning protocol in the unrestricted BSM gives a construction of a function $\pi$ with linear SM complexity (in the NOF model). If we additionally require that the computation on the prover is *local* (i.e. he only needs to look at small parts of the input), then $\pi$ has low complexity in the fully adaptive model. Finding a function with such properties is a longstanding open problem in communication complexity, and therefore this result can be viewed as a "negative" answer to the question posted in [16].

---

[1] Note that [35] uses the random oracle model, that we use in this work (in Sect. 4.1).

On a more positive side: we show some implications in the other direction. Namely, we prove that any function that has high communication complexity in the so-called "one-round almost SM model" (see Sect. 2.2 for the definition) can be transformed into a secure positioning protocol. The assumed hardness has to hold in a strong, randomized sense, i.e., the probability that any "adaptive SM" protocol computes the output correctly has to be negligible. Fortunately, we show a function that satisfies this requirement. Our function uses a hash function as a building block, and the security proof models this hash function as a random oracle (hence, our construction does not contradict the negative result mentioned above). The resulting positioning protocol is very simple: essentially, one verifier sends a long string $X$, the other verifiers send much shorter strings $Z_i$, and the output is the sub-string of $X$ on the positions determined by the hash of the concatenated $Z_i$'s.

We also construct positioning and position-based key agreement schemes from any function that has high complexity in the "fully adaptive SM model" (see Sect. 2.2). For our construction to work we need to assume even stronger hardness: the output of the function has to be "close to uniform" (in the sense of "statistical distance", see Sect. 2 for the definition). We show that the so-called "generalized inner product" function has this property. The resulting protocol does *not* have the "locality" property, i.e., the prover in the protocol needs to read its entire input. The good news is that this computation is very simple, can be performed very efficiently in an "online" fashion, and hence it may still be possible to implement it in practice.

## 2    Preliminaries

Let $A$ and $B$ be random variables distributed over set $\mathcal{A}$. The *statistical distance* between $A$ and $B$ is defined as $\Delta(A; B) := \frac{1}{2} \sum_{a \in \mathcal{A}} |\mathbb{P}(A = a) - \mathbb{P}(B = a)|$. The *statistical distance of $A$ from uniformity* is defined as $d(A) := \Delta(A; U_{\mathcal{A}})$, where $U_{\mathcal{A}}$ has uniform distribution over $\mathcal{A}$. The statistical distance of $A$ from uniformity *conditioned* on $B$ is defined as $d(A \mid B) = \Delta((A, B); (U_{\mathcal{A}}, B))$ (where $U_{\mathcal{A}}$ is uniform and independent from $B$). The *min-entropy* of a random variable $W$ is defined as $\mathbb{H}_{\infty}(W) := -\log_2(\max_w \mathbb{P}[W = w])$. We will use the following fact that can be viewed as a chain-rule for the statistical distance from uniformity (see, e.g., [19], Lemma 3).

**Lemma 1.** *For any random variables $X_1, \ldots, X_n$, and $Y$ we have that*

$$d(X_1, \ldots, X_n | Y) \leq \sum_{i=1}^{n} d(X_i | X_1, \ldots, X_{i-1}, Y).$$

We also have the following (see, e.g., [19], Lemma 1).

**Lemma 2.** *For every random variables $X$ and $Y$ taking values from $\mathcal{X}$ and $\mathcal{Y}$ (respectively) we have that $\max_{\alpha: \mathcal{Y} \to \mathcal{X}} (\mathbb{P}(X = \alpha(Y))) \leq d(X \mid Y) + 1/|\mathcal{X}|$. Moreover, if $\mathcal{X} = \{0, 1\}$, then $2 \max_{\alpha: \mathcal{Y} \to \mathcal{X}} (\mathbb{P}(X = \alpha(Y))) - 1 = d(X \mid Y)$.*

## 2.1   Guessing Bits from "compressed" Information

The following machinery will be needed in Sect. 4.1. Consider the following natural question. Suppose $X \leftarrow \{0,1\}^n$ is chosen uniformly at random. Let compress : $\{0,1\}^n \rightarrow \{0,1\}^{\beta n}$ be any function that "compresses" $X$, i.e., such that $\beta < 1$. Let us ask what is the maximal probability that given compress($X$) one can compute the substring consisting of $t$ random positions in $X$? More precisely, let guess : $\{1,\ldots,n\}^t \times \{0,1\}^{\beta n} \rightarrow \{0,1\}^t$ be any function that tries to "predict" these bits. We ask what is the maximal (over compress and guess) probability that guess($R$, compress($X$)) = $(X[R_1],\ldots,X[R_t])$, where $R = (R_1,\ldots,R_a) \leftarrow \{1,\ldots,n\}^t$ is random. This question was first answered by Nisan and Zuckerman [29]. In what follows, we use the presentation from [16] (which, in turn, is partly based on [36]). The following lemma can be derived from the discussion in Sect. 4.3 (p. 1306) of [16].

**Lemma 3 ([16, 29, 36]).**  *Take any $\beta < 1$. For every $t$ take $n$ such that $n > t$. Then for every* compress : $\{0,1\}^n \rightarrow \{0,1\}^{\beta n}$ *and* guess : $\{1,\ldots,n\}^t \times \{0,1\}^{\beta n} \rightarrow \{0,1\}^t$ *and a uniformly random $X \leftarrow \{0,1\}^n$ and $R = (R_1,\ldots,R_t) \leftarrow \{1,\ldots,n\}^t$ we have that*

$$\mathbb{P}\left(\text{guess}(R, \text{compress}(X)) = (X[R_1],\ldots,X[R_t])\right) \leq \text{negl}(t).$$

*Proof.* Simple inspection of the argument in Sect. 4.3 of [16]. Observe that EG in [16] is defined as $\text{EG}(X,R) := (X[Z_1],\ldots,X[Z_t])$. The argument in [16] uses parameters $\beta$ and $\delta$ in, where $\beta$ is defined as the "adversarial storage rate"(and is the same parameter as in our notation), and the $\delta$ is such that the min-entropy rate of $X$ is $\beta + \delta$. Since in our case $X$ is uniform, thus we can simply set $\delta := (1 - \beta)$. Observe that $\delta > 0$. In [16] the authors use a security parameter $\kappa$ and require that $t \geq (2/\delta)\kappa$. We can however also treat $t$ as the security parameter, and then set $\kappa := t\delta/2$. In [16] it is shown that the probability $p$ of guessing $\text{EG}(X,R)$ correctly is negligible in $\kappa$. Therefore it is also negligible in $t$ (as $\delta$ is a positive constant). $\qquad\square$

If $\mathcal{A}$ is a finite set, then $A \leftarrow \mathcal{A}$ denotes the fact that $A$ is sampled uniformly at random from $\mathcal{A}$. For a natural $q$ the symbol $\text{GF}(q)$ denotes the Galois field of order $q$. The "$||$" symbol denotes the concatenation of strings, and for $X = (X_1,\ldots,X_n) \in \mathcal{X}^n$ (for some set $\mathcal{X}$) and $i, j \in \{1,\ldots,n\}$ (such that $i \leq j$) by writing $X[i]$ we mean $X_i$, and by $X[i,\ldots,j]$ we mean $(X_i,\ldots,X_j)$. We will use the *random oracle model* (ROM) [7].

## 2.2   Multiparty Communication Complexity

A brief introduction to the multiparty complexity was already given in Sect. 1.1. We now introduce more formally the concrete computation models that are used later in this paper. A *protocol* is a tuple $\text{PROT} := (\text{PLR}_1,\ldots,\text{PLR}_k, \text{REF})$ of players (modeled as Turing machines) that interact with each other. We assume that the protocol is in the *public coins* model, i.e., the players have access to some common source of randomness. The *input of the protocol* is a tuple $(x_1, \ldots, x_k) \in \mathcal{X}_1 \times \cdots \times \mathcal{X}_k$ (where $\mathcal{X}_i$'s are some sets). Informally speaking, the goal of the players is to jointly compute some function $f : \mathcal{X}_1 \times \cdots \times \mathcal{X}_k \to \mathcal{Y}$ (where $\mathcal{Y}$ is some set). The models that are considered in the literature differ in terms of what access the players have to the input, and how can they communicate. The player REF is called the *referee* and typically takes no input. In the number-on-the-forehead (NOF) model each $\text{PLR}_i$ sees all inputs *except* $x_i$. We also impose some restrictions on the communication between the parties. We say that *the protocol* PROT *operates in fully adaptive simultaneous message (SM) model* if the parties communicate as follows.

1. Every player $\text{PLR}_i$ (for $i = 1$ to $k$) receives input $x_1, \ldots, x_{i-1}, x_{i+1}, \ldots, x_k$ (where each $x_i \in \mathcal{X}_i$), and the referee REF receives no input.
2. The computation is structured in some number of rounds. In the $j$th round the following happens:

    For $i = 1, \ldots, k$ every player $\text{PLR}_i$ (for $i = 1, \ldots, k$) broadcasts some value $w_i^j$, which is a function of his input variables and the messages broadcast by other players in the previous rounds.
3. Finally, REF computes the output of the protocol, denoted $\text{PROT}(x_1, \ldots, x_k)$, that is a function of the values $w_i^j$ that were broadcast by the $\text{PLR}_i$'s during the computation.

We say that the protocol operates in *one-round SM model* if the number of rounds in Step 2 above is 1 (in the literature this has also been called simply the "SM model"). The *one-round* almost SM *model* [31] is the same as the one-round SM model, except that one of the players, $\text{PLR}_k$, say, is the referee (and hence there is no need to specify REF separately, and we can write $\text{PROT} = (\text{PLR}_1, \ldots, \text{PLR}_k)$). Compared to the one-round SM model the only difference is in Step 3, that in case of the one-round almost SM model becomes:

**3'.** $\text{PLR}_k$ computes the output of the protocol, denoted $\text{PROT}(x_1, \ldots, x_k)$, that is a function of his own input $(x_1, \ldots, x_{k-1})$ and the values $w_i^j$ that were broadcast by the $\text{PLR}_i$'s during the computation.

Observe that in case of the one-round almost SM model we can assume that the message $w_k^1$ (sent by $\text{PLR}_k$) is empty, since the only receiver of this message is $\text{PLR}_k$ himself.

For a protocol PROT the maximal *total* length of the $w_i^j$'s (where the maximum is taken over all $(x_1, \ldots, x_k) \in \mathcal{X}_1 \times \cdots \times \mathcal{X}_k$) is called the *communication cost* of PROT. The communication complexity of a function $f$ is the minimum communication cost of any protocol computing $f$.

As explained above, we are mostly interested in the average-case complexity of the multiparty protocols.

**Definition 1.** *We say that a function* $f : \mathcal{X}_1 \times \cdots \times \mathcal{X}_k \to \mathcal{Y}$ *is* $(s, \varepsilon)$-*hard in the one-round SM model (or the fully adaptive model) if for every protocol* PROT *whose communication complexity is at most $s$, and that operates in the* *one-round SM model (or the fully adaptive model, respectively), the probability that* PROT *computes f correctly is at most ε, i.e.,*

$$\mathbb{P}\left(\text{PROT}(X_1, \ldots, X_k) = f(X_1, \ldots, X_k)\right) \leq \epsilon, \tag{1}$$

*where the probability is taken over $(X_1, \ldots, X_k) \leftarrow \mathcal{X}_1 \times \cdots \times \mathcal{X}_k$ and the public randomness available to the players (the probability in Eq. (1) is called the* correctness probability*).*

Observe that the adversary can always achieve $\epsilon = 1/|\mathcal{Y}|$. As we will be interested in protocols where $\epsilon$ is negligible, we will usually use $\mathcal{Y}$'s that are of size exponential in the security parameter $t$ (e.g., $\mathcal{Y} = \{0, 1\}^t$). We will also use a stronger notion of hardness that informally speaking requires that the information about $f(X_1, \ldots, X_k)$ obtained by a referee in a multiparty protocol with communication complexity $s$ is small.

**Definition 2.** *We say that a function $f : \mathcal{X}_1 \times \cdots \times \mathcal{X}_k \to \mathcal{Y}$ is $(s, \varepsilon)$-strongly-hard in the one-round SM model (or the fully adaptive model) if for every protocol* PROT *whose communication complexity is at most $s$, and that operates in the one-round SM model (or the fully adaptive model, respectively) we have that*

$$d\left(f(X_1, \ldots, X_k) \mid \{W_1^j, \ldots, W_k^j\}_{j=1}^t\right) \leq \epsilon, \tag{2}$$

*where the experiment in (2) consists of sampling $(X_1, \ldots, X_k) \leftarrow \mathcal{X}_1 \times \cdots \times \mathcal{X}_k$ and the public randomness of the players, and each $W_i^j$ is the message broadcast by $\text{PLR}_i$ in the jth round.*

To see why the notion defined in Definition 1 is at least as strong as the one from Definition 2, observe that, by Lemma 2, Eq. (2) implies that

$$\mathbb{P}\left(\text{PROT}(X_1, \ldots, X_k) = f(X_1, \ldots, X_k)\right) \leq 1/|\mathcal{Y}| + \epsilon$$

(see Eq. (1)), which is small for large $\mathcal{Y}$ (and small $\epsilon$).

### 2.3 Secure Positioning and the Position-Based Key Agreement

In this section we describe in details the model that was already informally discussed in Sect. 1 (for the full formal definition see [16]). A *secure positioning protocol in $D$ dimensions* is a tuple $\Pi = (\mathcal{V}_1, \ldots, \mathcal{V}_{D+1}, \mathcal{P})$, where the $\mathcal{V}_i$'s are the *verifiers* positioned in a $D$-dimensional space (and not lying on one $(D-1)$-dimensional hyperspace) and a $\mathcal{P}$ is a *prover*, positioned within the polytope determined by the verifiers. The protocol will be attacked be a set of adversaries $\{\mathcal{A}_1, \ldots, \mathcal{A}_t\}$, each $\mathcal{A}_i$ positioned in place $\widehat{\mathcal{A}}_i$. The $\mathcal{V}_i$'s, $\mathcal{A}_i$'s, and $\mathcal{P}$ are modeled as randomized Turing machines. We also assume that the $\mathcal{A}_i$'s have access to the common public randomness.

We assume that all the machines are equipped with perfect clocks and that their computation takes no time. Each machine is aware of its own position in space (more formally: it gets it as an auxiliary input). The position of each verifier $\mathcal{V}_i$ is denoted by $\widehat{\mathcal{V}}_i$. The verifiers also get as input a position $\widehat{\mathcal{P}}$ where the prover "claims to be". Their goal is to check if he indeed is in this position. The decision (yes/no) of the verifiers is communicated at the end of the protocol by one of them ($\mathcal{V}_1$, say).

The only messages that are sent are of a broadcast type (i.e. there are no directional antennas). A message sent by a machine positioned in point $U$ arrives to a machine in point $U'$ in time $\|UU'\|/c$, where $c$ is the speed of light. We assume that the adversary cannot block or delay the messages sent between the honest participants. It is clear that such an assumption is unavoidable, as, by blocking all the messages, the adversary can always prevent any protocol from succeeding. The communication links between the verifiers are secure (secret and authenticated), which can be achieved by standard cryptographic techniques.

As already highlighted in Sect. 1, the important difference between our model and the one of [16] is that we assume that if in some moment $T$ several messages $X_{i_1}, \ldots, X_{i_\ell}$ meet at point $\widehat{\mathcal{A}}_i$, then $\mathcal{A}_i$ can compute any joint function $\mathsf{adv}_i^T$ of $(X_{i_1}, \ldots, X_{i_\ell})$. Let $A_i^T$ be the result of this computation, and let $A$ be the random variable denoting the concatenation of all the $A_i^T$. We require that $|A| \leq s$, where $s$ is called the *retrieval bound*. Informally speaking, the adversary can either broadcast $A_i^T$ or store it in his memory, but to keep the model as simple as possible we will make no distinction between these two cases. Namely, we assume that (1) each adversary always broadcasts every value immediately after he computed it, and (2) each adversary stores every message broadcast by any adversary.[2] Hence a value of a function $\mathsf{adv}_i^T$ can depend on all the adversarial messages received by $\mathcal{A}_i$ at or before time $T$ (including the messages sent by $\mathcal{A}_i$ himself in time $T$).

We assume that several adversaries can be put in one place in space, but for simplicity we require that the adversaries that are in the same place do not broadcast messages at the same time (clearly, this assumption can be made without loss of generality, as such adversaries can be "simulated" by one).

We also assume that every adversary computes (and broadcasts) a value only once. Note that this also does not affect the generality of the model, as we do not put any restrictions on the number of adversaries, and moreover, several adversaries can be put in the same point in space. Therefore an adversary that computes $m$ values (in different moments in time), can be "simulated" by $m$ adversaries placed in the same point. We say that $\Pi$ *is an $(s, \rho)$-secure positioning protocol* if the following two conditions hold:

**correctness:** If the prover $\mathcal{P}$ is placed in the claimed position $\widehat{\mathcal{P}} \in \mathcal{G}$ then $\mathcal{V}_1$ produces as output "yes",

**security:** For any set of adversaries $\{\mathcal{A}_1, \ldots, \mathcal{A}_t\}$ with retrieval bound $s$ (such that no adversary or honest prover is in position $\widehat{\mathcal{P}}$), the verifier $\mathcal{V}_1$ produces as output "yes" with probability at most $\rho$. (If $\mathcal{V}_1$ produced "yes" then we say that the adversaries *broke the scheme*.)

---

[2] Observe that these assumptions can be made without loss of generality, as storing the computed values does not affect the retrieval bound.

Following [16], we also consider a stronger type of protocols called the *position-based key agreement*. In such a protocol the goal of the prover and the verifiers is to agree on a key $K \in \{0,1\}^m$. More formally, at the end of the execution the prover produces as output $K_{\mathcal{P}}$, and one of the verifiers, $\mathcal{V}_1$ (say) produces $K_{\mathcal{V}}$. We say that $\Pi$ *is an $(s, \rho)$-secure position-based key agreement protocol in $D$ dimensions* if the following two conditions hold (assuming the prover $\mathcal{P}$ is placed in the claimed position $\widehat{\mathcal{P}} \in \mathcal{G}$):

**correctness:** The agreed keys are identical, i.e., $K_{\mathcal{P}} = K_{\mathcal{V}}$.

**security:** For any set of adversaries $\{\mathcal{A}_1, \ldots, \mathcal{A}_t\}$ with retrieval bound $s$ (such that no adversary is in position $\widehat{\mathcal{P}}$) we have that $d(K_{\mathcal{P}} \mid A) \leq \rho$ (recall that $A$ is the random variable denoting all the information computed by the adversaries).[3]

For reasons explained in the introduction we are interested in protocols that have the following simple structure (let $T$ be some moment in time):

1. Each $\mathcal{V}_i$ sends a message $X_i \leftarrow \mathcal{X}_i$ (where $\mathcal{X}_i$ is some set) to $\mathcal{P}$ in time $T - \|\widehat{\mathcal{V}_i \mathcal{P}}\|/c$ (in this way all $X_i$'s arrive to $\mathcal{P}$ in time $T$).
2. $\mathcal{P}$ computes $Y = \pi(X_1, \ldots, X_{D+1})$ (for some function $\pi : \mathcal{X}_1 \times \cdots \times \mathcal{X}_{D+1} \to \mathcal{Y}$) and
   - **in case of the positioning protocols:** $\mathcal{P}$ broadcasts $Y$,
   - **in case of the key-agreement protocols:** $\mathcal{P}$ sets $K_{\mathcal{P}} = Y$.
3. In the last step the verifiers compute $\pi(X_1, \ldots, X_{D+1})$ in some way (e.g., they may simply send to one verifier all the inputs and let him compute the output). The details of this computation depend on the function that they compute. In many cases there also exist techniques that allow to save on the communication and space complexities of this procedure, e.g., each $X_i$ can be generated pseudorandomly from some seed $S_i$, in which case it is enough that the verifiers store and send to each other only the $S_i$'s. We write more about it when we consider the concrete implementations in Sect. 4.
   - **in case of the positioning protocols:** each $\mathcal{V}_i$ accepts the proof only if $y$ that he received is indeed equal to $\pi(X_1, \ldots, X_{D+1})$ and it arrived to him in time $T + \|\widehat{\mathcal{V}_i \mathcal{P}}\|/c$,
   - **in case of the key-agreement protocols:** the verifier $\mathcal{V}_1$ produces $K_{\mathcal{V}} = \pi(X_1, \ldots, X_{D+1})$ as the agreed key.

A protocol of this type will be called a *one-round protocol parametrized by $\pi$*. We say that a protocol is *for positions in the set $\mathcal{W} \subseteq \mathbb{R}^D$* if it works only if $\widehat{\mathcal{P}} \in \mathcal{W}$ (note, however, that we do *not* restrict the set of positions where the adversary can be placed). Let us also comment on the assumption that $X_i$ is sampled uniformly from some set. This is done mostly for the sake of simplicity,

---

[3] In [16] the security of a key agreement is defined using the "indistinguishability" paradigm (cf. Definition 2.2 in [16]): no adversary, after learning $A$, should be able to distinguish $K_{\mathcal{P}}$ from a uniformly random key, with advantage larger than $\rho$. It is easy to see that these definitions are equivalent.

and to keep our model consistent with the one in Sect. 2.2. We could also have a more general definition where the $X_i$'s would come from some more general class of distributions, e.g., the distributions with high min-entropy (as is done in [16]). For the equivalence results shown in Sect. 3 to hold, we would need to extend the hardness definitions in Sect. 2.2 to cover also the case when the $X_i$'s are not uniform, but this can be done in a straightforward way. Also our constructions can be easily generalized to cover the case when the inputs come from a high-min entropy source (this generalization will be described in the full version of this paper).

It is natural to ask how do these two primitives relate to each other. Obviously, every $(s, \rho)$-secure position-based key agreement protocol can be converted into an $(s, \rho')$-secure positioning protocol with $\rho' = 2^{-|K|} + \rho$ in the following way: let the prover send $K_{\mathcal{P}}$ to $\mathcal{V}_1$, and let $\mathcal{V}_1$ output "yes" only if $K_{\mathcal{P}} = K_{\mathcal{V}}$. It easily follows from Lemma 2 that if $\mathcal{P}$ is not in the position $\widehat{\mathcal{P}}$ then the probability that he can guess $K_{\mathcal{P}}$ is at most $\rho'$.

On the other hand, it is also possible to convert every secure $(s, \rho)$-secure positioning protocol (for some negligible $\rho$) into an $(s, \rho')$-secure position-based key agreement protocol (for negligible $\rho'$), at a cost of introducing computational assumptions. Concretely, pubilc-key encryption and non-malleable commitments, we refer to [16] (Sect. 6, p. 1311) for further details.

### 2.4   Prover's Efficiency

The function $\pi$ needs to be computed also by the prover $\mathcal{P}$, and it is important to choose $\pi$ such that this computation can be done efficiently. Note that the advantage of $\mathcal{P}$ over the adversaries is that he has simultaneous access to all the $\pi$'s inputs $X_1, \ldots, X_{D+1}$. Since the $X_i$'s are very long, we would ideally like to be able to compute $\pi$ by looking only on some small parts of the inputs (polylogaritmic in $|X|$, say). This property, called *locality*, was stated as an explicit requirement in [16]. It is also common in the previous papers on the bounded-storage model [3, 18, 20, 26]. One of our constructions in this paper (see Sect. 4.2) does not have this property (the one in Sect. 4.1 has it). Instead it has the property of being *online computable* which means that $\pi$ reads its input by just processing its input online in small memory. We remark that in some cases such algorithms may actually be easier to implement than some of the locally computable ones (think of a locally computable algorithm that is required to access many bits on its input that are located far away).

## 3   The Reductions

In this section we show strong connections between the two areas described in Sect. 2. We start (Sect. 3.1) with showing that a construction of a positioning protocol immediately gives a construction of a function with a high one-round SM complexity. Note that this means that a similar implication holds for position-based key agreement (since, as explained in Sect. 2.3, position-based key agreement is a stronger primitive than secure positioning). Then, in Sect. 3.2, we show an implication in the opposite direction, namely, we prove that every function with high one-round almost SM complexity gives rise to a secure positioning protocol, and every function with high fully adaptive SM complexity gives rise to a secure position-based key agreement protocol.

From an application point of view, the results in Sect. 3.1 are "negative", as they show that in order to construct secure positioning protocols (and the position-based key agreement protocols) we need to show multiparty functions that have high communication complexity, which seems to be non-trivial, especially if the locality is required (see end of Sect. 3.1 for a discussion on this). On the other hand, the results from Sect. 3.2 can be viewed as "positive", since they provide a way to construct secure positioning (and position-based key agreement) protocols. Notice that these positive results yield a constructive use of lower bounds in communication complexity. We instantiate these constructions with concrete protocols is Sect. 4.

### 3.1  Secure Positioning in the BRM Implies Lower Bounds for SM Complexity

We now show that existence of a one-round protocol for secure positioning implies lower bounds for the multiparty communication complexity. Note that, as described in Sect. 2.3, the secure positioning protocols are a weaker primitive than the position-based key agreement protocols, and a similar implication also holds for the position-based key agreement. To keep the exposition simple we address only the case when the verifiers are placed on vertices of a regular $D$-dimensional simplex, but it should be clear that our argument can be easily extended to more general cases. The statement of the lemma assumes that $D = 2$ or $D = 3$. This is because, obviously, the case of $D > 3$ has no practical relevance, and for $D = 1$ the function $\pi$ has only two arguments, so, as described in the introduction, it makes little sense to talk about the NOF complexity. Recall that a regular 2-dimensional simplex is an equilateral triangle, and a regular 3-dimensional simplex is a regular tetrahedron. We now have the following theorem.

**Theorem 1.** *Suppose $\Pi$ is an $(s, \rho)$-secure one-round positioning protocol in $D$ dimensions (for $D = 2$ or $D = 3$) parametrized by $\pi : \mathcal{X}_1 \times \cdots \times \mathcal{X}_{D+1} \to \mathcal{Y}$ with verifiers positioned on vertices of a regular $D$-dimensional simplex. Then $\pi$ is $(s, \rho)$-hard in the 1-round SM model.*

*Proof.* Let $a$ denote the length of the edge of the simplex, or, in other words, the distance between any pair of verifiers. For the sake of contradiction suppose $\pi$ can be computed in a one-round SM model by a protocol PROT $= (\text{PLR}_1, \ldots, \text{PLR}_{D+1}, \text{REF})$ with communication complexity $s$ and correctness probability $\rho' > \rho$. For every $\text{PLR}_j \in \{\text{PLR}_1, \ldots, \text{PLR}_{D+1}\}$ let $\text{Msg}_j = \text{Msg}_j(X_1, \ldots, X_{j-1}, X_{j+1}, \ldots, X_{D+1})$ denote the message computed by $\text{PLR}_j$, and let $\text{Ref}(\text{Msg}_1, \ldots, \text{Msg}_{D+1})$ be the value computed by the referee REF

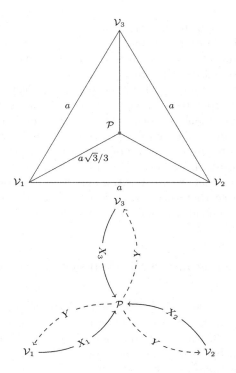

**Fig. 1.** On the left: the configuration of the prover and the verifiers for in the two-dimensional case. On the right: the execution of the positioning protocol in this configuration. The dashed lines indicate the messages sent back by the prover. Note that the $X_i$'s and $Y$ are broadcast (there are no directional antennas in our model), and the lines are only indicating the communication that matters for the protocol.

(equal to $\pi(X_1, \ldots, X_{D+1})$ with probability $\rho'$). We now show a set of adversaries $\mathcal{A}_1, \ldots, \mathcal{A}_{D+1}, \mathcal{B}_1, \ldots, \mathcal{B}_{D+1}$ with retrieval bound $s$ that break $\Pi$ with probability $\rho'$ (and none of them is positioned in position $\widehat{\mathcal{P}}$).

We assume that position $\widehat{\mathcal{P}}$ is the center of mass of the simplex determined by the verifiers. Hence, $\widehat{\mathcal{P}}$ is in the same distance to all the verifiers, and therefore all the messages $X_i$ are sent in the same moment $U = T - \|\widehat{\mathcal{P}}\widehat{\mathcal{V}}_1\|/c$, where (as it can be easily verified using basic geometric arguments) $\|\widehat{\mathcal{P}}\widehat{\mathcal{V}}_1\|$ is equal to $a\sqrt{3}/3$ (if $D = 2$) and is equal to $a\sqrt{6}/4$ (if $D = 3$). This situation is depicted on Fig. 1 for the case $D = 2$.

Obviously, all the verifiers expect to receive the answer from the prover in time $T + \|\widehat{\mathcal{P}}\widehat{\mathcal{V}}_1\|/c = U + 2\|\widehat{\mathcal{P}}\widehat{\mathcal{V}}_1\|/c$. The adversaries $\mathcal{A}_1, \ldots, \mathcal{A}_{D+1}, \mathcal{B}_1, \ldots, \mathcal{B}_{D+1}$ behave in the following way (see Fig. 2).

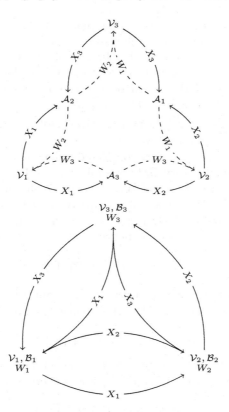

**Fig. 2.** On the left: the actions of the $\mathcal{A}_i$'s, on the right: the actions of the $\mathcal{B}_i$'s (recall that each $W_i$ is a function of all the $X_j$'s except of $X_i$).

– Each $\mathcal{A}_j$ is positioned in point $\widehat{\mathcal{A}}_j$ defined as follows: $\widehat{\mathcal{A}}_j$ is the center of mass of the facet determined by the points $\widehat{\mathcal{V}}_1, \ldots, \widehat{\mathcal{V}}_{j-1}, \widehat{\mathcal{V}}_{j+1}, \ldots, \widehat{\mathcal{V}}_{D+1}$. This facet is either a line segment—in case $D = 2$, or an equilateral triangle—in case $D = 3$. From the regularity of this facet we get that the messages $X_1, \ldots, X_{j-1}, X_{j+1}, \ldots, X_{D+1}$ (sent by the verifiers $\mathcal{V}_1, \ldots, \mathcal{V}_{j-1}, \mathcal{V}_{j+1}, \ldots, \mathcal{V}_{D+1}$) arrive to point $\widehat{\mathcal{A}}_j$ in the same moment. In the moment when they arrive there, the adversary $\mathcal{A}_j$ computes $W_j = \mathrm{Msg}_j(X_1, \ldots, X_{j-1}, X_{j+1}, \ldots, X_{D+1})$ and broadcasts the result. This happens in time $U + \|\widehat{\mathcal{A}}_j \widehat{\mathcal{V}}_i\|/c$.
– Each $\mathcal{B}_i$ is positioned in point $\widehat{\mathcal{V}}_i$.[4] He does the following:
  • When the messages $X_1, \ldots, X_{i-1}, X_{i+1}, \ldots, X_{D+1}$ arrive to him (observe that, from the regularity of the simplex, they all arrive in the same

---

[4] The reader may object that it is not realistic to assume that an adversary is positioned at zero distance from a verifier. At the end of the proof we argue that $\mathcal{B}_i$ can actually be put at some place far from any verifier. We decided to assume that $\mathcal{B}_i$ is positioned exactly in point $\widehat{\mathcal{V}}_i$ to keep the exposition simple.

moment $T' = U + a/c$) he computes $W_i := \mathrm{Msg}_i(X_1, \ldots, X_{i-1}, X_{i+1}, \ldots, X_{D+1})$ and stores the result.

- He also stores each message $W_j$ broadcast by $\mathcal{A}_j$ (for $j \in \{1, \ldots, i - 1, i+1, \ldots, D+1\}$) when it arrives to him. This happens in time $T'' = U + \|\widehat{\mathcal{A}_j \mathcal{V}_i}\|/c + \|\widehat{\mathcal{A}_j \mathcal{B}_i}\|/c$ (where $\widehat{\mathcal{B}_i}$ is the position of $\mathcal{B}_i$, which is equal to $\widehat{\mathcal{V}_i}$). Hence $T''$ is equal to $U + 2\|\widehat{\mathcal{A}_j \mathcal{V}_i}\|/c$.

  Additionally since $\|\widehat{\mathcal{A}_j \mathcal{B}_i}\|$ is nonnegative, it follows that $\|\widehat{\mathcal{A}_j \mathcal{V}_i}\| + \|\widehat{\mathcal{A}_j \mathcal{B}_i}\| \geq \|\widehat{\mathcal{A}_j \mathcal{V}_i}\| = a$, and therefore $T'' \geq T'$.

- After the two steps above are completed (which happens in time $\max(T', T'') = T''$) the adversary $\mathcal{B}_i$ knows all $W_1, \ldots, W_{D+1}$ and he can simply compute the output $Y$ as $\mathrm{Ref}(W_1, \ldots, W_{D+1})$, and pass it $\mathcal{V}_i$ (which takes zero time, since $\mathcal{B}_i$ is positioned exactly in $\widehat{\mathcal{V}_i}$). Moreover, he can do it exactly in time $U + 2\|\widehat{\mathcal{P} \mathcal{V}_1}\|/c$ when $\mathcal{V}_i$ expects to receive $y$. This is possible, because (as we show below)

$$T'' < U + 2\|\widehat{\mathcal{P} \mathcal{V}_1}\|/c. \tag{3}$$

We now show (3). Let us start with case $D = 2$. Since in this case each facet of the simplex is a line segment of length $a$, hence $\|\widehat{\mathcal{A}_j \mathcal{V}_i}\| = a/2$. Therefore (3) becomes

$$U + a/c < U + 2a\sqrt{3}/(3c), \tag{4}$$

which holds because $1 < 2\sqrt{3}/3$. In case $D = 3$ each facet is a regular triangle with edge of length $a$. Thus $\|\widehat{\mathcal{A}_j \mathcal{V}_i}\| = \sqrt{3}/3$, and therefore (3) becomes

$$U + 2a\sqrt{3}/(3c) < U + 2a\sqrt{6}/(4c), \tag{5}$$

which holds because $2\sqrt{3}/3 < 2\sqrt{6}/4$. Clearly the adversaries constructed this way compute function $\pi$ correctly with exactly the same probability $\sigma'$ as the SM protocol computes it. It remains to calculate how much communication was generated by the adversaries. Observe that each $\mathrm{Msg}_j$ is computed by each $\mathcal{A}_j$ and $\mathcal{B}_j$, respectively. Each $\mathcal{B}_j$ can compute the final answer by storing $\mathrm{Msg}_j$ and receiving $\{\mathrm{Msg}_i\}_{i \neq j}$, hence the total amount of retrieved information is $\sum_{i=1}^{D+1} \mathrm{Msg}_i = s$. This finishes the proof.

Finally, note that both inequalities (4) and (5) are sharp, and the differences between the left hand sides and the right hand sides are non-negligible. This means that $\mathcal{B}_i$ has to wait some noticeable amount of time before he sends $y$ to the verifier $\mathcal{V}_i$. Hence, it is also ok to place $\mathcal{B}_i$ in some position $\widehat{\mathcal{B}_i}$ further away from $\mathcal{V}_i$ (as long as the $\widehat{\mathcal{B}_i}$ is in equal distance to the remaining verifiers). □

Recall that according to the standard definitions (see Sect. 2.4) we want function $\pi$ to be locally computable, which means that it should be possible to compute it by looking only at a polylogarithmic number of bits of its input $(X_1, \ldots, X_{D+1})$. It is easy to see that such an algorithm is trivial to implement by a multiparty protocol that has polylogarithmic communication complexity in the fully adaptive settings. On the other hand, function $\pi$, by Theorem 1, needs to have a linear complexity in the one-round SM model. Since finding such functions is an open problem we view this result as an indication why showing one-round positioning protocols in the unrestricted BSM model is hard. The reader may object that typically the communication complexity literature is more focused on deterministic functions that compute one bit, while here we consider randomized functions (with small correctness probability) with multi-bit output. This is not a problem for the following reasons: (1) it is easy to see that a lower bound on the communication complexity of our multi-bit output randomized function also implies a lower bound on a single-bit output functions (since there has to be at least one bit of output that is hard to guess with good probability), and (2) randomized lower bounds imply the deterministic ones.

## 3.2   Lower Bounds for SM Complexity Imply Results for PBC

In this section we show implications in the other direction than in Sect. 3.1, i.e., we show how to build positioning and position-based key agreement protocols from functions that have high communication complexity. Unlike in case of Sect. 3.1 we consider these two cases separately (the first one in Theorem 2), and the second one in Theorem 3. Although in principle the second construction would suffice for showing the general implication (as the key agreement is a stronger primitive than the positioning), such a separation makes sense, since the requirements for the communication complexity that we need in Theorem 2 are weaker (and hence Theorem 2 does not directly follow from Theorem 3). Also the conditions on the position of the prover $\mathcal{P}$ are more restrictive in Theorem 3. First, we need the following geometric fact (see [16]).

**Lemma 4.** *Suppose $D \in \{2, 3\}$. Consider pairwise distinct points $\widehat{\mathcal{V}}_1, \ldots, \widehat{\mathcal{V}}_{D+1}$ positioned in a $D$-dimensional space, and let $\widehat{\mathcal{P}}$ be any point within the $D$-dimensional simplex $S$ whose vertices are in points $\widehat{\mathcal{V}}_1, \ldots, \widehat{\mathcal{V}}_{D+1}$. Then, for any point $\widehat{\mathcal{A}} \neq \widehat{\mathcal{P}}$ there exists $i$ such that $\|\widehat{\mathcal{V}}_i \widehat{\mathcal{A}}\| > \|\widehat{\mathcal{V}}_i \widehat{\mathcal{P}}\|$.*

We now have the following.

**Theorem 2.** *Suppose $D \in \{2, 3\}$. Let $\pi : \mathcal{X}_1 \times \cdots \times \mathcal{X}_{D+1} \to \mathcal{Y}$ be an $(s, \rho)$-hard function in the one-round almost SM model. Let $\Pi$ be a one-round positioning protocol parametrized by $\pi$. Then $\Pi$ is $(s, \rho)$-secure for positions within the $D$-dimensional simplex whose vertices are the positions of the verifiers $\widehat{\mathcal{V}}_1, \ldots, \widehat{\mathcal{V}}_{D+1}$.*

*Moreover, something slightly stronger holds, namely the protocol $\Pi$ is secure even if only $\mathcal{V}_k$ (i.e.: the arbiter in the almost adaptive NOF protocol) receives the message from the prover.*

*Proof.* We say that an adversary $\mathcal{A}_i$ *directly computes* on some $X_j$ if he produces his output exactly when $X_j$ passes through $\widehat{\mathcal{A}}_i$. We also recursively define a partial order *dependence* relation "$\preceq$" among the verifiers and the adversaries as follows:

- $\mathcal{V}_i \preceq \mathcal{A}_j$ if the value broadcast by $\mathcal{V}_i$ reaches $\mathcal{A}_j$ not later than when $\mathcal{A}_j$ produces his output. More precisely let $T_i$ be the time when $\mathcal{V}_i$ broadcast $X_i$ and let $T_j$ be the time when $\mathcal{A}_j$ computes his function, then $\mathcal{V}_i \preceq \mathcal{A}_j$ if $\|\widehat{\mathcal{A}_j}\widehat{\mathcal{V}_i}\|/c \le T_j - T_i$.
- analogously $\mathcal{A}_i \preceq \mathcal{A}_j$ if the value computed by $\mathcal{A}_i$ reaches $\mathcal{A}_j$ not later than when $\mathcal{A}_j$ produces his output.

(Clearly the dependence relation is a partial order.) Set $k := D + 1$. Let $\mathcal{P}$ be the prover, and $\mathcal{V}_1, \ldots, \mathcal{V}_{D+1}$ be the verifiers. Assume the position $\widehat{\mathcal{P}}$ of $\mathcal{P}$ is within the $D$-dimensional simplex whose vertices are the positions of the verifiers $\widehat{\mathcal{V}}_1, \ldots, \widehat{\mathcal{V}}_{D+1}$. For the sake of contradiction assume that $\Pi$ can be broken by adversaries with retrieval bound $s$ with probability $\rho' > \rho$. This means that one of the adversaries is able to send to the verifier $\mathcal{V}_k$ a message $Y$ equal to $\pi(X_1, \ldots, X_k)$ with probability $\rho'$ (assuming $(X_1, \ldots, X_k) \leftarrow \mathcal{X}_1 \times \cdots \times \mathcal{X}_k$), and this message arrived to $\mathcal{V}_k$ in time $T + \|\widehat{\mathcal{V}_k}\widehat{\mathcal{P}}\|/c$, where $T$ is the time where all the $X_i$'s arrive to point $\widehat{\mathcal{P}}$. We now show a one-round almost adaptive protocol for computing $\pi$ with probability $\rho'$ and communication complexity $s$. The protocol works as follows.

Let $Adv^1$ be the set of all adversaries $\mathcal{A}_i$ that depend on some proper subset of verifiers. Our protocol (in the first round) computes all $A_i$'s such that $\mathcal{A}_i \in Adv^1$. This can clearly be done since each such $A_i$ is a function of some proper subset of the input variables $X_\ell$.

Let $Adv^2$ be the set of all the remaining adversaries. Take any $\mathcal{A}_i \in Adv^2$. We know that $\mathcal{A}_i$ depends on *all* the verifiers (as otherwise it would be in $Adv^1$). Let $\widehat{\mathcal{A}}_i$ be the position of this adversary. By Lemma 4 it has to be the case that for some $\widehat{\mathcal{V}}_j$ we have

$$\|\widehat{\mathcal{V}_j}\widehat{\mathcal{A}_i}\| > \|\widehat{\mathcal{V}_j}\widehat{\mathcal{P}}\|. \tag{6}$$

Any $\mathcal{A}_i$ which depends on $\widehat{\mathcal{V}}_j$ must produce its output after receiving $X_j$. Therefore (6) implies that the time $T_i$ when $\mathcal{A}_i$ produces its output is such that

$$T_i > T. \tag{7}$$

Consider some $\mathcal{A}_i \in Adv^2$ that is positioned *further* away from $\mathcal{V}_k$ than $\mathcal{P}$. By (7) the output of such $A_i$ will not reach $\mathcal{V}_k$ before time $T + \|\widehat{\mathcal{V}_k}\widehat{\mathcal{P}}\|/c$, and hence it is irrelevant for the protocol.

Therefore what remains is to consider the adversaries $\mathcal{A}_i \in Adv^2$ that are *closer* to $\mathcal{V}_k$ than $\mathcal{P}$. From (7) we have that the computation of such $\mathcal{A}_i$ happens *after* $X_k$ passed through $A_i$, and therefore $\mathcal{A}_i$ does not compute on $X_k$ directly. Thus, every computation performed by the $\mathcal{A}_i$'s from $Adv^2$ (that are closer to $\mathcal{V}_k$ than $\mathcal{P}$) can be performed if one knows the set $X_1, \ldots, X_{k-1}$ plus the outputs of the $\mathcal{A}_j$'s from $Adv^1$. Hence, it can be done by $\text{PLR}_k$ acting as a referee.

Since the SM protocol that we constructed simply simulates the adversaries $\mathcal{A}_i$ by computing their outputs, its communication complexity is $s$. This completes the proof.     $\square$

We now show Theorem 3 that is similar to Theorem 2, but it holds for position-based key agreement. Observe that for the lemma to hold we need a stronger assumption than in Theorem 2, namely that $\pi$ is hard in the fully-adaptive SM model. Also, unlike in Theorem 2, we do not specify explicitly what geometric configurations of the verifiers and the prover are allowed. Instead, we simply say that they need to be such that the messages sent by the verifier (see Sect. 2.3) never "meet" at any place other than the position $\widehat{\mathcal{P}}$ of the prover. More precisely, we require that there does not exist time $U$ and place $\widehat{\mathcal{Z}} \neq \widehat{\mathcal{P}}$ such that at time $U$ all the $X_i$'s are in $\widehat{\mathcal{Z}}$. We refer the reader to [16], Sect. 7.3.1 as to what these valid configurations for the parties are. We now prove the following theorem.

**Theorem 3.** *Suppose $D \in \{2,3\}$. Let $\pi : \mathcal{X}_1 \times \cdots \times \mathcal{X}_{D+1} \to \mathcal{Y}$ be an $(s,\rho)$-strongly-hard function in the fully adaptive SM model. Let $\Pi$ be a one-round key-agreement protocol in $D$ dimensions parametrized by $\pi$. Then $\Pi$ is a $(s,\rho)$-secure key-agreement protocol assuming all the messages sent by the verifiers never meet at any other place than the position $\widehat{\mathcal{P}}$ of the prover.*

*Proof.* For the sake of contradiction suppose $\Pi$ is not $(s,\rho)$-secure, i.e. there exists adversaries $\mathcal{A}_1, \ldots, \mathcal{A}_t$, each positioned in $\widehat{\mathcal{A}}_i, \ldots, \widehat{\mathcal{A}}_t$ (resp.), such that

$$d(\pi(X_1, \ldots, X_{D+1}) \mid A) = \rho' > \rho, \tag{8}$$

where $X_1, \ldots, X_{D+1} \leftarrow \mathcal{X}_1 \times \cdots \times \mathcal{X}_{D+1}$ are the input variables, and $A$ is a concatenation of the outputs $A_i^T$ of the $\mathsf{adv}_i^T$ functions computed by the adversaries when the protocol $\Pi$ is executed on input $(X_1, \ldots, X_{D+1})$. To finish the proof we show an NOF protocol with communication complexity $s$ such that

$$d(\pi(X_1, \ldots, X_{D+1}) \mid W) = \rho', \tag{9}$$

where $W$ is a concatenation of the messages sent by the players when the NOF protocol is executed on variables $(X_1, \ldots, X_{D+1})$. Clearly, showing (9) will contradict the assumption that $\pi$ is $(s,\rho)$-strongly-hard in the NOF model.

Let $\preceq$ be the partial order from the proof of Lemma 2. The NOF protocol simply computes all the $A_i^T$ starting least $\mathcal{A}_i$'s in the "$\preceq$" order, and maintaining the invariant that a given $A_j^T$ can be computed only if the $\mathcal{A}_\ell$'s that precede $\mathcal{A}_j$ in this order were computed. By our assumption, its never the case that a $\mathcal{A}_i$ computes directly on all the $X_i$'s. Therefore this computation can be performed by a (fully adaptive) NOF protocol. It is also easy to see that the output $W$ of this protocol has identical distribution to $A$. This finishes the proof.  □

## 4    Concrete Constructions

In this section we provide two concrete constructions of positioning and position-based key agreement protocols. This is done using the theory developed in Sect. 3.2, i.e., we first prove that some function $\pi$ has high communication complexity, and then use this function to construct a position-based protocol. We start with a construction of a positioning protocol that has the "locality" property (see Sect. 2.4), and works in the random oracle model. Note, that using the techniques from [16], this positioning protocol can be transformed into a position-based key agreement, using the computational assumptions discussed in Sect. 2.3. Then, in Sect. 4.2, we show a construction of a position-based key agreement in the plain model (i.e. without a random oracle assumption). This second construction comes without the locality property, i.e., the prover has to read the entire random strings $X_i$ that are sent to him by the verifiers. On the other hand, it has the *on-line-computability* property, i.e., the $X_i$'s need to be read only once in an on-line fashion, by an a machine with very small memory (see Sect. 2.4).

### 4.1   Protocols in the Random Oracle Model

As proven in Sect. 3.2 (see Theorem 2), to construct such a protocol it is enough to show a function $\pi : \mathcal{X}_1 \times \cdots \times \mathcal{X}_k \to \mathcal{Y}$ whose one-round almost SM complexity is high. Let $t$ be a security parameter. We assume that the parties have access to $t$ random oracles containing functions $\{H_j : \{0,1\}^* \to \{1, \ldots, n\}\}_{j=1}^t$ (let $\mathcal{H}$ denote this family of functions). The function $\pi$ will depend on the functions in $\mathcal{H}$. Also every party will have access to the functions in $\mathcal{H}$. More concretely, let $\pi_{k,n}^{\mathcal{H},t} : (\{0,1\}^t)^{k-1} \times \{0,1\}^n \to \{0,1\}^t$ be a function defined as: $\pi_{k,n}^{\mathcal{H},t}(Z_1, \ldots, Z_{k-1}, X) := (X[H_1(Z)], \ldots, X[H_t(Z)])$, where $Z = (Z_1 || \cdots || Z_{k-1})$.

  Our positioning protocol $\Pi_{D,n}^{\mathcal{H},t}$ in $D$ dimensions (for $D \in \{2,3\}$) is simply the one-round positioning protocol parametrized by $\pi_{D+1,n}^{\mathcal{H},t}$ (see Sect. 2.3). More concretely: it consists of $D+1$ verifiers $\mathcal{V}_1, \ldots, \mathcal{V}_{D+1}$ (positioned in $\widehat{\mathcal{V}}_1, \ldots, \widehat{\mathcal{V}}_{D+1}$, resp.). Each $\mathcal{V}_i$ (for $i \leq D$) sends a random $Z_i \leftarrow \{0,1\}^t$ in time $T - \|\widehat{\mathcal{V}}_i \widehat{\mathcal{P}}\|/c$ (where $\widehat{\mathcal{P}}$ is the claimed position of the prover), and $\mathcal{V}_{D+1}$ sends a random $X \leftarrow \{0,1\}^n$ (in time $T - \|\widehat{\mathcal{V}}_{D+1} \widehat{\mathcal{P}}\|/c$). All the messages arrive to $\mathcal{P}$ in time $T$. Then, $\mathcal{P}$ computes $X[H_1(Z)], \ldots, X[H_t(Z)]$, and sends the result back to $\mathcal{V}_{D+1}$, who checks if the result is correct (at the end of this section we discuss how this check can be done very efficiently). The security of $\Pi_{D,n}^{\mathcal{H},t}$ follows directly from Theorem 3, and the following fact.

**Lemma 5.** *Consider an almost adaptive one-round SM protocol* $\mathrm{PLR}_1, \ldots, \mathrm{PLR}_k$ *with* $\mathrm{PLR}_k$ *being the referee, and every player having random oracle access to the functions in* $\mathcal{H}$. *Let* $\beta n$ *denote the total communication complexity of this protocol (where* $n \in \mathbb{N}$ *and* $\beta < 1$ *is some constant) and let* $q$ *be the number of times the parties query the random oracles. Assume* $q$ *is polynomial in* $t$ *and* $n$ *is any function of* $t$ *such that* $n \geq t$. *Let* $Y$ *denote the output of* $\mathrm{PLR}_k$. *Then we have*

$$\mathbb{P}\left(Y = \pi_{k,n}^{\mathcal{H},t}(Z_1, \ldots, Z_{k-1}, X)\right) \leq \mathsf{negl}(t), \tag{10}$$

*where* $\mathsf{negl}$ *denotes a negligible function, the probability in (10) is taken over random* $X \leftarrow \{0,1\}^n$, $(Z_1, \ldots, Z_{k-1}) \leftarrow (\{0,1\}^t)^{k-1}$, *and the random choice of the functions on* $\mathcal{H}$.

*Proof.* Suppose we have an almost adaptive one-round SM protocol $\text{PLR}_1, \ldots,$ $\text{PLR}_k$ (with $\text{PLR}_k$ being the referee) such that the probability in (10) is non-negligible. Recall the guessing game from Sect. 2.1. We now show how to use $\text{PLR}_1, \ldots, \text{PLR}_k$ to construct a pair of functions $\mathsf{compress} : \{0,1\}^n \to \{0,1\}^{\beta n}$ and $\mathsf{guess} : \{1, \ldots, n\}^t \times \{0,1\}^{\beta n} \to \{0,1\}^t$ such that the probability that $\mathsf{guess}(R, \mathsf{compress}(X)) = (X[R_1], \ldots, X[R_t])$ is non-negligible in $t$, where $X \leftarrow \{0,1\}^n$ and $R = (R_1, \ldots, R_t) \leftarrow \{1, \ldots, n\}^t$. Since by Lemma 3 we know that this is impossible, we will obtain that the probability in (10) has to be negligible.

The functions $\mathsf{compress}$ and $\mathsf{guess}$ that we construct are randomized, i.e., they depend on some external fresh randomness. In particular, we will assume that the hash functions $\mathcal{H}$ that the players have access to (via the random oracle) were sampled in advance. Of course, such sampling cannot be done efficiently (since the set of all such functions is of exponential size), but this is ok, since our construction is anyway information-theoretic (note that Lemma 3 does not involve any complexity-theoretic assumptions). We will later argue why the assumption about the availability of external randomness can be done without loss of generality. First, however, let us present the definitions of the functions $\mathsf{compress}$ and $\mathsf{guess}$.

The function $\mathsf{compress}$ is defined as follows. First it samples $(Z_1, \ldots, Z_{k-1}) \leftarrow (\{0,1\}^t)^{k-1}$. Then, on input $(X, R_1, \ldots, R_{k-1})$ it produces as output a tuple $(V_1, \ldots, V_{k-1})$, where each $V_i$ is equal to the output of player $\text{PLR}_i$ on input $(R_1, \ldots, R_{i-1}, R_{i+1}, \ldots, R_{k-1}, X)$ (recall that in this model the referee $\text{PLR}_k$ does not produce any output in the first phase). Note that simulating the $\text{PLR}_i$'s may require replying to their random oracle queries. We reply to each such query using the hash functions $\mathcal{H}$ that were sampled beforehand. Observe that $|(V_1, \ldots, V_{k-1})| \le \beta n$, and therefore $\mathsf{compress}$ can fit this output in the set $\{0,1\}^{\beta n}$.

On input $(R_1, \ldots, R_t)$ and $X$ the function $\mathsf{guess}$ does the following. It simulates the referee $\text{PLR}_k$ on input $(Z_1, \ldots, Z_{k-1})$ (which are the values that were already sampled by $\mathsf{compress}$). It answers all the random oracle queries using $\mathcal{H}$, with one important exception. Namely, every query of a form $(Z_1|| \cdots ||Z_{k-1})$ to an oracle containing a hash function $H_j$ (for $j = 1, \ldots, t$) is answered with $R_j$.

Now, let $\mathcal{E}$ denote the event that it never happened that any of the $\text{PLR}_1, \ldots,$ $\text{PLR}_{k-1}$ queried any of the random oracles on $(Z_1|| \cdots ||Z_{k-1})$. It is easy to see that we have the following:

$$\mathbb{P}\left(Y = \pi_{k,n}^{\mathcal{H},t}(Z_1, \ldots, Z_{k-1}, X) \mid \mathcal{E}\right)$$
$$= \mathbb{P}\left(\mathsf{guess}(R, \mathsf{compress}(X)) = (X[R_1], \ldots, X[R_t]) \mid \mathcal{E}\right). \tag{11}$$

This is because if $\mathcal{E}$ occurred then the functions $\mathsf{compress}$ and $\mathsf{guess}$ perfectly "emulated" the execution of $\text{PLR}_1, \ldots, \text{PLR}_k$. Observe that here we use the assumption that the $R_j$'s are uniform, which implies that our answers to the "$(Z_1|| \cdots ||Z_{k-1})$" queries are indistinguishable from the answers of the "real" random oracle. Of course, this would not be true if such a query was earlier asked by one of $\text{PLR}_1, \ldots, \text{PLR}_{k-1}$, but this did not happen, since in (11) we condition on the event $\mathcal{E}$.

On the other hand, it is clear that $\mathbb{P}(\neg\mathcal{E}) \leq q/2^t$. This is because querying the oracle on "$(Z_1||\cdots||Z_{k-1})$" requires the knowledge of all the $Z_i$'s, and every $\text{PLR}_i$ (for $i = 1, \ldots, k-1$) does not know one of them. Hence the probability that any $\text{PLR}_i$ guesses "$(Z_1||\cdots||Z_{k-1})$" in one query is $2^{-t}$ (remember that each of them is uniformly random on $\{0,1\}^t$). Consequently, the probability that it guesses it in *at least one* of its $q$ queries is at most $q/2^t$. Since we assumed that $q$ is polynomial in $t$, thus we get that $\mathbb{P}(\neg\mathcal{E}) \leq \mathsf{negl}(t)$. Combining it with (11) we obtain

$$\mathbb{P}\left(Y = \pi_{k,n}^{\mathcal{H},t}(Z_1, \ldots, Z_{k-1}, X)\right) \tag{12}$$
$$\leq \mathbb{P}\left(\mathsf{guess}(R, \mathsf{compress}(X)) = (X[R_1], \ldots, X[R_t])\right) + \mathsf{negl}(t). \tag{13}$$

Thus, since we assumed that (12) is non-negligible, we obtain that the probability in (13) is non-negligible.

What remains is to describe how to "derandomize" the compress and guess functions that we constructed. This can be done via a very standard argument. Since the inequality (13) holds when the probability is computed *including* the internal randomness $\rho$ of compress and guess thus there has to exist a concrete value $\rho_0$ such that (13) holds if we fix $\rho$ to $\rho_0$. We can therefore derandomize these functions by simply "hardwiring" these randomness into them. This finishes the proof.     □

Let us also discuss the nature of the $\pi_{k,n}^{\mathcal{H},t}$ function, focusing on the (simplest) case when $t = 1$, i.e., only one bit is produced as output. The reader familiar with the communication complexity literature may observe that this function is similar to so-called *shift function* [28], and more general notion called the *general addressing function (GAF)* [4,31]. The shift function is defined very similarly to $\pi_{k,n}^{\mathcal{H},1}$, except that the $Z_i$'s take values in the $\mathbb{Z}_n$ group, and $H_1$ is defined as $H(Z_1, \ldots, Z_n) := X[Z_1 + \cdots Z_{k-1}]$ (in case of GAF we can also have groups other than $\mathbb{Z}_n$). Somewhat surprisingly it appears very hard to prove the lower bounds for the SM complexity in this model. The only known non-trivial lower bound in the shift function is $\Omega(n^{1/k})$ [28,31]. Moreover, sublinear upper bounds on this complexity are known [1,2,30,31]. The hardness of this problem can in some sense serve as a justification for the use of the random oracles in our construction. Theorem 3 and Lemma 5 together imply the following.

**Corollary 1.** *For any $\beta < 1$ and for $n > t$ the protocol $\Pi_{D,n}^{\mathcal{H},t}$ is a $(\beta n, \mathsf{negl}(t))$-secure positioning protocol for positions within the $D$-dimensional simplex whose vertices are the positions of the protocol's verifiers.*

Let us also now mention that in a practical implementation one can let the verifiers choose the $Z_i$'s in advance. Therefore $\mathcal{V}_{D+1}$ can compute $H_i(Z_i)$'s and store only the $X[H_i(Z_i)]$'s. Thus, the storage requirements of this protocol are very low.

## 4.2   Protocols in the Plain Model

In this section we propose an alternative construction of positioning and key agreement protocols. The protocols presented in this section are online computable (see Sect. 2.4), and do not require the random oracle assumption. Let us first recall the definition of the generalized inner product function [5]. Let $\mathbb{F} = \mathsf{GF}(2^m)$ be a finite field (for simplicity we restrict ourselves to the Galois fields of order $2^m$, but our results can be generalized to arbitrary finite fields). For some natural parameters $\ell$ and $k$ (such that $k \geq 2$) define the *generalized inner product (GIP)* function as $\mathsf{GIP}_{\ell,k} : (\mathbb{F}^\ell)^k \to \mathbb{F}$ as $\mathsf{GIP}^{\mathbb{F}}_{\ell,k}((x_1^1, \ldots, x_\ell^1), \ldots, (x_1^k, \ldots, x_\ell^k)) = \sum_{i=1}^{\ell} \prod_{j=1}^{k} x_i^j$.

The positioning and the position-based key agreement protocols (in $D \in \{2, 3\}$ dimensions), denoted $\Gamma^{\mathsf{pos}}_{\ell,D,t}$ and $\Gamma^{\mathsf{ka}}_{\ell,D,t}$ (resp.), are simply the one-round protocols parameterized by $\mathsf{GIP}^{\mathbb{F}}_{\ell,D+1}$ (see Sect. 2.3), i.e., the verifiers $\mathcal{V}_1, \ldots, \mathcal{V}_{D+1}$ broadcast random strings $X_i \leftarrow \mathbb{F}^\ell$, and the prover computes $\mathsf{GIP}(X_1, \ldots, X_{D+1})$, which he either keeps as the agreed key, or broadcasts back to the verifiers (depending on whether the protocol is for key agreement or for positioning). The verifiers compute $\mathsf{GIP}(X_1, \ldots, X_{D+1})$ and keep it as the agreed key (in the first case), or simply check if it is identical to what they got from the prover (in the second case). We now have the following lemma that states that GIP is hard in the fully adaptive model. Note that this lemma implies hardness in the almost adaptive one-round SM model (since this model is more restrictive), and hence, together with Theorems 2 and 3, implies security of the $\Gamma^{\mathsf{pos}}_{\ell,D,t}$ and $\Gamma^{\mathsf{ka}}_{\ell,D,t}$ protocols. The communication complexity of the GIP function has been studied in multiple papers [5,6,22,23,32], but up to our knowledge, not in the strong randomized settings that we need in this work. Our proof is a rather straightforward adaptation of the techniques from this prior work.

**Lemma 6.** *Suppose* $\mathbb{F} = \mathsf{GF}(2^m)$ *(for any* $m$ *such that* $2^m \geq k^{1+\xi}$ *for some* $\xi > 0$*). Then for every* $\ell, k$*, the* $\mathsf{GIP}^{\mathbb{F}}_{\ell,k}$ *function is* $(s, \delta)$*-strongly hard in the fully adaptive model, for some* $s = \Omega(m\ell/2^k)$ *and* $\delta = \mathsf{negl}(\ell)$*.*

*Proof.* Consider an arbitrary fully adaptive protocol $(\mathrm{PLR}_1, \ldots, \mathrm{PLR}_k)$. Let $s$ denote its communication complexity. Suppose that $\vec{X}^1, \ldots, \vec{X}^k$ are sampled uniformly and independently, each from $\mathbb{F}^\ell$. Let $V$ denote the sequence of all the messages that were broadcast by the parties during the execution of the protocol on input $(\vec{X}^1, \ldots, \vec{X}^k)$. Let $Y := \mathsf{GIP}^{\mathbb{F}}_{\ell,k}(\vec{X}^1, \ldots, \vec{X}^k)$. We will now treat $Y \in \mathsf{GF}(2^m)$ as bit-strings of length $m$. We start with the following.

*Claim 1.* For any $i \in 1, \ldots, m$ and $s = \Omega(m\ell/2^k)$ we have that

$$d(Y[i] \mid Y[1, \ldots, i-1], V)) \leq \mathsf{negl}(\ell). \tag{14}$$

*Proof (Proof of the Claim).* We use the results of [5] which introduced the so-called *multiparty communication complexity with help*. More precisely, in [5] the authors consider protocols where the players can obtain an extra "help" from an external entity in a form of a function $H$ that gets as input all the inputs of all the players, the only restriction being that the output of $H$ has to be one bit shorter than the output of the computed function. Hence, in our case $H$ is any function of a type $H : (\mathbb{F}^\ell)^k \to \{0,1\}^{m-1}$. What they prove in their Lemma 3.3 can be translated to our notation as follows:

*For any protocol whose communication complexity is at most*

$$\log\left(\frac{1/2 - \epsilon}{\Gamma(f,\mathcal{C})}\right) \tag{15}$$

*(we will comment on the "$\Gamma(f,\mathcal{C})$" term in a moment) and for any $H :$ $(\mathbb{F}^\ell)^k \to \{0,1\}^{m-1}$ and any function $\alpha$ we have that*

$$\mathbb{P}\left(\mathsf{GIP}^{\mathbb{F}}_{\ell,k}(\vec{X}^1,\dots,\vec{X}^k) = \alpha(H(\vec{X}^1,\dots,\vec{X}^k),V)\right) \le 1 - \epsilon. \tag{16}$$

*(provided $2^m \ge k^{1+\xi}$ for some $\xi > 0$).*

Above $\Gamma(f,\mathcal{C})$ is a value called *the strong discrepancy of $f$ in $\mathcal{C}$* (for this discussion it is irrelevant what $\mathcal{C}$ is). Moreover, as inspection of the proof of Corollary 4.12 [5] shows we have that

$$\log(1/\Gamma(f,\mathcal{C})) \ge \Omega(m\ell/2^k). \tag{17}$$

Now, set $\epsilon := 1/2 - \sqrt{\Gamma(f,\mathcal{C})}$. It is easy to see that (15) now becomes equal to

$$\log(1/\sqrt{\Gamma(f,\mathcal{C})}) \ge \Omega(m\ell/2^k).$$

This also implies that $\epsilon - 1/2$ is negligible in $\ell$. Moreover, by Lemma 2, we have that

$$d(\mathsf{GIP}^{\mathbb{F}}_{\ell,k}(\vec{X}^1,\dots,\vec{X}^k) \mid H(\vec{X}^1,\dots,\vec{X}^k),V) \le 2(1 - \epsilon) - 1 \le \mathsf{negl}(\ell), \tag{18}$$

Now set $H(\vec{X}^1,\dots,\vec{X}^k) := (Y[1,\dots,i-1],Y[i+1],\dots,Y[m])$. Then, (18) becomes

$$\mathsf{negl}(\ell) \ge d(Y \mid Y[1,\dots,i-1],Y[i+1],\dots,Y[m],V)$$
$$\ge d(Y[i] \mid Y[1,\dots,i-1],V), \tag{19}$$

where (19) follows from Lemma 2. Hence (14) is proven.

To finish the proof of Lemma 6 we just apply the chain-rule for the statistical distance (Lemma 1), obtaining

$$d(Y \mid V) \le m \cdot \mathsf{negl}(\ell) = \mathsf{negl}(\ell).$$

We therefore obtain that for any protocol with the communication complexity $\Omega(m\ell/2^k)$ we have $d(\mathsf{GIP}^{\mathbb{F}}_{\ell,k}(\vec{X}^1,\dots,\vec{X}^k) \mid V) \le \mathsf{negl}(\ell)$, and the lemma is proven.                                                                                   □

Now, combining Lemma 6 with Theorems 2 and 3 we obtain the following.

**Corollary 2.** *For $D \in \{2,3\}$ and for $k, m$, and $\ell$ as in Lemma 6, we have that $\Gamma^{\mathsf{pos}}_{\ell,D,t}$ is one-round $(\Omega(m\ell), \mathsf{negl}(\ell))$-secure positioning protocol in $D$ dimensions for positions inside of a simplex determined by the verifiers, and $\Gamma^{\mathsf{ka}}_{\ell,D,t}$ is a one-round $(\Omega(m\ell), \mathsf{negl}(\ell))$-secure key agreement protocol in $D$ dimensions for positions such that the messages sent by the verifiers never meet at any other position than the one claimed by the prover (see [16], Sect. 7.3.1).*

Since the generalized inner product is a multi-source extractor, the reader might be tempted to think that our construction works when $\mathsf{GIP}^{\ell,k}$ is replaced with any $k$-source extractor. We note that this is not the case, as the generalized inner product has additional properties, that multi-source extractors do not have. Namely the multi-source extractors require that their inputs are fully independent (conditioned on adversary's information), which is not the case for GIP.

### 4.3   Practical Considerations for the GIP-based Protocol

Note that, unlike in the case of protocol $\Pi^{\mathcal{H},t}_{D,n}$ (see remark after Corollary 1), there is no simple trick to avoid the need for the verifiers to store large amounts of data (the $X_i$'s), as long as we want the protocols to be information-theoretically secure. However, if we move to the "computational world" we can simply let the $X_i$'s be generated pseudorandomly: for $i = 1, \ldots, D+1$ sample a short random seed $S_i$, and let $X_i := \mathsf{prg}(S_i)$, where $\mathsf{prg}$ is a pseudorandom generator. In this case, the verifiers need to store only the $S_i$'s. Also, instead of sending the $X_i$'s (via a private channel) to each other, they can just send the $S_i$.

# References

1. Ambainis, A.: Upper bounds on multiparty communication complexity of shifts. In: Puech, C., Reischuk, R. (eds.) STACS 1996. LNCS, vol. 1046, pp. 631–642. Springer, Heidelberg (1996). doi:10.1007/3-540-60922-9_51
2. Ambainis, A., Lokam, S.V.: Improved upper bounds on the simultaneous messages complexity of the generalized addressing function. In: Gonnet, G.H., Viola, A. (eds.) LATIN 2000. LNCS, vol. 1776, pp. 207–216. Springer, Heidelberg (2000). doi:10.1007/10719839_21
3. Aumann, Y., Rabin, M.O.: Information theoretically secure communication in the limited storage space model. In: Wiener, M. (ed.) CRYPTO 1999. LNCS, vol. 1666, pp. 65–79. Springer, Heidelberg (1999). doi:10.1007/3-540-48405-1_5
4. Babai, L., Gál, A., Kimmel, P.G., Lokam, S.V.: Communication complexity of simultaneous messages. SIAM J. Comput. **33**(1), 137–166 (2004)
5. Babai, L., Hayes, T.P., Kimmel, P.G.: The cost of the missing bit: communication complexity with help. Combinatorica **21**(4), 455–488 (2001)
6. Babai, L., Nisan, N., Szegedy, M.: Multiparty protocols, pseudorandom generators for logspace, and time-space trade-offs. J. Comput. Syst. Sci. **45**(2), 204–232 (1992)
7. Bellare, M., Rogaway, P.: Random oracles are practical: a paradigm for designing efficient protocols. In: Ashby, V. (ed.) ACM CCS 1993, Fairfax, Virginia, USA, pp. 62–73. ACM Press, 3–5 November 1993

8. Brands, S., Chaum, D.: Distance-bounding protocols. In: Helleseth, T. (ed.) EURO-CRYPT 1993. LNCS, vol. 765, pp. 344–359. Springer, Heidelberg (1994). doi:10.1007/3-540-48285-7_30

9. Brassard, G.: Quantum information: the conundrum of secure positioning. Nature **479**, 307–308 (2011)

10. Buhrman, H., Chandran, N., Fehr, S., Gelles, R., Goyal, V., Ostrovsky, R., Schaffner, C.: Position-based quantum cryptography: impossibility and constructions. SIAM J. Comput. **43**(1), 150–178 (2014)

11. Cachin, C., Maurer, U.: Unconditional security against memory-bounded adversaries. In: Kaliski, B.S. (ed.) CRYPTO 1997. LNCS, vol. 1294, pp. 292–306. Springer, Heidelberg (1997). doi:10.1007/BFb0052243

12. Capkun, S., Hubaux, J.-P.: Secure positioning of wireless devices with application to sensor networks. In: Proceedings of the 24th Annual Joint Conference of the IEEE Computer and Communications Societies, INFOCOM 2005, vol. 3, pp. 1917–1928. IEEE, March 2005

13. Cash, D., Ding, Y.Z., Dodis, Y., Lee, W., Lipton, R., Walfish, S.: Intrusion-resilient key exchange in the bounded retrieval model. In: Vadhan, S.P. (ed.) TCC 2007. LNCS, vol. 4392, pp. 479–498. Springer, Heidelberg (2007). doi:10.1007/978-3-540-70936-7_26

14. Chakraborty, K., Leverrier, A.: Practical position-based quantum cryptography. Phys. Rev. A **92**, 052304 (2015)

15. Chandra, A.K., Furst, M.L., Lipton, R.J.: Multi-party protocols. In: Proceedings of the 15th Annual ACM Symposium on the Theory of Computing, pp. 94–99 (1983)

16. Chandran, N., Goyal, V., Moriarty, R., Ostrovsky, R.: Position-based cryptography. SIAM J. Comput. **43**(4), 1291–1341 (2014)

17. Dziembowski, S.: Intrusion-resilience via the bounded-storage model. In: Halevi, S., Rabin, T. (eds.) TCC 2006. LNCS, vol. 3876, pp. 207–224. Springer, Heidelberg (2006). doi:10.1007/11681878_11

18. Dziembowski, S., Maurer, U.M.: Tight security proofs for the bounded-storage model. In: 34th ACM STOC, pp. 341–350, Montréal, Québec, Canada. ACM Press, 19–21 May 2002

19. Dziembowski, S., Maurer, U.M.: Optimal randomizer efficiency in the bounded-storage model. J. Crypt. **17**(1), 5–26 (2004)

20. Dziembowski, S., Pietrzak, K.: Intrusion-resilient secret sharing. In 48th FOCS, Providence, USA, pp. 227–237. IEEE Computer Society Press, 20–23 October 2007

21. Dziembowski, S., Zdanowicz, M.: Position-based cryptography from noisy channels. In: Pointcheval, D., Vergnaud, D. (eds.) AFRICACRYPT 2014. LNCS, vol. 8469, pp. 300–317. Springer, Cham (2014). doi:10.1007/978-3-319-06734-6_19

22. Ford, J., Gál, A.: Hadamard tensors and lower bounds on multiparty communication complexity. Comput. Complex. **22**(3), 595–622 (2013)

23. Graham, F.C.: Quasi-random hypergraphs revisited. Random Struct. Algorithms **40**(1), 39–48 (2012)

24. Kushilevitz, E., Nisan, N.: Communication Complexity. Cambridge University Press, Cambridge (1997)

25. Lu, C.-J.: Encryption against storage-bounded adversaries from on-line strong extractors. J. Crypt. **17**(1), 27–42 (2004)

26. Maurer, U.M.: Conditionally-perfect secrecy and a provably-secure randomized cipher. J. Crypt. **5**(1), 53–66 (1992)

27. Moran, T., Shaltiel, R., Ta-Shma, A.: Non-interactive timestamping in the bounded-storage model. J. Crypt. **22**(2), 189–226 (2009)

28. Nisan, N., Wigderson, A.: Rounds in communication complexity revisited. In: 23rd ACM STOC, New Orleans, Louisiana, USA, pp. 419–429. ACM Press, 6–8 May 1991
29. Nisan, N., Zuckerman, D.: Randomness is linear in space. J. Comput. Syst. Sci. **52**(1), 43–52 (1996)
30. Pudlák, P.: Unexpected upper bounds on the complexity of some communication games. In: Abiteboul, S., Shamir, E. (eds.) ICALP 1994. LNCS, vol. 820, pp. 1–10. Springer, Heidelberg (1994). doi:10.1007/3-540-58201-0_53
31. Pudlk, P., Rödl, V., Sgall, J.: Boolean circuits, tensor ranks, and communication complexity. SIAM J. Comput. **26**(3), 605–633 (1997)
32. Raz, R.: The BNS-Chung criterion for multi-party communication complexity. Comput. Complex. **9**(2), 113–122 (2000)
33. Sastry, N., Shankar, U., Wagner, D.: Secure verification of location claims. In: Proceedings of the 2nd ACM Workshop on Wireless Security, WiSe 2003, pp. 1–10. ACM, New York (2003)
34. Schaffner, C.: Position-based quantum cryptography. Webpage. http://homepages.cwi.nl/schaffne/positionbasedqcrypto.php. Accessed 17 Feb 2016
35. Unruh, D.: Quantum position verification in the random oracle model. In: Garay, J.A., Gennaro, R. (eds.) CRYPTO 2014. LNCS, vol. 8617, pp. 1–18. Springer, Heidelberg (2014). doi:10.1007/978-3-662-44381-1_1
36. Vadhan, S.P.: Constructing locally computable extractors and cryptosystems in the bounded-storage model. J. Crypt. **17**(1), 43–77 (2004)
37. Vora, A., Nesterenko, M.: Secure location verification using radio broadcast. In: Higashino, T. (ed.) OPODIS 2004. LNCS, vol. 3544, pp. 369–383. Springer, Heidelberg (2005). doi:10.1007/11516798_27

# When Does Functional Encryption Imply Obfuscation?

Sanjam Garg[1], Mohammad Mahmoody[2], and Ameer Mohammed[2(✉)]

[1] UC Berkeley, Berkeley, USA
sanjamg@berkeley.edu
[2] University of Virginia, Charlottesville, USA
{mohammad,ameer}@virginia.edu

**Abstract.** Realizing indistinguishablility obfuscation (IO) based on well understood computational assumptions is an important open problem. Recently, realizing functional encryption (FE) has emerged as a promising direction towards that goal. This is because: (1) compact single-key FE (where the functional secret-key is of length double the ciphertext length) is known to imply IO [Anath and Jain, CRYPTO 2015; Bitansky and Vaikuntanathan, FOCS 2015] and (2) several strong variants of single-key FE are known based on various standard computation assumptions.

In this work, we study *when* FE can be used for obtaining IO. We show any single-key FE for function families with "short" enough outputs (specifically the output is less than ciphertext length by a value at least $\omega(n+\kappa)$, where $n$ is the message length and $\kappa$ is the security parameter) is insufficient for IO even when non-black-box use of the underlying FE is allowed to some degree. Namely, our impossibility result holds even if we are allowed to plant FE sub-routines as gates inside the circuits for which functional secret-keys are issued (which is exactly how the known FE to IO constructions work).

Complementing our negative result, we show that our condition of "short" enough is almost tight. More specifically, we show that any compact single-key FE with functional secret-key output length strictly larger than ciphertext length is sufficient for IO. Furthermore, we show that non-black-box use of the underlying FE is necessary for such a construction, by ruling out any fully black-box construction of IO from FE even with arbitrary long output.

S. Garg—University of California, Berkeley. Research supported in part from 2017 AFOSR YIP Award, DARPA/ARL SAFEWARE Award W911NF15C0210, AFOSR Award FA9550-15-1-0274, NSF CRII Award 1464397, and research grants by the Okawa Foundation, Visa Inc., and Center for Long-Term Cybersecurity (CLTC, UC Berkeley). The views expressed are those of the author and do not reflect the official policy or position of the funding agencies.

M. Mahmoody—Supported by NSF CAREER award CCF-1350939.

A. Mohammed—Supported by University of Kuwait.

Y. Kalai and L. Reyzin (Eds.): TCC 2017, Part I, LNCS 10677, pp. 82–115, 2017.
https://doi.org/10.1007/978-3-319-70500-2_4

# 1   Introduction

The goal of program obfuscation is to make computer programs "unintelligible" while preserving their functionality. Over the past four years, we have come a long way from believing that obfuscation is impossible [BGI+01, GK05] to having plausible candidate constructions [GGH+13b, BR14, BGK+14, AGIS14, MSW14, AB15, GGH15, Zim15, GLSW15, BMSZ16, GMM+16], [DGG+16, Lin16a, LV16, AS16, Lin16b, LT17]. Furthermore, together with one-way functions, obfuscation has been shown to have numerous consequences, e.g. [GGH+13b, SW14, GGHR14, BZ14, BPR15].

However, all these constructions are based on the conjectured security of new computational assumptions [GGH13a, CLT13, GGH15] the security of which is not very well-understood [GGH13a, CHL+15, CGH+15, CLLT15, HJ16, MSZ16, CGH16, CLLT16, ADGM16]. In light of this, it is paramount that we base security of IO on better understood assumptions. Towards this goal, one of the suggested approaches is to first realize some kind of a Functional Encryption (FE) scheme based on standard computational assumptions and then use that to realize IO. This directions is particularly promising because of the following.

1. *Compact single-key FE is known to imply IO.* Recent results by Ananth and Jain [AJ15] and Bitansky and Vaikuntanathan [BV15] show how to base IO on a compact FE scheme — namely, a single-key FE scheme for which the encryption circuit is independent of the function circuit for which the functional secret-key is given out. Furthermore, these results can even be realized starting with FE for which at most one functional secret-key can be given out (i.e., the functional encryption scheme is single-key secure, and this is what we refer to by FE all along this paper). Furthermore, the construction works even if the ciphertext is weakly compact, i.e. the length of the ciphertext grows sub-linearly in the circuit size but is allowed to grow arbitrarily with the depth of the circuit.

2. *Positive results on single-key FE.* The construction of IO from compact single-key FE puts us in close proximity to primitives known from standard assumptions. One prominent work, is the single-key functional encryption scheme of Goldwasser et al. [GKP+13] that is based on LWE. Interestingly, this encryption scheme is *weakly compact* for boolean circuits. However, in this scheme the ciphertext grows additionally with the output length of the circuit for which the functional secret-key is given out. Hence, it doesn't imply IO.

In summary, the gap between the known single-key FE constructions from LWE and the single-key FE schemes known to imply IO (for the same ciphertext length properties) is only in the output length of circuit for which the functional secret-key is issued. In light of this, significant research continues to be invested towards realizing IO starting with various kinds of FE schemes (e.g. [BNPW16, BLP16]). This brings us to the following question.

**Main Question:** *What kind of FE schemes are sufficient for IO?*

## 1.1   Our Results

The main result of this work is to show that single-key FE schemes that support only functions with 'short output' are incapable of producing IO even when non-black-box use of the FE scheme is allowed in certain ways. The non-black-box use of FE is modeled in a way similar to prior works by Brakerski et al. [BKSY11], Asharov and Segev [AS15], and Garg et al. [GMM17]. We specifically use the *monolithic* framework of [GMM17] which is equivalent to the fully black-box framework of [IR89, RTV04] applied to *monolithic primitives* (that can include all of their subroutines as gates inside circuits given to them as input). This monolithic model captures the most commonly used non-black-box techniques in cryptography, including the ones used by Ananth and Jain [AJ15] and Bitansky and Vaikunthanathan [BV15] for realizing IO from FE. More formally, we prove the following theorem.

**Theorem 1 (Main Result–Informal).** *Assuming one-way functions exist and* **NP** $\not\subseteq$ **coAM***, there is no construction of IO from "short" output single-key FE where one is allowed to plant FE gates arbitrarily inside the circuits that are given to FE as input. An FE scheme is said to be "short" output if*

$$t(n, \kappa) \leq p(n, \kappa) - \omega(n + \kappa),$$

*where $n$ is the plaintext length, $\kappa$ is the security parameter, $p$ is the ciphertext length (for messages of length $n$) and $t$ is the output length of the functions evaluated on messages of length $n$.*

As a special case, the above result implies that single-key FE for boolean circuits and other single-key FE schemes known from standard assumptions are insufficient for IO in an monolithic black-box way.

**"Long-output" FE implies IO.** Complementing this negative result, we show that above condition on ciphertext length $t$ is almost tight. In particular, we show that a "long output" single-key FE — namely, a single-key FE scheme with $t = p + 1$ (supporting an appropriate class of circuits) is sufficient for realizing IO. This construction is non-black-box (or, monolithic to be precise) and is obtained as a simple extension of the previous results of Ananth and Jain [AJ15] and Bitansky and Vaikuntanathan [BV15]. We refer the reader to the full version of this paper for this result.

**Fully Black-Box Separation of IO from FE.** Finally, we show that some form of non-black-box techniques (beyond the fully black-box framework of [RTV04]) is necessary for getting IO from FE, *regardless* of the output lengths. Namely, we prove a fully black-box separation from FE to IO. Previously, Lin [Lin16a] (Corollary 1 there) showed that the existence of such fully black-box construction from FE to IO would imply a construction of IO from LWE and constant-degree PRGs. Our result shows that no such fully black-box construction exists (but the possibility of IO from LWE and constant-degree PRGs remains open). We refer the reader to the full version of this paper for this result.

## 1.2 Comparison with Known Lower Bounds on IO

Sequence of works [AS15, CKP15, Pas15, MMN15, BBF16, MMN+16a], [MMN+16b], under reasonable complexity assumptions,[1] proved lower bounds for building IO in a black-box manner from one-way functions, collision resistant hash functions, trapdoor permutations or even constant degree graded encoding oracles. Building on these work, authors [GMM17] showed barriers to realizing IO based on non-black-box use of "all-or-nothing encryption" primitives — namely, encryption primitives where the provided secret-keys either allow for complete decryption, or keep everything hidden. This includes encryption primitives such as attribute-based encryption [GVW13], predicate encryption [GVW15], and fully homomorphic encryption [Gen09, BV11b, BV11a, GSW13]. In comparison, this work aims to show barriers to getting IO through a non-black-box use of single-key FE, an encryption primitive that is not all-or-nothing, but has been previously shown to imply IO in certain settings. The work of Asharov and Segev [AS15] proved lower bounds on the complexity of assumptions behind IO *with* oracle gates (in our terminology, restricted monolithic) which is a stronger primitive than IO.[2]

**On the Relation to [GMM17, GKP+13].** Note that, as mentioned above, the work [GMM17] rules out the existence of monolithic IO constructions from attribute-based encryption (ABE) and the existence of monolithic IO constructions from fully homomorphic encryption (FHE). Furthermore, this result can be further broadened to separate IO from ABE *and* FHE in a monolithic way. One can then ask why the result in this paper does not follow as a corollary from [GMM17, GKP+13], where they construct single-key (non-compact) FE for general circuits from ABE and FHE.

We note that our result does not follow from the above observation for two reasons. First, the single-key FE construction of [GKP+13] also uses a garbling scheme in order to garble circuits with FHE decryption gates, whereas the impossibility of [GMM17] does not capture such garbling mechanisms in the monolithic model. However, if one could improve the result of [GMM17] in the monolithic model by adding a garbling subroutine that can accept ABE and FHE gates, then we can compose the results of [GMM17, GKP+13] and obtain an impossibility of IO from $t$-bit output (non-compact) FE. Secondly, we note that this resulting $t$-bit output FE scheme has the property that $t \leq p/\operatorname{poly}(\kappa)$ (i.e. the ciphertext size is a (polynomial) multiplicative factor of the output length of the function), whereas in this work we show the stronger impossibility of basing IO on single-key FE for output-length $t \leq p - \omega(\kappa)$.

**Other Non-Black-Box Separations.** Proving separations for non-black-box constructions are usually very hard. However, there are several works that go

---

[1] Note that since statistically secure IO exists if $\mathbf{P} = \mathbf{NP}$, therefore we need computational assumptions for proving lower bounds for assumptions implying IO.

[2] In fact, their separation is unconditional, while statistical IO can be built if $\mathbf{P} = \mathbf{NP}$. So any separation for IO needs to rely on computational assumptions before proving $\mathbf{P} \neq \mathbf{NP}$.

done this line. The work of Pass et al. [PTV11] showed that, under believable assumptions, there are no non-black-box constructions of certain cryptographic primitives (e.g., one-way permutations) from one-way functions, as long as the security reductions are black-box. Pass [Pas11] and Gentry and Wichs [GW11] proved further separations in this model by separating certain primitives from any falsifiable assumptions [Nao03], again, as long as the security proof is black-box. Finally, the recent work of Dachman-Soled [Dac16] showed that certain classes of constructions with some carefully defined non-black-box power are not capable of basing public-key encryption on one way functions.

### 1.3 Technical Overview

In order to demonstrate the ideas behind our impossibility, we start by recalling the constructions of IO from FE [AJ15,BV15]. The key point here is that their IO constructions crucially rely on the ability of the underlying FE scheme to generate functional secret keys for functions that generate outputs of sizes that are larger than the ciphertexts that are decrypted using these functional secret keys. In particular, when evaluating the obfuscation of some circuit $C$ on some input $x = (x_1, ..., x_n)$, they would need to decrypt a ciphertext using a functional secret key for a function that generates *two* ciphertexts – which is an output that is double the size of the input. Then, by successively decrypting $c_{x_1,...,x_i}$ for all $i$ under a functional secret key that has the property described above to get two encryptions $(c_{x_1,...,x_i,0}, c_{x_1,...,x_i,1})$ where $c_y$ is an encryption of $y$, the evaluator will obtain a ciphertext of the entire input $x$ that it wants to evaluate the obfuscated circuit on. The obtained $c_{x_1,...,x_n}$ is then decrypted using one final functional secret key that corresponds to the circuit $C$ to get $C(x)$.

On the other hand, in case the output of a functional secret key is "sufficiently smaller" than a ciphertext, then this explosion in number of ciphertexts does not seem possible anymore. This is also the key to our impossibility. Roughly speaking, at the core of the proof of our impossibility result is to show that in this "small" output setting, the total number of ciphertexts that an evaluator can compute remains polynomially bounded. Turning this high level intuition into an impossibility proof requires several new ideas that we now elaborate upon below.

**The Details of the Proof of Separation.** As mentioned before, monolithic constructions of IO from FE are the same as fully black-box constructions of IO from *monolithic* FE which is a primitive that is similar to FE but it allows FE gates to be used in the circuits for which keys are issued. Therefore, to prove the separation, we can still use oracle separation techniques from the literature on black-box constructions [IR89].

In fact, for any candidate construction $IO^{(\cdot)}$ of indistinguishability obfuscation from monolithic FE, we construct an oracle $O$ relative to which secure monolithic FE exists but the construction $IO^O$ becomes insecure (against polynomial-query attackers). In order to do this, we will employ an intermediate primitive:

a variant of functional witness encryption defined by Boyle et al. [BCP14]. We call this variant customized FWE (cFWE for short) and show that (1) relative to our oracle cFWE exists, (2) cFWE implies monolithic FE in a black-box way, and that (3) the construction $\text{IO}^O$ is insecure. We opted to work with this intermediate primitive of cFWE since it is conceptually easier to work with than an ideal FE oracle and allows us to leverage the previous results of [GMM17] to prove our separation in a modular way. Now in order to get (1) we directly define our oracle $O$ to be an idealized version of cFWE. To get (2) we use the power of cFWE.[3] To get (3) we rely on the fact that cFWE is *weakened* in a careful way so that it does not imply IO. Below, we describe more details about our idealized oracle for cFWE and how to break the security of a given candidate IO construction relative to this oracle. We first recap the general framework for proving separations for IO.

**General Recipe for Proving Separations for IO.** Let $\mathcal{I}$ be our idealized cFWE oracle. A general technique developed over the last few years [CKP15, MMN+16b, GMM17] for breaking $\text{IO}^{\mathcal{I}}$ using a polynomial number of queries to the oracle (i.e. the step (3) above) is to "compile out" the oracle $\mathcal{I}$ from the obfuscation scheme and get a new secure obfuscator $\text{IO}' = (\text{iO}', \text{Ev}')$ in the *plain-model* that is only *approximately-correct*. Namely, by obfuscating $\text{iO}'(C) = B$ and running $B$ over a *random* input we get the correct answer with probability $99/100$. By the result of [BBF16], doing so implies a polynomial query attacker against $\text{IO}^{\mathcal{I}}$ in model $\mathcal{I}$. Note that this compiling out process (of $\mathcal{I}$ from $\text{IO}^{\mathcal{I}}$) is not independent of the oracle being removed since different oracles may require different approaches to be emulated. However, the general high-level of the compiler that is used in previous work [CKP15, MMN+16b, GMM17], and we use as well, is the same: The new plain-model obfuscator $\text{iO}'$, given a circuit $C$ to obfuscate would work in two steps. The first step of $\text{iO}'$ is to emulate $\text{iO}^{\mathcal{I}}(C)$ (by simulating the oracle $\mathcal{I}$) to get an ideal-model obfuscation $B$, making sure to 'lazily' evaluate (emulate) any queries issued to $\mathcal{I}$. The second step of the compiler is to learn the queries that are likely to be asked by $\text{Ev}^{\mathcal{I}}(B, x)$ for a uniformly random input $x$, denote by $Q_B$, which can be found by by emulating $\text{Ev}^{\mathcal{I}}(B, x_i)$ enough number of times for different uniformly random $x_i$. Finally, the output of $\text{iO}'$ is the plain-model obfuscation $B' = (B, Q_B)$, where $B$ is the ideal-model obfuscation and $Q_B$ is the set of learned queries. To evaluate the obfuscation over a new random input $x$, we simply execute $\text{Ev}'(B, x) = \text{Ev}^{\mathcal{I}}(B, x)$ while emulating any queries to $\mathcal{I}$ consistently relative to $Q_B$. Any compiler (for removing $\mathcal{I}$ from IO) that uses the approach describe above is in fact secure, because we only send emulated queries to the evaluator that could be simulated in the ideal world $\mathcal{I}$. The challenge, however, is to prove the correctness of the new obfuscator. So we shall prove that, by having enough iterations of the learning process (in the learning step of $\text{iO}'$), the probability that we ask an unlearned emulation query occurs with sufficiently small probability.

---

[3] In fact, as shown in [BCP14], without our customization, the original FWE implies, not just IO itself, but even di-IO.

**The Challenge Faced for Compiling Out Our Customized Functional Witness Encryption Oracle.** When $\mathcal{I}$ is defined to be our idealized cFWE oracle, in order to prove the approximate correctness of the plain-model obfuscator, we face two problems.

1. **The Fuzzy Nature of FWE:** Unlike 'all-or-nothing' primitives such as witness encryption and predicate encryption, functional witness encryption mechanisms allow for more relaxed decryption functionalities. In particular, decrypting a ciphertext does not necessarily reveal the whole message $m$. In fact, the decryptor will learn only $f(w, m)$, which is a function of the encrypted message and witness. As a result, even after many learning steps, when the actual execution of the obfuscated circuit starts, we might aim for evaluating a ciphertext (generated during the obfuscation phase) on a *new* function. This challenge did not exist in the previous separations of [GMM17] that deals with the 'all-or-nothing' primitives, because the probability of *not* decrypting a ciphertext during all the learning steps and then suddenly trying to decrypt it during the final evaluation phase could be bounded to be arbitrary small. However, here we might try to decrypt this ciphertext in all these steps, every time with a different function, which could make the information gathered during the learning step useless for the final evaluation.

2. **Unlearnable Hidden Queries:** To get *monolithic* FE from our cFWE (step (2) above), our cFWE needs to be *restricted monolithic*. Namely, we allow the functions evaluated by cFWE to accept circuits with all possible gates that compute the subroutines of cFWE itself. However, for technical reasons, we limit how the witness verification is done in cFWE to only accept one-way function gates. Now, since we are dealing with an oracle that is an ideal version of our cFWE primitive, the function $f^{\mathrm{cFWE}}(m, w)$ may also issue queries of their own. The challenge is that there could be many such indirect/hidden queries asked during the obfuscation phase (in particular during the learning step) that we *cannot* send over to the final evaluator simply because these queries are *not* suitable in the ideal world.

**Resolving Challenges.** Here we describe main ideas to resolve the challenges above.

1. To resolve the first challenge, we add a specific feature to cFWE so that no ciphertext $c = \mathrm{Enc}(x = (a, m))$ would be decrypted more than once by the same person. More formally, we add a subroutine to FWE (as part of our cFWE) that reveals the message $x = (a, m)$ fully, if one can provide two correct witnesses $w_1 \neq w_2$ for the attribute $a$. This way, the second time that we want to decrypt $c$, instead we can recover the whole message $x$ and run the function $f$ on our own! By this trick, we will not have to worry about the fuzzy nature of FWE, as each message is now decryped at most once. In fact, adding this subroutine is the exact reason that cFWE is a *weaker* primitive than FWE.

2. To resolve the second challenge, we rely on an information theoretic argument. Suppose for simplicity that the encryption algorithm does not take an input other than the message[4] $x$. Suppose we use a random (injective) function $\mathsf{Enc} \colon x \mapsto c$ for encryption, mapping strings of length $n$ to strings of length $p = p(n)$. Then, if $p \gg n$, information theoretically, any $q$ query algorithm who has no special advice about the oracle has a chance of $\approx q \cdot 2^{n-p}$ to find a valid ciphertext. If $p \gg n$ this probability is very small, so intuitively we would need about $p - n - \log(q)$ bits of advice to find such ciphertext. On the other hand, any decryption query over a ciphertext $c$ will only return $t = t(n)$ bits, which in our paper is assumed to be $t \ll p - n$. Therefore, if we interpret the decryption like a 'trade' of information, we need to spend $\approx \Omega(p - n)$ bits to get back only $s \leq o(p - n)$ bits. This is the main idea behind our argument showing that during the learning phase, we will not discover more than a polynomial number of new ciphertexts, unless we have encrypted them! By running the learning step of the compiler enough number of times, we will learn all such queries and can successfully finish the final evaluation.

By the using above two ideas, we can successfully compile out our oracle $\mathcal{I}$ from any $\mathsf{IO}^{\mathcal{I}}$ construction. The compilation process itself consists of two steps. The first step being compiling out just the decryption queries where we face and resolve the challenges that we described above. Once we do that, we get an approximate obfuscator in a new oracle model $\mathcal{I}'$ that is actually a variant of an idealized witness encryption oracle. The second step would be to compile out the oracle $\mathcal{I}'$, which was already shown by [GMM17], to get the desired approximate obfuscator in the plain model.

## 2 Preliminaries

In this section we define the primitives that we deal with in this work and are defined prior to our work. We also give a brief background on black-box constructions and their monolithic variants.

**Notation.** We use "|" to concatenate strings and we use "," for attaching strings in a way that they could be retrieved. Namely, one can uniquely identify $x$ and $y$ from $(x, y)$. For example $(00|11) = (0011)$, but $(0, 011) \neq (001, 1)$. When writing the probabilities, by putting an algorithm $A$ in the subscript of the probability (e.g., $\Pr_A[\cdot]$) we mean the probability is over $A$'s randomness. We will use $n$ or $\kappa$ to denote the security parameter. We call an efficient algorithm $\mathsf{V}$ a verifier for an **NP** relation $R$ if $\mathsf{V}(w, a) = 1$ iff $(w, a) \in R$. We call $L_R = L_\mathsf{V} = \{a \mid \exists w, (a, w) \in R\}$ the corresponding **NP** language. By PPT we mean a probabilistic polynomial time algorithm. By an *oracle* PPT/algorithm we mean a PPT that might make oracle calls.

---

[4] This is not true as the encryption is randomized, but allows us to explain the idea more easily.

## 2.1   Obfuscation

The definition of IO below has a subroutine for evaluating the obfuscated code. The reason for defining the evaluation as a subroutine of its own is that when we want to construct IO in oracle/idealized models, we allow the obfuscated circuit to call the oracle as well. Having an evaluator subroutine to run the obfuscated code allows to have such oracle calls in the framework of black-box constructions of [RTV04] where each primitive $\mathcal{Q}$ is simply a class of acceptable functions that we (hope to) efficiently implement given oracle access to implementations of another primitive $\mathcal{P}$ (see Definition 12).

**Definition 1 (Indistinguishability Obfuscation (IO)).** *An Indistinguishability Obfuscation (IO) scheme consists of two subroutines:*

- *Obfuscator* iO *is a PPT that takes as inputs a circuit $C$ and a security parameter $1^\kappa$ and outputs a "circuit" $B$.*
- *Evaluator* Ev *takes as input $(B, x)$ and outputs $y$ (supposedly, equal to $C(x)$).*

*The completeness and soundness conditions assert that:*

- *Completeness: For every $C$, with probability $1$ over the randomness of $O$, we get $B \leftarrow iO(C, 1^\kappa)$ such that: For all $x$ it holds that $\mathrm{Ev}(B, x) = C(x)$.*
- *Security: For every distinguisher $D$ there exists a negligible function $\mu(\cdot)$ such that for every two circuits $C_0, C_1$ that are of the same size and compute the same function, we have:*

$$|\Pr_{iO}[D(iO(C_0, 1^\kappa)) = 1] - \Pr_{iO}[D(iO(C_1, 1^\kappa)) = 1]| \le \mu(\kappa)$$

**Definition 2 (Approximate IO).** *For function $0 < \varepsilon(n) \le 1$, an $\varepsilon$-approximate IO scheme is defined similarly to an IO scheme with a relaxed completeness condition:*

- *$\varepsilon$-Approximate Completeness. For every $C$ and $n$ we have:*

$$\Pr_{x, iO}[B = iO(C, 1^\kappa), \mathrm{Ev}(B, x) = C(x)] \ge 1 - \varepsilon(\kappa)$$

## 2.2   Functional Encryption

We will mainly be concerned with single-key functional encryption schemes which we define below so in the rest of this work whenever we refer to functional encryption, it is of the single-key type. We define a single-key functional encryption for function family $\mathsf{F} = \{\mathsf{F}_n\}_{n \in \mathbb{N}}$ (represented as a circuit family) as follows:

**Definition 3 (Single-Key Functional Encryption [BV15]).** *A single-key functional encryption (FE) for function family $\mathsf{F}$ consists of three PPT algorithms* (Setup, Enc, Dec) *defined as follows:*

- Setup($1^\kappa$): *Given as input the security parameter $1^\kappa$, it outputs a master public key and master secret key pair* $(\mathsf{MPK}, \mathsf{MSK})$.
- KGen($\mathsf{MSK}, f$): *Given master secret key $\mathsf{MSK}$ and function $f \in \mathsf{F}$, outputs a decryption key* $\mathsf{SK}_f$.
- Enc($\mathsf{MPK}, x$): *Given the master public key $\mathsf{MPK}$ and message $x$, outputs ciphertext* $c \in \{0,1\}^p$.
- Dec($\mathsf{SK}_f, c$): *Given a secret key $\mathsf{SK}_f$ and a ciphertext $c \in \{0,1\}^m$, outputs a string* $y \in \{0,1\}^s$.

*The following completeness and security properties must be satisfied:*

- **Completeness:** *For any security parameter $\kappa$, any $f \in \mathsf{F}$ with domain $\{0,1\}^n$ and message $x \in \{0,1\}^n$, the following holds:*

$$\mathrm{Dec}(\mathsf{SK}_f, \mathrm{Enc}(\mathsf{MPK}, x)) = f(x)$$

*where* $(\mathsf{MPK}, \mathsf{MSK}) \leftarrow \mathrm{Setup}(1^\kappa)$ *and* $\mathsf{SK}_f \leftarrow \mathrm{KGen}(\mathsf{MSK}, f)$
- **Security:** *For any PPT adversary $A$, there exists a negligible function $\mathrm{negl}(\cdot)$ such that:*

$$\Pr[IND_A^{1FE}(1^\kappa) = 1] \leq \frac{1}{2} + \mathrm{negl}(\kappa),$$

*where $IND_A^{1FE}$ is the following experiment.*

---

**Experiment $IND_A^{1FE}(1^\kappa)$:**
1. $(\mathsf{MSK}, \mathsf{MPK}) \leftarrow \mathrm{Setup}(1^\kappa)$
2. $(f, x_0, x_1) \leftarrow A(\mathsf{MPK})$ *where* $|x_0| = |x_1|$ *and* $f(x_0) = f(x_1)$
3. $b \xleftarrow{\$} \{0,1\}, c \leftarrow \mathrm{Enc}(\mathsf{MPK}, x_b), \mathsf{SK}_f \leftarrow \mathrm{KGen}(\mathsf{MSK}, f)$
4. $b' \leftarrow A(\mathsf{MPK}, \mathsf{SK}_f, c)$
5. *Output 1 if $b = b'$ and 0 otherwise.*

---

- **Efficiency:** *We define two notions of efficiency for single-key FE supporting the function family $\mathsf{F}$:*
    - **Compactness:** *An FE scheme is said to be* compact *if the size of the encryption circuit is bounded by some fixed polynomial $\mathrm{poly}(n, \kappa)$ where $n$ is the size of the message, independent of the function $f$ chosen by the adversary.*[5]
    - **Function Output Length:** *An FE scheme is said to be $t$-bit-output if $\mathsf{outlen}(f) \leq t(n, \kappa)$ for any $f \in \mathsf{F}$, where $\mathsf{outlen}(f)$ denotes the output length of $f$. Given ciphertext length $p(n, \kappa)$, we say an FE scheme is* long-output *if it is $(p + i)$-bit-output for some $i \geq 1$ and* short-output *if it is only $(p - \omega(n + \kappa))$-bit-output where $n$ is the size of the message.*

---

[5] A couple of other weaker notions of compactness for FE have also been considered in the literature. However, all these notions are known to be monolithically equivalent to compact single-key FE. Therefore, we restrict our discussion just to compact single-key FE.

**Definition 4 (Functional Witness Encryption (FWE) [BCP14]).** *Let* $\mathsf{V}$ *be a PPT algorithm that takes as input an instance-message pair* $x = (a, m)$ *and witness* $w$ *then outputs a bit. Furthermore, let* $\mathsf{F}$ *be a PPT Turing machine that accepts as input a witness* $w$ *and a message* $m$ *then outputs a string* $y \in \{0, 1\}^s$. *For any given security parameter* $\kappa$, *a* functional witness encryption *scheme consists of two PPT algorithms* $P = (\mathrm{Enc}, \mathrm{Dec}_{\mathsf{V},\mathsf{F}})$ *defined as follows:*

- $\mathrm{Enc}(1^\kappa, a, m)$ : *given an instance* $a \in \{0, 1\}^*$, *message* $m \in \{0, 1\}^*$, *and security parameter* $\kappa$, *outputs* $c \in \{0, 1\}^*$.
- $\mathrm{Dec}_{\mathsf{V},\mathsf{F}}(w, c)$ : *given ciphertext* $c$ *and "witness" string* $w \in \{0, 1\}^*$, *outputs a message* $m' \in \{0, 1\}^*$.

*A functional witness encryption scheme satisfies the following completeness and security properties:*

- **Correctness:** *For any security parameter* $\kappa$, *any* $m \in \{0, 1\}^*$, *and any* $(w, (a, m))$ *such that* $\mathsf{V}^P(w, a) = 1$, *it holds that*

$$\Pr_{\mathrm{Enc},\mathrm{Dec}}[\mathrm{Dec}_{\mathsf{V},\mathsf{F}}(w, \mathrm{Enc}(1^\kappa, a, m)) = \mathsf{F}^P(w, m)] = 1$$

- **Extractability:** *For any PPT adversary* $A$ *and polynomial* $p_1(.)$, *there exists a PPT extractor* $E$ *and a polynomial* $p_2(.)$ *such that for any security parameter* $\kappa$, *any* $a$ *for which* $\mathsf{V}^P(w, a) = 1$ *for some* $w$, *and any* $m_0, m_1$ *where* $|m_0| = |m_1|$, *if:*

$$\Pr\left[A(1^\kappa, c) = b \mid b \xleftarrow{\$} \{0, 1\}, c \leftarrow \mathrm{Enc}(1^\kappa, a, m_b)\right] \geq \frac{1}{2} + p_1(\kappa)$$

*Then:*

$$\Pr\left[E^A(1^\kappa, a, m_0, m_1) = w : \mathsf{V}^P(w, a) = 1 \wedge \mathsf{F}^P(w, m_0) \neq \mathsf{F}^P(w, m_1)\right] \geq p_2(\kappa)$$

### 2.3 Background on Black-Box Constructions

**Definition 5 (Cryptographic Primitive [RTV04]).** *A primitive* $\mathcal{P} = (\mathcal{F}, \mathcal{R})$ *is defined as set of functions* $\mathcal{F}$ *and a relation* $\mathcal{R}$ *between functions. A (possibly inefficient) function* $F \in \{0, 1\}^* \rightarrow \{0, 1\}^*$ *is a correct implementation of* $\mathcal{P}$ *if* $F \in \mathcal{F}$, *and a (possibly inefficient) adversary* $A$ *breaks an implementation* $F \in \mathcal{F}$ *if* $(A, F) \in \mathcal{R}$. *We sometimes refer to an implementation* $F \in \mathcal{F}$ *as a set of* $t$ *functions (or subroutines)* $F = \{F_1, ..., F_t\}$.

**Definition 6 (Indexed primitives).** *Let* $\mathcal{W}$ *be a set of (possibly inefficient) functions. An* $\mathcal{W}$-*indexed primitive* $\mathcal{P}[\mathcal{W}]$ *is indeed a set of primitives* $\{\mathcal{P}[W]\}_{W \in \mathcal{W}}$ *indexed by* $W \in \mathcal{W}$ *where, for each* $W \in \mathcal{W}$, $\mathcal{P}[W] = (\mathcal{F}[W], \mathcal{R}[W])$ *is a primitive according to Definition 5.*

**Definition 7 (Restrictions of indexed primitives).** *For* $\mathcal{P}[\mathcal{W}] = \{(\mathcal{F}[W], \mathcal{R}[W])\}_{W \in \mathcal{W}}$ *and* $\mathcal{P}'[\mathcal{W}'] = \{(\mathcal{F}'[W], \mathcal{R}'[W])\}_{W \in \mathcal{W}'}$, *we say* $\mathcal{P}'[\mathcal{W}']$ *is a* restriction *of* $\mathcal{P}[\mathcal{W}]$ *if the following conditions hold: (1)* $\mathcal{W}' \subseteq \mathcal{W}$, *and (2) for all* $W \in \mathcal{W}'$, $\mathcal{F}'[W] \subseteq \mathcal{F}[W]$, *and (3) for all* $W \in \mathcal{W}'$, $\mathcal{R}'[W] = \mathcal{R}[W]$.

We now proceed to apply the above definition of restrictions on indexed primitives to give the definition of monolithic (and restricted monolithic) primitives. We will then apply them to the case of functional encryption. We refer the reader to [GMM17] for a more in-depth study of the monolithic framework.

**Definition 8 (Universal Circuit Evaluator).** *We call an oracle algorithm* $w^{(\cdot)}$ *a* universal circuit evaluator *if it accepts a pair of inputs* $(C, x)$ *where* $C^{(\cdot)}$ *is an* oracle-aided *circuit and* $x$ *is a string in the domain of* $C$ *then outputs* $C^{(\cdot)}(x)$ *by forwarding all of* $C$'s *oracle queries to its own oracle.*

**Definition 9 (Monolithic Primitive [GMM17]).** *We call the restricted primitive* $\mathcal{P}'[\mathcal{W}'] = \{(\mathcal{F}'[W], \mathcal{R}[W])\}_{W \in \mathcal{W}'}$ *the* monolithic *variant of* $\mathcal{P}[\mathcal{W}] = \{(\mathcal{F}[W], \mathcal{R}[W])\}_{W \in \mathcal{W}}$ *if the following holds:*

– *For any* $F$ *and* $W \in \mathcal{W}$, *if* $W = w^F$ *for some universal circuit evaluator* $w^{(\cdot)}$ *and* $F \in \mathcal{F}[W]$ *then* $W \in \mathcal{W}'$ *and* $F \in \mathcal{F}'[W]$.

**Definition 10 (Restricted Monolithic Primitive [GMM17]).** *We call the restricted primitive* $\mathcal{P}'[\mathcal{W}'] = \{(\mathcal{F}'[W], \mathcal{R}[W])\}_{W \in \mathcal{W}'}$ *the* restricted monolithic *variant of* $\mathcal{P}[\mathcal{W}] = \{(\mathcal{F}[W], \mathcal{R}[W])\}_{W \in \mathcal{W}}$ *if is satisfies Definition 9 but the condition is replaced with the following:*

– *For any* $F$ *and* $W \in \mathcal{W}$, *if* $W = w^{F'}$ *for some universal circuit evaluator* $w^{(\cdot)}$, $F' \subset F \in \mathcal{F}[W]$ *then* $W \in \mathcal{W}'$ *and* $F \in \mathcal{F}'[W]$.

*That is, the subroutines of* $F$ *that* $w^{(\cdot)}$ *may call are a strict subset of all the subroutines contained in implementation* $F$.

**Definition 11 (Monolithic Functional Encryption).** *A* monolithic *functional encryption scheme* FE = (FE. Setup, FE. Enc, FE. Keygen, FE. Dec) *for the function family* F *is defined the same as Definition 3 except that, for any* $f \in$ F, $f$ *is an oracle-aided circuit that can call any subroutine of* FE.

**Definition 12 (Black-box Construction [RTV04]).** *A (fully) black-box construction of a primitive* $\mathcal{Q}$ *from a primitive* $\mathcal{P}$ *consists of two PPT algorithms* $(Q, S)$:

1. *Implementation: For any oracle* $P$ *that implements* $\mathcal{P}$, $Q^P$ *implements* $\mathcal{Q}$.
2. *Security reduction: for any oracle* $P$ *implementing* $\mathcal{P}$ *and for any (computationally unbounded) oracle adversary* $A$ *successfully breaking the security of* $Q^P$, *it holds that* $S^{P,A}$ *breaks the security of* $P$.

**Definition 13 (Monolithic Construction of IO from FE).** *A monolithic construction of IO from FE is a fully black-box construction of IO from monolithic FE.*

## 2.4   Tools for Lower Bounds of IO

**Definition 14 (Sub-models).** *We call the idealized model/oracle $\mathcal{O}$ a sub-model of the idealized oracle $\mathcal{I}$ with subroutines $(\mathcal{I}_1, \ldots, \mathcal{I}_k)$, denoted by $\mathcal{O} \sqsubseteq \mathcal{I}$, if there is a (possibly empty) $S \subseteq \{1, \ldots, k\}$ such that the idealized oracle $\mathcal{O}$ works as follows:*

- *First sample $I \leftarrow \mathcal{I}$ where the subroutines are $I = (I_1, \ldots, I_k)$.*
- *Provide access to subroutine $I_i$ iff $i \in S$.*

*If $S = \varnothing$ then the oracle $\mathcal{O}$ will be empty and we will be back to the plain model.*

**Definition 15 (Simulatable Compiling Out Procedures for IO).** *Suppose $\mathcal{O} \sqsubset \mathcal{I}$. We say that there is a simulatable compiler from IO in idealized model $\mathcal{I}$ into idealized model $\mathcal{O}$ with correctness error $\varepsilon$ if the following holds.*

*For every implementation $P_\mathcal{I} = (\mathrm{iO}_\mathcal{P}, \mathrm{Ev}_\mathcal{P})$ of $\delta$-approximate IO in idealized model $\mathcal{I}$ there is a implementation $P_\mathcal{O} = (\mathrm{iO}_\mathcal{O}, \mathrm{Ev}_\mathcal{O})$ of $(\delta + \varepsilon)$-approximate IO in idealized model $\mathcal{O}$ such that the security of the two are related as follows:*

**Simulation:** *There is an efficient PPT simulator $S$ and a negligible function $\mu(\cdot)$ such that for any $C$:*

$$\Delta(S(\mathrm{iO}^\mathcal{I}(C, 1^\kappa)), \mathrm{iO}^\mathcal{O}(C, 1^\kappa)) \leq \mu(\kappa)$$

*where $\Delta(., .)$ denotes the statistical distance between any two given random variables.*

**Lemma 1 (Lower Bounds for IO using Oracle Compilers [GMM17]).** *Suppose $\varnothing = \mathcal{I}_0 \sqsubseteq \mathcal{I}_1 \cdots \sqsubseteq \mathcal{I}_k = \mathcal{I}$ for constant $k = O(1)$ are a sequence of idealized models. Suppose for every $i \in [k]$ there is a simulatable compiler for IO in model $\mathcal{I}_i$ into model $\mathcal{I}_{i-1}$ with correctness error $\varepsilon_i < 1/(100k)$. Also suppose primitive $\mathcal{P}$ can be black-box constructed in the idealized model $\mathcal{I}$. Then there is no fully black-box construction of IO from $\mathcal{P}$.*

## 3   Monolithic Separation of IO from Short-Output FE

In this section, we prove our main impossibility result which states that we cannot construct an IO scheme in a monolithic way from any single-key functional encryption scheme that is restricted to handling only functions of "short" output length. More formally, we prove the following theorem.

**Theorem 2.** *Assume the existence of one-way functions and that* **NP** $\not\subseteq$ **co-NP**. *Then there exists no monolithic construction of IO from any single-key $t$-bit-output functional encryption scheme where $t(n, \kappa) \leq p(n, \kappa) - \omega(n + \kappa)$, $n$ is the message length, $p$ is the ciphertext length, and $\kappa$ is the security parameter of the functional encryption scheme.*

To prove Theorem 2, we will apply Lemma 1 for the idealized functional witness encryption model $\Gamma$ (formally defined in Sect. 3.1) to prove that there is no black-box construction of IO from any primitive $\mathcal{P}$ that can be black-box constructed from the $\Gamma$. In particular, we will do so for $\mathcal{P}$ that is the monolithic functional encryption primitive. Our task is thus twofold: **(1)** to prove that $\mathcal{P}$ can black-box constructed from $\Gamma$ and **(2)** to show a simulatable compilation procedure that compiles out $\Gamma$ from any IO construction. The first task is proven in Sect. 3.2 and the second task is proven in Sect. 3.3. By Lemma 1, this would imply the separation result of IO from $\mathcal{P}$ and prove Theorem 2.

Our oracle, which is more formally defined in Sect. 3.1, acts an idealized version of a single-key short-output functional encryption scheme, which makes the construction of secure FE quite straightforward. As a result, the main challenge lies in showing a simulatable compilation procedure for IO that satisfies Definition 15 in this idealized model, and therefore, it is instructive to look at how the compilation process works and what challenges are faced with dealing with oracle $\Gamma$.

### 3.1 The Ideal Model

In this section, we define the distribution of our idealized (randomized) oracle that can be used to realize (restricted-monolithic) functional witness encryption. We also provide several definitions regarding the algorithms in this model and the types of queries that these algorithms can make.

**Definition 16 (Randomized Functional Witness Encryption Oracle).**
*Let $\mathsf{V}$ be a PPT algorithm that takes as input $(w, a)$, outputs $b \in \{0, 1\}$ and runs in time $\mathrm{poly}(|a|)$. Also, let $\mathsf{F}$ be a PPT algorithm that accepts as input a witness $w$ and a message $m$ then outputs a string $y \in \{0, 1\}^s$. We denote the random $(\mathsf{V}, \mathsf{F}, p)$-functional witness encryption (rFWE) oracle as $\overline{\Gamma}_{\mathsf{V}, \mathsf{F}, p} = \{\overline{\Gamma}_{\mathsf{V}, \mathsf{F}, p}\}_{n \in \mathbb{N}}$ where $\overline{\Gamma}_{\mathsf{V}, \mathsf{F}, p} = (\mathrm{Enc}, \mathrm{Dec}_{\mathsf{V}, \mathsf{F}}, \mathrm{RevAtt}, \mathrm{RevMsg}_{\mathsf{V}})$ is defined as follows:*

- *$\mathrm{Enc} \colon \{0, 1\}^n \mapsto \{0, 1\}^{p(n)}$ is a random injective function mapping strings $x \in \{0, 1\}^n$ to "ciphertexts" $c \in \{0, 1\}^p$ where $p(n) \geq n$.*
- *$\mathrm{Dec}_{\mathsf{V}, \mathsf{F}} \colon \{0, 1\}^\ell \mapsto \{0, 1\}^n \cup \{\bot\}$: Given $(w, c) \in \{0, 1\}^\ell$ as input where $c \in \{0, 1\}^{p(n)}$, $\mathrm{Dec}_{\mathsf{V}, \mathsf{F}}(w, c)$ allows us to decrypt the ciphertext $c = \mathrm{Enc}(x)$ to get back $x$, parse it as $x = (a, m)$, then get $\mathsf{F}(w, m)$ as long as the predicate test is satisfied on $(w, a)$. More formally, the following steps are performed:*
  1. *If $\nexists \, x$ such that $\mathrm{Enc}(x) = c$, output $\bot$. Otherwise, continue to the next step.*
  2. *Find $x$ such that $\mathrm{Enc}(x) = c$, and parse it as $x = (a, m)$.*
  3. *If $\mathsf{V}(w, a) = 1$, output $\mathsf{F}(w, m)$. Otherwise, output $\bot$.*

- RevAtt: $\{0,1\}^{p(n)} \mapsto \{0,1\}^* \cup \{\bot\}$ *is a function that, given an input* $c \in \{0,1\}^{p(n)}$, *would output the corresponding attribute* $a \in \{0,1\}^*$ *for which* $\mathrm{Enc}((a,m)) = c$. *If there is no such* $a$ *then output* $\bot$.
- $\mathrm{RevMsg}_V \colon \{0,1\}^{\ell'} \mapsto \{0,1\}^* \cup \{\bot\}$: *Given* $(w_1, w_2, c)$ *where* $w_1 \neq w_2$ *and* $c \in \{0,1\}^{p(n)}$, *if there exist* $x = (a,m)$ *such that* $\mathrm{Enc}(x) = c$ *and* $V(w_i, a) = 1$ *for* $i \in \{1,2\}$ *then reveal* $m$. *Otherwise, output* $\bot$.

*When it is clear from context, we sometimes omit the subscripts from* $\mathrm{Dec}_{V,F}$, $\mathrm{RevMsg}_V$, *and* $\overline{\Gamma}_{V,F}$ *and simply write them as* $\mathrm{Dec}$, $\mathrm{RevMsg}$, *and* $\overline{\Gamma}$, *respectively. Furthermore, we denote any query-answer pair* $(q, \beta)$ *asked by some oracle algorithm* $A$ *to a subroutine* $T \in \{\mathrm{Enc}, \mathrm{Dec}, \mathrm{RevAtt}, \mathrm{RevMsg}\}$ *as* $(q \mapsto \beta)_T$.

**Definition 17 (Restricted-Monolithic Randomized Functional Witness Encryption Oracle).** *We define a randomized restricted-monolithic functional witness encryption oracle* $\Gamma_{V,F,p}$ *as an rFWE oracle* $\overline{\Gamma}_{V,F,p} = (\mathrm{Enc}, \mathrm{Dec}_{V,F}, \mathrm{RevAtt}, \mathrm{RevMsg})$ *where* $V$ *and* $F$ *satisfy the following properties:*

- $V$ *is a PPT oracle algorithm that takes as input* $(w, a)$, *interprets* $a^{(\cdot)}$ *as an oracle-aided circuit that can only make* $\mathrm{Enc}$ *calls, then outputs* $a^{\mathrm{Enc}}(w)$.
- $F$ *is a PPT oracle algorithm that takes as input* $(w, m)$, *parses* $w = (z_1, z_2)$, *interprets* $z_1^{(\cdot)}$ *as an oracle-aided circuit that can make calls to any subroutine in* $\Gamma = (\mathrm{Enc}, \mathrm{Dec}, \mathrm{RevAtt}, \mathrm{RevMsg})$, *then outputs* $z_1^{\Gamma}(m)$.

While the above oracle shares similar traits to a restricted-monolithic primitive (see Definition 10), the actual functionality of $F$ is slightly modified to simplify the notion of using only part of $w$. For the purposes of this section, we will use the restricted-monolithic rFWE $\Gamma$ in order to prove our separation result of IO from monolithic functional encryption - mainly because this oracle is sufficient for getting monolithic FE. Nevertheless, we will still make use of $\overline{\Gamma}$ later on in in the full version of this paper to prove the fully black-box separation of IO from (non-monolithic) functional encryption.

Next, we present the following definition of canonical executions that is a property of algorithms in this ideal model. This normal form of algorithms helps us in reducing the query cases to analyze since there are useless queries whose answers can be computed without needing to ask the oracle.

**Definition 18 (Canonical executions).** *We define an oracle algorithm* $A^{\Gamma}$ *relative to the restricted-monolithic rFWE oracle to be in canonical form if the following conditions are satisfied:*

- *If* $A$ *has issued a query of the form* $\mathrm{Enc}(x) = c$, *then it will not ask* $\mathrm{Dec}_{V,F}(., c)$, $\mathrm{RevAtt}(c)$, *or* $\mathrm{RevMsg}_V(.,.,c)$ *as it can compute the answers of these queries on its own. In particular, for* $\mathrm{Dec}_{V,F}$ *and* $\mathrm{RevMsg}_V$ *queries, it would run* $V$ *and* $F$ *directly to compute the query answers correctly.*
- *Before asking any* $\mathrm{Dec}_{V,F}(w, c)$ *query where* $\mathrm{Enc}(x) = c$ *for some* $x = (a, m)$, $A$ *would go through the following steps first:*

- $A$ would get $a \leftarrow$ RevAtt($c$) then run $\mathsf{V}^{\mathrm{Enc}}(w, a)$ on its own, making sure to answer any queries of $\mathsf{V}$ using Enc. If $\mathsf{V}^{\mathrm{Enc}}(w, a) = 0$ then do not issue $\mathrm{Dec}_{\mathsf{V},\mathsf{F}}(w, c)$ to $\Gamma$ and use $\bot$ as the answer instead. Otherwise, continue to the next step.
- If $A$ has beforehand ran $\mathsf{V}^{\mathrm{Enc}}(w', a) = 1$ for some $w' \neq w$ then it does not ask $\mathrm{Dec}_{\mathsf{V},\mathsf{F}}(w, c)$ and instead computes the answer to this query on its own. That is, it first gets $m \leftarrow$ RevMsg($w, w', c$), computes on its own $\mathsf{F}^{\Gamma}(w, m)$ and outputs $\mathsf{F}^{\Gamma}(w, m)$ if $\mathsf{V}^{\mathrm{Enc}}(w, a) = 1$ or otherwise $\bot$.
- If $A$ has not asked $\mathrm{Dec}_{\mathsf{V},\mathsf{F}}(w', c)$ for any $w' \neq w$ (or did but it received $\bot$ as the answer) then it directly asks $\mathrm{Dec}_{\mathsf{V},\mathsf{F}}(w, c)$ from the oracle.
- Before asking any RevMsg$_{\mathsf{V}}(w_1, w_2, c)$ query where Enc($x$) $= c$ for some $x = (a, m)$, $A$ would go through the following steps first:
  - $A$ would get $a \leftarrow$ RevAtt($c$) then run $\mathsf{V}^{\mathrm{Enc}}(w_i, a)$ for all $i \in \{1, 2\}$ on its own, making sure to answer any queries of $\mathsf{V}$ using Enc. If $\mathsf{V}^{\mathrm{Enc}}(w_i, a) = 0$ for some $i$ then do not issue RevMsg$_{\mathsf{V}}(w_1, w_2, c)$ to $\Gamma$ and use $\bot$ as the answer instead. Otherwise, continue to the next step.
  - After issuing RevMsg$_{\mathsf{V}}(w_1, w_2, c)$ to $\Gamma$ and getting back an answer $m \neq \bot$, ask the query Enc($x$) where $x = (a, m)$ then run $\mathsf{F}^{\Gamma}(w_1, m)$ and $\mathsf{F}^{\Gamma}(w_2, m)$.

*Note that any oracle algorithm $A$ can be easily modified into a canonical form by increasing its query complexity by at most a polynomial factor assuming that $\mathsf{F}$ has extended polynomial query complexity.*

*Remark 1.* We observe the following useful property regarding the number of queries of a specific type that a canonical algorithm in the $\Gamma$ oracle model can make. Namely, given a canonical $A$, for any ciphertext $c = $ Enc($x$) where $x = (a, m)$ for which $A$ has not asked Enc($x$) before, $A$ would ask at most one query of the form RevAtt($c$), at most one query of the form $\mathrm{Dec}_{\mathsf{V},\mathsf{F}}(w, c)$ for which $\mathsf{V}^{\mathrm{Enc}}(w, a) = 1$, and at most one query of the form RevMsg$_{\mathsf{V}}(w_1, w_2, c)$ for which $\mathsf{V}^{\mathrm{Enc}}(w_i, a) = 1$ where $i \in \{1, 2\}$. Furthermore, $A$ would never ask a query if $\mathsf{V}^{\mathrm{Enc}}(w, a) = 0$ since this condition can be verified independently by $A$ and the answer can be simulated as it would invariably be $\bot$.

Looking ahead, we will use this property later on to prove an upper bound on the number of ciphertexts that an adversary can decrypt without knowing the underlying message. Furthermore, we stress that this property holds specifically due to the presence of the RevMsg subroutine which leaks the entire message of a given ciphertext once two different valid witnesses are provided. As a result, this shows that decrypting a ciphertext more than once (under different witnesses) does not help as the message could be revealed instead.

We also provide the following definitions to classify the ciphertext and query types. This would simplify our discussion and clarify some aspects of the details later in the proof.

**Definition 19 (Ciphertext Types).** *Let $A$ be a canonical algorithm in the $\Gamma$ ideal model and suppose that $Q_A$ is the set of query-answer pairs that $A$*

*asks during its execution. For any q of the form* $\text{Dec}_{\mathsf{V},\mathsf{F}}(w, c)$, $\text{RevAtt}(c)$, *or* $\text{RevMsg}_{\mathsf{V}}(w_1, w_2, c)$, *we say that c is* valid *if there exists x such that* $c = \text{Enc}(x)$, *and we say that c is* unknown *if the query-answer pair* $(x \mapsto c)_{\text{Enc}}$ *is not in* $Q_A$.

**Definition 20 (Query Types).** *Let A be a canonical algorithm in the $\Gamma$ ideal model and let $Q_A$ be the query-answer pairs that it has asked so far. For any query new query q issued to $\Gamma$, we define several properties that such a query might have:*

- **Determined:** *We say q is determined with respect to $Q_A$ if there exists $(q \mapsto \beta)_T \in Q_A$ for some answer $\beta$ or there exists some query $(q' \mapsto \beta')_T \in Q_A$ that determines that answer of q without needing to issue q to $\Gamma$.*
- **Direct:** *We say q is a* direct *query if A issues this query to $\Gamma$ to get back some answer $\beta$. The answers to such queries are said to be* visible *to A.*
- **Indirect:** *We say q is an indirect query if q is issued by $\mathsf{F}^{\Gamma}$ during a Dec query that was issued by A. The answers to such queries are said to be* hidden *from A.*

### 3.2  Monolithic Functional Encryption Exists Relative to $\Gamma$

In this section, we show how to construct a semantically-secure monolithic FE scheme. Namely, we prove the following:

**Lemma 2.** *There exists a correct and subexponentially-secure implementation of monolithic functional encryption in the $\Gamma$ oracle model with measure one of oracles.*

We do this in two steps: we first show how to construct a restricted-monolithic variant of a functional witness encryption from the ideal oracle $\Gamma$ and then show how to use it to construct the desired functional encryption scheme. Our variant of FWE that we will construct is defined as follows.

**Definition 21 (Customized Functional Witness Encryption (CFWE)).** *Given any one-way function R, let $\mathsf{V}$ be a PPT oracle algorithm that takes as input an instance-message pair $x = (a, m)$ and witness w, interprets a as an oracle circuit then outputs $a^R(w)$ while only making calls to R. Furthermore, let $\mathsf{F}$ be a PPT oracle algorithm that accepts as input a string $w = (z_1, z_2)$ and a message m, interprets $z_1$ as a circuit then outputs a string $y = z_1(m)$. For any given security parameter $\kappa$, a customized functional witness encryption scheme defined by $\mathsf{V}$ and $\mathsf{F}$ consists of three PPT algorithms $P = (\text{Enc}, \text{Dec}_{\mathsf{V},\mathsf{F}}, \text{RevAtt})$ defined as follows:*

- Enc$(1^{\kappa}, a, m)$: *given an instance $a \in \{0,1\}^*$, message $m \in \{0,1\}^*$, and security parameter $\kappa$, outputs $c \in \{0,1\}^*$.*
- RevAtt$(c)$: *given a ciphertext c, outputs the corresponding attribute a under which the message is encrypted.*
- Dec$_{\mathsf{V},\mathsf{F}}(w, c)$: *given ciphertext c and "witness" string $w \in \{0,1\}^*$, outputs a message $m' \in \{0,1\}^*$.*

*A customized functional witness encryption scheme satisfies the following completeness and security properties:*

- **Correctness:** *For any security parameter $\kappa$, any $m \in \{0,1\}^*$, and any $(w, (a, m))$ such that $w$ and $\mathsf{V}^R(w, a) = 1$, it holds that*

$$\Pr_{\mathrm{Enc, Dec}}[\mathsf{Dec}_{\mathsf{V},\mathsf{F}}(w, \mathrm{Enc}(1^\kappa, a, m)) = \mathsf{F}^P(w, m)] = 1$$

- **Instance-Revealing:** *For any security parameter $\kappa$, any $m \in \{0,1\}^*$, and any $(w, (a, m))$ such that $\mathsf{V}^R(w, a) = 1$, it holds that*

$$\Pr[\mathrm{RevAtt}(\mathrm{Enc}(1^\kappa, a, m)) = a] = 1$$

- **Weak Extractability:** *For any PPT adversary $A$ and polynomial $p_1(.)$, there exists a PPT extractor $E$ and a polynomial $p_2(.)$ such that for any security parameter $\kappa$, any $a$ for which $\mathsf{V}^R(w, a) = 1$ for some $w$, and any $m_0, m_1$ where $|m_0| = |m_1|$, if:*

$$\Pr\left[A(1^\kappa, c) = b \mid b \xleftarrow{\$} \{0,1\}, c \leftarrow \mathrm{Enc}(1^\kappa, a, m_b)\right] \geq \frac{1}{2} + p_1(\kappa)$$

*Then:*

$$\Pr\left[\begin{array}{c} E^A(1^\kappa, a, m_0, m_1) = w : \mathsf{V}^R(w, a) = 1 \wedge \mathsf{F}^P(w, m_0) \neq \mathsf{F}^P(w, m_1) \\ \vee \\ E^A(1^\kappa, a, m_0, m_1) = (w_1, w_2) : w_1 \neq w_2 \wedge \mathsf{V}^R(w_1, a) = 1 \wedge \mathsf{V}^R(w_2, a) = 1 \end{array}\right] \geq p_2(\kappa)$$

**Customized FWE in the $\Gamma$ Ideal Model.** Here we provide the construction of customized FWE using the $\Gamma_{\mathsf{V},\mathsf{F}}$ oracle. We note that $\Gamma$ can be thought of as an ideal customized FWE and hence the construction of the CFWE primitive is straightforward.

**Construction 3 (Customized Functional Witness Encryption).** *Let $\mathsf{V}$ and $\mathsf{F}$ be as defined in Definition 21. For any security parameter $\kappa$ and oracle $\Gamma_{\mathsf{V},\mathsf{F}}$ sampled according to Definition 17, we will implement a customized FWE scheme $P$ defined by $\mathsf{V}$ and function class $\mathsf{F}$ as follows:*

- *CFWE.Enc$(1^\kappa, a, m)$: Given $a \in \{0,1\}^*$, message $m \in \{0,1\}^{n'}$ and security parameter $1^\kappa$, let $n = \Theta(n' + |a| + \kappa)$. Sample $r \leftarrow \{0,1\}^\kappa$ uniformly at random then output $c = \mathrm{Enc}(x)$ where $x = (a, (m, r))$.*
- *CFWE.Dec$(w, c)$: Given string $w$ and ciphertext $c \in \{0,1\}^p$, get $y \leftarrow \mathrm{Dec}_{\mathsf{V},\mathsf{F}}(w, c)$, then output $y$.*
- *CFWE.Rev$(c)$: Given ciphertext $c \in \{0,1\}^p$, outputs $\mathrm{RevAtt}(c)$.*

**Lemma 3.** *Construction 3 is a correct and subexponentially-secure implementation of customized functional witness encryption in the $\Gamma$ oracle model with measure one.*

For the proof of correctness and security for this construction, we refer the reader to the full version of this paper.

**From CFWE to Functional Encryption**

**Construction 4 (Functional Encryption).** *Let* $P_F$ = (FE. Setup, FE. Keygen, FE. Enc, FE. Dec) *be the functional encryption scheme for the function family* F *that we would like to construct. Suppose* Sig = (Sig.Gen, Sig.Sign, Sig.Ver) *is a secure signature scheme.*

*Define a language* $L$ *with an associated PPT verifier* V *such that an instance* $a$ *of the language corresponds to the signature verification circuit* Sig.Ver$(vk, .)$ *that takes as input* $w = (f, sk_f)$ *so that* $V(w, a) = a(w) = 1$ *if and only if* Sig.Ver$(vk, w) = 1$ *for some oracle-aided* $f \in F$, $sk_f \leftarrow$ Sig.Sign$(sk, f)$, *and* $(sk, vk) \leftarrow$ Sig.Gen$(1^\kappa)$. *Furthermore, let* F' *be a PPT algorithm that takes as input* $w = (f, sk_f)$ *and a message* $m$ *then outputs* $y = F'(w, m) = f(m)$.

*Given a customized functional witness encryption scheme* CFWE = (CFWE.Enc, CFWE.Dec$_{V,F'}$, CFWE.Rev) *for* V *and* F' *defined above, signature scheme* Sig, *and security parameter* $\kappa$, *we implement the monolithic FE scheme* $P_F$ *as follows:*

- FE. Setup$(1^\kappa)$: *Generate* $(sk, vk) \leftarrow$ Sig.Gen$(1^\kappa)$. *Output* (MPK, MSK) *where* MPK = $vk$ *and* MSK = $sk$.
- FE. Keygen(MSK, $f$): *Given* MSK = $sk$ *and* $f \in F$, *output* SK$_f$ = $(f, sk_f)$ *where* $sk_f \leftarrow$ Sig.Sign(MSK, $f$).
- FE. Enc(MPK, $m$): *Given* MPK $\in \{0,1\}^\kappa$ *and message* $m \in \{0,1\}^{n'}$, *output* *ciphertext* $c =$ CFWE.Enc$(1^\kappa, $MPK$, m)$.
- FE. Dec(SK$_f$, $c$): *Given* SK$_f$ = $(f, sk_f)$ *and ciphertext* $c \in \{0,1\}^p$, *call and output the value returned by* CFWE.Dec$_{V,F'}$(SK$_f$, $c$).

**Lemma 4.** *Construction 4 is a fully black-box construction of monolithic functional encryption from customized FWE.*

*Proof.* We first show that the construction is correct. Given (MPK, MSK) $\leftarrow$ FE. Setup$(1^\kappa)$, for any encryption $c \leftarrow$ FE. Enc(MPK, $m$) of a message $m \in \{0,1\}^{n'}$ and functional decryption key SK$_f \leftarrow$ FE. Keygen(MSK, $f$) for a function $f \in \mathcal{F}$, we get that, if $V(w, a) = a^{\text{Sig}}(w) = $ Sig.Ver$(vk, (f, sk_f)) = 1$ then:

$$\text{FE. Dec}(\text{SK}_f, c) = \text{CFWE.Dec}_{V,F'}((f, sk_f), c) = F'((f, sk_f), m) = f^{P_F}(m)$$

Note that, since this is an monolithic construction, $f$ can have oracle gates to any subroutine in $P_F$. As a result, we need to make sure that V are F' are specified in a way so that all monolithic computations are valid. First, V only has one Sig.Ver gate which is supported by OWFs. Furthermore, F' calls $f$ which has oracle gates to any subroutine in $P_F$. Nevertheless, we can reduce each gate to $P_F$ to CFWE or OWF gates. In particular, FE. Setup can be reduced to Sig.Gen gates, FE. Keygen can be reduced to Sig.Sign gates, FE. Enc can be reduced to CFWE.Enc gates, and FE. Dec can be reduced to CFWE.Dec gates. Thus, all gates in F' can be reduced to those in FWE or one-way functions.

Next, we prove the security of the scheme by reducing it to the underlying security of CFWE and Sig. Let $A$ be a computationally bounded adversary that asks one functional secret key query and breaks the security of the FE scheme. That is, for some non-negligible $\varepsilon(.)$:

$$\Pr[\text{IND}_A^{1\text{FE}}(1^\kappa) = 1] \geq \frac{1}{2} + \varepsilon(\kappa)$$

where $\text{IND}_A^{1\text{FE}}$ is the experiment of Definition 3.

Towards contradiction, we will now show that, given $A$, we can build an attacker $B$ that can break the strong existential unforgeability of the signature scheme under chosen message attack. On receiving the public-key MPK from the (signature game) challenger, $B$ forwards MPK to $A$ and upon receiving $(f, m_0, m_1)$, requests the signature for $f$ and then randomly chooses a message to encrypt. Note that, since FE.Enc(MPK, $m_b$) = CFWE.Enc($1^\kappa$, MPK, $m_b$), $B$ can use $A$ to build a distinguisher $A'$ against CFWE. $B$ then runs the black-box straight-line extractor $E^{A'}$ (guaranteed to exist by the security definition of CFWE) where at least one of the following events will happen with non-negligible probability:

- The extractor returns a single witness $w^* = (f^*, sk_{f^*})$ such that $\mathsf{V}(w^*, \mathsf{MPK})$ outputs 1 and $\mathsf{F}'(w^*, m_0) \neq \mathsf{F}'(w^*, m_1) \implies f^*(m_0) \neq f^*(m_1)$. Note that this implies that $sk_{f^*}$ is a valid forgery since $f^*$ cannot be the function $f$ that $A$ requests the signature for (because $f(m_0) = f(m_1)$ in that case) and $w^*$ passed verification thus violating the security of the signature scheme.
- The extractor returns a pair of witnesses $(w_1^*, w_2^*)$ such that $w_1^* \neq w_2^*$ and $\mathsf{V}(w_1^*, \mathsf{MPK}) = \mathsf{V}(w_2^*, \mathsf{MPK}) = 1$. This either implies that $w_i^* = (f^*, sk_{f^*})$ for some $i \in \{1, 2\}$ is a valid witness and $f^* \neq f$ in which case we have a signature forgery, or it implies that $w_i^* = (f, sk_f')$ for some $i \in \{1, 2\}$ and hence $sk_f' \neq sk_f$ (since even if $w_{i-1}^* = (f, sk_f)$ we have that $w_i^* \neq w_{i-1}^*$) which is also signature forgery.

In both of the above cases, an attack against the FE scheme results in an attack against the underlying signature scheme.

### 3.3 Compiling Out $\Gamma$ from IO

In this section, we show a simulatable compiler for compiling out $\Gamma_{\mathsf{V},\mathsf{F}}$ when $\mathsf{F}$ is short-output. We adapt the approach outlined in Sect. 2 to the restricted-monolithic rFWE oracle $\Gamma_{\mathsf{V},\mathsf{F}} = (\text{Enc}, \text{Dec}_{\mathsf{V},\mathsf{F}}, \text{RevAtt}, \text{RevMsg}_{\mathsf{V}})$ while making use of Lemma 1, which allows us to compile out $\Gamma_{\mathsf{V},\mathsf{F}}$ in two phases: we first compile out part of $\Gamma_{\mathsf{V},\mathsf{F}}$ to get an approximately-correct obfuscator $\widehat{O}^\Theta$ in the random instance-revealing witness encryption model (that produces an obfuscation $\widehat{B}^\Theta$ in the $\Theta$-model), and then use the previous result of [GMM17] to compile out $\Theta$ and get an obfuscator $O'$ in the plain-model. Since we are applying this lemma only a constant number of times, security should still be preserved. Specifically, we will prove the following lemma:

**Lemma 5.** *Let* F *be a PPT oracle Turing machine that accepts as input a witness $w$ and a message $m$ then outputs a string $y \in \{0,1\}^s$ where $s(n) \leq t(n)$. Let $\Theta$ be a random instance-revealing witness encryption oracle. Then for any $\Gamma_{V,F,p}$ satisfying $t(n) \leq p(n) - \omega(n)$ and for $\Theta \sqsubseteq \Gamma_{V,F,p}$, the following holds:*

- *For any IO in the $\Gamma_{V,F,p}$ ideal model, there exists a simulatable compiler with correctness error $\varepsilon < 1/200$ for it that outputs a new obfuscator in the random instance-revealing witness encryption oracle $\Theta$ model.*
- *[GMM17] For any IO in the $\Theta$ oracle model, there exists a simulatable compiler with correctness error $\varepsilon < 1/200$ for it that outputs a new obfuscator in the plain model.*

We observe that by compiling out only the Dec queries of $\Gamma$, we will end up with queries only to Enc, RevAtt, and RevMsg. However, we note that Enc and RevAtt already are part of $\Theta$ and RevMsg can in fact be interpreted as the decryption subroutine of $\Theta$ where $w' = (w_1, w_2)$ is defined as the witness to the decryption subroutine. Therefore, the second part of Lemma 5 follows directly by [GMM17], where they showed how to compile out the ideal witness encryption oracle from any IO scheme, and thus we focus on proving the first part of the lemma. We will present the construction of the obfuscator in the random instance-revealing witness encryption model that, given an obfuscator in the $\Gamma$ model, would compile out and emulate queries to Dec, while forwarding any Enc, RevAtt, RevMsg queries to $\Theta$. Throughout this section, for simplicity of notation, we will denote $\Gamma = \Gamma_{V,F,p}$ to be the oracle satisfying $t(n) \leq p(n) - \omega(n)$.

*Remark 2.* For simplicity of exposition, we assume that the compiler only asks the oracle for queries from $\Gamma_n$. However, our argument directly extends to handle arbitrary calls to the oracle $\Gamma$ using the following standard technique. As we will show, the "error" in our poly-query compiler in the ideal model will be at most $\text{poly}(q)/2^n$ (where $q = \text{poly}(\kappa)$ is a fixed polynomial over the security parameter $\kappa$ of the IO construction) when we only call $\Gamma_n$. It is also the case that this error adds up when we work with several input lengths $n_1, n_2, \ldots$, but it is still bounded by union bound. Therefore, the total error of the transformation will be at most $O(\text{poly}(n_1)/2^{n_1})$ where $n_1$ is the smallest integer for which $\Gamma_{n_1}$ is queried at some point. To make $n_1$ large enough (to keep the error small enough) we can modify all the parties to query $\Gamma$ on *all* oracle queries up to input parameter $n_1 = c(\log(\kappa))$ for sufficiently large $c$. (Note that this will be a polynomial number of queres in total.)

**The new obfuscator $\widehat{O}^{\Theta}$ in the instance-revealing witness encryption model.** Given a $\delta$-approximate obfuscator $O = (\text{iO}, \text{Ev})$ in the rFWE oracle model, we construct an $(\delta + \varepsilon)$-approximate obfuscator $\widehat{O} = (\widehat{\text{iO}}, \widehat{\text{Ev}})$ in the $\Theta$ oracle model. Throughout this process, we can assume that iO and Ev are in their canonical form as in Definition 18.

---

**Algorithm 1.** EmulateCall

---

**Input**: Query-answer set $Q$, query $q$ to a subroutine of
$\quad\quad T \in \{\text{Enc}, \text{Dec}, \text{RevAtt}, \text{RevMsg}\}$ of $\Gamma$
**Oracle**: Random Instance-Revealing Witness Encryption Oracle
$\quad\quad \Theta = (\text{WEnc}, \text{WDec}, \text{WRevAtt})$
**Output**: A query-answer pair $\rho_q$, and the set $W$ of hidden queries
**Begin:**
**if** $\exists\, (q \mapsto \beta)_T \in Q$ for some answer $\beta$ **then**
$\quad|\quad$ Set $\rho_q = (q \mapsto \beta)_T$
**end**
**if** $q = x$ is a query to Enc **then**
$\quad|\quad$ Set $\rho_q = (x \mapsto \text{WEnc}(x))_{\text{Enc}}$
**end**
**if** $q = c$ is a query to RevAtt **then**
$\quad|\quad$ Set $\rho_q = (c \mapsto \text{WRevAtt}(c))_{\text{Enc}}$
**end**
**if** $q = (w_1, w_2, c)$ is a query to $\text{RevMsg}_V$ **then**
$\quad|\quad$ Set $\rho_q = (x \mapsto \text{WDec}_{V'}((w_1, w_2), c))_{\text{Enc}}$
**end**
/* We simulate Dec queries */
**if** $q = (w, c)$ is a query to $\text{Dec}_{V,F}$ **then**
$\quad|\quad$ Let $a_R$ be the attribute returned by EmulateCall$(Q, q_R)$ where $q_R$ is the
$\quad|\quad$ query $\text{RevAtt}(c)$
$\quad|\quad$ Emulate $b \leftarrow V^{\text{Enc}}(w, a_R)$ while emulating any queries using EmulateCall
$\quad|\quad$ **if** $b = 1$ and $\exists\, ((a, m) \mapsto c)_{\text{Enc}} \in Q$ **then**
$\quad|\quad\quad|\quad$ Emulate $y \leftarrow F^{\Gamma}(w, m)$ while simulating any queries using EmulateCall
$\quad|\quad\quad|\quad$ Set $W$ to be the set of query-answer pairs asked by $F$
$\quad|\quad\quad|\quad$ Set $\rho_q = ((w, c) \mapsto y)_{\text{Dec}}$
$\quad|\quad$ **else**
$\quad|\quad\quad|\quad$ Set $\rho_q = ((w, c) \mapsto \perp)_{\text{Dec}}$
$\quad|\quad$ **end**
**end**
Return $(\rho_q, W)$

---

## Subroutine $\widehat{\text{iO}}^{\Theta}(C)$:

1. *Emulation phase*: Emulate $\text{iO}^{\Gamma}(C)$. Initialize $Q_O = \varnothing$ to be the set of query-answer pairs asked by the obfuscation algorithm iO. For every query $q$ asked by $\text{iO}^{\Gamma}(C)$, call $(\rho_q, W) \leftarrow$ EmulateCall$^{\Theta}(Q_O, q)$ and add $\rho_q$ to $Q_O$.
2. *Learning phase*: Set $Q_B = \varnothing$ to be the set of direct (visible) query-answer pairs asked during this phase (so far) and $Q_B^h = \varnothing$ to be the set of indirect (hidden) query-answer pairs (see Definition 20). Let $k = (\ell_O + \kappa)/\varepsilon$ where $\ell_O \leq |\text{iO}|$ represents the number of queries asked by iO. Choose $\lambda \xleftarrow{\$} [k]$ uniformly at random then for $i = \{1, ..., \lambda\}$ do the following:
   - Choose $z_i \xleftarrow{\$} \{0, 1\}^{|C|}$ uniformly at random
   - Run $\text{Ev}^{\Gamma}(B, z_i)$. For every query $q$ asked by $\text{Ev}^{\Gamma}(B, z_i)$, run $(\rho_q, W) \leftarrow$ EmulateCall$^{\Theta}(Q_O \cup Q_B \cup Q_B^h, q)$, then add $\rho_q$ to $Q_B$ and $W$ to $Q_B^h$.

3. The output of the $\Theta$-model obfuscation algorithm $\widehat{\text{iO}}^{\Theta}(C)$ will be $\widehat{B} = (B, Q_B)$.

**Subroutine $\widehat{\text{Ev}}^{\Theta}(\widehat{B}, z)$:** Initialize $Q_{\widehat{B}} = \varnothing$ to be the set of queries asked when evaluating $\widehat{B}$. To evaluate $\widehat{B} = (B, Q_B)$ on a new random input $z$ we simply emulate $\text{Ev}^{\Gamma}(B, z)$ as follows. For every query $q$ asked by $\text{Ev}^{\Gamma}(B, z)$, run and set $(\rho_q, W) = \texttt{EmulateCall}^{\Theta}(Q_B \cup Q_{\widehat{B}}, q)$ then add $(\rho_q \cup W)$ to $Q_{\widehat{B}}$.

**The running time of $\widehat{iO}$.** We note that the running time of the new obfuscator $\widehat{iO}$ remains polynomial time since we are emulating the original obfuscation once followed by a polynomial number $\lambda$ of learning iterations. Furthermore, since we are working with the restricted-monolithic oracle (see Definition 17), the way that F is defined (as a universal circuit evaluator) makes it so that the number of recursive calls that appear due to emulating $\text{F}^{\Gamma}$ is upper-bounded by some polynomial (in fact even quadratic).

**Proving Approximate Correctness.** Define $Q_{\widehat{B}}^h$ to be the set of hidden queries asked during the final execution phase. Set $Q_T = Q_O \cup Q_B \cup Q_B^h \cup Q_{\widehat{B}} \cup Q_{\widehat{B}}^h$ to be the set of all (visible and hidden) query-answer pairs asked during all the phases. We consider two distinct experiments that construct the $\Theta$ oracle model obfuscator exactly as described above but differ when evaluating $\widehat{B}$:

- **Real Experiment:** $\widehat{\text{Ev}}^{\Theta}(\widehat{B}, z)$ emulates $\text{Ev}^{\Gamma}(B, z)$ on a random input $z$ and answers any queries using $\texttt{EmulateCall}$.
- **Ideal Experiment:** $\widehat{\text{Ev}}^{\Gamma}(\widehat{B}, z)$ executes $\text{Ev}^{\Gamma}(B, z)$ and answers all the queries of $\text{Ev}^{\Gamma}(B, z)$ using the actual oracle $\Gamma$.

Note that the actual emulation of the new obfuscator is statistically close to an ideal emulation of the obfuscation and learning phases using $\Gamma$ and so it suffices to compare only the real and ideal final execution phases. In essence, in the real experiment, we can think of the execution as $\text{Ev}^{\widehat{\Gamma}}(B, z)$ where $\widehat{\Gamma}$ is the oracle simulated using the learned query-answer pairs $Q_B$ and oracle $\Theta$. We will compare the real experiment with the ideal experiment and show that the statistical distance between these two executions is at most $\varepsilon$. In order to achieve this, we will identify the events that make the executions $\text{Ev}^{\Gamma}(B, z)$ and $\text{Ev}^{\widehat{\Gamma}}(B, z)$ diverge (i.e. without them happening, they proceed statistically the same).

Let $q$ be a new query that is being asked by $\text{Ev}^{\widehat{\Gamma}}(B, z)$ (i.e. in the real experiment) and handled using $\texttt{EmulateCall}^{\Theta}(Q_B \cup Q_{\widehat{B}}, q)$. The following are the cases that should be handled:

1. If $q$ is a query of type $\text{Enc}(x)$, then the answer to $q$ will be distributed the same in both experiments as they will be both answered using the subroutine $\text{WEnc}(c)$ of $\Theta$.

2. If $q$ is a query of type $\text{RevAtt}(c)$, then the answer to $q$ will be distributed the same in both experiments as they will be both answered using the subroutine $\text{WRevAtt}(c)$ of $\Theta$.

3. If $q$ is a query of type $\text{RevMsg}_V(w_1, w_2, c)$, then the answer to $q$ will be distributed the same in both experiments as they will be both answered using the subroutine $\text{WDec}_{V'}(w', c)$ where $w' = (w_1, w_2)$.

4. If $q$ is a query of type $\text{Dec}_{V,F}(w, c)$ whose answer is determined by $Q_B \cup Q_{\widehat{B}}$ in the real experiment then it is also determined by $Q_T \supseteq (Q_B \cup Q_{\widehat{B}})$ in the ideal experiment and the answers are therefore distributed the same.

5. Suppose $q$ is a query of type $\text{Dec}_{V,F}(w, c)$ that is not determined by $Q_B \cup Q_{\widehat{B}}$ in the real experiment. Then the answer returned by `EmulateCall` is $\perp$ since the underlying encryption query $((a, m) \mapsto c)_{\text{Enc}}$ is not known. In that case, we have to consider three different counterparts in the ideal experiment:

   (a) **Bad Event 1:** If $q$ is not determined by $Q_T$ in the ideal experiment then this implies that the ideal execution $\text{Ev}^\Gamma(B, z)$ is for the first time hitting a valid ciphertext that was never generated by an encryption query asked during any of the phases. In that case, since Enc is injective, the answer returned by $\Gamma$ would be $\perp$ with overwhelming probability.

   (b) **Bad Event 2:** The query $q$ is determined by $Q_T \setminus (Q_B \cup Q_{\widehat{B}})$ in the ideal experiment and the ideal execution $\text{Ev}^\Gamma(B, z)$ has hit a valid unknown ciphertext that was generated by an encryption query in the obfuscation phase that was never learned. In this case, the answer will be $\text{F}^\Gamma(w, m)$ if the verification passes and $\perp$ otherwise.

   (c) **Bad Event 3:** The query $q$ is determined by $Q_T \setminus (Q_B \cup Q_{\widehat{B}})$ in the ideal experiment then and the ideal execution $\text{Ev}^\Gamma(B, z)$ has hit a valid unknown ciphertext that was generated as a hidden query (i.e. issued by inner F executions) during the learning or evaluation phases. In this case, the answer will be $\text{F}^\Gamma(w, m)$ if the verification passes and $\perp$ otherwise.

   Notice that the answer to such a query in the ideal experiment differs from that in the real experiment (which always outputs $\perp$). However, we will show below that such an event is unlikely to occur.

For circuit input $z$, let $E(z)$ be the event that either one of Cases 5a, 5b, or 5c happen. More specifically, this is the event that $\text{Ev}^{\widehat{F}}(B, z)$ asks a query $q$ of the form $\text{Dec}_{V,F}(w, c)$ where $c$ is a valid ciphertext that was either (i) never generated before during any of the phases, (ii) generated during the obfuscation phase, or (iii) generated by a hidden query in the learning and/or final evaluation phases. Assuming that event $E(z)$ does not happen, both experiments will proceed identically the same and the output distributions of $\text{Ev}^\Gamma(B, z)$ and $\text{Ev}^{\widehat{F}}(B, z)$ will be statistically close. More formally, the probability of correctness for $\widehat{iO}$ is:

$$\Pr_z[\text{Ev}^{\widehat{F}}(B, z) \neq C(z)] = \Pr_z[\text{Ev}^{\widehat{F}}(B, z) \neq C(z) \wedge \neg E(z)] + \Pr_z[\text{Ev}^{\widehat{F}}(B, z) \neq C(z) \wedge E(z)]$$

$$\leq \Pr_z[\text{Ev}^{\widehat{F}}(B, z) \neq C(z) \wedge \neg E(z)] + \Pr_z[E(z)]$$

By the approximate functionality of iO, we have that:

$$\Pr_z[\text{iO}^\Gamma(C)(z) \neq C(z)] = \Pr_z[\text{Ev}^\Gamma(B, z) \neq C(z)] \leq \delta(\kappa)$$

Therefore,

$$\Pr_z[\text{Ev}^{\widehat{\Gamma}}(B, z) \neq C(z) \wedge \neg E(z)] = \Pr_z[\text{Ev}^\Gamma(B, z) \neq C(z) \wedge \neg E(z)] \leq \delta \qquad (1)$$

We are thus left to show that $\Pr[E(z)] \leq \varepsilon$. Since both experiments proceed the same up until $E$ happens, the probability of $E$ happening is the same in both worlds and we will thus choose to bound this bad event in the ideal world.

**Proof Intuition.** At a high-level, in order to show that $E$ is unlikely, we will show that the learning procedure and final execution phases, when treated as a single non-uniform query-adaptive algorithm $A$, will only ask a bounded number of queries for valid ciphertexts whose corresponding underlying message is unknown to this algorithm. Then, given this upper bound on such queries, we ensure that by running the learning procedure for sufficient number of times, the final execution phase will not ask such queries to unknown ciphertexts with high probability and we maintain the approximate correctness of the obfuscation.

In order to prove this upper bound on the number of ciphertexts that will be hit, we start with the query-adaptive $A$ which consists of the *combination* of the learning and final execution phases that accepts as input an obfuscation $B$ in the $\Gamma$ oracle model and is able to adaptively query $\Gamma$ when running $B$ on multiple randomly chosen inputs. We then show through a sequence of reductions to other adversaries that the advantage of such an attacker in hitting a specific number of unknown ciphertexts is upper bounded by the advantage of a different non-adaptive attacker $\widehat{A}$ in hitting the same number of ciphertexts (up to some factor). We then finally show that $\widehat{A}$ has a negligible advantage in succeeding.

We begin by defining the notion of query adaptivity for oracle algorithms and specify what it means for an adversary to hit a ciphertext.

**Definition 22 (Query Adaptivity).** *Let $A$ be a poly-query randomized oracle algorithm that asks $\tau$ queries to some idealized oracle $\mathcal{I}$. Suppose $Q$ is the set of queries that $A$ will ask. We define the level of query adaptivity of $A$ as being one of two possible levels:*

- *Non-adaptive: $Q$ consists of $\tau$ queries, possibly from different domains, and chosen by $A$ before it issues any query and/or independently of the answers of any previous query.*
- *Fully adaptive: $Q = (q_1, ..., q_\tau)$ consists of $\tau$ queries possibly from different domains where, for each $i \in [\tau]$, $q_{i+1}$ is determined by the answer returned by $q_i$.*

**Definition 23 (Ciphertext Hit).** *Let $A$ be a $\tau$-query oracle algorithm that has access to $\Gamma$. We say that $A$ has hit a ciphertext $c$ if it queries $\text{Dec}(., c)$, $\text{RevAtt}(c)$, or $\text{RevMsg}(., ., c)$ and $c$ is a valid unknown ciphertext (that is, $A$ has never asked $\text{Enc}(x) = c$). We denote the set of ciphertexts that $A$ has hit by $H_A$.*

Our goal is to prove the following lemma which provides the desired upper bound on the number of ciphertexts that an attacker $A$ can hit.

**Lemma 6 (Hitting Ciphertexts).** *Let $\Gamma_{V,F}$ be as in Definition 17, $n$ be a fixed number, and $t(n) \leq p(n) - \omega(n)$, where $t$ is the upper bound on the output length of $F$ and $p$ is the ciphertext length. Let $A$ be an adaptive $\tau$-query oracle algorithm that takes as input $z$ and has access to $\Gamma_{V,F}$. Let $H_A$ be the set of unknown valid ciphertexts that $A$ hits. Then for security parameter (of the obfuscation scheme) $\kappa$, $n \geq \lg \kappa$, $\tau \leq \text{poly}(\kappa) \leq \kappa^{O(1)}$ we have that for any $s \leq \tau$:*

$$\Pr[|H_A| \geq s] \leq O(2^{\alpha - (t + \omega(n))s})$$

*where $\alpha = |z| + (t + 2n)s$.*

*Proof.* We will define a sequence of adversaries and show reductions between them in order to prove the upper bound stated above. Throughout, we assume that the algorithms are in canonical form (see Definition 18).

1. **Attacker $A$:** This is the original adaptive $\tau$-query attacker as defined in the statement of the lemma where it will receive some input $z$ and can ask $\tau$ queries to $\Gamma$. The goal of the adversary is to hit at least $s$ unknown valid ciphertexts via queries to Dec, RevAtt or RevMsg.
2. **Attacker $A_u$:** This is the same attacker as $A$ but does not accept any input and is modified as follows. For any Dec, RevAtt or RevMsg queries asked to $\Gamma$ with some answer $y \neq \bot$, $A_u$ will instead use an answer that is part of some fixed string $u \in \{0,1\}^\alpha$ hardcoded within $A_u$ where $\alpha = |z| + (t + 2n)s$. The Enc queries are handled normally as before. The goal of this adversary is to hit at least $s$ unknown valid ciphertexts via queries to Dec, RevAtt or RevMsg.
3. **Attacker $A'$:** This is the same attacker as $A_u$ for any fixed $u$. However, aside from Enc queries which are handled normally using $\Gamma$, the other query types are instead replaced with a single subroutine Test that takes as input a ciphertext $c$ and outputs 1 if $c$ is valid, and 0 otherwise. The goal of this adversary is to hit at least $s$ unknown valid ciphertexts via queries to Test.
4. **Attacker $\widehat{A}$:** This is the *non-adaptive* attacker where it will ask all its queries at once at the start of the experiment. Furthermore, it will *not* ask any Enc queries but will be constrained to asking only Test queries. The goal of this adversary is to hit at least $s$ unknown valid ciphertexts via queries to Test.

**Lemma 7.** *For every $A$, there exists some $u \in \{0,1\}^\alpha$ such that $\Pr[|H_A| \geq s] \leq 2^\alpha \Pr[|H_{A_u}| \geq s]$*

*Proof.* Recall that $A$ accepts $z$ as input and, when it hits $s$ ciphertexts, it would receive back at most $(t + 2n)$ since we can either get back $t$ bits information as a result of getting back an answer from $\text{Dec}_{V,F}$ or at most $n$ bits of information from queries of RevAtt and $\text{RevMsg}_V$. Furthermore, by the canonicalization of $A$, it can ask for any $c$ at most one query of each type $\text{Dec}_{V,F}$, RevAtt, and $\text{RevMsg}_V$. Thus, in order to say that $A_u$ would succeed at hitting $s$ with the same amount of information, the length of $u$ has to be $\alpha = |z| + (t + 2n)s$. Now, by a union bound over all $u$, the probability of success for $A$ is given as follows:

$$\Pr[|H_A| \geq s] \leq \Pr[\exists\, u : |H_{A_u}| \geq s] \leq \sum_u \Pr[|H_{A_u}| \geq s] \leq 2^\alpha \Pr[|H_{A_u}| \geq s]$$

**Lemma 8.** *For any $u \in \{0,1\}^\alpha$, $\Pr[|H_{A_u}| \geq s] = \Pr[|H_{A'}| \geq s]$*

*Proof.* Since $A_u$ does not obtain any information regarding the actual answers to the Dec, RevAtt and RevMsg queries that it asks, we can think of these subroutines simply as a testing procedure that $A_u$ can use to determine whether any given ciphertext $c$ is valid or not, and this is signaled by whether the oracle returns $\bot$ or not to any of these queries. Therefore, we can interpret $A_u$ as an adversary $A'$ that simply calls Test instead of Dec, RevAtt and RevMsg queries as this yields the same result.

**Lemma 9.** $\Pr[|H_{A'}| \geq s] \leq \Pr[|H_{\widehat{A}}| \geq s]$

*Proof.* Given attacker $A'$ we can define $\widehat{A}$ that uses $A'$ and only issues Test queries (non-adaptively). Any Enc queries that $A'$ asks (from a specific Enc domain of size $n$) can be lazily evaluated (emulated) by $\widehat{A}$. Furthermore, any Test queries that $A'$ asks will be answered using one of $\widehat{A}$'s pre-issued Test queries while remaining consistent with the previous Enc queries that were issued.

Lastly, we state and prove the following lemma which will be used to bound the number of ciphertexts that any (poly-query) non-adaptive algorithm might obtain and use for its decryption and/or reveal queries.

**Lemma 10 (Hitting Ciphertexts for Non-Adaptive Learners).** *Let $\Gamma$ be as in Definition 16 and $t(n) \leq p(n) - \omega(n)$ where $t$ is an upper bound on the output length of $F$ and $p$ is the ciphertext length. Let $\widehat{A}$ be a non-adaptive $\tau$-query canonical algorithm as defined above and $H_{\widehat{A}}$ be the set of unknown valid ciphertexts that $\widehat{A}$ hits via Test queries. Then for security parameter $\kappa$, fixed $n \geq \lg \kappa$, $\tau \leq \mathrm{poly}(\kappa)$, we have that for any $s \leq \tau$:*

$$\Pr[|H_{\widehat{A}}| \geq s] \leq O(2^{-(t+\omega(n))s})$$

*Proof.* Suppose $t \leq p - dn$ for $d = \omega(1)$ and let $\tau \leq \kappa^{d'} = 2^{d' \lg \kappa} \leq 2^{d'n}$ where $d' = d/2 = \omega(1)$ for the purposes of upper-bounding the probability for all poly-query algorithms $\widehat{A}$. Recall that the function Enc(.) is injective and maps messages $x \in \{0,1\}^n$ to ciphertexts $c \in \{0,1\}^{p(n)}$. For simplicity, assume that we want to compute the probability that $|H_{\widehat{A}}| = s$. For any set of $s$ ciphertexts that are in the image of some fixed $s$-sized set of the domain Enc(.), the probability that the $\tau$ queries will hit these $s$ ciphertexts is given by $\binom{\tau}{s} / \binom{2^p}{s}$. By a union bound over all the different $s$-sized sub-domains of Enc(.), we find that for sufficiently large security parameter $\kappa$:

$$\Pr[|H_{\widehat{A}}| = s] \leq \binom{2^n}{s} \frac{\binom{\tau}{s}}{\binom{2^p}{s}} \leq \frac{\left(\frac{2^n e}{s}\right)^s \left(\frac{\tau e}{s}\right)^s}{\left(\frac{2^p}{s}\right)^s} \leq \left(\frac{\frac{2^n e}{s} \times \frac{2^{d'} n e}{s}}{\frac{2^p}{s}}\right)^s \leq \left(\frac{2^{n(1+d')} e^2}{2^p s}\right)^s$$

$$\leq \left(\frac{2^{n(1+d/2)} e^2}{2^p}\right)^s \leq O(2^{-(t+\omega(n))s})$$

The last inequality follows from the short-output property, that is $t \leq p - d \cdot n$ for some $d = \omega(1)$. Note that $\Pr[|H_{\widehat{A}}| = s + 1] \leq \Pr[|H_{\widehat{A}}| = s]$ and therefore $\Pr[|H_{\widehat{A}}| \geq s]$ is dominated by the largest term represented by $\Pr[|H_{\widehat{A}}| = s]$.

**Putting things together.** By Lemmas 7, 8, and 9, and using Lemma 10, we find that:

$$\Pr[|H_A| \geq s] \leq O(2^{\alpha - (t+\omega(n))s})$$

Note that, for simplicity, Lemma 6 only considers hitting unknown ciphertexts from some fixed domain of size $n$. However, we observe that this argument can be extended for learners that can ask queries for different domain sizes as well.

**Lemma 11.** $\Pr[E(x)] \leq \varepsilon + \text{negl}(\kappa)$

*Proof.* Let $A$ to be an adaptive non-uniform oracle algorithm in the ideal hybrid that has access to $\Gamma$ and works as follows:

– Initialize the query-answer set $Q_A = \varnothing$
– For $i = \{1, ..., k\}$, run $\text{Ev}^\Gamma(B, z_i)$. For any query $q$ asked by $\text{Ev}^\Gamma(B, z_i)$, if $(q \mapsto a)_T \in Q_A$ for subroutine $T$ then answer with $a$. Otherwise, handle the query in the canonical form as in Definition 18, and if a query was sent to $\Gamma$, add the new query-answer pair $(q \mapsto a)_T$ to $Q_A$.
– Output $\text{Ev}^\Gamma(B, z_k)$

In essence, $A$ would run the learning and final execution phases (in total $k$ executions) making sure to only forward to $\Gamma$ the queries that are distinct and which cannot be computed from $Q_A$ so far. Given the above canonical $A$, we observe that for any unknown valid ciphertext $c = \text{Enc}(x)$ where $x = (a, m)$, $A$ would ask at most one query of the form $\text{RevAtt}(c)$, at most one query of the form $\text{Dec}(w, c)$ for which $V^{\text{Enc}}(w, a) = 1$, and at most one query of the form $\text{RevMsg}(w_1, w_2, c)$ for which $V^{\text{Enc}}(w_i, a) = 1$ where $i \in \{1, 2\}$. Furthermore, $A$ would never ask a query if $V^{\text{Enc}}(w, a) = 0$ since this condition can be verified independently by $A$ and the answer can be simulated as it would invariably be $\bot$.

Given $A$, we can bound the number of distinct unknown ciphertexts that the $k$ executions will hit, which we denote by $|H_B| = \left|\bigcup_{i=1}^{k} H_{B_i}\right|$ where $H_{B_i}$ is the set of ciphertexts hit by the $i$th evaluation $\mathrm{Ev}^\Gamma(B, z_i)$. Note that the total number of queries that will be asked across all executions is $k\ell_B = \mathrm{poly}(\kappa)$ where $\ell_B$ is the circuit size of $\mathrm{Ev}(B, .)$. It is straightforward to see that, for any $s$, $\Pr[|H_A| \geq s] = \Pr[|H_B| \geq s]$ since whenever one of the $k$ executions hits an unknown ciphertext $c$ for this first time, $A$ will also forward it to the oracle and hit it for the first time as well.

Since $A$ accepts as input the obfuscated circuit of size $|iO| = \ell_O$, by Lemma 6, the probability that $A$ hits at least $s = (\ell_O + \kappa)$ ciphertexts is at most $2^{\ell_O - \omega(n)s} \leq 2^{-\omega(n)\kappa} = \mathrm{negl}(\kappa)$. Therefore, the $k\ell_B$-query algorithm $A$ will hit at most $s = (\ell_O + \kappa)$ new unknown ciphertexts with overwhelming probability. Therefore we have that,

$$\Pr[|H_B| \geq s] = \Pr[|H_A| \geq s] \leq 2^{\ell_O - \omega(n)s}$$

Since the maximum possible number of learning iterations $k > s$ and $\bigcup_{j=1}^{i} H_{B_j} \subseteq \bigcup_{j=1}^{i+1} H_{B_j}$ for any $i$, the number of learning iterations that increase the size of the set $H_B$ of unknown ciphertext hits (via one of the bad event queries) is at most $s$. A ciphertext that was hit could have its encryption query generated during the obfuscation phase or as one of the hidden queries issued by $\mathsf{F}$ during one of the $k$ executions. We say $\lambda \overset{\$}{\leftarrow} [k]$ is bad if it is the case that $\bigcup_{j=1}^{\lambda} H_{B_j} \subsetneq \bigcup_{j=1}^{\lambda+1} H_{B_j}$ (i.e. $\lambda$ is an index of a learning iteration that increases the size of the hit ciphertexts). This would imply that after $\lambda$ learning iterations in the ideal experiment, the final execution with $H_{\widehat{B}} := \bigcup_{j=1}^{\lambda+1} H_{B_j}$ would contain an unknown ciphertext that it we will hit for this first time and for which we cannot consistently answer the queries that reference it. Thus, given that we have set $k = (\ell_O + \kappa)/\varepsilon$, the probability (over the selection of $\lambda$) that $\lambda$ is bad is at most $s/k < \varepsilon$.

**Proving Security.** To show that the resulting obfuscator is secure, it suffices to show that the compilation process represented as the new obfuscator's construction is simulatable. We show a simulator $\mathsf{Sim}$ (with access to $\Gamma$) that works as follows: given an obfuscated circuit $B$ in the $\Gamma$ ideal model, it runs the learning procedure as shown in Step 2 of the new obfuscator $\widehat{iO}$ to learn the heavy queries $Q_B$ then outputs $\widehat{B} = (B, Q_B)$. Note that this distribution is statistically close to the output of the real execution of $\widehat{iO}$ and, therefore, security follows.

# References

[AB15]    Applebaum, B., Brakerski, Z.: Obfuscating circuits via composite-order graded encoding. In: Dodis, Y., Nielsen, J.B. (eds.) TCC 2015. LNCS, vol. 9015, pp. 528–556. Springer, Heidelberg (2015). https://doi.org/10.1007/978-3-662-46497-7_21

[ADGM16]  Apon, D., Döttling, N., Garg, S., Mukherjee, P.: Cryptanalysis of indistinguishability obfuscations of circuits over ggh13. Cryptology ePrint Archive, Report 2016/1003 (2016). http://eprint.iacr.org/2016/1003

[AGIS14] Ananth, P.V., Gupta, D., Ishai, Y., Sahai, A.: Optimizing obfuscation: avoiding Barrington's theorem. In: Ahn, G.-J., Yung, M., Li, N. (eds.) ACM CCS 2014: 21st Conference on Computer and Communications Security, Scottsdale, AZ, USA, 3–7 November 2014, pp. 646–658. ACM Press (2014)

[AJ15] Ananth, P., Jain, A.: Indistinguishability obfuscation from compact functional encryption. In: Gennaro, R., Robshaw, M. (eds.) CRYPTO 2015. LNCS, vol. 9215, pp. 308–326. Springer, Heidelberg (2015). https://doi.org/10.1007/978-3-662-47989-6_15

[AS15] Asharov, G., Segev, G.: Limits on the power of indistinguishability obfuscation and functional encryption. In: 2015 IEEE 56th Annual Symposium on Foundations of Computer Science (FOCS), pp. 191–209. IEEE (2015)

[AS16] Ananth, P., Sahai, A.: Projective arithmetic functional encryption and indistinguishability obfuscation from degree-5 multilinear maps. Cryptology ePrint Archive, Report 2016/1097 (2016). http://eprint.iacr.org/2016/1097

[BBF16] Brakerski, Z., Brzuska, C., Fleischhacker, N.: On statistically secure obfuscation with approximate correctness. Cryptology ePrint Archive, Report 2016/226 (2016). http://eprint.iacr.org/

[BCP14] Boyle, E., Chung, K.-M., Pass, R.: On extractability obfuscation. In: Lindell, Y. (ed.) TCC 2014. LNCS, vol. 8349, pp. 52–73. Springer, Heidelberg (2014). https://doi.org/10.1007/978-3-642-54242-8_3

[BGI+01] Barak, B., Goldreich, O., Impagliazzo, R., Rudich, S., Sahai, A., Vadhan, S., Yang, K.: On the (im)possibility of obfuscating programs. In: Kilian, J. (ed.) CRYPTO 2001. LNCS, vol. 2139, pp. 1–18. Springer, Heidelberg (2001). https://doi.org/10.1007/3-540-44647-8_1

[BGK+14] Barak, B., Garg, S., Kalai, Y.T., Paneth, O., Sahai, A.: Protecting obfuscation against algebraic attacks. In: Nguyen, P.Q., Oswald, E. (eds.) EUROCRYPT 2014. LNCS, vol. 8441, pp. 221–238. Springer, Heidelberg (2014). https://doi.org/10.1007/978-3-642-55220-5_13

[BKSY11] Brakerski, Z., Katz, J., Segev, G., Yerukhimovich, A.: Limits on the power of zero-knowledge proofs in cryptographic constructions. In: Ishai, Y. (ed.) TCC 2011. LNCS, vol. 6597, pp. 559–578. Springer, Heidelberg (2011). https://doi.org/10.1007/978-3-642-19571-6_34

[BLP16] Bitansky, N., Lin, H., Paneth, O.: On removing graded encodings from functional encryption. Cryptology ePrint Archive, Report 2016/962 (2016). http://eprint.iacr.org/2016/962

[BMSZ16] Badrinarayanan, S., Miles, E., Sahai, A., Zhandry, M.: Post-zeroizing obfuscation: new mathematical tools, and the case of evasive circuits. In: Fischlin, M., Coron, J.-S. (eds.) EUROCRYPT 2016. LNCS, vol. 9666, pp. 764–791. Springer, Heidelberg (2016). https://doi.org/10.1007/978-3-662-49896-5_27

[BNPW16] Bitansky, N., Nishimaki, R., Passelègue, A., Wichs, D.: From cryptomania to obfustopia through secret-key functional encryption. In: Hirt, M., Smith, A. (eds.) TCC 2016. LNCS, vol. 9986, pp. 391–418. Springer, Heidelberg (2016). https://doi.org/10.1007/978-3-662-53644-5_15

[BPR15] Bitansky, N., Paneth, O., Rosen, A.: On the cryptographic hardness of finding a Nash equilibrium. In: Guruswami, V. (ed.) 56th Annual Symposium on Foundations of Computer Science, Berkeley, CA, USA, 17–20 October 2015, pp. 1480–1498. IEEE Computer Society Press (2015)

[BR14] Brakerski, Z., Rothblum, G.N.: Virtual black-box obfuscation for all circuits via generic graded encoding. In: Lindell, Y. (ed.) TCC 2014. LNCS, vol. 8349, pp. 1–25. Springer, Heidelberg (2014). https://doi.org/10.1007/978-3-642-54242-8_1

[BV11a] Brakerski, Z., Vaikuntanathan, V.: Efficient fully homomorphic encryption from (standard) LWE. In: Ostrovsky, R. (ed.) 52nd Annual Symposium on Foundations of Computer Science, Palm Springs, CA, USA, 22–25 October 2011, pp. 97–106, IEEE Computer Society Press (2011)

[BV11b] Brakerski, Z., Vaikuntanathan, V.: Fully homomorphic encryption from ring-LWE and security for key dependent messages. In: Rogaway, P. (ed.) CRYPTO 2011. LNCS, vol. 6841, pp. 505–524. Springer, Heidelberg (2011). https://doi.org/10.1007/978-3-642-22792-9_29

[BV15] Bitansky, N., Vaikuntanathan, V.: Indistinguishability obfuscation from functional encryption. In: Guruswami, V. (ed.) 56th Annual Symposium on Foundations of Computer Science, Berkeley, CA, USA, 17–20 October 2015, pp. 171–190. IEEE Computer Society Press (2015)

[BZ14] Boneh, D., Zhandry, M.: Multiparty key exchange, efficient traitor tracing, and more from indistinguishability obfuscation. In: Garay, J.A., Gennaro, R. (eds.) CRYPTO 2014. LNCS, vol. 8616, pp. 480–499. Springer, Heidelberg (2014). https://doi.org/10.1007/978-3-662-44371-2_27

[CGH+15] Coron, J.-S., Gentry, C., Halevi, S., Lepoint, T., Maji, H.K., Miles, E., Raykova, M., Sahai, A., Tibouchi, M.: Zeroizing without low-level zeroes: new MMAP attacks and their limitations. In: Gennaro, R., Robshaw, M. (eds.) CRYPTO 2015. LNCS, vol. 9215, pp. 247–266. Springer, Heidelberg (2015). https://doi.org/10.1007/978-3-662-47989-6_12

[CGH16] Chen, Y., Gentry, C., Halevi, S.: Cryptanalyses of candidate branching program obfuscators. Cryptology ePrint Archive, Report 2016/998 (2016). http://eprint.iacr.org/2016/998

[CHL+15] Cheon, J.H., Han, K., Lee, C., Ryu, H., Stehlé, D.: Cryptanalysis of the multilinear map over the integers. In: Oswald, E., Fischlin, M. (eds.) EUROCRYPT 2015. LNCS, vol. 9056, pp. 3–12. Springer, Heidelberg (2015). https://doi.org/10.1007/978-3-662-46800-5_1

[CKP15] Canetti, R., Kalai, Y.T., Paneth, O.: On obfuscation with random oracles. In: Dodis, Y., Nielsen, J.B. (eds.) TCC 2015. LNCS, vol. 9015, pp. 456–467. Springer, Heidelberg (2015). https://doi.org/10.1007/978-3-662-46497-7_18

[CLLT15] Coron, J.-S., Lee, M.S., Lepoint, T., Tibouchi, M.: Cryptanalysis of GGH15 multilinear maps. Cryptology ePrint Archive, Report 2015/1037 (2015). http://eprint.iacr.org/2015/1037

[CLLT16] Coron, J.-S., Lee, M.S., Lepoint, T., Tibouchi, M.: Zeroizing attacks on indistinguishability obfuscation over clt13. Cryptology ePrint Archive, Report 2016/1011 (2016). http://eprint.iacr.org/2016/1011

[CLT13] Coron, J.-S., Lepoint, T., Tibouchi, M.: Practical multilinear maps over the integers. In: Canetti, R., Garay, J.A. (eds.) CRYPTO 2013. LNCS, vol. 8042, pp. 476–493. Springer, Heidelberg (2013). https://doi.org/10.1007/978-3-642-40041-4_26

[Dac16] Dachman-Soled, D.: Towards non-black-box separations of public key encryption and one way function. In: Hirt, M., Smith, A. (eds.) TCC 2016. LNCS, vol. 9986, pp. 169–191. Springer, Heidelberg (2016). https://doi.org/10.1007/978-3-662-53644-5_7

[DGG+16] Döttling, N., Garg, S., Gupta, D., Miao, P., Mukherjee, P.: Obfuscation from low noise multilinear maps. Cryptology ePrint Archive, Report 2016/599 (2016). http://eprint.iacr.org/2016/599

[Gen09] Gentry, C.: Fully homomorphic encryption using ideal lattices. In: Mitzenmacher, M. (ed.) 41st Annual ACM Symposium on Theory of Computing, Bethesda, MD, USA, 31 May–2 June 2009, pp. 169–178. ACM Press (2009)

[GGH13a] Garg, S., Gentry, C., Halevi, S.: Candidate multilinear maps from ideal lattices. In: Johansson, T., Nguyen, P.Q. (eds.) EUROCRYPT 2013. LNCS, vol. 7881, pp. 1–17. Springer, Heidelberg (2013). https://doi.org/10.1007/978-3-642-38348-9_1

[GGH+13b] Garg, S., Gentry, C., Halevi, S., Raykova, M., Sahai, A., Waters, B.: Candidate indistinguishability obfuscation and functional encryption for all circuits. In: 54th Annual Symposium on Foundations of Computer Science, Berkeley, CA, USA, 26–29 October 2013, pp. 40–49. IEEE Computer Society Press (2013)

[GGH15] Gentry, C., Gorbunov, S., Halevi, S.: Graph-induced multilinear maps from lattices. In: Dodis, Y., Nielsen, J.B. (eds.) TCC 2015. LNCS, vol. 9015, pp. 498–527. Springer, Heidelberg (2015). https://doi.org/10.1007/978-3-662-46497-7_20

[GGHR14] Garg, S., Gentry, C., Halevi, S., Raykova, M.: Two-round secure MPC from indistinguishability obfuscation. In: Lindell, Y. (ed.) TCC 2014. LNCS, vol. 8349, pp. 74–94. Springer, Heidelberg (2014). https://doi.org/10.1007/978-3-642-54242-8_4

[GK05] Goldwasser, S., Kalai, Y.T.: On the impossibility of obfuscation with auxiliary input. In: 46th Annual Symposium on Foundations of Computer Science, Pittsburgh, PA, USA, 23–25 October 2005, pp. 553–562. IEEE Computer Society Press (2005)

[GKP+13] Goldwasser, S., Kalai, Y.T., Popa, R.A., Vaikuntanathan, V., Zeldovich, N.: Reusable garbled circuits and succinct functional encryption. In: Boneh, D., Roughgarden, T., Feigenbaum, J. (eds.) 45th Annual ACM Symposium on Theory of Computing, Palo Alto, CA, USA, 1–4 June 2013, pp. 555–564. ACM Press (2013)

[GLSW15] Gentry, C., Lewko, A.B., Sahai, A., Waters, B.: Indistinguishability obfuscation from the multilinear subgroup elimination assumption. In: Guruswami, V. (ed.) 56th Annual Symposium on Foundations of Computer Science, Berkeley, CA, USA, 17–20 October 2015, pp. 151–170. IEEE Computer Society Press (2015)

[GMM+16] Garg, S., Miles, E., Mukherjee, P., Sahai, A., Srinivasan, A., Zhandry, M.: Secure obfuscation in a weak multilinear map model. In: Hirt, M., Smith, A. (eds.) TCC 2016. LNCS, vol. 9986, pp. 241–268. Springer, Heidelberg (2016). https://doi.org/10.1007/978-3-662-53644-5_10

[GMM17] Garg, S., Mahmoody, M., Mohammed, A.: Lower bounds on obfuscation from all-or-nothing encryption primitives. In: Katz, J., Shacham, H. (eds.) CRYPTO 2017. LNCS, vol. 10401, pp. 661–695. Springer, Cham (2017). https://doi.org/10.1007/978-3-319-63688-7_22

[GSW13] Gentry, C., Sahai, A., Waters, B.: Homomorphic encryption from learning with errors: conceptually-simpler, asymptotically-faster, attribute-based. In: Canetti, R., Garay, J.A. (eds.) CRYPTO 2013. LNCS, vol. 8042, pp. 75–92. Springer, Heidelberg (2013). https://doi.org/10.1007/978-3-642-40041-4_5

[GVW13]  Gorbunov, S., Vaikuntanathan, V., Wee, H.: Attribute based encryption for circuits. In: Boneh, D., Roughgarden, T., Feigenbaum, J. (eds.) 45th Annual ACM Symposium on Theory of Computing, Palo Alto, CA, USA, 1–4 June 2013, pp. 545–554. ACM Press (2013)

[GVW15]  Gorbunov, S., Vaikuntanathan, V., Wee, H.: Predicate encryption for circuits from LWE. In: Gennaro, R., Robshaw, M. (eds.) CRYPTO 2015. LNCS, vol. 9216, pp. 503–523. Springer, Heidelberg (2015). https://doi.org/10.1007/978-3-662-48000-7_25

[GW11]  Gentry, C., Wichs, D.: Separating succinct non-interactive arguments from all falsifiable assumptions. In: Fortnow, L., Vadhan, S.P. (eds.) STOC. ACM (2011)

[HJ16]  Hu, Y., Jia, H.: Cryptanalysis of GGH map. In: Fischlin, M., Coron, J.-S. (eds.) EUROCRYPT 2016. LNCS, vol. 9665, pp. 537–565. Springer, Heidelberg (2016). https://doi.org/10.1007/978-3-662-49890-3_21

[IR89]  Impagliazzo, R., Rudich, S.: Limits on the provable consequences of one-way permutations. In: 21st Annual ACM Symposium on Theory of Computing, Seattle, WA, USA, 15–17 May 1989, pp. 44–61. ACM Press (1989)

[Lin16a]  Lin, H.: Indistinguishability obfuscation from constant-degree graded encoding schemes. In: Fischlin, M., Coron, J.-S. (eds.) EUROCRYPT 2016. LNCS, vol. 9665, pp. 28–57. Springer, Heidelberg (2016). https://doi.org/10.1007/978-3-662-49890-3_2

[Lin16b]  Lin, H.: Indistinguishability obfuscation from ddh on 5-linear maps and locality-5 prgs. Cryptology ePrint Archive, Report 2016/1096 (2016). http://eprint.iacr.org/2016/1096

[LT17]  Lin, H., Tessaro, S.: Indistinguishability obfuscation from bilinear maps and block-wise local prgs. Cryptology ePrint Archive, Report 2017/250 (2017). http://eprint.iacr.org/2017/250

[LV16]  Lin, H., Vaikuntanathan, V.: Indistinguishability obfuscation from DDH-like assumptions on constant-degree graded encodings. In: Dinur, I. (ed.) 57th Annual Symposium on Foundations of Computer Science, New Brunswick, NJ, USA, 9–11 October 2016, pp. 11–20. IEEE Computer Society Press (2016)

[MMN15]  Mahmoody, M., Mohammed, A., Nematihaji, S.: More on impossibility of virtual black-box obfuscation in idealized models. Cryptology ePrint Archive, Report 2015/632 (2015). http://eprint.iacr.org/

[MMN+16a]  Mahmoody, M., Mohammed, A., Nematihaji, S., Pass, R., Shelat, A.: A note on black-box separations for indistinguishability obfuscation. Cryptology ePrint Archive, Report 2016/316 (2016). http://eprint.iacr.org/2016/316

[MMN+16b]  Mahmoody, M., Mohammed, A., Nematihaji, S., Pass, R., Shelat, A.: Lower bounds on assumptions behind indistinguishability obfuscation. In: Kushilevitz, E., Malkin, T. (eds.) TCC 2016. LNCS, vol. 9562, pp. 49–66. Springer, Heidelberg (2016). https://doi.org/10.1007/978-3-662-49096-9_3

[MSW14]  Miles, E., Sahai, A., Weiss, M.: Protecting obfuscation against arithmetic attacks. Cryptology ePrint Archive, Report 2014/878 (2014). http://eprint.iacr.org/2014/878

[MSZ16]  Miles, E., Sahai, A., Zhandry, M.: Annihilation attacks for multilinear maps: cryptanalysis of indistinguishability obfuscation over GGH13. In: Robshaw, M., Katz, J. (eds.) CRYPTO 2016. LNCS, vol.

9815, pp. 629–658. Springer, Heidelberg (2016). https://doi.org/10.1007/978-3-662-53008-5_22

[Nao03] Naor, M.: On cryptographic assumptions and challenges. In: Boneh, D. (ed.) CRYPTO 2003. LNCS, vol. 2729, pp. 96–109. Springer, Heidelberg (2003). https://doi.org/10.1007/978-3-540-45146-4_6

[Pas11] Pass, R.: Limits of provable security from standard assumptions. In: Proceedings of the Forty-third Annual ACM Symposium on Theory of Computing, pp. 109–118. ACM (2011)

[Pas15] Pass, R., Shelat, A.: Impossibility of VBB obfuscation with ideal constant-degree graded encodings. Cryptology ePrint Archive, Report 2015/383 (2015). http://eprint.iacr.org/

[PTV11] Pass, R., Tseng, W.-L.D., Venkitasubramaniam, M.: Towards non-black-box lower bounds in cryptography. In: Ishai, Y. (ed.) TCC 2011. LNCS, vol. 6597, pp. 579–596. Springer, Heidelberg (2011). https://doi.org/10.1007/978-3-642-19571-6_35

[RTV04] Reingold, O., Trevisan, L., Vadhan, S.: Notions of reducibility between cryptographic primitives. In: Naor, M. (ed.) TCC 2004. LNCS, vol. 2951, pp. 1–20. Springer, Heidelberg (2004). https://doi.org/10.1007/978-3-540-24638-1_1

[SW14] Sahai, A., Waters, B.: How to use indistinguishability obfuscation: deniable encryption, and more. In: Shmoys, D.B. (ed.) 46th Annual ACM Symposium on Theory of Computing, New York, NY, USA, 31 May–June 3 2014, pp. 475–484. ACM Press (2014)

[Zim15] Zimmerman, J.: How to obfuscate programs directly. In: Oswald, E., Fischlin, M. (eds.) EUROCRYPT 2015. LNCS, vol. 9057, pp. 439–467. Springer, Heidelberg (2015). https://doi.org/10.1007/978-3-662-46803-6_15

# Obfuscation

# Limits on the Locality of Pseudorandom Generators and Applications to Indistinguishability Obfuscation

Alex Lombardi$^{(\boxtimes)}$ and Vinod Vaikuntanathan

MIT, Cambridge, USA
{alexjl,vinodv}@mit.edu

**Abstract.** Lin and Tessaro (ePrint 2017) recently proposed indistinguishability obfuscation (IO) and functional encryption (FE) candidates and proved their security based on two assumptions: a standard assumption on bilinear maps and a non-standard assumption on "Goldreich-like" pseudorandom generators. In a nutshell, their second assumption requires the existence of pseudorandom generators $G : [q]^n \rightarrow \{0,1\}^m$ for some $\mathrm{poly}(n)$-size alphabet $q$, each of whose output bits depend on at most two in put alphabet symbols, and which achieve sufficiently large stretch. We show polynomial-time attacks against such generators, invalidating the security of the IO and FE candidates. Our attack uses tools from the literature on two-source extractors (Chor and Goldreich, SICOMP 1988) and efficient refutation of random 2-XOR instances (Charikar and Wirth, FOCS 2004).

## 1 Introduction

There has been much recent progress on constructing indistinguishability obfuscation (IO) schemes [BGI+01, GR07] starting from the work of Garg et al. [GGH+16]. Most recently, Lin [Lin16a] and Lin et al. [LV16, Lin16b, AS16, LT17] showed a pathway to constructing IO schemes using two ingredients: multilinear maps of constant degree and pseudorandom generators of constant locality. In particular, Lin and Tessaro [LT17] construct an IO candidate from standard assumptions on *bilinear maps* and non-standard assumptions on "Goldreich-like" pseudorandom generators [Gol00] with "blockwise" locality 2.

This is a remarkable development: until recently, we had IO candidates based on constant degree (most recently, degree 5) multilinear maps and

A. Lombardi—Supported by an Akamai Presidential Fellowship and the grants of the second author.

V. Vaikuntanathan—Research supported in part by NSF Grants CNS-1350619 and CNS-1414119, Alfred P. Sloan Research Fellowship, Microsoft Faculty Fellowship, the NEC Corporation, a Steven and Renee Finn Career Development Chair from MIT. This work was also sponsored in part by the Defense Advanced Research Projects Agency (DARPA) and the U.S. Army Research Office under contracts W911NF-15-C-0226 and W911NF-15-C-0236.

Y. Kalai and L. Reyzin (Eds.): TCC 2017, Part I, LNCS 10677, pp. 119–137, 2017.
https://doi.org/10.1007/978-3-319-70500-2_5

constant locality (most recently, locality 5) PRGs. We did not have any candidates for the degree 5 multilinear maps that satisfied the required assumptions (namely, a version of the decisional Diffie-Hellman assumption); however, we did have candidates for locality 5 PRGs that are known to resist a large class of attacks [OW14, AL16]. The Lin-Tessaro result dramatically changed the landscape by shifting the burden of existence from degree 5 multilinear maps to pseudorandom generators with (so-called) blockwise locality 2 and polynomial stretch. In other words, we have candidates for degree 2 multilinear maps (also known as bilinear maps) [BF03, Jou02, Jou00]; however, there are no locality 2 PRGs, and the security of blockwise locality 2 PRGs is highly questionable. (For the formal definitions of all these technical terms, see below and Sect. 2.)

In this work, we show a polynomial-time attack against the pseudorandom generators required for the Lin-Tessaro construction. As such, this constitutes a break of the Lin-Tessaro IO (as well as functional encryption) constructions that use bilinear maps.

We remark that our attacks do not apply to the Lin-Tessaro IO construction based on 3-linear maps. This leaves us in a curious state of affairs regarding constructions of IO from multilinear maps.

- There is a construction [LT17] of IO from trilinear maps (whose existence is questionable) and "blockwise 3-local PRGs" (for which we have plausible candidates); and
- There is a construction [LT17] of IO from bilinear maps (for which we have candidates that have been around for almost two decades) and "blockwise 2-local PRGs" (which are broken in this work).

Since cryptographically secure trilinear maps have so far eluded us, it is not surprising that the difficulty of achieving IO arises from the gap between bilinear and trilinear maps. However, we find it quite surprising that this transition appears to be related to the pseudorandomness of 2-local functions and 3-local functions (over a large alphabet, no less)!

*Goldreich's PRGs with Blockwise 2-Local Predicates.* We start by describing the object we attack. Let $P$ be a predicate from $\Sigma^2$ to $\{0,1\}$, for some polynomial size alphabet $|\Sigma| = q = \text{poly}(n)$. Let $H$ be a (directed) graph with $n$ vertices and $m$ edges; we will refer to $H$ as the constraint graph. The pseudorandom generator $G_{H,P} : \Sigma^n \rightarrow \{0,1\}^m$ is defined in the following way. Let $e = (i,j)$ be a directed edge in $G$. Then, the $e^{th}$ bit of the output of the generator is computed as $P(x_i, x_j)$. We call this an $(n, m, q)$-*Goldreich-like* pseudorandom generator since it uses predicates over a large alphabet.

This construction can also be thought of as a "blockwise local" pseudorandom generator, a terminology that Lin and Tessaro introduce and use [LT17]. In an $(L, w)$-block-wise PRG, the $nw$-bit input is divided into blocks of size $w$ bits each, and each output bit of the PRG can depend on at most $L$ blocks. It is easy to see that a Goldreich PRG as defined above with alphabet size $q$ is a $(2, \lceil \log q \rceil)$-block-wise PRG. In fact, Lin and Tessaro's definition of block-wise PRGs is more general in that it allowed each output bit to be computed using a different (publicly known) predicate. However, their candidate PRG used the same predicate to compute all the output bits.

With this terminology, we are ready to state our main result.

**Theorem 1.** *There is a poly$(n, q)$ time algorithm $\mathcal{D}$ which, for any $m \geq \tilde{\Omega}(q \cdot n)$, any predicate $P : [q]^2 \to \{0, 1\}$, and any graph $H$ with $n$ vertices and $m$ edges, distinguishes between a uniformly random string $z \leftarrow U_m$ and a random output $z \leftarrow G_{H,P}(U_{n,q})$ (with a constant distinguishing advantage).*

*The Lin-Tessaro Theorem and Connection to Goldreich-like PRGs.* Lin and Tessaro [LT17], building on earlier work [BV15, AJ15, Lin16a, LV16, Lin16b, AS16] showed an IO candidate based on the hardness of standard assumptions on bilinear maps and the existence of a Goldreich-like PRG with blockwise locality 2 and *sufficiently large* stretch. That is, they show:

> Under standard assumptions on bilinear maps and the existence of a subexponentially secure $(n, m, q)$-Goldreich-like PRG with $q = \mathsf{poly}(n)$ and $m = (nq^3)^{1+\epsilon}$ for some constant $\epsilon > 0$, there is an IO scheme. Assuming the existence of such a generator with quasipolynomial security, there is a compact FE scheme.

In a nutshell, they utilize the reductions of Ananth and Jain [AJ15] and Bitansky and Vaikuntanathan [BV15] who show how to construct an IO scheme from any sub-exponentially secure *compact* FE scheme. By compact FE, roughly speaking, we mean a functional encryption scheme for functions of large *output* size $k$ with ciphertexts of size $k^{1-\epsilon}$ for some absolute constant $\epsilon > 0$. Such ciphertexts simply do not have enough space to hold the function output, so they, in a sense, have to do non-trivial computation as part of the FE decryption process. Since IO is the ultimate truth-table compression algorithm, the moral bottomline of [AJ15, BV15], formalized in [LPST16], is that "any compression implies the ultimate compression". On the other hand, non-compact FE schemes can be constructed essentially from any public-key encryption scheme [SS10, GVW12].

Thus, [LT17] construct a compact functional encryption scheme using their ingredients. Using their bootstrapping theorem, it turns out to be sufficient to construct an FE scheme that encrypts the seed of a PRG (which they instantiate with a Goldreich-like PRG as defined above) and whose functional key corresponds to the computation of the PRG itself (plus some). In a high level, their encryption algorithm takes as input the seed $\mathbf{x} = x_1 x_2 \ldots x_n \in [q]^n$, precomputes all possible monomials on the bits of each alphabet symbol $x_i \in [q]$ $(i = 1, \ldots, n)$, of which there are roughly $q$, and includes it in the ciphertext. Computing the PRG output, then, can be written as a degree-2 computation which can be performed using a bilinear map (leveraging on an earlier result of Lin [Lin16b]). Thus, the number of bits being encrypted is $n \cdot q$. To achieve sublinear compactness which, by the above discussion, is necessary to apply the FE-to-IO transformations, they need the output length of the PRG $m$ to be large enough, namely $m = \Omega((nq)^{1+\epsilon})$ for some constant $\epsilon > 0$. In fact, since they need to support computations that are a bit more complex than simply computing the PRG, they need the stretch to be $\Omega((nq^3)^{1+\epsilon})$.

Our main theorem (Theorem 1) now implies that a natural class of candidates for such PRGs, proposed and analyzed in [LT17], can be broken in polynomial-time. In fact, we show something stronger: even a potential extension of the Lin-Tessaro theorem that requires only blockwise 2-local PRGs with minimal expansion, namely $m = \tilde{\Omega}(nq)$, can be broken using our attack.

*Comparison to* [BBKK17]. The presentation of this work has changed significantly since the original preprint [LV17]. We originally proved the following weaker version of Theorem 1; see also the first line of Fig. 1.

**Theorem 2.** *There is a poly$(n, q)$ time algorithm $\mathcal{D}$ which, for any $m \geq \tilde{\Omega}(q \cdot n)$, any predicate $P : [q]^2 \to \{0, 1\}$, and a $(1 - o(1))$ fraction of graphs $H$ with $n$ vertices and $m$ edges, distinguishes between a uniformly random string $z \leftarrow U_m$ and a random output $z \leftarrow G_{H,P}(U_{n,q})$ (with a constant distinguishing advantage).*

In a concurrent work, Barak et al. [BBKK17] showed a completely different attack on a blockwise 2-local PRG with different parameter settings. Barak et al. show how to attack blockwise 2-local PRGs for *worst-case graphs* and a *worst-case collection of possibly different predicates* for each output bit. However, they need to assume that the PRG had a larger stretch, namely that $m = \tilde{\Omega}(q^2 \cdot n)$. They also achieve a threshold of $m = \tilde{\Omega}(q \cdot n)$ for the restricted case of *random* graphs and *random, single* predicate. See the second and third line of Fig. 1.

Our main theorem draws inspiration from [BBKK17] and applies our main technique that we refer to as *alphabet reduction* in a different way than we originally conceived. See the fourth line of Fig. 1.

There is a gap between our main theorem, namely Theorem 1, and a complete break of the [LT17] candidate: Theorem 1 breaks blockwise 2-local PRGs in which the predicate computing each output bit is the same. This breaks Lin and Tessaro's concrete PRG candidate. However, their theorem can be instantiated with more general block-wise local PRGs where each output bit is computed using a different predicate, a setting that [BBKK17] break. We remark here that our techniques (to be described below) can also be used to break this multiple-predicate variant at the cost of the same worse distinguishing threshold, namely $m \geq \tilde{\Omega}(nq^2)$.

On the negative side, we provide evidence that our own technique is unlikely to achieve a better threshold than $m \geq \tilde{\Omega}(q^2 \cdot n)$ for worst-case graphs and worst-case multiple predicates; it would be very interesting to understand the limits of the techniques in [BBKK17].

The current state of attacks against blockwise 2-local PRGs is summarized in Fig. 1. As one can see from the table, there is a very narrow set of possibilities that neither our attack nor [BBKK17] rule out just yet. Namely, we cannot rule out the possibility that (a) the Lin-Tessaro theorem could be improved to work with stretch $\Omega((nq)^{1+\epsilon})$; and (b) there is a PRG with such a stretch that

| Stretch | Worst-case vs. Random Predicate | Worst-case vs. Random Graph | Different vs. Same Predicate Per Output | Reference |
|---|---|---|---|---|
| $m = \tilde{\Omega}(q \cdot n)$ | Worst-case | Random | Same | This Work [LV17], as originally posted |
| $m = \tilde{\Omega}(q \cdot n)$ | Random | Random | Same | [BBKK17] |
| $m = \tilde{\Omega}(q^2 \cdot n)$ | Worst-case | Worst-case | Different | [BBKK17] |
| $m = \tilde{\Omega}(q \cdot n)$ | Worst-case | Worst-case | Same | This Work |
| $m = \tilde{\Omega}(q \cdot n)$ | Worst-case | Worst-case | Different | Open |

**Fig. 1.** The state of the art on attacks against blockwise 2-local PRGs.

necessarily has to employ a specially tailored graph and different predicates for each output bit. An exceedingly narrow window, indeed!

### 1.1 Outline of Our Attack

We start with a description of our original attack, namely the proof of Theorem 2, which exploited the well-known connection between our problem of distinguishing a Goldreich PRG output from a uniform string and problems studied in the setting of random constraint satisfaction (CSP). In particular, we utilized a result of Allen et al. [AOW15] who developed a polynomial-time algorithm for a problem related to ours, namely that of *refutation of random CSPs*.

Any graph $H$ with $n$ nodes and $m$ edges, any predicate $P$, and any string $z \in \{0,1\}^m$ together define an instance $\mathcal{I}$ of the following constraint satisfaction problem with predicates $P$ and $\neg P$.

$$P(x_i, x_j) = 1 \qquad \text{for every } e = (i,j) \text{ where } z_e = 1$$
$$\neg P(x_i, x_j) = 1 \qquad \text{for every } e = (i,j) \text{ where } z_e = 0$$

The task of breaking the PRG $G_{H,P}$ can be thought of as distinguishing CSP instances $\mathcal{I}$ in which the negations of $P$ are chosen uniformly at random from instances $\mathcal{I}$ in which the negations of $P$ are determined by a random planted solution $x \in [q]^n$.

Allen et al. [AOW15] developed a polynomial time algorithm for a different problem, namely that of *random CSP refutation*. In their setting (specialized to 2-CSPs), a random instance $\mathcal{I}$ is generated by choosing a random graph $H$ along with *random negation patterns* $(a_e, b_e) \in \mathbb{Z}_q^2$ for each edge $e = (i,j) \in E(H)$, and including constraints

$$P(x_i + a_e, x_j + b_e) = 1$$

Their algorithm can certify that $\text{Opt}(\mathcal{I})$, the largest fraction of constraints satisfied by any input, is less than 1 provided at least $\tilde{\Omega}(n \cdot \text{poly}(q))$ constraints (for an unspecified polynomial poly). Namely, their algorithm outputs 1 with probability $1 - o(1)$, but never outputs 1 if $\mathcal{I}$ is satisfiable. Clearly, this suffices to distinguish satisfiable instances $\mathcal{I}$ from uniformly random instances.[1] In fact, they achieve a much stronger property called *strong refutation* which will turn out to be crucial for us: given $\tilde{\Omega}(\frac{n}{\epsilon^2} \cdot \text{poly}(q))$ constraints, their algorithm outputs 1 with probability $1 - o(1)$, but never outputs 1 if $\mathcal{I}$ is "somewhat close" to being satisfiable, that is, if $\text{Opt}(\mathcal{I}) \geq 1/2 + \epsilon$ (when $P$ is balanced). Finally, we note that their result only holds over random graphs $H$, but analogous results in the so-called *semi-random setting*, in which the graph $H$ is worst-case but negation patterns are still random, have been shown in, e.g., [Wit17].

The most glaring difference between our setting and that of random CSP refutation [AOW15] is that our CSP instance has an "outer negation pattern" (randomly negating the predicate $P$) while theirs have an "inner negation pattern" as described above. However, it turns out that a refutation algorithm for the random CSP model of [AOW15] can nevertheless be turned into a distinguishing algorithm, but at a cost; the resulting algorithm requires $m \geq \tilde{\Omega}(n \cdot \text{poly}(q))$ for some large polynomial (roughly $q^2$ times the unspecified polynomial in [AOW15]).

Such a result is already nontrivial in the PRG setting, although it is far from the $m \geq \tilde{\Omega}(q \cdot n)$ threshold that we would like to achieve. This is the major challenge that this paper overcomes: how can we reduce this potentially large $\text{poly}(q)$-dependence to an explicit, small $\text{poly}(q)$-dependence?

Our main idea called alphabet reduction now comes to the rescue. Alphabet reduction is a way to convert our CSP on an alphabet of size $q$ to a related CSP on a *new alphabet whose size is an absolute constant independent of $q$*. If the original CSP is random, so is the new CSP. If the original CSP is satisfiable, the new one is "somewhat close to being satisfiable", that is, there is an assignment that satisfies at least $1/2 + \Omega(1/\sqrt{q})$ of its clauses. We then leverage the "strong refutation" property of the algorithm in [AOW15] to break the pseudorandomness of $G_{H,P}$ by certifying that a random CSP with *constant-sized predicate $Q$* is not $1/2 + \Omega(1/\sqrt{q})$-satisfiable, which can be done using the algorithm of [AOW15] with only $\tilde{\Omega}(n \cdot q'/\epsilon^2) = \tilde{\Omega}(n \cdot q)$ clauses, since $q' = O(1)$ and $\epsilon = \Omega(1/\sqrt{q})$. In other words, we traded a dependence on $q$ in the number of required clauses for a dependence on $q$ in the error parameter $\epsilon = \Omega(1/\sqrt{q})$; since the required number of clauses is proportional to $1/\epsilon^2$, this reduces the overall dependence on $q$ to linear.

We achieve alphabet reduction by showing that any predicate $P : [q]^2 \to \{0,1\}$ is $(1/2 + \Omega(1/\sqrt{q}))$-correlated to another predicate $P' : [q]^2 \to \{0,1\}$ which "depends on only one bit of each input". This uses, and refines, a classical lower bound due to Chor and Goldreich [CG88] on 2-source extractors.

If our alphabet reduction produced a CSP instance whose alphabet size was some large constant, then this would be the end of the story. However, we can actually reduce to the *binary alphabet*. In the binary alphabet setting, it turns out that we can use the old MAX-2-XOR approximation algorithm of Charikar and

---

[1] We note that refutation seems to give us a significantly stronger guarantee than distinguishing. An analogous "refutation algorithm" in our PRG setting would be able to distinguish a random string $z \leftarrow \{0,1\}^m$ from $z \leftarrow G_{H,P}(x)$ for *any* distribution of the input $x$, not just the uniformly random one.

Wirth [CW04] which achieves the following guarantee: for stretch $m = \tilde{\Omega}(\frac{n}{\epsilon^2})$, it can distinguish between a random string $z \leftarrow U_m$ and *any string* $z \in \{0,1\}^m$ which is within $\frac{1}{2} - \epsilon$ (fractional) Hamming distance of the image $G(\{0,1\}^n)$ of the PRG.[2] This allows us to obtain a much simpler algorithm (making a single black box call to the [CW04] algorithm instead of the [AOW15] algorithm) achieving the same $m = \tilde{\Omega}(n \cdot q)$ threshold, even for worst-case graphs.

*Organization of the Paper.* We start with some basic preliminaries in Sect. 2. Our alphabet reduction technique is presented in Sect. 3, and our attack which combines alphabet reduction with the 2-XOR algorithm of [CW04] is presented in Sect. 4.

## 2    Preliminaries

*Notation.* We let $U_n$ denote the uniform distribution on $\{0,1\}^n$. Additionally, we let $U_{n,q}$ denote the uniform distribution on the set $[q]^n$. Let $\mathsf{negl}(n) : \mathbb{N} \to \mathbb{R}$ denote a function that is smaller than any inverse polynomial in $n$. That is, we require that for every polynomial $p$, there is an $n_p \in \mathbb{N}$ such that $\mathsf{negl}(n) < 1/p(n)$ for all $n > n_p$.

### 2.1    Pseudorandom Generators

We say that a function $G : \{0,1\}^n \to \{0,1\}^m$ is a *pseudorandom generator* (PRG) if it has the following properties: (1) $G$ is computable in (uniform) time $\mathrm{poly}(n)$, and (2) for any probabilistic polynomial time adversary $A : \{0,1\}^m \to \{0,1\}$, there is a negligible function $\mathsf{negl}$ such that

$$\left| \mathop{\mathbf{E}}_{x \leftarrow U_n}[A(G(x))] - \mathop{\mathbf{E}}_{z \leftarrow U_m}[A(z)] \right| = \mathsf{negl}(n)$$

We say that a PRG $G : \{0,1\}^n \to \{0,1\}^m$ has *stretch* $m - n = m(n) - n$. In this paper, we focus on the *polynomial stretch* regime, namely where $m = O(n^c)$ for some constant $c > 1$.

If $G$ is computable in $\mathrm{NC}^0$, we define the *locality* of $G$ to be the maximum number of input bits on which any output bit of $G$ depends.

### 2.2    Goldreich's Candidate (Blockwise) Local PRG

Goldreich's candidate pseudorandom generator, first introduced in [Gol00] (then as a candidate one-way function), can be instantiated with any $k$-ary predicate $P : [q]^k \to \{0,1\}$ and any $k$-uniform (directed) hypergraph $H$ on $n$ vertices and $m$ hyperedges. (To the best of our knowledge, the generalization to predicates $P$ that take symbols from a larger alphabet was first considered by Lin and Tessaro

---

[2] The problem in the PRG setting that Charikar-Wirth solves is called the *image refutation* problem for $G$.

under the name of "block-wise local" PRGs). Given $H$ and $P$, we identify each vertex in $H$ with an index in $[n]$ and each hyperedge with an index $i \in [m]$. For each $i \in [m]$, let $\Gamma_H(i) \in [n]^k$ be the sequence of $k$ vertices in the $i$th hyperedge.

**Definition 1.** *Given a predicate $P$ and hypergraph $H$, Goldreich's PRG is the function from $[q]^n$ to $\{0,1\}^m$ defined by*

$$G_{H,P}(x) = \big(P(x|_{\Gamma_H(i)})\big)_{i \in [m]}.$$

*That is, the $i$th bit of $G_{H,P}(x)$ is the output of $P$ when given the $\Gamma_H(i)$-restriction of $x$ as input.*

Goldreich's function is often instantiated with a *uniformly random* choice of hypergraph $H$; in this setting, we say that "Goldreich's function instantiated with $P$ is a PRG" for some predicate $P$ if for a random $k$-uniform hypergraph $H$, $G_{H,P}$ is a PRG with probability $1 - o(1)$. Often, instead of proving hardness results for random hypergraphs it suffices to use hypergraphs with "good expansion" for varying definitions of expansion [AL16, OW14, ABR12]. For a more in-depth survey and discussion of Goldreich's PRG, see [App16].

For the rest of the paper, we specialize to the case of $k = 2$, that is, blockwise 2-local PRGs. Ultimately, the attacks on $G_{H,P}$ that we describe in this paper hold for *all* graphs $H$, rather than just random graphs.

Finally, we note that one can analogously define $G_{H,\vec{P}}$ for a collection of $m$ predicates $P_1, ..., P_m$ (in which the $i$th output bit of $G_{H,\vec{P}}$ is obtained using $P_i$).

## 3   Alphabet Reduction

Our main result relies on a technique that we call *alphabet reduction* which reduces the problem of distinguishing the Goldreich PRG that uses a predicate $P : \Sigma^2 \to \{0,1\}$ to that of distinguishing the PRG that uses a different predicate $Q : \Sigma'^2 \to \{0,1\}$ that acts on a smaller alphabet $\Sigma'$. In this section, we show the existence of such a suitable predicate $Q$ (for every predicate $P$) and in the next, we use it to break the PRG. We start with the definition of alphabet reduction.

**Definition 2 $((\Sigma, \Sigma', \delta)$-Alphabet Reduction).** *Let $P : \Sigma^2 \to \{0,1\}$ be a balanced predicate in two variables. A $(\Sigma, \Sigma', \delta)$-alphabet reduction for $P$ is defined to be a tuple $(Q, f, g)$ where $Q : \Sigma'^2 \to \{0,1\}$ is a balanced predicate defined on an alphabet $\Sigma'$, and $f$ and $g$ are (exactly) $\frac{|\Sigma|}{|\Sigma'|}$-to-one maps from $\Sigma$ to $\Sigma'$, and*

$$\mathop{\mathbf{E}}_{(x,y) \xleftarrow{\$} \Sigma^2} [P(x,y) \oplus Q(f(x), g(y))] < \delta.$$

*In other words, $P(x,y)$ is nontrivially correlated to the decomposed predicate $Q(f(x), g(y))$. We use the shorthand "$(q', \delta)$-alphabet reduction" when $|\Sigma'| = q'$.*

Note that if $P(x, y)$ is perfectly correlated to $P'(x, y) := Q(f(x), g(y))$, then the expectation defined above is 0, and if they are perfectly uncorrelated, it is $1/2$. In words, this definition asks for a way to approximately compute $P$ by first compressing the two inputs $x$ and $y$ independently, and then computing a different predicate $Q$ on the compressed inputs.

In this section, we prove a feasibility result for alphabet reduction: namely, that any predicate $P : \Sigma^2 \rightarrow \{0, 1\}$ has a $(\Sigma, \Sigma', 1/2 - \Omega(1/\sqrt{|\Sigma|}))$-alphabet reduction where $\Sigma' = \{0, 1\}$ is an alphabet of size two. In other words $Q(f(x), g(y))$ is mildly, but non-trivially, correlated to $P$. The predicate $Q$ as well as the compression functions $f$ and $g$ are efficently computable given the truth table of $P$. Our result is a refinement of a lower bound on the possible error of two-source extractors, due to Chor and Goldreich [CG88].

**Theorem 3.** *Suppose that $P : \Sigma^2 \rightarrow \{0, 1\}$ is a balanced predicate and $|\Sigma|$ is divisible by 2. Then, there exists a $(\Sigma, \Sigma', 1/2 - c/\sqrt{|\Sigma|})$-alphabet reduction $(Q, f, g)$ for $P$, for some universal constant $c$. Moreover, given $P$ we can find such a triple $(Q, f, g)$ in (expected) poly$(|\Sigma|)$ time.*

*Proof.* Throughout this proof, we will equate $\Sigma$ with the set $[q]$ (so that $|\Sigma| = q$) and $\Sigma'$ with the set $\{0, 1\}$ (so that $|\Sigma'| = 2$). Also, for ease of exposition, we consider $P$ taking values in $\{\pm 1\}$ instead of $\{0, 1\}$.

Given $P : [q]^2 \rightarrow \{\pm 1\}$, consider $P$ as a $\pm 1$-valued $q \times q$ matrix. At a high level, the proof goes as follows: we first find a $\frac{q}{2} \times \frac{q}{2}$ submatrix of $P$ with substantially more $+1$s than $-1$s in it (or vice-versa). Such a submatrix is not hard to construct: picking a random collection $T$ of $\frac{q}{2}$ columns and then choosing the collection $S$ of $\frac{q}{2}$ rows optimizing the number of $+1$s (or $-1$s) in the $S \times T$ submatrix suffices. Then, we pick $f$ (a function of the $q$ rows) and $g$ (a function of the $q$ columns) to be indicator functions for $S$ and $T$ respectively; there then turns out to be a choice of function $Q : \{0, 1\} \times \{0, 1\} \rightarrow \{\pm 1\}$ (in particular, with $Q(1, 1)$ set to be the majority value of $P$ in the submatrix $S \times T$) such that $(Q, f, g)$, with outputs transformed back to $\{0, 1\}$, is a valid alphabet reduction for $P$.

We now proceed with the full proof. For each $x \in [q]$ and subset $T \subset [q]$, define

$$B(x, T) = \left| \sum_{y \in T} P(x, y) \right|,$$

that is, the absolute value of the $T$-partial row sum of row $x$. In [CG88] (Lemma 2), Chor and Goldreich show that if we choose $T$ to be a uniformly random subset of $\frac{q}{2}$ columns, then for every $x$,

$$\Pr_{T \subset [q], |T| = \frac{q}{2}} \left[ B(x, T) \geq \sqrt{\frac{q}{2}} \right] \geq \frac{1}{8}.$$

Therefore, we have that

$$\mathbf{E}_{T \subset [q], |T| = \frac{q}{2}} \left[ \frac{1}{q} \cdot \# \left\{ x \in [q] : B(x, T) \geq \sqrt{\frac{q}{2}} \right\} \right] \geq \frac{1}{8}.$$

Since the random variable $\frac{1}{q} \cdot \# \left\{ x \in [q] : B(x,T) \geq \sqrt{\frac{q}{2}} \right\}$ takes values in the interval $[0,1]$ and has expectation at least $\frac{1}{8}$, we conclude by Markov's inequality that

$$\Pr_{T \subset [q], |T| = \frac{q}{2}} \left[ \frac{1}{q} \cdot \# \left\{ x \in [q] : B(x,T) \geq \sqrt{\frac{q}{2}} \right\} \leq \frac{1}{16} \right] \leq \frac{14}{15},$$

so that with probability $\geq \frac{1}{15}$ over the choice of $T$, there will be at least $\frac{q}{16}$ rows $x \in [q]$ such that $B(x,T) \geq \sqrt{\frac{q}{2}}$. Fixing any such set $T$, we then have that

$$\sum_{x \in [q]} B(x,T) \geq \frac{q\sqrt{q}}{16\sqrt{2}}.$$

Now, let $S \subset [q]$ be the set of $\frac{q}{2}$ rows $x_1, ..., x_{\frac{q}{2}}$ with the largest values of $\tilde{B}(x,T) := \sum_{y \in T} P(x,y)$. We claim that

$$\left| \sum_{x \in S} \tilde{B}(x,T) \right| + \left| \sum_{x \notin S} \tilde{B}(x,T) \right| \geq \frac{q\sqrt{q}}{48\sqrt{2}},$$

that is, we claim that a significant fraction of the $\tilde{B}(x,T)$ terms do not cancel with each other when we sum over $x \in S$ and $x \notin S$ separately. To see this, let

$$C_1 = \sum_{x : \tilde{B}(x,T) \geq 0} B(x,T)$$

and

$$C_2 = \sum_{x : \tilde{B}(x,T) < 0} B(x,T)$$

so that $C_1 + C_2 = \sum_{x \in [q]} B(x,T)$. We note that without loss of generality, we have that $\tilde{B}(x,T) \geq 0$ for all $x \in S$, so that

$$\left| \sum_{x \in S} \tilde{B}(x,T) \right| + \left| \sum_{x \notin S} \tilde{B}(x,T) \right| = \sum_{x \in S} B(x,T) + \max(\sum_{x \notin S} \tilde{B}(x,T), -\sum_{x \notin S} \tilde{B}(x,T))$$

$$\geq \max(C_1 - C_2, C_2) \geq \frac{1}{3}(C_1 - C_2) + \frac{2}{3}C_2 \geq \frac{q\sqrt{q}}{48\sqrt{2}}.$$

as desired. Thus, either the submatrix $S \times T$ or $([q] - S) \times T$ has the intermediate property we were looking for.

Finally, we can construct $Q, f$, and $g$ as follows: let $S_0 = S, S_1 = [q] - S$, $T_0 = T, T_1 = [q] - T$, and for $i, j \in \{0,1\}$ we define

$$E_{ij} = \frac{1}{q^2} \sum_{(x,y) \in S_i \times T_j} P(x,y).$$

For $i, j \in \{0, 1\}$, define $Q(i, j) = 1$ if $E_{ij}$ is one of the two largest elements of the (multi)set $\{E_{ij}, i, j \in \{0, 1\}\}$ (and $Q(i, j) = -1$ otherwise). Moreover, we define $f(x) = i$ if and only if $x \in S_i$, and we define $g(y) = j$ if and only if $y \in T_j$. Intuitively, for $(x, y) \in S_i \times T_j$ we want to set $Q(f(x), g(y))$ to be the majority value of $P(x', y')$ for $(x', y') \in S_i \times T_j$, but to make $Q$ a balanced predicate we may have to disagree with this majority function on some inputs.

By essentially the same argument about cancellation as before, we will show that $P(x, y)$ is $\frac{1}{2} + \Omega(\frac{1}{\sqrt{q}})$-correlated to $Q(f(x), g(y))$. That is, we show that

$$\underset{(x,y) \leftarrow U_{2,q}}{\mathbf{E}} [P(x, y)Q(f(x), g(y))] \geq \frac{1}{2} (|E_{00}| + |E_{01}| + |E_{10}| + |E_{11}|) = \Omega(\frac{1}{\sqrt{q}}).$$

To see this, re-order the four numbers $E_{ij}$ into $E_1 \leq E_2 \leq E_3 \leq E_4$; we know that $E_1 + E_2 + E_3 + E_4 = 0$ since $P(x, y)$ is balanced. If exactly two of these four numbers are negative, then the expected value above is exactly equal to $|E_1| + |E_2| + |E_3| + |E_4|$, so we are done. On the other hand, it may be that three of $\{E_1, E_2, E_3, E_4\}$ have the same sign; suppose without loss of generality that $E_3 \leq 0$. Then, we see that

$$\underset{(x,y) \leftarrow U_{2,q}}{\mathbf{E}} [P(x, y)Q(f(x), g(y))] = |E_1| + |E_2| - |E_3| + |E_4|$$

$$\geq |E_4| = \frac{1}{2} (|E_1| + |E_2| + |E_3| + |E_4|),$$

completing the existence proof. Moreover, our existence proof above is constructive: to find a valid triple $(Q, f, g)$, we repeatedly choose $T \subset [q]$ of size $\frac{q}{2}$ uniformly at random, check if $\sum_{x \in [q]} B(x, T) = \Omega(q\sqrt{q})$ (for suitably chosen constant $c$), and proceed to construct $S$, $Q$, $f$, and $g$ as described. In expectation only a constant number of sets $T$ will be selected before $S$, $Q$, $f$, and $g$ are successfully constructed, so we are done. □

## 3.1 Limits of Alphabet Reduction

Alphabet reduction is one of the two main ingredients to our distinguishing algorithm. In order to obtain distinguishers for an even larger class of PRGs, namely, instantiations of Goldreich's PRG in which $m$ possibly different predicates $P^{(1)}, P^{(2)}, ..., P^{(m)}$ are used instead of a repeated single predicate, one can analogously define an "average case alphabet reduction" for an $m$-tuple of predicates $\vec{P}$.

**Definition 3 (Average Case $(\Sigma, \Sigma', \delta)$-Alphabet Reduction).** Let $P^{(1)}$, $P^{(2)}, \ldots, P^{(m)} : \Sigma^2 \to \{0, 1\}$ be a collection of balanced predicates in two variables. A $(\Sigma, \Sigma', \delta)$-average case alphabet reduction for $\vec{P}$ is defined to be a tuple $(\vec{Q}, f, g)$ such that each $Q^{(i)} : \Sigma'^2 \to \{0, 1\}$ is a balanced predicate defined on an alphabet of size $q'$, $f$ and $g$ are (exactly) $\frac{q}{q'}$-to-one maps from $\Sigma \to \Sigma'$, and

$$\underset{(x,y) \xleftarrow{\$} \Sigma^2, i \xleftarrow{\$} [m]}{\mathbf{E}} [P^{(i)}(x, y) \oplus Q^{(i)}(f(x), g(y))] < \delta.$$

*In other words, $P^{(i)}(x,y)$ is nontrivially correlated to $Q^{(i)}(f(x),g(y))$ on average over the choice of $i$. We use the shorthand "$(q',\delta)$-average case alphabet reduction" for $\vec{P}$ when $|\Sigma'| = q'$.*

Note that we require the same alphabet reduction functions $f$ and $g$ to work for all the predicates $P^{(i)}$ *simultaneously*.

It turns out that average case alphabet reduction is significantly more difficult to achieve than alphabet reduction. In general, one cannot find a constant size average case alphabet reduction with $\delta < \frac{1}{2} - \tilde{O}(\frac{1}{q})$.

In particular, when $\vec{P}$ is a good 3-*source extractor* $\vec{P} : [q] \times [q] \times [m] \to \{0,1\}$, no such alphabet reduction can be done. Our impossibility result for alphabet reduction boils down to a (slightly modified) folklore construction of 3-source extractors, which we include for completeness.

**Theorem 4.** *Let $\vec{P} = (P_{ij}^{(k)})$ be a uniformly random $\pm 1$-entry $q \times q \times m$ 3-tensor subject to the contraint that $P^{(k)}$ is balanced for every $k$, and suppose that $q \leq m$. Then, for any constant $C$, we have that with overwhelming probability, every $\frac{q}{C} \times \frac{q}{C} \times \frac{m}{C}$ subtensor $\vec{P}|_{S \times T \times U}$ of $\vec{P}$ has discrepancy $\left| \sum_{(i,j,k) \in S \times T \times U} \vec{P}_{ij}^{(k)} \right| = O(\frac{\log(mq)}{q})$.*

**Corollary 1.** *If $\vec{P}$ is a uniformly random collection of $m$ balanaced predicates $P^{(i)} : [q]^2 \to \{0,1\}$, then for any constant $C$, there is no $\left( C, \frac{1}{2} - O(\frac{\log(mq)}{q}) \right)$-average case alphabet reduction for $\vec{P}$ with overwhelming probability.*

*Proof.* First, consider any fixed subtensor $\vec{P}|_{S \times T \times U}$ of size $\frac{q}{C} \times \frac{q}{C} \times \frac{m}{C}$, and suppose that $(P_{ij}^{(k)})$ is a uniformly random tensor (not constrained to be balanced). Then, $\vec{P}|_{S \times T \times U}$ is a uniformly random $\pm 1$-tensor whose discrepancy is governed by the Chernoff bound:

$$\Pr \left[ \left| \sum_{i \in S, j \in T, k \in U} P_{ij}^{(k)} \right| \geq \epsilon \right] \leq 2 \cdot 2^{-\Omega(\frac{mq^2}{C^3} \epsilon^2)}.$$

The number of subtensors we are considering is $\binom{m}{\frac{m}{C}}\binom{q}{\frac{q}{C}}\binom{q}{\frac{q}{C}}$, and the probability that a random tensor $\vec{P}$ has the property that $P^{(k)}$ is balanced for all $k$ is bounded by $(\Omega(\frac{1}{q}))^m$ (as the discrepancy of each $P^{(k)}$ follows the distribution Binomial($q^2, \frac{1}{2}$)). Thus, the probability that a random $\vec{P}$ satisfies this $\epsilon$-discrepancy property after conditioning on balanced is bounded by

$$O(q)^m \binom{m}{\frac{m}{C}} \binom{q}{\frac{q}{C}}^2 \cdot 2^{-\Omega(\frac{mq^2}{C^3} \epsilon^2)}.$$

Choosing $\epsilon = O(\frac{C^{1.5} \log(mq)}{q})$ suffices to make this probability negligible, so we are done.    $\square$

As a result of Theorem 4, it is unlikely for alphabet reduction to be sufficient for breaking $G_{H,\vec{P}}$ with $m = \tilde{\Omega}(q \cdot n)$ output length, because the refutation algorithms with which we combine predicate reduction have a $\frac{1}{\epsilon^2}$ dependence in the required output length for $\epsilon$-refutation (and this dependence is typical). Therefore, it is unlikely for average case alphabet reduction to lead to a distinguisher for $G_{H,\vec{P}}$ when the output length $m = |E(H)|$ is less than $q^2 n$.

However, we note for completeness' sake that Theorem 4 is tight up to log factors; that is, $\left(\frac{1}{2} - \Omega(\frac{1}{q})\right)$-average case alphabet reduction is possible. The construction is as follows: pick sets $S, T$ uniformly at random (of size $\frac{|\Sigma|}{2}$), choose $f, g : \Sigma \to \{0, 1\}$ to be indicator functions for $S$ and $T$, as before, and for each $\ell \in [m]$ define $Q^{(\ell)}(i, j)$ to be 1 if and only if the average value $E_{i,j}^{(\ell)}$ is in the top two out of four $E_{\cdot,\cdot}^{(\ell)}$, as before. Using average-case alphabet reduction, one can distinguish multiple-predicate Goldreich PRGs $G_{H,\vec{P}}$ when $m \geq \tilde{\Omega}(q^2 \cdot n)$; we will elaborate on this in Sect. 4.2.

# 4 From Small Alphabet Refutation to Large Alphabet Distinguishing

We now describe how alphabet reduction is used to obtain distinguishing algorithms for the (single predicate) Goldreich PRG $G_{H,P}$; combining this section with Theorem 3 yields Theorem 1. The cleanest interpretation of our application of alphabet reduction uses the notion of an "image refutation algorithm" for a function $G : [q]^n \to \{0, 1\}^m$, which was formally defined in [BBKK17]. Interpreted in this language, our result says that *any* image refutation algorithm for Goldreich's PRG can be converted into a distinguishing algorithm for Goldreich's PRG with a significantly improved dependence on the alphabet size. The new distinguishing threshold is a simple function of the quality of the alphabet reduction that was used and the refutation threshold for the image refutation algorithm.

**Definition 4 (Image Refutation).** *Let $G : [q]^n \to \{0, 1\}^m$ be any function. An* image refutation algorithm *for $G$ is an algorithm $\mathcal{A}$ which receives $G$ and a string $z \in \{0, 1\}^m$ as input, with the following properties:*

1. *(Soundness) If $z \in G([q]^n)$, then $\mathcal{A}(G, z) =$ "fail".*
2. *(Completeness) If $z \leftarrow U_m$, then $\mathcal{A}(G, z) =$ "z is not in the image of $G$" with probability $1 - o(1)$.*

*Furthermore, $\mathcal{A}$ is an $(\frac{1}{2} - \delta)$-image refutation algorithm for $G$ if it has the following properties:*

1. *(Strong Soundness) If $z$ has Hamming distance less than or equal to $(\frac{1}{2} - \delta)m$ from $G([q]^n)$, then $\mathcal{A}(G, z) =$ "fail".*
2. *(Strong Completeness) If $z \leftarrow U_m$, then $\mathcal{A}(G, z) =$ "z is $(\frac{1}{2} - \delta)$-far from the image of $G$" with probability $1 - o(1)$.*

Given this definition, we are ready to state our reduction theorem.

**Theorem 5.** *Let $P : [q]^2 \to \{0,1\}$ be a predicate. Assume the existence of the following two ingredients:*

- *An efficiently computable $(q', \frac{1}{2} - \epsilon)$-alphabet reduction for $P$ that produces a tuple $(Q, f, g)$ where $Q : [q']^2 \to \{0,1\}$; and*
- *An image refutation algorithm $\mathcal{A}$ that runs in $\mathsf{poly}(n, m, q', \frac{1}{\delta})$ time and does $(\frac{1}{2} - \delta)$-image refutation for the function $G_{H,Q}$ for any predicate $Q : [q']^2 \to \{0,1\}$, any $\delta > 0$ and any graph $H$ satisfying $m = |E(H)| \geq T(n, q', \delta)$ for some threshold function $T(\cdot)$.*

*Then, there is a distingusher $\mathcal{D}$ that, for any graph $H$ with $m = |E(H)| \geq T(2n, q', \epsilon - O(\sqrt{\frac{n}{m}}))$, runs in $\mathsf{poly}(n, q, \frac{1}{\epsilon})$ time and distinguishes a random string $z \leftarrow U_m$ from a random output $z \leftarrow G_{H,P}(U_{n,q})$ of $G_{H,P}$.*

In particular, since Theorem 3 efficiently produces a $(2, \frac{1}{2} - \Omega(\frac{1}{\sqrt{q}}))$-alphabet reduction for any balanced predicate $P$, Theorem 5 implies that any strong image refutation algorithm for Goldreich's PRG over the *binary* alphabet immediately yields a distinguishing algorithm for Goldreich's PRG over larger alphabets.

*Image Refutation Algorithms for Goldreich's PRG.* We originally combined an alphabet reduction (with $q' = O(1)$) with the random CSP refutation algorithm of [AOW15] in place of a PRG image refutation algorithm, which turned out to be sufficient to obtain a distinguisher for $G_{H,P}$ over random graphs for all $m = \tilde{\Omega}(q \cdot n)$.

However, with an alphabet reduction using $q' = 2$, the state of affairs is much simpler; indeed, the Charikar-Wirth algorithm [CW04] directly gives us a PRG image refutation algorithm which can then be used to obtain a distinguisher for worst case graphs and worst case single predicates for $m = \tilde{\Omega}(q \cdot n)$ (for a sufficiently large logarithmic factor). This is because Charikar-Wirth $(\frac{1}{2} - \epsilon)$-refutes random 2-XOR instances with $m = \tilde{\Omega}(\frac{n}{\epsilon^2})$ constraints, and strongly refuting Goldreich's PRG instantiated with a balanced predicate $Q : \{0,1\}^2 \to \{0,1\}$ is exactly the same as strongly refuting a random 2-XOR instance (or a random 1-XOR instance, which is even easier). In particular, a balanced predicate $Q : \{0,1\}^2 \to \{0,1\}$ is either $Q(x,y) = x$, $Q(x,y) = y$, $Q(x,y) = x \oplus y$, or a negation of the previous three examples. Thus, any Goldreich PRG $G_{H,Q}$ defines a random 2-XOR instance or a random 1-XOR instance, either of which can be efficiently (strongly) refuted.

In the *multiple predicate* case, a Goldreich PRG $G_{H,\vec{Q}}$ (still over the binary alphabet) defines both a random 2-XOR instance and a random 1-XOR instance. It is not hard to see that if $m$ is sufficiently large, at least one of these two CSP instances will be above its refutation threshold, yielding the necessary strong image refutation algorithm for $G_{\tilde{H},\vec{Q}}$. We will use this stronger fact for Theorem 6.

Furthermore, we note that this theorem can still be useful in regimes where general alphabet reduction is impossible; it says that if a predicate

$P : [q]^2 \to \{0,1\}$ happens to have an alphabet reduction, then $G_{H,P}$ may be less secure than one would expect for the given alphabet size $q$.

We now prove Theorem 5. The intuition is quite simple: given an alphabet reduction $(Q, f, g)$ for $P$ and an image $z = G_{H,P}(x)$ for a random $x$, one would expect that $z$ is noticeably closer to the point $G_{H,P'}(x)$ for $P'(x, y) = Q(f(x), g(y))$. Indeed, this is true in expectation over $x$, and holds with high probability by a concentration argument. Therefore, a strong refutation algorithm for the predicate $Q$ should be able to distinguish $G_{H,P}(x)$ from a random string.

### 4.1  Proof of Theorem 5

Fix any predicate $P : [q]^2 \to \{0,1\}$, efficiently computable $(q', \delta)$-alphabet reduction $(Q, f, g)$,[3] and graph $H$ with $n$ vertices and $m$ edges. Let $G_{H,P} : [q]^n \to \{0,1\}^m$ be Goldreich's PRG instantiated with $P$ and $H$. We want to construct a distinguisher $\mathcal{D}(H, P, z)$ which, given $P, H$, and a string $z \in \{0,1\}^m$ (where $m$ is the number of edges in $H$), outputs a bit $b \in \{0,1\}$ such that $\underset{z \leftarrow U_m}{\mathbf{E}} [\mathcal{D}(P, H, z)]$ is noticeably different from $\underset{z \leftarrow G_{H,P}(U_n)}{\mathbf{E}} [\mathcal{D}(P, H, z)]$. Our distinguisher $\mathcal{D}$ is defined as follows.

1. Compute $(Q, f, g)$ given $P$.
2. Let $\tilde{H}$ be the bipartite double-cover of $H$, i.e. a graph with vertex set $[n] \times \{0,1\}$ and edges from $(i, 0)$ to $(j, 1)$ for every $(i, j) \in E(H)$.
3. Call $\mathcal{A}(\tilde{H}, Q, \epsilon - 5\sqrt{\frac{n}{m}}, z)$.
4. Return 1 if and only if the call to $\mathcal{A}$ returns "$z$ is $(\frac{1}{2} - \epsilon + 5\sqrt{\frac{n}{m}})$-far from the image of $G_{\tilde{H},Q}$".

Note that by assumption on $\mathcal{A}$, for $z \leftarrow U_m$, $\mathcal{D}(P, H, z)$ will output 1 with probability $1 - o(1)$ as long as $m \geq T(2n, q', \epsilon - 5\sqrt{\frac{n}{m}})$. What remains is to analyze the "pseudorandom" case.

**Lemma 1.** *With constant probability over* $\mathbf{x} \leftarrow U_{n,q}$, $z = G_{H,P}(\mathbf{x})$ *will have Hamming distance at most* $(\frac{1}{2} - \epsilon + 5\sqrt{\frac{n}{m}})m$ *from* $G_{\tilde{H},Q}(\tilde{\mathbf{x}})$, *where* $\tilde{\mathbf{x}} \in (\mathbb{Z}_2^n)^2$ *is defined by* $\tilde{x}_{i,0} = f(x_i)$ *and* $\tilde{x}_{i,1} = g(x_i)$.

Since the call to $\mathcal{A}(\tilde{H}, Q, \epsilon - 5\sqrt{\frac{n}{m}}, z)$ must return "fail" whenever $z$ has Hamming distance at most $(\frac{1}{2} - \epsilon + 5\sqrt{\frac{n}{m}})m$ from $G_{\tilde{H},Q}(\mathbb{Z}_{q'}^n)$ (again for $m \geq T(2n, q', \epsilon - 5\sqrt{\frac{n}{m}}))$, Lemma 1 suffices to prove that

$$\underset{\mathbf{x} \leftarrow U_{n,q}}{\mathbf{E}} [\mathcal{D}(H, P, G_{H,P}(\mathbf{x}))] = 1 - \Omega(1).$$

*Proof.* Let $P'(x, y) = Q(f(x), g(y))$ so that $\underset{(x,y) \leftarrow U_{2,q}}{\Pr} [P(x, y) = P'(x, y)] = \alpha \geq \frac{1}{2} + \epsilon$, as guaranteed by the fact that $(Q, f, g)$ is a $(\frac{1}{2} - \epsilon)$-alphabet reduction for

---

[3] This alphabet reduction may be randomized; this does not affect the proof.

$P$. We are interested in the quantity $d_H(z, G_{\tilde{H},Q}(\tilde{\mathbf{x}})) = d_H(z, G_{H,P'}(\mathbf{x}))$, where $d_H$ denotes fractional Hamming distance. First, we note that in expectation over $\mathbf{x} \leftarrow U_{n,q}$,

$$
\begin{aligned}
E := 1 - \underset{\mathbf{x} \leftarrow U_{n,q}}{\mathbf{E}} &[d_H(G_{H,P}(\mathbf{x}), G_{\tilde{H},Q}(\tilde{\mathbf{x}}))] \\
&= \underset{\mathbf{x} \leftarrow U_{n,q}}{\mathbf{E}} \left[ \Pr_{(i,j) \overset{\$}{\leftarrow} E(H)} [P'(x_i, x_j) = P(x_i, x_j)] \right] \\
&\geq \alpha - \frac{n}{m} \\
&\geq \frac{1}{2} + \epsilon - \frac{n}{m},
\end{aligned}
$$

where the $\frac{n}{m}$ term comes from the fraction of edges in $H$ which are self loops (we cannot say that $P(x_i, x_i)$ is necessarily correlated to $P'(x_i, x_i)$). Now, we compute the variance (over $\mathbf{x}$) of this quantity to be

$$
\underset{\mathbf{x} \leftarrow U_{n,q}}{\text{Var}} [1 - d_H(G_{H,P}(\mathbf{x}), G_{\tilde{H},Q}(\tilde{\mathbf{x}}))]
$$

$$
= \underset{\mathbf{x} \leftarrow U_{n,q}}{\mathbf{E}} \left[ \left( \Pr_{(i,j) \overset{\$}{\leftarrow} E(H)} [P'(x_i, x_j) = P(x_i, x_j)] \right)^2 \right] - E^2
$$

$$
= \underset{\mathbf{x} \leftarrow U_{n,q}}{\mathbf{E}} \left[ \frac{1}{m^2} \sum_{\substack{(i,j) \in E(H) \\ (k,l) \in E(H)}} \chi\left(P'(x_i, x_j) = P(x_i, x_j)\right) \chi\left(P'(x_k, x_l) = P(x_k, x_l)\right) \right] - E^2
$$

$$
= \frac{1}{m^2} \sum_{\substack{(i,j) \in E(H) \\ (k,l) \in E(H)}} \underset{\mathbf{x} \leftarrow U_{n,q}}{\Pr} \left[ P'(x_i, x_j) = P(x_i, x_j) \text{ and } P'(x_k, x_l) = P(x_k, x_l) \right] - E^2.
$$

Note that if the edges $(i,j), (k,l) \in E(H)$ have no vertices in common, the events "$P'(x_i, x_j) = P(x_i, x_j)$" and "$P'(x_k, x_l) = P(x_k, x_l)$" are independent. This means that our variance is upper bounded by

$$
\frac{1}{m^2} \sum_{\substack{(i,j) \in E(H) \\ (k,l) \in E(H)}} \Pr_{\mathbf{x}} \left[ P'(x_i, x_j) = P(x_i, x_j) \right] \Pr_{\mathbf{x}} \left[ P'(x_k, x_l) = P(x_k, x_l) \right] + \frac{m_{\text{bad}}}{m^2} - E^2
$$

$$
= \frac{m_{\text{bad}}}{m^2},
$$

where $m_{\text{bad}}$ is defined to be the number of pairs of edges $((i,j), (k,l))$ which have a vertex in common. This is bounded by the quantity

$$
m_{\text{bad}} \leq \sum_{i \in [n]} \deg_H(i)^2 \leq 2n \cdot \sum_{i \in [n]} \deg_H(i) = 4mn.
$$

Therefore, we conclude that

$$
\underset{\mathbf{x} \leftarrow U_{n,q}}{\text{Var}} [1 - d_H(G_{H,P}(\mathbf{x}), G_{\tilde{H},Q}(\tilde{\mathbf{x}}))] \leq \frac{4n}{m}.
$$

By Chebyshev's inequality, this means that with constant probability over $\mathbf{x} \leftarrow U_{n,q}$, we have that

$$1 - d_H(G_{H,P}(\mathbf{x}), G_{H,\tilde{Q}}(\tilde{\mathbf{x}})) \geq \alpha - \frac{n}{m} - 4\sqrt{\frac{n}{m}} \geq \frac{1}{2} + \epsilon - 5\sqrt{\frac{n}{m}},$$

so that $d_H(G_{H,P}(\mathbf{x}), G_{H,\tilde{Q}}(\tilde{\mathbf{x}})) \leq \frac{1}{2} - \epsilon + 5\sqrt{\frac{n}{m}}$, completing the proof of the lemma. □

Lemma 1 tells us that for $m \geq T(2n, q', \epsilon - 5\sqrt{\frac{n}{m}})$, with constant probability over $\mathbf{x} \leftarrow G_{n,q}$ the call made to $\mathcal{A}$ will return "fail", and so

$$\mathop{\mathbf{E}}_{\mathbf{x} \leftarrow G_{n,q}}[\mathcal{D}(H, P, G_{H,P}(\mathbf{x}))] = 1 - \Omega(1).$$

Thus, we conclude that $\mathcal{D}$ achieves a constant distinguishing advantage between the "truly random $z$" case and the "pseudorandom $z$" case, completing the proof of Theorem 5.

### 4.2  Generalization of Theorem 5 to Multiple Predicates

We note that the proof of Theorem 5 does not fundamentally use the fact that the predicates used in Goldreich's PRG $G_{H,P}$ are identical. Indeed, the following result holds by the same argument.

**Theorem 6.** *Let $P^{(1)}, P^{(2)}, \ldots, P^{(m)} : [q]^2 \to \{0, 1\}$ be a collection of $m$ predicates. Assume the existence of the following two ingredients:*

- *An efficiently computable $(q', \frac{1}{2} - \epsilon)$-average case alphabet reduction for $\vec{P}$ that produces a tuple $(\vec{Q}, f, g)$ where each $Q^{(\ell)} : [q']^2 \to \{0, 1\}$; and*
- *An image refutation algorithm $\mathcal{A}$ that runs in $\mathrm{poly}(n, m, q', \frac{1}{\delta})$ time and does $(\frac{1}{2} - \delta)$-image refutation for the function $G_{H,\vec{Q}}$ for any predicate collection $Q^{(\ell)} : [q']^2 \to \{0, 1\}$, any $\delta > 0$ and any graph $H$ satisfying $m = |E(H)| \geq T(n, q', \delta)$ for some threshold function $T(\cdot)$.*

*Then, there is a distingusher $\mathcal{D}$ that, for any graph $H$ with $m = |E(H)| \geq T(2n, q', \epsilon - O(\sqrt{\frac{n}{m}}))$, runs in $\mathrm{poly}(n, q, \frac{1}{\epsilon})$ time and distinguishes a random string $z \leftarrow U_m$ from a random output $z \leftarrow G_{H,\vec{P}}(U_{n,q})$ of $G_{H,\vec{P}}$.*

Theorem 6, combined with the Charikar-Wirth algorithm and an average-case alphabet reduction with correlation $\Omega(\frac{1}{q})$, gives us a distinguisher for multiple predicate Goldreich PRGs $G_{H,\vec{P}} : [q]^n \to \{0, 1\}^m$ for all $m \geq \tilde{\Omega}(q^2 n)$.

**Acknowledgements.** We thank Gil Cohen, Dana Moshkovitz and Prasad Raghavendra for their quick responses to our oracle calls about two-source extractors and CSPs. We also thank our anonymous TCC reviewers for their helpful comments and suggestions.

# References

[ABR12]  Applebaum, B., Bogdanov, A., Rosen, A.: A dichotomy for local small-bias generators. In: Cramer, R. (ed.) TCC 2012. LNCS, vol. 7194, pp. 600–617. Springer, Heidelberg (2012). doi:10.1007/978-3-642-28914-9_34

[AJ15]  Ananth, P., Jain, A.: Indistinguishability obfuscation from compact functional encryption. In: Gennaro, R., Robshaw, M. (eds.) CRYPTO 2015. LNCS, vol. 9215, pp. 308–326. Springer, Heidelberg (2015). doi:10.1007/978-3-662-47989-6_15

[AL16]  Applebaum, B., Lovett, S.: Algebraic attacks against random local functions and their countermeasures. In: Proceedings of the 48th Annual ACM SIGACT Symposium on Theory of Computing, pp. 1087–1100. ACM (2016)

[AOW15]  Allen, S.R., O'Donnell, R., Witmer, D.: How to refute a random CSP. In: 2015 IEEE 56th Annual Symposium on Foundations of Computer Science (FOCS), pp. 689–708. IEEE (2015)

[App16]  Applebaum, B.: Cryptographic hardness of random local functions. Comput. Complex. **25**(3), 667–722 (2016)

[AS16]  Prabhanjan, A., Amit, S.: Projective arithmetic functional encryption and indistinguishability obfuscation from degree-5 multilinear maps. IACR Cryptology ePrint Archive 2016:1097 (2016)

[BBKK17]  Barak, B., Brakerski, Z., Komargodski, I., Kothari, P.K.: Limits on low-degree pseudorandom generators (or: Sum-of-squares meets program obfuscation) (2017). http://eprint.iacr.org/2017/312. Version 20170411:133059. Submitted 9 April 2017

[BF03]  Boneh, D., Franklin, M.: Identity-based encryption from the weil pairing. SIAM J. Comput. **32**(3), 586–615 (2003)

[BGI+01]  Barak, B., Goldreich, O., Impagliazzo, R., Rudich, S., Sahai, A., Vadhan, S., Yang, K.: On the (im)possibility of obfuscating programs. In: Kilian, J. (ed.) CRYPTO 2001. LNCS, vol. 2139, pp. 1–18. Springer, Heidelberg (2001). doi:10.1007/3-540-44647-8_1

[BV15]  Bitansky, N., Vaikuntanathan, V.: Indistinguishability obfuscation from functional encryption. In: Guruswami, V. (ed.) IEEE 56th Annual Symposium on Foundations of Computer Science, FOCS 2015, Berkeley, CA, USA, 17–20 October 2015, pp. 171–190. IEEE Computer Society (2015)

[CG88]  Chor, B., Goldreich, O.: Unbiased bits from sources of weak randomness and probabilistic communication complexity. SIAM J. Comput. **17**(2), 230–261 (1988)

[CW04]  Charikar, M., Wirth, A.: Maximizing quadratic programs: extending Grothendieck's inequality. In: Proceedings of the 45th Annual IEEE Symposium on Foundations of Computer Science, pp. 54–60. IEEE (2004)

[GGH+16]  Garg, S., Gentry, C., Halevi, S., Raykova, M., Sahai, A., Waters, B.: Candidate indistinguishability obfuscation and functional encryption for all circuits. SIAM J. Comput. **45**(3), 882–929 (2016)

[Gol00]  Goldreich, O.: Candidate one-way functions based on expander graphs. IACR Cryptology ePrint Archive 2000:63 (2000)

[GR07]  Goldwasser, S., Rothblum, G.N.: On best-possible obfuscation. In: Vadhan, S.P. (ed.) TCC 2007. LNCS, vol. 4392, pp. 194–213. Springer, Heidelberg (2007). doi:10.1007/978-3-540-70936-7_11

[GVW12]  Gorbunov, S., Vaikuntanathan, V., Wee, H.: Functional encryption with bounded collusions via multi-party computation. In: Safavi-Naini, R., Canetti, R. (eds.) CRYPTO 2012. LNCS, vol. 7417, pp. 162–179. Springer, Heidelberg (2012). doi:10.1007/978-3-642-32009-5_11

[Jou00]  Joux, A.: A one round protocol for tripartite Diffie-Hellman. In: Bosma, W. (ed.) ANTS 2000. LNCS, vol. 1838, pp. 385–393. Springer, Heidelberg (2000). doi:10.1007/10722028_23

[Jou02]  Joux, A.: The weil and tate pairings as building blocks for public key cryptosystems. In: Fieker, C., Kohel, D.R. (eds.) ANTS 2002. LNCS, vol. 2369, pp. 20–32. Springer, Heidelberg (2002). doi:10.1007/3-540-45455-1_3

[Lin16a]  Lin, H.: Indistinguishability obfuscation from constant-degree graded encoding schemes. In: Fischlin, M., Coron, J.-S. (eds.) EUROCRYPT 2016. LNCS, vol. 9665, pp. 28–57. Springer, Heidelberg (2016). doi:10.1007/978-3-662-49890-3_2

[Lin16b]  Lin, H.: Indistinguishability obfuscation from DDH on 5-linear maps and locality-5 PRGs (2016). Preprint: http://eprint.iacr.org/2016/1096.pdf

[LPST16]  Lin, H., Pass, R., Seth, K., Telang, S.: Indistinguishability obfuscation with non-trivial efficiency. In: Cheng, C.-M., Chung, K.-M., Persiano, G., Yang, B.-Y. (eds.) PKC 2016. LNCS, vol. 9615, pp. 447–462. Springer, Heidelberg (2016). doi:10.1007/978-3-662-49387-8_17

[LT17]  Lin, H., Tessaro, S.: Indistinguishability obfuscation from bilinear maps and block-wise local PRGs. IACR Cryptology ePrint Archive 2017:250 (2017). Version 20170320:142653

[LV16]  Lin, H., Vaikuntanathan, V.: Indistinguishability obfuscation from DDH-like assumptions on constant-degree graded encodings. In: 2016 IEEE 57th Annual Symposium on Foundations of Computer Science (FOCS), pp. 11–20. IEEE (2016)

[LV17]  Lombardi, A., Vaikuntanathan, V.: On the non-existence of blockwise 2-local PRGs with applications to indistinguishability obfuscation. Cryptology ePrint Archive, Report 2017/301 (2017). http://eprint.iacr.org/2017/301. Version 20170409:183008. Submitted 6 April 2017

[OW14]  O'Donnell, R., Witmer, D.: Goldreich's PRG: evidence for near-optimal polynomial stretch. In: 2014 IEEE 29th Conference on Computational Complexity (CCC), pp. 1–12. IEEE (2014)

[SS10]  Sahai, A., Seyalioglu, H.: Worry-free encryption: functional encryption with public keys. In: Al-Shaer, E., Keromytis, A.D., Shmatikov, V. (eds.) Proceedings of the 17th ACM Conference on Computer and Communications Security, CCS 2010, Chicago, Illinois, USA, 4–8 October 2010, pp. 463–472. ACM (2010)

[Wit17]  Witmer, D.: Refutation of random constraint satisfaction problems using the sum of squares proof system. Ph.D. thesis, Carnegie Mellon University (2017)

# Decomposable Obfuscation: A Framework for Building Applications of Obfuscation from Polynomial Hardness

Qipeng Liu$^{(\boxtimes)}$ and Mark Zhandry

Princeton University, Princeton, USA
qipengl@cs.princeton.edu

**Abstract.** There is some evidence that indistinguishability obfuscation (iO) requires either exponentially many assumptions or (sub)exponentially hard assumptions, and indeed, all known ways of building obfuscation suffer one of these two limitations. As such, any application built from iO suffers from these limitations as well. However, for most applications, such limitations do not appear to be inherent to the application, just the approach using iO. Indeed, several recent works have shown how to base applications of iO instead on functional encryption (FE), which can in turn be based on the polynomial hardness of just a few assumptions. However, these constructions are quite complicated and recycle a lot of similar techniques.

In this work, we unify the results of previous works in the form of a weakened notion of obfuscation, called *Decomposable Obfuscation*. We show (1) how to build decomposable obfuscation from functional encryption, and (2) how to build a variety of applications from decomposable obfuscation, including all of the applications already known from FE. The construction in (1) hides most of the difficult techniques in the prior work, whereas the constructions in (2) are much closer to the comparatively simple constructions from iO. As such, decomposable obfuscation represents a convenient new platform for obtaining more applications from polynomial hardness.

## 1 Introduction

Program obfuscation has recently emerged as a powerful cryptographic concept. An obfuscator is a compiler for programs, taking an input program, and scrambling it into an equivalent output program, but with all internal implementation details obscured. Indistinguishability obfuscation (iO) is the generally-accepted notion of security for an obfuscator, which says that the obfuscations of equivalent programs are computationally indistinguishable.

In the last few years since the first candidate indistinguishability obfuscator of Garg et al. [GGH+13], obfuscation has been used to solve many new amazing tasks such as deniable encryption [SW14], multiparty non-interactive key agreement [BZ14], polynomially-many hardcore bits for any one-way function [BST14], and much more. Obfuscation has also been shown to imply most

© International Association for Cryptologic Research 2017
Y. Kalai and L. Reyzin (Eds.): TCC 2017, Part I, LNCS 10677, pp. 138–169, 2017.
https://doi.org/10.1007/978-3-319-70500-2_6

traditional cryptographic primitives[1] such as public key encryption [SW14], zero knowledge [BP15], trapdoor permutations [BPW16], and even fully homomorphic encryption [CLTV15]. This makes obfuscation a "central hub" in cryptography, capable of solving almost any cryptographic task, be it classical or cutting edge. Even more, obfuscation has been shown to have important connections to other areas of computer science theory, from demonstrating the hardness of finding Nash equilibrium [BPR15] to the hardness of certain tasks in differential privacy [BZ14, BZ16].

The power of obfuscation in part comes from the power of the underlying tools, but its power also lies in the *abstraction*, by hiding away the complicated implementation details underneath a relatively easy to use interface. In this work, we aim to build a similarly powerful abstraction that avoids some of the limitations of iO.

## 1.1   The Sub-exponential Barrier in Obfuscation

Indistinguishability obfuscation (iO), as an assumption, has different flavor than most assumptions in cryptography. Most cryptographic assumptions look like

"Distribution $A$ is computationally indistinguishable from distribution $B$," or
"Given a sample $a$ from distribution $A$, it is computationally infeasible
to compute a value $b$ such that $a, b$ satisfy some given relation."

Such assumptions are often referred to as falsifiable [Nao03], or more generally as complexity assumptions [GT16]. In contrast, iO has the form

"*For  every  pair  of  circuits  $C_0, C_1$  that  are  functionally  equivalent*,
iO$(C_0)$ is computationally indisitnguishable from iO$(C_1)$."

In other words, for each pair of equivalent circuits $C_0, C_1$, there is an instance of a complexity assumption: that iO$(C_0)$ is indistinguishable from iO$(C_1)$. iO then is really a *collection* of exponentially-many assumptions made simultaneously, one per pair of equivalent circuits. iO is violated if *a single* assumption in the collection is false. This is a serious issue, as the security of many obfuscators relies on new assumptions that essentially match the schemes. To gain confidence in the security of the schemes, it would seem like we need to investigate the iO assumption for every possible pair of circuits, which is clearly infeasible.

Progress has been made toward remedying this issue. Indeed, Gentry et al. [GLSW15] show how to build obfuscation from a single assumption—multilinear subgroup elimination—on multilinear maps. Unfortunately, the security reduction loses a factor exponential in the number of input bits to the program. As such, in order for the reduction to be meaningful, the multilinear subgroup elimination problem must actually be *sub-exponentially* hard. Similarly, Bitansky and Vaikuntanathan [BV15] and Ananth and Jain [AJ15] demonstrate how to construct iO from a tool called functional encryption (FE).

---

[1] With additional mild assumptions such as the existence of one-way functions.

In turn, functional encryption can be based on simple assumptions on multilinear maps [GGHZ16]. However, while the construction of functional encryption can be based on the polynomial hardness of just a couple multilinear map assumptions, the construction of iO from FE incurs an exponential loss. This means the FE scheme, and hence the underlying assumptions on multilinear maps, still need to be *sub-exponentially* secure.

All current techniques for building iO suffer one of these two limitations: either security is based on an exponential number of assumptions, or the reduction incurs an exponential loss. Unfortunately, this means every application of iO also suffers from the same limitations. As iO is the only known instantiation of many new cryptographic applications, an important research direction is to devise new instantiations that avoid this exponential loss.

### 1.2   Breaking the Sub-exponential Barrier

A recent line of works starting with Garg et al. [GPS16] and continued by [GPSZ16, GS16] have shown how to break the sub-exponential barrier for certain applications. Specifically, these works show how to base certain applications on functional encryption, where the loss of the reduction is just polynomial. Using [GGHZ16], this results in basing the applications on the polynomial hardness of a few multilinear map assumptions. The idea behind these works is to compose the FE-to-iO conversion of [BV15, AJ15] with the iO-to-Application conversion to get an FE-to-Application construction. While this construction requires an exponential loss (due to the FE-to-iO conversion), by specializing the conversion to the particular application and tweaking things appropriately, the reduction can be accomplished with a polynomial loss. Applications treated in this way include: the hardness of computing Nash equilibria, trapdoor permutations, universal samplers, multiparty non-interactive key exchange, and multi-key functional encryption[2].

While the above works represent important progress, the downside is that, in order to break the sub-exponential barrier, they also break the convenient obfuscation abstraction. Both the FE-to-iO and iO-to-Application conversions are non-trivial, and the FE-to-iO conversion is moreover non-black box. Add to that the extra modifications to make the combined FE-to-Application conversion be polynomial, and the resulting constructions and analyses become reasonably cumbersome. This makes translating the techniques to new applications rather tedious—not to mention potentially repetitive given the common FE-to-iO core—and understanding the limits of this approach almost impossible.

### 1.3   A New Abstraction: Decomposable Obfuscation

In this work, we define a new notion of obfuscation, called *Decomposable Obfuscation*, or dO, that addresses the limitations above. This notion abstracts away

---

[2] The kind of functional encryption that is used as a starting point only allows for a single secret key query.

many of the common techniques in [GPS16, GPSZ16, GS16]; we use those techniques to build dO from the *polynomial* hardness of functional encryption. Then we can show that the dO can be used to build the various applications. With our new notion in hand, the dO-to-Application constructions begin looking much more like the original iO-to-Application constructions, with easily identifiable modifications that are necessary to prove security using our weaker notion.

## The Idea

*Functional Encryption (FE).* As in the works of [GPS16, GPSZ16, GS16], we will focus on obtaining our results from the starting point of polynomially-secure functional encryption. Functional encryption is similar to regular public key encryption, except now the secret key holder can produce function keys corresponding to arbitrary functions. Given a function key for a function $f$ and a ciphertext encrypting $m$, one can learn $f(m)$. Security requires that even given the function key for $f$, encryptions of $m_0$ and $m_1$ are indistinguishable, so long as $f(m_0) = f(m_1)^3$.

*The FE-to-iO Conversion.* The FE-to-iO conversions of [BV15, AJ15] can be thought of very roughly as follows. To obfuscate a circuit $C$, we generate the keys for an FE scheme, and encrypt the description of $C$ under the FE scheme's public key, obtaining $c$. We also produce function keys $\mathsf{fk}_i$ for particular functions $f_i$ that we will describe next. The obfuscated program consists of $c$ and the $\mathsf{fk}_i$.

To evaluate the program on input $x$, we first use $\mathsf{fk}_1$ and $c$ to learn $f_1(C)$. $f_1(C)$ is defined to produce two ciphertexts $c_0, c_1$, encrypting $(C, 0)$ and $(C, 1)$, respectively. We keep $c_{x_1}$, discarding the other ciphertext. Now, we actually define $\mathsf{fk}_1$ to encrypt $(C, 0)$ and $(C, 1)$ using the functional encryption scheme itself—therefore, we can continue applying function keys to the resulting plaintexts. We use $\mathsf{fk}_2$ and $c_{x_1}$ to learn $f_2(C, x_1)$. $f_2(C, b)$ is defined to produce two ciphertexts $c_{b0}, c_{b1}$, encrypting $(C, b0)$ and $(C, b1)$. Again, these ciphertexts will be encrypted using the functional encryption scheme. We will repeat this process until we obtain the encryption $c_x$ of $(C, x)$. Finally, we apply the last function key for the function $f_{n+1}$, which is the universal circuit evaluating $C(x)$.

This procedure implicitly defines a complete binary tree of all strings of length at most $2^n$, where a string $x$ is the parent of the two string $x\|0$ and $x\|1$. At each node $y \in \{0, 1\}^{\leq n}$, consider running the evaluation above for the first $|y|$ steps, obtaining a ciphertext $c_y$ encrypting $(C, y)$. We then assign the circuit $C$ to the node $y$, according the circuit that is encrypted in $c_y$. The root is *explicitly* assigned $C$ by handing out the ciphertext $c$ since we explicitly encrypt $C$ to obtain $c$. All subsequent nodes are *implicitly* assigned $C$ as $c_y$ is derived from $c$ during evaluation time. Put another way, by explicitly assigning a circuit $C$ to a node (in this case, the root) we implicitly assign the same circuit $C$ to

---

[3] The two encryptions would clearly be distinguishable if $f(m_0) \neq f(m_1)$ just by decrypting using the secret function key. Thus, this is the best one can hope for with an indistinguishability-type definition.

all of its descendants. The exception is the leaves: if we were to assign a circuit $C$ to a leaf $x$, we instead assign the output $C(x)$. In this way, the leaves contain the truth table for $C$.

Now, we start from an obfuscation of $C_0$ (assigning $C_0$ to the root of the tree) and we wish to change the obfuscation to an obfuscation of $C_1$ (assigning $C_1$ to the root). We cannot do this directly, but the functional encryption scheme does allow us to do the following: un-assign a circuit $C$ from any internal node $y$[4], and instead *explicitly* assign $C$ to the two children of that node. This is accomplished by changing $c_y$ to encrypt $(\perp, x)$, explicitly constructing the ciphertexts $c_{y\|0}$ and $c_{y\|1}$, and embedding $c_{y\|0}, c_{y\|1}$ in the function key $\mathsf{fk}_{|y|}$ in a particular way. If the children are leaves, explicitly assign the outputs of $C$ on those leaves. Note that this process does not change the values assigned to the leaves; as such, the functionality of the tree remains unchanged, so this change cannot be detected by functionality alone. The security of functional encryption shows that, in fact, the change is undetectable to any polynomial-time adversary.

The security reduction works by performing a depth-first traversal of the binary tree. When processing a node $y$ on the way down the tree, we un-assign $C_0$ from $y$ and instead explicitly assign $C_0$ to the children of $y$. When we get to a leaf, notice that by functional equivalence, we actually simultaneously have the output of $C_0$ and $C_1$ assigned. Therefore, when processing a node $y$ on our way up the tree from the leaves, we can perform the above process in reverse but for $C_1$ instead of $C_0$. We can un-assign $C_1$ from the children of $y$, and then explicitly assign $C_1$ to $y$. In this way, when the search is complete, we explicitly assign $C_1$ to the root, which implicitly assigns $C_1$ to all nodes in the tree. At this point, we are obfuscating $C_1$. By performing a depth-first search, we ensure that the number of explicitly assigned nodes never exceeds $n + 1$, which is crucial for the efficiency of the obfuscator, as we pay for explicit assignments (since they correspond to explicit ciphertexts embedded in the function keys) but not implicit ones (since they are computed on the fly). Note that while the obfuscator itself is polynomial, the number of steps in the proof is exponential: we need to un-assign and re-assign every internal node in the tree, which are exponential in number. This is the source of the exponential loss.

*Shortcutting the Conversion Process.* The key insight in the works of [GPS16, GPSZ16, GS16] is to modify the constructions in a way so that it is possible to re-assign certain internal nodes in a single step, without having to re-assign all of its descendants. By doing this it is possible to shortcut our way across an exponential number of steps using just a few steps.

In these prior works, the process is different for each application. In this work, we generalize the conditions needed for and the process of shortcutting in a very natural way. To see how shortcutting might work, we introduce a slightly different version of the above assignment setting. Like before, every node can be assigned a circuit. However, now the circuit assigned to a node $u$ of length $k$ must work on inputs of length $n - k$; essentially, it is the circuit that is "left

---

[4] By assigning $\perp$ instead, which does *not* propagate down the tree.

over" after reading the first $k$ bits and which operates on the remaining $n - k$ bits.

If we explicitly assign a circuit $C_y$ to a node $y$, its children are implicitly assigned the *partial evaluations* of $C_y$ on 0 and 1. That is, the circuit $C_{y||b}$ assigned to $y||b$ is $C_y(b, \cdot)$. We will actually use $C_y(b, \cdot)$ to denote the circuit obtained by hard-coding $b$ as the first input bit, and then simplifying using simple rules: (1) any unary gate with a constant input wire is replaced with an appropriate input wire, (2) any binary gate with a constant input is replaced with just a unary gate (a passthrough or a NOT) or a hardwired output according to the usual rules, (3) any wire that is not used is deleted, and (4) this process is repeated until there are no gates with hardwired inputs and no unused wires. An important observation is that our rules guarantee that circuits assigned to leaves are always constants, corresponding to the output of the circuit at that point.

Now when we obfuscate by assigning $C$ to the root, the internal nodes are implicitly assigned the simplified partial evaluations of $C$ on the prefix corresponding to that node: node $y$ is assigned $C(y, \cdot)$ (simplified). The move we are allowed to make is now to un-assign $C$ from a node where $C$ was explicit, and instead explicitly assign the simplified circuits $C(0, \cdot)$ and $C(1, \cdot)$ to its children. We call the partial evaluations $C(0, \cdot)$ and $C(1, \cdot)$ *fragments* of $C$, and we call this process of un-assigning the parent and assigning the fragments to the children *decomposing* the node to its children fragments. The reverse of decomposing is *merging*.

This simple transformation to the binary tree rules allows for, in some instances, the necessary shortcutting to avoid an exponential loss. When transforming $C_0$ to $C_1$, the crucial observation is that if any fragment $C_0(x, \cdot)$ is equal to $C_1(x, \cdot)$ *as circuits* (after simplification), it suffices to stop when we explicitly assign a circuit to $x$; we do not need to continue all the way down to the leaves. Indeed, once we explicitly assign the fragment $C_0(y, \cdot)$ to a node $y$, $y$ already happens to be assigned the fragment $C_1(y, \cdot)$ as well, and all of its descendants are therefore implicitly assigned the corresponding partial evaluations of $C_1$ as well. By not traversing all the way to the leaves, we cut out potentially exponentially many steps. For certain circuit pairs, it may therefore be possible to transform $C_0$ to $C_1$ in only polynomially-many steps.

*Our New Obfuscation Notion.* Our new obfuscation notion stems naturally from the above discussion. Consider two circuits $C_0, C_1$ of the same size, and consider assigning $C_0$ to the root of the binary tree. Suppose there is a set $S$ of tree nodes of size $\tau$ that (1) exactly cover all of the leaves[5], and (2) for every nodes $x \in S$, the (simplified) fragments $C_0(y, \cdot)$ and $C_1(y, \cdot)$ are identical *as circuits*. Then we say the circuits $C_0, C_1$ are $\tau$-decomposing equivalent. Our new obfuscation notion, called *decomposable obfuscation*, is parameterized by $\tau$ and says, roughly, that the obfuscations of two $\tau$-decomposing equivalent circuits must be indistinguishable.

---

[5] In the sense that for each leaf, the path from root to leaf contains exactly one element in $S$.

## 1.4 Our Results

Our results are as follows:

- We show how to use (compact, single key) functional encryption to attain our notion of dO. The construction is similar to the FE-to-iO conversion, with the key difference that each step simplifies the circuit as must as possible; this implements the new tree rules we need for shortcutting.

  The number of steps in the process of converting $C_0$ to $C_1$, and hence the loss in the security reduction is proportional to $\tau$. However, we show that by performing the decompose/merge steps in the right order, we can make sure the number of explicitly assigned nodes is always at most $n + 1$, independent of $\tau$. This means the obfuscator itself does not depend on $\tau$, and therefore $\tau$ can be taken to be an arbitrary polynomial or even exponential and the obfuscator will still be efficient. If we restrict $\tau$ to a polynomial, we obtain dO from polynomially secure FE. Our results also naturally generalize to larger $\tau$: we obtain dO for quasipolynomial $\tau$ from quasipolynomially secure FE, and we obtain dO for exponential $\tau$ from (sub)exponentially secure FE.

- We note that by setting $\tau$ to be $2^n$, $\tau$-decomposing equivalence corresponds to standard functional equivalence, since we can take the set $S$ of nodes to consist of all leaf nodes. Then dO coincides with the usual notion of indistinguishability obfuscation, giving us iO from sub-exponential FE. This re-derives the results of [BV15, AJ15]. In our reduction, the loss is $O(2^n)$.

- We then show how to obtain several applications of obfuscation from dO with *polynomial* $\tau$. Thus, for all these applications, we obtain the application from the polynomial hardness of FE, re-deriving several known results. In these applications, there is a single input, or perhaps several inputs, for which the computation must be changed from using the original circuit to using a hard-coded value. This is easily captured by decomposing equivalence: by decomposing each node from the root to the leaf for a particular input $x$, the result is that that the program's output on $x$ is hard-coded into the obfuscation. Applications include:
  - Proving the hardness of finding Nash equilibria (in the full version [LZ17]; Nash hardness from FE was originally shown in [GPS16])
  - Trapdoor Permutations (originally shown in [GPSZ16])
  - Universal Samplers (Sect. 3.3; originally shown in [GPSZ16])
  - Short Signatures (Sect. 3.2; not previously known from functional encryption, though known from obfuscation [SW14])
  - Multi-key functional encryption (in the full version [LZ17]; originally shown in [GS16])

  We note that Nash, universal samplers, and short signatures only require (polynomially hard) dO and one-way functions. In contrast, trapdoor permutations and multi-key functional encryption both additionally require public key encryption. If basing the application on public key functional encryption, this assumption is redundant. However, unlike the case for full-fledged iO, we do not know how to obtain public key functional encryption from just polynomially hard dO and one-way functions (more on this below). We do show that a weaker multi-key *secret key* functional encryption scheme does follow from dO and one-way functions.

Thus, we unify the techniques underlying many of the applications of FE—namely iO, Nash, trapdoor permutations, universal samplers, short signatures, and multi-key FE—under a single concept, dO. The constructions and proofs starting from dO are much simpler than the original proofs using functional encryption, due to the convenient dO abstraction hiding many of the common details. We hope that dO will also serve as a starting point for further constructions based on polynomially-hard assumptions.

## 1.5   Discussion

A natural question to ask is: what are the limits of these techniques? Could they be used to give full iO from polynomially-hard assumptions? Or at least all known applications from polynomial hardness? Here, we discuss several difficulties that arise.

*Difficulties in Breaking the Sub-exponential Barrier.* First, exponential loss may be inherent to constructing iO. Indeed, the following informal argument is adapted from Garg et al. [GGSW13]. Suppose we can prove iO from a single fixed assumption. This means that for every pair of equivalent circuits $C_0, C_1$, we prove under this assumption that $iO(C_0)$ is indistinguishable from $iO(C_1)$. Fix two circuits $C_0, C_1$, and consider the proof for those circuits. If $C_0$ is equivalent to $C_1$, then the proof succeeds. However, if $C_0$ is *not* equivalent to $C_1$, then the proof *must* fail: let $x$ be a point such that $C_0(x) \neq C_1(x)$. Then a simple adversary with $x$ hard-coded can distinguish $iO(C_0)$ from $iO(C_1)$ simply by running the obfuscated program on $x$.

This intuitively means that the proof must some how decide whether $C_0$ and $C_1$ are equivalent. Since the proof consists of an *efficient* algorithm $R$ reducing breaking the assumption to distinguishing $iO(C_0)$ from $iO(C_1)$, it seems that $R$ must be efficiently deciding circuit equivalence. Assuming $P \neq NP$, such a reduction should not exist.[6]

The reductions from iO to functional encryption/simple multilinear map assumptions avoid this argument by not being efficient. Indeed, the reductions traverse the entire tree of $2^n$ nodes as described above. In essence, the proof in each step just needs to check a local condition such as $C_0(x) = C_1(x)$ for some

---

[6] One may wonder whether the same arguments apply to the seemingly similar setting of zero knowledge, where zero knowledge must hold for true instances, but soundness must hold for false instances. The crucial difference is that soundness does not prevent the zero knowledge simulator from working on false instances. Therefore, a reduction from a hard problem to zero knowledge does not need to determine whether the instance is in the language. In contrast, for iO, the security property must apply to equivalent circuits, but correctness implies that it *cannot* apply to inequivalent circuits.

particular $x$—which can be done efficiently—as opposed to checking equivalence for all inputs.

While this argument is far from a proof of impossibility, it does represent an significant inherent difficulty in building full-fledged iO from polynomial hardness. We believe that overcoming this barrier, or showing that it is insurmountable, is an important and fascinating open question. For example, imagine translating the arguments above to iO for computational models with unbounded input lengths such as Turing machines. In this case, equivalence is not only inefficient, but *undecidable*. As such, the above arguments demonstrate a barrier to basing Turing machine obfuscation on a finite number of even (sub)exponentially hard assumptions. An important open question is whether it is possible to build iO from Turing machines from iO for circuits; we believe achieving this goal will likely require techniques that can also be used to overcome the sub-exponential barrier.

For the remainder of the discussion, we will assume that building iO from polynomial hardness is beyond reach without significant breakthroughs.

*Avoiding the Barrier.* We observe that poly-decomposing equivalence is an $NP$ relation: the polynomial-sized set of nodes where the fragments are identical provides a witness that two circuits are equivalent: it is straightforward to check that a collection of nodes covers all of the leaves and that the fragments at those nodes are identical. In contrast, general circuit equivalence is *co-NP*-complete, and therefore unlikely to be in $NP$ unless the polynomial hierarchy collapses. This distinction is exactly what allows us to avoid the sub-exponential barrier.

Our security reduction has access to the witness for equivalence, which guides how the reduction operates. The reduction can use the witness to trivially verify that the two circuits are equivalent; if the witness is not supplied or is invalid, the reduction does not run. The sub-exponential barrier therefore no longer applies in this setting.

More generally, the sub-exponential barrier will not apply to circuit pairs for which there is a witness proving equivalence; in other words, languages of circuit pairs in $NP \cap co\text{-}NP$[7]. Any languages outside $NP \cap co\text{-}NP$ are likely to run into the same sub-exponential barrier as full iO since witnesses for equivalence do not exist, and meanwhile there remains some hope that languages inside might be obfuscatable without a sub-exponential loss by feeding the witness to the reduction.

In fact, almost all applications of obfuscation we are aware of can be modified so that the pairs of circuits in question have a witness proving equivalence. For example, consider obtaining public key encryption from one-way functions using obfuscation [SW14]. The secret key is the seed $s$ for a PRG, and the public key is the corresponding output $x$. A ciphertext encrypting message $m$ is an obfuscation of the program $P_{x,m}$, which takes as input a seed $s'$ and checks that $\mathsf{PRG}(s') = x$. If the check fails, it aborts and outputs 0. Otherwise if the check

---

[7] Circuit equivalence is trivially in *co-NP*; a point on which the two circuits differ is a witness that they are not equivalent.

passes, it outputs $m$. To decrypt using $s$, simply evaluate obfuscated program on $s$.

In the security proof, iO is used for the following two programs: $P_{x,m}$ where $x$ *is a truly random element in the co-domain of* PRG, and $Z$, the trivial program that always outputs 0. We note that since PRG is expanding, with high probability $x$ will not have a pre-image, and therefore $P_{x,m}$ will also output 0 everywhere. Therefore, $P_{x,m}$ and $Z$ are (with high probability) functionally equivalent.

For general PRGs, there is no witness for equivalence of these two programs. However, by choosing the right PRG, we can remedy this. Let $P$ be a one-way permutation, and let $h$ be a hardcore bit for $P$. Now let $\mathsf{PRG}(s) = (P(s), h(s))$. Instead of choosing $x$ randomly, we choose $x$ as $P(s), 1 \oplus h(s)$ for a random seed $s^8$. This guarantees that $x$ has no pre-image under PRG. Moreover, $s$ serves as a witness that $x$ has no pre-image. Therefore, the programs $P_{x,m}$ and $Z$ have a witness for equivalence.

*Limits of the dO Approach.* Unfortunately, decomposable obfuscation is not strong enough to prove security in many settings. In fact, we demonstrate (Sect. 4) that $\tau$-decomposing equivalence can be decided in time proportional to $\tau$, meaning poly-decomposing equivalence is actually in $P$. However, for example, the equivalence of programs $P_{x,m}$ and $Z$ above cannot possibly be in $P$— otherwise we could break the PRG: on input $x$, check if $P_{x,m}$ is equivalent to $Z$. A random output will yield equivalence with probability $1/2$, whereas a PRG sample will never yield equivalence circuits. In other words, $P_{x,m}$ and $Z$ are provably *not* poly-decomposing equivalent, despite being functionally equivalent programs.

One can also imagine generalizing dO to encompass more general paths through the binary tree of prefixes. For example, one could decompose the circuit into fragments, partially merge some of the fragments back together, decompose again, etc. We show that this seemingly more general *path* decomposing equivalence is in fact equivalent to (standard) decomposing equivalence. Therefore, this path dO is equivalent to (standard) dO, and only works for pairs of circuits that can be easily verified as equivalent.

Unsurprisingly then, all the applications we obtain using poly-decomposable obfuscation obfuscate circuits for which it is easy to verify equivalence. This presents some interesting limitations relative to iO:

- All known ways of getting public key encryption from iO and one-way functions suffer from a similar problem, and cannot to our knowledge be based on poly-dO. In other words, unlike iO, dO might not serve as a bridge between Minicrypt and Cryptomania. Some of our applications—namely multi-key functional encryption and trapdoor permutations—imply public key encryption; for these applications, we actually have to use public key encryption as an additional ingredient. Note that if we are instantiating dO from functional

---

[8] This is no longer a random element in the codomain of the PRG, but it suffices for the security proof.

encryption, we get public key encryption for free. However, if we are interested in placing dO itself in the complexity landscape, the apparent inability to give public key encryption is an interesting barrier.

More generally, a fascinating question is whether any notion of obfuscation that works only for efficiently-recognizable equivalent circuits can imply public key encryption, assuming additionally just one-way functions.

- While iO itself does not imply one-way functions[9], iO can be used in conjunction with a worst-case complexity assumption, roughly $NP \not\subseteq BPP$, to obtain one-way functions [KMN+14]. The proof works by using a hypothetical inverter to solve the circuit equivalence problem; assuming the circuit equivalence problem is hard, they reach a contradiction. The solver works exactly because iO holds for the equivalent circuits.

  This strategy simply does not work in the context of dO. Indeed, dO only applies to circuits for which equivalence is easily decidable anyway, meaning no contradiction is reached. In order to obtain any results analogous to [KMN+14] for restricted obfuscation notions, the notion must always work for at least some collection of circuit pairs for which circuit equivalence is hard to decide. Put another way, dO could potentially exist in Pessiland.

- More generally, dO appears to roughly capture the most general form of the techniques in [GPS16,GPSZ16,GS16], and therefore it appears that these techniques will not extend to the case of non-efficiently checkable equivalence. Many constructions using obfuscation fall in this category of non-checkable equivalence: deniable encryption and non-interactive zero knowledge [SW14], secure function evaluation with optimal communication complexity [HW15], adaptively secure universal samples [HJK+16], and more.

We therefore leave some interesting open questions:

- Build iO for a class of circuit pairs for which equivalence is not checkable in polynomial time, but for which security can be based on the polynomial hardness of just a few assumptions.
- Modify the constructions in deniable encryption/NIZK/function evaluation/etc so that obfuscation is only ever applied on program pairs for which equivalence can be easily verified—ideally, the circuits would be decomposing equivalent.
- Prove that for some applications, obfuscation *must* be applied to program pairs with non-efficiently checkable equivalence.

## 2   Decomposing Equivalence and dO Definitions

In this section, we define several basic definitions including decomposing equivalence and dO.

---

[9] If $P = NP$, one-way functions do not exist but circuit minimization can be used to obfuscate.

## 2.1 Partial Evaluation on Circuits

**Definition 1.** *Consider a circuit $C$ defined on inputs of length $n > 0$, for any bit $b \in \{0,1\}$, a **partial evaluation** of $C$ on **bit** $b$ denoted as $C(b, \cdot)$ is a circuit defined on inputs of length $n - 1$, where we hardcode the input bit $x_1$ to $b$, and then simplify. To simplify, while there is a gate that has a hard-coded input, replace it with the appropriate gate or wire in the usual way (e.g. $\mathsf{AND}(1, b)$ gets replaced with the pass-through wire $b$, and $\mathsf{AND}(0, b)$ gets replaced with the constant $0$). Then remove all unused wires.*

*Also we can define a partial evaluation of a circuit $C$ on a **string** $x$ which is repeatedly applying partial evaluations and simplifying bit by bit.*

From now on, whenever we use the expression $C(x, \cdot)$, we always refer to the result of simplifying $C$ after hardcoding the prefix $x$.

## 2.2 Circuit Assignments

A binary tree $T_n$ is a tree of depth $n + 1$ where the root is labeled $\varepsilon$ (an empty string), and for any node that is not a root whose parent is labeled as $x$, it is labeled $x||0$ if it is a left-child of its parent; it is labeled as $x||1$ if it is a right-child of its parent.

**Definition 2 (Tree Covering).** *We say a set of binary strings $\{x_i\}_{i=1}^{\ell}$ is a **tree covering** for all strings of length $n$ if the following holds: for every string $x \in \{0,1\}^n$, there exists exactly one $x_j$ in the set such that $x_j$ is a prefix of $x$.*

*A tree covering $\{x_i\}_{i=1}^{\ell}$ also can be viewed as a set of nodes in $T_n$ such that for every leaf in the tree, the path from root $\varepsilon$ to this leaf will pass exactly one node in the set.*

*Yet another equivalent formulation is that a tree covering is either (1) a set consisting of the root node of the tree, or (2) the union of two tree coverings for the two subtrees rooted at the children of the root node.*

**Definition 3 (Circuit Assignment).** *We say $L = \{(x_i, C_{x_i})\}_{i=1}^{\ell}$ is a **circuit assignment** with size $\ell$ where $\{x_i\}_{i=1}^{\ell}$ is a tree covering for $T_n$ and $\{C_{x_i}\}_{i=1}^{\ell}$ is a set of circuits where $C_{x_i}$ is assigned to the node $x_i$ in the covering.*

*We say a circuit assignment is valid if for each $C_{x_i}$, it is defined on input length $n - |x_i|$.*

*An evaluation of $L$ on input $x$ is defined as: find the unique $x_j$ which is a prefix of $x = x_j||x_{-j}$ and return $C_{x_j}(x_{-j})$.*

*We call each circuit in the assignment a **fragment**. The **cardinality** of the circuit assignment is the size of the tree covering, and the **circuit size** is the maximum size of any fragment in the assignment.*

A circuit assignment $L = \{(x_i, C_{x_i})\}_{i=1}^{\ell}$ naturally corresponds to a function: on input $y \in \{0,1\}^n$, scan the prefix of $y$ from left to right until we find the smallest $i$ such that $y_{[i]}$ equals to some $x_j$, output $C_{x_j}(y_{[i+1\cdots n]})$. We will override the notation and write this function as $L(x)$.

We associate a circuit $C$ with the assignment $L_C = \{(\varepsilon, C)\}$ which assigns $C$ to the root of the tree. Notice that $L_C$ and $C$ are equivalent as functions.

**Definition 4 (one shot decomposing equivalent).** *Given two circuits $C_0, C_1$ defined on inputs of length $n$, we say they are $\tau$-one shot decomposing equivalent or simply $\tau$-decomposing equivalent if the following hold:*

- *There exists a tree covering $\mathcal{X} = \{x_i\}_i$ of size at most $\tau$;*
- *For all $x_i \in \mathcal{X}$, $C_0(x_i, \cdot) = C_1(x_i, \cdot)$ as circuits (they are exactly the same circuit).*

**Definition 5.** dO *with two PPT algorithms* {dO.ParaGen, dO.Eval} *is a $\tau(n, s, \kappa)$-decomposing obfuscator if the following conditions hold*

- **Efficiency:** dO.ParaGen, dO.Eval *are efficient algorithms;*
- **Functionality preserving:** dO.ParaGen *takes as input a security parameter $\kappa$ and a circuit $C$, and outputs the description $\hat{C}$ of an obfuscated program. For all $\kappa$ and all circuit $C$, for all input $x \in \{0,1\}^n$, we have* dO.Eval(dO.ParaGen($1^\kappa, C$), $x$) $= C(x)$;
- **Decomposing indistinguishability:** *Consider a pair of PPT adversaries (Samp, D) where Samp outputs a tuple $(C_0, C_1, \sigma)$ where $C_0, C_1$ are circuits of the same size $s = s(\kappa)$ and input length $n = n(\kappa)$. We require that, for any such PPT (Samp, D), if*

$$\Pr[C_0 \text{ is } \tau\text{-decomposing equivalent to } C_1 : (C_0, C_1, \sigma) \leftarrow Samp(\kappa)] = 1$$

*then there exists a negligible function negl($\kappa$) such that*

$$|\Pr[D(\sigma, \mathsf{dO.ParaGen}(1^\kappa, C_0)) = 1]$$
$$- \Pr[D(\sigma, \mathsf{dO.ParaGen}(1^\kappa, C_1)) = 1]| \leq \mathsf{negl}(\kappa)$$

Note that the size of parameters generated by dO.ParaGen is bounded by poly($n, \kappa, \tau, |C|$). But however you will see later that $\tau$ can always be replaced by $n$ so even if $\tau = \Omega(2^n)$, the size is still bounded by poly($n, \kappa, |C|$) (but you will have $\tau$-loss in the security analysis).

And in the next section we will discuss about the applications of dO and later come back to more discussions about dO including constructions and relations between different iO.

## 3   Applications

### 3.1   Notations

Before all the applications, let us first introduce several definitions for convenience.

First let us look at some operations defined on circuits (or circuit assignments).

1. Decompose($L, x$) takes a circuit assignment $L$ and a string $x$ as parameters. This operation is invalid if $x$ is not in the tree covering. The new circuit assignment has a slightly different tree covering: the new tree covering includes $x||0$ and $x||1$ but not $x$. It decomposes the fragment $C_x$ into two fragments $C_x(0, \cdot)$ and $C_x(1, \cdot)$ and assigns them to $x||0$ and $x||1$ respectively.

2. CanonicalMerge($L, x$) operates on an assignment $L$ where the tree covering includes both children of node $x$ but not $x$ itself. It takes two circuits $C_{x||0}, C_{x||1}$ assigned to the node $x||0$ and $x||1$ and merge them to get the following circuit $C_x(b, y) = (b \wedge C_{x||0}(y)) \vee (\overline{b} \wedge C_{x||1}(y))$ (Here we assume the output length of both circuits is 1. It is straightforward to extend the definition to circuits with any output length). The new tree covering has $x$ but not $x||0$ or $x||1$.

   One observation is that for any circuit assignment whose tree covering has $x||0$ and $x||1$ but not $x$ and $C_{x||0}, C_{x||1}$ can not be simplified any further, Decompose(CanonicalMerge($L, x$), $x$) = $L$.

3. DecomposeTo($L, TC$): It takes a circuit assignment $L$ (if the first parameter is a circuit $C$, then $L = \{(C, \varepsilon)\}$) and a tree covering $TC$ where $TC$ is below the covering in $L$. This procedure keeps taking the lexicographically first circuit fragment $C_x$ which $x$ is not in $TC$ and do Decompose($L, x$). Because the covering in $L$ is above $TC$, the procedure halts when the covering in the new circuit assignment is exactly $TC$.

   We can also define DecomposeTo($L, x$) = DecomposeTo($L, TC_x$) where $TC_x$ is a tree covering that consists all the nodes adjacent to the path from root to node $x$, in other words, $TC_x = \{\neg x_1, x_1 \neg x_2, x_1 x_2 \neg x_3, \cdots, x_{|x|-1} \neg x_{|x|}, x\}$ (a full description is in Sect. 4).

4. CanonicalMerge($L$): it canonically merges all the way to the root. In other words, the procedure keeps taking the lexicographically first circuit fragment pair $C_{x||0}$ and $C_{x||1}$ and doing CanonicalMerge($L, x$) until the tree covering in the circuit assignment is $\{\varepsilon\}$, in other words, it becomes a single circuit.

Note that the functionality of a circuit assignment is preserved under applying any valid operation above.

   We now define an decomposing compatible pseudo random function. The construction [GGM86] automatically satisfies the definition below.

**Definition 6.** *An decomposing compatible pseudo random function* DPRF *consists the following algorithms* DPRF.KeyGen *and* DPRF.Eval *where*

- DPRF.Eval *takes a input of length $n$ and the output is of length $p(n)$ where $p$ is a fixed polynomial;*
- *(PRF **Security**). For any poly sized adversary $\mathcal{A}$, there exists a negligible function* negl, *for any string $y_0 \in \{0,1\}^n$ and any $\kappa$,*

$$|\Pr[\mathcal{A}(\text{DPRF.Eval}(S, y_0)) = 1] - \Pr[\mathcal{A}(r) = 1]| \leq \text{negl}(\kappa)$$

*where $S \leftarrow$ DPRF.KeyGen($1^\kappa$) and $r \in \{0,1\}^{p(n)}$ is a uniformly random string.*

- *(EPRF **Security**). Consider the following game, let* Game$_{\kappa, \mathcal{A}, b}$ *be*
  - *The challenger prepares $S \leftarrow$ DPRF.KeyGen($1^\kappa$);*
  - *The adversary makes queries about $x$ and gets DPRF.Eval($S, x$) back from the challenger;*
  - *The adversary gives a tree covering $TC$ and $y^* \in TC$ to the challenger where $y^*$ is not a prefix of any $x$ that has been asked;*

- *The challenger sends the distribution $D_b$ back to the adversary $\mathcal{A}$ where*
  * $D_0$: *let the circuit $D$ to be $D(\cdot)$ = DPRF.Eval$(S, \cdot)$ defined on $\{0,1\}^n$, the circuit assignment is DecomposeTo$(D, TC)$. We observe that the fragment corresponding to $y$ is DPRF.Eval$(S, y, \cdot)$ defined on $\{0,1\}^{n-|y|}$.*
  * $D_1$: *For each $y \neq y^* \in TC$, let the fragment corresponding to $y$ be $D_y(\cdot)$ = DPRF.Eval$(S, y, \cdot)$ defined on $\{0,1\}^{n-|y|}$ and for $y^*$, $D_{y^*}(\cdot)$ = DPRF.Eval$(S', y^*, \cdot)$ defined on $\{0,1\}^{n-|y^*|}$ where $S' \leftarrow$ DPRF.KeyGen$(1^\kappa)$.*
- *The adversary can keep making queries about $x$ which does not have prefix $y^*$ and gets DPRF.Eval$(S, x)$ back from the challenger;*
- *The output of this game is the output of $\mathcal{A}$.*

*For any poly sized adversary $\mathcal{A}$, there exists a negligible function* negl *such that:*

$$|\Pr[\mathsf{Game}_{\kappa, \mathcal{A}, 0} = 1] - \Pr[\mathsf{Game}_{\kappa, \mathcal{A}, 1} = 1]| \leq \mathsf{negl}(\kappa)$$

Let us define an another operation on a circuit assignment and a circuit.

**Definition 7.** *By given a circuit $C$ and a circuit assignment $L$ where $C$ takes two inputs $x$ and $L(x)$, $C(\cdot, L(\cdot))$ is a circuit assignment defined below:*

- *Let $TC$ be the tree covering inside $L = \{(x, D_x)\}_{x \in TC}$.*
- *Let $L' = $ DecomposeTo$(C, TC) = \{(x, C_x)\}_{x \in TC}$.*
- *For each fragment in the output circuit assignment corresponding to $x \in TC$, it is $C_x(\cdot, D_x(\cdot))$ simplified, which is defined on $\{0,1\}^{n-|x|}$.*

*We can also define similar operations on several circuit assignments and one circuit as long as these circuit assignments have the same tree covering. In other words, let $L_1, \cdots, L_m (L_i = \{(x, D_x^i)\})$ are circuit assignments with the same tree covering $TC$, then $C(\cdot, L_1(\cdot), L_2(\cdot), \cdots, L_m(\cdot))$ is a circuit assignment whose fragment corresponding to $y \in TC$ is $C(y, \cdot, D_y^1(\cdot), \cdots, D_y^m(\cdot))$ simplified.*

Then we have the following lemma:

**Lemma 1.** *For any two circuits $C, D$ where $D$ takes a single input $x$ and $C$ takes two inputs $x$ and $D(x)$, for any tree covering $TC$, we have*

$$\mathsf{DecomposeTo}(C(\cdot, D(\cdot)), TC) = C(\cdot, [\mathsf{DecomposeTo}(D, TC)](\cdot))$$

*For $m + 1$ circuits $C, D_1, D_2, \cdots, D_m$, where $D_1, \cdots, D_m$ take a single input $x$ and $C$ takes $x$ and $D_1(x) \cdots D_m(x)$ as inputs, we have*

$$\mathsf{DecomposeTo}(C(\cdot, D_1(\cdot), \cdots, D_m(\cdot)), TC)$$
$$= C(\cdot, \mathsf{DecomposeTo}(D_1, TC), \cdots, \mathsf{DecomposeTo}(D_m, TC))$$

**Proof.** Let us first look at the left side. It is a circuit assignment with the tree covering $TC$. For the fragment corresponding to $y \in TC$, it is the partial evaluation of $C(\cdot, D(\cdot))$ on $y$.

For the right side, we first have a circuit assignment $\mathsf{DecomposeTo}(D, TC)$ where the fragment corresponding to $y$ is $D(y, \cdot)$. So by the definition of our operation, the fragment corresponding to $y$ in the right side is $C(y, \cdot, D(y, \cdot))$ simplified.

Since each pair of fragments are the same, the left side is equal to the right side.

## 3.2  Short Signatures

Here, we show how to use $\mathsf{dO}$ to build short signatures, following [SW14]. As in [SW14], we will construct statically secure signatures.

The signature is simply of the following form $f(\mathsf{DPRF.Eval}(S, m))$ where $f$ is a one-way function.

**Definition 8.** *A signature scheme* $\mathsf{SS}$ *consists of the following algorithms:*

- $\mathsf{SS.Setup}(1^\kappa)$: *it outputs a verification key* $\mathsf{vk}$ *and a signature key* $\mathsf{sk}$;
- $\mathsf{SS.Sign}(\mathsf{sk}, m)$: *it is a deterministic procedure; it takes a signature key and a message, then outputs a signature* $\sigma$;
- $\mathsf{SS.Ver}(\mathsf{vk}, m, \sigma)$: *it is a deterministic algorithm; it takes a verification key, a message* $m$ *and a signature* $\sigma$, *it outputs* 1 *if it accepts;* 0 *otherwise.*

*We say a short signature scheme is correct if for any message* $m \in \{0, 1\}^\ell$:

$$\Pr\left[\mathsf{SS.Ver}(\mathsf{vk}, m, \sigma) = 1 \middle| \begin{array}{c} (\mathsf{vk}, \mathsf{sk}) \leftarrow \mathsf{SS.Setup}(1^\kappa) \\ \sigma \leftarrow \mathsf{SS.Sign}(\mathsf{sk}, m) \end{array}\right] = 1$$

We now define security for short signatures.

**Definition 9.** *We denote* $\mathsf{Game}_{\kappa, \mathcal{A}}$ *to be the following where* $\kappa$ *is the security parameter and* $\mathcal{A}$ *is an adversary:*

- *First* $\mathcal{A}$ *announces a message* $m^*$ *of length* $\ell$;
- *The challenger gets* $m^*$ *and prepares two keys* $\mathsf{sk}$ *and* $\mathsf{vk}$; *it then sends* $\mathsf{vk}$ *back to* $\mathcal{A}$;
- $\mathcal{A}$ *can keep making queries* $m'$ *to the challenger and gets* $\mathsf{Sign}(\mathsf{sk}, m')$ *back for any* $m' \neq m^*$;
- *Finally* $\mathcal{A}$ *sends a forged signature* $\sigma^*$ *and the output of the game is* $\mathsf{Ver}(\mathsf{vk}, m^*, \sigma^*)$.

We say $\mathsf{SS}$ is secure if for any polysized $\mathcal{A}$, there exists a negligible function $\mathsf{negl}$,

$$\Pr[\mathsf{Game}_{\kappa, \mathcal{A}} = 1] \leq \mathsf{negl}(\kappa)$$

---

**Algorithm 1.** Verification Algorithm

---

1: **procedure** $V(m, \sigma, \mathsf{DPRF.Eval}(S, m))$
2:      it computes $\sigma' \leftarrow \mathsf{DPRF.Eval}(S, m)$
3:      **if** $f(\sigma) = f(\sigma')$ **then**
4:          **return** 1
5:      **else**
6:          **return** 0
7:      **end if**
8: **end procedure**

---

**Construction.** We now give a signature scheme where signatures are short. The construction is similar with that in [SW14] but we use dO instead of iO. Our SS has the following algorithms:

- SS.Setup($1^\kappa$): it takes a security parameter $\kappa$ and prepares a key $S \leftarrow$ DPRF.KeyGen($1^\kappa$). $S$ is the secret key sk. Then it computes the verification key as vk $\leftarrow$ dO.ParaGen($1^\kappa, V(\cdot, \mathsf{DPRF.Eval}(S, \cdot))$) where $V$ is given in Algorithm 1 (we will pad programs to a length upper bound before applying dO).
- SS.Sign(sk, $m$) = DPRF.Eval($S, m$)
- SS.Ver(vk, $m, \sigma$) = dO.Eval(vk, $\{m, \sigma\}$)

It is straightforward to see that the construction satisfies correctness.

**Security**

**Theorem 1.** *If* dO *is a secure* poly-dO, DPRF *is a secure decomposing compatible* PRF, *and* $f$ *is a one-way function, then the construction above is a short secure signature scheme.*

**Proof.** Now prove security through a sequence of hybrid experiments.

- **Hyb 0:** In this hybrid, we are in $\mathsf{Game}_{\kappa, \mathcal{A}}$;
- **Hyb 1:** In this hybrid, since the challenger gets $m^*$ before it releases vk, we decompose the circuit to get $L = \mathsf{DecomposeTo}(V(\cdot, \mathsf{DPRF.}$ $\mathsf{Eval}(S, \cdot)), m^*)$. By Lemma 1, the circuit assignment is $V(\cdot, \mathsf{DecomposeTo}$ $(\mathsf{DPRF.Eval}(S, \cdot), m^*))$.
  Therefore we have that the distributions dO.ParaGen($1^\kappa, V(\cdot, \mathsf{DPRF.Eval}$ $(S, \cdot))$) and dO.ParaGen($1^\kappa, \mathsf{CanonicalMerge}(L)$) are indistinguishable, since these two circuits are $\ell + 1$-decomposing equivalent by applying dO.
- **Hyb 2:** This is the same as **Hyb 1**, except that we replace the fragment in DecomposeTo(DPRF.Eval($S, \cdot$), $m^*$) corresponding to $m^*$—which is "**return** DPRF.Eval($S, m^*$)"—by "**return** DPRF.Eval($S', m^*$)" where $S' \leftarrow$ DPRF.KeyGen($1^\kappa$) is a fresh random DPRF key that is independent of $S$. We call the new circuit assignment $L'$. **Hyb 1** and **Hyb 2** are indistinguishable because of the DPRF security.

- **Hyb 3:** This is the same as **Hyb 2**, except that we replace the fragment in $L'$, which is "**return** DPRF.Eval$(S', m^*)$" by "**return** $r^*$" where $r^*$ is a uniformly random string. We call the new circuit assignment $L''$. As we don't have $S'$ in the program anywhere except this fragment, **Hyb 2** and **Hyb 3** are indistinguishable because of the PRF security.

  We find that in CanonicalMerge$(L'')$, the fragment corresponding to $m^*$ is: on input $\sigma$, it returns 1 if $f(\sigma) = v^*$; 0 otherwise, where $v^* = f(r^*)$ for a uniformly random $r^*$.

**Lemma 2.** *If there exists a poly sized adversary $\mathcal{A}$ for Hyb 3, then we can break one-way function $f$.*

**Proof.** Given $z^*$ which is $f(r^*)$ for a truly random $r^*$, we can actually simulate **Hyb 3**. If we successfully find a forged signature for **Hyb 3** with non-negligible probability, it is actually a pre-image of $z^*$ which means we break one-way function with non-negligible probability.

This completes the security proof.

### 3.3 Universal Samplers

Here we construct universal samplers from dO. For the sake of simplicity, we will show how to construct samplers meeting the one-time static definition from [HJK+16]. However, note that the same techniques also can be used to construct the more complicated $k$-time interactive simulation notion of [GPSZ16].

Let US denote an universal sampler. It has the following procedures:

- params $\leftarrow$ US.Setup$(1^\kappa, 1^\ell, 1^t)$: the Setup procedure takes a security parameter $\kappa$, a program size upper bound $\ell$ and a output length $t$ and outputs an parameter params;
- US.Sample(params, $C$) is a deterministic procedure that takes a params and a sampler $C$ of length at most $\ell$ where $C$ outputs a sample of length $t$. This procedure outputs a sample $s$;
- params$'$ $\leftarrow$ US.Sim$(1^\kappa, 1^\ell, 1^t, C^*, s^*)$ takes a security parameter $\kappa$, a program size upper bound $\ell$ and a output length $t$, also a circuit $C^*$ and a sample $s^*$ in the image of $C^*$.

**Correctness.** For any $C^*$ and $s^*$ in the image of $C^*$, and for any $\ell \geq |C^*|$, and $t$ is a upper bound for $C^*$'s outputs, we have

$$\Pr\left[\text{US.Sample}(\text{params}', C^*)\right] = s^* \mid \text{params}' \leftarrow \text{US.Sim}(1^\kappa, 1^\ell, 1^t, C^*, s^*)] = 1$$

**Security.** For any $\ell$ and $t$, for any $C^*$ of size at most $\ell$ and output size at most $t$, for any poly sized adversary $\mathcal{A}$, there exists a negligible function negl, such that

$$\left| \Pr[\mathcal{A}(\text{params}, C^*) = 1 \mid \text{params} \leftarrow \text{US.Setup}(1^\kappa, 1^\ell, 1^t)] \right.$$
$$\left. - \Pr\left[\mathcal{A}(\text{params}', C^*) = 1 \mid \begin{array}{l} \text{params}' \leftarrow \text{US.Sim}(1^\kappa, 1^\ell, 1^t, C^*, s^*), \\ s^* \xleftarrow{R} C^*(\cdot) \end{array}\right] \right| \leq \text{negl}(\kappa)$$

where $s^* \underset{R}{\leftarrow} C^*(\cdot)$ means $s^*$ is a truly random sample from $C^*(\cdot)$.

**Construction.** Now we give the detailed construction for our universal sampler:

- Define $U$ to be the size upper bound among all the circuits being obfuscated in our proof (not the size of circuits fed into the universal sampler). It is straightforward to see that $U = \mathsf{poly}(\kappa, \ell, t)$; Whenever we mention dO.ParaGen($1^\kappa, C$), we will pad $C$ to have size $U$.
- For simplicity, we will assume circuits $C$ fed into the universal sampler will always be padded to length $\ell$ so that we can consider only circuits of a fixed size.
- US.Setup($1^\kappa, 1^\ell, 1^t$) randomly samples a key $S \leftarrow$ DPRF.KeyGen($1^\kappa$), and constructs a circuit Sampler (see Algorithm 2) as follows: on input circuit $C$ of size $\ell$, it outputs a sample based on the randomness generated by DPRF; and the output of the procedure US.Setup is params $=$ dO.ParaGen($1^\kappa$, Sampler($\cdot$, DPRF.Eval($S, \cdot$))).

---

**Algorithm 2.** Sampler Algorithm

1: **procedure** Sampler($C = c_1 c_2 \cdots c_\ell$, DPRF.Eval($S, C$))
2:     $r_C \leftarrow$ DPRF.Eval($S, C$)
3:     **return** $C(; r_C)$
4: **end procedure**

---

- US.Sample(params, $C$): it simply outputs dO.Eval(params, $C$);
- US.Sim($1^\kappa, 1^\ell, 1^t, C^*, s^*$): it randomly samples a key $S \leftarrow$ DPRF.KeyGen($1^\kappa$), let $L$ be a circuit assignment Sampler($\cdot$, DecomposeTo(DPRF.Eval($S, \cdot$), $C^*$)). And finally it replaces the fragment corresponding to $C^*$ in $L$ with "**return** $s^*$" instead of returning $C^*(;$ DPRF.Eval($S, C^*$)). Let Sampler$'$ $=$ CanonicalMerge($L$) and the output of US.Sim is params$'$ $=$ dO.ParaGen($1^\kappa$, Sampler$'$).

**Theorem 2.** *If* dO *and one-way functions exist, then there exists an universal sampler.*

**Proof.** First, it is straightforward that correctness is satisfied. Next we prove security. Fix a circuit $C^*$ and suppose there is an adversary $\mathcal{A}$ for the sampler security game for $C^*$. We prove the indistinguishability through a sequence of hybrids:

- **Hyb 0:** Here, the adversary receives params $\leftarrow$ US.Setup($1^\kappa, 1^\ell, 1^t$);
- **Hyb 1:** In this hybrid, let $s^* \leftarrow C^*(;$ DPRF.Eval($S, C^*$)). We get params$_1$ $\leftarrow$ US.Sim($1^\kappa, 1^\ell, 1^t, C^*, s^*$) where Sampler$_1$ is the circuit constructed in US.Sim where we are using the same $S$ in **Hyb 0**.
  It is straightforward that Sampler$_1$ and Sampler are $\ell + 1$-decomposing equivalent. Therefore params$_1$ $=$ dO.ParaGen($1^\kappa$, Sampler$_1$) and params $=$ dO.ParaGen($1^\kappa$, Sampler) are indistinguishable by dO security, meaning **Hyb 0** and **Hyb 1** are indistinguishable.

- **Hyb 2:** This is the same as **Hyb 1**, except we replace the fragment in DecomposeTo(DPRF.Eval$(S, \cdot), C^*$) corresponding to $C^*$ with the fragment "**return** DPRF.Eval$(S', C^*)$" where $S' \leftarrow$ DPRF.KeyGen$(1^\kappa)$ is a new key generated by a uniformly random string. We call the new circuit assignment $L'$. The indistinguishability between **Hyb 1** and **Hyb 2** follows from the DPRF security.
- **Hyb 3:** In this hybrid, since the fragment in $L'$ corresponding to $C^*$ is now returning $C^*(; \text{DPRF.Eval}(S', C^*))$ and we don't have $S'$ in the program, by PRF security, we can replace the return value with $C(; r^*)$ where $r^*$ is a truly random string. This is equivalent to the adversary receiving params $\leftarrow$ US.Sim$(1^\kappa, 1^\ell, 1^t, C^*, s^*)$ for a fresh sample $s^* \leftarrow C^*$.

## 4  Constructions of dO

In this section, we give more discussions about decomposing equivalence and dO. And finally we give the constructions of dO from compact functional encryption schemes.

### 4.1  New Notions of Equivalence for Circuits

We will define a partial order $\preceq$ on nodes in a binary tree. We say that $x \preceq y$ (alternatively, $x$ is **above** $y$) if $x$ is a prefix of $y$. We also extend our partial order $\preceq$ to tree coverings. We say a tree covering $TC_0 \preceq TC_1$, or $TC_0$ is **above** $TC_1$, if for every node $u$ in $TC_1$, there exists a node $v$ in $TC_0$ such that $v \preceq u$ (that is, $v$ is equal to $u$ or an ancestor of $u$). A tree covering $TC_0$ is **below** $TC_1$ if $TC_1$ is above $TC_0$. It is straightforward that if $TC_0 \preceq TC_1$, then $|TC_0| \le |TC_1|$ where $|TC_0| = |TC_1|$ if and only if $TC_0 = TC_1$. We can also extend $\preceq$ to compare tree coverings to nodes. We have $u \preceq TC$ if there is a node $v \in TC$ such that $u \preceq v$. $TC \preceq u$ if there exists a $v \in TC$ such that $v \preceq u$.

We give more operations defined on circuits and circuit assignments for convenience.

- Decompose$(L, x)$: mentioned in Sect. 3.1.
- CanonicalMerge$(L, x)$: mentioned in Sect. 3.1.
- TargetedMerge$(L, x, C)$ operates on an assignment $L$ where the tree covering includes both children of node $x$ but not $x$ itself. This operation is invalid if either $C(0, \cdot) \ne C_{x||0}$ or $C(1, \cdot) \ne C_{x||1}$ as circuits. It takes the two circuits $C_{x||0}, C_{x||1}$ assigned to the node $x||0$ and $x||1$ and merges them to get $C_x = C$. The new tree covering has $x$ but not $x||0$ or $x||1$.
  We observe that
  - Decompose(TargetedMerge$(L, x, C), x) = L$ where $C_{x||0}$ and $C_{x||1}$ in $L$ can not be simplified any further, and all the operations are valid
  - TargetedMerge(Decompose$(L, x), x, C) = L$ where $C$ is the fragment at node $x$ in $L$ (as long as the operations are valid).

– DecomposeTo($L, x$): takes a circuit assignment $L$ and a string $x$ as parameters. The operation is valid if $TC \preceq x$, where $TC$ is the tree covering for $L$. Let $u$ be ancestor of $x$ in $TC$. Let $p_0 = u, p_1, \ldots, p_t = x$ be the path from $u$ to $x$. DecomposeTo first sets $L_0 = L$, and then runs $L_i \leftarrow$ Decompose($L_{i-1}, p_{i-1}$) for $i = 1, \ldots, t$. The output is the new circuit assignment $L' = L_t$. The new tree covering $TC'$ for $L'$ is the minimal $TC'$ that is both below $TC$ and contains $x$.

We will also extend DecomposeTo to operate on circuits in addition to assignments, by first interpreting the circuit as an assignment, and performing DecomposeTo on the assignment.

– DecomposeTo($L, TC$): mentioned in Sect. 3.1.
– CanonicalMerge($L, TC$): It takes a circuit assignment $L$ and a tree covering $TC$ where $TC$ is below the covering in $L$. It repeatedly performs CanonicalMerge($L, x$) at different $x$ until the tree covering in the assignment becomes $TC$. To make the merging truly canonical, we need to specify an order that nodes are merged in. We take the convention that the lowest nodes in the tree are merged first, and between nodes in the same level, the leftmost nodes are merged first.
– CanonicalMerge($L$) = CanonicalMerge($L, \{\varepsilon\}$): mentioned in Sect. 3.1.

### 4.2   Locally, Path, One Shot Decomposing Equivalence

We define two new equivalence notions for circuits based on the decomposing and merging operations defined above. First, we define a local equivalence condition on circuit assignments:

**Definition 10 (locally decomposing equivalent).** *We say two circuit assignments* $L_1 = \{(x_i, C_{x_i})\}, L_2 = \{(y_i, C'_{y_i})\}$ *are* $(\ell, s)$*-**locally decomposing equivalent** if the following hold:*

– *The circuit size of* $L_1, L_2$ *is at most* $s$;
– *The cardinality of* $L_1, L_2$ *is at most* $\ell$;
– $L_1$ *can be obtained from* $L_2$ *by applying* Decompose($L_2, x$) *for some* $x$ *or by applying* TargetedMerge($L_2, x, C$) *for some* $x$ *and* $C$ *is the fragment assigned in* $L_1$ *to the string (node)* $x$;

Local decomposing equivalence (Local DE) means that we can transform $L_1$ into $L_2$ by making just a single local change, namely decomposing a node or merging two nodes. Notice that since decomposing a node does not change functionality, local DE implies that $L_1$ and $L_2$ compute equivalent functions. For any $\ell, s$, $(\ell, s)$-local decomposing equivalence forms a graph, where nodes are circuit assignments and edges denote local decomposing equivalence. Next, we define a notion of *path* decomposing equivalence for circuits (which can be thought of as nodes in the graph), which says that two circuits are equivalent if they are connected by a reasonably short path through the graph.

**Definition 11 (path decomposing equivalent).** *We say two circuits $C_1, C_2$ are $(\ell, s, t)$-**path decomposing equivalent** if there exists at most $t - 1$ circuit assignments $L'_1, L'_2, \cdots, L'_{t-1}$ such that, for any $1 \leq i \leq t$, $L'_{i-1}$ and $L'_i$ are $(\ell, s)$-locally decomposing equivalent, where $L'_0 = \{(\varepsilon, C_1)\}$ and $L'_t = \{(\varepsilon, C_2)\}$.*

Now let's recall the definition of one shot decomposing equivalent which allows for exactly two steps to get between $C_1$ and $C_2$. Now the steps are not confined to be local, but instead the first step is allowed to decompose the root to a given tree covering, and the second then merges the tree covering all the way back to the root.

**Recall Definition 4 (one shot decomposing equivalent).** *Given two circuits $C_0, C_1$ defined on inputs of length $n$, we say they are $\tau$-**one shot decomposing equivalent** or simply $\tau$-**decomposing equivalent** if the following hold:*

- *There exists a tree covering $\mathcal{X} = \{x_i\}_i$ of size at most $\tau$;*
- *For all $x_i \in \mathcal{X}$, $C_0(x_i, \cdot) = C_1(x_i, \cdot)$ as circuits.*

*An equivalent definition for "$\tau$-one shot decomposing equivalent" is that there exists a tree covering $\mathcal{X}$ of size at most $\tau$, such that $\mathsf{DecomposeTo}(\{(\varepsilon, C_0)\}, \mathcal{X}) = \mathsf{DecomposeTo}(\{(\varepsilon, C_1)\}, \mathcal{X})$, in other words, the tree coverings are the same and the corresponding fragments for each node are the same.*

We note that since the operations defining path and one shot decomposing equivalence all preserve functionality, we have that these notions imply standard functional equivalence for the circuits:

**Lemma 3.** *If $C_0, C_1$ are $(\ell, s, t)$-path decomposing equivalent for any $\ell, s, t$, or if $C_0, C_1$ are $\tau$-one shot decomposing equivalent for any $\tau$, then $C_0, C_1$ compute equivalent functions $(C_0(x) = C_1(x), \forall x \in \{0,1\}^n)$.*

We also observe a partial converse:

**Lemma 4.** *Two circuits $C_0, C_1$ (defined on $n$ bits string) are $2^n$-one shot decomposing equivalent if and only if they are functionally equivalent $(C_0(x) = C_1(x), \forall x \in \{0,1\}^n)$.*

**Proof.** We only need to show the case that functional equivalence implies $2^n$-one shot decomposing equivalence. If $C_0, C_1$ are functionally equivalent, we can let the tree covering be $\mathcal{X} = \{0,1\}^n$. Because $C_0(x) = C_1(x)$ for all $x \in \{0,1\}^n = \mathcal{X}$, we have $\mathsf{DecomposeTo}(\{(\varepsilon, C_0)\}, \mathcal{X}) = \mathsf{DecomposeTo}(\{(\varepsilon, C_1)\}, \mathcal{X})$. Therefore $C_0, C_1$ are $2^n$-one shot decomposing equivalent.

### 4.3   Locally, One Shot dO

Here, we will recall decomposing obfuscation (dO) and give one more definition. Let us recall the definition of dO. Decomposable obfuscator, roughly, is an indistinguishability obfuscator, but where the indistinguishability security requirement only applies to pairs of circuits that are decomposing equivalent (as opposed to applying to all equivalent circuits).

**Recall Definition 5.** dO *wtih two PPT algorithms* {dO.ParaGen, dO.Eval} *is a* $\tau(n, s, \kappa)$*-decomposable obfuscator if the following conditions hold*

- **Efficiency:** dO.ParaGen, dO.Eval *are efficient algorithms;*
- **Functionality preserving:** dO.ParaGen *takes as input a security parameter* $\kappa$ *and a circuit* $C$, *and outputs the description* $\hat{C}$ *of an obfuscated program. For all* $\kappa$ *and all circuit* $C$, *for all input* $x \in \{0,1\}^n$, *we have* dO.Eval(dO.ParaGen($1^\kappa, C$), $x$) = $C(x)$;
- **Decomposing indistinguishability:** *Consider a pair of PPT adversaries* $(Samp, D)$ *where Samp outputs a tuple* $(C_0, C_1, \sigma)$ *where* $C_0, C_1$ *are circuits of the same size* $s = s(\kappa)$ *and input length* $n = n(\kappa)$. *We require that, for any such PPT* $(Samp, D)$, *if*

$$\Pr[C_0 \text{ is } \tau(n, s, \kappa)\text{-decomposing equivalent to } C_1 : (C_0, C_1, \sigma) \leftarrow Samp(\kappa)] = 1$$

*then there exists a negligible function* negl($\kappa$) *such that*

$$|\Pr[D(\sigma, \text{dO.ParaGen}(1^\kappa, C_0)) = 1]$$
$$- \Pr[D(\sigma, \text{dO.ParaGen}(1^\kappa, C_1)) = 1]| \le \text{negl}(\kappa)$$

Since $2^n$-equivalence corresponds to standard equivalence, $2^n$-dO is equivalent to the standard notion of iO. In this work, we will usually consider a much weaker setting, where $\tau$ is restricted to a polynomial.

The following tool, called *local* dO (ldO), will be used to help us build dO. Roughly, ldO is an obfuscator for *circuit assignments* with the property that local changes to the assignment (that is, decomposing operations) are computationally undetectable.

**Definition 12.** ldO *with two PPT algorithms* {ldO.ParaGen, ldO.Eval} *is a locally decomposable obfuscator if the following conditions hold*

- **Efficiency:** ldO.ParaGen, ldO.Eval *are efficient algorithms;*
- **Functionality preserving:** ldO.ParaGen *takes as input a security parameter* $\kappa$, *a circuit assignment* $L$, *a cardinality bound* $\ell$, *and a circuit size bound* $s$. *For all* $\kappa$ *and all circuit assignment* $L$ *with cardinality at most* $\ell$ *and circuit size at most* $s$, *for all input* $x \in \{0,1\}^n$, *we have* ldO.Eval(ldO.ParaGen($1^\kappa, L, \ell, s$), $x$) = $L(x)$;
- **Local decomposing indistinguishability:** *Consider polynomials* $\ell = \ell(\kappa)$ *and* $s = s(\kappa)$. *For any such polynomials, and any pair of PPT adversaries* $(Samp, D)$, *we require that if*

$$\Pr[L_0 \text{ is } (\ell(\kappa), s(\kappa))\text{-local decomp. equiv. to } L_1 : (L_0, L_1, \sigma) \leftarrow Samp(\kappa)] = 1$$

*then there exists a negligible function* negl($\kappa$) *such that*

$$|\Pr[D(\sigma, \text{ldO.ParaGen}(1^\kappa, L_0, \ell, s)) = 1]$$
$$- \Pr[D(\sigma, \text{ldO.ParaGen}(1^\kappa, L_1, \ell, s)) = 1]| \le \ell \cdot \text{negl}(\kappa)$$

We will also consider a stronger variant, called sub-exponentially secure local dO, where in the definition of local decomposing indistinguishability, the negligible function negl is replaced by a subexponential function subexp.

### 4.4   Locally dO Implies One Shot dO

**Lemma 5.** *If two circuits $C_0, C_1$ are $(t/2+1)$-one shot decomposing equivalent, then they are $(n+1, s, t)$-path decomposing equivalent where $s = \max\{|C_0|, |C_1|\}$.*

**Proof.** We start from the covering that has $C_0$ assigned to the root. We perform a depth-first traversal of the binary search tree consisting of the "bad" nodes: nodes for which the partial evaluations of $C_0$ and $C_1$ are different. Equivalently, we search over the ancestors of nodes in the tree covering. There are $t/2$ such nodes. When we first visit a node on our way down the tree, we Decompose the fragment at that node to its children. When we visit a node $x$ for the second time after processing both children, we merge the fragments in the two children, using a TargetedMerge toward the circuit $(C_1)_x$. This operation is always valid since for each child either: (1) the child is a "good" node, in which case the partial evaluations at that node is identical to the partial evaluation of $(C_1)_{x||b}$; or (2) the child is a "bad" node, in which case it was, by induction, already processed and replaced with the partial evaluation of $(C_1)_{x||b}$. The cardinality of any circuit assignment in this path is at most $n+1$ since we will only have fragments adjacent to the path from the root to the node we are visiting. The circuit size is moreover always bounded by $s = \max\{|C_0|, |C_1|\}$ because all the intermediate fragments are partial evaluations of either $C_0$ or $C_1$. Finally, the path performs an Decompose and TargetedMerge for each "bad" node, corresponding to $t$ operations.

Now we show that the existence of ldO implies the existence of dO.

**Lemma 6.** *If ldO exists, then $\tau$-dO exists, where the loss in the security reduction is $2(\tau - 1)$. In particular, if polynomially secure ldO exists, then $\tau$-dO exists for any polynomial function $\tau$. Moreover, if subexponentially secure ldO exists, then $2^n$-dO, and hence iO, exists.*

**Proof.** The construction of ldO from dO is the natural one: to obfuscate a circuit $C$, we simply consider the circuit as a circuit assignment with $C$ assigned to the root node, and obfuscate this circuit assignment. We take the maximum cardinality for ldO to be $n+1$ and the circuit size to be $|C|$.

- dO.ParaGen$(1^\kappa, C) = $ ldO.ParaGen$(1^\kappa, \{(\varepsilon, C)\}, n+1, |C|)$;
- dO.Eval$($params$, x) = $ ldO.Eval$($params$, x)$;

Efficiency and functionality preservation are straightforward to prove. Now we focus on security. Let (Samp, $D$) be two PPT adversaries, and $s, n$ be polynomials in $\kappa$. Suppose the circuits $C_0, C_1$ outputted by Samp$(\kappa)$ always have the same size $s(\kappa)$, same input length $n(\kappa)$, and are $\tau(n, s, \kappa)$-decomposing equivalent with probability 1. Then $C_0$ and $C_1$ are also $(n+1, s, 2(\tau - 1))$-path decomposing equivalent by Lemma 5. By the definition of path decomposing equivalence and Lemma 8 (which states that the minimum tree covering is efficiently computable), there exist $L'_1, L'_2, \cdots, L'_{2(\tau-2)}, L'_{2(\tau-1)-1}$ and

$L'_0 = \{(\varepsilon, C_0)\}, L'_{2(\tau-1)} = \{(\varepsilon, C_1)\}$ such that any two adjacent circuit assignments are $(n+1, s)$-locally decomposing equivalent. So we have that

$$|\Pr[D(\mathsf{dO.ParaGen}(1^\kappa, C_0))] - \Pr[D(\mathsf{dO.ParaGen}(1^\kappa, C_1))]|$$

$$\leq \sum_{i=1}^{2(\tau-1)} \left| \begin{array}{c} \Pr[D(\mathsf{ldO.ParaGen}(1^\kappa, L'_{i-1}), n+1, |C_0|)] \\ - \Pr[D(\mathsf{ldO.ParaGen}(1^\kappa, L'_i), n+1, |C_0|)] \end{array} \right|$$

$$\leq 2(\tau - 1) \cdot \epsilon(\kappa)$$

Here, $\epsilon$ is the advantage of the following adversary pair $(\mathsf{Samp}', D)$ in the local dO security game (where $D$ is from above). $\mathsf{Samp}'$ runs $(C_0, C_1, \sigma) \leftarrow \mathsf{Samp}'$, computes the path $L'_0, \cdots, L'_{2(\tau-1)}$, chooses a random $i \in [2(\tau-1)]$, and outputs $(L'_{i-1}, L'_i, \sigma)$.

Therefore, as desired, we get an adversary for the local dO where the loss is $2(\tau-1)$. If we assume the polynomial hardness of ldO, the adversary $(\mathsf{Samp}', D)$ must have negligible advantage $\epsilon$, and so we get $\tau - \mathsf{dO}$ for any polynomial $\tau$. If we assume the subexponential hardness of ldO, we can set $\kappa$ so that $\epsilon = 2^{-n}\mathsf{negl}(\kappa)$ for some negligible function $\mathsf{negl}$. In this case, we even get $2^n$-dO, which is equivalent to iO. In the regime of subexponential hardness, we can even set $\epsilon = 2^{-n}\mathsf{subexp}(\kappa)$ for some subexponential function $\mathsf{subexp}$, in which case we get subexponentially secure $2^n$-dO and hence subexponentially secure iO.     □

Next, we focus on constructing ldO, which we now know is sufficient for constructing dO.

## 4.5   Compact FE Implies dO

**Theorem 3.** *If compact single-key selective secure functional encryption schemes exist, then there exists local decomposable obfuscators ldO.*

With Theorem 3 and Lemma 6, we have the following Theorem 4.

**Theorem 4.** *If compact single-key selective secure functional encryption schemes exist, then there exist decomposable obfuscators dO.*

Now we prove Theorem 3.

**Proof.** Let us first give the construction of our ldO.ParaGen (see Algorithm 3) where FE is a compact functional encryption scheme, SKE is a symmetric key encryption scheme and PRG is a pseudo random generator.

For each function $f_i^{b, Z_i^b} (1 \leq i \leq n)$, it basically computes a partial evaluation of an input circuit and encrypts it under two different functional encryption schemes (See Algorithm 5). But instead of doing this, this function also allows us to cheat and output a result given a secret key.

For each function $f_{n+1}^b$, it is given a circuit with no input, and simply evaluates it (see Algorithm 6).

---

**Algorithm 3.** Locally decomposable obfuscator IdO.ParaGen

---

1: **procedure** IdO.ParaGen($1^\kappa, L = \{(x_i, C_{x_i})\}, \ell, s$)
2:     **for** $i = 1, 2, \cdots, n, n+1$ **do**
3:         $(\mathsf{mpk}_i^b, \mathsf{msk}_i^b) \leftarrow \mathsf{FE.Gen}(1^\kappa)$ for $b \in \{0, 1\}$
4:     **end for**
5:     prepare a list of secret keys $\mathsf{sk}_{i,j}^b \leftarrow \mathsf{SKE.KeyGen}(1^\kappa)$ for $1 \leq i \leq n, 1 \leq j \leq \ell$ and $b \in \{0, 1\}$
6:     prepare $Z_i^b = Z_{i,1}^b, Z_{i,2}^b, \cdots, Z_{i,\ell}^b$ for $1 \leq i \leq n$ and $b \in \{0, 1\}$ where $Z_{i,j}^b = \mathsf{SKE.Enc}(\mathsf{sk}_{i,j}^b, 0^{t_1})$ and $t_1$ is a length bound specified later;
7:     generate $c_0, c_1$ by calling a recursive algorithm $\mathsf{CGen}(\varepsilon, L)$
8:     **for** $i = 1, 2, \cdots, n$ **do**
9:         $\mathsf{fsk}_i^b \leftarrow \mathsf{FE.KeyGen}(\mathsf{msk}_i^b, f_i^{b, Z_i^b})$ for $b \in \{0, 1\}$
10:     **end for**
11:     $\mathsf{fsk}_{n+1}^b \leftarrow \mathsf{FE.KeyGen}(\mathsf{msk}_{n+1}^b, f_{n+1}^b)$ for $b \in \{0, 1\}$
12:     **return** the parameters $\{c_0, c_1, \{\mathsf{mpk}_i^0, \mathsf{mpk}_i^1\}_{i=1}^{n+1}, \{\mathsf{fsk}_i^0, \mathsf{fsk}_i^1\}_{i=1}^{n+1}\}$
13: **end procedure**

---

**Algorithm 4.** Generating $c_0, c_1$ recursively

---

1: **procedure** $\mathsf{CGen}(x, L)$
2:     **if** $L$ only contains one pair, it must be $(x, C_x)$ **then**
3:         Generate $K^b \leftarrow \{0, 1\}^\kappa$ for $b \in \{0, 1\}$
4:         $c_b \leftarrow \mathsf{FE.Enc}(\mathsf{mpk}_d^b, \langle C_x, K^b, 0, 0^{t_2}\rangle)$ for $b \in \{0, 1\}$, and $d = |x| + 1$
5:         **return** $c_0, c_1$
6:     **end if**
7:     Split $L$ into $L_0, L_1$ where $L_0$ contains all the pairs $(y, C_y)$ where $y$ starts with $x\|0$ and $L_1$ contains all the pairs $(y, C_y)$ where $y$ starts with $x\|1$
8:     $(c_0', c_1') \leftarrow \mathsf{CGen}(x\|0, L_0)$ and $(c_0'', c_1'') \leftarrow \mathsf{CGen}(x\|1, L_1)$
9:     Choose an integer $j_0$ randomly from 1 to $\ell$ that has not been used yet in $Z_d^0$ and replace $Z_{d,j_0}^0$ with $\mathsf{SKE.Enc}(\mathsf{sk}_{d,j_0}^0, \langle c_0', c_1'\rangle)$
10:     Choose $j_1$ in the same way and replace $Z_{d,j_1}^1$ with $\mathsf{SKE.Enc}(\mathsf{sk}_{d,j_1}^1, \langle c_0'', c_1''\rangle)$
11:     **return** $c_0, c_1$ where $c_0 = \mathsf{FE.Enc}(\mathsf{mpk}_d^0, \langle \bot, \bot, j_0, \mathsf{sk}_{d,j_0}^0\rangle)$ and $c_1 = \mathsf{FE.Enc}(\mathsf{mpk}_d^1, \langle \bot, \bot, j_1, \mathsf{sk}_{d,j_1}^1\rangle)$
12: **end procedure**

---

**Evaluation and Correctness.** Now let us look at how IdO.Eval works. By fixing the first two ciphers and keys, given a input $x \in \{0, 1\}^n$,

- It begins with $c_0, c_1$;
- For $i = 1, 2, \cdots, n$, it picks the function key $\mathsf{fsk}_i^{x_i}$ and $c_{x_i}$; then does the update: $(c_0, c_1) \leftarrow \mathsf{FE.Dec}(\mathsf{fsk}_i^{x_i}, c_{x_i})$;
- Finally we can either output $\mathsf{FE.Dec}(\mathsf{fsk}_{n+1}^0, c_0)$ or $\mathsf{FE.Dec}(\mathsf{fsk}_{n+1}^1, c_1)$;

IdO.Eval($c_0, c_1, \{\mathsf{mpk}_i^0, \mathsf{mpk}_i^1\}_{i=1}^{n+1}, \{\mathsf{fsk}_i^0, \mathsf{fsk}_i^1\}_{i=1}^{n+1}, \cdots$) actually has the same functionalities with the circuit assignment $L$ since basically on input $x$, it finds a fragment corresponding to a prefix $y$ of $x = y\|x'$ and keeps doing partial evaluations on each input bit of $x'$. Since the cardinality is at most $\ell$, $\ell$ different $Z_{i,j}^b$ in $Z_i^b$ are enough for use.

---

**Algorithm 5.** $f_i^{b, Z_i^b}$ for $1 \leq i \leq n$

---

1: **procedure** $f_i^{b, Z_i^b}(C, K, \sigma, \text{sk})$
2:  **Hardcoded :** $Z_i^b$
3:  **if** $\sigma \neq 0$ **then**
4:   **return** $\text{SKE.Dec}(\text{sk}, Z_{i,\sigma}^b)$
5:  **else**
6:   $C' \leftarrow C(b, \cdot)$ and pad $C'$ to have length $s$
7:   **return**  $\{\text{FE.Enc}(\text{mpk}_{i+1}^0, \langle C', K_{i+1}^0, 0, 0^{t_2}\rangle; r_1),$
8:               $\text{FE.Enc}(\text{mpk}_{i+1}^1 \langle C', K_{i+1}^1, 0, 0^{t_2}\rangle; r_2)\}$ where
9:               $K_{i+1}^0 \leftarrow r_3$
10:              $K_{i+1}^1 \leftarrow r_4$
11:              using randomness $r_1, r_2, r_3, r_4 \leftarrow \text{PRG}(K)$
12:  **end if**
13: **end procedure**

---

**Algorithm 6.** $f_{n+1}^b$

---

1: **procedure** $f_{n+1}^b(C, K, \sigma, \text{sk})$
2:  **return**  the evaluation of $C$ on an empty input
3: **end procedure**

---

**Efficiency.** Let us look at the parameter size. All the master keys $\{\text{mpk}_i^0, \text{mpk}_i^1\}_{i=1}^{n+1}$ are of length $\text{poly}(\kappa)$. $t_2$ is the length of a secret key for SKE scheme so it is also of $\text{poly}(\kappa)$. And we assume FE is a compact functional encryption scheme which means the size of ciphers $c_0, c_1$ is bounded by $O(\text{poly}(s, \log \ell, \kappa))$ and also the size of $f$ circuit is bounded by $O(\text{poly}(s, \ell, \kappa))$ which implies the size $\{\text{fsk}_i^b\}$ is bounded by $O(\text{poly}(s, \ell, \kappa))$. Finally $t_1$ is bounded by $O(\text{poly}(s, \log \ell, \kappa))$.

So IdO.ParaGen and IdO.Eval run in time $\text{poly}(s, \ell, n, \kappa)$.

**Security.** Without loss of generality, we have two circuit assignments $L_0$ and $L_1$ where $\text{Decompose}(L_0, x) = L_1$. We are going to prove the indistinguishability when we are given either $L_0$ or $L_1$.

- **Hyb 0:** Here, an adversary is given an instance $\text{IdO.ParaGen}(1^\kappa, L_0, \ell, s)$. In the process of generating $c_0, c_1$, we will get to CGen on $x$ and $L'$ where $L'$ is the current partial circuit assignment. Since $L'$ only contains $(x, C_x)$, CGen will return $\text{FE.Enc}(\text{mpk}_d^b, \langle C_x, K^b, 0, 0^{t_2}\rangle)$ for $b \in \{0, 1\}$ and $d = |x| + 1$; we denote them as $\hat{c}_0, \hat{c}_1$.
- **Hyb 1:** In this hybrid, we change $Z_d^b$. Assume $\hat{c}_{b,0}, \hat{c}_{b,1} = \text{FE.Dec}(\text{fsk}_d^b, \hat{c}_b)$. In IdO.ParaGen, $Z_d^b$ are assigned to an array of encryptions of $0^{t_1}$ before calling CGen. We instead choose random $j_0, j_1$ from the unused indices (not used in CGen process) and change $Z_{d,j_0}^0$ and $Z_{d,j_1}^1$ to encryptions of $\langle \hat{c}_{b,0}, \hat{c}_{b,1}\rangle$. Since an adversary does not have any secret key $\text{sk}_{i,j}^b$, SKE security means **Hyb 0** and **Hyb 1** are indistinguishable.

– **Hyb 2:** In this hybrid, we change the ciphertexts $\hat{c}_0, \hat{c}_1$ to

$$\hat{c}_b = \mathsf{FE.Enc}(\mathsf{mpk}_d^b, \langle \perp, \perp, j_b, \mathsf{sk}_{d,j_b}^b \rangle)$$

where $\perp$ means filling it with zeroes and $j_b$ are the indices chosen in **Hyb 1**. Notice that

$$f_d^{b,Z_d^b}(\perp, \perp, j_b, \mathsf{sk}_{d,j_b}^b) = f_d^{b,Z_d^b}(C_x, K^b, 0, 0^{t_2})$$

Therefore, FE security means **Hyb 1** and **Hyb 2** are indistinguishable.
– **Hyb 3:** In this hybrid, we change $Z_{d,j_0}^0$ and $Z_{d,j_1}^1$. In **Hyb 1**, $\hat{c}_{b,0}, \hat{c}_{b,1}$ were computed using the randomness from a pseudo random generator. In **Hyb 2**, we removed the seed feed to PRG. Therefore we can replace $\hat{c}_{b,0}, \hat{c}_{b,1}$ to be the values computed using uniformly chosen randomness. Indistinguishability from **Hyb 2** easily follows from PRG security. We observe that the distribution of the instances in **Hyb 3** is identical to the distribution of $\mathsf{IdO.ParaGen}(1^\kappa, L_1, \ell, s)$.

This completes our proof for Theorem 3.

## 5   Discussion

### 5.1   Deciding Decomposing Equivalence

**Definition 13.** *A* tree covering *$TC$ is a* witness *that $C_0 \equiv C_1$ if $TC$ satisfies* $\mathsf{DecomposeTo}(\{(\varepsilon, C_0)\}, \mathcal{X}) = \mathsf{DecomposeTo}(\{(\varepsilon, C_1)\}, \mathcal{X})$. *In other words, decomposing $C_0$ and $C_1$ to $TC$ give the same circuit assignment (as in, the circuit fragments themselves are identical).*

*$TC$ is an* minimal witness *if, for all other $TC'$ that are witnesses to $C_0 \equiv C_1$, we have that $TC \preceq TC'$. In particular, this means that $TC$ is strictly smaller than all other witnesses.*

We define a node $x$ as "good" for $C_0, C_1$ if $C_0(x, \cdot) = C_1(x, \cdot)$ as circuits. Notice that the children of a good node are also good. We say that a good node $x$ is "minimal" if its parent is not good.

**Lemma 7.** *For any two equivalent circuits $C_0, C_1$, there is always exactly one minimal witness $TC^*$, and it consists of all of the minimal good nodes for $C_0, C_1$.*

**Proof.** Since $C_0 \equiv C_1$, all the leaves are good, and at least the set of leaves form a tree covering that is a witness. Now, for each leaf, consider the path from the leaf to the root. There will be some node $x$ on the path such that all nodes in the path before $x$ are not good, but $x$ and all nodes after $x$ are good. Therefore, that $x$ is an minimal good node. Moreover, no minimal good node can be a descendant of any other minimal good node (since no minimal good node can be the descendant of *any* good node). Therefore, the set of minimal good nodes form a tree covering.

**Lemma 8.** *$\tau$-one shot decomposing equivalence can be decided deterministically in time $\tau \times \mathsf{poly}(n, \max\{|C_0|, |C_1|\})$. Moreover, if $C_0 \equiv C_1$, then the optimal witness $TC^*$ can also be computed in this time.*

**Proof.** The algorithm is simple: process the nodes in a depth-first manner, keeping a global list $R$. When processing a node $x$, if $C_0(x, \cdot) = C_1(x, \cdot)$ as circuits, add $x$ to $R$, and then do not recurse. Otherwise, recurse on the children as normal. If the list $R$ every grows to exceed $\tau$ elements, abort the search and report non-decomposing equivalence. If the search finishes with $|R| \leq \tau$, then report decomposing equivalence and output $R$.

The total running time is bounded by $O(n\tau \cdot \mathsf{poly}(\max\{|C_0|, |C_1|\}))$: at most $n\tau$ nodes are processed (the up to $\tau$ nodes in $R$, plus their ancestors), and processing each node takes time proportional to the sizes of $C_0, C_1$.

## 5.2   One Shot DE Is Equivalent to Path DE

We have already proved that path DE implies one shot DE. Now let us prove the converse.

**Lemma 9.** *If two circuits $C_0, C_1$ are $(\ell, s, t)$-path decomposing equivalent, then they are $(t/2 + 1)$-one shot decomposing equivalent*

**Proof.** If $C_0, C_1$ are $(\ell, s, t)$-path decomposing equivalent, there exists a minimal tree covering $TC^*$. We observe that, for each of the ancestors of nodes in $TC^*$, there must be a step in the path where that node is decomposed, and there must also be a step in the path where that node is merged. It is straightforward to show that the number of ancestors for any tree covering is exactly one less than the size of the covering. From this, we deduce that $|TC^*| \leq t/2 + 1$. Since $TC^*$ exists and the size is bounded by $t/2 + 1$, these two circuits are $(t/2 + 1)$-one shot decomposing equivalent.

We emphasize that the above lemma and proof were independent of the bounds $\ell$ and $s$. Putting together Lemmas 5 and 9, we find that the path equivalence definition is independent of the parameters $\ell, s$.

We also see that path decomposing equivalence can be computed efficiently, following Lemmas 5, 8, and 9.

## 5.3   One Shot DE Is Strictly Stronger Than Functional Equivalence

We then show that path/one-shot decomposing equivalence is a strictly stronger notion than standard functional equivalence, when a reasonable bound is placed on the path length/witness size. The rough idea is the use the fact that, say, polynomial decomposing equivalence can be decided in polynomial time, whereas in general deciding equivalence is hard.

**Lemma 10.** *For any $n$, there exist two circuits on $n$ bit inputs $C_0 \equiv C_1$ that are not $2^{n-1} - 1$-one-shot decomposing equivalent.*

**Proof.** Let $D_0, D_1$ be two equivalent but non-identical circuits on 2 input bits (for example, two different circuits computing the XOR). Let $TC^*$ be the tree covering consisting of all $2^{n-1}$ nodes in the layer just above the leaves. Let $L_b$ for $b = 0, 1$ be the circuit assignment assigning $D_b$ to every node in $TC^*$. Finally, Let $C_b$ be the result of canonically merging $L_b$ all the way to the root node.

Now, $TC^*$ is clearly the optimal witness that $C_0 \equiv C_1$. Therefore, any witness must have size at least $|TC^*| = 2^{n-1}$. Therefore, $C_0, C_1$ are not $2^{n-1} - 1$ one-shot decomposing equivalent.

Note that the above separation constructed exponentially-large $C_0, C_1$. We can even show a similar separation in the case where $C_0, C_1$ have polynomial size, assuming $P \neq NP$. Indeed, since poly-one shot decomposing equivalence is decidable in polynomial time, but functional equivalence is not (assuming $P \neq NP$), there must be circuits pairs that are equivalent but not poly-one shot decomposing equivalent.

Next, we even demonstrate an explicit ensemble of circuit pairs that are equivalent but not poly-decomposing equivalent, assuming one-way functions exist.

**Lemma 11.** *Assuming one-way functions exist, there is an explicit family of circuit pairs $(C_0, C_1)$ that are equivalent, but are not $\mathsf{poly}(n)$-decomposing equivalent for any polynomial $\mathsf{poly}(n)$.*

**Proof.** Let PRG be a length-doubling pseudorandom generator (which can be constructed from any one-way function). Let $C_0(x) = $ "**return** 0" and $C_1(x) = $ '**return** 1 if $\mathsf{PRG}(x) = v$; 0 otherwise'' where $v$ is uniformly chosen from $\{0, 1\}^{2\kappa}$. When $v$ is uniformly chosen, except with probability $\frac{1}{2^\kappa}$, $v$ has no pre-image under PRG. Therefore, with probability $1 - \frac{1}{2^\kappa}$, $C_0$ and $C_1$ are functionally equivalent.

Next, assume there exists a polynomial $\tau$ and a non-negligible probability $\delta$ such that $C_0$ and $C_1$ are $\tau$-decomposing equivalent with probability $\delta$. Now let us build an adversary $\mathcal{B}$ for this length-doubling PRG:

- The adversary $\mathcal{B}$ gets $u$ from the challenger;
- $\mathcal{B}$ prepares the following two circuits: $C_0(x) = $"**return** 0" and $C_1(x) = $ "**return** 1 if $\mathsf{PRG}(x) = u$; 0 otherwise".
- $\mathcal{B}$ runs the algorithm to see if they are $\tau$-decomposing equivalent. If the algorithm returns **true**, $\mathcal{B}$ guesses $u$ is a truly random string; otherwise it guesses $u$ is generated by PRG.

When $u$ is generated by PRG, it will always return the correct answer since $C_1$ does not return 0 at some point but $C_0$ does; when $u$ is truly random, the probability that $\mathcal{B}$ is correct equal to the probability $C_0$ and $C_1$ are $\tau$-decomposing equivalent which is a non-negligible $\delta$. So $\mathcal{B}$ has non-negligible advantage $\delta$ in breaking PRG.

# References

[AJ15] Ananth, P., Jain, A.: Indistinguishability obfuscation from compact functional encryption. In: Gennaro, R., Robshaw, M. (eds.) CRYPTO 2015. LNCS, vol. 9215, pp. 308–326. Springer, Heidelberg (2015). doi:10.1007/978-3-662-47989-6_15

[BP15] Bitansky, N., Paneth, O.: ZAPs and non-interactive witness indistinguishability from indistinguishability obfuscation. In: Dodis, Y., Nielsen, J.B. (eds.) TCC 2015. LNCS, vol. 9015, pp. 401–427. Springer, Heidelberg (2015). doi:10.1007/978-3-662-46497-7_16

[BPR15] Bitansky, N., Paneth, O., Rosen, A.: On the cryptographic hardness of finding a nash equilibrium. In: 2015 IEEE 56th Annual Symposium on Foundations of Computer Science (FOCS), pp. 1480–1498. IEEE (2015)

[BPW16] Bitansky, N., Paneth, O., Wichs, D.: Perfect structure on the edge of chaos. In: Kushilevitz, E., Malkin, T. (eds.) TCC 2016. LNCS, vol. 9562, pp. 474–502. Springer, Heidelberg (2016). doi:10.1007/978-3-662-49096-9_20

[BST14] Bellare, M., Stepanovs, I., Tessaro, S.: Poly-many hardcore bits for any one-way function and a framework for differing-inputs obfuscation. In: Sarkar, P., Iwata, T. (eds.) ASIACRYPT 2014. LNCS, vol. 8874, pp. 102–121. Springer, Heidelberg (2014). doi:10.1007/978-3-662-45608-8_6

[BV15] Bitansky, N., Vaikuntanathan, V.: Indistinguishability obfuscation from functional encryption. In: 2015 IEEE 56th Annual Symposium on Foundations of Computer Science (FOCS), pp. 171–190. IEEE (2015)

[BZ14] Boneh, D., Zhandry, M.: Multiparty key exchange, efficient traitor tracing, and more from indistinguishability obfuscation. In: Garay, J.A., Gennaro, R. (eds.) CRYPTO 2014. LNCS, vol. 8616, pp. 480–499. Springer, Heidelberg (2014). doi:10.1007/978-3-662-44371-2_27

[BZ16] Bun, M., Zhandry, M.: Order-revealing encryption and the hardness of private learning. In: Kushilevitz, E., Malkin, T. (eds.) TCC 2016. LNCS, vol. 9562, pp. 176–206. Springer, Heidelberg (2016). doi:10.1007/978-3-662-49096-9_8

[CLTV15] Canetti, R., Lin, H., Tessaro, S., Vaikuntanathan, V.: Obfuscation of probabilistic circuits and applications. In: Dodis, Y., Nielsen, J.B. (eds.) TCC 2015. LNCS, vol. 9015, pp. 468–497. Springer, Heidelberg (2015). doi:10.1007/978-3-662-46497-7_19

[GGH+13] Garg, S., Gentry, C., Halevi, S., Raykova, M., Sahai, A., Waters, B.: Candidate indistinguishability obfuscation and functional encryption for all circuits. In: Proceedings of the 2013 IEEE 54th Annual Symposium on Foundations of Computer Science, FOCS 2013, Washington, DC, USA, pp. 40–49. IEEE Computer Society (2013)

[GGHZ16] Garg, S., Gentry, C., Halevi, S., Zhandry, M.: Functional encryption without obfuscation. In: Kushilevitz, E., Malkin, T. (eds.) TCC 2016. LNCS, vol. 9563, pp. 480–511. Springer, Heidelberg (2016). doi:10.1007/978-3-662-49099-0_18

[GGM86] Goldreich, O., Goldwasser, S., Micali, S.: How to construct random functions. J. ACM (JACM) 33(4), 792–807 (1986)

[GGSW13] Garg, S., Gentry, C., Sahai, A., Waters, B.: Witness encryption and its applications. In: Proceedings of the Forty-Fifth Annual ACM Symposium on Theory of Computing, STOC 2013, pp. 467–476. ACM, New York (2013)

[GLSW15] Gentry, C., Lewko, A.B., Sahai, A., Waters, B.: Indistinguishability obfuscation from the multilinear subgroup elimination assumption. In: Proceedings of the 2015 IEEE 56th Annual Symposium on Foundations of Computer Science (FOCS), FOCS 2015, Washington, DC, USA, pp. 151–170. IEEE Computer Society (2015)

[GPS16] Garg, S., Pandey, O., Srinivasan, A.: Revisiting the cryptographic hardness of finding a nash equilibrium. In: Robshaw, M., Katz, J. (eds.) CRYPTO 2016. LNCS, vol. 9815, pp. 579–604. Springer, Heidelberg (2016). doi:10.1007/978-3-662-53008-5_20

[GPSZ16] Garg, S., Pandey, O., Srinivasan, A., Zhandry, M.: Breaking the subexponential barrier in obfustopia. Technical report, Cryptology ePrint Archive, Report 2016/102 (2016). http://eprint.iacr.org/2016/102

[GS16] Garg, S., Srinivasan, A.: Single-key to multi-key functional encryption with polynomial loss. In: Hirt, M., Smith, A. (eds.) TCC 2016. LNCS, vol. 9986, pp. 419–442. Springer, Heidelberg (2016). doi:10.1007/978-3-662-53644-5_16

[GT16] Goldwasser, S., Tauman Kalai, Y.: Cryptographic assumptions: a position paper. In: Kushilevitz, E., Malkin, T. (eds.) TCC 2016. LNCS, vol. 9562, pp. 505–522. Springer, Heidelberg (2016). doi:10.1007/978-3-662-49096-9_21

[HJK+16] Hofheinz, D., Jager, T., Khurana, D., Sahai, A., Waters, B., Zhandry, M.: How to generate and use universal samplers. In: Cheon, J.H., Takagi, T. (eds.) ASIACRYPT 2016. LNCS, vol. 10032, pp. 715–744. Springer, Heidelberg (2016). doi:10.1007/978-3-662-53890-6_24

[HW15] Hubacek, P., Wichs, D.: On the communication complexity of secure function evaluation with long output. In: Proceedings of the 2015 Conference on Innovations in Theoretical Computer Science, ITCS 2015, pp. 163–172. ACM, New York (2015)

[KMN+14] Komargodski, I., Moran, T., Naor, M., Pass, R., Rosen, A., Yogev, E.: One-way functions and (im)perfect obfuscation. In: 2014 IEEE 55th Annual Symposium on Foundations of Computer Science (FOCS), pp. 374–383, October 2014

[LZ17] Liu, Q., Zhandry, M.: Exploding obfuscation: a framework for building applications of obfuscation from polynomial hardness. Cryptology ePrint Archive, Report 2017/209 (2017). http://eprint.iacr.org/2017/209

[Nao03] Naor, M.: On cryptographic assumptions and challenges. In: Boneh, D. (ed.) CRYPTO 2003. LNCS, vol. 2729, pp. 96–109. Springer, Heidelberg (2003). doi:10.1007/978-3-540-45146-4_6

[SW14] Sahai, A., Waters, B.: How to use indistinguishability obfuscation: deniable encryption, and more. In: Proceedings of the 46th Annual ACM Symposium on Theory of Computing, pp. 475–484. ACM (2014)

# Functional Encryption

# Functional Encryption for Bounded Collusions, Revisited

Shweta Agrawal[1(✉)] and Alon Rosen[2]

[1] IIT Madras, Chennai, India
shweta.a@cse.iitm.ac.in
[2] Efi Arazi School of Computer Science, IDC Herzliya, Herzliya, Israel
alon.rosen@idc.ac.il

**Abstract.** We provide a new construction of functional encryption (FE) for circuits in the bounded collusion model. In this model, security of the scheme is guaranteed as long as the number of colluding adversaries can be a-priori bounded by some polynomial $Q$. Our construction supports *arithmetic* circuits in contrast to all prior work which support Boolean circuits. The ciphertext of our scheme is sublinear in the circuit size for the circuit class $\mathsf{NC}_1$; this implies the first construction of arithmetic reusable garbled circuits for $\mathsf{NC}_1$.

Additionally, our construction achieves several desirable features:

- Our construction for reusable garbled circuits for $\mathsf{NC}_1$ achieves the optimal "full" simulation based security.
- When generalised to handle $Q$ queries for any fixed polynomial $Q$, our ciphertext size grows additively with $Q^2$. In contrast, previous works that achieve full security [5,39] suffered a multiplicative growth of $Q^4$.
- The ciphertext of our scheme can be divided into a succinct data dependent component and a non-succinct data independent component. This makes it well suited for optimization in an *online-offline model* that allows a majority of the computation to be performed in an offline phase, before the data becomes available.

Security of our reusable garbled circuits construction for $\mathsf{NC}_1$ is based on the Ring Learning With Errors assumption (RLWE), while the bounded collusion construction (with non-succinct ciphertext) may also be based on the standard Learning with Errors (LWE) assumption. To achieve our result, we provide new public key and ciphertext evaluation algorithms. These algorithms are general, and may find application elsewhere.

## 1 Introduction

Functional encryption (FE) [52,53] generalizes public key encryption to allow fine grained access control on encrypted data. In functional encryption, a secret key $\mathsf{SK}_f$ corresponds to a function $f$, and a ciphertext $\mathsf{CT}_\mathbf{x}$ corresponds to some input $\mathbf{x}$ from the domain of $f$. Given $\mathsf{SK}_f$ and $\mathsf{CT}_\mathbf{x}$, functionality posits that the

© International Association for Cryptologic Research 2017
Y. Kalai and L. Reyzin (Eds.): TCC 2017, Part I, LNCS 10677, pp. 173–205, 2017.
https://doi.org/10.1007/978-3-319-70500-2_7

user may run the decryption procedure to learn the value $f(\mathbf{x})$, while security guarantees that nothing about $\mathbf{x}$ beyond $f(\mathbf{x})$ can be learned.

Recent years have witnessed significant progress towards constructing functional encryption for advanced functionalities [3, 4, 11, 13, 15, 16, 21, 25, 31, 32, 35, 40–42, 45, 46, 54]. However, for the most general notion of functional encryption – one that allows the evaluation of arbitrary efficient functions and is secure against general adversaries, the only known constructions rely on indistinguishability obfuscation (iO) [31] or on the existence of multilinear maps [33]. For full-fledged functional encryption, reliance on such strong primitives is not a co-incidence, since functional encryption has been shown to imply indistinguishability obfuscation [7, 8, 12].

Unfortunately, all known candidate multi-linear map constructions [27, 30, 34] as well as some candidates of indistinguishability obfuscation have recently been broken [22–24, 26, 43, 49]. To support general functionalities and base hardness on standard assumptions, a prudent approach is to consider principled relaxations of the security definition, as studied in [37, 39, 41].

The notion of *bounded collusion functional encryption*, inspired from the domain of secure multiparty computation (MPC), was introduced by Gorbunov, Vaikuntanathan and Wee [39]. This notion assumes that the number of colluding adversaries against a scheme can be upper bounded by some polynomial $Q$, which is known at the time of system design. It is important to note that $Q$-bounded security does not impose any restriction on the functionality of FE – in particular, it does not disallow the system from issuing an arbitrary number of keys. It only posits, à la MPC, that security is guaranteed as long as any collusion of attackers obtains at most $Q$ keys. Note that multiple independent collusions of size at most $Q$ are supported.

The notion of $Q$-bounded FE is appealing – proving security under the assumption that not too many parties are dishonest is widely accepted as reasonable in protocol design. Even in the context of FE, for the special case of Identity Based Encryption (IBE), bounded collusion security has been considered in a number of works [28, 29, 38].

*Structure versus Generality.* Gorbunov et al. [39] showed that $Q$-bounded FE can be constructed generically from *any* public key encryption (PKE) scheme by leveraging ideas from multiparty computation. Considering that most constructions of FE for general functionalities rely on the existence of sophisticated objects such as multilinear maps or indistinguishability obfuscation, basing a meaningful relaxation of FE on an assumption as generic and mild as PKE is both surprising, and aesthetically appealing. However, this generality comes at the cost of efficiency and useful structural properties. The ciphertext of the scheme is large and grows multiplicatively as $O(Q^4)$ to support collusions of size $Q$. Additionally, the entire ciphertext is data dependent, making the scheme unsuitable for several natural applications of FE, as discussed below.

## 1.1   Our Results

In this work, we provide a new construction of bounded key functional encryption. Our construction makes use of the recently developed Functional Encryption for Linear Functions [1,5], denoted by LinFE, and combines this with techniques developed in the context of Fully Homomorphic Encryption (FHE)[1] [18,19]. Since LinFE and FHE can be based on LWE/Ring LWE, our construction inherits the same hardness assumption. Our construction offers several advantages:

1. Our construction supports *arithmetic* circuits as against Boolean circuits.
2. The ciphertext of our scheme is succinct for circuits in $NC_1$ under Ring LWE and any constant depth under standard LWE. This gives the first construction of arithmetic reusable garbled circuits. We note that even single use arithmetic garbled circuits have only been constructed recently [10].
3. Our construction achieves the optimal "full" simulation based security.
4. When generalised to handle $Q$ queries for any fixed polynomial $Q$, our ciphertext size grows additively with $Q^2$. In contrast, previous works that achieve full security [5,39] suffered a multiplicative growth of $Q^4$.
5. The ciphertext of our scheme can be divided into a succinct data dependent component and a non-succinct data independent component. This makes it well suited for optimization in an *online-offline model* that allows a majority of the computation to be performed in an offline phase, before the data becomes available. This is followed by an efficient online phase which is performed after the data is available.

## 1.2   Related Work

The first functional encryption scheme for circuits was provided by Gorbunov, Vaikuntanathan and Wee [39]. Surprisingly, the security of this construction may be based only on the existence of public key encryption. However, the ciphertext size of this construction is large and does not enjoy the online-offline property described above. The online component of [39] depends on the circuit size and the number of queries in addition to the message size, whereas that of our scheme depends only on the message size. Additionally, the overall ciphertext size of [39] grows multiplicatively with $Q^4$, whereas that in our scheme grows *additively* with $Q^2$. More recently, Agrawal et al. [5] provided a construction for bounded collusion FE. However, their ciphertext size grows as $O(Q^6)$ and does not support online-offline computation.

*Concurrent and Subsequent Work.* Subsequent to our work, Agrawal [2] also constructed $Q$ collusion Functional Encryption where the ciphertext size grows additively with $O(Q^2)$. However, this construction only achieves semi-adaptive rather than full security in a weak security game where the attacker must announce all

---

[1] We emphasise that we do not rely on FHE in a black box way, but rather adapt techniques developed in this domain to our setting.

176 S. Agrawal and A. Rosen

Q queries "in one shot". Additionally, it supports Boolean rather than arithmetic circuits and makes black box use of "heavy machinery" such fully homomorphic encryption and attribute based encryption.

In another recent work, Canetti and Chen [20] provide a new construction for single key FE for $NC_1$ achieving full security. However, their construction supports Boolean rather than arithmetic circuits, which is the main focus of this work. Moreover, to generalise this construction to support $Q$ queries, one must rely on the [39] compiler, which incurs a multiplicative blowup of $O(Q^4)$ in the ciphertext size. For more details about related work, please see Appendix A.

## 1.3 Techniques

In this section, we describe our techniques. We begin by outlining the approach taken by previous work. [39] begin with a single key FE scheme for circuits [51] and generalize this to a $Q$ query scheme for $NC_1$ circuits. This is the most sophisticated part of the construction, and leverages techniques from multiparty computation. Then, the $Q$ query FE for $NC_1$ is bootstrapped to $Q$ query FE for all circuits by replacing the circuit in the key by a tuple of low degree polynomials admitted by computational randomized encodings [9].

Recently, Agrawal et al. [5] observe that a different construction for bounded collusion FE can be obtained by replacing the single key FE [51] and its generalisation to $Q$ query FE for $NC_1$, with an FE that computes inner products modulo some prime $p$. Such a scheme, which we denote by LinFE, was constructed by [1,5] and computes the following functionality: the encryptor provides a ciphertext $CT_x$ for some vector $x \in F_p^\ell$, the key generator provides a key $SK_v$ for some vector $v \in F_p^\ell$, and the decryptor, given $CT_x$ and $SK_v$ can compute $\langle x, v \rangle$ mod $p^2$. Since the bootstrapping theorem in [39] only requires FE for degree 3 polynomials, and FE for linear functions trivially implies FE for bounded degree polynomials simply by linearizing the message terms $x$ and encrypting each monomial $x_i x_j x_k$ separately, LinFE may be used to compute degree 3 polynomials.

Thus, in [5], the challenge of supporting multiplication is "brute-forced" by merely having the encryptor encrypt each monomial separately so that the FE must only support linear functions in order to achieve bounded degree polynomials. This brute force approach has several disadvantages: the ciphertext is not online-offline and its size grows as $O(Q^6)$. See Appendix A for more details.

*Our Approach.* In this work, we observe that viewing functional encryption through the lens of fully homomorphic encryption (FHE) enables a more sophisticated application of the Linear FE scheme LinFE, resulting in a bounded collusion FE scheme for circuits that is decomposable, online-succinct as well as achieves ciphertext dependence of $O(Q^2)$ additively on $Q$.

---

[2] We note that the FE scheme by Abdalla et al. [1] also supports linear functions but only over $\mathbb{Z}$, while the bounded collusion FE of [5] requires an FE scheme that supports $\mathbb{Z}_p$. Also note the difference from Inner Product *orthogonality testing* schemes [4,45] which test whether $\langle x, v \rangle = 0$ mod $p$ or not.

We begin on FE for quadratic polynomials for ease of exposition. Additionally, here and in the rest of the paper, we present our construction from Ring-LWE rather than standard LWE, for notational convenience and clarity. Our construction can be ported to the standard LWE setting, by performing standard transformations such as replacing ring products by vector tensor products. Details are provided in the full version [6].

Consider the ring LWE based symmetric key FHE scheme by Brakerski and Vaikuntanathan [19]. Recall that the ciphertext of this scheme, as in [50], is structured as $(u, c)$ where $c = u \cdot s + 2 \cdot \mu + x$. Here, $s$ is the symmetric key chosen randomly over an appropriate ring $R$, $u$ is an element chosen by the encryptor randomly over $R$, $x$ is a message bit and $\mu$ is an error term chosen by the encryptor from an appropriate distribution over $R$. Given secret key $s$, the decryptor may compute $c - u \cdot s \mod 2$ to recover the bit $x$.

The main observation in [19] was that if:

$$c_i = u_i \cdot s + 2 \cdot \mu_i + x_i$$
$$c_j = u_j \cdot s + 2 \cdot \mu_j + x_j$$

then the decryption equation can be written as

$$x_i x_j \approx c_i c_j + (u_i u_j)s^2 - (u_j c_i)s - (u_i c_j)s$$

Thus, the 3 tuple $(c_i c_j, \; u_i c_j + u_j c_i, \; u_i u_j)$ is a legitimate level 2 FHE ciphertext, decryptable by the secret key $s$. [19] observed that it is sufficient to add one ciphertext element per level of the circuit to propagate the computation.

In the context of FE, things are significantly more complex even for quadratic polynomials, since we must return a key that allows the decryptor to learn $x_i x_j$ and nothing else. Hence, providing $s$ to the decryptor is disastrous for FE security. Here we use our first trick: observe that in the above equation, the parenthesis can be shifted so that:

$$x_i x_j \approx c_i c_j + u_i u_j(s^2) - u_j(c_i s) - u_i(c_j s)$$

Now, if we use the Linear FE scheme to encrypt the terms in parenthesis, then we can have the decryptor recover the term $u_i u_j(s^2) - u_j(c_i s) - u_i(c_j s)$. More formally, let $|\mathbf{x}| = w$. Now if,

$$\mathsf{CT} = \mathsf{LinFE.Enc}(s^2, c_1 s, \ldots, c_w s)$$
$$\mathsf{SK}_{ij} = \mathsf{LinFE.KeyGen}(u_i u_j, -0-, u_i, -0-, u_j, -0-)$$

then, $\mathsf{LinFE.Dec}(\mathsf{SK}_{ij}, \mathsf{CT})$ should yield the above term by correctness. Since $c_1, \ldots, c_w$ may be provided directly in the ciphertext, the decryptor may itself compute the term $c_i c_j$. Now, LinFE decryption yields $u_i u_j(s^2) - u_j(c_i s) - u_i(c_j s)$, so the decryptor may recover (approximately) $x_i x_j$ as desired[3].

A bit more abstractly, we observe that a quadratic plaintext $x_i x_j$ can be represented as a quadratic polynomial which is quadratic in *public* terms $c_i, c_j$,

---

[3] As in FHE, approximate recovery is enough since the noise can be modded out.

and only *linear* in secret terms $c_i s$. In particular, since the number of secret terms $c_i s$ which must be encrypted is only linear in $|\mathbf{x}|$, we appear to avoid the quadratic blowup caused by linearization.

This intuition, while appealing, is very misleading. To begin, note that if we permit the decryptor to learn the term $u_i u_j s^2 - u_j c_i s - u_i c_j s$ exactly, then he can recover exact quadratic equations in the secret $s$, completely breaking the security of the scheme. To handle this, we resort to our second trick: add noise *artificially* to the decryption equation. This takes care of the above attack, but to handle $Q$ queries, we need $Q$ fresh noise terms to be encrypted in the ciphertext. This step introduces the dependence of the ciphertext size on $Q$. Providing a proof of security requires crossing several additional hurdles. The details of the proof are provided in Sect. 3.

*New Public Key and Ciphertext Evaluation Algorithms.* To generalize our construction to $\mathsf{NC}_1$, we develop new algorithms to compute on the public key and ciphertext. Designing these algorithms is the most challenging part of our work. Intuitively, the ciphertext evaluation algorithm enables the decryptor to compute a "functional" ciphertext $\mathsf{CT}_{f(\mathbf{x})}$ encoding $f(\mathbf{x})$ on the fly, using the function description $f$, and encodings of $\mathbf{x}$ provided by the encryptor obliviously of $f$. The public key evaluation algorithm enables the key generator to compute the "functional" public key $\mathsf{PK}_f$ given the public key $\mathsf{PK}$ and the function $f$, obliviously of $\mathbf{x}$ so that the functional public key $\mathsf{PK}_f$ *matches* the functional ciphertext $\mathsf{CT}_{f(\mathbf{x})}$ enabling the key generator to provide a functional secret key which allows decryption of $\mathsf{CT}_{f(\mathbf{x})}$.

We note that a previous work by Boneh et al. [14] also provided a ciphertext evaluation algorithm which enables computing $\mathsf{CT}_{f(\mathbf{x})}$ given $\mathsf{CT}_\mathbf{x}$ and $f$, but this algorithm crucially requires the evaluator to have some knowledge of $\mathbf{x}$ in order to support multiplications. In more detail, the evaluator must know at least one of encoded values $x_1, x_2$ in the clear in order to compute an encoding of $x_1 \cdot x_2$. In contrast, our ciphertext evaluation algorithm is completely oblivious of $\mathbf{x}$ even for multiplication gates.

We give a brief description of our approach below. Recall that the "level 1" encodings $\mathbf{c}$ of message $\mathbf{x}$ along with "level 2" encodings of message $\mathbf{c} \cdot s$ in the LinFE ciphertext were sufficient to compute encodings of degree two polynomials in $\mathbf{x}$. Generalizing, we get that at any level $k$ in the circuit, given an encoding $\mathbf{c}^{k-1}$ of message $f^{k-1}(\mathbf{x})$ where $f^{k-1}$ is the output of the circuit at level $k-1$, as well as encodings of $\mathbf{c}^{k-1} \cdot s$, we would be in a position to compute encodings $\mathbf{c}^k$ of level $k$ output of the circuit using the method to evaluate quadratic polynomials described above.

This intuition is complicated by the fact that the encryptor may not provide $\mathbf{c}^{k-1}$ directly as this depends on $f$ which it does not know. Thus, the encryptor must provide *advice* which enables the decryptor to compute $\mathbf{c}^{k-1}$ on the fly. Moreover, this advice must be sublinear in the size of the circuit. We design advice encodings that enable a decryptor to compute functional ciphertexts dynamically via *nested FHE decryptions*. Please see Sect. 4 for more details.

*Organization of the paper.* We provide preliminaries in Sect. 2. Our bounded collusion functional encryption scheme for quadratic polynomials is described in Sect. 3. To generalize our method beyond quadratic polynomials, we describe our public key and ciphertext evaluation procedures in Sect. 4. The succinct single key FE using these procedures is constructed in Sect. 5. The bounded collusion scheme is provided in Sect. 6, and parameters in Appendix B.

## 2  Preliminaries

In this section, we define the preliminaries we require for our constructions.

### 2.1  Functional Encryption

Let $\mathcal{X} = \{\mathcal{X}_\lambda\}_{\lambda \in \mathbb{N}}$ and $\mathcal{Y} = \{\mathcal{Y}_\lambda\}_{\lambda \in \mathbb{N}}$ denote ensembles where each $\mathcal{X}_\lambda$ and $\mathcal{Y}_\lambda$ is a finite set. Let $\mathcal{C} = \{\mathcal{C}_\lambda\}_{\lambda \in \mathbb{N}}$ denote an ensemble where each $\mathcal{C}_\lambda$ is a finite collection of circuits, and each circuit $C \in \mathcal{C}_\lambda$ takes as input a string $\mathbf{x} \in \mathcal{X}_\lambda$ and outputs $C(\mathbf{x}) \in \mathcal{Y}_\lambda$.

A functional encryption scheme $\mathcal{F}$ for $\mathcal{C}$ consists of four algorithms $\mathcal{F} = $ (FE.Setup, FE.Keygen, FE.Encrypt, FE.Decrypt) defined as follows.

- FE.Setup$(1^\lambda)$ is a p.p.t. algorithm takes as input the unary representation of the security parameter and outputs the master public and secret keys (PK, MSK).
- FE.Keygen(MSK, $C$) is a p.p.t. algorithm that takes as input the master secret key MSK and a circuit $C \in \mathcal{C}_\lambda$ and outputs a corresponding secret key SK$_C$.
- FE.Encrypt(PK, $\mathbf{x}$) is a p.p.t. algorithm that takes as input the master public key PK and an input message $\mathbf{x} \in \mathcal{X}_\lambda$ and outputs a ciphertext CT$_\mathbf{x}$.
- FE.Decrypt(SK$_C$, CT$_\mathbf{x}$) is a deterministic algorithm that takes as input the secret key SK$_C$ and a ciphertext CT$_\mathbf{x}$ and outputs $C(\mathbf{x})$.

**Definition 2.1 (Correctness).** *A functional encryption scheme $\mathcal{F}$ is correct if for all $C \in \mathcal{C}_\lambda$ and all $x \in \mathcal{X}_\lambda$,*

$$\Pr \left[ \begin{array}{l} (\mathsf{PK, MSK}) \leftarrow \mathsf{FE.Setup}(1^\lambda); \\ \mathsf{FE.Decrypt}\Big(\mathsf{FE.Keygen}(\mathsf{MSK}, C), \mathsf{FE.Encrypt}(\mathsf{PK}, \mathbf{x})\Big) \neq C(\mathbf{x}) \end{array} \right] = \mathrm{negl}(\lambda)$$

*where the probability is taken over the coins of* FE.Setup, FE.Keygen, *and* FE.Encrypt.

### 2.2  Simulation Based Security for Single Key FE

In this section, we define simulation based security for single key FE, as in [37, Definition 4.1].

**Definition 2.2 (FULL-SIM Security).** *Let $\mathcal{F}$ be a functional encryption scheme for a circuit family $\mathcal{C}$. For every stateful p.p.t. adversary* Adv *and a stateful p.p.t. simulator* Sim, *consider the following two experiments:*

| $\mathsf{Exp}^{\mathsf{real}}_{\mathcal{F},\mathsf{Adv}}(1^\lambda):$ | $\mathsf{Exp}^{\mathsf{ideal}}_{\mathcal{F},\mathsf{Sim}}(1^\lambda):$ |
|---|---|
| 1: $(\mathsf{PK}, \mathsf{MSK}) \leftarrow \mathsf{FE.Setup}(1^\lambda)$ | 1: $(\mathsf{PK}, \mathsf{MSK}) \leftarrow \mathsf{FE.Setup}(1^\lambda)$ |
| 2: $C \leftarrow \mathsf{Adv}(1^\lambda, \mathsf{PK})$ | 2: $C \leftarrow \mathsf{Adv}(1^\lambda, \mathsf{PK})$ |
| 3: $\mathsf{SK}_C \leftarrow \mathsf{FE.Keygen}(\mathsf{MSK}, C)$ | 3: $\mathsf{SK}_C \leftarrow \mathsf{FE.Keygen}(\mathsf{MSK}, C)$ |
| 4: $\mathbf{x} \leftarrow \mathsf{Adv}(\mathsf{SK}_C)$ | 4: $\mathbf{x} \leftarrow \mathsf{Adv}(\mathsf{SK}_C)$ |
| 5: $\mathsf{CT}_\mathbf{x} \leftarrow \mathsf{FE.Encrypt}(\mathsf{PK}, \mathbf{x})$ | 5: $\mathsf{CT}_\mathbf{x} \leftarrow \mathsf{Sim}(1^\lambda, 1^{|\mathbf{x}|}, \mathsf{PK}, C, \mathsf{SK}_C, C(\mathbf{x}))$ |
| 6: $\alpha \leftarrow \mathsf{Adv}(\mathsf{CT}_\mathbf{x})$ | 6: $\alpha \leftarrow \mathsf{Adv}(\mathsf{CT}_\mathbf{x})$ |
| 7: Output $(\mathbf{x}, \alpha)$ | 7: Output $(\mathbf{x}, \alpha)$ |

The functional encryption scheme $\mathcal{F}$ is then said to be FULL-SIM-secure if there is an admissible stateful p.p.t. simulator Sim such that for every stateful p.p.t. adversary Adv, the following two distributions are computationally indistinguishable.

$$\left\{ \mathsf{Exp}^{\mathsf{real}}_{\mathcal{F},\mathsf{Adv}}(1^\lambda) \right\}_{\lambda \in \mathbb{N}} \stackrel{c}{\approx} \left\{ \mathsf{Exp}^{\mathsf{ideal}}_{\mathcal{F},\mathsf{Sim}}(1^\lambda) \right\}_{\lambda \in \mathbb{N}}$$

In the bounded collusion variant of the above definition, the adversary is permitted an a-priori fixed $Q$ queries in Step 2, and $Q$ is input to the FE.Setup algorithm.

### 2.3 Lattice Preliminaries

An $m$-dimensional lattice $\Lambda$ is a full-rank discrete subgroup of $\mathbb{R}^m$. A basis of $\Lambda$ is a linearly independent set of vectors whose span is $\Lambda$.

**Gaussian distributions.** Let $L$ be a discrete subset of $\mathbb{Z}^n$. For any vector $\mathbf{c} \in \mathbb{R}^n$ and any positive parameter $\sigma \in \mathbb{R}_{>0}$, let $\rho_{\sigma,\mathbf{c}}(\mathbf{x}) := \mathsf{Exp}\left(-\pi \|\mathbf{x} - \mathbf{c}\|^2/\sigma^2\right)$ be the Gaussian function on $\mathbb{R}^n$ with center $\mathbf{c}$ and parameter $\sigma$. Let $\rho_{\sigma,\mathbf{c}}(L) := \sum_{\mathbf{x} \in L} \rho_{\sigma,\mathbf{c}}(\mathbf{x})$ be the discrete integral of $\rho_{\sigma,\mathbf{c}}$ over $L$, and let $\mathcal{D}_{L,\sigma,\mathbf{c}}$ be the discrete Gaussian distribution over $L$ with center $\mathbf{c}$ and parameter $\sigma$. Specifically, for all $\mathbf{y} \in L$, we have $\mathcal{D}_{L,\sigma,\mathbf{c}}(\mathbf{y}) = \frac{\rho_{\sigma,\mathbf{c}}(\mathbf{y})}{\rho_{\sigma,\mathbf{c}}(L)}$. For notational convenience, $\rho_{\sigma,0}$ and $\mathcal{D}_{L,\sigma,0}$ are abbreviated as $\rho_\sigma$ and $\mathcal{D}_{L,\sigma}$, respectively.

The following lemma gives a bound on the length of vectors sampled from a discrete Gaussian.

**Lemma 2.3 ([48, Lemma 4.4]).** *Let $\Lambda$ be an $n$-dimensional lattice, let $\mathbf{T}$ be a basis for $\Lambda$, and suppose $\sigma \geq \|\mathbf{T}\|_{\mathsf{GS}} \cdot \omega(\sqrt{\log n})$. Then for any $\mathbf{c} \in \mathbb{R}^n$ we have*

$$\Pr\left[\|\mathbf{x} - \mathbf{c}\| > \sigma\sqrt{n} : \mathbf{x} \xleftarrow{\mathrm{R}} \mathcal{D}_{\Lambda,\sigma,\mathbf{c}}\right] \leq \mathsf{negl}(n)$$

**Lemma 2.4 (Flooding Lemma).** [36] *Let $n \in \mathbb{N}$. For any real $\sigma = \omega(\sqrt{\log n})$, and any $\mathbf{c} \in \mathbb{Z}^n$,*

$$\mathsf{SD}(\mathcal{D}_{\mathbb{Z}^n,\sigma}, \mathcal{D}_{\mathbb{Z}^n,\sigma,\mathbf{c}}) \leq \|\mathbf{c}\|/\sigma$$

### 2.4 Hardness Assumptions

Our main construction of arithmetic reusable garbled circuits for $\mathsf{NC}_1$ is based on the hardness of Ring Learning with Errors, defined below. Our bounded collusion construction for circuits may also be based on the standard Learning with Errors problem, but we defer this discussion to the full version [6].

*Ring Learning with Errors.* Let $R = \mathbb{Z}[x]/(\phi)$ where $\phi = x^n + 1$ and $n$ is a power of 2. Let $R_q \triangleq R/qR$ where $q$ is a large prime satisfying $q = 1 \mod 2n$. Let $\chi$ be a probability distribution on $R_q$. For $s \in R_q$, let $A_{s,\chi}$ be the probability distribution on $R_q \times R_q$ obtained by choosing an element $a \in R_q$ uniformly at random, choosing $e \leftarrow \chi$ and outputting $(a, a \cdot s + e)$.

**Definition 2.5 (Ring Learning With Errors- $\mathsf{RLWE}_{\phi,q,\chi}$).** [47,50] *The decision $R$-$\mathsf{LWE}_{\phi,q,\chi}$ problem is: for $s \leftarrow R_q$, given a $\mathrm{poly}(n)$ number of samples that are either (all) from $A_{s,\chi}$ or (all) uniformly random in $R_q \times R_q$, output 0 if the former holds and 1 if the latter holds.*

The hardness of the ring LWE problem was studied in [47] and is summarised in the following theorem.

**Theorem 2.6 ([47]).** *Let $r \geq \omega(\sqrt{\log n})$ be a real number and let $R, q$ be as above. Then, there is a randomized reduction from $2^{\omega(\log n)} \cdot (q/r)$ approximate RSVP to $\mathsf{RLWE}_{\phi,q,\chi}$ where $\chi$ is the discrete Gaussian distribution with parameter $r$. The reduction runs in time $\mathrm{poly}(n, q)$.*

# 3  Warm-Up: Bounded Query Functional Encryption for Quadratic Polynomials

As a warm-up, we present our bounded key FE for the special case of quadratic functions, which we denote by QuadFE. Our construction will make use of the linear functional encryption scheme, denoted by LinFE, constructed by [1,5].

Our construction makes use of two prime moduli $p_0 < p_1$ where $p_0$ serves as the message space for QuadFE, and $p_1$ serves as the message space for LinFE. Let $L = |1 \leq j \leq i \leq w|$. Below, let distributions $\mathcal{D}_0, \mathcal{D}_1$ be discrete Gaussians with width $\sigma_0, \sigma_1$ respectively. Please see Appendix B for parameters.

For ease of exposition, our key generation algorithm receives the index of the requested key as input. This restriction can be removed using standard tricks, see the full version [6] for details. Additionally, we present our construction using Ring-LWE. This is both for efficiency and ease of exposition. The transformation to standard LWE follows standard machinery, please see the full version [6] for details.

FE.Setup($1^\lambda, 1^w, 1^Q$): On input a security parameter $\lambda$, a parameter $w$ denoting the length of message vectors and a parameter $Q$ denoting the number of keys supported, do:
  1. Invoke LinFE.Setup($1^\lambda, 1^{w+1+Q}$) to obtain LinFE.PK and LinFE.MSK.
  2. Sample $\mathbf{u} \leftarrow R_{p_1}^w$.
  3. Output PK = (LinFE.PK, $\mathbf{u}$), MSK = (LinFE.MSK).

FE.Enc(PK, $\mathbf{x}$): On input public parameters PK, and message vector $\mathbf{x} \in R_{p_0}^w$ do:
  1. Sample $s_1 \leftarrow R_{p_1}$ and $\boldsymbol{\mu} \leftarrow \mathcal{D}_0^w$, and compute an encoding of the message as:
$$\mathbf{c} = \mathbf{u} \cdot s_1 + p_0 \cdot \boldsymbol{\mu} + \mathbf{x} \in R_{p_1}^w.$$

2. For $i \in [Q]$, sample $\eta_i \leftarrow \mathcal{D}_1$ and let $\boldsymbol{\eta} = (\eta_1, \ldots, \eta_Q)$.
3. Let $\mathbf{b} = \mathsf{LinFE.Enc}\,(s_1^2, c_1 s_1, \ldots, c_w s_1, p_0 \cdot \boldsymbol{\eta})$.
4. Output $\mathsf{CT} = (\mathbf{c}, \mathbf{b})$.

$\mathsf{FE.KeyGen}(\mathsf{PK}, \mathsf{MSK}, k, \mathbf{g})$: On input the public parameters $\mathsf{PK}$, the master secret key $\mathsf{MSK}$, a counter $k \in [Q]$ denoting the index of the requested function key and a function $\mathbf{g} = \sum\limits_{1 \leq j \leq i \leq w} g_{ij} x_i x_j$, represented as a coefficient vector $(g_{ij}) \in \mathbb{Z}_{p_0}^L$ do:

1. Let $\mathbf{e}_k$ denote the binary unit vector with a 1 in the $k^{th}$ position and 0 elsewhere. Compute

$$\mathbf{u_g} = \Big( \sum_{1 \leq j \leq i \leq w} g_{ij}\,(u_i u_j, 0....0, -u_i, 0...0, -u_j, 0...0) \Big) \in R_{p_1}^{w+1}.$$

2. Compute $\mathsf{SK_g} = \mathsf{LinFE.KeyGen}\big(\mathsf{LinFE.PK}, \mathsf{LinFE.MSK}, (\mathbf{u_g}\|\mathbf{e}_k)\big)$ and output it.

$\mathsf{FE.Dec}(\mathsf{PK}, \mathsf{SK_g}, \mathsf{CT_x})$: On input the public parameters $\mathsf{PK}$, a secret key $\mathsf{SK_g}$ for polynomial $\sum\limits_{1 \leq j \leq i \leq w} g_{ij} x_i x_j$, and a ciphertext $\mathsf{CT_x} = (\mathbf{c}, \mathbf{b})$, compute

$$\sum_{1 \leq j \leq i \leq w} g_{ij} c_i c_j + \mathsf{LinFE.Dec}(\mathbf{b}, \mathsf{SK_g}) \bmod p_1 \bmod p_0$$

and output it.

### 3.1   Correctness

We establish correctness of the above scheme. Let $1 \leq j \leq i \leq w$. Let us assume $\mathbf{g}$ is the $k^{th}$ key constructed by $\mathsf{KeyGen}$, where $k \in [Q]$. By definition

$$x_i + p_0 \cdot \mu_i = c_i - u_i s_1 \mod p_1, \qquad x_j + p_0 \cdot \mu_j = c_j - u_j s_1 \mod p_1$$

Letting $\mu_{ij} = x_i \mu_j + x_j \mu_i + p_0 \mu_i \mu_j$, we have

$$x_i x_j + p_0 \cdot \mu_{ij} = c_i c_j - c_i u_j s_1 - c_j u_i s_1 + u_i u_j s_1^2 \mod p_1 \qquad (3.1)$$

By correctness of the linear scheme $\mathsf{LinFE}$, we have that

$$\mathsf{LinFE.Dec}(\mathbf{b}, \mathsf{SK_g}) = \sum_{1 \leq j \leq i \leq w} g_{ij}\big( - c_i u_j s_1 - c_j u_i s_1 + u_i u_j s_1^2 \big) + p_0 \cdot \eta_k$$

Therefore we have, $\quad \sum\limits_{1 \leq j \leq i \leq w} g_{ij} c_i c_j + \mathsf{LinFE.Dec}(\mathbf{b}, \mathsf{SK_g})$

$$= \sum_{1 \leq j \leq i \leq w} g_{ij} \Big( c_i c_j - c_i u_j s_1 - c_j u_i s_1 + u_i u_j s_1^2 \Big) + p_0 \cdot \eta_k$$

$$= \sum_{1 \leq j \leq i \leq w} g_{ij} \big( x_i x_j + p_0 \cdot \mu_{ij} \big) + p_0 \cdot \eta_k$$

$$= \sum_{1 \leq j \leq i \leq w} g_{ij}\, x_i x_j \bmod p_1 \bmod p_0 \text{ as desired.} \qquad (3.2)$$

## 3.2  Security

**Theorem 3.7.** *The construction in Sect. 3 achieves full simulation based security as per Definition 2.2.*

**Proof.** We describe our simulator.

*Simulator* $\mathsf{Sim}\big(\ 1^\lambda, 1^{|\mathbf{x}|}, \mathsf{PK}, \{\mathbf{g}_k, \mathsf{SK}_{\mathbf{g}_k}, \mathbf{g}_k(\mathbf{x})\}_{k\in[Q]}\ \big)$. The simulator given input the security parameter, length of message $\mathbf{x}$, the functions $\mathbf{g}_1, \dots, \mathbf{g}_Q$, the secret keys $\mathsf{SK}_{\mathbf{g}_1}, \dots, \mathsf{SK}_{\mathbf{g}_Q}$ and the values $\mathbf{g}_1(\mathbf{x}), \dots, \mathbf{g}_Q(\mathbf{x})$ does the following:

1. It picks the ciphertext $\mathbf{c} \leftarrow R_{p_1}^w$ randomly.
2. It parses $\mathbf{g}_k = \sum\limits_{1\leq j\leq i\leq w} g_{k,ij}\, x_i x_j$ for some $g_{k,ij} \in R_{p_0}$. For $k \in [Q]$, it samples
   $\eta_k \leftarrow \mathcal{D}_1$ and computes $d_k = \sum\limits_{1\leq j\leq i\leq w} g_{k,ij}\big(x_i x_j - c_i c_j\big) + p_0 \cdot \eta_k$.
3. It invokes the $Q$ key $\mathsf{LinFE}$ simulator with input $\mathbf{d} = (d_1, \dots, d_Q)$. It sets as $\mathbf{b}$ the output received by the $\mathsf{LinFE}$ simulator.
4. It outputs $\mathsf{CT}_{\mathbf{x}} = (\mathbf{c}, \mathbf{b})$.

We will prove that the output of the simulator is indistinguishable from the real world via a sequence of hybrids.

*The Hybrids.* Our Hybrids are described below.

*Hybrid 0.* This is the real world.

*Hybrid 1.* In this hybrid, the only thing that is different is that $\mathbf{b}$ is computed using the $\mathsf{LinFE}$ simulator as $\mathbf{b} = \mathsf{LinFE}.\mathsf{Sim}\big(1^\lambda, 1^{w+1+Q}, \{\mathbf{g}_k, \mathsf{SK}_{\mathbf{g}_k}, d_k\}_{k\in[Q]}\big)$ where

$$d_k = \sum_{1\leq j\leq i\leq w} g_{k,ij}\big(x_i x_j - c_i c_j\big) + p_0 \cdot \Big( \sum_{1\leq j\leq i\leq w} g_{k,ij}\mu_{ij} + \eta_k\Big)\ \forall\ k \in [Q]$$

Above, $\mu_{ij}$ is as defined in Eq. 3.1.

*Hybrid 2.* In this hybrid, let $d_k = \sum\limits_{1\leq j\leq i\leq w} g_{k,ij}\big(x_i x_j - c_i c_j\big) + p_0 \cdot \eta_k$ for $k \in [Q]$.

*Hybrid 3.* In this hybrid, sample $\mathbf{c}$ at random. This is the simulated world.

*Indistinguishability of Hybrids.* Below we establish that consecutive hybrids are indistinguishable.

*Claim.* Hybrid 0 is indistinguishable from Hybrid 1 assuming that $\mathsf{LinFE}$ is secure.

**Proof.** Recall that for $j \leq i \leq w$, we have:

$$x_i x_j + p_0 \cdot \mu_{ij} = c_i c_j - c_i u_j s_1 - c_j u_i s_1 + u_i u_j s_1^2$$

$$\therefore \sum_{j \leq i \leq w} g_{k,ij}(x_i x_j + p_0 \cdot \mu_{ij}) = \sum_{j \leq i \leq w} g_{k,ij}(c_i c_j + u_i u_j s_1^2 - u_j c_i s_1 - u_i c_j s_1)$$

This implies, $\displaystyle\sum_{j \leq i \leq w} g_{k,ij}(x_i x_j - c_i c_j) + p_0 \cdot \Big(\sum_{j \leq i \leq w} g_{k,ij}\mu_{ij} + \eta_k\Big)$

$$= \sum_{j \leq i \leq w} g_{k,ij}(u_i u_j s_1^2 - u_j c_i s_1 - u_i c_j s_1) + p_0 \cdot \eta_k$$

In Hybrid 0, we have by Eq. 3.2 that the output of LinFE decryption is:

$$\sum_{1 \leq j \leq i \leq w} g_{ij}(-c_i u_j s_1 - c_j u_i s_1 + u_i u_j s_1^2) + p_0 \cdot \eta_k$$

$$= \sum_{j \leq i \leq w} g_{k,ij}(x_i x_j - c_i c_j) + p_0 \cdot \Big(\sum_{j \leq i \leq w} g_{k,ij}\mu_{ij} + \eta_k\Big)$$

In Hybrid 1, the LinFE simulator is invoked with the above value, hence by security of LinFE, Hybrids 0 and 1 are indistinguishable.

*Claim.* Hybrid 1 and Hybrid 2 are statistically indistinguishable.

**Proof.** This follows by our choice of parameters since for $k \in [Q]$, we have

$$\mathsf{SD}\Big(\sum_{1 \leq j \leq i \leq w} g_{k,ij}\mu_{ij} + \eta_k, \eta_k\Big) = \mathrm{negl}(\lambda)$$

Hybrid 2 and Hybrid 3 are indistinguishable assuming the hardness of ring LWE. In more detail, we show:

*Claim.* Assume Regev public key encryption is semantically secure. Then, Hybrid 2 is indistinguishable from Hybrid 3.

**Proof.** Recall that by semantic security of Regev's (dual) public key encryption, we have that the ciphertext $\mathbf{c} = \mathbf{u} \cdot s_1 + p_0 \cdot \boldsymbol{\mu} + \mathbf{x}$ is indistinguishable from random, where $\mathbf{u}$ is part of the public key and $\boldsymbol{\mu} \leftarrow \mathcal{D}_0$ is suitably chosen noise. We refer the reader to [35] for more details.

Given an adversary $\mathcal{B}$ who distinguishes between Hybrid 2 and Hybrid 3, we build an adversary $\mathcal{A}$ who breaks the semantic security of Regev public key encryption. The adversary $\mathcal{A}$ receives $\mathsf{PK} = \mathbf{u}$ and does the following:

- Run LinFE.Setup to obtain LinFE.PK and LinFE.MSK. Return PK = (LinFE.PK, $\mathbf{u}$) to $\mathcal{B}$.
- When $\mathcal{B}$ requests a key $\mathbf{g}_k$ for $k \in [Q]$, construct it honestly as in Hybrid 0.
- When $\mathcal{B}$ outputs challenge $\mathbf{x}$, $\mathcal{A}$ outputs the same.

- $\mathcal{A}$ receives $\mathbf{c}$ where $\mathbf{c} = \mathbf{u} \cdot s_1 + p_0 \cdot \boldsymbol{\mu} + \mathbf{x}$ or random.
- $\mathcal{A}$ samples $\eta_1, \ldots, \eta_Q$ as in Hybrid 2 and computes $d_k = \sum\limits_{1 \leq j \leq i \leq w} g_{k,ij}(x_i x_j - c_i c_j) + p_0 \cdot \eta_k$. It invokes $\mathsf{LinFE.Sim}(1^\lambda, 1^{w+1+Q}, \{\mathbf{g}_k, \mathsf{SK}_{\mathbf{g}_k}, d_k\}_{k \in [Q]})$ and receives $\mathsf{LinFE}$ ciphertext $\mathbf{b}$. It returns $(\mathbf{c}, \mathbf{b})$ to $\mathcal{B}$.
- $\mathcal{B}$ may request more keys (bounded above by $Q$) which are handled as before. Finally, when $\mathcal{B}$ outputs a guess bit $b$, $\mathcal{A}$ outputs the same.

Clearly, if $b = 0$, then $\mathcal{B}$ sees the distribution of Hybrid 2, whereas if $b = 1$, it sees the distribution of Hybrid 3. Hence the claim follows.

## 4   Public Key and Ciphertext Evaluation Algorithms

In this section, we provide the tools to extend our construction for quadratic polynomials to circuits in $\mathsf{NC}_1$. Throughout this section, we assume circular security of LWE. This is for ease of exposition as well as efficiency. This assumption can be removed by choosing new randomness $s_i$ for each level $i$ as in levelled fully homomorphic encryption. Since the intuition was discussed in Sect. 1, we proceed with the technical overview and construction.

*Notation.* To begin, it will be helpful to set up some notation. We will consider circuits of depth $d$, consisting of alternate addition and multiplication layers. Each layer of the circuit is associated with a modulus $p_k$ for level $k$. For an addition layer at level $k$, the modulus $p_k$ will be the same as the previous modulus $p_{k-1}$; for a multiplication layer at level $k$, we require $p_k > p_{k-1}$. This results in a tower of moduli $p_0 < p_1 = p_2 < p_3 = \ldots < p_d$. The smallest modulus $p_0$ is associated with the message space of the scheme.

We define encoding functions $\mathcal{E}^k$ for $k \in [d]$ such that $\mathcal{E}^k : R_{p_{k-1}} \to R_{p_k}$. At level $k$, the encryptor will provide $L^k$ encodings $\mathcal{C}^k$ for some $L^k = O(2^k)$. For $i \in [L^k]$ we define

$$\mathcal{E}^k(y_i) = u_i^k \cdot s + p_{k-1} \cdot \eta_i^k + y_i \mod p_k$$

Here $u_i^k \in R_{p_k}$, $\eta_i^k \leftarrow \chi_k$ and $y_i \in R_{p_{k-1}}$. The RLWE secret $s$ is reused across all levels as discussed above, hence is chosen at the first level, i.e. $s \leftarrow R_{p_1}$. We will refer to $\mathcal{E}^k(y_i)$ as the Regev encoding of $y_i$. At level $k$, the decryptor will be able to compute a Regev encoding of $f^k(\mathbf{x})$ where $f^k$ is the circuit $f$ restricted to level $k$.

It will be convenient for us to denote encodings of functional values at every level, i.e. $f^k(\mathbf{x})$ by $c^k$, i.e. $c^k = \mathcal{E}^k(f^k(\mathbf{x}))$. Here, $c^k$ are encodings computed on the fly by the decryptor whereas $\mathcal{C}^k$ (described above) are a *set* of level $k$ encodings provided by the encryptor to enable the decryptor to compute $c^k$. We will denote the public key or label of an encoding $\mathcal{E}^k(\cdot)$ (resp. $c^k$) by $\mathsf{PK}(\mathcal{E}^k(\cdot))$ (resp. $\mathsf{PK}(c^k)$).

In our construction, we will compose encodings, so that encodings at a given level are messages to encodings at the next level. We refer to such encodings as *nested encodings.* In nested encodings at level $k + 1$, messages may be level $k$ encodings *or* level $k$ encodings times the RLWE secret $s$. We define the notions of nesting level and nested message degree as follows.

**Definition 4.1 (Nesting level and Nested Message Degree).** *Given a composition of successive encodings, i.e. a nested encoding of the form $\mathcal{E}^k(\mathcal{E}^{k-1}(\dots(\mathcal{E}^{\ell+1}(\mathcal{E}^{\ell}(y) \cdot s) \cdot s)\dots \cdot s) \cdot s)$, we will denote as nesting level the value $k - \ell$, the nested message of the encoding as $y$, and the nested message degree of the encoding as the degree of the innermost polynomial $y$.*

Note that in the above definition of nested message, we consider the message in the innermost encoding and ignore the multiplications by $s$ between the layers.
    We prove the following theorem.

**Theorem 4.2.** *There exists a set of encodings $\mathcal{C}^i$ for $i \in [d]$, such that:*

1. **Encodings have size sublinear in circuit.** $\forall i \in [d] \; |\mathcal{C}^i| = O(2^i)$.
2. **Efficient public key and ciphertext evaluation algorithms.** *There exist efficient algorithms $\mathsf{Eval_{PK}}$ and $\mathsf{Eval_{CT}}$ so that for any circuit $f$ of depth $d$, if $\mathsf{PK}_f = \mathsf{Eval_{PK}}(\mathsf{PK}, f)$ and $\mathsf{CT}_{(f(\mathbf{x}))} = \mathsf{Eval_{CT}}(\bigcup_{i \in [d]} \mathcal{C}^i, f)$, then $\mathsf{CT}_{(f(\mathbf{x}))}$ is a "Regev encoding" of $f(\mathbf{x})$ under public key $\mathsf{PK}_f$. Specifically, for some LWE secret $s$, we have:*

$$\mathsf{CT}_{(f(\mathbf{x}))} = \mathsf{PK}_f \cdot s + p_{d-1} \cdot \eta_f^{d-1} + \mu_{f(\mathbf{x})} + f(\mathbf{x}) \tag{4.1}$$

*where $p_{d-1} \cdot \eta_f^{d-1}$ is RLWE noise and $\mu_{f(\mathbf{x})} + f(\mathbf{x})$ is the desired message $f(\mathbf{x})$ plus some noise $\mu_{f(\mathbf{x})}$[4]. Here, $\mu_{f(\mathbf{x})} = p_{d-2} \cdot \eta_f^{d-2} + \dots p_0 \cdot \eta_f^0$ for some noise terms $\eta_f^{d-2}, \dots, \eta_f^0$.*

3. **Ciphertext and public key structure.** *The structure of the functional ciphertext is as:*

$$\mathsf{CT}_{f(\mathbf{x})} = \mathsf{Poly}_f(\mathcal{C}^1, \dots, \mathcal{C}^{d-1}) + \langle \mathsf{Lin}_f, \mathcal{C}^d \rangle \tag{4.2}$$

*where $\mathsf{Poly}_f(\mathcal{C}^1, \dots, \mathcal{C}^{d-1}) \in R_{p_{d-1}}$ is a high degree polynomial value obtained by computing a public $f$-dependent function on level $k \leq d - 1$ encodings $\{\mathcal{C}^k\}_{k \in [d-1]}$ and $\mathsf{Lin}_f \in R_{p_d}^{L_d}$ is an $f$-dependent linear function. We also have*

$$f(\mathbf{x}) + \mu_{f(\mathbf{x})} = \mathsf{Poly}_f(\mathcal{C}^1, \dots, \mathcal{C}^{d-1}) + \langle \mathsf{Lin}_f, \mathcal{M}^d \rangle \tag{4.3}$$

*where $\mathcal{M}^d$ are the messages encoded in $\mathcal{C}^d$ and $\mu_{f(\mathbf{x})}$ is functional noise. The public key for the functional ciphertext is structured as:*

$$\mathsf{PK}(\mathsf{CT}_{f(\mathbf{x})}) = \Big\langle \mathsf{Lin}_f, \big(\mathsf{PK}(\mathcal{C}_1^d), \dots, \mathsf{PK}(\mathcal{C}_{L_d}^d)\big) \Big\rangle \tag{4.4}$$

---

[4] Here $\mu_{f(\mathbf{x})}$ is clubbed with the message $f(\mathbf{x})$ rather than the RLWE noise $p_{d-1} \cdot \eta_f^{d-1}$ since $\mu_{f(\mathbf{x})} + f(\mathbf{x})$ is what will be recovered after decryption of $\mathsf{CT}_{f(\mathbf{x})}$, whereas $p_{d-1} \cdot \eta_f^{d-1}$ will be removed by the decryption procedure. This is merely a matter of notation.

*The Encodings.* We define $\mathcal{C}^k$ recursively as follows:

1. $\mathcal{C}^1 \triangleq \{\mathcal{E}^1(x_i), \mathcal{E}^1(s)\}$
2. If $k$ is a multiplication layer, $\mathcal{C}^k = \{\mathcal{E}^k(\mathcal{C}^{k-1}), \mathcal{E}^k(\mathcal{C}^{k-1} \cdot s), \mathcal{E}^k(s^2)\}$. If $k$ is an addition layer, let $\mathcal{C}^k = \mathcal{C}^{k-1}$.

We prove that:

**Lemma 4.3.** *Assume that $k$ is a multiplication layer. Given $\mathcal{C}^k$ for any $2 < k < d$,*

1. *Level $k$ encodings $\mathcal{E}^k(c^{k-1} \cdot s)$ and $\mathcal{E}^k(c^{k-1})$ may be expressed as quadratic polynomials in level $k-1$ encodings and level $k$ advice encodings $\mathcal{C}^k$. In particular, the polynomials are linear in terms $\mathcal{C}^k$ and quadratic in level $k-1$ encodings $\mathcal{E}^{k-1}(y_i)\mathcal{E}^{k-1}(y_j)$. The messages $y_i, y_j$ of the form $c_\ell^{k-3}$ or $c_\ell^{k-3} \cdot s$ for some level $k-3$ ciphertext $c_\ell^{k-3}$.*
   *Since the exact value of the coefficients is not important, we express this as:*

$$\mathcal{E}^k(c^{k-1} \cdot s), \mathcal{E}^k(c^{k-1}) = \mathsf{LinComb}\left( \mathcal{C}^k, \mathcal{E}^{k-1}(y_i)\mathcal{E}^{k-1}(y_j) \right) \; \forall \, i, j \qquad (4.5)$$

2. *We can compute $c^k$ and $c^{k+1}$ as a linear combination of quadratic terms in level $k-1$ encodings and linear in level $k$ encodings $\mathcal{C}^k$. In particular,*

$$c^k = \mathsf{CT}(f^k(\mathbf{x}) + \mu^k_{f(\mathbf{x})}) = \langle \mathsf{Lin}_{f^k}, \mathcal{C}^k \rangle + \mathsf{LinComb}(\mathsf{Quad}(\mathcal{E}^{k-1}(y_i)\,\mathcal{E}^{k-1}(y_j)))$$
$$= \langle \mathsf{Lin}_{f^k}, \mathcal{C}^k \rangle + \mathsf{Poly}_{f^k}(\mathcal{C}^1, \ldots, \mathcal{C}^{k-1})$$

Proof by induction.

*Base Case.* While the quadratic scheme described in Sect. 3 suffices as a base case, we work out an extended base case for level 4 circuits, since this captures the more general case. Moreover polynomials of degree 4 suffice for computing randomized encodings of circuits in P [44], which we use in our general construction.

We claim that $\mathcal{C}^4$ defined according to the above rules, permits the evaluator to compute :

1. $\mathcal{E}^4(c^3 \cdot s)$ and $\mathcal{E}^4(c^3)$ by taking linear combinations of elements in $\mathcal{C}^4$ and adding to this a quadratic term of the form $\mathcal{E}^3(y_i)\mathcal{E}^3(y_j)$ where $\mathcal{E}^3(y_i)\mathcal{E}^3(y_j) \in \mathcal{C}^3 = \mathcal{C}^2$. We note that since $k-1$ is an addition layer, $\mathcal{C}^3 = \mathcal{C}^2$.
2. Encodings of level 4 functions of $\mathbf{x}$, namely $c^4$.

Note that our level 2 ciphertext may be written as:

$$c_{i,j}^2 = \mathcal{E}^2(x_i x_j + p_0 \cdot \mu_{ij}) = \mathcal{E}^2(c_i^1 c_j^1 + u_i^1 u_j^1(s^2) - u_j^1(c_i^1 s) - u_i^1(c_j^1 s))$$
$$= \mathcal{E}^2(x_i x_j + p_0 \cdot \mu_{ij}) = c_i^1 c_j^1 + \mathcal{E}^2(u_i^1 u_j^1(s^2) - u_j^1(c_i^1 s) - u_i^1(c_j^1 s))$$
$$= c_i^1 c_j^1 + u_i^1 u_j^1 \, \mathcal{E}^2(s^2) - u_j^1 \, \mathcal{E}^2(c_i^1 s) - u_i^1 \, \mathcal{E}^2(c_j^1 s) \quad \in R_{p_2} \qquad (4.6)$$

In the above, the first equality follows by additive malleability of RLWE: here, $c_i^1 c_j^1 \in R_{p_1}$ is a message added to the encoding $\mathcal{E}^2(u_i^1 u_j^1(s^2) - u_j^1(c_i^1 s) - u_i^1(c_j^1 s))$ .

The second equality follows by additive homomorphism of the encodings. Additionally, the public key and the noise of the resultant encoding may be computed as:

$$u_\ell^2 \triangleq \text{PK} \left(\mathcal{E}^2(x_ix_j + p_0 \cdot \mu_{ij})\right) = u_i^1 u_j^1 \text{ PK } \left(\mathcal{E}^2(s^2)\right) - u_j^1 \text{ PK } \left(\mathcal{E}^2(c_i^1 s)\right) - u_i^1 \text{ PK } \left(\mathcal{E}^2(c_j^1 s)\right)$$

$$\text{Nse}_\ell^2 \triangleq \text{Nse} \left(\mathcal{E}^2(x_ix_j + p_0 \cdot \mu_{ij})\right) = u_i^1 u_j^1 \text{ Nse } \left(\mathcal{E}^2(s^2)\right) - u_j^1 \text{ Nse } \left(\mathcal{E}^2(c_i^1 s)\right) - u_i^1 \text{ Nse } \left(\mathcal{E}^2(c_j^1 s)\right)$$

Above, $\text{Nse}(\mathcal{E}^2(\cdot))$ refers to the noise level in the relevant encoding. Note that even though $u_i^1$ are chosen uniformly in $R_{p_1}$, they do not blow up the noise in the above equation since the above noise is relative to the larger ring $R_{p_2}$. This noise growth can be controlled further by using the bit decomposition trick [17,18] – we do not do this here for ease of exposition.

*The Quadratic Method.* Thus, we may compute a level 2 encoding as:

$$\mathcal{E}^2(x_ix_j + p_0 \cdot \mu_{ij}) = \mathcal{E}^1(x_i)\mathcal{E}^1(x_j) + u_i^1 u_j^1 \mathcal{E}^2(s^2) - u_j^1 \mathcal{E}^2(\mathcal{E}^1(x_i) \cdot s) - u_i^1 \mathcal{E}^2(\mathcal{E}^1(x_j) \cdot s) \quad (4.7)$$

Note that the above equation allows us to express the encoding of the desired product at level 2, namely (a noisy version of) $x_ix_j$, as a quadratic polynomial of the following form: level 1 encodings are in the quadratic terms and level 2 encodings are in the linear terms. This equation will be used recursively in our algorithms below, and will be referred to as the "quadratic method".

The key point is that our level 2 ciphertext has the exact same structure as a level 1 encoding, namely it is a Regev encoding using some secret $s$, some label and noise as computed in Eq. 4.7. Thus, letting $y_\ell = x_ix_j$, we may write

$$\mathcal{E}^2(y_\ell) = u_\ell^2 \cdot s + \text{Nse}_\ell^2 + y_\ell \quad \in R_{p_2} \quad (4.8)$$

**Addition (Level 3).** To add two encoded messages $y_\ell = x_ix_j + p_0 \cdot \mu_{ij}$ and $y_{\ell'} = x_{i'}x_{j'} + p_0 \cdot \mu_{i'j'}$, it is easy to see that adding their encodings suffices. The resultant public key and noise is just the summation of the individual public keys and noise terms. Thus, if the $\ell^{th}$ wire is the sum of the $i^{th}$ and $j^{th}$ wires, we have:

$$c_\ell^3 = c_i^2 + c_j^2 \quad (4.9)$$

and

$$\text{PK}(c_\ell^3) = \text{PK}(c_i^2) + \text{PK}(c_j^2) \quad (4.10)$$

**Multiplication (Level 4).** The nontrivial case is that of multiplication. We next compute an encoding for the product of $y_\ell = x_ix_j + x_mx_t + p_0 \cdot \mu_\ell^4$ and $y_{\ell'} = x_{i'}x_{j'} + x_{m'}x_{t'} + p_0 \cdot \mu_{\ell'}^4$ where $\mu_\ell^4, \mu_{\ell'}^4$ are level 4 noise terms computed as $\mu_\ell^4 = \mu_{ij} + \mu_{mt}$ (analogously for $\mu_{\ell'}^4$). Let $c_\ell^3$ and $c_{\ell'}^3$ denote the encodings of $y_\ell$ and $y_{\ell'}$ computed using the first three levels of evaluation. As before, we have by the quadratic method:

$$c_t^4 = \mathcal{E}^4(y_\ell y_{\ell'}) = c_\ell^3 c_{\ell'}^3 + \mathcal{E}^4 \left(u_\ell^3 u_{\ell'}^3 (s^2) - u_{\ell'}^3 (c_\ell^3 s) - u_\ell^3 (c_{\ell'}^3 s)\right) \in R_{p_4}$$

$$= c_\ell^3 c_{\ell'}^3 + u_\ell^3 u_{\ell'}^3 \mathcal{E}^4(s^2) - u_{\ell'}^3 \mathcal{E}^4(c_\ell^3 s) - u_\ell^3 \mathcal{E}^4(c_{\ell'}^3 s) \quad (4.11)$$

By correctness of first three levels of evaluation as described above, the decryptor can compute the encoding of $y_\ell$, namely $c_\ell^3$ correctly, hence the quadratic term $c_\ell^3 c_{\ell'}^3$ may be computed. It remains to compute the terms $\mathcal{E}^4(c_\ell^3 s)$. Note that the encryptor may not provide the encodings $\mathcal{E}^4(c_\ell^3 s)$ directly and preserve succinctness because $c_\ell^3 = \mathcal{E}^2(x_i\, x_j + p_0 \cdot \mu_{ij}) + \mathcal{E}^2(x_m\, x_t + p_0 \cdot \mu_{mt})$ and $\mathcal{E}^2(x_i\, x_j + p_0 \cdot \mu_{ij})$ contains the cross term $c_i^1 c_j^1$ as shown by Eq. 4.6.

Consider the term $\mathcal{E}^4(c_\ell^3 s)$. In fact, we will only be able to compute a noisy version of this encoding, i.e. $\mathcal{E}^4(c_\ell^3 s + p_1 \cdot \mu_\ell^3)$ for some $p_1 \cdot \mu_\ell^3$.

$$\mathcal{E}^4(c_\ell^3 s) = \mathcal{E}^4\big((\mathcal{E}^2(x_i\, x_j + p_0 \cdot \mu_{ij}) + \mathcal{E}^2(x_m\, x_t + p_0 \cdot \mu_{mt})) \cdot s\big)$$
$$= \mathcal{E}^4\Big(\big((c_i^1 c_j^1 + u_i^1 u_j^1\, \mathcal{E}^2(s^2) - u_j^1\, \mathcal{E}^2(c_i^1 s) - u_i^1\, \mathcal{E}^2(c_j^1 s)\,) \cdot s\big)$$
$$+ \mathcal{E}^4\Big(\big((c_m^1 c_t^1 + u_m^1 u_t^1\, \mathcal{E}^2(s^2) - u_t^1\, \mathcal{E}^2(c_m^1 s) - u_m^1\, \mathcal{E}^2(c_t^1 s)\,) \cdot s\big)$$
$$= \mathcal{E}^4(c_i^1 c_j^1 s) + \mathcal{E}^4(u_i^1 u_j^1\, \mathcal{E}^2(s^2)\, s) - \mathcal{E}^4(u_j^1\, \mathcal{E}^2(c_i^1 s)\, s) - \mathcal{E}^4(u_i^1\, \mathcal{E}^2(c_j^1 s)\, s)$$
$$+ \mathcal{E}^4(c_m^1 c_t^1 s) + \mathcal{E}^4(u_m^1 u_t^1\, \mathcal{E}^2(s^2)\, s) - \mathcal{E}^4(u_t^1\, \mathcal{E}^2(c_m^1 s) s) - \mathcal{E}^4(u_m^1\, \mathcal{E}^2(c_t^1 s)\, s)$$
$$= \mathcal{E}^4(c_i^1 c_j^1 s) + u_i^1 u_j^1\, \mathcal{E}^4(\mathcal{E}^2(s^2)\, s) - u_j^1\, \mathcal{E}^4(\mathcal{E}^2(c_i^1 s)\, s) - u_i^1\, \mathcal{E}^4(\mathcal{E}^2(c_j^1 s)\, s)$$
$$+ \mathcal{E}^4(c_m^1 c_t^1 s) + u_m^1 u_t^1\, \mathcal{E}^4(\mathcal{E}^2(s^2)\, s) - u_t^1\, \mathcal{E}^4(\mathcal{E}^2(c_m^1 s)s) - u_m^1\, \mathcal{E}^4(\mathcal{E}^2(c_t^1 s)\, s) \quad (4.12)$$

Thus, to compute $\mathcal{E}^4(c_\ell^3 s)$ by additive homomorphism, it suffices to compute the encodings $\mathcal{E}^4(c_i^1 c_j^1 s)$, $\mathcal{E}^4(\mathcal{E}^2(s^2)\, s)$ and $\mathcal{E}^4(\mathcal{E}^2(c_j^1 s)\, s)$ for all $i, j$. Note that by definition of $\mathcal{C}^4$, we have that for $m \in [w]$,

$$\left\{ \mathcal{E}^4(\mathcal{E}^2(s^2)\, s), \quad \mathcal{E}^4(\mathcal{E}^2(c_m^1 s)s) \right\} \subseteq \mathcal{C}^4 \qquad (4.13)$$

Note that since level 3 is an addition layer, $\mathcal{E}^3 = \mathcal{E}^2$.

The only terms above not accounted for are $\mathcal{E}^4(c_i^1 c_j^1 s)$ and $\mathcal{E}^4(c_m^1 c_t^1 s)$, which are symmetric. Consider the former. To compute this, we view $c_i^1 c_j^1 s$ as a quadratic term in $c_i^1$ and $c_j^1 \cdot s$ and re-apply the quadratic method given in Eq. 4.7. This will enable us to compute a noisy version of $\mathcal{E}^4(c_i^1 c_j^1 s)$, namely $\mathcal{E}^4(c_i^1 c_j^1 s + p_1 \cdot \mu_{ij}^2)$ for some noise $\mu_{ij}^2$.

*Applying the Quadratic Method (Eq. 4.7):* Given $\mathcal{E}^2(c_i^1)$, $\mathcal{E}^2(c_j^1 \cdot s)$ along with $\mathcal{E}^4(\mathcal{E}^2(c_i^1)\, s)$ and $\mathcal{E}^4(\mathcal{E}^2(c_j^1 \cdot s)\, s)$ we may compute $\mathcal{E}^4(c_i^1 c_j^1 s + p_1 \cdot \mu_{ij}^2)$ using the quadratic method. In more detail, we let

$$d_i \triangleq \mathcal{E}^2(c_i^1), \quad h_j \triangleq \mathcal{E}^2(c_j^1 \cdot s) \in R_{p_2} \quad \text{and} \quad \hat{d}_i \triangleq \mathcal{E}^4(\mathcal{E}^2(c_i^1)\, s), \quad \hat{h}_j \triangleq \mathcal{E}^4(\mathcal{E}^2(c_j^1 \cdot s)\, s) \in R_{p_4}$$

Then, we have:

$$\mathcal{E}^4(c_i^1 c_j^1 s + p_1 \cdot \mu_{ij}^2) = d_i h_j + \mathsf{PK}(\mathcal{E}^2(c_i^1))\, \mathsf{PK}(\mathcal{E}^2(c_j^1 \cdot s))\, \mathcal{E}^4(s^2) \qquad (4.14)$$
$$- \mathsf{PK}(\mathcal{E}^2(c_i^1))\, \hat{h}_j - \mathsf{PK}(\mathcal{E}^2(c_j^1 \cdot s))\, \hat{d}_i \ \in R_{p_4}$$

where $\mu_{ij}^2 = c_i^1 \cdot \mathsf{Nse}(\mathcal{E}^2(c_j^1 \cdot s)) + c_j^2 \cdot s \cdot \mathsf{Nse}(\mathcal{E}^2(c_i^1)) + p_1 \cdot \mathsf{Nse}(\mathcal{E}^2(c_j^1 \cdot s)) \cdot \mathsf{Nse}(\mathcal{E}^2(c_i^1))$.

Again, note that though $c_i$ are large in $R_{p_1}$, they are small in $R_{p_2}$ upwards, and may be clubbed with noise terms as done above.

Also, the public key for $\mathcal{E}^4(c_i^1 c_j^1 s + p_1 \cdot \mu_{ij}^2)$ may be computed as:

$$\mathsf{PK}(\mathcal{E}^4(c_i^1 c_j^1 s + p_1 \cdot \mu_{ij}^2)) = \mathsf{PK}(\mathcal{E}^2(c_i^1)) \, \mathsf{PK}(\mathcal{E}^2(c_j^1 \cdot s)) \, \mathsf{PK}(\mathcal{E}^4(s^2)) \qquad (4.15)$$
$$- \mathsf{PK}(\mathcal{E}^2(c_i^1)) \, \mathsf{PK}(\hat{h}_j) - \mathsf{PK}(\mathcal{E}^2(c_j^1 \cdot s)) \, \mathsf{PK}(\hat{d}_i)$$

Thus we have, $\mathcal{E}^4(c_\ell^3 s + p_1 \cdot \mu_\ell^3)$ is a Regev encoding with public key

$$\mathsf{PK}(\mathcal{E}^4(c_\ell^3 s + p_1 \cdot \mu_\ell^3))$$
$$= \mathsf{PK}\Big(\mathcal{E}^4(c_i^1 c_j^1 s + p_1 \cdot \mu_{ij}^2) \; + u_i^1 u_j^1 \, \mathcal{E}^4(\mathcal{E}^2(s^2) \, s) \; - u_j^1 \, \mathcal{E}^4(\mathcal{E}^2(c_i^1 s) \, s) - u_i^1 \, \mathcal{E}^4(\mathcal{E}^2(c_j^1 s) \, s)$$
$$+ \mathcal{E}^4((c_m^1 c_t^1 s + p_1 \cdot \mu_{mt}^2) \; + u_m^1 u_t^1 \, \mathcal{E}^4(\mathcal{E}^2(s^2) \, s) - u_t^1 \, \mathcal{E}^4(\mathcal{E}^2(c_m^1 s)s) - u_m^1 \, \mathcal{E}^4(\mathcal{E}^2(c_t^1 s) \, s)\Big)$$
$$= \mathsf{PK}(\mathcal{E}^4(c_i^1 c_j^1 s + p_1 \cdot \mu_{ij}^2)) \; + u_i^1 u_j^1 \, \mathsf{PK}(\mathcal{E}^4(\mathcal{E}^2(s^2) \, s)) \; - u_j^1 \, \mathsf{PK}(\mathcal{E}^4(\mathcal{E}^2(c_i^1 s) \, s))$$
$$- u_i^1 \, \mathsf{PK}(\mathcal{E}^4(\mathcal{E}^2(c_j^1 s) \, s)) + \mathsf{PK}(\mathcal{E}^4((c_m^1 c_t^1 s + p_1 \cdot \mu_{mt}^2)) \; + u_m^1 u_t^1 \, \mathsf{PK}(\mathcal{E}^4(\mathcal{E}^2(s^2) \, s))$$
$$- u_t^1 \, \mathsf{PK}(\mathcal{E}^4(\mathcal{E}^2(c_m^1 s)s)) - u_m^1 \, \mathsf{PK}(\mathcal{E}^4(\mathcal{E}^2(c_t^1 s) \, s)) \qquad (4.16)$$

Above $\mathsf{PK}(\mathcal{E}^4(c_i^1 c_j^1 s + p_1 \cdot \mu_{ij}^2))$ may be computed by Eq. 4.15 and the remaining public keys are provided in $\mathcal{C}^4$ as described in Eq. 4.13. Also, we have $\mu_\ell^3 = \mu_{ij}^2 + \mu_{mt}^2$.

By Eqs. 4.12, 4.13 and 4.14, we may compute $\mathcal{E}^4(c_\ell^3 s + p_1 \cdot \mu_\ell^3)$ for any $\ell$. Note that,

$$\mathcal{E}^4(c_\ell^3 s + p_1 \cdot \mu_\ell^3) = \mathsf{LinComb}\Big(\mathcal{E}^2(c_i^1) \cdot \mathcal{E}^2(c_j^1 \cdot s), \mathcal{E}^4(\mathcal{E}^2(c_i^1) \, s), \, \mathcal{E}^4(\mathcal{E}^2(c_j^1 \cdot s) \, s)\Big)$$
$$= \langle \mathsf{Lin}_{f^4}, \, \mathcal{C}^4 \rangle + \mathsf{Quad}(\mathcal{E}^2(c_i^1) \cdot \mathcal{E}^2(c_j^1 \cdot s))$$

for some linear function $\mathsf{Lin}_{f^4}$.

## 4.1   Ciphertext and Public Key Structure

By Eq. 4.11, we then get that

$$c_t^4 = c_\ell^3 \, c_{\ell'}^3 + u_\ell^3 \, u_{\ell'}^3 \mathcal{E}^4(s^2) - u_\ell^3 \left(\langle \mathsf{Lin}'_{f^4}, \, \mathcal{C}^4 \rangle + \mathsf{Quad}'(\mathcal{E}^2(c_i^1) \cdot \mathcal{E}^2(c_j^1 \cdot s))\right)$$
$$- u_{\ell'}^3 \left(\langle \mathsf{Lin}''_{f^4}, \, \mathcal{C}^4 \rangle + \mathsf{Quad}''(\mathcal{E}^2(c_i^1) \cdot \mathcal{E}^2(c_j^1 \cdot s))\right)$$
$$= \langle \mathsf{Lin}'''_{f^4}, \, \mathcal{C}^4 \rangle + \mathsf{Poly}_{f^4}(\mathcal{C}^1, \mathcal{C}^2, \mathcal{C}^3)$$

for some linear functions $\mathsf{Lin}'_{f^4}, \mathsf{Lin}''_{f^4}, \mathsf{Lin}'''_{f^4}$ and quadratic functions $\mathsf{Quad}', \mathsf{Quad}''$ and polynomial $\mathsf{Poly}_{f^4}$.

Thus, we have computed $\mathcal{E}^4(c_\ell^3 s + p_1 \cdot \mu_\ell^3)$ and hence, $c^4$ by Eq. 4.11. The final public key for $c^4$ is given by:

$$\mathsf{PK}(c^4) = u_\ell^3 u_{\ell'}^3 \, \mathsf{PK}(\mathcal{E}^4(s^2)) - u_{\ell'}^3 \, \mathsf{PK}(\mathcal{E}^4(c_\ell^3 s)) - u_\ell^3 \, \mathsf{PK}(\mathcal{E}^4(c_{\ell'}^3 s)) \qquad (4.17)$$

$\mathcal{E}^4(c^3)$ and $\mathcal{E}^4(c_i^1 c_j^1)$ are computed analogously. Thus, we have established correctness of the base case.

**Note.** In the base case, we see that each time the quadratic method is applied to compute an encoding of a product of two messages, we get an encoding of the desired product plus noise.

*Induction Step.* Assume that the claim is true for level $k-1$. Then we establish that it is true for level $k$.

By the I.H, we have that:

1. We can compute $\mathcal{E}^{k-1}(c^{k-2} \cdot s)$ and $\mathcal{E}^{k-1}(c^{k-2})$ by taking linear combinations of elements in $\mathcal{C}^{k-1}$ and quadratic terms of the form $\mathcal{E}^{k-2}(y_i)\mathcal{E}^{k-2}(y_j)$ for some $y_i, y_j$ of the form $c_i^{k-4}$, $c_j^{k-4}$ s.
2. We can compute $c^{k-1}$.

To compute $c^k$ using the quadratic method, it suffices to compute $\mathcal{E}^k(c^{k-1} \cdot s)$.

*Computing* $\mathcal{E}^k(c^{k-1} \cdot s)$. We claim that:

*Claim.* The term $\mathcal{E}^k(c_\ell^{k-1}s)$ (hence $c^k$) can be computed as a linear combination of elements in $\mathcal{C}^k$ and quadratic terms of the form $\mathcal{E}^{k-1}(\cdot) \cdot \mathcal{E}^{k-1}(\cdot)$.

**Proof.** The term $\mathcal{E}^k(c^{k-1} \cdot s)$ may be written as:

$$\mathcal{E}^k(c^{k-1} \cdot s)$$
$$= \mathcal{E}^k\left( \left( c_i^{k-2} c_j^{k-2} - u_i^{k-2}\mathcal{E}^{k-1}(c_j^{k-2} \cdot s) - u_j^{k-2}\mathcal{E}^{k-1}(c_i^{k-2} \cdot s) + u_i^{k-2}u_j^{k-2}\mathcal{E}^{k-1}(s^2) \right) \cdot s \right)$$
$$= \mathcal{E}^k(c_i^{k-2} c_j^{k-2} s) - u_i^{k-2}\mathcal{E}^k\left( \mathcal{E}^{k-1}(c_j^{k-2} \cdot s) \cdot s \right)$$
$$- u_j^{k-2}\mathcal{E}^k\left( \mathcal{E}^{k-1}(c_i^{k-2} \cdot s) \cdot s \right) + u_i^{k-2}u_j^{k-2}\mathcal{E}^k\left( \mathcal{E}^{k-1}(s^2) \cdot s \right) \qquad (4.18)$$

Consider $\mathcal{E}^k\left( \mathcal{E}^{k-1}(s^2) \cdot s \right)$. Since $\mathcal{E}^{k-1}(s^2) \in \mathcal{C}^{k-1}$ and $\mathcal{E}^k\left( \mathcal{C}^{k-1} \cdot s \right)$ is contained in $\mathcal{C}^k$, we have that $\mathcal{E}^k\left( \mathcal{E}^{k-1}(s^2) \cdot s \right) \in \mathcal{C}^k$.

Consider the term $\mathcal{E}^k(c_i^{k-2} c_j^{k-2} s)$. We may compute $\mathcal{E}^k(c_i^{k-2} c_j^{k-2} s)$ using the quadratic method with messages $c_i^{k-2}$ and $c_j^{k-2}$ s as:

$$\mathcal{E}^k(c_i^{k-2} c_j^{k-2} s)$$
$$= \left( \mathcal{E}^{k-1}(c_i^{k-2}) \cdot \mathcal{E}^{k-1}(c_j^{k-2} \cdot s) \right) + \mathsf{PK}(\mathcal{E}^{k-1}(c_i^{k-2}))\mathsf{PK}(\mathcal{E}^{k-1}(c_j^{k-2} \cdot s)) \, \mathcal{E}^k(s^2)$$
$$- \mathsf{PK}(\mathcal{E}^{k-1}(c_i^{k-2})) \left( \mathcal{E}^k\left( \mathcal{E}^{k-1}(c_j^{k-2} \cdot s) \cdot s \right) \right) - \mathsf{PK}(\mathcal{E}^{k-1}(c_j^{k-2} \cdot s)) \left( \mathcal{E}^k\left( \mathcal{E}^{k-1}(c_i^{k-2}) \cdot s \right) \right)$$
$$(4.19)$$

Thus, to compute $\mathcal{E}^k(c^{k-1} \cdot s)$, it suffices to compute the term $\mathcal{E}^k(c_i^{k-2} c_j^{k-2} s)$ since the additional terms such as $\mathcal{E}^k\left( \mathcal{E}^{k-1}(c_i^{k-2} \cdot s) \cdot s \right)$ that appear in Eq. 4.18 also appear in Eq. 4.19 and will be computed in the process of computing $\mathcal{E}^k(c_i^{k-2} c_j^{k-2} s)$.

**Note.** We observe that in Eq. 4.19, by "factoring out" the quadratic term $\mathcal{E}^{k-1}(c_i^{k-2}) \cdot \mathcal{E}^{k-1}(c_j^{k-2} \cdot s)$ (which can be computed by I.H.), we reduce the computation of $\mathcal{E}^k(c^{k-1} \cdot s)$ to $\mathcal{E}^k(\mathcal{E}^{k-1}(c_j^{k-2} \cdot s) \cdot s)$ where the latter value has half the nested message degree (ref. Definition 4.1) of the former at the cost of adding one more level of nesting and a new multiplication by $s$. By recursively applying Eq. 4.19, we will obtain $O(k)$ quadratic encodings in level $k-1$ and a linear term in level $k$ advice encodings $\mathcal{C}^k$.

Proceeding, we see that to compute $\mathcal{E}^k(c_i^{k-2} c_j^{k-2} s)$, we are required to compute the following terms:

1. $\mathcal{E}^{k-1}(c_i^{k-2})$ and $\mathcal{E}^{k-1}(c_j^{k-2} \cdot s)$. These can be computed by the induction hypothesis using linear combinations of elements in $\mathcal{C}^{k-1}$ and quadratic terms of the form $\mathcal{E}^{k-2}(y_i)\mathcal{E}^{k-2}(y_j)$ for some $y_i, y_j$. Since the precise linear coefficients are not important, we shall denote:

$$\mathcal{E}^{k-1}(c_j^{k-2} \cdot s) = \mathsf{LinComb}(\mathcal{C}^{k-1}, \mathcal{E}^{k-2}(\cdot)\mathcal{E}^{k-2}(\cdot)) \tag{4.20}$$

2. $\mathcal{E}^k(\mathcal{E}^{k-1}(c_i^{k-2}) \cdot s)$ and $\mathcal{E}^k(\mathcal{E}^{k-1}(c_j^{k-2} \cdot s) \cdot s)$: Consider the latter term (the former can be computed analogously).

By the induction hypothesis,

$$\mathcal{E}^k(\mathcal{E}^{k-1}(c_j^{k-2} \cdot s) \cdot s)$$
$$= \mathcal{E}^k\left(\mathsf{LinComb}(\mathcal{C}^{k-1}, \mathcal{E}^{k-2}(\cdot)\mathcal{E}^{k-2}(\cdot)) \cdot s\right)$$
$$= \mathcal{E}^k\left(\mathsf{LinComb}(\mathcal{C}^{k-1} \cdot s)\right) + \mathcal{E}^k\left(\mathsf{LinComb}(\mathcal{E}^{k-2}(y_a)\mathcal{E}^{k-2}(y_b) \cdot s)\right)$$
$$= \mathsf{LinComb}\left(\mathcal{E}^k(\mathcal{C}^{k-1} \cdot s)\right) + \mathsf{LinComb}\left(\mathcal{E}^k(\mathcal{E}^{k-2}(y_a)\mathcal{E}^{k-2}(y_b) \cdot s)\right) \tag{4.21}$$

Again, we note that the terms $\mathcal{E}^k(\mathcal{C}^{k-1} \cdot s) \in \mathcal{C}^k$ by definition hence it remains to construct $\mathcal{E}^k\left((\mathcal{E}^{k-2}(y_a)\mathcal{E}^{k-2}(y_b)) \cdot s\right)$ for some $y_a, y_b \in \{c_a^{k-3}, c_b^{k-3} \cdot s\}$.
To proceed, again, we will consider $z_a = \mathcal{E}^{k-2}(y_a)$ and $z_b = \mathcal{E}^{k-2}(y_b) \cdot s$ as messages and apply the quadratic method to compute an encoding of their product. In more detail,

$$\mathcal{E}^k\left((\mathcal{E}^{k-2}(y_a)\mathcal{E}^{k-2}(y_b)) \cdot s\right)$$
$$= \mathsf{LinComb}\Big(\mathcal{E}^{k-1}(\mathcal{E}^{k-2}(y_a)) \cdot \mathcal{E}^{k-1}(\mathcal{E}^{k-2}(y_b) \cdot s),$$
$$\mathcal{E}^k(\mathcal{E}^{k-1}(\mathcal{E}^{k-2}(y_a)) \cdot s), \ \mathcal{E}^k(\mathcal{E}^{k-1}(\mathcal{E}^{k-2}(y_b) \cdot s) \cdot s)\Big) \tag{4.22}$$

Thus, we are required to compute:
(a) $\mathcal{E}^{k-1}(\mathcal{E}^{k-2}(y_a)), \mathcal{E}^{k-1}(\mathcal{E}^{k-2}(y_b) \cdot s)$: These can be computed via the induction hypothesis.

(b) $\mathcal{E}^k\left(\mathcal{E}^{k-1}(\mathcal{E}^{k-2}(y_a))\cdot s\right)$ and $\mathcal{E}^k\left(\mathcal{E}^{k-1}(\mathcal{E}^{k-2}(y_b)\cdot s)\cdot s\right)$: Consider the latter term (the former may be computed analogously). Note that

$$\mathcal{E}^{k-2}(y_b) = \mathsf{LinComb}\left(\mathcal{C}^{k-2}, \mathcal{E}^{k-3}(\cdot)\mathcal{E}^{k-3}(\cdot)\right)$$

$$\therefore \mathcal{E}^k\left(\mathcal{E}^{k-1}(\mathcal{E}^{k-2}(y_b)\cdot s)\cdot s\right) = \mathcal{E}^k\left(\mathcal{E}^{k-1}(\mathsf{LinComb}(\mathcal{C}^{k-2}, \mathcal{E}^{k-3}(\cdot)\mathcal{E}^{k-3}(\cdot)))\cdot s)\cdot s\right)$$

Again, $\mathcal{E}^k(\mathcal{E}^{k-1}(\mathcal{C}^{k-2}\cdot s)\cdot s) \in \mathcal{C}^k$ so we are left to compute:

$$\mathcal{E}^k\left(\mathcal{E}^{k-1}(\mathcal{E}^{k-3}(\cdot)\mathcal{E}^{k-3}(\cdot)\cdot s)\cdot s\right)$$
$$= \mathcal{E}^k\left(\mathsf{LinComb}\left(\mathcal{E}^{k-2}(\mathcal{E}^{k-3}(\cdot)\cdot s)\cdot \mathcal{E}^{k-2}(\mathcal{E}^{k-3}(\cdot)),\right.\right.$$
$$\left.\left.\mathcal{E}^{k-1}(\mathcal{E}^{k-2}(\mathcal{E}^{k-3}(\cdot)\cdot s)\cdot s)\right)\right)$$
$$= \mathsf{LinComb}\left(\mathcal{E}^{k-1}(\mathcal{E}^{k-2}(\mathcal{E}^{k-3}(\cdot)\cdot s))\cdot \mathcal{E}^{k-1}(\mathcal{E}^{k-2}(\mathcal{E}^{k-3}(\cdot)\cdot s)\cdot s),\right.$$
$$\left.\mathcal{E}^k\left(\mathcal{E}^{k-1}(\mathcal{E}^{k-2}(\mathcal{E}^{k-3}(\cdot)\cdot s)\cdot s)\cdot s\right)\cdot s\right)$$

Thus, again by "factoring out" quadratic term $\mathcal{E}^{k-1}(\mathcal{E}^{k-2}(\mathcal{E}^{k-3}(\cdot)\cdot s))\cdot \mathcal{E}^{k-1}(\mathcal{E}^{k-2}(\mathcal{E}^{k-3}(\cdot)\cdot s)\cdot s)$, we have reduced computation of $\mathcal{E}^k\left(\mathcal{E}^{k-1}(\mathcal{E}^{k-2}(y_b)\cdot s)\cdot s\right)$ to $\mathcal{E}^k\left(\mathcal{E}^{k-1}(\mathcal{E}^{k-2}(\mathcal{E}^{k-3}(\cdot)\cdot s)\cdot s)\cdot s\right)$ which has half the nested message degree of the former at the cost of one additional nesting (and multiplication by $s$)[5].

Proceeding recursively, we may factor out a quadratic term for each level, to be left with a term which has half the nested message degree and one additional level of nesting. At the last level, we obtain nested encodings which are contained in $\mathcal{C}^k$ by construction. Hence we may compute $\mathcal{E}^k(c^{k-1}\cdot s)$ as a linear combination of quadratic terms of the form $\mathcal{E}^{k-1}(\cdot)\mathcal{E}^{k-1}(\cdot)$ and linear terms in $\mathcal{C}^k$. Please see Fig. 1 for a graphical illustration.

Note that the public key $\mathsf{PK}(\mathcal{E}^k(c^{k-1}\cdot s))$ can be computed as a linear combination of the public keys $\mathsf{PK}(\mathcal{C}^k)$, as in Eq. 4.16.

$$\mathsf{PK}(\mathcal{E}^k(c^{k-1}\cdot s)) = \mathsf{LinComb}(\mathsf{PK}(\mathcal{C}^k)) \qquad (4.23)$$

Note that for the public key computation, the higher degree encoding computations are not relevant as these form the message of the final level $k$ encoding.

*Computing level $k$ ciphertext.* Next, we have that:

$$c_t^k = c_\ell^{k-1}c_{\ell'}^{k-1} + \mathcal{E}^k\left(u_\ell^{k-1}u_{\ell'}^{k-1}(s^2) - u_{\ell'}^{k-1}(c_\ell^{k-1}s) - u_\ell^{k-1}(c_{\ell'}^{k-1}s)\right)$$
$$= c_\ell^{k-1}c_{\ell'}^{k-1} + u_\ell^{k-1}u_{\ell'}^{k-1}\,\mathcal{E}^k(s^2) - u_{\ell'}^{k-1}\,\mathcal{E}^k(c_\ell^{k-1}s) - u_\ell^{k-1}\,\mathcal{E}^k(c_{\ell'}^{k-1}s) \qquad (4.24)$$

---

[5] We note that the multiplication by $s$ does not impact the nested message degree, number of nestings or growth of the expression as we proceed down the circuit.

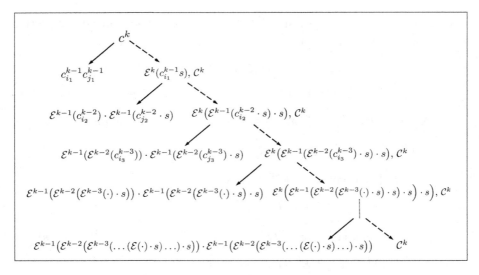

**Fig. 1.** Computing level $k$ functional ciphertext $c^k$ encoding $f^k(\mathbf{x})$ using induction. A term in any node is implied by a quadratic polynomial in its children, quadratic in the terms of the left child, and linear in the terms of the right child. The solid arrows on the left indicate quadratic terms that are computed by the induction hypothesis. The dashed arrows to the right point to terms whose *linear* combination suffices, along with the high degree terms in the left sibling, to compute the parent. The terms in the right child may be further decomposed into quadratic polynomials in its children, quadratic in left child terms and linear in right child terms, until we reach the last level, where the terms in the right child are provided directly by the encryptor as advice encodings $\mathcal{C}^k$. The functional ciphertext at level $k$, namely the root $c^k$ is thus ultimately linear in $\mathcal{C}^k$, while being high degree in lower level encodings $\mathcal{C}^1, \ldots, \mathcal{C}^{k-1}$.

Similarly,

$$\mathsf{PK}(c_t^k) = u_\ell^{k-1} u_{\ell'}^{k-1} \, \mathsf{PK}(\mathcal{E}^k(s^2)) - u_{\ell'}^{k-1} \, \mathsf{PK}(\mathcal{E}^k(c_\ell^{k-1}s)) - u_\ell^{k-1} \, \mathsf{PK}(\mathcal{E}^k(c_{\ell'}^{k-1}s)) \tag{4.25}$$

*Public Key, Ciphertext and Decryption Structure.* From the above, we claim:

*Claim.* The public key for $c_t^k$ (for any $t$) is a publicly computable linear combination of public keys of level $k$ encodings $\mathsf{PK}(\mathcal{E}^k(s^2))$ and $\mathsf{PK}(\mathcal{E}^k(c_\ell^{k-1}s))$ for all $\ell$.

Regarding the ciphertext, since we computed $\mathcal{E}^k(c_\ell^{k-1}s)$ from $\mathcal{C}^k$ above, and $c^{k-1}$ may be computed via the induction hypothesis, we may compute $c^k$ as desired. Moreover, since $\mathcal{E}^k(c_\ell^{k-1}s)$ is linear in level $k$ encodings and has quadratic terms in level $k-1$ encodings, we get by unrolling the recursion that $\mathcal{E}^k(c_\ell^{k-1}s)$

and hence level $k$ ciphertext $c^k$ is linear in level $k$ encodings and polynomial in lower level encodings $\mathcal{C}^1, \ldots, \mathcal{C}^{k-1}$. Hence, we have that:

$$c^k = \mathsf{CT}(f^k(\mathbf{x}) + \mu_{f(\mathbf{x})}^k) = \langle \mathsf{Lin}_{f^k}, \mathcal{C}^k \rangle + \mathsf{LinComb}\big(\mathsf{Quad}(\mathcal{E}^{k-1}(y_i)\, \mathcal{E}^{k-1}(y_j))\big)$$

$$= \langle \mathsf{Lin}_{f^k}, \mathcal{C}^k \rangle + \mathsf{Poly}_{f^k}\big(\mathcal{C}^1, \ldots, \mathcal{C}^{k-1}\big)$$

Moreover, note that the computation of the functional message embedded in a level $k$ ciphertext $c^k$ can be viewed as follows. By Eq. 4.6, we see that the message embedded in $c^k$ equals the *encoding* in the left child plus a linear combination of the *messages* embedded in the right child. At the next level, we see that the message in the right child at level 2 (from the top) again equals the encoding in the left child plus a linear combination of the messages embedded in the right child. At the last level, we get that the message embedded in $c^k$ is a quadratic polynomial in all the left children in the tree, and a linear combination of level $k$ messages $\mathcal{M}^k$. Thus, we have as desired that:

$$f(\mathbf{x}) \approx \mathsf{Poly}_f(\mathcal{C}^1, \ldots, \mathcal{C}^{d-1}) + \langle \mathsf{Lin}_f, \mathcal{M}^d \rangle$$

*The Public Key and Ciphertext Evaluation Algorithms.* Our evaluation algorithms $\mathsf{Eval}_{\mathsf{PK}}$ and $\mathsf{Eval}_{\mathsf{CT}}$ are defined recursively, so that to compute the functional public key and functional ciphertext at level $k$, the algorithms require the same for level $k-1$. Please see Figs. 2 and 3 for the formal descriptions.

---

**Algorithm $\mathsf{Eval}_{\mathsf{PK}}^k(\underset{i \in [k]}{\cup} \mathsf{PK}(\mathcal{C}^i), \ell)$**

To compute the label for the $\ell^{th}$ wire in the level $k$ circuit, do:

1. If the $\ell^{th}$ wire at level $k$ is the addition of the $i^{th}$ and $j^{th}$ wire at level $k-1$, then do the following:
   - If $k = 3$ (base case), then compute $\mathsf{PK}(c_\ell^3) = \mathsf{PK}(c_i^2) + \mathsf{PK}(c_j^2)$ as in Equation 4.10.
   - Let $\mathsf{PK}_i^{k-1} = \mathsf{Eval}_{\mathsf{PK}}^{k-1}(\underset{j \in [k-1]}{\cup} \mathsf{PK}(\mathcal{C}^j), i)$ and $\mathsf{PK}_j^{k-1} = \mathsf{Eval}_{\mathsf{PK}}^{k-1}(\underset{i \in [k-1]}{\cup} \mathsf{PK}(\mathcal{C}^i), j)$,
   - Let $\mathsf{PK}_\ell^k = \mathsf{PK}_i^{k-1} + \mathsf{PK}_j^{k-1}$
2. If the $\ell^{th}$ wire at level $k$ is the multiplication of the $i^{th}$ and $j^{th}$ wire at level $k-1$, then do the following:
   - If $k = 4$ (base case), then compute $\mathsf{PK}_\ell^k$ as described in Equation 4.17.
   - Let $u_i^{k-1} = \mathsf{Eval}_{\mathsf{PK}}^{k-1}(\underset{j \in [k-1]}{\cup} \mathsf{PK}(\mathcal{C}^j), i)$ and $u_j^{k-1} = \mathsf{Eval}_{\mathsf{PK}}^{k-1}(\underset{i \in [k-1]}{\cup} \mathsf{PK}(\mathcal{C}^i), j)$
   - Let $\mathsf{PK}(c_\ell^k) = u_i^{k-1} u_j^{k-1}\ \mathsf{PK}(\mathcal{E}^k(s^2)) - u_j^{k-1}\ \mathsf{PK}(\mathcal{E}^k(c_i^{k-1}s)) - u_i^{k-1}\, \mathsf{PK}(\mathcal{E}^k(c_j^{k-1}s))$ as in Equation 4.25.
   Here $\mathsf{PK}(\mathcal{E}^k(s^2))$, $\mathsf{PK}(\mathcal{E}^k(c_i^{k-1}s))$ and $\mathsf{PK}(\mathcal{E}^k(c_j^{k-1}s))$ are computed using $\mathcal{C}^k$ as described in Equation 4.16, 4.23.

---

**Fig. 2.** Algorithm to evaluate on public key.

---

**Algorithm $\mathsf{Eval}_{\mathsf{CT}}^k(\underset{i\in[k]}{\cup}\,\mathcal{C}^i,\ell)$**

To compute the encoding for the $\ell^{th}$ wire in the level $k$ circuit, do:

1. If the $\ell^{th}$ wire at level $k$ is the addition of the $i^{th}$ and $j^{th}$ wire at level $k-1$, then do the following:
   - If $k=3$ (base case), then compute $c_\ell^3 = c_i^2 + c_j^2$ as in Equation 4.9.
   - Let $\mathsf{CT}_i^{k-1} = \mathsf{Eval}_{\mathsf{CT}}^{k-1}(\underset{j\in[k-1]}{\cup}\,\mathcal{C}^j,i)$ and $\mathsf{CT}_j^{k-1} = \mathsf{Eval}_{\mathsf{CT}}^{k-1}(\underset{i\in[k-1]}{\cup}\,\mathcal{C}^i,j)$,
   - Let $\mathsf{CT}_\ell^k = \mathsf{CT}_i^{k-1} + \mathsf{CT}_j^{k-1}$
2. If the $\ell^{th}$ wire at level $k$ is the multiplication of the $i^{th}$ and $j^{th}$ wire at level $k-1$, then do the following:
   - If $k=4$ (base case) then compute $c_\ell^4$ (for any $\ell$) using Equations 4.11 and 4.12.
   - Let $c_i^{k-1} = \mathsf{Eval}_{\mathsf{CT}}^{k-1}(\underset{j\in[k-1]}{\cup}\,\mathcal{C}^j,i)$ and $c_j^{k-1} = \mathsf{Eval}_{\mathsf{CT}}^{k-1}(\underset{i\in[k-1]}{\cup}\,\mathcal{C}^i,j)$,
   - Let $c_\ell^k = c_i^{k-1}c_j^{k-1} + u_i^{k-1}u_j^{k-1}\,\mathcal{E}^k(s^2) - u_j^{k-1}\,\mathcal{E}^k(c_i^{k-1}s) - u_i^{k-1}\,\mathcal{E}^k(c_j^{k-1}s)$ as in Equation 4.24. Here, the terms $\mathcal{E}^k(s^2)$, $\mathcal{E}^k(c_i^{k-1}s)$ and $\mathcal{E}^k(c_j^{k-1}s)$ are computed using $\mathcal{C}^k$ as described in claim 4.1

---

**Fig. 3.** Algorithm to evaluate on ciphertext.

## 5    Succinct Functional Encryption for $\mathsf{NC}_1$

In this section, we extend the construction for quadratic functional encryption provided in Sect. 3 to circuits of depth $O(\log n)$. The construction generalises directly the $\mathsf{QuadFE}$ scheme using the public key and ciphertext evaluation algorithms from the previous section. We make black box use of the $\mathsf{LinFE}$ scheme [1,5].

We proceed to describe the construction.

$\mathsf{NC}_1.\mathsf{Setup}(1^\lambda, 1^w, 1^d)$: Upon input the security parameter $\lambda$, the message dimension $w$, and the circuit depth $d$, do:
1. For $k \in [d]$, let $L_k = |\mathcal{C}^k|$ where $\mathcal{C}^k$ is as defined in Theorem 4.2. For $k \in [d-1]$, $i \in [L_k]$, choose uniformly random $u_{i,k} \in R_{p_k}$. Denote $\mathbf{u}_k = (u_{i,k}) \in R_{p_k}^{L_k}$.
2. Invoke $\mathsf{LinFE}.\mathsf{Setup}(1^\lambda, 1^{L_d+1}, p_d)$ to obtain $\mathsf{PK} = \mathsf{LinFE}.\mathsf{PK}$ and $\mathsf{MSK} = \mathsf{LinFE}.\mathsf{MSK}$.
3. Output $\mathsf{PK} = (\mathsf{LinFE}.\mathsf{PK}, \mathbf{u}_1, \ldots, \mathbf{u}_{d-1})$ and $\mathsf{MSK} = \mathsf{LinFE}.\mathsf{MSK}$.

$\mathsf{NC}_1.\mathsf{KeyGen}(\mathsf{MSK}, f))$: Upon input the master secret key $\mathsf{MSK}$ and a circuit $f$ of depth $d$, do:
1. Let $\mathsf{Lin}_f \in R_{p_d}^{L_d}$ be an $f$ dependent linear function output by the algorithm $\mathsf{Eval}_{\mathsf{PK}}(\mathsf{PK}, f)$. as described in claim 4.1.
2. Compute $\mathsf{SK}_{\mathsf{Lin}} = \mathsf{LinFE}.\mathsf{KeyGen}(\mathsf{MSK}, (\mathsf{Lin}_f\|1))$ and output it.

$\mathsf{NC}_1.\mathsf{Enc}(\mathbf{x}, \mathsf{PK})$: Upon input the public key and the input $\mathbf{x}$, do:
1. Compute the encodings $\mathcal{C}^k$ for $k \in [d-1]$ as defined in Theorem 4.2.
2. Sample flooding noise $\eta$ as described in Appendix B.
3. Define $\mathcal{M}^d = (\ \mathcal{C}^{d-1},\ \mathcal{C}^{d-1}\cdot s,\ \mathcal{E}^d(s^2)\ ) \in R_{p_d}^{L_d}$. Compute $\mathsf{CT}_{\mathsf{Lin}} = \mathsf{LinFE}.\mathsf{Enc}(\ \mathsf{PK}, (\mathcal{M}^d\|\eta)\ )$
4. Output $\mathsf{CT}_{\mathbf{x}} = (\{\mathcal{C}^k\}_{k\in[d-1]}, \mathsf{CT}_{\mathsf{Lin}})$.

$\mathsf{NC}_1.\mathsf{Dec}(\mathsf{PK}, \mathsf{CT_x}, \mathsf{SK}_f)$: Upon input a ciphertext $\mathsf{CT_x}$ for vector $\mathbf{x}$, and a secret
   key $\mathsf{SK}_f = \mathbf{k}_f$ for circuit $f$, do:
   1. Compute $\mathsf{Poly}_f(\mathcal{C}^1, \ldots, \mathcal{C}^{d-1})$ as described in Sect. 4 by running
      $\mathsf{Eval}_{\mathsf{CT}}(\{\mathcal{C}^k\}_{k \in [d-1]}, f)$.
   2. Compute $\mathsf{LinFE.Dec}(\mathsf{CT_{Lin}}, \mathsf{SK_{Lin}}) + \mathsf{Poly}_f(\mathcal{C}^1, \ldots, \mathcal{C}^{d-1}) \bmod p_d$
      $\bmod p_{d-1} \ldots \bmod p_0$ and output it.

Correctness follows from correctness of $\mathsf{Eval}_{\mathsf{PK}}$, $\mathsf{Eval}_{\mathsf{CT}}$ and $\mathsf{LinFE}$. In more
detail, we have by Theorem 4.2 that,

$$f(\mathbf{x}) + \mu_{f(\mathbf{x})} = \mathsf{Poly}_f(\mathcal{C}^1, \ldots, \mathcal{C}^{d-1}) + \langle \mathsf{Lin}_f, \mathcal{M}^d \rangle$$

Since $\mathsf{CT_{Lin}}$ is a $\mathsf{LinFE}$ encryption of $(\mathcal{M}^d \| \eta)$ and $\mathsf{SK_{Lin}}$ is a $\mathsf{LinFE}$ functional key
for $(\mathsf{Lin}_f \| 1)$, we have by correctness of $\mathsf{LinFE}$ that $\mathsf{LinFE.Dec}(\mathsf{CT_{Lin}}, \mathsf{SK_{Lin}}) = \langle \mathsf{Lin}_f, \mathcal{M}^d \rangle + \eta \bmod p_d$. By correctness of $\mathsf{Eval}_{\mathsf{CT}}$, we have that
$\mathsf{Poly}_f(\mathcal{C}^1, \ldots, \mathcal{C}^{d-1}) + \langle \mathsf{Lin}_f, \mathcal{M}^d \rangle$ outputs $f(\mathbf{x}) + \mu_{f(\mathbf{x})} + \eta$. Since $\mu_{f(\mathbf{x})}$ as well
as $\eta$ is a linear combination of noise terms which are multiples of moduli $p_i$ for
$i \in [0, \ldots, d-1]$, i.e. $\mu_{f(\mathbf{x})} = p_{d-1} \cdot \beta_{d-1}^f + \ldots + p_0 \cdot \beta_0^f$ for some $\beta_i^f$, and $f(\mathbf{x}) \in R_{p_0}$,
we have that $f(\mathbf{x}) + \mu_{f(\mathbf{x})} + \eta = f(\mathbf{x}) \bmod p_d \bmod p_{d-1} \ldots \bmod p_0$, as desired.

*Analysis of Ciphertext Structure.* Note that the ciphertext consists of encodings
$\mathcal{C}^k$ for $k \in [d-1]$ and $\mathsf{LinFE}$ ciphertext for $(\mathcal{M}^d \| \eta)$. Since each message-dependent
encoding depends only on a single bit of the message, the ciphertext is decom-
posable, and enjoys local-updates: if a single bit of the message changes, then
only $O(d)$ encodings need updating, not the entire ciphertext. Also, since the
$\mathsf{LinFE}$ ciphertext is succinct, the message-dependent component of our ciphertext is also succinct. The ciphertext is *not* succinct overall, since we need to
encode a fresh noise term per requested key.

**Theorem 5.4.** *The construction in Sect. 5 achieves full simulation based security as per Definition 2.2.*

**Proof.** We describe our simulator.

*Simulator* $\mathsf{NC}_1.\mathsf{Sim}(1^\lambda, 1^{|\mathbf{x}|}, \mathsf{PK}, f, \mathsf{SK}_f, f(\mathbf{x}))$. The simulator given input the
security parameter, length of message $\mathbf{x}$, the circuit $f$, the secret key $\mathsf{SK}_f$ and
the value $f(\mathbf{x})$ does the following:

1. It computes $\mathsf{Lin}_f = \mathsf{Eval}_{\mathsf{PK}}(\mathsf{PK}, f)$. Note that by claim 4.1 that $\mathsf{Lin}_f \in R_{p_d}^{L_d}$.
2. It samples all encodings upto level $d-1$ randomly, i.e. $\mathcal{C}^k \leftarrow R_{p_k}^{L_k}$ for $k \in [d-1]$.
3. It samples $\eta \leftarrow \mathcal{D}_d$ as described in Appendix B and computes $d' = f(\mathbf{x}) + \eta - \mathsf{Poly}_f(\mathcal{C}^1, \ldots, \mathcal{C}^{d-1})$.
4. It invokes the single key $\mathsf{LinFE}$ simulator as

$$\mathsf{CT_{Lin}} = \mathsf{LinFE.Sim}(1^\lambda, 1^{L_d}, \mathsf{PK}, \mathsf{Lin}_f, \mathsf{SK}(\mathsf{Lin}_f), d')$$

5. It outputs $\mathsf{CT_x} = (\{\mathcal{C}^k\}_{k \in [d-1]}, \mathsf{CT_{Lin}})$.

We will prove that the output of the simulator is indistinguishable from the
real world via a sequence of hybrids.

*The Hybrids.* Our Hybrids are described below.

*Hybrid 0.* This is the real world.

*Hybrid 1.* In this hybrid, the only thing that is different is that $\mathsf{CT_{Lin}}$ is computed using the $\mathsf{LinFE}$ simulator. In more detail,

- It computes $\mathsf{Poly}_f(\mathcal{C}^1, \ldots, \mathcal{C}^{d-1}) = \mathsf{Eval_{CT}}(\{\mathcal{C}^k\}_{k \in [d-1]}, f)$.
- It computes $f(\mathbf{x}) + \mu_{f(\mathbf{x})} = \mathsf{Poly}_f(\mathcal{C}^1, \ldots, \mathcal{C}^{d-1}) + \langle \mathcal{M}^d, \mathsf{Lin}_f \rangle$
- It samples $\eta$ such that

$$\mathsf{SD}\big(\eta + \mu_{f(\mathbf{x})}, \eta\big) \leq \mathrm{negl}(\lambda) \qquad (5.1)$$

- It invokes the single key $\mathsf{LinFE}$ simulator with input $f(\mathbf{x}) + \mu_{f(\mathbf{x})} + \eta - \mathsf{Poly}_f(\mathcal{C}^1, \ldots, \mathcal{C}^{d-1})$.

*Hybrid 2.* In this hybrid, invoke the $\mathsf{LinFE}$ simulator with $f(\mathbf{x}) + \eta - \mathsf{Poly}_f(\mathcal{C}^1, \ldots, \mathcal{C}^{d-1})$.

*Hybrid 3.* In this hybrid, sample $\mathcal{C}^k$ for $k \in [d-1]$ at random. This is the simulated world.

Indistinguishability of Hybrids proceeds as in Sect. 3. Indistinguishability of Hybrids 0 and 1 follows from security of $\mathsf{LinFE}$. It is easy to see that Hybrids 1 and 2 are statistically indistinguishable by Eq. 5.1. Hybrids 2 and 3 are indistinguishable due to semantic security of Regev encodings $\mathcal{C}^k$ for $k \in [d-1]$.

In the full version [6], we describe how to generalize the above construction to bounded collusion FE scheme for all circuits in P, for any a-priori fixed polynomial bound $Q$. The approach follows the (by now) standard bootstrapping method of using low depth randomized encodings to represent any polynomial sized circuit [39]. The ciphertext of the final scheme enjoys additive quadratic dependence on the collusion bound $Q$.

# 6   Bounded Collusion FE for All Circuits

In this section, we describe how to put together the pieces from the previous sections to build a bounded collusion FE scheme for all circuits in P, denoted by $\mathsf{BddFE}$. The approach follows the (by now) standard bootstrapping method of using low depth randomized encodings to represent any polynomial sized circuit. This approach was first suggested by Gorbunov et al. [39], who show that $q$ query FE for degree three polynomials can be bootstrapped to $q$ query FE for all circuits.

At a high level, their approach can be summarized as follows. Let $\mathcal{C}$ be a family of polynomial sized circuits. Let $C \in \mathcal{C}$ and let $\mathbf{x}$ be some input. Let $\tilde{C}(\mathbf{x}, R)$ be a randomized encoding of $C$ that is computable by a constant depth circuit with respect to inputs $x$ and $R$. Then consider a new family of circuits $\mathcal{G}$ defined by:

$$G_{C,\Delta}(\mathbf{x}, R_1, \ldots, R_S) = \tilde{C}\left(\mathbf{x}; \bigoplus_{a \in \Delta} R_a\right)$$

Note that $G_{C,\Delta}(\cdot, \cdot)$ is computable by a degree three polynomial, one for each output bit. Given an FE scheme for $\mathcal{G}$, one may construct a scheme for $\mathcal{C}$ by having the decryptor first recover the output of $G_{C,\Delta}(\mathbf{x}, R_1, \ldots, R_S)$ and then applying the decoder for the randomized encoding to recover $C(\mathbf{x})$. Since our construction from Sect. 5 is capable of evaluating degree 3 polynomials, it suffices for bootstrapping, to yield $q$-query FE for all circuits. We will denote this scheme by PolyFE as against $\mathsf{NC}_1\mathsf{FE}$ to emphasize that it needs to only compute degree 3 polynomials.

As in [5,39], let $(S, v, m)$ be parameters to the construction. Let $\Delta_i$ for $i \in [q]$ be a uniformly random subset of $[S]$ of size $v$. To support $q$ queries, the key generator identifies the set $\Delta_i \subseteq [S]$ with query $i$. If $v = O(\lambda)$ and $S = O(\lambda \cdot q^2)$ then the sets $\Delta_i$ are cover free with high probability as shown by [39]. Let $L \triangleq (\ell^3 + S \cdot m)$.

BddFE.Setup$(1^\lambda, 1^\ell)$: Upon input the security parameter $\lambda$ and the message space $\{0,1\}^\ell$, invoke $(\mathsf{mpk}, \mathsf{msk}) = \mathsf{PolyFE.Setup}(1^\lambda, 1^L)$ and output it.
BddFE.KeyGen$(\mathsf{msk}, C))$: Upon input the master secret key and a circuit $C$, do:
1. Choose a uniformly random subset $\Delta \subseteq [S]$ of size $v$.
2. Express $C(\mathbf{x})$ by $G_{C,\Delta}(\mathbf{x}, R_1, \ldots, R_S)$, which in turn can be expressed as a sequence of degree 3 polynomials $P_1, \ldots, P_k$, where $k \in \mathsf{poly}(\lambda)$.
3. Set $\mathsf{BddFE.SK}_C = \{\mathsf{SK}_i = \mathsf{PolyFE.KeyGen}(\mathsf{PolyFE.msk}, P_i)\}_{i \in [k]}$ and output it.
BddFE.Enc$(\mathbf{x}, \mathsf{mpk})$: Upon input the public key and the input $\mathbf{x}$, do:
1. Choose $R_1, \ldots, R_S \leftarrow \{0,1\}^m$, where $m$ is the size of the random input in the randomized encoding.
2. Set $\mathsf{CT}_\mathbf{x} = \mathsf{PolyFE.Enc}(\mathsf{PolyFE.mpk}, \mathbf{x}, R_1, \ldots, R_s)$ and output it.
BddFE.Dec$(\mathsf{mpk}, \mathsf{CT}_\mathbf{x}, \mathsf{SK}_C)$: Upon input a ciphertext $\mathsf{CT}_\mathbf{x}$ for vector $\mathbf{x}$, and a secret key $\mathsf{SK}_C$ for circuit $C$, do the following:
1. Compute $G_{C,\Delta}(\mathbf{x}, R_1, \ldots, R_S) = \mathsf{PolyFE.Dec}(\mathsf{CT}_\mathbf{x}, \mathsf{SK}_C)$.
2. Run the Decoder for the randomized encoding to recover $C(\mathbf{x})$ from $G_{C,\Delta}(\mathbf{x}, R_1, \ldots, R_S)$.

Correctness follows immediately from the correctness of PolyFE and the correctness of randomized encodings. The proof of security follows easily from the security of randomized encodings and of the PolyFE scheme. Please see the full version [6] for details.

**Acknowledgements.** We thank Damien Stehlé and Chris Peikert for helpful discussions.

# Appendix

# A    Previous Constructions for Bounded Collusion FE

**The GVW12 Construction.** The scheme of [39] can be summarized as follows.

- The first ingredient they need is a single key FE scheme for all circuits. A construction for this was provided by Sahai and Seyalioglu in [51].
- Next, the single FE scheme is generalized to a $q$ query scheme for $NC_1$ circuits. This gerenalization is fairly complex, we provide an outline here. At a high level, they run $N$ copies of the single key scheme, where $N = O(q^4)$. The encryptor encrypts the views of the BGW MPC protocol for $N$ parties, computing some functionality related to $C$. They rely on the fact that BGW is non-interactive when used to compute bounded degree functions. To generate a secret key, KeyGen chooses a random subset of the single query FE keys, where the parameters are set so that the subsets have small pairwise intersections. This subset of keys enables the decryptor to recover sufficiently many shares of $C(x)$ which allows him to recover $C(x)$. [39] argue that an attacker with $q$ keys only learns a share $x_i$ when two subsets of keys intersect, but since the subsets were chosen to have small pairwise intersections, this does not occur often enough to recover enough shares of $x$. Finally, by the security of secret sharing, $x$ remains hidden.
- As the last step they "bootstrap" the $q$ query FE for $NC_1$ to $q$ query FE for all circuits using computational randomized encodings [9]. They must additionally use cover free sets to ensure that fresh randomness is used for each randomized encoding.

Thus, to encrypt a message $x$, the encryptor must secret share it into $N = O(q^4)$ shares, and encrypt each one with the one query FE. Since they use Shamir secret sharing with polynomial of degree $t$ and $t = O(q^2)$, note that at most $O(q^2)$ shares can be generated offline, since $t + 1$ points will determine the polynomial. Hence $O(q^4)$ shares must be generated in the online phase. This results in an online encryption time that degrades as $O(q^4)$.

**The ALS16 construction.** [5] provide a conceptually simpler way to build $q$-query Functional Encryption for all circuits. Their construction replaces steps 1 and 2 described above with a inner product modulo $p$ FE scheme, and then uses step 3 as in [39]. Thus, the construction of single key FE in step 1 by Sahai and Seyalioglu, and the nontrivial "MPC in the head" of step 2 can both be replaced by the simple abstraction of an inner product FE scheme. For step 3, observe that the bootstrapping theorem of [39] provides a method to bootstrap an FE for $NC_1$ that handles $q$ queries to an FE for all polynomial-size circuits that is also secure against $q$ queries. The bootstrapping relies on the result of Applebaum et al. [9, Theorem 4.11] which states that every polynomial time computable function $f$ admits a perfectly correct computational randomized encoding of degree 3.

In more detail, let $\mathcal{C}$ be a family of polynomial-size circuits. Let $C \in \mathcal{C}$ and let $x$ be some input. Let $\widetilde{C}(x, R)$ be a randomized encoding of $C$ that is computable by a constant depth circuit with respect to inputs $x$ and $R$. Then consider a new family of circuits $\mathcal{G}$ defined by:

$$G_{C,\Delta}(x, R_1, \ldots, R_S) = \left\{ \widetilde{C}\left(x; \underset{a \in \Delta}{\oplus} R_a\right) : C \in \mathcal{C}, \ \Delta \subseteq [S] \right\},$$

for some sufficiently large $S$ (quadratic in the number of queries $q$). As observed in [39], circuit $G_{C,\Delta}(\cdot, \cdot)$ is computable by a constant degree polynomial (one for each output bit). Given an FE scheme for $\mathcal{G}$, one may construct a scheme for $\mathcal{C}$ by having the decryptor first recover the output of $G_{C,\Delta}(x, R_1, \ldots, R_S)$ and then applying the decoder for the randomized encoding to recover $C(x)$.

However, to support $q$ queries the decryptor must compute $q$ randomized encodings, each of which needs fresh randomness. This is handled by hardcoding $S$ random elements in the ciphertext and using random subsets $\Delta \subseteq [S]$ (which are cover-free with overwhelming probability) to compute fresh randomness $\underset{a \in \Delta}{\oplus} R_a$ for every query. [5] observe that bootstrapping only requires support for the particular circuit class $\mathcal{G}$ described above. This circuit class, being computable by degree 3 polynomials, may be supported by a linear FE scheme, via linearization of the degree 3 polynomials.

Putting it together, the encryptor encrypts all degree 3 monomials in the inputs $R_1, \ldots, R_S$ and $x_1, \ldots, x_\ell$. Note that this ciphertext is polynomial in size. Now, for a given circuit $C$, the keygen algorithm samples some $\Delta \subseteq [S]$ and computes the symbolic degree 3 polynomials which must be released to the decryptor. It then provides the linear FE keys to compute the same. By correctness and security of Linear FE as well as the randomizing polynomial construction, the decryptor learns $C(x)$ and nothing else.

Note that in this construction the challenge of supporting multiplication is sidestepped by merely having the encryptor encrypt each monomial $x_i x_j$ separately so that the FE need only support addition. This "brute force" approach incurs several disadvantages. For instance, decomposability is lost – even though the ciphertext can be decomposed into $|\mathbf{x}|^2$ components, any input bit $x_1$ (say) must feature in $|\mathbf{x}|$ ciphertext components $x_1 x_2, \ldots, x_1 x_w$, where $w = |\mathbf{x}|$. This makes the scheme inapplicable for all applications involving distributed data, where a centre or a sensor device knows a bit $x_i$ but is oblivious to the other bits. Additionally, the scheme is not online-offline, since all the ciphertext components depend on the data, hence the entire encryption operation must be performed after the data becomes available. For applications where a centre or sensor must transmit data-dependent ciphertext after the data is observed, this incurs a significant cost in terms of bandwidth. Indeed, the work performed by the sensor device in computing the data dependent ciphertext becomes proportional to the size of the function being computed on the data, which may be infeasible for weak devices.

Another approach to obtain bounded collusion FE is to compile the single key FE of Goldwasser et al. [37] with the compiler of [39] to support $Q$ queries. Again, this approach yields succinct CTs but the CT grows as $O(q^4)$ rather than $O(q^2)$ as in our scheme.

# B    Parameters

In this section, we discuss the parameters for our constructions. We denote the magnitude of noise used in the level $i$ encodings by $B_i$. We require $B_i \leq O(p_i/4)$ at every level for correct decryption. We have that the message space for level 1 encodings $\mathcal{E}^1$ is $R_{p_0}$ and encoding space is $R_{p_1}$. Then message space for $\mathcal{E}^2$ is $O(p_0^2 + B_1^2) = O(B_1^2)$ since the noise at level 1 is a multiple of $p_0$. Then, $p_2$ must be chosen as $O(B_1^2)$. At the next multiplication level, i.e. level 4, we have the message space as $O(p_2^2 + B_2^2) = O(B_1^4)$. In general, for $d$ levels, it suffices to set $p_d = O(B^{2^d})$. We require all the distinct moduli to be relatively prime, hence we choose all the moduli to be prime numbers of the aforementioned size.

We must also choose the size of the noise that is added for flooding. As described in Sect. 3, for quadratic polynomials we require $\frac{L \cdot p_0 \cdot \sigma_0^2}{\sigma_1} = \mathrm{negl}(\lambda)$ where $\sigma_1$ is the standard deviation for the noise $\eta_i$ for $i \in [Q]$ encoded in the cipher-text. For depth $d$ (Sect. 5), we require $\dfrac{L_d \cdot \prod\limits_{i \in [0,d]} p_i \cdot B^{2^d}}{\sigma} = \mathrm{negl}(\lambda)$ where $\sigma$ is the standard deviation of the noise $\eta$ encoded in the ciphertext. Since $L_d = \mathrm{poly}(\lambda)$ by definition, we require $\sigma \geq O(\mathrm{poly}(\lambda)B^{2^{d+1}})$.

We may set $p_0 = n$ with initial noise level as $B_1 = \mathrm{poly}(n)$ and any $B_i, p_i = O(B_1^{2^i})$. Also, the number of encodings provided at level $d$ is $L_d = O(2^d)$, so in general we may let $d = O(\log n)$, thus supporting the circuit class $\mathsf{NC}_1$. Note that unlike FHE constructions [18,19], computation in our case proceeds UP a ladder of moduli rather than down, and we may add fresh noise at each level. Hence we never need to rely on subexponential modulus to noise ratio, and may support circuits in $\mathsf{NC}_1$ even without modulus switching tricks.

We note that by the definition of efficiency of reusable garbled circuits [37], it suffices to have ciphertext size that is sublinear in circuit size, which is achieved by our construction.

# References

1. Abdalla, M., Bourse, F., De Caro, A., Pointcheval, D.: Simple functional encryption schemes for inner products. In: Katz, J. (ed.) PKC 2015. LNCS, vol. 9020, pp. 733–751. Springer, Heidelberg (2015). doi:10.1007/978-3-662-46447-2_33
2. Agrawal, S.: Stronger security for reusable garbled circuits, general definitions and attacks. In: Katz, J., Shacham, H. (eds.) CRYPTO 2017. LNCS, vol. 10401, pp. 3–35. Springer, Cham (2017). doi:10.1007/978-3-319-63688-7_1
3. Agrawal, S., Boneh, D., Boyen, X.: Efficient Lattice (H)IBE in the Standard Model. In: Gilbert, H. (ed.) EUROCRYPT 2010. LNCS, vol. 6110, pp. 553–572. Springer, Heidelberg (2010). doi:10.1007/978-3-642-13190-5_28
4. Agrawal, S., Freeman, D.M., Vaikuntanathan, V.: Functional encryption for inner product predicates from learning with errors. In: Lee, D.H., Wang, X. (eds.) ASIACRYPT 2011. LNCS, vol. 7073, pp. 21–40. Springer, Heidelberg (2011). doi:10.1007/978-3-642-25385-0_2
5. Agrawal, S., Libert, B., Stehlé, D.: Fully secure functional encryption for linear functions from standard assumptions, and applications. In: CRYPTO (2016). https://eprint.iacr.org/2015/608

6. Agrawal, S., Rosen, A.: Functional encryption for bounded collusions, revisited. Eprint (2016). https://eprint.iacr.org/2016/361.pdf

7. Ananth, P., Jain, A.: Indistinguishability obfuscation from compact functional encryption. In: Gennaro, R., Robshaw, M. (eds.) CRYPTO 2015. LNCS, vol. 9215, pp. 308–326. Springer, Heidelberg (2015). doi:10.1007/978-3-662-47989-6_15

8. Ananth, P., Jain, A., Sahai, A.: Indistinguishability obfuscation from functional encryption for simple functions. Eprint 2015/730 (2015)

9. Applebaum, B., Ishai, Y., Kushilevitz, E.: Computationally private randomizing polynomials and their applications. Comput. Complex. **15**(2), 115–162 (2006)

10. Applebaum, B., Ishai, Y., Kushilevitz, E.: How to garble arithmetic circuits. In: IEEE 52nd Annual Symposium on Foundations of Computer Science, FOCS 2011, Palm Springs, CA, USA, 22–25 October 2011, pp. 120–129 (2011)

11. Bethencourt, J., Sahai, A., Waters, B.: Ciphertext-policy attribute-based encryption. In: IEEE Symposium on Security and Privacy, pp. 321–334 (2007)

12. Bitansky, N., Vaikuntanathan, V.: Indistinguishability obfuscation from functional encryption. IACR Cryptology ePrint Archive 2015, p. 163 (2015). http://eprint.iacr.org/2015/163

13. Boneh, D., Franklin, M.: Identity-based encryption from the weil pairing. In: Kilian, J. (ed.) CRYPTO 2001. LNCS, vol. 2139, pp. 213–229. Springer, Heidelberg (2001). doi:10.1007/3-540-44647-8_13

14. Boneh, D., Gentry, C., Gorbunov, S., Halevi, S., Nikolaenko, V., Segev, G., Vaikuntanathan, V., Vinayagamurthy, D.: Fully key-homomorphic encryption, arithmetic circuit abe and compact garbled circuits. In: Nguyen, P.Q., Oswald, E. (eds.) EUROCRYPT 2014. LNCS, vol. 8441, pp. 533–556. Springer, Heidelberg (2014). doi:10.1007/978-3-642-55220-5_30

15. Boneh, D., Waters, B.: Conjunctive, subset, and range queries on encrypted data. In: Vadhan, S.P. (ed.) TCC 2007. LNCS, vol. 4392, pp. 535–554. Springer, Heidelberg (2007). doi:10.1007/978-3-540-70936-7_29

16. Boyen, X., Waters, B.: Anonymous hierarchical identity-based encryption (without random oracles). In: Dwork, C. (ed.) CRYPTO 2006. LNCS, vol. 4117, pp. 290–307. Springer, Heidelberg (2006). doi:10.1007/11818175_17

17. Brakerski, Z., Gentry, C., Vaikuntanathan, V.: (Leveled) fully homomorphic encryption without bootstrapping. In: Proceedings of ITCS, pp. 309–325 (2012)

18. Brakerski, Z., Vaikuntanathan, V.: Efficient fully homomorphic encryption from (standard) LWE. In: IEEE 52nd Annual Symposium on Foundations of Computer Science, FOCS 2011, Palm Springs, CA, USA, 22–25 October 2011, pp. 97–106 (2011)

19. Brakerski, Z., Vaikuntanathan, V.: Fully homomorphic encryption from ring-LWE and security for key dependent messages. In: Rogaway, P. (ed.) CRYPTO 2011. LNCS, vol. 6841, pp. 505–524. Springer, Heidelberg (2011). doi:10.1007/978-3-642-22792-9_29

20. Canetti, R., Chen, Y.: Constraint-hiding constrained PRFs for NC1 from LWE. In: Eurocrypt (2017)

21. Cash, D., Hofheinz, D., Kiltz, E., Peikert, C.: Bonsai trees, or how to delegate a lattice basis. In: Gilbert, H. (ed.) EUROCRYPT 2010. LNCS, vol. 6110, pp. 523–552. Springer, Heidelberg (2010). doi:10.1007/978-3-642-13190-5_27

22. Cheon, J.H., Han, K., Lee, C., Ryu, H., Stehlé, D.: Cryptanalysis of the multilinear map over the integers. In: Oswald, E., Fischlin, M. (eds.) EUROCRYPT 2015. LNCS, vol. 9056, pp. 3–12. Springer, Heidelberg (2015). doi:10.1007/978-3-662-46800-5_1

23. Cheon, J.H., Fouque, P.-A., Lee, C., Minaud, B., Ryu, H.: Cryptanalysis of the new CLT multilinear map over the integers. In: Fischlin, M., Coron, J.-S. (eds.) EUROCRYPT 2016. LNCS, vol. 9665, pp. 509–536. Springer, Heidelberg (2016). doi:10.1007/978-3-662-49890-3_20

24. Cheon, J.H., Jeong, J., Lee, C.: An algorithm for ntru problems and cryptanalysis of the ggh multilinear map without a low level encoding of zero. Eprint 2016/139

25. Cocks, C.: An identity based encryption scheme based on quadratic residues. In: Proceedings of 8th International Conference on IMA, pp. 360–363 (2001)

26. Coron, J.-S., Gentry, C., Halevi, S., Lepoint, T., Maji, H.K., Miles, E., Raykova, M., Sahai, A., Tibouchi, M.: Zeroizing without low-level zeroes: new mmap attacks and their limitations. In: Gennaro, R., Robshaw, M. (eds.) CRYPTO 2015. LNCS, vol. 9215, pp. 247–266. Springer, Heidelberg (2015). doi:10.1007/978-3-662-47989-6_12

27. Coron, J.-S., Lepoint, T., Tibouchi, M.: Practical multilinear maps over the integers. In: Canetti, R., Garay, J.A. (eds.) CRYPTO 2013. LNCS, vol. 8042, pp. 476–493. Springer, Heidelberg (2013). doi:10.1007/978-3-642-40041-4_26

28. Cramer, R., Hanaoka, G., Hofheinz, D., Imai, H., Kiltz, E., Pass, R., Shelat, A., Vaikuntanathan, V.: Bounded CCA2-secure encryption. In: Kurosawa, K. (ed.) ASIACRYPT 2007. LNCS, vol. 4833, pp. 502–518. Springer, Heidelberg (2007). doi:10.1007/978-3-540-76900-2_31

29. Dodis, Y., Katz, J., Xu, S., Yung, M.: Key-insulated public key cryptosystems. In: Knudsen, L.R. (ed.) EUROCRYPT 2002. LNCS, vol. 2332, pp. 65–82. Springer, Heidelberg (2002). doi:10.1007/3-540-46035-7_5

30. Garg, S., Gentry, C., Halevi, S.: Candidate multilinear maps from ideal lattices. In: Johansson, T., Nguyen, P.Q. (eds.) EUROCRYPT 2013. LNCS, vol. 7881, pp. 1–17. Springer, Heidelberg (2013). doi:10.1007/978-3-642-38348-9_1

31. Garg, S., Gentry, C., Halevi, S., Raykova, M., Sahai, A., Waters, B.: Candidate indistinguishability obfuscation and functional encryption for all circuits. In: FOCS (2013). http://eprint.iacr.org/

32. Garg, S., Gentry, C., Halevi, S., Sahai, A., Waters, B.: Attribute-based encryption for circuits from multilinear maps. In: Canetti, R., Garay, J.A. (eds.) CRYPTO 2013. LNCS, vol. 8043, pp. 479–499. Springer, Heidelberg (2013). doi:10.1007/978-3-642-40084-1_27

33. Garg, S., Gentry, C., Halevi, S., Zhandry, M.: Fully secure functional encryption without obfuscation. In: IACR Cryptology ePrint Archive, p. 666 (2014). http://eprint.iacr.org/2014/666

34. Gentry, C., Gorbunov, S., Halevi, S.: Graph-induced multilinear maps from lattices. In: Dodis, Y., Nielsen, J.B. (eds.) TCC 2015. LNCS, vol. 9015, pp. 498–527. Springer, Heidelberg (2015). doi:10.1007/978-3-662-46497-7_20

35. Gentry, C., Peikert, C., Vaikuntanathan, V.: Trapdoors for hard lattices and new cryptographic constructions. In: STOC, pp. 197–206 (2008)

36. Goldwasser, S., Kalai, Y.T., Peikert, C., Vaikuntanathan, V.: Robustness of the learning with errors assumption. In: ITCS (2010)

37. Goldwasser, S., Kalai, Y.T., Popa, R.A., Vaikuntanathan, V., Zeldovich, N.: Reusable garbled circuits and succinct functional encryption. In: STOC, pp. 555–564 (2013)

38. Goldwasser, S., Lewko, A., Wilson, D.A.: Bounded-collusion IBE from key homomorphism. In: Cramer, R. (ed.) TCC 2012. LNCS, vol. 7194, pp. 564–581. Springer, Heidelberg (2012). doi:10.1007/978-3-642-28914-9_32

39. Gorbunov, S., Vaikuntanathan, V., Wee, H.: Functional encryption with bounded collusions via multi-party computation. In: Safavi-Naini, R., Canetti, R. (eds.) CRYPTO 2012. LNCS, vol. 7417, pp. 162–179. Springer, Heidelberg (2012). doi:10. 1007/978-3-642-32009-5_11

40. Gorbunov, S., Vaikuntanathan, V., Wee, H.: Attribute based encryption for circuits. In: STOC (2013)

41. Gorbunov, S., Vaikuntanathan, V., Wee, H.: Predicate encryption for circuits from LWE. In: Gennaro, R., Robshaw, M. (eds.) CRYPTO 2015. LNCS, vol. 9216, pp. 503–523. Springer, Heidelberg (2015). doi:10.1007/978-3-662-48000-7_25

42. Goyal, V., Pandey, O., Sahai, A., Waters, B.: Attribute-based encryption for fine-grained access control of encrypted data. In: ACM Conference on Computer and Communications Security, pp. 89–98 (2006)

43. Hu, Y., Jia, H.: Cryptanalysis of GGH map. In: Fischlin, M., Coron, J.-S. (eds.) EUROCRYPT 2016. LNCS, vol. 9665, pp. 537–565. Springer, Heidelberg (2016). doi:10.1007/978-3-662-49890-3_21

44. Ishai, Y., Kushilevitz, E.: Perfect constant-round secure computation via perfect randomizing polynomials. In: Widmayer, P., Eidenbenz, S., Triguero, F., Morales, R., Conejo, R., Hennessy, M. (eds.) ICALP 2002. LNCS, vol. 2380, pp. 244–256. Springer, Heidelberg (2002). doi:10.1007/3-540-45465-9_22

45. Katz, J., Sahai, A., Waters, B.: Predicate encryption supporting disjunctions, polynomial equations, and inner products. In: Smart, N. (ed.) EUROCRYPT 2008. LNCS, vol. 4965, pp. 146–162. Springer, Heidelberg (2008). doi:10.1007/ 978-3-540-78967-3_9

46. Lewko, A., Okamoto, T., Sahai, A., Takashima, K., Waters, B.: Fully secure functional encryption: attribute-based encryption and (hierarchical) inner product encryption. In: Gilbert, H. (ed.) EUROCRYPT 2010. LNCS, vol. 6110, pp. 62–91. Springer, Heidelberg (2010). doi:10.1007/978-3-642-13190-5_4

47. Lyubashevsky, V., Peikert, C., Regev, O.: On ideal lattices and learning with errors over rings. In: Gilbert, H. (ed.) EUROCRYPT 2010. LNCS, vol. 6110, pp. 1–23. Springer, Heidelberg (2010). doi:10.1007/978-3-642-13190-5_1

48. Micciancio, D., Regev, O.: Worst-case to average-case reductions based on gaussian measures. SIAM J. Comput. **37**(1), 267–302 (2007). Extended abstract in FOCS 2004

49. Miles, E., Sahai, A., Zhandry, M.: Annihilation attacks for multilinear maps: cryptanalysis of indistinguishability obfuscation over GGH13. In: Robshaw, M., Katz, J. (eds.) CRYPTO 2016. LNCS, vol. 9815, pp. 629–658. Springer, Heidelberg (2016). doi:10.1007/978-3-662-53008-5_22

50. Regev, O.: On lattices, learning with errors, random linear codes, and cryptography. In: STOC 2005 (Extended Abstract), J. ACM 56(6) (2009)

51. Sahai, A., Seyalioglu, H.: Worry-free encryption: Functional encryption with public keys. In: Proceedings of the 17th ACM Conference on Computer and Communications Security, CCS 2010 (2010)

52. Sahai, A., Waters, B.: Functional encryption: beyond public key cryptography. Power Point Presentation (2008). http://userweb.cs.utexas.edu/bwaters/ presentations/files/functional.ppt

53. Sahai, A., Waters, B.: Fuzzy identity-based encryption. In: Cramer, R. (ed.) EUROCRYPT 2005. LNCS, vol. 3494, pp. 457–473. Springer, Heidelberg (2005). doi:10. 1007/11426639_27

54. Waters, B.: Functional encryption for regular languages. In: Crypto (2012)

# Attribute-Hiding Predicate Encryption in Bilinear Groups, Revisited

Hoeteck Wee[✉]

CNRS and ENS, Paris, France
wee@di.ens.fr

**Abstract.** We present new techniques for achieving strong attribute-hiding in prime-order bilinear groups under the standard $k$-Linear assumption. Our main result is a "partially hiding" predicate encryption scheme for functions that compute an arithmetic branching program on public attributes, followed by an inner product predicate on private attributes. This constitutes the first "best of both worlds" result in bilinear groups that simultaneously generalizes existing attribute-based encryption schemes and inner product predicate encryption. Our scheme achieves a variant of simulation-based security in the semi-adaptive setting. Along the way, we introduce a conceptually simpler and more modular approach towards achieving the strong attribute-hiding guarantee.

## 1 Introduction

Predicate encryption is a novel paradigm for public-key encryption that enables both fine-grained access control and selective computation on encrypted data [12,23,26,34]. In a predicate encryption scheme, ciphertexts are associated with descriptive attributes $x$ and a plaintext $M$, secret keys are associated with boolean functions $f$, and a secret key decrypts the ciphertext to recover $M$ if $f(x)$ is true, corresponding to a so-called authorized key. The most basic security guarantee for predicate encryption stipulates that $M$ should remain private if $f(x)$ is false. A stronger security guarantee is *attribute-hiding*, which stipulates that the attribute $x$ remains hidden apart from leaking whether $f(x)$ is true or false and it comes in two flavors: (i) weak attribute-hiding which guarantees privacy of $x$ provided the adversary only gets unauthorized keys for which $f(x)$ is false; and (ii) strong attribute-hiding where the adversary can get both authorized and unauthorized keys. Henceforth, we use attribute-based encryption (ABE) to refer to schemes which only satisfy the basic guarantee, and reserve predicate encryption for schemes which are attribute-hiding.[1] Throughout, we

---

H. Wee—INRIA and Columbia University. Supported in part by ERC Project aSCEND (H2020 639554) and NSF Award CNS-1445424.

[1] Some early works around 2010–2011 use functional encryption (FE) to refer to ABE. Some more recent works also use predicate encryption to refer to ABE. For instance, we clarify here that the OT10 "KP-FE Scheme" in [29] for boolean formula with inner product gates is in fact an ABE and does not provide any attribute-hiding guarantee.

Y. Kalai and L. Reyzin (Eds.): TCC 2017, Part I, LNCS 10677, pp. 206–233, 2017.
https://doi.org/10.1007/978-3-319-70500-2_8

also require that the keys are resilient to collusion attacks, namely any group of users holding different secret keys learns nothing beyond what each of them could individually learn.

Over the past decade, tremendous progress has been made towards realizing *expressive* ABE and weak attribute-hiding predicate encryption [14,21–23,25, 29]; along the way, we developed extremely powerful techniques for building these primitives under standard assumptions in bilinear groups and lattices. However, much less is known for strong attribute-hiding predicate encryption schemes: the only examples we have are for very simple functionalities related to the inner product predicate [12,26,31,32], and we only have instantiations from bilinear groups. And for the more important setting of prime-order bilinear groups, the only instantiations are the works of Okamoto and Takashima [31,32].

There is good reason why strong attribute-hiding predicate encryption schemes, even in the simpler selective setting, are so elusive. The security definition requires that we reason about an adversary that gets hold of authorized keys, something that is forbidden for both ABE (even adaptively secure ones) and for weak attribute-hiding, and which we do not have a good grasp of. Moreover, we now know that strong attribute-hiding for sufficiently expressive predicates, namely $NC^1$, imply indistinguishability obfuscation for circuits, the new holy grail of cryptography [6,10,20]. For this, selective security already suffices; in any case, there is a generic transformation from selective to adaptive security for this class [7].

## 1.1  Our Contributions

We present new techniques for achieving strong attribute-hiding in prime-order bilinear groups under the standard $k$-Linear assumption. We achieve a variant of simulation-based security in a semi-adaptive setting [17], the latter a strengthening of selective security where the adversary can choose its encryption challenge after seeing mpk. We proceed to describe the new schemes that we obtain using these techniques, and then our new approach and techniques for strong attribute-hiding.

**New Schemes.** Our main result is a "partially hiding" predicate encryption (PHPE) scheme that compute an arithmetic branching program (ABP) on public attributes $x$, followed by an inner product predicate on private attributes $z$. This simultaneously generalizes ABE for boolean formula and ABPs and attribute-hiding predicate encryption for inner product. This means that we can support richer variants of prior applications captured by inner product predicate encryption, as we can support more complex pre-processing on public attributes before a simple computation on private attributes; see Sect. 4.1 for some concrete examples. Our result constitutes one of the most expressive classes we have to date for predicate encryption based on static assumptions in bilinear groups. See Fig. 1 for a comparison of our results with prior works in the context of expressiveness.

Our scheme achieves simulation-based security, but with respect to an unbounded simulator [4] (which is nonetheless still a strengthening of indistinguishability-based security). Prior results for inner product predicate encryption in [26,31,32] only achieve indistinguishability-based security. Our scheme also enjoys short ciphertexts whose size grows linearly with the total length of the attributes (as with prior selectively secure ABE for boolean formula and branching programs [23,25]) but independent of the size of $f$.

Along the way, we also obtain the following additional results:

- A scheme for inner product functional encryption –where ciphertexts and keys are associated with vectors $\mathbf{z}, \mathbf{y}$ and decryption recovers $\langle \mathbf{z}, \mathbf{y} \rangle$, provided the value falls in a polynomially bounded domain [1]– that achieves simulation-based security (cf. Appendix B). Prior works like [1,5] only achieve indistinguishability-based security, and in fact, our scheme is essentially the same as the adaptively secure scheme in [5] (our techniques can also be extended to yield a slightly different proof of adaptive security). This scheme has already been used as a building block for a multi-input functional encryption scheme (MIFE) for the inner product functionality based on the $k$-Linear assumption in prime-order bilinear groups [2].

- A simple and direct construction of a strongly attribute-hiding inner product predicate encryption scheme with constant-size keys (cf. Sect. 5.1). The previous prime-order schemes with constant-size keys in [31,32] are fairly complex: they start with a scheme with linear-size keys, and then use carefully crafted subgroups of sparse matrices [30] to compress the keys.

**Our Approach.** We introduce a conceptually simpler and more modular approach towards achieving the strong attribute-hiding guarantee. In particular, we deviate from the "two parallel sub-systems" paradigm introduced in [26] (cf. Sect. 4.3) and used in all subsequent works on inner product predicate encryption [31,32].

The main challenge in designing and proving security of strongly attribute-hiding predicate encryption schemes is that the following two invariants must be satisfied throughout the proof of security: (1) all secret keys (including simulated ones) must satisfy decryption correctness with respect to freshly and honestly generated ciphertexts; and (2) authorized secret keys must correctly decrypt the challenge ciphertext. Note that (1) already arises in ABE, whereas (2) does not.

To overcome this challenge, we follow a "private-key to public-key" paradigm [11,18,27,36], which in turn builds on Waters' dual system encryption methodology [28,35], introduced in the context of adaptively secure ABE. That is, we will start by building a private-key scheme where encryption requires the private key msk, and for security, the adversary gets a single ciphertext and no mpk, but an unbounded number of secret keys, and then provide a "compiler" from the private-key scheme to a public-key one. The advantage of working with a private-key scheme is that we need not worry about satisfying the first invariant, since an adversary cannot generate ciphertexts by itself in the private-key setting. Roughly speaking, the first invariant would be handled by the compiler, which ensures that if decryption correctness holds for honestly generated keys in the private-key scheme, then decryption correctness holds for both honestly generated and simulated keys in the public-key scheme.

In the case of building ABE schemes or weak attribute-hiding schemes as in prior works, then we are basically done at this point, since the security game does not allow the adversary access to authorized keys, and the second invariant is moot. Indeed, the main conceptual and technical novelty of this work lies in combining prior compilers with a new analysis to handle the second invariant.

**The Compiler and Our Analysis.** We proceed to describe the compiler and our analysis in a bit more detail. The compiler relies on the $k$-Linear (and more generally MDDH assumption) in prime-order groups, which says that $([\mathbf{A}], [\mathbf{As}]) \approx_c ([\mathbf{A}], [\mathbf{c}])$, where $\mathbf{A} \leftarrow_R \mathbb{Z}_q^{k \times (k+1)}, \mathbf{s} \leftarrow_R \mathbb{Z}_q^k, \mathbf{c} \leftarrow_R \mathbb{Z}_q^{k+1}$, and $[\cdot]$ corresponds to exponentiation.

Suppose we have a private-key scheme where the private key is given by $w_1, \ldots, w_n \in \mathbb{Z}_q$. We require that encryption and key generation be linear with respect to the private key. As with prior compilers, the private key in the "compiled" public-key scheme is given by vectors $\mathbf{w}_1, \ldots, \mathbf{w}_n \in \mathbb{Z}_q^{k+1}$ and the public key is given by:

$$\mathsf{mpk} := [\mathbf{A}], [\mathbf{A}^\top \mathbf{w}_1], \ldots, [\mathbf{A}^\top \mathbf{w}_n]$$

The new ciphertexts and secret keys are defined as follows:

- Encryption now samples $\mathbf{s} \leftarrow_R \mathbb{Z}_q^k$ and the new ciphertext is essentially the original ciphertext with $[\mathbf{s}^\top \mathbf{A}^\top \mathbf{w}_1], \ldots, [\mathbf{s}^\top \mathbf{A}^\top \mathbf{w}_n]$ as the private key, along with $[\mathbf{As}]$. For instance, if the original ciphertext was $2w_1 + w_2 \in \mathbb{Z}_q$, then the new ciphertext is $[\mathbf{As}], [\mathbf{s}^\top \mathbf{A}^\top (2\mathbf{w}_1 + \mathbf{w}_2)]$.
- Key generation outputs the original secret key with $\mathbf{w}_1, \ldots, \mathbf{w}_n$ as the private key. For instance, if the original secret key was $w_1 + 2w_2 \in \mathbb{Z}_q$, then the new secret key is $\mathbf{w}_1 + 2\mathbf{w}_2 \in \mathbb{Z}_q^k$.

The first step in the security proof is to use the MDDH assumption to replace $[\mathbf{As}]$ in the challenge ciphertext with $[\mathbf{c}]$ where $\mathbf{c} \leftarrow \mathbb{Z}_q^{k+1}$. Now, the challenge ciphertext is a ciphertext in the private-key scheme with

$$\mathsf{msk}^* := ([\mathbf{c}^\top \mathbf{w}_1], \ldots, [\mathbf{c}^\top \mathbf{w}_n])$$

as the private key. A key observation is that given mpk, the private key $\mathsf{msk}^*$ is completely random, since $\mathbf{A}, \mathbf{c}$ are linearly independent and forms a full basis (with overwhelming probability). We can then leverage the security of the underlying private-key scheme with $\mathsf{msk}^*$ as the private key.

What we have done so far is similar to prior works (e.g. [11,18,27]) and this is where the difference begins. Given a secret key sk in the new scheme (think of it as a column vector over $\mathbb{Z}_q$), we define:

$$(\mathsf{sk}^1, \mathsf{sk}^2) = (\mathbf{A}^\top \mathsf{sk}, \mathbf{c}^\top \mathsf{sk})$$

Since $\mathbf{A}, \mathbf{c}$ form a full basis, we have that $(\mathsf{sk}^1, \mathsf{sk}^2)$ completely determine $\mathsf{sk}$ (a weaker statement, for instance, already suffices for the ABE schemes in [18][2]) and it is essentially sufficient to reason about $\mathsf{sk}^1, \mathsf{sk}^2$. We observe that by linearity:

- $\mathsf{sk}^1$ is a secret key in the private-key scheme with $\mathbf{A}^\top \mathbf{w}_1, \ldots, \mathbf{A}^\top \mathbf{w}_n$ as the private key, and is therefore completely determined given $\mathsf{mpk}$. This means that the adversary learns nothing given $\mathsf{sk}^1$ beyond what it already learns from $\mathsf{mpk}$.
- $\mathsf{sk}^2$ is a secret key in the private-key scheme with $\mathbf{c}^\top \mathbf{w}_1, \ldots, \mathbf{c}^\top \mathbf{w}_n$ (i.e., $\mathsf{msk}^*$) as the private key.

That is, the view of the adversary given challenge ciphertext together with $\mathsf{sk}^2$ is essentially the same as the view of the adversary in the private-key scheme with $\mathsf{msk}^*$ as the private key! Therefore, we may then deduce the security of the compiled public-key scheme from the security of the original private-key scheme. In particular,

- if the original private-key scheme achieves selective security for a single challenge ciphertext and many secret keys, then the ensuing public-key scheme achieves semi-adaptive security with many secret keys. (The strengthening from selective to semi-adaptive comes from the fact that $\mathsf{msk}^*$ is completely hidden given $\mathsf{mpk}$.)
- if the original private-key scheme achieves simulation-based security, then the ensuing public-key scheme also achieves simulation-based security.

**Building Private-Key Schemes.** To complete the construction, we provide a brief overview of the corresponding private-key schemes achieving selective security for a single challenge ciphertext and many secret keys; we refer the reader to Sect. 2 for a more detailed technical overview.

As it turns out, the private-key scheme for inner product functional encryption is fairly straight-forward and can be realized unconditionally. Here, the ciphertext is associated with a vector $\mathbf{z} \in \mathbb{Z}_q^n$, and the secret key with a vector $\mathbf{y} \in \mathbb{Z}_q^n$, and decryption recovers $\langle \mathbf{z}, \mathbf{y} \rangle$:

$$\mathsf{msk} := \mathbf{w} \leftarrow_R \mathbb{Z}_q^n, \quad \mathsf{ct} := \mathbf{w} + \mathbf{z}, \quad \mathsf{sk}_\mathbf{y} := \langle \mathbf{w}, \mathbf{y} \rangle$$

The private-key scheme for inner product predicate encryption requires DDH in cyclic groups (without pairings) in order to (computationally) hide the value of

---

[2] Consider ABE in composite-order groups of order $p_1 p_2$. It is sufficient to show that the $p_2$-component of the encapsulated key accompanying the challenge ciphertext is completely hidden in the final hybrid, since we can always hash the encapsulated key, even if the $p_1$-component is completely leaked. In the case of strong attribute-hiding predicate encryption, it is not okay to leak the private attribute modulo $p_1$, even if the $p_2$-component is completely hidden. For this reason, we need to ensure that there is no leakage in $\mathsf{sk}$ beyond $\mathsf{sk}^1, \mathsf{sk}^2$, which means that $\mathsf{sk}^1, \mathsf{sk}^2$ need to completely determine $\mathsf{sk}$.

$\langle \mathbf{z}, \mathbf{y} \rangle$ beyond whether it is zero or non-zero. Together, these partially explain why in the public-key setting, the former does not require pairings whereas the latter does and why constructions for the former are much simpler (cf. [1] vs [26]).

The private-key scheme for the class $\mathcal{F}_{\mathsf{ABP} \circ \mathsf{IP}}$ of functions considered in our main result, namely an arithmetic branching program on public attributes, followed by an inner product predicate on private attribute, is more involved. We briefly mention that our private-key scheme builds upon the information-theoretic "partial" garbling schemes for $\mathcal{F}_{\mathsf{ABP} \circ \mathsf{IP}}$ in [25]. Our construction exploits the fact that for, these schemes enjoy so-called linear reconstruction (analogous to linear reconstruction for secret-sharing schemes). Using these partial garbling schemes, it is easy to build a private-key scheme for $\mathcal{F}_{\mathsf{ABP} \circ \mathsf{IP}}$ that is unconditionally secure for a single ciphertext and a single secret key, but where the ciphertext size grows with the size of the function (or alternatively, if we impose a read-once condition where each attribute variable appears once in the function). We then rely on the DDH assumption to (i) compress the ciphertext [3,17] so that it is linear in the length of the attribute rather than the size of the function, and (ii) to achieve security against many secret keys. To abstract some of these technical issues, we present a somewhat modular approach by appealing to a notion similar to "pair encodings" [3,8] developed in the context of adaptively secure ABE; see Sect. 4.

| Scheme | public $x$ | private $z$ | predicate $f$ |
|---|---|---|---|
| GPSW06 [23] | $\{0,1\}^n$ | — | boolean formula |
| OT10, IW14 [29, 25] | $\mathbb{Z}_q^n$ | — | arithmetic branching programs $\overset{?}{=} 0$ |
| KSW08, OT12 [26, 31, 32] | — | $\mathbb{Z}_q^n$ | inner product $\overset{?}{=} 0$ |
| this work | $\mathbb{Z}_q^{n'}$ | $\mathbb{Z}_q^n$ | ABP ∘ inner product $\overset{?}{=} 0$ |

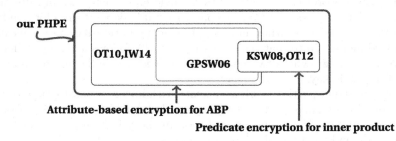

**Fig. 1.** Comparison amongst attribute-based and predicate encryption over bilinear groups. Recall that arithmetic branching programs (ABP) simultaneously generalize boolean and arithmetic formulas and branching programs with a small constant blowup in representation size.

## 1.2   Discussion

**On Simulation-Based Security.** There are now several results ruling out simulation-based predicate encryption [4,13,33], but none of which applies to the selective or semi-adaptive setting with a single ciphertext and unbounded secret key queries, as considered in this work. De Caro et al. [15] gave a feasibility result for all circuits in this setting, but under non-standard assumptions. Our work is the first to achieve simulation-based security in this setting for a nontrivial class of functions under standard cryptographic assumptions.

**Perspective.** Our (admittedly subjective) perspective is that developing strong attribute-hiding techniques from lattices is a promising route towards basing indistinguishability obfuscation on well-understood cryptographic assumptions. As a first small step towards this goal, we believe (again, admittedly subjective) that it would be useful to gain a better grasp of strongly attribute-hiding techniques in prime-order bilinear groups that work with vectors and matrices of group elements, with a minimal requirement on orthogonality relations amongst these vectors; indeed, this is the case for the schemes in this work (which rely on the "associative relation" framework introduced in [16,18]), but not for the prior works based on dual vector pairing spaces.

**Open Problems.** We conclude with a number of open problems:

- Our work clarifies functional encryption for linear functions as studied in [1,5] – the reason why this is much easier than inner product predicate is that it is very easy to construct a private-key scheme that is information-theoretically secure against unbounded number of secret key queries. This raises a number of questions pertaining to quadratic functions: (1) Is there a private-key functional encryption scheme for quadratic functions that is information-theoretically secure with a single ciphertext and an unbounded number of secret keys? (2) Can we construct public-key schemes for quadratic functions in to achieve either semi-adaptive or simulation-based security in the standard model? Note that the construction in [9] follows a "two parallel subsystems" strategy where two copies of the selective challenge are embedded into the public key.
- Can we construct partial garbling schemes with linear reconstruction for functions outside of $\mathcal{F}_{\mathsf{ABP} \circ \mathsf{IP}}$? It is easy to see that for linear reconstruction, we can only support degree one computation in the private input, so we cannot hope to extend substantially beyond $\mathcal{F}_{\mathsf{ABP} \circ \mathsf{IP}}$.
- Can we construct PHPE schemes for $\mathcal{F}_{\mathsf{ABP} \circ \mathsf{IP}}$ that are adaptively secure under standard assumptions (extending [31])? A first step would be to make the private-key scheme adaptively secure.

## 2   Detailed Technical Overview

We provide a more detailed technical overview in this section for the inner product functional and predicate encryption schemes.

*Notation.* Throughout, we fix a pairing group $(\mathbb{G}_1, \mathbb{G}_2, \mathbb{G}_T)$ with $e : \mathbb{G}_1 \times \mathbb{G}_2 \to \mathbb{G}_T$ of prime order $q$, and rely on implicit representation notation for group elements: for fixed generators $g_1$ and $g_2$ of $\mathbb{G}_1$ and $\mathbb{G}_2$, respectively, and for a matrix $\mathbf{M}$ over $\mathbb{Z}_q$, we define $[\mathbf{M}]_1 := g_1^{\mathbf{M}}$ and $[\mathbf{M}]_2 := g_2^{\mathbf{M}}$, where exponentiation is carried out component-wise. In addition, we will rely on the $k$-Linear (and more generally MDDH assumption) which says that $\left( [\mathbf{A}]_1, [\mathbf{As}]_1 \right) \approx_c \left( [\mathbf{A}]_1, [\mathbf{c}]_1 \right)$, where $\mathbf{A} \leftarrow \mathcal{D}_k, \mathbf{s} \leftarrow_\mathrm{R} \mathbb{Z}_q^k, \mathbf{c} \leftarrow_\mathrm{R} \mathbb{Z}_q^{k+1}$.

## 2.1   Inner Product Functional Encryption

For the inner product functional encryption, the ciphertext is associated with a vector $\mathbf{z} \in \mathbb{Z}_q^n$, and the secret key with a vector $\mathbf{y} \in \mathbb{Z}_q^n$, and decryption recovers $\langle \mathbf{z}, \mathbf{y} \rangle$, provided the value falls in a polynomially bounded domain.

**Private-Key Variant.** We present a private-key scheme where the ciphertexts and secret keys are over $\mathbb{Z}_q$ and which achieves information-theoretic security (for a single challenge ciphertext and many secret keys):

$$\mathsf{msk} := \mathbf{w} \leftarrow_\mathrm{R} \mathbb{Z}_q^n$$
$$\mathsf{ct} := \mathbf{w} + \mathbf{z}$$
$$\mathsf{sk_y} := \langle \mathbf{w}, \mathbf{y} \rangle$$

Decryption simply returns $\langle \mathsf{ct}, \mathbf{y} \rangle - \mathsf{sk_y}$.

For security, fix the selective challenge $\mathbf{z}^*$. The simulator picks $\tilde{\mathbf{w}} \leftarrow_\mathrm{R} \mathbb{Z}_q^n$ uniformly at random, and program

$$\tilde{\mathbf{w}} = \mathbf{w} + \mathbf{z}^*$$

Then, we can rewrite $\mathsf{ct}, \mathsf{sk_y}$ in terms of $\tilde{\mathbf{w}}$ as

$$\mathsf{ct} = \tilde{\mathbf{w}}, \quad \mathsf{sk_y} = \langle \tilde{\mathbf{w}}, \mathbf{y} \rangle - \langle \mathbf{z}^*, \mathbf{y} \rangle$$

It is clear that we can simulate an unbounded number of $\mathsf{sk_y}$ given just $\tilde{\mathbf{w}}, \mathbf{y}$ and the output of the ideal functionality $\langle \mathbf{z}^*, \mathbf{y} \rangle$.

**The Actual Scheme.** To transform the warm-up scheme into one that remains secure even if the adversary sees $\mathsf{mpk}$, we apply the "compiler" described in Sect. 1.1 where we replace $\mathbf{w} \in \mathbb{Z}_q^n$ with a matrix $\mathbf{W} \in \mathbb{Z}_q^{(k+1) \times n}$, upon which we arrive at the following public-key scheme:

$$\mathsf{msk} := \mathbf{W} \leftarrow_\mathrm{R} \mathbb{Z}_q^{(k+1) \times n}$$
$$\mathsf{mpk} := \left( [\mathbf{A}]_1, [\mathbf{A}^\top \mathbf{W}]_1 \right)$$
$$\mathsf{ct} := \left( [\mathbf{s}^\top \mathbf{A}^\top]_1, [\mathbf{s}^\top \mathbf{A}^\top \mathbf{W} + \mathbf{z}^\top]_1 \right)$$
$$\mathsf{sk_y} := \mathbf{W}\mathbf{y}$$

Decryption computes $[\langle \mathbf{z}, \mathbf{y} \rangle]_1 = [(\mathbf{s}^\top \mathbf{A}^\top \mathbf{W} + \mathbf{z}^\top)\mathbf{y}]_1 \cdot ([\mathbf{s}^\top \mathbf{A}^\top \mathbf{W}\mathbf{y}])^{-1}$ and uses brute-force discrete log to recover $\langle \mathbf{z}, \mathbf{y} \rangle$ as in [1]. We refer to Appendix B for the security proof.

**On Adaptive Security.** As alluded to in the introduction, the same proof plus one small observation essentially yields indistinguishability-based adaptive security as shown in [5] with a somewhat different argument (the approach here was used in the follow-up work [2]). Observe that the private-key scheme achieves perfect indistinguishability-based security in the selective setting (as implied by perfect simulation-based security); by complexity leveraging, this implies indistinguishability-based security in the adaptive setting. Moreover, it is straight-forward to verify that the adaptive security is preserved by the "compiler" since the use of the MDDH Assumption in the first step to switch $[\mathbf{As}]_1$ to $[\mathbf{c}]_1$ is oblivious to selective vs adaptive security.

## 2.2    Inner Product Predicate Encryption

We define predicate encryption in the framework of key encapsulation. For the inner product predicate, the ciphertext is associated with a vector $\mathbf{z}$, and the secret key with a vector $\mathbf{y}$, and decryption is possible iff $\langle \mathbf{z}, \mathbf{y} \rangle = 0$. In particular, decryption only leaks the predicate $\langle \mathbf{z}, \mathbf{y} \rangle \overset{?}{=} 0$ and not the exact value of $\langle \mathbf{z}, \mathbf{y} \rangle$.

**Private-Key Variant.** We present a private-key scheme where the ciphertexts are over $\mathbb{Z}_q$ and secret keys are over $\mathbb{G}_2$ and which achieves simulation-based security under the DDH assumption in $\mathbb{G}_2$. Roughly speaking, we start with the inner product functional encryption scheme, with an additional $u$ in the ciphertext (i.e. $u\mathbf{z} + \mathbf{w}$ instead of $\mathbf{z} + \mathbf{w}$) to hide any leakage beyond $\langle \mathbf{z}, \mathbf{y} \rangle \overset{?}{=} 0$; this would already be secure if there was only one secret key (since we cannot reuse the masking factor $u$). To achieve security against unbounded number of secret keys, we randomize the secret keys and rely on the DDH assumption.

$$\mathsf{msk} := \big( u, \mathbf{w}, \kappa \big) \leftarrow_{\mathrm{R}} \mathbb{Z}_q \times \mathbb{Z}_q^n \times \mathbb{Z}_q$$
$$(\mathsf{ct}, \mathsf{kem}) := \big( u\mathbf{z} + \mathbf{w}, [\kappa]_2 \big)$$
$$\mathsf{sk}_\mathbf{y} := \big( [\kappa - \langle \mathbf{w}, \mathbf{y} \rangle r]_2, [r]_2 \big), \quad r \leftarrow_{\mathrm{R}} \mathbb{Z}_q$$

Decryption recovers

$$[ \quad \overbrace{\kappa + ur\langle \mathbf{z}, \mathbf{y} \rangle}^{(\kappa - \langle \mathbf{w}, \mathbf{y} \rangle r) + \langle u\mathbf{z}+\mathbf{w}, \mathbf{y} \rangle r} \quad ]_2,$$

which equals $[\kappa]_2$ when $\langle \mathbf{z}, \mathbf{y} \rangle = 0$ and uniformly random otherwise.

For security, fix the selective challenge $\mathbf{z}^*$. The simulator picks $\tilde{\mathbf{w}} \leftarrow_{\mathrm{R}} \mathbb{Z}_q^n$ uniformly at random, and program

$$\tilde{\mathbf{w}} = u\mathbf{z}^* + \mathbf{w}$$

Then, we can rewrite $\mathsf{ct}, \mathsf{sk}_\mathbf{y}$ in terms of $\tilde{\mathbf{w}}$ as

$$\mathsf{ct} = \tilde{\mathbf{w}}$$
$$\mathsf{sk}_\mathbf{y} = \big( [\kappa + ur\langle \mathbf{z}^*, \mathbf{y} \rangle - \langle \tilde{\mathbf{w}}, \mathbf{y} \rangle r]_2, [r]_2 \big)$$
$$\approx_c \big( [\kappa + \boxed{\delta} \langle \mathbf{z}^*, \mathbf{y} \rangle - \langle \tilde{\mathbf{w}}, \mathbf{y} \rangle r]_2, [r]_2 \big), \delta \leftarrow_{\mathrm{R}} \mathbb{Z}_q$$

where we applied the DDH assumption to replace $([ur]_2, [r]_2)$ with $([\delta]_2, [r]_2)$. Now, we can easily simulate $\mathsf{sk_y}$ given $\kappa + \delta\langle \mathbf{z}^*, \mathbf{y}\rangle$ (which we can easily simulate given the output from the ideal functionality) along with $\mathbf{y}, \tilde{\mathbf{w}}$.

To achieve security under the $k$-Lin assumption, we replace $u, r$ with $\mathbf{u}, \mathbf{r} \leftarrow_{\mathrm{R}} \mathbb{Z}_q^k$, as well as $\mathbf{w}$ with $\mathbf{w}_1, \ldots, \mathbf{w}_n \leftarrow_{\mathrm{R}} \mathbb{Z}_q^k$. For the public-key variant, we then end up replacing $u$ with $\mathbf{U} \leftarrow_{\mathrm{R}} \mathbb{Z}_q^{(k+1) \times k}$, $\mathbf{w}$ with $\mathbf{W}_1, \ldots, \mathbf{W}_n \leftarrow_{\mathrm{R}} \mathbb{Z}_q^{(k+1) \times k}$, and $\kappa$ with $\boldsymbol{\kappa} \leftarrow_{\mathrm{R}} \mathbb{Z}_q^{k+1}$.

# 3  Preliminaries

**Notation.** We denote by $s \leftarrow_{\mathrm{R}} S$ the fact that $s$ is picked uniformly at random from a finite set $S$. By PPT, we denote a probabilistic polynomial-time algorithm. Throughout, we use $1^\lambda$ as the security parameter. We use lower case boldface to denote (column) vectors and upper case boldcase to denote matrices. We use $\equiv$ to denote two distributions being identically distributed.

**Arithmetic Branching Programs.** A *branching program* is defined by a directed acyclic graph $(V, E)$, two special vertices $v_0, v_1 \in V$ and a labeling function $\phi$. A *arithmetic branching program* (ABP), where $q \geq 2$ is a prime power, computes a function $f : \mathbb{F}_q^{n'} \to \mathbb{F}_q$. Here, $\phi$ assigns to each edge in $E$ an affine function in some input variable or a constant, and $f(x)$ is the sum over all $v_0$-$v_1$ paths of the product of all the values along the path. We refer to $|V| + |E|$ as the *size* of $\Gamma$.

We note that there is a linear-time algorithm that converts any boolean formula, boolean branching program or arithmetic formula to an arithmetic branching program with a constant blow-up in the representation size. Thus, ABPs can be viewed as a stronger computational model than all of the above. Recall also that branching programs and boolean formulas correspond to the complexity classes LOGSPACE and $NC_1$ respectively.

## 3.1  Cryptographic Assumptions

We follow the notation and algebraic framework for Diffie-Hellman-like assumptions in [19]. We fix a pairing group $(\mathbb{G}_1, \mathbb{G}_2, \mathbb{G}_T)$ with $e : \mathbb{G}_1 \times \mathbb{G}_2 \to \mathbb{G}_T$ of prime order $q$, where $q$ is a prime of $\Theta(\lambda)$ bits.

**$k$-Linear and MDDH Assumptions.** The $k$-Linear Assumption in $\mathbb{G}_1$ —more generally, the Matrix Decisional Diffie-Hellman (MDDH) Assumption— specifies an efficiently samplable distribution $\mathcal{D}_k$ over full-rank matrices in $\mathbb{Z}_q^{(k+1) \times k}$, and asserts that

$$\left( [\mathbf{A}]_1, [\mathbf{As}]_1 \right) \approx_c \left( [\mathbf{A}]_1, [\mathbf{c}]_1 \right)$$

where $\mathbf{A} \leftarrow \mathcal{D}_k, \mathbf{s} \leftarrow_R \mathbb{Z}_q^k, \mathbf{c} \leftarrow_R \mathbb{Z}_q^{k+1}$. We use $\mathsf{Adv}_{\mathbb{G}_1,\mathcal{A}}^{\mathrm{MDDH}}(\lambda)$ to denote the distinguishing advantage of an adversary $\mathcal{A}$ for the above distributions, and we define $\mathsf{Adv}_{\mathbb{G}_2,\mathcal{A}}^{\mathrm{MDDH}}(\lambda)$ analogously for $\mathbb{G}_2$. For the $k$-Linear assumption, the distribution $\mathcal{D}_k$ is given by

$$\begin{pmatrix} 1 & 1 & 1 & \cdots & 1 \\ a_1 & 0 & 0 & \cdots & 0 \\ 0 & a_2 & 0 & \cdots & 0 \\ 0 & 0 & a_3 & & 0 \\ \vdots & & & \ddots & \\ 0 & 0 & 0 & \cdots & a_k \end{pmatrix}$$

where $a_1, \ldots, a_k \leftarrow_R \mathbb{Z}_q^*$. Another example of $\mathcal{D}_k$ is the uniform distribution over full-rank matrices in $\mathbb{Z}_q^{(k+1) \times k}$.

## 3.2 Partially Hiding Predicate Encryption

We define PHPE for arithmetic functionalities with non-boolean output, in the framework of key encapsulation. Following [14,22,26], we associate $= 0$ with being true, and $\neq 0$ with being false.

**Syntax.** A *partially-hiding predicate encryption (PHPE) scheme* for a family $\mathcal{F} = \{f : \mathbb{Z}_q^{n'} \times \mathbb{Z}_q^n \to \mathbb{Z}_q\}$ consists of four algorithms (**setup, enc, keygen, dec**):

**setup**$(1^\lambda, 1^{n'+n}) \to (\mathsf{mpk}, \mathsf{msk})$. The setup algorithm gets as input the security parameter $\lambda$ and the attribute length $n'+n$ and outputs the public parameter $\mathsf{mpk}$, and the master key $\mathsf{msk}$. All the other algorithms get $\mathsf{mpk}$ as part of its input.

**enc**$(\mathsf{mpk}, (x, z)) \to (\mathsf{ct}, \mathsf{kem})$. The encryption algorithm gets as input $\mathsf{mpk}$, an attribute $(x, z) \in \mathbb{Z}_q^{n'} \times \mathbb{Z}_q^n$. It outputs a ciphertext $\mathsf{ct}$ and a symmetric-key $\mathsf{kem} \in \mathcal{M}$.

**keygen**$(\mathsf{msk}, f) \to \mathsf{sk}_f$. The key generation algorithm gets as input $\mathsf{msk}$ and a function $f \in \mathcal{F}$. It outputs a secret key $\mathsf{sk}_f$.

**dec**$((\mathsf{sk}_f, f), (\mathsf{ct}, x)) \to \mathsf{kem}$. The decryption algorithm gets as input $\mathsf{sk}_f$ and $\mathsf{ct}$, along with $f$ and $x$. It outputs a symmetric key $\mathsf{kem}$.

For notational simplicity, we often write **dec**$(\mathsf{sk}_f, \mathsf{ct})$ and omit the inputs $f, x$ to **dec**. Alternatively, we can think of $x$ and $f$ as part of the descriptions of $\mathsf{ct}$ and $\mathsf{sk}_f$ respectively.

**Correctness.** We require that for all $(x, z) \in \mathbb{Z}_q^{n'} \times \mathbb{Z}_q^n, f \in \mathcal{F}$ and for all $(\mathsf{mpk}, \mathsf{msk}) \leftarrow$ **setup**$(1^\lambda, 1^{n'})$ and $\mathsf{sk}_f \leftarrow$ **keygen**$(\mathsf{msk}, f)$,

- (authorized) if $f(x, z) = 0$, then $\Pr[(\mathsf{ct}, \mathsf{kem}) \leftarrow$ **enc**$(\mathsf{mpk}, (x, z));$ **dec**$((\mathsf{sk}_f, f), \mathsf{ct}) = \mathsf{kem}] = 1$;
- (unauthorized) if $f(x, z) \neq 0$, then **dec**$((\mathsf{sk}_f, f), \mathsf{ct})$ is uniformly distributed over $\mathcal{M}$, where $(\mathsf{ct}, \mathsf{kem}) \leftarrow$ **enc**$(\mathsf{mpk}, (x, z))$.

where both probability distributions are taken over the coins of **enc**.

**Security Definition.** The security definition for *semi-adaptively partially (strong) attribute-hiding* stipulates that there exists a randomized simulator $(\mathbf{setup}^*, \mathbf{enc}^*, \mathbf{keygen}^*)$ such that for every efficient stateful adversary $\mathcal{A}$,

$$
\begin{bmatrix}
(\mathsf{mpk}, \mathsf{msk}) \leftarrow \mathbf{setup}(1^\lambda, 1^{n'}); \\
(x^*, z^*) \leftarrow \mathcal{A}(\mathsf{mpk}); \\
(\mathsf{ct}, \mathsf{kem}) \leftarrow \mathbf{enc}(\mathsf{mpk}, (x^*, z^*)); \\
\text{output } \mathcal{A}^{\mathbf{keygen}(\mathsf{msk}, \cdot)}(\mathsf{mpk}, \mathsf{ct}, \mathsf{kem});
\end{bmatrix}
\approx_c
\begin{bmatrix}
(\mathsf{mpk}, \mathsf{msk}^*) \leftarrow \mathbf{setup}^*(1^\lambda, 1^{n'}); \\
(x^*, z^*) \leftarrow \mathcal{A}(\mathsf{mpk}); \\
\mathsf{ct} \leftarrow \mathbf{enc}^*(\mathsf{msk}^*, x^*); \mathsf{kem} \leftarrow_{\mathrm{R}} \mathcal{M}; \\
\text{output } \mathcal{A}^{\mathbf{keygen}^*(\mathsf{msk}^*, x^*, \cdot, \cdot)}(\mathsf{mpk}, \mathsf{ct}, \mathsf{kem});
\end{bmatrix}
$$

such that whenever $\mathcal{A}$ makes a query $f$ to **keygen**, the simulator **keygen**$^*$ gets $f$ along with

– kem if $f$ is authorized (i.e., $f(x^*, z^*) = 0$), and
– $\perp$ if $f$ is unauthorized (i.e., $f(x^*, z^*) \neq 0$), and

*Remark 1 (security definition).* Note that the security definition is the straightforward adaptation of strongly attribute-hiding from [12,26,32] to PHPE, in the semi-adaptive setting. This simulation-based definition implies the indistinguishability-based formulation of strongly attribute-hiding. Also, working with key encapsulation simplifies the security definition, since the adversary may as well receive the challenge ciphertext before making any secret key queries (indeed, this phenomenon was first noted in the context of CCA security).

## 4    $\mathcal{F}_{\mathsf{ABPoIP}}$ and Encodings

In this section, we formally describe the class $\mathcal{F}_{\mathsf{ABPoIP}}$ which our PHPE supports, as well as the encoding algorithm $\mathbf{rE}_f$ used in the PHPE scheme. Throughout, we work over $\mathbb{Z}_q$ where $q$ is prime.

### 4.1    The Class $\mathcal{F}_{\mathsf{ABPoIP}}$

We consider the class

$$
\mathcal{F}_{\mathsf{ABPoIP}} = \left\{ \, f : \mathbb{Z}_q^{n'} \times \mathbb{Z}_q^n \to \mathbb{Z}_q \, \right\}
$$

where $f$ on input $\mathbf{x} = (x_1, \dots, x_{n'}) \in \mathbb{Z}_q^{n'}$ and $\mathbf{z} = (z_1, \dots, z_n) \in \mathbb{Z}_q^n$ outputs

$$
f_1(\mathbf{x}) z_1 + \cdots + f_n(\mathbf{x}) z_n
$$

where $f_1, \dots, f_n : \mathbb{Z}_q^{n'} \to \mathbb{Z}_q$ are ABPs which are part of the description of $f$. We should think of $\mathbf{x}$ as the "public attribute", and $\mathbf{z}$ as the "private attribute". We will also use $m$ to denote the ABP size of $f$, which is the total number of edges and vertices in the underlying DAG.

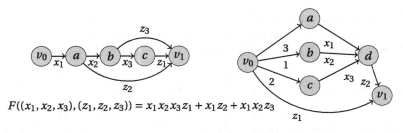

$$F((x_1, x_2, x_3), (z_1, z_2, z_3)) = x_1 x_2 x_3 z_1 + x_1 z_2 + x_1 x_2 z_3$$

$$F((x_1, x_2, x_3), (z_1, z_2)) = z_2(3x_1 + x_2 + 2x_3) + z_1$$

**Fig. 2.** Examples of functions in $\mathcal{F}_{\mathsf{ABP\circ IP}}$

**Examples.** It is clear that $\mathcal{F}_{\mathsf{ABP\circ IP}}$ contains both standard branching programs with public attributes by setting $n = 1, z_1 = 1$, as well as inner product with private attributes by setting $n' = 0$ and $f_1, \ldots, f_n$ to output constants $y_1, \ldots, y_n$. We refer to Fig. 2 for additional examples.

Next, we outline two concrete examples of new functionalities captured by our PHPE for $\mathcal{F}_{\mathsf{ABP\circ IP}}$:

- conjunctive comparison predicates [12, Sect. 3.1]: secret keys are associated with boolean functions $P_{a_1,\ldots,a_n}$ that compute

$$P_{a_1,\ldots,a_n}(z_1, \ldots, z_n) = \bigwedge_{i=1}^{n} (z_i \geq a_i)$$

Here, the $a_i$'s and $z_i$'s lie in polynomial-size domains. With inner product predicate encryption, $a_1, \ldots, a_n$ are fixed constants that are specified in the secret key. With PHPE for $\mathcal{F}_{\mathsf{ABP\circ IP}}$, we can carry out more complex computation where $a_1, \ldots, a_n$ are derived as the output of an ABP computation on public ciphertext attribute $x$. (Fixed $a_1, \ldots, a_n$ are a special case since we can have ABPs that ignore $x$ and output the fixed constant.)
- polynomial evaluation [26, Sect. 5.3]: secret keys are associated with polynomials in $z$ of degree less than $n$. With inner product predicate encryption, the coefficients of the polynomial are fixed constants that are specified in the secret key. With PHPE for $\mathcal{F}_{\mathsf{ABP\circ IP}}$, we may derive the coefficients as the output of an ABP computation on public ciphertext attribute $x$.

### 4.2 Encodings $\mathsf{rE}_f$ for $\mathcal{F}_{\mathsf{ABP\circ IP}}$

Suppose we want to build a private-key PHPE for $\mathcal{F}_{\mathsf{ABP\circ IP}}$ secure against a single ciphertext and a single secret key. Our ciphertext corresponding to public attribute $\mathbf{x} \in \mathbb{Z}_q^{n'}$ and private attribute $\mathbf{z} \in \mathbb{Z}_q^{n}$ will be of the form:

$$\left\{ u'_j x_i + v'_{ij} \right\}_{i \in [n'], j \in [m]}, \ \left\{ z_i + w'_i \right\}_{i \in [n]}$$

where $u'_j, v'_{ij}, w'_i$ are part of the private key. In particular, the ciphertext size grows linearly with $n' + n$ and is independent of the function $f \in \mathcal{F}_{\mathsf{ABP\circ IP}}$. Then, we can think of the output of $\mathbf{rE}_f$ as a secret key for $f$ that combined with the ciphertext, allows us to learn $\kappa + f(\mathbf{x}, \mathbf{z})$, where $\kappa$ is the "master secret key" which is used to mask the plaintext.

**The Encoding $\mathbf{rE}_f$.** We require a randomized algorithm $\mathbf{rE}_f$ parameterized by a function $f \in \mathcal{F}_{\mathsf{ABPoIP}}$ that takes as input

$$\kappa, \left\{ w_i' \right\}_{i \in [n]}, \left\{ u_j' \right\}_{j \in [m]}, \left\{ v_{ij}' \right\}_{i \in [n'], j \in [m]} \in \mathbb{Z}_q,$$

along randomness $\mathbf{t} \leftarrow_{\mathrm{R}} \mathbb{Z}_q^{m+n}$, which satisfies the following properties:

- **linearity:** $\mathbf{rE}_f$ computes a linear function of its inputs and randomness over $\mathbb{Z}_q$;
- **reconstruction:** there exists an efficient algorithm **rec** that on input

$$f, \mathbf{x}, \mathbf{rE}_f \big( \kappa, \left\{ w_i' \right\}_{i \in [n]}, \left\{ u_j' \right\}_{j \in [m]}, \left\{ v_{ij}' \right\}_{i \in [n'], j \in [m]}; \mathbf{t} \big),$$
$$\left\{ u_j' x_i + v_{ij}' \right\}_{i \in [n'], j \in [m]}, \left\{ z_i + w_i' \right\}_{i \in [n]}$$

  outputs $\kappa + f(\mathbf{x}, \mathbf{z})$. This holds for all $f, \mathbf{x}, \mathbf{z}, \kappa, \mathbf{t}$. Moreover, $\mathbf{rec}(f, \mathbf{x}, \cdot)$ computes a linear function of the remaining inputs.
- **privacy:** there exists an efficient simulator **sim** such that for all $f, \mathbf{x}, \mathbf{z}, \kappa$, the output of $\mathbf{sim}(f, \mathbf{x}, \kappa + f(\mathbf{x}, \mathbf{z}))$ is identically distributed to that of

$$\mathbf{rE}_f \big( \kappa, \left\{ -z_i \right\}_{i \in [n]}, \left\{ \delta_j \right\}_{j \in [m]}, \left\{ -\delta_j x_i \right\}_{i \in [n'], j \in [m]}; \mathbf{t} \big),$$

  where $\left\{ \delta_j \leftarrow_{\mathrm{R}} \mathbb{Z}_q \right\}_{j \in [m]}, \mathbf{t} \leftarrow_{\mathrm{R}} \mathbb{Z}_q^{m+n}$ are random.

We defer the description of the algorithm to Appendix A, which builds upon the "partial garbling scheme" for $\mathcal{F}_{\mathsf{ABPoIP}}$ from [24,25] in a somewhat straight-forward manner.

**Extension to Vectors.** In the scheme, we will run $\mathbf{rE}_f$ with vectors instead of scalars as inputs, by applying $\mathbf{rE}_f$ to each coordinate. That is, $\mathbf{rE}_f$ takes as input

$$\boldsymbol{\kappa}, \left\{ \mathbf{w}_i' \right\}_{i \in [n]}, \left\{ \mathbf{u}_j' \right\}_{j \in [m]}, \left\{ \mathbf{v}_{ij}' \right\}_{i \in [n'], j \in [m]} \in \mathbb{Z}_q^k,$$

along randomness $\mathbf{T} \leftarrow_{\mathrm{R}} \mathbb{Z}_q^{k \times (m+n)}$, and outputs

$$\left( \boldsymbol{\kappa} + \boldsymbol{\tau}, \left\{ \boldsymbol{\sigma}_i - \mathbf{w}_i' \right\}_{i \in [n]}, \left\{ \boldsymbol{\beta}_j + \mathbf{u}_j', \boldsymbol{\gamma}_j + \mathbf{v}_{\rho(j)j}' \right\}_{j \in [m]} \right) \in \mathbb{Z}_q^{k \times (1+n+m)}$$

The first row of the output is obtained by applying $\mathbf{rE}_f$ to the first coordinate/row of each input, etc. Linearity (as captured by left-multiplication by a matrix) is clearly preserved, whereas we will only invoke reconstruction and privacy for scalar inputs.

# 5   Our PHPE Construction

In this section, we present our partially-hiding predicate encryption scheme for the class

$$\mathcal{F}_{\mathsf{ABPoIP}} = \{\, f : \mathbb{Z}_q^{n'} \times \mathbb{Z}_q^n \to \mathbb{Z}_q \,\}$$

defined in Sect. 4. We also fix a pairing group $(\mathbb{G}_1, \mathbb{G}_2, \mathbb{G}_T)$ with $e : \mathbb{G}_1 \times \mathbb{G}_2 \to \mathbb{G}_T$ of prime order $q$.

## 5.1   Warm-Up I: Inner Product Predicate, i.e. $n' = 0$

As a warm-up, we sketch the scheme and the proof for inner product predicate encryption, corresponding to the special case:

$$n' = 0, \ f_{\mathbf{y}}(\mathbf{z}) = \langle \mathbf{y}, \mathbf{z} \rangle, \ \mathbf{rE}_f\big(\kappa, \mathbf{w}r_0, \dots\big) = \kappa - \langle \mathbf{w}r_0, \mathbf{y} \rangle.$$

That is, the ciphertext is associated with a vector $\mathbf{z}$, and the secret key with a vector $\mathbf{y}$, and decryption is possible iff $\langle \mathbf{z}, \mathbf{y} \rangle = 0$. We refer the reader to the private-key variant in Sect. 2.2.

*The scheme.* The scheme is as follows:

$$\mathsf{msk} := \big(\, \mathbf{U}, \mathbf{W}_1, \dots, \mathbf{W}_n, \boldsymbol{\kappa} \,\big) \leftarrow_{\mathrm{R}} \mathbb{Z}_q^{(k+1) \times k} \times \cdots \times \mathbb{Z}_q^{(k+1) \times k} \times \mathbb{Z}_q^{k+1}$$

$$\mathsf{mpk} := \big(\, [\mathbf{A}]_1, [\mathbf{A}^{\mathsf{T}} \mathbf{U}]_1, \{\, [\mathbf{A}^{\mathsf{T}} \mathbf{W}_i]\,\}_{i \in [n']}, [\mathbf{A}^{\mathsf{T}} \boldsymbol{\kappa}]_T \,\big)$$

$$(\mathsf{ct}, \mathsf{kem}) := \big(\, \big( [\mathbf{s}^{\mathsf{T}} \mathbf{A}^{\mathsf{T}}]_1, \{\, [\mathbf{s}^{\mathsf{T}} \mathbf{A}^{\mathsf{T}} (z_i \mathbf{U} + \mathbf{W}_i)]_1 \,\}_{i \in [n]} \big), [\mathbf{s}^{\mathsf{T}} \mathbf{A}^{\mathsf{T}} \boldsymbol{\kappa}]_T \,\big)$$

$$\mathsf{sk}_{\mathbf{y}} := \big(\, [\boldsymbol{\kappa} - \sum_{i=1}^{n} y_i \mathbf{W}_i \mathbf{r}]_2, [\mathbf{r}]_2 \big), \quad \mathbf{r} \leftarrow_{\mathrm{R}} \mathbb{Z}_q^k$$

Decryption relies on the fact that whenever $\langle \mathbf{z}, \mathbf{y} \rangle = 0$, we have

$$\mathbf{s}^{\mathsf{T}} \mathbf{A}^{\mathsf{T}} \cdot (\boldsymbol{\kappa} - \sum_{i=1}^{n} y_i \mathbf{W}_i \mathbf{r}) + \sum_{i=1}^{n} y_i \cdot (\mathbf{s}^{\mathsf{T}} \mathbf{A}^{\mathsf{T}} (z_i \mathbf{U} + \mathbf{W}_i)) \cdot \mathbf{r} = \mathbf{s}^{\mathsf{T}} \mathbf{A}^{\mathsf{T}} \boldsymbol{\kappa}$$

*Proof sketch.* The proof of security follows a series of games:

**Game 1.** Switch $(\mathsf{ct}, \mathsf{kem})$ to

$$\big(\, \big( [\, \mathbf{c}^{\mathsf{T}}]_1, \{\, [\, \mathbf{c}^{\mathsf{T}} (z_i \mathbf{U} + \mathbf{W}_i)]_1 \,\}_{i \in [n]} \big), [\, \mathbf{c}^{\mathsf{T}} \boldsymbol{\kappa}]_T \,\big)$$

where $\mathbf{c} \leftarrow_{\mathrm{R}} \mathbb{Z}_q^{k+1}$. That is, we used the MDDH assumption in $\mathbb{G}_1$ to replace $[\mathbf{A}\mathbf{s}]_1$ with $[\mathbf{c}]_1$.

**Game 2.** Given the semi-adaptive challenge $\mathbf{z}^*$, the simulator picks $\tilde{\mathbf{W}}_i \leftarrow_R \mathbb{Z}_q^{(k+1)\times k}, \hat{\mathbf{s}} \leftarrow_R \mathbb{Z}_q^k$, and programs

$$\mathbf{c}^\top \mathbf{U} = \hat{\mathbf{s}}^\top, \ \ \tilde{\mathbf{W}}_i = \mathbf{W}_i + z_i^* \mathbf{a}^\perp \hat{\mathbf{s}}^\top$$

where $\mathbf{a}^\perp \in \mathbb{Z}_q^{k+1}$ satisfies $\mathbf{A}^\top \mathbf{a}^\perp = \mathbf{0}, \mathbf{c}^\top \mathbf{a}^\perp = 1$. Note that $\mathbf{A}^\top \mathbf{W}_i = \mathbf{A}^\top \tilde{\mathbf{W}}_i$, which allows us to program $z_i^*$ into $\tilde{\mathbf{W}}_i$ even though $z_i^*$ is chosen after the adversary sees mpk. This parallels the step in the private-key variant where we program $\tilde{w} = uw + \mathbf{z}^*$. Now, we can rewrite (ct, kem) and $\mathsf{sk_y}$ as

$$(\mathsf{ct}, \mathsf{kem}) := \left( \left( [\mathbf{c}^\top]_1, \left\{ [\mathbf{c}^\top \tilde{\mathbf{W}}_i]_1 \right\}_{i\in[n]} \right), [\mathbf{c}^\top \boldsymbol{\kappa}]_T \right)$$

$$\mathsf{sk_y} := \left( [\boldsymbol{\kappa} + \langle \mathbf{z}^*, \mathbf{y} \rangle \mathbf{a}^\perp \hat{\mathbf{s}}^\top \mathbf{r} - \sum_{i=1}^n y_i \tilde{\mathbf{W}}_i \mathbf{r}]_2, [\mathbf{r}]_2 \right)$$

**Game 3.** We use the MDDH assumption in $\mathbb{G}_2$ to replace $([\hat{\mathbf{s}}^\top \mathbf{r}]_2, [\mathbf{r}]_2)$ in $\mathsf{sk_y}$ with $([\delta]_2, [\mathbf{r}]_2)$: that is, we switch $\mathsf{sk_y}$ to

$$\mathsf{sk_y} := \left( [\boldsymbol{\kappa} + \langle \mathbf{z}^*, \mathbf{y} \rangle \mathbf{a}^\perp \boxed{\delta} - \sum_{i=1}^n y_i \tilde{\mathbf{W}}_i \mathbf{r}]_2, [\mathbf{r}]_2 \right), \delta \leftarrow_R \mathbb{Z}_q$$

This parallels the step in the private-key variant where we applied the DDH assumption to switch $ur$ to $\delta$.

**Game 4.** To complete the proof, it suffices to show that we can simulate $\boldsymbol{\kappa} + \langle \mathbf{z}^*, \mathbf{y} \rangle \mathbf{a}^\perp \delta$ (and thus $\mathsf{sk_y}$) given $a = \mathbf{c}^\top \boldsymbol{\kappa} + \delta \langle \mathbf{z}^*, \mathbf{y} \rangle$ (which we can simulate given the output from the ideal functionality). This follows from the fact that we can compute

$$[\mathbf{A} \mid \mathbf{c}]^\top (\boldsymbol{\kappa} + \langle \mathbf{z}^*, \mathbf{y} \rangle \mathbf{a}^\perp \delta) = \begin{bmatrix} \mathbf{A}^\top \boldsymbol{\kappa} \\ a \end{bmatrix}$$

and then invert $[\mathbf{A} \mid \mathbf{c}]$.

### 5.2   Warm-Up II: A Private-Key Scheme

We sketch a private-key PHPE scheme for $\mathcal{F}_{\mathsf{ABPoIP}}$ where the ciphertexts are over $\mathbb{Z}_q$ and secret keys are over $\mathbb{G}_2$ and which achieves simulation-based security for a single challenge ciphertext and many secret keys under the DDH assumption in $\mathbb{G}_2$.

*The scheme.* The scheme uses the algorithm $\mathbf{rE}_f$ described in the previous section.

$$\mathsf{msk} := \left( u, \{ w_i \}_{i\in[n]}, \{ v_i \}_{i\in[n']}, \boldsymbol{\kappa} \right) \leftarrow_R \mathbb{Z}_q \times \mathbb{Z}_q^n \times \mathbb{Z}_q^{n'} \times \mathbb{Z}_q$$

$$(\mathsf{ct}, \mathsf{kem}) := \left( \{ uz_i + w_i \}_{i\in[n']}, \{ ux_i + v_i \}_{i\in[n]}, [\boldsymbol{\kappa}]_2 \right)$$

$$\mathsf{sk}_f := \left( [\mathbf{rE}_f( \boldsymbol{\kappa}, \{ w_i r_0 \}_{i\in[n]}, \{ u r_j \}_{j\in[m]}, \{ v_i r_j \}_{i\in[n'], j\in[m]}; \mathbf{t} )]_2, [r_0]_2, \{ [r_j]_2 \}_{j\in[m]} \right)$$

Decryption computes **rec** "in the exponent" over $\mathbb{G}_2$ to recover $[\boldsymbol{\kappa}]_2$. The proof is similar to that for the private-key inner product predicate encryption; we omit the details here since we will directly prove security of the public-key scheme.

## 5.3   Our PHPE Scheme

Our PHPE scheme for $\mathcal{F}_{\mathsf{ABP\circ IP}}$ also uses the algorithm $\mathbf{rE}_f$ described in the previous section:

$\mathbf{setup}(1^\lambda, 1^{n'+n})$ :   pick   $\mathbf{A} \leftarrow \mathcal{D}_k$,   $\mathbf{U}, \mathbf{W}_1, \dots, \mathbf{W}_n, \mathbf{V}_1, \dots, \mathbf{V}_{n'} \leftarrow_R$ $\mathbb{Z}_q^{(k+1)\times k}, \boldsymbol{\kappa} \leftarrow \mathbb{Z}_q^{k+1}$ and output

$$\mathsf{mpk} := \Big( [\mathbf{A}]_1, [\mathbf{A}^\top \mathbf{U}]_1, \big\{ [\mathbf{A}^\top \mathbf{W}_i]_1 \big\}_{i\in[n]}, \big\{ [\mathbf{A}^\top \mathbf{V}_i]_1 \big\}_{i\in[n']}, [\mathbf{A}^\top \boldsymbol{\kappa}]_T \Big),$$

$$\mathsf{msk} := \Big( \boldsymbol{\kappa}, \mathbf{U}, \big\{ \mathbf{W}_i \big\}_{i\in[n]}, \big\{ \mathbf{V}_i \big\}_{i\in[n']} \Big)$$

$\mathbf{enc}(\mathsf{mpk}, (\mathbf{x}, \mathbf{z}))$ : pick $\mathbf{s} \leftarrow_R \mathbb{Z}_q^k$ and output

$$\mathsf{ct} := \Big( \overbrace{[\mathbf{s}^\top \mathbf{A}^\top]_1}^{C_0}, \big\{ \overbrace{[\mathbf{s}^\top \mathbf{A}^\top (\mathbf{U} z_i + \mathbf{W}_i)]_1}^{C_{1,i}} \big\}_{i\in[n]}, \big\{ \overbrace{[\mathbf{s}^\top \mathbf{A}^\top (\mathbf{U} x_i + \mathbf{V}_i)]_1}^{C_{2,i}} \big\}_{i\in[n']} \Big)$$

$$\mathsf{kem} := [\mathbf{s}^\top \mathbf{A}^\top \boldsymbol{\kappa}]_T$$

$\mathbf{keygen}(\mathsf{msk}, f)$ : pick $\mathbf{r}_0, \mathbf{r}_1, \dots, \mathbf{r}_m \leftarrow_R \mathbb{Z}_q^k$, sample $\mathbf{T}$, and output

$$\mathsf{sk}_f := \Big( [\mathbf{rE}_f(\boldsymbol{\kappa}, \{\mathbf{W}_i \mathbf{r}_0\}_{i\in[n]}, \{\mathbf{U}\mathbf{r}_j\}_{j\in[m]}, \{\mathbf{V}_i \mathbf{r}_j\}_{i\in[n'],j\in[m]}; \mathbf{T})]_2, [\mathbf{r}_0]_2, \{[\mathbf{r}_j]_2\}_{j\in[m]} \Big)$$

$\mathbf{dec}((\mathsf{sk}_f, f), (\mathsf{ct}, \mathbf{x}))$ :   parse   $\mathsf{ct} = \big( C_0, \{C_{1,i}\}_{i\in[n]}, \{C_{2,i}\}_{i\in[n']} \big), \mathsf{sk}_f =$ $\big( D_0, [\mathbf{r}_0]_2, \{[\mathbf{r}_j]_2\}_{j\in[m]} \big)$, and output

$$\mathbf{rec}\big( f, \mathbf{x}, e(C_0, D_0), \{e(C_{2,i}, [\mathbf{r}_j]_2)\}_{i\in[n'],j\in[m]}, \{e(C_{1,i}, [\mathbf{r}_0]_2)\}_{i\in[n]} \big)$$

where $\mathbf{rec}$ is computed "in the exponent" over $\mathbb{G}_T$.

## 5.4   Analysis

**Theorem 1.** *Our PHPE scheme for $\mathcal{F}_{\mathsf{ABP\circ IP}}$ described in Sect. 5.3 achieves simulation-based semi-adaptively partially (strongly) attribute-hiding under the MDDH assumption in $\mathbb{G}_1$ and in $\mathbb{G}_2$, with an unbounded simulator.*

Note that unbounded simulation as considered in [4] implies (and is therefore stronger than) indistinguishability-based security.

**Correctness.** By the linearity and reconstruction properties for $\mathbf{rE}_f$, we have

$$\mathbf{rec}\big( \overbrace{\mathbf{s}^\top \mathbf{A}}^{C_0} \cdot \overbrace{\mathbf{rE}_f(\boldsymbol{\kappa}, \mathbf{W}_i \mathbf{r}_0, \mathbf{U}\mathbf{r}_j, \mathbf{V}_i \mathbf{r}_j)}^{D_0}, \{\overbrace{\mathbf{s}^\top \mathbf{A}(\mathbf{U} x_i + \mathbf{V}_i) \cdot \mathbf{r}_j}^{C_{2,i}}\}_{i\in[n'],j\in[m]}, \{\overbrace{\mathbf{s}^\top \mathbf{A}(\mathbf{U} z_i + \mathbf{W}_i) \cdot \mathbf{r}_0}^{C_{1,i}}\}_{i\in[n]} \big)$$

$$= \mathbf{rec}\big( \mathbf{rE}_f(\mathbf{s}^\top \mathbf{A}\boldsymbol{\kappa}, \mathbf{s}^\top \mathbf{A}\mathbf{W}_i \mathbf{r}_0, \mathbf{s}^\top \mathbf{A}\mathbf{U}\mathbf{r}_j, \mathbf{s}^\top \mathbf{A}\mathbf{V}_i \mathbf{r}_j), (\mathbf{s}^\top \mathbf{A}(\mathbf{U} x_i + \mathbf{V}_i)\mathbf{r}_j), (\mathbf{s}^\top \mathbf{A}(\mathbf{U} z_i + \mathbf{W}_i)\mathbf{r}_0) \big)$$

$$= \mathbf{s}^\top \mathbf{A}\boldsymbol{\kappa} + \mathbf{r}_0 f(\mathbf{x}, (\mathbf{s}^\top \mathbf{A}\mathbf{U})\mathbf{z})$$

$$= \mathbf{s}^\top \mathbf{A}\boldsymbol{\kappa} + \mathbf{s}^\top \mathbf{A}\mathbf{U}\mathbf{r}_0 \cdot f(\mathbf{x}, \mathbf{z})$$

Therefore, $\mathbf{dec}$ outputs $[\mathbf{s}^\top \mathbf{A}\boldsymbol{\kappa}]_T$ if $f(\mathbf{x}, \mathbf{z}) = 0$ and a uniformly random value in $\mathbb{G}_T$ otherwise.

## 5.5   Simulator

We start by describing the simulator for our scheme. Fix the semi-adaptive challenge $\mathbf{x}^*, \mathbf{z}^*$. Recall that for a query $f$ to **keygen**, the simulated **keygen**$^*$ gets kem from the ideal functionality if $f(\mathbf{x}^*, \mathbf{z}^*) = 0$, and $\bot$ otherwise. In the first case, we assume that **keygen**$^*$ gets kem as a value in $\mathbb{Z}_q$ instead of $G_T$, in which case it can be implemented efficiently. Otherwise, we would have an unbounded simulator (that computes discrete log via brute force) as considered in [4], which still implies indistinguishability-based security. In fact, to avoid the case analysis, we assume that the simulator gets $\mathsf{kem} + \delta_0 f(\mathbf{z}^*, \mathbf{z}^*)$ where a fresh $\delta_0 \leftarrow_R \mathbb{Z}_q$ is chosen for each $f$; it is easy to simulate this quantity given the output of the ideal functionality.

**setup**$^*(1^\lambda, 1^{n'+n})$ : pick $\mathbf{A} \leftarrow \mathcal{D}_k$, $\widetilde{\mathbf{W}}_1, \ldots, \widetilde{\mathbf{W}}_n, \widetilde{\mathbf{V}}_1, \ldots, \widetilde{\mathbf{V}}_{n'} \leftarrow_R \mathbb{Z}_q^{(k+1) \times k}$, $\widetilde{\mathbf{U}} \leftarrow_R \mathbb{Z}_q^{k \times k}, \boldsymbol{\kappa} \leftarrow \mathbb{Z}_q^{k+1}$, $\mathbf{c} \leftarrow_R \mathbb{Z}_q^{k+1}$ and output

$$\mathsf{mpk} := \left( [\mathbf{A}]_1, [\mathbf{A}^\top \widetilde{\mathbf{U}}]_1, \left\{ [\mathbf{A}^\top \widetilde{\mathbf{W}}_i]_1 \right\}_{i \in [n]}, \left\{ [\mathbf{A}^\top \widetilde{\mathbf{V}}_i]_1 \right\}_{i \in [n']}, [\mathbf{A}^\top \boldsymbol{\kappa}]_T \right),$$

$$\mathsf{msk}^* := \left( \boldsymbol{\kappa}, \widetilde{\mathbf{U}}, \left\{ \widetilde{\mathbf{W}}_i \right\}_{i \in [n]}, \left\{ \widetilde{\mathbf{V}}_i \right\}_{i \in [n']}, \mathbf{c}, \mathbf{C}^\bot, \mathbf{a}^\bot \right)$$

where $(\mathbf{A}|\mathbf{c})^\top (\mathbf{C}^\bot|\mathbf{a}^\bot) = \mathbf{I}_{k+1}$. In particular, $\mathbf{A}^\top \mathbf{a}^\bot = \mathbf{0}, \mathbf{c}^\top \mathbf{C}^\bot = \mathbf{0}, \mathbf{c}^\top \mathbf{a}^\bot = 1$.

**enc**$^*(\mathsf{msk}^*, \mathbf{x}^*)$ : output

$$\mathsf{ct} := \left( [\mathbf{c}^\top]_1, \left\{ [\mathbf{c}^\top \widetilde{\mathbf{W}}_i]_1 \right\}_{i \in [n]}, \left\{ [\mathbf{c}^\top \widetilde{\mathbf{V}}_i]_1 \right\}_{i \in [n']} \right)$$

$$\mathsf{kem} := [\mathbf{c}^\top \boldsymbol{\kappa}]_T$$

**keygen**$^*(\mathsf{msk}^*, \mathbf{x}^*, f, a = \mathbf{c}^\top \boldsymbol{\kappa} + \delta_0 f(\mathbf{x}^*, \mathbf{z}^*))$ : pick $\mathbf{r}_0, \mathbf{r}_1, \ldots, \mathbf{r}_m \leftarrow_R \mathbb{Z}_q^k$, sample $\mathbf{T}$, and output

$$\mathsf{sk}_f := \left( [\mathbf{r}\mathbf{E}_f(\mathbf{0}, \{ \widetilde{\mathbf{W}}_i \mathbf{r}_0 \}_{i \in [n]}, \{ \mathbf{C}^\bot \widetilde{\mathbf{U}} \mathbf{r}_j \}_{j \in [m]}, \{ \widetilde{\mathbf{V}}_i \mathbf{r}_j \}_{i \in [n'], j \in [m]}; \mathbf{T})]_2 \right.$$

$$\left. + [\mathbf{C}^\bot \cdot \mathbf{r}\mathbf{E}_f(\mathbf{A}^\top \boldsymbol{\kappa}, 0, 0, 0; \widetilde{\mathbf{T}}) + \mathbf{a}^\bot \cdot \mathsf{sim}(f, \mathbf{x}^*, a)]_2, [\mathbf{r}_0]_2, \{ [\mathbf{r}_j]_2 \}_{j \in [m]} \right)$$

## 5.6   Security Proof

We show that for any adversary $\mathcal{A}$ against the scheme, there exist adversaries $\mathcal{A}_1, \mathcal{A}_2$ whose running times are essentially the same as that of $\mathcal{A}$, such that

$$\mathsf{Adv}_{\mathcal{A}}^{\mathrm{PHPE}}(\lambda) \leq \mathsf{Adv}_{\mathbb{G}_1, \mathcal{A}_1}^{\mathrm{MDDH}}(\lambda) + \mathsf{Adv}_{\mathbb{G}_2, \mathcal{A}_2}^{\mathrm{MDDH}}(\lambda) + 2^{-\Omega(\lambda)}$$

We proceed via a series of games and we use $\mathsf{Adv}_i$ to denote the advantage of $\mathcal{A}$ in Game $i$.

**Game 0.** Real game.

**Game 1.** We replace $[\mathbf{As}]_1$ in $\mathbf{enc}(\mathsf{mpk}, (\mathbf{x}^*, \mathbf{z}^*))$ with $[\mathbf{c}]_1$ where $\mathbf{c} \leftarrow_R \mathbb{Z}_q^{k+1}$. That is, the challenge ciphertext is now given by

$$\mathsf{ct} := \left( [\mathbf{c}^\top]_1, \left\{ [\mathbf{c}^\top (\mathbf{U} z_i^* + \mathbf{W}_i)]_1 \right\}_{i \in [n]}, \left\{ [\mathbf{c}^\top (\mathbf{U} x_i^* + \mathbf{V}_i)]_1 \right\}_{i \in [n']} \right)$$

$$\mathsf{kem} := [\mathbf{c}^\top \boldsymbol{\kappa}]_T$$

This follows readily from the MDDH Assumption (cf. Sect. 3.1), so we have

$$|\mathsf{Adv}_0 - \mathsf{Adv}_1| \le \mathsf{Adv}_{\mathbb{G}_1, \mathcal{A}_1}^{\mathsf{MDDH}}(\lambda)$$

**Game 2.** We sample $\hat{\mathbf{s}} \leftarrow_R \mathbb{Z}_q^k$ and replace **setup, enc** with **setup**\*, **enc**\* and **keygen** with **keygen**$_2^*$ where

**keygen**$_2^*$(msk, $f$, $\mathbf{x}^*$): pick $\mathbf{r}_0, \mathbf{r}_1, \ldots, \mathbf{r}_m \leftarrow_R \mathbb{Z}_q^k$, sample $\mathbf{T}$, and output

$$\mathsf{sk}_f := \left( \left[ \mathbf{r} \mathbf{E}_f \left( \boldsymbol{\kappa}, \left\{ \widetilde{\mathbf{W}}_i \mathbf{r}_0 - z_i^* \mathbf{a}^\perp \hat{\mathbf{s}}^\top \mathbf{r}_0 \right\}_{i \in [n]}, \left\{ \mathbf{C}^\perp \widetilde{\mathbf{U}} \mathbf{r}_j - \mathbf{a}^\perp \hat{\mathbf{s}}^\top \mathbf{r}_j \right\}_{j \in [m]}, \right. \right. \right.$$
$$\left. \left. \left. \left\{ \widetilde{\mathbf{V}}_i \mathbf{r}_j - x_i^* \mathbf{a}^\perp \hat{\mathbf{s}}^\top \mathbf{r}_j \right\}_{i \in [n'], j \in [m]}; \mathbf{T} \right) \right]_2, [\mathbf{r}_0]_2, \left\{ [\mathbf{r}_j]_2 \right\}_{j \in [m]} \right)$$

The differences between **keygen** and **keygen**$_2^*$ is that we have replaced occurrences of $(\mathbf{U}, \mathbf{W}_i, \mathbf{V}_i)$ with those of $(\widetilde{\mathbf{U}}, \widetilde{\mathbf{W}}_i, \widetilde{\mathbf{V}}_i)$ and introduced additional terms involving $\mathbf{a}^\perp$ and the semi-adaptive challenge $\mathbf{x}^*, \mathbf{z}^*$.

The change from Game 1 to Game 2 follows from the following change of variables which embeds the semi-adaptive challenge into the $\mathbf{U}, \mathbf{W}_i, \mathbf{V}_i$:

$$\mathbf{U} \mapsto \mathbf{C}^\perp \widetilde{\mathbf{U}} + \mathbf{a}^\perp \hat{\mathbf{s}}^\top$$
$$\mathbf{W}_i \mapsto \widetilde{\mathbf{W}}_i - z_i^* \mathbf{a}^\perp \hat{\mathbf{s}}^\top$$
$$\mathbf{V}_i \mapsto \widetilde{\mathbf{V}}_i - x_i^* \mathbf{a}^\perp \hat{\mathbf{s}}^\top$$

which in particular implies that

$$\left( \mathbf{c}^\top (\mathbf{U} z_i^* + \mathbf{W}_i), \mathbf{c}^\top (\mathbf{U} x_i^* + \mathbf{V}_i), \mathbf{c}^\top \boldsymbol{\kappa} \right) = \left( \mathbf{c}^\top \widetilde{\mathbf{W}}_i, \mathbf{c}^\top \widetilde{\mathbf{V}}_i, \mathbf{c}^\top \boldsymbol{\kappa} \right),$$

where the LHS corresponds to **enc** and the RHS to **enc**\* and we use the fact that $(\mathbf{A} \mid \mathbf{c})^\top (\mathbf{C}^\perp \mid \mathbf{a}^\perp) = \mathbf{I}_{k+1}$.

For semi-adaptive security, we crucially rely on the fact that the terms $\left( \widetilde{\mathbf{U}}, \mathbf{A}^\top \widetilde{\mathbf{W}}_i, \mathbf{A}^\top \widetilde{\mathbf{V}}_i \right)$ in mpk in Game 2 only depends on $\widetilde{\mathbf{U}}, \widetilde{\mathbf{W}}_i, \widetilde{\mathbf{V}}_i$ (since $\mathbf{A}^\top \mathbf{a}^\perp = \mathbf{0}$), which allows us to embed the semi-adaptive challenge even though it may depend on mpk. Formally, to justify the change of variables, observe that for all $\mathbf{A}, \mathbf{C}^\perp, \mathbf{a}^\perp, \hat{\mathbf{s}}, \mathbf{x}^*, \mathbf{z}^*$, we have

$$\left( \mathbf{A}^\top \mathbf{U}, \mathbf{A}^\top \mathbf{W}_i, \mathbf{A}^\top \mathbf{V}_i, \mathbf{U}, \mathbf{W}_i, \mathbf{V}_i \right)$$
$$\equiv \left( \widetilde{\mathbf{U}}, \mathbf{A}^\top \widetilde{\mathbf{W}}_i, \mathbf{A}^\top \widetilde{\mathbf{V}}_i, \widetilde{\mathbf{U}} + \mathbf{a}^\perp \hat{\mathbf{s}}^\top, \widetilde{\mathbf{W}}_i - z_i^* \mathbf{a}^\perp \hat{\mathbf{s}}^\top, \widetilde{\mathbf{V}}_i - x_i^* \mathbf{a}^\perp \hat{\mathbf{s}}^\top \right)$$

where the distributions are taken over the random choices of $\mathbf{U}, \mathbf{W}_i, \mathbf{V}_i$, $\widetilde{\mathbf{U}}, \widetilde{\mathbf{W}}_i, \widetilde{\mathbf{V}}_i$. Then, by a complexity leveraging argument, we have that the distributions are identically distributed even if $(\mathbf{x}^*, \mathbf{z}^*)$ is adaptively chosen after seeing the first three terms in these distributions, as is the case for semi-adaptive security. Therefore, we have

$$\mathsf{Adv}_1 = \mathsf{Adv}_2$$

**Game 3.** We replace **keygen**$_2^*$ with **keygen**$_3^*$ where

**keygen**$_3^*$(msk, $f, \mathbf{x}^*$): pick $\mathbf{r}_0, \mathbf{r}_1, \ldots, \mathbf{r}_m \leftarrow_R \mathbb{Z}_q^k, \delta_0, \delta_1, \ldots, \delta_m \leftarrow_R \mathbb{Z}_q$, sample $\mathbf{T}$, and output

$$\mathsf{sk}_f := \Big( \big[ \mathbf{rE}_f \big( \kappa, \{ \widetilde{\mathbf{W}}_i \mathbf{r}_0 - z_i^* \mathbf{a}^{\perp} \boxed{\delta_0} \}_{i \in [n]}, \{ \mathbf{C}^{\perp} \widetilde{\mathbf{U}} \mathbf{r}_j - \mathbf{a}^{\perp} \boxed{\delta_j} \}_{j \in [m]},$$
$$\{ \widetilde{\mathbf{V}}_i \mathbf{r}_j - x_i^* \mathbf{a}^{\perp} \boxed{\delta_j} \}_{i \in [n'], j \in [m]}; \mathbf{T} \big) \big]_2, [\mathbf{r}_0]_2, \{ [\mathbf{r}_j]_2 \}_{j \in [m]} \Big)$$

where the grayed terms indicate the changes from **keygen**$_2^*$. This follows from the MDDH Assumption (cf. Sect. 3.1), which tells us that

$$\big( [ \boxed{\hat{\mathbf{s}}^{\top} \mathbf{r}_0} ]_2, [\mathbf{r}_0]_2, \{ [ \boxed{\hat{\mathbf{s}}^{\top} \mathbf{r}_j} ]_2, [\mathbf{r}_j]_2 \}_{j \in [m]} \big) \approx_c \big( [ \boxed{\delta_0} ]_2, [\mathbf{r}_0]_2, \{ [ \boxed{\delta_j} ]_2, [\mathbf{r}_j]_2 \}_{j \in [m]} \big)$$

In fact, this tightly reduces to the MDDH Assumption [19] (think of the concatenation of $\mathbf{r}_0, \mathbf{r}_1, \ldots, \mathbf{r}_m$ as a uniformly random matrix in $\mathbb{Z}_q^{k \times (m+1)}$, corresponding to the matrix $\mathbf{A}^{\top}$ in the original MDDH formulation).

Therefore, we have

$$|\mathsf{Adv}_2 - \mathsf{Adv}_3| \leq \mathsf{Adv}_{\mathbb{G}_2, \mathcal{A}_2}^{\text{MDDH}}(\lambda)$$

**Game 4.** We replace **keygen**$_3^*$ with **keygen**. By linearity of $\mathbf{rE}_f$, we can write the output of **keygen**$_3^*$ as

$$\mathsf{sk}_f := \Big( \big[ \mathbf{rE}_f \big( \mathbf{0}, \{ \widetilde{\mathbf{W}}_i \mathbf{r}_0 \}_{i \in [n]}, \{ \mathbf{C}^{\perp} \widetilde{\mathbf{U}} \mathbf{r}_j \}_{j \in [m]}, \{ \widetilde{\mathbf{V}}_i \mathbf{r}_j \}_{i \in [n'], j \in [m]}; \mathbf{0} \big) \big]_2$$
$$+ \mathbf{rE}_f \big( \kappa, \{ -z_i^* \mathbf{a}^{\perp} \delta_0 \}_{i \in [n]}, \{ -\mathbf{a}^{\perp} \delta_j \}_{j \in [m]}, \{ -x_i^* \mathbf{a}^{\perp} \delta_j \}_{i \in [n'], j \in [m]}; \mathbf{T} \big) \big]_2,$$
$$[\mathbf{r}_0]_2, \{ [\mathbf{r}_j]_2 \}_{j \in [m]} \Big)$$

Write $\mathbf{T} = \mathbf{C}\widetilde{\mathbf{T}} + \mathbf{a}^{\perp} \mathbf{t}$ where $\widetilde{\mathbf{T}}, \mathbf{t}$ are uniformly random and independent. Then, again by linearity, we have

$$\mathbf{A}^{\top} \cdot \mathbf{rE}_f \big( \kappa, \{ -z_i^* \mathbf{a}^{\perp} \delta_0 \}_{i \in [n]}, \{ -\mathbf{a}^{\perp} \delta_j \}_{j \in [m]}, \{ -x_i^* \mathbf{a}^{\perp} \delta_j \}_{i \in [n'], j \in [m]}; \mathbf{T} \big)$$
$$= \mathbf{rE}_f \big( \mathbf{A}^{\top} \kappa, 0, 0, 0; \widetilde{\mathbf{T}} \big)$$
$$\mathbf{c}^{\top} \cdot \mathbf{rE}_f \big( \kappa, \{ -z_i^* \mathbf{a}^{\perp} \delta_0 \}_{i \in [n]}, \{ -\mathbf{a}^{\perp} \delta_j \}_{j \in [m]}, \{ -x_i^* \mathbf{a}^{\perp} \delta_j \}_{i \in [n'], j \in [m]}; \mathbf{T} \big)$$
$$= \mathbf{rE}_f \big( \mathbf{c}^{\top} \kappa, \{ -z_i^* \delta_0 \}_{i \in [n]}, \{ -\delta_j \}_{j \in [m]}, \{ -x_i^* \delta_j \}_{i \in [n'], j \in [m]}; \mathbf{t} \big)$$
$$\equiv \mathbf{sim}(f, \mathbf{x}^*, \mathbf{c}^{\top} \kappa + f(\mathbf{x}^*, \delta_0 \mathbf{z}^*))$$
$$\equiv \mathbf{sim}(f, \mathbf{x}^*, \mathbf{c}^{\top} \kappa + \delta_0 f(\mathbf{x}^*, \mathbf{z}^*))$$

And therefore,

$$\mathbf{rE}_f\left(\,\kappa, \left\{\, -z_i^* \mathbf{a}^\perp \delta_0 \,\right\}_{i\in[n]}, \left\{\, -\mathbf{a}^\perp \delta_j \,\right\}_{j\in[m]}, \left\{\, -x_i^* \mathbf{a}^\perp \delta_j \,\right\}_{i\in[n'], j\in[m]}; \mathbf{T}\,\right)$$
$$\equiv \mathbf{C}^\perp \cdot \mathbf{rE}_f\left(\,\mathbf{A}^\top \kappa, 0, 0, 0; \tilde{\mathbf{T}}\,\right) + \mathbf{a}^\perp \cdot \mathbf{sim}(f, \mathbf{x}^*, \mathbf{c}^\top \kappa + \delta_0 f(\mathbf{x}^*, \mathbf{z}^*))$$

where the latter is exactly as computed in **keygen**\*. This means

$$\mathsf{Adv}_3 = \mathsf{Adv}_4$$

**Acknowledgments.** I would like to thank the anonymous reviewers for helpful feedback.

# A    Instantiating $\mathbf{rE}_f$ for $\mathcal{F}_{\mathsf{ABPoIP}}$

In this section, we present our encoding algorithm $\mathbf{rE}_f$.

## A.1    Partial Garbling for $\mathcal{F}_{\mathsf{ABPoIP}}$

Our encoding algorithm $\mathbf{rE}_f$ uses as a building block the "partial garbling scheme" for $\mathcal{F}_{\mathsf{ABPoIP}}$ from [24,25]. Informally, a partial garbling scheme for each $f \in \mathcal{F}_{\mathsf{ABPoIP}}$ takes as input as a secret $\kappa$ along with $(\mathbf{x}, \mathbf{z})$ and randomness $\mathbf{t}$ and outputs a collection of $m + n + 1$ shares

$$\left(\,\kappa + \tau, \left\{\, z_i + \sigma_i \,\right\}_{i\in[n]}, \left\{\, \beta_j x_{\rho(j)} + \gamma_j \,\right\}_{j\in[m]}\,\right), \text{where } \rho : [m] \to [n']$$

Here, $m, \rho$ depends only on $f$, and $\tau, \sigma_i, \beta_j, \gamma_j$ depend on both $f$ and $\mathbf{t}$. Given the shares along with $f, \mathbf{x}$, we should be able to recover $\kappa + f(\mathbf{x}, \mathbf{z})$ but learn nothing else about $\kappa, \mathbf{z}$.

**Syntax and Properties of pgb.** We will rely on a randomized algorithm **pgb** that takes as input $f \in \mathcal{F}_{\mathsf{ABPoIP}}$ and randomness $\mathbf{t} \in \mathbb{Z}_q^{m+n}$ and outputs

$$\mathbf{pgb}(f; \mathbf{t}) = \left(\,\tau, \left\{\, \sigma_i \,\right\}_{i\in[n]}, \left\{\, \beta_j, \gamma_j \,\right\}_{j\in[m]}\,\right) \in \mathbb{Z}_q^{1+n+m}.$$

Together with $\mathbf{x}, \mathbf{z}, \kappa$, this specifies a collection of $m + n + 1$ "shares"

$$\left(\,\kappa + \tau, \left\{\, z_i + \sigma_i \,\right\}_{i\in[n]}, \left\{\, \beta_j x_{\rho(j)} + \gamma_j \,\right\}_{j\in[m]}\,\right), \text{where } \rho : [m] \to [n'] \quad (1)$$

Here, $m$ is the ABP size of $f$ and $\rho$ is deterministically derived from $f$. The algorithm satisfies the following properties:

- **linearity**: for a fixed $f$, $\mathbf{pgb}(f; \cdot)$ computes a linear function of its randomness over $\mathbb{Z}_q$.
- **reconstruction**: there exists an efficient algorithm **rec** that on input $f, x$ and the shares in (1), outputs $\kappa + f(\mathbf{x}, \mathbf{z})$. This holds for all $f, \mathbf{x}, \mathbf{z}, \kappa$. Moreover, $\mathbf{rec}(f, \mathbf{x}, \cdot)$ computes a linear function of the shares.
- **privacy**: there exists an efficient simulator **sim** such that for all $f, \mathbf{x}, \mathbf{z}, \kappa$, the output of $\mathbf{sim}(f, \mathbf{x}, \kappa + f(\mathbf{x}, \mathbf{z}))$ is identically distributed to the shares in (1) (for a random $\mathbf{t}$).

**The Algorithm.** For completeness, we sketch the algorithm **pgb** from [25]; we omit the analysis for reconstruction and privacy which follows from [25, Theorem 3, Corollary 1] with $t = 1$.

1. Let $f'$ denote the ABP computing $(\mathbf{x}, \mathbf{z}, \kappa) \mapsto \kappa + f(\mathbf{x}, \mathbf{z})$ as shown in Fig. 3, such that $\kappa, \mathbf{z}$ only appear on edges leading into the sink node.

2. Compute the matrix representation $\mathbf{L}_{\mathbf{x},\mathbf{z},\kappa} \in \mathbb{Z}_q^{(m+n+1) \times (m+n+1)}$ of $f'$ using the algorithm in [25, Lemma 1], where $\mathbf{L}_{\mathbf{x},\mathbf{z},\kappa}$ satisfies the following properties as shown in Fig. 3:
   - $\det(\mathbf{L}_{\mathbf{x},\mathbf{z},\kappa}) = \kappa + f(\mathbf{x}, \mathbf{z})$.

   - for $j = 1, \ldots, m$, each entry in its $j$'th row is an affine function in $x_{\rho(j)}$, where $\rho : [n'] \to [m]$.[3]

   - $\mathbf{L}_{\mathbf{x},\mathbf{z},\kappa}$ contains only 1's in the second diagonal (the diagonal below the main diagonal) and 0's below the second diagonal.

   - the last column of $\mathbf{L}_{\mathbf{x},\mathbf{z},\kappa}$ is $(0, \ldots, 0, z_1, \ldots, z_n, \kappa)^\top$.

   Specifically, $\mathbf{L}_{\mathbf{x},\mathbf{z},\kappa}$ is obtained by removing the first column and the last row in the matrix $\mathbf{A}_{f'} - \mathbf{I}$, where $\mathbf{A}_{f'}$ is the adjacency matrix for the ABP computing $f'$.

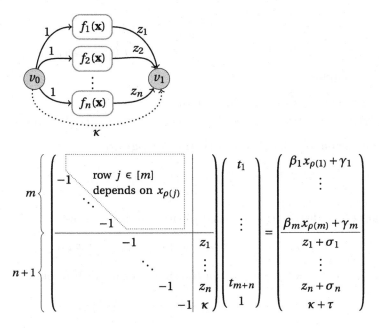

**Fig. 3.** The figure at the top shows an ABP computing $f_1(\mathbf{x})z_1 + \cdots + f_n(\mathbf{x})z_n + \kappa$. The figure at the bottom shows the corresponding partial garbling scheme.

---

[3] To achieve this, we need to also pre-process $f'$ by first replacing every edge $e$ for the public variable $\mathbf{x}$ with a pair of edges labeled 1 and $\phi(e)$.

3. Write $\mathbf{L}_{\mathbf{x},\mathbf{z},\kappa}\binom{t}{1}$ as

$$\left( \beta_1 x_{\rho(1)} + \gamma_1, \ldots, \beta_m x_{\rho(1)} + \gamma_m, z_1 + \sigma_1, \ldots, z_n + \sigma_n, \kappa + \tau \right)^{\top}$$

4. Output $\left( \tau, \left\{ \sigma_i \right\}_{i \in [n]}, \left\{ \beta_j \right\}_{j \in [m]}, \gamma_j \right)$.

It is straight-forward to verify that each of $\tau, \left\{ \sigma_i \right\}_{i \in [n]}, \left\{ \beta_j \right\}_{j \in [m]}, \gamma_j$ are indeed linear functions in $\mathbf{t}$.

**The Algorithm.** The algorithm $\mathbf{rE}_f$ proceeds as follows:

1. run $\mathbf{pgb}(f; \mathbf{t})$ to sample $\left( \tau, \left\{ \sigma_i \right\}_{i \in [n]}, \left\{ \beta_j, \gamma_j \right\}_{j \in [m]} \right)$
2. output

$$\left( \kappa + \tau, \left\{ \sigma_i - w'_i \right\}_{i \in [n]}, \left\{ \beta_j + u'_j, \gamma_j + v'_{\rho(j)j} \right\}_{j \in [m]} \right) \in \mathbb{Z}_q^{1+n+m}$$

We proceed to verify that $\mathbf{rE}_f$ satisfies the above properties:

- **linearity:** Linearity follows from that for $\mathbf{pgb}$.
- **reconstruction:** We are given

$$\begin{aligned}
&f, \mathbf{x}, \kappa + \tau, \\
&\left\{ \sigma_i - w'_i, z_i + w'_i \right\}_{i \in [n]}, \\
&\left\{ \beta_j + u'_j, \gamma_j + v'_{\rho(j)j}, u'_j x_i + v'_{ij} \right\}_{i \in [n'], j \in [m]}
\end{aligned}$$

We can compute

$$\begin{aligned}
z_i + \sigma_i &= (\sigma_i - w'_i) + (z_i + w'_i), & i \in [n] \\
\beta_j x_{\rho(j)} + \gamma_j &= (\beta_j + u'_j) x_{\rho(j)} + (\gamma_j + v'_{\rho(j)j}) - (u'_j x_{\rho(j)} + v'_{\rho(j)j}) & j \in [m]
\end{aligned}$$

We can then apply linear reconstruction for $\mathbf{pgb}$ to

$$\kappa + \tau, \left\{ z_i + \sigma_i \right\}_{i \in [n]}, \left\{ \beta_j x_{\rho(j)} + \gamma_j \right\}_{j \in [m]}$$

to recover $\kappa + f(\mathbf{x}, \mathbf{z})$.

- **privacy:** The distribution we need to simulate is given by

$$\kappa + \tau, \left\{ z_i + \sigma_i \right\}_{i \in [n]}, \left\{ \beta_j + \delta_j \right\}_{j \in [m]}, \left\{ \gamma_j - \delta_j x_{\rho(j)} \right\}_{j \in [m]}.$$

Given $f, \mathbf{x}, \kappa + f(\mathbf{x}, \mathbf{z})$, we can run the simulator for $\mathbf{pgb}$ to obtain

$$\kappa + \tau, \left\{ z_i + \sigma_i \right\}_{i \in [n]}, \left\{ \beta_j x_{\rho(j)} + \gamma_j \right\}_{j \in [m]}.$$

For each $j \in [m]$, we can simulate $\left( \beta_j + \delta_j, \gamma_j - \delta_j x_{\rho(j)} \right)$ given $x_{\rho(j)}, \beta_j x_{\rho(j)} + \gamma_j$ as follows:

- pick $\tilde{\delta}_j \leftarrow_{\mathrm{R}} \mathbb{Z}_q$;
- output $\left( \tilde{\delta}_j, (\beta_j x_{\rho(j)} + \gamma_j) - \tilde{\delta}_j x_{\rho(j)} \right)$.

# B    Our Inner Product Functional Encryption Scheme

In this section, we present our inner product functional encryption scheme. The ciphertext is associated with a vector $\mathbf{z} \in \mathbb{Z}_q^n$, and the secret key with a vector $\mathbf{y} \in \mathbb{Z}_q^n$, and decryption recovers $\langle \mathbf{z}, \mathbf{y} \rangle$, provided the value falls in a polynomially bounded domain. Our scheme achieves simulation-based security as defined in Sect. 3.2, where the simulator $\mathbf{keygen}^*$ gets $\mathbf{y}, \langle \mathbf{z}^*, \mathbf{y} \rangle$ whenever the adversary makes a query $\mathbf{y}$ to $\mathbf{keygen}$.

## B.1    Our Scheme

$\mathbf{setup}(1^\lambda, 1^n)$: pick $\mathbf{A} \leftarrow \mathcal{D}_k$, $\mathbf{W} \leftarrow_R \mathbb{Z}_q^{(k+1) \times n}$ and output

$$\mathsf{mpk} := \Big( [\mathbf{A}]_1, [\mathbf{A}^\top \mathbf{W}]_1 \Big),$$

$$\mathsf{msk} := \mathbf{W}$$

$\mathbf{enc}(\mathsf{mpk}, \mathbf{z})$: pick $\mathbf{s} \leftarrow_R \mathbb{Z}_q^k$ and output

$$\mathsf{ct} := \Big( \overbrace{[\mathbf{s}^\top \mathbf{A}^\top]_1}^{C_0}, \overbrace{[\mathbf{s}^\top \mathbf{A}^\top \mathbf{W} + \mathbf{z}^\top]_1}^{C_1} \Big)$$

$\mathbf{keygen}(\mathsf{msk}, \mathbf{y})$:

$$\mathsf{sk}_\mathbf{y} := \mathbf{W} \mathbf{y}$$

$\mathbf{dec}((\mathsf{sk}_\mathbf{y}, \mathbf{y}), ([C_0]_1, [C_1]_1))$: output the discrete log of

$$[C_1 \cdot \mathbf{y}]_1 \cdot [C_0 \cdot \mathsf{sk}_\mathbf{y}]_1^{-1}$$

## B.2    Analysis

**Theorem 2.** *Our Inner Product FE scheme described in Appendix B.1 achieves simulation-based semi-adaptively (strongly) attribute-hiding under the MDDH assumption in $\mathbb{G}_1$ with an efficient simulator.*

**Correctness.** Follows readily from

$$(\mathbf{s}^\top \mathbf{A} \mathbf{W} + \mathbf{z}^\top) \cdot \mathbf{y} - \mathbf{s}^\top \mathbf{A} \mathbf{W} \cdot \mathbf{y} = \langle \mathbf{z}, \mathbf{y} \rangle$$

## B.3    Simulator

$\mathbf{setup}^*(1^\lambda, 1^{n'+n})$ : pick $\mathbf{A} \leftarrow \mathcal{D}_k$, $\widetilde{\mathbf{W}} \leftarrow_R \mathbb{Z}_q^{(k+1) \times n}$, $\mathbf{c} \leftarrow_R \mathbb{Z}_q^{k+1}$ and output

$$\mathsf{mpk} := \Big( [\mathbf{A}]_1, [\mathbf{A}^\top \widetilde{\mathbf{W}}]_1 \Big),$$

$$\mathsf{msk}^* := (\mathbf{A}, \widetilde{\mathbf{W}}, \mathbf{c}, \mathbf{a}^\perp)$$

where $\mathbf{a}^\perp \in \mathbb{Z}_q^{k+1}$ satisfies $\mathbf{A}^\top \mathbf{a}^\perp = \mathbf{0}$, $\mathbf{c}^\top \mathbf{a}^\perp = 1$.

**enc**\*(msk\*) : output

$$\text{ct} := \big( [\mathbf{c}^\top]_1, [\mathbf{c}^\top \widetilde{\mathbf{W}}]_1 \big)$$

**keygen**\*(msk\*, $\mathbf{y}$, $a = \langle \mathbf{z}^*, \mathbf{y} \rangle$) : output

$$\text{sk}_{\mathbf{y}} := \widetilde{\mathbf{W}} \mathbf{y} - a \cdot \mathbf{a}^\perp$$

## B.4   Security Proof

We proceed via a series of games.

**Game 0.** Real game.

**Game 1.** We replace $[\mathbf{As}]_1$ in **enc**(mpk, $\mathbf{z}^*$) with $[\mathbf{c}]_1$ where $\mathbf{c} \leftarrow_R \mathbb{Z}_q^{k+1}$. That is, the challenge ciphertext is now given by

$$\text{ct} := \big( [\mathbf{c}^\top]_1, [\mathbf{c}^\top \mathbf{W} + (\mathbf{z}^*)^\top]_1 \big)$$

This follows readily from the MDDH Assumption (cf. Sect. 3.1), so we have

$$|\mathsf{Adv}_0 - \mathsf{Adv}_1| \le \mathsf{Adv}_{\mathbb{G}_1, \mathcal{A}_1}^{\text{MDDH}}(\lambda)$$

**Game 2.** We switch to the simulated game. The change from Game 1 to Game 2 follows from the following change of variables which embeds the semi-adaptive challenge $\mathbf{z}^*$ into the $\mathbf{W}$:

$$\widetilde{\mathbf{W}} = \mathbf{W} + \mathbf{a}^\perp (\mathbf{z}^*)^\top$$

which in particular implies that

$$\mathbf{A}^\top \mathbf{W} = \mathbf{A}^\top \widetilde{\mathbf{W}}$$
$$\mathbf{c}^\top \mathbf{W} + (\mathbf{z}^*)^\top = \mathbf{c}^\top \widetilde{\mathbf{W}}$$
$$\mathbf{W} \mathbf{y} = \widetilde{\mathbf{W}} \mathbf{y} - \mathbf{a}^\perp \cdot \langle \mathbf{z}^*, \mathbf{y} \rangle$$

Formally, to justify the change of variables, observe that for all $\mathbf{A}, \mathbf{z}^*$, we have

$$\Big( \mathbf{A}^\top \mathbf{W}, \mathbf{W} + \mathbf{a}^\perp (\mathbf{z}^*)^\top \Big)$$
$$\equiv \Big( \mathbf{A}^\top \widetilde{\mathbf{W}}, \widetilde{\mathbf{W}} \Big)$$

where the distributions are taken over the random choices of $\mathbf{W}, \widetilde{\mathbf{W}}$. Then, by a complexity leveraging argument, we have that the distributions are identically distributed even if $\mathbf{z}^*$ is adaptively chosen after seeing the first term in these distributions, as is the case for semi-adaptive security. Therefore, we have

$$\mathsf{Adv}_1 = \mathsf{Adv}_2$$

# References

1. Abdalla, M., Bourse, F., De Caro, A., Pointcheval, D.: Simple functional encryption schemes for inner products. In: Katz, J. (ed.) PKC 2015. LNCS, vol. 9020, pp. 733–751. Springer, Heidelberg (2015). doi:10.1007/978-3-662-46447-2_33
2. Abdalla, M., Gay, R., Raykova, M., Wee, H.: Multi-input inner-product functional encryption from pairings. In: Coron, J.-S., Nielsen, J.B. (eds.) EUROCRYPT 2017. LNCS, vol. 10210, pp. 601–626. Springer, Cham (2017). doi:10.1007/978-3-319-56620-7_21
3. Agrawal, S., Chase, M.: A study of pair encodings: predicate encryption in prime order groups. In: Kushilevitz, E., Malkin, T. (eds.) TCC 2016. LNCS, vol. 9563, pp. 259–288. Springer, Heidelberg (2016). doi:10.1007/978-3-662-49099-0_10
4. Agrawal, S., Gorbunov, S., Vaikuntanathan, V., Wee, H.: Functional encryption: new perspectives and lower bounds. In: Canetti, R., Garay, J.A. (eds.) CRYPTO 2013. LNCS, vol. 8043, pp. 500–518. Springer, Heidelberg (2013). doi:10.1007/978-3-642-40084-1_28. Also, Cryptology ePrint Archive, Report 2012/468
5. Agrawal, S., Libert, B., Stehlé, D.: Fully secure functional encryption for inner products, from standard assumptions. In: Robshaw, M., Katz, J. (eds.) CRYPTO 2016. LNCS, vol. 9816, pp. 333–362. Springer, Heidelberg (2016). doi:10.1007/978-3-662-53015-3_12
6. Ananth, P., Jain, A.: Indistinguishability obfuscation from compact functional encryption. In: Gennaro, R., Robshaw, M. (eds.) CRYPTO 2015. LNCS, vol. 9215, pp. 308–326. Springer, Heidelberg (2015). doi:10.1007/978-3-662-47989-6_15
7. Ananth, P., Brakerski, Z., Segev, G., Vaikuntanathan, V.: From selective to adaptive security in functional encryption. In: Gennaro, R., Robshaw, M. (eds.) CRYPTO 2015. LNCS, vol. 9216, pp. 657–677. Springer, Heidelberg (2015). doi:10.1007/978-3-662-48000-7_32
8. Attrapadung, N.: Dual system encryption via doubly selective security: framework, fully secure functional encryption for regular languages, and more. In: Nguyen, P.Q., Oswald, E. (eds.) EUROCRYPT 2014. LNCS, vol. 8441, pp. 557–577. Springer, Heidelberg (2014). doi:10.1007/978-3-642-55220-5_31
9. Baltico, C.E.Z., Catalano, D., Fiore, D., Gay, R.: Practical functional encryption for quadratic functions with applications to predicate encryption. Cryptology ePrint Archive, Report 2017/151 (2017)
10. Bitansky, N., Vaikuntanathan, V.: Indistinguishability obfuscation from functional encryption. In: FOCS (2015)
11. Blazy, O., Kiltz, E., Pan, J.: (Hierarchical) identity-based encryption from affine message authentication. In: Garay, J.A., Gennaro, R. (eds.) CRYPTO 2014. LNCS, vol. 8616, pp. 408–425. Springer, Heidelberg (2014). doi:10.1007/978-3-662-44371-2_23
12. Boneh, D., Waters, B.: Conjunctive, subset, and range queries on encrypted data. In: Vadhan, S.P. (ed.) TCC 2007. LNCS, vol. 4392, pp. 535–554. Springer, Heidelberg (2007). doi:10.1007/978-3-540-70936-7_29
13. Boneh, D., Sahai, A., Waters, B.: Functional encryption: definitions and challenges. In: Ishai, Y. (ed.) TCC 2011. LNCS, vol. 6597, pp. 253–273. Springer, Heidelberg (2011). doi:10.1007/978-3-642-19571-6_16
14. Boneh, D., Gentry, C., Gorbunov, S., Halevi, S., Nikolaenko, V., Segev, G., Vaikuntanathan, V., Vinayagamurthy, D.: Fully key-homomorphic encryption, arithmetic circuit ABE and compact garbled circuits. In: Nguyen, P.Q., Oswald, E. (eds.) EUROCRYPT 2014. LNCS, vol. 8441, pp. 533–556. Springer, Heidelberg (2014). doi:10.1007/978-3-642-55220-5_30

15. De Caro, A., Iovino, V., Jain, A., O'Neill, A., Paneth, O., Persiano, G.: On the achievability of simulation-based security for functional encryption. In: Canetti, R., Garay, J.A. (eds.) CRYPTO 2013. LNCS, vol. 8043, pp. 519–535. Springer, Heidelberg (2013). doi:10.1007/978-3-642-40084-1_29

16. Chen, J., Wee, H.: Fully, (almost) tightly secure IBE and dual system groups. In: Canetti, R., Garay, J.A. (eds.) CRYPTO 2013. LNCS, vol. 8043, pp. 435–460. Springer, Heidelberg (2013). doi:10.1007/978-3-642-40084-1_25

17. Chen, J., Wee, H.: Semi-adaptive attribute-based encryption and improved delegation for boolean formula. In: Abdalla, M., De Prisco, R. (eds.) SCN 2014. LNCS, vol. 8642, pp. 277–297. Springer, Cham (2014). doi:10.1007/978-3-319-10879-7_16

18. Chen, J., Gay, R., Wee, H.: Improved dual system ABE in prime-order groups via predicate encodings. In: Oswald, E., Fischlin, M. (eds.) EUROCRYPT 2015. LNCS, vol. 9057, pp. 595–624. Springer, Heidelberg (2015). doi:10.1007/978-3-662-46803-6_20

19. Escala, A., Herold, G., Kiltz, E., Ràfols, C., Villar, J.: An algebraic framework for diffie-hellman assumptions. In: Canetti, R., Garay, J.A. (eds.) CRYPTO 2013. LNCS, vol. 8043, pp. 129–147. Springer, Heidelberg (2013). doi:10.1007/978-3-642-40084-1_8

20. Garg, S., Gentry, C., Halevi, S., Raykova, M., Sahai, A., Waters, B.: Candidate indistinguishability obfuscation and functional encryption for all circuits. In: FOCS, pp. 40–49. Also, Cryptology ePrint Archive, Report 2013/451 (2013)

21. Gorbunov, S., Vaikuntanathan, V., Wee, H.: Attribute-based encryption for circuits. In: STOC, pp. 545–554. Also, Cryptology ePrint Archive, Report 2013/337 (2013)

22. Gorbunov, S., Vaikuntanathan, V., Wee, H.: Predicate encryption for circuits from LWE. In: Gennaro, R., Robshaw, M. (eds.) CRYPTO 2015. LNCS, vol. 9216, pp. 503–523. Springer, Heidelberg (2015). doi:10.1007/978-3-662-48000-7_25

23. Goyal, V., Pandey, O., Sahai, A., Waters, B.: Attribute-based encryption for fine-grained access control of encrypted data. In: ACM Conference on Computer and Communications Security, pp. 89–98 (2006)

24. Ishai, Y., Kushilevitz, E.: Perfect constant-round secure computation via perfect randomizing polynomials. In: Widmayer, P., Eidenbenz, S., Triguero, F., Morales, R., Conejo, R., Hennessy, M. (eds.) ICALP 2002. LNCS, vol. 2380, pp. 244–256. Springer, Heidelberg (2002). doi:10.1007/3-540-45465-9_22

25. Ishai, Y., Wee, H.: Partial garbling schemes and their applications. In: Esparza, J., Fraigniaud, P., Husfeldt, T., Koutsoupias, E. (eds.) ICALP 2014. LNCS, vol. 8572, pp. 650–662. Springer, Heidelberg (2014). doi:10.1007/978-3-662-43948-7_54. Also, Cryptology ePrint Archive, Report 2014/995

26. Katz, J., Sahai, A., Waters, B.: Predicate encryption supporting disjunctions, polynomial equations, and inner products. In: Smart, N. (ed.) EUROCRYPT 2008. LNCS, vol. 4965, pp. 146–162. Springer, Heidelberg (2008). doi:10.1007/978-3-540-78967-3_9

27. Kiltz, E., Wee, H.: Quasi-adaptive NIZK for linear subspaces revisited. In: Oswald, E., Fischlin, M. (eds.) EUROCRYPT 2015. LNCS, vol. 9057, pp. 101–128. Springer, Heidelberg (2015). doi:10.1007/978-3-662-46803-6_4

28. Lewko, A.B., Waters, B.: New techniques for dual system encryption and fully secure HIBE with short ciphertexts. In: Micciancio, D. (ed.) TCC 2010. LNCS, vol. 5978, pp. 455–479. Springer, Heidelberg (2010). doi:10.1007/978-3-642-11799-2_27

29. Okamoto, T., Takashima, K.: Fully secure functional encryption with general relations from the decisional linear assumption. In: Rabin, T. (ed.) CRYPTO 2010. LNCS, vol. 6223, pp. 191–208. Springer, Heidelberg (2010). doi:10.1007/978-3-642-14623-7_11

30. Okamoto, T., Takashima, K.: Achieving short ciphertexts or short secret-keys for adaptively secure general inner-product encryption. In: Lin, D., Tsudik, G., Wang, X. (eds.) CANS 2011. LNCS, vol. 7092, pp. 138–159. Springer, Heidelberg (2011). doi:10.1007/978-3-642-25513-7_11

31. Okamoto, T., Takashima, K.: Adaptively attribute-hiding (hierarchical) inner product encryption. In: Pointcheval, D., Johansson, T. (eds.) EUROCRYPT 2012. LNCS, vol. 7237, pp. 591–608. Springer, Heidelberg (2012). doi:10.1007/978-3-642-29011-4_35

32. Okamoto, T., Takashima, K.: Efficient (hierarchical) inner-product encryption tightly reduced from the decisional linear assumption. IEICE Trans. **96–A**(1), 42–52 (2013)

33. O'Neill, A.: Definitional issues in functional encryption. Cryptology ePrint Archive, Report 2010/556 (2010)

34. Sahai, A., Waters, B.: Fuzzy identity-based encryption. In: Cramer, R. (ed.) EUROCRYPT 2005. LNCS, vol. 3494, pp. 457–473. Springer, Heidelberg (2005). doi:10.1007/11426639_27

35. Waters, B.: Dual system encryption: realizing fully secure IBE and HIBE under simple assumptions. In: Halevi, S. (ed.) CRYPTO 2009. LNCS, vol. 5677, pp. 619–636. Springer, Heidelberg (2009). doi:10.1007/978-3-642-03356-8_36

36. Wee, H.: Dual system encryption via predicate encodings. In: Lindell, Y. (ed.) TCC 2014. LNCS, vol. 8349, pp. 616–637. Springer, Heidelberg (2014). doi:10.1007/978-3-642-54242-8_26

# Constrained PRFs

# Constrained Keys for Invertible Pseudorandom Functions

Dan Boneh, Sam Kim[(⊠)], and David J. Wu

Stanford University, Stanford, USA
skim13@cs.stanford.edu

**Abstract.** A constrained pseudorandom function (PRF) is a secure PRF for which one can generate constrained keys that can only be used to evaluate the PRF on a subset of the domain. Constrained PRFs are used widely, most notably in applications of indistinguishability obfuscation ($i\mathcal{O}$). In this paper we show how to constrain an *invertible* PRF (IPF), which is significantly harder. An IPF is a secure *injective* PRF accompanied by an inversion algorithm. A constrained key for an IPF can only be used to evaluate the IPF on a subset $S$ of the domain, and to invert the IPF on the image of $S$. We first define the notion of a constrained IPF and then give two main constructions: one for puncturing an IPF and the other for (single-key) circuit constraints. Both constructions rely on recent work on *private* constrained PRFs. We also show that constrained pseudorandom permutations for many classes of constraints are impossible under our definition.

## 1 Introduction

Pseudorandom functions (PRFs) [34] and pseudorandom permutations (PRPs) [41] have found numerous applications in cryptography, such as encryption, data integrity, user authentication, key derivation, and others. Invertible PRFs are a natural extension that borrows features from both concepts. An invertible PRF (IPF) is an efficiently-computable *injective* function $\mathsf{F} : \mathcal{K} \times \mathcal{X} \to \mathcal{Y}$ equipped with an efficient inversion algorithm $\mathsf{F}^{-1} : \mathcal{K} \times \mathcal{Y} \to \mathcal{X} \cup \{\bot\}$. The inversion algorithm is required to satisfy the following two properties for all $k \in \mathcal{K}$:

- (1) $\mathsf{F}^{-1}\big(k, \, \mathsf{F}(k, x)\big) = x$ for all $x \in \mathcal{X}$.
- (2) $\mathsf{F}^{-1}(k, y) = \bot$ whenever $y$ is not in the image of $f(x) := \mathsf{F}(k, x)$.

We say that an IPF $\mathsf{F}$ is secure if no poly-bounded adversary can distinguish the following two experiments. In one experiment the adversary is given oracles for the function $f(x) := \mathsf{F}(k, x)$ and its inverse $f^{-1}(x) := \mathsf{F}^{-1}(k, x)$, where $k$ is randomly chosen in $\mathcal{K}$. In the other experiment, the adversary is given oracles for a *random* injective function $g : \mathcal{X} \to \mathcal{Y}$ and its inverse $g^{-1} : \mathcal{Y} \to \mathcal{X} \cup \{\bot\}$. These two experiments should be indistinguishable. We define this in detail in

---

The full version of this paper is available at https://eprint.iacr.org/2017/477.pdf.

© International Association for Cryptologic Research 2017
Y. Kalai and L. Reyzin (Eds.): TCC 2017, Part I, LNCS 10677, pp. 237–263, 2017.
https://doi.org/10.1007/978-3-319-70500-2_9

Sect. 3. Note that when $\mathcal{X} = \mathcal{Y}$, an IPF is the same as a strong pseudorandom permutation [41].

IPFs come up naturally in the context of deterministic authenticated encryption (DAE) [50], as discussed below. A closely related concept called a *pseudorandom injection* (PRI) [50] is similar to an IPF except for some syntactic differences (an IPF is a pseudorandom injection without additional length constraints and with an empty header).

*Constrained PRFs.* In this paper we define and construct constrained IPFs. It is helpful to first review constrained PRFs [19,21,40]. Recall that a PRF $\mathsf{F} : \mathcal{K} \times \mathcal{X} \to \mathcal{Y}$ is said to be a constrained PRF if one can derive constrained keys from the master PRF key $k$. A constrained key $k_g$ is associated with a predicate $g \colon \mathcal{X} \to \{0,1\}$, and this $k_g$ enables one to evaluate $F(k,x)$ for all $x \in \mathcal{X}$ where $g(x) = 1$, but at no other points of $\mathcal{X}$. A constrained PRF is secure if given constrained keys for predicates $g_1, \ldots, g_Q$ of the adversary's choosing, the adversary cannot distinguish the PRF from a random function at points not covered by the given keys, namely at points $x$ where $g_1(x) = \cdots = g_Q(x) = 0$. We review the precise definition in Sect. 3.1.

Constrained PRFs have found numerous applications in cryptography [19,21,40]: they imply identity-based key exchange and broadcast encryption, and are a crucial ingredient in many applications of indistinguishability obfuscation ($i\mathcal{O}$) [51].

The simplest non-trivial constraint is a *puncturing* constraint, a constraint that enables one to evaluate the function on its entire domain except for one point. For $x \in \mathcal{X}$ we denote by $k_x$ a *punctured key* that lets one evaluate the PRF at all points in $\mathcal{X}$, except for the punctured point $x$. Given the key $k_x$, the adversary should be unable to distinguish $F(k,x)$ from a random element in $\mathcal{Y}$. PRFs supporting puncturing constraints can be easily constructed from the tree-based PRF of [34], as discussed in [19,21,40].

*Constrained IPFs.* Given the wide applicability of constrained PRFs, it is natural to look at constraining other symmetric primitives such as PRPs and, more generally, IPFs. A constrained key $k_g$ for an IPF enables one to evaluate the IPF at all points $x \in \mathcal{X}$ for which $g(x) = 1$, and invert at all points $y = \mathsf{F}(k,x') \in \mathcal{Y}$ for which $g(x') = 1$. Security for a constrained IPF is defined as for a PRF: the adversary is given a number of constrained keys and tries to distinguish the IPF from a random injective function at points not covered by any of the given keys. See Sect. 3.1 for more details.

We first show in Sect. 3.3 that constrained PRPs for many constraint classes do not exist in our model. However constrained IPFs, where the range can be larger than the domain, can exist. The challenge is to construct them. Surprisingly, constraining an IPF is significantly harder than constraining a PRF, even for simple puncturing constraints. For example, it is not difficult to see that puncturing a Luby-Rackoff cipher by puncturing the underlying PRFs does not work.

In this paper, we present constrained IPFs for both puncturing constraints and for arbitrary circuit constraints. Both constructions make use of a recent primitive called a *private constrained* PRF [18] that can be constructed from the learning with errors (LWE) problem [15,22,24]. Roughly speaking, a private constrained PRF is a constrained PRF where a constrained key $k_g$ reveals nothing about the constraint $g$. Before we describe our constructions, let us first look at an application.

*IPFs and deterministic encryption.* While constrained IPFs are interesting in their own right, they come up naturally in the context of deterministic encryption. IPFs are related to the concept of *deterministic authenticated encryption* (DAE) introduced by Rogaway and Shrimpton [50] where encryption is deterministic and does not take a nonce as input. A DAE provides the same security guarantees as (randomized) authenticated encryption, as long as all the messages encrypted under a single key are distinct. Rogaway and Shrimpton show that an IPF whose range is sufficiently larger than its domain is equivalent to a secure DAE. They further require that the length of the IPF output depend only on the length of the input, and this holds for all our constructions. Hence, our constrained IPFs give the ability to constrain keys in a DAE encryption scheme: the constrained key holder can only encrypt/decrypt messages that satisfy a certain predicate.

## 1.1  Building Constrained IPFs

In Sect. 4, we present two constructions for constrained IPFs on a domain $\mathcal{X} = \{0,1\}^n$. Our first construction, a warm-up, only supports puncturing constraints. Our second construction gives a constrained IPF for arbitrary circuit constraints, but is only secure if a single constrained key is released. Here we give the main ideas behind the constructions. Both rely heavily on the recent development of private constrained PRFs. In Sect. 5, we show how to instantiate our constructions from the LWE assumption. In Sect. 7, we also show that using $i\mathcal{O}$, it is possible to construct a multi-key, circuit-constrained IPF.

*A puncturable IPF.* Let $\mathsf{F}_1 \colon \mathcal{K}_1 \times \mathcal{X} \to \mathcal{V}$ and $\mathsf{F}_2 \colon \mathcal{K}_2 \times \mathcal{V} \to \mathcal{X}$ be two secure PRFs. Define the following IPF $\mathsf{F}$ on domain $\mathcal{X}$ using a key $k = (k^{(1)}, k^{(2)}) \in \mathcal{K}_1 \times \mathcal{K}_2$:

$$
\mathsf{F}\big((k^{(1)}, k^{(2)}),\, x\big) := \qquad\qquad \mathsf{F}^{-1}\big((k^{(1)}, k^{(2)}),\, (y_1, y_2)\big) :=
$$

$$
\left\{
\begin{array}{l}
y_1 \leftarrow \mathsf{F}_1(k^{(1)}, x) \\
y_2 \leftarrow x \oplus \mathsf{F}_2(k^{(2)}, y_1) \\
\text{output } (y_1, y_2)
\end{array}
\right\}
\qquad
\left\{
\begin{array}{l}
x \leftarrow \mathsf{F}_2(k^{(2)}, y_1) \oplus y_2 \\
\text{if } \mathsf{F}_1(k^{(1)}, x) \neq y_1 \\
\quad \text{then } x \leftarrow \bot \\
\text{output } x
\end{array}
\right\}
\qquad (1.1)
$$

It is not difficult to show that $\mathsf{F}$ is a secure IPF. In fact, one can view this IPF as an instance of a DAE construction called SIV (Synthetic-IV) [50].

The question is how to securely puncture $\mathsf{F}$. As a first attempt, suppose $\mathsf{F}_1$ is a puncturable PRF, say constructed from the tree-based GGM construction [34].

To puncture the IPF $F$ at a point $x \in \mathcal{X}$, one can puncture $F_1$ at $x$ to obtain the IPF punctured key $k_x := (k_x^{(1)}, k^{(2)})$. This key $k_x$ prevents the evaluation $F$ at the point $x$, as required. However, this is completely insecure. To see why, observe that given $k_x$, the adversary can easily distinguish $F(k, x)$ from a random pair in $\mathcal{V} \times \mathcal{X}$: given a challenge value $(y_1, y_2)$ for $F(k, x)$, the adversary can simply test if $x = F_2(k^{(2)}, y_1) \oplus y_2$. This will be satisfied by $F(k, x)$, but is unlikely to be satisfied by a random pair in $\mathcal{V} \times \mathcal{X}$.

To properly puncture $F$ at $x$ we must puncture $F_1$ at $x$ *and* puncture $F_2$ at $y_1 := F_1(k^{(1)}, x)$. The punctured key for $F$ is then $k_x := (k_x^{(1)}, k_{y_1}^{(2)})$. Here, it is vital that the punctured key $k_{y_1}^{(2)}$ reveal nothing about the punctured point $y_1$. Otherwise, it is again easy to distinguish $F(k, x) = (y_1, y_2)$ from a random pair in $\mathcal{V} \times \mathcal{X}$ using the exposed information about $y_1$. To ensure that $y_1$ is hidden, we must use a *private puncturable* PRF for $F_2$. Currently the best constructions for a private puncturable PRF rely on the LWE assumption [15,22,24]. It is not known how to construct a private puncturable PRF from one-way functions. We show in Theorem 4.3 that with this setup, the puncturable IPF in (1.1) is secure.

*A constrained IPF for circuit constraints.* Next we generalize (1.1) to support an arbitrary circuit constraint $g$. As a first step we can constrain $k^{(1)}$ to $g$ so that the IPF constrained key is $k_g := (k_g^{(1)}, k^{(2)})$. We can use for $F_1$ any of the candidate circuit-constrained PRFs [19,23].

As before, this is insecure: for security we must also constrain $F_2$. However we immediately run into a problem. Following the blueprint in (1.1) we must puncture $F_2$ at all points $F_1(k^{(1)}, x)$ where $g(x) = 0$. However, because the size of this set can be super-polynomial, we would need to constrain $F_2$ to a set containing super-polynomially-many pseudorandom points. The difficulty is that $F_2$ cannot efficiently test if an input $v \in \mathcal{V}$ satisfies $v = F_1(k^{(1)}, x)$ with $g(x) = 0$. Because $F_1$ is not invertible, this cannot be done even given $k^{(1)}$.

We solve this problem by replacing $F_1(k^{(1)}, x)$ with a CCA-secure public-key encryption $\mathsf{PKE.Encrypt}(\mathsf{pk}, x; r_x)$, where the randomness $r_x = F_1(k^{(1)}, x)$ is derived from $F_1$ and $\mathsf{pk}$ is the public key. In this case, the input to $F_2$ is a ciphertext $\mathsf{ct}$ that encrypts the point $x$. The output of the IPF is the pair $(\mathsf{ct}, F_2(k^{(2)}, \mathsf{ct}) \oplus x)$. When constraining $F_2$, we embed the secret decryption key $\mathsf{sk}$ for the public-key encryption scheme in the constrained key. Then, on an input ciphertext $\mathsf{ct}$, the constraint function first decrypts $\mathsf{ct}$ (using $\mathsf{sk}$) to obtain a value $x \in \mathcal{X}$, and then checks if $g(x) = 1$. Because knowledge of $\mathsf{sk}$ allows one to invert on *all* points, it is *critical* that the constrained key hides $\mathsf{sk}$. Here, we rely on a strong simulation-based notion of constraint privacy [15,24]. In Theorem 4.7, we show that as long as the underlying PKE scheme is CCA-secure and $F_2$ is a (single-key) *private* constrained PRF, then the resulting scheme is a (single-key) secure circuit-constrained IPF.

By design, our circuit-constrained IPF provides two ways to invert: the "honest" method where on input $(\mathsf{ct}, y_2)$, the evaluator uses the PRF key $k^{(2)}$ to compute a (candidate) preimage $x \leftarrow F_2(k^{(2)}, \mathsf{ct}) \oplus y_2$, and the "trapdoor" method where an evaluator who holds the decryption key for the public-key encryption scheme simply decrypts ct to recover the (candidate) preimage $x$. The inversion trapdoor plays an important role in the security analysis of our circuit-constrained IPF because it enables the reduction algorithm to properly simulate the inversion oracle queries in the IPF security game. We refer to the full version of this paper [16] for the complete details.

Theorems 4.3 and 4.7 state that our puncturable IPF and circuit-constrained IPF are secure assuming the security (and privacy) of the underlying constrained PRFs (and in the latter case, CCA-security of the public-key encryption scheme). While it may seem that security of the IPF should directly follow from security of the underlying puncturable (or constrained) PRFs, several complications arise in the security analysis because we give the adversary access to an IPF inversion oracle in the security game. As a result, our security analysis requires a more intricate hybrid argument where we appeal to the security of the underlying constrained PRFs multiple times. We provide the complete proofs in the full version [16].

*A multi-key constrained IPFs from iO.* In Sect. 7, we also show that an indistinguishability obfuscation of the puncturable IPF from (1.1) gives a multi-key circuit-constrained IPF. This construction parallels the Boneh-Zhandry construction of multi-key circuit-constrained PRFs from standard puncturable PRFs and indistinguishability obfuscation [20].

*Supporting key-delegation.* Several constrained PRF constructions support a mechanism called key-delegation [19,26,27], where the holder of a constrained PRF key can further constrain the key. For instance, the holder of a constrained key $k_f$ for a function $f$ can further constrain the key to a function of the form $f \wedge g$ where $(f \wedge g)(x) = 1$ if and only if $f(x) = g(x) = 1$. In Sect. 6, we describe how our circuit-constrained IPF can be extended to support key-delegation.

*Open problems.* Our impossibility results for constrained PRPs rule out any constraint class that enables evaluation on a non-negligible fraction of the domain. For example, this rules out the possibility of a puncturable PRP. Can we build constrained PRPs for constraint families that allow evaluation on a more restricted subset of the domain? For instance, do prefix-constrained PRPs exist?

Our circuit-constrained IPF from LWE is secure only if a *single* constrained key is issued. In Sect. 6, we show how to modify our construction to support giving out a pre-determined number of keys, provided that each successive key adds a further constraint on the previous key (i.e., via key delegation). Is there an IPF that supports multiple constrained keys for an arbitrary set of circuit constraints (and does not rely on strong assumptions such as $iO$ or multilinear maps)? A positive answer would also give a circuit-constrained PRF that supports multiple keys, which is currently an open problem.

Our circuit-constrained IPF relies on the LWE assumption. Can we build constrained IPFs from one-way functions? For example, the tree-based PRF of [34] gives a prefix-constrained PRF from one-way functions. Can we build a prefix-constrained IPF from one-way functions?

## 1.2   Related Work

Authenticated encryption was first formalized over a sequence of works [10,11, 39,48,49]. Deterministic authenticated encryption, and the notion of a pseudo-random injection, were introduced in [50]. These notions have been further studied in [37,38]. Our circuit-constrained IPF relies on derandomizing a public-key encryption scheme. Similar techniques have been used in the context of constructing deterministic public-key encryption [6,7,12,31]. Note however that an IPF is a *secret-key* primitive, so in our setting, the randomness used for encryption can be derived using a PRF on the message rather than as a publicly-computable function on the input. This critical difference eliminates the need to make entropic assumptions on the inputs.

Since the introduction of constrained PRFs in [19,21,40], numerous works have studied constraining other cryptographic primitives such as verifiable random functions (VRFs) [26,27,29] and signatures [8,21]. Other works have focused on constructing adaptively-secure constrained PRFs [30,35,36] and constrained PRFs for inputs of unbounded length [27,28].

## 2   Preliminaries

For a positive integer $n$, we write $[n]$ to denote the set $\{1, 2, \ldots, n\}$. For a distribution $\mathcal{D}$, we write $x \leftarrow \mathcal{D}$ to denote that $x$ is sampled from $\mathcal{D}$; for a finite set $S$, we write $x \xleftarrow{\text{R}} S$ to denote that $x$ is sampled uniformly from $S$. Throughout this work, we write $\lambda$ for the security parameter. We say a function $f(\lambda)$ is negligible in $\lambda$ if $f(\lambda) = o(1/\lambda^c)$ for all $c \in \mathbb{N}$. We denote this by writing $f(\lambda) = \text{negl}(\lambda)$. We say that an algorithm is efficient if it runs in probabilistic polynomial time in the length of its input. We write $\text{poly}(\lambda)$ to denote a quantity that is bounded by some polynomial in $\lambda$. We say that an event occurs with overwhelming probability if its complement occurs with negligible probability, and that it occurs with noticeable probability if it occurs with non-negligible probability. We say that two families of distributions $\mathcal{D}_1$ and $\mathcal{D}_2$ are computationally indistinguishable if no efficient algorithm can distinguish between $\mathcal{D}_1$ and $\mathcal{D}_2$, except with negligible probability. We say that $\mathcal{D}_1$ and $\mathcal{D}_2$ are statistically indistinguishable if the statistical distance between $\mathcal{D}_1$ and $\mathcal{D}_2$ is negligible.

*Function families.* For two sets $\mathcal{X}$, $\mathcal{Y}$, we write $\mathsf{Funs}[\mathcal{X}, \mathcal{Y}]$ to denote the set of functions from $\mathcal{X}$ to $\mathcal{Y}$. We write $\mathsf{InjFuns}[\mathcal{X}, \mathcal{Y}]$ to denote the set of *injective* functions from $\mathcal{X}$ to $\mathcal{Y}$. For an injective function $f \in \mathsf{InjFuns}[\mathcal{X}, \mathcal{Y}]$, we denote by $f^{-1} : \mathcal{Y} \to \mathcal{X} \cup \{\bot\}$ the function where $f^{-1}(y) = x$ if $y = f(x)$, and $\bot$ if there is no such $x \in \mathcal{X}$. We sometimes refer to $f^{-1}$ as the (generalized) inverse of $f$. When the domain and range are the same, the set $\mathsf{InjFuns}[\mathcal{X}, \mathcal{X}]$ is precisely the set of permutations on $\mathcal{X}$.

## 2.1   CCA-Secure Public-Key Encryption

A PKE scheme consists of three algorithms PKE = (PKE.Setup, PKE.Encrypt, PKE.Decrypt) over a message space $\mathcal{M}$ and a ciphertext space $\mathcal{T}$ with the following properties:

- PKE.Setup($1^\lambda$) $\rightarrow$ (pk, sk): On input the security parameter $\lambda$, the setup algorithm generates a public key pk and a secret key sk.
- PKE.Encrypt(pk, $m$) $\rightarrow$ ct: On input a public key pk and a message $m \in \mathcal{M}$, the encryption algorithm returns a ciphertext ct $\in \mathcal{T}$.
- PKE.Decrypt(sk, ct) $\rightarrow m$: On input a secret key sk and a ciphertext ct $\in \mathcal{T}$, the decryption algorithm outputs a message $m \in \mathcal{M} \cup \{\bot\}$.

We say that a PKE scheme is correct if for all keys (pk, sk) $\leftarrow$ PKE.Setup($1^\lambda$), and for all messages $m \in \mathcal{M}$, we have that

$$\Pr[\mathsf{PKE.Decrypt(sk, PKE.Encrypt(pk}, m))] = m] = 1.$$

**Definition 2.1 (CCA-Security [43,46]).** *Let* PKE $=$ (PKE.Setup, PKE.Encrypt, PKE.Decrypt) *be a PKE scheme with message space $\mathcal{M}$ and ciphertext space $\mathcal{T}$, and let $\mathcal{A}$ be an efficient adversary. For a security parameter $\lambda$ and a bit $b \in \{0,1\}$, we define the CCA-security experiment* $\mathsf{Expt}^{(\mathsf{CCA})}_{\mathcal{A},\mathsf{PKE}}(\lambda, b)$ *as follows. The challenger first samples* (pk, sk) $\leftarrow$ PKE.Setup($1^\lambda$). *The adversary can then issue decryption oracle queries and up to one challenge oracle query.[1] Depending on the bit $b \in \{0,1\}$, the challenger responds to each query as follows:*

- **Decryption oracle.** *On input a ciphertext* ct $\in \mathcal{T}$, *the challenger responds with the decryption $m \leftarrow$ PKE.Decrypt(sk, ct).*
- **Challenge oracle.** *On input two messages $m_0, m_1 \in \mathcal{M}$, the challenger responds with the ciphertext* ct$^* \leftarrow$ PKE.Encrypt(pk, $m_b$).

*At the end of the experiment, the adversary $\mathcal{A}$ outputs a bit $b' \in \{0,1\}$ which is the output of the experiment. An adversary $\mathcal{A}$ is admissible if $\mathcal{A}$ does not submit the ciphertext* ct$^*$ *it received from the challenge oracle to the decryption oracle. We say that* PKE *is secure against chosen-ciphertext attacks (CCA-secure) if for all efficient and admissible adversaries $\mathcal{A}$,*

$$\left| \Pr[\mathsf{Expt}^{(\mathsf{CCA})}_{\mathcal{A},\mathsf{PKE}}(\lambda, 0) = 1] - \Pr[\mathsf{Expt}^{(\mathsf{CCA})}_{\mathcal{A},\mathsf{PKE}}(\lambda, 1) = 1] \right| = \mathrm{negl}(\lambda).$$

---

[1] In the public-key setting, security against adversaries that make a single challenge query implies security against adversaries that make multiple challenge queries (via a standard hybrid argument).

*Smoothness.* In our security analysis, we require that our public-key encryption scheme satisfy an additional smoothness property. We say that a public-key encryption scheme is smooth if every message can encrypt to a super-polynomial number of potential ciphertexts. This property is satisfied by most natural public-key encryption schemes. After all, if the adversary can find a message $m$ that has only polynomially-many ciphertexts, then the adversary can trivially break semantic security of the scheme. Of course, it is possible to craft public-key encryption schemes [9] where there exist (hard-to-find) messages that encrypt to only polynomially-many ciphertexts. We give the formal definition of smoothness in Definition 2.2.

**Definition 2.2 (Smoothness** [9, adapted]**).** *A* PKE *scheme* PKE = (PKE.Setup, PKE.Encrypt, PKE.Decrypt) *with message space* $\mathcal{M}$ *and ciphertext space* $\mathcal{T}$ *is* smooth *if for all messages* $m \in \mathcal{M}$ *and all strings* $\mathsf{ct} \in \mathcal{T}$,

$$\Pr\left[(\mathsf{pk}, \mathsf{sk}) \leftarrow \mathsf{PKE.Setup}(1^\lambda) : \mathsf{PKE.Encrypt}(\mathsf{pk}, m) = \mathsf{ct}\right] = \mathrm{negl}(\lambda),$$

*where the probability is taken over the randomness in* PKE.Setup *and* PKE.Encrypt.

## 3   Invertible PRFs

In this section, we introduce the notion of an invertible pseudorandom function (IPF). We then extend our notions to that of a *constrained* IPF. We begin by recalling the definition of a pseudorandom function (PRF) [34].

**Definition 3.1 (Pseudorandom Function** [34]**).** *A pseudorandom function (PRF) with key-space* $\mathcal{K}$, *domain* $\mathcal{X}$, *and range* $\mathcal{Y}$ *is a function* $\mathsf{F} \colon \mathcal{K} \times \mathcal{X} \to \mathcal{Y}$ *that can be computed by a deterministic polynomial-time algorithm. A PRF can also include a setup algorithm* $\mathsf{F.Setup}(1^\lambda)$ *that on input the security parameter* $\lambda$, *outputs a key* $k \in \mathcal{K}$. *A function* $\mathsf{F}$ *is a secure PRF if for all efficient adversaries* $\mathcal{A}$,

$$\left| \Pr\left[k \leftarrow \mathsf{F.Setup}(1^\lambda) : \mathcal{A}^{\mathsf{F}(k,\cdot)}(1^\lambda) = 1\right] \right.$$
$$\left. - \Pr\left[\mathsf{R} \xleftarrow{\mathrm{R}} \mathsf{Funs}[\mathcal{X}, \mathcal{Y}] : \mathcal{A}^{\mathsf{R}(\cdot)}(1^\lambda) = 1\right]\right| = \mathrm{negl}(\lambda).$$

An invertible pseudorandom function (IPF) is an injective PRF whose inverse function can be computed efficiently (given the secret key). This requirement that the inverse be efficiently computable is the key distinguishing factor between IPFs and injective PRFs. For instance, injective PRFs can be constructed by composing a sufficiently-expanding PRF with a pairwise-independent hash function. However, it is unclear how to invert such a PRF. We now give the definition of an IPF.

**Definition 3.2 (Invertible Pseudorandom Functions).** *An invertible pseudorandom function (IPF) with key-space* $\mathcal{K}$, *domain* $\mathcal{X}$, *and range* $\mathcal{Y}$ *consists of two functions* $\mathsf{F} \colon \mathcal{K} \times \mathcal{X} \to \mathcal{Y}$ *and* $\mathsf{F}^{-1} \colon \mathcal{K} \times \mathcal{Y} \to \mathcal{X} \cup \{\bot\}$. *An IPF can also include a setup algorithm* $\mathsf{F.Setup}(1^\lambda)$ *that on input the security parameter* $\lambda$, *outputs a key* $k \in \mathcal{K}$. *The functions* $\mathsf{F}$ *and* $\mathsf{F}^{-1}$ *satisfy the following properties:*

- *Both* F *and* $F^{-1}$ *can be computed by deterministic polynomial-time algorithms.*
- *For all security parameters* $\lambda$ *and all keys* $k$ *output by* F.Setup($1^\lambda$), *the function* F($k, \cdot$) *is an injective function from* $\mathcal{X}$ *to* $\mathcal{Y}$. *Moreover, the function* $F^{-1}(k, \cdot)$ *is the (generalized) inverse of* F($k, \cdot$).

**Definition 3.3 (Pseudorandomness).** *An IPF* F $: \mathcal{K} \times \mathcal{X} \to \mathcal{Y}$ *is secure if for all efficient adversaries* $\mathcal{A}$,

$$\left| \Pr\left[ k \leftarrow \text{F.Setup}(1^\lambda) : \mathcal{A}^{F(k, \cdot),\, F^{-1}(k, \cdot)}(1^\lambda) \right] \right.$$
$$\left. - \Pr\left[ R \xleftarrow{\text{R}} \text{InjFuns}[\mathcal{X}, \mathcal{Y}] : \mathcal{A}^{R(\cdot),\, R^{-1}(\cdot)}(1^\lambda) \right] \right| = \text{negl}(\lambda).$$

*Remark 3.4 (Strong vs. Weak Pseudorandomness).* The pseudorandomness requirement for an IPF (Definition 3.3) requires that the outputs of an IPF be indistinguishable from random against adversaries that can query the IPF in both the forward direction as well as the backward direction. We can also consider a weaker notion of pseudorandomness where the adversary is given access to an evaluation oracle F($k, \cdot$), but not an inversion oracle $F^{-1}(k, \cdot)$. Motivated by the applications we have in mind, in this work, we focus exclusively on building IPFs satisfying the *strong* notion of pseudorandomness from Definition 3.3, where the adversary can evaluate the IPF in both directions.

### 3.1 Constrained PRFs and IPFs

We next review the notion of a constrained PRF [19,21,40] and then extend these definitions to constrained IPFs.

**Definition 3.5 (Constrained PRF [19,21,40]).** *A PRF* F $: \mathcal{K} \times \mathcal{X} \to \mathcal{Y}$ *is said to be constrained with respect to a predicate family* $\mathcal{F} = \{f : \mathcal{X} \to \{0, 1\}\}$ *if there are two additional algorithms* (F.Constrain, F.Eval) *with the following properties:*

- F.Constrain($k, f$) $\to k_f$: *On input a PRF key* $k \in \mathcal{K}$ *and a function* $f \in \mathcal{F}$, *the constraining algorithm outputs a constrained key* $k_f$.
- F.Eval($k_f, x$) $\to y$: *On input a constrained key* $k_f$ *and a point* $x \in \mathcal{X}$, *the evaluation algorithm outputs a value* $y \in \mathcal{Y}$.

*We say that a constrained PRF is correct for a function family* $\mathcal{F}$ *if for all* $k \leftarrow$ F.Setup($1^\lambda$), *every function* $f \in \mathcal{F}$, *and every input* $x \in \mathcal{X}$ *where* $f(x) = 1$, *we have that*

$$\text{F.Eval}(\text{F.Constrain}(k, f), x) = \text{F}(k, x).$$

**Definition 3.6 (Constrained PRF Security Experiment).** *Let* F $: \mathcal{K} \times \mathcal{X} \to \mathcal{Y}$ *be a constrained PRF with respect to a function family* $\mathcal{F}$, *and let* $\mathcal{A}$ *be an efficient adversary. In the constrained PRF security experiment* $\text{Expt}_{\mathcal{A}, F}^{(\text{PRF})}(\lambda, b)$ *(parameterized by a security parameter* $\lambda$ *and a bit* $b \in \{0, 1\}$), *the challenger begins by sampling a key* $k \leftarrow$ F.Setup($1^\lambda$) *and a random function* $R \xleftarrow{\text{R}}$ Funs[$\mathcal{X}, \mathcal{Y}$]. *The adversary is allowed to make constrain, evaluation, and challenge oracle queries. Depending on the value of the bit* $b \in \{0, 1\}$, *the challenger responds to each oracle query as follows:*

- **Constrain oracle.** *On input a function* $f \in \mathcal{F}$, *the challenger responds with a constrained key* $k_f \leftarrow$ F.Constrain$(k, f)$.
- **Evaluation oracle.** *On input a point* $x \in \mathcal{X}$, *the challenger returns* $y =$ F$(k, x)$.
- **Challenge oracle.** *On input a point* $x \in \mathcal{X}$, *the challenger returns* $y =$ F$(k, x)$ *to* $\mathcal{A}$ *if* $b = 0$ *and* $y =$ R$(x)$ *if* $b = 1$.

*Finally, at the end of the experiment, the adversary* $\mathcal{A}$ *outputs a bit* $b' \in \{0, 1\}$ *which is also the output of the experiment.*

**Definition 3.7 (Constrained PRF Security).** *Let* F $: \mathcal{K} \times \mathcal{X} \rightarrow \mathcal{Y}$ *be a constrained PRF for a function family* $\mathcal{F}$. *We say that an adversary* $\mathcal{A}$ *is admissible for the constrained PRF security experiment (Definition 3.6) if the following conditions hold:*

- *For all constrain queries* $f \in \mathcal{F}$ *and challenge queries* $x^* \in \mathcal{X}$ *the adversary makes,* $f(x^*) = 0$.
- *For all evaluation queries* $x \in \mathcal{X}$ *and challenge queries* $x^* \in \mathcal{X}$ *the adversary makes,* $x \neq x^*$.

*We say that* F *is a secure constrained PRF if for all efficient and admissible adversaries* $\mathcal{A}$,

$$\left| \Pr[\mathsf{Expt}_{\mathcal{A},\mathsf{F}}^{(\mathsf{PRF})}(\lambda, 0) = 1] - \Pr[\mathsf{Expt}_{\mathcal{A},\mathsf{F}}^{(\mathsf{PRF})}(\lambda, 1) = 1] \right| = \mathrm{negl}(\lambda).$$

*Without loss of generality, we restrict the adversary to make at most one challenge query in the constrained PRF security experiment.*[2]

*Remark 3.8 (Selective vs. Adaptive Security).* The constrained PRF security game (Definition 3.6) allows the adversary to *adaptively* choose the challenge point after making constrain and evaluation queries. We can also define a *selective* notion of security where the adversary must commit to its challenge query at the beginning of the security game (before it starts making queries). Using a standard technique called *complexity leveraging* [13], selective security implies adaptive security at the expense of a super-polynomial loss in the security reduction. For instance, this is the technique used in [19] in the context of constrained PRFs.

*Remark 3.9 (Single-Key Security).* Brakerski and Vaikuntanathan [23] considered another relaxation of Definition 3.7 where in the constrained PRF security game (Definition 3.6), the adversary is restricted to making a single query to the constrain oracle. In the single-key setting, we can consider the notion of *selective-function* security, where the adversary must commit to its constrain oracle query at the beginning of the security experiment. Thus, in this setting, there are two different notions of selectivity: the usual notion where the adversary commits

---

[2] As noted in [19], a standard hybrid argument shows that security against adversaries making a single challenge query implies security against adversaries making multiple challenge queries.

to the challenge point (Remark 3.8) and selective-function security where the adversary commits to the function. Many of the lattice-based (single-key) constrained PRF constructions [15, 22–24] are selectively secure in the choice of the constraint function, but adaptively secure in the choice of the challenge point.

**Definition 3.10 (Constrained IPF).** *An IPF* $(\mathsf{F}, \mathsf{F}^{-1})$ *with key-space* $\mathcal{K}$, *domain* $\mathcal{X}$, *and range* $\mathcal{Y}$ *is said to be constrained with respect to a function family* $\mathcal{F} = \{f : \mathcal{X} \to \{0, 1\}\}$ *if there are three additional algorithms* $(\mathsf{F.Constrain},$ $\mathsf{F.Eval}, \mathsf{F.Eval}^{-1})$ *with the following properties:*

- $\mathsf{F.Constrain}(k, f) \to k_f$: *On input a PRF key* $k \in \mathcal{K}$ *and a function* $f \in \mathcal{F}$, *the constraining algorithm outputs a constrained key* $k_f$.
- $\mathsf{F.Eval}(k_f, x) \to y$: *On input a constrained key* $k_f$ *and a value* $x \in \mathcal{X}$, *the evaluation algorithm outputs a value* $y \in \mathcal{Y}$.
- $\mathsf{F.Eval}^{-1}(k_f, y) \to x$: *On input a constrained key* $k_f$ *and a value* $y \in \mathcal{Y}$, *the evaluation algorithm outputs a value* $x \in \mathcal{X} \cup \{\bot\}$.

*We say that a constrained IPF is correct for a function family* $\mathcal{F}$ *if for all keys* $k \leftarrow \mathsf{F.Setup}(1^\lambda)$, *every function* $f \in \mathcal{F}$, *and* $k_f \leftarrow \mathsf{F.Constrain}(k, f)$, *the following two properties hold:*

- *For all inputs* $x \in \mathcal{X}$ *where* $f(x) = 1$, $\mathsf{F.Eval}(k_f, x) = \mathsf{F}(k, x)$.
- *For all inputs* $y \in \mathcal{Y}$ *where there exists* $x \in \mathcal{X}$ *such that* $\mathsf{F}(k, x) = y$ *and* $f(x) = 1$, *then* $\mathsf{F.Eval}^{-1}(k_f, y) = \mathsf{F}^{-1}(k, y)$.

**Definition 3.11 (Constrained IPF Security Experiment).** *Let* $(\mathsf{F}, \mathsf{F}^{-1})$ *be an IPF with key-space* $\mathcal{K}$, *domain* $\mathcal{X}$, *range* $\mathcal{Y}$, *and constrained with respect to a function family* $\mathcal{F}$. *Let* $\mathcal{A}$ *be an efficient adversary. The constrained IPF security experiment* $\mathsf{Expt}_{\mathcal{A}, \mathsf{F}}^{(\mathsf{IPF})}(\lambda, b)$ *is defined exactly as the constrained PRF security experiment* $\mathsf{Expt}_{\mathcal{A}, \mathsf{F}}^{(\mathsf{PRF})}(\lambda, b)$ *(except with the IPF in place of the PRF and the random function* $\mathsf{R}$ *is sampled from* $\mathsf{InjFuns}[\mathcal{X}, \mathcal{Y}]$), *and in addition to the constrain, evaluation, and challenge oracles, the adversary is also given access to an inversion oracle:*

- **Inversion oracle.** *On input a point* $y \in \mathcal{Y}$, *the challenger returns* $\mathsf{F}^{-1}(k, y)$.

*At the end of the experiment, the adversary* $\mathcal{A}$ *outputs a bit* $b' \in \{0, 1\}$, *which is the output of the experiment.*

**Definition 3.12 (Constrained IPF Security).** *Let* $(\mathsf{F}, \mathsf{F}^{-1})$ *be an IPF with key-space* $\mathcal{K}$, *domain* $\mathcal{X}$, *range* $\mathcal{Y}$, *and constrained with respect to a function family* $\mathcal{F}$. *We say that an adversary* $\mathcal{A}$ *is admissible for the constrained IPF security experiment (Definition 3.11) if the following conditions hold:*

- *For all constrain queries* $f \in \mathcal{F}$ *and challenge queries* $x^* \in \mathcal{X}$ *the adversary makes,* $f(x^*) = 0$.
- *For all evaluation queries* $x \in \mathcal{X}$ *and challenge queries* $x^* \in \mathcal{X}$ *the adversary makes,* $x \neq x^*$.

– *For all inversion queries* $y \in \mathcal{Y}$ *the adversary makes,* $y \notin \mathcal{Y}^*$, *where* $\mathcal{Y}^*$
*is the set of responses to the adversary's challenge oracle queries from the*
*challenger.*

*We say that* F *is a secure constrained IPF if for all efficient and admissible*
*adversaries* $\mathcal{A}$,

$$\left| \Pr[\mathsf{Expt}_{\mathcal{A},\mathsf{F}}^{(\mathsf{IPF})}(\lambda, 0) = 1] - \Pr[\mathsf{Expt}_{\mathcal{A},\mathsf{F}}^{(\mathsf{IPF})}(\lambda, 1) = 1] \right| = \mathrm{negl}(\lambda).$$

*As in Definition 3.7, we restrict the adversary to making at most one challenge*
*query in the constrained IPF security experiment.*

**Remark 3.13 (Selective vs. Adaptive Security for IPFs).** As with constrained
PRFs, we can define a notion of selective security for IPFs, where the adversary
commits to its challenge query at the beginning of the constrained IPF security
experiment (Remark 3.8). Similarly, we can consider a single-key variant of the
security game, where the adversary makes a single constrain oracle query. In this
case, we can also define the corresponding notion of selective-function security
(Remark 3.9).

*Puncturable PRFs and IPFs.* An important subclass of constrained PRFs is
the class of punctured PRFs [19,21,40]. A punctured PRF over a domain
$\mathcal{X}$ is a PRF constrained with respect to the family of point functions: $\mathcal{F} = \{f_{x^*} : \mathcal{X} \to \{0,1\} \mid x^* \in \mathcal{X}\}$, where $f_{x^*}(x) = 1$ for all $x \neq x^*$ and $f_{x^*}(x^*) = 0$.
For notational convenience, when working with a puncturable PRF F : $\mathcal{K} \times \mathcal{X} \to \mathcal{Y}$, we replace the F.Constrain algorithm with the F.Puncture algorithm that takes
as input a PRF key $k$ and a point $x^* \in \mathcal{X}$ and outputs a punctured key $k_{x^*}$ (a
key constrained to the point function $f_{x^*}$). We extend these notions accordingly
to puncturable IPFs.

## 3.2    Private Constrained PRFs

One of the key primitives we will need to build constrained IPFs is a *private*
constrained PRF [18]. A *private* constrained PRF is a constrained PRF with
the additional property that the constrained keys hide the underlying constraining function. Boneh et al. [18] showed how to construct private constrained
PRFs for all circuits using indistinguishability obfuscation. Recently, a number
of works have shown how to construct private constrained PRFs for puncturing
constraints [15], NC$^1$ constraints [24], and general circuit constraints [22] from
standard lattice assumptions. We now review the simulation-based notion of
privacy considered in [15,24].

**Definition 3.14 (Single-Key Constraint Privacy [15,24]).** *Let* F : $\mathcal{K} \times \mathcal{X} \to \mathcal{Y}$ *be a constrained PRF with respect to a function family* $\mathcal{F}$. *We say that* F *is
a single-key, selectively-private constrained PRF for* $\mathcal{F}$ *if for all efficient adver-
saries* $\mathcal{A} = (\mathcal{A}_1, \mathcal{A}_2)$, *there exists a stateful simulator* $\mathcal{S} = (\mathcal{S}_1, \mathcal{S}_2)$ *such that the
following two distributions are computationally indistinguishable:*

---

**Experiment $\mathsf{Real}_{\mathcal{A},\mathsf{F}}(\lambda)$:**

- $(f, \mathsf{st}_{\mathcal{A}}) \leftarrow \mathcal{A}(1^{\lambda})$
- $k \leftarrow \mathsf{F.Setup}(1^{\lambda})$
- $k_f \leftarrow \mathsf{F.Constrain}(k, f)$
- $b \leftarrow \mathcal{A}^{\mathsf{F}(k,\cdot)}(k_f, \mathsf{st}_{\mathcal{A}})$
- *Output b*

**Experiment $\mathsf{Ideal}_{\mathcal{A},\mathcal{S},\mathsf{F}}(\lambda)$:**

- $(f, \mathsf{st}_{\mathcal{A}}) \leftarrow \mathcal{A}(1^{\lambda})$
- $(k_f, \mathsf{st}_{\mathcal{S}}) \leftarrow \mathcal{S}_1(1^{\lambda})$
- $b \leftarrow \mathcal{A}^{\mathcal{O}_{\mathsf{Eval}}(\cdot)}(k_f, \mathsf{st}_{\mathcal{A}})$, *where the ideal evaluation oracle $\mathcal{O}_{\mathsf{Eval}}(\cdot)$ takes as input a point $x \in \mathcal{X}$, computes $(y, \mathsf{st}_{\mathcal{S}}) \leftarrow \mathcal{S}_2(x, f(x), \mathsf{st}_{\mathcal{S}})$, and returns $y$*
- *Output b*

---

Observe that the simulator $(\mathcal{S}_1, \mathcal{S}_2)$ in the ideal experiment is not given the function $f$ as input. Nevertheless, the simulator can simulate $k_f$ as in the real experiment. This implies that the adversary learns nothing about $f$ from $k_f$ beyond the value of $f$ at points $x \in \mathcal{X}$ where the adversary asks for $\mathsf{F}(k, x)$. Leaking this minimal information about $f$ is unavoidable.

### 3.3   Special Cases: PRPs and Constrained PRPs

Invertible pseudorandom functions can be viewed as a generalization of pseudorandom permutations (PRPs) where we allow the range of the function to be larger than its domain. A PRP is an IPF where the domain and range are identical. Our definitions for constrained IPFs can be similarly adapted to the setting of constrained PRPs. In this section, we make several observations on the (non)-existence of constrained PRPs, as well as discuss some possible relaxations of the security requirements to circumvent the impossibility results. We first show that constrained PRPs (for any family of constraints) on polynomial-size domains do not exist. Next, we show that even over large domains, security for many natural classes of constraints, including puncturing, is impossible to achieve. Our argument here can be extended to derive a lower bound on the size of the range of any IPF that supports puncturing constraints (or more generally, any constraint that enables evaluation a non-negligible fraction of the domain).

*Remark 3.15 (Small-Domain Constrained PRPs are Insecure).* No constrained PRP over a polynomial-size domain can be secure under the standard pseudorandomness definition of Definition 3.12. This follows from the fact that a PRP is easily distinguishable from a PRF when the domain is small—given even a single input-output pair $(x^*, y^*)$ for the PRP, the adversary already learns something about the values of the PRP at any point $x \neq x^*$ (namely, the value of the PRP at $x$ cannot be $y^*$). Thus, the adversary can distinguish the real output of the PRP at $x \neq x^*$ (which cannot be $y^*$) from a uniformly random value (which can be $y^*$ with noticeable probability when the domain is small).

**Theorem 3.16 (Limitations on Constrained PRPs).** *Let $\mathsf{F} : \mathcal{K} \times \mathcal{X} \to \mathcal{X}$ be a PRP constrained with respect to a predicate family $\mathcal{F}$. For each predicate*

$f \in \mathcal{F}$, let $S_f = \{x \in \mathcal{X} : f(x) = 1\}$ *denote the set of allowable points for* $f$. *If there exists* $f \in \mathcal{F}$ *where the quantity* $|S_f| / |\mathcal{X}|$ *is non-negligible, then* F *cannot be secure in the sense of Definition 3.12.*

*Proof.* Suppose there exists $f \in \mathcal{F}$ where $|S_f| / |\mathcal{X}|$ is non-negligible. We construct the following adversary for the constrained security game:

1. First, $\mathcal{A}$ makes a constrain query for $f$ and a challenge query on an arbitrary $x^* \in \mathcal{X}$ where $f(x^*) = 0$. It receives from the challenger a punctured key $k_f$ and a challenge value $y^*$.
2. Then, $\mathcal{A}$ computes $x \leftarrow \mathsf{F.Eval}^{-1}(k_f, y^*)$, and outputs 1 if either of the following conditions hold:
   – if $f(x) = 0$, or
   – if $\mathsf{F.Eval}(k_f, x) \neq y^*$.
   Otherwise, $\mathcal{A}$ outputs 0.

To complete the analysis, we compute the probability that $\mathcal{A}$ outputs 1:

– Suppose $y^* = \mathsf{F}(k, x^*)$. Consider the case where $f(x) = 1$. Note in particular that this means $x \neq x^*$. By correctness of F, we have that $\mathsf{F.Eval}(k_f, x) = \mathsf{F}(k, x)$. Moreover, since $\mathsf{F}(k, \cdot)$ is a permutation, it follows that $\mathsf{F}(k, x) \neq \mathsf{F}(k, x^*) = y^*$. Thus, in this case, either $f(x) = 0$ or $\mathsf{F.Eval}(k_f, x) \neq y^*$, so we conclude that $\mathcal{A}$ outputs 1 with probability 1.
– Suppose $y^*$ is uniformly random over $\mathcal{X}$. Let $\hat{x} = \mathsf{F}^{-1}(k, y^*)$. Suppose that $f(\hat{x}) = 1$. Then, by correctness of F, we have that

$$x = \mathsf{F.Eval}^{-1}(k_f, y^*) = \mathsf{F}^{-1}(k, y^*) = \hat{x}.$$

Moreover, since $f(\hat{x}) = 1$, we have

$$\mathsf{F.Eval}(k_f, x) = \mathsf{F.Eval}(k_f, \hat{x}) = \mathsf{F}(k, \hat{x}) = y^*.$$

Thus, whenever $f(\hat{x}) = 1$, adversary $\mathcal{A}$ outputs 1 with probability 0. Since $y^*$ is uniformly random over $\mathcal{X}$ and $\mathsf{F}(k, \cdot)$ is a permutation,

$$\Pr[\mathcal{A} \text{ outputs } 1] \leq \Pr[f(\hat{x}) = 0] = 1 - |S_f| / |\mathcal{X}|.$$

We conclude that $\mathcal{A}$ breaks the constrained security of F with advantage $|S_f| / |\mathcal{X}|$, which is non-negligible by assumption.        □

**Corollary 3.17 (Puncturable PRPs are Insecure).** *Let* $\mathsf{F} : \mathcal{K} \times \mathcal{X} \to \mathcal{X}$ *be a puncturable PRP. Then,* F *is insecure in the sense of Definition 3.12.*

*Proof.* The set of allowable points $S_f$ for a puncturing constraint $f$ is always $|\mathcal{X}| - 1$, so the ratio $|S_f| / |\mathcal{X}|$ is always non-negligible. The claim then follows from Theorem 3.16.        □

*Remark 3.18 (Constrained PRPs for Very Restricted Constraint Classes).*
Theorem 3.16 rules out any constrained PRP that supports issuing constrained keys that can be used to evaluate on a non-negligible fraction of the domain. It does leave open the possibility of building constrained PRPs where each constrained key can only be used to evaluate on a *negligible* fraction of the domain. A natural class of constraints that satisfies this property is the class of *prefix-constrained PRPs* (for a prefix of super-logarithmic size). We leave it as an open problem to construct a prefix-constrained PRP, or more generally, a constrained PRP where all of the constrained keys can only be used to evaluate on a negligible fraction of the domain.

*Remark 3.19 (Constrained IPFs Must be Expanding).* The attack from the proof of Theorem 3.16 also extends to the setting where $F : \mathcal{K} \times \mathcal{X} \to \mathcal{Y}$ is a constrained *IPF* with a small range. Specifically, if $|\mathcal{Y}| \leq |\mathcal{X}| \cdot \mathrm{poly}(\lambda)$, and $F$ supports issuing a constrained key for a function $f : \mathcal{X} \to \{0, 1\}$ where $|S_f| / |\mathcal{X}|$ is non-negligible, then $F$ cannot be secure in the sense of Definition 3.12. In this setting, we would modify the distinguisher in the proof of Theorem 3.16 to additionally output 1 if $x = \perp$. With this modification, the distinguishing advantage of the attack only decreases by a polynomial factor $|\mathcal{X}| / |\mathcal{Y}| = 1/\mathrm{poly}(\lambda)$. Therefore, any constrained IPF that admits a constraint that can be used to evaluate the IPF on a non-negligible fraction of the domain must necessarily have a range that is larger than the domain by at least a super-polynomial factor. Concretely, a puncturable IPF must have a range that is super-polynomially larger than the domain.

*Remark 3.20 (Weaker Security Relations).* The lower bound in Theorem 3.16 only applies when we require that the IPF value at a constrained point appear pseudorandom given the constrained key. One way to circumvent the lower bound is to consider a weaker security notion where we just require the IPF value at a constrained point to be *unpredictable* rather than pseudorandom (given the constrained key). In other words, no efficient adversary should be able to predict $F(k, x)$ given a constrained key $k_f$ that does not allow evaluation at $x$. While the weaker security properties are potentially satisfiable, they may not be sufficient for specific applications.

# 4    Constructing Constrained IPFs

We now turn to constructing constrained IPFs and give two main constructions in this section. Our main constructions use private constrained (non-invertible) PRFs as the primary tool. As a warm-up, we first construct a puncturable IPF from a private puncturable PRF in Sect. 4.1. We then show how the basic IPF construction can be extended to obtain a (single-key) circuit-constrained IPF in Sect. 4.2. In Sect. 7, we also show that an indistinguishability obfuscation of the basic puncturable IPF gives a *multi-key* circuit-constrained IPF.

## 4.1   Warm-Up: Puncturable IPF from Private Puncturable PRFs

We begin by showing how to construct a puncturable IPF on a domain $\mathcal{X}$ from a private puncturable PRF on $\mathcal{X}$. We describe the construction and then show in Theorems 4.2 and 4.3 that it is a secure puncturable IPF.

**Construction 4.1.** *Fix a domain $\mathcal{X} = \{0,1\}^n$ where $n = n(\lambda)$. Let $\mathsf{F}_1 \colon \mathcal{K}_1 \times \mathcal{X} \to \mathcal{V}$ be an injective puncturable PRF with key-space $\mathcal{K}_1$ and range $\mathcal{V}$. Let $\mathsf{F}_2 \colon \mathcal{K}_2 \times \mathcal{V} \to \mathcal{X}$ be a private puncturable PRF with key-space $\mathcal{K}_2$. The puncturable IPF $\mathsf{F} \colon \mathcal{K} \times \mathcal{X} \to \mathcal{Y}$ with key-space $\mathcal{K} = \mathcal{K}_1 \times \mathcal{K}_2$, domain $\mathcal{X}$, and range $\mathcal{Y} = \mathcal{V} \times \mathcal{X}$ is defined as follows:*

- *The IPF key is a pair of keys $k = (k^{(1)}, k^{(2)}) \in \mathcal{K}_1 \times \mathcal{K}_2$ for the puncturable PRFs $\mathsf{F}_1$ and $\mathsf{F}_2$.*
- *On input $k = (k^{(1)}, k^{(2)}) \in \mathcal{K}_1 \times \mathcal{K}_2 = \mathcal{K}$, and $x \in \mathcal{X}$ the IPF is defined as the pair*

$$\mathsf{F}\big((k^{(1)}, k^{(2)}),\ x\big) := \Big( \mathsf{F}_1(k^{(1)}, x),\ \ x \oplus \mathsf{F}_2(k^{(2)}, \mathsf{F}_1(k^{(1)}, x)) \Big).$$

- *On input $k = (k^{(1)}, k^{(2)}) \in \mathcal{K}_1 \times \mathcal{K}_2 = \mathcal{K}$, and $y = (y_1, y_2) \in \mathcal{V} \times \mathcal{X} = \mathcal{Y}$, the inversion algorithm $\mathsf{F}^{-1}(k, y)$ first computes $x \leftarrow \mathsf{F}_2(k^{(2)}, y_1) \oplus y_2$ and outputs*

$$\mathsf{F}^{-1}(k, (y_1, y_2)) := \begin{cases} x & \text{if } y_1 = \mathsf{F}_1(k^{(1)}, x) \\ \bot & \text{otherwise.} \end{cases}$$

*Next, we define the setup and constraining algorithms for $(\mathsf{F}, \mathsf{F}^{-1})$.*

- *$\mathsf{F}.\mathsf{Setup}(1^\lambda)$: On input the security parameter $\lambda$, the setup algorithm samples two puncturable PRF keys $k^{(1)} \leftarrow \mathsf{F}_1.\mathsf{Setup}(1^\lambda)$ and $k^{(2)} \leftarrow \mathsf{F}_2.\mathsf{Setup}(1^\lambda)$. The setup algorithm outputs the IPF key $k = (k^{(1)}, k^{(2)})$.*
- *$\mathsf{F}.\mathsf{Puncture}(k, x^*)$: On input the IPF key $k = (k^{(1)}, k^{(2)})$ and a point $x^* \in \mathcal{X}$ to be punctured, the puncturing algorithm first computes $v^* \leftarrow \mathsf{F}_1(k^{(1)}, x^*)$. It then generates two punctured keys $k_{x^*}^{(1)} \leftarrow \mathsf{F}_1.\mathsf{Puncture}(k^{(1)}, x^*)$ and $k_{v^*}^{(2)} \leftarrow \mathsf{F}_2.\mathsf{Puncture}(k^{(2)}, v^*)$ and returns $k_{x^*} = \big(k_{x^*}^{(1)}, k_{v^*}^{(2)}\big)$.*
- *$\mathsf{F}.\mathsf{Eval}(k_{x^*}, x)$: On input the punctured key $k_{x^*} = (k_{x^*}^{(1)}, k_{v^*}^{(2)})$ and a point $x \in \mathcal{X}$, the evaluation algorithm first computes $y_1 \leftarrow \mathsf{F}_1.\mathsf{Eval}(k_{x^*}^{(1)}, x)$ and returns $y = (y_1, \mathsf{F}_2.\mathsf{Eval}(k_{v^*}^{(2)}, y_1) \oplus x)$.*
- *$\mathsf{F}.\mathsf{Eval}^{-1}(k_{x^*}, y)$: On input the punctured key $k_{x^*} = (k_{x^*}^{(1)}, k_{v^*}^{(2)})$, and $y = (y_1, y_2) \in \mathcal{V} \times \mathcal{X} = \mathcal{Y}$, the inversion algorithm begins by computing the quantity $x \leftarrow \mathsf{F}_2.\mathsf{Eval}(k_{v^*}^{(2)}, y_1) \oplus y_2$. It returns $x$ if $\mathsf{F}_1.\mathsf{Eval}(k_{x^*}^{(1)}, x) = y_1$ and $\bot$ otherwise.*

We now state our correctness and security theorems. We provide the formal proofs in the full version [16].

**Theorem 4.2.** *Suppose $\mathsf{F}_1$ is an injective puncturable PRF and $\mathsf{F}_2$ is a puncturable PRF. Then, the IPF $(\mathsf{F}, \mathsf{F}^{-1})$ from Construction 4.1 is correct.*

**Theorem 4.3.** *Suppose* $\mathsf{F}_1$ *is a selectively-secure puncturable PRF,* $\mathsf{F}_2$ *is a selectively-secure, private puncturable PRF, and* $|\mathcal{X}|/|\mathcal{V}| = \mathrm{negl}(\lambda)$. *Then* $(\mathsf{F}, \mathsf{F}^{-1})$ *from Construction 4.1 is a selectively-secure puncturable IPF.*

*Remark 4.4 (Adaptive Security).* Theorem 4.3 shows that if the underlying puncturable PRFs in Construction 4.1 are selectively secure, then the resulting IPF is selectively secure. We note that if we instantiate the underlying PRFs with an adaptively-secure (private) puncturable PRF (for instance, the construction due to Canetti and Chen [24]), then the resulting IPF can also be shown to be adaptively secure (following a similar argument as that used in the proof of Theorem 4.3).

### 4.2 Circuit-Constrained IPF from Private Circuit-Constrained PRFs

In this section, we show how to extend our puncturable IPF construction from Sect. 4.1 to obtain a (single-key) constrained IPF for arbitrary circuit constraints. Our security analysis for our circuit-constrained IPF construction relies critically on the assumption that one of the underlying PRFs is a circuit-constrained PRF satisfying a strong simulation-based notion of privacy (Definition 3.14). Canetti and Chen [24] previously showed that even a 2-key private constrained PRF satisfying this simulation-based notion of privacy implies virtual black-box (VBB) obfuscation for the same underlying circuit class. Since VBB obfuscation for all circuits is impossible in the standard model [5], our construction is instantiatable only in the single-key setting, and thus, we present our construction in the single-key setting.

**Construction 4.5.** *Fix a domain* $\mathcal{X} = \{0,1\}^n$ *where* $n = n(\lambda)$. *Our circuit-constrained IPF construction for* $\mathsf{NC}^1$ *(resp.,* $\mathsf{P}/\mathsf{poly}$) *relies on several primitives:*

- *Let* $\mathsf{PKE} = (\mathsf{PKE.Setup}, \mathsf{PKE.Encrypt}, \mathsf{PKE.Decrypt})$ *be a PKE scheme with message space* $\mathcal{X}$, *ciphertext space* $\mathcal{T}$, *and whose decryption function can be computed in* $\mathsf{NC}^1$ *(resp.,* $\mathsf{P}/\mathsf{poly}$). *Let* $\mathcal{PK}$ *and* $\mathcal{SK}$ *denote the space of public keys and the space of secret keys, respectively, for* $\mathsf{PKE}$. *Let* $\mathcal{V}$ *denote the space from which the randomness for encryption is sampled.*
- *Let* $\mathsf{F}_1 : \mathcal{K}_1 \times \mathcal{X} \to \mathcal{V}$ *be a circuit-constrained PRF for* $\mathsf{NC}^1$ *(resp.,* $\mathsf{P}/\mathsf{poly}$).
- *Let* $\mathsf{F}_2 : \mathcal{K}_2 \times \mathcal{T} \to \mathcal{X}$ *be a private circuit-constrained PRF for* $\mathsf{NC}^1$ *(resp.,* $\mathsf{P}/\mathsf{poly}$).[3]

---

[3] To simplify the presentation, we implicitly assume that the PRFs $\mathsf{F}_1$ and $\mathsf{F}_2$ support general circuit constraints (i.e., $\mathsf{NC}^1$ constraints or $\mathsf{P}/\mathsf{poly}$ constraints). However, we can also instantiate our construction using private constrained PRFs for weaker constraint classes, provided that the constraint class is expressive enough to include the decryption algorithm for a CCA-secure public-key encryption scheme (see Remark 4.8).

*The constrained IPF* $F : \mathcal{K} \times \mathcal{X} \rightarrow \mathcal{Y}$ *with key-space* $\mathcal{K} = \mathcal{K}_1 \times \mathcal{K}_2 \times \mathcal{PK} \times \mathcal{SK}$, *domain* $\mathcal{X}$, *and range* $\mathcal{Y} \subseteq \mathcal{T} \times \mathcal{X}$ *is defined as follows:*

- *The IPF key consists of two PRF keys* $(k^{(1)}, k^{(2)}) \in \mathcal{K}_1 \times \mathcal{K}_2$ *for* $F_1$ *and* $F_2$, *respectively, and a public/secret key-pair* $(\mathsf{pk}, \mathsf{sk}) \in \mathcal{PK} \times \mathcal{SK}$ *for the public-key encryption scheme* PKE.
- *On input a key* $k = (k^{(1)}, k^{(2)}, \mathsf{pk}, \mathsf{sk}) \in \mathcal{K}$, *and* $x \in \mathcal{X}$, *the IPF* $F(k, x)$ *computes randomness* $r_x \leftarrow F_1(k^{(1)}, x)$, *a ciphertext* $\mathsf{ct} \leftarrow \mathsf{PKE.Encrypt}(\mathsf{pk}, x; r_x)$, *and outputs*

$$F(k, x) := \Big( \mathsf{ct}, \ F_2(k^{(2)}, \mathsf{ct}) \oplus x \Big).$$

*Note that the public key* pk *can also be included as part of the public parameters for the IPF.*

- *On input a key* $k = (k^{(1)}, k^{(2)}, \mathsf{pk}, \mathsf{sk}) \in \mathcal{K}$, *and* $(y_1, y_2) \in \mathcal{Y}$, *the inversion function* $F^{-1}(k, (y_1, y_2))$ *first computes* $x \leftarrow F_2(k^{(2)}, y_1) \oplus y_2$ *and* $r_x \leftarrow F_1(k^{(1)}, x)$. *Finally, it outputs*

$$F^{-1}(k, (y_1, y_2)) := \begin{cases} x & \textit{if } y_1 = \mathsf{PKE.Encrypt}(\mathsf{pk}, x; r_x) \\ \perp & \textit{otherwise.} \end{cases}$$

- *The range of the IPF* $\mathcal{Y}$ *is defined to be the space* $\mathcal{T}' \times \mathcal{X}$ *where* $\mathcal{T}' = \{\mathsf{PKE.Encrypt}(\mathsf{pk}, x; r)\}_{x \in \mathcal{X}, r \in \mathcal{V}}$ *is the subset of ciphertexts that correspond to a valid encryption of some message under the public key* pk.

*Next, we define the setup and constraining algorithms for* $(F, F^{-1})$.

- F.Setup($1^\lambda$): *On input the security parameter* $\lambda$, *the setup algorithm samples two PRF keys* $k^{(1)} \leftarrow F_1.\mathsf{Setup}(1^\lambda)$, $k^{(2)} \leftarrow F_2.\mathsf{Setup}(1^\lambda)$, *and a public/secret key-pair for the PKE scheme:* $(\mathsf{pk}, \mathsf{sk}) \leftarrow \mathsf{PKE.Setup}(1^\lambda)$. *It outputs the IPF key* $k = (k^{(1)}, k^{(2)}, \mathsf{pk}, \mathsf{sk})$.
- F.Constrain($k, f$): *On input the IPF key* $k = (k^{(1)}, k^{(2)}, \mathsf{pk}, \mathsf{sk})$ *and a constraint function* $f \in \mathcal{F}$, *the algorithm first constrains* $k_f^{(1)} \leftarrow F_1.\mathsf{Constrain}(k^{(1)}, f)$. *Then, it defines the function* $F_{\mathsf{sk}, f} : \mathcal{T} \rightarrow \{0, 1\}$ *as follows:*

$$F_{\mathsf{sk}, f}(\mathsf{ct}) := \begin{cases} 1 & \textit{if } \mathsf{PKE.Decrypt}(\mathsf{sk}, \mathsf{ct}) \neq \perp \textit{ and } f(\mathsf{PKE.Decrypt}(\mathsf{sk}, \mathsf{ct})) = 1 \\ 0 & \textit{otherwise.} \end{cases}$$

$$(4.1)$$

*The constrain algorithm constrains the key* $k^{(2)}$ *to* $F_{\mathsf{sk}, f}$ *and obtains* $k_F^{(2)} \leftarrow F_2.\mathsf{Constrain}(k^{(2)}, F_{\mathsf{sk}, f})$. *It then defines and returns the constrained key* $k_f = (k_f^{(1)}, k_F^{(2)}, \mathsf{pk})$. *Note that if* PKE.Decrypt($\mathsf{sk}, \cdot$) *can be computed in* $\mathsf{NC}^1$ *(resp.,* P/poly*), then the function* $F_{\mathsf{sk}, f}$ *can also be computed in* $\mathsf{NC}^1$ *(resp.,* P/poly*).*
- F.Eval($k_f, x$): *On input the constrained key* $k_f = (k_f^{(1)}, k_F^{(2)}, \mathsf{pk})$, *and a point* $x \in \mathcal{X}$, *the algorithm first computes* $r_x \leftarrow F_1.\mathsf{Eval}(k_f^{(1)}, x)$. *Then, it encrypts* $\mathsf{ct} \leftarrow \mathsf{PKE.Encrypt}(\mathsf{pk}, x; r_x)$ *and returns the tuple* $y = \Big( \mathsf{ct}, \ F_2.\mathsf{Eval}(k_F^{(2)}, \mathsf{ct}) \oplus x \Big)$.

– $\mathsf{F.Eval}^{-1}(k_f, y)$: *On input the constrained key* $k_f = (k_f^{(1)}, k_F^{(2)}, \mathsf{pk})$, *and a point* $y = (y_1, y_2) \in \mathcal{Y}$, *the algorithm first computes* $x \leftarrow \mathsf{F_2.Eval}(k_F^{(2)}, y_1) \oplus y_2$. *Then, it computes* $r_x \leftarrow \mathsf{F_1.Eval}(k_f^{(1)}, x)$ *and* $\mathsf{ct} \leftarrow \mathsf{PKE.Encrypt}(\mathsf{pk}, x; r_x)$. *If* $y_1 = \mathsf{ct}$, *then the algorithm returns* $x$. *Otherwise, it returns* $\bot$.

We now state our correctness and security theorems. We provide the formal proofs in the full version [16].

**Theorem 4.6.** *Suppose* $\mathsf{PKE}$ *is a public-key encryption scheme, and* $\mathsf{F_1}, \mathsf{F_2}$ *are circuit-constrained PRFs for* $\mathsf{NC}^1$ *(resp.,* $\mathsf{P/poly}$*). Then, the IPF* $(\mathsf{F}, \mathsf{F}^{-1})$ *from Construction 4.5 is a circuit-constrained IPF for* $\mathsf{NC}^1$ *(resp.,* $\mathsf{P/poly}$*).*

**Theorem 4.7.** *Suppose* $\mathsf{PKE}$ *is a smooth, CCA-secure public-key encryption scheme,* $\mathsf{F_1}$ *is a single-key selective-function-secure circuit-constrained PRF for* $\mathsf{NC}^1$ *(resp.,* $\mathsf{P/poly}$*), and* $\mathsf{F_2}$ *is a single-key, selective-function-secure private circuit-constrained PRF for* $\mathsf{NC}^1$ *(resp.,* $\mathsf{P/poly}$*). Then,* $(\mathsf{F}, \mathsf{F}^{-1})$ *from Construction 4.5 is a single-key, selective-function-secure circuit-constrained IPF for* $\mathsf{NC}^1$ *(resp.,* $\mathsf{P/poly}$*).*

*Remark 4.8 (Weaker Constraint Classes).* While Construction 4.5 gives a circuit-constrained IPF from private circuit-constrained PRFs, the same construction also applies for building constrained PRFs that support a weaker class of constraints. Specifically, given a private constrained PRF for some constraint family $\mathcal{F}$, if $\mathcal{F}$ is expressive enough to support the decryption operation of a CCA-secure PKE scheme (composed with the constraining function), then the constrained PRF for $\mathcal{F}$ can be leveraged to construct an IPF for the family $\mathcal{F}$ (via Construction 4.5).

*Remark 4.9 (Computational Notion of Smoothness).* As stated, Theorem 4.7 imposes an additional smoothness requirement (Definition 2.2) on the underlying public-key encryption scheme. While most semantically-secure public-key encryption schemes naturally satisfy this property, a weaker notion of "computational smoothness" also suffices for Theorem 4.7. In particular, we say a public-key encryption scheme $\mathsf{PKE} = (\mathsf{PKE.Setup}, \mathsf{PKE.Encrypt}, \mathsf{PKE.Decrypt})$ with message space $\mathcal{M}$ and ciphertext space $\mathcal{T}$ satisfies computational smoothness if for all messages $m \in \mathcal{M}$ output by an efficient adversary (on input the security parameter $\lambda$ and the public key $\mathsf{pk}$), and all strings $\mathsf{ct} \in \mathcal{T}$, $\Pr[\mathsf{PKE.Encrypt}(\mathsf{pk}, m) = \mathsf{ct}] = \mathsf{negl}(\lambda)$. Clearly, if $\mathsf{PKE}$ is semantically secure, then $\mathsf{PKE}$ satisfies computational smoothness. It is straightforward to modify the proof of Theorem 4.7 to rely on the computational version of smoothness. In this case, we can use any CCA-secure public-key encryption scheme to instantiate Construction 4.5.

# 5    Concrete Instantiations of Constrained IPFs

In this section, we describe how to concretely instantiate Constructions 4.1 and 4.5 using existing lattice-based private constrained PRFs [15, 22, 24] to obtain puncturable IPFs and circuit-constrained IPFs (for both $\mathsf{NC}^1$ and $\mathsf{P/poly}$), respectively, from standard lattice assumptions.

*Puncturable IPFs from lattices.* To apply Construction 4.1, we require an injective puncturable PRF and a private puncturable PRF. As shown in [51], (statistically) injective puncturable PRFs[4] can be built from any one-way function. Next, the recent works of [15,22,24] show how to construct private puncturable PRFs from standard lattice assumptions. Thus, applying Construction 4.1, we obtain puncturable IPFs from standard lattice assumptions. In fact, the construction of Canetti and Chen [24] gives an adaptively-secure private puncturable PRF from the (polynomial) hardness of the learning with errors (LWE) problem [47], and so, combining their construction with Theorem 4.3, we obtain an adaptively-secure puncturable IPF from the (polynomial) hardness of LWE with subexponential error rate.

*Circuit-constrained IPFs from lattices.* Starting from (single-key) private circuit-constrained PRFs for $\mathsf{NC}^1$ [24] and $\mathsf{P/poly}$ [22], we can leverage Construction 4.5 to obtain (single-key) circuit-constrained IPFs for $\mathsf{NC}^1$ and $\mathsf{P/poly}$, respectively. We give two candidate instantiations based on standard lattice assumptions:

- To construct a circuit-constrained IPF for $\mathsf{NC}^1$-constraints, we require a private circuit-constrained PRF for $\mathsf{NC}^1$ and a CCA-secure public-key encryption scheme with an $\mathsf{NC}^1$ decryption circuit. We can instantiate the private circuit-constrained PRF for $\mathsf{NC}^1$ using the construction of Canetti and Chen [24]. The CCA-secure encryption scheme with $\mathsf{NC}^1$ decryption can be instantiated using existing lattice-based CCA-secure PKE schemes [42,44,45] or by applying the Boneh et al. [14] transformation to a suitable identity-based encryption (IBE) scheme [1,2,25,33] and a message authentication code (MAC) with verification in $\mathsf{NC}^1$, which can be built from lattice-based PRFs [3,4,17]. Putting these pieces together, we obtain a (single-key) circuit-constrained IPF for $\mathsf{NC}^1$ constraints from standard lattice assumptions.
- To construct a circuit-constrained IPF for $\mathsf{P/poly}$, we primarily require a private constrained PRF for $\mathsf{P/poly}$. We instantiate the private circuit-constrained PRF using the recent construction of Brakerski et al. [22], and the CCA-secure public key encryption as above. This yields a secure (single-key) circuit-constrained IPF for general predicates from standard lattice assumptions.

*Remark 5.1 (Relaxed Notions of Correctness).* Several lattice-based constrained PRF constructions [15,22,23] satisfy a weaker "computational" notion of correctness which roughly states that an efficient adversary with a constrained key $k_f$ cannot find an input $x$ where $\mathsf{F.Eval}(k_f, x) \neq \mathsf{F}(k, x)$, where $k$ is the PRF key. If we instantiate Constructions 4.1 and 4.5 with a constrained PRF that satisfies

---

[4] A statistically injective puncturable PRF is a puncturable PRF $\mathsf{F}$ where $\mathsf{F}(k, \cdot)$ is injective with overwhelming probability over the choice of coins used for sampling the key $k \leftarrow \mathsf{F.Setup}(1^\lambda)$.

a computational notion of correctness, then the resulting constrained IPF also achieves computational correctness. It is straightforward to modify the correctness analysis (Theorems 4.2 and 4.6) to work under a computational notion of correctness. The security analysis remains unchanged since none of the proofs rely on perfect correctness of the underlying constrained PRFs.

# 6    An Extension: Supporting Delegation

In a delegatable constrained IPF, the holder of a constrained IPF key $k_f$ for a function $f$ can further constrain the key to some function $g$ (i.e., construct a key $k_{f \wedge g}$ that allows IPF evaluation only on points $x$ where $f(x) = g(x) = 1$). Many constrained PRF constructions either support or can be modified to support some flavor of key delegation [19,26,27]. In this section, we describe (informally) how to extend our constrained IPF construction from Sect. 4.2 to support key delegation.

*Delegatable constrained PRFs.* A constrained PRF that supports one level of delegation can be generically constructed from any constrained PRF by defining the PRF output to be the xor of the outputs of two constrained PRFs. For instance, we can define a PRF $\mathsf{F}$ as follows:

$$\mathsf{F}((k_1, k_2), x) := \mathsf{F}_1(k^{(1)}, x) \oplus \mathsf{F}_2(k^{(2)}, x),$$

where $\mathsf{F}_1$ and $\mathsf{F}_2$ are constrained PRFs. The master secret key is $k^{(1)}$ and $k^{(2)}$, and the constrained key for a function $f$ is $(k_f^{(1)}, k^{(2)})$ where $k^{(1)} \leftarrow \mathsf{F}_1.\mathsf{Constrain}(k^{(1)}, f)$. The holder of the constrained key $(k_f^{(1)}, k^{(2)})$ can further constrain to a function of the form $f \wedge g$ by computing $(k_f^{(1)}, k_g^{(2)})$ where $k_g^{(2)} \leftarrow \mathsf{F}_2.\mathsf{Constrain}(k^{(2)}, g)$. Security of this construction follows by a simple hybrid argument. This general technique can be extended to support any a priori polynomially-bounded delegation depth.

*Delegatable constrained IPFs.* We can define a similar notion of key delegation for constrained IPFs. However, the above method of xoring together the outputs of several constrained IPFs does not directly give a delegatable constrained IPF. In fact, xoring together the outputs of several IPFs may not even give an injective function, let alone an efficiently invertible one. Thus, to support delegation for a constrained IPF, we need a different construction. One method is to use a variant of the xoring trick in conjunction with Construction 4.5. We describe a construction for achieving one level of delegation here. Our construction relies on a CCA-secure public-key encryption scheme $\mathsf{PKE}$, three constrained PRFs $\mathsf{F}_1, \mathsf{F}_2, \mathsf{F}_3$, and a constrained IPF $\mathsf{IPF}$. The master secret key consists of keys $k^{(1)}, k^{(2)}, k^{(3)}$ for $\mathsf{F}_1, \mathsf{F}_2$, and $\mathsf{F}_3$, respectively, a key $k^{(\mathsf{IPF})}$ for $\mathsf{IPF}$, and the public/secret key-pair pk, sk for the PKE scheme. Our delegatable IPF works as follows:

$$
F((k^{(1)}, k^{(2)}, k^{(3)}, k^{(\mathsf{IPF})}, \mathsf{pk}, \mathsf{sk}),\ x) := \left\{ \begin{array}{l} r \leftarrow \mathsf{F}_1(k^{(1)}, x) \oplus \mathsf{F}_3(k^{(3)}, x) \\ \mathsf{ct} \leftarrow \mathsf{PKE.Encrypt}(\mathsf{pk}, x; r) \\ z \leftarrow \mathsf{F}_2(k^{(2)}, \mathsf{ct}) \oplus \mathsf{IPF}(k^{(\mathsf{IPF})}, x) \\ \text{output } (\mathsf{ct}, z) \end{array} \right\}
$$

$$
F^{-1}((k^{(1)}, k^{(2)}, k^{(3)}, k^{(\mathsf{IPF})}, \mathsf{pk}, \mathsf{sk}),\ (\mathsf{ct}, z)) := \left\{ \begin{array}{l} x \leftarrow \mathsf{IPF}^{-1}(k^{(\mathsf{IPF})}, z \oplus \mathsf{F}_2(k^{(2)}, \mathsf{ct})) \\ r \leftarrow \mathsf{F}_1(k^{(1)}, x) \oplus \mathsf{F}_3(k^{(3)}, x) \\ \text{if } \mathsf{ct} \neq \mathsf{PKE.Encrypt}(\mathsf{pk}, x; r) \\ \quad \text{then } x \leftarrow \perp \\ \text{output } x \end{array} \right\}
$$

To constrain a key $(k^{(1)}, k^{(2)}, k^{(3)}, k^{(\mathsf{IPF})}, \mathsf{pk}, \mathsf{sk})$ to a function $f$, we first constrain the PRF keys $k^{(1)}$, $k^{(2)}$ exactly as described in Construction 4.5. In particular, the constrain algorithm computes $k_f^{(1)} \leftarrow \mathsf{F}_1.\mathsf{Constrain}(k^{(1)}, f)$ and $k_F^{(2)} \leftarrow \mathsf{F}_2.\mathsf{Constrain}(k^{(2)}, F_{\mathsf{sk},f})$, where $F_{\mathsf{sk},f}$ is defined as in Eq. (4.1). The constrained key is the tuple $k_f = (k_f^{(1)}, k_F^{(2)}, k^{(3)}, k^{(\mathsf{IPF})}, \mathsf{pk})$. To further constrain (that is, delegate) to a function $g$, we constrain $\mathsf{F}_3$ and $\mathsf{IPF}$ to $g$. In other words, we compute $k_g^{(3)} \leftarrow \mathsf{F}_3.\mathsf{Constrain}(k^{(3)}, g)$ and $k_g^{(\mathsf{IPF})} \leftarrow \mathsf{IPF}.\mathsf{Constrain}(k^{(\mathsf{IPF})}, g)$. The constrained key $k_{f \wedge g}$ for the function $f \wedge g$ is defined to be $k_{f \wedge g} := (k_f^{(1)}, k_F^{(2)}, k_g^{(3)}, k_g^{(\mathsf{IPF})}, \mathsf{pk})$. Security of this construction follows by a similar argument as that used in the proof of Theorem 4.7 (namely, by appealing to security of $\mathsf{F}_1$ and privacy as well as security of $\mathsf{F}_2$), in addition to security of $\mathsf{F}_3$ and the underlying IPF. Our construction can be viewed as taking a standard constrained IPF (that does not support key delegation), and constructing a constrained IPF that supports one level of delegation. Iterating this construction multiple times yields an IPF that can support any a priori bounded number of delegations.

## 7    Multi-key Constrained IPF from Obfuscation

In this section, we construct a *multi-key* circuit-constrained IPF from (polynomially-hard) indistinguishability obfuscation and one-way functions. Our construction of a circuit-constrained IPF from $i\mathcal{O}$ (and one-way functions) mirrors the Boneh-Zhandry construction [20] of a circuit-constrained PRF from $i\mathcal{O}$ (and one-way functions). More precisely, Boneh and Zhandry show that obfuscating a puncturable PRF effectively gives a circuit-constrained PRF. Similarly, our construction works by obfuscating our punctured IPF construction (Construction 4.1) using $i\mathcal{O}$. In our construction, each constrained IPF key contains two obfuscated programs: one for evaluating the IPF, and one for inverting the IPF. The constraint function $f$ is embedded within the obfuscated evaluation and inversion programs. We now describe our scheme more formally. First, we review the standard definition of indistinguishability obfuscation [5,32].

**Definition 7.1 (Indistinguishability Obfuscation [5,32]).** *An indistinguishability obfuscator $i\mathcal{O}$ for a circuit class $\mathcal{C}$ is a uniform and efficient algorithm satisfying the following requirements:*

– **Correctness.** *For all security parameter $\lambda \in \mathbb{N}$, all circuits $C \in \mathcal{C}$, and all inputs $x$, we have that*

$$
\Pr[C' \leftarrow i\mathcal{O}(C) : C'(x) = C(x)] = 1.
$$

- **Indistinguishability.** *For all security parameter* $\lambda \in \mathbb{N}$, *and any two circuits* $C_0, C_1 \in \mathcal{C}_\lambda$, *if* $C_0(x) = C_1(x)$ *for all inputs* $x$, *then for all efficient adversaries* $\mathcal{A}$, *we have that*

$$|\Pr[\mathcal{A}(i\mathcal{O}(C_0)) = 1] - \Pr[\mathcal{A}(i\mathcal{O}(C_1)) = 1]| = \text{negl}(\lambda).$$

**Construction 7.2.** *Fix a domain* $\mathcal{X} = \{0,1\}^n$ *where* $n = n(\lambda)$. *Let* $\mathsf{F}_1 \colon \mathcal{K}_1 \times \mathcal{X} \to \mathcal{V}$ *be a puncturable PRF with key-space* $\mathcal{K}_1$ *and range* $\mathcal{V}$. *Let* $\mathsf{F}_2 \colon \mathcal{K}_2 \times \mathcal{V} \to \mathcal{X}$ *be a puncturable PRF with key-space* $\mathcal{K}_2$. *The constrained IPF* $\mathsf{F} : \mathcal{K} \times \mathcal{X} \to \mathcal{Y}$ *with key-space* $\mathcal{K} = \mathcal{K}_1 \times \mathcal{K}_2$, *domain* $\mathcal{X}$, *and range* $\mathcal{Y} = \mathcal{V} \times \mathcal{X}$ *is defined as follows:*

- *The IPF key is a pair of keys* $k = (k^{(1)}, k^{(2)}) \in \mathcal{K}_1 \times \mathcal{K}_2 = \mathcal{K}$. *On input a key* $(k^{(1)}, k^{(2)})$ *and an input* $x \in \mathcal{X}$, *the value of the IPF is defined to be*

$$\mathsf{F}(k, x) := \left( \mathsf{F}_1(k^{(1)}, x), \ \mathsf{F}_2(k^{(2)}, \mathsf{F}_1(k^{(1)}, x)) \oplus x \right).$$

- *On input* $k = (k^{(1)}, k^{(2)}) \in \mathcal{K}_1 \times \mathcal{K}_2 = \mathcal{K}$, *and* $y = (y_1, y_2) \in \mathcal{V} \times \mathcal{X} = \mathcal{Y}$, *the inversion algorithm* $\mathsf{F}^{-1}(k, y)$ *first computes* $x \leftarrow \mathsf{F}_2(k^{(2)}, y_1) \oplus y_2$ *and outputs*

$$\mathsf{F}^{-1}(k, (y_1, y_2)) := \begin{cases} x & \text{if } y_1 = \mathsf{F}_1(k^{(1)}, x) \\ \perp & \text{otherwise.} \end{cases}$$

*Next, we define the setup and constraining algorithms for the IPF* $(\mathsf{F}, \mathsf{F}^{-1})$.

- $\mathsf{F}.\mathsf{Setup}(1^\lambda)$: *On input the security parameter* $\lambda$, *the setup algorithm samples two puncturable PRF keys* $k^{(1)} \leftarrow \mathsf{F}_1.\mathsf{Setup}(1^\lambda)$ *and* $k^{(2)} \leftarrow \mathsf{F}_2.\mathsf{Setup}(1^\lambda)$, *and outputs* $k = (k^{(1)}, k^{(2)})$.
- $\mathsf{F}.\mathsf{Constrain}(k, f)$: *On input the IPF key* $k = (k^{(1)}, k^{(2)})$ *and a constraint function* $f \in \mathcal{F}$, *the constrain algorithm outputs two obfuscated programs* $P_0 = i\mathcal{O}(P^{\mathsf{Eval}}[f, k^{(1)}, k^{(2)}])$ *and* $P_1 = i\mathcal{O}(P^{\mathsf{Inv}}[f, k^{(1)}, k^{(2)}])$ *where the programs* $P^{\mathsf{Eval}}[f, k^{(1)}, k^{(2)}]$ *and* $P^{\mathsf{Inv}}[f, k^{(1)}, k^{(2)}]$ *are defined in Figs. 1 and 2. Note that the programs* $P^{\mathsf{Eval}}$ *and* $P^{\mathsf{Inv}}$ *are padded to the maximum size of any program that appears in the proof of Theorem 7.4.*
- $\mathsf{F}.\mathsf{Eval}(k_f, x)$: *On input the constrained key* $k_f = (P_1, P_2)$, *and a point* $x \in \mathcal{X}$, *the evaluation algorithm outputs* $P_1(x)$.
- $\mathsf{F}.\mathsf{Eval}^{-1}(k_f, y)$: *On input the constrained key* $k_f = (P_1, P_2)$, *and a point* $y \in \mathcal{Y}$, *the inversion algorithm outputs* $P_2(y)$.

We now state our correctness and security theorems. We provide the formal proofs in the full version [16].

**Theorem 7.3.** *Suppose* $\mathsf{F}_1$ *and* $\mathsf{F}_2$ *are puncturable PRFs, and* $i\mathcal{O}$ *is an indistinguishability obfuscator. Then, the IPF* $(\mathsf{F}, \mathsf{F}^{-1})$ *from Construction 7.2 is correct.*

**Theorem 7.4.** *Suppose* $\mathsf{F}_1$ *and* $\mathsf{F}_2$ *are selectively-secure puncturable PRFs,* $i\mathcal{O}$ *is an indistinguishability obfuscator, and* $|\mathcal{X}| / |\mathcal{V}| = \text{negl}(\lambda)$. *Then* $(\mathsf{F}, \mathsf{F}^{-1})$ *from Construction 7.2 is a selectively-secure circuit-constrained IPF.*

***Constants:*** *a function* $f \in \mathcal{F}$, *and two keys* $k^{(1)}$ *and* $k^{(2)}$ *for* $\mathsf{F}_1$ *and* $\mathsf{F}_2$, *respectively.*

*On input* $x \in \mathcal{X}$:

1. *If* $f(x) = 0$, *output* $\perp$.
2. *Otherwise, output* $\mathsf{F}(k, x) = \big(\mathsf{F}_1(k^{(1)}, x), \mathsf{F}_2(k^{(2)}, \mathsf{F}_1(k^{(1)}, x)) \oplus x\big)$.

**Fig. 1.** The program $P^{\mathsf{Eval}}[f, k^{(1)}, k^{(2)}]$

***Constants:*** *a function* $f \in \mathcal{F}$, *and two keys* $k^{(1)}$ *and* $k^{(2)}$ *for* $\mathsf{F}_1$ *and* $\mathsf{F}_2$, *respectively.*

*On input* $y = (y_1, y_2) \in \mathcal{V} \times \mathcal{X}$

1. *Compute* $x \leftarrow \mathsf{F}_2(k^{(2)}, y_1) \oplus y_2$.
2. *If* $f(x) = 0$ *or* $y_1 \neq \mathsf{F}_1(k^{(1)}, x)$, *output* $\perp$.
3. *Otherwise, output* $x$.

**Fig. 2.** The program $P^{\mathsf{Inv}}[f, k^{(1)}, k^{(2)}]$

**Acknowledgments.** We thank the anonymous TCC reviewers for helpful comments on this work. This work was funded by NSF, the DARPA/ARL SAFEWARE project, a grant from ONR, and the Simons Foundation. Opinions, findings and conclusions or recommendations expressed in this material are those of the authors and do not necessarily reflect the views of DARPA.

# References

1. Agrawal, S., Boneh, D., Boyen, X.: Efficient lattice (H)IBE in the standard model. In: Gilbert, H. (ed.) EUROCRYPT 2010. LNCS, vol. 6110, pp. 553–572. Springer, Heidelberg (2010). https://doi.org/10.1007/978-3-642-13190-5_28
2. Agrawal, S., Boneh, D., Boyen, X.: Lattice basis delegation in fixed dimension and shorter-ciphertext hierarchical IBE. In: Rabin, T. (ed.) CRYPTO 2010. LNCS, vol. 6223, pp. 98–115. Springer, Heidelberg (2010). https://doi.org/10.1007/978-3-642-14623-7_6
3. Banerjee, A., Peikert, C.: New and improved key-homomorphic pseudorandom functions. In: Garay, J.A., Gennaro, R. (eds.) CRYPTO 2014. LNCS, vol. 8616, pp. 353–370. Springer, Heidelberg (2014). https://doi.org/10.1007/978-3-662-44371-2_20

4. Banerjee, A., Peikert, C., Rosen, A.: Pseudorandom functions and lattices. In: Pointcheval, D., Johansson, T. (eds.) EUROCRYPT 2012. LNCS, vol. 7237, pp. 719–737. Springer, Heidelberg (2012). https://doi.org/10.1007/978-3-642-29011-4_42

5. Barak, B., Goldreich, O., Impagliazzo, R., Rudich, S., Sahai, A., Vadhan, S.P., Yang, K.: On the (im)possibility of obfuscating programs. In: Kilian, J. (ed.) CRYPTO 2001. LNCS, vol. 2139, pp. 1–18. Springer, Heidelberg (2001). https://doi.org/10.1007/3-540-44647-8_1

6. Bellare, M., Boldyreva, A., O'Neill, A.: Deterministic and efficiently searchable encryption. In: Menezes, A. (ed.) CRYPTO 2007. LNCS, vol. 4622, pp. 535–552. Springer, Heidelberg (2007). https://doi.org/10.1007/978-3-540-74143-5_30

7. Bellare, M., Fischlin, M., O'Neill, A., Ristenpart, T.: Deterministic encryption: definitional equivalences and constructions without random oracles. In: Wagner, D. (ed.) CRYPTO 2008. LNCS, vol. 5157, pp. 360–378. Springer, Heidelberg (2008). https://doi.org/10.1007/978-3-540-85174-5_20

8. Bellare, M., Fuchsbauer, G.: Policy-based signatures. In: Krawczyk, H. (ed.) PKC 2014. LNCS, vol. 8383, pp. 520–537. Springer, Heidelberg (2014). https://doi.org/10.1007/978-3-642-54631-0_30

9. Bellare, M., Hofheinz, D., Kiltz, E.: Subtleties in the definition of IND-CCA: when and how should challenge decryption be disallowed? J. Cryptol. **28**(1), 29–48 (2015)

10. Bellare, M., Namprempre, C.: Authenticated encryption: relations among notions and analysis of the generic composition paradigm. In: Okamoto, T. (ed.) ASIACRYPT 2000. LNCS, vol. 1976, pp. 531–545. Springer, Heidelberg (2000). https://doi.org/10.1007/3-540-44448-3_41

11. Bellare, M., Rogaway, P.: Encode-then-encipher encryption: how to exploit nonces or redundancy in plaintexts for efficient cryptography. In: Okamoto, T. (ed.) ASIACRYPT 2000. LNCS, vol. 1976, pp. 317–330. Springer, Heidelberg (2000). https://doi.org/10.1007/3-540-44448-3_24

12. Boldyreva, A., Fehr, S., O'Neill, A.: On notions of security for deterministic encryption, and efficient constructions without random oracles. In: Wagner, D. (ed.) CRYPTO 2008. LNCS, vol. 5157, pp. 335–359. Springer, Heidelberg (2008). https://doi.org/10.1007/978-3-540-85174-5_19

13. Boneh, D., Boyen, X.: Efficient selective-ID secure identity-based encryption without random oracles. In: Cachin, C., Camenisch, J.L. (eds.) EUROCRYPT 2004. LNCS, vol. 3027, pp. 223–238. Springer, Heidelberg (2004). https://doi.org/10.1007/978-3-540-24676-3_14

14. Boneh, D., Canetti, R., Halevi, S., Katz, J.: Chosen-ciphertext security from identity-based encryption. SIAM J. Comput. **36**(5), 1301–1328 (2007)

15. Boneh, D., Kim, S., Montgomery, H.: Private puncturable PRFs from standard lattice assumptions. In: Coron, J.-S., Nielsen, J.B. (eds.) EUROCRYPT 2017. LNCS, vol. 10210, pp. 415–445. Springer, Cham (2017). https://doi.org/10.1007/978-3-319-56620-7_15

16. Boneh, D., Kim, S., Wu, D.J.: Constrained keys for invertible pseudorandom functions. Cryptology ePrint Archive, Report 2017/477 (2017). http://eprint.iacr.org/2017/477

17. Boneh, D., Lewi, K., Montgomery, H.W., Raghunathan, A.: Key homomorphic PRFs and their applications. In: Canetti, R., Garay, J.A. (eds.) CRYPTO 2013. LNCS, vol. 8042, pp. 410–428. Springer, Heidelberg (2013). https://doi.org/10.1007/978-3-642-40041-4_23

18. Boneh, D., Lewi, K., Wu, D.J.: Constraining pseudorandom functions privately. In: Fehr, S. (ed.) PKC 2017. LNCS, vol. 10175, pp. 494–524. Springer, Heidelberg (2017). https://doi.org/10.1007/978-3-662-54388-7_17

19. Boneh, D., Waters, B.: Constrained pseudorandom functions and their applications. In: Sako, K., Sarkar, P. (eds.) ASIACRYPT 2013. LNCS, vol. 8270, pp. 280–300. Springer, Heidelberg (2013). https://doi.org/10.1007/978-3-642-42045-0_15

20. Boneh, D., Zhandry, M.: Multiparty key exchange, efficient traitor tracing, and more from indistinguishability obfuscation. In: Garay, J.A., Gennaro, R. (eds.) CRYPTO 2014. LNCS, vol. 8616, pp. 480–499. Springer, Heidelberg (2014). https://doi.org/10.1007/978-3-662-44371-2_27

21. Boyle, E., Goldwasser, S., Ivan, I.: Functional signatures and pseudorandom functions. In: Krawczyk, H. (ed.) PKC 2014. LNCS, vol. 8383, pp. 501–519. Springer, Heidelberg (2014). https://doi.org/10.1007/978-3-642-54631-0_29

22. Brakerski, Z., Tsabary, R., Vaikuntanathan, V., Wee, H.: Private constrained PRFs (and more) from LWE. In: TCC (2017)

23. Brakerski, Z., Vaikuntanathan, V.: Constrained key-homomorphic PRFs from standard lattice assumptions - or: how to secretly embed a circuit in your PRF. In: Dodis, Y., Nielsen, J.B. (eds.) TCC 2015. LNCS, vol. 9015, pp. 1–30. Springer, Heidelberg (2015). https://doi.org/10.1007/978-3-662-46497-7_1

24. Canetti, R., Chen, Y.: Constraint-hiding constrained PRFs for $NC^1$ from LWE. In: Coron, J.-S., Nielsen, J.B. (eds.) EUROCRYPT 2017. LNCS, vol. 10210, pp. 446–476. Springer, Cham (2017). https://doi.org/10.1007/978-3-319-56620-7_16

25. Cash, D., Hofheinz, D., Kiltz, E., Peikert, C.: Bonsai trees, or how to delegate a lattice basis. In: Gilbert, H. (ed.) EUROCRYPT 2010. LNCS, vol. 6110, pp. 523–552. Springer, Heidelberg (2010). https://doi.org/10.1007/978-3-642-13190-5_27

26. Chandran, N., Raghuraman, S., Vinayagamurthy, D.: Constrained pseudorandom functions: verifiable and delegatable. IACR Cryptology ePrint Archive 2014 (2014)

27. Datta, P., Dutta, R., Mukhopadhyay, S.: Constrained pseudorandom functions for unconstrained inputs revisited: achieving verifiability and key delegation. In: Fehr, S. (ed.) PKC 2017. LNCS, vol. 10175, pp. 463–493. Springer, Heidelberg (2017). https://doi.org/10.1007/978-3-662-54388-7_16

28. Deshpande, A., Koppula, V., Waters, B.: Constrained pseudorandom functions for unconstrained inputs. In: Fischlin, M., Coron, J.-S. (eds.) EUROCRYPT 2016. LNCS, vol. 9666, pp. 124–153. Springer, Heidelberg (2016). https://doi.org/10.1007/978-3-662-49896-5_5

29. Fuchsbauer, G.: Constrained verifiable random functions. IACR Cryptology ePrint Archive 2014 (2014)

30. Fuchsbauer, G., Konstantinov, M., Pietrzak, K., Rao, V.: Adaptive security of constrained PRFs. In: Sarkar, P., Iwata, T. (eds.) ASIACRYPT 2014. LNCS, vol. 8874, pp. 82–101. Springer, Heidelberg (2014). https://doi.org/10.1007/978-3-662-45608-8_5

31. Fuller, B., O'Neill, A., Reyzin, L.: A unified approach to deterministic encryption: new constructions and a connection to computational entropy. In: Cramer, R. (ed.) TCC 2012. LNCS, vol. 7194, pp. 582–599. Springer, Heidelberg (2012). https://doi.org/10.1007/978-3-642-28914-9_33

32. Garg, S., Gentry, C., Halevi, S., Raykova, M., Sahai, A., Waters, B.: Candidate indistinguishability obfuscation and functional encryption for all circuits. In: FOCS (2013)

33. Gentry, C., Peikert, C., Vaikuntanathan, V.: Trapdoors for hard lattices and new cryptographic constructions. In: STOC (2008)

34. Goldreich, O., Goldwasser, S., Micali, S.: How to construct random functions. In: FOCS (1984)
35. Hofheinz, D.: Fully secure constrained pseudorandom functions using random oracles. IACR Cryptology ePrint Archive 2014 (2014)
36. Hohenberger, S., Koppula, V., Waters, B.: Adaptively secure puncturable pseudorandom functions in the standard model. In: Iwata, T., Cheon, J.H. (eds.) ASIACRYPT 2015. LNCS, vol. 9452, pp. 79–102. Springer, Heidelberg (2015). https://doi.org/10.1007/978-3-662-48797-6_4
37. Iwata, T., Yasuda, K.: BTM: a single-key, inverse-cipher-free mode for deterministic authenticated encryption. In: Jacobson, M.J., Rijmen, V., Safavi-Naini, R. (eds.) SAC 2009. LNCS, vol. 5867, pp. 313–330. Springer, Heidelberg (2009). https://doi.org/10.1007/978-3-642-05445-7_20
38. Iwata, T., Yasuda, K.: HBS: a single-key mode of operation for deterministic authenticated encryption. In: Dunkelman, O. (ed.) FSE 2009. LNCS, vol. 5665, pp. 394–415. Springer, Heidelberg (2009). https://doi.org/10.1007/978-3-642-03317-9_24
39. Katz, J., Yung, M.: Unforgeable encryption and chosen ciphertext secure modes of operation. In: Goos, G., Hartmanis, J., van Leeuwen, J., Schneier, B. (eds.) FSE 2000. LNCS, vol. 1978, pp. 284–299. Springer, Heidelberg (2001). https://doi.org/10.1007/3-540-44706-7_20
40. Kiayias, A., Papadopoulos, S., Triandopoulos, N., Zacharias, T.: Delegatable pseudorandom functions and applications. In: ACM CCS (2013)
41. Luby, M., Rackoff, C.: How to construct pseudorandom permutations from pseudorandom functions. SIAM J. Comput. **17**(2), 373–386 (1988)
42. Micciancio, D., Peikert, C.: Trapdoors for lattices: simpler, tighter, faster, smaller. In: Pointcheval, D., Johansson, T. (eds.) EUROCRYPT 2012. LNCS, vol. 7237, pp. 700–718. Springer, Heidelberg (2012). https://doi.org/10.1007/978-3-642-29011-4_41
43. Naor, M., Yung, M.: Public-key cryptosystems provably secure against chosen ciphertext attacks. In: STOC (1990)
44. Peikert, C.: Bonsai trees (or, arboriculture in lattice-based cryptography). IACR Cryptology ePrint Archive 2009 (2009)
45. Peikert, C., Waters, B.: Lossy trapdoor functions and their applications. In: STOC (2008)
46. Rackoff, C., Simon, D.R.: Non-interactive zero-knowledge proof of knowledge and chosen ciphertext attack. In: Feigenbaum, J. (ed.) CRYPTO 1991. LNCS, vol. 576, pp. 433–444. Springer, Heidelberg (1992). https://doi.org/10.1007/3-540-46766-1_35
47. Regev, O.: On lattices, learning with errors, random linear codes, and cryptography. In: STOC (2005)
48. Rogaway, P.: Authenticated-encryption with associated-data. In: ACM CCS (2002)
49. Rogaway, P., Bellare, M., Black, J.: OCB: a block-cipher mode of operation for efficient authenticated encryption. ACM Trans. Inf. Syst. Secur. (TISSEC) **6**(3), 365–403 (2003)
50. Rogaway, P., Shrimpton, T.: Deterministic authenticated encryption: a provable-security treatment of the key-wrap problem. In: EUROCRYPT (2006)
51. Sahai, A., Waters, B.: How to use indistinguishability obfuscation: deniable encryption, and more. In: STOC (2014)

# Private Constrained PRFs (and More) from LWE

Zvika Brakerski[1], Rotem Tsabary[1], Vinod Vaikuntanathan[2(✉)], and Hoeteck Wee[3]

[1] Weizmann Institute of Science, Rehovot, Israel
[2] MIT, Cambridge, USA
vinodv@mit.edu
[3] CNRS and ENS, Paris, France

**Abstract.** In a constrained PRF, the owner of the PRF key $K$ can generate constrained keys $K_f$ that allow anyone to evaluate the PRF on inputs $x$ that satisfy the predicate $f$ (namely, where $f(x)$ is "true") but reveal no information about the PRF evaluation on the other inputs. A private constrained PRF goes further by requiring that the constrained key $K_f$ hides the predicate $f$.

Boneh, Kim and Montgomery (EUROCRYPT 2017) recently presented a construction of private constrained PRF for point function constraints, and Canetti and Chen (EUROCRYPT 2017) presented a completely different construction for more general $NC^1$ constraints. In this work, we show two constructions of LWE-based constraint-hiding constrained PRFs for *general predicates* described by polynomial-size circuits.

The two constructions are based on two distinct techniques that we show have further applicability, by constructing weak attribute-hiding predicate encryption schemes. In a nutshell, the first construction imports the technique of *modulus switching* from the FHE world into the domain of trapdoor extension and homomorphism. The second construction shows how to use the duality between FHE secret-key/randomness and ABE randomness/secret-key to construct a scheme with *dual use* of the same values for both FHE and ABE purposes.

## 1 Introduction

Lattice-based cryptography, and in particular the construction of cryptographic primitives based on the learning with errors (LWE) assumption [Reg05], has seen

---

Z. Brakerski and R. Tsabary—Supported by the Israel Science Foundation (Grant No. 468/14), Binational Science Foundation (Grants No. 2016726, 2014276) and ERC Project 756482 REACT.

V. Vaikuntanathan—Research supported in part by NSF Grants CNS-1350619 and CNS-1414119, Alfred P. Sloan Research Fellowship, Microsoft Faculty Fellowship and by the Defense Advanced Research Projects Agency (DARPA) and the U.S. Army Research Office under contracts W911NF-15-C-0226 and W911NF-15-C-0236.

H. Wee—Supported in part by ERC Project aSCEND (H2020 639554) and NSF Award CNS-1445424.

Y. Kalai and L. Reyzin (Eds.): TCC 2017, Part I, LNCS 10677, pp. 264–302, 2017.
https://doi.org/10.1007/978-3-319-70500-2_10

a significant leap in recent years. Most notably, we now have a number of constructions of cryptographic primitives that "compute on encrypted data". For example, fully homomorphic encryption (FHE) [Gen09, BV11, BGV12, GSW13], which enables arbitrary computation on encrypted data without knowledge of the secret key; attribute-based encryption (ABE) [SW05, GPSW06, GVW13, BGG+14], which supports fine-grained access control of encrypted data via the creation of restricted secret keys; new forms of pseudo-random functions (PRF) such as constrained PRFs [BW13, KPTZ13, BGI14]; and many more.

In this paper, we continue this line of inquiry and develop two new constructions of weak attribute-hiding predicate encryption schemes [BW07, KSW08, BSW11, O'N10] and two new constructions of private constrained PRFs [BLW17]. These are private variants of ABE and constrained PRFs respectively, that take us further along in the quest to extend the limits of computing on encrypted data using LWE-based techniques. Our private constrained PRFs support polynomial-time computable constraints, generalizing the recent results of Boneh, Kim and Montgomery [BKM17] for point functions and Canetti and Chen [CC17] for $NC^1$ functions.

In constructing these schemes, we develop two new techniques that we believe are as interesting in their own right as the end results themselves. We proceed to introduce the protagonists of our work and describe our results and techniques.

*Predicate Encryption.* Predicate Encryption (PE) is a strengthening of ABE with additional privacy guarantees [BW07, KSW08, BSW11, O'N10]. In a predicate encryption scheme, ciphertexts are associated with descriptive attributes $x$ and a plaintext $M$; secret keys are associated with Boolean functions $f$; and a secret key decrypts the ciphertext to recover $M$ if $f(x)$ is true (henceforth, for convenience of notation later in the paper, we denote this by $f(x) = 0$).

The most basic security guarantee for attribute-based encryption as well as predicate encryption, called *payload hiding*, stipulates that $M$ should remain private given its encryption under attributes $x^*$ and an unbounded number of *unauthorized* keys, namely secret keys $\mathsf{sk}_f$ where $f(x^*)$ is false (we denote this by $f(x^*) = 1$). The additional requirement in predicate encryption refers to hiding the attribute $x^*$ (beyond leaking whether $f(x^*)$ is true or false). It turns out that this requirement, called attribute-hiding, can be formalized in two ways. The first is the definition of *weak attribute-hiding*, which stipulates that $x^*$ remains hidden given an unbounded number of *unauthorized* keys. The second, called *strong attribute-hiding*, stipulates that $x^*$ remains hidden given an unbounded number of keys, which may comprise of both authorized and unauthorized keys. Both these requirements can be formalized using simulation-based and indistinguishability-based definitions (simulation based strong attribute hiding is known to be impossible [AGVW13]); jumping ahead, we remark that our constructions will achieve the stronger simulation-based definition but for weak attribute hiding.

A sequence of works showed the surprising power of strong attribute-hiding predicate encryption [BV15a, AJ15, BKS16]. A strong attribute-hiding PE scheme (for sufficiently powerful classes of predicates) gives us a functional encryption scheme [BSW11], which in turn can be used to build an indistinguishability obfuscation (IO) scheme [BV15a, AJ15], which in turn has emerged as a very powerful "hub of cryptography" [GGH+16, SW14].

The only strong attribute-hiding predicate encryption schemes we have under standard cryptographic assumptions are for very simple functionalities related to the inner product predicate [KSW08, BW07, OT12], and build on bilinear groups. On the other hand, Gorbunov, Vaikuntanathan and Wee (GVW) [GVW15a] recently constructed a weak attribute-hiding predicate encryption scheme for all circuits (of an a-priori bounded polynomial depth) from the LWE assumption. They also pointed out two barriers, two sources of leakage, that prevent their construction from achieving the strong attribute-hiding guarantee. Indeed, Agrawal [Agr16] showed that both sources of leakage can be exploited to recover the private attribute $x^*$ in the GVW scheme, under strong attribute-hiding attacks (that is, using both authorized and unauthorized secret keys).[1]

*Private Constrained PRFs (CPRFs).* Constrained Pseudorandom Functions, denoted CPRFs, [BW13, KPTZ13, BGI14] are pseudorandom functions (PRF) where it is possible to delegate the computation of the PRF on a subset of the inputs. Specifically, an adversary can ask for a constrained key $\sigma_f$ corresponding to a function $f$, which is derived from the (global) seed $\sigma$. Using $\sigma_f$ it is possible to compute $\mathsf{PRF}_\sigma(x)$ for all $x$ where $f(x)$ is true (in our notation, again, $f(x) = 0$). However, if $f(x) = 1$ then $\mathsf{PRF}_\sigma(x)$ is indistinguishable from uniform even for an adversary holding $\sigma_f$. The original definition considers the case of unbounded collusion, i.e. security against an adversary that can ask for many different $\sigma_{f_i}$, but this is currently only achievable for very simple function classes or under strong assumptions such as multilinear maps or indistinguishability obfuscation. Many of the applications of CPRFs (e.g. for broadcast encryption [BW13] and identity based key exchange [HKKW14]) rely on collusion resilience, but some (such as the puncturing paradigm [SW14]) only require releasing a single key. Brakerski and Vaikuntanathan [BV15b] showed that single-key CPRF is achievable for all functions with a priori depth bound and non-uniformity bound under the LWE assumption.

Boneh, Lewi and Wu [BLW17] recently considered *constraint hiding* CPRFs (CH-CPRF or private CPRFs) where the constrained key $\sigma_f$ does not reveal $f$ (so, in a sense, the constrained key holder cannot tell whether it is computing the right value or not). They showed various applications for this new primitive, as well as constructions from multilinear maps and obfuscation for various function classes. Very recently, Boneh, Kim and Montgomery [BKM17] showed how to construct single-key private CPRFs for point functions, and Canetti and Chen [CC17] showed how to construct a single-key private CPRF for the class of $NC^1$ circuits (i.e. polynomial-size formulae). Both their constructions are secure

---

[1] In addition, we also have several constructions of *functional encryption* schemes for computing inner products over large fields [ABCP15, BJK15, ALS16] (as opposed to the inner product predicate) and for quadratic functions [Lin16, Gay16] from standard assumptions.

under the LWE assumption. They also showed that even collusion resistance against 2-keys would imply indistinguishability obfuscation.

The technical core of these constructions is lattice-based constructions of PRFs, initiated by Banerjee, Peikert and Rosen [BPR12] and developed in a line of followup works [BP14, BLMR15, BFP+15, BV15b].

## 1.1 Our Results

In this work, we present two new techniques for achieving the attribute-hiding guarantee from the LWE assumption. We exemplify the novelty and usefulness of our techniques by showing that they can be used to derive new predicate encryption schemes and new constraint-hiding constrained PRFs [BLW17, CC17]. In particular, under the (polynomial hardness of the subexponential noise rate) LWE assumption, we construct:

– Two single-key constraint-hiding constrained PRF families for all circuits (of an a-priori bounded polynomial depth). This generalizes recent results of [BKM17] who handle point functions and [CC17] who handle NC$^1$ circuits. Our new techniques allow us to handle arbitrary polynomial-time constraints (of an a-priori bounded depth), which does not seem to follow from previous PE techniques, e.g., [GVW15a]. We describe constrained PRFs, constraint-hiding and our constructions in more detail in the sequel.
– Two new predicate encryption schemes that achieve the weak attribute-hiding security guarantee. Our predicate secret keys are shorter than in [GVW15a] by a poly($\lambda$) factor. They also avoid the first source of leakage identified in [GVW15a, Agr16]. We will describe these features in more detail in the sequel.

**Technical Background.** Following [GVW15a] (henceforth GVW), we build a predicate encryption scheme starting from an FHE and an ABE, following the "FHE+ABE" paradigm introduced in [GVW12, GKP+13] for the setting of a-priori bounded collusions. The idea is to first use FHE to produce an encryption $\Psi$ of the attribute $x$, and use $\Psi$ as the attribute in an ABE. This paradigm allows us to reduce the problem of protecting arbitrary polynomial-time computation $f$ on a private attribute $x$ to protecting a fixed computation, namely FHE decryption, on the FHE secret key. Henceforth, we suppress the issue of carrying out FHE homomorphic evaluation on the encrypted attribute, which can be handled via the underlying ABE as in [GVW15a], and focus on the issue of FHE decryption, which is where we depart from prior works.

With all LWE-based FHE schemes [BV11, BGV12, GSW13, BV14, AP14], decryption corresponds to computing an inner product modulo $q$ followed by a threshold function. While constructing a *strongly* attribute hiding PE scheme for this function class is still beyond reach,[2] GVW construct an LWE-based weakly

---

[2] There are constructions for function classes that semantically seem astonishingly similar, such as inner product *over the integers* (and not modulo $q$) followed by rounding [ALS16] but there appears to be a big technical gap between these classes.

attribute hiding scheme by extending previous works [AFV11, GMW15], and show how to attach it to the end of the decryption process of [BGG+14] ABE. Specifically, Agrawal, Freeman and Vaikuntanathan [AFV11] showed how to construct weakly attribute hiding PE for orthogonality checking modulo $q$, i.e. the class where attributes $\mathbf{x}$ and functions $f_{\mathbf{y}}$ correspond to vectors and decryption is possible if $\langle \mathbf{x}, \mathbf{y} \rangle = 0 \pmod{q}$. GVW rely on an additional feature of LWE-based FHE: that the value to be rounded after the inner product can be made polynomially bounded. Thus inner product plus rounding can be interpreted as a sequence of shifted inner products that are supported by [AFV11]. This in particular means that an authorized decryptor learns which of the shifts had been the successful one, a value that depends on the FHE randomness. This is one of the reasons why the GVW scheme is not strongly attribute hiding; there are others as described in [Agr16]. Interestingly, these shifts are also what prevent us from combining the PE techniques in [GVW15a] with the "constrained PRF from ABE" paradigm of [BV15b] to obtain constraint-hiding constrained PRFs.

**First New Technique: Dual Use.** In this technique, we use the same LWE secret for the FHE and the ABE.[3] Our main observation is that the structure of the [BGG+14] ABE scheme and that of the [GSW13] FHE scheme are so very similar that we can use the same LWE secret in both schemes. This can be viewed as encrypting the attribute under some FHE key, and then providing partly decrypted pieces as the ABE ciphertext. The PE decryption process first "puts the pieces together" according to the FHE homomorphic evaluation function, which makes the ABE ciphertext decrypt its own FHE component, leaving us with an ABE ciphertext which is ready to be decrypted using the ABE key. Proving security for this approach requires to delicately argue about the randomness used in the FHE encryption.

**Second New Technique: Modulus Switching and HNF Lattice Trapdoors.** In this technique, we attempt to implement the rounding post innerproduct straightforwardly by rounding the resulting ciphertext. This does not work since the attribute is encoded in the ciphertext in a robust way, so it is not affected by rounding (this is why more sophisticated methods were introduced in the past). However, we show how to homomorphically modify the rounding in a way that makes it effective for small noise, and yet preserves the most significant bits properly encoded. We note that a similar idea was also used in [BKM17]. Interestingly, for the proof of security of our PE scheme, we utilize the ability of generating trapdoors for LWE lattices of the form $[\mathbf{I} \| \mathbf{A}]$ (which corresponds to Hermite Normal Form), even when generating a trapdoor for $\mathbf{A}$ itself is not possible.

We first construct predicate encryption schemes using our techniques, on the way to our main result, namely constructions of constraint-hiding CPRFs for general constraints. With this executive summary, we move on to a more in-depth technical discussion of our results and techniques.

---

[3] An LWE instance contains multiple samples of the form $(\mathbf{a}_i, \mathbf{s}\mathbf{a}_i + e_i)$, the vector $\mathbf{s}$ is referred to as the LWE secret.

## 2    Technical Overview

We provide a brief overview of the GVW predicate encryption scheme, along with our constructions, focusing on the points where they differ and suppressing many technical details.

### 2.1    The [GVW15a] Scheme

We will largely ignore how ciphertexts and keys are generated and instead start by looking at what happens when one decrypts an encryption with respect to attribute $x$ using the secret key for a function (predicate) $f$. The decryption algorithm computes a vector over $\mathbb{Z}_q$ of the form:

$$\mathbf{s}^T[\mathbf{A}\|\mathbf{A}_f - (f(x) \cdot t + \delta)\mathbf{G}] + \mathsf{noise} \tag{1}$$

where $\mathbf{s}$ is the LWE secret (chosen as part of the encryption algorithm) and the matrix $\mathbf{A}_f$ is deterministically derived from the public parameters and the predicate $f$ (the precise derivation is not relevant for the overview). An additional component of the ciphertext, not described here, carries the encrypted message. For this overview, the only property we require is that the message is recoverable given a *lattice trapdoor* for the lattice defined by $[\mathbf{A}\|\mathbf{A}_f - (f(x) \cdot t + \delta)\mathbf{G}]$. A lattice trapdoor allows to sample low norm vectors in the kernel of the respective matrix.

The first thing we will zoom into is the term $f(x) \cdot t + \delta$ which corresponds to the inner product of an FHE ciphertext (upon homomorphic evaluation) and the corresponding secret key. Here, $\delta$ is a small noise value bounded by $B$, and $t \gg B$ is a large constant, most commonly $t = \lfloor \frac{q}{2} \rceil$ (but we will also use other values, see below). As usual in LWE-based constructions, the vector $\mathbf{s}$ is an "LWE secret", and we use $\mathsf{noise}$ to denote non-specific low norm noise that is added to the ciphertext and accumulates as it is processed.[4]

Decryption should be permitted when $f(x) = 0$, which indicates that the policy $f$ accepts the attribute $x$ (and forbidden when $f(x) = 1$). Therefore, in the GVW scheme, $\mathsf{sk}_f$ contains trapdoors for the $2B + 1$ lattices

$$[\mathbf{A}\|\mathbf{A}_f - \beta\mathbf{G}], \quad \forall|\beta| \leq B,$$

and decryption tries all trapdoors until one works. This is called the "lazy OR" evaluation in [GVW15a] and has at least two problems: (1) In the context of a predicate encryption scheme, this ruins security by letting a successful decryption leak the FHE noise $\delta$; and (2) Looking ahead, in the context of a constraint-hiding CPRF scheme (where one switches the function $f$ and the input $x$), it ruins even correctness, preventing the holder of a constrained key from recovering the PRF

---

[4] A knowledgeable reader might notice that in [GVW15a] there is a plus sign in Eq. (1) instead of the minus sign. This alternative notation is equivalent and will be more useful for us.

value $\mathbf{s}^T[\mathbf{A}\|\mathbf{A}_x]$;[5] rather, she only gets $\mathbf{s}^T[\mathbf{A}\|\mathbf{A}_x - \beta\mathbf{G}]$ for some small noise term $\beta = \beta(f, x)$.

Moving on, in the proof of security, a simulator needs to generate secret keys whenever $f(x^*) = 1$ where $x^*$ is the challenge attribute. To this end, the reduction knows a short $\mathbf{R}_f$ for which

$$\mathbf{AR}_f = \mathbf{A}_f - (f(x^*) \cdot t + \delta^*)\mathbf{G} \tag{2}$$

where $\delta^*$ is the noise that results from decrypting a homomorphically evaluated encryption of $f(x^*)$ using the FHE secret key. We can then rewrite

$$[\mathbf{A}\|\mathbf{A}_f - \beta\mathbf{G}] = [\mathbf{A}\|\mathbf{AR}_f + (t + \delta^* - \beta)\mathbf{G}]$$

and since $\delta^* + t - \beta \neq 0$, we will be able to generate trapdoors for this lattice knowing only $\mathbf{R}_f$, using the trapdoor extension techniques of [ABB10b, MP12].

## 2.2  Dual-Use of Secret and Randomness

Our first technique hinges on the key observation that the structure of the [BGG+14] ABE scheme and that of the [GSW13] FHE scheme are so very similar that we can use the same LWE secret in both schemes; we refer to this as the "dual use" technique.

Let us consider the [GSW13] homomorphic encryption scheme (using the later "gadget" formulation). In this scheme, the public key is of the form $\left(\begin{smallmatrix}\mathbf{B}\\\mathbf{s}^T\mathbf{B}+\mathbf{e}\end{smallmatrix}\right)$, the secret key is the vector $(\mathbf{s}^T, -1)$ (note that $(\mathbf{s}^T, -1) \cdot \left(\begin{smallmatrix}\mathbf{B}\\\mathbf{s}^T\mathbf{B}+\mathbf{e}\end{smallmatrix}\right) \approx 0$). A ciphertext $\Psi$ encrypting the message $\mu$ is of the form $\Psi = \left(\begin{smallmatrix}\mathbf{B}\\\mathbf{s}^T\mathbf{B}+\mathbf{e}\end{smallmatrix}\right)\mathbf{R} + \mu\mathbf{G}$, and has the property that $(\mathbf{s}^T, -1) \cdot \Psi \approx \mu \cdot (\mathbf{s}^T, -1)\mathbf{G}$. The structure of the secret key suggests that it might be beneficial to treat the bottom row of $\Psi$ differently than the other rows. Let us denote $\Psi = \left(\begin{smallmatrix}\overline{\Psi}\\\underline{\Psi}\end{smallmatrix}\right)$ and likewise $\mathbf{G} = \left(\begin{smallmatrix}\overline{\mathbf{G}}\\\underline{\mathbf{G}}\end{smallmatrix}\right)$. It follows that $(\mathbf{s}^T, -1) \cdot \Psi = \mathbf{s}^T\overline{\Psi} - \underline{\Psi} \approx \mu\mathbf{s}^T\overline{\mathbf{G}} - \mu\underline{\mathbf{G}}$. Specifically when $\mu = 0$ we have $\mathbf{s}^T\overline{\Psi} \approx \underline{\Psi}$. We note that the chopped gadget $\overline{\mathbf{G}}$ has all of the useful properties of $\mathbf{G}$ itself.

Back to our predicate encryption construction, instead of (1), we will compute a vector of the form

$$\mathbf{s}^T[\mathbf{B}\|\mathbf{B}_f - \overline{\Psi}_f] + \text{noise}, \tag{3}$$

where $\overline{\Psi}_f$ is the matrix containing the top rows of a known matrix $\Psi_f$ which in turn is an encryption of $f(x)$ under the key $(\mathbf{s}^T, -1)$.[6]

---

[5] In the constrained PRF setting, the role of the function $f$ and input $x$ are reversed, and hence $\mathbf{A}_x$.

[6] We use $\mathbf{B}$ instead of $\mathbf{A}$ to denote the public matrices here. This is since actually the matrix $\mathbf{A}$ is analogous to $\left(\begin{smallmatrix}\mathbf{B}\\\mathbf{s}^T\mathbf{B}+\mathbf{e}\end{smallmatrix}\right)$ (as is hinted from $\mathbf{B}$ being matching in dimension to $\overline{\Psi}, \overline{\mathbf{G}}$). In fact, the dual use technique can be viewed as a method for working with $\mathbf{A}$ which is different for every ciphertext.

If we can compute such a vector from our ciphertexts, then it will follow that if $f(x) = 0$ then

$$\mathbf{s}^T[\mathbf{B}\|\mathbf{B}_f - \overline{\mathit{\Psi}}_f] + \mathsf{noise} = \mathbf{s}^T[\mathbf{B}\|\mathbf{B}_f] + [0\|\underline{\mathit{\Psi}}_f] + \mathsf{noise},$$

and thus we can define $\mathsf{sk}_f$ as containing a trapdoor for $\mathbf{s}^T[\mathbf{B}\|\mathbf{B}_f - \mathbf{G}]$ (note that the value $[0\|\underline{\mathit{\Psi}}_f]$ can easily be subtracted off since $\mathit{\Psi}_f$ is known).

It is left to explain first how to define the ciphertext to allow computing a vector of this form, and second how to prove security.

**Compactification.** The problem of defining ciphertexts that will allow computing the term in Eq. (3) is almost solved by previous works [BGG+14, GVW15a]. As in GVW, given an attribute $x$, we create an ABE ciphertext with respect to the FHE encryption of the bits of $x$. Then, using techniques from [BGG+14], these bits can be manipulated to apply the FHE homomorphic evaluation of $f$ on the attribute bits. All in all, these techniques show how to create ciphertexts with respect to a hidden attribute $x$ that can be processed into vectors of the form:

$$\mathbf{s}^T[\mathbf{B}\|\mathbf{B}_{f_j} - \psi_{f,j}\overline{\mathbf{G}}] + \mathsf{noise} \tag{4}$$

where $\psi_{f,j} \in \mathbb{Z}_q$ are the entries of $\overline{\mathit{\Psi}}_j$, and we work with respect to the truncated gadget matrix $\overline{\mathbf{G}}$ instead of $\mathbf{G}$. This means that we can formally write $\mathit{\Psi}_f$ as

$$\mathit{\Psi}_f = \sum_j \psi_{f,j} \cdot \mathbf{E}_j$$

where $\mathbf{E}_j$ is a $0, 1$-matrix whose $j$'th entry is 1 and 0 everywhere else. This suggests the following manipulation:

$$\mathbf{B}_f + \overline{\mathit{\Psi}}_f = \sum_j (\mathbf{B}_{f_j} - \psi_{f,j}\overline{\mathbf{G}}) \cdot \overline{\mathbf{G}}^{-1}(\mathbf{E}_j),$$

can be applied to the vectors from Eq. (4), thus creating the value from Eq. (3).

**Dual Use Decryption.** As explained above, the secret key for $f$ is a trapdoor for the lattice $[\mathbf{B}\|\mathbf{B}_f]$. We now explain how to set up the parameters of the scheme so as to be able to generate secret keys whenever $f(x) = 1$ in the proof of security (i.e. without being able to decrypt the challenge ciphertext or generate keys when $f(x) = 0$). Given an LWE instance $\binom{\mathbf{B}}{\mathbf{s}^T\mathbf{B}+\mathbf{e}}$, we will generate all parameters of the scheme such that for all $f$, the reduction can compute a short $\mathbf{W}_f$ for which

$$\mathbf{B}\mathbf{W}_f = \mathbf{B}_f - \overline{\mathit{\Psi}}_f.$$

We can then rewrite

$$[\mathbf{B}\|\mathbf{B}_f] = [\mathbf{B}\|\mathbf{B}\mathbf{W}_f + \overline{\mathit{\Psi}}_f].$$

However, $\mathit{\Psi}_f$ is an encryption of $f(x) = 1$ under public key $\binom{\mathbf{B}}{\mathbf{s}^T\mathbf{B}+\mathbf{e}}$, i.e. $\mathit{\Psi}_f = \binom{\mathbf{B}}{\mathbf{s}^T\mathbf{B}+\mathbf{e}}\mathbf{R}_f + \mathbf{G}$, which means that $\overline{\mathit{\Psi}}_f = \mathbf{B}\mathbf{R}_f + \overline{\mathbf{G}}$, and so

$$[\mathbf{B}\|\mathbf{B}_f] = [\mathbf{B}\|\mathbf{B}\mathbf{W}_f + \overline{\mathit{\Psi}}_f] = [\mathbf{B}\|\mathbf{B}(\mathbf{W}_f + \mathbf{R}_f) + \overline{\mathbf{G}}]$$

and we will be able to generate trapdoors for this lattice knowing only $\mathbf{R}_f, \mathbf{W}_f$.

### 2.3 Modulus Switching and Trapdoor Extension in Hermite Normal Form

The crux of this technique is to replace Eq. (1) with a computation producing a vector of the form

$$\mathbf{s}^T[\mathbf{A}'\|\mathbf{A}'_f - f(x)\mathbf{G}'] + \text{noise} \tag{5}$$

where $\mathbf{G}'$ is a different gadget matrix and $\mathbf{A}'_f$ is again deterministically derived from the public parameters and $f$. We will also make sure to sample a small $\mathbf{s}$, specifically from the LWE noise distribution (this is known as LWE in *Hermite Normal Form* (HNF) and was shown equivalent to the standard form [ACPS09]), the reason for doing so will be clear in a little bit. Next, we will address two challenges: first, how to arrive at a vector of this form, and second, how to generate secret keys for such vectors, both of which require new techniques.

**Modulus Switching.** We first describe how to get to Eq. (5) starting from Eq. (1) (to get to the latter, we will proceed as in GVW). We would like to use the magnitude gap between $t$ and $\delta$, and, inspired by modulus switching techniques in FHE [BV11,BGV12], "divide by $t$" to remove the dependence on $\delta$. This seems odd at first since $t \cdot \mathbf{G}$ and $\delta \cdot \mathbf{G}$ actually have the same magnitude, so dividing by $t$ will not eliminate the $\delta$ component. Therefore we will first find a linear transformation that maps $\delta\mathbf{G}$ into a matrix of small entries, while mapping $t \cdot \mathbf{G}$ into a gadget matrix with big entries. Recall that eventually this transformation is to be applied to the processed ciphertext from Eq. (1), so due to the noise component, we are only allowed linear operations with small coefficients (or more explicitly, multiplying on the right by a matrix with small values).

As we pointed out $\delta\mathbf{G}$ and $t\mathbf{G}$ have the same magnitude so it might seem odd that a low-magnitude linear transformation can shift them so far apart. However, since $\mathbf{G}$ is a matrix with public trapdoor, it is possible to convert $\mathbf{G}$ into any other matrix $\mathbf{M}$ using a small magnitude linear transformation which is denoted by $\mathbf{G}^{-1}(\mathbf{M})$ (note that this is just a formal notation, since $\mathbf{G}$ doesn't have an actual inverse). Specifically, we will multiply by $\mathbf{G}^{-1}(\mathbf{G}_p)$, where $\mathbf{G}_p$ is the gadget matrix w.r.t a smaller modulus $p = q/t$ (we assume that $p$ is integer). Recall that our conceptual goal is to divide by $t$, and end up with a ciphertext in $\mathbb{Z}_p$, we can now reveal that indeed $\mathbf{G}' = \mathbf{G}_p$. Applying this transformation to the ciphertext results in

$$\mathbf{s}^T[\mathbf{A}\|\mathbf{A}_f\mathbf{G}^{-1}(\mathbf{G}_p) - f(x)t\mathbf{G}_p] - [0\|\delta\mathbf{s}^T\mathbf{G}_p] + \text{noise}, \tag{6}$$

and indeed, since we use low-norm $\mathbf{s}$, we have that $\|\delta\mathbf{s}^T\mathbf{G}_p\| \ll q$, and we can now think about it as part of the noise. However, $t\mathbf{G}_p$ is still not a valid gadget matrix over $\mathbb{Z}_q$. Still, we can now divide the entire expression by $t$ which results in

$$\mathbf{s}^T\big[\underbrace{\lfloor\mathbf{A}/t\rfloor}_{\mathbf{A}'} \| \underbrace{\lfloor\mathbf{A}_f\mathbf{G}^{-1}(\mathbf{G}_p)/t\rfloor}_{\mathbf{A}'_f} - f(x)\mathbf{G}_p\big] + \text{noise} \quad (\text{mod } p), \tag{7}$$

as in Eq. (5). This technique is reminiscent of the one used by Boneh, Kim and Montgomery [BKM17] in constructing a private CPRF for point functions (but was obtained independently of theirs).

**HNF Trapdoor Extension.** The standard way to generate keys that decrypt whenever $f(x) = 0$ is to provide a trapdoor for $[\mathbf{A}' \| \mathbf{A}'_f]$ (over $\mathbb{Z}_p$) as in previous ABE schemes. Indeed, this will provide the required functionality, but introduce problems in the proof. As in Eq. (2), the simulator can find a low-magnitude $\mathbf{R}_f$ s.t. $\mathbf{A}\mathbf{R}_f = \mathbf{A}_f + (t + \delta^*)\mathbf{G}$, however, when applying our modulus switching from above, we get

$$\mathbf{A}'\mathbf{R}'_f = \mathbf{A}'_f - \mathbf{G}_p - \mathbf{E},$$

where $\mathbf{E}$ is a low-magnitude error matrix which is the result of the bias introduced by $\delta^*$ and various rounding errors (note that $\mathbf{E}$ is easily computable given $\mathbf{R}'_f$). Therefore, we have that

$$[\mathbf{A}' \| \mathbf{A}'_f] = [\mathbf{A}' \| \mathbf{A}'\mathbf{R}'_f + \mathbf{G}_p + \mathbf{E}],$$

which is no longer a form for which we can find a trapdoor using $\mathbf{R}'_f$.

To resolve this, we observe that we *can* find a trapdoor for the matrix $[\mathbf{I} \| \mathbf{A}' \| \mathbf{A}'_f] = [\mathbf{I} \| \mathbf{A}' \| \mathbf{A}'\mathbf{R}'_f + \mathbf{G}_p + \mathbf{E}]$, which corresponds to generating trapdoors for *lattices* in Hermite Normal Form. This follows from the trapdoor extension methods of [ABB10b, MP12] since

$$[\mathbf{I} \| \mathbf{A}' \| \mathbf{A}'\mathbf{R}'_f + \mathbf{G}_p + \mathbf{E}] \cdot \begin{bmatrix} -\mathbf{E} \\ -\mathbf{R}'_f \\ \mathbf{I} \end{bmatrix} = \mathbf{G}_p.$$

We will therefore change the way secret keys are generated in our scheme, and generate them as trapdoors for $[\mathbf{I} \| \mathbf{A}' \| \mathbf{A}'_f]$ instead of trapdoors for $[\mathbf{A}' \| \mathbf{A}'_f]$. This might seem problematic because our ciphertext processes to $\mathbf{s}^T[\mathbf{A}' \| \mathbf{A}'_f - f(x)\mathbf{G}'] + \mathsf{noise}$ as in Eq. (5) and not to $\mathbf{s}^T[\mathbf{I} \| \mathbf{A}' \| \mathbf{A}'_f - f(x)\mathbf{G}'] + \mathsf{noise}$. However, since $\mathbf{s}$ is short, the zero vector itself has the form $\mathbf{0} = \mathbf{s}^T\mathbf{I} + \mathsf{noise}$ (with noise $= -\mathbf{s}^T$), and therefore we can always extend our ciphertext to this new form just by concatenating the zero vector.

*Comparison with GVW15 Predicate Encryption.* [GVW15a] pointed out that there are two barriers to achieving strongly attribute-hiding predicate encryption from LWE. First, multiple shifts approach to handle threshold inner product for FHE decryption leaks the exact inner product and therefore cannot be used to achieve full attribute-hiding. That is, authorized keys leak the FHE decryption key and in turn the private attribute $x$. Second, we do not currently know of a fully attribute-hiding inner product encryption scheme under the LWE assumption. Here, authorized keys leak the error terms used in the ciphertext. Indeed, Agrawal [Agr16] showed that both sources of leakage can be exploited to recover the private attribute $x$ in the GVW scheme. Both of our new constructions do not explicitly contain the first source of leakage.

## 2.4   From PE to Constraint Hiding CPRF

It was shown in [BV15b] that the [BGG+14] ABE structure can be used to construct constrained PRFs for arbitrary bounded-uniformity bounded-depth functions, without collusion. Namely, a pseudorandom function where it is possible to produce a constrained key $\sigma_f$ for a function $f$ whose description length is a-priori bounded by $\ell$ and its depth is a-priori bounded by $d$, s.t. the constrained key can be used to compute $\mathsf{PRF}(x)$ for all $x$ where $f(x) = 0$. At a high level, they considered a set of public parameters for the ABE scheme, and some ciphertext randomness $\mathbf{s}$ (currently not corresponding to any concrete ciphertext). To compute the PRF at point $x$, they considered the circuit $\mathcal{U}_x$ which is the universal circuit that takes an $\ell$-bit long description of a depth-$d$ function, and evaluates it on $x$. Now, they compute $\mathsf{PRF_s}(x) = \left\lfloor \frac{\mathbf{s}^T \mathbf{A}_{\mathcal{U}_x}}{T} \right\rceil$ for a sufficiently large $T$. This essentially the deterministic variant to setting $\mathsf{PRF_s}(x) = \mathbf{s}^T \mathbf{A}_{\mathcal{U}_x} + \mathsf{noise}$ except here the noise is deterministic since the PRF computation needs to be deterministic. The matrix $\mathbf{A}_{\mathcal{U}_x}$ is exactly the matrix that would be computed in the ABE decryption process if given a key $\mathsf{sk}_{\mathcal{U}_x}$. The constrained key corresponds to an ABE ciphertext encrypting the description of $f$ Therefore, constrained keys can be processed like ABE ciphertexts into the form $\mathbf{s}^T(\mathbf{A}_{\mathcal{U}_x} - \mathcal{U}_x(f)\mathbf{G}) + \mathsf{noise}$, for any circuit $\mathcal{U}_x$. Indeed, when $f(x) = 0$ the constrained key can be used to compute $\mathsf{PRF}(x)$. The construction itself is more complicated and contains additional features to ensure pseudorandomness in all of the points that cannot be computed using the constrained key.

This seems to be readily extendable to the PE setting, where the attribute hiding property should guarantee the constraint hiding of the CPRF. Indeed, now as in Eq. (1), the constrained key will only process to $\mathbf{s}^T(\mathbf{A}_{\mathcal{U}_x} - (tf(x) + \delta)\mathbf{G}) + \mathsf{noise}$. When $f(x) = 0$ this is equal to $\mathbf{s}^T(\mathbf{A}_{\mathcal{U}_x} - \delta\mathbf{G}) + \mathsf{noise}$ which does not allow to compute the correct value.

However, it is easy to see how using either of our new methods it is possible to overcome this issue. In a sense, in both methods the FHE noise which is embodied in the $\delta$ term is made small enough to be conjoined with the noise. The modulus switching technique allows to remove the $\delta$ term via multiplication by $\mathbf{G}^{-1}(\mathbf{G}_p)$ and dividing by $t$, and in the dual use method, the FHE noise is not multiplied by $\mathbf{G}$ to begin with. There are many other technical details to be dealt with, but they are resolved in ways inspired by [BV15b]. One technical difference between our solution and [BV15b] is that we do not use admissible hash functions to go from unpredictability to pseudorandomness, but instead we "compose" with the Banerjee-Peikert [BP14] pseudorandom function, which saves some complication as well as tightens the reduction somewhat. This could be used even in the setting of [BV15b] when constraint hiding is not sought.

*Organization of the Paper.* We start the rest of this paper with background information on lattices, LWE, trapdoors and FHE schemes in Sect. 3. Our first technique, namely dual-use, and the resulting PE and private CPRF scheme are presented in Sect. 4. Our second technique, namely HNF trapdoors and modulus switching, and the resulting PE and private CPRF schemes are presented in

Sect. 5. These two sections can be read independently of each other. In each section, we first present the PE scheme and then the private CPRF scheme.

# 3 Preliminaries

## 3.1 Constrained Pseudo-Random Functions

In a constrained PRF family [BW13, BGI14, KPTZ13], the owner of a PRF key $\sigma$ can compute a constrained PRF key $\sigma_f$ corresponding to any Boolean circuit $f$. Given $\sigma_f$, anyone can compute the PRF on inputs $x$ such that $f(x) = 0$. (As described before, our convention throughout this paper is that $f(x) = 0$ corresponds to the predicate $f$ being satisfied). Furthermore, $\sigma_f$ does not reveal any information about the PRF values at the other locations. A constrained PRF family is *constraint-hiding* if $\sigma_f$ does not reveal any information about the internals of $f$. This requirement can be formalized through either an indistinguishability-based or simulation-based definition [BLW17, CC17, BKM17]. Below, we present the definition of a constrained PRF adapted from [BV15b].

**Definition 1 (Constrained PRF).** *A* constrained *pseudo-random function (PRF) family is defined by algorithms* (KeyGen, Eval, Constrain, ConstrainEval) *where:*

- *KeyGen$(1^\lambda, 1^\ell, 1^d, 1^r)$ is a* PPT *algorithm that takes as input the security parameter $\lambda$, a circuit max-length $\ell$, a circuit max-depth $d$ and an output space $r$, and outputs a PRF key $\sigma$ and public parameters* pp.
- *Eval$_{pp}(\sigma, x)$ is a deterministic algorithm that takes as input a key $\sigma$ and a string $x \in \{0,1\}^*$, and outputs $y \in \mathbb{Z}_r$;*
- *Constrain$_{pp}(\sigma, f)$ is a* PPT *algorithm that takes as input a PRF key $\sigma$ and a circuit $f : \{0,1\}^* \to \{0,1\}$, and outputs a constrained key $\sigma_f$;*
- *ConstrainEval$_{pp}(\sigma_f, x)$ is a deterministic algorithm that takes as input a constrained key $\sigma_f$ and a string $x \in \{0,1\}^*$, and outputs either a string $y \in \mathbb{Z}_r$ or $\perp$.*

Previous works define and analyze the correctness, pseudorandomness and constraint hiding properties separately. However, for our purposes it will be easiest to define a single game that captures all of these properties at the same time. This definition is equivalent to computational correctness and selective punctured pseudorandomness [BV15b], and selective constraint hiding [BLW15].

**Definition 2.** *Consider the following game between a PPT adversary $\mathcal{A}$ and a challenger:*

1. *$\mathcal{A}$ sends $1^\ell, 1^d$ and $f_0, f_1 \in \{0,1\}^\ell$ to the challenger.*
2. *The challenger generates $(pp, seed) \leftarrow$ Keygen$(1^\lambda, 1^\ell, 1^d, 1^r)$. It flips three coins $b_1, b_2, b_3 \xleftarrow{\$} \{0,1\}$, intuitively $b_1$ selects whether $f_0$ or $f_1$ are used for the constraint, $b_2$ selects whether a real or random value is returned on queries*

*non-constrained queries, and $b_3$ selects whether the actual or constrained value is returned on constrained queries.*
*The challenger creates $seed_f \leftarrow$ Constrain$_{pp}(seed, f_{b_1})$, and sends $(pp, seed_f)$ to $\mathcal{A}$.*

3. *$\mathcal{A}$ adaptively sends unique queries $x \in \{0,1\}^*$ to the challenger (i.e. no $x$ is queried more than once). The challenger returns:*

$$y = \begin{cases} \bot, & \text{if } f_0(x) \neq f_1(x). \\ U(\mathbb{Z}_r), & \text{if } (f_0(x) = f_1(x) = 1) \wedge (b_2 = 1). \\ \text{ConstrainEval}_{pp}(\sigma_f, x), & \text{if } (f_0(x) = f_1(x) = 0) \wedge (b_3 = 0). \\ \text{Eval}_{pp}(\sigma, x), & \text{otherwise.} \end{cases}$$

4. *$\mathcal{A}$ sends a guess $(i, b')$.*

*The advantage of the adversary in this game is $\text{Adv}[\mathcal{A}] = |\Pr[b' = b_i] - 1/2|$. A family of PRFs (KeyGen, Eval, Constrain, ConstrainEval) is a single-key constraint-hiding selective-function constrained PRF if for every PPT adversary $\mathcal{A}$, $\text{Adv}[\mathcal{A}] = \text{negl}(\lambda)$.*

### 3.2   Weakly Attribute Hiding Predicate Encryption

Following prior works, we associate $C(x) = 0$ as true and authorized, and $C(x) \neq 0$ as false and unauthorized.

*Syntax.* A Predicate Encryption scheme PE for input universe $\mathcal{X}$, a predicate universe $\mathcal{C}$, a message space $\mathcal{M}$, consists of four algorithms (PE.Setup, PE.Enc, PE.KeyGen, PE.Dec):

PE.Setup$(1^\lambda, \mathcal{X}, \mathcal{C}, \mathcal{M}) \to (\text{mpk}, \text{msk})$. The setup algorithm gets as input the security parameter $\lambda$ and a description of $(\mathcal{X}, \mathcal{C}, \mathcal{M})$ and outputs the public parameter mpk, and the master key msk.

PE.Enc$(\text{mpk}, x, \mu) \to \text{ct}$. The encryption algorithm gets as input mpk, an attribute $x \in \mathcal{X}$ and a message $\mu \in \mathcal{M}$. It outputs a ciphertext ct.

PE.KeyGen$(\text{msk}, C) \to \text{sk}_C$. The key generation algorithm gets as input msk and a predicate $C \in \mathcal{C}$. It outputs a secret key $\text{sk}_C$.

PE.Dec$((\mathbf{sk}_C, C), \text{ct}) \to \mu$. The decryption algorithm gets as input the secret key $\text{sk}_C$, a predicate $C$, and a ciphertext ct. It outputs a message $\mu \in \mathcal{M}$ or $\bot$.

*Correctness.* We require that for all PE.Setup$(1^\lambda, \mathcal{X}, \mathcal{C}, \mathcal{M}) \to (\text{mpk}, \text{msk})$, for all $(x, C) \in \mathcal{X} \times \mathcal{C}$ such that $C(x) = 0$, for all $\mu \in \mathcal{M}$,

$$\Pr\left[\text{PE.Dec}((\text{sk}_C, C), \text{ct}) = \mu\right] \geq 1 - \text{negl}(\lambda),$$

where the probabilities are taken over the coins of the setup algorithm PE.Setup, secret keys $\text{sk}_C \leftarrow \text{PE.KeyGen}(\text{msk}, C)$ and ciphertexts $\text{ct} \leftarrow \text{PE.Enc}(\text{mpk}, x, \mu)$.

**Definition 3 (PE (Weak) Attribute-Hiding).** *Fix a predicate encryption scheme* (PE.Setup, PE.Enc, PE.KeyGen, PE.Dec). *For every stateful PPT adversary Adv, and a PPT simulator Sim, consider the following two experiments:*

<table>
<tr><td>

$\exp_{\mathcal{PE},\mathrm{Adv}}^{\mathsf{real}}(1^\lambda)$:

</td><td>

$\exp_{\mathcal{PE},\mathrm{Sim}}^{\mathsf{ideal}}(1^\lambda)$:

</td></tr>
<tr><td>

*1:* $x \leftarrow \mathrm{Adv}(1^\lambda, \mathcal{X}, \mathcal{C}, \mathcal{M})$
*2:* $(mpk, msk) \leftarrow$
  $\mathrm{PE.Setup}(1^\lambda, \mathcal{X}, \mathcal{C}, \mathcal{M})$
*3:* $\mu \leftarrow \mathrm{Adv}^{\mathrm{PE.KeyGen}(msk, \cdot)}(mpk)$
*4:* $ct \leftarrow \mathrm{PE.Enc}(mpk, x, \mu)$
*5:* $\alpha \leftarrow \mathrm{Adv}^{\mathrm{PE.KeyGen}(msk, \cdot)}(ct)$
*6: Output* $(x, \mu, \alpha)$

</td><td>

*1:* $x \leftarrow \mathrm{Adv}(1^\lambda, \mathcal{X}, \mathcal{C}, \mathcal{M})$
*2:* $(mpk, msk) \leftarrow$
  $\mathrm{PE.Setup}(1^\lambda, \mathcal{X}, \mathcal{C}, \mathcal{M})$
*3:* $\mu \leftarrow \mathrm{Adv}^{\mathrm{PE.KeyGen}(msk, \cdot)}(mpk)$
*4:* $ct \leftarrow \mathrm{Sim}(mpk, \mathcal{X}, \mathcal{M})$
*5:* $\alpha \leftarrow \mathrm{Adv}^{\mathrm{PE.KeyGen}(msk, \cdot)}(ct)$
*6: Output* $(x, \mu, \alpha)$

</td></tr>
</table>

*We say an adversary Adv is admissible if all oracle queries that it makes* $C \in \mathcal{C}$ *satisfy* $C(x) \neq 0$ *(i.e. false). The Predicate Encryption scheme* $\mathcal{PE}$ *is then said to be* (weak) attribute-hiding *if there is a PPT simulator Sim such that for every stateful PPT adversary Adv, the following two distributions are computationally indistinguishable:*

$$\left\{ \exp_{\mathcal{PE},\mathrm{Adv}}^{\mathsf{real}}(1^\lambda) \right\}_{\lambda \in \mathbb{N}} \overset{c}{\approx} \left\{ \exp_{\mathcal{PE},\mathrm{Sim}}^{\mathsf{ideal}}(1^\lambda) \right\}_{\lambda \in \mathbb{N}}$$

### 3.3 Learning with Errors

The *Learning with Errors* (LWE) problem was introduced by Regev [Reg05]. Our scheme relies on the hardness of its decisional version.

**Definition 4 (Decisional LWE (DLWE) [Reg05] and its HNF [ACPS09]).** *Let* $\lambda$ *be the security parameter,* $n = n(\lambda)$ *and* $q = q(\lambda)$ *be integers and let* $\chi = \chi(\lambda)$ *be a probability distribution over* $\mathbb{Z}$. *The* $\mathrm{DLWE}_{n,q,\chi}$ *problem states that for all* $m = \mathrm{poly}(n)$, *letting* $\mathbf{A} \leftarrow \mathbb{Z}_q^{n \times m}$, $\mathbf{s} \leftarrow \mathbb{Z}_q^n$, $\mathbf{e} \leftarrow \chi^m$, *and* $\mathbf{u} \leftarrow \mathbb{Z}_q^m$, *it holds that* $(\mathbf{A}, \mathbf{s}^T \mathbf{A} + \mathbf{e})$ *and* $(\mathbf{A}, \mathbf{u})$ *are computationally indistinguishable. The problem is equally hard in its "Hermite Normal Form": when sampling* $\mathbf{s} \leftarrow \chi^n$.

In this work we only consider the case where $q \leq 2^n$. Recall that $\mathsf{GapSVP}_\gamma$ is the (promise) problem of distinguishing, given a basis for a lattice and a parameter $d$, between the case where the lattice has a vector shorter than $d$, and the case where the lattice doesn't have any vector shorter than $\gamma \cdot d$. $\mathsf{SIVP}$ is the search problem of finding a set of "short" vectors. The best known algorithms for $\mathsf{GapSVP}_\gamma$ ([Sch87]) require at least $2^{\tilde{\Omega}(n/\log \gamma)}$ time. We refer the reader to [Reg05, Pei09] for more information.

There are known reductions between $\mathrm{DLWE}_{n,q,\chi}$ and those problems, which allows us to appropriately choose the LWE parameters for our scheme. We summarize in the following corollary (which addresses the regime of sub-exponential modulus-to-noise ratio).

**Corollary 1 ([Reg05, Pei09, MM11, MP12, BLP+13]).** *For any function* $B = B(n) \geq \widetilde{O}(\sqrt{n})$ *there exists a $B$-bounded distribution ensemble* $\chi = \chi(n)$ *over the integers s.t. for all* $q = q(n)$, *letting* $\gamma = \widetilde{O}(\sqrt{n}q/B)$, *it holds that* $\mathrm{DLWE}_{n,q,\chi}$ *is at least as hard as the quantum hardness of* $\mathsf{GapSVP}_\gamma$ *and* $\mathsf{SIVP}_\gamma$. *Classical hardness* $\mathsf{GapSVP}_\gamma$ *follows if* $q(n) \geq 2^{n/2}$ *or for other values of $q$ for* $\widetilde{\Omega}(\sqrt{n})$ *dimensional lattices and approximation factor* $q/B \cdot \mathrm{poly}(n\lceil \log q \rceil)$.

### 3.4 Trapdoors and Discrete Gaussians

Let $n, q \in \mathbb{Z}$,
$$\mathbf{g} = (1, 2, 4, \dots, 2^{\lceil \log q \rceil - 1}) \in \mathbb{Z}_q^{\lceil \log q \rceil}$$
and $m = n\lceil \log q \rceil$. The *gadget matrix* $\mathbf{G}$ is defined as the diagonal concatenation of $\mathbf{g}$ $n$ times. Formally, $\mathbf{G} = \mathbf{g} \otimes \mathbf{I}_n \in \mathbb{Z}_q^{n \times m}$. For any $t \in \mathbb{Z}$, the function $\mathbf{G}^{-1} : \mathbb{Z}_q^{n \times t} \to \{0,1\}^{m \times t}$ expands each entry $a \in \mathbb{Z}_q$ of the input matrix into a column of size $\lceil \log q \rceil$ consisting of the bit-representation of $a$. For any matrix $\mathbf{A} \in \mathbb{Z}_q^{n \times t}$, it holds that $\mathbf{G} \cdot \mathbf{G}^{-1}(\mathbf{A}) = \mathbf{A} \pmod{q}$.

The (centered) discrete Gaussian distribution over $\mathbb{Z}^m$ with parameter $\tau$, denoted $D_{\mathbb{Z}^m, \tau}$, is the distribution over $\mathbb{Z}^m$ where for all $\mathbf{x}$, $\Pr[\mathbf{x}] \propto e^{-\pi \|\mathbf{x}\|^2 / \tau^2}$.

Let $n, m, q \in \mathbb{N}$ and consider a matrix $\mathbf{A} \in \mathbb{Z}_q^{n \times m}$. For all $\mathbf{v} \in \mathbb{Z}_q^n$ we let $\mathbf{A}_\tau^{-1}(\mathbf{v})$ denote the random variable whose distribution is the Discrete Gaussian $D_{\mathbb{Z}^m, \tau}$ conditioned on $\mathbf{A} \cdot \mathbf{A}_\tau^{-1}(\mathbf{v}) = \mathbf{v} \pmod{q}$. If $\mathbf{h} \xleftarrow{\$} \mathbf{A}_\tau^{-1}(\mathbf{v})$ then $\|\mathbf{h}\| \leq k\tau\sqrt{m}$ with probability at least $1 - e^{-\Omega(k^2)}$.

A $\tau$-trapdoor for $\mathbf{A}$ is a procedure that can sample from a distribution within $2^{-n}$ statistical distance of $\mathbf{A}_\tau^{-1}(\mathbf{v})$ in time $\mathrm{poly}(n, m, \log q)$, for any $\mathbf{v} \in \mathbb{Z}_q^n$. We denote a $\tau$-trapdoor for $\mathbf{A}$ by $\mathbf{T}_{\mathbf{A}}^\tau$. The following properties have been established in a long sequence of works.

**Corollary 2 (Trapdoor Generation [Ajt96, MP12]).** *There is a probabilistic polynomial-time algorithm* $\mathsf{TrapGen}(1^n, q, m)$ *that for all* $m \geq m_0 = m_0(n,q) = O(n \log q)$, *outputs* $(\mathbf{A}, \mathbf{T}_{\mathbf{A}}^{\tau_0})$ *s.t.* $\mathbf{A} \in \mathbb{Z}_q^{n \times m}$ *is within statistical distance* $2^{-n}$ *from uniform and* $\tau_0 = O(\sqrt{n \log q \log n})$.

We use the most general form of trapdoor extension as formalized in [MP12].

**Theorem 1 (Trapdoor Extension [ABB10b, MP12]).** *Given* $\mathbf{A} \in \mathbb{Z}_q^{n \times m}$, *with a trapdoor* $\mathbf{T}_{\mathbf{A}}^\tau$, *and letting* $\mathbf{B} \in \mathbb{Z}_q^{n \times m'}$ *be s.t.* $\mathbf{A} = \mathbf{B}\mathbf{S} \pmod{q}$ *where* $\mathbf{S} \in \mathbb{Z}^{m' \times m}$ *with largest singular value* $s_1(\mathbf{S}) \leq \sigma$, *then* $(\mathbf{T}_{\mathbf{A}}^\tau, \mathbf{S})$ *can be used to sample from* $\mathbf{B}_{\sigma\tau}^{-1}$.

Note that since only an upper bound on the singular value is required, this theorem implies that $\mathbf{T}_{\mathbf{A}}^{\tau'}$ is derived from $\mathbf{T}_{\mathbf{A}}^\tau$ whenever $\tau \leq \tau'$. A few additional important corollaries are derived from this theorem. We recall that $s_1(\mathbf{S}) \leq \sqrt{nm} \|\mathbf{S}\|_\infty$ and that a trapdoor $\mathbf{T}_{\mathbf{G}}^{O(1)}$ is trivial.

The first is a trapdoor extension that follows by taking $\mathbf{S} = [\mathbf{I} \| \mathbf{0}]$.

**Corollary 3.** *Given* $\mathbf{A} \in \mathbb{Z}_q^{n \times m}$, *with a trapdoor* $\mathbf{T}_{\mathbf{A}}^{\tau}$, *it is efficient to sample from* $[\mathbf{A} \| \mathbf{B}]_{\tau}^{-1}$ *for all* $\mathbf{B}$.

Next is a trapdoor extension that had been used extensively in prior work. It follows from Theorem 1 with $\mathbf{S} = [-\mathbf{R}^T \| \mathbf{I}]^T$.

**Corollary 4.** *Given* $\bar{\mathbf{A}} \in \mathbb{Z}_q^{n \times m'}$, *and* $\mathbf{R} \in \mathbb{Z}^{m' \times m}$ *with* $m = n\lceil \log q \rceil$, *it is efficient to sample from* $[\bar{\mathbf{A}} \| \bar{\mathbf{A}}\mathbf{R} + \mathbf{G}]_{\tau}^{-1}$ *for* $\tau = O(\sqrt{mm'} \|\mathbf{R}\|_{\infty})$.

Note that by taking $\bar{\mathbf{A}}$ uniform and $\mathbf{R}$ to be a high entropy small matrix, e.g. uniform in $\{-1, 0, 1\}$ and relying on the leftover hash lemma, Corollary 2 is in fact a special case of this one.

The following shows a different method for trapdoor extension which corresponds to matrices in Hermite Normal Form. This trapdoor generation method is mentioned in passing in [MP12] as a method for improving parameters by relying on computational assumptions. Our use of this property is quite different. Technically it follows from Theorem 1 with $\mathbf{S} = [-\mathbf{E}^T \| - \mathbf{R}^T \| \mathbf{I}]^T$.

**Corollary 5 (Trapdoor Extension in HNF).** *Let* $n, q, m' \geq 1$ *and let* $m = n\lceil \log q \rceil$. *Given* $\bar{\mathbf{A}} \xleftarrow{\$} \mathbb{Z}_q^{n \times m'}$, $\mathbf{R} \in \mathbb{Z}^{m' \times m}$ *and* $\mathbf{E} \in \mathbb{Z}^{n \times m}$, *the trapdoor* $\mathbf{T}_{[\mathbf{I} \| \bar{\mathbf{A}} \| \bar{\mathbf{A}}\mathbf{R} + \mathbf{G} + \mathbf{E}]}^{\tau}$ *is efficiently computable for* $\tau = O(\sqrt{mm'} \|\mathbf{R}\|_{\infty} + \sqrt{mn} \|\mathbf{E}\|_{\infty})$.

### 3.5 Lattice Evaluation

The following is an abstraction of the evaluation procedure in recent LWE based FHE and ABE schemes that developed in a long sequence of works [ABB10b, MP12, GSW13, AP14, BGG+14, GVW15b]. We use a similar formalism as in [BV15b, BCTW16] but slightly rename the functions.

**Theorem 2.** *There exist efficient deterministic algorithms* EvalF *and* EvalFX *such that for all* $n, q, \ell \in \mathbb{N}$, *and for any sequence of matrices* $(\mathbf{A}_1, \ldots, \mathbf{A}_\ell) \in (\mathbb{Z}_q^{n \times n\lceil \log q \rceil})^\ell$, *for any depth-d Boolean circuit* $f : \{0,1\}^\ell \to \{0,1\}$ *and for every* $\mathbf{x} = (x_1, \ldots, x_\ell) \in \{0,1\}^\ell$, *the following properties hold.*

- *The outputs* $\mathbf{H}_f = $ EvalF$(f, \mathbf{A}_1, \ldots, \mathbf{A}_\ell)$ *and* $\mathbf{H}_{f,x} = $ EvalFX$(f, x, \mathbf{A}_1, \ldots, \mathbf{A}_\ell)$ *are both matrices in* $\mathbb{Z}^{(\ell n\lceil \log q \rceil) \times n\lceil \log q \rceil}$;
- *It holds that* $\|\mathbf{H}_f\|_{\infty}, \|\mathbf{H}_{f,x}\|_{\infty} \leq (n \log q)^{O(d)}$.
- *It holds that*

$$[\mathbf{A}_1 - x_1\mathbf{G} \| \mathbf{A}_2 - x_2\mathbf{G} \| \ldots \| \mathbf{A}_\ell - x_\ell\mathbf{G}] \cdot \mathbf{H}_{f,\mathbf{x}}$$
$$= [\mathbf{A}_1 \| \mathbf{A}_2 \| \ldots \| \mathbf{A}_\ell] \cdot \mathbf{H}_f - f(\mathbf{x})\mathbf{G} \pmod{q} \qquad (8)$$

*We will call this the "key equation" for matrix evaluation.*

For a proof of this theorem, we refer the reader to [BV15b]. This evaluation method was extended by [AFV11, GVW15a] to show that in the case of the inner product function it is possible to compute EvalFX with only one of the two operands.

**Theorem 3.** *There exist efficient deterministic algorithms* EvalF$^{ip}$ *and* EvalFX$^{ip}$ *as follows. Let* $n, q, \ell, \vec{\mathbf{A}} = (\mathbf{A}_1, \ldots, \mathbf{A}_\ell), \mathbf{x}$ *be as above. Let* $\ell' \in \mathbb{N}$ *and* $\vec{\mathbf{B}} = (\mathbf{B}_1, \ldots, \mathbf{B}_{\ell'}) \in (\mathbb{Z}_q^{n \times n \lceil \log q \rceil})^{\ell'}$, *and let* $f : \{0, 1\}^\ell \to \{0, 1\}^{\ell'}$ *be a depth $d$ boolean circuit with $\ell'$ output bits. Then:*

- $\mathbf{H}_f = $ EvalF$^{ip}(f, \vec{\mathbf{A}}, \vec{\mathbf{B}})$ *and* $\mathbf{H}_{f,x} = $ EvalFX$^{ip}(f, \mathbf{x}, \vec{\mathbf{A}}, \vec{\mathbf{B}})$ *are both in*
  $\mathbb{Z}^{((\ell+\ell')n\lceil \log q \rceil) \times n \lceil \log q \rceil}$;
- *It holds that* $\|\mathbf{H}_f\|_\infty, \|\mathbf{H}_{f,x}\|_\infty \le \ell'(n \log q)^{O(d)}$;
- *It holds that for all* $\mathbf{y} \in \mathbb{Z}^{\ell'}$

$$\left([\vec{\mathbf{A}}\|\vec{\mathbf{B}}] - [\mathbf{x}\|\mathbf{y}] \otimes \mathbf{G}\right) \cdot \mathbf{H}_{f,x} = [\vec{\mathbf{A}}\|\vec{\mathbf{B}}] \cdot \mathbf{H}_f - \langle f(\mathbf{x}), \mathbf{y}\rangle \mathbf{G} \pmod{q}, \quad (9)$$

*where the inner product is over the integers (or equivalently modulo $q$).*

We note that EvalFX$^{ip}$ does not take $\mathbf{y}$ as input and furthermore that $\mathbf{y}$ can have arbitrary integer values (not necessarily binary). We will later extend these theorems to functions that output matrices in Sect. 4.1.

### 3.6    Fully Homomorphic Encryption (FHE)

A (secret-key) homomorphic encryption (HE) scheme w.r.t a function class $\mathcal{F}$ is a semantically secure encryption scheme adjoined with an additional PPT algorithm Eval s.t. for all $f \in \mathcal{F}$ and $\mathbf{x} \in \{0, 1\}^\ell$ it holds that if sk is properly generated and $\mathsf{ct}_i = \mathsf{Enc_{sk}}(x_i)$, then $\mathsf{Dec_{sk}}(\mathsf{Eval}(f, \mathsf{ct}_1, \ldots, \mathsf{ct}_\ell)) = f(\mathbf{x})$ with all but negligible probability. The following is a corollary of the [GSW13] encryption scheme. We note that the common use of the scheme is with $t = q/2$ but we will use $t \approx \sqrt{q}$ in this work.

**Lemma 1 (Leveled FHE [GSW13]).** *Let* $q, n, t, d \ge 1$ *and let* $\chi$ *be $B$-bounded. If* $q > 2t \ge 4B(n\lceil \log q \rceil)^{O(d)}$ *then there exists an FHE scheme for the class $\mathcal{F}_d$ of depth $d$ circuits based on* DLWE$_{n,q,\chi}$ *with the following properties.*

- *The ciphertext length is* $\ell_c = \mathrm{poly}(n\lceil \log q \rceil)$.
- *Decryption involves (i) preprocessing the ciphertext (independently of the secret key) into a* binary *vector* $\mathbf{c} \in \{0, 1\}^{\ell_s}$ *for* $\ell_s = \mathrm{poly}(n\lceil \log q \rceil)$; *(ii) taking inner product* $\langle \mathbf{c}, \mathbf{s}\rangle \pmod{q}$ *for an integer secret-key vector $\mathbf{s}$, which results in $t\mu + \delta$ with $|\delta| \le B(n\lceil \log q \rceil)^{O(d)}$; (iii) extracting the output $\mu$ from the above expression.*
  *Moreover, for any $f \in \mathcal{F}_d$, the depth of $f'(\cdot) = $ FHE.Eval$(f, \cdot)$ is at most $d' = d \cdot \mathrm{polylog}(n\lceil \log q \rceil)$.*

### 3.7    The Banerjee-Peikert Pseudorandom Function

Banerjee and Peikert [BP14] introduced an LWE-based key homomorphic pseudorandom function which was the basis for the [BV15b] constrained PRF. While [BV15b] only drew from the ideas in [BP14], we use their construction explicitly as a building block, which simplifies our analysis. We present their construction using our instance evaluation terminology.

For all $x \in \{0,1\}^\ell$, consider the circuit (more precisely, arithmetic formula) $\mathcal{T}_x(y_0, y_1)$ which computes the product $\prod_{i \in [\ell]} y_{x_i}$ using a balanced binary multiplication tree. Note that we are never actually computing $\mathcal{T}_x$ on any input. We are only using its formal combinatorial structure for the purpose of evolution as described next.

**Corollary 6 (follows from [BP14, Theorems 3.7 and 3.8]).** *Let $n, p, \ell \geq 1$ be integers, let $\chi$ be $B$-bounded and assume $\mathrm{DLWE}_{n,p,\chi}$. Then there exists an efficiently computable randomized function $E : \{0,1\}^\ell \to \mathbb{Z}^{n\lceil \log p \rceil}$ with bounded norm $\|E\|_\infty \leq B\sqrt{\ell} \cdot (n\lceil \log p \rceil)^{\log \ell}$, such that, letting $\mathbf{C}_0, \mathbf{C}_1 \xleftarrow{\$} \mathbb{Z}_p^{n \times n\lceil \log p \rceil}$ and denoting $\vec{\mathbf{C}} = (\mathbf{C}_0, \mathbf{C}_1)$, $\mathbf{C}_x = \mathsf{EvalF}(\mathcal{T}_x, \vec{\mathbf{C}})$ for all $x$.*

$$F_{\mathbf{s}}(x) = \mathbf{s}^T \mathbf{C}_x + E(x) \pmod{p}$$

*is pseudorandom, where $\mathbf{s} \xleftarrow{\$} \mathbb{Z}_p^n$. Furthermore, the same holds for*

$$F'_{\mathbf{d}}(x) = \mathbf{d}^T \mathbf{G}_p^{-1}(\mathbf{C}_x) + E(x) \pmod{p}$$

*where $\mathbf{d} \xleftarrow{\$} \mathbb{Z}_p^{n\lceil \log p \rceil}$ and $\mathbf{C}_x, E$ as above.*

# 4    Our First Construction: The Dual-Use Technique

In this section, we present the *dual-use technique* and construct a new weakly attribute-hiding PE scheme and a constraint-hiding constrained PRF based on LWE. We will use the machinery for lattice evaluation developed in Sect. 3.5. First, in Sect. 4.1, we extend this machinery to work for computations that output not just scalars but matrices. Then, in Sects. 4.2 and 4.3, we describe our weakly attribute-hiding PE scheme and a constraint-hiding constrained PRF scheme, respectively.

## 4.1    Lattice Evaluation of Matrix-Valued Functions

We first extend evaluation of matrices from Sect. 3.5 to deal with functions whose output is a matrix instead of a bit (we still treat the input as bits).

*Notation.* Given a matrix $\mathbf{X} \in \mathbb{Z}_q^{n \times n \log q}$, we will index its $n^2 \log q$ entries by numbers, for convenience of notation (as opposed to the standard practice of using a pair of numbers to index the row and column separately). We use $x_{j,\tau} \in \{0,1\}$ where $j \in [n^2 \log q], \tau \in [\log q]$ to denote the $\tau$'th bit of the $j$'th entry of $\mathbf{X}$. This means that we can write

$$\mathbf{X} = \sum_{j,\tau} x_{j,\tau} \cdot 2^\tau \mathbf{E}_j$$

where $\mathbf{E}_j$ is a $0, 1$-matrix whose $j$'th entry is 1 and 0 everywhere else. Throughout, we use $j \in [n^2 \log q], \tau \in [\log q]$ and $i \in [\ell]$ and we avoid explicitly quantifying over these variables.

*Matrix Computation.* Suppose $f : x_1, \ldots, x_\ell \mapsto \mathbf{X}_f$ where these matrices have the same dimensions as $\mathbf{A}_1, \mathbf{A}_2, \ldots, \mathbf{A}_\ell$. Then, we require the following key relation between $\mathbf{H}_f$ and $\mathbf{H}_{f,\mathbf{x}}$:

$$\left[\mathbf{A}_1 - x_1\mathbf{G}\middle|\ \cdots\ \middle|\mathbf{A}_\ell - x_\ell\mathbf{G}\right] \cdot \mathbf{H}_{f,\mathbf{x}} = \left[\mathbf{A}_1\middle|\ \cdots\ \middle|\mathbf{A}_\ell\right] \cdot \mathbf{H}_f - \mathbf{X}_f \qquad (10)$$

*Constructing $\mathbf{H}_{f,\mathbf{x}}$ and $\mathbf{H}_f$.* Let $f_{j,\tau} : x_1, \ldots, x_\ell \mapsto \{0,1\}$ denote the function that outputs $\tau$'th bit of the $j$'th entry of $\mathbf{X}_f$. Then, we define $\mathbf{H}_f$ as follows.

$$\mathbf{H}_{f,j,\tau} := \mathsf{EvalF}(f_{j,\tau}, \{\mathbf{A}_i\}), \qquad \mathbf{H}_f := \sum_{j,\tau} \mathbf{H}_{f,j,\tau} \cdot \mathbf{G}^{-1}(2^\tau \mathbf{E}_j)$$

Then, the key relation (Eq. 10) follows readily from the following relations:

$$\left[\mathbf{A}_1 - x_1\mathbf{G}\middle|\ \cdots\ \middle|\mathbf{A}_\ell - x_\ell\mathbf{G}\right] \cdot \mathbf{H}_{f,j,\tau,\mathbf{x}} = \left[\mathbf{A}_1\middle|\ \cdots\ \middle|\mathbf{A}_\ell\right] \cdot \mathbf{H}_{f,j,\tau} - x_{f,j,\tau}\mathbf{G}$$

$$\text{and} \quad \sum_{j,\tau} x_{f,j,\tau}\mathbf{G} \cdot \mathbf{G}^{-1}(2^\tau \mathbf{E}_j) = \mathbf{X}_f$$

where the first equation is the key relation for functions with scalar output. These two relations together show us that the setting of

$$\mathbf{H}_f := \sum_{j,\tau} \mathbf{H}_{f,j,\tau}\mathbf{G}^{-1}(2^\tau \mathbf{E}_j), \quad \mathbf{H}_{f,\mathbf{x}} := \sum_{j,\tau} \mathbf{H}_{f,j,\tau,\mathbf{x}}\mathbf{G}^{-1}(2^\tau \mathbf{E}_j)$$

satisfies Eq. 10.

## 4.2    Weakly Attribute-Hiding Predicate Encryption

In this section, we describe the dual use technique and use it to construct a weakly attribute-hiding predicate encryption scheme.

*Notation.* We use gadget matrices $\mathbf{G} \in \mathbb{Z}_q^{(n+1)\times(n+1)\log q}$ and we write $\overline{\mathbf{G}} \in \mathbb{Z}_q^{n\times(n+1)\log q}$ to denote all but the last row of $\mathbf{G}$. Given a circuit computing a function $f : \{0,1\}^\ell \to \{0,1\}$, and GSW FHE encryptions $\mathit{\Psi} := (\mathit{\Psi}_1, \ldots, \mathit{\Psi}_\ell)$ of $x_1, \ldots, x_\ell$, we write $\mathit{\Psi}_f$ to denote $\mathsf{FHE.Eval}(f, \mathit{\Psi})$. Noting that $\mathit{\Psi}_f$ is a matrix, we let $\underline{\mathit{\Psi}}_f$ denote the last row of $\mathit{\Psi}_f$, and $\overline{\mathit{\Psi}}_f$ to denote all but the last row of $\mathit{\Psi}_f$. In addition, we write $\hat{f}$ to denote the circuit that computes $\mathit{\Psi} \mapsto \overline{\mathit{\Psi}}_f$, namely it takes as input the bits of $\mathit{\Psi}$ and outputs the matrix $\overline{\mathit{\Psi}}_f$.

We let $\mathbf{e} \xleftarrow{\sigma} \mathbb{Z}^m$ denote the process of sampling a vector $\mathbf{e}$ where each of its entries is drawn independently from the discrete Gaussian with mean 0 and standard deviation $\sigma$ over $\mathbb{Z}$.

Our predicate encryption scheme works as follows.

- Setup($1^\lambda, 1^\ell, 1^d$): sample $(\mathbf{B}, \mathbf{T_B})$ where $\mathbf{B} \in \mathbb{Z}_q^{n \times (n+1) \log q}$ and $\mathbf{T_B}$ denotes the trapdoor for $\mathbf{B}$. Pick $\mathbf{B}_j \xleftarrow{\$} \mathbb{Z}_q^{n \times (n+1) \log q}$ and $\mathbf{p} \xleftarrow{\$} \mathbb{Z}_q^n$. Output

$$\mathsf{mpk} := \Big( \mathbf{B}, \{\mathbf{B}_j\}_{j \in [L]}, \mathbf{p} \Big),$$
$$\mathsf{msk} := \Big( \mathbf{T_B} \Big)$$

where $L = \ell \cdot (n+1)^2 \log^2 q$.
- Enc($\mathsf{mpk}, \mathbf{x}, M \in \{0,1\}$): pick $\mathbf{s} \xleftarrow{\$} \mathbb{Z}_q^n, \mathbf{e}, \mathbf{e}_0, \mathbf{e}_j \xleftarrow{\sigma} \mathbb{Z}^m, e' \xleftarrow{\sigma} \mathbb{Z}, \mathbf{R}_i \in \{0,1\}^{(n+1) \log q \times (n+1) \log q}$ and compute

$$\Psi_i := \begin{pmatrix} \mathbf{B} \\ \mathbf{s}^T \mathbf{B} + \mathbf{e}^T \end{pmatrix} \mathbf{R}_i + x_i \mathbf{G}$$

Let $\psi_1, \ldots, \psi_L$ denote the binary representation of $\Psi := [\Psi_1 \mid \cdots \mid \Psi_\ell]$. Compute

$$\mathbf{c}_0^T := \mathbf{s}^T \mathbf{B} + \mathbf{e}_0^T, \qquad \mathbf{c}_j^T := \mathbf{s}^T [\mathbf{B}_j - \psi_j \overline{\mathbf{G}}] + \mathbf{e}_j^T$$

and $\kappa := \mathbf{s}^T \mathbf{p} + e' + M \cdot \lfloor q/2 \rfloor \pmod{q}$.
The PE ciphertext consists of the FHE ciphertext $\Psi$ and the ABE ciphertexts computed as above. That is,

$$\mathsf{ct} := \Big( \Psi, \mathbf{c}_0, \{\mathbf{c}_j\}_{j \in [L]}, \kappa \Big)$$

- KeyGen($\mathsf{msk}, f$): Let $\hat{f}$ denote the circuit computing $\Psi \mapsto \overline{\Psi}_f$ and

$$\mathbf{H}_{\hat{f}} := \mathsf{EvalF}(\hat{f}, \{\mathbf{B}_j\}_{j \in [L]}), \quad \mathbf{B}_{\hat{f}} := [\mathbf{B}_1 \mid \cdots \mid \mathbf{B}_L] \cdot \mathbf{H}_{\hat{f}}$$

Sample a short $\mathsf{sk}_f$ using $\mathbf{T_B}$ such that

$$[\mathbf{B} \mid \mathbf{B}_{\hat{f}}] \cdot \mathsf{sk}_f = \mathbf{p}$$

Output $\mathsf{sk}_f$.
- Dec($(\mathsf{sk}_f, f), \mathsf{ct}$): Let $\hat{f}$ denote the circuit computing $\Psi \mapsto \overline{\Psi}_f$ and parse the ciphertext $\mathsf{ct}$ as $(\Psi, \mathbf{c}_0, \{\mathbf{c}_j\}_{j \in L}, \kappa)$. Compute:

$$\Psi_f := \hat{f}(\Psi)$$
$$\mathbf{H}_{\hat{f}, \Psi} := \mathsf{EvalFX}(\hat{f}, \Psi, \{\mathbf{B}_j\}_{j \in [L]})$$
$$\mathbf{c}_{\hat{f}} := [\mathbf{c}_1 \mid \cdots \mid \mathbf{c}_L] \cdot \mathbf{H}_{\hat{f}, \Psi} + \underline{\Psi}_f$$

Compute

$$\kappa' := [\mathbf{c}_0 \mid \mathbf{c}_{\hat{f}}] \cdot \mathsf{sk}_f$$

and output the MSB of $\kappa - \kappa'$.

We now analyze the correctness of the PE scheme (in the process setting the parameters) and prove its (selective) security under the polynomial hardness of LWE with a sub-exponential modulus-to-noise ratio.

**Theorem 4 (Correctness).** *The PE construction above is correct as per Definition 3.*

*Proof.* The key relation tells us that

$$[\mathbf{B}_1 - \psi_1 \overline{\mathbf{G}} \mid \cdots \mid \mathbf{B}_L - \psi_L \overline{\mathbf{G}}] \cdot \mathbf{H}_{\hat{f}, \psi} = [\mathbf{B}_1 \mid \cdots \mid \mathbf{B}_L] \cdot \mathbf{H}_{\hat{f}} - \overline{\Psi}_f = \mathbf{B}_{\hat{f}} - \overline{\Psi}_f$$

Multiplying both sides by $\mathbf{s}^T$, we have

$$\begin{aligned}
\mathbf{c}_{\hat{f}} &\approx \mathbf{s}^T [\mathbf{B}_1 - \psi_1 \overline{\mathbf{G}} \mid \cdots \mid \mathbf{B}_L - \psi_L \overline{\mathbf{G}}] \cdot \mathbf{H}_{\hat{f}, \psi} + \underline{\Psi}_f \\
&= \mathbf{s}^T \mathbf{B}_{\hat{f}} - \mathbf{s}^T \overline{\Psi}_f + \underline{\Psi}_f \\
&= \mathbf{s}^T \mathbf{B}_{\hat{f}} - [\mathbf{s}^T \mid -1] \cdot \Psi_f \\
&\approx \mathbf{s}^T \mathbf{B}_{\hat{f}} - f(\mathbf{x}) \cdot [\mathbf{s}^T \mid -1] \cdot \mathbf{G}
\end{aligned}$$

where the first approximate equality is because of the accumulated error which is a product of the LWE errors and the low-norm matrix $\mathbf{H}_{\hat{f}, \psi}$, the second equality is because of the key relation, and the final approximate equality is because of the decryption equation of the GSW FHE scheme. Then, when $f(\mathbf{x}) = 0$,

$$\kappa' := [\mathbf{c}_0 \mid \mathbf{c}_{\hat{f}}] \cdot \mathsf{sk}_f \approx \mathbf{s}^T [\mathbf{B} \mid \mathbf{B}_{\hat{f}}] \cdot \mathsf{sk}_f = \mathbf{s}^T \mathbf{p}$$

Now, decryption succeeds in recovering $M$ since $\kappa := \mathbf{s}^T \mathbf{p} + e' + M \cdot \lfloor q/2 \rfloor \pmod{q}$.

**Setting Parameters.** The error growth on FHE evaluation is by a multiplicative factor of $(n \log q)^{O(d_f)}$ where $d_f$ is the depth of the circuit computing $f$. Furthermore, the error growth on ABE evaluation has magnitude at most $(n \log q)^{O(d_{\hat{f}})}$ where $d_{\hat{f}}$ is the depth of the circuit that performs GSW FHE evaluation for the function $f$. We know that $d_{\hat{f}} = d \cdot \mathsf{poly}(\log n, \log \log q)$. The total error growth thus has magnitude $(n \log q)^{d \cdot \mathsf{poly}(\log n, \log \log q)}$ which should be at most $q/4$ for correctness.

On the other hand, we would like to set $q = O(2^{n^\epsilon})$ for some constant $\epsilon$ so as to rely on the hardness of sub-exponential-error LWE. It is possible to find a setting of parameters that satisfy all these conditions, analogous to Sect. 5.1.

**Theorem 5 (Security).** *The scheme PE is secure as per Definition 3 under the $\mathsf{LWE}_{n,q,\chi}$ assumption, and thus under the worst case hardness of approximating $\mathsf{GapSVP}, \mathsf{SIVP}$ to within a $2^{\widetilde{O}(n^\epsilon)}$ factor in polynomial time.*

*Proof.* We provide a proof sketch for selective security of the PE scheme.

First, we describe a set of auxiliary algorithms consisting of alternative algorithms $(\mathsf{Setup}^*, \mathsf{KeyGen}^*, \mathsf{Enc}^*)$ that will be used in the proof of security. We are given $\mathbf{A} = \binom{\mathbf{B}}{\mathbf{c}}, \mathbf{p}, p'$ and the selective challenge $\mathbf{x}^*$. Here, $(\mathbf{c}, p')$ is either $(\mathbf{s}^T \mathbf{B} + \mathbf{e}, \mathbf{s}^T \mathbf{p} + e')$ or uniformly random.

Setup$^*(\mathbf{B}, \mathbf{p}, \mathbf{x}^*)$: Pick $\mathbf{W}'_j \overset{\$}{\leftarrow} \{0,1\}^{n \times (n+1) \log q}, \mathbf{R}_i \in \{0,1\}^{(n+1) \log q \times (n+1) \log q}$.
  Compute

$$\Psi_i := \mathbf{A}\mathbf{R}_i + x_i^* \mathbf{G}$$
$$\mathbf{B}_j = \mathbf{B}\mathbf{W}'_j + \psi_j \overline{\mathbf{G}}$$

where, as before, $\psi_j$ denote the bits of $\Psi = [\Psi_1 \mid \cdots \mid \Psi_\ell]$. Output

$$\mathsf{mpk} := \left( \mathbf{B}, \{\mathbf{B}_j\}_{j \in [L]}, \mathbf{p} \right),$$
$$\mathsf{msk}^* := \left( \{\mathbf{W}'_j\}_{j \in [L]} \right)$$

Enc$^*(\mathbf{B}, \mathbf{p}, \mathbf{x}^*)$: Compute

$$\mathbf{c}_0^T := \mathbf{c}^T, \qquad \mathbf{c}_j^T := \mathbf{c}^T \mathbf{W}'_j$$

Output

$$\mathsf{ct} := \left( \Psi, \mathbf{c}_0, \{\mathbf{c}_j\}_{j \in [L]}, p' + M \cdot q/2 \right)$$

KeyGen$^*(\mathsf{msk}^*, f)$: On input $f$ such that $f(\mathbf{x}^*) \neq 0$,

$$\mathbf{B}_{\hat{f}} = [\mathbf{B}\mathbf{W}'_1 + \psi_1 \overline{\mathbf{G}} \mid \cdots \mid \mathbf{B}\mathbf{W}'_L + \psi_L \overline{\mathbf{G}}] \cdot \mathbf{H}_{\hat{f}}$$
$$= [\mathbf{B}\mathbf{W}'_1 \mid \cdots \mid \mathbf{B}\mathbf{W}'_L] \cdot \mathbf{H}_{\hat{f}, \Psi} + \overline{\Psi}_f$$
$$= \mathbf{B}(\mathbf{W}'_{\hat{f}} + \mathbf{R}_f) + f(\mathbf{x}^*)\overline{\mathbf{G}}$$

where

$$\mathbf{W}'_{\hat{f}} := [\mathbf{W}'_1 \mid \cdots \mid \mathbf{W}'_L] \cdot \mathbf{H}_{\hat{f}, \Psi}, \quad \Psi_f = \mathbf{A}\mathbf{R}_f + f(\mathbf{x}^*)\mathbf{G}$$

We can then sample a short $\mathsf{sk}_f$ using $\mathbf{W}'_{\hat{f}} + \mathbf{R}_f$ such that

$$[\mathbf{B} \mid \mathbf{B}_{\hat{f}}] \cdot \mathsf{sk}_f = \mathbf{p}$$

Output $\mathsf{sk}_f$.

We now proceed to describe a sketch of the proof of security through a sequence of games, using the auxiliary algorithms described above.

*Hybrid $\mathcal{H}_0$.* Real world.

*Hybrid $\mathcal{H}_1$.* Switch to Setup$^*$, Enc$^*$ that are given $\mathbf{A} = \binom{\mathbf{B}}{\mathbf{c}}$ and use $\mathbf{W}'_j$. When $\mathbf{c}$ is the LWE vector relative to $\mathbf{B}$, game 0 and game 1 are statistically close by an application of the leftover hash lemma. (In this proof sketch, we ignore the issue of smoothing the errors in the ciphertext, which can be done by noise flooding). Note that in this game, the challenger does not know the LWE secret $\mathbf{s}$.

*Hybrid $\mathcal{H}_2$.* Switch to KeyGen* that uses $(\mathbf{W}'_j, \mathbf{R}_i)$ instead of $\mathbf{T_B}$. The difference between game 1 and game 2 is that in the former, secret keys are generated using $\mathbf{T_B}$ whereas in the latter, they are generated using $\mathbf{W}'_{\hat{f}} + \mathbf{R}_f$, by employing the ABB trick [ABB10a]. Thus, games 1 and 2 are statistically indistinguishable.

*Hybrid $\mathcal{H}_3$.* Switch $\mathbf{c}$ in $\mathbf{A}$ from $\mathbf{s}^T\mathbf{B} + \mathbf{e}$ to a random $\mathbf{c}$ (this changes both abe.ct and $\Psi$). Games 2 and 3 are computationally indistinguishable by the LWE assumption.

*Hybrid $\mathcal{H}_4$.* Switch from KeyGen* back to KeyGen. Games 3 and 4 are statistically indistinguishable by the same argument as Games 1 versus 2.

Now, in game 4, we argue that $x_1^*, \ldots, x_n^*$ is information-theoretically hidden, as follows:

- First, note that the distribution of the NO keys only depends on $[\mathbf{B} \mid \mathbf{B}_{\hat{f}}]$, that is, on $(\mathsf{mpk}, f, \mathbf{T_B})$, and leak no information about the FHE encryption randomness $\mathbf{R}_1, \ldots, \mathbf{R}_n$.
- Secondly, mpk and the ciphertext depend on the $\psi_i$'s and the $\mathbf{W}'_j$'s, but not on the FHE encryption randomness $\mathbf{R}_1, \ldots, \mathbf{R}_n$.
- Using these two observations, we argue that $\psi_i$ hides $x_i^*$. Indeed, by left-over hash lemma, we know that $\mathbf{AR}_i$ is statistically close to uniform given $\mathbf{A} = \binom{\mathbf{B}}{\mathbf{c}}$, and therefore completely hides $x_i^*$.

*Remark: Relation to the GVW15 Security Proof.* Many of the steps in the proof are analogous to what happens in GVW15. The crucial difference is that in GVW15, the leftover hash lemma (LHL) was used to hide the FHE secret key which is embedded as part of the ABE attributes. Using the fact that NO keys do not leak any information about *the randomness $\mathbf{W}_j$ used to simulate the ABE ciphertext*, one can apply LHL to this randomness and therefore, hide the FHE secret key, and consequently, hiding the attributes. In our scheme, LHL is applied to *the randomness $\mathbf{R}_j$ used for FHE encryption*, and not on the randomness $\mathbf{W}'_j$ used to simulate the ABE ciphertext.

### 4.3   Constraint Hiding Constrained PRF

We now present a Constraint Hiding CPRF construction that relies on the [BV15b] CPRF together with the dual use technique from Sect. 4.2.

Our constraint hiding CPRF scheme works as follows.

- CPRF.Keygen$(1^\lambda, 1^\ell, 1^{\ell_x}, 1^d)$ takes as input the security parameter $\lambda$, the maximum description length $\ell$ of constraint functions, their input length $\ell_x$ and depth $d$, and outputs public parameters pp and a secret key $\sigma$ for the CPRF scheme. Let $L = \ell \cdot (n+1)^2 \log^2 q$.
   Sample $\mathbf{B}, \mathbf{B}_1, \ldots, \mathbf{B}_L \xleftarrow{\$} \mathbb{Z}_q^{n \times (n+1)\log q}$ and $\mathbf{D}, \mathbf{C}_1, \ldots, \mathbf{C}_{\ell_x} \in \mathbb{Z}_q^{n \times m}$ for some

$m = \Omega(n \log q)$. Sample a uniformly random vector $\mathbf{s} \in \mathbb{Z}_q^n$. Output

$$\mathsf{pp} := \Big( \mathbf{B}, \{\mathbf{B}_j\}_{j \in [L]}, \{\mathbf{C}_j\}_{j \in [\ell_x]}, \mathbf{D} \Big),$$
$$\sigma := \mathbf{s}$$

– CPRF.Eval$_{\mathsf{pp}}(\sigma, x)$ outputs the evaluation of the PRF on an input $x$.
Let $\mathcal{U}_x : \{0,1\}^\ell \to \{0,1\}$ be the circuit that takes as input a description of a function $f$ and outputs $f(x)$. Now consider the circuit $\widehat{\mathcal{U}}_x : \{0,1\}^L \to \mathbb{Z}_q^{n \times (n+1) \log q}$ that takes as input a GSW encryption $\hat{f}$ of the description of $f$ and outputs $\overline{\Psi}_{\mathbf{x}}$ where $\Psi_{\mathbf{x}} = \mathsf{FHE.Eval}(\mathcal{U}_x, \hat{f})$.
Let $\widehat{\mathcal{U}}_x$ denote the circuit computing $\Psi \mapsto \overline{\Psi}_{\mathbf{x}}$ and

$$\mathbf{H}_{\widehat{\mathcal{U}}_x} := \mathsf{EvalF}(\widehat{\mathcal{U}}_x, \{\mathbf{B}_j\}_{j \in [L]}), \quad \mathbf{B}_{\widehat{\mathcal{U}}_x} := [\mathbf{B}_1 \mid \cdots \mid \mathbf{B}_L] \cdot \mathbf{H}_{\widehat{\mathcal{U}}_x}$$

Compute $\mathbf{C}_x = \mathsf{EvalF}(\mathcal{T}_x, \mathbf{C}_1, \ldots, \mathbf{C}_{\ell_x})$ (as defined in Sect. 3.7) and fix $\mathbf{M}_x = \mathbf{DG}^{-1}(\mathbf{C}_x)$. The PRF output is

$$y = \left\lfloor \mathbf{s}^T \cdot \mathbf{B}_{\widehat{\mathcal{U}}_x} \mathbf{G}^{-1}(\mathbf{M}_x) \right\rceil.$$

– CPRF.Constrain$_{\mathsf{pp}}(\sigma, f)$ outputs a constrained key $\sigma_f$.
Pick $\mathbf{e}, \mathbf{e}_0, \mathbf{e}_j \xleftarrow{\sigma} \mathbb{Z}^m, \mathbf{R}_i \in \{0,1\}^{(n+1) \log q \times (n+1) \log q}$ and compute GSW ciphertexts

$$\Psi_i := \begin{pmatrix} \mathbf{B} \\ \mathbf{s}^T \mathbf{B} + \mathbf{e}^T \end{pmatrix} \mathbf{R}_i + f_i \mathbf{G}$$

where $(f_1, \ldots, f_\ell)$ is the description of the function $f$.
Let $\psi_1, \ldots, \psi_L$ denote the binary representation of $\Psi := [\Psi_1 \mid \cdots \mid \Psi_\ell]$. Compute

$$\mathbf{c}_0^T := \mathbf{s}^T \mathbf{B} + \mathbf{e}_0^T, \qquad \mathbf{c}_j^T := \mathbf{s}^T [\mathbf{B}_j - \psi_j \overline{\mathbf{G}}] + \mathbf{e}_j^T$$

The constrained key consists of the FHE ciphertext $\Psi$ and the "ABE ciphertexts" computed as above. That is,

$$\mathsf{ct} := \Big( \Psi, \mathbf{c}_0, \{\mathbf{c}_j\}_{j \in [L]} \Big)$$

– CPRF.ConstrainEval$_{\mathsf{pp}}(\sigma_f, x)$ takes as input a constrained key $\sigma_f$ and an input $x$ and outputs a (potential) PRF output.
Let $\hat{f}$ denote the circuit computing $\Psi \mapsto \overline{\Psi}_{\mathbf{x}}$ (as above) and parse the constrained key $\mathsf{ct}$ as $(\Psi, \mathbf{c}_0, \{\mathbf{c}_j\}_{j \in L})$. Compute:

$$\overline{\Psi}_{\mathbf{x}} := \widehat{\mathcal{U}}_x(\Psi)$$
$$\mathbf{H}_{\widehat{\mathcal{U}}_x, \Psi} := \mathsf{EvalFX}(\widehat{\mathcal{U}}_x, \Psi, \{\mathbf{B}_j\}_{j \in [L]})$$
$$\mathbf{c}_{\widehat{\mathcal{U}}_x} := [\mathbf{c}_1 \mid \cdots \mid \mathbf{c}_L] \cdot \mathbf{H}_{\widehat{\mathcal{U}}_x, \Psi} + \underline{\Psi}_{\mathbf{x}}$$

Output

$$y' = \left\lfloor \mathbf{c}_{\widehat{\mathcal{U}}_x} \mathbf{G}^{-1}(\mathbf{M}_x) \right\rceil$$

**Theorem 6 (Correctness, Pseudorandomness, Constraint Hiding).**
*Under the* $\mathrm{DLWE}_{n,q,\chi}$ *hardness assumption, CPRF is correct, pseudorandom and constraint hiding.*

*Proof.* Correctness follows from a computation similar to the one in Sect. 4.2. In particular, the key relation tells us that

$$[\mathbf{B}_1 - \psi_1 \overline{\mathbf{G}} \mid \cdots \mid \mathbf{B}_L - \psi_L \overline{\mathbf{G}}] \cdot \mathbf{H}_{\widehat{\mathcal{U}}_x, \Psi} = [\mathbf{B}_1 \mid \cdots \mid \mathbf{B}_L] \cdot \mathbf{H}_{\widehat{\mathcal{U}}_x} - \overline{\Psi}_{\mathbf{x}} = \mathbf{B}_{\widehat{\mathcal{U}}_x} - \overline{\Psi}_{\mathbf{x}}$$

Multiplying both sides by $\mathbf{s}^T$, we have

$$\begin{aligned}
\mathbf{c}_{\widehat{\mathcal{U}}_x} &\approx \mathbf{s}^T [\mathbf{B}_1 - \psi_1 \overline{\mathbf{G}} \mid \cdots \mid \mathbf{B}_L - \psi_L \overline{\mathbf{G}}] \cdot \mathbf{H}_{\widehat{\mathcal{U}}_x, \Psi} + \underline{\Psi}_{\mathbf{x}} \\
&= \mathbf{s}^T \mathbf{B}_{\widehat{\mathcal{U}}_x} - \mathbf{s}^T \overline{\Psi}_{\mathbf{x}} + \underline{\Psi}_{\mathbf{x}} \\
&= \mathbf{s}^T \mathbf{B}_{\widehat{\mathcal{U}}_x} - [\mathbf{s}^T \mid -1] \cdot \Psi_{\mathbf{x}} \\
&\approx \mathbf{s}^T \mathbf{B}_{\widehat{\mathcal{U}}_x} - f(\mathbf{x}) \cdot [\mathbf{s}^T \mid -1] \cdot \mathbf{G}
\end{aligned}$$

Then, when $f(\mathbf{x}) = 0$, the constrained evaluation algorithm outputs

$$y = \left\lfloor \mathbf{c}_{\widehat{\mathcal{U}}_x} \mathbf{G}^{-1}(\mathbf{M}_x) \right\rceil = \left\lfloor \mathbf{s}^T \mathbf{B}_{\widehat{\mathcal{U}}_x} \mathbf{G}^{-1}(\mathbf{M}_x) \right\rceil$$

which is indeed the PRF output on $\mathbf{x}$. The error growth behaves as in the PE scheme and thus, the parameters are set as in Theorem 4.

The proof of security closely follows the outline of Theorem 9 for our modulus-switching based private CPRF construction. We omit the details from this version.

# 5   Our Second Technique: Modulus Switching in HNF

This section contains our PE and CH-CPRF constructions based on the modulus switching method. We start with a technical lemma that explains how rounding is used to push the FHE noise into the ABE noise, as explained in the introduction. This is followed by our construction of a Weakly Attribute Hiding Predicate Encryption in Sect. 5.1 and our construction of Constraint Hiding Constrained PRF in Sect. 5.2.

Throughout this section we denote $\lfloor x \rceil_p = \left\lfloor \frac{x}{q/p} \right\rceil$ when the operand is $x \in \mathbb{Z}_q$ and output in $\mathbb{Z}_p$, for $q, p$ that will be defined appropriately in the relevant sections. We extend this operator to vectors and matrices by applying it element-wise. We start with the aforementioned rounding lemma.

**Lemma 2.** *Let* $n, m', t, p$ *be integers and consider* $q = t \cdot p$. *Let* FHE *be the scheme guaranteed in Lemma 1, with some depth bound* $d$, *let* $d', B$ *as in the lemma statement, and assume that* $t$ *conforms with the conditions of the lemma. Denote* $m = n \lceil \log q \rceil$.

Let $sk \in \mathbb{Z}_q^{\ell_s} \leftarrow$ FHE.$Keygen(1^\lambda)$ and $\tilde{x} \in \mathbb{Z}_q^{\ell_p} \leftarrow$ FHE.$Enc(sk, x)$ for some $x \in \{0, 1\}^\ell$, and for any circuit $f : \{0, 1\}^\ell \to \{0, 1\}$ define the circuit $f' : \{0, 1\}^{\ell_p} \to \{0, 1\}^{\ell_s}$ as $f'(\cdot) =$ FHE.$Eval(f, \cdot)$. Let $\mathbf{M} \in \mathbb{Z}_p^{n \times m'}, \vec{\mathbf{A}} \in \mathbb{Z}_q^{n \times \ell_p m}, \vec{\mathbf{B}} \in \mathbb{Z}_q^{n \times \ell_s m}$. Denote

$$\mathbf{A}_f := [\vec{\mathbf{A}} \parallel \vec{\mathbf{B}}] \cdot \mathbf{H}_f$$
$$\Psi_f := [\vec{\mathbf{A}} - \tilde{x} \otimes \vec{\mathbf{G}} \parallel \vec{\mathbf{B}} - sk \otimes \vec{\mathbf{G}}] \cdot \mathbf{H}_{f,\mathbf{x}}$$

where $\mathbf{H}_f = \mathsf{EvalF}^{ip}(f', \vec{\mathbf{A}}, \vec{\mathbf{B}})$ and $\mathbf{H}_{f,\mathbf{x}} = \mathsf{EvalFX}^{ip}(f', \tilde{x}, \vec{\mathbf{A}}, \vec{\mathbf{B}})$ as in Theorem 3. Then

1. $\Psi_f = \mathbf{A}_f - (f(x) \cdot t + e)\mathbf{G}$ where $|e| \le B_{\mathrm{FHE}} = B(n\lceil \log q\rceil)^{O(d)}$.
2. $\lfloor \Psi_f \mathbf{G}^{-1}(\mathbf{M}) \rceil_p = \lfloor \mathbf{A}_f \mathbf{G}^{-1}(\mathbf{M}) \rceil_p - f(x)\mathbf{M} + \mathbf{E}$ where $\|\mathbf{E}\|_\infty \le 2 + \frac{B_{\mathrm{FHE}}\|\mathbf{M}\|_\infty}{t}$.

*Proof.* By Theorem 3,

$$\Psi_f = \left[\vec{\mathbf{A}} - \tilde{x} \otimes \vec{\mathbf{G}} \parallel \vec{\mathbf{B}} - sk \otimes \vec{\mathbf{G}}\right] \cdot \mathbf{H}_{f,\mathbf{x}}$$
$$= [\vec{\mathbf{A}}\|\vec{\mathbf{B}}] \cdot \mathbf{H}_f - \langle f'(\tilde{x}), sk\rangle \mathbf{G}$$
$$= \mathbf{A}_f - \langle \text{FHE.Eval}(f, \tilde{x}), sk\rangle \mathbf{G}$$

where by Lemma 1, $\langle$FHE.Eval$(f, \tilde{x}), sk\rangle = t \cdot f(x) + e$ with $|e| \le B(n\lceil\log q\rceil)^{O(d)}$, so (1) follows. Moreover,

$$\lfloor \Psi_f \mathbf{G}^{-1}(\mathbf{M}) \rceil_p = \lfloor (\mathbf{A}_f - (t \cdot f(x) + e)\mathbf{G})\mathbf{G}^{-1}(\mathbf{M}) \rceil_p$$
$$= \lfloor \mathbf{A}_f \mathbf{G}^{-1}(\mathbf{M}) - t \cdot f(x)\mathbf{M} - e\mathbf{M} \rceil_p$$
$$= \lfloor \mathbf{A}_f \mathbf{G}^{-1}(\mathbf{M}) - e\mathbf{M} \rceil_p - f(x)\mathbf{M}$$
$$= \lfloor \mathbf{A}_f \mathbf{G}^{-1}(\mathbf{M}) \rceil_p - f(x)\mathbf{M} - \mathbf{E}$$

where $\mathbf{E} = (e/t)\mathbf{M} + \boldsymbol{\Delta}$ for a rounding-errors matrix $\|\boldsymbol{\Delta}\|_\infty \le 2$, and therefore $\|\mathbf{E}\|_\infty \le 2 + |e| \cdot (\|\mathbf{M}\|_\infty /t)$.

## 5.1 Weakly Attribute Hiding Predicate Encryption

The scheme is parameterized by $\epsilon \in (0, 1)$ which governs the lattice hardness assumption that underly the construction. Essentially, with parameter $\epsilon$ the scheme will be secure under the polynomial hardness of approximating lattice problems to within a $2^{\widetilde{O}(n^\epsilon)}$-factor.

- PE.Setup$(1^\lambda, 1^d) \to$ (mpk, msk). Define $\ell = \lambda$ (this is the supported attribute length). Set $n = (\lambda d)^{1/\epsilon}$. Let $\chi$ be the $B = \widetilde{O}(\sqrt{n})$-bounded distribution from Corollary 1. Let $p, \tau$ be integer parameters set such that $\tau \ge z_1, p \ge 4z_2 \cdot \tau$ for parameters $z_1, z_2 = 2^{d \cdot \mathrm{polylog}(n)}$ that will be specified throughout the analysis. Let $t = \Theta(p)$ and $q = p \cdot t$. Denote $m = n\lceil \log q\rceil$. Recall Corollary 2 and let $m_0 = m_0(n, q)$ as in the corollary statement. Let FHE be the scheme from Lemma 1 with depth parameter $d$, define $\ell_s, \ell_c, d'$ as in the lemma statement, and let $\ell_p = \ell \cdot \ell_c$.

Recall Corollary 2 and let $m_0 = m_0(n, p)$ as in the corollary statement. Consider $m' = \max\{(n+1)\lceil \log q \rceil + 2\lambda, m_0\}$ (note that $m_0$ is w.r.t $p$ but $m'$ needs to be larger than $(n+1)\lceil \log q \rceil$). Generate a matrix with a trapdoor $(\mathbf{A}, \mathbf{T_A}) \leftarrow \mathsf{TrapGen}(1^n, p, m')$, i.e. $\mathbf{A} \in \mathbb{Z}_p^{n \times m'}$. Sample a uniform $\mathbf{v} \overset{\$}{\leftarrow} \mathbb{Z}_p^n$. Generate uniform $\vec{\mathbf{A}} \overset{\$}{\leftarrow} (\mathbb{Z}_q^{n \times m})^{\ell_p}$ and $\vec{\mathbf{B}} \overset{\$}{\leftarrow} (\mathbb{Z}_q^{n \times m})^{\ell_s}$.

Output $\mathsf{msk} := \mathbf{T_A}$ and $\mathsf{mpk} := (\mathbf{A}, \mathbf{v}, \vec{\mathbf{A}}, \vec{\mathbf{B}})$.

- $\mathsf{PE.Enc}(\mathsf{mpk}, \mu, x) \to \mathsf{ct}$. Generate $\mathsf{sk} \leftarrow \mathsf{FHE.Keygen}(1^\lambda)$, s.t. $\mathsf{sk} \in \mathbb{Z}_p^{\ell_s}$ and compute $\tilde{\mathbf{x}} \leftarrow \mathsf{FHE.Enc}(\mathsf{sk}, x)$. Sample a vector $\mathbf{s} \overset{\$}{\leftarrow} \chi^n$, an error vector $\mathbf{e} \overset{\$}{\leftarrow} \chi^{m'}$ and an error scalar $e \overset{\$}{\leftarrow} \chi$. Sample $\mathbf{R}_A \overset{\$}{\leftarrow} \{0,1\}^{m' \times m\ell_p}$ and $\mathbf{R}_B \overset{\$}{\leftarrow} \{0,1\}^{m' \times m\ell_s}$. Sample a matrix $\mathbf{A}_t \overset{\$}{\leftarrow} \mathbb{Z}_t^{n \times m'}$ and a vector $\mathbf{v}_t \overset{\$}{\leftarrow} \mathbb{Z}_t^n$. Encrypt as follows:

$$\mathbf{u}_0 := \mathbf{s}^T \mathbf{A} + \lfloor \mathbf{s}^T \mathbf{A}_t + \mathbf{e} \rceil_p \qquad (\bmod\ p)$$

$$\mathbf{u}_\mu := \mathbf{s}^T \mathbf{v} + \lfloor \mathbf{s}^T \mathbf{v}_t + e \rceil_p + \mu \lfloor p/2 \rceil \qquad (\bmod\ p)$$

$$\vec{\mathbf{a}} := \mathbf{s}^T (\vec{\mathbf{A}} - \tilde{\mathbf{x}} \otimes \mathbf{G}_q) + \mathbf{e} \mathbf{R}_A \qquad (\bmod\ q)$$

$$\vec{\mathbf{b}} := \mathbf{s}^T (\vec{\mathbf{B}} - \mathsf{sk} \otimes \mathbf{G}_q) + \mathbf{e} \mathbf{R}_B \qquad (\bmod\ q)$$

Output $\mathsf{ct} := (\tilde{\mathbf{x}}, \mathbf{u}_0, \mathbf{u}_\mu, \vec{\mathbf{a}}, \vec{\mathbf{b}})$.

- $\mathsf{PE.Keygen}(\mathsf{msk}, f) \to \mathsf{sk}_f$. Define $f'(\cdot) := \mathsf{FHE.Eval}(f, \cdot)$ and compute $\mathbf{A}_f := [\vec{\mathbf{A}} \| \vec{\mathbf{B}}] \cdot \mathbf{H}_f$, where $\mathbf{H}_f \leftarrow \mathsf{EvalF}^{ip}(f', \vec{\mathbf{A}}, \vec{\mathbf{B}})$. Compute $\widehat{\mathbf{A}}_f := \lfloor \mathbf{A}_f \mathbf{G}^{-1}(\mathbf{G}_p) \rceil_p$. Use $\mathbf{T_A}$ to sample $[\mathbf{h}_f \| \mathbf{k}_f] := [\mathbf{I} \| \mathbf{A} \| \widehat{\mathbf{A}}_f]_\tau^{-1}(\mathbf{v})$, i.e. s.t. $[\mathbf{A} \| \widehat{\mathbf{A}}_f] \mathbf{k}_f = \mathbf{v} - \mathbf{h}_f$ $(\bmod\ p)$. Output $\mathsf{sk}_f := \mathbf{k}_f$.

- $\mathsf{PE.Dec}(\mathsf{mpk}, \mathsf{ct}, \mathsf{sk}_f) \to \mu$. Compute $\mathbf{H}_{f,x} \leftarrow \mathsf{EvalFX}^{ip}(f', \tilde{\mathbf{x}}, \vec{\mathbf{A}}, \vec{\mathbf{B}})$ and set $\mathbf{a}_{f,x} := [\vec{\mathbf{a}} \| \vec{\mathbf{b}}] \cdot \mathbf{H}_{f,x}$. Compute $\widehat{\mathbf{a}}_{f,x} := (1/t)(\mathbf{a}_{f,x} \mathbf{G}^{-1}(\mathbf{G}_p))$ and $b' := \mathbf{u}_\mu - [\mathbf{u}_0 \| \widehat{\mathbf{a}}_{f,x}] \mathbf{k}_f$ $(\bmod\ p)$. Return 0 if $|b'| < \frac{p}{4}$ and 1 otherwise.

**Analysis.** Correctness and security are stated and proven next. We note that since $q \leq 2^n$ regardless of the exact manner we choose $p, \tau$ we have that any polynomial of the form $\mathsf{poly}(\lambda, B, (n\lceil \log q \rceil)^{O(d')})$ is upper bounded by a function of the form $2^{d \cdot \mathsf{polylog}(n)}$. This is since $n\lceil \log q \rceil \leq n^2$, $\lambda < n$ and $d' = d \cdot \mathsf{polylog}(n\lceil \log q \rceil) = d \cdot \mathsf{polylog}(n)$.

**Theorem 7 (Correctness).** *The PE construction above is correct as per Definition 3.*

*Proof.* Let $\mathsf{ct}$ be an encryption of message $\mu$ under attribute $x$ and let $\mathbf{k}_f$ be a secret key for a function $f$. Let $\mathbf{H}_f := \mathsf{EvalF}^{ip}(f', \vec{\mathbf{A}}, \vec{\mathbf{B}})$, $\mathbf{H}_{f,\mathbf{x}} := \mathsf{EvalFX}^{ip}(f', \vec{\mathbf{A}}, \vec{\mathbf{B}})$, $\mathbf{A}_f := [\vec{\mathbf{A}} \| \vec{\mathbf{B}}] \cdot \mathbf{H}_f$, and denote $\Psi_f := [\vec{\mathbf{A}} - \tilde{\mathbf{x}} \otimes \mathbf{G}_q \| \vec{\mathbf{B}} -$

$\mathsf{sk} \otimes \mathbf{G}_q] \cdot \mathbf{H}_{f,\mathbf{x}}$. By Lemma 2, $\Psi_f = \mathbf{A}_f - (f(x) \cdot t + e)\mathbf{G}$ where $|e| \le B_{\mathrm{FHE}} = B(n\lceil \log q \rceil)^{O(d)}$. Then

$$
\begin{aligned}
\mathbf{a}_{f,x} &= [\vec{\mathbf{a}} \| \vec{\mathbf{b}}]\mathbf{H}_{f,x} \\
&= \left(\mathbf{s}^T([\vec{\mathbf{A}} \| \vec{\mathbf{B}}] - [\tilde{\mathbf{x}} \| \mathsf{sk}] \otimes \mathbf{G}) + \mathbf{e}[\mathbf{R}_A \| \mathbf{R}_B]\right)\mathbf{H}_{f,x} \\
&= \mathbf{s}^T \Psi_f + \mathbf{e}[\mathbf{R}_A \| \mathbf{R}_B]\mathbf{H}_{f,x} \\
&= \mathbf{s}^T\left(\mathbf{A}_f - (f(x) \cdot t + e)\mathbf{G}\right) + \mathbf{e}[\mathbf{R}_A \| \mathbf{R}_B]\mathbf{H}_{f,x}
\end{aligned}
$$

Therefore,

$$
\begin{aligned}
\widehat{\mathbf{a}}_{f,x} &= \frac{\mathbf{a}_{f,x}\mathbf{G}^{-1}(\mathbf{G}_p)}{t} \\
&= \frac{\mathbf{s}^T\left(\mathbf{A}_f - (f(x) \cdot t + e)\mathbf{G}\right)\mathbf{G}^{-1}(\mathbf{G}_p)}{t} + \underbrace{\frac{\mathbf{e}[\mathbf{R}_A \| \mathbf{R}_B]\mathbf{H}_{f,x}\mathbf{G}^{-1}(\mathbf{G}_p)}{t}}_{\mathbf{e}_1} \\
&= \frac{\mathbf{s}^T\mathbf{A}_f\mathbf{G}^{-1}(\mathbf{G}_p)}{t} - f(x)\mathbf{s}^T\mathbf{G}_p \underbrace{-(e/t)\mathbf{s}^T\mathbf{G}_p}_{\mathbf{e}_2} + \mathbf{e}_1 \\
&= \mathbf{s}^T \cdot \left\lfloor \frac{\mathbf{A}_f\mathbf{G}^{-1}(\mathbf{G}_p)}{t} \right\rceil - f(x)\mathbf{s}^T\mathbf{G}_p + \mathbf{e}_1 + \mathbf{e}_2 + \underbrace{\mathbf{s}^T \mathbf{\Delta}}_{\mathbf{e}_3},
\end{aligned}
$$

where $\mathbf{\Delta}$ is the matrix of rounding errors, i.e. $\|\mathbf{\Delta}\|_\infty \le 1/2$. We can bound the error $\mathbf{e}' = \mathbf{e}_1 + \mathbf{e}_2 + \mathbf{e}_3$ as follows: $\|\mathbf{e}_1\|_\infty \le Bm'(\ell_p + \ell_s)(n\lceil \log q \rceil)^{O(d')}n\lceil \log p \rceil/t$, $\|\mathbf{e}_2\|_\infty \le nBp(n\lceil \log q \rceil)^{O(d)}/t$, $\|\mathbf{e}_3\|_\infty \le nB/2$. Note that $\ell_p, \ell_s = \mathrm{poly}(n\lceil \log q \rceil)$, hence $\|\mathbf{e}'\|_\infty \le \mathrm{poly}(\lambda, B, (n\lceil \log q \rceil)^{O(d')})$.

It follows that if indeed $f(x) = 0$ then $\widehat{\mathbf{a}}_{f,x} = \mathbf{s}^T\widehat{\mathbf{A}}_f + \mathbf{e}'$. Now, recall that the distribution of $\mathbf{k}_f, \mathbf{h}_f$ is Gaussian with parameter $\tau$ subject to $[\mathbf{A} \| \widehat{\mathbf{A}}_f]\mathbf{k}_f = \mathbf{v} - \mathbf{h}_f \pmod{p}$. Therefore $\|\mathbf{k}_f\|_\infty \le \tau\sqrt{\lambda(m + m')}$ and $\|\mathbf{h}_f\|_\infty \le \tau\sqrt{\lambda n}$ with all but $2^{-\lambda} = \mathrm{negl}(\lambda)$ probability. By definition,

$$
\mathbf{u}_0 = \mathbf{s}^T\mathbf{A} + \left\lfloor \mathbf{s}^T\mathbf{A}_t + \mathbf{e} \right\rceil_p, \quad \mathbf{u}_\mu = \mathbf{s}^T\mathbf{v} + \left\lfloor \mathbf{s}^T\mathbf{v}_t + \mathbf{e} \right\rceil_p + \mu\lfloor p/2 \rceil
$$

Denote $\mathbf{e}_0 = \left\lfloor \mathbf{s}^T\mathbf{A}_t + \mathbf{e} \right\rceil_p$ and $e_\mu = \left\lfloor \mathbf{s}^T\mathbf{v}_t + \mathbf{e} \right\rceil_p$, then $\|\mathbf{e}_0\|_\infty, |e_\mu| \le (n + 1)B$. Therefore,

$$
\begin{aligned}
b' &= \mathbf{u}_\mu - [\mathbf{u}_0 \| \widehat{\mathbf{a}}_{f,x}]\mathbf{k}_f \\
&= \mathbf{s}^T\mathbf{v} + e_\mu + \mu\lfloor p/2 \rceil - \mathbf{s}^T[\mathbf{A} \| \widehat{\mathbf{A}}_f - f(x)\mathbf{G}_p]\mathbf{k}_f - [\mathbf{e}_0 \| \mathbf{e}']\mathbf{k}_f \\
&= \mu\lfloor p/2 \rceil + \underbrace{e_\mu - \mathbf{s}^T\mathbf{h}_f - [\mathbf{e}_0 \| \mathbf{e}']\mathbf{k}_f}_{e''} + f(x)\mathbf{s}^T[\mathbf{0} \| \mathbf{G}_p]\mathbf{k}_f
\end{aligned}
$$

where $|e''| < \tau \cdot \mathrm{poly}(\lambda, B, (n\lceil \log q \rceil)^{O(d')})$. Therefore there exists some $z_2 = 2^{d\mathrm{polylog}(n)}$ s.t. when we set $p > 4z_2\tau$ we get that $|e''| < \frac{p}{4}$. Hence, if $f(x) = 0$ then $b' = \mu\lfloor p/2 \rceil + e'' \in \mu\lfloor p/2 \rceil \pm \frac{p}{4}$ and in particular $\mu = 0$ implies $|b'| < \frac{p}{4}$ and $\mu = 1$ implies $|b'| > \frac{p}{4}$.  $\square$

**Theorem 8 (Security).** *The scheme* PE *is secure as per Definition 3 under the* $\text{LWE}_{n,q,\chi}$ *assumption, and thus under the worst case hardness of approximating* GapSVP, SIVP *to within a* $2^{\tilde{O}(n^\varepsilon)}$ *factor in polynomial time.*

*Proof (Sketch).* Define the simulator $\text{Sim}(\text{mpk}) \to \text{ct}$ that generates a ciphertext $\text{ct} = (\tilde{x}, \mathbf{u}_0, \mathbf{u}_\mu, \vec{\mathbf{a}}, \vec{\mathbf{b}})$ by computing $\tilde{x} \leftarrow \text{FHE.Enc}(\text{sk}, 0^\ell)$ and sampling all the other ct parts uniformly from $\mathbb{Z}_q$ as required. We now show a sequence of hybrids, where the first hybrid corresponds to $\exp_{real}$ and the last hybrid corresponds to $\exp_{ideal}$ with the simulator Sim we just defined.

*Hybrid* $\mathcal{H}_0$. This is $\exp_{real}$.

*Hybrid* $\mathcal{H}_1$. We change the Setup algorithm, specifically the generation of $\vec{\mathbf{A}}, \vec{\mathbf{B}}$: Let $x$ be the attribute declared by the adversary. Generate $\text{sk} \leftarrow \text{FHE.Keygen}(1^\lambda)$ and compute $\tilde{x} \leftarrow \text{FHE.Enc}(\text{sk}, x)$. Sample $\mathbf{R}_A \xleftarrow{\$} \{0,1\}^{m' \times (m\ell_p)}$ and $\mathbf{R}_B \xleftarrow{\$} \{0,1\}^{m' \times (m\ell_s)}$, and define

$$\vec{\mathbf{A}} := (t\mathbf{A} + \mathbf{A}_t)\mathbf{R}_A + \tilde{\mathbf{x}} \otimes \mathbf{G}_q, \qquad \vec{\mathbf{B}} := (t\mathbf{A} + \mathbf{A}_t)\mathbf{R}_B + \text{sk} \otimes \mathbf{G}_q.$$

$\mathbf{A}$ is statistically close to uniform in $\mathbb{Z}_p^{n \times m'}$ and $\mathbf{A}_t$ is uniform in $\mathbb{Z}_t^{n \times m'}$, therefore the matrix $t\mathbf{A} + \mathbf{A}_t$ is close to uniform in $\mathbb{Z}_q$. Since each $\mathbf{R}_A, \mathbf{R}_B$ are sampled uniformly and independently and $m' \geq (n+1)\lceil \log q \rceil + 2\lambda$, indistinguishability follows from the extended leftover hash lemma.

*Hybrid* $\mathcal{H}_2$. We change the Enc algorithm. Sample $\mathbf{s} \leftarrow \chi_q^n$, $\mathbf{e} \leftarrow \chi_q^{m'}$ and $e \leftarrow \chi_q$ as in the original encryption algorithm, then compute

$$\mathbf{u}_0' := \mathbf{s}^T(t\mathbf{A} + \mathbf{A}_t) + \mathbf{e}, \qquad \mathbf{u}_\mu' := \mathbf{s}^T(t\mathbf{v} + \mathbf{v}_t) + e.$$

Encrypt as follows:

$$\mathbf{u}_0 := \lfloor \mathbf{u}_0' \rceil_p, \qquad \mathbf{u}_\mu := \lfloor \mathbf{u}_\mu' \rceil_p, \qquad \vec{\mathbf{a}} := \mathbf{u}_0' \mathbf{R}_A, \qquad \vec{\mathbf{b}} := \mathbf{u}_0' \mathbf{R}_B.$$

The distributions remain as in the original scheme so statistical indistinguishability is maintained:

$$\mathbf{u}_0 = \lfloor \mathbf{u}_0' \rceil_p = \lfloor \mathbf{s}^T(t\mathbf{A} + \mathbf{A}_t) + \mathbf{e} \rceil_p = \mathbf{s}^T \mathbf{A} + \lfloor \mathbf{s}^T \mathbf{A}_t + \mathbf{e} \rceil_p$$

$$\mathbf{u}_\mu = \lfloor \mathbf{u}_\mu' \rceil_p = \lfloor \mathbf{s}^T(t\mathbf{v} + \mathbf{v}_t) + e \rceil_p = \mathbf{s}^T \mathbf{v} + \lfloor \mathbf{s}^T \mathbf{v}_t + e \rceil_p$$

$$\vec{\mathbf{a}} = \mathbf{u}_0' \mathbf{R}_A = (\mathbf{s}^T(t\mathbf{A} + \mathbf{A}_t) + \mathbf{e})\mathbf{R}_A = \mathbf{s}^T(\vec{\mathbf{A}} - \tilde{\mathbf{x}} \otimes \mathbf{G}_q) + \mathbf{e}\mathbf{R}_A$$

$$\vec{\mathbf{b}} = \mathbf{u}_0' \mathbf{R}_B = (\mathbf{s}^T(t\mathbf{A} + \mathbf{A}_t) + \mathbf{e})\mathbf{R}_B = \mathbf{s}^T(\vec{\mathbf{B}} - \text{sk} \otimes \mathbf{G}_q) + \mathbf{e}\mathbf{R}_B$$

*Hybrid* $\mathcal{H}_3$. We change the Keygen algorithm. We're only required to generate keys for $f$ s.t. $f(x) = 1$, otherwise the adversary is not admissible. Recall that in PE.Keygen we sample from $[\mathbf{I}\|\mathbf{A}\|\widehat{\mathbf{A}}_f]_\tau^{-1}(\mathbf{v})$, where $\widehat{\mathbf{A}}_f = \lfloor \mathbf{A}_f \mathbf{G}^{-1}(\mathbf{G}_p) \rceil_p$ and $\mathbf{A}_f = [\vec{\mathbf{A}}\|\vec{\mathbf{B}}] \cdot \mathbf{H}_f$. Using the notation

$$\Psi_f := [\vec{\mathbf{A}} - \tilde{x} \otimes \mathbf{G}_q \| \vec{\mathbf{B}} - \text{sk} \otimes \mathbf{G}_q] \cdot \mathbf{H}_{f,\mathbf{x}},$$

after the changes that were made in the previous hybrid, we have:

$$\Psi_f = [\tilde{\mathbf{A}} - \tilde{x} \otimes \mathbf{G}_q \| \tilde{\mathbf{B}} - \mathsf{sk} \otimes \mathbf{G}_q] \cdot \mathbf{H}_{f,x} = (t\mathbf{A} + \mathbf{A}_t)[\mathbf{R}_A \| \mathbf{R}_B] \cdot \mathbf{H}_{f,x}.$$

so

$$
\begin{aligned}
\left\lfloor \Psi_f \mathbf{G}^{-1}(\mathbf{G}_p) \right\rfloor_p &= \left\lfloor (t\mathbf{A} + \mathbf{A}_t)[\mathbf{R}_A \| \mathbf{R}_B] \cdot \mathbf{H}_{f,x} \mathbf{G}^{-1}(\mathbf{G}_p) \right\rfloor_p \\
&= \mathbf{A}[\mathbf{R}_A \| \mathbf{R}_B] \cdot \mathbf{H}_{f,x} \mathbf{G}^{-1}(\mathbf{G}_p) + \left\lfloor \mathbf{A}_t[\mathbf{R}_A \| \mathbf{R}_B] \cdot \mathbf{H}_{f,x} \mathbf{G}^{-1}(\mathbf{G}_p) \right\rfloor_p \\
&= \mathbf{A}[\mathbf{R}_A \| \mathbf{R}_B] \cdot \mathbf{H}_{f,x} \mathbf{G}^{-1}(\mathbf{G}_p) + \mathbf{E}' \qquad \|\mathbf{E}'\|_\infty \leq (n \lceil \log q \rceil)^{O(d')}
\end{aligned}
$$

and by Lemma 2,

$$\left\lfloor \Psi_f \mathbf{G}^{-1}(\mathbf{G}_p) \right\rfloor_p = \left\lfloor \mathbf{A}_f \mathbf{G}^{-1}(\mathbf{G}_p) \right\rfloor_p - f(x)\mathbf{G}_p + \mathbf{E} \qquad \|\mathbf{E}\|_\infty \leq 2 + \frac{B_{\mathrm{FHE}} \cdot p}{t}$$

Therefore, when $f(x) = 1$,

$$
\begin{aligned}
\widehat{\mathbf{A}}_f = \left\lfloor \mathbf{A}_f \mathbf{G}^{-1}(\mathbf{G}_p) \right\rfloor_p &= \left\lfloor \Psi_f \mathbf{G}^{-1}(\mathbf{G}_p) \right\rfloor_p + \mathbf{G}_p - \mathbf{E} \\
&= \mathbf{A}[\mathbf{R}_A \| \mathbf{R}_B] \cdot \mathbf{H}_{f,x} \mathbf{G}^{-1}(\mathbf{G}_p) + \mathbf{G}_p + \mathbf{E}' - \mathbf{E}
\end{aligned}
$$

where $\|\mathbf{E}' - \mathbf{E}\|_\infty \leq \mathrm{poly}(\lambda, B, (n \lceil \log q \rceil)^{O(d')})$. Given $[\mathbf{R}_A \| \mathbf{R}_B]\mathbf{H}_{f,x}\mathbf{G}^{-1}(\mathbf{G}_p)$ we can also compute $\mathbf{E}' - \mathbf{E}$, and then, by Corollary 5, we can compute the trapdoor $[\mathbf{I}\|\mathbf{A}\|\widehat{\mathbf{A}}_f]_\tau^{-1}$ for any $\tau \geq z_1$ for

$$
\begin{aligned}
z_1 &= O(\sqrt{mm'} \left\| [\mathbf{R}_A \| \mathbf{R}_B]\mathbf{H}_{f,x}\mathbf{G}^{-1}(\mathbf{G}_p) \right\|_\infty + \sqrt{mn} \left\| \mathbf{E}' - \mathbf{E} \right\|_\infty) \\
&\leq \mathrm{poly}(\lambda, B, (n \lceil \log q \rceil)^{O(d')}) \leq 2^{d \cdot \mathrm{polylog}(n)}.
\end{aligned}
$$

We will choose our parameters so that indeed $\tau \geq z_1$ which will allow us to sample from $[\mathbf{I}_n \| \mathbf{A} \| \widehat{\mathbf{A}}_f]_\tau^{-1}(\mathbf{v})$. Note that in this hybrid $\mathbf{T_A}$ is no longer used.

*Hybrid* $\mathcal{H}_4$. In Setup: Generate $\mathbf{A}$ uniformly instead of generating it with a trapdoor. Statistical indistinguishability holds by Corollary 2.

*Hybrid* $\mathcal{H}_5$. In Enc: Generate $\mathbf{u}_0', \mathbf{u}_\mu'$ uniformly in $\mathbb{Z}_q^n, \mathbb{Z}_q$ respectively. This is indistinguishable assuming hardness of $\mathrm{DLWE}_{q,n,\chi}$. Note that now $\mathbf{u}_0 = \lfloor \mathbf{u}_0' \rfloor_p$ and $\mathbf{u}_\mu = \lfloor \mathbf{u}_\mu' \rfloor_p$ are uniform in $\mathbb{Z}_p^n, \mathbb{Z}_p$ as well.

*Hybrid* $\mathcal{H}_6$. In Enc: Generate $\vec{a}$ and $\vec{b}$ uniformly from $\mathbb{Z}_p^m$. This is indistinguishable by the extended leftover hash lemma since $\mathbf{u}_0'$ is uniform, $\mathbf{R}_A, \mathbf{R}_B$ were randomly and independently generated and $m' \geq (n+1)\lceil \log q \rceil + 2\lambda$. The only information that ct reveals now is $\tilde{x}$.

*Hybrid* $\mathcal{H}_7$. In Setup: Generate $\mathbf{A}$ together with a trapdoor (the opposite of Hybrid 4). Statistical indistinguishability holds by Corollary 2.

*Hybrid* $\mathcal{H}_8$. In Keygen: Generate keys with $\mathbf{T_A}$ (the opposite of Hybrid 3). Indistinguishability holds since the keys are sampled from the same distribution.

*Hybrid* $\mathcal{H}_9$. In Setup: Generate the matrices $\vec{\mathbf{A}}, \vec{\mathbf{B}}$ as in the real Setup algorithm (the opposite of Hybrid 1). Indistinguishability holds by the leftover hash lemma.

*Hybrid* $\mathcal{H}_{10}$. Change $\tilde{x}$ to $\tilde{x} \leftarrow$ FHE.Enc(sk, $0^\ell$). By Lemma 1, those hybrids are indistinguishable under $\text{DLWE}_{n,q,\chi}$. In this hybrid the Enc algorithm is equivalent to the simulator Sim that was defined at the beginning of the proof, therefore it is equivalent to $\exp_{ideal}$.                                                      $\square$

## 5.2  Constraint Hiding Constrained PRF

We present a constraint hiding constrained PRF scheme that supports all functions expressible by boolean circuits of depth $d$, input length $k$ and description length $\ell$, for predefined polynomials $\ell, k, d$. We will rely on the hardness of LWE with sub-exponential noise to modulus ratio, as in our predicate encryption scheme. Working with a predefined polynomial input length $k$ makes the analysis much simpler than [BV15b], however we note that relying on a different hardness assumption (a variant of one dimensional SIS) it is possible to support a-priori unbounded inputs as in [BV15b].

– CPRF.Keygen$(1^\lambda, 1^\ell, 1^k, 1^d) \rightarrow (\text{pp}, \sigma)$. We let $n$ be a parameter to be chosen later as a function of $\lambda, \ell, k, d$. We let $q = p \cdot t$ and $t'$ be s.t. $t'|p$. If we wish to rely on the hardness of lattice problems with approximation ratio $2^{\tilde{O}(n^\varepsilon)}$, then all values $p, t, t'$ will be of size $2^{\tilde{O}(n^\varepsilon)}$ as well. The resulting constrained PRF scheme will support constraint functions of description length $\ell$, input length $k$ and depth $d$. The PRF itself outputs random elements in $\mathbb{Z}_{p/t'}$, i.e. $\log(p/t')$ bits of randomness.
  Denote $m = n\lceil \log q \rceil$ and $m' = n\lceil \log p \rceil$. Let FHE be the scheme from Lemma 1 with depth parameter $d$, define $\ell_c, \ell_s, d'$ as in the lemma statement, where $\ell_c$ is the FHE ciphertext length, $\ell_s$ is the FHE key length and $d'$ is the max depth of FHE.Eval$_{\text{pp}}(f, \cdot)$ for any $f$ of depth at most $d$. Denote $\ell_p = \ell \cdot \ell_c$. Let $\mathbf{G}_q$ and $\mathbf{G}_p$ denote the gadget matrices of dimensions $n \times n\lceil \log q \rceil$ and $n \times n\lceil \log p \rceil$ respectively.
  Generate $\vec{\mathbf{A}} \xleftarrow{\$} (\mathbb{Z}_q^{n \times m})^{\ell_p}$ and $\vec{\mathbf{B}} \xleftarrow{\$} (\mathbb{Z}_q^{n \times m})^{\ell_s}$. Generate $\mathbf{D} \xleftarrow{\$} \mathbb{Z}_p^{n \times m'}$ and $\vec{\mathbf{C}} = [\mathbf{C}_0 \| \mathbf{C}_1] \xleftarrow{\$} (\mathbb{Z}_p^{n \times m'})^2$. Sample a vector $\mathbf{s} \xleftarrow{\$} \chi^n$ and compute sk $\leftarrow$ FHE.Keygen$(1^\lambda)$. Sample an error vector $\mathbf{e}_b \xleftarrow{\$} \chi^{m \ell_s}$ and let $\vec{\mathbf{b}} = \mathbf{s}^T (\vec{\mathbf{B}} - \text{sk} \otimes \mathbf{G}_q) + \mathbf{e}_b$. The public parameters are pp $= (\vec{\mathbf{A}}, \vec{\mathbf{B}}, \vec{\mathbf{C}}, \mathbf{D}, \vec{\mathbf{b}})$ and the master seed is $\sigma = (\mathbf{s}, \text{sk})$.
– CPRF.Eval$_{\text{pp}}(\sigma, x) \rightarrow y \in \mathbb{Z}_{p/t'}$. Let $\mathcal{U}_x : \{0,1\}^\ell \rightarrow \{0,1\}$ be the circuit that takes as input a description of a function $f$ and outputs $f(x)$. Now consider the circuit $\mathcal{U}'_x : \{0,1\}^{\ell_p} \rightarrow \{0,1\}^{\ell_s}$ that takes as input an encryption of a description of $f$, i.e. $\tilde{f} = $ FHE.Enc(sk, $f$), and outputs FHE.Eval$(\mathcal{U}_x, \tilde{f})$, i.e. an FHE encryption of $f(x)$. Compute $\mathbf{A}_x := [\vec{\mathbf{A}} \| \vec{\mathbf{B}}] \cdot \mathbf{H}_x$, where $\mathbf{H}_x \leftarrow$

$\mathsf{EvalF}^{ip}(\mathcal{U}'_x, \vec{\mathbf{A}}, \vec{\mathbf{B}})$. Compute $\mathbf{C}_x := \mathsf{EvalF}(\mathcal{T}_x, \vec{\mathbf{C}})$ (as defined in Sect. 3.7) and fix $\mathbf{M}_x := \mathbf{D}\mathbf{G}_p^{-1}(\mathbf{C}_x) \mod p$. Output

$$y := \left\lfloor \mathbf{s}^T \cdot \frac{\mathbf{A}_x \mathbf{G}_q^{-1}(\mathbf{M}_x)}{t' \cdot t} \right\rceil .$$

- $\mathsf{CPRF.Constrain}_{\mathsf{pp}}(\sigma, f) \to \sigma_f$. Compute $\tilde{f} := \mathsf{FHE.Enc}(\mathsf{sk}, f)$. Sample an error vector $\mathbf{e}_a \xleftarrow{\$} \chi^{m\ell_p}$ and compute $\vec{\mathbf{a}} := \mathbf{s}^T(\vec{\mathbf{A}} - \tilde{f} \otimes \mathbf{G}_q) + \mathbf{e}_a$. Output $\sigma_f := (\vec{\mathbf{a}}, \tilde{f})$.
- $\mathsf{CPRF.ConstrainEval}_{\mathsf{pp}}(\sigma_f, x) \to y' \in \mathbb{Z}_r$. Compute $\mathbf{a}_{f,x} := [\vec{\mathbf{a}} \| \vec{\mathbf{b}}] \cdot \mathbf{H}_{f,x}$, where $\mathbf{H}_{f,x} \leftarrow \mathsf{EvalFX}^{ip}(\mathcal{U}'_x, \tilde{f}, \vec{\mathbf{A}}, \vec{\mathbf{B}})$, and output

$$y' := \left\lfloor \frac{\mathbf{a}_{f,x} \mathbf{G}_q^{-1}(\mathbf{M}_x)}{t' \cdot t} \right\rceil$$

**Analysis.** The following will be useful in the security and correctness proof.

**Lemma 3.** *Let $d'$ denote the depth of the circuit $\mathcal{U}'_x$. Consider $\mathbf{a}_{f,x}$ and $\mathbf{A}_x$ as defined in CPRF.ConstrainEval and CPRF.Eval, then:*

$$\frac{\mathbf{a}_{f,x} \mathbf{G}_q^{-1}(\mathbf{M}_x)}{t} = \mathbf{s}^T \frac{\mathbf{A}_x \mathbf{G}_q^{-1}(\mathbf{M}_x)}{t} - f(x)\mathbf{s}^T \mathbf{M}_x + \mathbf{e}''$$

*where $\|\mathbf{e}''\|_\infty \le \mathrm{poly}(\lambda, B, (n\lceil \log q\rceil)^{O(d')})$.*

*Proof.* Recall that $\|[\mathbf{e}_a \| \mathbf{e}_b]\|_\infty \le B$ and $\|\mathbf{H}_{f,x}\|_\infty \le (n\lceil \log q\rceil)^{O(d')}$. Hence

$$\begin{aligned} \mathbf{a}_{f,x} &= [\vec{\mathbf{a}} \| \vec{\mathbf{b}}] \cdot \mathbf{H}_{f,x} \\ &= \mathbf{s}^T \underbrace{[\vec{\mathbf{A}} - \tilde{f} \otimes \mathbf{G}_q \| \vec{\mathbf{B}} - \mathsf{sk} \otimes \mathbf{G}_q] \cdot \mathbf{H}_{f,x}}_{\Psi_x} + \underbrace{[\mathbf{e}_a \| \mathbf{e}_b] \cdot \mathbf{H}_{f,x}}_{\mathbf{e}} \end{aligned}$$

where $\|\mathbf{e}\|_\infty \le \mathrm{poly}(\lambda, B, (n\lceil \log q\rceil)^{O(d')})$. Therefore

$$\frac{\mathbf{a}_{f,x} \mathbf{G}_q^{-1}(\mathbf{M}_x)}{t} = \frac{(\mathbf{s}^T \Psi_x + \mathbf{e})\mathbf{G}_q^{-1}(\mathbf{M}_x)}{t} = \mathbf{s}^T \cdot \frac{\Psi_x \mathbf{G}_q^{-1}(\mathbf{M}_x)}{t} + \underbrace{\mathbf{e}/t \cdot \mathbf{G}_q^{-1}(\mathbf{M}_x)}_{\mathbf{e}'} \tag{11}$$

where $\|\mathbf{e}'\|_\infty \le \mathrm{poly}(\lambda, B, (n\lceil \log q\rceil)^{O(d')})$.

By Lemma 2, $\Psi_x = \mathbf{A}_x - (f(x) \cdot t + e)\mathbf{G}_q$ where $|e| \le B_{\mathsf{FHE}} = B(n\lceil \log q\rceil)^{O(d)}$, therefore

$$\frac{\Psi_x \mathbf{G}_q^{-1}(\mathbf{M}_x)}{t} = \frac{\mathbf{A}_x \mathbf{G}_q^{-1}(\mathbf{M}_x)}{t} - f(x)\mathbf{M}_x - \underbrace{e/t \mathbf{M}_x}_{\mathbf{E}} \qquad \|\mathbf{E}\|_\infty \le B_{\mathsf{FHE}} \cdot (p/t) \tag{12}$$

From Eqs. 11 and 12, we get

$$
\begin{aligned}
\frac{\mathbf{a}_{f,x}\mathbf{G}_q^{-1}(\mathbf{M}_x)}{t} &= \mathbf{s}^T \cdot \frac{\Psi_x \mathbf{G}_q^{-1}(\mathbf{M}_x)}{t} + \mathbf{e}' \\
&= \mathbf{s}^T \cdot \left( \frac{\mathbf{A}_x \mathbf{G}_q^{-1}(\mathbf{M}_x)}{t} - f(x)\mathbf{M}_x - \mathbf{E} \right) + \mathbf{e}' \\
&= \mathbf{s}^T \frac{\mathbf{A}_x \mathbf{G}_q^{-1}(\mathbf{M}_x)}{t} - f(x)\mathbf{s}^T \mathbf{M}_x + \underbrace{-\mathbf{s}^T \mathbf{E} + \mathbf{e}'}_{\mathbf{e}''}
\end{aligned}
$$

where $\|\mathbf{e}''\|_\infty \le \mathrm{poly}(\lambda, B, (n\lceil \log q\rceil)^{O(d')})$.

**Theorem 9 (Correctness, Pseudorandomness, Constraint Hiding).**
*Under the $\mathrm{DLWE}_{n,q,\chi}$ hardness assumption, CPRF is correct, pseudorandom and constraint hiding.*

*Proof.* Let $\mathcal{A}$ be a PPT adversary against CPRF and consider the game from Definition 2. The proof proceeds with a sequence of hybrids.

*Hybrid $\mathcal{H}_0$.* The game from the definition.

*Hybrid $\mathcal{H}_1$.* Change the way that the vectors $\vec{a}$ and $\vec{b}$ are computed in Constrain and Keygen respectively: Define the matrices $\widehat{\mathbf{A}} := \vec{\mathbf{A}} - \tilde{f} \otimes \mathbf{G}_q$ and $\widehat{\mathbf{B}} := \vec{\mathbf{B}} - \mathsf{sk} \otimes \mathbf{G}_q$. Then let $\vec{a} := \mathbf{s}^T \widehat{\mathbf{A}} + \mathbf{e}_a$ and $\vec{b} := \mathbf{s}^T \widehat{\mathbf{B}} + \mathbf{e}_b$ where $\mathbf{e}_a \overset{\$}{\leftarrow} \chi^{m\ell_p}$, $\mathbf{e}_b \overset{\$}{\leftarrow} \chi^{m\ell_s}$. This is simply a change in notation.

*Hybrid $\mathcal{H}_2$.* Change the Eval algorithm. Up to this hybrid, in Eval we computed $\mathbf{M}_x := \mathbf{D}\mathbf{G}_p^{-1}(\mathbf{C}_x)$ and the output was

$$
y := \left\lfloor \mathbf{s}^T \cdot \frac{\mathbf{A}_x \mathbf{G}_q^{-1}(\mathbf{M}_x)}{t' \cdot t} \right\rceil .
$$

Consider the vector $\mathbf{d} := \mathbf{s}^T \mathbf{D} + \mathbf{e}_d$ where $\mathbf{e}_d \leftarrow \chi^{n\lceil \log p\rceil}$. In this hybrid the output of Eval will be

$$
y^* := \left\lfloor \frac{\mathbf{v}}{t'} \right\rceil \qquad \text{where} \qquad \mathbf{v} := \frac{\mathbf{a}_{f,x}\mathbf{G}_q^{-1}(\mathbf{M}_x)}{t} + f(x)\left( \mathbf{d}\mathbf{G}_p^{-1}(\mathbf{C}_x) + E(x) \right)
$$

and $E(\cdot)$ is the function from Corollary 6, and in particular $|E(x)| \le B\sqrt{k} \cdot (n\lceil \log p\rceil)^{\log k}$.

We analyse now the event that $y^* \ne y$. Note that

$$
\mathbf{d}\mathbf{G}_p^{-1}(\mathbf{C}_x) = \mathbf{s}^T \underbrace{\mathbf{D}\mathbf{G}_p^{-1}(\mathbf{C}_x)}_{\mathbf{M}_x} + \underbrace{\mathbf{e}_d \mathbf{G}_p^{-1}(\mathbf{C}_x)}_{\mathbf{e}} = \mathbf{s}^T \mathbf{M}_x + \mathbf{e} \qquad \|\mathbf{e}\|_\infty \le B \cdot n\lceil \log p\rceil
$$

By Lemma 3,

$$\frac{\mathbf{a}_{f,x}\mathbf{G}^{-1}(\mathbf{M}_x)}{t} = \mathbf{s}^T \cdot \frac{\mathbf{A}_x\mathbf{G}^{-1}(\mathbf{M}_x)}{t} - f(x)\mathbf{s}^T\mathbf{M}_x + \mathbf{e}''$$

where $\|\mathbf{e}''\|_\infty \leq \mathrm{poly}(\lambda, B, (n\lceil\log q\rceil)^{O(d')})$. Hence

$$
\begin{aligned}
y &= \left\lfloor \mathbf{s}^T \cdot \frac{\mathbf{A}_x\mathbf{G}^{-1}(\mathbf{M}_x)}{t' \cdot t} \right\rceil \\
&= \left\lfloor \frac{1}{t'} \left( \frac{\mathbf{a}_{f,x}\mathbf{G}^{-1}(\mathbf{M}_x)}{t} + f(x)\mathbf{s}^T\mathbf{M}_x - \mathbf{e}'' \right) \right\rceil \\
&= \left\lfloor \frac{1}{t'} \left( \frac{\mathbf{a}_{f,x}\mathbf{G}^{-1}(\mathbf{M}_x)}{t} + f(x)\left(\mathbf{dG}_p^{-1}(\mathbf{C}_x) - \mathbf{e}\right) - \mathbf{e}'' \right) \right\rceil \\
&= \left\lfloor \frac{1}{t'} \left( \frac{\mathbf{a}_{f,x}\mathbf{G}^{-1}(\mathbf{M}_x)}{t} + f(x)\left(\mathbf{dG}_p^{-1}(\mathbf{C}_x) + E(x)\right) - \underbrace{\left(f(x)E(x) + f(x)\mathbf{e} + \mathbf{e}''\right)}_{\mathbf{e}'''} \right) \right\rceil \\
&= \left\lfloor \frac{1}{t'}\left(\mathbf{v} - \mathbf{e}'''\right) \right\rceil
\end{aligned}
$$

where $\|\mathbf{e}'''\|_\infty$ is bounded by a value $E' = \mathrm{poly}(\lambda, B, (n\lceil\log q\rceil)^{O(d')}, B\sqrt{k} \cdot (n\lceil\log p\rceil)^{\log k})$. Therefore $y^* \neq y$ only when there exists $i \in [n\lceil\log p\rceil]$ such that the $i$th entry of the vector $\mathbf{v}$ is $E'$-close to $t'\mathbb{Z} + t'/2$, i.e. when the $i$th entry of the vector $t\mathbf{v}$ is $tE'$-close to $(t \cdot t')\mathbb{Z} + (t \cdot t')/2$. Let Borderline$_x$ denote this event, then $\neg$Borderline$_x \implies y^* = y$. We can bound the advantage in distinguishing between this hybrid and the previous one by the probability of Borderline $= \bigvee_x$ Borderline$_x$:

$$|\mathrm{Adv}_{\mathcal{H}_2}(\mathcal{A}) - \mathrm{Adv}_{\mathcal{H}_1}(\mathcal{A})| \leq \Pr_{\mathcal{H}_2}[\text{Borderline}]$$

**Lemma 4.** *The following holds:*

$$\Pr\left[ \bigvee_{x\in\{0,1\}^k} \text{Borderline}_x \right] \leq n\lceil\log p\rceil 2^k E'/t' = \mathrm{negl}(\lambda), \tag{13}$$

*where the probability is over the randomness of the key generation algorithm in $\mathcal{H}_2$.*

*Proof.* Fix an arbitrary value for $x$ and some coordinate $i \in [n\lceil\log p\rceil]$ and note that

$$t\mathbf{v} = \mathbf{a}_{f,x}\mathbf{G}_q^{-1}(\mathbf{M}_x) + f(x)t\left(\mathbf{dG}_p^{-1}(\mathbf{C}_x) + E(x)\right)$$

where $\mathbf{a}_{f,x} = [\vec{\mathbf{a}}\|\vec{\mathbf{b}}]\mathbf{H}_{f,x} = \mathbf{s}^T[\widehat{\mathbf{A}}\|\widehat{\mathbf{B}}]\mathbf{H}_{f,x} + [\mathbf{e}_a\|\mathbf{e}_b]\mathbf{H}_{f,x}$. Recall that $\|\mathbf{s}\|_\infty \leq B < t < p$, where $p, t$ are prime and $q = p \cdot t$, so each entry of $\mathbf{s}$ is a unit in $\mathbb{Z}_q$. Similarly, $\|\mathbf{H}_{f,x}\mathbf{G}_q^{-1}(\mathbf{M}_x)\| \leq (n\lceil\log q\rceil)^{O(d')} < t \leq p$ and so each entry of $\mathbf{H}_{f,x}\mathbf{G}_q^{-1}(\mathbf{M}_x)$ is a unit in $\mathbb{Z}_q$.

Since $[\widehat{\mathbf{A}}\|\widehat{\mathbf{B}}]$ is uniform over $\mathbb{Z}_q^{n\times m(\ell_p+\ell_s)}$, it follows that each entry of the vector $\mathbf{s}^T[\widehat{\mathbf{A}}\|\widehat{\mathbf{B}}]\mathbf{H}_{f,x}\mathbf{G}_q^{-1}(\mathbf{M}_x)$ is uniform over $\mathbb{Z}_q$ and so the marginal distribution of the $i$th entry of $t\mathbf{v}$ as a function of the randomness of Keygen is uniform over $\mathbb{Z}_q$. Therefore, the probability of this value being $tE'$-close to $(t \cdot t')\mathbb{Z} + (t \cdot t')/2$ is at most $E'/t'$. Applying the union bound over all possible values of $x$ and $i$, the lemma follows.

Note that in this hybrid, if $f(x) = 0$ then the output of Eval is identical to the output of ConstrainEval, so the adversary has no advantage in guessing $b_3$.

*Hybrid $\mathcal{H}_3$.* Change $\mathbf{d}$: sample it uniformly from $\mathbb{Z}_p^{n\lceil \log p \rceil}$. This change is computationally indistinguishable under $\text{DLWE}_{n,p,\chi}$.

*Hybrid $\mathcal{H}_4$.* Change again Eval: compute $\mathbf{v}$ by first sampling a vector $\mathbf{u}_x \xleftarrow{\$} \mathbb{Z}_p^m$ and setting

$$\mathbf{v} := \frac{\mathbf{a}_{f,x}\mathbf{G}_q^{-1}(\mathbf{M}_x)}{t} + f(x)\mathbf{u}_x.$$

Recall that the adversary can query each distinct $x$ once. By Corollary 6, those hybrids are indistinguishable under $\text{DLWE}_{n,p,\chi}$.

In this hybrid, if $f(x) = 1$ then the output of Eval is uniformly distributed over $\mathbb{Z}_p^m$, so the adversary has no advantage in guessing $b_2$.

*Hybrid $\mathcal{H}_5$.* Change Constrain: compute $\tilde{f}$ as $\tilde{f} \leftarrow \text{FHE.Enc}(\text{sk}, 0)$. By Lemma 1, those hybrids are indistinguishable under $\text{DLWE}_{n,q,\chi}$. At this stage the adversary has no information about $f$ and therefore it has no advantage in guessing $b_1$, which completes the proof.

*Choice of Parameters.* In order to satisfy the requirements in the above proof, we require that $n\lceil \log p \rceil 2^k E'/t' = \text{negl}(\lambda)$. For the sake of concreteness, we will set $\text{negl}(\lambda)$ to $2^{-\lambda}$. Recalling that $E' = \text{poly}(\lambda, B, (n\lceil \log q \rceil)^{O(d')}, B\sqrt{k} \cdot (n\lceil \log p \rceil)^{\log k})$, we get $t' \geq 2^{O(\lambda+k+(d+\log k)\cdot\text{polylog}(n))}$. This can be satisfied by setting $n = (\lambda kd)^{1/\epsilon}$ and setting $t' = 2^{\tilde{O}(n^\epsilon)}$ appropriately. Then $p, t$ can be chosen to be polynomially related in size to $t'$ s.t. $t, t', p/t'$ are prime.

# References

[ABB10a] Agrawal, S., Boneh, D., Boyen, X.: Efficient lattice (H)IBE in the standard model. In: Gilbert, H. (ed.) EUROCRYPT 2010. LNCS, vol. 6110, pp. 553–572. Springer, Heidelberg (2010). doi:10.1007/978-3-642-13190-5_28

[ABB10b] Agrawal, S., Boneh, D., Boyen, X.: Lattice basis delegation in fixed dimension and shorter-ciphertext hierarchical IBE. In: Rabin, T. (ed.) CRYPTO 2010. LNCS, vol. 6223, pp. 98–115. Springer, Heidelberg (2010). doi:10.1007/978-3-642-14623-7_6

[ABCP15] Abdalla, M., Bourse, F., Caro, A., Pointcheval, D.: Simple functional encryption schemes for inner products. In: Katz, J. (ed.) PKC 2015. LNCS, vol. 9020, pp. 733–751. Springer, Heidelberg (2015). doi:10.1007/978-3-662-46447-2_33

[ACPS09] Applebaum, B., Cash, D., Peikert, C., Sahai, A.: Fast cryptographic primitives and circular-secure encryption based on hard learning problems. In: Halevi, S. (ed.) CRYPTO 2009. LNCS, vol. 5677, pp. 595–618. Springer, Heidelberg (2009). doi:10.1007/978-3-642-03356-8_35

[AFV11] Agrawal, S., Freeman, D.M., Vaikuntanathan, V.: Functional encryption for inner product predicates from learning with errors. In: Lee, D.H., Wang, X. (eds.) ASIACRYPT 2011. LNCS, vol. 7073, pp. 21–40. Springer, Heidelberg (2011). doi:10.1007/978-3-642-25385-0_2

[Agr16] Agrawal, S.: Interpolating predicate and functional encryption from learning with errors. IACR Cryptology ePrint Archive, 2016:654 (2016)

[AGVW13] Agrawal, S., Gorbunov, S., Vaikuntanathan, V., Wee, H.: Functional encryption: new perspectives and lower bounds. In: Canetti, R., Garay, J.A. (eds.) CRYPTO 2013. LNCS, vol. 8043, pp. 500–518. Springer, Heidelberg (2013). doi:10.1007/978-3-642-40084-1_28

[AJ15] Ananth, P., Jain, A.: Indistinguishability obfuscation from compact functional encryption. In: Gennaro, R., Robshaw, M. (eds.) CRYPTO 2015. LNCS, vol. 9215, pp. 308–326. Springer, Heidelberg (2015). doi:10.1007/978-3-662-47989-6_15

[Ajt96] Ajtai, M.: Generating hard instances of lattice problems (extended abstract). In: STOC, pp. 99–108 (1996)

[ALS16] Agrawal, S., Libert, B., Stehlé, D.: Fully secure functional encryption for inner products, from standard assumptions. In: Robshaw, M., Katz, J. (eds.) CRYPTO 2016. LNCS, vol. 9816, pp. 333–362. Springer, Heidelberg (2016). doi:10.1007/978-3-662-53015-3_12

[AP14] Alperin-Sheriff, J., Peikert, C.: Faster bootstrapping with polynomial error. In: Garay, J.A., Gennaro, R. (eds.) CRYPTO 2014. LNCS, vol. 8616, pp. 297–314. Springer, Heidelberg (2014). doi:10.1007/978-3-662-44371-2_17

[BCTW16] Brakerski, Z., Cash, D., Tsabary, R., Wee, H.: Targeted homomorphic attribute-based encryption. In: Hirt, M., Smith, A. (eds.) TCC 2016. LNCS, vol. 9986, pp. 330–360. Springer, Heidelberg (2016). doi:10.1007/978-3-662-53644-5_13

[BFP+15] Banerjee, A., Fuchsbauer, G., Peikert, C., Pietrzak, K., Stevens, S.: Key-homomorphic constrained pseudorandom functions. In: Dodis, Y., Nielsen, J.B. (eds.) TCC 2015. LNCS, vol. 9015, pp. 31–60. Springer, Heidelberg (2015). doi:10.1007/978-3-662-46497-7_2

[BGG+14] Boneh, D., Gentry, C., Gorbunov, S., Halevi, S., Nikolaenko, V., Segev, G., Vaikuntanathan, V., Vinayagamurthy, D.: Fully key-homomorphic encryption, arithmetic circuit abe and compact garbled circuits. In: Nguyen, P.Q., Oswald, E. (eds.) EUROCRYPT 2014. LNCS, vol. 8441, pp. 533–556. Springer, Heidelberg (2014). doi:10.1007/978-3-642-55220-5_30

[BGI14] Boyle, E., Goldwasser, S., Ivan, I.: Functional signatures and pseudorandom functions. In: Krawczyk, H. (ed.) PKC 2014. LNCS, vol. 8383, pp. 501–519. Springer, Heidelberg (2014). doi:10.1007/978-3-642-54631-0_29

[BGV12] Brakerski, Z., Gentry, C., Vaikuntanathan, V.: (Leveled) fully homomorphic encryption without bootstrapping. In: ITCS (2012)

[BJK15] Bishop, A., Jain, A., Kowalczyk, L.: Function-hiding inner product encryption. In: Iwata, T., Cheon, J.H. (eds.) ASIACRYPT 2015. LNCS, vol. 9452, pp. 470–491. Springer, Heidelberg (2015). doi:10.1007/978-3-662-48797-6_20

[BKM17] Boneh, D., Kim, S., Montgomery, H.: Private puncturable PRFs from standard lattice assumptions. In: Coron, J.-S., Nielsen, J.B. (eds.) EUROCRYPT 2017. LNCS, vol. 10210, pp. 415–445. Springer, Cham (2017). doi:10.1007/978-3-319-56620-7_15

[BKS16] Brakerski, Z., Komargodski, I., Segev, G.: Multi-input functional encryption in the private-key setting: stronger security from weaker assumptions. In: Fischlin, M., Coron, J.-S. (eds.) EUROCRYPT 2016. LNCS, vol. 9666, pp. 852–880. Springer, Heidelberg (2016). doi:10.1007/978-3-662-49896-5_30

[BLMR15] Boneh, D., Lewi, K., Montgomery, H.W., Raghunathan, A.: Key homomorphic PRFs and their applications. IACR Cryptology ePrint Archive, 2015:220 (2015)

[BLP+13] Brakerski, Z., Langlois, A., Peikert, C., Regev, O., Stehlé, D.: Classical hardness of learning with errors. In: Boneh, D., et al. (eds.) [BRF13], pp. 575–584 (2013)

[BLW15] Boneh, D., Lewi, K., David, J.W.: Constraining pseudorandom functions privately. IACR Cryptology ePrint Archive, 2015:1167 (2015)

[BLW17] Boneh, D., Lewi, K., Wu, D.J.: Constraining pseudorandom functions privately. In: Fehr, S. (ed.) PKC 2017. LNCS, vol. 10175, pp. 494–524. Springer, Heidelberg (2017). doi:10.1007/978-3-662-54388-7_17

[BP14] Banerjee, A., Peikert, C.: New and improved key-homomorphic pseudorandom functions. In: Garay, J.A., Gennaro, R. (eds.) CRYPTO 2014. LNCS, vol. 8616, pp. 353–370. Springer, Heidelberg (2014). doi:10.1007/978-3-662-44371-2_20

[BPR12] Banerjee, A., Peikert, C., Rosen, A.: Pseudorandom functions and lattices. In: Pointcheval, D., Johansson, T. (eds.) EUROCRYPT 2012. LNCS, vol. 7237, pp. 719–737. Springer, Heidelberg (2012). doi:10.1007/978-3-642-29011-4_42

[BRF13] Boneh, D., Roughgarden, T., Feigenbaum, J. (eds.) Symposium on Theory of Computing Conference, STOC 2013, Palo Alto, CA, USA. ACM, 1–4 June 2013

[BSW11] Boneh, D., Sahai, A., Waters, B.: Functional encryption: definitions and challenges. In: Ishai, Y. (ed.) TCC 2011. LNCS, vol. 6597, pp. 253–273. Springer, Heidelberg (2011). doi:10.1007/978-3-642-19571-6_16

[BV11] Brakerski, Z., Vaikuntanathan, V.: Efficient fully homomorphic encryption from (standard) LWE. In: FOCS (2011)

[BV14] Brakerski, Z., Vaikuntanathan, V.: Lattice-based FHE as secure as PKE. In: Naor, M. (ed.) Innovations in Theoretical Computer Science, ITCS 2014, Princeton, NJ, USA, pp. 1–12. ACM, 12–14 January 2014

[BV15a] Bitansky, N., Vaikuntanathan, V.: Indistinguishability obfuscation from functional encryption. In: Guruswami, V. (ed.) IEEE 56th Annual Symposium on Foundations of Computer Science, FOCS 2015, Berkeley, CA, USA, pp. 171–190. IEEE Computer Society, 17–20 October 2015

[BV15b] Brakerski, Z., Vaikuntanathan, V.: Constrained key-homomorphic PRFs from standard lattice assumptions. In: Dodis, Y., Nielsen, J.B. (eds.) TCC 2015. LNCS, vol. 9015, pp. 1–30. Springer, Heidelberg (2015). doi:10.1007/978-3-662-46497-7_1

[BW07] Boneh, D., Waters, B.: Conjunctive, subset, and range queries on encrypted data. In: Vadhan, S.P. (ed.) TCC 2007. LNCS, vol. 4392, pp. 535–554. Springer, Heidelberg (2007). doi:10.1007/978-3-540-70936-7_29

[BW13] Boneh, D., Waters, B.: Constrained pseudorandom functions and their applications. In: Sako, K., Sarkar, P. (eds.) ASIACRYPT 2013. LNCS, vol. 8270, pp. 280–300. Springer, Heidelberg (2013). doi:10.1007/978-3-642-42045-0_15

[CC17] Canetti, R., Chen, Y.: Constraint-hiding constrained PRFs for $NC^1$ from LWE. In: Coron, J.-S., Nielsen, J.B. (eds.) EUROCRYPT 2017. LNCS, vol. 10210, pp. 446–476. Springer, Cham (2017). doi:10.1007/978-3-319-56620-7_16

[CHKP12] Cash, D., Hofheinz, D., Kiltz, E., Peikert, C.: Bonsai trees, or how to delegate a lattice basis. J. Crypt. **25**(4), 601–639 (2012)

[Gay16] Gay, R.: Functional encryption for quadratic functions, and applications to predicate encryption. IACR Cryptology ePrint Archive, 2016:1106 (2016)

[Gen09] Gentry, C.: Fully homomorphic encryption using ideal lattices. In: Mitzenmacher, M. (ed.) Proceedings of the 41st Annual ACM Symposium on Theory of Computing, STOC 2009, Bethesda, MD, USA, pp. 169–178. ACM, 31 May–2 June 2009

[GGH+16] Garg, S., Gentry, C., Halevi, S., Raykova, M., Sahai, A., Waters, B.: Candidate indistinguishability obfuscation and functional encryption for all circuits. SIAM J. Comput. **45**(3), 882–929 (2016)

[GKP+13] Goldwasser, S., Kalai, Y.T., Popa, R.A., Vaikuntanathan, V., Zeldovich, N.: Reusable garbled circuits and succinct functional encryption. In: STOC, pp. 555–564 (2013)

[GMW15] Gay, R., Méaux, P., Wee, H.: Predicate encryption for multi-dimensional range queries from lattices. In: Katz, J. (ed.) PKC 2015. LNCS, vol. 9020, pp. 752–776. Springer, Heidelberg (2015). doi:10.1007/978-3-662-46447-2_34

[GPSW06] Goyal, V., Pandey, O., Sahai, A., Waters, B.: Attribute-based encryption for fine-grained access control of encrypted data. In: Juels, A., Wright, R.N., De Capitani di Vimercati, S. (eds.) Proceedings of the 13th ACM Conference on Computer and Communications Security, CCS 2006, Alexandria, VA, USA, pp. 89–98. ACM, 30 October–3 November 2006

[GPV08] Gentry, C., Peikert, C., Vaikuntanathan, V.: Trapdoors for hard lattices and new cryptographic constructions. In: Dwork, C. (ed.) Proceedings of the 40th Annual ACM Symposium on Theory of Computing, Victoria, British Columbia, Canada, pp. 197–206. ACM, 17–20 May 2008

[GSW13] Gentry, C., Sahai, A., Waters, B.: Homomorphic encryption from learning with errors: conceptually-simpler, asymptotically-faster, attribute-based. In: Canetti, R., Garay, J.A. (eds.) CRYPTO 2013. LNCS, vol. 8042, pp. 75–92. Springer, Heidelberg (2013). doi:10.1007/978-3-642-40041-4_5

[GVW12] Gorbunov, S., Vaikuntanathan, V., Wee, H.: Functional encryption with bounded collusions via multi-party computation. In: Safavi-Naini, R., Canetti, R. (eds.) CRYPTO 2012. LNCS, vol. 7417, pp. 162–179. Springer, Heidelberg (2012). doi:10.1007/978-3-642-32009-5_11

[GVW13] Gorbunov, S., Vaikuntanathan, V., Wee, H.: Attribute-based encryption for circuits. In Boneh, D., et al. (eds.) [BRF13], pp. 545–554 (2013)

[GVW15a] Gorbunov, S., Vaikuntanathan, V., Wee, H.: Predicate encryption for circuits from LWE. In: Gennaro, R., Robshaw, M. (eds.) CRYPTO 2015. LNCS, vol. 9216, pp. 503–523. Springer, Heidelberg (2015). doi:10.1007/978-3-662-48000-7_25

[GVW15b] Gorbunov, S., Vaikuntanathan, V., Wichs, D.: Leveled fully homomorphic signatures from standard lattices. In: Servedio, R.A., Rubinfeld, R. (eds.) Proceedings of the Forty-Seventh Annual ACM on Symposium on Theory of Computing, STOC 2015, Portland, OR, USA, pp. 469–477. ACM, 14–17 June 2015

[HKKW14] Hofheinz, D., Kamath, A., Koppula, V., Waters, B.: Adaptively secure constrained pseudorandom functions. Cryptology ePrint Archive, Report 2014/720 (2014)

[KPTZ13] Kiayias, A., Papadopoulos, S., Triandopoulos, N., Zacharias, T.: Delegatable pseudorandom functions and applications. In: Sadeghi, A.-R., Gligor, V.D., Yung, M. (eds.) 2013 ACM SIGSAC Conference on Computer and Communications Security, CCS 2013, Berlin, Germany, pp. 669–684. ACM, 4–8 November 2013

[KSW08] Katz, J., Sahai, A., Waters, B.: Predicate encryption supporting disjunctions, polynomial equations, and inner products. In: Smart, N. (ed.) EURO-CRYPT 2008. LNCS, vol. 4965, pp. 146–162. Springer, Heidelberg (2008). doi:10.1007/978-3-540-78967-3_9

[Lin16] Lin, H.: Indistinguishability obfuscation from constant-degree graded encoding schemes. IACR Cryptology ePrint Archive 2016:257 (2016)

[MM11] Micciancio, D., Mol, P.: Pseudorandom knapsacks and the sample complexity of LWE search-to-decision reductions. In: Rogaway, P. (ed.) CRYPTO 2011. LNCS, vol. 6841, pp. 465–484. Springer, Heidelberg (2011). doi:10.1007/978-3-642-22792-9_26

[MP12] Micciancio, D., Peikert, C.: Trapdoors for lattices: simpler, tighter, faster, smaller. In: Pointcheval, D., Johansson, T. (eds.) EUROCRYPT 2012. LNCS, vol. 7237, pp. 700–718. Springer, Heidelberg (2012). doi:10.1007/978-3-642-29011-4_41

[O'N10] O'Neill, A.: Definitional issues in functional encryption. Cryptology ePrint Archive, Report 2010/556 (2010)

[OT12] Okamoto, T., Takashima, K.: Adaptively attribute-hiding (hierarchical) inner product encryption. In: Pointcheval, D., Johansson, T. (eds.) EURO-CRYPT 2012. LNCS, vol. 7237, pp. 591–608. Springer, Heidelberg (2012). doi:10.1007/978-3-642-29011-4_35

[Pei09] Peikert, C.: Public-key cryptosystems from the worst-case shortest vector problem: extended abstract. In: Proceedings of the 41st Annual ACM Symposium on Theory of Computing, STOC 2009, Bethesda, MD, USA, pp. 333–342, 31 May–2 June 2009

[Reg05] Regev, O.: On lattices, learning with errors, random linear codes, and cryptography. In: Proceedings of the 37th Annual ACM Symposium on Theory of Computing, Baltimore, MD, USA, pp. 84–93, 22–24 May 2005

[Sch87] Schnorr, C.-P.: A hierarchy of polynomial time lattice basis reduction algorithms. Theor. Comput. Sci. **53**, 201–224 (1987)

[SW05] Sahai, A., Waters, B.: Fuzzy identity-based encryption. In: Cramer, R. (ed.) EUROCRYPT 2005. LNCS, vol. 3494, pp. 457–473. Springer, Heidelberg (2005). doi:10.1007/11426639_27

[SW14] Sahai, A., Waters, B.: How to use indistinguishability obfuscation: deniable encryption, and more. In: Shmoys, D.B. (ed.) Symposium on Theory of Computing, STOC 2014, pp. 475–484. ACM, New York, 31 May–03 June 2014

# Encryption

# The Edited Truth

Shafi Goldwasser[1,2], Saleet Klein[1(✉)], and Daniel Wichs[3]

[1] MIT, Cambridge, MA, USA
{shafi,saleet}@csail.mit.edu
[2] Weizmann Institute of Science, Rehovot, Israel
[3] Northeastern University, Boston, MA, USA
wichs@ccs.neu.edu

**Abstract.** We introduce two new cryptographic notions in the realm of public and symmetric key encryption.

- *Encryption with invisible edits* is an encryption scheme with two tiers of users: "privileged" and "unprivileged". Privileged users know a key pair $(\mathsf{pk}, \mathsf{sk})$ and "unprivileged" users know a key pair $(\mathsf{pk}_e, \mathsf{sk}_e)$ which is associated with an underlying edit $e$ to be applied to messages encrypted. When an unprivileged user attempts to decrypt a ciphertext generated by a privileged user of an underlying plaintext $m$, it will be decrypted to an edited $m' = \mathsf{Edit}(m, e)$. Here, $\mathsf{Edit}$ is a supported edit function and $e$ is a description of the particular edit. A user shouldn't be able to tell whether he's an unprivileged or a privileged user.
- An *encryption with deniable edits* is an encryption scheme which allows a user who owns a ciphertext $c$ encrypting a large corpus of data $m$ under a secret key $\mathsf{sk}$, to generate an alternative but legitimate looking secret key $\mathsf{sk}_{c,e}$ that decrypts $c$ to an "edited" version of the data $m' = \mathsf{Edit}(m, e)$. This generalizes classical receiver deniable encryption, which is a special case of deniable edits where the edit function completely replaces the original data. The new flexibility allows to design solutions with much smaller key sizes than required in classical receiver deniable encryption allowing the key size to only scale with the description size of the edit $e$ which can be much smaller than the plaintext data $m$.

We construct encryption schemes with deniable and invisible edits for any polynomial-time computable edit function under minimal assumptions: in the public-key setting we require the existence of standard public-key encryption and in the symmetric-key setting require the existence of one-way functions.

The solutions to both problems use common ideas, however there is a significant conceptual difference between deniable edits and invisible edits. Whereas encryption with deniable edits enables a user to modify the meaning of a single ciphertext in hindsight, the goal of encryption with invisible edits is to enable ongoing modifications of multiple ciphertexts.

© International Association for Cryptologic Research 2017
Y. Kalai and L. Reyzin (Eds.): TCC 2017, Part I, LNCS 10677, pp. 305–340, 2017.
https://doi.org/10.1007/978-3-319-70500-2_11

# 1    Introduction

In this paper, we introduce two novel cryptographic notions in the realm of public and symmetric key encryption: *Encryption with invisible edits (IEdit)* and *Encryption with deniable edits (DEdit)*.

We construct both asymmetric and symmetric key versions of IEdit and DEdit schemes, under minimal assumptions using the machinery of garbled circuits. In particular, we can get such schemes in the public-key setting using only public key encryption and in the symmetric-key setting using only one-way functions. Our constructions rely on a simple but delicate use of functional encryption (FE), further illustrating the incredible versatility of this powerful abstraction.

We proceed to describe the new notions and our constructions.

## 1.1    Invisible Edits

Alice is a company boss and her secretary Bob is in charge of going through her e-mail (which is naturally all encrypted) and responding to routine requests. However, sometimes other bosses will send e-mails containing information that Bob should not see, for example discussing layoffs among the secretarial staff. Alice would like to give Bob a secret key which will invisibly introduce some careful edits to all such e-mails (e.g., replaces the word "layoffs" with "bonuses"), even ones sent in the future. Ideally, Bob should not know anything about what edits are being introduced and should even be oblivious to the fact that he does not have Alice's real secret key which decrypts all e-mails correctly.

*Encryption with Invisible Edits.* To solve the above problem, we introduce a new cryptographic primitive that we call encryption with *invisible edits* (IEdit). IEdit is an encryption system which allows dispensing computationally indistinguishable decryption keys which each decrypt a ciphertext to a different "edited" plaintexts. A user cannot tell whether or not his decryption key is introducing edits.

In more detail, such a scheme allows us to create "privileged" encryption/decryption key pairs (pk, sk) and "unprivileged" encryption/decryption key pairs (pk$_e$, sk$_e$) tied to some edit $e$. Both key pairs individually work correctly, meaning that a message encrypted under pk (resp. pk$_e$) will decrypt correctly under sk (resp. sk$_e$). However, when a privileged user encrypts some message $m$ under pk, the unprivileged user will decrypt it to $m' = \mathsf{Edit}(m, e)$ under sk$_e$. Here, we think of Edit as some edit function which is specified as part of the scheme and $e$ is the description of the particular edit that should be applied. For example, we might consider an edit function that performs a small number of insertions and deletions on blocks of the data, as specified by $e$. Alternatively, the edit function could be a complex suite of image-editing tools and $e$ could specify a series of transformations (e.g., crop, rotate, blur, airbrush, etc.) to be performed on the encrypted image. More generally, we can think of the edit $e$

as a Turing Machine and the edit function as a universal Turing Machine which runs $e(m)$.

A user shouldn't be able to tell whether he is privileged or unprivileged. In particular, the user can't tell whether he's an unprivileged user that has $(\mathsf{pk}_e, \mathsf{sk}_e)$ and is receiving ciphertexts from privileged users that are encrypting some messages $m_i$ under $\mathsf{pk}$ while he is decrypting the edited versions $m_i' = \mathsf{Edit}(m_i, e)$, or whether he is a privileged user that gets $(\mathsf{pk}, \mathsf{sk})$ and is receiving ciphertexts from other privileged users that are really encrypting $m_i'$ under $\mathsf{pk}$.

In addition to considering the problem of invisible edits in the public-key setting, we also consider a symmetric-key variant of the problem where the key $\mathsf{sk}$ (resp. $\mathsf{sk}_e$) is used for both encryption and decryption. In the symmetric-key case, we consider two potential variants.

**Dual-Key Variant.** In the dual key variant, the privileged/unprivileged keys $\mathsf{sk}$ and $\mathsf{sk}_e$ look indistinguishable and a user cannot tell which key he has.

**Dual-Scheme Variant.** In the dual scheme variant, the privileged and unprivileged users have completely different keys and even encryption/decryption procedures. Therefore users can tell whether they are privileged or unprivileged. However, unprivileged users still cannot tell whether their key always decrypts all ciphertexts correctly or whether it is introducing edits to data encrypted by privileged users.

Intuitively, the dual-key variant is more desirable.

*Invisible Edits: Our Results.* We construct encryption with invisible edits in the public-key setting, under the minimal assumption that public-key encryption exists. In the symmetric-key setting, we construct the weaker dual-scheme variant under one-way functions but leave it as an interesting open problem to also construct the stronger dual-key variant under one-way functions or show that it requires public key encryption.

The secret key (and public key) size of our schemes is linear in the edit description size $|e|$. The run-time of the encryption/decryption procedures and the ciphertext size are linear in the circuit size of the edit function. In the public-key setting, we can use identity based encryption (IBE) to further reduce the public-key size to only depend on the security parameter.

## 1.2   Deniable Edits

DEdit is a different but technically related notion to IEdit, which extends the classical notion of receiver deniable encryption [CDNO97] to allow the legal owner (and originator) of a secret key to produce an alternative computationally indistinguishable secret key under which a targeted ciphertext decrypts to an "edited" plaintext. The description size of the edits to be applied to the original plaintext can be much smaller than the size of the plaintext itself. This will allow us to design solutions, where the secret key size is only proportional to the description size of the edit, but can be much smaller than the message size.

As a motivating scenario, consider Alice who is an owner of a private server hosting a large corpus of data which is encrypted under a small secret key held by Alice on a separate device. Circumstances cause Alice to become the subject of scrutiny, the server is seized by investigators, and Alice must hand over her secret key. Although most of the data is innocuous, the server might contain a few private photos, confidential recommendation letters, etc. Alice wants to comply, but give a different secret key which looks legitimate but decrypts the data to a "lightly edited" version where the sensitive content is appropriately modified. Typically, the description of the edits to be broadly applied can be succinctly summarized and is much smaller than the size of the data.

*New Primitive: Encryption with Deniable Edits.* To solve the above problem, we introduce a new cryptographic primitive that we call encryption with *deniable edits*. Such a scheme can be used to encrypt a potentially huge message $m$ using a relatively short secret key $\mathsf{sk}$ to derive a ciphertext $c$. Later, it should be possible to come up with a legitimate looking secret key $\mathsf{sk}_{c,e}$ that decrypts the ciphertext $c$ to an edited message $m' = \mathsf{Edit}(m, e)$, where $\mathsf{Edit}$ is some "edit function" specified by the scheme and $e$ is a description of the particular edit that should be applied. We envision that the description-size of the edit $|e|$ is relatively small, and much smaller than the potentially huge message size $|m|$. Therefore, although we necessarily need to allow the secret key size $|\mathsf{sk}|$ to grow with the edit description size $|e|$, we do not want it to depend on the message size $|m|$. The exact same notion can be defined in either public or symmetric key settings.

*Relation to Deniable Encryption and its Limitations.* One can think of encryption with deniable edits as a more flexible version of *receiver deniable encryption*, introduced by Canetti et al. [CDNO97]. In receiver deniable encryption, it is possible to come up with a secret key $\mathsf{sk}_{c,m'}$ that decrypts a ciphertext $c$ to an arbitrary message $m'$. However, the size of the secret key in deniable encryption schemes must necessarily be at least as large as the message size. This makes such schemes unsuitable for encrypting a large messages such as the entire hard-disk contents. Encryption with deniable edits provides flexibility by allowing the secret key size to only scale with the edit description size which can potentially be much smaller than the message size. Naturally, we can recover the notion of receiver deniable encryption as a special case by taking the edit function $\mathsf{Edit}(m, e) = e$ which simply overwrites the encrypted message $m$ with the value $e$, of size $|e| = |m|$. We discuss the relevant literature on deniable encryption and its relation to our work in Sect. 1.5.

Since encryption with deniable edits generalizes receiver deniable encryption, it also *inherits its limitations*. In particular, Bedlin et al. [BNNO11] show that the most natural definition of deniability, where the original secret key $\mathsf{sk}$ can be used to create a legitimate-looking $\mathsf{sk}'$ which is indistinguishable from $\mathsf{sk}$ but decrypts a selected ciphertext $c$ differently, cannot be achieved. Instead, we consider two potential ways to weaken the definition:

**Dual-Key Variant.** The key-generation algorithm outputs a secret decryption key sk along with a secret denying key dk. Most users can immediately discard dk since it is not needed for decryption. However, users that keep dk (e.g., hidden in their basement) can use it to later produce a modified secret key $sk_{c,e}$ which looks legitimate but decrypts a selected ciphertext $c$ to an edited message.

**Dual-Scheme Variant.** There are two entirely different encryption schemes: a "default" scheme and a "denying" scheme. Most users are expected to use the default scheme. However, if a user instead uses the denying scheme, she can take her secret key sk and a ciphertext $c$ and produce a secret key $sk_{c,e}$ which makes it look as though she was using the default scheme but $c$ decrypts to an edited message.[1]

Intuitively, one can think of the dual-key variant as a special case of the dual-scheme variant, where the default and denying schemes are essentially identical, except that in the latter the user keeps both (sk, dk) while in the former she only keeps sk. Therefore, we view the dual-key variant as more desirable. In the public-key setting, it turns out that the two variants are essentially identical and therefore we can only consider the more compelling dual-key variant. However, we do not know if equivalence holds in the symmetric-key setting and therefore consider both variants there.

*Deniable Edits: Our Results.* We construct encryption with deniable edits for arbitrary polynomial-time edit functions under essentially minimal assumptions. In the public-key setting, we construct such a scheme from any standard public-key encryption. In the symmetric-key setting, we show how to construct the dual-scheme variant under the minimal assumption that one-way functions exist. However, we leave it as an interesting open problem whether one can also construct the stronger dual-key variant under one-way functions or whether it requires public key encryption.

The secret key (and public key) size of our schemes is linear in the edit description size $|e|$. The run-time of the encryption/decryption procedures and the ciphertext size are linear in the circuit size of the edit function. In the public-key setting, we can use identity based encryption (IBE) to further reduce the public-key size to only depend on the security parameter.

We also discuss an extension of our schemes to deniably editing some bounded number of ciphertexts (rather than just one) at the cost of having the secret key size scale with this bound. Furthermore we show how to extend our schemes to be able to deniably produce not just a secret key but also the randomness of the key generation algorithm (see Sect. 4.4).

### 1.3 Comparison: Deniable Edits, Invisible Edits and Functional Encryption

It is useful to compare the notions of deniable edits, invisible edits and functional encryption. For concreteness, we consider the comparison in the public-key

---

[1] This variant was also called multi-distributional deniable encryption in recent works.

setting. In all three cases, we can produce a secret key tied to some edit $e$ and ensure that it decrypts encrypted data $m$ to some modified value $\mathsf{Edit}(m, e)$. However, there are crucial differences between the three primitives.

- In functional encryption, we are not hiding the fact that the secret key $\mathsf{sk}_e$ is introducing edits to the encrypted data. In fact, a user that has the (master) public key $\mathsf{pk}$ will be immediately aware of the fact that when he encrypts a message $m$ via $\mathsf{pk}$ and decrypts via $\mathsf{sk}_e$ he gets an edited value $m' = \mathsf{Edit}(m, e)$. This is in contrast to both encryption with deniable and invisible edits, where we do want to hide the fact that edits are being introduced.
- In encryption with deniable edits, we create a secret key $\mathsf{sk}_{c,e}$ which only introduces edits to the decryption of a single specified ciphertext $c$. Therefore, even if a user has $\mathsf{pk}$ and can create his own ciphertexts, he will not observe any edits being introduced.
- In encryption with invisible edits, we hide the fact that the secret key $\mathsf{sk}_e$ is introducing edits by also creating a matching public key $\mathsf{pk}_e$. Encryptions under $\mathsf{pk}_e$ decrypt correctly (with no edits) under $\mathsf{sk}_e$ and therefore a user that has $(\mathsf{pk}_e, \mathsf{sk}_e)$ cannot tell that edits are being introduced. However, if other users encrypt data under $\mathsf{pk}$, it will consistently decrypt to an edited version under $\mathsf{sk}_e$.

Despite the major differences between the three primitives, we will use functional encryption (based on garbled circuits) as a tool to get relatively simple constructions of the other two primitives.

We can think of using a scheme with invisible edits, which targets multiple ciphertexts, in scenarios involving deniability. In particular, consider the case where Alice is running an e-mail server storing a large corpus of individually encrypted e-mails $c_1 = \mathsf{Enc}_{\mathsf{pk}}(m_1), \ldots, c_T = \mathsf{Enc}_{\mathsf{pk}}(m_T)$. She comes under an investigation and wants to give a secret key that applies some simple edit across *all* the e-mails (e.g., replaces one word with a different word). Using an encryption scheme with deniable edits this would only be possible if all of the e-mails were encrypted simultaneously in one ciphertext, but that's not the case here. Using encryption with invisible edits, we can solve the problem at the cost of Alice having to be able to convincingly hand over to the investigators not only her modified secret key (giving $\mathsf{sk}_e$ instead of $\mathsf{sk}$) but also her modified encryption key (giving $\mathsf{pk}_e$ instead of $\mathsf{pk}$). This makes sense in the symmetric-key setting if we think of the encryption key $\mathsf{pk}$ as also being private or even in scenarios where Alice gives her encryption key $\mathsf{pk}$ to a small circle of semi-trusted parties but does not publish it widely.

## 1.4   Our Techniques

All of our constructions rely on simple but delicate use of functional encryption (FE), further illustrating the versatility of this powerful abstraction. A public-key FE scheme for some function $F(x, y)$ comes with a master public key $\mathsf{mpk}$ that can be used to generate ciphertexts $c \leftarrow \mathsf{Enc}_{\mathsf{mpk}}(x)$ encrypting some values $x$, and a master secret key msk that can be used to generate secret keys $sk_y \leftarrow Gen_{msk}(y)$ associated with values $y$. When we decrypt the ciphertext $c$ with the secret key $sk_y$ we get $Dec_{sk_y}(c) = F(x, y)$. We only need FE schemes that are secure in the setting where the adversary sees a single secret key, which we know how to construct under minimal assumptions using the machinery of garbled circuits. In particular, we can get such schemes in the public-key setting using only public key encryption and in the symmetric-key setting using only one-way functions by the work of Sahai and Seyalioglu [SS10]

*Invisible Edits.* Let us start with our construction of public-key encryption with invisible edits, for some edit function $Edit(m, e)$.

As an initial idea, we might consider taking a functional encryption scheme for the function $F(m, e) = Edit(m, e)$ where ciphertexts encrypt messages $m$ and secret keys are associated with edits $e$, and set the privileged secret key $sk_{id}$ to be a secret key for the identity edit id such that $Edit(m, id) = m$, whereas unprivileged secret key pair would be $sk_e$ such that $Dec_{sk_e}(c) = Edit(m, e)$. Unfortunately, this initial idea does not work since it's easy to distinguish $sk_e$ from $sk_{id}$ by generating encryptions of known plaintexts and seeing how they decrypt.

To fix the above idea, we take a functional encryption scheme for a more complicated function $F(x, y)$ which interprets $x = (m, k)$ and tests if $y \oplus k$ is of the form $0^\lambda || e$ where $\lambda$ is the security parameter; if so it outputs $Edit(m, e)$ and else it outputs $m$. A "privileged" key pair consists of a public key $(mpk, k)$ and secret key $sk_y$ where $k, y$ are random and independent. To encrypt a message $m$, we use the FE scheme to encrypt the tuple $x = (m, k)$ where $k$ comes from the public key. An "unprivileged" key pair consists of a public key $(mpk, k')$ and a secret key $sk_{y'}$ where $k'$ is random and $y' = (0^\lambda || e) \oplus k$.

Notice that the privileged and unprivileged key pairs are individually identically distributed, but there is a correlation between them. If we encrypt a message $m$ with a privileged (resp. unprivileged) public-key and then decrypt the resulting ciphertext with a privileged (resp. unprivileged) secret key than since $k, y$ (resp. $k', y'$) are random and independent we decrypt the correct value $F(x, y) = m$ with all but negligible probability. However, if we encrypt a message $m$ with a privileged public key which corresponds to an FE encryption of $x = (m, k)$ and then decrypt with an unprivileged secret key $sk_{y'}$ then we get $F(x, y') = Edit(m, e)$.

We argue that one cannot distinguish between having a privileged key pair $((mpk, k), sk_y)$ and seeing privileged encryptions of $m' = Edit(m, e)$ which corresponds to FE encryptions of $x' = (m', k)$, versus having an unprivileged key pair $((mpk, k'), sk_{y'})$ and seeing privileged encryptions of $m$ which corresponds to FE encryptions of $x = (m, k)$. In particular, since the key pairs are identically distributed, the only difference between these games is the conditional distribution of $x$ versus $x'$, but since $F(x', y) = F(x, y') = m'$, this difference is hidden by FE security.

Our solution for symmetric-key encryption with invisible edits is again analogous, but relying on symmetric-key FE instead of public-key FE.

*Deniable Edits.* As an initial idea, we might consider taking a functional encryption scheme for the function $F(m, e) = \mathsf{Edit}(m, e)$ where ciphertexts encrypt messages $m$ and secret keys are associated with edits $e$. We set the public-key of our scheme to be the FE master public-key $\mathsf{mpk}$ and the secret key $\mathsf{sk_{id}}$ would be a secret key for the identity edit $\mathsf{id}$ such that $\mathsf{Edit}(m, \mathsf{id}) = m$. A user that wants to be able to deny in the future would also keep a "denying key" $\mathsf{dk}$ which we set to be the FE master secret key $\mathsf{dk} = \mathsf{msk}$. To later claim that some ciphertext $c$ encrypting a message $m$ is really an encryption of $m' = \mathsf{Edit}(m, e)$ the user would use $\mathsf{dk} = \mathsf{msk}$ to generate the secret key $\mathsf{sk}_e$ for the edit $e$. Unfortunately, this initial idea does not work since it's easy to distinguish $\mathsf{sk}_e$ from $\mathsf{sk_{id}}$ by generating encryptions of known plaintexts and seeing how they decrypt. What we really need is for the denying procedure to output a secret key that only edits the value in one particular targeted ciphertext $c$, but otherwise decrypts all other ciphertexts correctly.

To fix the above, we use a similar idea as in the case of invisible edits. We take a functional encryption scheme for a more complicated function $F(x, y)$ which interprets $x = (m, k)$ and tests if $y \oplus k$ is of the form $0^\lambda || e$ where $\lambda$ is the security parameter; if so it outputs $\mathsf{Edit}(m, e)$ and else it outputs $m$. We set the public-key of our encryption scheme to be $\mathsf{mpk}$, the secret key to be $\mathsf{sk}_y$ for a uniformly random value $y$, and the denying key to be $\mathsf{dk} = \mathsf{msk}$. To encrypt a message $m$, the encryption procedure chooses a fresh value $k$ on each invocation (this is in contrast to the invisible edits construction where $k$ was part of the public key) and uses the FE scheme to encrypt the tuple $x = (m, k)$ resulting in some ciphertext $c$. Notice that, since $k, y$ are random and independent, $y \oplus k$ is not of the form $0^\lambda || e$ except with negligible probability and therefore decrypting the ciphertext $c$ with the key $\mathsf{sk}_y$ results in the correct value $F(x, y) = m$. If the user wants to later claim that this particular ciphertext $c$ is really an encryption of $m' = \mathsf{Edit}(m, e)$, she would use $\mathsf{dk} = \mathsf{msk}$ to generate a secret key $\mathsf{sk}_{y'}$ for the value $y' = (0^\lambda || e) \oplus k$ which decrypts $c$ to $F(x, y') = \mathsf{Edit}(m, e)$. Notice that the original key $\mathsf{sk}_y$ and the new key $\mathsf{sk}_{y'}$ are identically distributed. We claim that one cannot distinguish between seeing $(c, \mathsf{sk}_{y'})$ and $(c', \mathsf{sk}_y)$ where $c'$ is an actual encryption of $m' = \mathsf{Edit}(m, e)$, meaning that it is an FE encryption of $x' = (m', k')$ for a uniform $k'$. Since $y$ and $y'$ are individually identically distributed, the only difference between these tuples is the conditional distribution of $x$ vs. $x'$, but since $F(x', y) = F(x, y') = m'$, this difference is hidden by FE security.

Our solution for symmetric-key encryption with deniable edits is analogous, but relying on symmetric-key FE instead of public-key FE.

## 1.5    Related Work

The notion of *deniable encryption* was introduced by Canetti et al. [CDNO97]. They considered two separate facets of this notion: *sender deniability* considers the scenario where the encryptor is coerced to produce the random coins of the encryption algorithm, whereas *receiver deniability* considers the scenario where the decryptor is coerced to produce the secret key (or even the random coins of the key generation algorithm). As noted in several prior works, it is easy to protect against sender coercion by simply having senders erase the randomness they use after each encryption operation, and similarly the receiver can erase the randomness of the key generation algorithm. However, the receiver needs to keep her secret key for the long term in order to decrypt. Therefore, we view receiver deniability, where the receiver is coerced to produce her secret key, as the most important deniability scenario and focus on this in our work. Nevertheless, we mention that the other notions of deniability are also interesting and meaningful in settings where erasure is not technically or legally feasible.

Canetti et al. [CDNO97] construct both sender and receiver deniable public-key encryption schemes where it is possible to distinguish between the real key/randomness and the fake key/randomness with an inverse polynomial advantage. The work of Sahai and Waters [SW14] constructs a sender deniable with negligible distinguishing advantage using indistinguishability obfuscation. Bedlin et al. [BNNO11] show that a negligible distinguishing advantage cannot be achieved for receiver deniability if we consider the most natural notion where, given a secret key $\mathsf{sk}$ and a honestly generated ciphertext $c$ encrypting some message $m$, it is possible to generate a secret key $\mathsf{sk}_{c,m'}$ that decrypts $c$ to an arbitrarily different message $m'$. Although they show this for public-key encryption, the result also naturally extends to CPA secure symmetric-key encryption (but not for one-time encryption, where the one-time pad is optimally deniable).

As we discussed, it is possible to circumvent the results of Bedlin et al. [BNNO11] by relaxing the notion of receiver deniability and considering dual-key or dual-scheme (also called multi-distributional) variants. The work of O'Neill et al. [OPW11] constructs a dual-scheme deniable public-key encryption which is simultaneously sender and receiver deniable (bi-deniable). The work of [DIO16] construct both dual-scheme and dual-key variants of receiver deniable *functional encryption*. Whereas in that work, functionality and deniability were orthogonal properties (i.e., the goal was to get a scheme which is simultaneously a functional encryption scheme and deniable), one can see our notion of deniable edits as a type of functional-deniability where the fake secret key invisibly applies a function to the encrypted message.

Deniable encryption is also very related to the concept of non-committing encryption [CFGN96, DN00, CDMW09]. On a very high level, the latter notion only requires the ability to equivocate ciphertexts that were specially generated by a simulator whereas the former notion requires the ability to equivocate honestly generated ciphertexts.

In both receiver-deniable and non-committing encryption, the secret key size is necessarily at least as large as the message size [Nie02]. This is because for every possible message $m'$, there has to be a different secret key $\mathsf{sk}_{c,m'}$ that decrypts the given ciphertext $c$ to $m'$. Our work *flexibly circumvents this lower bound in the setting of deniable encryption* by restricting the set of messages $m'$ to which we can open the ciphertext to only be values of the type $m' = \mathsf{Edit}(m, e)$ where $m$ is the message that was originally encrypted and $e$ is the description of an edit. This allows the secret key size to only scale with the edit description size $|e|$ instead of the message size $|m|$.

The idea of restricting the set of messages to which a ciphertext can be opened in order to reduce the secret key size has been considered in several other prior works, both in the context of deniability and non-committing encryption. For example, the notions of *plan-ahead deniability* [CDNO97, OPW11] and *somewhat-non committing encryption* [GWZ09] fix a small set of messages to which a ciphertext can be opened at encryption time. In *somewhere equivocal (non-committing) encryption* [HJO+16] it is possible to modify a few blocks of the encrypted data. Perhaps the closest concept to our work is the notion of *functionally equivocal (non-committing) encryption* from the recent work of Canetti et al. [CPV16]. In that work, it's possible to open a simulated encryption to any message $m' = f(x)$ which is in the range of some function $f$, where $f$ can be an expanding function and the secret key size is only proportional to $|x|$ rather than to $|m'|$. The main differences with our work on deniable edits are: (1) we study deniability rather than the non-committing setting, meaning that we start with a real ciphertext of some message $m$ rather than a simulated ciphertext, (2) we want to open the ciphertext to an edited messages $m' = \mathsf{Edit}(m, e)$ that depends on the original value $m$ rather than just an arbitrary value in the range of some fixed function $f$.

## 2    Preliminaries

We introduce several preliminaries including notation and definitions of functional encryption. See Appendix A for additional standard cryptographic definitions.

*Notation.* We denote by $[n]$ the set $\{1, \ldots, n\}$. For a string $x \in \{0, 1\}^*$ we denote by $x[i]$ the $i$-th bit of $x$. If $X$ is a random variable, a probability distribution, or a randomized algorithm we let $x \leftarrow X$ denote the process of sampling $x$ according to $X$. If $\mathcal{X}$ is a set, we let $x \leftarrow \mathcal{X}$ denote the process of sampling $x$ uniformly at random from $\mathcal{X}$.

### 2.1    Single-Key Functional-Encryption

We now present definition of public and symmetric key functional encryption. We only require a weak notions of security where (1) the adversary only sees at most a single secret key and (2) the adversary has to selectively choose the secret key before it gets the challenge ciphertext.

**Definition 1 (Single-Key PK FE).** *A single-key public-key functional-encryption scheme (PK FE) for a function* $F : \{0,1\}^{n_1(\lambda)} \times \{0,1\}^{n_2(\lambda)} \to \{0,1\}^{n_3(\lambda)}$ *consists of PPT algorithms* (Setup, Gen, Enc, Dec) *with the following syntax:*

- (mpk, msk) ← Setup($1^\lambda$) *generates a master secret-key* msk *and master public key* mpk.
- $\mathsf{sk}_y$ ← Gen$_{\mathsf{msk}}(y)$ *takes an input* $y \in \{0,1\}^{n_2(\lambda)}$, *generates a secret-key* $\mathsf{sk}_y$.

– $c \leftarrow \mathsf{Enc_{mpk}}(x)$ *takes an input* $x \in \{0,1\}^{n_1(\lambda)}$, *outputs an encryption of* $x$.
– $F(x,y) = \mathsf{Dec_{sk_y}}(c)$ *outputs* $F(x,y) \in \{0,1\}^{n_3(\lambda)}$.

*The scheme should satisfy the following properties:*

**Correctness.** *For every security parameter* $\lambda$, *message* $x \in \{0,1\}^{n_1(\lambda)}$, *and* $y \in \{0,1\}^{n_2(\lambda)}$:

$$\Pr\left[F(x,y) = \mathsf{Dec_{sk_y}}(\mathsf{Enc_{mpk}}(x)) \,\middle|\, \begin{array}{l} (\mathsf{mpk},\mathsf{msk}) \leftarrow \mathsf{Setup}(1^\lambda) \\ \mathsf{sk}_y \leftarrow \mathsf{Gen_{msk}}(y) \end{array}\right] = 1.$$

**Single-Key PK FE Security.** *We define the "single-key public-key functional encryption game"* $\mathsf{FEGame}_{\mathcal{A}}^b(\lambda)$ *between an adversary* $\mathcal{A}$ *and a challenger with a challenge bit* $b \in \{0,1\}$ *as follows:*

– *Sample* $(\mathsf{mpk},\mathsf{msk}) \leftarrow \mathsf{Setup}(1^\lambda)$ *and send* $\mathsf{mpk}$ *to* $\mathcal{A}$.
– *The adversary* $\mathcal{A}$ *chooses* $y \in \{0,1\}^{n_2(\lambda)} \cup \{\bot\}$.
– *If* $y \neq \bot$, *sample* $\mathsf{sk}_y \leftarrow \mathsf{Gen_{msk}}(y)$ *and send* $\mathsf{sk}_y$ *to* $\mathcal{A}$.
– *The adversary* $\mathcal{A}$ *chooses messages* $x_0, x_1 \in \{0,1\}^{n_1(\lambda)}$ *such that if* $y \neq \bot$ *then* $F(x_0, y) = F(x_1, y)$.
– *The adversary* $\mathcal{A}$ *gets a challenge* $\mathsf{Enc_{mpk}}(x_b)$ *and eventually outputs a bit* $b'$ *which we define as the output of the game.*

*We require that for all PPT adversary* $\mathcal{A}$ *we have*

$$|\Pr[\mathsf{FEGame}_{\mathcal{A}}^0(\lambda) = 1] - \Pr[\mathsf{FEGame}_{\mathcal{A}}^1(\lambda) = 1]| \leq \mathsf{negl}(\lambda).$$

**Definition 2 (Single-Key SK FE).** *A single-key symmetric-key functional-encryption scheme (SK FE) for a function* $F : \{0,1\}^{n_1(\lambda)} \times \{0,1\}^{n_2(\lambda)} \to \{0,1\}^{n_3(\lambda)}$ *consists of PPT algorithms* $(\mathsf{Setup}, \mathsf{Gen}, \mathsf{Enc}, \mathsf{Dec})$ *with the following syntax:*

– $\mathsf{msk} \leftarrow \mathsf{Setup}(1^\lambda)$ *generates a master secret-key* $\mathsf{msk}$.
– $\mathsf{sk}_y \leftarrow \mathsf{Gen_{msk}}(y)$ *takes an input* $y \in \{0,1\}^{n_2(\lambda)}$, *generates a functional secret-key* $\mathsf{sk}_y$.
– $c \leftarrow \mathsf{Enc_{msk}}(x)$ *takes an input* $x \in \{0,1\}^{n_1(\lambda)}$, *outputs an encryption of* $x$
– $F(x,y) = \mathsf{Dec_{sk_y}}(c)$ *outputs a message* $F(x,y) \in \{0,1\}^{n_3(\lambda)}$.

*The scheme should satisfy the following properties:*

**Correctness.** *For every security parameter* $\lambda$, *message* $x \in \{0,1\}^{n_1(\lambda)}$, *and* $y \in \{0,1\}^{n_1(\lambda)}$:

$$\Pr\left[F(x,y) = \mathsf{Dec_{sk_y}}(\mathsf{Enc_{msk}}(x)) \,\middle|\, \begin{array}{l} \mathsf{msk} \leftarrow \mathsf{Setup}(1^\lambda) \\ \mathsf{sk}_y \leftarrow \mathsf{Gen_{msk}}(y) \end{array}\right] = 1.$$

**Single-Key SK FE Security.** *We define the "single-key secret-key functional encryption game"* $\mathsf{FEGame}_{\mathcal{A}}^b(\lambda)$ *between an adversary* $\mathcal{A}$ *and a challenger with a challenge bit* $b \in \{0,1\}$ *as follows:*

– *Sample* $\mathsf{msk} \leftarrow \mathsf{Setup}(\lambda)$ *and let* $\mathcal{O}(\cdot)$ *be an encryption oracle* $\mathcal{O}(\cdot) := \mathsf{Enc_{msk}}(\cdot)$

- *The adversary gets access to the encryption oracle $\mathcal{A}^{\mathcal{O}}$ and eventually chooses $y \in \{0,1\}^{n_2(\lambda)} \cup \{\bot\}$.*
- *If $y \neq \bot$, sample $\mathsf{sk}_y \leftarrow \mathsf{Gen}_{\mathsf{msk}}(y)$ and send $\mathsf{sk}_y$ to $\mathcal{A}$*
- *The adversary $\mathcal{A}^{\mathcal{O}}(\mathsf{sk}_y)$ gets further access to the encryption oracle and eventually chooses messages $x_0, x_1$ such that if $y \neq \bot$ then $F(x_0, y) = F(x_1, y)$.*
- *The adversary $\mathcal{A}^{\mathcal{O}}(\mathsf{sk}_y, c)$ gets a challenge message $c \leftarrow \mathsf{Enc}_{\mathsf{msk}}(x_b)$ and further access to the encryption oracle, and eventually outputs a bit $b'$ which we define as the output of the game.*

*We require that for all PPT adversary $\mathcal{A}$ we have*

$$|\Pr[\mathsf{FEGame}^0_{\mathcal{A}}(\lambda) = 1] - \Pr[\mathsf{FEGame}^1_{\mathcal{A}}(\lambda) = 1]| \leq \mathsf{negl}(\lambda).$$

*Special Encryption/Decryption.* We will require two additional properties from our FE schemes. Informally, a symmetric-key FE with a *special encryption* allows one to encrypt given a secret-key $\mathsf{sk}_y$ instead of $\mathsf{msk}$ while ensuring that the two methods are indistinguishable even given $\mathsf{sk}_y$. A symmetric-key or public-key FE with *special decryption* allows one to decrypt with $\mathsf{msk}$ to recover the entire value $x$.

**Definition 3 (Special Encryption).** *We say that a symmetric-key functional encryption scheme* $\mathsf{FE} = (\mathsf{Setup}, \mathsf{Gen}, \mathsf{Enc}, \mathsf{Dec})$ *has a special encryption if the syntax of the $\mathsf{Enc}$ algorithm can be extended to work with a secret key $\mathsf{sk}_y$ instead of a master secret key $\mathsf{msk}$, and for all PPT adversary $\mathcal{A}$ we have*

$$|\Pr[\mathsf{EncGame}^0_{\mathcal{A}}(\lambda) = 1] - \Pr[\mathsf{EncGame}^1_{\mathcal{A}}(\lambda) = 1]| \leq \mathsf{negl}(\lambda).$$

*where $\mathsf{EncGame}^b_{\mathcal{A}}(\lambda)$ is a game between an adversary and a challenger with a challenge bit $b \in \{0,1\}$, defined as follows:*

- *The adversary $\mathcal{A}$ chooses $y \in \{0,1\}^{n_2(\lambda)}$*
- *Sample $\mathsf{msk} \leftarrow \mathsf{Setup}(\lambda)$ and $\mathsf{sk}_y \leftarrow \mathsf{Gen}_{\mathsf{msk}}(y)$, and let $\mathcal{O}(\cdot)$ be an encryption oracle*
- *The adversary $\mathcal{A}^{\mathcal{O}}(\mathsf{sk}_y)$ gets access to the encryption oracle and the secret key, and eventually outputs a bit $b'$ which we define as the output of the game.*

**Definition 4 (Special Decryption).** *We say that a symmetric-key functional encryption scheme* $\mathsf{FE} = (\mathsf{Setup}, \mathsf{Gen}, \mathsf{Enc}, \mathsf{Dec})$ *has a special decryption if the syntax of the $\mathsf{Dec}$ algorithm can be extended to work with a master secret key $\mathsf{msk}$ instead of a secret key $\mathsf{sk}$, and for every security parameter $\lambda$ and message $x \in \{0,1\}^{n(\lambda)}$:*

$$\Pr\left[\mathsf{Dec}_{\mathsf{msk}}(\mathsf{Enc}_{\mathsf{msk}}(x)) = x \,\middle|\, \mathsf{msk} \leftarrow \mathsf{Setup}(1^{\lambda})\right] = 1$$

*Similarly, we say that a public-key functional encryption scheme* $\mathsf{FE} = (\mathsf{Setup}, \mathsf{Gen}, \mathsf{Enc}, \mathsf{Dec})$ *has a special decryption if the syntax of the $\mathsf{Dec}$ algorithm can be extended to work with a master secret key $\mathsf{msk}$ instead of a secret key $\mathsf{sk}$, and for every security parameter $\lambda$ and message $x \in \{0,1\}^{n(\lambda)}$:*

$$\Pr\left[\mathsf{Dec}_{\mathsf{msk}}(\mathsf{Enc}_{\mathsf{mpk}}(x)) = x \,\middle|\, (\mathsf{mpk}, \mathsf{msk}) \leftarrow \mathsf{Setup}(1^{\lambda})\right] = 1$$

*Constructions.* We now summarize what is known about FE schemes as defined above. The following theorem essentially follows from prior work [SS10,GVW12] using the machinery of garbled circuits and, for completeness, we describe the constructions in Appendix B.

**Theorem 1.** *Under the assumption that standard public-key encryption schemes exist, there exists a single-key public-key functional-encryption scheme with the special decryption property for any polynomial-time function F. Under the assumption that one-way functions exist, there exists a single-key symmetric-key functional-encryption scheme with the special encryption and special decryption properties for any polynomial-time function F.*

*There is some fixed polynomial $\mathsf{poly}(\lambda)$ such that for a function $F : \{0,1\}^{n_1(\lambda)} \times \{0,1\}^{n_2(\lambda)} \to \{0,1\}^{n_3(\lambda)}$ with circuit size $s(\lambda)$, the resulting FE schemes have a master public key $\mathsf{mpk}$ (in the case of public-key FE), master secret key $\mathsf{msk}$, and secret keys $\mathsf{sk}_y$ of size $n_2(\lambda)\mathsf{poly}(\lambda)$ and encryption/decryption time and ciphertext size $s(\lambda)\mathsf{poly}(\lambda)$. Assuming identity-based encryption (IBE) we can further reduce the size of $\mathsf{mpk}$ to be just $\mathsf{poly}(\lambda)$.*

See Appendix B for a proof of the above.

# 3   Invisible-Edits

We begin by defining and constructing encryption schemes with invisible edits. We start with the public key setting and then move on to the symmetric-key setting.

## 3.1   Public-Key Invisible-Edits

Our definition of public-key encryption with invisible edits follows the *dual-key* paradigm. The key generation algorithm outputs a "privileged" key pair $(\mathsf{pk}, \mathsf{sk})$ along with an edit key $\mathsf{ek}$. The edit key can be used to generate an "unprivileged" key pair $(\mathsf{pk}_e, \mathsf{sk}_e) \leftarrow \mathsf{InvEdit}_{\mathsf{ek}}(e)$ corresponding to some edit $e$. An encryption of a message $m$ encrypted under $\mathsf{pk}$ will decrypt to $m' = \mathsf{Edit}(m, e)$ under $\mathsf{sk}_e$. A user cannot tell the difference between the following two scenarios:

- The user is an unprivileged user that gets $(\mathsf{pk}_e, \mathsf{sk}_e)$ and sees encryptions $c_i \leftarrow \mathsf{Enc}_{\mathsf{pk}}(m_i)$ of messages $m_i$ under the privileged public key $\mathsf{pk}$ which he decrypts incorrectly to $m'_i = \mathsf{Edit}(m_i, e)$ under $\mathsf{sk}_e$.
- The user is a privileged user that gets $(\mathsf{pk}, \mathsf{sk})$ and sees encryptions $c_i \leftarrow \mathsf{Enc}_{\mathsf{pk}}(m'_i)$ of messages $m'_i = \mathsf{Edit}(m_i, e)$ under the privileged public key $\mathsf{pk}$ which he decrypts correctly to $m'_i$ under $\mathsf{sk}$.

The above even holds under chosen message attack where the user can choose the messages $m_i$. Note that since $(\mathsf{pk}, \mathsf{sk})$ and $(\mathsf{pk}_e, \mathsf{sk}_e)$ are indistinguishable it implies that correctness must hold when using the latter key pair and for any $m$ with all but negligible probability $\mathsf{Dec}_{\mathsf{sk}_e}(\mathsf{Enc}_{\mathsf{pk}_e}(m)) = m$ since otherwise it would be easy to distinguish $(\mathsf{pk}_e, \mathsf{sk}_e)$ from $(\mathsf{pk}, \mathsf{sk})$.

**Definition 5 (Public-Key Invisible Edits).** *An* Edit-*invisible public-key encryption with message-length* $n = n(\lambda)$, *edit description length* $\ell = \ell(\lambda)$, *and edit function* Edit $: \{0,1\}^{n(\lambda)} \times \{0,1\}^{\ell(\lambda)} \to \{0,1\}^{n(\lambda)}$ *consists of PPT algorithms* (Gen, Enc, Dec, InvEdit) *with the following syntax:*

- $(\mathsf{pk}, \mathsf{sk}, \mathsf{ek}) \leftarrow \mathsf{Gen}(1^\lambda)$ *generates a public-key* pk, *secret-key* sk, *and edit key* ek.
- $c \leftarrow \mathsf{Enc}_{\mathsf{pk}}(m), m = \mathsf{Dec}_{\mathsf{sk}}(c)$ *have the standard syntax of public-key encryption and decryption.*
- $(\mathsf{pk}_e, \mathsf{sk}_e) \leftarrow \mathsf{InvEdit}_{\mathsf{ek}}(e)$ *takes as input an edit* e *and outputs a public/secret key pair* $\mathsf{pk}_e, \mathsf{sk}_e$.

*The scheme should satisfy the following properties:*

**Correctness & Encryption Security.** *The scheme* (Gen, Enc, Dec) *satisfies the standard notions of public-key encryption correctness and semantic security (see Definition 12) if we ignore the edit-key* ek.

**Invisibility of Edits.** *We define the "invisible edits game"* $\mathsf{InvGame}_{\mathcal{A}}^b(\lambda)$ *between an adversary* $\mathcal{A}$ *and a challenger with a challenge bit* $b \in \{0,1\}$ *as follows:*

- *The adversary* $\mathcal{A}$ *chooses an edit function* $e \in \{0,1\}^\ell$.
- *Sample* $(\mathsf{pk}, \mathsf{sk}, \mathsf{ek}) \leftarrow \mathsf{Gen}(1^\lambda)$ *and* $(\mathsf{pk}_e, \mathsf{sk}_e) \leftarrow \mathsf{InvEdit}_{\mathsf{ek}}(e)$. *If* $b = 0$, *give* $(\mathsf{pk}, \mathsf{sk})$ *to* $\mathcal{A}$ *and let* $\mathcal{O}(\cdot) := \mathsf{Enc}_{\mathsf{pk}}(\mathsf{Edit}(\cdot, e))$, *else if* $b = 1$ *give* $(\mathsf{pk}_e, \mathsf{sk}_e)$ *to* $\mathcal{A}$ *and let* $\mathcal{O}(\cdot) := \mathsf{Enc}_{\mathsf{pk}}(\cdot)$.
- $\mathcal{A}^{\mathcal{O}}$ *gets access to the oracle* $\mathcal{O}$ *and eventually outputs a bit* $b'$ *which we define as the output of the game.*

*We require that for all PPT adversary* $\mathcal{A}$ *we have* $|\Pr[\mathsf{InvGame}_{\mathcal{A}}^0(\lambda) = 1] - \Pr[\mathsf{InvGame}_{\mathcal{A}}^1(\lambda) = 1]| \leq \mathsf{negl}(\lambda)$.

**Construction.** We now present our construction of public-key invisible encryption using public-key FE. The construction follows the outline presented in the introduction. Before we give the construction, we define the function $F_{\mathsf{Edit}}$ which will be used throughout the paper.

**Definition 6.** *For every polynomial-time edit function* Edit $: \{0,1\}^{n(\lambda)} \times \{0,1\}^{\ell(\lambda)} \to \{0,1\}^{n(\lambda)}$, *we define the function* $F_{\mathsf{Edit}} : \{0,1\}^{n(\lambda)+(\lambda+\ell(\lambda))} \times \{0,1\}^{\lambda+\ell(\lambda)} \to \{0,1\}^{n(\lambda)}$ *as follows:*

$$F_{\mathsf{Edit}}(x = (m, k), y) := \begin{cases} \mathsf{Edit}(m, e) & \text{if } \exists e \text{ s.t. } y \oplus k = (0^\lambda, e) \\ m & \text{otherwise} \end{cases}$$

*where we parse* $x = (m, k)$ *with* $m \in \{0,1\}^{n(\lambda)}$ *and* $k \in \{0,1\}^{\lambda+\ell(\lambda)}$.

**Construction 2 (Public-Key Invisible Edits).** *For any polynomial-time edit function* Edit $: \{0,1\}^{n(\lambda)} \times \{0,1\}^{\ell(\lambda)} \to \{0,1\}^{n(\lambda)}$, *we construct an* Edit-*invisible public-key encryption using a single-key public-key functional encryption* FE = (Setup, Gen, Enc, Dec) *for the function* $F_{\mathsf{Edit}}$ *(Definition 6). The construction proceeds as follows.*

- IEdit.Gen$(1^\lambda)$:
  - $(\mathsf{mpk}, \mathsf{msk}) \leftarrow \mathsf{FE.Setup}(1^\lambda)$
  - *Select uniform* $(y, k) \leftarrow \{0,1\}^{\lambda+\ell} \times \{0,1\}^{\lambda+\ell}$
  - $\mathsf{sk}_y \leftarrow \mathsf{FE.Gen}_{\mathsf{msk}}(y)$
  - *Output* $(\mathsf{pk} := (\mathsf{mpk}, k), \mathsf{sk} := \mathsf{sk}_y, \mathsf{ek} := (\mathsf{mpk}, k, \mathsf{msk}))$
- IEdit.Enc$_{\mathsf{pk}}(m)$:
  - *Output* $c \leftarrow \mathsf{FE.Enc}_{\mathsf{mpk}}((m, k))$
- IEdit.Dec$_{\mathsf{sk}}(c)$:
  - *Output* $m = \mathsf{FE.Dec}_{\mathsf{sk}_y}(c)$
- IEdit.InvEdit$_{\mathsf{ek}}(e)$:
  - *Select uniform* $k' \leftarrow \{0,1\}^{\lambda+\ell}$
  - $\mathsf{sk}_{y'} \leftarrow \mathsf{FE.Gen}_{\mathsf{msk}}(y')$ *where* $y' = k \oplus (0^\lambda, e)$
  - *Output* $(\mathsf{pk}_e := (\mathsf{mpk}, k'), \mathsf{sk}_e := \mathsf{sk}_{y'})$

**Theorem 3.** *The scheme* IEdit *given in the above Construction 2 is a secure Edit-invisible public-key encryption if* FE *is a single-key public-key functional encryption for the function* $F_{\mathsf{Edit}}$. *In particular, the construction only relies on the existence of standard public-key encryption.*

*Proof.* We now prove that the above Construction 2 satisfies the properties of Edit-invisible public-key encryption in Definition 5.

**Correctness:** For every security parameter $\lambda$, and message $m \in \{0,1\}^n$:

$$\Pr\left[m = \mathsf{IEdit.Dec}_{\mathsf{sk}}(\mathsf{IEdit.Enc}_{\mathsf{pk}}(m)) \,\middle|\, (\mathsf{pk}, \mathsf{sk}, \mathsf{dk}) \leftarrow \mathsf{IEdit.Gen}(1^\lambda)\right]$$

$$= \Pr\left[m = \mathsf{FE.Dec}_{\mathsf{sk}_y}(\mathsf{FE.Enc}_{\mathsf{pk}}((m, k))) \,\middle|\, \begin{array}{l} (k, y) \leftarrow \{0,1\}^{\lambda+\ell} \times \{0,1\}^{\lambda+\ell} \\ (\mathsf{mpk}, \mathsf{msk}) \leftarrow \mathsf{FE.Setup}(1^\lambda) \\ \mathsf{sk}_y \leftarrow \mathsf{FE.Gen}_{\mathsf{msk}}(y) \end{array}\right]$$

$$= \Pr\left[m = F((m, k), y) \,\middle|\, (k, y) \leftarrow \{0,1\}^{\lambda+\ell} \times \{0,1\}^{\lambda+\ell}\right]$$

$$= 1 - \Pr\left[y \oplus k = (0^\lambda, r) \,\middle|\, \begin{array}{l} (k, y) \leftarrow \{0,1\}^{\lambda+\ell} \times \{0,1\}^{\lambda+\ell} \\ r \in \{0,1\}^\ell \end{array}\right]$$

$$= 1 - \frac{1}{2^\lambda}$$

**Encryption Security:** We want to show that for any PPT adversary $\mathcal{A}$:

$$|\Pr[\mathsf{CPAGame}_{\mathcal{A}}^0(\lambda) = 1] - \Pr[\mathsf{CPAGame}_{\mathcal{A}}^1(\lambda) = 1]| \leq \mathsf{negl}(\lambda).$$

This follows since an adversary $\mathcal{A}$ who breaks the CPA security also wins in the single-key public-key functional-encryption security game FEGame (with no secret key, when $y = \bot$).

**Invisibility of Edits.** We want to show that for any PPT adversary $\mathcal{A}$:

$$|\Pr[\mathsf{InvGame}_{\mathcal{A}}^0(\lambda) = 1] - \Pr[\mathsf{InvGame}_{\mathcal{A}}^1(\lambda) = 1]| \leq \mathsf{negl}(\lambda).$$

Informally, an adversary $\mathcal{A}$ who wins the "invisible edits game" $\mathsf{InvGame}_{\mathcal{A}}^b(\lambda)$ with an edit $e$ and oracle queries $m_i$, wins the single-key public-key functional-encryption security game with a random $y \leftarrow \{0,1\}^{\lambda+\ell}$, and messages $x_0 = (\mathsf{Edit}(m_i, e), k)$ and $x_1 = (m_i, k')$ where $k \leftarrow \{0,1\}^{\lambda+\ell}$ and $k' = y \oplus (0^\lambda, e)$.

Formally, we prove it by a sequence of $q$ hybrids where $q$ is a bound of the number of queries that $\mathcal{A}$ makes to its oracle $\mathcal{O}$. We define the hybrid games $\mathsf{HybGame}_{\mathcal{A}}^j(\lambda)$ for $j = 0, \dots, q$ by modifying $\mathsf{InvGame}_{\mathcal{A}}^b(\lambda)$ and defining the encryption oracle $\mathcal{O}^j$ and the challenge key pair $(\mathsf{pk}, \mathsf{sk})$ given to the adversary as follows:

$$\mathcal{O}^j(\cdot) := \begin{cases} \mathsf{FE.Enc}_{\mathsf{mpk}}(\mathsf{Edit}(\cdot, e), k) & i > j \\ \mathsf{FE.Enc}_{\mathsf{mpk}}(\cdot, k') & i \le j \end{cases}$$

$$(\mathsf{pk}, \mathsf{sk}) := ((\mathsf{mpk}, k), \mathsf{sk}_y)$$

where $y, k \leftarrow \{0,1\}^{\lambda+\ell}$, $k' = y \oplus (0^\ell, e)$, and $i$ is the index of the current query.

Observe that $\mathsf{HybGame}_{\mathcal{A}}^0(\lambda) \equiv \mathsf{InvGame}_{\mathcal{A}}^0(\lambda)$. This is because the value $k$ used by the encryption oracle $\mathcal{O}$ matches the one in $\mathsf{pk}$, the value $y$ is random and independent of $k$, and the encryption oracle is encrypting edited messages.

Also observe that $\mathsf{HybGame}_{\mathcal{A}}^q(\lambda) \equiv \mathsf{InvGame}_{\mathcal{A}}^1(\lambda)$. This is because the value $k'$ used by the encryption oracle is independent of the value $k$ given in $\mathsf{pk}$, the value $y$ contained in $\mathsf{sk}$ is correlated to the value $k'$ used by the encryption oracle via the relationship $y \oplus k' = (0^\ell, e)$, and the encryption oracle is encrypting un-edited messages.

Therefore, is suffices to show that for each $j$, the hybrids $\mathsf{HybGame}_{\mathcal{A}}^j(\lambda)$ and $\mathsf{HybGame}_{\mathcal{A}}^{j+1}(\lambda)$ are indistinguishable. This follows directly by public-key functional-encryption security. In particular, the only difference between the games is whether query $(j+1)$ to $\mathcal{O}$ is answered as $\mathsf{FE.Enc}_{\mathsf{mpk}}(\mathsf{Edit}(\cdot, e), k)$ or $\mathsf{FE.Enc}_{\mathsf{mpk}}(\cdot, k')$. But, since for any $m$ we have $F(x_0, y) = F(x_1, y)$ where $x_0 = (\mathsf{Edit}(m, e), k)$, $x_1 = (m, k')$, this is indistinguishable by functional-encryption security.

## 3.2    Symmetric-Key Invisible-Edits

In the symmetric-key setting, we present two different definitions of encryption with invisible edits.

First, we present a definition that follows the *dual-key* paradigm and can be seen as a direct analogue of our public-key definition for the symmetric-key setting. We can always interpret a public-key encryption with invisible edits as a symmetric-key scheme and therefore we can achieve this definition assuming the existence of standard public-key encryption using the results from the previous section. However, it remains as a fascinating open problem whether one can construct symmetric-key encryption with invisible edits following the dual-key paradigm by relying only one one-way functions or whether public-key encryption is necessary.

**Definition 7 (Dual-Key Invisible Edits).** *A* dual-key Edit-*invisible symmetric-key encryption scheme with message-length* $n = n(\lambda)$, *edit descrip-tion length* $\ell = \ell(\lambda)$, *and edit function* Edit : $\{0,1\}^n \times \{0,1\}^\ell \rightarrow \{0,1\}^n$ *consists of PPT algorithms* (Gen, Enc, Dec, InvEdit) *with the following syntax:*

- (sk, ek) ← Gen($1^\lambda$) *generates a secret-key* sk *and edit key* ek.
- $c \leftarrow$ Enc$_{sk}(m), m =$ Dec$_{sk}(c)$ *have the standard syntax of symmetric-key encryption and decryption.*
- sk$_e$ ← InvEdit$_{ek}(e)$ *takes as input an edit* $e$ *and outputs a secret key* sk$_e$.

*The scheme should satisfy the following properties:*

**Correctness & Encryption Security.** *The scheme* (Gen, Enc, Dec) *satisfies the standard notions of symmetric-key encryption correctness and CPA security (see Definition 13) if we ignore the edit-key* ek.

**Invisibility of Edits.** *We define the "invisible edits game"* InvGame$_\mathcal{A}^b(\lambda)$ *between an adversary* $\mathcal{A}$ *and a challenger with a challenge bit* $b \in \{0,1\}$ *as follows:*

- *The adversary* $\mathcal{A}$ *chooses an edit function* $e \in \{0,1\}^\ell$.
- *Sample* (sk, ek) ← Gen($1^\lambda$) *and* sk$_e$ ← InvEdit$_{ek}(e)$. *If* $b = 0$, *let* $\mathcal{O}(\cdot) :=$ Enc$_{sk}($Edit$(\cdot, e))$ *and if* $b = 1$ *let* $\mathcal{O}(\cdot) :=$ Enc$_{sk}(\cdot)$.
- $\mathcal{A}^\mathcal{O}$ *gets the secret key* sk *if* $b = 0$, *and* sk$_e$ *if* $b = 1$ *together with an access to the oracle* $\mathcal{O}$. *Eventually* $\mathcal{A}$ *outputs a bit* $b'$ *which we define as the output of the game.*

*We require that for all PPT adversary* $\mathcal{A}$ *we have* $|\Pr[$InvGame$_\mathcal{A}^0(\lambda) = 1] - \Pr[$InvGame$_\mathcal{A}^1(\lambda) = 1]| \leq$ negl($\lambda$).

Below, we present a definition of symmetric-key encryption with invisible edits that follows the weaker *dual-scheme* paradigm. In this case there are two different encryption schemes: an *unprivileged* scheme (Gen, Enc, Dec) and a *privileged* scheme (PrivGen, PrivEnc, PrivDec). Given a secret key sk* for the privileged scheme, it's possible to create a secret key sk$_e$ ← InvEdit$_{sk*}(e)$ that looks like a legitimate secret key of the unprivileged scheme but is tied to some edit $e$. An encryption of a message $m$ encrypted under sk* will decrypt to $m' =$ Edit$(m, e)$ under sk$_e$. A user cannot tell the difference between the following two scenarios:

- The user is an unprivileged user that gets sk$_e$ ← InvEdit$_{sk*}(e)$ and sees encryptions $c_i$ ← Enc$_{sk*}(m_i)$ of messages $m_i$ under the privileged secret key sk* which he decrypts incorrectly to $m_i' =$ Edit$(m_i, e)$ under sk$_e$.
- The user is an unprivileged user that gets sk ← Gen($1^\lambda$) created using the legitimate unprivileged key generation algorithm and sees encryptions $c_i$ ← Enc$_{sk}(m_i')$ of messages $m_i' =$ Edit$(m_i, e)$ under the unprivileged secret key sk which he then decrypts correctly to $m_i'$ using the same sk.

In other words, the user can tell that he's unprivileged. But he does't know whether everyone else is also unprivileged and he's correctly decrypting the messages they are sending or whether some other users are privileged and he's decrypting edited messages.

**Definition 8 (Dual-Scheme Invisible Edits).** *A dual-scheme* Edit-*invisible symmetric-key encryption scheme with message-length* $n = n(\lambda)$, *edit description length* $\ell = \ell(\lambda)$, *and edit function* Edit : $\{0,1\}^n \times \{0,1\}^\ell \rightarrow \{0,1\}^n$ *consists of PPT algorithms* Gen, Enc, Dec, PrivGen, PrivEnc, PrivDec, InvEdit. *The schemes* (Gen, Enc, Dec), (PrivGen, PrivEnc, PrivDec) *have the usual symmetric-key encryption syntax. The algorithm* $\mathsf{sk}_e \leftarrow \mathsf{InvEdit}_{\mathsf{sk}}(e)$ *takes as input an edit e and a privileged secret key* sk *and outputs an unprivileged secret key* $\mathsf{sk}_e$ *tied to an edit e.*

**Correctness & Encryption Security.** *The schemes* (Gen, Enc, Dec) *and* (PrivGen, PrivEnc, PrivDec) *satisfy the standard notions of symmetric-key encryption correctness and CPA security (Definition 13).*

**Invisibility of Edits.** *We define the "invisible edits game"* $\mathsf{InvGame}_{\mathcal{A}}^b(\lambda)$ *between an adversary* $\mathcal{A}$ *and a challenger with a challenge bit* $b \in \{0,1\}$ *as follows:*

- *The adversary* $\mathcal{A}$ *chooses an edit function* $e \in \{0,1\}^\ell$.
- *If* $b = 0$ *sample* $\mathsf{sk} \leftarrow \mathsf{Gen}(1^\lambda)$ *and if* $b = 1$ *sample* $\mathsf{sk}^* \leftarrow \mathsf{PrivGen}(1^\lambda)$ *and* $\mathsf{sk}_e \leftarrow \mathsf{InvEdit}_{\mathsf{sk}^*}(e)$. *If* $b = 0$, *let* $\mathcal{O}(\cdot) := \mathsf{Enc}_{\mathsf{sk}}(\mathsf{Edit}(\cdot, e))$ *and if* $b = 1$ *let* $\mathcal{O}(\cdot) := \mathsf{PrivEnc}_{\mathsf{sk}^*}(\cdot)$.
- *The adversary* $\mathcal{A}^{\mathcal{O}}$ *gets the secret key* sk *if* $b = 0$, *or* $\mathsf{sk}_e$ *if* $b = 1$. *It also gets oracle access to* $\mathcal{O}(\cdot)$ *and eventually it outputs a bit* $b'$ *which we define as the output of the game.*

*We require that for all PPT adversary* $\mathcal{A}$ *we have* $|\Pr[\mathsf{InvGame}_{\mathcal{A}}^0(\lambda) = 1] - \Pr[\mathsf{InvGame}_{\mathcal{A}}^1(\lambda) = 1]| \leq \mathsf{negl}(\lambda)$.

**Construction.** Our construction for the dual-scheme symmetric-key encryption with invisible edits roughly follows the same outline as the public-key construction with the main difference that we rely on symmetric-key rather than public-key FE.

**Construction 4 (Dual-Scheme Invisible Edits).** *For any polynomial time edit function* Edit : $\{0,1\}^{n(\lambda)} \times \{0,1\}^{\ell(\lambda)} \rightarrow \{0,1\}^{n(\lambda)}$, *we construct a dual-scheme* Edit-*invisible symmetric-key encryption* DSInvE = (Gen, Enc, Dec, PrivGen, PrivEnc, PrivDec, InvEdit), *using a single-key symmetric-key functional encryption* FE = (Setup, Gen, Enc, Dec) *with special encryption (see Definition 3) for the function* $F := F_{\mathsf{Edit}}$ *(see Definition 6). The construction proceeds as follows.*

- DSInvE.PrivGen($1^\lambda$):
  - FE.msk $\leftarrow$ FE.Setup($1^\lambda$)
  - *Select uniform* $k^* \leftarrow \{0,1\}^{\lambda+\ell}$
  - *Output* $\mathsf{sk}^* = (\mathsf{FE.msk}, k^*)$
- DSInvE.PrivEnc$_{\mathsf{sk}^*}(m)$:
  - *Output* $c \leftarrow \mathsf{FE.Enc}_{\mathsf{msk}}((m, k^*))$
- DSInvE.PrivDec$_{\mathsf{sk}^*}(c)$:
  - $(m, k^*) = \mathsf{FE.Dec}_{\mathsf{msk}}(c)$

- *Output m*
- DSInvE.Gen$(1^\lambda)$:
  - FE.msk $\leftarrow$ FE.Setup$(1^\lambda)$
  - *Select uniform* $y \leftarrow \{0,1\}^{\lambda+\ell}$
  - FE.sk$_y \leftarrow$ FE.Gen$_{\mathsf{msk}}(y)$
  - *Output* sk $=$ FE.sk$_y$
- DSInvE.Enc$_{\mathsf{sk}}(m)$:
  - *Select uniform* $k \leftarrow \{0,1\}^{\lambda+\ell}$
  - *Output* $c \leftarrow$ FE.Enc$_{\mathsf{sk}_y}((m,k))$
- DSInvE.Dec$_{\mathsf{sk}}(c)$:
  - *Output* $m =$ FE.Dec$_{\mathsf{sk}_y}(c)$
- DSInvE.InvEdit$_{\mathsf{sk}^*}(e)$:
  - FE.sk$_{y'} \leftarrow$ FE.Gen$_{\mathsf{msk}}(y')$ *where* $y' = k^* \oplus (0^\lambda, e)$
  - *Output* sk$_e =$ FE.sk$_{y'}$

**Theorem 5.** *The scheme* DSInvE *given in the above Construction 4 is a secure dual-scheme* Edit-*invisible symmetric-key encryption if* FE *is a single-key symmetric-key functional encryption scheme with special encryption for the function* $F_{\mathsf{Edit}}$. *In particular, the construction only relies on the existence of one-way functions.*

*Proof.* We now prove that Construction 4 satisfies the properties of *dual-scheme* Edit-*invisible symmetric-key encryption* in Definition 8.

**Correctness.** For every security parameter $\lambda$, and message $m \in \{0,1\}^n$:

$$\Pr\left[m = \mathsf{DSInvE.Dec_{sk}(DSInvE.Enc_{sk}}(m)) \,\middle|\, \mathsf{sk} \leftarrow \mathsf{DSInvE.Gen}(1^\lambda)\right]$$

$$= \Pr\left[m = \mathsf{FE.Dec_{sk_y}(FE.Enc_{sk_y}}((m,k))) \,\middle|\, \begin{array}{l} (k,y) \leftarrow \{0,1\}^{\lambda+\ell} \times \{0,1\}^{\lambda+\ell} \\ \mathsf{msk} \leftarrow \mathsf{FE.Setup}(1^\lambda) \\ \mathsf{sk}_y \leftarrow \mathsf{FE.Gen_{msk}}(y) \end{array}\right]$$

$$= \Pr\left[m = F((m,k),y) \,\middle|\, (k,y) \leftarrow \{0,1\}^{\lambda+\ell} \times \{0,1\}^{\lambda+\ell}\right]$$

$$= 1 - \Pr\left[\exists e \in \{0,1\}^\ell : y \oplus k = (0^\lambda, e) \,\middle|\, (k,y) \leftarrow \{0,1\}^{\lambda+\ell} \times \{0,1\}^{\lambda+\ell}\right]$$

$$= 1 - \frac{1}{2^\lambda}$$

Therefore, the scheme (DSInvE.Gen, DSInvE.Enc, DSInvE.Dec) is correct. Moreover, for every security parameter $\lambda$, and message $m \in \{0,1\}^n$:

$$\Pr\left[m = \mathsf{DSInvE.PrivDec_{sk^*}(DSInvE.PrivEnc_{sk}^*}(m)) \,\middle|\, \mathsf{sk}^* \leftarrow \mathsf{DSInvE.PrivGen}(1^\lambda)\right]$$

$$= \Pr\left[m = \mathsf{FE.Dec_{msk}(FE.Enc_{msk}}((m,k^*))) \,\middle|\, \begin{array}{l} k^* \leftarrow \{0,1\}^{\lambda+\ell} \\ \mathsf{msk} \leftarrow \mathsf{FE.Setup}(1^\lambda) \end{array}\right]$$

$$= 1$$

Thus, also the scheme(DSInvE.PrivGen, DSInvE.PrivEnc, DSInvE.PrivDec) is correct.

**Encryption Security.** The scheme $(\mathsf{DSInvE.PrivGen}, \mathsf{DSInvE.PrivEnc}, \mathsf{DSInvE.}$
$\mathsf{PrivDec})$ is symmetrically secure (i.e., CPA secure). Namely, for every PPT
adversary $\mathcal{A}$ there exists a negligible function $\mathsf{negl}(\cdot)$ such that for every security parameter $\lambda$,

$$|\Pr[\mathsf{CPAGame}_{\mathcal{A}}^0(\lambda) = 1] - \Pr[\mathsf{CPAGame}_{\mathcal{A}}^1(\lambda) = 1]| \leq \mathsf{negl}(\lambda).$$

A PPT adversary $\mathcal{A}$ who wins the CPA security also wins the single-key
symmetric-key functional-encryption security game $\mathsf{FEGame}$ (with no secret
key).

The scheme $(\mathsf{DSInvE.Gen}, \mathsf{DSInvE.Enc}, \mathsf{DSInvE.Dec})$ is also symmetrically
secure. The underline functional encryption scheme $\mathsf{FE}$ has a special encryption, therefore no PPT can distinguish between the CPA game $\mathsf{CPAGame}_{\mathcal{A}}^b(\lambda)$
and the hybrid game $\mathsf{HybGame}_{\mathcal{A}}^b(\lambda)$ where the encryption oracle and the challenge ciphertext instead of:

$$\mathcal{O}(\cdot) := \mathsf{FE.Enc}_{\mathsf{sk}_y}((\cdot, k))_{k \leftarrow \{0,1\}^{\lambda+\ell}}$$
$$c \leftarrow \mathsf{DSInvE.Enc}_{\mathsf{sk}}(\cdot) := \mathsf{FE.Enc}_{\mathsf{sk}_y}((m_b, k))_{k \leftarrow \{0,1\}^{\lambda+\ell}}$$

are replaced with:

$$\mathcal{O}(\cdot) := \mathsf{FE.Enc}_{\mathsf{msk}}((\cdot, k))_{k \leftarrow \{0,1\}^{\lambda+\ell}}$$
$$c \leftarrow \mathsf{DSInvE.Enc}_{\mathsf{sk}}(\cdot) := \mathsf{FE.Enc}_{\mathsf{msk}}((m_b, k))_{k \leftarrow \{0,1\}^{\lambda+\ell}}$$

The $\mathsf{HybGame}$ game is the same as the $\mathsf{FEGame}$ (with no secret-key, when
$y = \bot$).

**Invisibility of Edits.** For any PPT adversary $\mathcal{A}$ there exists a negligible function $\mathsf{negl}(\cdot)$, such that for every security parameter $\lambda$

$$|\Pr[\mathsf{InvGame}_{\mathcal{A}}^0(\lambda) = 1] - \Pr[\mathsf{InvGame}_{\mathcal{A}}^1(\lambda) = 1]| \leq \mathsf{negl}(\lambda).$$

An PPT adversary who wins the"invisible edits game" $\mathsf{InvGame}_{\mathcal{A}}^b(\lambda)$ with
an edit $e$ and an oracle query $m_i$, wins the single-key symmetric-key functional encryption security with a random $y \leftarrow \{0,1\}^{\lambda+\ell}$ and messages $m_0 =
(\mathsf{Edit}(m_{\tilde{q}}, e), k)$ and $m_1 = (m_{\tilde{q}}, k^*)$ where $k \leftarrow \{0,1\}^{\lambda+\ell}$ and $k^* = y \oplus (0^\ell, e)$.
Formally, we prove it by a sequence of $(q+1)$ hybrids where $q$ is a bound of
the number of query messages that $\mathcal{A}$ is able to make.

We define the hybrid game $\mathsf{HybGame}_{\mathcal{A}}^{\tilde{q},b}(\lambda)$ (a modification of $\mathsf{InvGame}_{\mathcal{A}}^b$), in
which the encryption oracle $\mathcal{O}(\cdot)$ and challenge $\mathsf{sk}$ are:

$$\mathcal{O}_b^{\tilde{q}}(\cdot) := \begin{cases} \mathsf{FE.Enc}_{\mathsf{msk}}(\mathsf{Edit}(\cdot, e), k)_{k \leftarrow \{0,1\}^{\lambda+\ell}} & i < \tilde{q} \\ \mathsf{FE.Enc}_{\mathsf{msk}}(\mathsf{Edit}(m_{\tilde{q}}, e), k)_{k \leftarrow \{0,1\}^{\lambda+\ell}} & b = 0 \land i = \tilde{q} \\ \mathsf{FE.Enc}_{\mathsf{msk}}(m_{\tilde{q}}, k^*) & b = 1 \land i = \tilde{q} \\ \mathsf{FE.Enc}_{\mathsf{msk}}(\cdot, k^*) & i > \tilde{q} \end{cases}$$

$$\mathsf{sk} \leftarrow \mathsf{FE.Gen}_{\mathsf{msk}}(y)$$

where $y \leftarrow \{0,1\}^{\lambda+\ell}$, $k^* = y \oplus (0^\ell, e)$, and $i$ is the number of queries that
were asked.

By the public-key functional-encryption security[2] it holds that for every $\tilde{q} \in [q]$ and every PPT adversary $\mathcal{A}$ there exists a negligible function $\mathsf{negl}(\cdot)$, such that for every security parameter $\lambda$

$$| \Pr[\mathsf{HybGame}_{\mathcal{A}}^{\tilde{q},0}(\lambda) = 1] - \Pr[\mathsf{HybGame}_{\mathcal{A}}^{\tilde{q},1}(\lambda) = 1]| \leq \mathsf{negl}(\lambda). \qquad (1)$$

Note that syntactically for every $\tilde{q}$:

$$\mathsf{HybGame}_{\mathcal{A}}^{\tilde{q},1}(\lambda) = \mathsf{HybGame}_{\mathcal{A}}^{(\tilde{q}-1),0}(\lambda). \qquad (2)$$

**Hybrid 0:** we start with the invisibility game with $b = 0$, $\mathsf{InvGame}_{\mathcal{A}}^{0}(\lambda)$. The encryption oracle and challenge are:

$$\mathcal{O}(\cdot) := \mathsf{IEdit.Enc}_{\mathsf{sk}}(\mathsf{Edit}(\cdot, e)) \quad = \mathsf{FE.Enc}_{\mathsf{sk}_y}(\mathsf{Edit}(\cdot, e), k)_{k \leftarrow \{0,1\}^{\lambda+\ell}}$$
$$\mathsf{sk} \leftarrow \mathsf{IEdit.Gen}(1^\lambda) \quad = \mathsf{sk}_y$$

where $y \leftarrow \{0,1\}^{\lambda+\ell}$, $\mathsf{sk}_y \leftarrow \mathsf{FE.Gen}_{\mathsf{msk}}(y)$, and $\mathsf{msk} \leftarrow \mathsf{FE.Setup}(1^\lambda)$.

**Hybrid 1:** we move to a the hybrid game $\mathsf{HybGame}_{\mathcal{A}}^{q,0}(\lambda)$ in which we encrypt using $\mathsf{FE.Enc}_{\mathsf{msk}}$ (instead of using $\mathsf{FE.Enc}_{\mathsf{sk}_y}$). The encryption oracle and the challenge are:

$$\mathcal{O}(\cdot) := \mathsf{FE.Enc}_{\mathsf{msk}}(\mathsf{Edit}(\cdot, e), k)_{k \leftarrow \{0,1\}^{\lambda+\ell}}$$
$$\mathsf{sk} := \mathsf{FE.Gen}_{\mathsf{msk}}(y)$$

where $y \leftarrow \{0,1\}^{\lambda+\ell}$, and $\mathsf{msk} \leftarrow \mathsf{FE.Setup}(1^\lambda)$. By the special encryption property[3],

$$\mathsf{InvGame}_{\mathcal{A}}^{0}(\lambda) \overset{c}{\approx} \mathsf{HybGame}_{\mathcal{A}}^{q,0}(\lambda)$$

**Hybrid 2:** we move to the hybrid game $\mathsf{HybGame}_{\mathcal{A}}^{1,1}(\lambda)$ by a sequence of $q$ hybrids (each start with Eq. (1) and follows by Eq. (2)). Namely,

$$\mathsf{HybGame}_{\mathcal{A}}^{q,0}(\lambda) \overset{c}{\approx} \mathsf{HybGame}_{\mathcal{A}}^{q,1}(\lambda) = \mathsf{HybGame}_{\mathcal{A}}^{(q-1),0}(\lambda)$$
$$\mathsf{HybGame}_{\mathcal{A}}^{(q-1),0}(\lambda) \overset{c}{\approx} \mathsf{HybGame}_{\mathcal{A}}^{(q-1),1}(\lambda) = \mathsf{HybGame}_{\mathcal{A}}^{(q-2),0}(\lambda)$$

$$\vdots$$

$$\mathsf{HybGame}_{\mathcal{A}}^{1,0}(\lambda) \overset{c}{\approx} \mathsf{HybGame}_{\mathcal{A}}^{1,1}(\lambda)$$

Observe that $\mathsf{HybGame}_{\mathcal{A}}^{1,1}(\lambda) = \mathsf{InvGame}_{\mathcal{A}}^{1}(\lambda)$ in which the encryption oracle $\mathcal{O}$ and challenge $\mathsf{sk}$ are:

$$\mathcal{O}(\cdot) := \mathsf{IEdit.PrivEnc}_{\mathsf{sk}^*}(\cdot) \quad = \mathsf{FE.Enc}_{\mathsf{msk}}(\cdot, k^*)$$
$$\mathsf{sk}_e \leftarrow \mathsf{IEdit.InvEdit}_{\mathsf{sk}^*}(e) \quad = \mathsf{FE.Gen}_{\mathsf{msk}}(y)$$

where $y = k^* \oplus (0^\ell, e)$, $k^* \leftarrow \{0,1\}^{\lambda+\ell}$, and $\mathsf{msk} \leftarrow \mathsf{FE.Setup}(1^\lambda)$.

---

[2] With random $y \leftarrow \{0,1\}^{\lambda+\ell}$ and $m_0 = (\mathsf{Edit}(m_{\tilde{q}}, e), k), m_1 = (m_{\tilde{q}}, k^*)$ where $y, k \leftarrow \{0,1\}^{\lambda+\ell}$ and $k^* = y \oplus (0^\ell, e)$.

[3] See Definition 3.

## 3.3  Efficiency

For an edit function $\mathsf{Edit} : \{0,1\}^{n(\lambda)} \times \{0,1\}^{\ell(\lambda)} \to \{0,1\}^{n(\lambda)}$ with $n(\lambda)$ size message, $\ell(\lambda)$ edit description size, and where the circuit size of $\mathsf{Edit}$ is $s(\lambda)$ the efficiency of our public-key and symmetric-key $\mathsf{Edit}$-invisible encryption schemes given in Constructions 2 and 4 is summarized as follows. There is some fixed polynomial $\mathsf{poly}(\lambda)$ such that:

- The secret key size is $\ell(\lambda)\mathsf{poly}(\lambda)$.
- The run-time of the encryption/decryption procedures and the ciphertext size $s(\lambda)\mathsf{poly}(\lambda)$.
- In the case of public-key deniable encryption, the public-keys size is $\ell(\lambda)\mathsf{poly}(\lambda)$. If we're willing to use a stronger assumption of *identity-based encryption* (IBE) we can use a more efficient FE instantiation in our construction which reduces the public-key size to just $\mathsf{poly}(\lambda)$.

One open problem would be to reduce the encryption time and the ciphertext size to only depend on the message size $n(\lambda)$ rather than the circuit size $s(\lambda)$ without increasing the secret key size. However, we envision that most interesting $\mathsf{Edit}$ functions that we'd want to apply anyway have relatively small circuit size which is roughly linear in the message size $s(\lambda) = O(n(\lambda))$.

## 4  Deniable-Edits

We now define and construct encryption schemes with deniable edits. We start with the public key setting and then move on to the symmetric-key setting.

### 4.1  Public-Key Deniable-Edits

Our definition of public-key encryption with deniable edits follows the *dual-key* paradigm outlined in the introduction. The key generation algorithm outputs a secret decryption key $\mathsf{sk}$ and denying key $\mathsf{dk}$, and most users are expected to discard $\mathsf{dk}$ since it is not needed for decryption. In particular, this means that users might be later coerced to give up their secret key $\mathsf{sk}$ which they need to keep for decryption but we assume they cannot be coerced to give up $\mathsf{dk}$ since they can plausibly claim they discarded it. Users that keep $\mathsf{dk}$ can use it to later "deny" the contents of a particular ciphertext $c$ encrypting some message $m$ by producing a legitimate secret key $\mathsf{sk}_{c,e} \leftarrow \mathsf{Deny}_{\mathsf{dk}}(c,e)$ that decrypts $c$ to $m' = \mathsf{Edit}(m,e)$. Given a ciphertext $c$ and a secret key $\mathsf{sk}^*$, the coercer cannot distinguish whether $c$ is really an encryption of $m'$ and $\mathsf{sk}^* = \mathsf{sk}$ is the original secret key output by the key generation algorithm or whether $c$ is an encryption of $m$ and $\mathsf{sk}^* = \mathsf{sk}_{c,e}$ is the modified secret key output by the denying algorithm.

**Definition 9 (Public-Key Deniable Edits).** *An* $\mathsf{Edit}$*-deniable public-key encryption with message-length* $n(\lambda)$, *edit description length* $\ell(\lambda)$, *and a PPT edit function* $\mathsf{Edit} : \{0,1\}^{n(\lambda)} \times \{0,1\}^{\ell(\lambda)} \to \{0,1\}^{n(\lambda)}$ *consists of PPT algorithms* $(\mathsf{Gen}, \mathsf{Enc}, \mathsf{Dec}, \mathsf{Deny})$ *having the following syntax:*

- $(\mathsf{pk}, \mathsf{sk}, \mathsf{dk}) \leftarrow \mathsf{Gen}(1^\lambda)$ *generates a public-key* $\mathsf{pk}$, *secret-key* $\mathsf{sk}$ *and denying key* $\mathsf{dk}$.
- $c \leftarrow \mathsf{Enc}_{\mathsf{pk}}(m), m = \mathsf{Dec}_{\mathsf{sk}}(c)$ *have the standard syntax of public-key encryption and decryption.*
- $\mathsf{sk}_{c,e} \leftarrow \mathsf{Deny}_{\mathsf{dk}}(c, e)$ *takes as input some ciphertext* $c$ *encrypting data* $m$ *along with an edit* $e$ *and outputs a secret key* $\mathsf{sk}_{c,e}$ *that decrypts* $c$ *to* $m' = \mathsf{Edit}(m, e)$.

*The scheme should satisfy the following properties:*

**Encryption Correctness & Security:** *The scheme* (Gen, Enc, Dec) *should satisfy the standard correctness and CPA security definitions of public-key encryption (see Definition 12), if we ignore the denying key* $\mathsf{dk}$.

**Deniability Security.** *We define the "deniability game"* $\mathsf{DenGame}^b_{\mathcal{A}}(\lambda)$ *between an adversary* $\mathcal{A}$ *and a challenger with a challenge bit* $b \in \{0, 1\}$ *as follows:*
- *Sample* $(\mathsf{pk}, \mathsf{sk}, \mathsf{dk}) \leftarrow \mathsf{Gen}(1^\lambda)$ *and give* $\mathsf{pk}$ *to* $\mathcal{A}$.
- $\mathcal{A}$ *chooses a message* $m \in \{0, 1\}^{n(\lambda)}$ *and an edit* $e \in \{0, 1\}^{\ell(\lambda)}$.
- *If* $b = 0$, *sample* $c \leftarrow \mathsf{Enc}_{\mathsf{pk}}(\mathsf{Edit}(m, e))$ *and give* $(\mathsf{sk}, c)$ *to* $\mathcal{A}$.
  *If* $b = 1$, *sample* $c \leftarrow \mathsf{Enc}_{\mathsf{pk}}(m)$, $\mathsf{sk}_{c,e} \leftarrow \mathsf{Deny}_{\mathsf{dk}}(c, e)$ *and give* $(\mathsf{sk}_{c,e}, c)$ *to* $\mathcal{A}$.
- $\mathcal{A}$ *outputs a bit* $b'$ *which we define as the output of the game.*

*For all PPT adversary* $\mathcal{A}$, *we require*

$$|\Pr[\mathsf{DenGame}^0_{\mathcal{A}}(\lambda) = 1] - \Pr[\mathsf{DenGame}^1_{\mathcal{A}}(\lambda) = 1]| \leq \mathsf{negl}(\lambda).$$

**Construction.** The construction of public-key encryption with deniable edits is similar to our earlier construction of public-key encryption with invisible edits. The main difference is that we previously chose a random value $k$ in the public key and use it for all encryptions whereas we now chose a fresh random value $k$ during each encryption operation. The secret key $\mathsf{sk}_y$ is associated with a random value $y$. When we want to deny a particular ciphertext $c$ which was created using $k$, we create a new secret key $\mathsf{sk}_{y'}$ with $y' = k \oplus (0^\lambda, e)$. This ensures that the edit is applied when decrypting the ciphertext $c$ via $\mathsf{sk}_{y'}$.

**Construction 6 (Public-Key Deniable Edit).** *For any polynomial-time edit function* $\mathsf{Edit} : \{0, 1\}^{n(\lambda)} \times \{0, 1\}^{\ell(\lambda)} \to \{0, 1\}^{n(\lambda)}$, *we construct an Edit-deniable public-key encryption* $\mathsf{DEdit} = (\mathsf{Gen}, \mathsf{Enc}, \mathsf{Dec}, \mathsf{Deny})$ *using a single-key public-key functional encryption* $\mathsf{FE} = (\mathsf{Setup}, \mathsf{Gen}, \mathsf{Enc}, \mathsf{Dec})$ *with special decryption (see Definition 4) for the function* $F := F_{\mathsf{Edit}}$ *(see Definition 6). The construction proceeds as follows.*

- $\mathsf{DEdit.Gen}(1^\lambda)$:
  - $(\mathsf{mpk}, \mathsf{msk}) \leftarrow \mathsf{FE.Setup}(1^\lambda)$
  - *Select uniform* $y \leftarrow \{0, 1\}^{\lambda + \ell}$
  - $\mathsf{sk}_y \leftarrow \mathsf{FE.Gen}_{\mathsf{msk}}(y)$
  - *Output* $(\mathsf{pk} := \mathsf{mpk}, \mathsf{sk} := \mathsf{sk}_y, \mathsf{dk} := \mathsf{msk})$
- $\mathsf{DEdit.Enc}_{\mathsf{pk}}(m)$:
  - *Select uniform* $k \leftarrow \{0, 1\}^{\lambda + \ell}$

- *Output* $c \leftarrow \mathsf{FE.Enc_{mpk}}((m, k))$
- $\mathsf{DEdit.Dec_{sk}}(c)$:
  - *Output* $m := \mathsf{FE.Dec_{sk_y}}(c)$
- $\mathsf{DEdit.Deny_{dk}}(c, e)$:
  - $(m, k) = \mathsf{FE.Dec_{msk}}(c)$
  - $\mathsf{sk}_y \leftarrow \mathsf{FE.Gen_{msk}}(y)$ *where* $y = k \oplus (0^\lambda, e)$
  - *Output* $\mathsf{sk}_{c,e} := \mathsf{sk}_y$

**Theorem 7.** *The scheme* $\mathsf{DEdit}$ *given in the above Construction 6 is a secure* $\mathsf{Edit}$-*deniable public-key encryption if* $\mathsf{FE}$ *is a single-key public-key functional encryption with special decryption for the function* $F_{\mathsf{Edit}}$. *In particular, the construction only relies on the existence of standard public-key encryption.*

*Proof.* We now prove that Construction 6 satisfies the properties in Definition 9

**Correctness:** For every security parameter $\lambda$, and message $m \in \{0,1\}^n$:

$$\Pr\left[m = \mathsf{DEdit.Dec_{sk}}(\mathsf{DEdit.Enc_{pk}}(m)) \,\big|\, (\mathsf{pk}, \mathsf{sk}, \mathsf{dk}) \leftarrow \mathsf{DEdit.Gen}(1^\lambda)\right]$$

$$= \Pr\left[m = \mathsf{FE.Dec_{sk_y}}(\mathsf{FE.Enc_{mpk}}((m, k))) \,\middle|\, \begin{array}{l} (k, y) \leftarrow \{0,1\}^{\lambda+\ell} \times \{0,1\}^{\lambda+\ell} \\ (\mathsf{mpk}, \mathsf{msk}) \leftarrow \mathsf{FE.Setup}(1^\lambda) \\ \mathsf{sk}_y \leftarrow \mathsf{FE.Gen_{msk}}(y) \end{array}\right]$$

$$= \Pr\left[m = F((m, k), y) \,\big|\, (k, y) \leftarrow \{0,1\}^{\lambda+\ell} \times \{0,1\}^{\lambda+\ell}\right]$$

$$= 1 - \Pr\left[\exists e \in \{0,1\}^\ell : y \oplus k = (0^\lambda, e) \,\big|\, (k, y) \leftarrow \{0,1\}^{\lambda+\ell} \times \{0,1\}^{\lambda+\ell}\right]$$

$$= 1 - \frac{1}{2^\lambda}$$

**Encryption Security:** We want to show that for any PPT adversary $\mathcal{A}$:

$$|\Pr[\mathsf{CPAGame}^0_{\mathcal{A}}(\lambda) = 1] - \Pr[\mathsf{CPAGame}^1_{\mathcal{A}}(\lambda) = 1]| \leq \mathsf{negl}(\lambda).$$

This follows since an adversary $\mathcal{A}$ who breaks the CPA security also breaks the single-key public-key functional-encryption security game $\mathsf{FEGame}$ (with no secret key, when $y = \perp$).

**Deniability Security.** We want to show that for any PPT adversary $\mathcal{A}$:

$$|\Pr[\mathsf{DenGame}^0_{\mathcal{A}}(\lambda) = 1] - \Pr[\mathsf{DenGame}^1_{\mathcal{A}}(\lambda) = 1]| \leq \mathsf{negl}(\lambda).$$

This follows since an adversary $\mathcal{A}$ who wins the deniability game $\mathsf{DenGame}$ with message $m$ and edit $e$, also wins the single-key public-key functional-encryption security game $\mathsf{FEGame}$ with random $y \leftarrow \{0,1\}^{\lambda+\ell}$, and messages $x_0 = (m, k)$ and $x_1 = (\mathsf{Edit}(m, e), k')$ where $k = y \oplus (0^{\lambda+\ell}, e)$, and $k' \leftarrow \{0,1\}^{\lambda+\ell}$. Note that $F_{\mathsf{Edit}}(x_0, y) = F_{\mathsf{Edit}}(x_1, y) = \mathsf{Edit}(m, e)$ unless $k' \oplus y = (0^\lambda, e')$ for some $e'$ which happens with negligible probability. Formally, we construct $\mathcal{A}'$ (who uses an adversary $\mathcal{A}$ that wins in the $\mathsf{DenGame}$) to win the $\mathsf{FEGame}$:

- The challenger samples $(\mathsf{mpk}, \mathsf{msk}) \leftarrow \mathsf{FE.Setup}(\lambda)$ and sends $\mathsf{mpk}$ to $\mathcal{A}'$. The adversary $\mathcal{A}'$ chooses a random $y \leftarrow \{0,1\}^{\lambda+\ell}$.

– The challenger samples $\mathsf{sk}_y \leftarrow \mathsf{FE.Gen_{msk}}(y)$ and sends $\mathsf{sk}_y$ to $\mathcal{A}'$.
  The adversary $\mathcal{A}'$ forward $\mathsf{pk} := \mathsf{mpk}$ to $\mathcal{A}$ and receives back a message
  $m \in \{0,1\}^n$ and an edit $e \in \{0,1\}^\ell$. The adversary $\mathcal{A}'$ chooses two messages $x_0 = (m, k)$ and $x_1 = (\mathsf{Edit}(m, e), k')$ where $k' \leftarrow \{0,1\}^{\lambda+\ell}$ and
  $k = y \oplus (0^{\lambda+\ell}, e)$.
– The challenge samples a ciphertext $c \leftarrow \mathsf{FE.Enc_{mpk}}(m_b)$ and sends $c$ to $\mathcal{A}'$.
  The adversary $\mathcal{A}'$ forwards $(\mathsf{sk}_y, c)$ to $\mathcal{A}$ and receives back a bit $b'$ to
  output.

The advantage of $\mathcal{A}'$ in FEGame is the same as the advantage of $\mathcal{A}$ in DenGame,
up to the negligible probability that $k' \oplus y = (0^\lambda, e')$ for some $e'$.

## 4.2   Symmetric-Key Deniable-Edits

In the symmetric-key setting, we present two different definitions of encryption
with deniable edits analogously to our two definitions of symmetric-key encryption with invisible edits.

First, we present a definition that follows the *dual-key* paradigm and can
be seen as a direct analogue of our public-key definition for the symmetric-key
setting. In particular, the key generation algorithm outputs a secret decryption
key $\mathsf{sk}$ and denying key $\mathsf{dk}$ which can use it to later "deny" the contents of a particular ciphertext $c$ encrypting some message $m$ by producing a legitimate secret
key $\mathsf{sk}_{c,e} \leftarrow \mathsf{Deny_{dk}}(c, e)$ that decrypts $c$ to $m' = \mathsf{Edit}(m, e)$. For both encryption
security and deniability we assume that the adversary has access to an encryp-
tion oracle. We can always interpret a public-key deniable encryption scheme
as a symmetric-key one and therefore we can achieve this definition assuming
the existence of standard public-key encryption using the results from the previous section. However, it remains as a fascinating open problem whether one
can construct symmetric-key deniable encryption following the dual-key paradigm by relying only one one-way functions or whether public-key encryption is
necessary.

**Definition 10 (Dual-Key Deniable Edits).** *A* dual-key *Edit-deniable
symmetric-key encryption scheme with message-length $n(\lambda)$, edit description
length $\ell(\lambda)$, and edit function* $\mathsf{Edit} : \{0,1\}^{n(\lambda)} \times \{0,1\}^{\ell(\lambda)} \to \{0,1\}^{n(\lambda)}$ *consists
of PPT algorithms* $(\mathsf{Gen}, \mathsf{Enc}, \mathsf{Dec}, \mathsf{Deny})$ *with the following syntax:*

– $(\mathsf{sk}, \mathsf{dk}) \leftarrow \mathsf{Gen}(1^\lambda)$ *generates a secret-key $\mathsf{sk}$ and deniability key $\mathsf{dk}$.*
– $c \leftarrow \mathsf{Enc_{sk}}(m), m = \mathsf{Dec_{sk}}(c)$ *have the standard syntax of public-key encryption
  and decryption.*
– $\mathsf{sk}_{c,e} \leftarrow \mathsf{Deny_{dk}}(c, e)$ *takes as input some ciphertext $c$ encrypting data $m$ along
  with an edit $e$ and outputs a secret key $\mathsf{sk}_{c,e}$ that decrypts $c$ to $m' = \mathsf{Edit}(m, e)$.*

*The scheme should satisfy the following properties:*

**Correctness & Encryption Security.** *The scheme* $(\mathsf{Gen}, \mathsf{Enc}, \mathsf{Dec})$ *satisfies the
  standard notions of symmetric-key encryption correctness and CPA security
  (see Definition 13) if we ignore the key $\mathsf{dk}$.*

**Deniability.** *We define the "deniability game"* $\mathsf{DenGame}^b_{\mathcal{A}}(\lambda)$ *between an adversary* $\mathcal{A}$ *and a challenger with a challenge bit* $b \in \{0, 1\}$ *as follows:*

- *Sample* $(\mathsf{sk}, \mathsf{dk}) \leftarrow \mathsf{Gen}(1^\lambda)$.
- $\mathcal{A}^{\mathsf{Enc}_{\mathsf{sk}}(\cdot)}$ *gets access to the encryption oracle. Eventually, it chooses a message* $m \in \{0, 1\}^{n(\lambda)}$ *and an edit* $e \in \{0, 1\}^{\ell(\lambda)}$.
- *If* $b = 0$, *sample* $c \leftarrow \mathsf{Enc}_{\mathsf{sk}}(\mathsf{Edit}(m, e))$ *and give* $(\mathsf{sk}, c)$ *to* $\mathcal{A}$. *If* $b = 1$, *sample* $c \leftarrow \mathsf{Enc}_{\mathsf{sk}}(m)$, $\mathsf{sk}_{c,e} \leftarrow \mathsf{Deny}_{\mathsf{dk}}(c, e)$ *and give* $(\mathsf{sk}_{c,e}, c)$ *to* $\mathcal{A}$.
- $\mathcal{A}^{\mathsf{Enc}_{\mathsf{sk}}(\cdot)}$ *outputs a bit* $b'$ *which we define as the output of the game.*

*We require that for all PPT adversary* $\mathcal{A}$ *we have* $|\Pr[\mathsf{DenGame}^0_{\mathcal{A}}(\lambda) = 1] - \Pr[\mathsf{DenGame}^1_{\mathcal{A}}(\lambda) = 1]| \leq \mathsf{negl}(\lambda)$.

Below, we present a definition of symmetric-key encryption with deniable edits that follows the weaker *dual-scheme* paradigm. In this case there are two different encryption schemes: a *default* scheme $(\mathsf{Gen}, \mathsf{Enc}, \mathsf{Dec})$ and a *denying* scheme $(\mathsf{DenGen}, \mathsf{DenEnc}, \mathsf{DenDec})$. Most users are expected to use the default scheme. However, if a user decides to use the denying scheme instead, she can "deny" the contents of a particular ciphertext $c$ encrypting some message $m$ under $\mathsf{sk}$ by producing a secret key $\mathsf{sk}_{c,e} \leftarrow \mathsf{Deny}_{\mathsf{sk}}(c, e)$ that looks like a legitimate key for the default scheme and decrypts $c$ to $m' = \mathsf{Edit}(m, e)$. Even given access to an encryption oracle, a ciphertext $c$ and a key $\mathsf{sk}$, the coercer cannot tell whether (1) all ciphertexts are generated using the default scheme, $c$ is an encryption of $m'$, and $\mathsf{sk}$ is the honestly generated key of the default scheme, versus (2) all ciphertexts are generated using the denying scheme, $c$ is an encryption of $m$ and $\mathsf{sk} = \mathsf{sk}_{c,e}$ is the output of the Deny algorithm.

**Definition 11 (Dual-Scheme Deniable Edits).** *A* *dual-scheme* *Edit-deniable symmetric-key encryption scheme with message-length* $n = n(\lambda)$, *edit description length* $\ell = \ell(\lambda)$, *and edit function* $\mathsf{Edit}$ : $\{0, 1\}^{n(\lambda)} \times \{0, 1\}^{\ell(\lambda)} \rightarrow \{0, 1\}^{n(\lambda)}$ *consists of PPT algorithms* $(\mathsf{Gen}, \mathsf{Enc}, \mathsf{Dec}, \mathsf{DenGen}, \mathsf{DenEnc}, \mathsf{DenDec}, \mathsf{Deny})$. *The default scheme* $(\mathsf{Gen}, \mathsf{Enc}, \mathsf{Dec})$ *and the denying scheme* $(\mathsf{DenGen}, \mathsf{DenEnc}, \mathsf{DenDec})$ *have the usual symmetric-key encryption syntax. The algorithm* $\mathsf{sk}_{c,e} \leftarrow \mathsf{Deny}_{\mathsf{sk}}(c, e)$ *takes as input some ciphertext* $c$ *encrypting data* $m$ *under the denying scheme with secret key* $\mathsf{sk}$, *along with an edit* $e$ *and outputs a secret key* $\mathsf{sk}_{c,e}$ *that decrypts* $c$ *to* $m' = \mathsf{Edit}(m, e)$.

**Correctness & Encryption Security.** *The schemes* $(\mathsf{Gen}, \mathsf{Enc}, \mathsf{Dec})$ *and* $(\mathsf{DenGen}, \mathsf{DenEnc}, \mathsf{DenDec})$ *satisfy the standard notions of symmetric-key encryption correctness and CPA security (Definition 13).*

**Deniability.** *We define the "deniability game"* $\mathsf{DenGame}^b_{\mathcal{A}}(\lambda)$ *between an adversary* $\mathcal{A}$ *and a challenger with a challenge bit* $b \in \{0, 1\}$ *as follows:*

- *If* $b = 0$ *sample* $\mathsf{sk} \leftarrow \mathsf{Gen}(1^\lambda)$ *and if* $b = 1$ *sample* $\mathsf{sk}^* \leftarrow \mathsf{DenGen}(1^\lambda)$. *Let* $\mathcal{O}(\cdot)$ *be the encryption oracle with* $\mathcal{O}(\cdot) := \mathsf{Enc}_{\mathsf{sk}}(\cdot)$ *if* $b = 0$ *and* $\mathcal{O}(\cdot) := \mathsf{DenEnc}_{\mathsf{sk}^*}(\cdot)$ *if* $b = 1$.
- $\mathcal{A}^{\mathcal{O}}$ *gets access to the encryption oracle and eventually chooses a message* $m \in \{0, 1\}^{n(\lambda)}$ *and an edit* $e \in \{0, 1\}^{\ell(\lambda)}$.

- If $b = 0$, sample $c \leftarrow \mathsf{Enc}_{\mathsf{sk}}(\mathsf{Edit}(m, e))$ and give $(\mathsf{sk}, c)$ to $\mathcal{A}$.
  If $b = 1$, sample $c \leftarrow \mathsf{DenEnc}_{\mathsf{sk}^*}(m)$, $\mathsf{sk}_{c,e} \leftarrow \mathsf{Deny}_{\mathsf{sk}^*}(c, e)$ and give $(\mathsf{sk}_{c,e}, c)$ to $\mathcal{A}$.
- $\mathcal{A}^{\mathcal{O}}$ gets further access to the encryption oracle and eventually outputs a bit $b'$ which we define as the output of the game.

For all PPT adversary $\mathcal{A}$ we require

$$|\Pr[\mathsf{DenGame}_{\mathcal{A}}^0(\lambda) = 1] - \Pr[\mathsf{DenGame}_{\mathcal{A}}^1(\lambda) = 1]| \leq \mathsf{negl}(\lambda).$$

**Construction.** Our construction of dual-scheme symmetric-key encryption with deniable edits follows the same general approach as out public-key construction.

**Construction 8 (Dual-Scheme Deniable Edit).** *For any polynomial-time edit function* $\mathsf{Edit} : \{0,1\}^{n(\lambda)} \times \{0,1\}^{\ell(\lambda)} \to \{0,1\}^{n(\lambda)}$ *we construct a dual-scheme* $\mathsf{Edit}$-*deniable symmetric-key encryption* $\mathsf{DSDenE} = (\mathsf{Gen}, \mathsf{Enc}, \mathsf{Dec}, \mathsf{DenGen}, \mathsf{DenEnc}, \mathsf{DenDec}, \mathsf{Deny})$, *using a single-key symmetric-key functional encryption* $\mathsf{FE} = (\mathsf{Setup}, \mathsf{Gen}, \mathsf{Enc}, \mathsf{Dec})$ *with special encryption and decryption (Definitions 3 and 4) for the function* $F := F_{\mathsf{Edit}}$ *(Definition 6). The construction proceeds as follows.*

- $\mathsf{DSDenE.DenGen}(1^\lambda)$:
  - $\mathsf{msk} \leftarrow \mathsf{FE.Setup}(1^\lambda)$
  - *Output* $\mathsf{sk}^* := \mathsf{msk}$
- $\mathsf{DSDenE.DenEnc}_{\mathsf{sk}^*}(m)$:
  - *Select uniform* $k \leftarrow \{0,1\}^{\lambda+\ell}$
  - *Output* $c \leftarrow \mathsf{FE.Enc}_{\mathsf{msk}}((m, k))$
- $\mathsf{DSDenE.DenDec}_{\mathsf{sk}^*}(c)$:
  - $(m, k) = \mathsf{FE.Dec}_{\mathsf{msk}}(c)$
  - *Output* $m$
- $\mathsf{DSDenE.Gen}(1^\lambda)$:
  - $\mathsf{msk} \leftarrow \mathsf{FE.Setup}(1^\lambda)$
  - *Select uniform* $y \leftarrow \{0,1\}^{\lambda+\ell}$
  - $\mathsf{sk}_y \leftarrow \mathsf{FE.Gen}_{\mathsf{msk}}(y)$
  - *Output* $\mathsf{sk} := \mathsf{sk}_y$
- $\mathsf{DSDenE.Enc}_{\mathsf{sk}}(m)$:
  - *Select uniform* $k \leftarrow \{0,1\}^{\lambda+\ell}$
  - *Output* $c \leftarrow \mathsf{FE.Enc}_{\mathsf{sk}_y}((m, k))$
- $\mathsf{DSDenE.Dec}_{\mathsf{sk}}(c)$:
  - *Output* $m = \mathsf{FE.Dec}_{\mathsf{sk}_y}(c)$
- $\mathsf{DSDenE.Deny}_{\mathsf{sk}^*}(c, e)$:
  - $(m, k) = \mathsf{FE.Dec}_{\mathsf{msk}}(c)$
  - $\mathsf{sk}_y \leftarrow \mathsf{FE.Gen}_{\mathsf{msk}}(y)$ *where* $y = k \oplus (0^\lambda, e)$
  - *Output* $\mathsf{sk}_{c,e} = \mathsf{sk}_y$

**Theorem 9.** *The scheme* DSDenE *given in the above Construction 8 is a secure dual-scheme* Edit-*deniable symmetric-key encryption if* FE *is a single-key symmetric-key functional encryption with special encryption and decryption for the function* $F_{\mathsf{Edit}}$. *In particular, the construction only relies on the existence of one-way functions.*

*Proof.* We now prove that Construction 8 satisfies the properties of *dual-scheme* Edit-*deniable symmetric-key encryption* in Definition 11.

**Correctness.** For every security parameter $\lambda$, and message $m \in \{0,1\}^n$:

$$\Pr\left[m = \mathsf{DSDenE.Dec_{sk}}(\mathsf{DSDenE.Enc_{sk}}(m)) \,\middle|\, \mathsf{sk} \leftarrow \mathsf{DSDenE.Gen}(1^\lambda) \right]$$

$$= \Pr\left[m = \mathsf{FE.Dec_{sk_y}}(\mathsf{FE.Enc_{sk_y}}((m,k))) \,\middle|\, \begin{array}{l} (k,y) \leftarrow \{0,1\}^{\lambda+\ell} \times \{0,1\}^{\lambda+\ell} \\ \mathsf{msk} \leftarrow \mathsf{FE.Setup}(1^\lambda) \\ \mathsf{sk}_y \leftarrow \mathsf{FE.Gen_{msk}}(y) \end{array}\right]$$

$$= \Pr\left[m = F((m,k),y) \,\middle|\, (k,y) \leftarrow \{0,1\}^{\lambda+\ell} \times \{0,1\}^{\lambda+\ell}\right]$$

$$= 1 - \Pr\left[\exists e \in \{0,1\}^\ell : y \oplus k = (0^\lambda, e) \,\middle|\, (k,y) \leftarrow \{0,1\}^{\lambda+\ell} \times \{0,1\}^{\lambda+\ell}\right]$$

$$= 1 - \frac{1}{2^\lambda}$$

Therefore, the scheme (DSDenE.Gen, DSDenE.Enc, DSDenE.Dec) is correct. Moreover, for every security parameter $\lambda$, and message $m \in \{0,1\}^n$:

$$\Pr\left[m = \mathsf{DSDenE.DenDec_{sk^*}}(\mathsf{DSDenE.DenEnc_{sk^*}}(m)) \,\middle|\, \mathsf{sk}^* \leftarrow \mathsf{DSDenE.DenGen}(1^\lambda) \right]$$

$$= \Pr\left[(m,k) = \mathsf{FE.Dec_{msk}}(\mathsf{FE.Enc_{msk}}((m,k))) \,\middle|\, \begin{array}{l} k \leftarrow \{0,1\}^{\lambda+\ell} \\ \mathsf{msk} \leftarrow \mathsf{FE.Setup}(1^\lambda) \end{array}\right]$$

$$= 1$$

Thus, also the scheme (DSDenE.DenGen, DSDenE.DenEnc, DSDenE.DenDec) is correct.

**Encryption Security.** The scheme (DSDenE.DenGen, DSDenE.DenEnc, DSDenE.DenDec) is symmetrically secure (i.e., CPA secure). Namely, for every PPT adversary $\mathcal{A}$:

$$\left| \Pr[\mathsf{CPAGame}^0_{\mathcal{A}}(\lambda) = 1] - \Pr[\mathsf{CPAGame}^1_{\mathcal{A}}(\lambda) = 1]\right| \leq \mathsf{negl}(\lambda).$$

This holds because a PPT adversary $\mathcal{A}$ who breaks the CPA security also breaks the single-key symmetric-key functional-encryption security game FEGame (with no secret key, when $y = \bot$).

The scheme (DSDenE.Gen, DSDenE.Enc, DSDenE.Dec) is also CPA secure. To prove this we introduce two hybrid games $\mathsf{HybGame}^b_{\mathcal{A}}(\lambda)$ where, instead of using the encryption oracle and the challenge ciphertext defined as follows:

$$\mathcal{O}(\cdot) := \mathsf{DSDenE.Enc}(\cdot) = \mathsf{FE.Enc_{sk_y}}(\cdot, k)_{k \leftarrow \{0,1\}^{\lambda+\ell}}$$

$$c \leftarrow \mathsf{DSDenE.Enc}(m_b) = \mathsf{FE.Enc_{sk_y}}(m_b, k)_{k \leftarrow \{0,1\}^{\lambda+\ell}}$$

we replace them with the following modification:

$$\mathcal{O}(\cdot) := \mathsf{FE.Enc}_{\mathsf{msk}}(\cdot, k)_{k \leftarrow \{0,1\}^{\lambda+\ell}}$$

$$c \leftarrow \mathsf{FE.Enc}_{\mathsf{msk}}(m_b, k)_{k \leftarrow \{0,1\}^{\lambda+\ell}}$$

Now we argue that $\mathsf{CPAGame}^0$ is indistinguishable from $\mathsf{HybGame}^0$ which follows by the special encryption property of the FE scheme (Definition 3). Furthermore $\mathsf{HybGame}^0$ is indistinguishable from $\mathsf{HybGame}^1$ by the single-key symmetric-key functional-encryption security game $\mathsf{FEGame}$ (with no secret key, when $y = \bot$). Lastly $\mathsf{HybGame}^1$ is indistinguishable from $\mathsf{CPAGame}^1$ by the special encryption property.

**Deniability.** We want to show that for any PPT adversary $\mathcal{A}$:

$$|\Pr[\mathsf{DenGame}^0_{\mathcal{A}}(\lambda) = 1] - \Pr[\mathsf{DenGame}^1_{\mathcal{A}}(\lambda) = 1]| \leq \mathsf{negl}(\lambda).$$

This follows since an adversary $\mathcal{A}$ who wins the "deniability game" $\mathsf{DenGame}$ with message $m$ and edit $e$ also wins in the single-key symmetric-key functional-encryption security game $\mathsf{FEGame}$ with random $y \leftarrow \{0,1\}^{\lambda+\ell}$, and messages $x_0 = (\mathsf{Edit}(m, e), k)$ and $x_1 = (m, k')$ where $k \leftarrow \{0,1\}^{\lambda+\ell}$ and $k' = y \oplus (0^{\lambda+\ell}, e)$. Formally, we prove it by a sequence of hybrids where we change the distribution of the encryption oracle $\mathcal{O}(\cdot)$ and the challenge $(c, \mathsf{sk})$.

**Hybrid 0:** we starts with the deniability game with $b = 0$, $\mathsf{DenGame}^0_{\mathcal{A}}(\lambda)$. The encryption oracle and the challenge are:

$$\mathcal{O}(\cdot) := \mathsf{DSDenE.Enc}_{\mathsf{sk}}(\cdot) \qquad\qquad = \mathsf{FE.Enc}_{\mathsf{sk}_y}(\cdot, k)_{k \leftarrow \{0,1\}^{\lambda+\ell}}$$

$$(c, \mathsf{sk}) := (\mathsf{DSDenE.Enc}_{\mathsf{sk}}(\mathsf{Edit}(m, e)), \mathsf{sk}) \quad = (\mathsf{FE.Enc}_{\mathsf{sk}_y}(\mathsf{Edit}(m, e), k'), \mathsf{sk}_y)$$

and $(y, k') \leftarrow \{0,1\}^{\lambda+\ell} \times \{0,1\}^{\lambda+\ell}$.

**Hybrid 1:** we move to a hybrid game $\mathsf{HybGame}_{\mathcal{A}}(\lambda)$ (a modification of $\mathsf{DenGame}^0_{\mathcal{A}}(\lambda)$), in which we encrypt using $\mathsf{FE.Enc}_{\mathsf{msk}}$ (instead of using $\mathsf{FE.Enc}_{\mathsf{sk}_y}$). The encryption oracle and the challenge are:

$$\mathcal{O}(\cdot) := \mathsf{FE.Enc}_{\mathsf{msk}}(\cdot, k)_{k \leftarrow \{0,1\}^{\lambda+\ell}}$$

$$(c, \mathsf{sk}) := (\mathsf{FE.Enc}_{\mathsf{msk}}(\mathsf{Edit}(m, e), k'), \mathsf{sk}_y)$$

where $(y, k') \leftarrow \{0,1\}^{\lambda+\ell} \times \{0,1\}^{\lambda+\ell}$. By the special encryption property (Definition 3) of the underline functional encryption scheme,

$$\mathsf{DenGame}^0_{\mathcal{A}}(\lambda) \overset{c}{\approx} \mathsf{HybGame}_{\mathcal{A}}(\lambda)$$

**Hybrid 2:** we move to the deniability game with $b = 1$, $\mathsf{DenGame}^1_{\mathcal{A}}(\lambda)$. The encryption oracle and the challenge are:

$$\mathcal{O}(\cdot) := \mathsf{DSDenE.Enc}_{\mathsf{sk}}(\cdot)$$

$$= \mathsf{FE.Enc}_{\mathsf{msk}}(\cdot, k)_{k \leftarrow \{0,1\}^{\lambda+\ell}}$$

$$(c, \mathsf{sk}) := (\mathsf{DSDenE.Enc}_{\mathsf{msk}}(m), \mathsf{DSDenE.Deny}_{\mathsf{msk}}(c, e))$$

$$= (\mathsf{FE.Enc}_{\mathsf{msk}}(m, k'), \mathsf{sk}_y)$$

where $k' \leftarrow \{0,1\}^{\lambda+\ell}$ and $y := k' \oplus (0^\lambda, e)$. This is equivalent to $y \leftarrow \{0,1\}^{\lambda+\ell}$ and $k' := y \oplus (0^\lambda, e)$. By the security of the functional encryption[4].

$$\mathsf{HybGame}_{\mathcal{A}}(\lambda) \overset{c}{\approx} \mathsf{DenGame}^1_{\mathcal{A}}(\lambda)$$

### 4.3   Efficiency

We note that the efficiency of our public-key and symmetric-key encryption schemes with deniable edits are the same as the analogous constructions of schemes with invisible edits, see Sect. 3.3.

### 4.4   Extensions

We now briefly and informally describe two extensions of our deniable schemes.

*Bounded-Ciphertext Deniability.* Our notion of deniable edits allows us to edit the contents of a single targeted ciphertext $c$ via an edit $e$ by producing a legitimate looking secret key $\mathsf{sk}_{c,e}$. We can also extend our scheme to allowing us to edit the contents of some bounded number of ciphertexts $\boldsymbol{c} = (c_1, \ldots, c_t)$ via edits $\boldsymbol{e} = (e_1, \ldots, e_t)$ by producing a secret key $\mathsf{sk}_{c,e}$. The construction is essentially the same as before but we use an FE scheme for the function $F(x = (m,k), \boldsymbol{y} = (y_1, \ldots, y_t))$ which checks whether there exists some $y_i$ such that $k \oplus y_i = (0^\lambda || e)$ and if so outputs $\mathsf{Edit}(m,e)$ else outputs $m$. The key generation algorithm would output an FE secret key $\mathsf{sk}_{\boldsymbol{y}}$ for a uniformly random vector $\boldsymbol{y}$. To deny a vector of ciphertexts $\boldsymbol{c} = (c_1, \ldots, c_t)$ where each $c_i$ is an FE encryption of $x_i = (m_i, k_i)$ we would create an FE secret key for the vector $\boldsymbol{y} = (y_1, \ldots, y_t)$ where $y_i = (0^\lambda || e_i) \oplus k_i$. The cost of this construction is that now the secret key size scales with $\ell \cdot t$ where $\ell$ is the edit description size and $t$ is the number of ciphertexts.

We could also consider yet another variant where we want to edit the contents of $t$ ciphertexts $\boldsymbol{c} = (c_1, \ldots, c_t)$ via a single edit $e$ to be applied to all of them by creating a secret key $\mathsf{sk}_{c,e}$. In that case we could use an FE scheme for the function $F(x = (m,k), (y^*, y_1, \ldots, y_t))$ which checks if $k \oplus (y_i || y^*) = (0^\lambda || e)$ and if so output $\mathsf{Edit}(m,e)$ else $m$. Otherwise the scheme would be analogous to the previous one. The allows us to get a construction where the secret key size scales with $\ell + t$ instead of $\ell \cdot t$.

Later, when we consider invisible edits, we will be able to edit the contents of an unbounded number of ciphertexts via an edit $e$ by generating a secret key $\mathsf{sk}_e$ of some fixed size. However, in that case we will also need to be able to also plausibly lie about the public key by giving out a modified public key $\mathsf{pk}_e$ instead of $\mathsf{pk}$. This is in contrast to bounded-ciphertext deniability discussed above where the secret key $\mathsf{sk}_{c,e}$ looks like a legitimate secret key for the original public key $\mathsf{pk}$.

---

[4] FE game with a random $y$ and messages $m_0 = (m, y \oplus (0^\lambda, e))$, $m_1 = (\mathsf{Edit}(m,e), k')$ for a random $k'$.

*Denying Randomness of Key Generation.* For simplicity, we previously assumed that the coercing adversary can only ask the user for her secret key but not for the randomness of the key generation algorithm which the user can plausibly delete. However, it would be relatively easy to also allow the user to deniably generate fake randomness for the key generation algorithm as well. We briefly sketch this extension.

Let's start by considering this extension in the public-key setting. The way we defined the syntax of deniable public-key encryption, we had a single key generation algorithm that outputs $(\mathsf{pk}, \mathsf{sk}, \mathsf{dk}) \leftarrow \mathsf{Gen}(1^\lambda)$. In order for the above extension to be possible we must now consider two algorithms (moving us closer to the two-scheme rather than two-key setting), a default one that outputs $(\mathsf{pk}, \mathsf{sk}) \leftarrow \mathsf{Gen}(1^\lambda)$ and a deniable one that outputs $(\mathsf{pk}, \mathsf{sk}, \mathsf{dk}) \leftarrow \mathsf{DenGen}(1^\lambda)$. Given $\mathsf{dk}, c, e$ where $c = \mathsf{Enc}_{\mathsf{pk}}(m)$, the denying procedure should now output $r \leftarrow \mathsf{Deny}_{\mathsf{dk}}(c, e)$ such that if we run $\mathsf{sk}_{c,e} = \mathsf{Gen}(1^\lambda; r)$ then $\mathsf{Dec}_{\mathsf{sk}_{c,e}}(c) = \mathsf{Edit}(m, e)$. Security is defined analogously except that the adversary gets the key generation randomness $r$ rather than $\mathsf{sk}$.

It turns out that our construction (Construction 6) already essentially achieves this if we start with a *simulatable Functional Encryption* scheme where it's possible to obliviously generate $(\mathsf{mpk}, \mathsf{sk}_y) = \mathsf{OGen}(1^\lambda, y; r)$ without knowing $\mathsf{msk}$ so that even given the randomness $r$ one cannot distinguish encryptions of $x_0, x_1$ if $F(x_0, y) = F(x_1, y)$. Moreover given $\mathsf{mpk}, \mathsf{msk}$ and $\mathsf{sk}_y$ it's possible to come up with legitimate looking random coins $r$ such that $(\mathsf{mpk}, \mathsf{sk}_y) \leftarrow \mathsf{OGen}(1^\lambda; r)$. Using this type of FE we can modify the $\mathsf{DEdit.Gen}$ algorithm to run $\mathsf{FE.OGen}$. Using $\mathsf{dk} = \mathsf{msk}$ we'd then be able to sample legitimate looking random coins for $\mathsf{OGen}$.

It furthermore turns out that the construction of FE from PKE already gives us the simulatable FE property if we start with a simulatable PKE [DN00].

The same idea also works in the symmetric key setting analogously, using only one-way functions.

**Acknowledgment.** Thanks to Omer Paneth for interesting discussions on the topics of this work.

Shafi Goldwasser was supported by NSF MACS - CNS-1413920, DARPA IBM - W911NF-15-C-0236, SIMONS Investigator award Agreement Dated 6-5-12. Saleet Klein was supported by an Akamai Presidential Fellowship and NSF MACS - CNS-1413920, DARPA IBM - W911NF-15-C-0236, SIMONS Investigator award Agreement Dated 6-5-12. Daniel Wichs was supported by NSF grants CNS-1314722, CNS-1413964.

# A   Standard Cryptographic Definitions

## A.1   Encryption Scheme Definitions

**Definition 12 (Public-Key Encryption).** *A public-key encryption consists of PPT algorithms* $(\mathsf{Gen}, \mathsf{Enc}, \mathsf{Dec})$ *with the following syntax:*

- $(\mathsf{pk}, \mathsf{sk}) \leftarrow \mathsf{Gen}(1^\lambda)$.
- $c \leftarrow \mathsf{Enc_{pk}}(m)$ *outputs an encryption of* $m$.
- $m \leftarrow \mathsf{Dec_{sk}}(c)$ *outputs a message* $m$.

*The scheme should satisfy the following properties:*

**Correctness:** *For every security parameter* $\lambda$ *and message* $m$,

$$\Pr[\mathsf{Dec_{sk}}(\mathsf{Enc_{pk}}(m)) = m | (\mathsf{pk}, \mathsf{sk}) \leftarrow \mathsf{Gen}(1^\lambda)] = 1 - \mathsf{negl}(\lambda)$$

**CPA Security.** *We define the "CPA game"* $\mathsf{CPAGame}_{\mathcal{A}}^b(\lambda)$ *between an adversary* $\mathcal{A}$ *and a challenger with a challenge bit* $b\{0, 1\}$ *as follows:*
  - *Sample* $(\mathsf{pk}, \mathsf{sk}) \leftarrow \mathsf{Gen}(1^\lambda)$ *and give* $\mathsf{pk}$ *to* $\mathcal{A}$.
  - *The adversary* $\mathcal{A}$ *chooses two messages* $m_0, m_1 \in \{0, 1\}^n$
  - *The adversary* $\mathcal{A}$ *gets a challenge* $c \leftarrow \mathsf{Enc_{sk}}(m_b)$, *and eventually outputs a bit* $b'$ *which we define as the output of the game.*

*We require that for all PPT adversary* $\mathcal{A}$ *we have* $| \Pr[\mathsf{CPAGame}_{\mathcal{A}}^0(\lambda) = 1] - \Pr[\mathsf{CPAGame}_{\mathcal{A}}^1(\lambda) = 1] | \leq \mathsf{negl}(\lambda)$.

**Definition 13 (Symmetric-Key Encryption).** *A* symmetric-key encryption *consists of PPT algorithms* $(\mathsf{Gen}, \mathsf{Enc}, \mathsf{Dec})$ *with the following syntax:*

- $\mathsf{sk} \leftarrow \mathsf{Gen}(1^\lambda)$.
- $c \leftarrow \mathsf{Enc_{sk}}(m)$ *outputs an encryption of* $m$.
- $m \leftarrow \mathsf{Dec_{sk}}(c)$ *outputs a message* $m$.

*The scheme should satisfy the following properties:*

**Correctness:** *For every security parameter* $\lambda$ *and message* $m$,

$$\Pr[\mathsf{Dec_{sk}}(\mathsf{Enc_{sk}}(m)) = m | \mathsf{sk} \leftarrow \mathsf{Gen}(1^\lambda)] = 1 - \mathsf{negl}(\lambda)$$

**CPA Security.** *We define the "CPA game"* $\mathsf{CPAGame}_{\mathcal{A}}^b(\lambda)$ *between an adversary* $\mathcal{A}$ *and a challenger with a challenge bit* $b\{0, 1\}$ *as follows:*
  - *Sample* $\mathsf{sk} \leftarrow \mathsf{Gen}(1^\lambda)$.
  - *The adversary* $\mathcal{A}^{\mathsf{Enc_{sk}}(\cdot)}$ *gets the encryption oracle. Eventually, it chooses two messages* $m_0, m_1 \in \{0, 1\}^n$
  - *The adversary* $\mathcal{A}$ *gets a challenge* $c \leftarrow \mathsf{Enc_{sk}}(m_b)$ *and further access to the encryption oracle* $\mathcal{A}^{\mathsf{Enc_{sk}}(\cdot)}(c)$, *and eventually output a bit* $b'$ *which we define as the output of the game.*

*We require that for all PPT adversary* $\mathcal{A}$ *we have* $| \Pr[\mathsf{CPAGame}_{\mathcal{A}}^0(\lambda) = 1] - \Pr[\mathsf{CPAGame}_{\mathcal{A}}^1(\lambda) = 1] | \leq \mathsf{negl}(\lambda)$.

### A.2    Garbled Circuits

**Definition 14 (Garbling).** *A* garbling scheme *for a class of circuits* $\mathcal{C} = \{C : \{0, 1\}^{n_1(\lambda)} \rightarrow \{0, 1\}^{n_2(\lambda)}\}$ *consists of PPT algorithms* $(\mathsf{Setup}, \mathsf{Garble}, \mathsf{Encode}, \mathsf{Eval})$ *with the following syntax:*

- $\mathbf{K} \leftarrow \mathsf{Setup}(1^\lambda)$ *generates* $\mathbf{K} = \{k_{i,b} : i \in [n_1(\lambda)], b \in \{0,1\}\}$
- $\hat{C} \leftarrow \mathsf{Garble}(C, \mathbf{K})$ *outputs a garbled circuit of the circuit* $C$.
- $\mathbf{K}_x \leftarrow \mathsf{Encode}(x, \mathbf{K})$ *outputs an encoding of the input* $x \in \{0,1\}^{n_1(\lambda)}$, $\mathbf{K}_x = \{k_{i,x[i]}\}_{i \in [n_1(\lambda)]}$ *where* $x[i]$ *is the* $i$-*th bit of* $x$.
- $C(x) = \mathsf{Eval}(\hat{C}, \mathbf{K}_x)$ *outputs* $C(x) \in \{0,1\}^{n_2(\lambda)}$.

*The scheme should satisfy the following properties:*

**Correctness.** *For every security parameter* $\lambda$, *circuit* $C : \{0,1\}^{n_1(\lambda)} \to \{0,1\}^{n_2(\lambda)}$, *and input* $x \in \{0,1\}^{n_1(\lambda)}$:

$$\Pr\left[ C(x) = \mathsf{Eval}(\hat{C}, \mathbf{K}_x) \,\middle|\, \begin{array}{l} \mathbf{K} \leftarrow \mathsf{Setup}(1^\lambda) \\ \hat{C} \leftarrow \mathsf{Garble}(C, \mathbf{K}) \\ \mathbf{K}_x \leftarrow \mathsf{Encode}(x, \mathbf{K}) \end{array} \right] = 1.$$

**Security.** *For every security parameter* $\lambda$, *circuit* $C : \{0,1\}^{n_1(\lambda)} \to \{0,1\}^{n_2(\lambda)}$, *and pair of inputs* $x_0, x_1 \in \{0,1\}^{n_1(\lambda)}$ *such that* $C(x_0) = C(x_1)$:

$$\left\{ \hat{C}, \mathbf{K}_{x_0} \,\middle|\, \mathbf{K}_{x_0} \leftarrow \mathsf{Encode}(x_0, \mathbf{K}) \right\} \overset{c}{\approx} \left\{ \hat{C}, \mathbf{K}_{x_1} \,\middle|\, \mathbf{K}_{x_1} \leftarrow \mathsf{Encode}(x_1, \mathbf{K}) \right\}$$

*where* $\hat{C} \leftarrow \mathsf{Garble}(C, \mathbf{K})$ *and* $\mathbf{K} \leftarrow \mathsf{Setup}(1^\lambda)$.

# B    Constructions of Single-Key Functional-Encryption Schemes

*Notation: Garbling Two-Input Circuits.* It will be useful for us to define some notation for garbling circuits $C(x, y)$ that take two inputs. Let $\mathsf{GC} = (\mathsf{Setup}, \mathsf{Garble}, \mathsf{Encode}, \mathsf{Eval})$ be a garbling scheme for a class of circuits $\mathcal{C} = \{C : \{0,1\}^{n_1(\lambda)} \times \{0,1\}^{n_2(\lambda)} \to \{0,1\}^{n_3(\lambda)}\}$, and let $\mathbf{K} \leftarrow \mathsf{GC.Setup}(1^\lambda)$. Recall $\mathbf{K} = \{k_{i,b} : i \in [n_1 + n_2], b \in \{0,1\}\}$.

We denote by $k_{i,b}^1 = k_{i,b}$ for every $i \in [n_1(\lambda)]$, by $k_{i,b}^2 = k_{(n_1(\lambda)+i),b}$ for every $i \in [n_2(\lambda)]$, by $\mathbf{K}^1$ the sets of keys for the first input, and by $\mathbf{K}^2$ the sets of keys for the second input i.e.,

$$\mathbf{K}^1 = \{k_{i,b}^1 : i \in [n_1(\lambda)], b \in \{0,1\}\} = \{k_{i,b} : i \in [n_1(\lambda)], b \in \{0,1\}\}$$
$$\mathbf{K}^2 = \{k_{i,b}^2 : i \in [n_2(\lambda)], b \in \{0,1\}\} = \{k_{(n_1(\lambda)+i),b} : i \in [n_2(\lambda)], b \in \{0,1\}\}.$$

Moreover, if $(\mathbf{K}^1, \mathbf{K}^2) \leftarrow \mathsf{GC.Setup}(1^\lambda)$, we also define notation for encoding part of the input $\mathbf{K}_x^1 \leftarrow \mathsf{GC.Encode}(x, \mathbf{K}^1)$ and similarly $\mathbf{K}_y^2 \leftarrow \mathsf{GC.Encode}(y, \mathbf{K}^2)$.

## B.1    Single-Key Public-Key Functional-Encryption Construction

**Construction 10 (Single-Key PK FE).** *We construct* $\mathsf{FE} = (\mathsf{Setup}, \mathsf{Gen}, \mathsf{Enc}, \mathsf{Dec})$ *a single-key public-key functional-encryption for a function* $F : \{0,1\}^{n_1(\lambda)} \times \{0,1\}^{n_2(\lambda)} \to \{0,1\}^{n_3(\lambda)}$ *that has a special decryption algorithm using* $\mathsf{PKE} = (\mathsf{Gen}, \mathsf{Enc}, \mathsf{Dec})$ *a public-key encryption scheme and* $\mathsf{GC} =$

(Setup, Garble, Encode, Eval) *a garbling scheme for a class of circuits* $\mathcal{C} = \{C : \{0,1\}^{n_1(\lambda)+n_2(\lambda)} \to \{0,1\}^{n_3(\lambda)}\}$.

We denote by $n_1 = n_1(\lambda), n_2 = n_2(\lambda)$ and $n_3 = n_3(\lambda)$, and abuse notation and denote by $F$ the circuit that compute the function $F$.

- FE.Setup($1^\lambda$):
  - *For* $i \in [n_2], b \in \{0,1\}$: *select* $(\mathsf{sk}_{i,b}, \mathsf{pk}_{i,b}) \leftarrow \mathsf{PKE.Gen}(1^\lambda)$.
  - *Output* $(\mathsf{mpk} := \{\mathsf{pk}_{i,b}\}_{i\in[n_2],b\in\{0,1\}}, \mathsf{msk} := \{\mathsf{sk}_{i,b}\}_{i\in[n_2],b\in\{0,1\}})$.
- FE.Gen$_{\mathsf{msk}}(y)$:
  - *Output* $\mathsf{sk}_y := \{\mathsf{sk}_{i,y[i]} : i \in [n_2]\}$.
- FE.Enc$_{\mathsf{mpk}}(x)$:
  - $(\mathbf{K}^1, \mathbf{K}^2) \leftarrow \mathsf{GC.Setup}(1^\lambda)$.
  - $\hat{F} \leftarrow \mathsf{GC.Garble}(F, (\mathbf{K}^1, \mathbf{K}^2))$.
  - $\mathbf{K}_x^1 \leftarrow \mathsf{GC.Encode}(x, \mathbf{K}^1)$.
  - *For* $i \in [n_2], b \in \{0,1\}$: *select* $c_{i,b} \leftarrow \mathsf{PKE.Enc}_{\mathsf{pk}_{i,b}}(k_{i,b}^2)$.
  - *Output* $c = (\hat{F}, \mathbf{K}_x^1, \{c_{i,b} : i \in [n_2], b \in \{0,1\}\})$.
- FE.Dec$_{\mathsf{sk}_y}(c)$ :
  - *For every* $i \in [n_2] : k_{i,y[i]}^2 = \mathsf{PKE.Dec}_{\mathsf{sk}_{i,y[i]}}(c_{i,y[i]})$.
  - $\mathbf{K}_y^2 = \{k_{i,y[i]}^2 : i \in [n_2]\}$.
  - *Output* $F(x,y) = \mathsf{GC.Eval}(\hat{F}, (\mathbf{K}_x^1, \mathbf{K}_y^2))$.

The correctness and security (as in Definition 1) of Construction 10 follows directly from the security of the garbling and public-key encryption schemes.[5] Additionally, a simple modification for the construction above results a scheme with a special decryption algorithm. We change the encryption algorithm to garble the circuit $F_{\mathsf{special}}$ (instead of $F$) where $F_{\mathsf{special}} : \{0,1\}^{n_1} \times \{0,1\}^{n_2+1} \to \{0,1\}^{\max\{n_1,n_3\}}$,

$$F_{\mathsf{special}}(x, (y,b)) := \begin{cases} x & \text{If } (y,b) = (0^{n_2}, 0) \\ F(x,y) & \text{otherwise} \end{cases}$$

To make the output length the same in both cases, pad with zeros.

*Using an IBE scheme.* We change the construction above to work with an *identity based encryption* scheme $\mathsf{IBE} = (\mathsf{Setup}, \mathsf{Gen}, \mathsf{Enc}, \mathsf{Dec})$ to reduce the master public-key size $\mathsf{mpk}$. In the resulting scheme the master public-key is of the same size as the master public-key in the IBE scheme.

Instead of generating for every $(i,b) \in [n_2] \times \{0,1\}$ a pair of public-key and secret-key, the setup algorithm generates a pair of master public-key and master secret-key for an IBE scheme, $(\mathsf{mpk}, \mathsf{msk}) \leftarrow \mathsf{IBE.Setup}(1^\lambda)$. In addition, the key generating algorithm generates $n_2$ private-keys of the IBE scheme, namely for each identity $(i, y[i])_{i\in[n_2]}$ generates an IBE private-key, $\mathsf{sk}_{i,y[i]} \leftarrow \mathsf{IBE.Gen}_{\mathsf{msk}}(\mathsf{id} = (i, y[i]))$. Further, the FE encryption algorithm now samples $c_{i,b} \leftarrow \mathsf{IBE.Enc}_{\mathsf{mpk}}(\mathsf{id} = (i,b), k_{i,b}^2)$ using the IBE encryption algorithm.

---

[5] If we assume perfect correctness of the underline GC and PKE, also the constructed FE has a perfect correctness (as in Definition 1).

## B.2    Single-Key Symmetric-Key Functional-Encryption Construction

**Construction 11 (Single-Key SK FE).** *We construct* FE $=$ (Setup, Gen, Enc, Dec) *a single-key symmetric-key functional-encryption for a function* $F :$ $\{0,1\}^{n_1(\lambda)} \times \{0,1\}^{n_2(\lambda)} \rightarrow \{0,1\}^{n_3(\lambda)}$ *that has a special encryption and decryption algorithm using* Sym $=$ (Gen, Enc, Dec) *a symmetric-key encryption scheme with pseudorandom ciphertexts and* GC $=$ (Setup, Garble, Encode, Eval) *a garbling scheme for a class of circuits* $\mathcal{C} = \{C : \{0,1\}^{n_1(\lambda)+n_2(\lambda)} \rightarrow \{0,1\}^{n_3(\lambda)}\}$.

*We denote by* $n_1 = n_1(\lambda), n_2 = n_2(\lambda)$ *and* $n_3 = n_3(\lambda)$, *and abuse notation and denote by* $F$ *the circuit that compute the function* $F$.

- FE.Setup$(1^\lambda)$:
  - *For* $i \in [n_2], b \in \{0,1\}$: *select* $(\mathsf{sk}_{i,b}) \leftarrow$ Sym.Gen$(1^\lambda)$.
  - *Output* (msk $:= \{\mathsf{sk}_{i,b} : i \in [n_2], b \in \{0,1\}\}$.)
- FE.Gen$_{\mathsf{msk}}(y)$:
  - *Output* $\mathsf{sk}_y := \{\mathsf{sk}_{i,y[i]} : i \in [n_2]\}$.
- FE.Enc$_{\mathsf{msk}}(x)$:
  - $(\mathbf{K}^1, \mathbf{K}^2) \leftarrow$ GC.Setup$(1^\lambda)$.
  - $\hat{F} \leftarrow$ GC.Garble$(F, (\mathbf{K}^1, \mathbf{K}^2))$.
  - $\mathbf{K}^1_x \leftarrow$ GC.Encode$(x, \mathbf{K}^1)$.
  - *For* $i \in [n_2], b \in \{0,1\}$: *select* $c_{i,b} \leftarrow$ PKE.Enc$_{\mathsf{sk}_{i,b}}(k^2_{i,b})$.
  - *Output* $c = (\hat{F}, \mathbf{K}^1_x, \{c_{i,b} : i \in [n_2], b \in \{0,1\}\})$.
- FE.Dec$_{\mathsf{sk}_y}(c)$ :
  - *For every* $i \in [n_2] : k^2_{i,y[i]} =$ PKE.Dec$_{\mathsf{sk}_{i,y[i]}}(c_{i,y[i]})$.
  - $\mathbf{K}^2_y = \{k^2_{i,y[i]} : i \in [n_2]\}$.
  - *Output* $F(x,y) =$ GC.Eval$(\hat{F}, (\mathbf{K}^1_x, \mathbf{K}^2_y))$.

The correctness and security (as in Definition 2) of Construction 11 follows directly from the security of the garbling and symmetric-key encryption schemes (see footnote 5). If ciphertexts of the underline symmetric-key encryption are computationally indistinguishable from random strings, then we also get a symmetric-key functional encryption with a special encryption algorithm. In particular, to encrypt with $\mathsf{sk}_y$, the encryption algorithm outputs uniformly random strings in place of $c_{i,1-y[i]} \leftarrow$ Sym.Enc$_{\mathsf{sk}_{i,(1-y[i])}}[k^2_{i,(1-y[i])}]$ for every $i \in [n_2]$. Additionally, we cam use the same trick we did in the public-key case to get the special decryption property.

## References

[BNNO11] Bendlin, R., Nielsen, J.B., Nordholt, P.S., Orlandi, C.: Lower and upper bounds for deniable public-key encryption. In: Lee, D.H., Wang, X. (eds.) ASIACRYPT 2011. LNCS, vol. 7073, pp. 125–142. Springer, Heidelberg (2011). doi:10.1007/978-3-642-25385-0_7

[CDMW09] Choi, S.G., Dachman-Soled, D., Malkin, T., Wee, H.: Improved non-committing encryption with applications to adaptively secure protocols. In: Matsui, M. (ed.) ASIACRYPT 2009. LNCS, vol. 5912, pp. 287–302. Springer, Heidelberg (2009). doi:10.1007/978-3-642-10366-7_17

[CDNO97] Canetti, R., Dwork, C., Naor, M., Ostrovsky, R.: Deniable encryption. In: Kaliski, B.S. (ed.) CRYPTO 1997. LNCS, vol. 1294, pp. 90–104. Springer, Heidelberg (1997). doi:10.1007/BFb0052229

[CFGN96] Canetti, R., Feige, U., Goldreich, O., Naor, M.: Adaptively secure multi-party computation. In: 28th Annual ACM Symposium on Theory of Computing, Philadephia, PA, USA, 22–24 May 1996, pp. 639–648. ACM Press (1996)

[CPV16] Canetti, R., Poburinnaya, O., Venkitasubramaniam, M.: Equivocating yao: Constant-round adaptively secure multiparty computation in the plain model. Cryptology ePrint Archive, Report 2016/1190 (2016). http://eprint.iacr.org/2016/1190

[DIO16] De Caro, A., Iovino, V., O'Neill, A.: Deniable functional encryption. In: Cheng, C.-M., Chung, K.-M., Persiano, G., Yang, B.-Y. (eds.) PKC 2016. LNCS, vol. 9614, pp. 196–222. Springer, Heidelberg (2016). doi:10.1007/978-3-662-49384-7_8

[DN00] Damgård, I., Nielsen, J.B.: Improved non-committing encryption schemes based on a general complexity assumption. In: Bellare, M. (ed.) CRYPTO 2000. LNCS, vol. 1880, pp. 432–450. Springer, Heidelberg (2000). doi:10.1007/3-540-44598-6_27

[GVW12] Gorbunov, S., Vaikuntanathan, V., Wee, H.: Functional encryption with bounded collusions via multi-party computation. In: Safavi-Naini, R., Canetti, R. (eds.) CRYPTO 2012. LNCS, vol. 7417, pp. 162–179. Springer, Heidelberg (2012). doi:10.1007/978-3-642-32009-5_11

[GWZ09] Garay, J.A., Wichs, D., Zhou, H.-S.: Somewhat non-committing encryption and efficient adaptively secure oblivious transfer. In: Halevi, S. (ed.) CRYPTO 2009. LNCS, vol. 5677, pp. 505–523. Springer, Heidelberg (2009). doi:10.1007/978-3-642-03356-8_30

[HJO+16] Hemenway, B., Jafargholi, Z., Ostrovsky, R., Scafuro, A., Wichs, D.: Adaptively secure garbled circuits from one-way functions. In: Robshaw, M., Katz, J. (eds.) CRYPTO 2016. LNCS, vol. 9816, pp. 149–178. Springer, Heidelberg (2016). doi:10.1007/978-3-662-53015-3_6

[Nie02] Nielsen, J.B.: Separating random oracle proofs from complexity theoretic proofs: the non-committing encryption case. In: Yung, M. (ed.) CRYPTO 2002. LNCS, vol. 2442, pp. 111–126. Springer, Heidelberg (2002). doi:10.1007/3-540-45708-9_8

[OPW11] O'Neill, A., Peikert, C., Waters, B.: Bi-deniable public-key encryption. In: Rogaway, P. (ed.) CRYPTO 2011. LNCS, vol. 6841, pp. 525–542. Springer, Heidelberg (2011). doi:10.1007/978-3-642-22792-9_30

[SS10] Sahai, A., Seyalioglu, H.: Worry-free encryption: functional encryption with public keys. In: Al-Shaer, E., Keromytis, A.D., Shmatikov, V. (eds.) ACM CCS 2010: 17th Conference on Computer and Communications Security, Chicago, Illinois, USA, 4–8 October 2010, pages 463–472. ACM Press (2010)

[SW14] Sahai, A., Waters, B.: How to use indistinguishability obfuscation: deniable encryption, and more. In: Shmoys, D.B. (ed.) 46th Annual ACM Symposium on Theory of Computing, 31 May–3 June 2014, pp. 475–484. ACM Press, New York (2014)

# A Modular Analysis of the Fujisaki-Okamoto Transformation

Dennis Hofheinz[1], Kathrin Hövelmanns[2(✉)], and Eike Kiltz[2]

[1] Karlsruhe Institute of Technology, Karlsruhe, Germany
Dennis.Hofheinz@kit.edu
[2] Ruhr Universität Bochum, Bochum, Germany
{Kathrin.Hoevelmanns,Eike.Kiltz}@rub.de

**Abstract.** The Fujisaki-Okamoto (FO) transformation (CRYPTO 1999 and Journal of Cryptology 2013) turns any weakly secure public-key encryption scheme into a strongly (i.e., IND-CCA) secure one in the random oracle model. Unfortunately, the FO analysis suffers from several drawbacks, such as a non-tight security reduction, and the need for a perfectly correct scheme. While several alternatives to the FO transformation have been proposed, they have stronger requirements, or do not obtain all desired properties.

In this work, we provide a fine-grained and modular toolkit of transformations for turning weakly secure into strongly secure public-key encryption schemes. All of our transformations are robust against schemes with correctness errors, and their combination leads to several tradeoffs among tightness of the reduction, efficiency, and the required security level of the used encryption scheme. For instance, one variant of the FO transformation constructs an IND-CCA secure scheme from an IND-CPA secure one with a tight reduction and very small efficiency overhead. Another variant assumes only an OW-CPA secure scheme, but leads to an IND-CCA secure scheme with larger ciphertexts.

We note that we also analyze our transformations in the quantum random oracle model, which yields security guarantees in a post-quantum setting.

**Keywords:** Public-Key Encryption · Fujisaki-Okamoto transformation · Tight reductions · Quantum Random Oracle Model

## 1 Introduction

The notion of <u>IND</u>istinguishability against <u>C</u>hosen-<u>C</u>iphertext <u>A</u>ttacks (IND-CCA) [34] is now widely accepted as the standard security notion for asymmetric encryption schemes. Intuitively, IND-CCA security requires that no efficient adversary can recognize which of two messages is encrypted in a given ciphertext, even if the two candidate messages are chosen by the adversary himself. In contrast to the similar but weaker notion of <u>IND</u>istinguishability against <u>C</u>hosen-<u>P</u>laintext <u>A</u>ttacks (IND-CPA), an IND-CCA adversary is given access to a decryption oracle throughout the attack.

© International Association for Cryptologic Research 2017
Y. Kalai and L. Reyzin (Eds.): TCC 2017, Part I, LNCS 10677, pp. 341–371, 2017.
https://doi.org/10.1007/978-3-319-70500-2_12

GENERIC TRANSFORMATIONS ACHIEVING IND-CCA SECURITY. While IND-CCA security is in many applications the desired notion of security, it is usually much more difficult to prove than IND-CPA security. Thus, several transformations have been suggested that turn a public-key encryption (PKE) scheme with weaker security properties into an IND-CCA one generically. For instance, in a seminal paper, Fujisaki and Okamoto [23,24] proposed a generic transformation (FO transformation) combining any One-Way (OW-CPA) secure asymmetric encryption scheme with any one-time secure symmetric encryption scheme into a Hybrid encryption scheme that is (IND-CCA) secure in the random oracle model [7]. Subsequently, Okamoto and Pointcheval [32] and Coron et al. [18] proposed two more generic transformations (called REACT and GEM) that are considerably simpler but require the underlying asymmetric scheme to be One-Way against Plaintext Checking Attacks (OW-PCA). OW-PCA security is a non-standard security notion that provides the adversary with a plaintext checking oracle $Pco(c, m)$ that returns 1 iff decryption of ciphertext $c$ yields message $m$. A similar transformation was also implicitly used in the "Hashed ElGamal" encryption scheme by Abdalla et al. [1].

KEMs. In his "A Designer's Guide to KEMs" paper, Dent [20] provides "more modern" versions of the FO [20, Table 5] and the REACT/GEM [20, Table 2] transformations that result in IND-CCA secure key-encapsulation mechanisms (KEMs). Recall that any IND-CCA secure KEM can be combined with any (one-time) chosen-ciphertext secure symmetric encryption scheme to obtain a IND-CCA secure PKE scheme [19]. Due to their efficiency and versatility, in practice one often works with such hybrid encryption schemes derived from a KEM. For that reason the primary goal of our paper will be constructing IND-CCA secure KEMs.

We remark that all previous variants of the FO transformation require the underlying PKE scheme to be $\gamma$-spread [23], which essentially means that ciphertexts (generated by the probabilistic encryption algorithm) have sufficiently large entropy.

SECURITY AGAINST QUANTUM ADVERSARIES. Recently, the above mentioned generic transformations have gathered renewed interest in the quest of finding an IND-CCA secure asymmetric encryption scheme that is secure against quantum adversaries, i.e., adversaries equipped with a quantum computer. In particular, the NIST announced a competition with the goal to standardize new asymmetric encryption systems [31] with security against quantum adversaries. Natural candidates base their IND-CPA security on the hardness of certain problems over lattices and codes, which are generally believed to resists quantum adversaries. Furthermore, quantum computers may execute all "offline primitives" such as hash functions on arbitrary superpositions, which motivated the introduction of the quantum (accessible) random oracle model [11]. Targhi and Unruh recently proved a variant of the FO transformation secure in the quantum random oracle model [38]. Helping to find IND-CCA secure KEM with provable (post-quantum) security will thus be an important goal in this paper.

DISCUSSION. Despite their versatility, the above FO and REACT/GEM transformations have a couple of small but important disadvantages.

- **Tightness.** The security reduction of the FO transformation [23,24] in the random oracle model is not tight, i.e., it loses a factor of $q_G$, the number of random oracle queries. A non-tight security proof requires to adapt the system parameters accordingly, which results in considerably less efficient schemes. The REACT/GEM transformations have a tight security reduction, but they require the underlying encryption scheme to be OW-PCA secure. As observed by Peikert [33], due to their decision/search equivalence, many natural lattice-based encryption scheme are not OW-PCA secure and it is not clear how to modify them to be so. In fact, the main technical difficulty is to build an IND-CPA or OW-PCA secure encryption scheme from an OW-CPA secure one, with a tight security reduction.
- **Correctness error.** The FO, as well as the REACT/GEM transformation require the underlying asymmetric encryption scheme to be perfectly correct, i.e., not having a decryption error. In general, one cannot exclude the fact that even a (negligibly) small decryption error could be exploited by a concrete IND-CCA attack against FO-like transformed schemes.
  Dealing with imperfectly correct schemes is of great importance since many (but not all) practical lattice-based encryption schemes have a small correctness error, see, e.g., DXL [21], Peikert [33], BCNS [14], New Hope [3], Frodo [13], Lizard [17], and Kyber [12].[1]

These deficiencies were of little or no concern when the FO and REACT/GEM transformations were originally devised. Due to the emergence of large-scale scenarios (which benefit heavily from tight security reductions) and the increased popularity of lattice-based schemes with correctness defects, however, we view these deficiencies as acute problems.

## 1.1   Our Contributions

Our main contribution is a modular treatment of FO-like transformations. That is, we provide fine-grained transformations that can be used to turn an OW-CPA secure PKE scheme into an IND-CCA secure one in several steps. For instance, we provide separate OW-CPA → OW-PCA and OW-PCA → IND-CCA transformations that, taken together, yield the original FO transformation. However, we also provide variants of these individual transformations that achieve different security goals and tightness properties. All of our individual transformations are

---

[1] Lattice-based encryption schemes can be made perfectly correctness by putting a limit on the noise and setting the modulus of the LWE instance large enough, see e.g. [9,27]. But increasing the size of the modulus makes the LWE problem easier to solve in practice, and thus the dimension of the problem needs to be increased in order to obtain the same security levels. Larger dimension and modulus increase the public-key and ciphertext length.

robust against PKE schemes with correctness errors (in the sense that the correctness error of the resulting schemes can be bounded by the correctness error of the original scheme).

The benefit of our modular treatment is not only a conceptual simplification, but also a larger variety of possible combined transformations (with different requirements and properties). For instance, combining two results about our transformations T and $U^{\not\perp}$, we can show that the original FO transformation yields IND-CCA security from IND-CPA security with a *tight* security reduction. Combining $S^\ell$ with T and $U^{\not\perp}$, on the other hand, yields tight IND-CCA security from the weaker notion of OW-CPA security, at the expense of a larger ciphertext. (See Fig. 1 for an overview.)

**Our Transformations in Detail.** In the following, we give a more detailed overview over our transformations. We remark that all our transformations require a PKE scheme (and not a KEM). We view it as an interesting open problem to construct similar transformations that only assume (and yield) KEMs, since such transformations have the potential of additional efficiency gains.

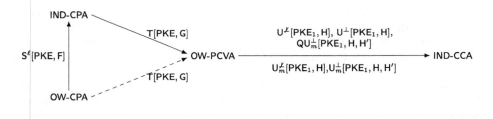

| Transformation | Security implication | QROM? | ROM Tightness? | Requirements |
|---|---|---|---|---|
| $PKE_1 = T[PKE, G]$ (§3.1) | OW-CPA $\Rightarrow$ OW-PCA | ✓ | — | none |
| $PKE_1 = T[PKE, G]$ (§3.1) | IND-CPA $\Rightarrow$ OW-PCA | ✓ | ✓ | none |
| $PKE_1 = T[PKE, G]$ (§3.1) | OW-CPA $\Rightarrow$ OW-PCVA | ✓ | — | $\gamma$-spread |
| $PKE_1 = T[PKE, G]$ (§3.1) | IND-CPA $\Rightarrow$ OW-PCVA | — | ✓ | $\gamma$-spread |
| $KEM^{\not\perp} = U^{\not\perp}[PKE_1, H]$ (§3.2) | OW-PCA $\Rightarrow$ IND-CCA | — | ✓ | none |
| $KEM^{\perp} = U^{\perp}[PKE_1, H]$ (§3.2) | OW-PCVA $\Rightarrow$ IND-CCA | — | ✓ | none |
| $KEM_m^{\not\perp} = U_m^{\not\perp}[PKE_1, H]$ (§3.2) | OW-CPA $\Rightarrow$ IND-CCA | — | ✓ | det. $PKE_1$ |
| $KEM_m^{\perp} = U_m^{\perp}[PKE_1, H]$ (§3.2) | OW-VA $\Rightarrow$ IND-CCA | — | ✓ | det. $PKE_1$ |
| $QKEM_m^{\perp} = QU_m^{\perp}[PKE_1, H, H']$ (§4.3) | OW-PCA $\Rightarrow$ IND-CCA | ✓ | ✓ | none |
| $PKE_\ell = S^\ell[PKE, F]$ (§3.4) | OW-CPA $\Rightarrow$ IND-PCA | — | ✓ | none |

**Fig. 1.** Our modular transformations. Top: solid arrows indicate tight reductions, dashed arrows indicate non-tight reductions. Bottom: properties of the transformations. The tightness row only refers to tightness in the standard random oracle model; all our reductions in the quantum random oracle model are non-tight.

T: FROM OW-CPA TO OW-PCA SECURITY ("DERANDOMIZATION" + "RE-ENCRYPTION"). T is the Encrypt-with-Hash construction from [6]: Starting from an encryption scheme PKE and a hash function G, we build a deterministic encryption scheme $PKE_1 = T[PKE, G]$ by defining

$$Enc_1(pk, m) := Enc(pk, m; G(m)),$$

where $G(m)$ is used as the random coins for Enc. Note that $Enc_1$ is deterministic. $Dec_1(sk, c)$ first decrypts $c$ into $m'$ and rejects if $Enc(pk, m'; G(m')) \neq c$ ("re-encryption"). Modeling G as a random oracle, OW-PCA security of $PKE_1$ non-tightly reduces to OW-CPA security of PKE and tightly reduces to IND-CPA security of PKE. If PKE furthermore is $\gamma$-spread (for sufficiently large $\gamma$), then $PKE_1$ is even OW-PCVA secure. OW-PCVA security[2] is PCA security, where the adversary is additionally given access to a validity oracle $Cvo(c)$ that checks $c$'s validity (in the sense that it does not decrypt to $\bot$, see also Definition 1).

$U^{\not\bot}$ ($U^\bot$): FROM OW-PCA (OW-PCVA) TO IND-CCA SECURITY ("HASHING"). Starting from an encryption scheme $PKE_1$ and a hash function H, we build a key encapsulation mechanism $KEM^{\not\bot} = U^{\not\bot}[PKE_1, H]$ with "implicit rejection" by defining

$$Encaps(pk) := (c \leftarrow Enc_1(pk, m), K := H(c, m)), \tag{1}$$

where $m$ is picked at random from the message space.

$$Decaps^{\not\bot}(sk, c) = \begin{cases} H(c, m) & m \neq \bot \\ H(c, s) & m = \bot \end{cases}, \tag{2}$$

where $m := Dec(sk, c)$ and $s$ is a random seed which is contained in $sk$. Modeling H as a random oracle, IND-CCA security of $KEM^{\not\bot}$ tightly reduces to OW-PCA security of $PKE_1$.

We also define $KEM^\bot = U^\bot[PKE_1, H]$ with "explicit rejection" which differs from $KEM^{\not\bot}$ only in decapsulation:

$$Decaps^\bot(sk, c) = \begin{cases} H(c, m) & m \neq \bot \\ \bot & m = \bot \end{cases}, \tag{3}$$

where $m := Dec(sk, c)$. Modeling H as a random oracle, IND-CCA of $KEM^\bot$ security tightly reduces to OW-PCVA security of $PKE_1$. We remark that transformation $U^\bot$ is essentially [20, Table 2], i.e., a KEM variant of the REACT/GEM transformations.

$U_m^{\not\bot}$ ($U_m^\bot$): FROM DETERMINISTIC OW-CPA (OW-VA) TO IND-CCA SECURITY ("HASHING"). We consider two more variants of $U^{\not\bot}$ and $U^\bot$, namely $U_m^{\not\bot}$ and $U_m^\bot$. Transformation $U_m^{\not\bot}$ ($U_m^\bot$) is a variant of $U^{\not\bot}$ ($U^\bot$), where $K = H(c, m)$ from Eqs. (1)–(3) is replaced by $K = H(m)$. We prove that IND-CCA security of $KEM_m^{\not\bot} := U_m^{\not\bot}[PKE_1, H]$ ($KEM_m^\bot := U_m^\bot[PKE_1, H]$) in the random oracle model tightly reduces to IND-CPA (IND-VA[3]) security of $PKE_1$, if encryption of $PKE_1$ is deterministic.

---

[2] OW-PCVA security is called OW-CPA$^+$ security with access to a Pco oracle in [20].

[3] OW-VA security is OW-CPA security, where the adversary is given access to a validity oracle $Cvo(c)$ that checks $c$'s validity (cf. Definition 1).

$QU_m^\perp$: FROM OW-PCA TO IND-CCA SECURITY IN THE QUANTUM ROM.
We first prove that transformation T also works in the quantum random oracle
model. Next, to go from OW-PCA to IND-CCA in the QROM, we build a key
encapsulation mechanism $QKEM_m^\perp = QU_m^\perp[PKE_1, H, H']$ with explicit rejection
by defining

$$QEncaps_m(pk) := ((c \leftarrow Enc_1(pk, m), d := H'(m)), K := H(m)),$$

where $m$ is picked at random from the message space.

$$QDecaps_m^\perp(sk, c, d) = \begin{cases} H(m') & m' \neq \perp \\ \perp & m' = \perp \vee H'(m') \neq d \end{cases},$$

where $m' := Dec(sk, c)$. $QU_m^\perp$ differs from $U_m^{\not\perp}$ only in the additional hash value
$d = H'(m)$ from the ciphertext and $H'$ is a random oracle with matching domain
and image. This trick was introduced in [40] and used in [38] in the context of the
FO transformation. Modeling H and $H'$ as a quantum random oracles, IND-CCA
security of KEM reduces to OW-PCA security of $PKE_1$.

**The Resulting FO Transformations.** Our final transformations $FO^{\not\perp}$ ("FO
with implicit rejection"), $FO^\perp$ ("FO with explicit rejection"), $FO_m^{\not\perp}$ ("FO with
implicit rejection, $K = H(m)$"), $FO_m^\perp$ ("FO with explicit rejection, $K = H(m)$"),
and $QFO_m^\perp$ ("Quantum FO with explicit rejection, $K = H(m)$") are defined in
the following table.

| Transformation | QROM? | ROM Tightness? | Requirements |
|---|---|---|---|
| $FO^{\not\perp}[PKE, G, H] := U^{\not\perp}[T[PKE, G], H]$ | — | ✓ | none |
| $FO^\perp[PKE, G, H] := U^\perp[T[PKE, G], H]$ | — | ✓ | $\gamma$-spread |
| $FO_m^{\not\perp}[PKE, G, H] := U_m^{\not\perp}[T[PKE, G], H]$ | — | ✓ | none |
| $FO_m^\perp[PKE, G, H] := U_m^\perp[T[PKE, G], H]$ | — | ✓ | $\gamma$-spread |
| $QFO_m^\perp[PKE, G, H, H'] := QU_m^\perp[T[PKE, G], H, H']$ | ✓ | ✓ | none |

As corollaries of our modular transformation we obtain that IND-CCA secu-
rity of $FO^{\not\perp}[PKE, G, H]$, $FO^\perp[PKE, G, H]$, $FO_m^{\not\perp}[PKE, G, H]$, and $FO_m^\perp[PKE, G, H]$
non-tightly reduces to the OW-CPA security of PKE, and tightly reduces to the
IND-CPA security of PKE, in the random oracle model. We remark that transformation $FO_m^\perp$ essentially recovers a KEM variant [20, Table 5] of the original
FO transformation [23]. Whereas the explicit rejection variants $FO^\perp$ and $FO_m^\perp$
require PKE to be $\gamma$-spread, there is no such requirement on $FO^{\not\perp}$ and $FO_m^{\not\perp}$. Further, IND-CCA security of $QFO_m^\perp[PKE, G, H, H']$ reduces to the OW-CPA security
of PKE, in the quantum random oracle model. Our transformation $QFO_m^\perp$ essentially recovers a KEM variant of the modified FO transformation by Targhi and
Unruh [38]. As it is common in the quantum random oracle model, all our reductions are (highly) non-tight. We leave it as an open problem to derive a tighter
security reduction of T, for example to IND-CPA security of PKE.

CORRECTNESS ERROR. We stress that all our security reductions also take non-zero correctness error into account. Finding the "right" definition of correctness that is achievable (say, by currently proposed lattice-based encryption schemes) and at the same time sufficient to prove security turned out to be a bit subtle. This is the reason why our definition of correctness (see Sect. 2.1) derives from the ones previously given in the literature (e.g. [10,22]). The concrete bounds of $FO^{\not\perp}$, $FO^{\perp}$, $FO_m^{\not\perp}$, and $FO_m^{\perp}$ give guidance on the required correctness error of the underlying PKE scheme. Concretely, for "$\kappa$ bits security", PKE requires a correctness error of $2^{-\kappa}$.

**Example Instantiations.** In the context of ElGamal encryption one can apply $\{FO^{\not\perp}, FO^{\perp}, FO_m^{\not\perp}, FO_m^{\perp}\}$ to obtain the schemes of [4,25,28] whose IND-CCA security non-tightly reduces to the CDH assumption, and tightly reduces to the DDH assumption. Alternatively, one can directly use $U^{\not\perp}/U^{\perp}$ to obtain the more efficient schemes of [1,18,32,36] whose IND-CCA security tightly reduces to the gap-DH (a.k.a. strong CDH) assumption. In the context of deterministic encryption schemes such as RSA, Paillier, etc., one can apply $U^{\not\perp}/U^{\perp}$ to obtain schemes mentioned in [20,36] whose IND-CCA security tightly reduces to one-way security. Finally, in the context of lattices-based encryption (e.g., [30,35]), one can apply $FO^{\not\perp}$, $FO^{\perp}$, $FO_m^{\not\perp}$, $FO_m^{\perp}$, and $QFO_m^{\perp}$ to achieve IND-CCA security.

**Transformation $S^\ell$: From OW-CPA to IND-CPA, Tightly.** Note that T requires PKE to be IND-CPA secure to achieve a tight reduction. In case one has to rely on OW-CPA security, transformation $S^\ell$ offers the following tradeoff between efficiency and tightness. It transforms an OW-CPA secure PKE into an IND-CPA secure $PKE_\ell$, where $\ell$ is a parameter. The ciphertext consists of $\ell$ independent PKE ciphertexts:

$$\mathsf{Enc}_\ell(pk, m) := (\mathsf{Enc}(pk, x_1), \ldots, \mathsf{Enc}(pk, x_\ell), m \oplus \mathsf{G}(x_1, \ldots, x_\ell)).$$

The reduction (to the OW-CPA security of PKE) loses a factor of $q_{\mathsf{G}}^{1/\ell}$, where $q_{\mathsf{G}}$ is the number of G-queries an adversary makes.

Observe that the only way to gather information about $m$ is to explicitly query $\mathsf{G}(x_1, \ldots, x_n)$, which requires to find all $x_i$. The reduction can use this observation to embed an OW-CPA challenge as one $\mathsf{Enc}(pk, x_{i^*})$ and hope to learn $x_{i^*}$ from the G-queries of a successful IND-CPA adversary. In this, the reduction will know all $x_i$ except $x_{i^*}$. The difficulty in this reduction is to identify the "right" G-query (that reveals $x_{i^*}$) in all of the adversary's G-queries. Intuitively, the more instances we have, the easier it is for the reduction to spot the G-query $(x_1, \ldots, x_\ell)$ (by comparing the $x_i$ for $i \neq i^*$), and the less guessing is necessary. Hence, we get a tradeoff between the number of instances $\ell$ (and thus the size of the ciphertext) and the loss of the reduction.

## 1.2   Related Work

As already pointed out, $FO_m^{\perp} = U_m^{\perp} \circ T$ is essentially a KEM variant of the Fujisaki-Okamoto transform from [20, Table 5]. Further, $U^{\perp}$ is a KEM variant

[20] of the GEM/REACT transform [1,18,32]. Our modular view suggest that the FO transform implicitly contains the GEM/REACT transform, at least the proof technique. With this more general view, the FO transform and its variants remains the only known transformation from CPA to CCA security. It is an interesting open problem to come up with alternative transformations that get rid of derandomization or that dispense with re-encryption (which preserving efficiency). Note that for the ElGamal encryption scheme, the "twinning" technique [15,16] does exactly this, but it uses non-generic zero-knowledge proofs that are currently not available for all schemes (e.g., for lattice-based schemes).

In concurrent and independent work, [2] considers the IND-CCA security of LIMA which in our notation can be described as $\mathsf{FO}_m^\perp[\mathsf{RLWE}, \mathsf{G}, \mathsf{H}]$. Here RLWE is a specific encryption scheme based on lattices associated to polynomial rings from [29], which is IND-CPA secure under the Ring-LWE assumption. As the main result, [2] provides a tight reduction of LIMA's IND-CCA security to the Ring-LWE assumption, in the random oracle model. The proof exploits "some weakly homomorphic properties enjoyed by the underlying encryption scheme" and therefore does not seem to be applicable to other schemes. The tight security reduction from Ring-LWE is recovered as a special case of our general security results on $\mathsf{FO}_m^\perp$. We note that the security reduction of [2] does not take the (non-zero) correctness error of RLWE into account.

## 2 Preliminaries

For $n \in \mathbb{N}$, let $[n] := \{1, \ldots, n\}$. For a set $S$, $|S|$ denotes the cardinality of S. For a finite set $S$, we denote the sampling of a uniform random element $x$ by $x \xleftarrow{\$} S$, while we denote the sampling according to some distribution $\mathfrak{D}$ by $x \leftarrow \mathfrak{D}$. For a polynomial $p(X)$ with integer coefficients, we denote by $\mathsf{Roots}(p)$ the (finite) set of (complex) roots of $p$. By $[\![B]\!]$ we denote the bit that is 1 if the Boolean Statement $B$ is true, and otherwise 0.

ALGORITHMS. We denote deterministic computation of an algorithm $A$ on input $x$ by $y := A(x)$. We denote algorithms with access to an oracle O by $\mathsf{A}^O$. Unless stated otherwise, we assume all our algorithms to be probabilistic and denote the computation by $y \leftarrow A(x)$.

RANDOM ORACLES. We will at times model hash functions $\mathsf{H} : \mathfrak{D}_\mathsf{H} \to \Im(\mathsf{H})$ as random oracles. To keep record of the queries issued to H, we will use a hash list $\mathfrak{L}_\mathsf{H}$ that contains all tuples $(x, \mathsf{H}(x))$ of arguments $x \in \mathfrak{D}_\mathsf{H}$ that H was queried on and the respective answers $\mathsf{H}(x)$. We make the convention that $\mathsf{H}(x) = \perp$ for all $x \notin \mathfrak{D}_\mathsf{H}$.

GAMES. Following [8,37], we use code-based games. We implicitly assume boolean flags to be initialized to false, numerical types to 0, sets to $\emptyset$, and strings to the empty string $\epsilon$. We make the convention that a procedure terminates once it has returned an output.

## 2.1  Public-Key Encryption

SYNTAX. A public-key encryption scheme $\mathsf{PKE} = (\mathsf{Gen}, \mathsf{Enc}, \mathsf{Dec})$ consists of three algorithms and a finite message space $\mathcal{M}$ (which we assume to be efficiently recognizable). The key generation algorithm $\mathsf{Gen}$ outputs a key pair $(pk, sk)$, where $pk$ also defines a randomness space $\mathcal{R} = \mathcal{R}(pk)$. The encryption algorithm $\mathsf{Enc}$, on input $pk$ and a message $m \in \mathcal{M}$, outputs an encryption $c \leftarrow \mathsf{Enc}(pk, m)$ of $m$ under the public key $pk$. If necessary, we make the used randomness of encryption explicit by writing $c := \mathsf{Enc}(pk, m; r)$, where $r \xleftarrow{\$} \mathcal{R}$ and $\mathcal{R}$ is the randomness space. The decryption algorithm $\mathsf{Dec}$, on input $sk$ and a ciphertext $c$, outputs either a message $m = \mathsf{Dec}(sk, c) \in \mathcal{M}$ or a special symbol $\bot \notin \mathcal{M}$ to indicate that $c$ is not a valid ciphertext.

CORRECTNESS. We call a public-key encryption scheme $\mathsf{PKE}$ $\delta$-correct if

$$\mathbf{E}[\max_{m \in \mathcal{M}} \Pr\left[\mathsf{Dec}(sk, c) \neq m \mid c \leftarrow \mathsf{Enc}(pk, m)\right]] \leq \delta,$$

where the expectation is taken over $(pk, sk) \leftarrow \mathsf{Gen}$. Equivalently, $\delta$-correctness means that for all (possibly unbounded) adversaries $\mathsf{A}$, $\Pr[\mathsf{COR}_{\mathsf{PKE}}^{\mathsf{A}} \Rightarrow 1] \leq \delta$, where the correctness game $\mathsf{COR}$ is defined as in Fig. 2 (left). That is, an (unbounded) adversary obtains the public and the secret key and wins if it finds a message inducing a correctness error. Note that our definition of correctness slightly derives from previous definitions (e.g. [10,22]) but it has been carefully crafted such that it is sufficient to prove our main theorems (i.e., the security of the Fujisaki-Okamoto transformation) and at the same time it is fulfilled by all recently proposed lattice-based encryption schemes with correctness error.

If $\mathsf{PKE} = \mathsf{PKE}^\mathsf{G}$ is defined relative to a random oracle $\mathsf{G}$, then defining correctness is a bit more subtle as the correctness bound might depend on the number of queries to $\mathsf{G}$.[4] We call a public-key encryption scheme $\mathsf{PKE}$ in the random oracle model $\delta(q_\mathsf{G})$-correct if for all (possibly unbounded) adversaries $\mathsf{A}$ making at most $q_\mathsf{G}$ queries to random oracle $\mathsf{G}$, $\Pr[\mathsf{COR\text{-}RO}_{\mathsf{PKE}}^{\mathsf{A}} \Rightarrow 1] \leq \delta(q_\mathsf{G})$, where the correctness game $\mathsf{COR\text{-}RO}$ is defined as in Fig. 2 (right). If $\mathsf{PKE}$ is defined relative to two random oracles $\mathsf{G}$, $\mathsf{H}$, then the correctness error $\delta$ is a function in $q_\mathsf{G}$ and $q_\mathsf{H}$.

Note that our correctness definition in the standard model is a special case of the one in the random oracle model, where the number of random oracle queries is zero and hence $\delta(q_\mathsf{G})$ is a constant.

MIN-ENTROPY. [24] For $(pk, sk) \leftarrow \mathsf{Gen}$ and $m \in \mathcal{M}$, we define the *min-entropy* of $\mathsf{Enc}(pk, m)$ by $\gamma(pk, m) := -\log \max_{c \in \mathcal{C}} \Pr_{r \leftarrow \mathcal{R}}[c = \mathsf{Enc}(pk, m; r)]$. We say that $\mathsf{PKE}$ is $\gamma$-*spread* if, for every key pair $(pk, sk) \leftarrow \mathsf{Gen}$ and every message $m \in \mathcal{M}$, $\gamma(pk, m) \geq \gamma$. In particular, this implies that for every possible ciphertext $c \in \mathcal{C}$, $\Pr_{r \leftarrow \mathcal{R}}[c = \mathsf{Enc}(pk, m; r)] \leq 2^{-\gamma}$.

SECURITY. We now define three security notions for public-key encryption: One-Wayness under Chosen Plaintext Attacks (OW-CPA), One-Wayness under

---

[4] For an example why the number of random oracle queries matters in the context of correctness, we refer to Theorem 1.

| GAME COR: | GAME COR-RO: |
|---|---|
| 01 $(pk, sk) \leftarrow$ Gen | 05 $(pk, sk) \leftarrow$ Gen |
| 02 $m \leftarrow A(sk, pk)$ | 06 $m \leftarrow A^{G(\cdot)}(sk, pk)$ |
| 03 $c \leftarrow$ Enc$(pk, m)$ | 07 $c \leftarrow$ Enc$(pk, m)$ |
| 04 **return** $[\![$Dec$(sk, c) = m]\!]$ | 08 **return** $[\![$Dec$(sk, c) = m]\!]$ |

**Fig. 2.** Correctness game COR for PKE in the standard model (left) and COR-RO for PKE defined relative to a random oracle G (right).

| GAME OW-ATK: | Pco$(m \in \mathcal{M}, c)$ |
|---|---|
| 09 $(pk, sk) \leftarrow$ Gen | 14 **return** $[\![$Dec$(sk, c) = m]\!]$ |
| 10 $m^* \xleftarrow{\$} \mathcal{M}$ | |
| 11 $c^* \leftarrow$ Enc$(pk, m^*)$ | Cvo$(c \neq c^*)$ |
| 12 $m' \leftarrow A^{O_{ATK}}(pk, c)$ | 15 $m := $ Dec$(sk, c)$ |
| 13 **return** Pco$(m', c^*)$ | 16 **return** $[\![m \in \mathcal{M}]\!]$ |

**Fig. 3.** Games OW-ATK (ATK $\in \{$CPA, PCA, VA, PCVA$\}$) for PKE, where $O_{ATK}$ is defined in Definition 1. Pco$(\cdot, \cdot)$ is the $\underline{P}$laintext $\underline{C}$hecking $\underline{O}$racle and Cvo$(\cdot)$ is the $\underline{C}$iphertext $\underline{V}$alidity $\underline{O}$racle.

$\underline{P}$laintext $\underline{C}$hecking $\underline{A}$ttacks (OW-PCA) and $\underline{O}$ne-$\underline{W}$ayness under $\underline{P}$laintext and $\underline{V}$alidity $\underline{C}$hecking $\underline{A}$ttacks (OW-PCVA).

**Definition 1** *(OW-ATK).* *Let* PKE $= ($Gen, Enc, Dec$)$ *be a public-key encryption scheme with message space* $\mathcal{M}$. *For* ATK $\in \{$CPA, PCA, VA, PCVA$\}$, *we define* OW-ATK *games as in Fig. 3, where*

$$O_{ATK} := \begin{cases} - & ATK = CPA \\ Pco(\cdot, \cdot) & ATK = PCA \\ Cvo(\cdot) & ATK = VA \\ Pco(\cdot, \cdot), Cvo(\cdot) & ATK = PCVA \end{cases}.$$

*We define the* OW-ATK *advantage function of an adversary* A *against* PKE *as* $\text{Adv}_{PKE}^{OW\text{-}ATK}(A) := \Pr[OW\text{-}ATK_{PKE}^A \Rightarrow 1]$.

A few remarks are in place. Our definition of the plaintext checking oracle Pco$(m, c)$ (c.f. Fig. 3) implicitly disallows queries on messages $m \in \mathcal{M}$. (With the convention that Pco$(m \notin \mathcal{M}, c)$ yields $\bot$.) This restriction is important since otherwise the ciphertext validity oracle Cvo$(\cdot)$ could be simulated as Cvo$(m) = $ Pco$(\bot, c)$. Similarly, the ciphertext validity oracle Cvo$(c)$ implicitly disallows queries on the challenge ciphertext $c^*$.

Usually, the adversary wins the one-way game iff its output $m'$ equals the challenge message $m^*$. Instead, in game OW-ATK the correctness of $m'$ is checked using the Pco oracle, i.e., it returns 1 iff Dec$(sk, c^*) = m'$. The two games have statistical difference $\delta$, if PKE is $\delta$-correct.

Additionally, we define $\underline{I}$n$\underline{d}$istinguishability under $\underline{C}$hosen $\underline{P}$laintext $\underline{A}$ttacks (IND-CPA).

**Definition 2** *(IND-CPA). Let* $\mathsf{PKE} = (\mathsf{Gen}, \mathsf{Enc}, \mathsf{Dec})$ *be a public-key encryption scheme with message space* $\mathcal{M}$. *We define the* $\mathsf{IND\text{-}CPA}$ *game as in Fig. 4, and the* $\mathsf{IND\text{-}CPA}$ *advantage function of an adversary* $\mathsf{A} = (\mathsf{A}_1, \mathsf{A}_2)$ *against* $\mathsf{PKE}$ *(such that* $\mathsf{A}_2$ *has binary output) as* $\mathrm{Adv}_{\mathsf{PKE}}^{\mathsf{IND\text{-}CPA}}(\mathsf{A}) := |\Pr[\mathsf{IND\text{-}CPA}^{\mathsf{A}} \Rightarrow 1] - 1/2|$.

We also define OW-ATK and IND-CPA security in the random oracle model, where PKE and adversary A are given access to a random oracle H. We make the convention that the number $q_{\mathsf{H}}$ of the adversary's random oracle queries count the total number of times H is executed in the experiment. That is, the number of A explicit queries to $\mathsf{H}(\cdot)$ plus the number of implicit queries to $\mathsf{H}(\cdot)$ made by the experiment.

It is well known that IND-CPA security of PKE with sufficiently large message space implies its OW-CPA security.

**Lemma 1.** *For any adversary* B *there exists an adversary* A *with the same running time as that of* B *such that* $\mathrm{Adv}_{\mathsf{PKE}}^{\mathsf{OW\text{-}PCA}}(\mathsf{B}) \leq \mathrm{Adv}_{\mathsf{PKE}}^{\mathsf{IND\text{-}CPA}}(\mathsf{A}) + 1/|\mathcal{M}|$.

### 2.2 Key Encapsulation

SYNTAX. A key encapsulation mechanism $\mathsf{KEM} = (\mathsf{Gen}, \mathsf{Encaps}, \mathsf{Decaps})$ consists of three algorithms. The key generation algorithm Gen outputs a key pair $(pk, sk)$, where $pk$ also defines a finite key space $\mathcal{K}$. The encapsulation algorithm Encaps, on input $pk$, outputs a tuple $(K, c)$ where $c$ is said to be an encapsulation of the key $K$ which is contained in key space $\mathcal{K}$. The deterministic decapsulation algorithm Decaps, on input $sk$ and an encapsulation $c$, outputs either a key $K := \mathsf{Decaps}(sk, c) \in \mathcal{K}$ or a special symbol $\perp \notin \mathcal{K}$ to indicate that $c$ is not a valid encapsulation. We call KEM $\delta$-*correct* if

$$\Pr\left[\mathsf{Decaps}(sk, c) \neq K \mid (pk, sk) \leftarrow \mathsf{Gen}; (K, c) \leftarrow \mathsf{Encaps}(pk)\right] \leq \delta.$$

Note that the above definition also makes sense in the random oracle model since KEM ciphertexts do not depend on messages.

SECURITY. We now define a security notion for key encapsulation: <u>In</u>distinguishability under <u>C</u>hosen <u>C</u>iphertext <u>A</u>ttacks (IND-CCA).

**Definition 3** *(IND-CCA). We define the* $\mathsf{IND\text{-}CCA}$ *game as in Fig. 4 and the* $\mathsf{IND\text{-}CCA}$ *advantage function of an adversary* A *(with binary output) against* KEM *as* $\mathrm{Adv}_{\mathsf{KEM}}^{\mathsf{IND\text{-}CCA}}(\mathsf{A}) := |\Pr[\mathsf{IND\text{-}CCA}^{\mathsf{A}} \Rightarrow 1] - 1/2|$ .

## 3 Modular FO Transformations

In Sect. 3.1, we will introduce T that transforms any OW-CPA secure encryption scheme PKE into a OW-PCA secure encryption scheme $\mathsf{PKE}_1$. If PKE is furthermore IND-CPA, then the reduction is tight. Furthermore, if PKE is $\gamma$-spread, then $\mathsf{PKE}_1$ even satisfied the stronger security notion of OW-PCVA security. Next, in Sect. 3.2, we will introduce transformations $\mathsf{U}^{\not\perp}$, $\mathsf{U}_m^{\not\perp}$

| GAME IND-CPA | GAME IND-CCA | DECAPS($c \neq c^*$) |
|---|---|---|
| 01 $(pk, sk) \leftarrow$ Gen | 07 $(pk, sk) \leftarrow$ Gen | 13 $K :=$ Decaps$(sk, c)$ |
| 02 $b \xleftarrow{\$} \{0, 1\}$ | 08 $b \xleftarrow{\$} \{0, 1\}$ | 14 **return** $K$ |
| 03 $(m_0^*, m_1^*, st) \leftarrow A_1(pk)$ | 09 $(K_0^*, c^*) \leftarrow$ Encaps$(pk)$ | |
| 04 $c^* \leftarrow$ Enc$(pk, m_b^*)$ | 10 $K_1^* \xleftarrow{\$} \mathcal{K}$ | |
| 05 $b' \leftarrow A_2(pk, c^*, st)$ | 11 $b' \leftarrow A^{\text{DECAPS}}(c^*, K_b^*)$ | |
| 06 **return** $[\![b' = b]\!]$ | 12 **return** $[\![b' = b]\!]$ | |

**Fig. 4.** Games IND-CPA for PKE and IND-CCA game for KEM.

($U^\perp$, $U_m^\perp$) that transform any OW-PCA (OW-PCVA) secure encryption scheme $\text{PKE}_1$ into an IND-CCA secure KEM. The security reduction is tight. Transformations $U_m^{\not\perp}$ and $U_m^\perp$ can only be applied for deterministic encryption schemes. Combining T with $\{U^{\not\perp}, U_m^{\not\perp}, U^\perp, U_m^\perp\}$, in Sect. 3.3 we provide concrete bounds for the IND-CCA security of the resulting KEMs. Finally, in Sect. 3.4 we introduce $S^\ell$ that transforms any OW-CPA secure scheme into an IND-CPA secure one, offering a tradeoff between tightness and ciphertext size.

### 3.1 Transformation T: From OW-CPA/IND-CPA to OW-PCVA

T transforms an OW-CPA secure public-key encryption scheme into an OW-PCA secure one.

THE CONSTRUCTION. To a public-key encryption scheme PKE = (Gen, Enc, Dec) with message space $\mathcal{M}$ and randomness space $\mathcal{R}$, and random oracle $G : \mathcal{M} \rightarrow \mathcal{R}$, we associate $\text{PKE}_1 = \text{T}[\text{PKE}, G]$. The algorithms of $\text{PKE}_1 = (\text{Gen}, \text{Enc}_1, \text{Dec}_1)$ are defined in Fig. 5. Note that $\text{Enc}_1$ deterministically computers the ciphertext as $c := \text{Enc}(pk, m; G(m))$.

| $\text{Enc}_1(pk, m)$ | $\text{Dec}_1(sk, c)$ |
|---|---|
| 01 $c := \text{Enc}(pk, m; G(m))$ | 03 $m' := \text{Dec}(sk, c)$. |
| 02 **return** $c$ | 04 **if** $m' = \perp$ **or** $\text{Enc}(pk, m'; G(m')) \neq c$ |
| | 05     **return** $\perp$ |
| | 06 **else return** $m'$ |

**Fig. 5.** OW-PCVA-secure encryption scheme $\text{PKE}_1 = \text{T}[\text{PKE}, G]$ with deterministic encryption.

NON-TIGHT SECURITY FROM OW-CPA. The following theorem establishes that OW-PCVA security of $\text{PKE}_1$ (cf. Definition 1) non-tightly reduces to the OW-CPA security of PKE, in the random oracle model, given that PKE is $\gamma$-spread (for sufficiently large $\gamma$). If PKE is not $\gamma$-spread, then $\text{PKE}_1$ is still OW-PCA secure.

**Theorem 1** (PKE OW-CPA $\overset{\text{ROM}}{\Rightarrow}$ PKE$_1$ OW-PCVA ). *If* PKE *is $\delta$-correct, then* PKE$_1$ *is $\delta_1$-correct in the random oracle model with $\delta_1(q_G) = q_G \cdot \delta$. Assume* PKE *to be $\gamma$-spread. Then, for any* OW-PCVA *adversary* B *that issues at most* $q_G$ *queries to the random oracle* G, $q_P$ *queries to a plaintext checking oracle* Pco, *and* $q_V$ *queries to a validity checking oracle* Cvo, *there exists an* OW-CPA *adversary* A *such that*

$$\mathrm{Adv}^{\mathsf{OW\text{-}PCVA}}_{\mathsf{PKE}_1}(\mathsf{B}) \leq q_G \cdot \delta + q_V \cdot 2^{-\gamma} + (q_G + 1) \cdot \mathrm{Adv}^{\mathsf{OW\text{-}CPA}}_{\mathsf{PKE}}(\mathsf{A})$$

*and the running time of* A *is about that of* B.

The main idea of the proof is that since Enc$_1$ is deterministic, the PCA$(\cdot, \cdot)$ oracle can be equivalently implemented by "re-encryption" and the Cvo$(\cdot)$ oracle by controlling the random oracles. Additional care has to be taken to account for the correctness error.

*Proof.* To prove correctness, consider an adversary A playing the correctness game COR-RO (Fig. 2) of PKE$_1$ in the random oracle model. Game COR-RO makes at most $q_G$ (distinct) queries $G(m_1), \ldots, G(m_{q_G})$ to G. We call such a query $G(m_i)$ *problematic* iff it exhibits a correctness error in PKE$_1$ (in the sense that $\mathsf{Dec}(sk, \mathsf{Enc}(pk, m_i; G(m_i))) \neq m_i$). Since G outputs independently random values, each $G(m_i)$ is problematic with probability at most $\delta$ (averaged over $(pk, sk)$), since we assumed that PKE is $\delta$-correct. Hence, a union bound shows that the probability that at least one $G(m_i)$ is problematic is at most $q_G \cdot \delta$. This proves $\Pr[\mathsf{COR\text{-}RO}^{\mathsf{A}} \Rightarrow 1] \leq q_G \cdot \delta$ and hence PKE$_1$ is $\delta_1$-correct with $\delta_1(q_G) = q_G \cdot \delta$.

To prove security, let B be an adversary against the OW-PCVA security of PKE$_1$, issuing at most $q_G$ queries to G, at most $q_P$ queries to Pco, and at most $q_V$ queries to Cvo. Consider the sequence of games given in Fig. 6.

GAME $G_0$. This is the original OW-PCVA game. Random oracle queries are stored in set $\mathfrak{L}_G$ with the convention that $G(m) = r$ iff $(m, r) \in \mathfrak{L}_G$. Hence,

$$\Pr[G_0^{\mathsf{B}} \Rightarrow 1] = \mathrm{Adv}^{\mathsf{OW\text{-}PCVA}}_{\mathsf{PKE}_1}(\mathsf{B}).$$

GAME $G_1$. In game $G_1$ the ciphertext validity oracle Cvo$(c \neq c^*)$ is replaced with one that first computes $m' = \mathsf{Dec}(sk, c)$ and returns 1 iff there exists a previous query $(m, r)$ to G such that $\mathsf{Enc}(pk, m; r) = c$ and $m = m'$.

Consider a single query Cvo$(c)$ and define $m' := \mathsf{Dec}(sk, c)$. If Cvo$(c) = 1$ in $G_1$, then $G(m') = G(m) = r$ and hence $\mathsf{Enc}(pk, m'; G(m')) = c$, meaning Cvo$(c) = 1$ in $G_0$. If Cvo$(c) = 1$ in $G_0$, then we can only have Cvo$(c) = 0$ in $G_1$ only if $G(m')$ was not queried before. This happens with probability $2^{-\gamma}$, where $\gamma$ is the parameter from the $\gamma$-spreadness of PKE. By the union bound we obtain

$$|\Pr[G_1^{\mathsf{B}} \Rightarrow 1] - \Pr[G_0^{\mathsf{B}} \Rightarrow 1]| \leq q_V \cdot 2^{-\gamma}.$$

GAME $G_2$. In game $G_2$ we replace the plaintext checking oracle Pco$(m, c)$ and the ciphertext validity oracle Cvo$(c)$ by a simulation that does not check whether $m = m'$ anymore, where $m' = \mathsf{Dec}(sk, c)$

```
GAMES G₀-G₃                              Pco(m ∈ M, c)
01  (pk, sk) ← Gen                       14  m' := Dec(sk, c)                        // G₀-G₁
02  m* ←$ M                              15  return ⟦m' = m⟧
03  c* ← Enc(pk, m*)                         and ⟦Enc(pk, m'; G(m')) = c⟧           // G₀-G₁
04  m' ← B^{G(·),Pco(·,·),Cvo(·)}(pk, c*) 16  return ⟦Enc(pk, m, G(m)) = c⟧         // G₂-G₃
05  return ⟦m' = m*⟧

G(m)                                     Cvo(c ≠ c*)
06  if ∃r s. th.(m, r) ∈ 𝔏_G             17  m' := Dec(sk, c)                        // G₀-G₁
07      return r                          18  return ⟦m' ∈ M⟧
08  if m = m*                     // G₃       and ⟦Enc(pk, m'; G(m')) = c⟧           // G₀
09      QUERY := true            // G₃   19  return ⟦∃(m, r) ∈ 𝔏_G
10      abort                    // G₃       and Enc(pk, m; r) = c and m' = m⟧       // G₁
11  r ←$ R                               20  return ⟦∃(m, r) ∈ 𝔏_G
12  𝔏_G := 𝔏_G ∪ {(m, r)}                    and Enc(pk, m; r) = c⟧                  // G₂-G₃
13  return r
```

Fig. 6. Games $G_0$-$G_3$ for the proof of Theorem 1.

We claim

$$|\Pr[G_2^B \Rightarrow 1] - \Pr[G_1^B \Rightarrow 1]| \leq q_G \cdot \delta. \tag{4}$$

To show Eq. (4), observe that the whole Game $G_1$ (and also the whole Game $G_2$) makes at most $q_G$ (distinct) queries $G(m_1), \ldots, G(m_{q_G})$ to $G$. Again, we call such a query $G(m_i)$ *problematic* iff it exhibits a correctness error in $PKE_1$ (in the sense that $Dec(sk, Enc(pk, m_i; G(m_i))) \neq m_i$). Clearly, if $B$ makes a problematic query, then there exists an adversary $F$ that wins the correctness game COR-RO in the random oracle model. Hence, the probability that at least one $G(m_i)$ is problematic is at most $\delta_1(q_G) \leq q_G \cdot \delta$.

However, conditioned on the event that no query $G(m_i)$ is problematic, Game $G_1$ and Game $G_2$ proceed identically (cf. Fig. 6). Indeed, the two games only differ if $B$ submits a Pco query $(m, c)$ or a Cvo query $c$ together with a $G$ query $m$ such that $G(m)$ is problematic and $c = Enc(pk, m; G(m))$. (In this case, $G_1$ will answer the query with 0, while $G_2$ will answer with 1.) This shows Eq. (4).

GAME $G_3$. In Game $G_3$, we add a flag QUERY in line 09 and abort when it is raised. Hence, $G_2$ and $G_3$ only differ if QUERY is raised, meaning that $B$ made a query $G$ on $m^*$, or, equivalently, $(m^*, \cdot) \in 𝔏_G$. Due to the difference lemma [37],

$$|\Pr[G_3^B \Rightarrow 1] - \Pr[G_2^B \Rightarrow 1]| \leq \Pr[QUERY].$$

We first bound $\Pr[G_3^B \Rightarrow 1]$ by constructing an adversary $C$ in Fig. 7 against the OW-CPA security of the original encryption scheme PKE. $C$ inputs $(pk, c^* \leftarrow Enc(pk, m^*))$ for random, unknown $m^*$, perfectly simulates game $G_3$ for $B$, and finally outputs $m' = m^*$ if $B$ wins in game $G_3$.

$$\Pr[G_3^B \Rightarrow 1] = Adv_{PKE}^{OW\text{-}CPA}(C).$$

| $C(pk, c^*)$ | $D(pk, c^*)$ |
|---|---|
| 01  $m' \leftarrow B^{G(\cdot), \text{Pco}(\cdot,\cdot)}(pk, c^*)$ | 03  $m \leftarrow B^{G(\cdot), \text{Pco}(\cdot,\cdot)}(pk, c^*)$ |
| 02  **return** $m'$ | 04  $(m', r') \xleftarrow{\$} \mathfrak{L}_G$ |
| | 05  **return** $m'$ |

**Fig. 7.** Adversaries C and D against OW-CPA for the proof of Theorem 1. Oracles Pco, Cvo are defined as in game $G_3$, and G is defined as in game $G_2$ of Fig. 6.

So far we have established the bound

$$\text{Adv}_{\text{PKE}_1}^{\text{OW-PCVA}}(B) \leq q_G \cdot \delta + q_V \cdot 2^{-\gamma} + \Pr[\text{QUERY}] + \text{Adv}_{\text{PKE}}^{\text{OW-CPA}}(C). \quad (5)$$

Finally, in Fig. 7 we construct an adversary D against the OW-CPA security of the original encryption scheme PKE, that inputs $(pk, c^* \leftarrow \text{Enc}(pk, m^*))$, perfectly simulates game $G_3$ for B. If flag QUERY is set in $G_3$ then there exists en entry $(m^*, \cdot) \in \mathfrak{L}_G$ and D returns the correct $m' = m^*$ with probability at most $1/q_G$. We just showed

$$\Pr[\text{QUERY}] \leq q_G \cdot \text{Adv}_{\text{PKE}}^{\text{OW-CPA}}(D).$$

Combining the latter bound with Eq. (5) and folding C and D into one single adversary A against OW-CPA yields the required bound of the theorem. □

By definition, OW-PCA security is OW-PCVA security with $q_V := 0$ queries to the validity checking oracle. Hence, the bound of Theorem 1 shows that $\text{PKE}_1$ is in particular OW-PCA secure, without requiring PKE to be $\gamma$-spread.

TIGHT SECURITY FROM IND-CPA. Whereas the reduction to OW-CPA security in Theorem 1 was non-tight, the following theorem establishes that OW-PCVA security of $\text{PKE}_1$ tightly reduces to IND-CPA security of PKE, in the random oracle model, given that PKE is $\gamma$-spread. If PKE is not $\gamma$-spread, then $\text{PKE}_1$ is still OW-PCA secure.

**Theorem 2** (PKE IND-CPA $\overset{\text{ROM}}{\Rightarrow}$ $\text{PKE}_1$ OW-PCVA). *Assume PKE to be $\delta$-correct and $\gamma$-spread. Then, for any OW-PCVA adversary B that issues at most $q_G$ queries to the random oracle G, $q_P$ queries to a plaintext checking oracle Pco, and $q_V$ queries to a validity checking oracle Cvo, there exists an IND-CPA adversary A such that*

$$\text{Adv}_{\text{PKE}_1}^{\text{OW-PCVA}}(B) \leq q_G \cdot \delta + q_V \cdot 2^{-\gamma} + \frac{2q_G + 1}{|\mathcal{M}|} + 3 \cdot \text{Adv}_{\text{PKE}}^{\text{IND-CPA}}(A)$$

*and the running time of A is about that of B.*

*Proof.* Considering the games of Fig. 6 from the proof of Theorem 1 we obtain by Eq. (5)

$$\text{Adv}_{\text{PKE}_1}^{\text{OW-PCVA}}(B) \leq q_G \cdot \delta + q_V \cdot 2^{-\gamma} + \Pr[\text{QUERY}] + \text{Adv}_{\text{PKE}}^{\text{OW-CPA}}(C)$$

$$\leq q_G \cdot \delta + q_V \cdot 2^{-\gamma} + \Pr[\text{QUERY}] + \frac{1}{|\mathcal{M}|} + \text{Adv}_{\text{PKE}}^{\text{IND-CPA}}(C),$$

| $D_1(pk)$ | $D_2(pk, c^*, st)$ |
|---|---|
| 06  $st := (m_0^*, m_1^*) \xleftarrow{\$} \mathcal{M}^2$ | 08  $m' \leftarrow B^{G(\cdot), Pco(\cdot), Cvo(\cdot)}(pk, c^*)$ |
| 07  **return** $st$ | 09  $b' := \begin{cases} 0 & \lvert \mathfrak{L}_G(m_0^*) \rvert > \lvert \mathfrak{L}_G(m_1^*) \rvert \\ 1 & \lvert \mathfrak{L}_G(m_1^*) \rvert < \lvert \mathfrak{L}_G(m_0^*) \rvert \\ \xleftarrow{\$} \{0,1\} & \text{otherwise} \end{cases}$ |
| | 10  **return** $b'$ |

**Fig. 8.** Adversary $D = (D_1, D_2)$ against IND-CPA for the proof of Theorem 2. For fixed $m \in \mathcal{M}$, $\mathfrak{L}_G(m)$ is the set of all $(m, r) \in \mathfrak{L}_G$. Oracles Pco, Cvo are defined as in game $G_3$, and G is defined as in game $G_2$ of Fig. 6.

where the last inequation uses Lemma 1.

In Fig. 8 we construct an adversary $D = (D_1, D_2)$ against the IND-CPA security of the original encryption scheme PKE that wins if flag QUERY is set in $G_3$. The first adversary $D_1$ picks two random messages $m_0^*, m_1^*$. The second adversary $D_2$ inputs $(pk, c^* \leftarrow \mathsf{Enc}(pk, m_b^*), st)$, for an unknown random bit $b$, and runs B on $(pk, c^*)$, simulating its view in game $G_3$. Note that by construction message $m_b^*$ is uniformly distributed.

Consider game IND-CPA$^D$ with random challenge bit $b$. Let BADG be the event that B queries random oracle G on $m_{1-b}^*$. Since $m_{1-b}^*$ is uniformly distributed and independent from B's view, we have $\Pr[\text{BADG}] \leq q_G/\lvert \mathcal{M} \rvert$. For the remainder of the proof we assume BADG did not happen, i.e. $\lvert \mathfrak{L}_G(m_{1-b}^*) \rvert = 0$.

If QUERY happens, then B queried the random oracle G on $m_b^*$, which implies $\lvert \mathfrak{L}_G(m_b^*) \rvert > 0 = \lvert \mathfrak{L}_G(m_{1-b}^*) \rvert$ and therefore $b = b'$. If QUERY does not happen, then B did not query random oracle G on $m_b^*$. Hence, $\lvert \mathfrak{L}_G(m_b^*) \rvert = \lvert \mathfrak{L}_G(m_{1-b}^*) \rvert = 0$ and $\Pr[b = b'] = 1/2$ since A picks a random bit $b'$. Overall, we have

$$\mathsf{Adv}_{\mathsf{PKE}}^{\mathsf{IND\text{-}CPA}}(D) + \frac{q_G}{\lvert \mathcal{M} \rvert} \geq \left\lvert \Pr[b = b'] - \frac{1}{2} \right\rvert$$

$$= \left\lvert \Pr[\text{QUERY}] + \frac{1}{2} \Pr[\neg \text{QUERY}] - \frac{1}{2} \right\rvert$$

$$= \frac{1}{2} \Pr[\text{QUERY}].$$

Folding C and D into one single IND-CPA adversary A yields the required bound of the theorem.

With the same argument as in Theorem 1, a tight reduction to OW-PCA security is implied without requiring PKE to be $\gamma$-spread.

### 3.2   Transformations $U^{\not\perp}$, $U_m^{\not\perp}$, $U^{\perp}$, $U_m^{\perp}$

In this section we introduce four variants of a transformation U, namely $U^{\not\perp}$, $U_m^{\not\perp}$, $U^{\perp}$, $U_m^{\perp}$, that convert a public-key encryption scheme PKE$_1$ into a key encapsulation mechanism KEM. Their differences are summarized in the following table.

| Transformation | Rejection of invalid ciphertexts | KEM key | $PKE_1$'s requirements |
|---|---|---|---|
| $U^{\not\perp}$ | implicit | $K = H(m, c)$ | OW-PCA |
| $U^{\perp}$ | explicit | $K = H(m, c)$ | OW-PCVA |
| $U_m^{\not\perp}$ | implicit | $K = H(m)$ | det. + OW-CPA |
| $U_m^{\perp}$ | explicit | $K = H(m)$ | det. + OW-VA |

**Transformation $U^{\perp}$ : From OW-PVCA to IND-CCA.** $U^{\perp}$ transforms an OW-PCVA secure public-key encryption scheme into an IND-CCA secure key encapsulation mechanism. The $\perp$ in $U^{\perp}$ means that decapsulation of an invalid ciphertext results in the rejection symbol $\perp$ ("explicit rejection").

THE CONSTRUCTION. To a public-key encryption scheme $PKE_1 = (Gen_1, Enc_1, Dec_1)$ with message space $\mathcal{M}$, and a hash function $H : \{0,1\}^* \rightarrow \{0,1\}^n$, we associate $KEM^{\perp} = U^{\perp}[PKE_1, H]$. The algorithms of $KEM^{\perp} = (Gen_1, Encaps, Decaps^{\perp})$ are defined in Fig. 9.

| $\underline{Encaps(pk)}$ | $\underline{Decaps^{\perp}(sk, c)}$ |
|---|---|
| 01 $m \xleftarrow{\$} \mathcal{M}$ | 05 $m' := Dec_1(sk, c)$ |
| 02 $c \leftarrow Enc_1(pk, m)$ | 06 **if** $m' = \perp$ **return** $\perp$ |
| 03 $K := H(m, c)$ | 07 **else return** |
| 04 **return** $(K, c)$ | $\quad K := H(m', c)$ |

**Fig. 9.** IND-CCA-secure key encapsulation mechanism $KEM^{\perp} = U^{\perp}[PKE_1, H]$.

SECURITY. The following theorem establishes that IND-CCA security of $KEM^{\perp}$ tightly reduces to the OW-PCVA security of $PKE_1$, in the random oracle model.

**Theorem 3** ($PKE_1$ OW-PCVA $\overset{ROM}{\Rightarrow}$ $KEM^{\perp}$ IND-CCA). *If $PKE_1$ is $\delta_1$-correct, so is $KEM^{\perp}$. For any IND-CCA adversary B against $KEM^{\perp}$, issuing at most $q_D$ queries to the decapsulation oracle $DECAPS^{\perp}$ and at most $q_H$ queries to the random oracle H, there exists an OW-PCVA adversary A against $PKE_1$ that makes at most $q_H$ queries both to the $PCO$ oracle and to the $CVO$ oracle such that*

$$Adv_{KEM^{\perp}}^{IND\text{-}CCA}(B) \leq Adv_{PKE_1}^{OW\text{-}PCVA}(A)$$

*and the running time of A is about that of B.*

The main idea of the proof is to simulate the decapsulation oracle without the secret-key. This can be done by answering decryption queries with a random key and then later patch the random oracle using the plaintext checking oracle $PCO(\cdot, \cdot)$ provided by the OW-PCVA game. Additionally, the ciphertext validity oracle $CVO(\cdot)$ is required to reject decapsulation queries with inconsistent ciphertexts.

```
GAMES G_0 - G_2                              H(m, c)
01  (pk, sk) ← Gen_1                          12  if ∃K such that (m, c, K) ∈ 𝔏_H
02  m* ←$ M                                   13      return K
03  c* ← Enc_1(pk, m*)                        14  K ←$ K
04  K_0* := H(m*, c*)                         15  if Dec_1(sk, c) = m               // G_1-G_2
05  K_1* ←$ {0, 1}^n                          16      if c = c*                     // G_2
06  b ←$ {0, 1}                               17          CHAL := true              // G_2
07  b' ← B^{DECAPS^⊥,H}(pk, c*, K_b*)         18          abort                     // G_2
08  return [[b' = b]]                         19  if ∃K' such that (c, K') ∈ 𝔏_D    // G_1-G_2
                                              20      K := K'                       // G_1-G_2
                                              21  else                              // G_1-G_2
                                              22      𝔏_D := 𝔏_D ∪ {(c, K)}          // G_1-G_2
                                              23  𝔏_H := 𝔏_H ∪ {(m, c, K)}
                                              24  return K

DECAPS^⊥(c ≠ c*)           // G_0    DECAPS^⊥(c ≠ c*)                              // G_1-G_2
09  m' := Dec_1(sk, c)               25  if ∃K s. th. (c, K) ∈ 𝔏_D
10  if m' = ⊥ return ⊥               26      return K
11  return K := H(m', c)            27  if Dec_1(sk, c) ∉ M
                                     28      return ⊥
                                     29  K ←$ K
                                     30  𝔏_D := 𝔏_D ∪ {(c, K)}
                                     31  return K
```

**Fig. 10.** Games $G_0$ - $G_2$ for the proof of Theorem 3.

*Proof.* It is easy to verify the correctness bound. Let B be an adversary against the IND-CCA security of KEM$^⊥$, issuing at most $q_D$ queries to DECAPS$^⊥$ and at most $q_H$ queries to H. Consider the games given in Fig. 10.

GAME $G_0$. Since game $G_0$ is the original IND-CCA game,

$$\left| \Pr[G_0^B \Rightarrow 1] - \frac{1}{2} \right| = \text{Adv}_{\text{KEM}^⊥}^{\text{IND-CCA}}(B).$$

GAME $G_1$. In game $G_1$, the oracles H and DECAPS$^⊥$ are modified such that they make no use of the secret key any longer except by testing if $\text{Dec}_1(sk', c) = m$ for given $(m, c)$ in line 15 and if $\text{Dec}_1(sk, c) \in M$ for given $c$ in line 27. Game $G_1$ contains two sets: hash list $\mathfrak{L}_H$ that contains all entries $(m, c, K)$ where H was queried on $(m, c)$, and set $\mathfrak{L}_D$ that contains all entries $(c, K)$ where either H was queried on $(m', c)$, $m' := \text{Dec}_1(sk', c)$, or DECAPS$^⊥$ was queried on $c$. In order to show that the view of B is identical in games $G_0$ and $G_1$, consider the following cases for a fixed ciphertext $c$ and $m' := \text{Dec}_1(sk', c)$.

– Case 1: $m' \notin M$. Since $\text{Cvo}(c) = 0$ is equivalent to $m' = ⊥$, DECAPS$^⊥(c)$ returns $⊥$ as in both games.
– Case 2: $m' \in M$. We will now show that H in game $G_1$ is "patched", meaning that it is ensures DECAPS$^⊥(c) = H(m', c)$, where $m' := \text{Dec}_1(sk, c)$, for all

ciphertexts $c$ with $m' \in \mathcal{M}$. We distinguish two sub-cases: B might either first query H on $(m', c)$, then DECAPS$^{\perp}$ on $c$, or the other way round.

- If H is queried on $(m', c)$ first, it is recognized that $\mathsf{Dec}_1(sk, c) = m$ in line 15. Since DECAPS was not yet queried on $c$, no entry of the form $(c, K)$ can already exist in $\mathfrak{L}_D$. Therefore, besides adding $(m, c, K \xleftarrow{\$} \mathcal{K})$ to $\mathfrak{L}_H$, H also adds $(c, K)$ to $\mathfrak{L}_D$ in line 22, thereby defining DECAPS$^{\perp}(c) := K = \mathsf{H}(m', c)$.

- If DECAPS$^{\perp}$ is queried on $c$ first, no entry of the form $(c, K)$ exists in $\mathfrak{L}_D$ yet. Therefore, DECAPS$^{\perp}$ adds $(c, K \xleftarrow{\$} \mathcal{K})$ to $\mathfrak{L}_D$, thereby defining DECAPS$^{\perp}(c) := K$. When queried on $(m', c)$ afterwards, H recognizes that $\mathsf{Dec}_1(sk, c) = m'$ in line 15 and that an entry of the form $(c, K)$ already exists in $\mathfrak{L}_D$ in line 19. By adding $(m, c, K)$ to $\mathfrak{L}_H$ and returning $K$, H defines $\mathsf{H}(m', c) := K = $ DECAPS$^{\perp}(c)$.

We have shown that B's view is identical in both games and

$$\Pr[G_1^{\mathsf{B}} \Rightarrow 1] = \Pr[G_0^{\mathsf{B}} \Rightarrow 1]|.$$

GAME $G_2$. From game $G_2$ on we proceed identical to the proof of Theorem 4. That is, we abort immediately on the event that B queries H on $(m^*, c^*)$. Denote this event as CHAL. Due to the difference lemma,

$$|\Pr[G_2^{\mathsf{B}} \Rightarrow 1] - \Pr[G_1^{\mathsf{B}} \Rightarrow 1]| \leq \Pr[\text{CHAL}].$$

In game $G_2$, $\mathsf{H}(m^*, c^*)$ will not be given to B; neither through a hash nor a decryption query, meaning bit $b$ is independent from B's view. Hence,

$$\Pr[G_2^{\mathsf{B}}] = \frac{1}{2}.$$

It remains to bound $\Pr[\text{CHAL}]$. To this end, we construct an adversary A against the OW-PCVA security of $\mathsf{PKE}_1$ simulating $G_2$ for B as in Fig. 11. Note that the simulation is perfect. Since CHAL implies that B queried $\mathsf{H}(m^*, c^*)$ which implies $(m^*, c^*, K') \in \mathfrak{L}_H$ for some $K'$, and A returns $m' = m^*$. Hence,

$$\Pr[\text{CHAL}] = \mathrm{Adv}_{\mathsf{PKE}}^{\mathsf{OW\text{-}PCVA}}(\mathsf{A}).$$

Collecting the probabilities yields the required bound.

**Transformation $\mathsf{U}^{\not\perp}$ : From OW-PCA to IND-CCA.** $\mathsf{U}^{\not\perp}$ is a variant of $\mathsf{U}^{\perp}$ with "implicit rejection" of inconsistent ciphertexts. It transforms an OW-PCA secure public-key encryption scheme into an IND-CCA secure key encapsulation mechanism.

THE CONSTRUCTION. To a public-key encryption scheme $\mathsf{PKE}_1 = (\mathsf{Gen}_1, \mathsf{Enc}_1, \mathsf{Dec}_1)$ with message space $\mathcal{M}$, and a random oracle $\mathsf{H} : \{0,1\}^* \rightarrow \mathcal{M}$ we associate $\mathsf{KEM}^{\not\perp} = \mathsf{U}^{\not\perp}[\mathsf{PKE}_1, \mathsf{H}] = (\mathsf{Gen}^{\not\perp}, \mathsf{Encaps}, \mathsf{Decaps}^{\not\perp})$. The algorithms of $\mathsf{KEM}^{\not\perp}$ are

| $\mathsf{A}^{\mathrm{Pco}(\cdot,\cdot)}(pk, c^*)$ | $\mathsf{H}(m, c)$ |
|---|---|
| 01 $K^* \xleftarrow{\$} \mathcal{K}$ | 07 **if** $\exists K$ such that $(m, c, K) \in \mathfrak{L}_H$ |
| 02 $b' \leftarrow \mathsf{B}^{\mathrm{Decaps}^\perp(\cdot),\mathsf{H}(\cdot,\cdot)}(pk, c^*, K^*)$ | 08     **return** $K$ |
| 03 **if** $\exists(m', c', K') \in \mathfrak{L}_H$ | 09 $K \xleftarrow{\$} \mathcal{K}$ |
|     s. th. $\mathrm{Pco}(m', c^*) = 1$ | 10 **if** $\mathrm{Pco}(m, c) = 1$ |
| 04     **return** $m'$ | 11     **if** $\exists K'$ such that $(c, K') \in \mathfrak{L}_D$ |
| 05 **else** | 12         $K := K'$ |
| 06     **abort** | 13     **else** |
| | 14         $\mathfrak{L}_D := \mathfrak{L}_D \cup \{(c, K)\}$ |
| | 15 $\mathfrak{L}_H := \mathfrak{L}_H \cup \{(m, c, K)\}$ |
| | 16 **return** $K$ |

**Fig. 11.** Adversary A against OW-PCVA for the proof of Theorem 3, where $\mathrm{Decaps}^\perp$ is defined as in Game $G_2$ of Fig. 10.

| $\mathsf{Gen}^{\cancel{\perp}}$ | $\mathsf{Encaps}(pk)$ | $\mathsf{Decaps}^{\cancel{\perp}}(sk, c)$ |
|---|---|---|
| 01 $(pk', sk') \leftarrow \mathsf{Gen}_1$ | 05 $m \xleftarrow{\$} \mathcal{M}$ | 09 Parse $sk = (sk', s)$ |
| 02 $s \xleftarrow{\$} \mathcal{M}$ | 06 $c \leftarrow \mathsf{Enc}_1(pk, m)$ | 10 $m' := \mathsf{Dec}_1(sk', c)$ |
| 03 $sk := (sk', s)$ | 07 $K := \mathsf{H}(m, c)$ | 11 **if** $m' \neq \perp$ |
| 04 **return** $(pk', sk)$ | 08 **return** $(K, c)$ | 12     **return** $K := \mathsf{H}(m', c)$ |
| | | 13 **else return** $K := \mathsf{H}(s, c)$ |

**Fig. 12.** IND-CCA-secure key encapsulation mechanism $\mathsf{KEM}^{\cancel{\perp}} = \mathsf{U}^{\cancel{\perp}}[\mathsf{PKE}_1, \mathsf{H}]$.

defined in Fig. 12, Encaps is the same as in $\mathsf{KEM}^\perp$ (Fig. 9). Note that $\mathsf{U}^\perp$ and $\mathsf{U}^{\cancel{\perp}}$ essentially differ in decapsulation: $\mathsf{Decaps}^\perp$ from $\mathsf{U}^\perp$ rejects if $c$ decrypts to $\perp$, whereas $\mathsf{Decaps}^{\cancel{\perp}}$ from $\mathsf{U}^{\cancel{\perp}}$ returns a pseudorandom key $K$.

SECURITY. The following theorem establishes that IND-CCA security of $\mathsf{KEM}^{\cancel{\perp}}$ tightly reduces to the OW-PCA security of $\mathsf{PKE}_1$, in the random oracle model.

**Theorem 4** ($\mathsf{PKE}_1$ OW-PCA $\overset{\mathrm{ROM}}{\Rightarrow}$ $\mathsf{KEM}$ IND-CCA). *If* $\mathsf{PKE}_1$ *is* $\delta_1$*-correct, then* $\mathsf{KEM}^{\cancel{\perp}}$ *is* $\delta_1$*-correct in the random oracle model. For any* IND-CCA *adversary* B *against* $\mathsf{KEM}^{\cancel{\perp}}$, *issuing at most* $q_D$ *queries to the decapsulation oracle* $\mathrm{Decaps}^{\cancel{\perp}}$ *and at most* $q_H$ *queries to the random oracle* H, *there exists an* OW-PCA *adversary* A *against* $\mathsf{PKE}_1$ *that makes at most* $q_H$ *queries to the* Pco *oracle such that*

$$\mathrm{Adv}^{\mathrm{IND\text{-}CCA}}_{\mathsf{KEM}^{\cancel{\perp}}}(\mathsf{B}) \leq \frac{q_H}{|\mathcal{M}|} + \mathrm{Adv}^{\mathrm{OW\text{-}PCA}}_{\mathsf{PKE}_1}(\mathsf{A})$$

*and the running time of* A *is about that of* B.

The proof is very similar to the one of Theorem 3. The only difference is the handling of decapsulation queries with inconsistent ciphertexts. Hence, we defer the proof to the full version [26].

**Transformations $U^{\not\perp_m}/U^{\perp_m}$ : From OW-CPA/OW-VA to IND-CCA for deterministic Encryption.** Transformation $U_m^\perp$ is a variant of $U^\perp$ that derives the KEM key as $K = H(m)$, instead of $K = H(m, c)$. It transforms a OW-VA secure public-key encryption scheme with deterministic encryption (e.g., the ones obtained via T from Sect. 3.1) into an IND-CCA secure key encapsulation mechanism. We also consider an implicit rejection variant $U_m^{\not\perp}$ that only requires OW-CPA security of the underlying encryption scheme PKE.

THE CONSTRUCTION. To a public-key encryption scheme $PKE_1 = (Gen_1, Enc_1, Dec_1)$ with message space $\mathcal{M}$, and a random oracle $H : \{0,1\}^* \rightarrow \{0,1\}^n$, we associate $KEM_m^{\not\perp} = U_m^{\not\perp}[PKE_1, H] = (Gen^{\not\perp}, Encaps_m, Decaps_m^{\not\perp})$ and $KEM_m^\perp = U_m^\perp[PKE_1, H] = (Gen_1, Encaps_m, Decaps_m^\perp)$. Algorithm $Gen^{\not\perp}$ is given in Fig. 12 and the remaining algorithms of $KEM_m^{\not\perp}$ and $KEM_m^\perp$ are defined in Fig. 13.

| $Encaps_m(pk)$ | $Decaps_m^{\not\perp}(sk, c)$ | $Decaps_m^\perp(sk, c)$ |
|---|---|---|
| 01 $m \xleftarrow{\$} \mathcal{M}$ | 05 Parse $sk = (sk', s)$ | 10 $m' := Dec_1(sk, c)$ |
| 02 $c := Enc_1(pk, m)$ | 06 $m' := Dec_1(sk', c)$ | 11 if $m' = \perp$ return $\perp$ |
| 03 $K := H(m)$ | 07 if $m' \neq \perp$ | 12 else return |
| 04 return $(K, c)$ | 08 $\quad$ return $K := H(m')$ | $\quad K := H(m')$ |
| | 09 else return $K := H(s, c)$ | |

**Fig. 13.** IND-CCA-secure key encapsulation mechanisms $KEM_m^{\not\perp} = U_m^{\not\perp}[PKE_1, H]$ and $KEM_m^\perp = U_m^\perp[PKE_1, H]$.

SECURITY OF $KEM_m^\perp$. The following theorem establishes that IND-CCA security of $KEM_m^\perp$ tightly reduces to the OW-VA security of $PKE_1$, in the random oracle model. Again, the proof is similar to the one of Theorem 3 and can be found in [26].

**Theorem 5 ($PKE_1$ OW-VA $\overset{ROM}{\Rightarrow}$ $KEM_m^\perp$ IND-CCA).** If $PKE_1$ is $\delta_1$-correct, then so is $KEM_m^\perp$. Let $G$ denote the random oracle that $PKE_1$ uses (if any), and let $q_{Enc_1, G}$ and $q_{Dec_1, G}$ denote an upper bound on the number of $G$-queries that $Enc_1$, resp. $Dec_1$ makes upon a single invocation. If $Enc_1$ is deterministic then, for any IND-CCA adversary $B$ against $KEM_m^\perp$, issuing at most $q_D$ queries to the decapsulation oracle $\text{DECAPS}_m^\perp$ and at most $q_G$, resp. $q_H$ queries to its random oracles $G$ and $H$, there exists an OW-VA adversary $A$ against $PKE_1$ that makes at most $q_D$ queries to the $\text{CVO}$ oracle such that

$$\text{Adv}_{KEM_m^\perp}^{IND\text{-}CCA}(B) \leq \text{Adv}_{PKE_1}^{OW\text{-}VA}(A) + \delta_1(q_G + (q_H + q_D)(q_{Enc_1, G} + q_{Dec_1, G}))$$

and the running time of $A$ is about that of $B$.

SECURITY OF $KEM_m^{\not\perp}$. The following theorem establishes that IND-CCA security of $KEM_m^{\not\perp}$ tightly reduces to the OW-CPA security of $PKE_1$, in the random oracle model. Its proof is easily obtained by combining the proofs of Theorems 4 and 5.

**Theorem 6** (PKE$_1$ OW-CPA $\overset{\text{ROM}}{\Rightarrow}$ KEM$_m^{\not{\perp}}$ IND-CCA). *If* PKE$_1$ *is* $\delta_1$-*correct, then so is* KEM$_m^{\not{\perp}}$. *Let* G *denote the random oracle that* PKE$_1$ *uses (if any), and let* $q_{\text{Enc}_1,\text{G}}$ *and* $q_{\text{Dec}_1,\text{G}}$ *denote an upper bound on the number of* G-*queries that* Enc$_1$, *resp.* Dec$_1$ *makes upon a single invocation. If* Enc$_1$ *is deterministic then, for any* IND-CCA *adversary* B *against* KEM$_m^{\not{\perp}}$, *issuing at most* $q_D$ *queries to the decapsulation oracle* DECAPS$_m^{\not{\perp}}$ *and at most* $q_G$, *resp.* $q_H$ *queries to its random oracles* G *and* H, *there exists an* OW-CPA *adversary* A *against* PKE$_1$ *such that*

$$\text{Adv}_{\text{KEM}_m^{\not{\perp}}}^{\text{IND-CCA}}(\text{B}) \leq \text{Adv}_{\text{PKE}_1}^{\text{OW-CPA}}(\text{A}) + \frac{q_D}{|\mathcal{M}|} + \delta_1(q_G + (q_H + q_D)(q_{\text{Enc}_1,\text{G}} + q_{\text{Dec}_1,\text{G}}))$$

*and the running time of* A *is about that of* B.

### 3.3   The Resulting KEMs

For completeness, we combine transformation T with $\{U^{\not{\perp}}, U^{\perp}, U_m^{\not{\perp}}, U_m^{\perp}\}$ from the previous sections to obtain four variants of the FO transformation FO $:= U^{\not{\perp}} \circ T$, FO$^{\perp} := U^{\perp} \circ T$, FO$_m^{\not{\perp}} := U_m^{\not{\perp}} \circ T$, and FO$_m^{\perp} := U_m^{\perp} \circ T$. To a public-key encryption scheme PKE = (Gen, Enc, Dec) with message space $\mathcal{M}$ and randomness space $\mathcal{R}$, and hash functions G $: \mathcal{M} \to \mathcal{R}$, H $: \{0,1\}^* \to \{0,1\}^n$ we associate

$$\text{KEM}^{\not{\perp}} = \text{FO}^{\not{\perp}}[\text{PKE}, \text{G}, \text{H}] := U^{\not{\perp}}[\text{T}[\text{PKE}, \text{G}], \text{H}] = (\text{Gen}^{\not{\perp}}, \text{Encaps}, \text{Decaps}^{\not{\perp}})$$
$$\text{KEM}^{\perp} = \text{FO}^{\perp}[\text{PKE}, \text{G}, \text{H}] := U^{\perp}[\text{T}[\text{PKE}, \text{G}], \text{H}] = (\text{Gen}, \text{Encaps}, \text{Decaps}^{\perp})$$
$$\text{KEM}_m^{\not{\perp}} = \text{FO}_m^{\not{\perp}}[\text{PKE}, \text{G}, \text{H}] := U_m^{\not{\perp}}[\text{T}[\text{PKE}, \text{G}], \text{H}] = (\text{Gen}^{\not{\perp}}, \text{Encaps}_m, \text{Decaps}_m^{\not{\perp}})$$
$$\text{KEM}_m^{\perp} = \text{FO}_m^{\perp}[\text{PKE}, \text{G}, \text{H}] := U_m^{\perp}[\text{T}[\text{PKE}, \text{G}], \text{H}] = (\text{Gen}, \text{Encaps}_m, \text{Decaps}_m^{\perp}) .$$

Their constituting algorithms are given in Fig. 14.

The following table provides (simplified) concrete bounds of the IND-CCA security of KEM $\in \{\text{KEM}^{\not{\perp}}, \text{KEM}^{\perp}, \text{KEM}_m^{\not{\perp}}, \text{KEM}_m^{\perp}\}$, directly obtained by combining Theorems 1−6. Here $q_{\text{RO}} := q_G + q_H$ counts the total number of B's queries

---

| $\underline{\text{Gen}^{\not{\perp}}}$ | $\underline{\text{Encaps}(pk)}$ $\boxed{\text{Encaps}_m(pk)}$ |
|---|---|
| 01 $(pk, sk) \leftarrow \text{Gen}$ | 09 $m \overset{\$}{\leftarrow} \mathcal{M}$ |
| 02 $s \overset{\$}{\leftarrow} \mathcal{M}$ | 10 $c := \text{Enc}(pk, m; \text{G}(m))$ |
| 03 $sk' := (sk, s)$ | 11 $K := \text{H}(m, c)$ $\boxed{K := \text{H}(m)}$ |
| 04 **return** $(pk, sk')$ | 12 **return** $(K, c)$ |
| | |
| $\underline{\text{Decaps}^{\perp}(sk, c)}$ $\boxed{\text{Decaps}_m^{\perp}(sk, c)}$ | $\underline{\text{Decaps}^{\not{\perp}}(sk' = (sk, s), c)}$ $\boxed{\text{Decaps}_m^{\not{\perp}}(sk'(sk, s), c)}$ |
| 05 $m' := \text{Dec}(sk, c)$ | 13 $m' := \text{Dec}(sk, c)$ |
| 06 **if** $c \neq \text{Enc}(pk, m'; \text{G}(m'))$ or $m' = \perp$ | 14 **if** $c \neq \text{Enc}(pk, m'; \text{G}(m'))$ or $m' = \perp$ |
| 07    **return** $\perp$ | 15    **return** $K := \text{H}(s, c)$ $\boxed{K := \text{H}(m')}$ |
| 08 **else return** $K := \text{H}(m', c)$ $\boxed{K := \text{H}(m')}$ | 16 **else return** $K := \text{H}(m', c)$ $\boxed{K := \text{H}(m')}$ |

**Fig. 14.** IND-CCA secure Key Encapsulation Mechanisms KEM$^{\not{\perp}}$ = (Gen$^{\not{\perp}}$, Encaps, Decaps$^{\not{\perp}}$), KEM$^{\perp}$ = (Gen, Encaps, Decaps$^{\perp}$), KEM$_m^{\not{\perp}}$ = (Gen$^{\not{\perp}}$, Encaps$_m$, Decaps$_m^{\not{\perp}}$), and KEM$_m^{\perp}$ = (Gen, Encaps$_m$, Decaps$_m^{\perp}$) obtained from PKE = (Gen, Enc, Dec).

to the random oracles G and H and $q_D$ counts the number of B's decryption queries. The left column provides the bounds relative to the OW-CPA advantage, the right column relative to the IND-CPA advantage.

| KEM | Concrete bounds on $Adv^{IND-CCA}_{KEM}(B) \leq$ | |
|---|---|---|
| $KEM^{\not\perp}$ | $q_{RO} \cdot \delta + \frac{2q_{RO}}{|\mathcal{M}|} + 2q_{RO} \cdot Adv^{OW-CPA}_{PKE}(A)$ | $q_{RO} \cdot \delta + \frac{3q_{RO}}{|\mathcal{M}|} + 3 \cdot Adv^{IND-CPA}_{PKE}(A')$ |
| $KEM^{\perp}$ | $q_{RO} \cdot (\delta + 2^{-\gamma}) + 2q_{RO} \cdot Adv^{OW-CPA}_{PKE}(A)$ | $q_{RO} \cdot \left(\delta + 2^{-\gamma}\right) + \frac{3q_{RO}}{|\mathcal{M}|} + 3 \cdot Adv^{IND-CPA}_{PKE}(A')$ |
| $KEM^{\not\perp}_m$ | $(2q_{RO} + q_D) \cdot \delta + \frac{2q_{RO}}{|\mathcal{M}|} + 2q_{RO} \cdot Adv^{OW-CPA}_{PKE}(A)$ | $(2q_{RO} + q_D) \cdot \delta + \frac{3q_{RO}}{|\mathcal{M}|} + 3 \cdot Adv^{IND-CPA}_{PKE}(A')$ |
| $KEM^{\perp}_m$ | $(2q_{RO} + q_D) \cdot \delta + q_{RO} \cdot 2^{-\gamma} + 2q_{RO} \cdot Adv^{OW-CPA}_{PKE}(A)$ | $(2q_{RO} + q_D) \cdot \delta + q_{RO} \cdot 2^{-\gamma} + 3 \cdot Adv^{IND-CPA}_{PKE}(A')$ |

CONCRETE PARAMETERS. For "$\kappa$ bits of security" one generally requires that for all adversaries B with advantage $Adv(B)$ and running in time $Time(B)$, we have

$$\frac{Time(B)}{Adv(B)} \geq 2^{\kappa}.$$

The table below gives recommendations for the information-theoretic terms $\delta$ (correctness error of PKE, $\gamma$ ($\gamma$-spreadness of PKE), and $\mathcal{M}$ (message space of PKE) appearing in the concrete security bounds above.

| Term in concrete bound | Minimal requirement for $\kappa$ bits security |
|---|---|
| $q_{RO} \cdot \delta$ | $\delta \leq 2^{-\kappa}$ |
| $q_{RO} \cdot 2^{-\gamma}$ | $\gamma \geq \kappa$ |
| $q_{RO}/|\mathcal{M}|$ | $|\mathcal{M}| \geq 2^{\kappa}$ |

For example, if the concrete security bound contains the term $q_{RO} \cdot \delta$, then with $\delta \leq 2^{-\kappa}$ one has

$$\frac{Time(B)}{Adv(B)} \geq \frac{q_{RO}}{q_{RO} \cdot \delta} = \frac{1}{\delta} \geq 2^{\kappa},$$

as required for $\kappa$ bits security.

## 3.4   $S^{\ell}$: From OW-CPA to IND-CPA Security, Tightly

$S^{\ell}$ transforms an OW-CPA secure public-key encryption scheme into an IND-CPA secure scheme. The security reduction has a parameter $\ell$ which allows for a trade-off between the security loss of the reduction and the compactness of ciphertexts.

THE CONSTRUCTION. Fix an $\ell \in \mathbb{N}$. To a public-key encryption scheme PKE = (Gen, Enc, Dec) with message space $\mathcal{M} = \{0,1\}^n$ and a hash function $F : \mathcal{M}^{\ell} \to \mathcal{R}$, we associate $PKE_{\ell} = S^{\ell}[PKE, F]$. The algorithms of $PKE_{\ell}$ are defined in Fig. 15.

SECURITY. The following theorem shows that $PKE_{\ell}$ is IND-CPA secure, provided that PKE is OW-CPA secure. The proof (sketched in the introduction) is postponed to [26].

| $\mathsf{Enc}_\ell(pk, m)$ | $\mathsf{Dec}_\ell(sk, c = (c_0, \ldots, c_\ell))$ |
|---|---|
| 01 $\mathbf{x} := (x_1, \ldots, x_\ell) \xleftarrow{\$} (\{0,1\}^n)^\ell$ | 06 **for** $i = 1$ **to** $\ell$ **do** |
| 02 $c_0 := m \oplus \mathsf{F}(\mathbf{x})$ | 07 $\quad x_i := \mathsf{Dec}(sk, c_i)$ |
| 03 **for** $i = 1$ **to** $\ell$ **do** | 08 $\mathbf{x} := (x_1, \ldots, x_\ell)$ |
| 04 $\quad c_i := \mathsf{Enc}(pk, x_i)$ | 09 **return** $c_0 \oplus \mathsf{F}(\mathbf{x})$ |
| 05 **return** $c := (c_0, \ldots, c_\ell)$ | |

**Fig. 15.** Tightly IND-CPA secure encryption $\mathsf{PKE}_\ell$ obtained from PKE.

**Theorem 7** (PKE OW-CPA $\Rightarrow$ $\mathsf{PKE}_\ell$ IND-CPA). *If* PKE *is $\delta$-correct (in the ROM), then $\mathsf{PKE}_\ell$ is $\ell \cdot \delta$-correct. Moreover, for any* IND-CPA *adversary* B *that issues at most* $q_\mathsf{F}$ *queries to random oracle* F, *there exists an* OW-CPA *adversary* A *such that*

$$\mathrm{Adv}_{\mathsf{PKE}_\ell}^{\mathsf{IND\text{-}CPA}}(\mathsf{B}) \leq q_\mathsf{F}^{1/\ell} \cdot \mathrm{Adv}_{\mathsf{PKE}}^{\mathsf{OW\text{-}CPA}}(\mathsf{A})$$

*and the running time of* A *is about that of* B.

# 4    Modular FO Transformation in the QROM

In this section, we will revisit our transformations in the quantum random oracle model. In Sect. 4.1, we give a short primer on quantum computation and define the quantum random oracle model (QROM). In Sect. 4.2, we will state that transformation T from Fig. 5 (Sect. 3.1) is also secure in the quantum random oracle model. Next, in Sect. 4.3 we will introduce $\mathsf{QU}_m^\perp$ ($\mathsf{QU}_m^{\not\perp}$), a variant of $\mathsf{U}_m^\perp$ ($\mathsf{U}_m^{\not\perp}$), which has provable security in the quantum random oracle model. Combining the two above transformations, in Sect. 4.4 we provide concrete bounds for the IND-CCA security of $\mathsf{QKEM}_m^\perp = \mathsf{QFO}_m^\perp[\mathsf{PKE}, \mathsf{G}, \mathsf{H}, \mathsf{H}']$ and $\mathsf{QKEM}_m^{\not\perp} = \mathsf{QFO}_m^{\not\perp}[\mathsf{PKE}, \mathsf{G}, \mathsf{H}, \mathsf{H}']$ in the QROM.

## 4.1    Quantum Computation

QUBITS. For simplicity, we will treat a *qubit* as a vector $|b\rangle \in \mathbb{C}^2$, i.e., a linear combination $|b\rangle = \alpha \cdot |0\rangle + \beta \cdot |1\rangle$ of the two *basis states* (vectors) $|0\rangle$ and $|1\rangle$ with the additional requirement to the probability amplitudes $\alpha, \beta \in \mathbb{C}$ that $|\alpha|^2 + |\beta|^2 = 1$. The basis $\{|0\rangle, |1\rangle\}$ is called *standard orthonormal computational basis*. The qubit $|b\rangle$ is said to be *in superposition*. Classical bits can be interpreted as quantum bits via the mapping $(b \mapsto 1 \cdot |b\rangle + 0 \cdot |1 - b\rangle)$.

QUANTUM REGISTERS. We will treat a quantum register as a collection of multiple qubits, i.e. a linear combination $\sum_{(b_1, \cdots, b_n) \in \{0,1\}^n} \alpha_{b_1 \cdots b_n} \cdot |b_1 \cdots b_n\rangle$, where $\alpha_{b_1, \cdots, b_n} \in \mathbb{C}^n$, with the additional restriction that $\sum_{(b_1, \cdots, b_n) \in \{0,1\}^n} |\alpha_{b_1 \cdots b_n}|^2 = 1$. As in the one-dimensional case, we call the basis $\{|b_1 \cdots b_n\rangle\}_{(b_1, \cdots, b_n) \in \{0,1\}^n}$ the *standard orthonormal computational basis*.

MEASUREMENTS. Qubits can be measured with respect to a basis. In this paper, we will only consider measurements in the standard orthonormal computational basis, and denote this measurement by $\text{MEASURE}(\cdot)$, where the outcome of $\text{MEASURE}(|b\rangle)$ is a single qubit $|b\rangle = \alpha \cdot |0\rangle + \beta \cdot |1\rangle$ will be $|0\rangle$ with probability $|\alpha|^2$ and $|1\rangle$ with probability $|\beta|^2$, and the outcome of measuring a qubit register $\sum\limits_{b_1,\cdots,b_n \in \{0,1\}} \alpha_{b_1\cdots b_n} \cdot |b_1 \cdots b_n\rangle$ will be $|b_1 \cdots b_n\rangle$ with probability $|\alpha_{b_1\cdots b_n}|^2$. Note that the amplitudes *collapse* during a measurement, this means that by measuring $\alpha \cdot |0\rangle + \beta \cdot |1\rangle$, $\alpha$ and $\beta$ are switched to one of the combinations in $\{\pm(1,0), \pm(0,1)\}$. Likewise, in the $n$-dimensional case, all amplitudes are switched to 0 except for the one that belongs to the measurement outcome and which will be switched to 1.

QUANTUM ORACLES AND QUANTUM ADVERSARIES. Following [5,11], we view a quantum oracle as a mapping

$$|x\rangle|y\rangle \mapsto |x\rangle|y \oplus \text{O}(x)\rangle,$$

where $\text{O} : \{0,1\}^n \to \{0,1\}^m$, $x \in \{0,1\}^n$ and $y \in \{0,1\}^m$, and model quantum adversaries A with access to O by the sequence $U \circ \text{O}$, where $U$ is a unitary operation. We write $\text{A}^{|\text{O}\rangle}$ to indicate that the oracles are quantum-accessible (contrary to oracles which can only process classical bits).

QUANTUM RANDOM ORACLE MODEL. We consider security games in the quantum random oracle model (QROM) as their counterparts in the classical random oracle model, with the difference that we consider quantum adversaries that are given **quantum** access to the random oracles involved, and **classical** access to all other oracles (e.g., plaintext checking or decapsulation oracles). Zhandry [41] proved that no quantum algorithm $\text{A}^{|f\rangle}$, issuing at most $q$ quantum queries to $|f\rangle$, can distinguish between a random function $f : \{0,1\}^m \to \{0,1\}^n$ and a $2q$-wise independent function. It allows us to view quantum random oracles as polynomials of sufficient large degree. That is, we define a quantum random oracle $|H\rangle$ as an oracle evaluating a random polynomial of degree $2q$ over the finite field $\mathbb{F}_{2^n}$.

CORRECTNESS OF PKE IN THE QROM. Similar to the classical random oracle model, we need to define correctness of encryption in the quantum random oracle model. If $\text{PKE} = \text{PKE}^\text{G}$ is defined relative to a random oracle $|G\rangle$, then again the correctness bound might depend on the number of queries to $|G\rangle$. We call a public-key encryption scheme PKE in the quantum random oracle model $\delta(q_\text{G})$-*correct* if for all (possibly unbounded, quantum) adversaries A making at most $q_\text{G}$ queries to quantum random oracle $|G\rangle$, $\Pr[\text{COR-QRO}_{\text{PKE}}^\text{A} \Rightarrow 1] \leq \delta(q_\text{G})$, where the correctness game COR-QRO is defined as in Fig. 16.

### 4.2   Transformation T: From **OW-CPA** to **OW-PCA** in the QROM

Recall transformation T from Fig. 5 of Sect. 3.1.

**Lemma 2.** *Assume* PKE *to be $\delta$-correct. Then* $\text{PKE}_1 = \text{T}[\text{PKE}, \text{G}]$ *is $\delta_1$-correct in the quantum random oracle model, where* $\delta_1 = \delta_1(q_\text{G}) \leq 8 \cdot (q_\text{G} + 1)^2 \cdot \delta$.

```
GAME COR-QRO:
10  (pk, sk) ← Gen
11  m ← A^{|G⟩}(sk, pk)
12  return [[Dec(sk, Enc(pk, m; G(m))) ≠ m]]
```

**Fig. 16.** Correctness game COR-QRO for $\mathsf{PKE}_1$ in the quantum random oracle model.

It can be shown that $\delta_1(q_\mathsf{G})$ can be upper bounded by the success probability of an (unbounded, quantum) adversary against a generic search problem. For more details, refer to the full version [26].

The following theorem (whose proof is loosely based on [38]) establishes that IND-PCA security of $\mathsf{PKE}_1$ reduces to the OW-CPA security of $\mathsf{PKE}$, in the quantum random oracle model.

**Theorem 8** (PKE OW-CPA $\overset{\mathrm{QROM}}{\Rightarrow}$ $\mathsf{PKE}_1$ OW-PCA). *Assume* $\mathsf{PKE}$ *to be* $\delta$-*correct. For any* OW-PCA *quantum adversary* B *that issues at most* $q_\mathsf{G}$ *queries to the quantum random oracle* $|\mathsf{G}⟩$ *and* $q_P$ *(classical) queries to the plaintext checking oracle* PCO, *there exists an* OW-CPA *quantum adversary* A *such that*

$$\mathrm{Adv}^{\mathsf{OW\text{-}PCA}}_{\mathsf{PKE}_1}(\mathsf{B}) \leq 8 \cdot \delta \cdot (q_\mathsf{G} + 1)^2 + (1 + 2q_\mathsf{G}) \cdot \sqrt{\mathrm{Adv}^{\mathsf{OW\text{-}CPA}}_{\mathsf{PKE}}(\mathsf{A})},$$

*and the running time of* A *is about that of* B.

Similar to the proof of Theorem 1, the proof first implements the PCA oracle via "re-encryption". Next, we apply an algorithmic adaption of OW2H from [39] to decouple the challenge ciphertext $c^* := \mathsf{Enc}(pk, m^*; \mathsf{G}(m^*))$ from the random oracle G. The decoupling allows for a reduction from OW-CPA security. Again, we defer to [26] for details.

## 4.3   Transformations $\mathsf{QU}^{\perp}_m$, $\mathsf{QU}^{\not\perp}_m$

**Transformation $\mathsf{QU}^{\perp}_m$: From OW-PCA to IND-CCA in the QROM.** $\mathsf{QU}^{\perp}_m$ transforms an OW-PCA secure public-key encryption scheme into an IND-CCA secure key encapsulation mechanism with explicit rejection.

THE CONSTRUCTION. To a public-key encryption scheme $\mathsf{PKE}_1 = (\mathsf{Gen}_1, \mathsf{Enc}_1, \mathsf{Dec}_1)$ with message space $\mathcal{M} = \{0,1\}^n$, and hash functions $\mathsf{H} : \{0,1\}^* \to \{0,1\}^n$ and $\mathsf{H}' : \{0,1\}^n \to \{0,1\}^n$, we associate $\mathsf{QKEM}^{\perp}_m = \mathsf{QU}^{\perp}_m[\mathsf{PKE}_1, \mathsf{H}, \mathsf{H}']$. The algorithms of $\mathsf{QKEM}^{\perp}_m = (\mathsf{QGen} := \mathsf{Gen}_1, \mathsf{QEncaps}_m, \mathsf{QDecaps}^{\perp}_m)$ are defined in Fig. 17. We stress that hash function $\mathsf{H}'$ has matching domain and range.

SECURITY. The following theorem (whose proof is again loosely based on [38] and is postponed to [26]) establishes that IND-CCA security of $\mathsf{QKEM}^{\perp}_m$ reduces to the OW-PCA security of $\mathsf{PKE}_1$, in the quantum random oracle model.

**Theorem 9** ($\mathsf{PKE}_1$ OW-PCA $\overset{\mathrm{QROM}}{\Rightarrow}$ $\mathsf{QKEM}^{\perp}_m$ IND-CCA). *If* $\mathsf{PKE}_1$ *is* $\delta_1$-*correct, so is* $\mathsf{QKEM}^{\perp}_m$. *For any* IND-CCA *quantum adversary* B *issuing at most* $q_D$ *(classical) queries to the decapsulation oracle* QDECAPS$^{\perp}_m$, *at most* $q_\mathsf{H}$ *queries to the*

| $\text{QEncaps}_m(pk)$ | $\text{QDecaps}_m^{\perp}(sk, c, d)$ |
|---|---|
| 01  $m \xleftarrow{\$} \mathcal{M}$ | 06  $m' := \text{Dec}_1(sk, c)$ |
| 02  $c \leftarrow \text{Enc}_1(pk, m)$ | 07  if $m' = \perp$ or $\text{H}'(m') \neq d$ |
| 03  $d := \text{H}'(m)$ | 08      return $\perp$ |
| 04  $K := \text{H}(m)$ | 09  else return $K := \text{H}(m')$ |
| 05  return $(K, c, d)$ | |

**Fig. 17.** IND-CCA-secure key encapsulation mechanism $\text{QKEM}_m^{\perp} = \text{QU}_m^{\perp}[\text{PKE}_1, \text{H}, \text{H}']$.

*quantum random oracle* $|\text{H}\rangle$ *and at most* $q_{\text{H}'}$ *queries to the quantum random oracle* $|\text{H}'\rangle$, *there exists an* OW-PCA *quantum adversary* A *issuing* $2q_D q_{\text{H}'}$ *queries to oracle* PCO *such that*

$$\text{Adv}_{\text{QKEM}_m^{\perp}}^{\text{IND-CCA}}(B) \leq (2q_{\text{H}'} + q_{\text{H}}) \cdot \sqrt{\text{Adv}_{\text{PKE}_1}^{\text{OW-PCA}}(A)},$$

*and the running time of* A *is about that of* B.

**Transformation $\text{QU}^{\not\perp}{}_m$: From OW-PCA to IND-CCA in the QROM.** $\text{QU}_m^{\not\perp}$ transforms an OW-PCA secure public-key encryption scheme into an IND-CCA secure key encapsulation mechanism with implicit rejection.

THE CONSTRUCTION. To a public-key encryption scheme $\text{PKE}_1 = (\text{Gen}_1, \text{Enc}_1, \text{Dec}_1)$ with message space $\mathcal{M} = \{0,1\}^n$, and hash functions $\text{H} : \{0,1\}^* \to \{0,1\}^n$ and $\text{H}' : \{0,1\}^n \to \{0,1\}^n$, we associate $\text{QKEM}_m^{\not\perp} = \text{QU}_m^{\not\perp}[\text{PKE}_1, \text{H}, \text{H}'] = (\text{QGen} := \text{Gen}^{\not\perp}, \text{QEncaps}_m, \text{QDecaps}_m^{\not\perp})$. Algorithm $\text{Gen}^{\not\perp}$ is given in Fig. 12 and the remaining algorithms of $\text{QKEM}_m^{\not\perp}$ are defined in Fig. 18. We stress again that hash function $\text{H}'$ has matching domain and range.

| $\text{QEncaps}_m(pk)$ | $\text{QDecaps}_m^{\not\perp}(sk' = (sk, s), c, d)$ |
|---|---|
| 01  $m \xleftarrow{\$} \mathcal{M}$ | 06  $m' := \text{Dec}_1(sk, c)$ |
| 02  $c \leftarrow \text{Enc}_1(pk, m)$ | 07  if $m' = \perp$ or $\text{H}'(m') \neq d$ |
| 03  $d := \text{H}'(m)$ | 08      return $K := \text{H}(s, c, d)$ |
| 04  $K := \text{H}(m)$ | 09  else return $K := \text{H}(m')$ |
| 05  return $(K, c, d)$ | |

**Fig. 18.** IND-CCA-secure key encapsulation mechanism $\text{QKEM}_m^{\not\perp} = \text{QU}_m^{\not\perp}[\text{PKE}_1, \text{H}, \text{H}']$.

SECURITY. The following theorem (whose proof is deferred to [26]) establishes that IND-CCA security of $\text{QKEM}_m^{\not\perp}$ reduces to the OW-PCA security of $\text{PKE}_1$, in the quantum random oracle model.

**Theorem 10** (PKE₁ OW-PCA $\overset{\text{QROM}}{\Longrightarrow}$ QKEM$_m^{\not\perp}$ IND-CCA). *If* $\text{PKE}_1$ *is* $\delta$-*correct, so is* $\text{QKEM}_m^{\not\perp}$. *For any* IND-CCA *quantum adversary* B *issuing at most* $q_D$ *(classical) queries to the decapsulation oracle* $\text{QDECAPS}_m^{\not\perp}$, *at most* $q_{\text{H}}$ *queries to the* quantum random oracle $|\mathsf{H}\rangle$ and at most $q_{\mathsf{H}'}$ queries to the quantum random oracle $|\mathsf{H}'\rangle$, there exists an OW-PCA quantum adversary A issuing $2q_Dq_{\mathsf{H}'}$ queries to oracle PCO such that

$$\mathrm{Adv}_{\mathsf{QKEM}_m^\perp}^{\mathsf{IND\text{-}CCA}}(\mathsf{B}) \le (2q_{\mathsf{H}'} + q_{\mathsf{H}}) \cdot \sqrt{\mathrm{Adv}_{\mathsf{PKE}_1}^{\mathsf{OW\text{-}PCA}}(\mathsf{A})},$$

and the running time of A is about that of B.

## 4.4   The Resulting KEMs

For concreteness, we combine transformations T and $\{\mathsf{QU}_m^\perp, \mathsf{QU}_m^{\not\perp}\}$ from the previous sections to obtain $\mathsf{QFO}_m^\perp = \mathsf{T} \circ \mathsf{QU}_m^\perp$ and $\mathsf{QFO}_m^{\not\perp} = \mathsf{T} \circ \mathsf{QU}_m^{\not\perp}$. To a public-key encryption scheme $\mathsf{PKE} = (\mathsf{Gen}, \mathsf{Enc}, \mathsf{Dec})$ with message space $\mathcal{M} = \{0,1\}^n$ and randomness space $\mathcal{R}$, and hash functions $\mathsf{G} : \mathcal{M} \to \mathcal{R}$, $\mathsf{H} : \{0,1\}^* \to \{0,1\}^n$ and $\mathsf{H}' : \{0,1\}^n \to \{0,1\}^n$, we associate

$$\begin{aligned}
\mathsf{QKEM}_m^\perp &= \mathsf{QFO}_m^\perp[\mathsf{PKE}, \mathsf{G}, \mathsf{H}, \mathsf{H}'] := \mathsf{QU}_m^\perp[\mathsf{T}[\mathsf{PKE}, \mathsf{G}], \mathsf{H}, \mathsf{H}'] \\
&= (\mathsf{Gen}, \mathsf{QEncaps}_m, \mathsf{QDecaps}_m^\perp) \\
\mathsf{QKEM}_m^{\not\perp} &= \mathsf{QFO}_m^{\not\perp}[\mathsf{PKE}, \mathsf{G}, \mathsf{H}, \mathsf{H}'] := \mathsf{QU}_m^{\not\perp}[\mathsf{T}[\mathsf{PKE}, \mathsf{G}], \mathsf{H}, \mathsf{H}'] \\
&= (\mathsf{Gen}^{\not\perp}, \mathsf{QEncaps}_m, \mathsf{QDecaps}_m^{\not\perp}).
\end{aligned}$$

Algorithm $\mathsf{Gen}^{\not\perp}$ is given in Fig. 12 and the remaining algorithms are given in Fig. 19.

| $\underline{\mathsf{QEncaps}_m(pk)}$ | $\underline{\mathsf{QDecaps}_m^\perp(sk, c, d)}$ |
|---|---|
| 01  $m \overset{\$}{\leftarrow} \mathcal{M}$ | 06  $m' := \mathsf{Dec}(sk, c)$ |
| 02  $c := \mathsf{Enc}(pk, m; \mathsf{G}(m))$ | 07  **if** $c = \mathsf{Enc}(pk, m', \mathsf{G}(m'))$ **and** $\mathsf{H}'(m') = d$ |
| 03  $K := \mathsf{H}(m)$ | 08      **return** $K := \mathsf{H}(m')$ |
| 04  $d := \mathsf{H}'(m)$ | 09  **else return** $\perp$ |
| 05  **return** $(K, c, d)$ | |
| | $\underline{\mathsf{QDecaps}_m^{\not\perp}(sk' = (sk, s), c, d)}$ |
| | 10  $m' := \mathsf{Dec}(sk, c)$ |
| | 11  **if** $c = \mathsf{Enc}(pk, m', \mathsf{G}(m'))$ **and** $\mathsf{H}'(m') = d$ |
| | 12      **return** $K := \mathsf{H}(m')$ |
| | 13  **else return** $K := \mathsf{H}(s, c, d)$ |

**Fig. 19.** IND-CCA secure $\mathsf{QKEM}_m^\perp$ and $\mathsf{QKEM}_m^{\not\perp}$ obtained from PKE.

The following table provides (simplified) concrete bounds of the IND-CCA security of $\mathsf{KEM} \in \{\mathsf{QKEM}_m^{\not\perp}, \mathsf{QKEM}_m^\perp\}$ in the quantum random oracle model, directly obtained by combining Theorems 8–10. Here $q_{\mathsf{RO}} := q_{\mathsf{G}} + q_{\mathsf{H}} + q_{\mathsf{H}}'$ counts the total number of (implicit and explicit) queries to the quantum random oracles G, H and H'.

| KEM | Concrete bound on $\mathrm{Adv}_{\mathsf{KEM}}^{\mathsf{IND\text{-}CCA}}(B) \leq$ |
|---|---|
| $\mathsf{QKEM}_m^{\not\perp}$, $\mathsf{QKEM}_m^{\perp}$ | $8q_{\mathsf{RO}}\sqrt{\delta \cdot q_{\mathsf{RO}}^2 + q_{\mathsf{RO}} \cdot \sqrt{\mathrm{Adv}_{\mathsf{PKE}}^{\mathsf{OW\text{-}CPA}}(A)}}$ |

**Acknowledgments.** We would like to thank Andreas Hülsing, Christian Schaffner, and Dominique Unruh for interesting discussions on the FO transformation in the QROM. We are also grateful to Krzysztof Pietrzak and Victor Shoup for discussions on Sect. 3.4. The first author was supported in part by ERC project PREP-CRYPTO (FP7/724307) and by DFG grants HO4534/4-1 and HO4534/2-2. The second author was supported by DFG RTG 1817/1 UbiCrypt. The third author was supported in part by ERC Project ERCC (FP7/615074) and by DFG SPP 1736 Big Data.

# References

1. Abdalla, M., Bellare, M., Rogaway, P.: The oracle Diffie-Hellman assumptions and an analysis of DHIES. In: Naccache, D. (ed.) CT-RSA 2001. LNCS, vol. 2020, pp. 143–158. Springer, Heidelberg (2001). https://doi.org/10.1007/3-540-45353-9_12

2. Albrecht, M.R., Orsini, E., Paterson, K.G., Peer, G., Smart, N.P.: Tightly secure Ring-LWE based key encapsulation with short ciphertexts. Cryptology ePrint Archive, Report 2017/354 (2017). http://eprint.iacr.org/2017/354

3. Alkim, E., Ducas, L., Pöppelmann, T., Schwabe, P.: Post-quantum key exchange - a new hope. In: 25th USENIX Security Symposium, USENIX Security 2016, Austin, TX, USA, pp. 327–343, 10–12 August 2016

4. Baek, J., Lee, B., Kim, K.: Secure length-saving ElGamal encryption under the computational Diffie-Hellman assumption. In: Dawson, E.P., Clark, A., Boyd, C. (eds.) ACISP 2000. LNCS, vol. 1841, pp. 49–58. Springer, Heidelberg (2000). https://doi.org/10.1007/10718964_5

5. Beals, R., Buhrman, H., Cleve, R., Mosca, M., Wolf, R.: Quantum lower bounds by polynomials. In: 39th FOCS, pp. 352–361. IEEE Computer Society Press, November 1998

6. Bellare, M., Boldyreva, A., O'Neill, A.: Deterministic and efficiently searchable encryption. In: Menezes, A. (ed.) CRYPTO 2007. LNCS, vol. 4622, pp. 535–552. Springer, Heidelberg (2007). https://doi.org/10.1007/978-3-540-74143-5_30

7. Bellare, M., Rogaway, P.: Random oracles are practical: a paradigm for designing efficient protocols. In: Ashby, V. (ed.) ACM CCS 1993, pp. 62–73. ACM Press, November 1993

8. Bellare, M., Rogaway, P.: The security of triple encryption and a framework for code-based game-playing proofs. In: Vaudenay, S. (ed.) EUROCRYPT 2006. LNCS, vol. 4004, pp. 409–426. Springer, Heidelberg (2006). https://doi.org/10.1007/11761679_25

9. Bernstein, D.J., Chuengsatiansup, C., Lange, T., van Vredendaal, C.: NTRU prime. Cryptology ePrint Archive, Report 2016/461 (2016). http://eprint.iacr.org/2016/461

10. Bitansky, N., Vaikuntanathan, V.: A note on perfect correctness by derandomization. In: Coron, J.-S., Nielsen, J.B. (eds.) EUROCRYPT 2017. LNCS, vol. 10211, pp. 592–606. Springer, Cham (2017). https://doi.org/10.1007/978-3-319-56614-6_20

11. Boneh, D., Dagdelen, Ö., Fischlin, M., Lehmann, A., Schaffner, C., Zhandry, M.: Random oracles in a quantum world. In: Lee, D.H., Wang, X. (eds.) ASIACRYPT 2011. LNCS, vol. 7073, pp. 41–69. Springer, Heidelberg (2011). https://doi.org/10.1007/978-3-642-25385-0_3

12. Bos, J., Ducas, L., Kiltz, E., Lepoint, T., Lyubashevsky, V., Schanck, J.M., Schwabe, P., Stehlé, D.: Crystals - Kyber: a CCA-secure module-lattice-based KEM. Cryptology ePrint Archive, Report 2017/634 (2017). http://eprint.iacr.org/2017/634

13. Bos, J.W., Costello, C., Ducas, L., Mironov, I., Naehrig, M., Nikolaenko, V., Raghunathan, A., Stebila, D.: Frodo: take off the ring! Practical, quantum-secure key exchange from LWE. In: Weippl, E.R., Katzenbeisser, S., Kruegel, C., Myers, A.C., Halevi, S. (eds.) ACM CCS 2016, pp. 1006–1018. ACM Press, October 2016

14. Bos, J.W., Costello, C., Naehrig, M., Stebila, D.: Post-quantum key exchange for the TLS protocol from the ring learning with errors problem. In: 2015 IEEE Symposium on Security and Privacy, pp. 553–570. IEEE Computer Society Press, May 2015

15. Cash, D., Kiltz, E., Shoup, V.: The twin Diffie-Hellman problem and applications. In: Smart, N. (ed.) EUROCRYPT 2008. LNCS, vol. 4965, pp. 127–145. Springer, Heidelberg (2008). https://doi.org/10.1007/978-3-540-78967-3_8

16. Cash, D., Kiltz, E., Shoup, V.: The twin Diffie-Hellman problem and applications. J. Cryptol. **22**(4), 470–504 (2009)

17. Cheon, J.H., Kim, D., Lee, J., Song, Y.: Lizard: Cut off the tail! Practical post-quantum public-key encryption from LWE and LWR. Cryptology ePrint Archive, Report 2016/1126 (2016). http://eprint.iacr.org/2016/1126

18. Coron, J.S., Handschuh, H., Joye, M., Paillier, P., Pointcheval, D., Tymen, C.: GEM: a generic chosen-ciphertext secure encryption method. In: Preneel, B. (ed.) CT-RSA 2002. LNCS, vol. 2271, pp. 263–276. Springer, Heidelberg (2002). https://doi.org/10.1007/3-540-45760-7_18

19. Cramer, R., Shoup, V.: Design and analysis of practical public-key encryption schemes secure against adaptive chosen ciphertext attack. SIAM J. Comput. **33**(1), 167–226 (2003)

20. Dent, A.W.: A designer's guide to KEMs. In: Paterson, K.G. (ed.) Cryptography and Coding 2003. LNCS, vol. 2898, pp. 133–151. Springer, Heidelberg (2003). https://doi.org/10.1007/978-3-540-40974-8_12

21. Ding, J., Xie, X., Lin, X.: A simple provably secure key exchange scheme based on the learning with errors problem. Cryptology ePrint Archive, Report 2012/688 (2012). http://eprint.iacr.org/2012/688

22. Dwork, C., Naor, M., Reingold, O.: Immunizing encryption schemes from decryption errors. In: Cachin, C., Camenisch, J.L. (eds.) EUROCRYPT 2004. LNCS, vol. 3027, pp. 342–360. Springer, Heidelberg (2004). https://doi.org/10.1007/978-3-540-24676-3_21

23. Fujisaki, E., Okamoto, T.: Secure integration of asymmetric and symmetric encryption schemes. In: Wiener, M. (ed.) CRYPTO 1999. LNCS, vol. 1666, pp. 537–554. Springer, Heidelberg (1999). https://doi.org/10.1007/3-540-48405-1_34

24. Fujisaki, E., Okamoto, T.: Secure integration of asymmetric and symmetric encryption schemes. J. Cryptol. **26**(1), 80–101 (2013)

25. Galindo, D., Martín, S., Morillo, P., Villar, J.L.: Fujisaki-Okamoto hybrid encryption revisited. Int. J. Inf. Secur. **4**(4), 228–241 (2005)

26. Hofheinz, D., Hövelmanns, K., Kiltz, E.: A modular analysis of the Fujisaki-Okamoto transformation. Cryptology ePrint Archive, Report 2017/604 (2017). https://eprint.iacr.org/2017/604

27. Howgrave-Graham, N., Silverman, J.H., Whyte, W.: Choosing parameter sets for NTRUEncrypt with NAEP and SVES-3. In: Menezes, A. (ed.) CT-RSA 2005. LNCS, vol. 3376, pp. 118–135. Springer, Heidelberg (2005). https://doi.org/10.1007/978-3-540-30574-3_10

28. Kiltz, E., Malone-Lee, J.: A general construction of IND-CCA2 secure public key encryption. In: Paterson, K.G. (ed.) Cryptography and Coding 2003. LNCS, vol. 2898, pp. 152–166. Springer, Heidelberg (2003). https://doi.org/10.1007/978-3-540-40974-8_13

29. Lyubashevsky, V., Peikert, C., Regev, O.: On ideal lattices and learning with errors over rings. In: Gilbert, H. (ed.) EUROCRYPT 2010. LNCS, vol. 6110, pp. 1–23. Springer, Heidelberg (2010). https://doi.org/10.1007/978-3-642-13190-5_1

30. Lyubashevsky, V., Peikert, C., Regev, O.: A toolkit for Ring-LWE cryptography. In: Johansson, T., Nguyen, P.Q. (eds.) EUROCRYPT 2013. LNCS, vol. 7881, pp. 35–54. Springer, Heidelberg (2013). https://doi.org/10.1007/978-3-642-38348-9_3

31. NIST: National institute for standards and technology. Postquantum crypto project (2017). http://csrc.nist.gov/groups/ST/post-quantum-crypto

32. Okamoto, T., Pointcheval, D.: REACT: rapid enhanced-security asymmetric cryptosystem transform. In: Naccache, D. (ed.) CT-RSA 2001. LNCS, vol. 2020, pp. 159–174. Springer, Heidelberg (2000). https://doi.org/10.1007/3-540-45353-9_13

33. Peikert, C.: Lattice cryptography for the internet. Cryptology ePrint Archive, Report 2014/070 (2014). http://eprint.iacr.org/2014/070

34. Rackoff, C., Simon, D.R.: Non-interactive zero-knowledge proof of knowledge and chosen ciphertext attack. In: Feigenbaum, J. (ed.) CRYPTO 1991. LNCS, vol. 576, pp. 433–444. Springer, Heidelberg (1992). https://doi.org/10.1007/3-540-46766-1_35

35. Regev, O.: On lattices, learning with errors, random linear codes, and cryptography. In: Gabow, H.N., Fagin, R. (eds.) 37th ACM STOC, pp. 84–93. ACM Press, May 2005

36. Shoup, V.: ISO 18033-2: An emerging standard for public-key encryption, December 2004. http://shoup.net/iso/std6.pdf. Final Committee Draft

37. Shoup, V.: Sequences of games: a tool for taming complexity in security proofs. Cryptology ePrint Archive, Report 2004/332 (2004). http://eprint.iacr.org/2004/332

38. Targhi, E.E., Unruh, D.: Post-quantum security of the Fujisaki-Okamoto and OAEP transforms. In: Hirt, M., Smith, A. (eds.) TCC 2016. LNCS, vol. 9986, pp. 192–216. Springer, Heidelberg (2016). https://doi.org/10.1007/978-3-662-53644-5_8

39. Unruh, D.: Revocable quantum timed-release encryption. In: Nguyen, P.Q., Oswald, E. (eds.) EUROCRYPT 2014. LNCS, vol. 8441, pp. 129–146. Springer, Heidelberg (2014). https://doi.org/10.1007/978-3-642-55220-5_8

40. Unruh, D.: Non-interactive zero-knowledge proofs in the quantum random oracle model. In: Oswald, E., Fischlin, M. (eds.) EUROCRYPT 2015. LNCS, vol. 9057, pp. 755–784. Springer, Heidelberg (2015). https://doi.org/10.1007/978-3-662-46803-6_25

41. Zhandry, M.: Secure identity-based encryption in the quantum random oracle model. In: Safavi-Naini, R., Canetti, R. (eds.) CRYPTO 2012. LNCS, vol. 7417, pp. 758–775. Springer, Heidelberg (2012). https://doi.org/10.1007/978-3-642-32009-5_44

# From Selective IBE to Full IBE and Selective HIBE

Nico Döttling[1,2]($\boxtimes$) and Sanjam Garg[2]

[1] Friedrich-Alexander-University Erlangen-Nürnberg, Nürnberg, Germany
nico.doettling@fau.de
[2] University of California, Berkeley, USA

**Abstract.** Starting with any selectively secure identity-based encryption (IBE) scheme, we give generic constructions of fully secure IBE and selectively secure hierarchical IBE (HIBE) schemes. Our HIBE scheme allows for delegation arbitrarily many times.

## 1 Introduction

Identity-based encryption schemes [Sha84, Coc01, BF01] (IBE) are public key encryption schemes [DH76, RSA78] for which arbitrary strings can serve as valid public keys, given short public parameters. Additionally, in such a system, given the master secret key corresponding to the public parameters, one can efficiently compute secret keys corresponding to any string id. A popular use case for this type of encryption is certificate management for encrypted email: A sender Alice can send an encrypted email to Bob at bob@iacr.org by just using the string "bob@iacr.org" and the public parameters to encrypt the message. Bob can decrypt the email using a secret-key corresponding to "bob@iacr.org" which he can obtain from the setup authority that holds the master secret key corresponding to the public parameters.

Two main security notions for IBE have been considered in the literature—selective security and full security. In the *selective* security experiment of identity-based encryption [CHK04], the adversary is allowed to first choose a *challenge identity* and may then obtain the public parameters and the identity secret keys for identities different from the challenge identity. The adversary's goal is to distinguish messages encrypted under the challenge identity, for which he is not allowed to obtain a secret key. On the other hand, in the *fully secure* notion [BF01], the (adversarial) choice of the challenge identity may depend arbitrarily on the public parameters. That is, the adversary may choose the challenge identity after seeing the public parameters and any number of identity secret keys of its choice. It is straightforward to see that any scheme that features

---

Research supported in part from AFOSR YIP Award, DARPA/ARL SAFEWARE Award W911NF15C0210, AFOSR Award FA9550-15-1-0274, NSF CRII Award 1464397, and research grants by the Okawa Foundation, Visa Inc., and Center for Long-Term Cybersecurity (CLTC, UC Berkeley). The views expressed are those of the author and do not reflect the official policy or position of the funding agencies.

© International Association for Cryptologic Research 2017
Y. Kalai and L. Reyzin (Eds.): TCC 2017, Part I, LNCS 10677, pp. 372–408, 2017.
https://doi.org/10.1007/978-3-319-70500-2_13

full security is also selectively secure. On the other hand, example IBE schemes that are selectively secure but trivially insecure in the full security sense can be constructed without significant effort.

The first IBE scheme was realized by Boneh and Franklin [BF01] based on bilinear maps. Soon after, Cocks [Coc01] provided the first IBE scheme based on quadratic residuocity assumption. However, the security of these constructions was argued in the random oracle model [BR93]. Subsequently, substantial effort was devoted to realizing IBE schemes without random oracles. The first constructions of IBE without random oracles were only proved to be selectively secure [CHK04, BB04a] and achieving full security for IBE without the random oracle heuristic required significant research effort. In particular, the first IBE scheme meeting the full security definition in the standard model were constructed by Boneh and Boyen [BB04b] and Waters [Wat05] using bilinear maps. Later, several other IBE schemes based on the learning with errors assumption [Reg05] were proposed [GPV08, AB09, CHKP10, ABB10a]. Very recently, constructions based on the security of the Diffie-Hellman Assumption and Factoring have also be obtained [DG17].

Basic IBE does not support the capability of delegating the power to issue identity secret keys. This property is captured by the notion of *hierarchical identity-based encryption* (HIBE) [HL02, GS02]. In a HIBE scheme, the owner of a master secret key can issue delegated master secret keys that enable generating identity secret keys for identities that start with a certain prefix. For instance, Alice may use a delegated master secret key to issue an identity secret key to her secretary for the identity "alice@iacr.org ‖ 05-24-2017", allowing the secretary to decrypt all her emails received on this day. While HIBE trivially implies IBE, the converse question has not been resolved yet. Abdalla, Fiore and Lyubashevsky [AFL12] provided constructions of fully secure HIBE from selective-pattern-secure *wildcarded identity-based encryption* (WIBE) schemes [ACD+06] and a construction of WIBE from HIBE schemes fulfilling the stronger notion of *security under correlated randomness*. Substantial effort has been devoted to realizing HIBE schemes based on specific assumptions [GS02, BB04b, BBG05, GH09, LW10, CHKP10, ABB10b, DG17].

The question whether selectively secure IBE generically implies fully secure IBE or HIBE remains open hitherto.

## 1.1   Our Results

In this work, we provide a generalization of the framework developed in [DG17]. Specifically, we replace the primitive chameleon encryption (or, chameleon hash function with encryption) from [DG17] with a weaker primitive which we call *one-time signatures with encryption* (OTSE). We show that this weaker primitive[1] also suffices for realizing fully secure IBE and selectively secure HIBE building on the techniques of [DG17]. We show that OTSE can be realized from

---

[1] Note that chameleon hash functions imply collision resistant hash functions which one-time signatures with encryption are not known to imply [AS15, MM16].

chameleon encryption, which, as shown in [DG17], can be based on the Computational Diffie-Hellman Assumption.

In the context of [DG17], OTSE can be seen as an additional layer of abstraction that further modularizes the IBE construction of [DG17]. More concretely, when plugging the construction of OTSE from chameleon encryption (Sect. 4) into the construction of HIBE from OTSE (Sect. 7), one obtains precisely the HIBE construction of [DG17][2].

The new insight in this work is that OTSE, unlike chameleon encryption, can be realized generically from any selectively secure IBE scheme. As a consequence, it follows that both fully secure IBE and selectively secure HIBE can also be constructed *generically* from any selectively secure IBE scheme. Prior works on broadening the assumptions sufficient for IBE and HIBE have focused on first realizing selectively secure IBE. Significant subsequent research has typically been needed for realizing fully secure IBE and HIBE. Having a generic construction immediately gives improvements over previously known results and makes it easier to achieve improvements in the future. For example, using the new IBE construction of Gaborit et al. [GHPT17] we obtain a new construction of HIBE from the rank-metric problem. As another example, we obtain a construction of selectively secure HIBE from LWE with compact public parameters, i.e. a HIBE scheme where the size of the public parameters does not depend on a maximum hierarchy depth [CHKP10, ABB10b].

## 1.2   Technical Outline

The results in this work build on a recent work of the authors [DG17], which provides an IBE scheme in groups without pairings. In particular, we will employ the tree-based bootstrapping technique of [DG17], which itself was inspired by the tree-based construction of *Laconic Oblivious Transfer*, a primitive recently introduced by Cho et al. [CDG+17]. Below, we start by recalling [DG17] and expand on how we generalize that technique to obtain our results.

*Challenge in Realizing the IBE Schemes.* The key challenge in realizing IBE schemes is the need to "somehow compress" public keys corresponding to all possible identities (which could be exponentially many) into small public parameters. Typically, IBE schemes resolve this challenge by generating the "identity specific" public keys in a correlated manner. Since these public keys are correlated they can all be described with succinct public parameters. However, this seems hard to do when relying on an assumption such as the Diffie-Hellman Assumption. Recently, [DG17] introduced new techniques for compressing multiple uncorrelated public keys into small public parameters allowing for a construction based on the Diffie-Hellman Assumption. Below we start by describing the notion of chameleon encryption and how the IBE scheme of [DG17] uses it.

---

[2] The IBE construction of [DG17] is optimized and does not fit nicely into the OTSE framework.

*Chameleon Encryption at a High Level.* At the heart of the [DG17] construction is a new chameleon hash function [KR98] with some additional encryption and decryption functionality. A (keyed) chameleon hash function $H_k$ : $\{0,1\}^n \times \{0,1\}^\lambda \rightarrow \{0,1\}^\lambda$ on input an $n$-bit string x (for $n > \lambda$) and random coins $r \in \{0,1\}^\lambda$ outputs a $\lambda$-bit string. The keyed hash function is such that a trapdoor t associated to k can be used to find collisions. In particular, given a trapdoor t for k, a pair of input and random coins $(x, r)$ and an alternative preimage x' it is easy to compute coins $r'$ such that $H_k(x; r) = H_k(x', r')$. Additionally, we require the following encryption and decryption procedures. The encryption function $Enc(k, (h, i, b), m)$ outputs a ciphertext c such that decryption $Dec(k, c, (x, r))$ yields the original message $m$ back as long as

$$h = H_k(x; r) \text{ and } x_i = b,$$

where $(h, i, b)$ are the values used in the generation of the ciphertext ct. In other words, the decryptor can use the knowledge of the preimage of h as the secret key to decrypt m as long as the $i^{th}$ bit of the preimage it can supply is equal to the value $b$ chosen at the time of encryption. Roughly, the security requirement of chameleon encryption is that

$$\{k, x, r, Enc(k, (h, i, 1 - x_i), 0)\} \stackrel{c}{\approx} \{k, x, r, Enc(k, (h, i, 1 - x_i), 1)\},$$

where $\stackrel{c}{\approx}$ denotes computational indistinguishability. In other words, if an adversary is given a preimage x of the hash value h, but the $i^{th}$ bit of h is different from the value $b$ used during encryption, then ciphertext indistinguishability holds.

*Realization of Chameleon Encryption.* [DG17] provide the following very natural realization of the Chameleon Encryption under the DDH assumption. Given a group $\mathbb{G}$ of prime order $p$ with a generator $g$, the hash function H is computed as follows:

$$H_k(x; r) = g^r \prod_{j \in [n]} g_{j, x_j},$$

where the key $k = (g, \{g_{j,0}, g_{j,1}\}_{j \in [n]})$, $r \in \mathbb{Z}_p$ and $x_j$ is the $j^{th}$ bit of $x \in \{0,1\}^n$.

Corresponding to this chameleon hash function the encryption procedure $Enc(k, (h, i, b), m)$ proceeds as follows. Sample a random value $\rho \stackrel{\$}{\leftarrow} \mathbb{Z}_p$ and output the ciphertext $ct = (e, c, c', \{c_{j,0}, c_{j,1}\}_{j \in [n] \setminus \{i\}})$, where $c := g^\rho$, $c' := h^\rho$, $\forall j \in [n] \setminus \{i\}$, $c_{j,0} := g_{j,0}^\rho$, $c_{j,1} := g_{j,1}^\rho$, and $e := m \oplus g_{i,b}^\rho$. It is easy to see that if $x_i = b$, then decryption $Dec(ct, (x, r))$ can be performed by computing

$$e \oplus \frac{c'}{c^r \prod_{j \in [n] \setminus \{i\}} c_{j, x_j}}.$$

However, if $x_i \neq b$ then the decryptor has access to the value $g_{i, x_i}^\rho$ but not $g_{i,b}^\rho$, and this prevents him from learning the message m. This observation can be formalized as a security proof based on the DDH assumption[3] and we refer the reader to [DG17] for the details.

*From Chameleon Encryption to Identity-Based Encryption [DG17].* As mentioned earlier, [DG17] provide a technique for compressing uncorrelated public keys. [DG17] achieve this compression using the above-mentioned hash function in a Merkle-hash-tree fashion. In particular, the public parameters of the [DG17] IBE scheme consist of the key of the hash function and the root of the Merkle-hash-tree hashing the public keys of all the parties. Note that the number of identities is too large (specifically it is exponential) to efficiently hash all the identity-specific public keys into short public parameters. Instead [DG17] use the chameleon property of the hash function to generate the tree top-down rather than bottom-up (as is typically done in a Merkle-tree hashing). We skip the details of this top-down Merkle tree generation and refer to [DG17].

A secret key for an identity id in the [DG17] scheme consists of the hash-values along the root-to-leaf path corresponding to the leaf node id in the Merkle-hash-tree. We also include the siblings of the hash-values provided and the random coins used. Moreover, it includes the secret key corresponding to the public key at the leaf-node id.

Encryption and decryption are based on the following idea. Let $\{Y_{j,0}, Y_{j,1}\}_{j \in [n]}$ be $2n$ *labels*. Given a hash-value h, an encryptor can compute the ciphertexts $c_{j,b} := \mathsf{Enc}(\mathsf{k}, (\mathsf{h}, j, b), Y_{j,b})$ for $j = 1, \ldots, n$ and $b \in \{0, 1\}$. Given the ciphertexts $\{c_{j,0}, c_{j,1}\}_{j \in [n]}$, a decryptor in possession of a message x and coins $r$ with $\mathsf{H}_\mathsf{k}(\mathsf{x}; r) = \mathsf{h}$ can now decrypt the ciphertexts $\{c_{j,\mathsf{x}_j}\}_{j \in [n]}$ and obtain the labels $Y_{j,\mathsf{x}_j} := \mathsf{Dec}(\mathsf{k}, (\mathsf{x}, r), c_{j,\mathsf{x}_j})$ for $j = 1, \ldots, n$. Due to the security of the chameleon encryption scheme, the decryptor will learn nothing about the labels $\{Y_{j,1-\mathsf{x}_j}\}_{j \in [n]}$.

This technique can be combined with a *projective garbling scheme* to help an encryptor provide a value C(x) to the decryptor, where C is an arbitrary circuit that knows some additional secrets chosen by the encryptor. The key point here being that the encryptor does not need to know the value x, but only a hash-value $\mathsf{h} = \mathsf{H}_\mathsf{k}(\mathsf{x}; r)$. The encryptor garbles the circuit C and obtains a garbled circuit $\tilde{\mathsf{C}}$ and labels $\{Y_{j,0}, Y_{j,1}\}$ for the input-wires of C. Encrypting the labels in the above fashion, (i.e. computing $c_{j,b} := \mathsf{Enc}(\mathsf{k}, (\mathsf{h}, j + \mathsf{id}_i \cdot \lambda, b), Y_{j,b}))$, we obtain a ciphertext $\mathsf{ct} := (\tilde{\mathsf{C}}, \{c_{j,0}, c_{j,1}\}_{j \in [n]})$.

Given such a ciphertext, by the above a decryptor can obtain the labels $\{Y_{j,\mathsf{x}_j}\}_{j \in [n]}$ corresponding to the input x and evaluate the garbled circuit $\tilde{\mathsf{C}}$ to obtain C(x). By the security property of the garbling scheme and the discussion above the decryptor will learn nothing about the circuit C but the output-value C(x).

The encryption procedure of the IBE scheme provided in [DG17] uses this technique as follows. It computes a sequence of garbled circuits $\tilde{\mathsf{Q}}^{(1)}, \ldots, \tilde{\mathsf{Q}}^{(n)}$, where the circuit $\mathsf{Q}^{(i)}$ takes as input a hash-value h, and returns chameleon encryptions $\{c_{j,0}, c_{j,1}\}_{j \in [n]}$ of the input-labels $\{Y_{j,0}^{(i+1)}, Y_{j,1}^{(i+1)}\}_{j \in [n]}$ of $\mathsf{Q}^{(i+1)}$,

---

[3] In fact, [DG17] show that a variant of this scheme can be proven secure under the computational Diffie-Hellman assumption.

where $c_{j,b} := \mathsf{Enc}(\mathsf{k}, (\mathsf{h}, j + \mathsf{id}_i \cdot \lambda, b), Y_{j,b}^{(i+1)})$. The last garbled circuit $\mathsf{Q}^{(n)}$ in this sequence outputs chameleon encryptions of the labels $\{T_{j,0}, T_{j,1}\}_{j \in [n]}$ of a garbled circuit $\mathsf{T}$, where the circuit $\mathsf{T}$ takes as input a public key $\mathsf{pk}$ of a standard public key encryption scheme $(\mathsf{KG}, \mathsf{E}, \mathsf{D})$ and outputs and encryption $\mathsf{E}(\mathsf{pk}, \mathsf{m})$ of the message $\mathsf{m}$. The IBE ciphertext consists of the chameleon encryptions $\{c_{j,0}^{(1)}, c_{j,1}^{(1)}\}_{j \in [n]}$ of the input labels of the first garbled circuit $\tilde{\mathsf{Q}}^{(1)}$, the garbled circuits $\tilde{\mathsf{Q}}^{(1)}, \ldots, \tilde{\mathsf{Q}}^{(n)}$ and the garbled circuit $\tilde{\mathsf{T}}$.

The decryptor, who is in possession of the siblings along the root-to-leaf path for identity $\mathsf{id}$, can now traverse the tree as follows. He starts by decrypting $\{c_{j,0}^{(1)}, c_{j,1}^{(1)}\}_{j \in [n]}$ to the labels corresponding the first pair of siblings, evaluating the garbled circuit $\tilde{\mathsf{Q}}^{(1)}$ on this input and thus obtain chameleon encryptions $\{c_{j,0}^{(2)}, c_{j,1}^{(2)}\}_{j \in [n]}$ of the labels of the next garbled circuit $\tilde{\mathsf{Q}}^{(2)}$. Repeating this process, the decryptor will eventually be able to evaluate the last garbled circuit $\tilde{\mathsf{T}}$ and obtain $\mathsf{E}(\mathsf{pk}_{\mathsf{id}}, \mathsf{m})$, an encryption of the message $\mathsf{m}$ under the leaf-public-key $\mathsf{pk}_{\mathsf{id}}$. Now this ciphertext can be decrypted using the corresponding leaf-secret-key $\mathsf{sk}_{\mathsf{id}}$.

Stated differently, the encryptor uses the garbled circuits $\tilde{\mathsf{Q}}^{(1)}, \ldots, \tilde{\mathsf{Q}}^{(n)}$ to help the decryptor traverse the tree to the leaf corresponding to the identity $\mathsf{id}$ and obtain an encryption of $\mathsf{m}$ under the leaf-public key $\mathsf{pk}_{\mathsf{id}}$ (which is not know to the encryptor).

Security of this scheme follows, as sketched above, from the security of the chameleon encryption scheme, the garbling scheme and the security of the public key encryption scheme $(\mathsf{KG}, \mathsf{E}, \mathsf{D})$.

*Connection to a Special Signature Scheme.* It is well-known that IBE implies a signature scheme—specifically, by interpreting the secret key for an identity $\mathsf{id}$ as the signature on the message $\mathsf{id}$. The starting point of our work is the observation that the [DG17] IBE scheme has similarities with the construction of a signature scheme from a one-time signature scheme [Lam79, NY89]. In particular, the chameleon hash function mimics the role of a one-time signature scheme which can then be used to obtain a signature scheme similar to the IBE scheme of [DG17]. Based on this intuition we next define a new primitive which we call *one-time signature with encryption* which is very similar to (though weaker than) chameleon encryption. Construction of one-time signature with encryption from chameleon encryption is provided in Sect. 4.

*One-Time Signatures with Encryption.* A one-time signature scheme [Lam79, NY89] is a signature scheme for which security only holds if a signing key is used at most once. In more detail, a one-time signature scheme consists of three algorithms $(\mathsf{SGen}, \mathsf{SSign}, \mathsf{Verify})$, where $\mathsf{SGen}$ produces a pair $(\mathsf{vk}, \mathsf{sk})$ of verification and signing keys, $\mathsf{SSign}$ takes a signing key $\mathsf{sk}$ and a message $\mathsf{x}$ and produces a signature $\sigma$, and $\mathsf{Verify}$ takes a message-signature pair $(\mathsf{x}, \sigma)$ and checks if $\sigma$ is a valid signature for $\mathsf{x}$. One-time security means that given a verification key $\mathsf{vk}$ and a signature $\sigma$ on a message of its own choice, an efficient adversary will not be able to concoct a valid signature $\sigma'$ on a different message $\mathsf{x}'$.

As with chameleon encryption, we will supplement the notion of one-time signature schemes with an additional encryption functionality. More specifically, we require additional encryption and decryption algorithms SEnc and SDec with the following properties. SEnc encrypts a message m using parameters $(vk, i, b)$, i.e. a verification key vk, an index $i$ and a bit $b$, and any message signature pair $(x, \sigma)$ satisfying "Verify$(vk, x, \sigma) = 1$ and $x_i = b$" can be used with SDec to decrypt the plaintext m. In terms of security, we require that given a signature $\sigma$ on a selectively chosen message x, it is infeasible to distinguish encryptions for which the bit $b$ is set to $1 - x_i$, i.e. SEnc$((vk, i, 1 - x_i), m_0)$ and SEnc$((vk, i, 1 - x_i), m_1)$ are indistinguishable for any pair of messages $m_0, m_1$.

Finally, we will have the additional requirement that the verification keys are succinct, i.e. the size of the verification keys does not depend on the length of the messages that can be signed.

In the following, we will omit the requirement of a verification algorithm Verify, as such an algorithm is implied by the SEnc and SDec algorithms[4].

Moreover, we remark that in the actual definition of OTSE in Sect. 3, we introduce additional public parameters pp that will be used to sample verification and signing keys.

In Sect. 4, we will provide a direct construction of an OTSE scheme from chameleon encryption [DG17]. We remark that the techniques used in this construction appear in the HIBE-from-chameleon-encryption construction of [DG17].

We will now sketch a construction of an OTSE scheme from any selectively secure IBE scheme. Assume henceforth that (Setup, KeyGen, Encrypt, Decrypt) is a selectively secure IBE scheme. We will construct an OTSE scheme (SGen, SSign, SDec) as follows. SGen runs the Setup algorithm and sets vk := mpk and sk := msk, i.e. the master public key mpk will serve as verification key vk and the master secret key msk will serve as signing key sk. To sign a message $x \in \{0, 1\}^n$, compute identity secret keys for the identities $x_j \| bin(j)$ for $j \in [n]$. Here, $x_j$ is the $j$-th bit of x, $\|$ is the string concatenation operator and $bin(j)$ is a $\lceil \log_2(n) \rceil$ bits representation of the index $j \in [n]$. Thus, a signature $\sigma$ of x is computed by

$$\sigma = SSign(sk, x) := \{KeyGen(msk, x_j \| bin(j))\}_{j \in [n]}.$$

It can be checked that this is a correct and secure one-time signature scheme. The encryption and decryption algorithms SEnc and SDec are obtained from the Encrypt and Decrypt algorithms of the IBE scheme. Namely, to encrypt a plaintext m using vk = mpk, $i, b$, compute the ciphertext

$$c = SEnc((vk, i, b), m) := Encrypt(mpk, b \| bin(i), m),$$

i.e. we encrypt m to the identity $b \| bin(i)$. Decryption using a signature $\sigma$ on a message x is performed by computing

$$m = SDec((\sigma, x), c) := Decrypt(sk_{x_i \| bin(i)}, c),$$

---

[4] To verify a signature $\sigma$ for a message x using SEnc and SDec, encrypt a random plaintext m using $(vk, i, x_i)$ for all indices $i$ and test whether decryption using $(x, \sigma)$ yields m.

which succeeds if $x_i = b$. The succinctness requirement is fulfilled, as the size of the verification keys (which are master public keys) depends only (polynomially) on the security parameter, but not on the actual number of identities.

Security can be based on the selective security of the IBE scheme by noting that if the $i$-th bit of the message $x$ for which a signature has been issued is different from $b$, then the identity secret key corresponding to the identity $b\|\mathrm{bin}(i)$ is not contained in $\sigma$ and we can use the selective security of the IBE scheme.

*Realizing Fully Secure IBE.* We will now show how an OTSE scheme can be bootstrapped into a fully secure IBE scheme. As mentioned before, we will use the tree based approach of the authors [DG17]. For the sake of simplicity, we will describe a stateful scheme, i.e. the key-generation algorithm keeps a state listing the identity secret keys that have been issued so far. The actual scheme, described in Sect. 6, will be a stateless version of this scheme, which can be obtained via pseudorandom functions.

We will now describe how identity secret keys are generated. The key generation algorithm of our scheme can be seen as an instance of the tree-based construction of a signature scheme from one-time signatures and universal one-way hash functions [NY89]. In fact, our OTSE scheme serves as one-time signature scheme with short verification keys in the construction of [NY89]. In [NY89], one-time signature scheme with short verification keys are used implicitly via a combination of one-time signatures and universal one-way hash functions.

Assume that identities are of length $n$ and that we have a binary tree of depth $n$. Nodes in this tree are labelled by binary strings $v$ that correspond to the path to this node from the root, and the root itself is labelled by the empty string $v_0 = \{\}$.

We will place public keys $\mathsf{lpk}_v$ of a standard $\mathsf{IND}^{\mathsf{CPA}}$-secure encryption scheme $(\mathsf{KG}, \mathsf{E}, \mathsf{D})$ into the leaf-nodes $v$ of the tree and a verification key $\mathsf{vk}_v$ of the OTSE scheme into every node $v$. The nodes are connected in the following manner. If $v$ is a node with two children $v\|0$ and $v\|1$, we will concatenate the keys $\mathsf{vk}_{v\|0}$ and $\mathsf{vk}_{v\|1}$ and sign them with the signing key $\mathsf{sk}_v$ (corresponding to the verification key $\mathsf{vk}_v$), i.e. define $x_v := \mathsf{vk}_{v\|0}\|\mathsf{vk}_{v\|1}$ and compute

$$\sigma_v := \mathsf{SSign}(\mathsf{sk}_v, x).$$

If $v$ is a leaf-node, compute

$$\sigma_v := \mathsf{SSign}(\mathsf{sk}_v, \mathsf{lpk}_v),$$

after padding $\mathsf{lpk}_v$ to the appropriate length.

The master public key $\mathsf{mpk}$ of our scheme consist of the verification key $\mathsf{vk}_{v_0}$ at the root node $v_0$. The identity secret key for a root-to-leaf path $v_0, \ldots, v_n$ consists of the root verification key $\mathsf{vk}_{v_0}$, the $x_{v_0}, \ldots, x_{v_n}$ (i.e. the verification keys for the siblings along the path), the signatures $\sigma_{v_0}, \ldots, \sigma_{v_n}$, and the leaf public and secrets keys $\mathsf{lpk}_{v_n}$ and $\mathsf{lsk}_{v_n}$.

We can think of the entire information in the identity secret key as public information, *except* the leaf secret key $\mathsf{lsk}_{v_n}$. That is, from a security perspective they could as well be made publicly accessible (they are not, due to the succinctness constraint of the master public key).

*Encryption and Decryption.* We will now describe how a plaintext is encrypted to an identity id and how it is decrypted using the corresponding identity secret key $\mathsf{sk}_{\mathsf{id}}$. The basic idea is, as in [DG17], that the encryptor delegates encryption of the plaintext m to the decryptor. More specifically, while the encryptor only knows the root verification key, the decryptor is in possession of all verification keys and signatures along the root-to-leaf path for the identity.

This delegation task will be achieved using garbled circuits along with the OTSE scheme. The goal of this delegation task is to provide a garbled circuit $\tilde{\mathsf{T}}$ with the leaf public key $\mathsf{lpk}_{\mathsf{id}}$ for the identity id. To ensure that the proper leaf public key is provided to $\tilde{\mathsf{T}}$, a sequence of garbled circuits $\tilde{\mathsf{Q}}^{(0)}, \ldots, \tilde{\mathsf{Q}}^{(n)}$ is used to *traverse* the tree from the root to the leaf id.

First consider a tree that consists of one single leaf-node v, i.e. in this case there is just one leaf public key $\mathsf{lpk}_v$ and one verification key $\mathsf{vk}_v$. The signature $\sigma$ is given by

$$\sigma := \mathsf{SSign}(\mathsf{sk}_v, \mathsf{lpk}_v)$$

The encryptor wants to compute an encryption of a plaintext m under $\mathsf{lpk}_v$, while only in possession of the verification key $\mathsf{vk}_v$. It will do so using a garbled circuit $\tilde{\mathsf{T}}$. The garbled circuit $\tilde{\mathsf{T}}$ has the plaintext m hardwired, takes as input a local public key lpk and outputs an encryption of the plaintext m under lpk, i.e. $\mathsf{E}(\mathsf{lpk}, \mathsf{m})$. Let $\{T_{j,0}, T_{j,1}\}_{j \in [\ell]}$ be the set of input labels for the garbled circuit $\tilde{\mathsf{T}}$. In this basic case, the ciphertext consists of the garbled circuit $\tilde{\mathsf{T}}$ and encryptions of the labels $\{T_{j,0}, T_{j,1}\}_{j \in [\ell]}$ under the OTSE scheme. More specifically, for all $j \in [\ell]$ and $b \in \{0,1\}$ the encryptor computes $c_{j,b} := \mathsf{SEnc}((\mathsf{vk}_v, j, b), T_{j,b})$ and sets the ciphertext to $\mathsf{ct} := (\tilde{\mathsf{T}}, \{c_{j,b}\}_{j,b})$.

To decrypt such a ciphertext ct given $\mathsf{lsk}_v$, $\mathsf{lpk}_v$ and a signature $\sigma_v$ of $\mathsf{lpk}_v$ we proceed as follows. First, the decryptor recovers the labels $\{T_{j,(\mathsf{lpk}_v)_j}\}_j$ (where $(\mathsf{lpk}_v)_j$ is the $j$-th bit of $\mathsf{lpk}_v$) by computing

$$T_{j,(\mathsf{lpk}_v)_j} := \mathsf{SDec}((\sigma, \mathsf{lpk}_v), c_{j,(\mathsf{lpk}_v)_j}).$$

By the correctness of the OTSE scheme it follows that these are indeed the correct labels corresponding to $\mathsf{lpk}_v$. Evaluating the garbled circuit $\tilde{\mathsf{T}}$ on these labels yields an encryption $\mathsf{f} = \mathsf{E}(\mathsf{lpk}_v, \mathsf{m})$ of the plaintext m. Now the secret key $\mathsf{lsk}_v$ can be used to decrypt f to the plaintext m.

For larger trees, the encryptor is not in possession of the verification key $\mathsf{vk}_v$ of the leaf-node v, and can therefore not compute the encryptions $c_{j,b} := \mathsf{SEnc}((\mathsf{vk}_v, j, b), T_{j,b})$ by herself. This task will therefore be delegated to a sequence of garbled circuits $\tilde{\mathsf{Q}}^{(0)}, \ldots, \tilde{\mathsf{Q}}^{(n)}$. For $i = 0, \ldots, n-1$, the garbled circuit $\tilde{\mathsf{Q}}^{(i)}$ has the bit $\mathsf{id}_{i+1}$ and the labels $\{X_{j,b}\}_{j,b}$ of the next garbled circuit $\tilde{\mathsf{Q}}^{(i+1)}$ hardwired, takes as input a verification key $\mathsf{vk}_v$ and outputs $\{c_{j,b}\}_{j,b}$, where $c_{j,b} := \mathsf{SEnc}((\mathsf{vk_v}, \mathsf{id}_{i+1} \cdot \ell + j, b), X_{j,b})$. The garbled circuit $\tilde{Q}^{(n)}$ has the labels $\{T_{j,b}\}_{j,b}$ of the garbled circuit $\tilde{T}$ hardwired, takes as input a verification key $\mathsf{vk_v}$ and outputs $\{c_{j,b}\}_{j,b}$, where $c_{j,b} := \mathsf{SEnc}((\mathsf{vk_v}, j, b), T_{j,b})$.

Thus, a decryptor who knows input labels for $\tilde{Q}^{(i)}$ corresponding to $\mathsf{vk_v}$ will be able to evaluate $\tilde{Q}^{(i)}$ and obtain the encrypted labels $\{c_{j,b}\}_{j,b}$, where $c_{j,b} = \mathsf{SEnc}((\mathsf{vk_v}, \mathsf{id}_{i+1} \cdot \ell + j, b), X_{j,b})$. If the decryptor is in possession of the values $\mathsf{x_v} = \mathsf{vk}_{\mathsf{v}_i \| 0} \| \mathsf{vk}_{\mathsf{v}_i \| 1}$ and a valid signature $\sigma_\mathsf{v}$ of $\mathsf{x_v}$ that verifies with respect to $\mathsf{vk_v}$, he will be able to compute

$$X_{j, (\mathsf{vk}_{\mathsf{v} \| \mathsf{id}_i})_j} := \mathsf{SDec}((\sigma_\mathsf{v}, \mathsf{x_v}), c_{j, (\mathsf{vk}_{\mathsf{v} \| \mathsf{id}_i})_j}).$$

These are the input labels of $\tilde{Q}^{(i+1)}$ corresponding to the input $\mathsf{vk}_{\mathsf{v} \| \mathsf{id}_{i+1}}$. Consequently, the decryptor will be able to evaluate $\tilde{Q}^{(i+1)}$ on input $\mathsf{vk}_{\mathsf{v} \| \mathsf{id}_{i+1}}$ and so forth.

Thus, in the full scheme a ciphertext $\mathsf{ct}$ consists of the input-labels of the garbled circuit $\tilde{Q}^{(0)}$, the sequence of garbled circuits $\tilde{Q}^{(0)}, \ldots, \tilde{Q}^{(n)}$ and a garbed circuit $\tilde{T}$. To decrypt this ciphertext, proceed as above starting with the garbled circuit $\tilde{Q}^{(0)}$ and traversing the tree to the leaf-node $\mathsf{id}$, where $\tilde{T}$ can be evaluated and the plaintext $\mathsf{m}$ be recovered as above.

In the security proof, we will replace the garbled circuits with simulated garbled circuits and change the encryptions to only encrypt labels for the next verification key in the sequence of nodes. One key idea here is that the security reduction knows all the verification keys and signatures in the tree, which as mentioned above is not private but not accessible to the real encryptor due to succinctness requirements of the public parameters. See Sect. 6 for details.

*Hierarchical IBE.* To upgrade the above scheme into a HIBE scheme, we will associate a local public key $\mathsf{lpk_{vv}}$ with each node $\mathsf{v}$ of the tree, i.e. each node of the tree may serve as a *leaf* in the above scheme if needed. This means each node will contain a signature of the verification keys of the two child nodes and the local public key, i.e. we set $\mathsf{x} := \mathsf{vk}_{\mathsf{v} \| 0} \| \mathsf{vk}_{\mathsf{v} \| 1} \| \mathsf{lpk_v}$ and compute

$$\sigma_\mathsf{v} := \mathsf{SSign}(\mathsf{sk_v}, \mathsf{x})$$

Moreover, we can make this scheme stateless using a pseudorandom function that supports the delegation of keys. In particular, the classic GGM construction [GGM86] supports delegation of PRF keys for subtrees when instantiated appropriately. We are only able to prove selective security of the obtained HIBE scheme, as in the HIBE experiment the delegation keys include PRF keys, something that was not needed to be done for the case of IBE.

## 2   Preliminaries

Let $\lambda$ denote the security parameter. We use the notation $[n]$ to denote the set $\{1, \ldots, n\}$. By PPT we mean a probabilistic polynomial time algorithm. For any set $S$, we use $x \xleftarrow{\$} S$ to denote that $x$ is sampled uniformly at random from the set $S$.[5] Alternatively, for any distribution $D$ we use $x \xleftarrow{\$} D$ to denote that $x$ is sampled from the distribution $D$. We use the operator $:=$ to represent assignment and $=$ to denote an equality check. For two strings $\mathsf{x}$ and $\mathsf{x}'$, we denote the concatenation of $\mathsf{x}$ and $\mathsf{x}'$ by $\mathsf{x}\|\mathsf{x}'$. For an integer $j \in [n]$, let $\mathsf{bin}(j)$ be the $\lceil \log_2(n) \rceil$ bits representation of $j$.

## 2.1 Public Key Encryption

**Definition 1 (Public Key Encryption).** *A public key encryption scheme consists of three PPT algorithms* $(\mathsf{KG}, \mathsf{E}, \mathsf{D})$ *with the following syntax.*

- $\mathsf{KG}(1^\lambda)$ *takes as input a security parameter* $1^\lambda$ *and outputs a pair of public and secret keys* $(\mathsf{pk}, \mathsf{sk})$.
- $\mathsf{E}(\mathsf{pk}, \mathsf{m})$ *takes as input a public key* $\mathsf{pk}$ *and a plaintext* $\mathsf{m}$ *and outputs a ciphertext* $c$.
- $\mathsf{D}(\mathsf{sk}, c)$ *takes as input a secret key* $\mathsf{sk}$ *and a ciphertext* $c$ *and outputs a plaintext* $\mathsf{m}$.

*We require the following properties to hold.*

- **Completeness:** *For every security parameter* $\lambda$ *and for all messages* $\mathsf{m}$, *it holds that*
$$\mathsf{D}(\mathsf{sk}, \mathsf{E}(\mathsf{pk}, \mathsf{m})) = \mathsf{m},$$
*where* $(\mathsf{pk}, \mathsf{sk}) := \mathsf{KG}(1^\lambda)$.
- $\mathsf{IND}^{\mathsf{CPA}}$ **Security:** *For any PPT adversary* $\mathcal{A} = (\mathcal{A}_1, \mathcal{A}_2)$, *there exists a negligible function* $\mathsf{negl}(\cdot)$ *such that the following holds:*
$$\Pr[\mathsf{IND}^{\mathsf{CPA}}(\mathcal{A}) = 1] \leq \frac{1}{2} + \mathsf{negl}(\lambda)$$
*where* $\mathsf{IND}^{\mathsf{CPA}}(\mathcal{A})$ *is shown in Fig. 1.*

This notion easily extends to multiple challenge-ciphertexts. A simple hybrid argument shows that if a PPT-adversary $\mathcal{A}$ breaks the $\mathsf{IND}^{\mathsf{CPA}}$-security in the $k$ ciphertext setting with advantage $\epsilon$, then there exists a PPT adversary $\mathcal{A}'$ that breaks single challenge-ciphertext $\mathsf{IND}^{\mathsf{CPA}}$-security with advantage $\epsilon/k$.

## 2.2 Identity-Based Encryption

Below we provide the definition of identity-based encryption (IBE).

**Definition 2 (Identity-Based Encryption (IBE) [Sha84,BF01]).** *An identity-based encryption scheme consists of four PPT algorithms* $(\mathsf{Setup}, \mathsf{KeyGen}, \mathsf{Encrypt}, \mathsf{Decrypt})$ *defined as follows:*

---

[5] We use this notion only when the sampling can be done by a PPT algorithm and the sampling algorithm is implicit.

---

**Experiment** $\mathsf{IND}^{\mathsf{CPA}}(\mathcal{A})$:

1. $(\mathsf{pk}, \mathsf{sk}) \xleftarrow{\$} \mathsf{KG}(1^\lambda)$
2. $(\mathsf{m}_0, \mathsf{m}_1) \xleftarrow{\$} \mathcal{A}_1(\mathsf{pk})$.
3. $b^* \xleftarrow{\$} \{0, 1\}$.
4. $\mathsf{m}^* := \mathsf{m}_b$
5. $c^* \xleftarrow{\$} \mathsf{E}(\mathsf{pk}, \mathsf{m}^*)$
6. $b' \xleftarrow{\$} \mathcal{A}_2(\mathsf{pk}, c^*)$
7. *Output* 1 *if* $b^* = b'$ *and* 0 *otherwise*.

---

**Fig. 1.** The $\mathsf{IND}^{\mathsf{CPA}}(\mathcal{A})$ experiment

- Setup($1^\lambda$): *given the security parameter, it outputs a master public key* mpk *and a master secret key* msk.
- KeyGen(msk, id): *given the master secret key* msk *and an identity* id $\in \{0, 1\}^n$, *it outputs the identity secret key* $\mathsf{sk}_{\mathsf{id}}$.
- Encrypt(mpk, id, m): *given the master public key* mpk, *an identity* id $\in \{0, 1\}^n$, *and a message* m, *it outputs a ciphertext* c.
- Decrypt($\mathsf{sk}_{\mathsf{id}}$, c): *given a secret key* $\mathsf{sk}_{\mathsf{id}}$ *for identity* id *and a ciphertext* c, *it outputs a plaintext* m.

*The following completeness and security properties must be satisfied:*

- **Completeness:** *For all security parameters* $\lambda$, *identities* id $\in \{0, 1\}^n$ *and messages* m, *the following holds:*

$$\mathsf{Decrypt}(\mathsf{sk}_{\mathsf{id}}, \mathsf{Encrypt}(\mathsf{mpk}, \mathsf{id}, \mathsf{m})) = \mathsf{m}$$

*where* $\mathsf{sk}_{\mathsf{id}} \leftarrow \mathsf{KeyGen}(\mathsf{msk}, \mathsf{id})$ *and* $(\mathsf{mpk}, \mathsf{msk}) \leftarrow \mathsf{Setup}(1^\lambda)$.
- **Selective Security** [CHK04]: *For any PPT adversary* $\mathcal{A} = (\mathcal{A}_1, \mathcal{A}_2, \mathcal{A}_3)$, *there exists a negligible function* $\mathsf{negl}(\cdot)$ *such that the following holds:*

$$\Pr[\mathsf{sel\text{-}IND}^{\mathsf{IBE}}(\mathcal{A}) = 1] \leq \frac{1}{2} + \mathsf{negl}(\lambda)$$

*where* $\mathsf{sel\text{-}IND}^{\mathsf{IBE}}(\mathcal{A})$ *is shown in Fig. 2, and for each key query* id *that* $\mathcal{A}$ *sends to the* KeyGen *oracle, it must hold that* id $\neq$ id$^*$.
- **Full Security:** *For any PPT adversary* $\mathcal{A} = (\mathcal{A}_1, \mathcal{A}_2)$, *there exists a negligible function* $\mathsf{negl}(\cdot)$ *such that the following holds:*

$$\Pr[\mathsf{IND}^{\mathsf{IBE}}(\mathcal{A}) = 1] \leq \frac{1}{2} + \mathsf{negl}(\lambda)$$

*where* $\mathsf{IND}^{\mathsf{IBE}}(\mathcal{A})$ *is shown in Fig. 3, and for each key query* id *that* $\mathcal{A}$ *sends to the* KeyGen *oracle, it must hold that* id $\neq$ id$^*$.

***Experiment*** sel-IND$^{\text{IBE}}(\mathcal{A})$:

1. id$^*$ := $\mathcal{A}_1(1^\lambda)$
2. (mpk, msk) $\overset{\$}{\leftarrow}$ Setup($1^\lambda$)
3. $(m_0, m_1) \overset{\$}{\leftarrow} \mathcal{A}_1^{\text{KeyGen(msk,.)}}(\text{mpk})$ *where* $|m_0| = |m_1|$ *and for each query* id *by* $\mathcal{A}_1$ *to* KeyGen(msk, .) *we have that* id $\neq$ id$^*$.
4. $b^* \overset{\$}{\leftarrow} \{0, 1\}$.
5. $m^* := m_b$
6. $c^* \overset{\$}{\leftarrow}$ Encrypt(mpk, id$^*$, m$^*$)
7. $b' \overset{\$}{\leftarrow} \mathcal{A}_2^{\text{KeyGen(msk,.)}}(\text{mpk}, c^*)$ *where for each query* id *by* $\mathcal{A}_2$ *to* KeyGen(msk, .) *we have that* id $\neq$ id$^*$.
8. *Output* 1 *if* $b^* = b'$ *and* 0 *otherwise.*

**Fig. 2.** The sel-IND$^{\text{IBE}}(\mathcal{A})$ experiment

*The selective security notion easily extends to multiple challenge ciphertexts with multiple challenge identities. A simple hybrid argument shows that if an PPT adversary $\mathcal{A}$ break* sel-IND$^{\text{IBE}}$ *security in the k ciphertext setting with advantage $\epsilon$, there exists a PPT adversary $\mathcal{A}'$ that breaks single challenge ciphertext* sel-IND$^{\text{IBE}}$ *with advantage $\epsilon/k$.*

### 2.3   Hierarchical Identity-Based Encryption (HIBE)

In a HIBE scheme, there exists an additional algorithm Delegate which allows to generate hierarchical secret-keys msk$_{\text{id}}^{\text{HIBE}}$ for any input identity id. The hierarchical key for an identity id allows a user holding it to generate regular (or hierarchical keys) for any identity with prefix id. The syntax of Delegate is as follows.

– Delegate(msk, id) takes as input a master secret key (or a delegated key) msk and an identity id and outputs a HIBE key msk$_{\text{id}}^{\text{HIBE}}$.

In terms of correctness, we require that our HIBE additionally has the property that identity secret keys computed from delegated master secret keys are identical to identity secret keys computed by the original master secret key, i.e. for all identities id and id$'$ it holds that

$$\text{KeyGen}(\text{msk}, \text{id}\|\text{id}') = \text{KeyGen}(\text{msk}_{\text{id}}^{\text{HIBE}}, \text{id}'),$$

$$\text{Delegate}(\text{msk}, \text{id}\|\text{id}') = \text{Delegate}(\text{msk}_{\text{id}}^{\text{HIBE}}, \text{id}'),$$

where msk$_{\text{id}}^{\text{HIBE}}$ := Delegate(msk, id). This correctness condition is stronger than what is typically defined for HIBE and we use this definition as it simplifies our

---

**Experiment** $\mathsf{IND}^{\mathsf{IBE}}(\mathcal{A})$:

1. $(\mathsf{mpk}, \mathsf{msk}) \xleftarrow{\$} \mathsf{Setup}(1^\lambda)$.
2. $(\mathsf{id}^*, \mathsf{m}_0, \mathsf{m}_1) \xleftarrow{\$} \mathcal{A}_1^{\mathsf{KeyGen}(\mathsf{msk},.)}(\mathsf{mpk})$ *where* $|\mathsf{m}_0| = |\mathsf{m}_1|$ *and for each query* $\mathsf{id}$ *by* $\mathcal{A}_1$ *to* $\mathsf{KeyGen}(\mathsf{msk},.)$ *we have that* $\mathsf{id} \neq \mathsf{id}^*$.
3. $b^* \xleftarrow{\$} \{0, 1\}$.
4. $\mathsf{m}^* := \mathsf{m}_b$
5. $c^* \xleftarrow{\$} \mathsf{Encrypt}(\mathsf{mpk}, \mathsf{id}^*, \mathsf{m}^*)$
6. $b' \xleftarrow{\$} \mathcal{A}_2^{\mathsf{KeyGen}(\mathsf{msk},.)}(\mathsf{mpk}, c^*)$ *where for each query* $\mathsf{id}$ *by* $\mathcal{A}_2$ *to* $\mathsf{KeyGen}(\mathsf{msk},.)$ *we have that* $\mathsf{id} \neq \mathsf{id}^*$.
7. *Output* 1 *if* $b^* = b'$ *and* 0 *otherwise.*

---

**Fig. 3.** The $\mathsf{IND}^{\mathsf{IBE}}(\mathcal{A})$ experiment

correctness analysis and the security definition. We note that if the distribution of the secret-key queries obtained via first computing delegation keys is different from the distribution of the secret-keys obtained directly, then a "complete" model of HIBE security is needed. This was introduced by [SW08].

The security property is analogous to the $\mathsf{sel\text{-}IND}^{\mathsf{IBE}}$ except that now $\mathcal{A}$ is also allowed to ask for any hierarchical secret-key queries as long as they are not sufficient for decrypting the challenge ciphertext. We only consider the notion of *selective security* for HIBE; namely, the adversary $\mathcal{A}$ is required to announce the challenge identity $\mathsf{id}^*$ before it can make any secret-key or hierarchical secret-key queries.

**Selective Security:** For any PPT adversary $\mathcal{A} = (\mathcal{A}_1, \mathcal{A}_2, \mathcal{A}_3)$, there exists a negligible function $\mathsf{negl}(\cdot)$ such that the following holds:

$$\Pr[\mathsf{sel\text{-}IND}^{\mathsf{HIBE}}(\mathcal{A}) = 1] \leq \frac{1}{2} + \mathsf{negl}(\lambda)$$

where $\mathsf{sel\text{-}IND}^{\mathsf{HIBE}}(\mathcal{A})$ is shown in Fig. 4. For each identity key query $\mathsf{id}$ that $\mathcal{A}$ sends to the KeyGen oracle, it must hold that $\mathsf{id} \neq \mathsf{id}^*$. Moreover, for each HIBE key query $\mathsf{id}$ that $\mathcal{A}$ sends to the Delegate oracle, it must hold that $\mathsf{id}$ is not a prefix of $\mathsf{id}^*$.

### 2.4 Chameleon Encryption

**Definition 3 (Chameleon Encryption [DG17]).** *A chameleon encryption scheme consists of five PPT algorithms* CGen, CHash, CHash$^{-1}$, CEnc, *and* CDec *with the following syntax.*

- CGen$(1^\lambda, n)$: *Takes the security parameter* $\lambda$ *and a message-length* $n$ *(with* $n = \mathsf{poly}(\lambda)$*) as input and outputs a key* k *and a trapdoor* t.

---

**Experiment sel-IND$^{\mathsf{HIBE}}(\mathcal{A})$:**

1. $\mathsf{id}^* := \mathcal{A}_1(1^\lambda)$
2. $(\mathsf{mpk}, \mathsf{msk}) \xleftarrow{\$} \mathsf{Setup}(1^\lambda)$
3. $(\mathsf{m}_0, \mathsf{m}_1) \xleftarrow{\$} \mathcal{A}_1^{\mathsf{KeyGen(msk,.),Delegate(msk,\cdot)}}(\mathsf{mpk})$ where $|\mathsf{m}_0| = |\mathsf{m}_1|$ and for each query id by $\mathcal{A}_1$ to $\mathsf{KeyGen(msk,.)}$ we have that $\mathsf{id} \neq \mathsf{id}^*$ and for each $\mathsf{Delegate(msk,.)}$ query we have that id is not a prefix of $\mathsf{id}^*$.
4. $b^* \xleftarrow{\$} \{0,1\}$.
5. $\mathsf{m}^* := \mathsf{m}_b$
6. $c^* \xleftarrow{\$} \mathsf{Encrypt}(\mathsf{mpk}, \mathsf{id}^*, \mathsf{m}^*)$
7. $b' \xleftarrow{\$} \mathcal{A}_2^{\mathsf{KeyGen(msk,.),Delegate(msk,\cdot)}}(\mathsf{mpk}, c^*)$ where for each query id by $\mathcal{A}_2$ to $\mathsf{KeyGen(msk,.)}$ we have that $\mathsf{id} \neq \mathsf{id}^*$ and for each $\mathsf{Delegate(msk,.)}$ query we have that id is not a prefix of $\mathsf{id}^*$.
8. Output 1 if $b^* = b'$ and 0 otherwise.

---

**Fig. 4.** The sel-IND$^{\mathsf{HIBE}}(\mathcal{A})$ experiment

- $\mathsf{CHash}(\mathsf{k}, \mathsf{x}; r)$: *Takes a key* $\mathsf{k}$, *a message* $\mathsf{x} \in \{0,1\}^n$, *and coins* $r$ *and outputs a hash value* $\mathsf{h}$, *where the size of* $\mathsf{h}$ *is* $\lambda$ *bits.*
- $\mathsf{CHash}^{-1}(\mathsf{t}, (\mathsf{x}, r), \mathsf{x}')$: *Takes a trapdoor* $\mathsf{t}$, *previously used message* $\mathsf{x} \in \{0,1\}^n$ *and coins* $r$, *and a message* $\mathsf{x}' \in \{0,1\}^n$ *as input and returns* $r'$.
- $\mathsf{CEnc}(\mathsf{k}, (\mathsf{h}, i, b), \mathsf{m})$: *Takes a key* $\mathsf{k}$, *a hash value* $\mathsf{h}$, *an index* $i \in [n]$, $b \in \{0,1\}$, *and a message* $\mathsf{m} \in \{0,1\}^*$ *and outputs a ciphertext* $\mathsf{ct}$.[6]
- $\mathsf{CDec}(\mathsf{k}, (\mathsf{x}, r), \mathsf{ct})$: *Takes a key* $\mathsf{k}$, *a message* $\mathsf{x}$, *coins* $r$ *and a ciphertext* $\mathsf{ct}$, *as input and outputs a value* $\mathsf{m}$ *(or* $\bot$).

*We require the following properties*

- **Uniformity:** *For* $\mathsf{x}, \mathsf{x}' \in \{0,1\}^n$ *the two distributions* $\mathsf{CHash}(\mathsf{k}, \mathsf{x}; r)$ *and* $\mathsf{CHash}(\mathsf{k}, \mathsf{x}'; r')$ *are statistically close (when* $r, r'$ *are chosen uniformly at random).*
- **Trapdoor Collisions:** *For every choice of* $\mathsf{x}, \mathsf{x}' \in \{0,1\}^n$ *and* $r$ *it holds that if* $(\mathsf{k}, \mathsf{t}) \xleftarrow{\$} \mathsf{CGen}(1^\lambda, n)$ *and* $r' := \mathsf{CHash}^{-1}(\mathsf{t}, (\mathsf{x}, r), \mathsf{x}')$, *then it holds that*

$$\mathsf{CHash}(\mathsf{k}, \mathsf{x}; r) = \mathsf{CHash}(\mathsf{k}, \mathsf{x}'; r'),$$

  *i.e.* $\mathsf{CHash}(\mathsf{k}, \mathsf{x}; r)$ *and* $\mathsf{CHash}(\mathsf{k}, \mathsf{x}'; r')$ *generate the same hash* $\mathsf{h}$. *Moreover, if* $r$ *is chosen uniformly at random, then* $r'$ *is also statistically close to uniform.*
- **Correctness:** *For any choice of* $\mathsf{x} \in \{0,1\}^n$, *coins* $r$, *index* $i \in [n]$ *and message* $\mathsf{m}$ *it holds that if* $(\mathsf{k}, \mathsf{t}) \xleftarrow{\$} \mathsf{CGen}(1^\lambda, n)$, $\mathsf{h} := \mathsf{CHash}(\mathsf{k}, \mathsf{x}; r)$, *and* $\mathsf{ct} \xleftarrow{\$} \mathsf{CEnc}(\mathsf{k}, (\mathsf{h}, i, \mathsf{x}_i), \mathsf{m})$ *then* $\mathsf{CDec}(\mathsf{k}, (\mathsf{x}, r), \mathsf{ct}) = \mathsf{m}$.

---

[6] ct is assumed to contain $(\mathsf{h}, i, b)$.

– **Security:** *For any PPT adversary* $\mathcal{A} = (\mathcal{A}_1, \mathcal{A}_2)$ *there exists a negligible function* $\mathsf{negl}(\cdot)$ *such that the following holds:*

$$\Pr[IND_{\mathcal{A}}^{CE}(1^\lambda) = 1] \leq \frac{1}{2} + \mathsf{negl}(\lambda)$$

*where* $IND_{\mathcal{A}}^{CE}$ *is shown in Fig. 5.*

---

**Experiment** $IND_{\mathcal{A}=(\mathcal{A}_1,\mathcal{A}_2)}^{CE}(1^\lambda)$:

1. $(\mathsf{k}, \mathsf{t}) \overset{\$}{\leftarrow} \mathsf{CGen}(1^\lambda, n)$.
2. $(\mathsf{x}, r, i \in [n]) \overset{\$}{\leftarrow} \mathcal{A}_1(\mathsf{k})$.
3. $b^* \overset{\$}{\leftarrow} \{0, 1\}$.
4. $\mathsf{ct} \overset{\$}{\leftarrow} \mathsf{CEnc}(\mathsf{k}, (\mathsf{CHash}(\mathsf{k}, \mathsf{x}; r), i, 1 - \mathsf{x}_i), b)$.
5. $b' \overset{\$}{\leftarrow} \mathcal{A}_2(\mathsf{k}, \mathsf{ct}, (\mathsf{x}, r))$.
6. *Output 1 if* $b^* = b'$ *and 0 otherwise.*

---

**Fig. 5.** The $IND_{\mathcal{A}}^{CE}$ experiment

## 2.5 Garbled Circuits

Garbled circuits were first introduced by Yao [Yao82] (see Lindell and Pinkas [LP09] and Bellare et al. [BHR12] for a detailed proof and further discussion). A projective circuit garbling scheme is a tuple of PPT algorithms $(\mathsf{Garble}, \mathsf{Eval})$ with the following syntax.

– $\mathsf{Garble}(1^\lambda, \mathsf{C})$ takes as input a security parameter $\lambda$ and a circuit $\mathsf{C}$ and outputs a *garbled circuit* $\tilde{\mathsf{C}}$ and labels $\mathsf{e}_C = \{X_{\iota,0}, X_{\iota,1}\}_{\iota \in [n]}$, where $n$ is the number of input wires of $\mathsf{C}$.
– Projective Encoding: To encode an $\mathsf{x} \in \{0,1\}^n$ with the input labels $\mathsf{e}_C = \{X_{\iota,0}, X_{\iota,1}\}_{\iota \in [n]}$, we compute $\tilde{\mathsf{x}} := \{X_{\iota,\mathsf{x}_\iota}\}_{\iota \in [n]}$.
– $\mathsf{Eval}(\tilde{\mathsf{C}}, \tilde{\mathsf{x}})$: takes as input a garbled circuit $\tilde{\mathsf{C}}$ and a garbled input $\tilde{\mathsf{x}}$, represented as a sequence of input labels $\{X_{\iota,\mathsf{x}_\iota}\}_{\iota \in [n]}$, and outputs an output $y$.

We will denote hardwiring of an input $s$ into a circuit $\mathsf{C}$ by $\mathsf{C}[s]$. The garbling algorithm $\mathsf{Garble}$ treats the hardwired input as a regular input and additionally outputs the garbled input corresponding to $s$ (instead of all the labels of the input wires corresponding to $s$). If a circuit $\mathsf{C}$ uses additional randomness, we will implicitly assume that appropriate random coins are hardwired in this circuit during garbling.

*Correctness.* For correctness, we require that for any circuit $\mathsf{C}$ and input $\mathsf{x} \in \{0,1\}^n$ we have that

$$\Pr\left[\mathsf{C}(\mathsf{x}) = \mathsf{Eval}(\tilde{\mathsf{C}}, \tilde{\mathsf{x}})\right] = 1$$

where $(\tilde{\mathsf{C}}, \mathsf{e}_C = \{X_{\iota,0}, X_{\iota,1}\}_{\iota \in [n]}) \overset{\$}{\leftarrow} \mathsf{Garble}(1^\lambda, \mathsf{C})$ and $\tilde{\mathsf{x}} := \{X_{\iota,\mathsf{x}_\iota}\}$.

*Security.* For security, we require that there is a PPT simulator GCSim such that for any circuit C and any input x, we have that

$$(\tilde{C}, \tilde{x}) \stackrel{\text{comp}}{\approx} \text{GCSim}(C, C(x))$$

where $(\tilde{C}, e_C = \{X_{\iota,0}, X_{\iota,1}\}_{\iota \in [n]}) := \text{Garble}(1^\lambda, C)$ and $\tilde{x} := \{X_{\iota, x_\iota}\}$.

## 2.6 Delegatable Pseudorandom Functions

In our HIBE construction we will need a PRF for which the inputs can be binary strings of unrestricted length and which supports the delegation of seeds for inputs that start with certain prefixes.

**Definition 4.** *A delegatable pseudorandom function consists of two algorithms F and F.Delegate with the following syntax.*

- *$F(s, x)$ takes as input a seed $s \in \{0,1\}^\lambda$ and a string $x \in \{0,1\}^*$ and outputs a value $u \in \{0,1\}^\lambda$.*
- *F.Delegate$(s, x)$ takes as input a seed $s$ and an input $x$ and outputs a seed $s_x$.*

*We require the following properties of a delegatable pseudorandom function.*

- **Delegatability:** *It holds for all inputs $x, x' \in \{0,1\}^*$ that*

$$F(s, x\|x') = F(s_x, x'),$$

*where $s_x := F.\text{Delegate}(s, x)$.*
- **Pseudorandomness:** *It holds for all PPT distinguishers $\mathcal{D}$ and every $x \in \{0,1\}^*$ of size at most polynomial in $\lambda$ that*

$$|\Pr[\mathcal{D}^{F(s,\cdot), \text{Delegate}(s,\cdot)}(1^\lambda) = 1] - \Pr[\mathcal{D}^{H(\cdot), \text{Delegate}(s,\cdot)}(1^\lambda) = 1]| \leq \text{negl}(\lambda)$$

*where $s \stackrel{\$}{\leftarrow} \{0,1\}^\lambda$ is chosen uniformly at random, $H$ is a function which is uniformly random on all prefixes of $x$ (including $x$) and identical to $F(s, \cdot)$ on all other inputs, and $\text{Delegate}(s, \cdot)$ delegates seeds for all inputs $x' \in \{0,1\}^*$ that are not a prefix of $x$.*

We will briefly sketch a simple variant of the GGM construction [GGM84] which satisfies the above definition. Let $G : \{0,1\}^\lambda \rightarrow \{0,1\}^{3\lambda}$ be a length-tripling pseudorandom generator and $G_0, G_1$ and $G_2$ be the $1 \ldots \lambda$, $\lambda + 1 \ldots 2\lambda$ and $2\lambda + 1 \ldots 3\lambda$ bits of the output of $G$, respectively. Now define a GGM-type pseudo-random function $F : \{0,1\}^\lambda \times \{0,1\}^* \rightarrow \{0,1\}^\lambda$ such that $F(s, x) := G_2(G_{x_n}(G_{x_{n-1}}(\ldots(G_{x_1}(s))\ldots)))$, where for each $i \in [n]$ $x_i$ is the $i^{th}$ bit of $x \in \{0,1\}^n$. $F.\text{Delegate}(s, x)$ computes and outputs $G_{x_n}(G_{x_{n-1}}(\ldots(G_{x_1}(s))\ldots))$.

# 3   One-Time Signatures with Encryption

In this Section, we will introduce a primitive we call *One-Time Signatures with Encryption* (OTSE). Syntactically, we will not require the existence of a verification algorithm for such signature schemes, but instead require the existence of accompanying encryption and decryption algorithms. Details follow.

**Definition 5.** *A One-Time Signature with Encryption (OTSE) scheme consists of five algorithms* (SSetup, SGen, SSign, SEnc, SDec) *with the following syntax.*

- SSetup$(1^\lambda, \ell)$: *Takes as input an unary encoding of the security parameter* $1^\lambda$ *and a message length parameter* $\ell$ *and outputs public parameters* pp.
- SGen(pp): *Takes as input public parameters* pp *and outputs a pair* (vk, sk) *of verification and signing keys.*
- SSign(pp, sk, x): *Takes as input public parameters* pp, *a signing key* sk *and a message* x *and outputs a signature* $\sigma$.
- SEnc(pp, (vk, $i, b$), m): *Takes as input public parameters* pp, *a verification key* vk, *an index* $i$, *a bit* $b$ *and a plaintext* m *and outputs a ciphertext* c. *We will generally assume that the index* $i$ *and the bit* $b$ *are included in* c.
- SDec(pp, (vk, $\sigma, x$), c): *Takes as input public parameters* pp, *a verification key* vk, *a signature* $\sigma$, *a message* x *and a ciphertext* c *and returns a plaintext* m.

*We require the following properties.*

- **Succinctness:** *For* pp := SSetup$(1^\lambda, \ell)$ *and* (vk, sk) := SGen(pp, $\ell$) *it holds that the size of* vk *is independent of* $\ell$, *only depending on* $\lambda$.
- **Correctness:** *It holds for all security parameters* $\lambda$, *every message* x *and every plaintext* m *that if* pp := Setup$(1^\lambda, \ell)$, (vk, sk) := SGen(pp) *and* $\sigma$ := SSign(sk, x) *then*

$$\text{SDec}(\text{pp}, (\text{vk}, \sigma, \text{x}), \text{SEnc}(\text{pp}, (\text{vk}, i.b), \text{m})) = \text{m}.$$

- **Selective Security:** *For any PPT adversary* $\mathcal{A} = (\mathcal{A}_1, \mathcal{A}_2, \mathcal{A}_3)$, *there exists a negligible function* negl$(\cdot)$ *such that the following holds:*

$$\Pr[\text{IND}^{\text{OTSE}}(\mathcal{A}) = 1] \leq \frac{1}{2} + \text{negl}(\lambda)$$

*where* $\text{IND}^{\text{OTSE}}(\mathcal{A})$ *is shown in Fig. 6.*

Again, we remark that multi-challenge security follows via a hybrid argument.

# 4   One-Time Signatures with Encryption from Chameleon Encryption

In this Section we provide a construction of an OTSE scheme from chameleon encryption.

---

**Experiment** $\mathsf{IND}^{\mathsf{OTSE}}(\mathcal{A})$:

1. $\mathsf{pp} := \mathsf{SSetup}(1^\lambda, \ell)$
2. $\mathsf{x} := \mathcal{A}_1(\mathsf{pp})$
3. $(\mathsf{vk}, \mathsf{sk}) := \mathsf{SGen}(\mathsf{pp})$
4. $\sigma := \mathsf{SSign}(\mathsf{pp}, \mathsf{sk}, \mathsf{x})$
5. $(i, \mathsf{m}_0, \mathsf{m}_1) := \mathcal{A}_2(\mathsf{pp}, \mathsf{vk}, \sigma)$
6. $b^* \xleftarrow{\$} \{0, 1\}$
7. $\mathsf{m}^* := \mathsf{m}_{b^*}$
8. $c^* := \mathsf{SEnc}(\mathsf{pp}, (\mathsf{vk}, i, 1 - \mathsf{x}_i), \mathsf{m}^*)$
9. $b' := \mathcal{A}_3(\mathsf{pp}, \mathsf{vk}, \sigma, c^*)$
10. *Output* 1 *if* $b' = b^*$ *and* 0 *otherwise.*

---

**Fig. 6.** The $\mathsf{IND}^{\mathsf{OTSE}}(\mathcal{A})$ experiment

$\mathsf{SSetup}(1^\lambda, \ell)$ : Compute $(K, \cdot) := \mathsf{CGen}(1^\lambda, \ell)$ and output $\mathsf{pp} := K$.

$\mathsf{SGen}(\mathsf{pp})$ : Compute $(\mathsf{k}, \mathsf{t}) := \mathsf{CGen}(1^\lambda, \lambda)$, sample $r' \xleftarrow{\$} \{0, 1\}^\lambda$, compute $\mathsf{h} := \mathsf{CHash}(\mathsf{k}, 0^\lambda; r')$. Set $\mathsf{vk} := (\mathsf{k}, h)$, $\mathsf{sk} := (\mathsf{t}, r')$ and output $(\mathsf{vk}, \mathsf{sk})$.

$\mathsf{SSign}(\mathsf{pp}, \mathsf{sk} = (\mathsf{t}, r'), \mathsf{x})$ : Compute $y := \mathsf{CHash}(K, \mathsf{x})$ and $r := \mathsf{CHash}^{-1}(\mathsf{t}, (0^\lambda, r'), y)$, output $\sigma := r$.

$\mathsf{SEnc}(\mathsf{pp} = K, (\mathsf{vk} = (\mathsf{k}, h), i, b), \mathsf{m})$ : Let $C$ be the following circuit.
- $C[K, i, b](y)$ : Compute and output $\mathsf{CEnc}(K, (y, i, b), \mathsf{m})$.
  $(\tilde{C}, e_C) := \mathsf{Garble}(1^\lambda, C[K, i, b])$
  Parse $e_C = \{Y_{\iota,0}, Y_{\iota,1}\}_{\iota \in [\lambda]}$
  $f_C := \{\mathsf{CEnc}(\mathsf{k}, (h, \iota, b'), Y_{\iota,b'})\}_{\iota \in [\lambda], b' \in \{0,1\}}$
  Output $\mathsf{ct} := (\tilde{C}, f_C)$.

$\mathsf{SDec}(\mathsf{pp} = K, (\mathsf{vk} = (\mathsf{k}, h), \sigma = r, \mathsf{x}), \mathsf{ct} = (\tilde{C}, f_C))$ :
  Parse $f_C = \{c_{\iota,b'}\}_{\iota \in [\lambda], b' \in \{0,1\}}$
  $y := \mathsf{CHash}(K, \mathsf{x})$
  $\tilde{y} := \{\mathsf{CDec}(\mathsf{k}, (y, r), c_{\iota, y_\iota})\}_{\iota \in [\lambda]}$
  $c' := \mathsf{Eval}(\tilde{C}, \tilde{y})$
  $\mathsf{m} := \mathsf{CDec}(K, \mathsf{x}, c')$
  Output $\mathsf{m}$

*Succinctness and Correctness.* By construction the size of $\mathsf{vk} = (\mathsf{k}, h)$ depends only on $\lambda$, so we have established the succinctness property. To see that the construction is correct, note that since the hash value $\mathsf{h} = \mathsf{CHash}(\mathsf{k}, y; r)$ and $c_{\iota,b'} = \mathsf{CEnc}(\mathsf{k}, (h, \iota, b'), Y_{\iota,b'})$, it holds by the correctness property of the chameleon encryption scheme $(\mathsf{CGen}, \mathsf{CHash}, \mathsf{CHash}^{-1}, \mathsf{CEnc}, \mathsf{CDec})$ that

$$\tilde{y} = \{\mathsf{CDec}(\mathsf{k}, (y, r), c_{\iota, y_\iota})\}_{\iota \in [\lambda]} = \{Y_{\iota, y_\iota}\}.$$

Therefore, as $(\tilde{C}, e_C) = \mathsf{Garble}(1^\lambda, C[K, i, b])$, it holds by the correctness of the garbling scheme $(\mathsf{Garble}, \mathsf{Eval})$ that

$$c' = \mathsf{Eval}(\tilde{C}, \tilde{y}) = C[K, i, b](y) = \mathsf{CEnc}(K, (y, i, b), m).$$

Finally, as $y = \mathsf{CHash}(K, x)$, it holds by the correctness of the of the chameleon encryption scheme $(\mathsf{CGen}, \mathsf{CHash}, \mathsf{CHash}^{-1}, \mathsf{CEnc}, \mathsf{CDec})$ that

$$\mathsf{CDec}(K, x, c') = m.$$

*Security.* We will now establish the $\mathsf{IND}^{\mathsf{OTSE}}$ security of $(\mathsf{SSetup}, \mathsf{SGen}, \mathsf{SSign}, \mathsf{SEnc}, \mathsf{SDec})$ from the $\mathsf{IND}^{\mathsf{CE}}$-security of $(\mathsf{CGen}, \mathsf{CHash}, \mathsf{CHash}^{-1}, \mathsf{CEnc}, \mathsf{CDec})$ and the security of the garbling scheme $(\mathsf{Garble}, \mathsf{Eval})$.

**Theorem 1.** *Assume that* $(\mathsf{CGen}, \mathsf{CHash}, \mathsf{CHash}^{-1}, \mathsf{CEnc}, \mathsf{CDec})$ *is* $\mathsf{IND}^{\mathsf{CE}}$*-secure and* $(\mathsf{Garble}, \mathsf{Eval})$ *is a secure garbling scheme. Then* $(\mathsf{SSetup}, \mathsf{SGen}, \mathsf{SSign}, \mathsf{SEnc}, \mathsf{SDec})$ *is* $\mathsf{IND}^{\mathsf{OTSE}}$*-secure.*

*Proof.* Let $\mathcal{A}$ be a PPT-adversary against $\mathsf{IND}^{\mathsf{OTSE}}$. Consider the following hybrid experiments.

*Hybrid $\mathcal{H}_0$.* This experiment is identical to $\mathsf{IND}^{\mathsf{OTSE}}(\mathcal{A})$.

*Hybrid $\mathcal{H}_1$.* This experiment is identical to $\mathcal{H}_0$, except that $f_C$ is computed by $f_C := \{\mathsf{CEnc}(k, (h, \iota, b'), Y_{\iota, y_\iota})\}_{\iota \in [\lambda], b' \in \{0,1\}}$ instead of by the expression $f_C := \{\mathsf{CEnc}(k, (h, \iota, b'), Y_{\iota, b'})\}_{\iota \in [\lambda], b' \in \{0,1\}}$. Computational indistinguishability between hybrids $\mathcal{H}_0$ and $\mathcal{H}_1$ follows by the $\mathsf{IND}^{\mathsf{CE}}$-security of $(\mathsf{CGen}, \mathsf{CHash}, \mathsf{CHash}^{-1}, \mathsf{CEnc}, \mathsf{CDec})$. Note that the security reduction has no access to the collision-trapdoor $t$. However, as the $\mathsf{IND}^{\mathsf{OTSE}}$-experiment is defined selectively, the reduction gets to see $x$ before it has to provide $vk$. Consequently, it can set $h := \mathsf{CHash}(k, \mathsf{CHash}(K, x); r)$, $vk := (k, h)$ and present $\sigma := r$ as a valid signature to the adversary without the need of a collision trapdoor.

*Hybrid $\mathcal{H}_2$.* This experiment is identical to $\mathcal{H}_1$, except that we compute $\tilde{C}$ and $\tilde{y}$ by $(\tilde{C}, \tilde{y}) := \mathsf{GCSim}(C, c)$, where $c := \mathsf{CEnc}(K, (y, i, b), m)$ instead of $(\tilde{C}, e_C) := \mathsf{Garble}(1^\lambda, C[K, i, b])$, where $e_C = \{Y_{\iota, b'}\}_{\iota \in [\lambda], b' \in \{0,1\}}$ and $\tilde{y} = \{Y_{\iota, y_\iota}\}$. Computational indistinguishability between hybrids $\mathcal{H}_1$ and $\mathcal{H}_2$ follows by the security of the garbling scheme $(\mathsf{Garble}, \mathsf{Eval})$. By the $\mathsf{IND}^{\mathsf{CE}}$-security of $(\mathsf{CGen}, \mathsf{CHash}, \mathsf{CHash}^{-1}, \mathsf{CEnc}, \mathsf{CDec})$ it follows that the advantage of $\mathcal{A}$ in $\mathcal{H}_2$ is negligible.

## 5 One-Time Signatures with Encryption from Selectively Secure IBE

We will now provide a construction of an OTSE scheme from selectively secure IBE. Let therefore $(\mathsf{Setup}, \mathsf{KeyGen}, \mathsf{Encrypt}, \mathsf{Decrypt})$ be an IBE scheme.

SSetup($1^\lambda, \ell$): Output pp := $\ell$.

SGen(pp): Compute (mpk, msk) := Setup($1^\lambda$), set vk := mpk and sk := msk and output (vk, sk).

SSign(pp, sk = msk, x): Compute and output $\sigma := \{\mathsf{KeyGen}(\mathsf{msk}, \mathsf{x}_\iota \| \mathsf{bin}(\iota))\}_{\iota \in [\ell]}$.

SEnc(pp, (vk = mpk, $i, b$), m): Compute                and                output $c := \mathsf{Encrypt}(\mathsf{mpk}, b \| \mathsf{bin}(i), \mathsf{m})$.

SDec(pp, (vk, $\sigma$, x), $c$): Parse $\sigma = \{\mathsf{sk}_{\mathsf{x}_\iota \| \mathsf{bin}(\iota)}\}_{\iota \in [\ell]}$. Compute and output m := $\mathsf{Decrypt}(\mathsf{sk}_{\mathsf{x}_i \| \mathsf{bin}(i)}, c)$.

*Succinctness and Correctness.* The succinctness property follows directly form the fact the size of the master public key mpk does not depend on this length of the identities, but is a fixed polynomial in c$\lambda$.

On the other hand, correctness follows from the correctness of the IBE scheme (Setup, KeyGen, Encrypt, Decrypt).

*Security.* We will now show that the $\mathsf{IND}^{\mathsf{OTSE}}$-security of (SSetup, SGen, SSign, SEnc, SDec) follows from the $\mathsf{sel\text{-}IND}^{\mathsf{IBE}}$-security of the IBE scheme (Setup, KeyGenEncrypt, Decrypt).

**Theorem 2.** *Assume that* (Setup, KeyGen, Encrypt, Decrypt) *is* $\mathsf{sel\text{-}IND}^{\mathsf{IBE}}$ *secure. Then* ($\cdot$, SGen, SSign, SEnc, SDec) *is* $\mathsf{IND}^{\mathsf{OTSE}}$-*secure.*

*Proof.* Let $\mathcal{A}$ be a PPT adversary that breaks the $\mathsf{IND}^{\mathsf{OTSE}}$-security of (SSetup, SGen, SSign, SEnc, SDec) with advantage $\epsilon$. We will provide a reduction $\mathcal{R}$ such that $\mathcal{R}^{\mathcal{A}}$ breaks the $\mathsf{sel\text{-}IND}^{\mathsf{IBE}}$-security of (Setup, KeyGen, Encrypt, Decrypt) with advantage $\epsilon$. $\mathcal{R}$ proceeds as follows. $\mathcal{R}$ first guesses a random index $i^* \xleftarrow{\$} [\ell]$. It then simulates the $\mathsf{IND}^{\mathsf{OTSE}}$-experiment with $\mathcal{A}$ until $\mathcal{A}$ outputs a message x (that is, $\mathcal{R}$ runs $\mathcal{A}_1(1^\lambda)$). $\mathcal{R}$ now declares its challenge identity id$^* := (1 - \mathsf{x}_{i^*}) \| \mathsf{bin}(i^*)$ to the $\mathsf{sel\text{-}IND}^{\mathsf{IBE}}$ experiment and also asks for identity secret keys corresponding to the identities $\{\mathsf{x}_\iota \| \mathsf{bin}(\iota)\}_{\iota \in [\ell]}$. $\mathcal{R}$ now receives the master public key mpk and the identity secret keys $\{\mathsf{sk}_{\mathsf{x}_\iota \| \mathsf{bin}(\iota)}\}_{\iota \in [\ell]}$. Next, $\mathcal{R}$ sets vk := mpk and $\sigma := \{\mathsf{sk}_{\mathsf{x}_\iota \| \mathsf{bin}(\iota)}\}_{\iota \in [\ell]}$ and provides vk and $\sigma$ to $\mathcal{A}$. $\mathcal{R}$ now continues the simulation until $\mathcal{A}$ outputs a triple ($i, \mathsf{m}_0, \mathsf{m}_1$). If $i \neq i^*$, $\mathcal{R}$ aborts the simulation and outputs a random bit. Otherwise, $\mathcal{R}$ sends ($\mathsf{m}_0, \mathsf{m}_1$) to the $\mathsf{sel\text{-}IND}^{\mathsf{IBE}}$-experiment, obtains a challenge ciphertext $c^*$ and forwards $c^*$ to $\mathcal{A}$. $\mathcal{R}$ now continues the simulation and outputs whatever $\mathcal{A}$ outputs.

We will now analyze the advantage of $\mathcal{R}^{\mathcal{A}}$. Clearly, if $i^* \neq i$, then the advantage of $\mathcal{R}^{\mathcal{A}}$ is 0. On the other hand, if $i^* = i$, then from the view of $\mathcal{A}$ the $\mathsf{IND}^{\mathsf{OTSE}}$-experiment is simulated perfectly, where the challenge bit of the simulated $\mathsf{IND}^{\mathsf{OTSE}}$-experiment is identical to the challenge bit $b^*$ of the $\mathsf{sel\text{-}IND}^{\mathsf{IBE}}$-experiment. Consequently, in this case the advantage of $\mathcal{R}^{\mathcal{A}}$ is identical to the advantage of $\mathcal{A}$. Since $i^*$ is chosen uniformly at random, it holds $i^* = i$ with probability $1/\ell$. We can conclude that the advantage of $\mathcal{R}^{\mathcal{A}}$ is

$$\mathsf{Adv}_{\mathsf{sel\text{-}IND}^{\mathsf{IBE}}}(\mathcal{R}^{\mathcal{A}}) = \frac{1}{\ell} \cdot \mathsf{Adv}_{\mathsf{IND}^{\mathsf{OTSE}}}(\mathcal{A}) = \frac{\epsilon}{\ell},$$

which concludes the proof.

# 6   Achieving Fully Secure IBE

Let in the following (SSetup, SGen, SSign, SEnc, SDec) be an OTSE scheme. Without loss of generality, we will assume that the signing algorithm SSign is deterministic. This can always be achieved by making an additional pseudorandom function seed part of the signing key and generating random coins for the signing algorithm as needed. Let $F$ be a pseudorandom function. We assume for convenience that the pseudorandom function $F$ has two output registers, $F_1$ and $F_2$. Moreover, let (KG, E, D) be a standard public key encryption scheme. Without loss of generality assume that the verification keys of (SSetup, SGen, SSign, SEnc, SDec) and the public keys of the public-key encryption scheme (KG, E, D) have the same length $\ell$. This can always be achieved by an appropriate padding.

As we are working with an exponentially sized tree, we will define two functions NodeGen and LeafGen that provide access to the keys and thus implicitly define the tree. The NodeGen function generates keys for the root node and all internal nodes, whereas the LeafGen function generates public and private keys for the leaf nodes. More specifically, the NodeGen function takes as input a node identifier $v$ and a pseudorandom function seed $s$ and outputs a verification key $vk_v$ for this node, a signature $\sigma_v$ authenticating the verification keys of its children and an auxiliary value $x_v$ which is the concatenation of the verification keys of the children of $v$.

Recall that $\|$ is the concatenation operator. In the rest of this Section and the next Section we will use the following convention. The variable $\iota$ will always run over the range $[l]$ and $b$ will always run over $\{0, 1\}$.

NodeGen(pp, v, s):
  $(vk_v, sk_v) := SGen(pp; F_1(s, v))$
  Compute $vk_{v\|0}$ and $vk_{v\|1}$ in the same way.
  $x_v := vk_{v\|0} \| vk_{v\|1}$
  $\sigma_v := SSign(pp, sk_v, x)$
  Output $(vk_v, \sigma_v, x_v)$

The function LeafGen takes as input public parameters pp, a node-identifier $v$ of a leaf-node and a pseudorandom function seed $s$ and outputs the verification key $vk_v$ of the leaf, a signature $\sigma_v$ authenticating the leaf public key, a leaf public key $lpk_v$ and a leaf secret key $lsk_v$.

LeafGen(pp, v, s)
  $(vk_v, sk_v) := SGen(pp; F_1(s, v))$
  $(lpk_v, lsk_v) := KG(1^\lambda; F_2(s, v))$
  $x_v := lpk_v$
  $\sigma_v := SSign(pp, sk_v, x_v)$
  Output $(vk_v, \sigma_v, lpk_v, lsk_v)$

We will now provide the construction of our IBE scheme (Setup, KeyGen, Encrypt, Decrypt).

Setup($1^\lambda, n$) : Choose a random seed $s$ for the PRF $F$. Compute the public parameters $\mathsf{pp} := \mathsf{SSetup}(1^\lambda, 2\ell)$ and $(\mathsf{vk}_{\mathsf{v}_0}, \cdot, \cdot) := \mathsf{NodeGen}(\mathsf{pp}, \mathsf{v}_0, s)$. Output $\mathsf{mpk} := (\mathsf{pp}, \mathsf{vk}_{\mathsf{v}_0})$ and $\mathsf{msk} := s$.

KeyGen($\mathsf{msk} = s, \mathsf{id} \in \{0,1\}^n$) : Let $\mathsf{v}_0, \mathsf{v}_1, \ldots, \mathsf{v}_n$ be the root-to-leaf path for the identity id, i.e. all the prefixes of id. For $j = 0, \ldots, n-1$ compute $(\cdot, \sigma_{\mathsf{v}_j}, \mathsf{x}_{\mathsf{v}_j}) := \mathsf{NodeGen}(\mathsf{pp}, \mathsf{v}_j, s)$. Further compute $(\cdot, \sigma_{\mathsf{id}}, \mathsf{lpk}_{\mathsf{id}}, \mathsf{lsk}_{\mathsf{id}}) := \mathsf{LeafGen}(\mathsf{pp}, \mathsf{v}_n, s)$. Output $\mathsf{sk}_{\mathsf{id}} := ((\sigma_{\mathsf{v}_0}, \mathsf{x}_{\mathsf{v}_0}), \ldots, (\sigma_{\mathsf{v}_n}, \mathsf{x}_{\mathsf{v}_n}), \sigma_{\mathsf{id}}, \mathsf{lpk}_{\mathsf{id}}, \mathsf{lsk}_{\mathsf{id}})$.

Encrypt($\mathsf{mpk} = (\mathsf{pp}, \mathsf{vk}_{\mathsf{v}_0}), \mathsf{id} \in \{0,1\}^n, \mathsf{m}$) : We will first describe two circuits that will be used by the encryption algorithm.

- $Q[\mathsf{pp}, \beta \in \{0,1\}, e_Q = \{(Y_{\iota,0}, Y_{\iota,1})\}_\iota](\mathsf{vk})$ : Compute and output $\{\mathsf{SEnc}(\mathsf{pp}, (\mathsf{vk}, \beta \cdot \ell + \iota, b), Y_{\iota,b})\}_{\iota,b}$
- $T[\mathsf{m}](\mathsf{lpk})$: Compute and output $E(\mathsf{lpk}, \mathsf{m})$.

$(\tilde{T}, e_T) := \mathsf{Garble}(1^\lambda, T[\mathsf{m}])$
$(\tilde{Q}^{(n)}, e_Q^{(n)}) := \mathsf{Garble}(1^\lambda, Q[\mathsf{pp}, 0, e_T])$
For $j = n-1, \ldots, 0$
$\quad (\tilde{Q}^{(j)}, e_Q^{(j)}) := \mathsf{Garble}(1^\lambda, Q[\mathsf{pp}, \mathsf{id}_{j+1}, e_Q^{(j+1)}])$
Parse $e_Q^{(0)} = \{Y_{\iota,0}, Y_{\iota,1}\}_\iota$
$y := \mathsf{vk}_{\mathsf{v}_0}$
$\tilde{y}^{(0)} := \{Y_{\iota, y_\iota}\}_\iota$
Output $c := (\tilde{y}^{(0)}, \tilde{Q}^{(0)}, \ldots, \tilde{Q}^{(n)}, \tilde{T})$

Decrypt($\mathsf{sk}_{\mathsf{id}} = ((\sigma_{\mathsf{v}_0}, \mathsf{x}_{\mathsf{v}_0}), \ldots, (\sigma_{\mathsf{v}_n}, \mathsf{x}_{\mathsf{v}_n}), \sigma_{\mathsf{id}}, \mathsf{lpk}_{\mathsf{id}}, \mathsf{lsk}_{\mathsf{id}}), c = (\tilde{y}^{(0)}, \tilde{Q}^{(0)}, \ldots, \tilde{Q}^{(n)}, \tilde{T})$)
$\quad$For $j = 0, \ldots, n-1$:
$\quad\quad \{c_{\iota,b}^{(j)}\}_{\iota,b} := \mathsf{Eval}(\tilde{Q}^{(j)}, \tilde{y}^{(j)})$
$\quad\quad \tilde{y}^{(j+1)} := \{\mathsf{SDec}(\mathsf{pp}, (\mathsf{vk}_{\mathsf{v}_j}, \sigma_{\mathsf{v}_j}, \mathsf{x}_{\mathsf{v}_j}), c_{\iota,(\mathsf{x}_{\mathsf{v}_j})_\iota}^{(j)})\}_\iota$
$\quad \{c_{\iota,b}^{(n)}\}_{\iota,b} := \mathsf{Eval}(\tilde{Q}^{(n)}, \tilde{y}^{(n)})$
$\quad z := \mathsf{lpk}_{\mathsf{id}}$
$\quad \tilde{z} := \{\mathsf{SDec}(\mathsf{pp}, (\mathsf{vk}_{\mathsf{v}_n}, \sigma_{\mathsf{id}}, z), c_{\iota,z_\iota}^{(n)})\}_\iota$
$\quad f := \mathsf{Eval}(\tilde{T}, \tilde{z})$
$\quad$Output $\mathsf{m} := D(\mathsf{lsk}_{\mathsf{id}}, f)$

### 6.1  Correctness

We will first show that our scheme is correct. Note that by correctness of the garbling scheme $(\mathsf{Garble}, \mathsf{Eval})$, we have that the evaluation of $\tilde{Q}^{(0)}$ on the labels $\tilde{y}^{(0)}$ yields correctly formed ciphertexts of the OTSE scheme $(\mathsf{SSetup}, \mathsf{SGen}, \mathsf{SSignSEnc}, \mathsf{SDec})$. Next, by the correctness of $(\mathsf{SSetup}, \mathsf{SGen}, \mathsf{SSign}, \mathsf{SEnc}, \mathsf{SDec})$, we get that the decrypted values $\tilde{y}^{(1)}$ are correct labels for the next garbled circuit $\tilde{Q}^{(1)}$. Repeating this argument, we can argue that all $\tilde{Q}^{(j)}$ output correct encryptions that are subsequently decrypted to correct input labels of the next garbled circuit in the sequence. Finally, the circuit $\tilde{Q}^{(n)}$ outputs correct encryptions of the input labels of $\tilde{T}$, which are again correctly decrypted to input labels for $\tilde{\mathsf{T}}$. Finally, the correctness of the garbling scheme $(\mathsf{Garble}, \mathsf{Eval})$ guarantees that $\tilde{\mathsf{T}}$ outputs a correct encryption of the plaintext $\mathsf{m}$ under the leaf public key $\mathsf{lpk_{id}}$, and the correctness of the public-key-encryption scheme $(\mathsf{KG}, \mathsf{E}, \mathsf{D})$ ensures that the decryption function $\mathsf{D}$ outputs the correct plaintext $\mathsf{m}$.

## 6.2   Proof of Security

We will now show that our scheme is fully secure.

**Theorem 3.** *Assume that* $(\mathsf{KG}, \mathsf{E}, \mathsf{D})$ *is an* $\mathsf{IND}^{\mathsf{CPA}}$*-secure public key encryption scheme,* $(\mathsf{SSetup}, \mathsf{SGen}, \mathsf{SSign}, \mathsf{SEnc}, \mathsf{SDec})$ *is a* $\mathsf{IND}^{\mathsf{OTSE}}$*-secure OTSE scheme and that* $(\mathsf{Garble}, \mathsf{Eval})$ *is a garbling scheme. Then the scheme* $(\mathsf{Setup}, \mathsf{KeyGen}, \mathsf{Encrypt}, \mathsf{Decrypt})$ *is a fully secure IBE scheme.*

We will split the proof of Theorem 3 into several lemmas. Let $\mathcal{A}$ be a PPT adversary with advantage $\epsilon$ against the fully secure $\mathsf{IND}^{\mathsf{IBE}}$-experiment and let in the following $\mathsf{v}_0, \ldots, \mathsf{v}_n$ always denote the root-to-leaf path for the challenge identity $\mathsf{id}^*$. Consider the following hybrids.

Hybrid $\mathcal{H}_0$ is identical to the real experiment $\mathsf{IND}^{\mathsf{IBE}}(\mathcal{A})$, except that we replace the pseudorandom function $F$ used for the generation of the identity keys by a lazily evaluated truly random function. In particular, each time we visit a new node during key generation we generate fresh keys for this node and store them. If these keys are needed later on, we retrieve them from a table of stored keys instead of generating new ones. By a standard argument it follows that the $\mathsf{IND}^{\mathsf{IBE}}(\mathcal{A})$-experiment and $\mathcal{H}_0$ are computationally indistinguishable, given that $F$ is a pseudorandom function.

In the remaining hybrids we will only change the way the challenge ciphertext $c^*$ is computed. First consider the computation of the challenge ciphertext $c^*$ in the extremal hybrids $\mathcal{H}_0$ and $\mathcal{H}_{2n+3}$ (Fig. 7). While in $\mathcal{H}_0$ all garbled circuits are computed by the garbling algorithm $\mathsf{Garble}$, in $\mathcal{H}_{2n+3}$ all garbled circuits are simulated. Moreover, in $\mathcal{H}_{2n+3}$ the messages encrypted in the ciphertexts computed by the garbled circuits do not depend on the bit $b$, i.e. decryption of these ciphertexts always yields the same labels, regardless of which message-signature pair has been used to decrypt the encrypted labels. Notice that in $\mathcal{H}_{2n+3}$ the garbled circuit $\tilde{\mathsf{T}}$ is simulated using $\mathsf{f} := \mathsf{E}(\mathsf{lpk_{id^*}}, \mathsf{m}^*)$, the encryption of the challenge message $\mathsf{m}^*$ under the leaf public key $\mathsf{lpk_{id^*}}$.

We will show indistinguishability of $\mathcal{H}_0$ and $\mathcal{H}_{2n+3}$ via the following hybrids. For $i = 0, \ldots, n-1$ define:

*Hybrid* $\mathcal{H}_{2i+1}$. This hybrid is the same as $\mathcal{H}_{2i}$, except that we change the way $\tilde{\mathsf{Q}}^{(i)}$ and $\tilde{\mathsf{y}}^{(i)}$ are computed. Compute $\tilde{\mathsf{Q}}^{(i)}$ and $\tilde{\mathsf{y}}^{(i)}$ by $(\tilde{\mathsf{Q}}^{(i)}, \tilde{\mathsf{y}}^{(i)}) := \mathsf{GCSim}(\mathsf{Q}, \mathsf{f}_{\mathsf{Q}}^{(i)})$.

*Hybrid* $\mathcal{H}_{2(i+1)}$. This hybrid is identical to $\mathcal{H}_{2i+1}$, except for the following change. Instead of computing $\mathsf{f}_{\mathsf{Q}}^{(i+1)} := \{\mathsf{SEnc}(\mathsf{pp}, (\mathsf{vk_{v_i}}, \mathsf{id}_{i+1}^* \cdot \ell + \iota, b), Y_{\iota,b})\}_{\iota,b}$ we compute $\mathsf{f}_{\mathsf{Q}}^{(i+1)} := \{\mathsf{SEnc}(\mathsf{pp}, (\mathsf{vk_{v_i}}, \mathsf{id}_{i+1}^* \cdot \ell + \iota, b), \tilde{\mathsf{y}}_\iota^{(i+1)})\}_{\iota,b}$.

$\mathcal{H}_0$:
$(\tilde{\mathsf{T}}, e_T) := \mathsf{Garble}(1^\lambda, \mathsf{T}[m^*])$
$(\tilde{\mathsf{Q}}^{(n)}, e_Q^{(n)}) := \mathsf{Garble}(1^\lambda, \mathsf{Q}[\mathsf{pp}, 0, e_T])$
For $j = n - 1, \ldots, 0$
  $\quad (\tilde{\mathsf{Q}}^{(j)}, e_Q^{(j)}) := \mathsf{Garble}(1^\lambda, \mathsf{Q}[\mathsf{pp}, \mathsf{id}_{j+1}, e_Q^{(j+1)}])$
$y := \mathsf{vk}_{v_0}$
$\tilde{y}^{(0)} := \{Y_{\iota, y_\iota}\}_\iota$
$c := (\tilde{y}^{(0)}, \tilde{\mathsf{Q}}^{(0)}, \ldots, \tilde{\mathsf{Q}}^{(n)}, \tilde{\mathsf{T}})$

$\mathcal{H}_{2n+3}$:
$f := \mathsf{E}(\mathsf{lpk}_{\mathsf{id}^*}, m^*)$
$(\tilde{\mathsf{T}}, \tilde{z}) := \mathsf{GCSim}(\mathsf{T}, f)$
$f_T := \{(\mathsf{SEnc}(\mathsf{pp}, (\mathsf{vk}_{\mathsf{id}^*}, \iota, b), \tilde{z}_\iota)\}_{\iota, b}$
$(\tilde{\mathsf{Q}}^{(n)}, \tilde{y}^{(n)}) := \mathsf{GCSim}(\mathsf{Q}, f_T)$
For $j = n - 1, \ldots, 0$
  $\quad f_Q^{(j)} := \{\mathsf{SEnc}(\mathsf{pp}, (\mathsf{vk}_{v_j}, \mathsf{id}_{j+1}^* \cdot \ell + \iota, b), \tilde{y}_\iota^{(j+1)})\}_{\iota, b}$
  $\quad (\tilde{\mathsf{Q}}^{(j)}, \tilde{y}^{(j)}) := \mathsf{GCSim}(\mathsf{Q}, f_Q^{(j)})$
Output $c := (\tilde{y}^{(0)}, \tilde{\mathsf{Q}}^{(0)}, \ldots, \tilde{\mathsf{Q}}^{(n)}, \tilde{\mathsf{T}})$

**Fig. 7.** The extremal hybrids $\mathcal{H}_0$ and $\mathcal{H}_{2n+3}$

The final 3 hybrids are given as follows.

*Hybrid* $\mathcal{H}_{2n+1}$. This hybrid is the same as $\mathcal{H}_{2n}$, except that we change the way $\tilde{\mathsf{Q}}^{(n)}$ and $\tilde{y}^{(n)}$ are computed. Compute $\tilde{\mathsf{Q}}^{(n)}$ and $\tilde{y}^{(n)}$ by $(\tilde{\mathsf{Q}}^{(n)}, \tilde{y}^{(n)}) := \mathsf{GCSim}(\mathsf{Q}, f_T)$, where $f_T = \{(\mathsf{SEnc}(\mathsf{pp}, (\mathsf{vk}_{\mathsf{id}^*}, \iota, b), Z_{\iota, b})\}_{\iota, b}$.

*Hybrid* $\mathcal{H}_{2n+2}$. This hybrid is the same as $\mathcal{H}_{2n+1}$, except that we change how $f_T$ is computed. Let $e_T = \{Z_{\iota, 0}, Z_{\iota, 1}\}_\iota$. Instead of computing $f_T$ by $f_T := \{(\mathsf{SEnc}(\mathsf{pp}, (\mathsf{vk}_{\mathsf{id}^*}, \iota, b), Z_{\iota, b})\}_{\iota, b}$ we compute $f_T := \{(\mathsf{SEnc}(\mathsf{pp}, (\mathsf{vk}_{\mathsf{id}^*}, \iota, b), \tilde{z}_\iota^{(n)})\}_{\iota, b}$.

*Hybrid* $\mathcal{H}_{2n+3}$. This hybrid is the same as $\mathcal{H}_{2n+2}$, except that we change the way $\tilde{\mathsf{T}}$ and $\tilde{z}$ are computed. Compute $\tilde{\mathsf{T}}$ and $\tilde{z}$ by $(\tilde{\mathsf{T}}, \tilde{z}) := \mathsf{GCSim}(\mathsf{Q}, f)$, where $f := \mathsf{E}(\mathsf{lpk}_{\mathsf{id}}, m)$.

**Lemma 1.** *We claim that for $i = 0, \ldots, n - 1$ the hybrids $\mathcal{H}_{2i}$ and $\mathcal{H}_{2i+1}$ are computationally indistinguishable, given that $(\mathsf{Garble}, \mathsf{Eval})$ is a secure garbling scheme.*

*Proof.* Assume towards contradiction that $\mathcal{A}$ distinguishes between $\mathcal{H}_{2i}$ and $\mathcal{H}_{2i+1}$ with non-negligible advantage $\epsilon$. We will construct a distinguisher $\mathcal{R}^\mathcal{A}$ that breaks the security of the garbling scheme with advantage $\epsilon$. $\mathcal{R}$ simulates the $\mathcal{H}_{2i}$ experiment faithfully with the adversary $\mathcal{A}$ until $\mathcal{A}$ requests a challenge ciphertext. Once $\mathcal{A}$ does request the challenge ciphertext, $\mathcal{R}$ computes

$\quad (\tilde{\mathsf{T}}, e_T) := \mathsf{Garble}(1^\lambda, \mathsf{T}[m^*])$
$\quad (\tilde{\mathsf{Q}}^{(n)}, e_Q^{(n)}) := \mathsf{Garble}(1^\lambda, \mathsf{Q}[\mathsf{pp}, 0, e_T])$
$\quad$ For $j = n - 1, \ldots, i + 1$
$\qquad (\tilde{\mathsf{Q}}^{(j)}, e_Q^{(j)}) := \mathsf{Garble}(1^\lambda, \mathsf{Q}[\mathsf{pp}, \mathsf{id}_{j+1}^*, e_Q^{(j+1)}]).$
$\quad (\tilde{\mathsf{Q}}^{(i)}, e_Q^{(i)}) := \mathsf{Garble}(1^\lambda, \mathsf{Q}[\mathsf{pp}, \mathsf{id}_{i+1}^*, e_Q^{(i+1)}])$

and sends the circuit $\mathsf{Q}[e_Q^{(i)}]$ and the input $y^{(i)}$ to the experiment. Once the experiment returns $\tilde{\mathsf{Q}}^{(i)}, \tilde{y}^{(i)}$, $\mathcal{R}$ computes

For $j = i - 1, \ldots, 0$
$$\mathsf{f}_Q^{(j)} := \{\mathsf{SEnc}(\mathsf{pp}, (\mathsf{vk}_{\mathsf{v}_j}, \mathsf{id}_{j+1}^* \cdot \ell + \iota, b), \tilde{\mathsf{y}}_\iota^{(j+1)})\}_{\iota, b}$$
$$(\tilde{\mathsf{Q}}^{(j)}, \tilde{\mathsf{y}}^{(j)}) := \mathsf{GCSim}(\mathsf{Q}, \mathsf{f}_Q^{(j)})$$
$$c^* := (\tilde{\mathsf{y}}^{(0)}, \tilde{\mathsf{Q}}^{(0)}, \ldots, \tilde{\mathsf{Q}}^{(n)}, \tilde{\mathsf{T}})$$

and returns $c^*$ to $\mathcal{A}$. $\mathcal{R}$ now continues the simulation of the $\mathcal{H}_{2i}$ experiment and outputs whatever the simulated $\mathcal{H}_{2i}$ experiment outputs.

Clearly, if $\mathcal{R}$'s challenge $\tilde{\mathsf{Q}}^{(i)}, \tilde{\mathsf{y}}^{(i)}$ is distributed according to the real distribution, then the view of $\mathcal{A}$ in $\mathcal{R}$'s simulation is identical to the view of $\mathcal{A}$ in $\mathcal{H}_{2i}$. On the other hand, if $\mathcal{R}$'s challenge is distributed according to the simulated distribution, then the view of $\mathcal{A}$ in $\mathcal{R}$'s simulation is identical to the view of $\mathcal{A}$ in $\mathcal{H}_{2i+1}$. We conclude that

$$\mathsf{Adv}(\mathcal{R}^{\mathcal{A}}) = |\Pr[\mathcal{H}_{2i}(\mathcal{A}) = 1] - \Pr[\mathcal{H}_{2i+1}(\mathcal{A}) = 1]| \leq \epsilon,$$

which contradicts the security of the garbling scheme $(\mathsf{Garble}, \mathsf{Eval})$.

**Lemma 2.** *We claim that for* $i = 0, \ldots, n-1$ *the hybrids* $\mathcal{H}_{2i+1}$ *and* $\mathcal{H}_{2(i+1)}$ *are computationally indistinguishable, given that* $(\mathsf{SSetup}, \mathsf{SGen}, \mathsf{SSign}, \mathsf{SEnc}, \mathsf{SDec})$ *is a selectively* $\mathsf{IND}^{\mathsf{OTSE}}$*-secure OTSE scheme.*

*Proof.* Let $q$ be the number of queries by $\mathcal{A}$ (including the challenge query), which gives us an upper bound for the number of distinct nodes visited at level $i$. We will construct an adversary $\mathcal{R}^{\mathcal{A}}$ that breaks the $\mathsf{IND}^{\mathsf{OTSE}}$-security of $(\mathsf{SSetup}, \mathsf{SGen}, \mathsf{SSign}, \mathsf{SEnc}, \mathsf{SDec})$ in the multi-challenge setting with advantage $\epsilon/q$. $\mathcal{R}$ first guesses an index $k^* \in [q]$. $\mathcal{R}$ then generates keys

$$(\mathsf{vk}_0^*, \mathsf{sk}_0^*) := \mathsf{SGen}(\mathsf{pp})$$
$$(\mathsf{vk}_1^*, \mathsf{sk}_1^*) := \mathsf{SGen}(\mathsf{pp})$$

and sets $\mathsf{x}^* := \mathsf{vk}_{\mathsf{v}_i \| 0} \| \mathsf{vk}_{\mathsf{v}_i \| 1}$ and sends the challenge message $\mathsf{x}^*$ to the $\mathsf{IND}^{\mathsf{OTSE}}$-experiment and receives a verification key $\mathsf{vk}$ and a signature $\sigma$ from the $\mathsf{IND}^{\mathsf{OTSE}}$-experiment.

$\mathcal{R}$ continues simulating the $\mathcal{H}_{2i+1}$ experiment. Once the $k^*$-th distinct node $\mathsf{v}^*$ on level $i$ is visited, $\mathcal{R}$ modifies the $\mathsf{NodeGen}$ function for this node as follows.

$\mathsf{vk}_{\mathsf{v}^*} := \mathsf{vk}$
$\mathsf{vk}_{\mathsf{v}^* \| 0} := \mathsf{vk}_0^*$
$\mathsf{sk}_{\mathsf{v}^* \| 0} := \mathsf{sk}_0^*$
$\mathsf{vk}_{\mathsf{v}^* \| 1} := \mathsf{vk}_1^*$
$\mathsf{sk}_{\mathsf{v}^* \| 1} := \mathsf{sk}_1^*$
$\mathsf{x}_{\mathsf{v}^*} := \mathsf{vk}_{\mathsf{v}^* \| 0} \| \mathsf{vk}_{\mathsf{v}^* \| 1}$
$\sigma_{\mathsf{v}^*} := \sigma$
Output $(\mathsf{vk}_{\mathsf{v}^*}, \sigma_{\mathsf{v}^*}, \mathsf{x}_{\mathsf{v}^*})$

When the corresponding signing keys are required for the NodeGen procedure on $v^* \| 0$ and $v^* \| 1$, use the corresponding signing keys $\mathsf{sk}_{v^* \| 0}$ and $\mathsf{sk}_{v^* \| 1}$ computed in the modified procedure above.

$\mathcal{R}$ now continues the simulation. Once $\mathcal{A}$ requests a challenge-ciphertext for an identity $\mathsf{id}^*$, $\mathcal{R}$ checks if $v^*$ is on the root-to-leaf path for $\mathsf{id}^*$ (i.e. if $v^*$ is a prefix of $\mathsf{id}^*$), and if not aborts and outputs a random bit. Otherwise, $\mathcal{R}$ generates the challenge ciphertext $c^*$ for $\mathcal{A}$ in the following way.

$$(\tilde{\mathsf{T}}, \mathsf{e}_T) := \mathsf{Garble}(1^\lambda, \mathsf{T}[m^*])$$
$$(\tilde{\mathsf{Q}}^{(n)}, \mathsf{e}_Q^{(n)}) := \mathsf{Garble}(1^\lambda, \mathsf{Q}[\mathsf{pp}, 0, \mathsf{e}_T])$$
For $j = n-1, \ldots, i+1$
$$\quad (\tilde{\mathsf{Q}}^{(j)}, \mathsf{e}_Q^{(j)}) := \mathsf{Garble}(1^\lambda, \mathsf{Q}[\mathsf{pp}, \mathsf{id}_{j+1}^*, \mathsf{e}_Q^{(j+1)}])$$
Parse $\mathsf{e}_Q^{(i+1)} = \{(Y_{\iota,0}, Y_{\iota,1})\}_\iota$

$\mathcal{R}$ now computes the messages $M_0^* := \{Y_{\iota, 1 - x_\iota^{(i+1)}}\}_\iota$ and $M_1^* := \{Y_{\iota, x_\iota^{(i+1)}}\}_\iota$, sends the challenge messages $(M_0^*, M_1^*)$ to the $\mathsf{IND}^{\mathsf{OTSE}}$ experiment and receives a challenge ciphertext $C^* = (C_1^*, \ldots, C_\ell^*)$. Now $\mathcal{R}$ computes $\mathsf{f}_Q^{(i+1)}$ by $\mathsf{f}_Q^{(i+1)} := \{C_{\iota, b}\}_\iota$, where $C_{\iota, x_\iota} := \mathsf{SEnc}(\mathsf{pp}, (\mathsf{vk}_{v_i}, \mathsf{id}_{i+1}^* \cdot \ell + \iota, x_\iota^{(i+1)}), Y_{\iota, x_\iota^{(i+1)}})$ and $C_{\iota, 1 - x_\iota} := C_\iota^*$. $\mathcal{R}$ continues the computation of the challenge ciphertext as follows.

$$(\tilde{\mathsf{Q}}^{(i)}, \tilde{\mathsf{y}}^{(i)}) := \mathsf{GCSim}(\mathsf{Q}, \mathsf{f}_Q^{(i)})$$
For $j = i-1, \ldots, 0$
$$\quad \mathsf{f}_Q^{(j)} := \{\mathsf{SEnc}(\mathsf{pp}, (\mathsf{vk}_{v_j}, \mathsf{id}_{j+1}^* \cdot \ell + \iota, b), \tilde{\mathsf{y}}_\iota^{(j+1)})\}_{\iota, b}$$
$$\quad (\tilde{\mathsf{Q}}^{(j)}, \tilde{\mathsf{y}}^{(j)}) := \mathsf{GCSim}(\mathsf{Q}, \mathsf{f}_Q^{(j)})$$
$$c^* := (\tilde{\mathsf{y}}^{(0)}, \tilde{\mathsf{Q}}^{(0)}, \ldots, \tilde{\mathsf{Q}}^{(n)}, \tilde{\mathsf{T}})$$

and returns $c^*$ to $\mathcal{A}$. $\mathcal{R}$ now continues the simulation of the $\mathcal{H}_{2i+1}$ experiment and outputs whatever the simulated $\mathcal{H}_{2i+1}$ experiment outputs.

We will now compute the advantage of $\mathcal{R}^{\mathcal{A}}$. First notice that the keys provided by $\mathcal{R}$ to $\mathcal{A}$ are distributed exactly as in $\mathcal{H}_{2i+1}$ (and therefore do not depend on $k^*$). If $\mathcal{R}$ guesses $k^*$ wrongly its advantage is 0. Let $\mathsf{E}$ be the event that $k^*$ has been guessed correctly. It clearly holds that $\Pr[\mathsf{E}] \geq 1/q$. Assume now that the event $\mathsf{E}$ holds. If the challenge bit $b^*$ of the $\mathsf{IND}^{\mathsf{OTSE}}$ experiment is 0, then the view of $\mathcal{A}$ in $\mathcal{R}$'s simulation is distributed exactly as in experiment $\mathcal{H}_{2i+1}$. On the other hand, if $b^* = 1$ then the view of $\mathcal{A}$ is distributed exactly as in experiment $\mathcal{H}_{2(i+1)}$. Thus we can conclude

$$\begin{aligned}
\mathsf{Adv}(\mathcal{R}^{\mathcal{A}}) &= \Pr[\mathsf{E}] \cdot |\Pr[\mathcal{H}_{2i+1}(\mathcal{A}) = 1] - \Pr[\mathcal{H}_{2(i+1)}(\mathcal{A}) = 1]| \\
&\geq \Pr[\mathsf{E}] \cdot \epsilon \\
&\geq \epsilon/q.
\end{aligned}$$

**Lemma 3.** *We claim that the hybrids $\mathcal{H}_{2n}$ and $\mathcal{H}_{2n+1}$ are computationally indistinguishable, given that $(\mathsf{Garble}, \mathsf{Eval})$ is a secure garbling scheme.*

The proof proceeds analogous to the proof of Lemma 1.

**Lemma 4.** *We claim that the hybrids $\mathcal{H}_{2n+1}$ and $\mathcal{H}_{2n+2}$ are computationally indistinguishable, given that the OTSE-scheme (SSetup, SGen, SSign, SEnc, SDec) is $\mathsf{IND}^{\mathsf{OTSE}}$-secure.*

The proof follows analogous to the proof of Lemma 2.

**Lemma 5.** *We claim that the hybrids $\mathcal{H}_{2n+2}$ and $\mathcal{H}_{2n+3}$ are computationally indistinguishable, given that (Garble, Eval, GCSim) is a secure garbling scheme.*

Again, the proof follows analogous to the proof of Lemma 1.

**Lemma 6.** *The advantage of $\mathcal{A}$ in $\mathcal{H}_{2n+3}$ is negligible, given that (KG, E, D) is $\mathsf{IND}^{\mathsf{CPA}}$-secure.*

*Proof.* We will construct an adversary $\mathcal{R}^{\mathcal{A}}$ that breaks the $\mathsf{IND}^{\mathsf{CPA}}$ security of (KG, E, D) with advantage $\epsilon$. $\mathcal{R}$ simulates $\mathcal{H}_{2n+3}$ faithfully, with the exception that it uses its own challenge public key $\mathsf{pk}^*$ as public key for the leaf $\mathsf{id}^*$, i.e. it sets $\mathsf{lpk}_{\mathsf{id}^*} := \mathsf{pk}^*$. It forwards $\mathcal{A}$'s challenge messages $\mathsf{m}_0$ and $\mathsf{m}_1$ to the $\mathsf{IND}^{\mathsf{CPA}}$ experiment and uses its own challenge ciphertext $c^*$ as the ciphertext $\mathsf{f}$ in the computation of the challenge ciphertext $c^*$. It follows that $\mathcal{R}$ simulates $\mathcal{H}_{4n+3}$ perfectly and therefore $\mathsf{Adv}_{\mathsf{IND}^{\mathsf{CPA}}}(\mathcal{R}^{\mathcal{A}}) = \mathsf{Adv}_{\mathcal{H}_{4n+3}}(\mathcal{A})$.

This concludes the proof of Theorem 3.

# 7   Achieving Selectively Secure HIBE

We will now add a delegation mechanism to the IBE scheme constructed in the last Section, yielding the construction of a hierarchical IBE scheme. The basic idea is as follows. Instead of putting the public keys of the $\mathsf{IND}^{\mathsf{CPA}}$-secure scheme only into the leaf nodes of the tree, we will put such public keys into every node of the tree. This means that every node of the (unbounded size) tree can effectively be used in the same way we used the leaf nodes in the scheme of the last Section.

Since we want to be able to delegate the ability to delegate HIBE keys for entire sub-trees, we need to work with a pseudorandom function supporting this kind of delegation. We therefore use the *delegatable pseudorandom functions* defined in Sect. 2.6 for this task.

In our scheme, the delegated master secret key for an identity $\mathsf{id}$ consist of the identity secret key for $\mathsf{id}$ and a delegated PRF seed $s_{\mathsf{id}}$. This enables the delegator to compute identity secret keys for all the nodes in the sub-tree of $\mathsf{id}$.

Let (SSetup, SGen, SSign, SEnc, SDec) be an $\mathsf{IND}^{\mathsf{OTSE}}$-secure OTSE scheme, $(F, F.\mathsf{Delegate})$ be a delegatable pseudorandom function and (KG, E, D) be a standard public key encryption scheme. We assume for convenience that the pseudorandom function $F$ has two output registers, $F_1$ and $F_2$. Assume that both the verification keys of (SSetup, SGen, SSign, SEnc, SDec) and the public keys of (KG, E, D) have length $\ell$ and let $d = 3\ell$.

Again, we will first define a function NodeGen that provides access to the keys stored in the tree. As mentioned above, we do not make distinctions between leaf nodes and non-leaf nodes anymore but store a local public key $\mathsf{lpk}_\mathsf{v}$ at every node v. NodeGen takes as input a node identifier v and a pseudorandom function seed $s$ and outputs a verification key $\mathsf{vk}_\mathsf{v}$, signatures $\sigma_\mathsf{v}$, auxiliary information $\mathsf{x}_\mathsf{v}$ and a secret key $\mathsf{lsk}_\mathsf{v}$. Again, we use the convention that the variable $\iota$ runs over $[\ell]$ and $b$ over $\{0, 1\}$.

NodeGen(pp, v, $s$):
   $(\mathsf{vk}_\mathsf{v}, \mathsf{sk}_\mathsf{v}) := \mathsf{SGen}(\mathsf{pp}; F_1(s, \mathsf{v}))$
   Compute $\mathsf{vk}_{\mathsf{v}\|0}$ and $\mathsf{vk}_{\mathsf{v}\|1}$ in the same way.
   $(\mathsf{lpk}_\mathsf{v}, \mathsf{lsk}_\mathsf{v}) := \mathsf{KG}(1^\lambda; F_2(s, \mathsf{v}))$
   $\mathsf{x}_\mathsf{v} := \mathsf{vk}_{\mathsf{v}\|0} \| \mathsf{vk}_{\mathsf{v}\|1} \| \mathsf{lpk}_\mathsf{v}$
   $\sigma_\mathsf{v} := \mathsf{SSign}(\mathsf{pp}, \mathsf{sk}_\mathsf{v}, \mathsf{x}_\mathsf{v})$
   Output $(\mathsf{vk}_\mathsf{v}, \sigma_\mathsf{v}, \mathsf{x}_\mathsf{v}, \mathsf{lsk}_\mathsf{v})$

The HIBE scheme (Setup, Delegate, KeyGen, Encrypt, Decrypt) is given by the following algorithms.

Setup($1^\lambda$) : Let $\mathsf{v}_0$ be the root-node. Choose a random seed $s$ for the pseudorandom function $F$. Compute $\mathsf{pp} := \mathsf{SSetup}(1^\lambda, 3 \cdot \ell)$ and $(\mathsf{vk}_{\mathsf{v}_0}, \cdot, \cdot, \cdot) := \mathsf{NodeGen}(\mathsf{pp}, \mathsf{v}_0, s)$. Output $\mathsf{mpk} := \mathsf{vk}_{\mathsf{v}_0}$ and $\mathsf{msk} := s$.

Delegate(msk $= s$, id $\in \{0, 1\}^*$): Set $n := |\mathsf{id}|$. Let $\mathsf{v}_0, \mathsf{v}_1, \ldots, \mathsf{v}_n$ be the root-to-leaf path for the identity id, i.e. all the prefixes of id. For $j = 0, \ldots, n - 1$ compute $(\cdot, \sigma_{\mathsf{v}_j}, \mathsf{x}_\mathsf{v}, \cdot) := \mathsf{NodeGen}(\mathsf{pp}, \mathsf{v}_j, s)$. Compute $s_\mathsf{id} := F.\mathsf{Delegate}(s, \mathsf{id})$.
   Output $((\sigma_{\mathsf{v}_0}, \mathsf{x}_{\mathsf{v}_0}), \ldots, (\sigma_{\mathsf{v}_n}, \mathsf{x}_{\mathsf{v}_n}), s_\mathsf{id})$[7]

KeyGen($\mathsf{msk}_{\mathsf{id}'}^{\mathsf{HIBE}} = ((\sigma_{\mathsf{v}_0}, \mathsf{x}_{\mathsf{v}_0}), \ldots, (\sigma_{\mathsf{v}_{|\mathsf{id}'|}}, \mathsf{x}_{\mathsf{v}_{|\mathsf{id}'|}}), s_{\mathsf{id}'})$, id $\in \{0, 1\}^*$) : Set $n := |\mathsf{id}|$. Let $\mathsf{v}_{|\mathsf{id}'|}, \ldots, \mathsf{v}_{|\mathsf{id}'|+|\mathsf{id}|}$ be the path from $\mathsf{id}'$ to $\mathsf{id}' \| \mathsf{id}$, i.e. $\mathsf{id}'$ concatenated with all the prefixes of id. For $j = |\mathsf{id}'|, \ldots, |\mathsf{id}'| + |\mathsf{id}| - 1$ compute $(\cdot, \sigma_{\mathsf{v}_j}, \mathsf{x}_\mathsf{v}, \mathsf{lsk}_\mathsf{v}) := \mathsf{NodeGen}(\mathsf{pp}, \mathsf{v}_j, s_{\mathsf{id}'})$. Output $\mathsf{sk}_\mathsf{id} := ((\sigma_{\mathsf{v}_0}, \mathsf{x}_{\mathsf{v}_0}), \ldots, (\sigma_{\mathsf{v}_{|\mathsf{id}'|+|\mathsf{id}|}}, \mathsf{x}_{\mathsf{v}_{|\mathsf{id}'|+|\mathsf{id}|}}), \sigma_\mathsf{id}, \mathsf{lsk}_\mathsf{id})$

Encrypt(mpk $= \mathsf{vk}_{\mathsf{v}_0}$, id $\in \{0, 1\}^*$, m) : We will first describe two circuits that will be used by the encryption algorithm. The mode $\beta = 2$ of the circuit Q targets a local public key.

  – $\mathsf{Q}[\mathsf{pp}, \beta \in \{0, 1, 2\}, e_Q = \{(Y_{\iota,0}, Y_{\iota,1})\}_\iota](\mathsf{vk})$ : Compute and then output $\{\mathsf{SEnc}(\mathsf{pp}, (\mathsf{vk}, \beta \cdot \ell + \iota, b), Y_{\iota,b})\}_{\iota,b}$
  – $\mathsf{T}[\mathsf{m}](\mathsf{lpk})$: Compute and output $E(\mathsf{lpk}, \mathsf{m})$.

   $n := |\mathsf{id}|$
   $(\tilde{\mathsf{T}}, e_T) := \mathsf{Garble}(1^\lambda, \mathsf{T}[\mathsf{m}])$
   $(\tilde{\mathsf{Q}}^{(n)}, e_Q^{(n)}) := \mathsf{Garble}(1^\lambda, \mathsf{Q}[\mathsf{pp}, 2, e_T])$
   For $j = n - 1, \ldots, 0$
      $(\tilde{\mathsf{Q}}^{(j)}, e_Q^{(j)}) := \mathsf{Garble}(1^\lambda, \mathsf{Q}[\mathsf{pp}, \mathsf{id}_{j+1}, e_Q^{(j+1)}])$

---

[7] To delegate keys from delegated keys at an identity id, treat id as a root node, compute the delegated keys, and the concatenate the root-to-node paths.

Parse $e_Q^{(0)} = \{Y_{\iota,0}, Y_{\iota,1}\}_\iota$
$y := \mathsf{mpk}_{v_0}$
$\tilde{y}^{(0)} := \{Y_{\iota,y_\iota}\}_\iota$
Output $c := (\tilde{y}^{(0)}, \tilde{Q}^{(0)}, \ldots, \tilde{Q}^{(n)}, \tilde{T})$

$\mathsf{Decrypt}(\mathsf{sk}_{id} = ((\sigma_{v_0}, x_{v_0}), \ldots, (\sigma_{v_n}, x_{v_n}), \sigma_{id}, \mathsf{lpk}_{id}, \mathsf{lsk}_{id}), c = (\tilde{y}^{(0)}, \tilde{Q}^{(0)}, \ldots, \tilde{Q}^{(n)}, \tilde{T}))$
    For $i = 0, \ldots, n-1$:
        $\{c_{\iota,b}^{(i)}\}_{\iota,b} := \mathsf{Eval}(\tilde{Q}^{(i)}, \tilde{y}^{(i)})$
        $\tilde{y}^{(i+1)} := \{\mathsf{SDec}(\mathsf{pp}, (\mathsf{vk}_{v_i}, \sigma_{v_i}, x_{v_i}), c_{\iota,(x_{v_i})_\iota}^{(i)})\}_\iota$
    $\{c_{\iota,b}^{(n)}\}_{\iota,b} := \mathsf{Eval}(\tilde{Q}^{(n)}, \tilde{y}^{(n)})$
    $z := \mathsf{lpk}_{id}$
    $\tilde{z} := \{\mathsf{SDec}(\mathsf{pp}, (\mathsf{vk}_{v_n}, \sigma_{id}, z), c_{\iota,z_\iota}^{(n)})\}_\iota$
    $c^\dagger := \mathsf{Eval}(\tilde{T}, \tilde{z})$
    Output $m := \mathsf{D}(\mathsf{lsk}_{id}, c^\dagger)$

## 7.1 Correctness

Correctness of the scheme follows by the same argument as for the scheme in Sect. 6. Moreover, correctness of the delegation mechanism follows directly from the the the correctness of the delegation mechanism $F.\mathsf{Delegate}$.

## 7.2 Proof of Security

We will now show that our scheme is sel-IND$^{\mathsf{HIBE}}$-secure.

**Theorem 4.** *Assume that* $(\mathsf{KG}, \mathsf{E}, \mathsf{D})$ *is an* IND$^{\mathsf{CPA}}$-*secure public-key-encryption scheme,* $(\mathsf{SSetup}, \mathsf{SGen}, \mathsf{SSign}, \mathsf{SEnc}, \mathsf{SDec})$ *is an* IND$^{\mathsf{OTSE}}$-*secure one-time signature with encryption scheme and that* $(\mathsf{Garble}, \mathsf{Eval})$ *is a garbling scheme. Then* $(\mathsf{Setup}, \mathsf{Delegate}, \mathsf{KeyGen}, \mathsf{Encrypt}, \mathsf{Decrypt})$ *is a* sel-IND$^{\mathsf{HIBE}}$-*secure HIBE scheme.*

We will split the proof of Theorem 4 into several lemmas. Let $\mathcal{A}$ be a PPT adversary with advantage $\epsilon$ against the sel-IND$^{\mathsf{HIBE}}$-experiment, let id$^*$ be the challenge identity, which is selectively chosen by $\mathcal{A}$ at the beginning of the experiment and let $n^* := |id^*|$ be the length of the challenge identity. Let in the following $v_0, \ldots, v_{n^*}$ always denote the root-to-leaf path for the challenge identity id$^*$.

We will start by providing an overview of the hybrids.

*Hybrid $\mathcal{H}_0$.* This hybrid is identical to the real experiment sel-IND$_{\mathcal{A}}^{\mathsf{HIBE}}$, except that on the challenge-path $v_0, \ldots, v_n$ we replace the pseudorandom function $F$ used for the generation of the identity keys by a function $H$, which is truly random on the path from the root to the challenge identity and identical to $F(s, \cdot)$ everywhere else. This means, in particular, that we can choose the all the keys on the path from the root to the challenge identity in advance and with truly random coins. It follows directly from the pseudorandomness property of the delegatable pseudorandom function $(F, F.\mathsf{Delegate})$ that the experiments $\mathsf{IND}^{\mathsf{IBE}}(\mathcal{A})$ and $\mathcal{H}_0$ are computationally indistinguishable.

In the remaining hybrids, we will only change the way the challenge ciphertext $c^*$ is computed. For $i = 0, \ldots, n^* - 1$ we define the hybrids $\mathcal{H}_0, \ldots, \mathcal{H}_{2n^*+3}$. As in the last Section, we will first provide an overview of the extremal hybrids $\mathcal{H}_0$ and $\mathcal{H}_{2n^*+3}$ in Fig. 8.

$\mathcal{H}_0$:
$(\tilde{\mathsf{T}}, e_T) := \mathsf{Garble}(1^\lambda, T[m^*])$
$(\tilde{\mathsf{Q}}^{(n^*)}, e_Q^{(n^*)}) := \mathsf{Garble}(1^\lambda, Q[\mathsf{pp}, 2, e_T])$
For $j = n^* - 1, \ldots, 0$
$\quad (\tilde{\mathsf{Q}}^{(j)}, e_Q^{(j)}) := \mathsf{Garble}(1^\lambda, Q[\mathsf{pp}, \mathsf{id}_{j+1}^*, e_Q^{(j+1)}])$
$y := \mathsf{pk}_{v_0}$
$\tilde{y}^{(0)} := \{Y_{\iota, y_\iota}\}_\iota$
$c := (\tilde{y}^{(0)}, \tilde{\mathsf{Q}}^{(0)}, \ldots, \tilde{\mathsf{Q}}^{(n^*)}, \tilde{\mathsf{T}})$

$\mathcal{H}_{2n^*+3}$:
$f := E(\mathsf{lpk}_{\mathsf{id}^*}, m^*)$
$(\tilde{\mathsf{T}}, \tilde{z}) := \mathsf{GCSim}(T, f)$
$f_T := \{(\mathsf{SEnc}(\mathsf{pp}, (\mathsf{vk}_{\mathsf{id}^*}, \iota, b), \tilde{z}_\iota)\}_{\iota, b}$
$(\tilde{\mathsf{Q}}^{(n^*)}, \tilde{y}^{(n^*)}) := \mathsf{GCSim}(Q, f_T)$
For $j = n^* - 1, \ldots, 0$
$\quad f_Q^{(j)} := \{\mathsf{SEnc}(\mathsf{pp}, (\mathsf{vk}_{v_j}, \mathsf{id}_{j+1}^* \cdot \ell + \iota, b), \tilde{y}_\iota^{(j+1)})\}_{\iota, b}$
$\quad (\tilde{\mathsf{Q}}^{(j)}, \tilde{y}^{(j)}) := \mathsf{GCSim}(Q, f_Q^{(j)})$
Output $c := (\tilde{y}^{(0)}, \tilde{\mathsf{Q}}^{(0)}, \ldots, \tilde{\mathsf{Q}}^{(n^*)}, \tilde{\mathsf{T}})$

**Fig. 8.** The extremal hybrids $\mathcal{H}_0$ and $\mathcal{H}_{2n^*+3}$

For $i = 0, \ldots, n^* - 1$ define the following hybrids.

*Hybrid $\mathcal{H}_{2i+1}$.* This hybrid is the same as $\mathcal{H}_{2i}$, except that we change the way $\tilde{\mathsf{Q}}^{(i)}$ and $\tilde{y}^{(i)}$ are computed. Compute $\tilde{\mathsf{Q}}^{(i)}$ and $\tilde{y}^{(i)}$ by $(\tilde{\mathsf{Q}}^{(i)}, \tilde{y}^{(i)}) := \mathsf{GCSim}(Q, f_Q^{(i)})$.

*Hybrid $\mathcal{H}_{2(i+1)}$.* This hybrid is identical to $\mathcal{H}_{2i+1}$, except for the following change. Instead of computing $f_Q^{(i+1)} := \{\mathsf{SEnc}(\mathsf{pp}, (\mathsf{vk}_{v_i}, \mathsf{id}_{i+1}^* \cdot \ell + \iota, b), Y_{\iota, b})\}_{\iota, b}$ we compute $f_Q^{(i+1)} := \{\mathsf{SEnc}(\mathsf{pp}, (\mathsf{vk}_{v_i}, \mathsf{id}_{i+1}^* \cdot \ell + \iota, b), \tilde{y}_\iota^{(i+1)})\}_{\iota, b}$
The final 3 hybrids are given as follows.

*Hybrid $\mathcal{H}_{2n^*+1}$.* This hybrid is the same as $\mathcal{H}_{2n^*}$, except that we change the way $\tilde{\mathsf{Q}}^{(n^*)}$ and $\tilde{y}^{(n^*)}$ are computed. Compute $\tilde{\mathsf{Q}}^{(n^*)}$ and $\tilde{y}^{(n^*)}$ by $(\tilde{\mathsf{Q}}^{(n^*)}, \tilde{y}^{(n^*)}) := \mathsf{GCSim}(Q, f_T)$.

*Hybrid $\mathcal{H}_{2n^*+2}$.* This hybrid is the same as $\mathcal{H}_{2n^*+1}$, except that we change how $f_T$ is computed. Let $e_T = \{Z_{\iota, 0}, Z_{\iota, 1}\}_\iota$. Instead of computing $f_T$ by $f_T := \{(\mathsf{SEnc}(\mathsf{pp}, (\mathsf{vk}\mathsf{vk}_{v_{n^*}}, \iota, b), Z_{\iota, b})\}_{\iota, b}$ we compute $f_T := \{(\mathsf{SEnc}(\mathsf{pp}, (\mathsf{vk}_{n^*}, \iota, b), \tilde{z}_\iota^{(n^*)})\}_{\iota, b}$.

*Hybrid $\mathcal{H}_{2n^*+3}$.* This hybrid is the same as $\mathcal{H}_{2n^*+2}$, except that we change the way $\tilde{\mathsf{T}}$ and $\tilde{z}$ are computed. Compute $\tilde{\mathsf{T}}$ and $\tilde{z}$ by $(\tilde{\mathsf{T}}, \tilde{z}) := \mathsf{GCSim}(Q, f)$, where $f := E(\mathsf{lpk}_{\mathsf{id}^*}, m^*)$.

**Lemma 7.** *We claim that for $i = 0, \ldots, n^* - 1$ the hybrids $\mathcal{H}_{2i}$ and $\mathcal{H}_{2i+1}$ are computationally indistinguishable, given that* (Garble, Eval) *is a secure garbling scheme.*

*Proof.* Assume towards contradiction that $\mathcal{A}$ distinguishes between $\mathcal{H}_{2i}$ and $\mathcal{H}_{2i+1}$ with non-negligible advantage $\epsilon$. We will construct a distinguisher $\mathcal{R}^{\mathcal{A}}$ that breaks the security of the garbling scheme with advantage $\epsilon$. $\mathcal{R}$ simulates the $\mathcal{H}_{2i}$ experiment faithfully with the adversary $\mathcal{A}$ until $\mathcal{A}$ requests a challenge ciphertext. Once $\mathcal{A}$ does request the challenge ciphertext, $\mathcal{R}$ computes

$$(\tilde{\mathsf{T}}, \mathsf{e}_T) := \mathsf{Garble}(1^\lambda, \mathsf{T}[\mathsf{m}^*])$$
$$(\tilde{\mathsf{Q}}^{(n^*)}, \mathsf{e}_Q^{(n^*)}) := \mathsf{Garble}(1^\lambda, \mathsf{Q}[\mathsf{pp}, 2, \mathsf{e}_T])$$
$$\text{For } j = n^* - 1, \ldots, i + 1$$
$$\quad (\tilde{\mathsf{Q}}^{(j)}, \mathsf{e}_Q^{(j)}) := \mathsf{Garble}(1^\lambda, \mathsf{Q}[\mathsf{pp}, \mathsf{id}^*_{j+1}, \mathsf{e}_Q^{(j+1)}]).$$
$$(\tilde{\mathsf{Q}}^{(i)}, \mathsf{e}_Q^{(i)}) := \mathsf{Garble}(1^\lambda, \mathsf{Q}[\mathsf{pp}, \mathsf{id}^*_{i+1}, \mathsf{e}_Q^{(i+1)}])$$

and sends the circuit $\mathsf{Q}[\mathsf{e}_Q^{(i)}]$ and the input $\mathsf{y}^{(i)}$ to the experiment. Once the experiment returns $\tilde{\mathsf{Q}}^{(i)}, \tilde{\mathsf{y}}^{(i)}$, $\mathcal{R}$ computes

$$\text{For } j = i - 1, \ldots, 0$$
$$\quad \mathsf{f}_Q^{(j)} := \{\mathsf{SEnc}(\mathsf{pp}, (\mathsf{vk}_{v_i}, \mathsf{id}^*_{j+1} \cdot \ell + \iota, b), \tilde{\mathsf{y}}_\iota^{(j+1)})\}_{\iota, b}$$
$$\quad (\tilde{\mathsf{Q}}^{(j)}, \tilde{\mathsf{y}}^{(j)}) := \mathsf{GCSim}(\mathsf{Q}, \mathsf{f}_Q^{(j)})$$
$$c^* := (\tilde{\mathsf{y}}^{(0)}, \tilde{\mathsf{Q}}^{(0)}, \ldots, \tilde{\mathsf{Q}}^{(n^*)}, \tilde{\mathsf{T}})$$

and returns $c^*$ to $\mathcal{A}$. $\mathcal{R}$ now continues the simulation of the $\mathcal{H}_{2i}$ experiment and outputs whatever the simulated $\mathcal{H}_{2i}$ experiment outputs.

Clearly, if $\mathcal{R}$'s challenge $\tilde{\mathsf{Q}}^{(i)}, \tilde{\mathsf{y}}^{(i)}$ is distributed according to the real distribution, then the view of $\mathcal{A}$ in $\mathcal{R}$'s simulation is identical to the view of $\mathcal{A}$ in $\mathcal{H}_{2i}$. On the other hand, if $\mathcal{R}$'s challenge is distributed according to the simulated distribution, then the view of $\mathcal{A}$ in $\mathcal{R}$'s simulation is identical to the view of $\mathcal{A}$ in $\mathcal{H}_{2i+1}$. We conclude that

$$\mathsf{Adv}(\mathcal{R}^{\mathcal{A}}) = |\Pr[\mathcal{H}_{2i}(\mathcal{A}) = 1] - \Pr[\mathcal{H}_{2i+1}(\mathcal{A}) = 1]| \leq \epsilon,$$

which contradicts the security of the garbling scheme (Garble, Eval).

**Lemma 8.** *We claim that for $i = 0, \ldots, n^* - 1$ the hybrids $\mathcal{H}_{2i+1}$ and $\mathcal{H}_{2(i+1)}$ are computationally indistinguishable, given that* (SSetup, SGen, SSign, SEnc, SDec) *is an* $\mathsf{IND}^{\mathsf{OTSE}}$*-secure IBE scheme.*

*Proof.* We will construct an adversary $\mathcal{R}^{\mathcal{A}}$ that breaks the multi-challenge $\mathsf{IND}^{\mathsf{OTSE}}$-security of (SSetup, SGen, SSign, SEnc, SDec) with advantage $\epsilon$. Let $\mathsf{v}^* = \mathsf{v}_i$ be the $i$-th node on the challenge-path. Let $\mathsf{pp}$ be the public parameters passed to $\mathcal{R}$. $\mathcal{R}$ first generates keys for the children $\mathsf{v}^*\|0$ and $\mathsf{v}^*\|1$ of $\mathsf{v}^*$ by

$$(\mathsf{vk}_b^*, \mathsf{sk}_b^*) := \mathsf{SGen}(\mathsf{pp})$$

if $v^*\|b$ is on the challenge path and

$$(vk_b^*, sk_b^*) := SGen(pp; F(s, v^*\|b))$$

otherwise. Next, $\mathcal{R}$ generates the local key $lpk_{v^*}$ by $(lpk^*, lsk^*) := KeyGen(1^\lambda)$. Now $\mathcal{R}$ sets $x^* := vk_{v^*\|0}\|vk_{v^*\|1}\|lpk_{v^*}$, sends the challenge message $x^*$ to the $IND^{OTSE}$-experiment and receives a verification key $vk$ and a signature $\sigma$.

$\mathcal{R}$ now chooses the keys for all nodes on the root-to-leaf path as in $\mathcal{H}_{2i+1}$, except for the keys of $v^*$, which are chosen as follows.

$vk_{v^*} := vk$
$vk_{v^*\|0} := vk_0^*$
$sk_{v^*\|0} := sk_0^*$
$vk_{v^*\|1} := vk_1^*$
$sk_{v^*\|1} := sk_1^*$
$x_{v^*} := vk_{v^*\|0}\|vk_{v^*\|1}\|lpk_{v^*}$
$\sigma_{v^*} := \sigma$
Output $(vk_{v^*}, \sigma_{v^*}, x_{v^*}, lsk_{v^*})$

When the corresponding secret keys are required for the NodeGen procedure on $v^*\|0$ and $v^*\|1$, use the corresponding secret keys $sk_{v^*\|0}$ and $sk_{v^*\|1}$ set above in the modified procedure above.

$\mathcal{R}$ now continues the simulation. Once $\mathcal{A}$ requests a challenge-ciphertext for the identity $id^*$, $\mathcal{R}$ generates the challenge ciphertext $c^*$ for $\mathcal{A}$ in the following way.

$(\tilde{T}, e_T) := Garble(1^\lambda, T[m^*])$
$(\tilde{Q}^{(n^*)}, e_Q^{(n^*)}) := Garble(1^\lambda, Q[pp, 2, e_T])$
For $j = n^* - 1, \ldots, i+1$
$\quad (\tilde{Q}^{(j)}, e_Q^{(j)}) := Garble(1^\lambda, Q[pp, id_{j+1}^*, e_Q^{(j+1)}])$
Parse $e_Q^{(i+1)} = \{(Y_{\iota,0}, Y_{\iota,1})\}_\iota$

$\mathcal{R}$ now computes the messages $M_0^* := \{Y_{\iota,1-x_\iota^{(i+1)}}\}_\iota$ and $M_1^* := \{Y_{\iota,x_\iota^{(i+1)}}\}_\iota$, sends the challenge messages $(M_0^*, M_1^*)$ to the $IND^{OTSE}$-experiment and receives a challenge ciphertext $C^* = (C_1^*, \ldots, C_\ell^*)$. Now $\mathcal{R}$ computes $f_Q^{(i+1)}$ by $f_Q^{(i+1)} := \{C_{\iota,b}\}_{\iota \in [\ell]}$, where $C_{\iota,x_\iota} := SEnc(pp, (vk_{v^*}, \beta \cdot \ell + \iota, x_\iota^{(i+1)}), Y_{\iota,x_\iota^{(i+1)}})$ and $C_{\iota,1-x_\iota} := C_\iota^*$.

$(\tilde{Q}^{(i)}, \tilde{y}^{(i)}) := GCSim(Q, f_Q^{(i)})$
For $j = i - 1, \ldots, 0$
$\quad f_Q^{(j)} := \{SEnc(pp, (vk_{v_j}, id_{j+1}^* \cdot \ell + \iota, b), \tilde{y}_\iota^{(j+1)})\}_{\iota,b}$
$\quad (\tilde{Q}^{(j)}, \tilde{y}^{(j)}) := GCSim(Q, f_Q^{(j)})$
$c^* := (\tilde{y}^{(0)}, \tilde{Q}^{(0)}, \ldots, \tilde{Q}^{(n^*)}, \tilde{T})$

and returns $c^*$ to $\mathcal{A}$. $\mathcal{R}$ now continues the simulation of the $\mathcal{H}_{2i+1}$ experiment and outputs whatever the simulated $\mathcal{H}_{2i+1}$ experiment outputs.

We will now compute the advantage of $\mathcal{R}^{\mathcal{A}}$. First notice that the keys provided by $\mathcal{R}$ to $\mathcal{A}$ are distributed exactly as in $\mathcal{H}_{2i+1}$ (and therefore do not depend on $i^*$). If the challenge bit $b^*$ of the $\mathsf{IND}^{\mathsf{OTSE}}$-experiment is 0, then the view of $\mathcal{A}$ in $\mathcal{R}$'s simulation is distributed exactly as in experiment $\mathcal{H}_{2i+1}$. On the other hand, if $b^* = 1$ then the view of $\mathcal{A}$ is distributed exactly as in experiment $\mathcal{H}_{2(i+1)}$. Thus we can conclude

$$\mathsf{Adv}(\mathcal{R}^{\mathcal{A}}) = |\Pr[\mathcal{H}_{2i+1}(\mathcal{A}) = 1] - \Pr[\mathcal{H}_{2(i+1)}(\mathcal{A}) = 1]| \geq \epsilon$$

**Lemma 9.** *We claim that the hybrids $\mathcal{H}_{2n}$ and $\mathcal{H}_{2n+1}$ are computationally indistinguishable, given that $(\mathsf{Garble}, \mathsf{Eval})$ is a secure garbling scheme.*

The proof proceeds analogous to the proof of Lemma 7.

**Lemma 10.** *We claim that the hybrids $\mathcal{H}_{2n+1}$ and $\mathcal{H}_{2n+2}$ are computationally indistinguishable, given that the OTSE scheme $(\mathsf{SSetup}, \mathsf{SGen}, \mathsf{SSign}, \mathsf{SEnc}, \mathsf{SDec})$ is $\mathsf{IND}^{\mathsf{OTSE}}$-secure.*

The proof follows analogous to the proof of Lemma 8.

**Lemma 11.** *We claim that the hybrids $\mathcal{H}_{2n+2}$ and $\mathcal{H}_{2n+3}$ are computationally indistinguishable, given that $(\mathsf{Garble}, \mathsf{Eval})$ is a secure garbling scheme.*

Again, the proof follows analogous to the proof of Lemma 7.

**Lemma 12.** *The advantage of $\mathcal{A}$ in $\mathcal{H}_{2n+3}$ is negligible, given that $(\mathsf{KG}, \mathsf{E}, \mathsf{D})$ is $\mathsf{IND}^{\mathsf{CPA}}$-secure.*

*Proof.* We will construct an adversary $\mathcal{R}^{\mathcal{A}}$ that breaks the $\mathsf{IND}^{\mathsf{CPA}}$-security of $(\mathsf{KG}, \mathsf{E}, \mathsf{D})$ with advantage $\epsilon$. $\mathcal{R}$ simulates $\mathcal{H}_{2n^*+3}$ faithfully, with the exception that it uses its own challenge public key $\mathsf{pk}^*$ as public key $\mathsf{lpk}_{\mathsf{id}^*}$ for the identity $\mathsf{id}^*$, i.e. it sets $\mathsf{lpk}_{\mathsf{id}^*} := \mathsf{pk}^*$. It forwards $\mathcal{A}$'s challenge messages $\mathsf{m}_0$ and $\mathsf{m}_1$ to the $\mathsf{IND}^{\mathsf{CPA}}$-experiment and uses its own challenge ciphertext $c^*$ as the ciphertext $\mathsf{f}$ in the computation of the challenge ciphertext $c^*$. It follow directly that $\mathcal{R}$ simulates $\mathcal{H}_{4n^*+3}$ perfectly and therefore $\mathsf{Adv}_{\mathsf{IND}^{\mathsf{CPA}}}(\mathcal{R}^{\mathcal{A}}) = \mathsf{Adv}_{\mathcal{H}_{4n^*+3}}(\mathcal{A})$.

This concludes the proof of Theorem 4.

# References

[AB09]  Agrawal, S., Boyen, X.: Identity-based encryption from lattices in the standard model (2009)

[ABB10a]  Agrawal, S., Boneh, D., Boyen, X.: Efficient lattice (H)IBE in the standard model. In: Gilbert, H. (ed.) EUROCRYPT 2010. LNCS, vol. 6110, pp. 553–572. Springer, Heidelberg (2010). https://doi.org/10.1007/978-3-642-13190-5_28

[ABB10b]  Agrawal, S., Boneh, D., Boyen, X.: Lattice basis delegation in fixed dimension and shorter-ciphertext hierarchical IBE. In: Rabin, T. (ed.) CRYPTO 2010. LNCS, vol. 6223, pp. 98–115. Springer, Heidelberg (2010). https://doi.org/10.1007/978-3-642-14623-7_6

[ACD+06] Abdalla, M., Catalano, D., Dent, A.W., Malone-Lee, J., Neven, G., Smart, N.P.: Identity-based encryption gone wild. In: Bugliesi, M., Preneel, B., Sassone, V., Wegener, I. (eds.) ICALP 2006. LNCS, vol. 4052, pp. 300–311. Springer, Heidelberg (2006). https://doi.org/10.1007/11787006_26

[AFL12] Abdalla, M., Fiore, D., Lyubashevsky, V.: From selective to full security: semi-generic transformations in the standard model. In: Fischlin, M., Buchmann, J., Manulis, M. (eds.) PKC 2012. LNCS, vol. 7293, pp. 316–333. Springer, Heidelberg (2012). https://doi.org/10.1007/978-3-642-30057-8_19

[AS15] Asharov, G., Segev, G.: Limits on the power of indistinguishability obfuscation and functional encryption. In: Guruswami, V. (ed.) 56th Annual Symposium on Foundations of Computer Science, Berkeley, CA, USA, 17–20 October 2015, pp. 191–209. IEEE Computer Society Press (2015)

[BB04a] Boneh, D., Boyen, X.: Efficient selective-ID secure identity-based encryption without random oracles. In: Cachin, C., Camenisch, J.L. (eds.) EUROCRYPT 2004. LNCS, vol. 3027, pp. 223–238. Springer, Heidelberg (2004). https://doi.org/10.1007/978-3-540-24676-3_14

[BB04b] Boneh, D., Boyen, X.: Secure identity based encryption without random oracles. In: Franklin, M. (ed.) CRYPTO 2004. LNCS, vol. 3152, pp. 443–459. Springer, Heidelberg (2004). https://doi.org/10.1007/978-3-540-28628-8_27

[BBG05] Boneh, D., Boyen, X., Goh, E.-J.: Hierarchical identity based encryption with constant size ciphertext. In: Cramer, R. (ed.) EUROCRYPT 2005. LNCS, vol. 3494, pp. 440–456. Springer, Heidelberg (2005). https://doi.org/10.1007/11426639_26

[BF01] Boneh, D., Franklin, M.: Identity-based encryption from the weil pairing. In: Kilian, J. (ed.) CRYPTO 2001. LNCS, vol. 2139, pp. 213–229. Springer, Heidelberg (2001). https://doi.org/10.1007/3-540-44647-8_13

[BHR12] Bellare, M., Hoang, V.T., Rogaway, P.: Foundations of garbled circuits. In: Yu, T., Danezis, G., Gligor, V.D. (eds.) 19th Conference on Computer and Communications Security, ACM CCS 2012, Raleigh, NC, USA, 16–18 October 2012, pp. 784–796. ACM Press (2012)

[BR93] Bellare, M., Rogaway, P.: Random oracles are practical: a paradigm for designing efficient protocols. In: Ashby, V. (ed.) 1st Conference on Computer and Communications Security, ACM CCS 1993, Fairfax, Virginia, USA, 3–5 November 1993, pp. 62–73. ACM Press (1993)

[CDG+17] Cho, C., Döttling, N., Garg, S., Gupta, D., Miao, P., Polychroniadou, A.: Laconic oblivious transfer and its applications. In: Katz, J., Shacham, H. (eds.) CRYPTO 2017. LNCS, vol. 10402, pp. 33–65. Springer, Cham (2017). https://doi.org/10.1007/978-3-319-63715-0_2

[CHK04] Canetti, R., Halevi, S., Katz, J.: Chosen-ciphertext security from identity-based encryption. In: Cachin, C., Camenisch, J.L. (eds.) EUROCRYPT 2004. LNCS, vol. 3027, pp. 207–222. Springer, Heidelberg (2004). https://doi.org/10.1007/978-3-540-24676-3_13

[CHKP10] Cash, D., Hofheinz, D., Kiltz, E., Peikert, C.: Bonsai trees, or how to delegate a lattice basis. In: Gilbert, H. (ed.) EUROCRYPT 2010. LNCS, vol. 6110, pp. 523–552. Springer, Heidelberg (2010). https://doi.org/10.1007/978-3-642-13190-5_27

[Coc01] Cocks, C.: An identity based encryption scheme based on quadratic residues. In: Honary, B. (ed.) Cryptography and Coding 2001. LNCS, vol. 2260, pp. 360–363. Springer, Heidelberg (2001). https://doi.org/10.1007/3-540-45325-3_32

[DG17] Döttling, N., Garg, S.: Identity-based encryption from the diffie-hellman assumption. In: Katz, J., Shacham, H. (eds.) CRYPTO 2017. LNCS, vol. 10401, pp. 537–569. Springer, Cham (2017). https://doi.org/10.1007/978-3-319-63688-7_18

[DH76] Diffie, W., Hellman, M.E.: New directions in cryptography. IEEE Trans. Inf. Theory **22**(6), 644–654 (1976)

[GGM84] Goldreich, O., Goldwasser, S., Micali, S.: How to construct random functions (extended abstract). In: 25th Annual Symposium on Foundations of Computer Science, Singer Island, Florida, 24–26 October 1984, pp. 464–479. IEEE Computer Society Press (1984)

[GGM86] Goldreich, O., Goldwasser, S., Micali, S.: How to construct random functions. J. ACM **33**(4), 792–807 (1986)

[GH09] Gentry, C., Halevi, S.: Hierarchical identity based encryption with polynomially many levels. In: Reingold, O. (ed.) TCC 2009. LNCS, vol. 5444, pp. 437–456. Springer, Heidelberg (2009). https://doi.org/10.1007/978-3-642-00457-5_26

[GHPT17] Gaborit, P., Hauteville, A., Phan, D.H., Tillich, J.-P.: Identity-based encryption from codes with rank metric. In: Katz, J., Shacham, H. (eds.) CRYPTO 2017. LNCS, vol. 10403, pp. 194–224. Springer, Cham (2017). https://doi.org/10.1007/978-3-319-63697-9_7

[GPV08] Gentry, C., Peikert, C., Vaikuntanathan, V.: Trapdoors for hard lattices and new cryptographic constructions. In: Ladner, R.E., Dwork, C. (eds.) 40th Annual ACM Symposium on Theory of Computing, Victoria, British Columbia, Canada, 17–20 May 2008, pp. 197–206. ACM Press (2008)

[GS02] Gentry, C., Silverberg, A.: Hierarchical ID-based cryptography. In: Zheng, Y. (ed.) ASIACRYPT 2002. LNCS, vol. 2501, pp. 548–566. Springer, Heidelberg (2002). https://doi.org/10.1007/3-540-36178-2_34

[HL02] Horwitz, J., Lynn, B.: Toward hierarchical identity-based encryption. In: Knudsen, L.R. (ed.) EUROCRYPT 2002. LNCS, vol. 2332, pp. 466–481. Springer, Heidelberg (2002). https://doi.org/10.1007/3-540-46035-7_31

[KR98] Krawczyk, H., Rabin, T.: Chameleon hashing and signatures. Cryptology ePrint Archive, Report 1998/010 (1998). http://eprint.iacr.org/1998/010

[Lam79] Lamport, L.: Constructing digital signatures from a one-way function. Technical report, October 1979

[LP09] Lindell, Y., Pinkas, B.: A proof of security of Yao's protocol for two-party computation. J. Cryptol. **22**(2), 161–188 (2009)

[LW10] Lewko, A., Waters, B.: New techniques for dual system encryption and fully secure HIBE with short ciphertexts. In: Micciancio, D. (ed.) TCC 2010. LNCS, vol. 5978, pp. 455–479. Springer, Heidelberg (2010). https://doi.org/10.1007/978-3-642-11799-2_27

[MM16] Mahmoody, M., Mohammed, A.: On the power of hierarchical identity-based encryption. In: Fischlin, M., Coron, J.-S. (eds.) EUROCRYPT 2016. LNCS, vol. 9666, pp. 243–272. Springer, Heidelberg (2016). https://doi.org/10.1007/978-3-662-49896-5_9

[NY89]  Naor, M., Yung, M.: Universal one-way hash functions and their cryptographic applications. In: 21st Annual ACM Symposium on Theory of Computing, Seattle, WA, USA, 15–17 May 1989, pp. 33–43. ACM Press (1989)

[Reg05]  Regev, O.: On lattices, learning with errors, random linear codes, and cryptography. In: Gabow, H.N., Fagin, R. (eds.) 37th Annual ACM Symposium on Theory of Computing, Baltimore, MA, USA, 22–24 May 2005, pp. 84–93. ACM Press (2005)

[RSA78]  Rivest, R.L., Shamir, A., Adleman, L.M.: A method for obtaining digital signature and public-key cryptosystems. Commun. Assoc. Comput. Mach. **21**(2), 120–126 (1978)

[Sha84]  Shamir, A.: Identity-based cryptosystems and signature schemes. In: Blakley, G.R., Chaum, D. (eds.) CRYPTO 1984. LNCS, vol. 196, pp. 47–53. Springer, Heidelberg (1985). https://doi.org/10.1007/3-540-39568-7_5

[SW08]  Shi, E., Waters, B.: Delegating capabilities in predicate encryption systems. In: Aceto, L., Damgård, I., Goldberg, L.A., Halldórsson, M.M., Ingólfsdóttir, A., Walukiewicz, I. (eds.) ICALP 2008. LNCS, vol. 5126, pp. 560–578. Springer, Heidelberg (2008). https://doi.org/10.1007/978-3-540-70583-3_46

[Wat05]  Waters, B.: Efficient identity-based encryption without random oracles. In: Cramer, R. (ed.) EUROCRYPT 2005. LNCS, vol. 3494, pp. 114–127. Springer, Heidelberg (2005). https://doi.org/10.1007/11426639_7

[Yao82]  Yao, A.C.-C.: Protocols for secure computations (extended abstract). In: 23rd Annual Symposium on Foundations of Computer Science, Chicago, Illinois, 3–5 November 1982, pp. 160–164. IEEE Computer Society Press (1982)

# Multi-key Authenticated Encryption
# with Corruptions: Reductions Are Lossy

Tibor Jager[1], Martijn Stam[2], Ryan Stanley-Oakes[2(✉)], and Bogdan Warinschi[2]

[1] Department of Computer Science, Paderborn University, Paderborn, Germany
tibor.jager@upb.de
[2] Department of Computer Science, University of Bristol, Bristol, UK
{martijn.stam,ryan.stanley-oakes,bogdan.warinschi}@bristol.ac.uk

**Abstract.** We study the security of symmetric encryption schemes in settings with multiple users and realistic adversaries who can adaptively corrupt encryption keys. To avoid confinement to any particular definitional paradigm, we propose a general framework for multi-key security definitions. By appropriate settings of the parameters of the framework, we obtain multi-key variants of many of the existing single-key security notions.

This framework is instrumental in establishing our main results. We show that for all single-key secure encryption schemes satisfying a minimal key uniqueness assumption and almost any instantiation of our general multi-key security notion, any reasonable reduction from the multi-key game to a standard single-key game necessarily incurs a linear loss in the number of keys. We prove this result for all three classical single-key security notions capturing confidentiality, authenticity and the combined authenticated encryption notion.

**Keywords:** Encryption · Multi-key · Corruption · Reductions · Tightness

## 1 Introduction

In theory, most symmetric and public key cryptosystems are considered by default in a single-key setting, yet in reality cryptographic ecosystems provide an abundance of keys—and hence targets—for an adversary to attack. Often one can construct a reduction that shows that single-key security implies multi-key security, but typically such a reduction is lossy: an adversary's multi-key advantage is roughly bounded by the single-key advantage times the number of keys $n$ in the ecosystem. The ramifications of such a loss can be debated [16], but undeniably in a concrete setting with perhaps $2^{30}$ to $2^{40}$ keys in circulation, an *actual* loss of 30 to 40 bits of security would be considerable. Therefore the natural question arises to what extent this loss in the reduction is inevitable.

This inevitable loss of reductions from multi-key to single-key has previously been addressed by Bellare et al. [6] when introducing multi-key security

© International Association for Cryptologic Research 2017
Y. Kalai and L. Reyzin (Eds.): TCC 2017, Part I, LNCS 10677, pp. 409–441, 2017.
https://doi.org/10.1007/978-3-319-70500-2_14

for public key schemes. Specifically, they provided a counterexample: namely a pathological encryption scheme that has a small chance (about $\frac{1}{n}$, where $n$ is a parameter) of leaking the key when used in a single-key environment. In a multi-key scenario, where there are $n$ key pairs, insecurity of the scheme is amplified to the point where it becomes a constant. It follows that any *generic* reduction, i.e. a reduction that works for any scheme, from the multi-key to single-key security must lose a factor of about $n$. A similar example can be concocted for symmetric schemes to conclude that there cannot be a tight generic reduction from a multi-key game to a single-key game for symmetric encryption, i.e. a reduction that works for *all* encryption schemes, since the reduction will not be tight when instantiated by the pathological scheme. However, this does not rule out all reductions, since a tighter reduction could exist that exploits specific features of a certain class of (non-pathological) schemes.

Consider a setting with a security notion G for primitives (e.g. pseudorandomness for blockciphers), a security notion H for constructions (e.g. ciphertext integrity for authenticated encryption), and suppose we are given a specific construction $C[\mathcal{E}]$ building on any instantiation $\mathcal{E}$ of the primitive. A reduction $\mathcal{R}$ would take adversary $\mathcal{A}$ against the H property of the construction and turn it into one against the G property of the primitive. To be *black-box*, the reduction $\mathcal{R}$ should not depend on $\mathcal{A}$, but instead only use $\mathcal{A}$'s input/output behaviour. However, when considering black-box reductions, it turns out there are many shades of black. Baecher et al. [4] presented a taxonomy of black-box reductions; the shades of black emerge when considering whether $\mathcal{R}$ may depend on the construction $C$ and/or the primitive $\mathcal{E}$ or not. A *fully* black-box (BBB) reduction works for all $C$ and $\mathcal{E}$, while partially black-box (NBN) reductions can depend on the specific choice of $C$ and $\mathcal{E}$.

The pathological encryption schemes used as counterexamples are by nature rather contrived and the one used by Bellare et al. is of dubious security even in the single-key setting [6]. The counterexamples suffice to rule out tight BBB reductions, but they do *not* rule out the existence of potentially large classes of encryption schemes—perhaps practical ones, or even all *secure* ones—for which a tight NBN reduction *does* exist. Clearly, such an NBN reduction could not be generic, but instead would have to exploit some feature of the specific primitive or construction under consideration. Even when the primitive is assumed 'ideal' as is common in symmetric cryptology, the relevant reductions typically still depend on the details of the construction at hand, and are therefore not fully (BBB) black-box. Concluding, for secure schemes the relation between single-key and multi-key security is still largely unsettled.

**Our Contribution.** Focusing on authenticated encryption (AE) schemes, we make two main contributions: a general multi-key security definition including corruptions and lower-bounds on the tightness of black-box (NBN) reductions from the multi-key security to the single-key security of AE schemes.

*General Security Definition.* The first complication we face is the choice of security notions. As we recall in more detail in Sect. 2.1, there are many different ways of defining single-key security for AE. For instance, confidentiality can be expressed in several (not necessarily equivalent) ways, including left-or-right indistinguishability (LRIND) and ciphertexts being indistinguishable from random strings (IND). Moreover there are different ways of treating nonces; each defines a slightly different security notion.

When moving to a multi-key setting, the water becomes even more muddied, especially when considering adaptive corruptions as we do. Adaptive corruptions allow an adversary to learn some of the keys during the course of the multi-key game; it models the real-life circumstance that not all keys will remain secret and some *will* leak. In this setting, security can be formulated in (at least) two ways: firstly using a hidden bit $b_i$ for each key $K_i$, with the adversary having to guess the bit $b_i$ for a key $K_i$ that has not been corrupted; and secondly, using a single hidden bit $b$ determining the 'challenge' oracles for all $n$ keys (e.g. left or right, real or random) with the adversary having to guess this bit $b$, under the restriction that no single key gets both corrupted and challenged.

As we explain in the full version of the paper [31], these two approaches do not appear to be tightly equivalent to each other. Furthermore, notions that used to be equivalent in the single-key setting suddenly start drifting apart, something previously observed in the multi-instance setting [8]. Again, this creates a bit of a conundrum as to what is the 'right' multi-key security notion, where we want to avoid a situation where we show that a reduction loss targeting one security notion is inevitable, while leaving the door open for tight reductions targeting another.

To avoid having to make a choice, we instead provide a general definition for multi-key security game (Definition 7) that allows us to plug in the 'flavour' of AE security we desire, and of which the two approaches for dealing with corruptions in a multi-key setting are special cases.

*Lower Bounds on the Loss for Simple Reductions.* Roughly speaking, we show that for any member $G^n$ of a large class of $n$-key security games that allow for adaptive corruptions and for most AE schemes $C[\mathcal{E}]$ built on a single-key secure AE scheme $\mathcal{E}$ (including $C[\mathcal{E}] = \mathcal{E}$), any black-box reduction from $G^n$ for $C[\mathcal{E}]$ to a standard single-key security game $H^1$ for $\mathcal{E}$ incurs a loss that is close to $n$. By 'black-box', we mean *at least* NBN: the reduction must be black-box with respect to the adversary against $G^n$ but can depend on $C$ and $\mathcal{E}$.

Figure 1 shows both the logic of our approach and the overall results. The main idea is to first consider a *very weak* $n$-key security game, $K^n$, and show that reductions from $K^n$ to $H^1$ are lossy. Then, for any $n$-key game $G^n$ that tightly implies $K^n$, the loss from $G^n$ to $H^1$ will have to match that from $K^n$ to $H^1$ (or a contradiction would appear when composing the reduction from $K^n$ to $G^n$ with that from $G^n$ to $H^1$). Our weak security notion $K^n$ is a 1-out-of-$n$ key recovery game where the adversary first sees encryptions of fixed messages under all $n$ keys, then corrupts all but one key and must try to guess the uncorrupted key. The choice for the three $H^1$ notions AE−PAS, IND−PAS, and CTI−CPA is inspired by their ubiquity in current AE literature (the naming convention is clarified in Sect. 2.1).

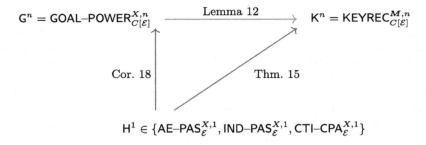

**Fig. 1.** A roadmap of our results, showing that some reductions between the security notions for authenticated encryption are necessarily lossy. A green arrow $G \to G'$ indicates that there is a non-lossy reduction from $G'$ to $G$ (so security in the sense of $G$ implies security in the sense of $G'$). A red arrow $G \to G'$ indicates that all reductions from $G'$ to $G$ have a loss that is linear in $n$. Theorem 15 and Corollary 18 concern $\mathsf{H}^1 = \mathsf{AE\text{-}PAS}_{\mathcal{E}}^{X,1}$; the other choices of $\mathsf{H}^1$ are treated in the full version of the paper [31]. (Color figure online)

To show for each choice of $\mathsf{H}^1$ that reductions from $\mathsf{K}^n$ for $C[\mathcal{E}]$ to $\mathsf{H}^1$ for $\mathcal{E}$ are lossy, we use three *meta-reductions*. Unlike using pathological schemes as counterexamples, meta-reductions can easily deal with NBN reductions that depend on the construction $C$ and scheme $\mathcal{E}$: a meta-reduction $\mathcal{M}$ *simulates* an ideal adversary $\mathcal{A}$ against $C[\mathcal{E}]$ for a reduction $\mathcal{R}$ and then uses $\mathcal{R}$ to break $\mathcal{E}$ [3, 14,19]. Then one finds the inevitable loss factor of $\mathcal{R}$ by bounding the advantage of $\mathcal{M}$ (in its interaction with $\mathcal{R}$) by the advantage of the best possible adversary against $\mathcal{E}$. We remark that this technique is vacuous for insecure schemes $\mathcal{E}$ as the resulting bound on the advantage of $\mathcal{M}$ is not meaningful.

More precisely, we show that for the three choices of $\mathsf{H}^1$, any black-box reduction running in time at most $t$ from $\mathsf{K}^n$ for $C[\mathcal{E}]$ to $\mathsf{H}^1$ for $\mathcal{E}$ must lose $\left(\frac{1}{n} + \epsilon\right)^{-1}$, where $\epsilon$ is essentially the maximum advantage in $\mathsf{H}^1$ of an adversary running in time $n \cdot t$. These results hold provided that $C[\mathcal{E}]$ is *key-unique*: given sufficient plaintext–ciphertext pairs the key is *always* uniquely determined. For almost all variants $G^n$ of our general $n$-key security game, there is a tight reduction from $\mathsf{K}^n$ to $G^n$ (Lemma 12); combining this tight reduction with the unavoidable loss from $\mathsf{K}^n$ to $\mathsf{H}^1$ shows that any black-box reduction from $G^n$ to $\mathsf{H}^1$ is lossy.

In summary, we show that for almost any variant $G^n$ of the general $n$-key security game and for $\mathsf{H}^1 \in \left\{\mathsf{AE\text{-}PAS}_{\mathcal{E}}^{X,1}, \mathsf{IND\text{-}PAS}_{\mathcal{E}}^{X,1}, \mathsf{CTI\text{-}CPA}_{\mathcal{E}}^{X,1}\right\}$, if $\mathcal{E}$ is "secure" in the sense of $\mathsf{H}^1$ and $C[\mathcal{E}]$ is key-unique, then any black-box reduction from $G^n$ to $\mathsf{H}^1$ with a "reasonable" runtime loses approximately $n$.

**Related Work.** The idea of using a weak auxiliary security game to prove that reductions are lossy for more meaningful games was pioneered by Bader et al. for public key primitives [3]. Bader et al. considered as their $\mathsf{H}^1$ notion a non-interactive assumption, whereas our $\mathsf{H}^1$ games are highly interactive. The main obstacle here is that our meta-reduction needs to simulate an appropriate environment towards $n$ *copies* of the reduction, while having access only to a single set of oracles for the considered single-key game. Thus we are forced to devise an additional mechanism that allows the meta-reduction to simulate responses to the oracle queries made by $\mathcal{R}$ and prove that $\mathcal{R}$ cannot distinguish this simulation from the real oracles in its game.

Multi-key security was first considered in the public key setting [6], extending the LRIND−CCA notion to a single-bit multi-key setting without corruptions. A simple hybrid argument shows the loss of security is at most linear in the number of keys; furthermore this loss is inevitable as demonstrated by a *counterexample*. Relatedly, for many schemes a generic key recovery attack exists whose success probability is linear in both time and the number of keys $n$ [10, 11, 22]. For schemes where this generic key recovery attack is actually the *best* attack (in both the single-key and $n$-key games), this shows that security in the $n$-key setting is indeed $n$ times less than in the single-key setting. However, even for very secure schemes it is unlikely that key recovery is the optimum strategy for e.g. distinguishing genuine ciphertexts from random strings.

The danger of ignoring the loss in reductions between security notions is by now widely understood [15, 16] and has served as motivation for work on improved security analysis that avoid the loss of generic reductions. Recent results include multi-user security for Even–Mansour [34], AES-GCM with nonce randomisation [9], double encryption [26], and block ciphers [42].

Tightness is better understood in the public key setting than in the symmetric setting. There are, for instance, many constructions of (identity-based) public-key encryption [6, 13, 17, 24, 28], digital signatures [1, 12, 27, 32, 33, 40], key exchange protocols [2], as well as several different types of lower bounds and impossibility results [18, 21, 23, 29, 36]. We emphasise that, for signature schemes and public key encryption schemes, 'tightly secure' means that the reduction from the scheme to some complexity assumption does not incur a multiplicative loss equal to *the number of signing or encryption queries*.

There exist several other previous works describing meta-reductions from interactive problems, such as the *one-more discrete logarithm* (OMDL) problem [19, 23, 36, 41]. However, all these works have in common that they consider a significantly simpler setting, where the reduction is rewound a much smaller number of times (typically only once), and with only a single oracle (the discrete logarithm oracle).

## 2    Preliminaries

**Notation.** For any integer $n \geq 1$ we use $[n]$ to denote the set $\{1, \ldots, n\}$ and for any $i \in [n]$ we use $[n \setminus i]$ to denote the set $[n] \setminus \{i\}$. For any finite set $S$ we write $x \leftarrow_\$ S$ to indicate that $x$ is drawn uniformly at random from $S$. In any security experiment, if an adversary $\mathcal{A}$ has worst-case runtime $t$, then we say $\mathcal{A}$ is a $t$-adversary. When $\mathcal{A}$ is clear from the context, we write $t_\mathcal{A}$ for its worst case runtime. Since our security notions are *concrete*, rather than asymptotic (as is standard for symmetric cryptography), we loosely use the term "secure" to mean that, for all reasonable values of $t$, the advantage of any $t$-adversary in the relevant security game is close to 0. Of course, what constitutes a "reasonable" runtime depends on the model of computation and is beyond the scope of this work.

## 2.1  Authenticated Encryption

**Syntax.** Both the syntax and security definitions for symmetric and then authenticated encryption have evolved over the years. We will use the modern perspective where encryption is deterministic and takes in not just a key and a message, but also a nonce, which could be used to provide an explicit form of randomization. Our syntax is summarised in Definition 1 and is a simplification of that used for subtle authenticated encryption [5]. For simplicity, we omit any associated data, though our later results could be extended to that setting; moreover we are not interested in the 'subtle' aspect, where decryption might 'leak', e.g. unverified plaintext or multiple error symbols.

**Definition 1 (Authenticated Encryption).** *An* authenticated encryption scheme *is a pair of deterministic algorithms* $(\mathcal{E}, \mathcal{D})$ *satisfying*

$$\mathcal{E} : \mathsf{K} \times \mathsf{N} \times \mathsf{M} \to \mathsf{C}$$
$$\mathcal{D} : \mathsf{K} \times \mathsf{N} \times \mathsf{C} \to \mathsf{M} \cup \{\bot\}$$

*where* $\mathsf{K}$, $\mathsf{M}$, $\mathsf{N}$ *and* $\mathsf{C}$ *are subsets of* $\{0,1\}^*$ *whose elements are called* keys, *messages,* nonces *and* ciphertexts *respectively. The unique failure symbol* $\bot$ *indicates that* $C$ *was not a valid encryption under the key* $K$ *with nonce* $N$.

As is customary, we abbreviate $\mathcal{E}(K, N, M)$ by $\mathcal{E}_K^N(M)$ and $\mathcal{D}(K, N, C)$ by $\mathcal{D}_K^N(C)$ and assume throughout that all authenticated encryption schemes satify, for all $K \in \mathsf{K}, N \in \mathsf{N}, M \in \mathsf{M}$ and all $C \in \mathsf{C}$, the following three properties:

1. *(correctness)* $\mathcal{D}_K^N\left(\mathcal{E}_K^N(M)\right) = M$,
2. *(tidiness)* $\mathcal{D}_K^N(C) \neq \bot \Rightarrow \mathcal{E}_K^N\left(\mathcal{D}_K^N(C)\right) = C$,
3. *(length-regularity)* $|\mathcal{E}_K^N(M)| = \mathsf{enclen}(|M|)$ for some fixed function $\mathsf{enclen}$.

Correctness and tidiness together imply that $\mathcal{D}$ is uniquely determined by $\mathcal{E}$, allowing us to refer to the pair $(\mathcal{E}, \mathcal{D})$ simply by $\mathcal{E}$ [35].

**Single-key Security Notions.** An authenticated encryption scheme should provide both *confidentiality* and *authenticity*. When defining an adversary's advantage, we separate these orthogonal properties by looking at the $\mathsf{IND-PAS}$ and $\mathsf{CTI-CPA}$ security games, while also considering their combination $\mathsf{AE-PAS}$ in a single game [38]. Below we discuss these notions in more detail, however we defer formal definitions of the relevant games and advantages to the next section, where they will be viewed as a special case of the *multi-key* games given in Definition 7 (cf. Remark 9).

The notions IND−PAS, CTI−CPA and AE−PAS are commonly called IND−CPA, for indistinguishability under chosen plaintext attack; INT−CTXT, for integrity of ciphertexts; and AE, for authenticated encryption (respectively). However, we adhere to the GOAL−POWER naming scheme [5]. It makes explicit that, in the first case, the adversary's goal is to distinguish between real ciphertexts and random strings (IND, for indistinguishability) without access to any additional oracles (PAS, for passive); in the second case, the adversary's goal is to forge a well-formed ciphertext (CTI, for ciphertext integrity) and has access to an 'always-real' encryption oracle (CPA, for chosen plaintext attack); and in the third case, the adversary tries to either distinguish real ciphertexts from random strings or forge a well-formed ciphertext (AE, for authenticated encryption), without having access to any additional oracles (PAS). For the notions above, we opted for minimal adversarial powers: it is often possible to trade queries to additional oracles (such as a true encryption oracle) for queries to the challenge oracle. We refer to Barwell et al. [5] for an overview of known relations between various notions.

*Nonce Usage Convention.* All three of the games above have variants according to how nonces may be used by the adversary in the game:

1. In the IV-based setting, denoted IV, the adversary is required to choose nonces uniformly at random for each encryption query.
2. In the nonce-respecting setting, denoted NR, the adversary chooses nonces adaptively for each encryption query, but may never use the same nonce in more than one encryption query.
3. In the misuse-resistant setting, denoted MR, the adversary chooses nonces adaptively for each encryption query and may use the same nonce in more than one encryption query.

*Remark 2.* The customary definition for IV-based security lets the game select the IVs [35]. We prefer the recent alternative [5] that provides the same interface across the various notions by restricting the class of valid adversaries in the IV-based setting to those who always provide uniformly random nonces in encryption queries. (Note that there is no need to check the distribution of nonces). This gives a subtly stronger notion, as a reduction will no longer be able to 'program' the IV, which it would be allowed to do in the classical definition (cf. [20,30]).

The results in this paper hold with the alternative, customary formulation of IV-based encryption, with only cosmetic changes to the proof (to take into account the changed interface).

*Different Confidentiality Goals.* Above we captured the confidentiality goal IND as distinguishing between real ciphertexts and random strings of the appropriate length. However, there are several competing notions to capture confidentiality, all captured by considering a different challenge encryption oracle:

- In left-or-right indistinguishability (LRIND) the challenge oracle is LR; on input $(M_0, M_1, N)$, this oracle returns $\mathcal{E}_K^N(M_b)$ (here $b$ is the hidden bit that the adversary must try to learn).
- In real-or-random indistinguishability the challenge oracle, on input $(M, N)$, returns either $\mathcal{E}_K^N(M)$ or $\mathcal{E}_K^N(\$)$, where $\$$ is a random string of the same length as $M$.
- In pseudorandom-injection indistinguishability the challenge oracle, on input $(M, N)$, returns either $\mathcal{E}_K^N(M)$ or $\rho^N(M)$, where $\rho$ is a suitably sampled family of random injections [25,38].

In the single-key setting, these four notions can be partitioned into two groups of two each, namely left-or-right and real-or-random on the one hand and IND and pseudorandom-injection indistinguishability on the other. Within each group, the two notions can be considered equivalent, as an adversary against one can be turned into an adversary against the other with the same resources and a closely related advantage. Furthermore, security in the IND setting trivially implies security in the LRIND setting, but not vice versa.

*Summary.* Thus, for each authenticated encryption scheme $\mathcal{E}$, we potentially obtain $5 \times 4 = 20$ security games (see Fig. 2) and for each we need to consider three classes of adversary depending on nonce usage behaviour. However, for single-key security, we will concentrate on *nine* notions only, namely $\mathsf{G}_{\mathcal{E}}^{X,1}$, where

$$\mathsf{G} \in \{\mathsf{AE-PAS}, \mathsf{IND-PAS}, \mathsf{CTI-CPA}\},$$
$$X \in \{\mathsf{IV}, \mathsf{NR}, \mathsf{MR}\}$$

and where the 1 in the superscript indicates that these are *single-key* security games.

*Remark 3.* In this paper we use meta-reductions to analyse reductions from multi-key games to single-key games for authenticated encryption. We show that, for any AE scheme that is secure in a single-key sense, any reduction from the multi-key game to the single-key game is lossy. We do not need to consider equivalent single-key notions separately, as any scheme that is secure according to one notion will be secure according to the other, and one can convert between the single-key games without (significant) additional loss. From this perspective, we can leverage known equivalences as mentioned above. However, the set $\{\mathsf{AE-PAS}, \mathsf{IND-PAS}, \mathsf{CTI-CPA}\}$ does not provide a comprehensive set of meta-reduction results; for that we would have to consider for example $\mathsf{LRIND-PAS}$ and $\mathsf{IND-CCA}$ as well (the full set would contain eight games). Nevertheless, our results capture the single-key notions that are most commonly used.

## 2.2   Black-Box Reductions

Informally, a *reduction* $\mathcal{R}$ is an algorithm that transforms an adversary $\mathcal{A}$ in some security game $\mathsf{G}$ into an adversary $\mathcal{R}(\mathcal{A})$ in a different security game $\mathsf{G}'$.

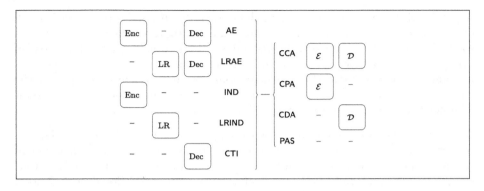

**Fig. 2.** The oracles available to the adversary for each GOAL−POWER security notion. Formal definitions of each oracle are given in Fig. 4. (Many thanks to Guy Barwell for providing this diagram.)

One hopes that, if the advantage $\mathsf{Adv}^{\mathsf{G}}(\mathcal{A})$ of $\mathcal{A}$ in $\mathsf{G}$ is high, then the advantage $\mathsf{Adv}^{\mathsf{G}'}(\mathcal{R}(\mathcal{A}))$ is also high. Here $\mathcal{R}$ breaks some scheme $\mathcal{E}$, given an adversary $\mathcal{A}$ that breaks a construction $C[\mathcal{E}]$ that uses $\mathcal{E}$. The construction $C$ is typically fixed, so the reduction $\mathcal{R}$ may depend on it (though to unclutter notation we leave this dependency implicit). On the contrary, when discussing the reduction $\mathcal{R}$, $\mathcal{E}$ is crucially quantified over some class of schemes $\mathcal{C}$.

Three properties of a reduction $\mathcal{R}$ are usually of interest: how the resources, specifically run-time, of the resulting adversary $\mathcal{R}(\mathcal{A})$ relate to those of $\mathcal{A}$; how the reduction translates the success of $\mathcal{A}$ to that of $\mathcal{R}(\mathcal{A})$; and how 'lossy' this translation is, i.e. how $\mathsf{Adv}^{\mathsf{G}'}(\mathcal{R}(\mathcal{A}))$ compares to $\mathsf{Adv}^{\mathsf{G}}(\mathcal{A})$. The overall picture for a reduction, especially its loss, strongly depends on the class $\mathcal{C}$ of schemes considered.

Formally, we take into account both the translation $\mathbb{S}$ and the relation $\mathbb{T}$ in runtime into account by considering the quotient of $\mathcal{A}$ and $\mathcal{R}(\mathcal{A})$'s *work factors*, themselves defined as the quotient of time over success probability (cf. [3]).

**Definition 4.** *We say that $\mathcal{R}$ is a $(\mathbb{S}, \mathbb{T})$ reduction from $\mathsf{G}$ to $\mathsf{G}'$ if for every $t_A$-adversary $\mathcal{A}$ against $\mathsf{G}$, $\mathcal{R}_\mathcal{A}$ is an $\mathbb{T}(t_A)$-adversary against $\mathsf{G}'$ and $\mathsf{Adv}^{\mathsf{G}'}(\mathcal{R}(\mathcal{A})) = \mathbb{S}(\mathsf{Adv}^{\mathsf{G}}(\mathcal{A}))$. Furthermore, the tightness of a reduction $\mathcal{R}$ relative to the class of schemes $\mathcal{C}$ is defined as*

$$\sup_{\mathcal{A},\mathcal{E}} \frac{\mathsf{Adv}^{\mathsf{G}}(\mathcal{A}) \cdot t_{\mathcal{R}(\mathcal{A})}}{\mathsf{Adv}^{\mathsf{G}'}(\mathcal{R}(\mathcal{A})) \cdot t_A} = \sup_{\mathcal{A},\mathcal{E}} \frac{\mathbb{T}(t_A) \cdot \mathsf{Adv}^{\mathsf{G}}(\mathcal{A})}{t_A \cdot \mathbb{S}(\mathsf{Adv}^{\mathsf{G}}(\mathcal{A}))}$$

*where the supremum is taken over all schemes $\mathcal{E}$ in $\mathcal{C}$ and all (valid) adversaries $\mathcal{A}$ against $\mathcal{E}$.*

*Remark 5.* Our quantification over *valid* adversaries only is inspired by the AE literature's reliance on only considering adversaries satisfying certain behaviour (e.g. to avoid trivial wins, or distinguish between IV, NR, and MR settings). In all cases, one can recast to a security game that incorporates checks and balances to deal with arbitrary adversarial behaviour. This recasting is without loss of generality as an adversary in this more general game will be 'aware' that it is making a 'bad' query *and* this bad behaviour does not influence the state of the game (cf. [7]). Of course, when determining $\mathbb{S}$ we do need to take into account whether the reduction $\mathcal{R}$ preserves validity.

In this paper we are concerned with *simple, black-box reductions*: these are reductions that have only black-box access to adversary $\mathcal{A}$, and that run $\mathcal{A}$ precisely once (without rewinding). For a $(\mathbb{S}, \mathbb{T})$ simple reduction $\mathcal{R}$ we have that $\mathbb{T}(t_{\mathcal{A}}) = t_{\mathcal{A}} + t_{\mathcal{R}}$, where $t_{\mathcal{R}}$ is the time taken for whatever additional work $\mathcal{R}$ does. Henceforth, we write $t_{\mathcal{R}}$ for this quantity, whenever $\mathcal{R}$ is a simple reduction.

These reductions compose in the obvious way: if $\mathcal{R}_1$ is a simple $(\mathbb{S}_1, \mathbb{T}_1)$ reduction from $\mathsf{G}_1$ to $\mathsf{G}_2$ and $\mathcal{R}_2$ is a simple $(\mathbb{S}_2, \mathbb{T}_2)$ reduction from $\mathsf{G}_2$ to $\mathsf{G}_3$, then we can construct a simple $(\mathbb{S}_3, \mathbb{T}_3)$ reduction $\mathcal{R}_3$ from $\mathsf{G}_1$ to $\mathsf{G}_3$, where $\mathbb{S}_3(\epsilon) = \mathbb{S}_2(\mathbb{S}_1(\epsilon))$ and $\mathbb{T}_3(t) = \mathbb{T}_2(\mathbb{T}_1(t))$.

*Bounding Tightness.* Precisely evaluating the tightness of a reduction can be difficult, yet to show that for schemes in $\mathcal{C}$ *any* simple reduction $\mathcal{R}$ loses *at least* some factor $L$, it suffices to show that for any $\mathcal{R}$ there exists a scheme $\mathcal{E} \in \mathcal{C}$ and a valid adversary $\mathcal{A}$ such that

$$\frac{\mathsf{Adv}^{\mathsf{G}}(\mathcal{A})}{\mathsf{Adv}^{\mathsf{G}'}(\mathcal{R}(\mathcal{A}))} \geq L. \tag{1}$$

Indeed, the desired lower bound follows since, for simple reductions, $\mathbb{T}(t_{\mathcal{A}}) \geq t_{\mathcal{A}}$.

We briefly discuss two distinct techniques to establish a bound such as the one above, in which the order of quantifiers is $(\forall \mathcal{R} \exists \mathcal{E} \exists \mathcal{A})$:

- *Counterexample ($\exists \mathcal{E} \forall \mathcal{A} \forall \mathcal{R}$).* Here, one shows that there exists a scheme $\mathcal{E} \in \mathcal{C}$ such that for any adversary $\mathcal{A}$ and any reduction $\mathcal{R}$, inequality 1 is satisfied. One drawback of such results is that they only imply the desired lowerbound for a class of schemes $\mathcal{C}$ containing $\mathcal{E}$; tighter reductions might be possible in the class $\mathcal{C}' := \mathcal{C} \setminus \{\mathcal{E}\}$. Moreover, if the counterexample scheme $\mathcal{E}$ is an artificially insecure scheme (e.g. the one used by Bellare et al. [6]), then the lowerbound might not hold within the class of *secure* schemes, which are obviously of greater significance in practice.
- *Meta-reduction Lowerbound ($\forall \mathcal{E} \exists \mathcal{A} \forall \mathcal{R}$).* For any $\mathcal{E} \in \mathcal{C}$, this technique constructs an idealised adversary $\mathcal{A}$ with advantage 1 and then shows, via a meta-reduction simulating $\mathcal{A}$, that any simple reduction interacting with $\mathcal{A}$ must have advantage at most $L^{-1}$, yielding inequality 1. Thus we show that the loss is a property of the reduction $\mathcal{R}$, and not of the particular choice of $\mathcal{E} \in \mathcal{C}$. The results in this paper, using the meta-reduction approach, hold when $\mathcal{C}$ is any non-empty subset of the class of secure schemes that satisfy the key uniqueness assumption. Since $\mathcal{C}$ could contain just one element $\mathcal{E}$, our

results show that even a reduction that is tailored to the specific details of $\mathcal{E}$ cannot be tight. On the other hand, our results are not directly comparable to those of Bellare et al. [6], since the artificially insecure scheme used in their counterexample does not belong to any class $\mathcal{C}$ we consider here.

*Remark 6.* An alternative definition of tightness might consider only 'reasonable' adversaries $\mathcal{A}$ in the supremum, namely those for which $t_{\mathcal{A}}$ is not too large. Our meta-reduction approach would not work in this setting, since the idealised adversary $\mathcal{A}$ we construct has an extremely large (and wholly unfeasible) runtime as it performs an exhaustive search over all possible keys. Nevertheless, reductions $\mathcal{R}$ that are black-box with respect to $\mathcal{A}$ have no way of 'excluding' such unrealistic adversaries and so we feel it is not reasonable to exclude them in the definition of tightness. We remark that unrealistic adversaries are not uncommon in the meta-reduction literature [3].

# 3    Multi-key Security Notions

**Multi-key Security with Adaptive Corruptions.** In the single-key case, the challenge oracles depend on a single hidden bit $b$ and it is the job of the adversary to try and learn $b$. The straightforward generalization [6] to a multi-key setting (with $n$ keys) is to enrich all the oracles to include the index $i \in [n]$ of the key $K_i$ that will then be used by the oracle. Thus the challenge oracles for distinct keys will all depend on the same single hidden bit $b$.

However, in a realistic multi-key setting, an adversary might well learn some of the keys. For instance, consider the situation where an attacker passively monitors millions of TLS connections and adaptively implants malware on particular endpoint devices in order to recover the session keys for those devices. We still want security for those keys that have not been compromised; the question is how to appropriately model multi-key security.

There are two natural approaches to model multi-key security games in the presence of an adaptive corruption oracle Cor that, on input $i \in [n]$, returns the key $K_i$. The approaches differ in how they avoid trivial wins that occur when the adversary corrupts a key that was used for a challenge query. In one approach, the same bit is used for the challenge queries throughout, but the adversary is prohibited from using the same index $i$ for both a corruption and challenge query (cf. [37]). In another approach, for each index $i$ there is an independent hidden bit $b_i$ to guess and the adversary has to specify for which uncorrupted index its guess $b'$ is intended (cf. [8]).

As far as we are aware, these two approaches have not been formally compared; moreover we could not easily establish a tight relationship between them. However, as we show, both options lead to a reduction loss linear in $n$. To do so, we will use a novel way of formalizing a multi-key security game with adaptive corruptions that encompasses *both* options mentioned above.

In our generalised game (Definition 7) there are $n$ independently, uniformly sampled random bits $b_1, \ldots, b_n$. Each challenge query from the adversary must

---

**Experiment** GOAL–POWER$_{\mathcal{E}}^{X,n}(\mathcal{A})$:

$K_1, \ldots, K_n \leftarrow_{\$} \mathsf{K}$

$b_1, \ldots, b_n \leftarrow_{\$} \{0,1\}$

$(j, b_j') \leftarrow \mathcal{A}^{\mathcal{O}}$

Return $(b_j' = b_j)$

---

**Fig. 3.** The GOAL–POWER$_{\mathcal{E}}^{X,n}$ games, where $X \in \{\mathsf{IV}, \mathsf{NR}, \mathsf{MR}\}$, $n \geq 1$, GOAL $\in$ $\{\mathsf{AE}, \mathsf{LRAE}, \mathsf{IND}, \mathsf{LRIND}, \mathsf{CTI}\}$ and POWER $\in \{\mathsf{CCA}, \mathsf{CPA}, \mathsf{CDA}, \mathsf{PAS}\}$. The oracles $\mathcal{O}$ available to the adversary always include the corruption oracle Cor; the other oracles depend on GOAL and POWER, as indicated in Fig. 2.

specify two indices, $i, j \in [n]$, such that the response to the query depends on key $K_i$ and hidden bit $b_j$. The two 'natural' multi-key games are special cases of this general game: in the single-bit game the adversary is restricted to challenge queries with $j = 1$, whereas in the multi-bit game only challenge queries with $i = j$ are allowed.

Our impossibility results hold regardless how the hidden bits are used: we only require that for any $i \in [n]$ there exists *some* $j \in [n]$ such that the adversary can make a challenge query corresponding to $K_i$ and $b_j$. In other words, our impossibility results hold provided that the adversary can win the game by 'attacking' any of the $n$ keys in the game, not just some subset of the keys.

**Definition 7 (Security of AE).** *Let* GOAL $\in \{\mathsf{AE}, \mathsf{LRAE}, \mathsf{IND}, \mathsf{LRIND}, \mathsf{CTI}\}$, POWER $\in \{\mathsf{CCA}, \mathsf{CPA}, \mathsf{CDA}, \mathsf{PAS}\}$, $X \in \{\mathsf{IV}, \mathsf{NR}, \mathsf{MR}\}$ *and* $n \geq 1$. *Then for any authenticated encryption scheme* $\mathcal{E}$ *and adversary* $\mathcal{A}$, *the advantage of* $\mathcal{A}$ *against* $\mathcal{E}$ *with respect to* GOAL–POWER$^{X,n}$ *is defined as*

$$\mathsf{Adv}_{\mathcal{E}}^{\mathsf{GOAL–POWER},X,n}(\mathcal{A}) := 2 \cdot \mathbf{Pr}\left[\mathsf{GOAL–POWER}_{\mathcal{E}}^{X,n}(\mathcal{A}) = 1\right] - 1 ,$$

*where the experiment* GOAL–POWER$_{\mathcal{E}}^{X,n}(\mathcal{A})$ *is defined in Fig. 3, with the oracles' behaviour shown in Fig. 4 and their* GOAL–POWER*-dependent availability in Fig. 2 (all games have access to* Cor*).*

Whenever the experiment $\mathsf{G} = \mathsf{GOAL–POWER}_{\mathcal{E}}^{X,n}(\mathcal{A})$ is clear from the context, we write $\mathsf{Adv}^{\mathsf{G}}(\mathcal{A})$ for the advantage of $\mathcal{A}$ in experiment $\mathsf{G}$.

The outline games are deliberately kept simple, but are trivial to win: if $\mathcal{A}$ corrupts a key $K_i$ and then issues a challenge query corresponding to $K_i$ and a hidden bit $b_j$, then it is trivial for $\mathcal{A}$ to compute $b_j$ from the response to the query; successfully 'guessing' $b_j$ does not represent a meaningful attack. In our formal syntax, we say $j$ is *compromised* iff there is some $i \in [n]$ such that $\mathcal{A}$ has issued a query Cor$(i)$ and $\mathcal{A}$ has also issued some challenge query of the form Enc$(i, j, -, -)$, LR$(i, j, -, -, -)$ or Dec$(i, j, -, -)$. We disallow such trivial wins.

Relatedly, we follow the AE literature in disallowing certain combinations of queries that lead to trivial wins (*prohibited queries*), or that are inconsistent

**Oracle** $\text{Enc}(i, j, M, N)$:
if $b_j = 0$, $C \leftarrow \mathcal{E}_{K_i}^N(M)$
else $C \leftarrow_{\$} \{0, 1\}^{\text{enclen}(|M|)}$
return $C$

**Oracle** $\mathcal{E}(i, M, N)$:
return $\mathcal{E}_{K_i}^N(M)$

**Oracle** $\text{LR}(i, j, M_0, M_1, N)$:
$C \leftarrow \mathcal{E}_{K_i}^N(M_{b_j})$
return $C$

**Oracle** $\mathcal{D}(i, C, N)$:
return $\mathcal{D}_{K_i}^N(C)$

**Oracle** $\text{Dec}(i, j, C, N)$:
if $b_j = 0$, $M \leftarrow \mathcal{D}_{K_i}^N(C)$
else $M \leftarrow \perp$
return $M$

**Oracle** $\text{Cor}(i)$:
return $K_i$

**Fig. 4.** Oracles for the $\text{GOAL–POWER}_{\mathcal{E}}^{X,n}$ security games. Without loss of generality, we assume that all oracles return $\xi$ if the input arguments do not belong to the relevant sets. For example, the $\mathcal{E}$ oracle will return $\xi$ on any input $(i, M, N)$ that is not a member of $[n] \times \mathsf{M} \times \mathsf{N}$.

with the nonce notion under consideration. Without loss of generality, we also disallow queries where the response from the oracle can be computed by the adversary directly without making the query, e.g. using correctness (*pointless queries*). The relevant—and standard—definitions are given in Combining the various restrictions leads to the notion of valid adversaries (cf. Remark 5), as summarised in Definition 8 below.

**Definition 8 (Valid Adversaries).** *An adversary against* $\text{GOAL–POWER}_{\mathcal{E}}^{X,n}$ *is* valid *iff:*

1. *it does not output* $(j, b_j')$ *where* $j$ *was* compromised;
2. *it does not make* pointless *or* prohibited *queries;*
3. *it uses nonces correctly with respect to* $X$.

*Remark 9 (Recovering the Single-Key Security Notions).* Setting $n = 1$ in Definition 7 yields formal definitions of the *single-key* security games for authenticated encryption, albeit with a more complicated interface than one is used to: the specification of $i$ and $j$ becomes redundant, as does the corruption oracle for valid adversaries. Indeed, to simplify notation in the case $n = 1$, we often omit $i$ and $j$ from the queries made, refer to the hidden bit $b_1$ as $b$, and only expect a simple guess $b'$ by an adversary.

**Relations Among Multi-key Notions.** We discuss the relations between different single-user and multi-user security notions in the full version of the paper [31].

---

**Experiment** $\mathsf{KEYREC}_{\mathcal{E}}^{M,n}(\mathcal{A})$:

$K_1, \ldots, K_n \leftarrow_{\$} \mathsf{K}$
for $i$ in $1, \ldots, n,$
  for $j$ in $1, \ldots, l,$
   $N_{i,j} \leftarrow_{\$} \mathsf{N}$
   $C_{i,j} \leftarrow \mathcal{E}_{K_i}^{N_{i,j}}(M_j)$
$(i^*, st) \leftarrow \mathcal{A}_1\left((C_{i,j}, N_{i,j})_{i \in [n], j \in [l]}\right)$
$K^* \leftarrow \mathcal{A}_2\left((K_i)_{i \in [n \setminus i^*]}, st\right)$
Return $(K_{i^*} = K^*)$

---

**Fig. 5.** Key recovery game with $n$ keys and the hard-coded messages $M_1, \ldots, M_l$. Without loss of generality, we separate the adversary $\mathcal{A}$ into two components $\mathcal{A}_1$ and $\mathcal{A}_2$.

**Key Recovery Notions.** For our meta-reduction, we use an auxiliary, key recovery game $\mathsf{KEYREC}_{\mathcal{E}}^{M,n}$ (Definition 10). Here there are $n$ unknown keys and the adversary is provided with encryptions under each of the keys of the hard-coded (and hence known) messages $M \in \mathsf{M}^l$, using known, yet random, nonces. Then the adversary provides an index $i^* \in [n]$, learns the $n - 1$ keys $(K_i)_{i \in [n \setminus i^*]}$ and tries to guess the uncorrupted key.

**Definition 10.** *For any integers $n, \ell \geq 1$, messages $M = (M_1, \ldots, M_\ell) \in \mathsf{M}^\ell$, AE scheme $\mathcal{E}$ and any adversary $\mathcal{A} = (\mathcal{A}_1, \mathcal{A}_2)$, the advantage of $\mathcal{A}$ against $\mathsf{KEYREC}_{\mathcal{E}}^{M,n}$ is defined as*

$$\mathsf{Adv}_{\mathcal{E}}^{\mathsf{KEYREC},M,n}(\mathcal{A}) := \mathbf{Pr}\left[\mathsf{KEYREC}_{\mathcal{E}}^{M,n}(\mathcal{A}) = 1\right],$$

*where the experiment $\mathsf{KEYREC}_{\mathcal{E}}^{M,n}(\mathcal{A})$ is given in Fig. 5.*

Of course, it might be the case that it is impossible to win the key recovery game with certainty, since there could be more than one key that 'matches' the messages, nonces and ciphertexts. For our tightness results, we need to assume that there is some reasonably small $l$ and some messages $M_1, \ldots, M_l$ such that the key recovery game corresponding to $M_1, \ldots, M_l$ *can* be won with certainty; we call this the *key uniqueness* property; its definition is below.

**Definition 11.** *Let $\mathcal{E}$ be an authenticated encryption scheme. Suppose there is some integer $l \geq 1$ and certain messages $M_1, \ldots, M_l \in \mathsf{M}$ such that, for all keys $K \in \mathsf{K}$ and all nonces $N_1, \ldots, N_l \in \mathsf{N}$,*

$$\left\{K' \in \mathsf{K} : \mathcal{E}_{K'}^{N_i}(M_i) = \mathcal{E}_{K}^{N_i}(M_i) \text{ for all } i \in 1, \ldots, l\right\} = \{K\}.$$

*Then we say $\mathcal{E}$ is $M$-key-unique, where $M = (M_1, \ldots, M_l) \in \mathsf{M}^l$. This means that encryptions of $M_1, \ldots, M_l$ under the same key uniquely determine the key, regardless of the nonces used.*

As mentioned above, $\mathsf{KEYREC}_{\mathcal{E}}^{M,n}$ corresponds to a very weak notion of security. In the following Lemma, we prove that this weak notion of security is implied, with only a small loss, by many of the more reasonable $n$-key security notions given in Definition 7. For succinctness we present the reduction in a compact way, but split the analysis in different cases (depending on the adversary goal and on the requirements to respect uniqueness or not).

**Lemma 12.** *Let* $\mathsf{GOAL} \in \{\mathsf{AE}, \mathsf{LRAE}, \mathsf{IND}, \mathsf{LRIND}, \mathsf{CTI}\}$, $\mathsf{POWER} \in \{\mathsf{CCA}, \mathsf{CPA}\}$ *and suppose* $\mathcal{E}$ *is* $M$-*key-unique. Then there exists an* $(\mathbb{S}, \mathbb{T})$ *simple reduction from* $\mathsf{KEYREC}_{\mathcal{E}}^{M,n}$ *to* $\mathsf{GOAL}-\mathsf{POWER}_{\mathcal{E}}^{X,n}$ *with* $\mathbb{T}(t_{\mathcal{A}}) = t_{\mathcal{A}} + (l + m_{\mathsf{GOAL}})t_{\mathcal{E}}$ *and* $\mathbb{S}(\epsilon_{\mathcal{A}}) = \delta_X \cdot \delta_{\mathsf{GOAL}} \cdot \epsilon_{\mathcal{A}}$, *where* $m_{\mathsf{IND}} = m \geq 1$, *an arbitrary integer;* $m_{\mathsf{GOAL}} = 1$ *if* $\mathsf{GOAL} \neq \mathsf{IND}$; $t_{\mathcal{E}}$ *is a bound on the runtime of a single encryption with* $\mathcal{E}$;

$$
\delta_X = \begin{cases} 1 - \frac{nl(l-1) + m_{\mathsf{GOAL}}(m_{\mathsf{GOAL}} + 2l - 1)}{2|\mathsf{N}|}, & \mathit{if}\ X = \mathsf{NR} \\ 1, & \mathit{if}\ X \neq \mathsf{NR} \end{cases}
$$

*and*

$$
\delta_{\mathsf{GOAL}} = \begin{cases} 1 - \frac{1}{2^m}, & \mathit{if}\ \mathsf{GOAL} = \mathsf{IND} \\ 1, & \mathit{if}\ \mathsf{GOAL} \neq \mathsf{IND}. \end{cases}
$$

Note that $\delta_X$ and $\delta_{\mathsf{GOAL}}$ are both close to 1: $m$ can be set arbitrarily large and, for useful encryption schemes, the nonce space $\mathsf{N}$ is very large.

*Remark 13.* We are unable to show a corresponding result for $\mathsf{POWER} = \mathsf{CDA}$ or $\mathsf{POWER} = \mathsf{PAS}$. This is because we need the 'always real' encryption oracle $\mathcal{E}$ to simulate the environment of $\mathcal{A}$ in the key recovery game. As a consequence, looking forward, our lower bounds for tightness of simple reductions hold only for $n$-key games with such an oracle. Nevertheless, we feel it is natural to give the $n$-key adversary access to the $\mathcal{E}$ oracle so that, for example, the adversary can use queries to this oracle to determine which keys to corrupt and which to challenge.

*Proof.* We construct $\mathcal{R}_{\mathcal{A}}$ that runs the key recovery adversary $\mathcal{A}$ to obtain the key used by the challenge oracle(s) and then uses it to guess the hidden bit $b_1$. Therefore $\mathcal{R}_{\mathcal{A}}$ will return $(1, b_1')$ and wins if $b_1' = b_1$.

For each $i \in [n]$ and $j \in [l]$, $\mathcal{R}_{\mathcal{A}}$ samples $N_{i,j} \leftarrow_{\$} \mathsf{N}$ and then queries the encryption oracle $\mathcal{E}$ on input $(i, M_j, N_{i,j})$, receiving $C_{i,j}$ (unless $\mathcal{R}_{\mathcal{A}}$ has made this query before, since this is a pointless query, in which case it just sets $C_{i,j}$ to be the response from the last time the query was made). Then $\mathcal{R}_{\mathcal{A}}$ passes $(C_{i,j}, N_{i,j})_{i \in [n], j \in [l]}$ to the key recovery adversary $\mathcal{A}$.

When $\mathcal{A}$ returns an index $i^*$, $\mathcal{R}_{\mathcal{A}}$ queries Cor on each $i \in [n \setminus i^*]$ and passes $(K_i)_{i \in [n \setminus i^*]}$ to $\mathcal{A}$.

When $\mathcal{A}$ returns a key $K^*$, $\mathcal{R}_{\mathcal{A}}$ checks if $\mathcal{E}_{K^*}^{N_{i^*,j}}(M_j) = C_{i^*,j}$ for each $j \in [l]$. If not, then $\mathcal{A}$ has been unsuccessful, so $\mathcal{R}_{\mathcal{A}}$ samples a random bit $b_1' \leftarrow_{\$} \{0,1\}$ and returns $(1, b_1')$. If the tests all succeed, then by $M$-key-uniqueness, $K^* = K_{i^*}$. Then $\mathcal{R}_{\mathcal{A}}$ does the following:

- If GOAL = IND, for $i = 1, 2, \ldots, m$ (for some "large" $m$), $\mathcal{R}_{\mathcal{A}}$ chooses random $M_i^* \leftarrow_{\$} \mathsf{M}$ and $N_i^* \leftarrow_{\$} \mathsf{N}$ such that $M_i^* \neq M_j$ for all $j \in [l]$. Then $\mathcal{R}_{\mathcal{A}}$ queries Enc on input $(i^*, 1, M_i^*, N_i^*)$, receiving $C_i^*$. If for all $i = 1, 2, \ldots, m$ it holds that $\mathcal{E}_{K^*}^{N_i^*}(M_i^*) = C^*$ then $\mathcal{R}_{\mathcal{A}}$ returns $(1, 0)$. Else, $\mathcal{R}_{\mathcal{A}}$ returns $(1, 1)$.
- If GOAL = LRIND, $\mathcal{R}_{\mathcal{A}}$ chooses random $M_0^*, M_1^* \leftarrow_{\$} \mathsf{M}$ and $N^* \leftarrow_{\$} \mathsf{N}$ such that $|M_0^*| = |M_1^*|$, $M_0^* \neq M_j$ and $M_1^* \neq M_j$ for all $j \in [l]$. Then $\mathcal{R}_{\mathcal{A}}$ queries LR on input $(i^*, 1, M_0^*, M_1^*, N^*)$, receiving $C^*$. If $\mathcal{E}_{K^*}^{N^*}(M_0^*) = C^*$, $\mathcal{R}_{\mathcal{A}}$ returns $(1, 0)$. Else, $\mathcal{R}_{\mathcal{A}}$ returns $(1, 1)$.
- If GOAL $\in$ {AE, LRAE, CTI}, $\mathcal{R}_{\mathcal{A}}$ chooses random $M^* \leftarrow_{\$} \mathsf{M}$ and $N^* \leftarrow_{\$} \mathsf{N}$ such that $M^* \neq M_j$ for all $j \in [l]$. Then $\mathcal{R}_{\mathcal{A}}$ computes $C^* \leftarrow \mathcal{E}_{K^*}^{N^*}(M^*)$ and queries Dec on input $(i^*, 1, C^*, N^*)$, receiving $M$. If $M \neq \bot$, $\mathcal{R}_{\mathcal{A}}$ returns $(1, 0)$. Else, $\mathcal{R}_{\mathcal{A}}$ returns $(1, 1)$.

For GOAL $\in$ {LRIND, AE, LRAE, CTI}, the adversary $\mathcal{R}_{\mathcal{A}}$ returns $(1, b)$ with $b = b_1$ whenever the adversary $\mathcal{A}$ against key recovery is successful.

For GOAL $\in$ {IND}, the adversary $\mathcal{R}_{\mathcal{A}}$ always returns the correct bit if $b_1 = 1$. It also returns the correct bit $b_1 = 0$, provided that the random ciphertexts $(C_i^*)_{i \in [m]}$ that oracle Enc returns do not *all* collide with the true ciphertexts $\mathcal{E}_{K^*}^{N_i^*}(M_i^*)$. This collision event occurs with probability at most $\frac{1}{2^m}$.

In other words, for GOAL $\in$ {IND, LRIND, AE, LRAE, CTI}, $\mathcal{R}$ succeeds whenever $\mathcal{A}$ succeeds if $b_1 = 0$, while, if $b_1 = 1$, then $\mathcal{R}$ succeeds with the same probability that $\mathcal{A}$ succeds multiplied by $\delta_{\mathsf{GOAL}}$, where $\delta_{\mathsf{GOAL}} = 1$ for GOAL $\in$ {LRIND, AE, LRAE, CTI} and $\delta_{\mathsf{GOAL}} = \left(1 - \frac{1}{2^m}\right)$ for GOAL = IND.

Whenever $\mathcal{A}$ does not recover $K^*$, $\mathcal{R}_{\mathcal{A}}$ guesses correctly with probability $\frac{1}{2}$. Putting it all together we get the following:

$$
\Pr\left[\mathsf{GOAL\text{-}POWER}_{\mathcal{E}}^{X,n}(\mathcal{R}_{\mathcal{A}}) = 1\right]
$$
$$
= \Pr\left[\mathsf{KEYREC}_{\mathcal{E}}^{M,n}(\mathcal{A}) = 1\right] \cdot \left(1 - \frac{1 - \delta_{\mathsf{GOAL}}}{2}\right)
$$
$$
+ \frac{1}{2} \cdot \left(1 - \Pr\left[\mathsf{KEYREC}_{\mathcal{E}}^{M,n}(\mathcal{A}) = 1\right]\right)
$$
$$
= \Pr\left[\mathsf{KEYREC}_{\mathcal{E}}^{M,n}(\mathcal{A}) = 1\right] \cdot \left(\frac{1}{2} - \frac{1 - \delta_{\mathsf{GOAL}}}{2}\right) + \frac{1}{2},
$$

from which we obtain

$$
\mathsf{Adv}_{\mathcal{E}}^{\mathsf{GOAL\text{-}POWER},X,n}(\mathcal{R}_{\mathcal{A}}) = 2\left(\Pr\left[\mathsf{GOAL\text{-}POWER}_{\mathcal{E}}^{X,n}(\mathcal{R}_{\mathcal{A}}) = 1\right] - \frac{1}{2}\right)
$$
$$
= \delta_{\mathsf{GOAL}} \cdot \Pr\left[\mathsf{KEYREC}_{\mathcal{E}}^{M,n}(\mathcal{A}) = 1\right]
$$
$$
= \delta_{\mathsf{GOAL}} \cdot \mathsf{Adv}_{\mathcal{E}}^{\mathsf{KEYREC},M,n}(\mathcal{A})
$$
$$
= \delta_{\mathsf{GOAL}} \cdot \epsilon_{\mathcal{A}}.
$$

Ignoring the time taken for random sampling, the runtime of $\mathcal{R}_{\mathcal{A}}$ is precisely the runtime of $\mathcal{A}$, plus the time taken for additional encryptions using $K^*$: if

GOAL = IND, there are $l + m$ additional encryptions and, if GOAL $\neq$ IND, there are $l + 1$ additional encryptions. It follows that

$$t_{\mathcal{R}_{\mathcal{A}}} = t_{\mathcal{A}} + (l + m_{\mathsf{GOAL}})t_{\mathcal{E}},$$

where $m_{\mathsf{IND}} = m$ and $m_{\mathsf{GOAL}} = 1$ for GOAL $\neq$ IND.

Moreover, $\mathcal{R}_{\mathcal{A}}$, doesn't compromise $b_1$ and makes no pointless or prohibited queries: no queries are repeated, the messages used to generate the challenge queries do not appear in any of the previous encryption queries under key $K_{i^*}$ and, in the LRIND case, the challenge messages are of equal length. It follows that $\mathcal{R}_{\mathcal{A}}$ is a valid adversary against GOAL$-$POWER$_{\mathcal{E}}^{X,n}$ for $X \in \{\mathsf{IV}, \mathsf{MR}\}$, since nonces are always chosen uniformly at random.

If $X = \mathsf{NR}$, $\mathcal{R}_{\mathcal{A}}$ might not be a valid adversary, since the randomly chosen nonces might accidentally collide. So we modify $\mathcal{R}_{\mathcal{A}}$ to abort and output a random bit whenever there is a collision among the $l$ randomly chosen nonces $(N_{i,j})_{j \in [l]}$ for each $i \in [n \setminus i^*]$, or among the $l + m_{\mathsf{GOAL}}$ randomly chosen nonces for encryptions under $K_{i^*}$: the $l + m$ nonces $(N_{i^*,j})_{j \in [l]}$ and $(N_i^*)_{i \in [m]}$, if GOAL $=$ IND, and the $l + 1$ nonces $(N_{i^*,j})_{j \in [l]}$ and $N^*$, if GOAL $\neq$ IND. Then $\mathcal{R}_{\mathcal{A}}$ is a valid adversary and its advantage is $\epsilon_{\mathcal{A}}$ multiplied by the probability that no such nonce collisions happen. By a simple union bound the probability of a collision among the $l$ randomly chosen nonces $(N_{i,j})_{j \in [l]}$ is at most $\frac{l(l-1)}{2|\mathsf{N}|}$ for each $i \in [n \setminus i^*]$ and the probability of a collision among the $l + m_{\mathsf{GOAL}}$ randomly chosen nonces for $i^*$ is at most $\frac{(l+m_{\mathsf{GOAL}})(l+m_{\mathsf{GOAL}}-1)}{2|\mathsf{N}|}$. Thus the probability of a collision among the nonces for any of the $n$ keys is at most

$$(n-1)\frac{l(l-1)}{2|\mathsf{N}|} + \frac{l + m_{\mathsf{GOAL}}(l + m_{\mathsf{GOAL}} - 1)}{2|\mathsf{N}|}$$

$$= \frac{nl(l-1) + m_{\mathsf{GOAL}}(m_{\mathsf{GOAL}} + 2l - 1)}{2|\mathsf{N}|}$$

$$= 1 - \delta_{\mathsf{NR}}.$$

Thus the advantage of $\mathcal{R}_{\mathcal{A}}$ is $\epsilon_{\mathcal{R}_{\mathcal{A}}} \geq \delta_{\mathsf{NR}} \cdot \delta_{\mathsf{GOAL}} \cdot \epsilon_{\mathcal{A}}$, as desired.     $\square$

*Remark 14.* In the proof, we assumed that the adversary is allowed to associate the bit $b_1$ with any of the $n$ keys $K_1, \ldots, K_n$. While this is permitted according to our definition of the GOAL$-$POWER$_{\mathcal{E}}^{n,X}$ game, in fact the result holds for more restrictive games: we only require that for all $i \in [n]$ there exists *some* $j \in [n]$ such that the adversary can associate the bit $b_j$ with the key $K_i$. In this case, $\mathcal{R}_{\mathcal{A}}$ uses the recovered key $K^*$ from $\mathcal{A}$ to determine the value of any hidden bit $b_j$ that can be associated with $K_{i^*}$.

## 4   Multi-key to Single-Key Reductions Are Lossy

In this section we present our main results: any simple black-box reduction from multi-key security (in its many definitional variants) to single-key security loses a linear factor in the number of keys. Two remarks are in order. First, we show the lower bound for reductions from the security of an arbitrary construction of an (authenticated) encryption scheme $C[\mathcal{E}]$ to that of $\mathcal{E}$ (and in particular for the case where $C[\mathcal{E}] = \mathcal{E}$). This more general setting encompasses interesting cases, e.g. where $C[\mathcal{E}]$ is *double encryption* with $\mathcal{E}$, i.e.

$$C[\mathcal{E}]_{(K_1,K_2)}^{(N_1,N_2)}(M) = \mathcal{E}_{K_2}^{N_2}\left(\mathcal{E}_{K_1}^{N_1}(M)\right),$$

which has been shown to have desirable multi-key properties [26]. Furthermore, showing the separation for $C[\mathcal{E}]$ and $\mathcal{E}$ also suggests how to circumvent the lower bound for the loss that we provide. Our lower bound requires that $C[\mathcal{E}]$ satisfies key-uniqueness. It may therefore be possible to start from a secure single-key security that satisfies key-uniqueness, and show a tight reduction from multi-key security of a *variant* $C[\mathcal{E}]$ of $\mathcal{E}$, provided that $C[\mathcal{E}]$ somehow avoids key uniqueness.

We consider separately reductions between different security flavours (authenticated encryption, privacy, integrity). For each case in turn, we proceed in two steps. First, we establish that if $\mathcal{E}$ is a (single-key) secure encryption scheme and $C[\mathcal{E}]$ is a key-unique encryption scheme, then all simple reductions from the multi-key key recovery game for $C[\mathcal{E}]$ to the single-key security game for $\mathcal{E}$ are lossy. Since by Lemma 12 there is a tight reduction from multi-key key recovery to multi-key security, it is an immediate corollary that there is no tight reduction from the multi-key security of $C[\mathcal{E}]$ to the single-key security of $\mathcal{E}$.

An interesting remark is that the bound on the inherent loss of simple reductions depends on the security of the scheme $\mathcal{E}$: the more secure the scheme, the tighter the bound. While our bound is therefore not meaningful for insecure schemes, this case is of little interest in practice.

*Authenticated Encryption.* We give the formal results for the case of authenticated encryption below.

**Theorem 15.** *Let $\mathcal{E}$ and $C[\mathcal{E}]$ be AE schemes such that $C[\mathcal{E}]$ is $M$-key-unique for some $M \in \mathsf{M}^l$. Then, for $X \in \{\mathsf{IV}, \mathsf{NR}, \mathsf{MR}\}$, any simple reduction $\mathcal{R}$ from $\mathsf{KEYREC}_{C[\mathcal{E}]}^{M,n}$ to $\mathsf{AE-PAS}_{\mathcal{E}}^{X,1}$ loses at least $\left(\frac{1}{n} + 2\epsilon\right)^{-1}$, where $\epsilon$ is the maximum advantage for a valid adversary against $\mathsf{AE-PAS}_{\mathcal{E}}^{X,1}$ running in time at most $nt_{\mathcal{R}} + 2l(n-1)t_{C[\mathcal{E}]}$ (where $t_{C[\mathcal{E}]}$ is an upper-bound on the runtime of a single encryption with $C[\mathcal{E}]$).*

We sketch the proof before giving its details below. The crucial idea, following [3], is to construct a *meta-reduction* $\mathcal{M}$ that *rewinds* the reduction $\mathcal{R}$ in order to simulate its interaction with an ideal adversary $\mathcal{A}$ against $\mathsf{KEYREC}_{C[\mathcal{E}]}^{M,n}$. If the simulation works correctly, then the output of $\mathcal{R}$ can be used by $\mathcal{M}$ to win the $\mathsf{AE-PAS}_{\mathcal{E}}^{X,1}$ game with probability $\epsilon_{\mathcal{R}}$. Then the (single-key) security of $\mathcal{E}$ yields an upper-bound on the success probability of $\mathcal{M}$, i.e. an upper-bound on $\epsilon_{\mathcal{R}}$.

We view $\mathcal{R}$ as a collection of three algorithms, $\mathcal{R} = (\mathcal{R}_1, \mathcal{R}_2, \mathcal{R}_3)$. The first, $\mathcal{R}_1$, makes oracle queries in the $\mathsf{AE-PAS}_{\mathcal{E}}^{X,1}$ game, then produces the ciphertexts and nonces that $\mathcal{A}$ expects to receive in the $\mathsf{KEYREC}^{M,n}_{C[\mathcal{E}]}$ game. The second, $\mathcal{R}_2$, receives an index $i^*$ from $\mathcal{A}$ and the state $st_1$ of the previous algorithm, $\mathcal{R}_1$. Then $\mathcal{R}_2$ makes oracle queries and eventually produces the vector of keys that $\mathcal{A}$ expects to receive in the $\mathsf{KEYREC}^{M,n}_{C[\mathcal{E}]}$ game. Finally, $\mathcal{R}_3$ receives a guessed key $K^*$ from $\mathcal{A}$ and the state $st_2$ of $\mathcal{R}_2$. Then $\mathcal{R}_3$ makes oracle queries and outputs a guessed bit $b'$.

$\mathcal{M}$ only rewinds $\mathcal{R}_2$: $\mathcal{M}$ executes $\mathcal{R}_2$ on each of the $n$ possible indices $i^*$ that could be returned by $\mathcal{A}$ and each $\mathcal{R}_2$ then returns a set of keys. Then $\mathcal{M}$ uses the keys returned by one execution of $\mathcal{R}_2$ to construct the input to a *different* execution of $\mathcal{R}_3$, i.e. $st_2$ given to $\mathcal{R}_3$ will not be from the same execution of $\mathcal{R}_2$ used to construct the 'guessed' key $K^*$.

The main obstacle in arguing that the above strategy works is that $\mathcal{M}$ needs to break $\mathsf{AE\!-\!PAS}^{X,1}_{\mathcal{E}}$, which is an *interactive* assumption. This is in contrast to the meta-reductions from [3], which are designed to violate a non-interactive complexity assumption. In our case, $\mathcal{M}$ needs to simulate an appropriate environment towards multiple copies of $\mathcal{R}$, each of which may make oracle queries, yet $\mathcal{M}$ has access to a single set of oracles for the $\mathsf{AE\!-\!PAS}^{X,1}_{\mathcal{E}}$ game. It is not obvious that $\mathcal{M}$ can simply forward queries from all copies of $\mathcal{R}$ to these oracles, since queries across different invocations of $\mathcal{R}$ may interfere with one-another and render $\mathcal{M}$ invalid. The key observation is that we can leverage the single-key security of $\mathcal{E}$: instead of forwarding queries, $\mathcal{M}$ simply simulates the Enc and Dec oracles by sampling random ciphertexts and returning $\perp$, respectively. We argue, based on the security of $\mathcal{E}$, that $\mathcal{R}$ cannot distinguish this simulation from the real oracles in its game.

*Proof.* For ease of notation, let $\mathsf{K}$, $\mathsf{M}$, $\mathsf{N}$ and $\mathsf{C}$ be the sets of keys, messages, nonces and ciphertexts, respectively, for the *construction* $C[\mathcal{E}]$ (even though they may differ from the corresponding sets for $\mathcal{E}$, but we shall not need to refer to those in the proof).

Consider the following (inefficient) adversary $\mathcal{A} = (\mathcal{A}_1, \mathcal{A}_2)$ in the game $\mathsf{KEYREC}^{M,n}_{C[\mathcal{E}]}$. On input

$$(C_{i,j}, N_{i,j})_{i \in [n], j \in [l]},$$

$\mathcal{A}_1$ first checks that each $C_{i,j} \in \mathsf{C}$ and each $N_{i,j} \in \mathsf{N}$. If this check fails, then $\mathcal{A}_1$ aborts (by outputting a random index $i^* \in [n]$ and recording an abort message in the state $st_{\mathcal{A}}$ for $\mathcal{A}_2$, triggering the latter to output $\perp$). If the check succeeds, then $\mathcal{A}_1$ chooses $i^* \in [n]$ uniformly at random, sets

$$st_{\mathcal{A}} \leftarrow \left( i^*, (C_{i,j}, N_{i,j})_{i \in [n], j \in [l]} \right)$$

and outputs $(i^*, st_{\mathcal{A}})$. On input $\left( (K_i)_{i \in [n \setminus i^*]}, st_{\mathcal{A}} \right)$, $\mathcal{A}_2$ checks that $K_i$ is *valid* for each $i \in [n \setminus i^*]$, that is:

1. $K_i \in \mathsf{K}$
2. For each $j \in [l]$, $C[\mathcal{E}]^{N_{i,j}}_{K_i}(M_j) = C_{i,j}$.

If this check fails, then $\mathcal{A}_2$ outputs $\perp$. If the check succeeds, then $\mathcal{A}_2$ uses exhaustive search to find some $K^* \in \mathsf{K}$ such that $C[\mathcal{E}]^{N_{i^*,j}}_{K^*}(M_j) = C_{i^*,j}$ for each $j \in [l]$. Since $C[\mathcal{E}]$ is $M$-key-unique, either $K^*$ exists and is unique, or the ciphertexts $C_{i^*,j}$ were not all encryptions of the messages $M_j$ with the nonces $N_{i^*,j}$ under the same key. So if $A_2$ does not find a $K^*$ with this property, it outputs $\perp$. Otherwise it outputs $K^*$.

It is clear that the advantage of $\mathcal{A}$ is $\epsilon_\mathcal{A} = 1$ since, in the real $\mathsf{KEYREC}^{M,n}_{C[\mathcal{E}]}$ game, all the checks performed by $\mathcal{A}$ will succeed and $K^*$ is uniquely defined.

We construct a meta-reduction $\mathcal{M}$ that simulates the environment of $\mathcal{R}$ in its interaction with this ideal adversary $\mathcal{A}$. Then $\mathcal{M}$ will use the output of $\mathcal{R}$ to play the $\mathsf{AE-PAS}^{X,1}_\mathcal{E}$ game. In what follows, we describe $\mathcal{M}$ in detail. A diagram showing the overall structure of the interaction between $\mathcal{M}$ and $\mathcal{R}$ is given in Fig. 6.

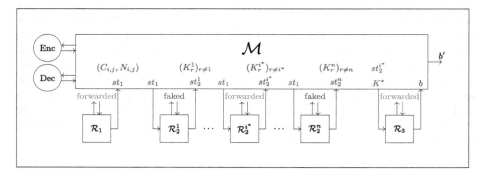

**Fig. 6.** An overview of the meta-reduction $\mathcal{M}$, which rewinds a reduction $\mathcal{R} = (\mathcal{R}_1, \mathcal{R}_2, \mathcal{R}_3)$. The inputs to each component of the reduction $\mathcal{R}$ are shown in teal, while the outputs are shown in blue. Some oracle queries from $\mathcal{R}$ are forwarded to the oracles in the game played by $\mathcal{M}$ and the responses sent back, while other oracle queries from $\mathcal{R}$ are faked by $\mathcal{M}$. (Color figure online)

First, $K^*$ is initialised to $\perp$. Then, $\mathcal{M}$ uses its oracles to simulate the oracles used by $\mathcal{R}_1$ by simply forwarding the queries from $\mathcal{R}_1$ and the responses from the oracles, until $\mathcal{R}_1$ returns

$$\left( (C_{i,j}, N_{i,j})_{i \in [n], j \in [l]}, st_1 \right).$$

Then $\mathcal{M}$ checks that each $C_{i,j} \in \mathsf{C}$ and each $N_{i,j} \in \mathsf{N}$. If this check fails, $\mathcal{M}$ 'aborts' just as $\mathcal{A}$ would. That is, $\mathcal{M}$ runs $\mathcal{R}_2$ on input $(i, st_1)$ for a random index $i^* \in [n]$, forwarding oracle queries and responses, receives $\left( (K_i)_{i \in [n \setminus i^*]}, st_2 \right)$ from $\mathcal{R}_2$, runs $\mathcal{R}_3$ on input $(\perp, st_2)$, receives a bit $b'$ and outputs this in its game. If, on the other hand, the check succeeds, then $\mathcal{M}$ chooses $i^*$ uniformly at random from $[n]$ and does the following for each $i \in [n]$:

1. $\mathcal{M}$ runs $\mathcal{R}_2$ on input $(i, st_1)$, which we call $\mathcal{R}_2^i$ for ease of readability.
2. When $\mathcal{R}_2^i$ makes oracle queries:
   (a) If $i = i^*$, $\mathcal{M}$ uses its oracles to honestly answer all oracle queries; forwarding the queries to its oracles and then forwarding the replies to $\mathcal{R}_2^{i^*}$.
   (b) If $i \neq i^*$, $\mathcal{M}$ simulates the 'fake' oracles, i.e. the oracles Enc and Dec in the case $b = 1$. Concretely, when $\mathcal{R}_2^i$ makes an encryption query $(M, N)$, $\mathcal{M}$ samples $C \leftarrow_\$ \{0, 1\}^{\mathsf{enclen}(|M|)}$ and returns this to $\mathcal{R}_2^i$.[1] When $\mathcal{R}_2^i$ makes a decryption query $(C, N)$, $\mathcal{M}$ returns $\perp$ to $\mathcal{R}_2^i$.
3. When $\mathcal{R}_2^i$ outputs $\left( (K_r^i)_{r \in [n \setminus i]}, st_2^i \right)$, if $i \neq i^*$ then $\mathcal{M}$ checks if $K_{i^*}^i$ is *valid*, i.e.
   (a) $K_{i^*}^i \in \mathsf{K}$,
   (b) For each $j \in [l]$, $C[\mathcal{E}]_{K_{i^*}^i}^{N_{i^*,j}}(M_j) = C_{i^*,j}$.

   If $K_{i^*}^i$ is valid, then $K^* \leftarrow K_{i^*}^i$. By $\mathcal{M}$-key-uniqueness, $K_{i^*}^i$ is the only key with this property.

At the end of these runs of $\mathcal{R}_2$, if $\mathcal{R}_2^{i^*}$ did not provide a full set of valid keys, i.e. $K_r^{i^*}$ is not valid for some $r \in [n \setminus i^*]$, then $\mathcal{M}$ sets $K^* \leftarrow \perp$ (mirroring the check performed by $\mathcal{A}_2$).

If $\mathcal{R}_2^{i^*}$ did provide a full set of valid keys, but $K^* = \perp$, (so none of the $\mathcal{R}_2, i \neq i^*$ provided a valid key $K_{i^*}^i$), $\mathcal{M}$ aborts the simulation and returns a random bit. We call this event BAD.

Otherwise, $\mathcal{M}$ runs $\mathcal{R}_3$ on input $\left( K^*, st_2^{i^*} \right)$, forwarding oracle queries from $\mathcal{R}_3$ to its oracles and sending back the responses.

When $\mathcal{R}_3$ outputs a bit $b'$, $\mathcal{M}$ returns this bit in its game.

Now we consider the resources of $\mathcal{M}$ and its advantage in the $\mathsf{AE-PAS}_\mathcal{E}^{X,1}$ game.

$\mathcal{M}$ performs $n$ runs of (part of) $\mathcal{R}$ and carries out $2(n-1)l$ encryptions with $C[\mathcal{E}]$ (checking validity of $K_{i^*}^i$ for each $i \neq i^*$ and checking validity of $K_r^{i^*}$ for each $r \neq i^*$), so if we ignore the time taken for random sampling and checking set membership, the runtime of $\mathcal{M}$ is at most $nt_\mathcal{R} + 2l(n-1)t_{C[\mathcal{E}]}$. Moreover, $\mathcal{M}$ makes at most $q_\mathcal{R}$ oracle queries, since it only forwards the queries from $\mathcal{R}_1$, $\mathcal{R}_2^{i^*}$ and $\mathcal{R}_3$.

Now consider the advantage $\epsilon_\mathcal{M}$ of $\mathcal{M}$ in $\mathsf{AE-PAS}_\mathcal{E}^{X,1}$. From the definition of a simple reduction, $\mathcal{R}$ must be a valid adversary in $\mathsf{AE-PAS}_\mathcal{E}^{X,1}$ whenever $\mathcal{A}$ is a valid adversary in $\mathsf{KEYREC}_{C[\mathcal{E}]}^{M,n}$. But all adversaries are automatically valid in $\mathsf{KEYREC}_{C[\mathcal{E}]}^{M,n}$, so $\mathcal{R}$ must always be a valid adversary against $\mathsf{AE-PAS}_\mathcal{E}^{X,1}$. Now the oracle queries $\mathcal{M}$ makes are exactly the same queries as $\left( \mathcal{R}_1, \mathcal{R}_2^{i^*}, \mathcal{R}_3 \right)$ makes in the same game. Since $\mathcal{R}$ is a valid adversary, this shows that $\mathcal{M}$ does not make pointless or prohibited queries and uses nonces correctly with respect to $X$. Therefore $\mathcal{M}$ is a valid adversary against $\mathsf{AE-PAS}_\mathcal{E}^{X,1}$ and so $\epsilon_\mathcal{M} \leq \epsilon$.

Note that for $\mathcal{R}_1, \mathcal{R}_2^{i^*}$ and $\mathcal{R}_3$, $\mathcal{M}$ answers the oracle queries honestly with its own oracles. Therefore $\mathcal{M}$ correctly simulates the view of $\left( \mathcal{R}_1, \mathcal{R}_2^{i^*}, \mathcal{R}_3 \right)$ in the

---

[1] Of course, here enclen refers to the lengths of ciphertexts from $\mathcal{E}$, not $C[\mathcal{E}]$.

game $\mathsf{AE-PAS}_{\mathcal{E}}^{X,1}$. However, $\mathcal{M}$ might not correctly simulate the responses from $\mathcal{A}$. Indeed, to correctly simulate $\mathcal{A}$, $\mathcal{M}$ requires that some $\mathcal{R}_2^i, i \neq i^*$ provides a valid key $K_{i^*}^i$, but the oracle queries from $\mathcal{R}_2^i, i \neq i^*$ are not handled honestly. The imperfect simulation of the view of $\mathcal{R}_2^i$ might make it less likely to provide a valid key $K_{i^*}^i$. We will therefore need to show that the change in behaviour of the $\mathcal{R}_2^i$ due to the imperfect simulation is small. The intuition for this claim is that if $\mathcal{R}_2^i$ could distinguish between the honest and the simulated oracles (having only received an index $i$ from the key-recovery adversary $\mathcal{A}$, not a key), then one can use $(\mathcal{R}_1, \mathcal{R}_2^i)$ directly, without $\mathcal{A}$, to win the single-key game $\mathsf{AE-PAS}_{\mathcal{E}}^{X,1}$.

Consider the three possible scenarios:

1. $\mathcal{R}_2^{i^*}$ did not provide a full set of valid keys.
2. $\mathcal{R}_2^{i^*}$ did provide a full set of valid keys and, for some $i \neq i^*$, $\mathcal{R}_2^i$ provided a valid key $K_{i^*}^i$.
3. $\mathcal{R}_2^{i^*}$ did provide a full set of valid keys, but, for each $i \neq i^*$, $\mathcal{R}_2^i$ did not provide a valid key $K_{i^*}^i$.

In the first case, both $\mathcal{M}$ and $\mathcal{A}$ submit $\bot$ to $\mathcal{R}_3$ as their 'key', so the simulation is correct. In the second case, both $\mathcal{M}$ and $\mathcal{A}$ submit a key $K^*$ to $\mathcal{R}_3$ that satisfies $C[\mathcal{E}]_{K^*}^{N_{i^*}, j}(M_j) = C_{i^*,j}$ for all $j \in [l]$, and $K^*$ is the only key with this property by the $\mathcal{M}$-key-uniqueness of $C[\mathcal{E}]$. So the simulation is correct in this case too.

The third case is the event $\mathsf{BAD}$ and is where the simulation fails. By construction $\mathcal{M}$ aborts the simulation if $\mathsf{BAD}$ occurs and outputs a random bit. Given that $\mathsf{BAD}$ does not occur, the view of $(\mathcal{R}_1, \mathcal{R}_2^{i^*}, \mathcal{R}_3)$ in its interaction with $\mathcal{A}$ and the $\mathsf{AE-PAS}_{\mathcal{E}}^{X,1}$ oracles is identical to its view in its interaction with $\mathcal{M}$ and $\mathcal{M}$ returns the bit $b'$ returned by $\mathcal{R}_3$. This shows that

$$\Pr\left[\mathsf{AE-PAS}_{\mathcal{E}}^{X,1}(\mathcal{R}) = 1\right] = \Pr\left[\mathsf{AE-PAS}_{\mathcal{E}}^{X,1}(\mathcal{M}) = 1 \mid \neg\mathsf{BAD}\right].$$

Write $\mathsf{W}^X(\mathcal{M})$ ('Win') for the event $\mathsf{AE-PAS}_{\mathcal{E}}^{X,1}(\mathcal{M}) = 1$. Then, as $\mathcal{M}$ outputs a random bit if $\mathsf{BAD}$ occurs, we have $\Pr\left[\mathsf{W}^X(\mathcal{M}) \mid \mathsf{BAD}\right] = \frac{1}{2}$ and it follows that:

$$\begin{aligned}
\Pr&\left[\mathsf{W}^X(\mathcal{M})\right] \\
&= \Pr\left[\mathsf{W}^X(\mathcal{M}) \cap \neg\mathsf{BAD}\right] + \Pr\left[\mathsf{W}^X(\mathcal{M}) \cap \mathsf{BAD}\right] \\
&= \Pr\left[\mathsf{W}^X(\mathcal{M}) \mid \neg\mathsf{BAD}\right](1 - \Pr[\mathsf{BAD}]) + \Pr\left[\mathsf{W}^X(\mathcal{M}) \mid \mathsf{BAD}\right]\Pr[\mathsf{BAD}] \\
&= \Pr\left[\mathsf{W}^X(\mathcal{M}) \mid \neg\mathsf{BAD}\right] - \Pr[\mathsf{BAD}]\left(\Pr\left[\mathsf{W}^X(\mathcal{M}) \mid \neg\mathsf{BAD}\right] - \frac{1}{2}\right).
\end{aligned}$$

Then,

$$\mathsf{Adv}_{\mathcal{E}}^{\mathsf{AE-PAS},X,1}(\mathcal{M}) = 2\left(\Pr\left[\mathsf{W}^X(\mathcal{M})\right] - \frac{1}{2}\right)$$

$$= 2\left[\Pr\left[\mathsf{W}^X(\mathcal{M}) \mid \neg\mathsf{BAD}\right] - \Pr\left[\mathsf{BAD}\right]\left(\Pr\left[\mathsf{W}^X(\mathcal{M}) \mid \neg\mathsf{BAD}\right] - \frac{1}{2}\right) - \frac{1}{2}\right]$$

$$= 2\left(\Pr\left[\mathsf{W}^X(\mathcal{M}) \mid \neg\mathsf{BAD}\right] - \frac{1}{2}\right) - \Pr\left[\mathsf{BAD}\right] \cdot 2\left(\Pr\left[\mathsf{W}^X(\mathcal{M}) \mid \neg\mathsf{BAD}\right] - \frac{1}{2}\right)$$

$$= (1 - \Pr\left[\mathsf{BAD}\right])\,\mathsf{Adv}_{\mathcal{E}}^{\mathsf{AE-PAS},X,1}(\mathcal{R}).$$

It follows that:

$$\mathsf{Adv}_{\mathcal{E}}^{\mathsf{AE-PAS},X,1}(\mathcal{M}) \geq \mathsf{Adv}_{\mathcal{E}}^{\mathsf{AE-PAS},X,1}(\mathcal{R}) - \Pr\left[\mathsf{BAD}\right].$$

To complete the proof we bound the probability of BAD (see the next lemma) by $\Pr\left[\mathsf{BAD}\right] \leq \frac{1}{n} + \epsilon$.

We therefore get that

$$\epsilon \geq \epsilon_{\mathcal{M}} \geq \epsilon_{\mathcal{R}} - \Pr\left[\mathsf{BAD}\right] \geq \epsilon_{\mathcal{R}} - \frac{1}{n} - \epsilon.$$

So, $\epsilon_{\mathcal{R}} \leq (\frac{1}{n} + 2\epsilon)$. Since $\epsilon_{\mathcal{A}} = 1$, we get that

$$\frac{\epsilon_{\mathcal{A}}}{\epsilon_{\mathcal{R}}} \geq \left(\frac{1}{n} + 2\epsilon\right)^{-1},$$

as required to show that $\mathcal{R}$ loses $\left(\frac{1}{n} + 2\epsilon\right)^{-1}$.    □

**Lemma 16**

$$\Pr\left[\mathsf{BAD}\right] \leq \frac{1}{n} + \epsilon.$$

*Proof.* Consider a meta-reduction $\mathcal{M}'$ in the $\mathsf{AE-PAS}_{\mathcal{E}}^{X,1}$ game that executes $\mathcal{R}_1$ and each $\mathcal{R}_2^i, i \in [n]$ exactly as $\mathcal{M}$ does, but without treating $\mathcal{R}_2^{i^*}$ differently. That is, encryption and decryption queries from $\mathcal{R}_2^{i^*}$ are 'faked' in the same way as for the other $\mathcal{R}_2^i, i \neq i^*$. Such an $\mathcal{M}'$ could have chosen $i^* \leftarrow_\$ [n]$ *after* executing each $\mathcal{R}_2^i$, simply by storing all the keys output by each $\mathcal{R}_2^i$, and then, once $i^*$ had been chosen, checking if $\mathcal{R}_2^{i^*}$ returned a full set of valid keys and if each $K_{i^*}^i$ was valid for $i \neq i^*$.

Note that the probability of BAD occuring for $\mathcal{M}'$ does not depend on whether $i^*$ was chosen at the start of executing the $\mathcal{R}_2^i$, or at the end, since $\mathcal{M}'$ runs each $\mathcal{R}_2^i$ in the same way. Moreover, after executing each $\mathcal{R}_2^i$, there can be at most one $j \in [n]$ such that $\mathcal{R}_2^j$ returned a full set of valid keys but for each $i \neq j$, $\mathcal{R}_2^i$ did not provide a full set of valid keys. Therefore there can be at most one $j \in [n]$ such that $\mathcal{R}_2^j$ returned a full set of valid keys but for each $i \neq j$, $\mathcal{R}_2^i$ did not provide a valid key $K_j^i$. Since $i^*$ was sampled uniformly from

$[n]$, the probability that $i^*$ has the latter property, i.e. that BAD occurs for $\mathcal{M}'$, is at most $\frac{1}{n}$.

Now we compare the probability that BAD occurs for the two meta-reductions $\mathcal{M}$ and $\mathcal{M}'$. Let $\mathsf{BAD}_{\mathcal{M}} = \mathsf{BAD}$ and let $\mathsf{BAD}_{\mathcal{M}'}$ be the event that BAD occurs in the game played by $\mathcal{M}'$.

Consider the hidden bit $b$ in the game played by $\mathcal{M}$ and $\mathcal{M}'$. If $b = 1$, then the views of $\mathcal{R}_1$ and each $\mathcal{R}_2^i$ are identically distributed in their interactions with $\mathcal{M}$ and $\mathcal{M}'$ (since $\mathcal{R}_2^{i^*}$ receives 'fake' responses to its queries, regardless of whether the meta-reduction forwards them to its own oracles or simulates the responses.) It follows that $\Pr\left[\mathsf{BAD}_{\mathcal{M}'} \mid b = 1\right] = \Pr\left[\mathsf{BAD}_{\mathcal{M}} \mid b = 1\right].$

Then

$$\Pr\left[\mathsf{BAD}\right] = \Pr\left[\mathsf{BAD}_{\mathcal{M}}\right] - \Pr\left[\mathsf{BAD}_{\mathcal{M}'}\right] + \Pr\left[\mathsf{BAD}_{\mathcal{M}'}\right]$$

$$\leq \Pr\left[\mathsf{BAD}_{\mathcal{M}}\right] - \Pr\left[\mathsf{BAD}_{\mathcal{M}'}\right] + \frac{1}{n}$$

$$= \frac{1}{2}\left(\Pr\left[\mathsf{BAD}_{\mathcal{M}} \mid b = 0\right] - \Pr\left[\mathsf{BAD}_{\mathcal{M}'} \mid b = 0\right]\right) + \frac{1}{n}.$$

Now we construct an adversary $\mathcal{B}$ that simulates the environment of $\mathcal{R}_1$ and the $\mathcal{R}_2^i$ in their interaction with either $\mathcal{M}$ or $\mathcal{M}'$, depending on the hidden bit $b'$ in the game played by $\mathcal{B}$. If BAD occurs, $\mathcal{B}$ will output 0. Otherwise $\mathcal{B}$ will output 1.

Consider $\mathcal{B}$ in the $\mathsf{AE\text{-}CCA}_{\mathcal{E}}^{X,1}$ game. That is, $\mathcal{B}$ has access to the usual challenge oracles Enc and Dec, but can also query the 'always real' oracles $\mathcal{E}$ and $\mathcal{D}$ (provided it does not make pointless or prohibited queries). But if $\mathcal{B}$ has significant advantage in this game, then there is another adversary, with the same resources as $\mathcal{B}$, that has significant advantage against $\mathsf{AE\text{-}PAS}_{\mathcal{E}}^{X,1}$:

**Lemma 17.** *Suppose $\mathcal{A}$ is a valid adversary against $\mathsf{AE\text{-}CCA}_{\mathcal{E}}^{X,1}$, where $X \in \{\mathsf{IV}, \mathsf{NR}, \mathsf{MR}\}$. Then*

$$\mathsf{Adv}_{\mathcal{E}}^{\mathsf{AE\text{-}CCA},X,1}(\mathcal{A}) \leq 2\epsilon,$$

*where $\epsilon$ is the maximum advantage of a valid adversary against $\mathsf{AE\text{-}PAS}_{\mathcal{E}}^{X,1}$ that runs in the same time as $\mathcal{A}$ and makes the same number of oracle queries as $\mathcal{A}$.*

The proof of Lemma 17 is in the full version of the paper [31]. We remark that a similar statement can be easily derived by combining results from an existing work [5]. However, this approach only shows that the advantage in $\mathsf{AE\text{-}CCA}_{\mathcal{E}}^{X,1}$ is at most *four times* the maximum advantage in $\mathsf{AE\text{-}PAS}_{\mathcal{E}}^{X,1}$, whereas proving the statement directly gives a tighter bound.

Now we describe the adversary $\mathcal{B}$ in the $\mathsf{AE\text{-}CCA}_{\mathcal{E}}^{X,1}$ game. First, $\mathcal{B}$ runs $\mathcal{R}_1$, but all queries are forwarded to the *genuine* oracles $\mathcal{E}$ and $\mathcal{D}$. Then $\mathcal{B}$ carries out the same checks as $\mathcal{M}$ (or $\mathcal{M}'$) and, if the checks succeed, $\mathcal{B}$ samples $i^* \leftarrow_\$ [n]$ and, for each $i \in [n]$, $\mathcal{B}$ runs $\mathcal{R}_2$ on input $(i, st_1)$.

When $\mathcal{R}_2^i$ makes oracle queries:

1. If $i = i^*$, $\mathcal{B}$ uses its *challenge* oracles Enc and Dec to honestly answer all oracle queries; forwarding the queries to its oracles and then forwarding the replies to $\mathcal{R}_2^{i^*}$.

2. If $i \neq i^*$, $\mathcal{B}$ simulates the 'fake' oracles, i.e. the oracles Enc and Dec with $b = 1$, just as $\mathcal{M}$ (or $\mathcal{M}'$) does.

Finally, $\mathcal{B}$ checks if BAD has occured. If so $\mathcal{B}$ outputs 0. Otherwise, $\mathcal{B}$ outputs 1.

Let $b'$ be the hidden bit in the game played by $\mathcal{B}$. So the oracle queries from $\mathcal{R}_1$ will always be 'real' (as they are for $\mathcal{M}$ and $\mathcal{M}'$, given that $b = 0$), the oracle queries from $\mathcal{R}_2^i$ for $i \neq i^*$ will always be 'fake' (as they are for $\mathcal{M}$ and $\mathcal{M}'$) and, depending on $b'$, the oracle queries from $\mathcal{R}_2^{i^*}$ will be real (like $\mathcal{M}$, given that $b = 0$), or fake (like $\mathcal{M}'$). It follows that $\Pr\left[0 \leftarrow \mathcal{B} \mid b' = 0\right] = \Pr\left[\mathsf{BAD}_{\mathcal{M}} \mid b = 0\right]$ and $\Pr\left[0 \leftarrow \mathcal{B} \mid b' = 1\right] = \Pr\left[\mathsf{BAD}_{\mathcal{M}'} \mid b = 0\right]$. Now,

$$\Pr\left[\mathsf{AE\text{--}CCA}_{\mathcal{E}}^{X,1}(\mathcal{B}) = 1\right] = \frac{1}{2}\left(\Pr\left[0 \leftarrow \mathcal{B} \mid b' = 0\right] + \Pr\left[1 \leftarrow \mathcal{B} \mid b' = 1\right]\right)$$
$$= \frac{1}{2}\left(\Pr\left[0 \leftarrow \mathcal{B} \mid b' = 0\right] - \Pr\left[0 \leftarrow \mathcal{B} \mid b' = 1\right]\right) + \frac{1}{2}$$

and so

$$\mathsf{Adv}_{\mathcal{E}}^{\mathsf{AE\text{--}CCA},X,1}(\mathcal{B}) = 2\left(\Pr\left[\mathsf{AE\text{--}CCA}_{\mathcal{E}}^{X,1}(\mathcal{B}) = 1\right] - \frac{1}{2}\right)$$
$$= \Pr\left[0 \leftarrow \mathcal{B} \mid b' = 0\right] - \Pr\left[0 \leftarrow \mathcal{B} \mid b' = 1\right]$$
$$= \Pr\left[\mathsf{BAD}_{\mathcal{M}} \mid b = 0\right] - \Pr\left[\mathsf{BAD}_{\mathcal{M}'} \mid b = 0\right]$$
$$\geq 2\left(\Pr\left[\mathsf{BAD}\right] - \frac{1}{n}\right).$$

Like $\mathcal{M}$ (or $\mathcal{M}'$), $\mathcal{B}$ performs $n$ runs of (part of) $\mathcal{R}$ and carries out $2(n-1)l$ encryptions to check if BAD has occured. So the runtime of $\mathcal{B}$ is at most $nt_{\mathcal{R}} + 2l(n-1)t_{C[\mathcal{E}]}$. Moreover $\mathcal{B}$ makes at most $q_{\mathcal{R}}$ oracle queries (only forwarding queries from $\mathcal{R}_1$ and $\mathcal{R}_2^{i^*}$).

Consider $\mathsf{Adv}_{\mathcal{E}}^{\mathsf{AE\text{--}CCA},X,1}(\mathcal{B})$. Firstly, note that $\mathcal{B}$ uses nonces correctly with respect to $X$, since any query to Enc or $\mathcal{E}$ is a query made to Enc by $\left(\mathcal{R}_1, \mathcal{R}_2^{i^*}, \mathcal{R}_3\right)$ and $\mathcal{R}$ is a valid adversary against $\mathsf{AE\text{--}PAS}_{\mathcal{E}}^{X,1}$. Also, $\mathcal{B}$ will not make pointless queries:

- A repeated query to $\mathcal{E}$ or $\mathcal{D}$ by $\mathcal{B}$ would be a repeated query to Enc or Dec from $\mathcal{R}_1$, which is a pointless or prohibited query in the game played by $\mathcal{R}$.
- A repeated query to Dec by $\mathcal{B}$ would be a repeated query to Dec from $\mathcal{R}_2^{i^*}$, which is a pointless query in the game played by $\mathcal{R}$.
- A query $\mathcal{D}(C, N)$ by $\mathcal{B}$, where $C$ was the response to a query $\mathcal{E}(M, N)$, would be a query $\mathrm{Dec}(C, N)$ from $\mathcal{R}_1$, where $C$ was the response to a query $\mathrm{Enc}(M, N)$, which is a prohibited query in the game played by $\mathcal{R}$.
- A query $\mathcal{E}(M, N)$ by $\mathcal{B}$, where $M \neq \perp$ was the response to a query $\mathcal{D}(C, N)$, would be a query $\mathrm{Enc}(M, N)$ from $\mathcal{R}_1$, where $M \neq \perp$ was the response to a query $\mathrm{Dec}(C, N)$, which is a pointless query in the game played by $\mathcal{R}$.
- Finally, suppose $\mathcal{B}$ makes a query $\mathcal{E}(M, N)$ or $\mathrm{Enc}(M, N)$, where $M \neq \perp$ was the response to a query $\mathrm{Dec}(C, N)$. The query $\mathrm{Dec}(C, N)$ from $\mathcal{B}$ would

correspond to a query $Dec(C, N)$ from $\mathcal{R}_2^{i^*}$ and so the subsequent encryption query would correspond to a query $Enc(M, N)$ from $\mathcal{R}_2^{i^*}$. But as $M \neq \bot$ this is a pointless query for $\mathcal{R}$.

Moreover, $\mathcal{B}$ will not make prohibited queries:

- A repeated query to Enc by $\mathcal{B}$ would be a repeated query to Enc from $\mathcal{R}_2^{i^*}$, which is a prohibited query in the game played by $\mathcal{R}$.
- Suppose $\mathcal{B}$ makes two queries of the form $Enc(M, N)$ and $\mathcal{E}(M, N)$. Each of these queries would correspond to the same query $Enc(M, N)$ from $\mathcal{R}$, which is prohibited in the game played by $\mathcal{R}$.
- A query $\mathcal{D}(C, N)$ from $\mathcal{B}$, where $C$ was the response to a query $Enc(M, N)$, is impossible since $\mathcal{B}$ only queries Enc and Dec after querying $\mathcal{E}$ and $\mathcal{D}$.
- A query $Dec(C, N)$ from $\mathcal{B}$, where $C$ was the response to a query $\mathcal{E}(M, N)$ or $Enc(M, N)$, would correspond to a query $Dec(C, N)$ from $\mathcal{R}_2^{i^*}$, where $C$ was the response to a query $Enc(M, N)$ from $\mathcal{R}_1$ or $\mathcal{R}_2^{i^*}$, which is a prohibited query in the game played by $\mathcal{R}$.
- A query $Enc(M, N)$ from $\mathcal{B}$, where $M \neq \bot$ was the response to a query $\mathcal{D}(C, N)$, would correspond to a query $Enc(M, N)$ from $\mathcal{R}_2^{i^*}$, where $M \neq \bot$ was the response to a query $Dec(C, N)$ from $\mathcal{R}_1$, which is a pointless query in the game played by $\mathcal{R}$.

It follows that $\mathcal{B}$ is a valid adversary against $\mathsf{Adv}_{\mathcal{E}}^{\mathsf{AE-CCA},X,1}(\mathcal{B})$. Then, by Lemma 17, we have

$$2 \left( \Pr[\mathsf{BAD}] - \frac{1}{n} \right) \leq \mathsf{Adv}_{\mathcal{E}}^{\mathsf{AE-CCA},X,1}(\mathcal{B}) \leq 2\epsilon,$$

from which the result follows.    □

Theorem 15 establishes that reductions from $\mathsf{KEYREC}_{C[\mathcal{E}]}^{M,n}$ to $\mathsf{AE-PAS}_{\mathcal{E}}^{X,1}$ are lossy. By Lemma 12, there exists a tight reduction from $\mathsf{KEYREC}_{C[\mathcal{E}]}^{M,n}$ to $\mathsf{GOAL-POWER}_{C[\mathcal{E}]}^{X',n}$ (for $\mathsf{POWER} \in \{\mathsf{CCA}, \mathsf{CPA}\}$); it immediately follows that reductions from $\mathsf{GOAL-POWER}_{C[\mathcal{E}]}^{X',n}$ to $\mathsf{AE-PAS}_{\mathcal{E}}^{X,1}$ must be lossy (for $\mathsf{POWER} \in \{\mathsf{CCA}, \mathsf{CPA}\}$). We formalise this intuition in the following corollary:

**Corollary 18.** *Let $\mathcal{E}$ and $C[\mathcal{E}]$ be AE schemes such that $C[\mathcal{E}]$ is $M$-key-unique for some $M \in \mathsf{M}^l$. Then for $\mathsf{GOAL} \in \{\mathsf{AE}, \mathsf{LRAE}, \mathsf{IND}, \mathsf{LRIND}, \mathsf{CTI}\}$, $\mathsf{POWER} \in \{\mathsf{CCA}, \mathsf{CPA}\}$, $X, X' \in \{\mathsf{IV}, \mathsf{NR}, \mathsf{MR}\}$ and $n > 1$, all simple reductions from $\mathsf{GOAL-POWER}_{C[\mathcal{E}]}^{X',n}$ to $\mathsf{AE-PAS}_{\mathcal{E}}^{X,1}$ must lose*

$$L = \delta_{\mathsf{GOAL}} \cdot \delta_{X'} \cdot \left( \frac{1}{n} + 2\epsilon \right)^{-1},$$

*where $\delta_{\mathsf{GOAL}}$ and $\delta_{X'}$ are as in Lemma 12 and $\epsilon$ is as given in Theorem 15.*

We emphasise that the 'nonce use' parameters $X', X \in \{\mathsf{IV}, \mathsf{NR}, \mathsf{MR}\}$ can differ between the $n$-key game and the single key game. While it is natural to consider $X' = X$ we prefer to state the result in full generality and show that a very large class of reductions are necessarily lossy. Note that multi-key games for POWER $\in$ {PAS, CDA} are not known to be (tightly) equivalent to those where POWER $\in$ {CCA, CPA} (see the full version of the paper [31]). It therefore remains an open problem to obtain tightness lowerbounds for POWER $\in$ {PAS, CDA}.

*Proof.* Recall from Lemma 12 the $(\mathbb{S}, \mathbb{T})$-simple reduction from $\mathsf{KEYREC}_{\mathcal{E}}^{M,n}$ to $\mathsf{GOAL-POWER}_{\mathcal{E}}^{X,n}$, where $\mathbb{S}(\epsilon_{\mathcal{A}}) = \delta_X \cdot \delta_{\mathsf{GOAL}} \cdot \epsilon_{\mathcal{A}}$ and $\mathbb{T}(t_{\mathcal{A}}) = t_{\mathcal{A}} + (l + m_{\mathsf{GOAL}})t_{\mathcal{E}}$. Relabelling, we obtain a $(\mathbb{S}', \mathbb{T}')$-simple reduction from $\mathsf{KEYREC}_{C[\mathcal{E}]}^{M,n}$ to $\mathsf{GOAL-POWER}_{C[\mathcal{E}]}^{X',n}$, where $\mathbb{S}'(\epsilon_{\mathcal{A}}) = \delta_{X'} \cdot \delta_{\mathsf{GOAL}} \cdot \epsilon_{\mathcal{A}}$ and $\mathbb{T}'(t_{\mathcal{A}}) = t_{\mathcal{A}} + (l + m_{\mathsf{GOAL}})t_{C[\mathcal{E}]}$, which we call $\mathcal{R}$.

We argue by contradiction. Suppose there is a simple reduction $\mathcal{R}'$ from $\mathsf{GOAL-POWER}_{C[\mathcal{E}]}^{X',n}$ to $\mathsf{AE-PAS}_{\mathcal{E}}^{X,1}$ such that, for all valid adversaries $\mathcal{B}$ against $\mathsf{AE-PAS}_{\mathcal{E}}^{X,n}$, $\epsilon_{\mathcal{R}'} > L^{-1}\epsilon_{\mathcal{B}}$.

Then we can form a simple reduction $\mathcal{R}''$ from $\mathsf{KEYREC}_{C[\mathcal{E}]}^{M,n}$ to $\mathsf{AE-PAS}_{\mathcal{E}}^{X,1}$: for any adversary $\mathcal{A}$ against $\mathsf{KEYREC}_{C[\mathcal{E}]}^{M,n}$, running $\mathcal{R}$ with $\mathcal{A}$ provides a valid adversary $\mathcal{B}$ against $\mathsf{GOAL-POWER}_{C[\mathcal{E}]}^{X',n}$ for $\mathcal{R}'$ to turn into a valid adversary against $\mathsf{AE-PAS}_{\mathcal{E}}^{X,1}$.

By construction, the advantage $\epsilon_{\mathcal{R}''}$ of $\mathcal{R}''$ is equal to the advantage of $\mathcal{R}'$ with access to an adversary with advantage $\epsilon_{\mathcal{R}}$, i.e. $\epsilon_{\mathcal{R}''} > L^{-1}\epsilon_{\mathcal{R}}$. Since $\epsilon_{\mathcal{R}} \geq \delta_{X'} \cdot \delta_{\mathsf{GOAL}} \cdot \epsilon_{\mathcal{A}}$ for all adversaries $\mathcal{A}$ against $\mathsf{KEYREC}_{C[\mathcal{E}]}^{M,n}$, we have

$$\epsilon_{\mathcal{R}''} > L^{-1} \cdot \delta_{X'} \cdot \delta_{\mathsf{GOAL}} \cdot \epsilon_{\mathcal{A}} = \left(\frac{1}{n} + 2\epsilon\right)\epsilon_{\mathcal{A}}.$$

But this is a contradiction since, by Theorem 15, for any simple reduction $\mathcal{R}''$ from $\mathsf{KEYREC}_{C[\mathcal{E}]}^{M,n}$ to $\mathsf{AE-PAS}_{\mathcal{E}}^{X,1}$, there exists an adversary $\mathcal{A}$ against $\mathsf{KEYREC}_{C[\mathcal{E}]}^{M,n}$ such that

$$\epsilon_{\mathcal{R}''} \leq \left(\frac{1}{n} + 2\epsilon\right)\epsilon_{\mathcal{A}}.$$

Thus for any simple reduction $\mathcal{R}'$ from $\mathsf{GOAL-POWER}_{C[\mathcal{E}]}^{X',n}$ to $\mathsf{AE-PAS}_{\mathcal{E}}^{X,1}$ there exists a valid adversary $\mathcal{B}$ against $\mathsf{GOAL-POWER}_{C[\mathcal{E}]}^{X',n}$ such that $\epsilon_{\mathcal{R}'} \leq L^{-1}\epsilon_{\mathcal{B}}$, i.e. $\mathcal{R}'$ loses $L$.  $\square$

*Privacy and Integrity.* The above results hold for notions of authenticated encryption schemes. It is natural to ask whether the loss for simple reductions from $\mathsf{GOAL-POWER}_{C[\mathcal{E}]}^{X',n}$ to $\mathsf{AE-PAS}_{\mathcal{E}}^{X,1}$ is an artefact of considering the two orthogonal single-key security properties of secrecy and authenticity at the same time. Perhaps it is possible to circumvent the loss when looking at these properties separately, e.g. there could there be non-lossy simple reductions from $\mathsf{GOAL-POWER}_{C[\mathcal{E}]}^{X',n}$ to $\mathsf{IND-PAS}_{\mathcal{E}}^{X,1}$ and from $\mathsf{GOAL-POWER}_{C[\mathcal{E}]}^{X',n}$ to $\mathsf{CTI-CPA}_{\mathcal{E}}^{X,1}$. We show that this is not the case.

We proceed as for the authenticated encryption case. For privacy and integrity, in turn, we show that reductions from multi-key recovery to single-key security are inherently lossy; the lower bound then follows by Lemma 12. We give the details in the full version of the paper [31].

*Other Single-Key Security Notions.* Given the results above concerning reductions from multi-key AE security notions to the single-key notions $\mathsf{AE-PAS}$, $\mathsf{IND-PAS}$ and $\mathsf{CTI-CPA}$, one can obtain analogous results for *equivalent or weaker* single key notions, such as where ciphertexts being indistinguishable from random strings (IND, AE) is replaced by (weaker) left-or-right indistinguishability (LRIND, LRAE). The idea is that if there were a tight reduction from an $n$-key game to single-key $\mathsf{LRAE-PAS}$, say, then this reduction could be combined with the tight reduction from $\mathsf{LRAE-PAS}$ to $\mathsf{AE-PAS}$ to obtain a tight reduction from the $n$-key game to $\mathsf{AE-PAS}$ that contradicts Corollary 18. However, "tight" is defined here with respect to a number of parameters including, crucially, $\epsilon$: the maximum advantage *in the $\mathsf{AE-PAS}$ game*. If $\epsilon$ is close to 1, then so is the "loss". In other words, the tightness lowerbounds that one can prove using our existing results for strictly weaker single-key security notions are only meaningful for schemes that are secure according to the stronger notions. This leaves open the possibility that tight multi-key to single-key reductions exist for schemes that achieve the weaker single-key security notions, but *not* the stronger ones. Moreover, our meta-reduction techniques cannot be directly applied to left-or-right indistinguishability, since the meta-reduction cannot correctly simulate left-or-right encryption queries during the rewinding phase without making its own (possibly prohibited) oracle queries (unlike for IND when the meta-reduction simply samples random strings of the appropriate length).

*Public Key Encryption.* It should be possible to adapt our existing techniques to the public key setting. Let $\mathsf{LRIND-CPA}$ be the standard game in which the adversary is given the public key and can query a left-or-right encryption oracle. Note that the honest encryption oracle is omitted as it is rendered superfluous by the public key. Since public key encryption is typically randomised rather than nonce-based, repeated left-or-right encryption queries are not prohibited, so a meta-reduction $\mathcal{M}$ can use its own left-or-right challenge oracle to correctly simulate left-or-right queries from the reduction $\mathcal{R}$ during the rewinding phase, without $\mathcal{M}$ becoming an invalid adversary. However, if $\mathcal{R}$ can also make decryption queries, then simulating these queries during the rewinding phase might force $\mathcal{M}$ to be invalid (such as if one instance of $\mathcal{R}$ attempts to decrypt the output of the left-or-right encryption oracle sent to an earlier instance of $\mathcal{R}$). In summary, it should be possible to show reductions from multi-key games to single-key $\mathsf{LRIND-CPA}$ are lossy for public key encryption schemes secure according to $\mathsf{LRIND-CPA}$, but to show an analogous result for $\mathsf{LRIND-CCA}$ one needs to additionally assume that ciphertexts are indistinguishable from random strings (which is a rather strong assumption in the public key setting). We leave formally proving these claims for future work.

## 5    Conclusion

We have presented a general family of multi-key security definitions for authenticated encryption, where the adversary can adaptively corrupt keys. We have shown, for a very large class of authenticated encryption schemes, for most members of our family of definitions and for widely-accepted single-key security definitions, that any black-box reduction from the $n$-key security of an encryption scheme to its single-key security will incur a loss close to $n$.

For practitioners who set security parameters based on provable guarantees, this shows that security reductions have an inherent shortcoming. Since keys are sampled independently, the corruption of one key should not affect the security of another, yet it is impossible in many cases to prove that security does not degrade from the single-key setting to the $n$-key setting. It appears that the loss of $n$ is an unfortunate, unavoidable artefact of the proof.

We have shown that the loss of reductions is inevitable for multi-key definitions where the adversary has access to an honest encryption oracle. We therefore left open the possibility that for security notions without such an oracle, tight reductions may be found. Furthermore, our impossibility results apply to schemes where ciphertexts are indistinguishable from random strings. It may be possible that tight reductions exist for schemes that achieve weaker forms of confidentiality, such as left-or-right indistinguishability. Historically, the community has tended to opt for stronger and stronger security notions, but perhaps a slightly weaker single-key notion would be preferred if it tightly implied a meaningful multi-key notion. Finally, it was pointed out by an anonymous reviewer that, in practice, the number of keys an adversary can corrupt is likely to be much smaller than the number of keys in use; it might be possible to find tighter multi-key to single-key reductions for multi-key games where the adversary can corrupt at most $q_c$ keys (with $q_c \ll n$). We leave these interesting open questions for future work.

**Acknowledgements.** This work was supported by an EPSRC Industrial CASE award and DFG grant JA 2445/1-1. The authors would also like to thank the anonymous TCC reviewers for their constructive comments on our paper.

## Appendix

## Valid Adversarial Behaviour for AE Games

*Pointless and Prohibited Queries.* Since encryption is deterministic, the response to certain oracle queries can be predicted in advance. Therefore the adversary learns nothing from these queries; we call them *pointless*. Without loss of generality we assume that valid adversaries do not make such queries. The following queries are pointless:

- Repeat a query to any oracle other than Enc(the Enc oracle sometimes samples random ciphertexts, but all other oracles are deterministic).
- Make a query $\mathcal{D}(i, C, N)$, where $C$ was the response to a query $\mathcal{E}(i, M, N)$ (since the response will be $M$, by correctness).
- Make a query $\mathcal{E}(i, M, N)$, where $M \neq \perp$ was the response to a query $\mathcal{D}(i, C, N)$ (since the response will be $C$, by tidiness).
- Make a query $\mathcal{E}(i, M, N)$ or $\mathrm{Enc}(i, j, M, N)$, where a query $\mathrm{Dec}(i, j, C, N)$ was made with response $M \neq \perp$ (since the response $M \neq \perp$ reveals $b_j = 0$ and $\mathcal{E}_{K_i}^N(M) = C$ by tidiness).

Some other queries lead to hidden bits being trivial to recover (without having to corrupt a key); we call these queries *prohibited*, since valid adversaries are not permitted to make them. The following queries are prohibited:

- Repeat a query $\mathrm{Enc}(i, j, M, N)$ (if the response to both queries is the same, then with very high probability $b_j = 0$ and otherwise $b_j = 1$).
- Make a query of the form $\mathrm{LR}(i, j, M_0, M_1, N)$ with $|M_0| \neq |M_1|$ (since the length of the ciphertext reveals the length of the plaintext, trivially revealing which of $M_0$ or $M_1$ was encrypted).
- Make two queries of the form $\mathrm{LR}(i, j, M_0, M_1, N)$, $\mathrm{LR}(i, j, M_0', M_1', N)$ such that $M_b = M_b'$ and $M_{1-b} \neq M_{1-b}'$ for some $b \in \{0, 1\}$ (if the response to both queries is the same, then $b_j = b$ by correctness, and otherwise $b_j = 1 - b$).
- Make two queries of the form $\mathrm{Enc}(i, j, M, N)$ and $\mathcal{E}(i, M, N)$, in any order (which trivially reveals $b_j$).
- Make two queries of the form $\mathrm{LR}(i, j, M_0, M_1, N)$ and $\mathcal{E}(i, M_b, N)$, in any order, for some $b \in \{0, 1\}$ (which trivially reveals $b_j$).
- Make a query $\mathcal{D}(i, C, N)$, where $C$ was the response to a query $\mathrm{Enc}(i, j, M, N)$ or $\mathrm{LR}(i, j, M_0, M_1, N)$ (which trivially reveals $b_j$, by correctness).
- Make a query $\mathrm{Dec}(i, j, C, N)$, where a query $\mathcal{E}(i, M, N)$, $\mathrm{Enc}(i, j, M, N)$ or $\mathrm{LR}(i, j, M_0, M_1, N)$ was previously made with response $C$ (which trivially reveals $b_j$, by correctness).
- Make a query $\mathrm{Enc}(i, j, M, N)$, $\mathrm{LR}(i, j, M, M_1, N)$ or $\mathrm{LR}(i, j, M_0, M, N)$, where $M \neq \perp$ was the response to a query $\mathcal{D}(i, C, N)$ (which trivially reveals $b_j$, by tidiness).

It is not necessary to prohibit queries being forwarded between the Enc and LR oracles, since we do not consider games where both these challenge oracles are present.

*Correct Nonce Use.* The parameter $X \in \{\mathsf{IV}, \mathsf{NR}, \mathsf{MR}\}$ determines how the adversary may use nonces in encryption queries. We say $\mathcal{A}$ uses nonces correctly with respect to $X$ if the following statements hold:

- If $X = \mathsf{IV}$, then for each query of the form $\mathcal{E}(-, -, N)$, $\mathrm{Enc}(-, -, -, N)$, or $\mathrm{LR}(-, -, -, -, N)$, $N$ is sampled uniformly at random from $\mathsf{N}$.

- If $X = $ NR, then each nonce appears in at most one encryption query *under the same key*. That is, for each $i \in [n]$, each nonce $N$ appears in at most one query of the form $\mathrm{Enc}(i, -, -, N)$, $\mathrm{LR}(i, -, -, -, N)$ or $\mathcal{E}(i, -, N)$.
- If $X = $ MR, then nonces may chosen be arbitrarily and repeated in different queries (modulo the pointless and prohibited queries specified above).

# References

1. Abdalla, M., Fouque, P.-A., Lyubashevsky, V., Tibouchi, M.: Tightly-secure signatures from lossy identification schemes. In: Pointcheval, D., Johansson, T. (eds.) EUROCRYPT 2012. LNCS, vol. 7237, pp. 572–590. Springer, Heidelberg (2012). doi:10.1007/978-3-642-29011-4_34
2. Bader, C., Hofheinz, D., Jager, T., Kiltz, E., Li, Y.: Tightly-secure authenticated key exchange. In: Dodis, Y., Nielsen, J.B. (eds.) TCC 2015. LNCS, vol. 9014, pp. 629–658. Springer, Heidelberg (2015). doi:10.1007/978-3-662-46494-6_26
3. Bader, C., Jager, T., Li, Y., Schäge, S.: On the impossibility of tight cryptographic reductions. In: Fischlin, M., Coron, J.-S. (eds.) EUROCRYPT 2016. LNCS, vol. 9666, pp. 273–304. Springer, Heidelberg (2016). doi:10.1007/978-3-662-49896-5_10
4. Baecher, P., Brzuska, C., Fischlin, M.: Notions of black-box reductions, revisited. In: Sako, K., Sarkar, P. (eds.) ASIACRYPT 2013. LNCS, vol. 8269, pp. 296–315. Springer, Heidelberg (2013). doi:10.1007/978-3-642-42033-7_16
5. Barwell, G., Page, D., Stam, M.: Rogue decryption failures: reconciling AE robustness notions. In: Groth, J. (ed.) IMACC 2015. LNCS, vol. 9496, pp. 94–111. Springer, Cham (2015). doi:10.1007/978-3-319-27239-9_6
6. Bellare, M., Boldyreva, A., Micali, S.: Public-key encryption in a multi-user setting: security proofs and improvements. In: Preneel, B. (ed.) EUROCRYPT 2000. LNCS, vol. 1807, pp. 259–274. Springer, Heidelberg (2000). doi:10.1007/3-540-45539-6_18
7. Bellare, M., Hofheinz, D., Kiltz, E.: Subtleties in the definition of IND-CCA: When and how should challenge decryption be disallowed? J. Cryptol. **28**(1), 29–48 (2015)
8. Bellare, M., Ristenpart, T., Tessaro, S.: Multi-instance security and its application to password-based cryptography. In: Safavi-Naini, R., Canetti, R. (eds.) CRYPTO 2012. LNCS, vol. 7417, pp. 312–329. Springer, Heidelberg (2012). doi:10.1007/978-3-642-32009-5_19
9. Bellare, M., Tackmann, B.: The multi-user security of authenticated encryption: AES-GCM in TLS 1.3. In: Robshaw, M., Katz, J. (eds.) CRYPTO 2016. LNCS, vol. 9814, pp. 247–276. Springer, Heidelberg (2016). doi:10.1007/978-3-662-53018-4_10
10. Biham, E.: How to decrypt or even substitute DES-encrypted messages in $2^{28}$ steps. Inf. Process. Lett. **84**(3), 117–124 (2002). doi:10.1016/S0020-0190(02)00269-7
11. Biryukov, A., Mukhopadhyay, S., Sarkar, P.: Improved time-memory trade-offs with multiple data. In: Preneel, B., Tavares, S. (eds.) SAC 2005. LNCS, vol. 3897, pp. 110–127. Springer, Heidelberg (2006). doi:10.1007/11693383_8
12. Blazy, O., Kakvi, S.A., Kiltz, E., Pan, J.: Tightly-secure signatures from chameleon hash functions. In: Katz, J. (ed.) PKC 2015. LNCS, vol. 9020, pp. 256–279. Springer, Heidelberg (2015). doi:10.1007/978-3-662-46447-2_12
13. Blazy, O., Kiltz, E., Pan, J.: (Hierarchical) Identity-based encryption from affine message authentication. In: Garay, J.A., Gennaro, R. (eds.) CRYPTO 2014. LNCS, vol. 8616, pp. 408–425. Springer, Heidelberg (2014). doi:10.1007/978-3-662-44371-2_23

14. Boneh, D., Venkatesan, R.: Breaking RSA may not be equivalent to factoring. In: Nyberg, K. (ed.) EUROCRYPT 1998. LNCS, vol. 1403, pp. 59–71. Springer, Heidelberg (1998). doi:10.1007/BFb0054117

15. Chatterjee, S., Koblitz, N., Menezes, A., Sarkar, P.: Another look at tightness II: Practical issues in cryptography. Cryptology ePrint Archive, Report 2016/360 (2016). http://eprint.iacr.org/2016/360

16. Chatterjee, S., Menezes, A., Sarkar, P.: Another look at tightness. In: Miri, A., Vaudenay, S. (eds.) SAC 2011. LNCS, vol. 7118, pp. 293–319. Springer, Heidelberg (2012). doi:10.1007/978-3-642-28496-0_18

17. Chen, J., Wee, H.: Fully, (Almost) tightly secure IBE and dual system groups. In: Canetti, R., Garay, J.A. (eds.) CRYPTO 2013. LNCS, vol. 8043, pp. 435–460. Springer, Heidelberg (2013). doi:10.1007/978-3-642-40084-1_25

18. Coron, J.-S.: Security proof for partial-domain hash signature schemes. In: Yung, M. (ed.) CRYPTO 2002. LNCS, vol. 2442, pp. 613–626. Springer, Heidelberg (2002). doi:10.1007/3-540-45708-9_39

19. Fischlin, M., Fleischhacker, N.: Limitations of the meta-reduction technique: the case of schnorr signatures. In: Johansson, T., Nguyen, P.Q. (eds.) EUROCRYPT 2013. LNCS, vol. 7881, pp. 444–460. Springer, Heidelberg (2013). doi:10.1007/978-3-642-38348-9_27

20. Fischlin, M., Lehmann, A., Ristenpart, T., Shrimpton, T., Stam, M., Tessaro, S.: Random oracles with(out) programmability. In: Abe, M. (ed.) ASIACRYPT 2010. LNCS, vol. 6477, pp. 303–320. Springer, Heidelberg (2010). doi:10.1007/978-3-642-17373-8_18

21. Fleischhacker, N., Jager, T., Schröder, D.: On tight security proofs for schnorr signatures. In: Sarkar, P., Iwata, T. (eds.) ASIACRYPT 2014. LNCS, vol. 8873, pp. 512–531. Springer, Heidelberg (2014). doi:10.1007/978-3-662-45611-8_27

22. Fouque, P.-A., Joux, A., Mavromati, C.: Multi-user collisions: applications to discrete logarithm, even-mansour and PRINCE. In: Sarkar, P., Iwata, T. (eds.) ASIACRYPT 2014. LNCS, vol. 8873, pp. 420–438. Springer, Heidelberg (2014). doi:10.1007/978-3-662-45611-8_22

23. Garg, S., Bhaskar, R., Lokam, S.V.: Improved bounds on security reductions for discrete log based signatures. In: Wagner, D. (ed.) CRYPTO 2008. LNCS, vol. 5157, pp. 93–107. Springer, Heidelberg (2008). doi:10.1007/978-3-540-85174-5_6

24. Gay, R., Hofheinz, D., Kiltz, E., Wee, H.: Tightly CCA-secure encryption without pairings. In: Fischlin, M., Coron, J.-S. (eds.) EUROCRYPT 2016. LNCS, vol. 9665, pp. 1–27. Springer, Heidelberg (2016). doi:10.1007/978-3-662-49890-3_1

25. Hoang, V.T., Krovetz, T., Rogaway, P.: Robust authenticated-encryption AEZ and the problem that it solves. In: Oswald, E., Fischlin, M. (eds.) EUROCRYPT 2015. LNCS, vol. 9056, pp. 15–44. Springer, Heidelberg (2015). doi:10.1007/978-3-662-46800-5_2

26. Hoang, V.T., Tessaro, S.: The multi-user security of double encryption. In: Coron, J.-S., Nielsen, J.B. (eds.) EUROCRYPT 2017. LNCS, vol. 10211, pp. 381–411. Springer, Cham (2017). doi:10.1007/978-3-319-56614-6_13

27. Hofheinz, D.: Algebraic partitioning: fully compact and (almost) tightly secure cryptography. In: Kushilevitz, E., Malkin, T. (eds.) TCC 2016. LNCS, vol. 9562, pp. 251–281. Springer, Heidelberg (2016). doi:10.1007/978-3-662-49096-9_11

28. Hofheinz, D., Jager, T.: Tightly secure signatures and public-key encryption. In: Safavi-Naini, R., Canetti, R. (eds.) CRYPTO 2012. LNCS, vol. 7417, pp. 590–607. Springer, Heidelberg (2012). doi:10.1007/978-3-642-32009-5_35

29. Hofheinz, D., Jager, T., Knapp, E.: Waters signatures with optimal security reduction. In: Fischlin, M., Buchmann, J., Manulis, M. (eds.) PKC 2012. LNCS, vol. 7293, pp. 66–83. Springer, Heidelberg (2012). doi:10.1007/978-3-642-30057-8_5

30. Hsiao, C.-Y., Reyzin, L.: Finding collisions on a public road, or do secure hash functions need secret coins? In: Franklin, M. (ed.) CRYPTO 2004. LNCS, vol. 3152, pp. 92–105. Springer, Heidelberg (2004). doi:10.1007/978-3-540-28628-8_6

31. Jager, T., Stam, M., Stanley-Oakes, R., Warinschi, B.: Multi-key authenticated encryption with corruptions: Reductions are lossy. Cryptology ePrint Archive, Report 2017/495 (2017). http://eprint.iacr.org/2017/495

32. Kakvi, S.A., Kiltz, E.: Optimal security proofs for full domain hash, revisited. In: Pointcheval, D., Johansson, T. (eds.) EUROCRYPT 2012. LNCS, vol. 7237, pp. 537–553. Springer, Heidelberg (2012). doi:10.1007/978-3-642-29011-4_32

33. Katz, J., Wang, N.: Efficiency improvements for signature schemes with tight security reductions. In: Jajodia, S., Atluri, V., Jaeger, T. (eds.) ACM CCS 2003, pp. 155–164. ACM Press, October 2003

34. Mouha, N., Luykx, A.: Multi-key security: The Even-Mansour construction revisited. In: Gennaro, R., Robshaw, M. (eds.) CRYPTO 2015. LNCS, vol. 9215, pp. 209–223. Springer, Heidelberg (2015). doi:10.1007/978-3-662-47989-6_10

35. Namprempre, C., Rogaway, P., Shrimpton, T.: Reconsidering generic composition. In: Nguyen, P.Q., Oswald, E. (eds.) EUROCRYPT 2014. LNCS, vol. 8441, pp. 257–274. Springer, Heidelberg (2014). doi:10.1007/978-3-642-55220-5_15

36. Paillier, P., Vergnaud, D.: Discrete-log-based signatures may not be equivalent to discrete log. In: Roy, B. (ed.) ASIACRYPT 2005. LNCS, vol. 3788, pp. 1–20. Springer, Heidelberg (2005). doi:10.1007/11593447_1

37. Panjwani, S.: Tackling adaptive corruptions in multicast encryption protocols. In: Vadhan, S.P. (ed.) TCC 2007. LNCS, vol. 4392, pp. 21–40. Springer, Heidelberg (2007). doi:10.1007/978-3-540-70936-7_2

38. Rogaway, P., Shrimpton, T.: A provable-security treatment of the key-wrap problem. In: Vaudenay, S. (ed.) EUROCRYPT 2006. LNCS, vol. 4004, pp. 373–390. Springer, Heidelberg (2006). doi:10.1007/11761679_23

39. Safavi-Naini, R., Canetti, R. (eds.): CRYPTO 2012. LNCS, vol. 7417. Springer, Heidelberg (2012). doi:10.1007/978-3-642-32009-5

40. Schäge, S.: Tight proofs for signature schemes without random oracles. In: Paterson, K.G. (ed.) EUROCRYPT 2011. LNCS, vol. 6632, pp. 189–206. Springer, Heidelberg (2011). doi:10.1007/978-3-642-20465-4_12

41. Seurin, Y.: On the exact security of Schnorr-type signatures in the random oracle model. In: Pointcheval, D., Johansson, T. (eds.) EUROCRYPT 2012. LNCS, vol. 7237, pp. 554–571. Springer, Heidelberg (2012). doi:10.1007/978-3-642-29011-4_33

42. Tessaro, S.: Optimally secure block ciphers from ideal primitives. In: Iwata, T., Cheon, J.H. (eds.) ASIACRYPT 2015. LNCS, vol. 9453, pp. 437–462. Springer, Heidelberg (2015). doi:10.1007/978-3-662-48800-3_18

# Moderately Hard Functions

# On the Depth-Robustness and Cumulative Pebbling Cost of Argon2i

Jeremiah Blocki$^{(\boxtimes)}$ and Samson Zhou

Department of Computer Science, Purdue University, West Lafayette, IN, USA
jblocki@purdue.edu, samsonzhou@gmail.com

**Abstract.** Argon2i is a data-independent memory hard function that won the password hashing competition. The password hashing algorithm has already been incorporated into several open source crypto libraries such as libsodium. In this paper we analyze the cumulative memory cost of computing Argon2i. On the positive side we provide a lower bound for Argon2i. On the negative side we exhibit an improved attack against Argon2i which demonstrates that our lower bound is nearly tight. In particular, we show that

(1) An Argon2i DAG is $\left(e, O\left(n^3/e^3\right)\right)$-reducible.
(2) The cumulative pebbling cost for Argon2i is at most $O\left(n^{1.768}\right)$. This improves upon the previous best upper bound of $O\left(n^{1.8}\right)$ [AB17].
(3) Argon2i DAG is $\left(e, \tilde{\Omega}\left(n^3/e^3\right)\right)$-depth robust. By contrast, analysis of [ABP17a] only established that Argon2i was $\left(e, \tilde{\Omega}\left(n^2/e^2\right)\right)$-depth robust.
(4) The cumulative pebbling complexity of Argon2i is at least $\tilde{\Omega}\left(n^{1.75}\right)$. This improves on the previous best bound of $\Omega\left(n^{1.66}\right)$ [ABP17a] and demonstrates that Argon2i has higher cumulative memory cost than competing proposals such as Catena or Balloon Hashing.

We also show that Argon2i has high *fractional* depth-robustness which strongly suggests that data-dependent modes of Argon2 are resistant to space-time tradeoff attacks.

## 1 Introduction

Memory-hard functions (MHFs) are a promising primitive to help protect low entropy user passwords against offline attacks. MHFs can generally be divided into two categories: data-dependent (dMHF) and data-independent (iMHF). A data-independent MHF (iMHF) is characterized by the property that the memory-access pattern induced by an honest evaluation algorithm is not dependent on the input to the function (e.g., the password). In contexts such as password hashing, iMHFs are useful for their resistance to side-channel attacks such as cache-timing [Ber][1].

---

[1] Unfortunately, this resistance to side-channel attacks has a price; we now know that the dMHFs `scrypt` enjoys strictly greater memory-hardness [ACP+17] than can possibly be achieved for a very broad class of iMHFs [AB16].

Y. Kalai and L. Reyzin (Eds.): TCC 2017, Part I, LNCS 10677, pp. 445–465, 2017.
https://doi.org/10.1007/978-3-319-70500-2_15

Both in theory and in practice, iMHFs (e.g.,[BDK16, CGBS16, CJMS14, Cox14, Wu15, Pin14, AABSJ14]) can be viewed as a directed acyclic graph (DAG) which describes how inputs and outputs of various calls to an underlying compression function are related. That is, the function $f_{G,h}$ can be fully specified in terms of a DAG $G$ and a round function $h$. The input to the function is the label of the source node(s) and the output of the function is the label of the sink node(s). The label of node $v$ is computed by applying the round function $h$ to the labels of $v$'s parents.

The goal of a MHF is to ensure that it is cost prohibitive for an attacker to evaluate $f_{G,t}$ millions or billions of times even if the attacker can use customized hardware (e.g., FPGAs, ASICs). Thus, we wish to lower bound the "cumulative memory complexity" or "amortized area-time complexity" of any algorithm that computes $f_{G,h}$.

## 1.1   iMHFs, Graph Pebbling and Depth-Robustness

In the parallel random oracle model, the memory hardness of the iMHF $f_{G,h}$ can be characterized using the parallel black pebbling game on the graph $G$ [AS15, CGBS16, FLW13]. In particular, the "cumulative memory complexity" or "amortized area-time complexity" of $f_{G,h}$ is (essentially) equivalent to the cumulative cost of any legal black pebbling of $G$ in the parallel Random Oracle Model (pROM) [AS15]. Given a directed acyclic graph (DAG) $G = (V, E)$, the goal of the (parallel) black pebbling game is to place pebbles on all sink nodes of $G$ (not necessarily simultaneously). The game is played in rounds and we use $P_i \subseteq V$ to denote the set of currently pebbled nodes on round $i$. Initially all nodes are unpebbled, $P_0 = \emptyset$, and in each round $i \geq 1$ we may only include $v \in P_i$ if all of $v$'s parents were pebbled in the previous configuration (parents($v$) $\subseteq P_{i-1}$) or if $v$ was already pebbled in the last round ($v \in P_{i-1}$). The cumulative cost of the pebbling is defined to be $|P_1| + \ldots + |P_t|$.

Graph pebbling is a particularly useful as a tool to analyze the security of an iMHF [AS15]. A pebbling of $G$ naturally corresponds to an algorithm to compute the iMHF. Alwen and Serbinenko [AS15] proved that in the parallel random oracle model (pROM) of computation, *any* algorithm evaluating such an iMHF could be reduced to a pebbling strategy with (approximately) the same cumulative memory cost.

Recently it has been shown that for a DAG $G$ to have high "amortized area-time complexity" it is both necessary [ABP17a] and sufficient [AB16] for $G$ to be very depth-robust, where an $(e, d, b)$-block depth robust DAG $G$ has the property that after removing any subset $S \subseteq V(G)$ of up to $e$ blocks of $b$-consecutive nodes (and adjacent edges) there remains a directed path of length $d$ in $G - S$ (when $b = 1$ we simply say that $G$ is $(e, d)$-depth robust). It is particularly important to understand the depth-robustness and cumulative pebbling cost of iMHF candidates.

## 1.2   Argon2i

Of particular importance is the iMHF candidate Argon2i [BDK15], winner of the password hashing competition. Argon2i is being considered for standardization by the Cryptography Form Research Group (CFRG) of the IRTF [BDKJ16][2].

While significant progress has been made in the last two years in understanding the depth-robustness and cumulative pebbling complexity of candidate iMHFs (e.g., see Table 1) there is still a large gap in the lower and upper bounds for Argon2i, which is arguably the most important iMHF candidate to understand. A table summarizing the asymptotic cumulative complexity of various iMHFs can be found in Table 1.

**Table 1.** Overview of the asymptotic cumulative complexity of various iMHF.

| Algorithm | Lowerbound | Upperbound | Appearing In |
|---|---|---|---|
| Argon2i-A | $\tilde{\Omega}\left(n^{1.\bar{6}}\right)$ | $\tilde{O}\left(n^{1.708}\right)$ | [ABP17a] |
| Argon2i-B | | $O\left(n^{1.8}\right)$ | [AB17] |
| Argon2i-B | $\tilde{\Omega}\left(n^{1.\bar{6}}\right)$ | | [ABP17a] |
| Argon2i-B | $\tilde{\Omega}\left(n^{1.75}\right)$ | $O\left(n^{1.767}\right)$ | This Work |
| Balloon-Hashing | $\tilde{\Omega}\left(n^{1.5}\right)$ | $\tilde{O}\left(n^{1.625}\right)$ | [ABP17a] |
| Balloon-Hashing: Single Buffer (SB) | $\tilde{\Omega}\left(n^{1.\bar{6}}\right)$ | $\tilde{O}\left(n^{1.708}\right)$ | [ABP17a] |
| Catena | $\tilde{\Omega}\left(n^{1.5}\right)$ | $\tilde{O}\left(n^{1.625}\right)$ | [ABP17a] |
| (Existential Result) | $\Omega\left(\frac{n^2}{\log n}\right)$ | | [ABP17a] |
| DRSample | $\Omega\left(\frac{n^2}{\log n}\right)$ | | [ABH17] |
| Arbitrary iMHF | | $O\left(\frac{n^2 \log\log n}{\log n}\right)$ | [AB16] |

## 1.3   Results

We first completely characterize the depth-robustness of Argon2i in Theorem 1, and then apply our bounds to develop (nearly tight) upper and lower bounds

---

[2] The specification of Argon2i has changed several times. Older versions of the specification constructed $G$ by sampling edges uniformly at random, while this distribution has been modified to a non-uniform distribution in newer versions. Following [AB17] we use Argon2i-A to refer to *all (older) versions* of the algorithm that used a uniform edge distribution. We use Argon2i-B to refer to all versions of the algorithm that use the new non-uniform edge distribution (including the current version that is being considered for standardization by the Cryptography Form Research Group (CFRG) of the IRTF [BDKJ16]). Since we are primarily interested in analyzing the current version of the algorithm we will sometimes simply write Argon2i instead of Argon2i-B. By contrast, we will always write Argon2i-A whenever we refer to the earlier version.

on the cumulative pebbling cost of Argon2i — see Theorems 2 and 3. For comparison, the previous best known upper bound for Argon2i was $O\left(n^{1.8}\right)$ and the best known lower bound was $\Omega\left(n^{5/3}\right)$. Our new bounds are $O\left(n^{1.7676}\right)$ and $\tilde{\Omega}\left(n^{7/4}\right)$ respectively.

Interestingly, Theorem 1 shows that Argon2i is more depth-robust than Argon2i-A as well as other competing iMHFs such as Catena [FLW13] or Balloon Hashing [CGBS16][3]. Furthermore, Theorem 2 in combination with attacks of Alwen et al. [ABP17a] show that Argon2i enjoys strictly greater cumulative memory complexity than Catena [FLW13] or Balloon Hashing [CGBS16] as well as the earlier version Argon2i-A.

**Theorem 1.** *Argon2i is* $\left(e, \tilde{\Omega}(n^3/e^3), \Omega(n/e)\right)$-*block depth robust with high probability.*

**Theorem 2.** *For any* $\epsilon > 0$ *the cumulative pebbling cost of a random Argon2i DAG $G$ is at most* $\Pi_{cc}^{\parallel}(G) = O(n^{1+a+\epsilon})$ *with high probability, where* $a = \frac{1/3+\sqrt{1+4/9}}{2} \approx 0.7676$.

**Theorem 3.** *With high probability, the cumulative pebbling cost of a random Argon2i DAG $G$ is at least* $\Pi_{cc}^{\parallel}(G) = \tilde{\Omega}\left(n^{7/4}\right)$ *with high probability.*

**Theorem 4.** *If $G$ contains all of the edges of the form $(i-1,i)$ for $1 < i \leq n$ and is $(e,d,b)$-block depth robust, then $G$ is $\left(\frac{e}{2}, d, \frac{eb}{2n}\right)$-fractional depth robust.*

*Techniques.* To upper bound the depth-robustness of Argon2i we use the layered attack of [AB16]. Once we know that Argon2i is depth-reducible for multiple different points $(e_i, d_i)$ along a curve, then we can apply a recursive pebbling attack of Alwen et al. [ABP17a] to obtain the upper bounds on cumulative pebbling complexity from Theorem 2.

Lower bounding the depth-robustness of Argon2i is significantly more challenging. We adapt and generalize techniques from Erdos et al. [EGS75] to reason about the depth-robustness of meta-graph $G_m$ of an Argon2i DAG $G$ (essentially, the meta-graph is formed by compressing each group of $m$ sequential nodes in $G$ into a single point to obtain a new graph with $n' = n/m$ nodes). We prove that for appropriate choice of $m$ and $r^*$ that the meta-graph is a local expander meaning that for every $r \geq r^*$ every node $x \leq (n/m) + 1 - 2r$ the sets $[x, x + r - 1]$ and $[x + r, x + 2r - 1]$ are connected by an expander graph. We then use local expansion to lower bound the depth-robustness of $G_m$. Finally, we can apply a result of Alwen et al. [ABP17a] to translate this bound to a lower bound on the block depth robustness of $G_m$.

Finally, we extend ideas from [ABP17a] to lower bound the cumulative pebbling complexity of an Argon2i DAG. Essentially, we show that any pebbling

---

[3] Argon2i is not as depth-robust as the theoretically optimal constructions of [ABP17a], but at the moment this construction is purely theoretical while Argon2i has been deployed in crypto libraries such as libsodium.

strategy must either keep $\tilde{\Omega}\left(n^{0.75}\right)$ pebbles on the graph during most pebbling rounds or repebble a $\left(\tilde{\Omega}\left(n^{0.75}\right), \tilde{\Omega}\left(n^{0.75}\right)\right)$-depth robust graph $\tilde{\Omega}\left(n^{0.25}\right)$ times. In the first case the cumulative cost is at least $\Omega\left(n \times n^{0.75}\right)$ since we have at least $n$ pebbling rounds and in the second case we also have that cumulative cost is at least $\Omega\left(n^{0.25} \times n^{1.5}\right)$ since the cost to repebble a $\left(e=\tilde{\Omega}\left(n^{0.75}\right), d=\tilde{\Omega}\left(n^{0.75}\right)\right)$-depth robust graph is at least $ed$ [ABP17a].

## 2   Related Work

[ABW03] noticed that that cache-misses are more egalitarian than computation and therefore proposed the use of functions which maximize the number of expensive cache misses, "memory-bound" functions. Percival [Per09] observed that memory costs seemed to be more stable across different architectures and proposed the use of memory-hard functions (MHFs) for password hashing. Since the cost of computing the function is primarily memory related (storing/retrieving data values) and cannot be significantly reduced by constructing an ASIC, there presently seems to be a consensus that memory hard functions are the "right tool" for constructing moderately expensive functions. In fact, all entrants in the password hashing competition claimed some form of memory hardness [PHC]. Percival [Per09] introduced a candidate memory hard function called scrypt, which has subsequently been shown to be vulnerable to side-channel attacks as its computation yields a memory access pattern that is data-dependent (i.e., depends on the secret input/password). On the positive side this function has been shown to require maximum possible cumulative memory complexity to evaluate [ACP+17].

Alwen and Blocki [AB16] gave an attack on Argon2i-A (an earlier version of Argon2i) with cumulative memory complexity $O(n^{1.75} \log n)$ as well as several other iMHF candidates. They later extended the attack to Argon2i-B (the current version) showing that the function has complexity $O(n^{1.8})$ [AB17]. Alwen and Blocki [AB16] also showed that any iMHF has cumulative memory complexity at most $O\left(\frac{n^2 \log \log n}{\log n}\right)$, and Alwen et al. [ABP17a] later constructed a graph with cumulative pebbling complexity at least $\Omega\left(\frac{n^2 \log \log n}{\log n}\right)$. Alwen et al. [ABP17a] also found a "recursive version" of the [AB16] attack which further reduced the cumulative memory complexity of Argon2i-A to $\tilde{O}\left(n^{1.708}\right)$. At the same time they established a lower bound of $\tilde{\Omega}\left(n^{1.\bar{6}}\right)$ for Argon2i-A and Argon2i-B.

Depth-robust graphs have found several applications in theoretical computer science e.g., proving lowerbounds on circuit complexity and Turing machine time [Val77, PR80, Sch82, Sch83]. [MMV13] constructed proofs of sequential work using depth-robust graph and more recently depth-robust graphs were used to prove lower bounds in the domain of proof complexity [AdRNV16]. Recent results [AB16, ABP17a] demonstrate that depth-robustness is a necessary and sufficient property for a secure iMHF. Several constructions of graphs with low indegree exhibiting this asymptotically optimally depth-robustness are given in the literature [EGS75, PR80, Sch82, Sch83, MMV13, ABP17b] but none of these constructions are suitable for practical deployment.

# 3   Preliminaries

Let $\mathbb{N}$ denote the set $\{0, 1, \ldots\}$ and $\mathbb{N}^+ = \{1, 2, \ldots\}$. Let $\mathbb{N}_{\geq c} = \{c, c+1, c+2, \ldots\}$ for $c \in \mathbb{N}$. Define $[n]$ to be the set $\{1, 2, \ldots, n\}$ and $[a, b] = \{a, a+1, \ldots, b\}$ where $a, b \in \mathbb{N}$ with $a \leq b$.

We say that a directed acyclic graph (DAG) $G = (V, E)$ has *size* $n$ if $|V| = n$. We shall assume that $G$ is labeled in topological order. A node $v \in V$ has indegree $\delta = \mathsf{indeg}(v)$ if there exist $\delta$ incoming edges $\delta = |(V \times \{v\}) \cap E|$. More generally, we say that $G$ has indegree $\delta = \mathsf{indeg}(G)$ if the maximum indegree of any node of $G$ is $\delta$. A node with indegree 0 is called a source node and a node with no outgoing edges is called a sink. We use $\mathsf{parents}_G(v) = \{u \in V : (u, v) \in E\}$ to denote the parents of a node $v \in V$. In general, we use $\mathsf{ancestors}_G(v) = \bigcup_{i \geq 1} \mathsf{parents}_G^i(v)$ to denote the set of all ancestors of $v$ — here, $\mathsf{parents}_G^2(v) = \mathsf{parents}_G(\mathsf{parents}_G(v))$ denotes the grandparents of $v$ and $\mathsf{parents}_G^{i+1}(v) = \mathsf{parents}_G(\mathsf{parents}_G^i(v))$. When $G$ is clear from context we will simply write $\mathsf{parents}$ ($\mathsf{ancestors}$). We denote the set of all sinks of $G$ with $\mathsf{sinks}(G) = \{v \in V : \nexists(v, u) \in E\}$ — note that $\mathsf{ancestors}(\mathsf{sinks}(G)) = V$. We often consider the set of all DAGs of equal size $\mathbb{G}_n = \{G = (V, E) : |V| = n\}$ and often will bound the maximum indegree $\mathbb{G}_{n, \delta} = \{G \in \mathbb{G}_n : \mathsf{indeg}(G) \leq \delta\}$. For directed path $p = (v_1, v_2, \ldots, v_z)$ in $G$, its length is the number of nodes it traverses, $\mathsf{length}(p) := z$. The depth $d = \mathsf{depth}(G)$ of DAG $G$ is the length of the longest directed path in $G$.

We will often consider graphs obtained from other graphs by removing subsets of nodes. Therefore if $S \subset V$, then we denote by $G - S$ the DAG obtained from $G$ by removing nodes $S$ and incident edges. The following is a central definition to our work.

**Definition 1 (Block Depth-Robustness).** *Given a node $v$, let $N(v, b) = \{v-b+1, \ldots, v\}$ denote a segment of $b$ consecutive nodes ending at $v$. Similarly, given a set $S \subseteq V$, let $N(S, b) = \cup_{v \in S} N(v, b)$. We say that a DAG $G$ is $(e, d, b)$-block-depth-robust if for every set $S \subseteq V$ of size $|S| \leq e$, we have $\mathsf{depth}(G - N(s, b)) \geq d$. If $b = 1$, we simply say $G$ is $(e, d)$-depth-robust and if $G$ is not $(e, d)$-depth-robust, we say that $G$ is $(e, d)$-depth-reducible.*

Observe when $b > 1$ $(e, d, b)$-block-depth robustness is a strictly stronger notion that $(e, d)$-depth-robustness since the set $N(S, b)$ of nodes that we remove may have size as large as $|N(S, b)| = eb$. Thus, $(e, d, b \geq 1)$-block depth robustness implies $(e, d)$-depth robustness. However, $(e, d)$-depth robustness only implies $(e/b, d, b)$-block depth robustness.

We fix our notation for the parallel graph pebbling game following [AS15].

**Definition 2 (Parallel/Sequential Graph Pebbling).** *Let $G = (V, E)$ be a DAG and let $T \subseteq V$ be a target set of nodes to be pebbled. A pebbling configuration (of $G$) is a subset $P_i \subseteq V$. A legal parallel pebbling of $T$ is a sequence*

$P = (P_0, \ldots, P_t)$ *of pebbling configurations of* $G$ *where* $P_0 = \emptyset$ *and which satisfies conditions 1 & 2 below.*

1. *At some step every target node is pebbled (though not necessarily simultaneously).*

$$\forall x \in T \; \exists z \leq t \; : \; x \in P_z.$$

2. *Pebbles are added only when their predecessors already have a pebble at the end of the previous step.*

$$\forall i \in [t] \; : \; x \in (P_i \setminus P_{i-1}) \; \Rightarrow \; \mathsf{parents}(x) \subseteq P_{i-1}.$$

*We denote with* $\mathcal{P}_{G,T}$ *(and* $\mathcal{P}_{G,T}^{\parallel}$*) the set of all legal (parallel) pebblings of* $G$ *with target set* $T$. *We will be mostly interested in the case where* $T = \mathsf{sinks}(G)$ *and then will simply write* $\mathcal{P}_G^{\parallel}$.

We remark that in the sequential black pebbling game, we face the additional restriction that at most one pebble is place in each step ($\forall i \in [t] \; : \; |P_i \setminus P_{i-1}| \leq 1$), while in the parallel black pebbling game there is no such restriction. The cumulative complexity of a pebbling $P = \{P_0, \ldots, P_t\} \in \mathcal{P}_G^{\parallel}$ is defined to be $\Pi_{cc}(P) = \sum_{i \in [t]} |P_i|$. The cumulative cost of pebbling a graph $G$ a target set $T \subseteq V$ is defined to be

$$\Pi_{cc}^{\parallel}(G, T) = \min_{P \in \mathcal{P}_{G,T}^{\parallel}} \Pi_{cc}(P) \; .$$

When $T = \mathsf{sinks}(G)$, we simplify notation and write $\Pi_{cc}^{\parallel}(G) = \min_{P \in \mathcal{P}_G^{\parallel}} \Pi_{cc}(P)$.

### 3.1  Edge Distribution of Argon2i-B

Definition 3 gives the edge distribution for the single-lane/single-pass version of Argon2i-B. The definition also captures the core of the Argon2i-B edge distribution for multiple lane/multiple-pass variants of Argon2i-B. While we focus on the single-lane/single-pass variant for ease of exposition, we stress that all of our results can be extended to multiple-lane/multiple-pass versions of Argon2i-B provided that the parameters $\tau, \ell = O(1)$ are constants. Here, $\ell$ is the number of lanes and $\tau$ is the number of passes and in practice these parameters $\ell$ and $\tau$ will be *always* be constants.

**Definition 3.** *The Argon2i-B is a graph* $G = (V = [n], E)$, *where* $E = \{(i, i + 1) \; : \; i \in [n-1]\} \cup \{(r(i), i)\}$, *where* $r(i)$ *is a random value distributed as follows:*

$$\Pr[r(i) = j] = \Pr_{x \in [N]} \left[ i \left( 1 - \frac{x^2}{N^2} \right) \in (j - 1, j] \right],$$

*since* $i \left( 1 - \frac{x^2}{N^2} \right)$ *is not always an integer. Note that we assume* $n \ll N$. *In the current Argon2i-B implementation we have,* $N = 2^{32}$. *By contrast, we will have* $n \leq 2^{24}$ *in practice.*

## 3.2   Metagraphs

We will use the notion of a metagraph in our analysis. Fix an arbitrary integer $m \in [n]$ and set $n' = \lfloor n/m \rfloor$. Given a DAG $G$, we will define a DAG $G_m$ called the metagraph of $G$. For this, we use the following sets. For all $i \in [n']$, let $M_i = [(i-1)m+1, im] \subseteq V$. Moreover, we denote the first and last thirds respectively of $M_i$ with

$$M_i^F = \left[ (i-1)m+1, (i-1)m + \left\lfloor \frac{m}{3} \right\rfloor \right] \subseteq M_i \ ,$$

and

$$M_i^L = \left[ (i-1)m + \left\lceil \frac{2m}{3} \right\rceil + 1, im \right] \subseteq M_i \ .$$

We define the metagraph $G_m = (V_m, E_m)$ as follows:

*Nodes:* $V_m$ contains one node $v_i$ per set $M_i$. We call $v_i$ the *simple node* and $M_i$ its *meta-node*.

*Edges:* If the end of a meta-node $M_i^L$ is connected to the beginning $M_j^F$ of another meta-node we connect their simple nodes.

$$V_m = \{v_i : i \in [n']\} \qquad\qquad E_m = \{(v_i, v_j) : E \cap (M_i^L \times M_j^F) \neq \emptyset\}.$$

Claim 1 is a simple extension of a result from [ABP17a], which will be useful in our analysis.

**Claim 1 ([ABP17a], Claim 1).** *If $G_m$ is $(e,d)$-depth robust, then $G$ is $\left( \frac{e}{2}, \frac{dm}{3}, m \right)$-block depth robust.*

# 4   Depth-Reducibility of Argon2iB

In this section, we show that the Argon2i-B is depth reducible with high probability. Then, using results from previous layered attacks (such as [AB16, ABP17a]), we show an upper bound on the computational complexity of Argon2i-B.

**Theorem 5.** *With high probability, the Argon2i-B graph is $\left( e, \Omega\left( \left( \frac{n}{e} \right)^3 \right) \right)$-depth reducible.*

*Proof.* Recall that for node $i$, Argon2i-B creates an edge from $i$ to parent node $i \left( 1 - \frac{x^2}{N^2} \right)$, where $x \in [N]$ is picked uniformly at random. Suppose we remove a node between every $g$ nodes, leaving gap size $g$. Suppose also that we have $L$

layers, each of size $\frac{n}{L}$. Let $i$ be in layer $\alpha$, so that $i \in [(\alpha-1)\frac{n}{L}, \alpha\frac{n}{L}]$. Then the probability that the parent of $i$ is also in layer $\alpha$, for $\alpha > 1$, is

$$
\begin{aligned}
\mathbf{Pr}\left[(\alpha-1)\frac{n}{L} \le i\left(1 - \frac{x^2}{N^2}\right)\right] &\le \mathbf{Pr}\left[(\alpha-1)\frac{n}{iL} \le \left(1 - \frac{x^2}{N^2}\right)\right] \\
&= \mathbf{Pr}\left[\left(\frac{x^2}{N^2}\right) \le \frac{iL - (\alpha-1)n}{iL}\right] \\
&\le \mathbf{Pr}\left[\left(\frac{x^2}{N^2}\right) \le \frac{\alpha n - (\alpha-1)n}{iL}\right] \\
&\le \mathbf{Pr}\left[\left(\frac{x^2}{N^2}\right) \le \frac{n}{(\alpha-1)n}\right] \\
&\le \frac{1}{\sqrt{\alpha-1}}
\end{aligned}
$$

Thus, the expected number of in-layer edges is at most

$$
\frac{n}{L}\left(1 + \frac{1}{\sqrt{1}} + \frac{1}{\sqrt{2}} + \frac{1}{\sqrt{3}} + \dots\right) < \frac{n}{L}\left(2\int_1^L \frac{1}{\sqrt{\alpha-1}}\,d\alpha\right) = 4\frac{n}{\sqrt{L}}.
$$

Hence, if we remove a node between every $g$ nodes, as well as all in-layer edges, we have $e = \frac{n}{g} + \frac{4n}{\sqrt{L}}$. We can apply standard concentration bounds to show that the number of in-layer edges is tightly concentrated around the mean. As a result, the depth is at most $g$ nodes each gap over all $L$ layers, $d = gL$. Therefore, Argon2i-B is $\left(\frac{n}{g} + \frac{4n}{\sqrt{L}}, gL\right)$ depth reducible. Setting $g = \sqrt{L}$ shows $\left(\frac{5n}{\sqrt{L}}, L^{3/2}\right)$ depth reducibility. Consequently, for $e = \frac{5n}{\sqrt{L}}$, then $L^{3/2} = \left(\frac{5n}{e}\right)^3$, and the result follows.

Given function $f$, we say that $G$ is $f$-reducible if $G$ is $(f(d), d)$-reducible for each value $d \in [n]$. Theorem 6, due to Alwen et al. [ABP17a], upper bounds $\Pi_{cc}^{\parallel}(G)$ for any $f$-reducible DAG.

**Theorem 6 ([ABP17a], Theorem 8).** *Let $G$ be a $f$-reducible DAG on $n$ nodes then if $f(d) = \tilde{O}\left(\frac{n}{d^b}\right)$ for some constant $0 < b \le \frac{2}{3}$ then for any constant $\epsilon > 0$, the cumulative pebbling cost of $G$ is at most $\Pi_{cc}^{\parallel}(G) = O(n^{1+a+\epsilon})$, where $a = \frac{1-2b+\sqrt{1+4b^2}}{2}$.*

**Reminder of Theorem 2.** *For any $\epsilon > 0$ the cumulative pebbling cost of a random Argon2i DAG $G$ is at most $\Pi_{cc}^{\parallel}(G) = O(n^{1+a+\epsilon})$ with high probability, where $a = \frac{1/3+\sqrt{1+4/9}}{2} \approx 0.7676$.*

**Proof of Theorem 2:** By Theorem 5, the Argon2i-B graph is $f$-reducible for $b = \frac{1}{3}$ with high probability, and the result follows. $\qquad\square$

# 5  Depth-Robustness for Argon2iB

In this section we show the general block-depth robustness curve of a random Argon2i-B DAG. We will ultimately use these results to lower bound the cumulative pebbling of an Argon2i-B DAG in Sect. 6. Interestingly, our lower bound from Theorem 1 matches the upper bound from Theorem 5 in the last section up to logarithmic factors. Thus, both results are essentially tight.

**Reminder of Theorem 1.** *Argon2i is $\left(e, \tilde{\Omega}(n^3/e^3), \Omega(n/e)\right)$-block depth robust with high probability.*

The notion of a $(\delta, r^*)$-local expander will be useful in our proofs. Definition 4 extends the basic notion of a $\delta$-local expander from [EGS75]. [EGS75] showed that for a sufficiently small constant $\delta$, any $\delta$-local expander is $(\Omega(n), \Omega(n))$-depth robust.

**Definition 4.** *A directed acyclic graph $G$ (with $n$ nodes) is a $(\delta, r^*)$-local expander if for all $r \geq r^*$ and for all $x \leq n-2r+1$ and all $A \subseteq \{x, \ldots, x+r-1\}$, $B \subseteq \{x+r, \ldots, x+2r-1\}$ such that $|A|, |B| \geq \delta r$, we have $E(G) \cap (A \times B) \neq \emptyset$. That is, there exists an edge from some node in $A$ to some node in $B$. If $r^* = 1$, then we say $G$ is a $\delta$-local expander.*

Proof Overview: We set $m = \Omega(n/e)$ and construct a metagraph $G_m$ for a random Argon2i-B graph, and bound the probability that two metanodes in $G_m$ are connected, using Claims 2 and 3. Using these bounds, we show that the metagraph $G_m$ for a random Argon2i-B graph is a $(\delta, r^*)$-local expander with high probability for $r^* = \tilde{\Omega}(e^3/n^2)$ (we will be interested in the realm where $e = \Omega(n^{2/3})$) and some suitably small constant $\delta > 0$. We then divide the metagraph into several layers. With respect to a set $S$, we call a layer "good" if $S$ does not remove too many elements from the layer. We then show that there exists a long path between these layers, which indicates that the remaining graph has high depth.

We now show that the Argon2i-B class of graphs is a $(\delta, r^*)$-local expander with high probability. Given a directed acyclic graph $G$ with $n$ nodes sampled from the Argon2i-B distribution, let $G_m$ be the graph with the metanodes of $G$, where each metanode has size $m = 6n^{1/3} \log n$, so that $G_m$ has $\frac{n}{m} = \frac{n^{2/3}}{6 \log n}$ nodes. First, given two metanodes $x, y \in G_m$ with $x < y$, we bound the probability that for node $i$ in metanode $y$, there exists an edge from $x$ to $i$.

**Claim 2.** *For each $x, y \in G_m$ with $y > x$ and node $i$ in metanode $y$, there exists an edge from the last third of metanode $x$ to node $i$ with probability at least $\frac{1}{12\sqrt{y}\sqrt{y-x+1}}$.*

**Claim 3.** *For any two metanodes $x, y \in G_m$ with $x < y$, the last third of $x$ is connected to the first third of $y$ with probability at least $\frac{m\sqrt{m}}{m\sqrt{m}+36\sqrt{n(y-x+1)}}$.*

This allows us to show that the probability there exist subsets $A \subseteq [x, x + r - 1]$ and $B \subseteq [x + r, x + 2r - 1]$ of size $\delta r$ such that $A$ has no edge to $B$ is at most $e^{-\delta r \log(1 + \sqrt{\log n})} \binom{r}{\delta r}^2$. We then use Stirling's approximation to show this term is negligible, and then apply the union bound over all vertices $x$ and all $r \geq r^*$, which shows that the metagraph $G_m$ (for Argon2i) is a $(\delta, r^*)$-local expander with high probability.

**Lemma 1.** *Let $m = n/(20000e)$ then for $r^* = \tilde{\Omega}(e^3/n^2) = \tilde{\Omega}(n/m^3)$ the meta-graph $G_m$ (for Argon2i) is a $(\delta, r^*)$-local expander with high probability.*

We now divide $G_m$ into layers $L_1, L_2, \ldots L_{n/(mr^*)}$ of size $r^*$ each. Say that a layer $L_i$ is $c$-good with respect to a subset $S \subseteq V(G_m)$ if for all $t \geq 0$ we have

$$\left| S \cap \left( \bigcup_{j=i}^{i+t-1} L_j \right) \right| \leq c \left| \left( \bigcup_{j=i}^{i+t-1} L_j \right) \right|, \text{ and } \left| S \cap \left( \bigcup_{j=i-t+1}^{i} L_j \right) \right| \leq c \left| \left( \bigcup_{j=i-t+1}^{i} L_j \right) \right|,$$

We ultimately want to argue that $G_m - S$ has a path through these good layers.

**Claim 4.** *If $|S| < n/(10000m)$ then at least half of the layers $L_1, L_2, \ldots L_{n/(mr^*)}$ are $(1/1000)$-good with respect to $S$.*

Fixing a set $S$ let $H_{1,S}, H_{2,S}, \ldots,$ denote the $c$-good layers and let $R_{1,S} = H_{1,S} - S$ and let $R_{i+1,S} = \{x \in H_{i+1,S} \mid x \text{ can be reached from some } y \in R_{i,S} \text{ in } G_m - S\}$.

**Lemma 2.** *Suppose that for any $S$ with $|S| \leq e$ and $i \leq n/(2mr^*)$, the set $R_{i,S} \neq \emptyset$. Then $G_m$ is $(e = n/(10000m), n/(2mr^*))$-depth robust and $G$ is $(e = n/(20000m), n/(6r^*), m)$-block depth robust.*

*Proof.* Removing any $e = n/(10000m)$ nodes from $G_m$, there is still a path passing through each good layer since $R_{i,S} \neq \emptyset$ and there are at least $n/(2mr^*)$ good layers. Thus, $G_m$ is $(e = n/(10000m), n/(2mr^*))$-depth robust. Then block depth robustness follows from Claim 1. Intuitively, removing $e = n/(20000m)$ blocks of nodes of size $m$ from $G$ can affect at most $n/(10000m)$ metanodes. Thus, there is a path of length $(m/3)n/(2mr^*) = n/(6r^*)$ through $G$, and so $G$ is $(e = n/(20000m), n/(6r^*), m)$-block depth robust. $\square$

We now show that the number of nodes in each reachable good layer $R_{i,S}$ is relatively high, which allows us to construct a path through the nodes in each of these layers. We first show that if two good layers $H_{i,S}$ and $H_{i+1,S}$ are close to each other, then no intermediate layer contains too many nodes in $S$, so we can use expansion to inductively argue that each intermediate layer has many reachable nodes from $R_{i,S}$, and it follows that $R_{i+1,S}$ is large. On the other hand, if $H_{i,S}$ and $H_{i+1,S}$ have a large number of intermediate layers in between, then the argument becomes slightly more involved. However, we can use local expansion to argue that most of the intermediate layers have the property that most of the nodes in that layer are reachable. We then use a careful argument to show that as we move close to layer $H_{i+1,S}$, the density of layers with this property increases. It then follows that $R_{i+1,S}$ is large. See Fig. 1 for example.

**Lemma 3.** *Suppose that $G_m$ is a $(\delta, r^*)$-local expander with $\delta = 1/16$ and let $S \subseteq V(G_m)$ be given such that $|S| \leq n/(10000m)$. Then, $|R_{i,S}| \geq 7r^*/8$.*

**Proof of Theorem** 1: Let $m = n/20000e$ and let $G$ be a random Argon2i DAG. Lemma 1 shows that the metagraph $G_m$ of a random Argon2i DAG $G$ is a $(\delta, r^*)$-local expander with high probability for $r^* = \tilde{\Omega}\left(e^3/n^2\right)$. Now fix any set $S \subseteq G_m$ of size $|S| \leq e$. Claim 4 now implies we have at least $n/(2mr^*)$ good layers $H_{1,S}, \ldots, H_{n/(2mr^*)}$. Theorem 1 now follows by applying Lemma 3 and Lemma 2. $\qquad\square$

## 6   Cumulative Pebbling Cost of Argon2iB

We now use the depth-robust results to show a lower bound on the cumulative pebbling complexity of Argon2iB. Given a pebbling of $G$, we show in Theorem 7 that if at any point the number of pebbles on $G$ is low, then we must completely re-pebble a depth-robust graph. We then appeal to a result which provides a lower bound on the cost of pebbling a depth-robust graph.

**Theorem 7.** *Suppose $G$ is a DAG that has an edge from $[i, i + b - 1]$ to $\left[j, j + \frac{128n \log n}{b}\right]$ for all $\frac{n}{2} \leq j \leq n - \frac{128n \log n}{b}$ and $1 \leq i \leq \frac{n}{2} - b + 1$. If the subgraph induced by nodes $\left[1, \frac{n}{2}\right]$ is $(e, d, b)$-block depth robust, then the cost to pebble $G$ is at least $\min\left(\frac{en}{8}, \frac{edb}{1024 \log n}\right)$.*

First, we exhibit a property which occurs if the number of pebbles on $G$ is low:

**Lemma 4.** *Suppose $G$ is a DAG that has an edge from $[i, i + b - 1]$ to $\left[j, j + \frac{128n \log n}{b}\right]$ for all $\frac{n}{2} \leq j \leq n - \frac{128n \log n}{b}$ and $1 \leq i \leq \frac{n}{2} - b + 1$. Suppose also that the subgraph induced by nodes $\left[1, \frac{n}{2}\right]$ is $(e, d, b)$-block depth robust. For a subset $S \subset \left[1, \frac{n}{2}\right]$, if $|S| < \frac{e}{2}$, then $H = \mathsf{ancestors}_{G-S}\left(\left[j, j + \frac{128n \log n}{b}\right]\right)$ is $\left(\frac{e}{2}, d\right)$-depth robust.*

*Proof.* Let $G_1$ denote the subgraph induced by first $\frac{n}{2}$ nodes. Note that $H$ contains the graph $W = G_1 - \bigcup_{x \in S}[x - b + 1, x]$ since there exists an edge from each interval $[x - b + 1, x]$. Moreover, $W$ is $\left(\frac{e}{2}, d, b\right)$-block depth robust since $G_1$ is $(e, d, b)$-block depth robust contains only $\frac{e}{2}$ additional blocks. Finally, since $W$ is a subgraph of $H$, then $H$ is $\left(\frac{e}{2}, d\right)$-depth robust.

**Lemma 5 ([ABP17a], Corollary 2).** *Given a DAG $G = (V, E)$ and subsets $S, T \subset V$ such that $S \cap T = \emptyset$, let $G' = G - (V/\mathsf{ancestors}_{G-S}(T))$. If $G'$ is $(e, d)$-depth robust, then the cost of pebbling $G - S$ with target set $T$ is $\Pi^{\parallel}_{cc}(G - S, T) > ed$.*

We now prove Theorem 7.

**Proof of Theorem 7:** For each interval of length $\frac{256n \log n}{b}$, let $t_1$ denote the first time we pebble the first node, let $t_2$ denote the first time we pebble the middle node of the interval, and let $t_3$ denote the first time we pebble the last node of the interval. We show $\sum_{t \in [t_1, t_3]} |P_t| \geq \min\{en \log(n)/(2b), ed/2\}$. Then a pebbling do at least one of the following:

1. Keep $\frac{e}{2}$ pebbles on $G$ for at least $\frac{128n \log n}{b}$ steps (i.e., during the entire interval $[t_1, t_2]$)
2. Pay $\left(\frac{e}{2}\right) d$ to repebble a $(e/2, d)$-depth robust DAG during before round $t_3$. (Lemma 4)

In the first case, $|P_t| \geq \frac{e}{2}$ for each $t \in [t_1, t_2]$, which is at least $\frac{128n \log n}{b}$ time steps. In the second case, there exists $t \in [t_1, t_2]$ such that $|P_t| < \frac{e}{2}$. Then by Lemmas 4 and 5, $\sum_{t \in [t_1, t_3]} |P_t| \geq \frac{ed}{2}$. The cost of the first case is $\frac{64en \log n}{b}$ and the cost of the second case is $\frac{ed}{2}$. Since the last $n/2$ nodes can be partitioned into $(n/2)/(256(n/b) \log n) = b/(512 \log n)$ such intervals, then the cost is at least $\left(\frac{b}{512 \log n}\right) \min \left(\frac{64en \log n}{2b}, \frac{ed}{2}\right)$, and the result follows. $\qquad\square$

We now provide a lower bound on the probability that there exists an edge between two nodes in the Argon2iB graph.

**Claim 5.** *Let $i, j \in [n]$ be given $(i \neq j)$ and let $G$ be a random Argon2iB DAG on $n$ nodes. There exists an edge from node $j$ to $i$ in $G$ with probability at least $\frac{1}{4n}$.*

Using the bound on the probability of two nodes being connected, we can also lower bound the probability that two intervals are connected in the Argon2iB graph.

**Lemma 6.** *Let $b \geq 1$ be a constant. Then with high probability, an Argon2iB DAG has the property that for all pairs $i, j$ such that $\frac{n}{2} \leq j \leq n - \frac{128n \log n}{b}$ and $1 \leq i \leq \frac{n}{2} - b + 1$ there is an edge from $[i, i + b - 1]$ to $\left[j, j + \frac{128n \log n}{b}\right]$.*

*Proof.* By Claim 5, the probability that there exists an edge from a specific node $y \in [i, i + b - 1]$ to a specific node $x \in \left[j, j + \frac{128n \log n}{b}\right]$ is at least $\frac{1}{4n}$. Then the expected number of edges from $[i, i + b - 1]$ to $\left[j, j + \frac{128n \log n}{b}\right]$ is at least $\frac{1}{4n}(128n \log n) = 32 \log n$. By Chernoff bounds, the probability that there exists no edge from $[i, i + b - 1]$ to $\left[j, j + \frac{128n \log n}{b}\right]$ is at most $\frac{1}{n^4}$. Taking a union bound over all possible intervals, the graph of Argon2iB is a DAG that has an edge from $[i, i + b - 1]$ to $\left[j, j + \frac{128n \log n}{b}\right]$ and all $\frac{n}{2} + j \leq n - \frac{128n \log n}{b}$ and $1 \leq i \leq \frac{n}{2} - b + 1$ with probability at least $1 - \frac{1}{n^2}$.

We now have all the tools to lower bound the computational complexity of Argon2iB.

**Reminder of Theorem 3.** *With high probability, the cumulative pebbling cost of a random Argon2i DAG $G$ is at least $\Pi_{cc}^{\|}(G) = \tilde{\Omega}\left(n^{7/4}\right)$ with high probability.*

**Proof of Theorem 3:** The result follows Theorem 7, Lemma 6, and setting $e = d = n^{3/4}$ and $b = n^{1/4}$. $\qquad\square$

# 7    Fractional Depth-Robustness

Thus far, our analysis has focused on Argon2i, the data-independent mode of operation for Argon2. In this section, we argue that our analysis of the depth-robustness of Argon2i has important security implications for both data-dependent modes of operation: Argon2 and Argon2id. In particular, we prove a generic relationship between block-depth robustness and fractional depth-robustness of any block-depth robust DAG such as Argon2i. Intuitively, fractional depth-robustness says that even if we delete $e$ vertices from the DAG that a large fraction of the remaining vertices have depth $\geq d$ in the remaining graph.

In the context of a dMHF fractional depth-robustness is a significant metric because the attacker will be repeatedly challenged for a random data-label. Intuitively, if the attacker reduces memory usage and only stores $e$ data labels, then there is a good chance that the attacker will need time $\geq d$ to respond to each challenge. It is known that SCRYPT has cumulative memory complexity $\Omega(n^2)$. However, SCRYPT allows for dramatic space-time trade-off attacks (e.g., attackers could evaluate SCRYPT with memory $O(1)$ if they are willing to run in time $O(n^2)$). Our results are compelling evidence for the hypothesis that similar time space-trade offs are not possible for Argon2 or Argon2id without incurring a dramatic increase in cumulative memory complexity (We believe that providing a formal proof of this claim could be a fruitful avenue of future research). In particular, our results provide strong evidence that any evaluation algorithm either (1) requires space $\Omega\left(n^{0.99}\right)$ for at least $n$ steps, or (2) has cumulative memory complexity $\omega\left(n^2\right)$ since it should take time $\tilde{\Omega}\left(n^3/e^3\right) = \tilde{\Omega}\left(n^{2\epsilon} \times \frac{n}{e}\right)$ on average to respond to a random challenge on with any configuration with space $e = O(n^{1-\epsilon})$. By contrast for SCRYPT, it may only take time $\Omega(n/e)$ to respond to a random challenge starting from a configuration with space $e$ — while this is sufficient to ensure cumulative memory complexity $\Omega(n^2)$, it does not prevent space-time trade-off attacks.

**Definition 5.** *Recall that the depth of a specific vertex $v$ in graph $G$, denoted $\mathsf{depth}(v, G)$ is the length of the longest path to $v$ in $G$. We say that a DAG $G = (V, E)$ is $(e, d, f)$-fractionally depth robust if for all $S \subseteq V$ with $|S| \leq e$, we have*

$$|\{v \in V : \mathsf{depth}(v, G - S) \geq d\}| \geq f \cdot n.$$

Then we have the following theorem which relates fractional depth-robustness and block depth-robustness.

**Reminder of Theorem 4.** *If $G$ contains all of the edges of the form $(i - 1, i)$ for $1 < i \leq n$ and is $(e, d, b)$-block depth robust, then $G$ is $\left(\frac{e}{2}, d, \frac{eb}{2n}\right)$-fractional depth robust.*

**Proof of Theorem 4:** Suppose, by way of contradiction, that $G$ is not $\left(\frac{e}{2}, d, \frac{eb}{2n}\right)$-fractionally depth robust. Then let $S$ be a set of size $\frac{e}{2}$ such that at most $\frac{eb}{2n}$ nodes in $G$ have depth at least $d$. Now consider the following procedure:

Let $S' = \emptyset$.

Repeat until $\mathsf{depth}\left(G - \left(\bigcup_{v \in S'}[v, v+b-1] \cup S\right)\right) < d$:

(1) Let $v$ be the topologically first node s.t

$$\mathsf{depth}\left(v, G - \left(S \cup \bigcup_{v \in S'}[v, v+b-1]\right)\right) \geq d .$$

(2) Set $S' = S' \cup \{v\}$.

Return $S' \cup \left(S \setminus \bigcup_{v \in S'}[v, v+b-1]\right)$.

We remark that during round $i$, the interval $[v, v+b-1]$ either (1) covers $b$ nodes at depth at least $d$ in $G - S_i$, or (2) covers some node in the set $S_0$. Since at most $\frac{eb}{2}$ nodes in $G - (S_i \cup S)$ have depth at least $d$ the first case can happen at most $e/2$ times. Similarly, the second case can happen at most $|S| = \frac{e}{2}$ times, and each time we hit this case we decrease the size of the set $\left|S \setminus \bigcup_{v \in S'}[v, v+b-1]\right|$ by *at least* one. Thus, the above procedure returns a set $S'$ of size $|S'| \leq e$ such that $\mathsf{depth}(G - \bigcup_{v \in S'}[v, v+b-1]) < d$. But then, the longest path in the resulting graph is at most $d - 1$, which contradicts that $G$ is $(e, d, b)$-block depth robust. $\qquad\square$

**Corollary 1.** *Argon2i is $\left(e, \tilde{\Omega}(n^3/e^3), \Omega(1)\right)$-fractional depth robust with high probability.*

**Acknowledgements.** We would like to thank Ling Ren and anonymous TCC reviewers for comments that have helped us to improve the presentation of the paper. The work was supported by the National Science Foundation under NSF Awards #1649515 and #1704587. The opinions expressed in this paper are those of the authors and do not necessarily reflect those of the National Science Foundation.

## A    Missing Proofs

**Reminder of Claim 2.** *For each $x, y \in G_m$ with $y > x$ and node $i$ in metanode $y$, there exists an edge from the last third of metanode $x$ to node $i$ with probability at least $\frac{1}{12\sqrt{y}\sqrt{y-x+1}}$.*

**Proof of Claim 2:** Recall that for node $i$, Argon2iB creates an edge from $i$ to parent node $i\left(1 - \frac{k^2}{N^2}\right)$, where $k \in [N]$ is picked uniformly at random. Thus, for nodes $i, j \in G$ with $i > j$, there exists an edge from node $j$ to $i$ with probability at least

$$\mathbf{Pr}\left[(x-1)m+1 \le i\left(1-\frac{k^2}{N^2}\right) \le \left(x-1+\frac{1}{3}\right)m\right]$$

$$= \mathbf{Pr}\left[\left(x-1+\frac{1}{6}\right)m \le ym\left(1-\frac{k^2}{N^2}\right) \le \left(x-1+\frac{1}{3}\right)m\right]$$

$$\ge \mathbf{Pr}\left[\frac{y-x+\frac{5}{6}}{y} \ge \frac{k^2}{N^2} \ge \frac{y-x+\frac{2}{3}}{y}\right]$$

$$\ge \sqrt{\frac{y-x+\frac{5}{6}}{y}} - \sqrt{\frac{y-x+\frac{2}{3}}{y}}$$

$$\ge \frac{1}{6\sqrt{y}(2\sqrt{y-x+1})} = \frac{1}{12\sqrt{y}\sqrt{y-x+1}}.$$

□

**Reminder of Claim 3.** *For any two metanodes $x, y \in G_m$ with $x < y$, the last third of $x$ is connected to the first third of $y$ with probability at least* $\frac{m\sqrt{m}}{m\sqrt{m}+36\sqrt{n(y-x+1)}}$.

**Proof of Claim 3:** Let $p$ be the probability that the final third of $x$ is connected to the first third of $y$. Let $E_i$ be the event that the $i^{th}$ node of metanode $y$ is the first node in $y$ to which there exists an edge from the last third of metanode $x$, so that by Claim 2, $\mathbf{Pr}[E_1] \ge \frac{1}{12\sqrt{y}\sqrt{y-x+1}}$. Note that furthermore, $\mathbf{Pr}[E_i]$ is the probability that there exists an edge from the last third of metanode $x$ to the $i^{th}$ node of metanode $y$ and no previous metanode of $y$. Hence, $\mathbf{Pr}[E_i] \ge \frac{1}{12\sqrt{y}\sqrt{y-x+1}}(1-p)$. Thus,

$$p = \mathbf{Pr}[E_1] + \mathbf{Pr}[E_2] + \ldots + \mathbf{Pr}[E_{m/3}]$$

$$\ge \left(\frac{m}{3}\right)\frac{1}{12\sqrt{y}\sqrt{y-x+1}}(1-p).$$

Setting $\alpha = \left(\frac{m}{3}\right)\frac{1}{12\sqrt{y}\sqrt{y-x+1}}$, then it follows that $p + \alpha p \ge \alpha$, so that $p \ge \frac{\alpha}{1+\alpha}$. Since $y \le \frac{n}{m}$,

$$p \ge \frac{m/36}{\sqrt{y(y-x+1)}+m/36} \ge \frac{m\sqrt{m}}{m\sqrt{m}+36\sqrt{n(y-x+1)}}$$

□

**Reminder of Lemma 1.** *Let $m = n/(20000e)$ then for $r^* = \tilde{\Omega}(e^3/n^2) = \tilde{\Omega}(n/m^3)$ the metagraph $G_m$ (for Argon2i) is a $(\delta, r^*)$-local expander with high probability.*

**Proof of Lemma 1:** Let $r \ge r^*$ and $A \subseteq \{x, \ldots, x+r-1\}$, $B \subseteq \{x+r, \ldots, x+2r-1\}$ be subsets of size $\delta r$, for some $x \le n-2r+1$. By Stirling's approximation,

$$\sqrt{2\pi}r^{r+1/2}e^{-r} \le r! \le er^{r+1/2}e^{-r}.$$

Then it follows that

$$\binom{r}{\delta r} \leq \frac{er^{r+1/2}e^{-r}}{2\pi(\delta r)^{\delta r+1/2}(r-\delta r)^{r-\delta r+1/2}e^{-r}}$$

$$\leq \frac{e}{2\pi\delta^{\delta r+1/2}(1-\delta)^{r-\delta r+1/2}\sqrt{r}}$$

$$= \frac{e^{1+\delta r\log\frac{1}{\delta}+(r-\delta r)\log\frac{1}{1-\delta}}}{2\pi\sqrt{r\delta(1-\delta)}}$$

For two specific metanodes in $A$ and $B$, the probability the pair is connected is at least $\frac{m\sqrt{m}}{m\sqrt{m}+36\sqrt{nr}}$ by Claim 3. For $36\sqrt{nr} \geq m\sqrt{m}$, the probability is at least $\frac{m\sqrt{m}}{72\sqrt{nr}}$ (otherwise, for $36\sqrt{nr} < m\sqrt{m}$, the probability is at least $\frac{1}{2} > \frac{m\sqrt{m}}{72\sqrt{nr}}$). Now, let $p$ be the probability that there exists an edge from $A$ to a specific metanode in $B$. Furthermore, let $E_i$ be the event that the $i^{th}$ metanode of $A$ is the first node from which there exists an edge from a specific metanode of $B$, so that, $\mathbf{Pr}\,[E_1] \geq \frac{m\sqrt{m}}{72\sqrt{nr}}$. For $E_i$ to occurs, that must exist an edge from the last third of metanode $x$ to the $i^{th}$ node of metanode $y$ and no previous metanode of $y$, so then $\mathbf{Pr}\,[E_i] \geq \frac{m\sqrt{m}}{72\sqrt{nr}}(1-p)$. Thus,

$$p = \mathbf{Pr}\,[E_1] + \mathbf{Pr}\,[E_2] + \ldots + \mathbf{Pr}\,[E_{|A|}]$$

$$\geq (\delta r)\frac{m\sqrt{m}}{72\sqrt{nr}}(1-p).$$

Since $r \geq r^* = \tilde{\Omega}(n/m^3)$, it follows for an appropriate choice of $r'$ that $p \geq \sqrt{\log n}(1-p)$. Thus, $p \geq \frac{\sqrt{\log n}}{1+\sqrt{\log n}}$ is the probability that there exists an edge from $A$ to a specific metanode in $B$.

Now, taking the probability over all $\delta r$ metanodes in $B$, the probability that $A$ and $B$ are not connected is at most

$$(1-p)^{\delta r} = \left(\frac{1}{1+\sqrt{\log n}}\right)^{\delta r}$$

$$= e^{-\delta r\log(1+\sqrt{\log n})}$$

Since there are $\binom{r}{\delta r}^2$ such sets $A$ and $B$, the probability that there exists $A$ and $B$ in the above intervals which are not connected by an edge is at most

$$e^{-\delta r\log(1+\sqrt{\log n})}\binom{r}{\delta r}^2$$

by a simple union bound. Then from the above Stirling approximation, the probability is at most

$$\exp\left(2 + 2\delta r\log\frac{1}{\delta} + 2(r-\delta r)\log\frac{1}{1-\delta} - \delta r\log(1+\sqrt{\log n})\right)\frac{1}{4\pi^2 r\delta(1-\delta)},$$

where $-\delta r \log(1 + \sqrt{\log n})$ is the dominant term in the exponent. Again taking $r \geq r^* = \Omega\left(\frac{n \log n}{m^3}\right)$, the probability that $G_m$ is not a $\delta$-local expander is at most

$$\mathbf{Pr}\left[\exists r \geq r^*, x, A, B \text{ with no edge}\right] \leq n \sum_{r \geq r^*} \frac{e^{-\Omega(r \log \log n)}}{4\pi^2 r \delta (1 - \delta)}$$

$$= o\left(\frac{1}{n}\right).$$

Thus, $G_m$ is a $\delta$-local expander with high probability.          $\square$

**Reminder of Claim 4.** *If $|S| < n/(10000m)$ then at least half of the layers $L_1, L_2, \ldots L_{n/(mr^*)}$ are $(1/1000)$-good with respect to $S$.*

**Proof of Claim 4:** Let $i_1$ be the index of the first layer $L_{i_1}$ such that for some $x_1 > 0$ we have $\left|S \cap \left(\bigcup_{t=i_1}^{i_1+x_1-1} L_t\right)\right| \geq c \left|\left(\bigcup_{t=i}^{i_1+x_1-1} L_t\right)\right|$. Once $i_1 < \ldots < i_{j-1}$ and $x_1, \ldots, x_{j-1}$ have been defined we let $i_j$ be the least layer such that $i_j > i_{j-1} + x_{j-1}$ and there exists $x_j > 0$ such that $\left|S \cap \left(\bigcup_{t=i_j}^{i_j+x_j-1} L_t\right)\right| \geq c \left|\left(\bigcup_{t=i_j}^{i_j+x_j-1} L_t\right)\right|$ (assuming that such a pair $i_j, x_j$ exists). Let $i_1 + x_1 < i_2$, $i_2 + x_2 < i_3, \ldots i_{k-1} + x_{k-1} < i_k$ denote a maximal such sequence and let

$$F = \bigcup_{t=1}^{k} [i_t, x_t - 1] .$$

Observe that by construction of $F$ we have $|S| \geq c \left|\bigcup_{j \in F} L_j\right| = c|F|r^*$, which means that $|F| \leq |S|/(cr^*) = n/(10000cmr^*)$. Similarly, we can define a maximal sequence $i_1^* > \ldots > i_{k^*}^*$ such that $i_j^* - x_j^* > i_{j+1}^*$ and $\left|S \cap \left(\bigcup_{t=i_j^*-x_j^*+1}^{i_j^*} L_t\right)\right| \geq c \left|\left(\bigcup_{t=i_j^*-x_j^*+1}^{i_j^*} L_t\right)\right|$ for each $j$. A similar argument shows that $|B| \leq |S|/(cr^*) = n/(10000cmr^*)$, where $B = \bigcup_{t=1}^{k} [i_t^* - x_t^* + 1, i_t^*]$. Finally, we note that if $L_i$ is not $c$-good then $i \in F \cup B$. Thus, at most $n/(5000cmr^*)$ layers are not $c$-good, which means that the number of $c = (1/1000)$-good layers is at least

$$\frac{n}{mr^*} - \frac{n}{5mr^*} \geq \frac{n}{2mr^*} .$$

$\square$

**Reminder of Lemma 3.** *Suppose that $G_m$ is a $(\delta, r^*)$-local expander with $\delta = 1/16$ and let $S \subseteq V(G_m)$ be given such that $|S| \leq n/(10000m)$. Then, $|R_{i,S}| \geq 7r^*/8$.*

**Proof of Lemma 3:** We prove by induction. For the base case, we set $R_1 = H_{1,S} - S$. Thus, $|R_1| = |H_{1,S} - S| \geq r^* - (1/1000)r^*$, since $H_{1,S}$ is $(1/1000)$-good with respect to $S$.

Now, suppose that $|R_j| \geq 7r^*/8$ for each $j \leq i$. If layers $H_{i,S}$ and $H_{i+1,S}$ are within 100 intermediate layers, then since $H_{i,S}$ is $(1/1000)$-good with respect to $S$, it follows that at most $100/1000 = 1/10$ of the nodes in $H_{i+1,S}$ are also in $S$. Moreover, since $G_m$ is a $(\delta, r^*)$-local expander with $\delta = 1/16$, then at most $\delta r^*$ additional nodes in $H_{i+1,S}$ are not reachable from $H_{i,S}$. Therefore,

$$|R_{i+1,S}| \geq |H_{i+1,S} - S| - \delta r^* \geq (1 - 1/1000 - 1/16)r^* \geq (7/8)r^* \ .$$

Otherwise, suppose more than 100 intermediate layers separate layers $H_{i,S}$ and $H_{i+1,S}$. Figure 1 provides a visual illustration of our argument in this second case. Let $Y_1, \ldots, Y_k$ denote the intermediate layers between $H_{i,S}$ and $H_{i+1,S}$, so that $k > 100$. Let $j$ be the integer such that $2^j \leq k < 2^{j+1}$. Since $H_{i,S}$ is $(1/1000)$-good with respect to $S$, at most $2^{j+1}r^*/1000$ nodes in $Y_1 \cup \ldots \cup Y_k$ can be in $S$. Thus, at least $(1/8)$-fraction of the nodes in $Y_{k-2^{j-1}}, \ldots, Y_{k-2^{j-2}+1}$ are reachable from $R_i$. We now show this is sufficient.

Suppose that at least $(1/8)$-fraction of the nodes in $Y_{k-2u}, \ldots, Y_{k-u-1}$ are reachable from $R_i$. Then at least $(7/8)$-fraction of nodes in $Y_{k-u}, \ldots, Y_{k-u/2}$ are reachable from $R_i$, since layer $H_{i+1}$ is both $(1/1000)$-good and a $(\delta, r^*)$-local expander with $\delta = 1/16$. (Note: we are now using layer $H_{i+1}$, *not layer* $H_i$). It follows that at least $(7/8)$-fraction of the nodes in $Y_k$ are reachable from $R_i$. Again,

$$|R_{i+1,S}| \geq |H_{i+1,S} - S| - \delta r^* \geq (1 - 1/1000 - 1/16)r^* \geq (7/8)r^* \ .$$

Thus, at least $(7/8)$-fraction of the nodes in $H_{i+1}$ are reachable, and so $|R_{i+1,S}| \geq (7/8)r^*$. $\qquad\square$

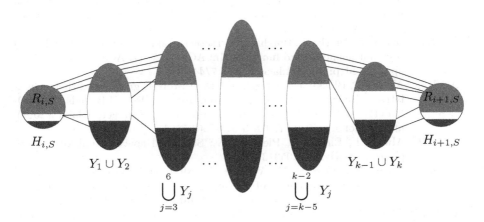

**Fig. 1.** The red area represents deleted nodes in the set $S \subseteq V(G_m)$. Because the layers $H_{i,S}$ and $H_{i+1,S}$ are both $(1/1000)$-good with respect to $S$ the number of deleted nodes in each oval cannot be too large. The green area in each oval represents nodes that are reachable from $R_{i,S}$ and are not in the deleted set $S$; other nodes are colored white. An inductive argument shows that the number of white nodes in each oval cannot be too large since $G_m$ is a local expander. (Color figure online)

**Reminder of Claim** 5. *Let $i, j \in [n]$ be given $(i \neq j)$ and let $G$ be a random Argon2iB DAG on $n$ nodes. There exists an edge from node $j$ to $i$ in $G$ with probability at least $\frac{1}{4n}$.*

**Proof of Claim** 5: Recall that for node $i$, Argon2iB creates an edge from $i$ to parent node $i\left(1 - \frac{x^2}{N^2}\right)$, where $x \in [N]$ is picked uniformly at random. Thus, for $i, j \in G$ with $i > j$, there exists an edge from node $j$ to $i$ with probability at least

$$\mathbf{Pr}\left[j \leq i\left(1 - \frac{x^2}{N^2}\right) \leq j + \frac{1}{2}\right] = \mathbf{Pr}\left[\frac{i-j}{i} \geq \frac{x^2}{N^2} \geq \frac{i-j-\frac{1}{2}}{i}\right]$$

$$\geq \mathbf{Pr}\left[1 \geq \frac{x^2}{N^2} \geq 1 - \frac{1}{2n}\right]$$

$$\geq \frac{1}{4n}. \qquad \square$$

# References

[AABSJ14] Almeida, L.C., Andrade, E.R., Barreto, P.S.L.M., Lyra Jr., M.A.S.: Password-based key derivation with tunable memory and processing costs. J. Cryptographic Eng. **4**(2), 75–89 (2014)

[AB16] Alwen, J., Blocki, J.: Efficiently computing data-independent memory-hard functions. In: Robshaw, M., Katz, J. (eds.) CRYPTO 2016. LNCS, vol. 9815, pp. 241–271. Springer, Heidelberg (2016). https://doi.org/10.1007/978-3-662-53008-5_9

[AB17] Alwen, J., Blocki, J.: Towards practical attacks on argon2i and balloon hashing. In: 2nd IEEE European Symposium on Security and Privacy (EuroS&P 2017) (2017)

[ABH17] Alwen, J., Blocki, J., Harsha, B.: Practical graphs for optimal side-channel resistant memory-hard functions. In: ACM CCS 17. ACM Press (2017, to appear). http://eprint.iacr.org/2017/443

[ABP17a] Alwen, J., Blocki, J., Pietrzak, K.: Depth-robust graphs and their cumulative memory complexity. In: Coron, J.-S., Nielsen, J.B. (eds.) EUROCRYPT 2017. LNCS, vol. 10212, pp. 3–32. Springer, Cham (2017). https://doi.org/10.1007/978-3-319-56617-7_1

[ABP17b] Alwen, J., Blocki, J., Pietrzak, K.: Sustained space complexity. arXiv preprint: arXiv:1705.05313 (2017)

[ABW03] Abadi, M., Burrows, M., Wobber, T.: Moderately hard, memory-bound functions. In: Proceedings of the Network and Distributed System Security Symposium, NDSS 2003, San Diego, California, USA (2003)

[ACP+17] Alwen, J., Chen, B., Pietrzak, K., Reyzin, L., Tessaro, S.: Scrypt is maximally memory-hard. In: Coron, J.-S., Nielsen, J.B. (eds.) EUROCRYPT 2017. LNCS, vol. 10212, pp. 33–62. Springer, Cham (2017). https://doi.org/10.1007/978-3-319-56617-7_2

[AdRNV16] Alwen, J., de Rezende, S.F., Nordstrm, J., Vinyals, M.: Cumulative space in black-white pebbling and resolution. In: Proceedings of the 2016 ACM Conference on Innovations in Theoretical Computer Science, Berkeley, California USA, pp. 9–11, January 2017

[AS15]    Alwen, J., Serbinenko, V.: High parallel complexity graphs and memory-hard functions. In: Proceedings of the Eleventh Annual ACM Symposium on Theory of Computing, STOC 2015 (2015). http://eprint.iacr.org/2014/238

[BDK15]   Biryukov, A., Dinu, D., Khovratovich, D.: Fast and tradeoff-resilient memory-hard functions for cryptocurrencies and password hashing. Cryptology ePrint Archive, Report 2015/430 (2015). http://eprint.iacr.org/2015/430

[BDK16]   Biryukov, A., Dinu, D., Khovratovich, D.: Argon2 password hash. Version 1.3 (2016). https://www.cryptolux.org/images/0/0d/Argon2.pdf

[BDKJ16]  Biryukov, A., Dinu, D., Khovratovich, D., Josefsson, S.: The memory-hard Argon2 password hash and proof-of-work function. Internet-Draft draft-irtf-cfrg-argon2-00, Internet Engineering Task Force, March 2016

[Ber]     Bernstein, D.J.: Cache-Timing Attacks on AES (2005). https://cr.yp.to/antiforgery/cachetiming-20050414.pdf

[CGBS16]  Corrigan-Gibbs, H., Boneh, D., Schechter, S.: Balloon hashing: Provably space-hard hash functions with data-independent access patterns. Cryptology ePrint Archive, Report 2016/027, Version: 20160601:225540 (2016). http://eprint.iacr.org/

[CJMS14]  Chang, D., Jati, A., Mishra, S., Sanadhya, S.K.: Rig: A simple, secure and flexible design for password hashing version 2.0. (2014)

[Cox14]   Cox, B.: Twocats (and skinnycat): A compute time and sequential memory hard password hashing scheme. Password Hashing Competition. v0 edn. (2014)

[EGS75]   Erdös, P., Graham, R.L., Szemeredi, E.: On sparse graphs with dense long paths. Technical report, Stanford, CA, USA (1975)

[FLW13]   Forler, C., Lucks, S., Wenzel, J.: Catena: A memory-consuming password scrambler. IACR Cryptology ePrint Archive 2013:525 (2013)

[MMV13]   Mahmoody, M., Moran, T., Vadhan, S.P.: Publicly verifiable proofs of sequential work. In: Kleinberg, R.D. (ed.) Innovations in Theoretical Computer Science, ITCS 2013, Berkeley, CA, USA, 9–12 January, 2013, pp. 373–388. ACM (2013)

[Per09]   Percival, C.: Stronger key derivation via sequential memory-hard functions. In: BSDCan 2009 (2009)

[PHC]     Password hashing competition. https://password-hashing.net/

[Pin14]   Pintér, K.: Gambit - A sponge based, memory hard key derivation function. Submission to Password Hashing Competition (PHC) (2014)

[PR80]    Paul, W.J., Reischuk, R.: On alternation II. A graph theoretic approach to determinism versus nondeterminism. Acta Inf. **14**, 391–403 (1980)

[Sch82]   Schnitger, G.: A family of graphs with expensive depth reduction. Theor. Comput. Sci. **18**, 89–93 (1982)

[Sch83]   Schnitger, G.: On depth-reduction and grates. In: 24th Annual Symposium on Foundations of Computer Science, Tucson, Arizona, USA, 7–9 November, 1983, pp. 323–328. IEEE Computer Society (1983)

[Val77]   Valiant, L.G.: Graph-theoretic arguments in low-level complexity. In: Gruska, J. (ed.) MFCS 1977. LNCS, vol. 53, pp. 162–176. Springer, Heidelberg (1977). https://doi.org/10.1007/3-540-08353-7_135

[Wu15]    Wu, H.: POMELO - A Password Hashing Algorithm (2015)

# Bandwidth Hard Functions for ASIC Resistance

Ling Ren[(⊠)] and Srinivas Devadas

Massachusetts Institute of Technology, Cambridge, MA, USA
{renling,devadas}@mit.edu

**Abstract.** Cryptographic hash functions have wide applications including password hashing, pricing functions for spam and denial-of-service countermeasures and proof of work in cryptocurrencies. Recent progress on ASIC (Application Specific Integrated Circuit) hash engines raise concerns about the security of the above applications. This leads to a growing interest in ASIC resistant hash function and ASIC resistant proof of work schemes, i.e., those that do not give ASICs a huge advantage. The standard approach towards ASIC resistance today is through memory hard functions or memory hard proof of work schemes. However, we observe that the memory hardness approach is an incomplete solution. It only attempts to provide resistance to an ASIC's area advantage but overlooks the more important energy advantage. In this paper, we propose the notion of bandwidth hard functions to reduce an ASIC's energy advantage. CPUs cannot compete with ASICs for energy efficiency in computation, but we can rely on memory accesses to reduce an ASIC's energy advantage because energy costs of memory accesses are comparable for ASICs and CPUs. We propose a model for hardware energy cost that has sound foundations in practice. We then analyze the bandwidth hardness property of ASIC resistant candidates. We find scrypt, Catena-BRG and Balloon are bandwidth hard with suitable parameters. Lastly, we observe that a capacity hard function is not necessarily bandwidth hard, with a stacked double butterfly graph being a counterexample.

## 1 Introduction

Cryptographic hash functions have a wide range of applications in both theory and practice. Two of the major applications are password protection and more recently proof of work. It is well known that service providers should store hashes of user passwords. This way, when a password hash database is breached, an adversary still has to invert the hash function to obtain user passwords. Proof of work, popularized by its usage in the Bitcoin cryptocurrency for reaching consensus [43], has earlier been used as "pricing functions" to defend against email spam and denial-of-service attacks [19, 30].

In the last few years, driven by the immense economic incentives in the Bitcoin mining industry, there has been amazing progress in the development of ASIC (Application Specific Integrated Circuit) hash units. These ASIC hash engines are specifically optimized for computing SHA-256 hashes and offer

© International Association for Cryptologic Research 2017
Y. Kalai and L. Reyzin (Eds.): TCC 2017, Part I, LNCS 10677, pp. 466–492, 2017.
https://doi.org/10.1007/978-3-319-70500-2_16

incredible speed and energy efficiency that CPUs cannot hope to match. A state-of-the-art ASIC Bitcoin miner [1] computes 13 trillion hashes at about 0.1 nJ energy cost per hash. This is roughly 200,000× faster and 40,000× more energy efficient than a state-of-the-art multi-core CPU. These ASIC hash engines call the security of password hashing and pricing functions into question. For ASIC-equipped adversaries, brute-forcing a password database seems quite feasible, and pricing functions are nowhere near deterrent if they are to stay manageable for honest CPU users. ASIC mining also raises some concerns about the decentralization promise of Bitcoin as mining power concentrates to ASIC-equipped miners.

As a result, there is an increasing interest in ASIC resistant hash functions and ASIC resistant proof of work schemes, i.e., those that do not give ASICs a huge advantage. For example, in the recent Password Hashing Competition [34], the winner Argon2 [21] and three of the four "special recognitions" — Catena [35], Lyra2 [9] and yescrypt [47] — claimed ASIC resistance. More studies on ASIC resistant hash function and proof of work include [10–15, 18, 23, 25, 39, 46, 49, 53].

The two fundamental advantages of ASICs over CPUs (or general purpose GPUs) are their smaller area and better energy efficiency when speed is normalized. The speed advantage can be considered as a derived effect of the area and energy advantage (cf. Sect. 3.1). A chip's area is approximately proportional to its manufacturing cost. From an economic perspective, this means when we normalize speed, an adversary purchasing ASICs can lower its initial investment (capital cost) due to area savings and its recurring electricity cost due to energy savings, compared to a CPU user. To achieve ASIC resistance is essentially to reduce ASICs' area and energy efficiency advantages.

Most prior works on ASIC resistance have thus far followed the *memory hard function* approach, first proposed by Percival [46]. This approach tries to find functions that require a lot of memory *capacity* to evaluate. To better distinguish from other notions later in the paper, we henceforth refer to memory hard functions as *capacity hard functions*. For a traditional hash function, an ASIC has a big area advantage because one hash unit occupies much smaller chip area than a whole CPU. The reasoning behind a capacity hard function is to reduce an ASIC's area advantage by forcing it to spend significant area on memory. Historically, the capacity hardness approach only attempts to resist the area advantage. We quote from Percival's paper [46]:

> A natural way to reduce the advantage provided by an attacker's ability to construct highly parallel circuits is to increase the size of the key derivation circuit — if a circuit is twice as large, only half as many copies can be placed on a given area of silicon ...

Very recently, some works [10, 11, 14] analyze capacity hard functions from an energy angle (though they try to show negative results). However, an energy model based on memory capacity cannot be justified from a hardware perspective. We defer a more detailed discussion to Sects. 6.2 and 6.3.

It should now be clear that the capacity hardness approach does not provide a full solution to ASIC resistance since it only attempts to address the area aspect, but not the energy aspect of ASIC advantage. Fundamentally, the relative importance of these two aspects depends on many economic factors, which is out of the scope of this paper. But it may be argued that the energy aspect is more important than the area aspect in many scenarios. Area advantage, representing lower capital cost, is a one-time gain, while energy advantage, representing lower electricity consumption, keeps accumulating with time. The goal of this paper is to fill in the most important but long-overlooked energy aspect of ASIC resistance.

## 1.1   Bandwidth Hard Functions

We hope to find a function $f$ that ensures the energy cost to evaluate $f$ on an ASIC cannot be much smaller than on a CPU. We cannot change the fact that ASICs have much superior energy efficiency for computation compared to CPUs. Luckily, to our rescue, off-chip memory accesses incur comparable energy costs on ASICs and CPUs, and there are reasons to believe that it will remain this way in the foreseeable future (cf. Sect. 6.1). Therefore, we would like an ASIC resistant function $f$ to be *bandwidth hard*, i.e., it requires a lot of off-chip memory accesses to evaluate $f$. Informally, if off-chip memory accesses account for a significant portion of the total energy cost to evaluate $f$, it provides an opportunity to bring the energy cost on ASICs and CPUs onto a more equal ground.

A capacity hard function is not necessarily bandwidth hard. Intuitively, an exception arises when a capacity hard function has good locality in its memory access pattern. In this case, an ASIC adversary can use some on-chip cache to "filter out" many off-chip memory accesses. This makes computation the energy bottleneck again and gives ASICs a big advantage in energy efficiency. A capacity hard function based on a stacked double butterfly graph is one such example (Sect. 5.4).

On the positive side, most capacity hard functions are bandwidth hard. Scrypt has a data-dependent and (pseudo-)random memory access pattern. A recent work shows that scrypt is also capacity hard even under amortization and parallelism [13]. Adapting results from the above work, we prove scrypt is also bandwidth hard in Sect. 5.1 with some simplifying assumptions. Thus, scrypt offers nearly optimal ASIC resistance from both the energy aspect and the area aspect. But scrypt still has a few drawbacks. First, scrypt is bandwidth hard only when its memory footprint (i.e., capacity requirement) is much larger than the adversary's cache size. In practice, we often see protocol designers adopt scrypt with too small a memory footprint (to be less demanding for honest users) [5], which completely undermines its ASIC resistance guarantee [6]. Second, in password hashing, a data-dependent memory access pattern is considered to be less secure for fear of side channel attacks [25]. Thus, it is interesting to also look for *data-independent* bandwidth hard functions, especially those that achieve bandwidth hardness with a smaller memory footprint.

To study data-independent bandwidth hard functions, we adopt the graph labeling framework in the random oracle model, which is usually modeled by the pebble game abstraction. The most common and simple pebble game is the black pebble game, which is often used to study space and time complexity. To model the cache/memory architecture that an adversary may use, we adopt the red-blue pebble game [33,50]. In a red-blue game, there are two types of pebbles. A red (hot) pebble models data in cache and a blue (cold) pebble models data in memory. Data in memory must be brought into the cache before being computed on. Accordingly, a blue pebble must be "turned into" a red pebble (i.e., brought into the cache) before being used by a computation unit. We incorporate an energy cost model into red-blue pebble games, and then proceed to analyze data-independent bandwidth hard function candidates. We show that Catena-BRG [35] and Balloon [25] are bandwidth hard in the pebbling model. But we could not show a reduction from graph labeling with random oracles to red-blue pebble games. Thus, all results on data-independent graphs are only in the pebbling mode. A reduction from labeling to pebbling remains interesting future work.

Our idea of using memory accesses resembles, and is indeed inspired by, a line of work called memory bound functions [8,29,31]. Memory bound functions predate capacity hard functions, but unfortunately have been largely overlooked by recent work on ASIC resistance. We mention one key difference between our work and memory bound functions here and defer a more detailed comparison in Sect. 2. Memory bound functions assume computation is free for an adversary and thus aim to put strict lower bounds on the number of memory accesses. We, on the other hand, assume computation is cheap but not free for an adversary (which we justify in Sect. 4.1). As a result, we just need to guarantee that an adversary who attempts to save memory accesses has to compensate with so much computation that it ends up increasing its energy consumption. This relaxation of "bandwidth hardness" leads to much more efficient and practical solutions than existing memory bound functions [8,29,31]. To this end, the term "bandwidth hard" and "memory hard" may be a little misleading as they do not imply strict lower bounds on bandwidth and capacity. Memory (capacity) hardness as defined by Percival [46] refers to a lower bound on the space-time product $ST$, while bandwidth hardness in this paper refers to a lower bound on an ASICs' energy consumption under our model.

## 1.2 Our Contributions

We observe that energy efficiency, as the most important aspect of ASIC resistance, has thus far not received much attention. To this end, we propose using bandwidth hard functions to reduce the energy advantage of ASICs. We propose a simple energy model and incorporate it into red-blue pebble games. We note that ASIC resistance is a complex real-world notion that involves low-level hardware engineering. Therefore, in this paper we go over the reasoning and basic concepts of ASIC resistance from a hardware perspective and introduce a model based on hardware architecture and energy cost in practice.

Based on the model, we study the limit of ASIC energy resistance. Roughly speaking, an ASIC adversary can always achieve an energy advantage that equals the ratio between a CPU's energy cost per random oracle evaluation and an ASIC's energy cost per memory access. We observe that if we use a hash function (e.g., SHA-256) as the random oracle, which is popular among ASIC resistant proposals, it is impossible to reduce an ASIC's energy advantage below 100× in today's hardware landscape. Fortunately, we may be able to improve the situation utilizing CPUs' AES-NI instruction extensions.

We then turn our attention to analyzing the bandwidth hardness properties of ASIC resistant candidate constructions. We prove in the pebbling model that scrypt [46], Catena-BRG [35] and Balloon [25] enjoy tight bandwidth hardness under suitable parameters. Lastly, we point out that a capacity hard function is not necessarily bandwidth hard, using a stacked double butterfly graph as a counterexample.

## 2   Related Work

***Memory (capacity) hard functions.*** Memory (capacity) hard functions are currently the standard approach towards ASIC resistance. The notion was first proposed by Percival [46] along with the scrypt construction. There has been significant follow-up that propose constructions with stronger notions of capacity hardness [9,15,21,25,35,39,49]. As we have noted, capacity hardness only addresses the area aspect of ASIC resistance. It is important to consider the energy aspect for a complete solution to ASIC resistance.

***Memory (capacity) hard proof of work.*** Memory (capacity) hard proofs of work [18,23,49,53] are proof of work schemes that require a prover to have a lot of memory capacity, but at the same time allow a verifier to check the prover's work with a small amount of space and time. The motivation is also ASIC resistance, and similarly, it overlooks the energy aspect of ASIC resistance.

***Memory bound functions.*** The notion of memory bound functions was first proposed by Abadi et al. [8] and later formalized and improved by Dwork et al. [29,31]. A memory bound function requires a lot of memory accesses to evaluate. Those works do not relate to an energy argument, but rather use speed and hence memory latency as the metrics. As we discuss in Sect. 3.1, using speed as the only metric makes it hard to interpret the security guarantee in a normalized sense. Another major difference is that memory bound functions assume computation is completely free and aim for strict lower bounds on bandwidth (the number of memory accesses), while we assume computation is cheap but not free. To achieve its more ambitious goal, memory bound function constructions involve traversing random paths in a big table of true random numbers. This results in a two undesirable properties. First, the constructions are inherently data-dependent, which raises some concerns for memory access pattern leakage in password hashing. Second, the big random table needs to be transferred over the network between a prover (who computes the function) and a verifier (who checks the prover's computation). A follow-up work [31] allows the big table to be filled by pebbling a rather complex graph (implicitly moving to our model where computation is cheap but not free), but still relies on the random walk in the table to enforce memory accesses. Our paper essentially achieves the same goal just through pebbling and from simpler graphs, thus eliminating the random walk and achieving better efficiency and data-independence.

***Parallel attacks.*** An impressive recent line of work has produced many interesting results regarding capacity hardness in the presence of parallel attacks. These works show that a parallel architecture can reduce the area-time product for any data independent capacity hard function [10,12,15]. The practical implications of these attacks are less clear and we defer a discussion to Sect. 6.3. We would also like to clarify a direct contradiction between some parallel attacks' claims [10,11,14] and our results. We prove that Catena-BRG [35] and Balloon [25] enjoy great energy advantage resistance while those works conclude the exact opposite. The contradiction is due to their energy model that we consider flawed, which we discuss in Sect. 6.3.

***Graph pebbling.*** Graph pebbling is a powerful tool in computer science, dating back at least to 1970s in studying Turing machines [27,36] and register allocation [51]. More recently, graph pebbling has found applications in various areas of cryptography [18,25,31–33,35,40,49,52]. Some of our proof techniques are inspired by seminal works in pebbling lower bounds and trade-offs by Paul and Tarjan [44] and Lengauer and Tarjan [38].

# 3 Preliminaries

## 3.1 A Hardware Perspective on ASIC Resistance

The first and foremost question we would like to answer is: what advantages of ASICs are we trying to resist? The most strongly perceived advantage of ASIC miners may be their incredible speed, which can be a million times faster than CPUs [1]. But if speed were the sole metric, we could just deploy a million CPUs in parallel to catch up on speed. Obviously, using a million CPUs would be at a huge disadvantage in two aspects: capital cost (or manufacturing cost) and power consumption. The manufacturing cost of a chip is often approximated by its area in theory [41]. Therefore, the metrics to compare hardware systems should be:

1. the area-speed ratio, or equivalently the area-time product, commonly referred to as $AT$ in the literature [10,11,22,41], and
2. the power-speed ratio, which is equivalent to energy cost per function evaluation.

Area and energy efficiency are the two major advantages of ASICs. The speed advantage can be considered as a derived effect from them. Because an ASIC hash unit is small and energy efficient, ASIC designers can pack thousands of them in a single chip and still have reasonable manufacturing cost and manageable power consumption and heat dissipation.

**Bandwidth hard functions to address both aspects.** Percival proposes using capacity hard functions to reduce ASIC area advantage [46]. With bandwidth hard functions, we hope to additionally reduce ASIC's energy advantage. We note that a bandwidth hard function also needs to be capacity hard. Thus, a hardware system evaluating it, be it a CPU or an ASIC, needs off-chip external memory. This has two important implications. First, a bandwidth hard function inherits the area advantage resistance from capacity hardness (though somewhat weakened by parallel attacks). Second, a bandwidth hard function forces an ASIC into making a lot of off-chip memory accesses, which limits the ASIC's energy advantage. To study hardware energy cost more formally, we need to introduce a hardware architecture model and an energy cost model.

**Hardware architecture model.** The adversary is allowed to have any cache policy on its ASIC chip, e.g., full associativity and optimal replacement [20]. Our proofs do not directly analyze cache hit rate, but the results imply that a bandwidth hard function ensures a low hit rate even for an optimal cache. We assume a one-level cache hierarchy for convenience. This does not affect the accuracy of the model. We do not charge the adversary for accessing data from the cache, so only the total cache size matters. Meanwhile, although modern CPUs are equipped with large caches, honest users cannot utilize it since a bandwidth hard function has very low cache hit rate. We simply assume a 0% cache hit rate for honest users.

**Energy cost model.** We assume it costs $c_b$ energy to transfer one bit of data between memory and cache, and $c_r$ energy to evaluate the random oracle on one bit of data in cache. If an algorithm transfers $B$ bits of data and queries the random oracle on $R$ bits of data in total, its energy cost is $\mathsf{ec} = c_b B + c_r R$. A compute unit and memory interface may operate at a much larger word granularity, but we define $c_b$ and $c_r$ to be amortized per bit for convenience. The two coefficients are obviously hardware dependent. We write $c_{b,\mathsf{cpu}}, c_{r,\mathsf{cpu}}$ and $c_{b,\mathsf{asic}}, c_{r,\mathsf{asic}}$ when we need to distinguish them. The values of these coefficients are determined experimentally or extracted from related studies or sources in Sect. 4.1. Additional discussions and justifications of the models are presented in Sect. 6.

**Energy fairness.** Our ultimate goal is to achieve *energy fairness* between CPUs and ASICs. For a function $f$, suppose honest CPU users adopt an algorithm with an energy cost $\mathsf{ec}_0 = c_{b,\mathsf{cpu}} B_0 + c_{r,\mathsf{cpu}} R_0$. Let $\overline{\mathsf{ec}} = \overline{\mathsf{ec}}(f, M, c_{b,\mathsf{asic}}, c_{r,\mathsf{asic}})$ be the minimum energy cost for an adversary to evaluate $f$ with cache size $M$ and ASIC energy parameters $c_{b,\mathsf{asic}}$ and $c_{r,\mathsf{asic}}$. Energy fairness is then measured by the energy advantage of an ASIC adversary over honest CPU users (under those parameters): $A_{ec} = ec_0/\overline{ec} > 1$ . A smaller $A_{ec}$ indicates a smaller energy advantage of ASICs, and thus better energy fairness between CPUs and ASICs.

We remark that while an ASIC's energy cost for computation $c_{r,asic}$ is small, we assume it is not strictly 0. It is assumed in some prior works that computation is completely free for the adversary [31,33]. In that model, we must find a function that simultaneously satisfies the following two conditions: (1) it has a trade-off-proof space lower bound (even an exponential computational penalty for space reduction is insufficient), and (2) it requires a comparable amount of computation and memory accesses. We do not know of any candidate data-independent construction that satisfies both conditions. We believe our assumption of a non-zero $c_{r,asic}$ is realistic, and we justify it in Sect. 4.1 with experimental values. In fact, our model may still be overly favorable to the adversary. It has been noted that the energy cost to access data from an on-chip a cache is roughly proportional to the square root of the cache size [16]. Thus, if an adversary employs a large on-chip cache, the energy cost of fetching data from this cache needs to be included in $c_{r,asic}$.

## 3.2   The Graph Labeling and Pebbling Framework

We adopt the graph labeling and pebbling framework that is common in the study of ASIC resistant [15,18,25,31,35].

*Graph labeling.* Graph labeling is a computational problem that evaluates a random oracle $\mathcal{H}$ in a directed acyclic graph (DAG) $G$. A vertex with no incoming edges is called a *source* and a vertex with no outgoing edges is called a *sink*. Vertices in $G$ are numbered, and each vertex $v_i$ is associated with a label $l(v_i)$, computed as:

$$l(v_i) = \begin{cases} \mathcal{H}(i,x) & \text{if } v_i \text{ is a source} \\ \mathcal{H}(i,l(u_1),\cdots,l(u_d)) & \text{otherwise, } u_1 \text{ to } u_d \text{ are } v_i\text{'s predecessors} \end{cases}$$

The output of the graph labeling problem are the labels of the sinks. It is common to hash the labels of all sinks into a final output (of the ASIC resistant function) to keep it short.

*Adversary.* We consider a deterministic adversary that has access to $\mathcal{H}$ that runs in rounds, starting from round 1. In round $i$, the adversary receives an input state $\sigma_i$ and produces an output state $\bar{\sigma}_i$. Each input state $\sigma_i = (\tau_i, \eta_i, h_i)$ consists of

- $\tau_i$, $M$ bits of data in cache,
- $\eta_i$, an arbitrary amount of data in memory, and
- a $w$-bit random oracle response $h_i$ if a random oracle query was issued in the previous round.

Each output state $\bar{\sigma}_i = (\bar{\tau}_i, \eta_i, q_i)$ consists of

- $\bar{\tau}_i$, $M$ bits of data in cache, which can be any deterministic function of $\sigma_i$ and $h_i$.
- $\eta_i$, data in memory, which is unchanged from the input state, and
- an operation $q_i$ that can either be a random oracle query or a data transfer operation between memory and cache.

If the operation $q_i$ is a random oracle query, then in the input state of the next round, the random oracle response is $h_{i+1} = \mathcal{H}(q_i)$ and the contents of the cache/memory is unchanged $(\sigma_{i+1}, \eta_{i+1}) = (\bar{\sigma}_i, \eta_i)$. If the operation $q_i$ is a data transfer operation, then it has the form $(x_i, y_i, z_i, b_i)$ in which $x_i$ is an offset in the cache, $y_i$ is an offset in memory, $z_i$ specifies whether the direction of the transfer is from cache to memory ($z_i = 0$) or from memory to cache ($z_i = 1$), and $b_i$ is the number of bits to be transfered. In the input state of the next round, the contents of the cache/memory $(\sigma_{i+1}, \eta_{i+1})$ are obtained by applying the data transfer operation on $(\bar{\sigma}_i, \eta_i)$, and $h_{i+1} = \bot$. The energy cost of the adversary is defined as follows. A random oracle call on $r_i = |q_i|$ bits if input costs $c_r r_i$ units of energy. A data transfer of $b_i$ bits in either direction costs $c_b b_i$ units of energy. Any other computation that happens during a round is free for the adversary. The total energy cost of the adversary is the sum of cost in all rounds.

***Pebble games.*** Graph labeling is often abstracted as a pebble game. Computing $l(v)$ is modeled as placing a pebble on vertex $v$. The goal of the pebble game in our setting is to place pebbles on the sinks. There exist several variants of pebble games. The simplest one is the *black* pebble game where there is only one type of pebbles. In each move, a pebble can be placed on vertex $v$ if $v$ is a source or if all predecessors of $v$ have pebbles on them. Pebbles can be removed from any vertices at any time.

***Red-blue pebble games.*** To model a cache/memory hierarchy, *red-blue* pebble games have been proposed [33,50]. In this game, there are two types of pebbles. A red (hot) pebble models data in cache, which can be computed upon immediately. A blue (cold) pebble models data in memory, which must first be brought into cache to be computed upon. The rule of a red-blue pebble game is naturally extended as follows:

1. A *red* pebble can be placed on vertex $v$ if $v$ is a source or if all predecessors of $v$ have *red* pebbles on them.
2. A red pebble can be placed on vertex $v$ if there is a blue pebble on $v$. A blue pebble can be placed on vertex $v$ if there is a red pebble on $v$.

We refer to the first type of moves as *red moves* and the second type as *blue moves*. Pebbles (red or blue) can be removed from any vertices at any time. A pebbling strategy can be represented as a sequence of transitions between pebble placement configurations on the graph, $\mathbf{P} = (P_0, P_1, P_2 \cdots, P_T)$. Each configuration consists of two vectors of size $|V|$, specifying for each vertex if a red pebble exists and if a blue pebble exists. The starting configuration $P_0$ does not have to be empty; pebbles may exist on some vertices in $P_0$. Each transition makes *either* a red move *or* a blue move, and then removes any number of pebbles for free.

We introduce some extra notations. If a pebble (red or blue) exists on a vertex $v$ in a configuration $P_i$, we say $v$ is *pebbled* in $P_i$. We say a sequence **P** pebbles a vertex $v$ if there exists $P_i \in$ **P** such that $v$ is pebbled in $P_i$. We say a sequence **P** pebbles a set of vertices if **P** pebbles every vertex in the set. Note that blue pebbles cannot be directly created on unpebbled vertices. If a vertex $v$ is not initially pebbled in $P_0$, then the first pebble that gets placed on $v$ in **P** must be a red pebble, and it must result from a red move.

**Energy cost of red-blue pebbling.** In red-blue pebbling, red moves model computation on data in cache and blue moves model data transfer between cache and memory. It is straightforward to adopt the energy cost model in Sect. 3.1 to a red-blue pebbling sequence **P**. We charge $c_b$ cost for each blue move. For each red move (i.e., random oracle call), we charge a cost proportional to the number of input vertices. Namely, if a vertex $v$ has $d$ predecessors, a red move on $v$ costs $c_r d$ units of cost. Similarly, we write $c_{b,\text{cpu}}, c_{r,\text{cpu}}$ and $c_{b,\text{asic}}, c_{r,\text{asic}}$ when we need to distinguish them. The energy coefficients in Sect. 3.1 are defined per bit and here they are per label. This is not a problem because only the ratio between these coefficients matter. As before, removing pebbles (red or blue) is free. If **P** uses $B$ blue moves and $R$ red moves each with $d$ predecessors, it incurs a total energy cost $\text{ec}(\mathbf{P}) = c_b B + c_r d R$.

The adversary's cache size $M$ translates to a bounded number of red pebbles at any given time, which we denote as $m$. For a graph $G$, given parameters $m$, $c_b$ and $c_r$, let $\overline{\text{ec}} = \overline{\text{ec}}(G, m, c_b, c_r)$ be the minimum cost to pebble $G$ in a red-blue pebble game starting with an empty initial configuration under those parameters. Let $\text{ec}_0$ be the cost of an honest CPU user. The energy advantage of an ASIC is $A_{\text{ec}} = \text{ec}_0 / \overline{\text{ec}}$.

**Definition of bandwidth hardness.** The ultimate goal of a bandwidth hard function is to achieve fairness between CPUs and ASICs in terms of energy cost. In the next section, we will establish $\overline{A_{\text{ec}}} = \frac{c_{b,\text{cpu}} + c_{r,\text{cpu}}}{c_{b,\text{asic}} + c_{r,\text{asic}}}$ as a lower bound on the adversary's energy advantage $A_{\text{ec}}$ for any function. We say a function *under a particular parameter setting* is bandwidth hard if it ensures $A_{\text{ec}} = \Theta(\overline{A_{\text{ec}}})$, i.e., if it upper bounds an adversary's energy advantage to a constant within the best we can hope for.

In the above definition, we emphasize "under a particular parameter setting" because we will frequently see that a function's bandwidth hardness kicks in only when its memory capacity requirement $n$ is sufficiently large compared to the adversary's cache size $m$. This should be as expected: if the entire memory footprint fits in cache, then a function must be computation bound rather than bandwidth bound. As an example, we will later show that scrypt is bandwidth hard when it requires sufficiently large memory capacity. But when scrypt is adopted in many practical systems (e.g., Litecoin), it is often configured to use much smaller memory, thus losing its bandwidth hardness and ASIC resistance.

*Connection between labeling and pebbling.* The labeling-to-pebbling reduction has been established for data-independent graphs [31,33] and for scrypt [13] when the metric is space complexity or cumulative complexity. Unfortunately, for bandwidth hard functions and energy cost, we do yet know how to reduce the graph labeling problem with a cache to the red-blue pebbling game without making additional assumptions. The difficulty lies in how to transform the adversary's data transfer between a memory and a cache into blue moves. Thus, all results for data-independent graphs in this paper will be in the red-blue pebbling model. This is equivalent to placing a restriction on the adversary that it can only transfer whole labels between cache and memory. Showing a reduction for data-independent graphs without the above restriction is an interesting open problem. We mention that for general data-dependent graphs and proofs of space [32], a reduction from labeling to black pebbling also remains open.

## 4    The Limit of Energy Fairness

While our goal is to upper bound the energy advantage $A_E$, it is helpful to first look at a lower bound to know how good a resistance we can hope for. Suppose honest users adopt an algorithm that transfers $B_0$ bits and queries $\mathcal{H}$ on $R_0$ bits in total. Even if an adversary does not have a better algorithm, it can simply adopt the honest algorithm but implements it on an ASIC. In this case, the adversary's energy advantage is

$$A_{ec} = \frac{c_{b,cpu}B_0 + c_{r,cpu}R_0}{c_{b,asic}B_0 + c_{r,asic}R_0} = \frac{c_{b,cpu} + c_{r,cpu}R_0/B_0}{c_{b,asic} + c_{r,asic}R_0/B_0}.$$

Since we expect $c_{r,cpu} \gg c_{r,asic}$ and $c_{b,cpu} \approx c_{b,asic}$, the above value is smaller when $R_0/B_0$ is smaller (more memory accesses and less computation). Any data brought into the cache must be consumed by the compute unit (random oracle) — otherwise, the data transfer is useless and should not have happened. Given that $B_0 \leq R_0$, the adversary can at least have an energy consumption advantage of:

$$A_{ec} \geq \frac{c_{b,cpu} + c_{r,cpu}}{c_{b,asic} + c_{r,asic}} = \overline{A_{ec}}.$$

In Sects. 5.2 and 5.3, we prove that bit reversal graphs and stacked expanders essentially reduce $A_{ec}$ very close to the lower bound $\overline{A_{ec}}$. So $\overline{A_{ec}}$ is quite tight and represents both the lower and upper limit of the energy advantage resistance we can achieve.

Since we expect $c_{r,asic}$ to be small, and $c_{b,cpu} \approx c_{b,asic}$, the above lower bound is approximately $1 + c_{r,cpu}/c_{b,cpu}$. So we hope $c_{r,cpu}$ to be small and $c_{b,cpu}$ to be large, in which case memory accesses account for a significant portion of the total energy cost on CPUs. It is often mentioned that computation is cheap compared to memory accesses even for CPUs, which seems to be in our favor. However, the situation is much less favorable for our scenario because a cryptographic hash is a complex function that involves thousands of operations. It would be unrealistic for us to assume $c_{r,\text{cpu}} \ll c_{b,\text{cpu}}$. To estimate the concrete value of $\overline{A_{\text{ec}}}$, in Sect. 4.1 we conduct experiments to measure $c_{r,\text{cpu}}$ and $c_{b,\text{cpu}}$ and cite estimates of $c_{r,\text{asic}}$ and $c_{b,\text{asic}}$ from reliable sources.

## 4.1 Experiments to Estimate Energy Cost Coefficients

All values we report here are approximates as their exact values depend on many low level factors (technology process, frequency, voltage, etc.). Nevertheless, they should allow us to estimate $A_{\text{ec}}$ to the correct order of magnitude.

We keep a CPU fully busy with the task under test, i.e., compute hashes and making memory accesses. We use Intel Power Gadget [4] to measure the CPU package energy consumption in a period of time, and then divide by the number of Bytes processed (hashed or transferred). We run tests on an Intel Core I7-4600U CPU in 22 nm technology clocked at 1.4 GHz. The operating system is Ubuntu 14.04 and we use Crypto++ Library 5.6.3 compiled with GCC 4.6.4.

**Table 1.** Measured energy cost (in nJ) per Byte for memory accesses and cryptographic operations on CPUs.

| Operation | Memory access | SHA-256 | AES-NI |
|---|---|---|---|
| Energy, CPU | 0.5 | 30 | 1.5 |
| Energy, ASIC | 0.3 | 0.0012 | / |

Table 1 reports the measured CPU energy cost per Bytes. For comparison, we take the memory access energy estimates for ASICs from two papers [37, 45], which have very close estimations. We take the SHA-256 energy cost for ASIC from the state-of-the-art Antminer S9 specification [1]. Antminer S9 spends 0.098 nJ to hash 80 Bytes, which normalizes to 0.0012 nJ/Byte.

## 4.2 Better Energy Fairness with AES-NI

From the above results, we have $c_{b,\text{cpu}} \approx 0.5$, $c_{b,\text{asic}} \approx 0.3$, and if we use SHA-256 to implement the random oracle $\mathcal{H}$, then $c_{r,\text{cpu}} \approx 30$ and $c_{r,\text{asic}} \approx 0.1$. With these parameters, any function in the graph labeling framework can at most reduce an ASIC's energy advantage to $\overline{A_{\text{ec}}} \approx (0.5 + 30)/(0.3 + 0.0012) \approx 100\times$. While this represents an improvement over plain SHA-256 hashing (which suffers from an energy advantage of roughly $30/0.0012 = 25,000\times$), $100\times$ is still a quite substantial advantage.

Is $100\times$ the limit of energy fairness or can we do better? To push $\overline{A_{\text{ec}}}$ lower, we need a smaller $c_{r,\text{cpu}}$. The AES-NI extension gives exactly what we need. AES-NI

(AES New Instructions) [3] is a set of new CPU instructions specifically designed to improve the speed and energy efficiency of AES operations on CPUs. Today AES-NI is available in all mainstream Intel processors. In fact, AES-NI is an ASIC-style AES circuit that Intel builds into its CPUs, which is why it reduces ASIC advantage. But also we cannot expect AES-NI to completely match stand-alone AES ASICs because it is subject to many design constrains imposed by Intel CPUs.

We repeat our previous experiments to measure the energy efficiency of AES operations on CPUs. As expected, AES-NI delivers much better energy efficiency, 1.5 nJ per Byte. We do not know for sure what $c_{r,\mathsf{asic}}$ would be for AES, but expect it to be no better than SHA-256 (and the bounds are insensitive to $c_{r,\mathsf{asic}}$ since $c_{b,\mathsf{asic}}$ dominates in the denominator). Therefore, if we use AES for pebbling, the lower bound drops to $\overline{A_{\mathsf{ec}}} \approx (0.5 + 1.5)/0.3 \approx 6.7\times$. It is worth noting that using AES for pebbling also reduces an ASIC's $AT$ advantage as it makes CPUs run faster (smaller $T$).

Great care needs to be taken when instantiating the random oracle with a concrete function. Boneh et al. [25] point out that the pebbling analogy breaks down if the random oracle $\mathcal{H}$ is instantiated with a cryptographic hash function based on the Merkle-Damgård construction [28,42]. The problem is that a Merkle-Damgård construction does not require its entire input to be present at the same time, but instead absorbs the input chunk by chunk. The same caveat exists when we use AES for pebbling. We leave a thorough study on pebbling with AES to future work. If we want even smaller $c_{r,\mathsf{cpu}}$ and $\overline{A_{\mathsf{ec}}}$ or to avoid the complication of using AES, we may have to count on Intel's SHA instruction extensions. Intel announced plans to add SHA extensions a few years ago [7], but no product has incorporated them so far.

## 5    Bandwidth Hardness of Candidate Constructions

Some candidate constructions we analyze in this section are based on a class of graphs called "sandwich graphs" [15,25]. A sandwich graph is a directed acyclic graph $G = (V \cup U, E)$ that has $2n$ vertices $V \cup U = (v_0, v_1, \cdots v_{n-1}) \cup (u_0, u_1, \cdots u_{n-1})$, and two types of edges:

- chain edges, i.e., $(v_i, v_{i+1})$ and $(u_i, u_{i+1})$ $\forall i \in [0..n-2]$, and
- cross edges from $V$ to $U$.

Figure 1 is a random sandwich graph with $n = 8$. In other words, a sandwich graph is a bipartite graph with the addition of chain edges. We call the path consisting of $(v_0, v_1), (v_1, v_2), \cdots (v_{n-2}, v_{n-1})$ the *input path*, and the path consisting of $(u_0, u_1), (u_1, u_2), \cdots (u_{n-2}, u_{n-1})$ the *output path*.

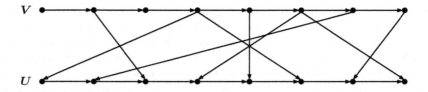

**Fig. 1.** A random sandwich graph with $n = 8$.

## 5.1  Scrypt

Scrypt [46] can be thought of as a sandwich graph where the cross edges are dynamically generated at random in a data-dependent fashion. Each vertex $u_i$ on the output path has one incoming cross edge from a vertex $v_j$ that is chosen uniformly random from the input path based on the previous label $l(u_{i-1})$ (or $l(v_{n-1})$ for $u_0$), and thus cannot be predicted beforehand.

The default strategy to compute scrypt is to first compute each $l(v_i)$ on the input path sequentially and store each one in memory, and then compute each $l(u_i)$ on the output path, fetching each $l(v_j)$ from memory as needed. The total cost of this strategy is $(c_r + c_b)n + (c_b + 2c_r)n = (2c_b + 3c_r)n$ (every node on the output path has in-degree 2).

To lower bound the energy cost, we make a simplifying assumption that if the adversary transfers data from memory to cache at all, it transfers at least $w$ bits where $w = |l(\cdot)|$ is the label size. We also invoke the "single-challenge time lower bound" theorem on scrypt [13], which we paraphrase below. The adversary can fill a cache of $M$ bits after arbitrary computation and preprocessing on the input path. The adversary then receives a challenge $j$ chosen uniformly at random from 0 to $n - 1$ and tries to find $l(v_j)$ using only the data in the cache. Let $t$ be the random variable that represents the number of *sequential* random oracle calls to $\mathcal{H}$ made by the adversary till it queries $\mathcal{H}$ with $l(v_j)$ for the first time.

**Theorem 1 (Alwen et al. [13]).** *For all but a negligible fraction of random oracles, the following holds: given a cache of $M$ bits, $\Pr[t > \frac{n}{2p}] > \frac{1}{2}$ where $p = (M + 1)/(w - 3 \log n + 1)$ and $w = |l(\cdot)|$ is the label size.*

The above theorem states that in the parallel random oracle model, with at least $1/2$ probability, an adversary needs $n/2p$ sequential random oracles to answer the random challenge. (Note that the above theorem does not directly apply to scrypt, since challenges in scrypt come from the random oracle rather than from an independent external source. This issue can be handled similarly as in [13].) A lower bound on the number of sequential random oracle calls in the parallel model is also a lower bound on the number of total random oracle calls in our sequential model. Theorem 1 states that if the adversary wishes to compute a label on the output path only using the $M$ bits in cache without fetching from memory, there is a $1/2$ chance that doing so requires $n/2p$ random oracle calls. If we choose a sufficiently large $n$ such that $c_r n/2p > c_b$, then making $n/2p$

random oracle calls is more expensive than simply fetching the challenged input label from memory. Since we assume the adversary fetches $w$ bits at a time, so if it fetches from memory at all, it rather fetches the challenged input label. Then, for any adversary, the expected cost to compute a label on the output path is at least $c_b/2$ and the energy advantage is at most $A_{ec} < \frac{2c_{b,cpu} + 3c_{r,cpu}}{0.5c_{b,asic}}$. This parameterization requires $n > 2p \cdot \frac{c_{b,asic}}{c_{r,asic}} > 2m \cdot \frac{c_{b,asic}}{c_{r,asic}}$, which means the capacity requirement of scrypt should be a few hundred times larger than an adversary's conceivable cache size.

## 5.2   Bit-Reversal Graphs

A bit-reversal graph is a sandwich graph where $n$ is a power of 2 and the cross edges $(v_i, u_j)$ follow the bit-reversal permutation, namely, the binary representation of $j$ reverses the bits of the binary representation of $i$. Figure 2 is a bit-reversal graph with $n = 8$. Catena-BRG [35] is based on bit-reversal graphs.

**Black pebbling complexity.** For a black pebble game, Lenguaer and Tarjan [38] showed an asymptotically tight space-time trade-off $ST = \Theta(n^2)$ for bit-reversal graphs.

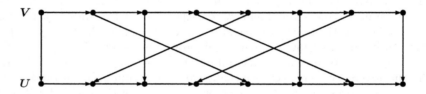

**Fig. 2.** A bit-reversal graph with $n = 8$.

**Red-Blue pebbling complexity.** For a red-blue pebble game, the default strategy is the same as the one for scrypt in Sect. 5.1 The total cost of this strategy is $(c_r + c_b)n + (c_b + 2c_r)n = (2c_b + 3c_r)n$. We now show a lower bound on the red-blue pebbling complexity for bit-reversal graphs. The techniques are similar to Lenguaer and Tarjan [38].

**Theorem 2.** *Let $G$ be a bit-reversal graph with $2n$ vertices, and $m$ be the number of red pebbles available. If $n > 2mc_b/c_r$, then the red-blue pebbling cost* $ec(G, m, c_b, c_r)$ *is lower bounded by* $(c_b + c_r)n(1 - \frac{2(m+1)c_b}{nc_r})$.

*Proof.* Suppose a sequence **P** pebbles $u_{n-1}$ of a bit-reversal graph starting from an empty initial configuration. Let $m'$ be the largest power of 2 satisfying $m' < nc_r/c_b$. We have $m' \geq nc_r/(2c_b) > m$.

Let the output path be divided into $n/m'$ intervals of length $m'$ each. Denote the $j$-th interval $I_j$, $j = 1, 2, \cdots, n/m'$. $I_j$ contains vertices

$u_{(j-1)m'}, u_{(j-1)m'+1}, \ldots, u_{jm'-1}$. The first time these intervals are pebbled must be in topological order, so $\mathbf{P}$ can be divided into $n/m'$ subsequences $(\mathbf{P}_1, \mathbf{P}_2, \cdots, \mathbf{P}_{n/m'})$ such that all vertices in $I_j$ are pebbled for the first time by $\mathbf{P}_j$. The red blue pebbling costs of subsequences are additive, so we can consider each $\mathbf{P}_j$ separately.

Suppose $\mathbf{P}_j$ uses $b$ blue moves. For any $I_j$, $1 \le j \le n/m'$, let $v_{j_1}, v_{j_2}, \ldots, v_{j_{m'}}$ be the immediate predecessors on the input path. Note that these immediate predecessors are $n/m'$ edges apart from each other due to the bit-reversal property. $\mathbf{P}_j$ must place red pebbles on all these immediate predecessors at some point during $\mathbf{P}_j$. An immediate predecessor $v$ may get its red pebble in one of the following three ways below:

1. $v$ has a red pebble on it at the beginning of $\mathbf{P}_j$.
2. $v$ has a "close" ancestor (can be itself) that gets a red pebble through a blue move, where being "close" means being less than $n/m'$ edges away. $\mathbf{P}_j$ can then place a red pebble on $v$ using less than $n/m'$ red moves utilizing its "close" ancestor.
3. $v$ gets its red pebble through a red move *and* has no "close" ancestor that gets a red pebble through a blue move. To place a red pebble on $v$, $\mathbf{P}_j$ must use at least $n/m'$ red moves (except for one $v$ that may be "close" to the source vertex $v_0$).

The first category accounts for at most $m$ immediate predecessors due to the cache size limit $m$. The second category accounts for at most $b$ immediate predecessors since each uses a blue move. If $b + m < m' - 1$, then $\mathbf{P}_j$ must use at least $n/m'$ red moves for each immediate predecessor in the third category. Under the conditions in the theorem, the cost of $n/m'$ red moves is greater than a blue move since $c_r n/m' > c_b$. Thus, the best strategy is to use blue moves over red moves for vertices on the input path whenever possible. Therefore,

$$\mathsf{ec}(\mathbf{P}_j) \ge c_r m' + c_b(m' - m - 1) > (c_b + c_r)(m' - m - 1)$$

$$\mathsf{ec}(\mathbf{P}) = \Sigma_{j=1}^{n/m'} \mathsf{ec}(\mathbf{P}_j) > (c_b + c_r)n(1 - \frac{2(m+1)c_b}{nc_r}). \qquad \square$$

When $n$ is sufficiently large, a bit-reversal graph is bandwidth hard. Its red-blue pebbling complexity has a lower bound close to $(c_b + c_r)n$. An ASIC's energy advantage is similar to that of scrypt, $A_{\mathsf{ec}} \approx \frac{2c_{b,\mathsf{cpu}} + 3c_{r,\mathsf{cpu}}}{c_{b,\mathsf{asic}} + c_{r,\mathsf{asic}}}$ and $A_{\mathsf{ec}} \approx 18$ with parameters in Table 1. The capacity requirement on bit-reversal graphs to remain bandwidth hard is also similar to the requirement for scrypt.

## 5.3   Stacked Expanders

An $(n, \alpha, \beta)$ bipartite expander $(0 < \alpha < \beta < 1)$ is a directed bipartite graph with $n$ sources and $n$ sinks such that any subset of $\alpha n$ sinks are connected to at least $\beta n$ sources. Prior work has shown that bipartite expanders for any $0 < \alpha < \beta < 1$ exist given sufficiently many edges. For example, Pinsker's construction [48] simply connects each sink to $d$ independent sources. It yields an

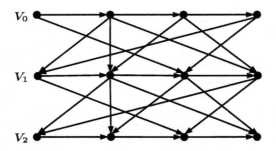

**Fig. 3.** A stacked random sandwich graph with $n = 4$, $k = 2$ and $d = 2$.

$(n, \alpha, \beta)$ bipartite expander for sufficiently large $n$ with overwhelming probability [25] if

$$d > \frac{\mathrm{H_b}(\alpha) + \mathrm{H_b}(\beta)}{-\alpha \log_2 \beta}$$

where $\mathrm{H_b}(\alpha) = -\alpha \log_2 \alpha - (1 - \alpha) \log_2(1 - \alpha)$.

An $(n, k, \alpha, \beta)$ stacked expander graph is constructed by stacking $k$ bipartite expanders back to back. It has $n(k + 1)$ vertices, partitioned into $k + 1$ sets each of size $n$, $V = \{V_0, V_1, V_2, \cdots, V_k\}$ with all edges are directed from $V_{i-1}$ to $V_i$ ($i \in [1..k]$). $V_{i-1}$ and $V_i$ plus all edges between them form an $(n, \alpha, \beta)$ bipartite expander $\forall i \in [1..k]$. The bipartite expanders at different layers can but do not have to be the same. Its maximum in-degree is the same as the underlying $(n, \alpha, \beta)$ bipartite expanders.

In the Balloon hashing algorithm, the vertices are furthered chained sequentially, i.e., there exist edges $(v_{i,j}, v_{i,j+1})$ for each $0 \le i \le k, 0 \le j \le n-2$ as well as an edge $(v_{i,n-1}, v_{i+1,0})$ for each $0 \le i \le k$. In other words, Balloon hashing uses a stacked random sandwich graph in which each vertex has $d > 1$ predecessors from the previous layer. Figure 3 is a stacked random sandwich graph with $n = 4$, $k = 2$ and $d = 2$. In the figure, two consecutive layers form a $(4, 4, \frac{1}{4}, \frac{1}{2})$ expander.

A large in-degree can be problematic for the pebbling abstraction since the random oracle in graph labeling cannot be based on a Merkle-Damgård construction. In the case of stacked expanders, we can apply a transformation to make the in-degree to be 2: we simply replace each $d$-to-1 connection with a binary tree where the $d$ predecessors are at the leaf level, the successor is the root and each edge in the tree points from a child to its parent. This transformation preserves the expanding property between layers and increases the cost of a red move by a factor of 2 at most (the number of edges in a binary tree is at most twice the number of its leaves).

We remark that the latest version of the Balloon hash paper [25] analyzes random sandwich graphs using a new "well-spread" property rather than the expanding property, in an attempt to tighten the required in-degree. We may be able to adopt their new framework to analyze bandwidth hardness, but we leave it to future work.

**Black pebbling complexity.** Black pebble games on stacked expanders have been well studied. Obviously, simply pebbling each expander in order and removing pebbles as they are no longer needed results in a sequence **P** that uses $2n$ space and $n(k + 1)$ moves. An exponentially sharp space-time trade-off in black pebble games is shown by Paul and Tarjan [44] and further strengthened by Ren and Devadas [49]. The result says that to pebble any subset of $\alpha n$ initially unpebbled sinks of $G$ requires either at least $(\beta - 2\alpha)n$ pebbles or at least $2^k$ moves.

**Red-blue pebbling complexity.** We now consider red-blue pebble games on stacked expanders. An honest user would simply pebble each expander in order in a straightforward way. First, for each vertex $v$ in the source layer $V_0$, the honest user places a red pebble on $v$ and then immediately replaces it with a blue pebble. Then, for each vertex $v \in V_1$, the honest user places red pebbles on its $d$ predecessors through blue moves, pebbles $v$ using a red move, replacing the red pebble with a blue pebble, and lastly removing all red pebbles. The cost to pebble each source vertex is $(c_b + c_r)$ and the cost to pebble each non-source vertex is $c_b(d + 1) + c_r d$. The total cost to pebble the entire graph is therefore $\approx nkd(c_b + c_r)$.

Following the proof of the sharp space-time trade-off in a black pebble game [44,49], we can similarly derive a sharp trade-off between red and blue moves in a red-blue pebble game. It will then lead to a lower bound on red-blue pebbling cost for stacked expander graph $G$.

**Theorem 3.** *Let $G$ be an $(n, k, \alpha, \beta)$ stacked expander. In a red-blue pebble game, if a sequence **P** pebbles any subset of $\alpha n$ sinks of $G$ through red moves, using at most $m$ red pebbles (plus an arbitrary number of blue pebbles) and at most $(\beta - 2\alpha)n - m$ blue moves, then **P** must use at least $2^k \alpha n$ red moves.*

Informally, if there is a strategy that pebbles any subset of $\alpha n$ vertices using at most $m$ red *pebbles* and at most $b$ blue *moves*, it implies a strategy that pebbles those $\alpha n$ vertices using at most $m + b$ black pebbles. The reason is that while there may be arbitrarily many blue pebbles, at most $b$ blue pebbles can be utilized since there are at most $b$ blue moves. Therefore, either $m + b \geq (\beta - 2\alpha)n$ or an exponential number of red moves are needed. Below is a rigorous proof.

*Proof.* The proof is similar to the inductive proof for the black pebble game trade-off [44,49]. For the base case $k = 0$, an $(n, 0, \alpha, \beta)$ stacked expander is simply a collection of $n$ isolated vertices with no edges. The theorem is trivially true since the $\alpha n$ are pebbled through red moves.

Now we show the inductive step for $k \geq 1$ assuming the theorem holds for $k - 1$. The $\alpha n$ sinks in $V_k$ that are pebbled through red moves collectively are connected to at least $\beta n$ predecessors in $V_{k-1}$ due to the $(n, \alpha, \beta)$ expander property. Each of these $\beta n$ vertices in $V_{k-1}$ must have a red pebble on it at some point to facilitate the red moves on the $\alpha n$ sinks. These $\beta n$ vertices may get their red pebbles in one of the three ways below. Up to $m$ of them may initially have red pebbles on them. Up to $(\beta - 2\alpha)n - m$ of them may initially have blue pebbles on them get red pebbles through blue moves. The remaining $2\alpha n$ of them must get their red pebbles through red moves. These $2\alpha n$ vertices in $V_{k-1}$ are sinks of an $(n, k-1, \alpha, \beta)$ stacked expander. Divide them into two groups of $\alpha n$ each in the order they get red pebbles in $\mathbf{P}$ for the first time. $\mathbf{P}$ can be then divided into two parts $\mathbf{P} = (\mathbf{P}_1, \mathbf{P}_2)$ where $\mathbf{P}_1$ places red pebbles on the first group ($\mathbf{P}_1$ does not place red pebbles on any vertices in the second group) and $\mathbf{P}_2$ places red pebbles on the second group. Both $\mathbf{P}_1$ and $\mathbf{P}_2$ use no more than $m$ red pebbles and $(\beta - 2\alpha)n - m$ blue moves. Due to the inductive hypothesis, both use at least $2^{k-1}\alpha n$ red moves. Therefore, $\mathbf{P}$ uses at least $2^k\alpha n$ red moves. $\qquad\square$

**Theorem 4.** *Let $G$ be an $(n, k, \alpha, \beta)$ stacked expander with in-degree $d$. Its red-blue pebbling complexity* $\mathsf{ec}(G, m, c_b, c_r)$ *is lower bounded by* $(c_b+c_r)\cdot((\beta-2\alpha)n - m) \cdot (k - \lceil\log_2(c_b/dc_r)\rceil)/\alpha$.

*Proof.* With the chain edges, if a sequence starts from an empty configuration, then it must pebble vertices in $G$ in topological order. For simplicity, let us assume each layer of $n$ vertices can be divided into an integer number of groups of size $\alpha n$ each (i.e., $\alpha n$ divides $n$). Now we can break up the sequence into $(k+1)n/\alpha n$ sub-sequences; each one pebbles the next consecutive $\alpha n$ vertices *for the first time*. Since the red-blue pebbling costs from multiple sub-sequences are additive, we analyze and lower bound them independently.

Consider a sub-sequence $\mathbf{P}'$ that pebbles $\alpha n$ vertices in $V_i$ for the first time. Theorem 3 shows a trade-off on the usage of red versus blue moves. We note that Theorem 3 can be generalized. If $\mathbf{P}'$ uses at most $m$ red pebbles (plus an arbitrary number of blue pebbles) and at most $(\beta - q\alpha)n - m$ blue moves, then $\mathbf{P}'$ must use at least $q^i\alpha n$ red moves. For a proof, simply notice that there will be $q\alpha n$ vertices in $V_{i-1}$ that need to get their red pebbles through red moves. The $q^i$ factor follows from a similar induction. This means $\mathbf{P}'$ must choose one of the following options:

- use at least $(\beta - 2\alpha)n - m$ blue moves, plus $\alpha n$ red moves;
- use less than $(\beta - 2\alpha)n - m$ but at least $(\beta - 3\alpha)n - m$ blue moves, plus at least $2^i\alpha n$ red moves;
- use less than $(\beta - 3\alpha)n - m$ but at least $(\beta - 4\alpha)n - m$ blue moves, plus at least $3^i\alpha n$ red moves;
- $\cdots$

Comparing these options, we see that in order to save $\alpha n$ blue moves, $\mathbf{P}'$ needs to compensate with $(2^i - 1)\alpha n$ more red moves. For $i > \lceil\log_2(c_b/dc_r)\rceil$, blue moves are not worth saving because $\alpha n$ blue moves cost $c_b\alpha n$ which is less than the cost of $2^i - 1$ red moves. To save $(q+1)\alpha n$ blue moves, $\mathbf{P}'$ needs to compensate with $(q^i - 1)\alpha n$ more red moves, which is even less economical. This means, for layers relatively deep, the best strategy is to use blue moves whenever possible. The cost of the first option is $\mathsf{ec}(\mathbf{P}') \geq c_b((\beta-2\alpha)n-m)+c_rd\alpha n > (c_b+c_r)((\beta-2\alpha)n-m)$. The latter inequality is due to $d\alpha > \beta - 2\alpha$, which is easy to check from the requirement on $d$ for expanders. Lastly, there are $(k - \lceil\log_2(c_b/dc_r)\rceil)$ layers $V_i$

satisfying $i > \lceil \log_2(c_b/dc_r) \rceil$ and each contains $1/\alpha$ vertex groups of size $\alpha n$. The bound in the theorem follows.     □

For a stacked expander graph to be bandwidth hard, we only need $n$ and $k$ to be a constant factor larger than $m/(\beta - 2\alpha)$ and $\lceil \log_2(c_b/dc_r) \rceil$, respectively, which can be much less space and time from honest users compared to scrypt and bit-reversal graphs under some parameters. When $n$ and $k$ are sufficiently large, an ASIC's advantage $A_{ec} \approx \frac{c_{b,cpu}+c_{r,cpu}}{c_{b,asic}+c_{r,asic}} \cdot \frac{d\alpha}{\beta-2\alpha} = \overline{A_{ec}} \cdot \frac{d\alpha}{\beta-2\alpha}$. For an example design point, if we can choose $\alpha = 0.01$ and $\beta = 0.05$, we have $d = 9$, $d\alpha/(\beta - 2\alpha) = 3$ and $A_{ec} \approx 20$.

## 5.4   Stacked Butterfly Graphs Are Not Bandwidth Hard

In this section, we demonstrate that a capacity hard function in the sequential model may not be bandwidth hard using a stacked double butterfly graph as a counterexample. A double butterfly graph consists of two fast Fourier transform graphs back to back. It has $n$ sources, $n$ sinks and $2n \log_2 n$ vertices in total for some $n$ that is a power of 2. The intermediate vertices form two smaller double butterfly graphs each with $n/2$ sources and $n/2$ sinks. Figure 4 shows an example double butterfly graph with $n = 8$. A stacked double butterfly graph further stacks copies of double butterfly graphs back to back (not shown in the figure).

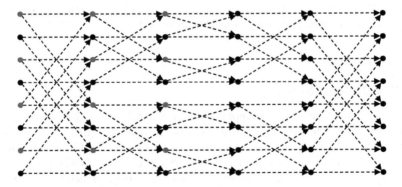

**Fig. 4.** A double butterfly graph with $n = 8$ sources and sinks. Vertices marked in red have locality assuming a cache size of $m = 4$. (Color figure online)

A double butterfly graph is a superconcentrator [26], and it has been shown that stacked superconcentrators have an exponentially sharp space-time trade-off in sequential pebble games [38]. However, a stacked double butterfly graph is not bandwidth hard due to locality in its memory access pattern. One can fetch a batch of operands into the cache and perform a lot of computation with them before swapping in another batch of operands. For example, in Fig. 4, one can pebble the red vertices layer by layer without relying on other vertices, since the red vertices only have incoming edges from themselves. If equipped with a cache of size $m$ (assume $m$ is a power of 2 for simplicity), we can adopt the following pebbling strategy to save blue moves without sacrificing red moves. We first place red pebbles on $m$ vertices in the same layer that are $n/m$ away from each other, possibly through blue moves. We then use red moves to proceed $\log_2 m$ layers horizontally, placing red pebbles on the $m$ vertices in the same horizontal positions. For a stacked double butterfly with $N$ vertices in total, this strategy uses $N$ red moves and only $N/\log_2 m$ blue moves. Its cost is therefore $(2c_r + c_b/\log_2 m)N$. As demonstrated in Sect. 4.1, $c_{r,\mathsf{cpu}}$ is larger or at least comparable to $c_{b,\mathsf{cpu}}$ while $c_{r,\mathsf{asic}} \ll c_{b,\mathsf{asic}}$. Therefore, the red-blue pebbling of a stacked double butterfly graph costs more than $2c_{r,\mathsf{cpu}}N$ on CPUs and roughly $c_{b,\mathsf{asic}}N/\log_2 m$ on ASICs. This results in an advantage proportional to $\log_2 m$.

Stacked double butterfly graphs are used by the capacity hard function Catena-DBG [35] and the capacity hard proof of work by Ateniese et al. [18]. We note that Catena-DBG designers further add chain edges within each layer [35]. These chain edges will prevent our proposed pebbling strategy, so Catena-DBG may not suffer from the $\log_2 m$ ASIC energy advantage. Our goal here is to show that capacity hard functions in the sequential model are not necessarily bandwidth hard, and a stacked double butterfly graph without chain edges serves as an example. We also remark that since stacked double butterfly graphs are not capacity hard under parallel attacks, it remains unclear whether parallel capacity hardness implies bandwidth hardness. But since capacity and bandwidth are quite different metrics, we currently do not expect that to be the case. (Bandwidth hardness certainly does not imply parallel capacity hardness with Catena-BRG and Balloon being counterexamples.)

## 6   Discussion

### 6.1   The Role of Memory

It is not a coincidence that memory plays a central role in both the area and the energy approach, and this point may be worth some further justification. As mentioned, CPUs are at a huge disadvantage over ASICs in computation because CPUs are general purpose while ASICs are specifically optimized for a certain task. Memory does not suffer from this problem because memory is, for the most part, intrinsically general purpose. Memory's job is to store bits and deliver them to the compute units regardless of what the computational task is. New technologies like 3D-stacked memory [24], high speed serial [2] and various types of non-volatile memory do not undermine this argument: they are also general purpose and will be adopted by both CPUs and ASICs when they become successful.

### 6.2   Capacity Hardness and Energy?

Here a reader may wonder whether we can make an energy argument for capacity hard functions. Specifically, one may argue that holding a large capacity of data in memory also costs energy, and it must be similar for ASICs and CPUs due to the general purpose nature of memory. The problem is that the energy cost of holding data in memory depends on the underlying memory technology, and can be extremely small. We call the power spent on holding data *idle power*, and the power spent on transferring data *busy power*. Volatile memory like DRAM needs to periodically refresh data and thus has a noticeable idle power consumption. For non-volatile memory/storage, idle power is negligible or even strictly 0, independent of memory capacity [54]. Think about hard disks in one's garage — they consume no energy no matter how much data they are holding. The energy argument for capacity hardness breaks down for non-volatile memory/storage. Energy consumption in non-volatile memory/storage only occurs when data transfer happens, which is exactly what our model assumes.

In fact, even with volatile memory like DRAM, the energy model cannot be solely based on memory capacity. While DRAM idle power is indeed proportional to memory capacity, idle power will never be the dominant part in a reasonable system. Section 6.3 further discusses this issue.

### 6.3   Implications of Parallel Attacks

***Parallel attacks and area.*** Percival [46] defines memory hard functions to be functions that (1) can be computed using $T_0$ time and $S_0 = O(T_0^{1-\epsilon})$ space, and (2) cannot be computed using $T$ time and $S$ space where $ST = O(T_0^{2-\epsilon})$. The $ST$ lower bound at the first glance makes intuitive sense as it lower bounds the $AT$ product assuming that memory rather than the compute unit dominates chip area. However, concerns have been raised about the above reasoning [10, 22]. Because a $ST$ lower bound allows space-time trade-off, a chip designer can reduce the amount of memory by a factor of $q$, and then use $q$ compute units in parallel to keep the running time at $T_0$. If $q$ is not too large, chip area may still be dominated by memory, so in theory this parallel architecture reduces the $AT$ product by roughly a factor of $q$. To address this issue, subsequent proposals introduce stronger notions of capacity hardness that, for example, require a linear space lower bound (in a computational sense) $S = cS_0$ [18, 25, 35]. But it is later uncovered that parallel architectures can asymptotically decrease the amortized $AT$ product of these constructions as well, and even stronger, the amortized $AT$ product of any data independent functions [10].

However, we would like to note that the above parallel attacks adopt an oversimplified hardware model [10, 12, 14, 15, 22]: most of them assume unlimited bandwidth for free. In practice, memory bandwidth is a scarce resource and is *the* major bottleneck in parallel computing, widely known as the "memory wall" [17]. Increasing memory bandwidth would inevitably in turn increase chip area and the more fundamental metric manufacturing cost. Only one paper presents simulation results with concrete bandwidth requirements [11]. We laud this effort, but unfortunately, the paper incorrectly chooses energy as the metric, as we explain below. The area model in those attacks [10] looks reasonable, though the memory bandwidth they assume is still too high. It would improve our understanding on this issue if the authors provide simulation results with area as the metric and for a wide range of bandwidth values from GB/s to TB/s.

***Parallel attacks and energy.*** We adopt a sequential model for bandwidth hard functions in which parallelism does not help by definition. We believe this model is reasonable because, to first-order effects, transferring data sequentially or in parallel should consume roughly the same amount of energy. However, some recent works [10, 12, 15] conclude that parallel attacks will have an asymptotic energy gain for any data independent function, bit-reversal graphs and stacked expanders included in particular, which is the exact opposite of our conclusion. Their conclusions result from a flawed energy model. They assume memory's idle power is proportional to its capacity, which is reasonable assuming volatile memory like DRAM. The flaw is that they explicitly assume that memory idle power keeps increasing with memory capacity to the extent that it eventually dwarfs all other power consumption. On a closer look, the energy advantage they obtain under this model is not due to a parallel ASIC architecture having superb energy efficiency, but rather because the sequential baseline has absurdly high memory idle energy cost (i.e., energy cost for holding data). Under their concrete parameterization [11], if we hash 1 GB of data using one CPU core, the memory idle power/energy will be 5000× greater than all other power/energy cost combined! The mistake in their concrete parameterization is that they incorrectly cite an estimated conversion rate for area density in a prior work [22] as a conversion rate for energy cost, which leads to an overestimate of memory idle power/energy by at least 100,000×. But if only the constant is off, asymptotically speaking, isn't it true that as DRAM capacity increases, eventually memory idle power/energy will dwarf other components? The answer is yes, but its implication is rather uninteresting and not concerning. It tells us that a computer with a single CPU core and Terabytes of DRAM will have terrible energy efficiency because it spends too much energy refreshing DRAM. Obviously, no manufacturer will produce and no user will buy such a computer — long before reaching this design point, manufacturers will switch to non-volatile memory or simply stop adding DRAM capacity.

## 7   Conclusion

ASIC resistance requires both theoretical advancement and accurate hardware understanding. With this work, we would like call attention to arguably the most important aspect of ASIC resistance: energy efficiency. We illustrate that the popular memory (capacity) hardness notion does not capture energy efficiency, and indeed a capacity hard function may not achieve energy fairness. We propose the notion of bandwidth hardness to achieve energy fairness between ASICs and CPUs. We analyze candidate constructions and show that scrypt, Catena-BRG and Balloon hashing provide good energy efficiency fairness with suitable parameters.

We conclude the paper with a summary of provable security of different constructions under different thread models. (1) If memory access pattern leakage is not a concern, then scrypt is a good option, since it enjoys capacity hardness under parallel attacks as well as bandwidth hardness (for which parallel attacks do not help). (2) If we assume the adversary has limited parallelism, then Balloon hash is a good choice since it achieves sequential capacity hardness and bandwidth hardness. (3) In some scenarios (e.g., Bitcoin mining), it may be argued that energy advantage resistance alone is sufficient to thwart ASIC attackers, in which case data-independent bandwidth hard functions (e.g., Catena-BRG and Balloon) can be used despite parallel attacks on their area resistance. (4) If both area and energy resistance are required, memory access pattern must be data-independent and additionally the adversary has extremely high parallelism, then we know of no good candidates. In this situation, area resistance alone must suffer poly-logarithmic loss. Furthermore, good parallel capacity hard constructions to date are highly complex and we have not been able to analyze their bandwidth behaviors. Lastly, we mention that in the first three models, a possible alternative is Argon2 [21], the winner of the Password Hashing Competition. We have not been able to analyze the bandwidth hardness of Argon2, and it remains interesting future work.

**Acknowledgements.** The authors are grateful to Krzysztof Pietrzak, Joël Alwen and Jeremiah Blocki for valuable discussions.

# References

1. Antminer S9 - Bitmain. https://shop.bitmain.com/market.htm?name=antminer_s9_asic_bitcoin_miner. Accessed 04 Feb 2017
2. High Speed Serial - Xilinx. https://www.xilinx.com/products/technology/high-speed-serial.html. Accessed 04 Feb 2017
3. Intel advanced encryption standard instructions (AES-NI). https://software.intel.com/en-us/articles/intel-advanced-encryption-standard-instructions-aes-ni. Accessed 04 Feb 2017
4. Intel power gadget. https://software.intel.com/en-us/articles/intel-power-gadget-20. Accessed 04 Feb 2017
5. Litecoin. https://litecoin.org/
6. Zoom Hash Scrypt ASIC. http://zoomhash.com/collections/asics. Accessed 20 May 2016
7. Intel SHA extensions (2013). https://software.intel.com/en-us/articles/intel-sha-extensions. Accessed 04 Feb 2017
8. Abadi, M., Burrows, M., Manasse, M., Wobber, T.: Moderately hard, memory-bound functions. ACM Trans. Internet Technol. **5**(2), 299–327 (2005)
9. Almeida, L.C., Andrade, E.R., Barreto, P.S.L.M., Simplicio Jr., M.A.: Lyra: password-based key derivation with tunable memory and processing costs. J. Cryptogr. Eng. **4**(2), 75–89 (2014)
10. Alwen, J., Blocki, J.: Efficiently computing data-independent memory-hard functions. In: Robshaw, M., Katz, J. (eds.) CRYPTO 2016. LNCS, vol. 9815, pp. 241–271. Springer, Heidelberg (2016). doi:10.1007/978-3-662-53008-5_9
11. Alwen, J., Blocki, J.: Towards practical attacks on Argon2i and balloon hashing. In: 2017 IEEE European Symposium on Security and Privacy (EuroS&P), pp. 142–157. IEEE (2017)
12. Alwen, J., Blocki, J., Pietrzak, K.: Depth-robust graphs and their cumulative memory complexity. In: Coron, J.-S., Nielsen, J.B. (eds.) EUROCRYPT 2017. LNCS, vol. 10212, pp. 3–32. Springer, Cham (2017). doi:10.1007/978-3-319-56617-7_1

13. Alwen, J., Chen, B., Pietrzak, K., Reyzin, L., Tessaro, S.: Scrypt is maximally memory-hard. In: Coron, J.-S., Nielsen, J.B. (eds.) EUROCRYPT 2017. LNCS, vol. 10212, pp. 33–62. Springer, Cham (2017). doi:10.1007/978-3-319-56617-7_2

14. Alwen, J., Gazi, P., Kamath, C., Klein, K., Osang, G., Pietrzak, K., Reyzin, L., Rolınek, M., Rybár, M.: On the memory-hardness of data-independent password-hashing functions. Cryptology ePrint Archive, Report 2016/783 (2016)

15. Alwen, J., Serbinenko, V.: High parallel complexity graphs and memory-hard functions. In: Proceedings of the Forty-Seventh Annual ACM on Symposium on Theory of Computing, pp. 595–603. ACM (2015)

16. Amrutur, B., Horowitz, M.: Speed and power scaling of SRAM's. IEEE J. Solid-State Circ. 35(2), 175–185 (2000)

17. Asanovic, K., Bodik, R., Catanzaro, B.C., Gebis, J.J., Husbands, P., Keutzer, K., Patterson, D.A., Plishker, W.L., Shalf, J., Williams, S.W. et al.: The landscape of parallel computing research: A view from berkeley. Technical report, Technical Report UCB/EECS-2006-183, EECS Department, University of California, Berkeley (2006)

18. Ateniese, G., Bonacina, I., Faonio, A., Galesi, N.: Proofs of space: when space is of the essence. In: Abdalla, M., De Prisco, R. (eds.) SCN 2014. LNCS, vol. 8642, pp. 538–557. Springer, Cham (2014). doi:10.1007/978-3-319-10879-7_31

19. Back, A.: Hashcash-a denial of service counter-measure (2002)

20. Belady, L.A.: A study of replacement algorithms for a virtual-storage computer. IBM Syst. J. 5(2), 78–101 (1966)

21. Biryukov, A., Dinu, D., Khovratovich, D.: Fast and tradeoff-resilient memory-hard functions for cryptocurrencies and password hashing (2015)

22. Biryukov, A., Khovratovich, D.: Tradeoff cryptanalysis of memory-hard functions. Cryptology ePrint Archive, Report 2015/227 (2015)

23. Biryukov, A., Khovratovich, D.: Equihash: asymmetric proof-of-work based on the generalized birthday problem. In: NDSS (2016)

24. Black, B., Annavaram, M., Brekelbaum, N., DeVale, J., Jiang, L., Loh, G.H., McCaule, D., Morrow, P., Nelson, D.W., Pantuso, D. et al.: Die stacking (3D) microarchitecture. In: Proceedings of the 39th Annual IEEE/ACM International Symposium on Microarchitecture, pp. 469–479. IEEE Computer Society (2006)

25. Boneh, D., Corrigan-Gibbs, H., Schechter, S.: Balloon hashing: a memory-hard function providing provable protection against sequential attacks. In: Cheon, J.H., Takagi, T. (eds.) ASIACRYPT 2016. LNCS, vol. 10031, pp. 220–248. Springer, Heidelberg (2016). doi:10.1007/978-3-662-53887-6_8

26. Bradley, W.F.: Superconcentration on a pair of butterflies. CoRR abs/1401.7263 (2014)

27. Cook, S.A.: An observation on time-storage trade off. In: Proceedings of the Fifth Annual ACM Symposium on Theory of Computing, pp. 29–33. ACM (1973)

28. Damgård, I.B.: A design principle for hash functions. In: Brassard, G. (ed.) CRYPTO 1989. LNCS, vol. 435, pp. 416–427. Springer, New York (1990). doi:10.1007/0-387-34805-0_39

29. Dwork, C., Goldberg, A., Naor, M.: On memory-bound functions for fighting spam. In: Boneh, D. (ed.) CRYPTO 2003. LNCS, vol. 2729, pp. 426–444. Springer, Heidelberg (2003). doi:10.1007/978-3-540-45146-4_25

30. Dwork, C., Naor, M.: Pricing via processing or combatting junk mail. In: Brickell, E.F. (ed.) CRYPTO 1992. LNCS, vol. 740, pp. 139–147. Springer, Heidelberg (1993). doi:10.1007/3-540-48071-4_10

31. Dwork, C., Naor, M., Wee, H.: Pebbling and proofs of work. In: Shoup, V. (ed.) CRYPTO 2005. LNCS, vol. 3621, pp. 37–54. Springer, Heidelberg (2005). doi:10.1007/11535218_3

32. Dziembowski, S., Faust, S., Kolmogorov, V., Pietrzak, K.: Proofs of space. In: Gennaro, R., Robshaw, M. (eds.) CRYPTO 2015. LNCS, vol. 9216, pp. 585–605. Springer, Heidelberg (2015). doi:10.1007/978-3-662-48000-7_29

33. Dziembowski, S., Kazana, T., Wichs, D.: One-time computable self-erasing functions. In: Ishai, Y. (ed.) TCC 2011. LNCS, vol. 6597, pp. 125–143. Springer, Heidelberg (2011). doi:10.1007/978-3-642-19571-6_9

34. Forler, C., List, E., Lucks, S., Wenzel, J.: Overview of the candidates for the password hashing competition. In: Mjølsnes, S.F. (ed.) PASSWORDS 2014. LNCS, vol. 9393, pp. 3–18. Springer, Cham (2015). doi:10.1007/978-3-319-24192-0_1

35. Forler, C., Lucks, S., Wenzel, J.: Catena : a memory-consuming password-scrambling framework. Cryptology ePrint Archive, Report 2013/525 (2013)

36. Hopcroft, J., Paul, W., Valiant, L.: On time versus space and related problems. In: 16th Annual Symposium on Foundations of Computer Science, pp. 57–64. IEEE (1975)

37. Horowitz, M.: Computing's energy problem (and what we can do about it). In: 2014 IEEE International Solid-State Circuits Conference Digest of Technical Papers (ISSCC), pp. 10–14. IEEE (2014)

38. Lengauer, T., Tarjan, R.E.: Asymptotically tight bounds on time-space trade-offs in a pebble game. J. ACM **29**(4), 1087–1130 (1982)

39. Lerner, S.D.: Strict memory hard hashing functions (preliminary v0. 3, 01–19-14)

40. Mahmoody, M., Moran, T., Vadhan, S.: Publicly verifiable proofs of sequential work. In: Proceedings of the 4th Conference on Innovations in Theoretical Computer Science, pp. 373–388. ACM (2013)

41. Mead, C.A., Rem, M.: Cost and performance of vlsi computing structures. IEEE Trans. Electron Devices **26**(4), 533–540 (1979)

42. Merkle, R.C.: One way hash functions and DES. In: Brassard, G. (ed.) CRYPTO 1989. LNCS, vol. 435, pp. 428–446. Springer, New York (1990). doi:10.1007/0-387-34805-0_40

43. Nakamoto, S.: Bitcoin: A peer-to-peer electronic cash system (2008)

44. Paul, W.J., Tarjan, R.E.: Time-space trade-offs in a pebble game. Acta Inf. **10**(2), 111–115 (1978)

45. Pedram, A., Richardson, S., Galal, S., Kvatinsky, S., Horowitz, M.: Dark memory and accelerator-rich system optimization in the dark silicon era. IEEE Des. Test **34**, 39–50 (2016)

46. Percival, C.: Stronger key derivation via sequential memory-hard functions (2009)

47. Peslyak, A.: yescrypt - a password hashing competition submission (2014). https://password-hashing.net/submissions/specs/yescrypt-v2.pdf. Accessed Aug 2016

48. Pinsker, M.S.: On the complexity of a concentrator. In: 7th International Telegraffic Conference, vol. 4 (1973)

49. Ren, L., Devadas, S.: Proof of space from stacked expanders. In: Hirt, M., Smith, A. (eds.) TCC 2016. LNCS, vol. 9985, pp. 262–285. Springer, Heidelberg (2016). doi:10.1007/978-3-662-53641-4_11

50. Savage, J.E.: Models of Computation. Addison-Wesley, Boston (1998)

51. Sethi, R.: Complete register allocation problems. SIAM J. Comput. **4**(3), 226–248 (1975)

52. Smith, A., Zhang, Y.: Near-linear time, leakage-resilient key evolution schemes from expander graphs. Cryptology ePrint Archive, Report 2013/864 (2013)

53. Tromp, J.: Cuckoo cycle: a memory-hard proof-of-work system (2014)
54. Xue, C.J., Sun, G., Zhang, Y., Yang, J.J., Chen, Y., Li, H.: Emerging non-volatile memories: opportunities and challenges. In: 2011 Proceedings of the 9th International Conference on Hardware/Software Codesign and System Synthesis, pp. 325–334. IEEE (2011)

# Moderately Hard Functions: Definition, Instantiations, and Applications

Joël Alwen[1] and Björn Tackmann[2]([✉])

[1] IST Austria, Vienna, Austria
jalwen@ist.ac.at
[2] IBM Research – Zurich, Rüschlikon, Switzerland
bta@zurich.ibm.com

**Abstract.** Several cryptographic schemes and applications are based on functions that are both reasonably efficient to compute and moderately hard to invert, including client puzzles for Denial-of-Service protection, password protection via salted hashes, or recent proof-of-work blockchain systems. Despite their wide use, a definition of this concept has not yet been distilled and formalized explicitly. Instead, either the applications are proven directly based on the assumptions underlying the function, or some property of the function is proven, but the security of the application is argued only informally. The goal of this work is to provide a (universal) definition that decouples the efforts of designing new moderately hard functions and of building protocols based on them, serving as an interface between the two.

On a technical level, beyond the mentioned definitions, we instantiate the model for four different notions of hardness. We extend the work of Alwen and Serbinenko (STOC 2015) by providing a general tool for proving security for the first notion of memory-hard functions that allows for provably secure applications. The tool allows us to recover all of the graph-theoretic techniques developed for proving security under the older, non-composable, notion of security used by Alwen and Serbinenko. As an application of our definition of moderately hard functions, we prove the security of two different schemes for proofs of effort (PoE). We also formalize and instantiate the concept of a non-interactive proof of effort (niPoE), in which the proof is not bound to a particular communication context but rather any bit-string chosen by the prover.

## 1 Introduction

Several cryptographic schemes and applications are based on (computational) problems that are "moderately hard" to solve. One example is hashing passwords with a salted, moderately hard-to-compute hash function and storing the hash in the password file of a login server. Should the password file become exposed through an attack, the increased hardness of the hash function relative to a standard one increases the effort that the attacker has to spend to recover the passwords in a brute-force attack [33,48,51]. Another widely-cited example of

© International Association for Cryptologic Research 2017
Y. Kalai and L. Reyzin (Eds.): TCC 2017, Part I, LNCS 10677, pp. 493–526, 2017.
https://doi.org/10.1007/978-3-319-70500-2_17

this approach originates in the work of Dwork and Naor [28], who suggested the use of a so-called *pricing function*, supposedly moderately hard to compute, as a countermeasure for junk mail: the sender of a mail must compute a moderately hard function (MoHF) on an input that includes the sender, the receiver, and the mail body, and send the function value together with the message, as otherwise the receiver will not accept the mail. This can be viewed as a proof of effort[1] (PoE), which, in a nutshell, is a 2-party (interactive) proof system where the verifier accepts if and only if the prover has exerted a moderate amount of effort during the execution of the protocol. Such a PoE can be used to meter access to a valuable resource like, in the case of [28], the attention of a mail receiver. As observed by the authors, requiring this additional effort would introduce a significant obstacle to any spammer wishing to flood many receivers with unsolicited mails. Security was argued only informally in the original work. A line of follow-up papers [1,27,29] provides a formal treatment and proves security for protocols that are intuitively based on functions that are moderately hard to compute on architectures with limited cache size.

PoEs have many applications beyond combatting spam mail. One widely discussed special case of PoE protocols are so-called cryptographic puzzles (or client puzzles, e.g. [12,21,22,36,37,40,52,54]), which are mainly targeted at protecting Internet servers from Denial-of-Service attacks by having the client solve the puzzle before the server engages in any costly operation. These PoEs have the special form of consisting of a single pair of challenge and response messages (i.e., one round of communication), and are mostly based on either inverting a MoHF [40], or finding an input to an MoHF that leads to an output with a certain number of trailing zeroes [2]. More recently, cryptocurrencies based on distributed transaction ledgers that are managed through a consensus protocol based on PoEs have emerged, most prominently Bitcoin [49] and Ethereum [19], and are again based on MoHFs. In a nutshell, to append a block of transactions to the ledger, a so-called *miner* has to legitimate the block by a PoE, and as long as miners that control a majority of a computing power are honest, the ledger remains consistent [34].

The notions of hardness underlying the MoHFs that have been designed for the above applications vary widely. The earliest and still most common one is computational hardness in terms of the number of computation steps that have to be spent to solve the problem [22,28,40,49]. Other proposals exploit the limited size of fast cache in current architectures and are aimed at forcing the processor to access the slower main memory [1,27,29], the use of large amounts of memory during the evaluation of the function [10,33,51], or even disk space [30].

Given the plethora of work (implicitly or explicitly) designing and using MoHFs, one question soon comes to mind: is it possible to use the MoHF designed in one work in the application context of another? The current answer is sobering. Either the security notion for the MoHF is not quite sufficient for

---

[1] We intentionally use the term *effort* instead of *work* since the latter is often associated with computational work, while a MoHF in our framework may be based on spending other types of resources such as memory.

proving the security of the targeted applications. Or security of the application is proven directly without separating out the properties used from the underlying MoHF.

For example, in the domain of memory-hard functions—an increasingly common type of MoHF first motivated by Percival in [51]—the security of MoHF applications is generally argued only informally. Indeed, this likely stems from the fact that proposed definitions seem inadequate for the task. As argued by Alwen and Serbinenko [10], the hardness notion used by Percival [51] and Forler *et al.* [33] is not sufficient in practical settings because it disregards that an attacker may amortize the effort over multiple evaluations of the function, or use inherently parallel computational capabilities as provided by a circuit. Yet the definition of [10], while taking these into account, is also not (known to be) useful in proving the security of higher-level protocols, because it requires high average-case, instead of worst-case, complexity. Worse, like all other MoHF definitions in the literature (e.g. [3,15]), it focuses only on the hardness of *evaluating* the function; indeed, in most cases the functions modified to append their inputs to their outputs would be considered to have the same complexity as the original ones, but become trivially invertible. However, all applications present the adversary with the task of *inverting* the MoHF in some form.

In other areas, where the application security *is* explicitly proven [1,27,29], this is done directly with out separating out the properties of the underlying MoHF. This means that (a) the MoHF (security) cannot easily be "extracted" from the paper and used in other contexts, and (b) the protocols cannot easily be instantiated with other MoHFs. Furthermore, the security definitions come with a hard-wired notion of hardness, so it is *a priori* even more difficult to replace the in-built MoHF with one for a different type of hardness.

Consequently, as already discussed by Naor in his 2003 invited lecture [50], what is needed is a unifying theory of MoHFs. The contribution of this paper is a step toward this direction. Our goal is to design an abstract notion of MoHF that is flexible enough to model various types of functions for various hardness notions considered in the literature, but still expressive enough to be useful in a wide range of applications. We propose such a definition, show (with varying degrees of formality) that existing constructions for various types of hardness instantiate it, and show how it can be used in various application scenarios. Not all proof-of-work schemes, however, fall into the mold of the ones covered in this work. For example the recently popular Equihash [16] has a different form.[2]

*More Details on Related Work.* We briefly summarize related papers beyond those referenced above. A detailed overview can be found in the full version [11].

---

[2] Nevertheless, we conjecture that Equihash could also be analyzed in out framework. In particular, if we can always model the underlying hash function used by Equihash as a (trivially secure) MoHF. Then, by assuming the optimality of Wagner's collision finding algorithm (as done in [16]) one could compute the parameters for which Equihash gives rise to our proof-of-effort definition in Sect. 6. We leave this line of reasoning for future work.

After the initial work of Dwork and Naor [28], most subsequent work on MoHFs is based on hash functions, such as using the plain hash function [2] or iterating the function to increase the hardness of inverting it. Iteration seems to first appear in the Unix crypt function [48] and analyzed by Yao and Yin [56] and Bellare *et al.* [14]. A prefixing scheme for iteration has been discussed and analyzed by Demay *et al.* [26]. The definitions of [14,26] are conceptually similar to ours, as they are also based on indifferentiability. Their definitions, however, are restricted to the complexity measure of counting the number of random-oracle invocations.

Based on memory-bound functions, which aim at forcing the processor to access the (slower) main memory because the data needed to compute the functions do not fit into the (fast but small) cache, proofs-of-effort have been developed and analyzed in [1,27,29]. The rough idea is that during the computation of the function one has to access various position in a random-looking array that is too large to fit into cache. We discuss the reduction that will be necessary to make those functions useful in our framework in Sect. 5.

For memory-hard functions, which rely on a notion of hardness aimed at ensuring that application-specific integrated circuits (ASICs) have as little advantage (in terms of dollar per rate of computation) over general-purpose hardware, the first security notion of memory-hard functions was given by Percival [51]. The definition asks for a lower bound on the product of memory and time used by an algorithm evaluating the function on any single input. This definition was refined by Alwen and Serbinenko [10] by modeling parallel algorithms as well as the amortized Cumulative Memory Complexity (aCMC) of the algorithms. aCMC was further refined by Alwen and Blocki [3] to account for possible trade-offs of decreasing memory consumption at the added cost of increased logic gates resulting in the notion of amortized Energy Complexity (aEC).

*Our Contributions and Outline of the Paper.* The starting point of our MoHF definition is the observation that—on the one hand—many instantiations of MoHFs are based on hash functions and analyzed in the random-oracle model, and—on the other hand—many applications also assume that a MoHF behaves like a random oracle. More concretely, we base our definition on indifferentiability from a random oracle [47], and describe each "real-world setting" according to the computational model underlying the MoHF.

Section 2 covers preliminaries; in particular we recall the notion of indifferentiability and introduce an abstract notion of computational cost and resource-bounded computation. In Sect. 3, we describe our new indifferentiability-based definition of MoHF in terms of the real and ideal models considered. Next, in Sect. 4, we instantiate the MoHF definition for the case of memory-hard functions. This section contains the main technical result of the paper, an extension of the pebbling reduction of Alwen and Serbinenko [10] to our stricter MoHF definition. In Sect. 5, we discuss then discuss how other types of moderately hard functions from the literature are captured in our framework, in particular weak memory-hard functions, memory-bound functions, and one-time computable functions. In Sect. 6, we describe a (composable) security definition for PoE. We present an ideal-world description of a PoE; a functionality where the prover can convince the verifier in a certain bounded number of sessions. As this definition starts from the ideal-world description of a MoHF as described above, it can be easily composed with every type of MoHF in our framework. We consider two types of PoE—one based on function inversion, and the other one on hash trail. In Sect. 7, we then continue to describing an analogous definition for a non-interactive proof of effort (niPoE), and again give an instantiation based on hash trail. In Sect. 8, we discuss the composition of the MoHF definition and the PoE and niPoE applications more concretely.

## 2 Preliminaries

We use the sets $\mathbb{N} := \{1, 2, \ldots\}$, and $\mathbb{Z}_{\geq c} := \{c, c+1, \ldots\} \cap \mathbb{Z}$ to denote integers greater than or equal to $c$. Similarly we write $[a, c]$ to denote $\{a, a+1, \ldots, c\}$ and $[c]$ for the set $[1, c]$. For a set $S$, we use the notation $x \leftarrow_\$ S$ to denote that $x$ is chosen uniformly at random from the set $S$. For arbitrary set $\mathbb{I}$ and $n \in \mathbb{N}$ we write $\mathbb{I}^{\times n}$ to denote the $n$-wise cross product of $\mathbb{I}$. We refer to sets of functions (or distributions) as *function (or distribution) families*.

### 2.1 Reactive Discrete Systems

For an input set $\mathbb{X}$ and an output set $\mathbb{Y}$, a *reactive discrete $(\mathbb{X}, \mathbb{Y})$-system* repeatedly takes as input a value (or query) $x_i \in \mathbb{X}$ and responds with a value $y_i \in \mathbb{Y}$, for $i \in \{1, 2, \ldots\}$. Thereby, each output $y_i$ may depend on all prior inputs $x_1, \ldots, x_i$. As discussed by Maurer [43], reactive discrete systems are exactly modeled by the notion of a *random system*, that is, the conditional distribution $\mathsf{p}_{Y_i | X^i Y^{i-1}}$ of each output (random variable) $Y_i \in \mathbb{Y}$ given all previous inputs $X_1, \ldots, X_i \in \mathbb{X}$ and outputs $Y_1, \ldots, Y_{i-1} \in \mathbb{Y}$ of the system.

Discrete reactive systems can have multiple interfaces, where each interface is labeled by an element in some set $\mathbb{I}$. We then formally consider $(\mathbb{I} \times \mathbb{X}, \mathbb{I} \times \mathbb{Y})$-systems, where providing an input $x \in \mathbb{X}$ at interface $i \in \mathbb{I}$ then means evaluating the system on input $(i, x) \in \mathbb{I} \times \mathbb{X}$, and the resulting output $(i', y) \in \mathbb{Y}$ means that the value $y$ is provided as a response at the interface $i' \in \mathbb{I}$. We generally denote reactive discrete systems by upper-case calligraphic letters such as $\mathcal{S}$ or $\mathcal{T}$ or by lower-case Greek letters such as $\pi$ or $\sigma$.

A *configuration of systems* is a set of systems which are connected via their interfaces. Any configuration of systems can again be seen as a system that provides all unconnected interfaces to its environment. Examples are shown in Fig. 1, where Fig. 1a shows a two-interface system $\pi$ connected to the single interface of another system $\mathcal{R}$, and Fig. 1b shows a two-interface system $\pi$ connected to the priv-interface of the system $\mathcal{S}$. The latter configuration is denoted by the term $\pi^{\mathrm{priv}} \mathcal{S}$. Finally, Fig. 1c shows a similar setting, but where additionally a distinguisher (or environment) $D$ is attached to both interfaces of $\sigma^{\mathrm{pub}} \mathcal{T}$. This setting is denoted as $D(\sigma^{\mathrm{pub}} \mathcal{T})$ and is further discussed in Sect. 2.2.

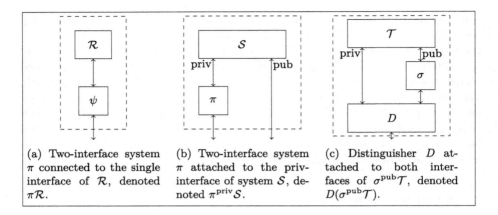

(a) Two-interface system $\pi$ connected to the single interface of $\mathcal{R}$, denoted $\pi\mathcal{R}$.

(b) Two-interface system $\pi$ attached to the priv-interface of system $\mathcal{S}$, denoted $\pi^{\mathrm{priv}}\mathcal{S}$.

(c) Distinguisher $D$ attached to both interfaces of $\sigma^{\mathrm{pub}}\mathcal{T}$, denoted $D(\sigma^{\mathrm{pub}}\mathcal{T})$.

**Fig. 1.** Examples for configurations of systems.

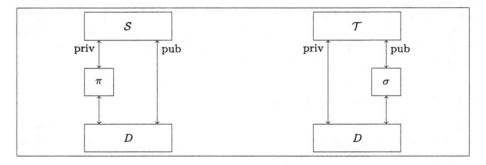

**Fig. 2.** Indifferentiability. **Left:** Distinguisher $D$ connected to protocol $\pi$ using the priv-interface of the real-world resource $\mathcal{S}$, denoted $D\left(\pi^{\mathrm{priv}}\mathcal{S}\right)$. **Right:** Distinguisher $D$ connected to simulator $\sigma$ attached to the pub-interface of the ideal-world resource $\mathcal{T}$, denoted $D\left(\sigma^{\mathrm{pub}}\mathcal{T}\right)$.

## 2.2 Indifferentiability

The main definitions in this work are based on the indifferentiability framework of Maurer *et al.* [46,47]. We define the indifferentiability notion in this section.

Indifferentiability of a protocol or scheme $\pi$, which using certain resources $\mathcal{S}$, from resource $\mathcal{T}$ requires that there exists a simulator $\sigma$ such that the two systems $\pi^{\mathrm{pub}}\mathcal{S}$ and $\sigma^{\mathrm{pub}}\mathcal{T}$ are indistinguishable, as depicted in Fig. 2. The indistinguishability is defined via a distinguisher $D$, a special system that interacts with either $\pi^{\mathrm{priv}}\mathcal{S}$ or $\sigma^{\mathrm{pub}}\mathcal{T}$ and finally outputs a bit. In the considered "real-world" setting with $\pi^{\mathrm{priv}}\mathcal{S}$, the distinguisher $D$ has direct access to the pub-interface of $\mathcal{S}$, but the priv-interface is accessible only through $\pi$. In the considered "ideal-world" setting with $\sigma^{\mathrm{pub}}\mathcal{T}$, $D$ has direct access to the priv-interface of $\mathcal{T}$, but the pub-interface is accessible only through $\sigma$. The advantage of the distinguisher is now defined to be the difference in the probability that $D$ outputs some fixed value, say 1, in the two settings, more formally,

$$\Delta^D\left(\pi^{\mathrm{priv}}\mathcal{S}, \sigma^{\mathrm{pub}}\mathcal{T}\right) = \left|\Pr\left[D(\pi^{\mathrm{priv}}\mathcal{S}) = 1\right] - \Pr\left[D(\sigma^{\mathrm{pub}}\mathcal{T}) = 1\right]\right|.$$

Intuitively, if the advantage is small, then, for the honest parties, the real-world resource $\mathcal{S}$ is at least as useful (when using it via $\pi$) as the ideal-world resource $\mathcal{T}$. Conversely, for the adversary the real world is at most as useful as the ideal world. Put differently, from the perspective of the honest parties, the real world is at least as safe as the ideal world. So any application that makes use of $\mathcal{T}$ can instead use $\pi^{\mathrm{priv}}\mathcal{S}$. This leads to the following definition.

**Definition 1 (Indifferentiability).** *Let $\pi$ be a protocol and $\mathcal{S}, \mathcal{T}$ be resources, and let $\varepsilon > 0$. Then $\pi^{\mathrm{priv}}\mathcal{S}$ is $\varepsilon$-indifferentiable from $\mathcal{T}$, if*

$$\exists \sigma : \pi^{\mathrm{priv}}\mathcal{S} \approx_\varepsilon \sigma^{\mathrm{pub}}\mathcal{T},$$

*with $\pi^{\mathrm{priv}}\mathcal{S} \approx_\varepsilon \sigma^{\mathrm{pub}}\mathcal{T}$ defined as $\forall D : \Delta^D\left(\pi^{\mathrm{priv}}\mathcal{S}, \sigma^{\mathrm{pub}}\mathcal{T}\right) \leq \varepsilon$.*

### 2.3   Oracle Functions and Oracle Algorithms

We explore several constructions of hard-to-compute functions that are defined via a sequence of calls to an oracle. To make this dependency explicit, we use the following notation. For sets $D$ and $R$, a *random oracle (RO)* $H$ is a random variable distributed uniformly over the function family $\mathbb{H} = \{h : D \to R\}$.

**Definition 2 (Oracle functions).** *For (implicit) oracle set $\mathbb{H}$, an oracle function $f^{(\cdot)}$ (with domain $D$ and range $R$), denoted $f^{(\cdot)} : D \to R$, is a set of functions indexed by oracles $h \in \mathbb{H}$ where each $f^h$ maps $D \to R$.*

We fix a concrete function in the set $f^{(\cdot)}$ by fixing an oracle $h \in \mathbb{H}$ to obtain function $f^h : D \to R$. More generally, if $\boldsymbol{f} = (f_1^{(\cdot)}, \ldots, f_n^{(\cdot)})$ is an $n$-tuple of oracle functions then we write $\boldsymbol{f}^h$ to denote the $n$-tuple $(f_1^h, \ldots, f_n^h)$.

For an algorithm A we write $\mathsf{A}^h$ to make explicit that A has access to oracle $h$ during its execution. We sometimes refer to algorithms that expect such access as *oracle algorithm*. We leave the precise model of computation for such algorithms unspecified for now as these will vary between concrete notions of MoHFs.

*Example 1.* The prefixed hash chain of length $c \in \mathbb{N}$ is an oracle function as

$$f_{\mathrm{HC},c}^h : \quad D \to R, \quad x \mapsto h\left(c\|h(c-1\|\ldots h(1\|x)\ldots)\right).$$

An algorithm $\mathsf{A}^{\mathrm{HC}}$ that computes a hash chain of length $c$ is described as initially evaluating $h$ at the input $1\|x$, and then iteratively $(c-1)$ times on the outputs of the previous round, prefixing with the round index.                    ◇

### 2.4   Computation and Computational Cost

One main goal of this paper is to introduce a unifying definitional framework for MoHFs. For any concrete type of MoHF, we have to quantify the (real-world) resources required for performing computations such as evaluating the function.

*Cost Measures.* For the remainder of this section, we let $(\mathcal{V}, 0, +, \leq)$ be a commutative group with a partial order $\leq$ such that the operation "$+$" is compatible with the partial order "$\leq$", meaning that $\forall a, b, c \in \mathcal{V} : a \leq b \Rightarrow a + c \leq b + c$. More concretely, we could consider $\mathcal{V} = \mathbb{Z}$ or $\mathcal{V} = \mathbb{R}$, but also $\mathcal{V} = \mathbb{R}^n$ for some $n \in \mathbb{N}$ if the computational cost cannot be quantified by a single value, for instance if we want to measure both the computational effort and the memory required to perform the task. We generally use the notation $\mathcal{V}_{\geq 0} := \{v \in \mathcal{V} : 0 \leq v\}$.

*The Cost of Computation.* We later describe several MoHFs for differing notions of effort, where the hardness is defined using the following complexity notion based on a generic cost function. Intuitively a cost function assigns a non-negative real number as a cost to a given execution of an algorithm $\mathsf{A}$. More formally, let $\mathbb{A}$ be some set of algorithms (in some fixed computational model). Then an $\mathbb{A}$-*cost function* has the form $\mathsf{cost} : \mathbb{A} \times \{0,1\}^* \times \{0,1\}^* \to \mathcal{V}_{\geq 0}$. The first argument is an algorithm, the second fixes the input to the execution and the third fixes the random coins of the algorithm (and, in the ROM, also the random coins of the RO). Thus any such triple completely determines an execution which is then assigned a cost. Concrete examples include measuring the number of RO calls made by $\mathsf{A}$ during the execution, the number of cache misses during the computation [27, 29] or the amount of memory (in bits) used to store intermediate values during the computation [10]. We write $y \xleftarrow{a} \mathsf{A}(x; \$)$ if the algorithm $\mathsf{A}$ computes the output $y \in \{0,1\}^*$, when given input $x \in \{0,1\}^*$ and random coins $\$ \leftarrow_\$ \{0,1\}^*$, with computation cost $a \in \mathcal{V}$.

For concreteness we continue developing the example of a hash-chain of length $c$ by defining an appropriate cost notion.

*Example 2.* Let $\mathsf{A}$ be an oracle algorithm as in Example 1. The cost of evaluating the algorithm $\mathsf{A}$ is measured by the number $b \in \mathbb{N} = \mathcal{V}$ of queries to the oracle that can be made during the evaluation of $\mathsf{A}$. Therefore, we write

$$y \xleftarrow{b}_{\#} \mathsf{A}^h(x)$$

if $\mathsf{A}$ computes $y$ from $x$ with $b$ calls to the oracle $h$. For the algorithm $\mathsf{A}^{\mathrm{HC}}$ computing the prefixed hash chain of length $c \in \mathbb{N}$, the cost of each evaluation is $c$ and therefore obviously independent of the choice of random oracle, so simply writing $y \xleftarrow{b}_{\#} \mathsf{A}^{\mathrm{HC}}(x)$ is well-defined.                    $\Diamond$

## 2.5   A Model for Resource-Bounded Computation

In this section, we describe generically how we model resource-bounded computation in the remainder of this work. The scenario we consider in the following section has a party specify an algorithm and evaluate it, possibly repeatedly on different inputs. We want to model that evaluating the algorithm incurs a certain computational cost and that the party has bounded resources to evaluate the algorithm—depending on the available resources—only for a bounded number of times, or maybe not at all. Our approach consists of specifying a *computation device* to which an algorithm A can be input. Then, one can evaluate the algorithm repeatedly by providing inputs $x_1, \ldots, x_k$ to the device, which evaluates the algorithm A on each of the inputs. Each such evaluation incurs a certain computational cost, and as long as there are still resources available for computation, the device responds with the proper outputs $y_1 = A(x_1), y_2 = A(x_2), \ldots$. Once the resources are exhausted, the device always responds with the special symbol $\perp$. In the subsequent part of this paper, we will often refer to the computation device as the "computation resource."

The above-described approach can be used to model arbitrary types of algorithms and computational resources. Examples for such resources include the memory used during the computation (memory-hardness) or the number of computational steps incurred during the execution (computational hardness). Resources may also come in terms of "oracles" or "sub-routines" called by the algorithms, such as a random oracle, where we may want to quantify the number of queries to the oracle (query hardness).

As a concrete example, we describe the execution of an algorithm whose use of resources accumulates over subsequent executions:[3]

1. Let $b \in \mathcal{V}$ be the resources available to the party and $j = 1$.
2. Receive input $x_j \in \{0, 1\}^*$ from the party.
3. Compute $y_j \xleftarrow{c} A(x_j)$, for $c \in \mathcal{V}$. If $c \geq b$ then set $b \leftarrow 0$ and output $\perp$. Otherwise, set $b \leftarrow b - c$ and output $y_j$. Set $j \leftarrow j + 1$ and go to step 2.

We denote the resource that behaves as described above for the specific case of oracle algorithms that are allowed to make a bounded number $b \in \mathbb{N}$ of oracle queries by $\mathcal{S}_b^{\mathrm{OA}}$. For concreteness we show how to define an appropriate computational resource for reasoning about the hash-chain example.

*Example 3.* We continue with the setting described in Examples 1 and 2, and consider the hash-chain algorithm $A^{\mathrm{HC}}$ with a computational resource that is specified by the overall number $b \in \mathcal{V} = \mathbb{N}$ that can be made to the oracle.

In more detail, we consider the resource $\mathcal{S}_b^{\mathrm{OA}}$ described above. Upon startup, $\mathcal{S}_b^{\mathrm{OA}}$ samples a uniform $h \leftarrow_\$ \mathbb{H}$. Upon input of the oracle algorithm A (the type described in Example 1) into the computation resource, the party can query $x_1, x_2, \ldots$ and the algorithm A is evaluated, with access to $h$, on all inputs until $b$ queries to $h$ have been made, and subsequently only returns $\perp$.

For algorithm $A^{\mathrm{HC}}$, chain length $c$, and resource $\mathcal{S}_b^{\mathrm{OA}}$ with $b \in \mathbb{N}$, the algorithm can be evaluated $\lfloor b/c \rfloor$ times before all queries are answered with $\perp$.     ◇

## 3   Moderately Hard Functions

In this section, we combine the concepts introduced in Sect. 2 and state our definition of moderately hard function. The existing definitions of MoHF can be

---

[3] An example of this type of resource restriction is the cumulative number of oracle calls that the algorithm can make. Other resources may have different characteristics, such as a bound on the maximum amount of simultaneous memory use during the execution of the algorithm; which does not accumulate over multiple executions.

seen as formalizing that, with a given amount of resources, the function can only be evaluated a certain (related) number of times. Our definition is different in that it additionally captures that even an arbitrary computation with the same amount of resources cannot provide more (useful) results about the function than making the corresponding number of evaluations. This stronger statement is essential for proving the security of applications.

We base the definition of MoHFs on the notion of indifferentiability discussed in Sect. 2.2. In particular, the definition is based on the indistinguishability of a *real* and an *ideal* execution that we describe below. Satisfying such a definition will then indeed imply the desired statement, i.e., that the best the adversary can do is evaluate the function in the forward direction, and additionally that for each of these evaluations it must spend a certain amount of resources.

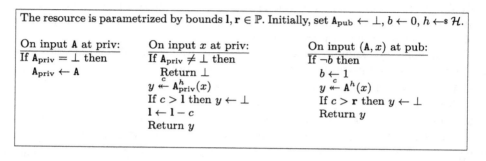

**Fig. 3.** Specification of the real-world resource $\mathcal{S}_{\mathbf{l},\mathbf{r}}$.

The *real-world resource* consists of resource-bounded computational devices that can be used to evaluate certain types of algorithms; one such resource at the priv- and one at the pub-interface. For such a resource $\mathcal{S}$ with bounds specified by $\mathbf{l}, \mathbf{r} \in \mathbb{P}$, for some parameter space $\mathbb{P}$ that is specified by $\mathcal{S}$, for the priv- and pub-interfaces, respectively, we usually write $\mathcal{S}_{\mathbf{l},\mathbf{r}}$. The protocol system $\pi$ used by the honest party initially inputs an algorithm naïve to $\mathcal{S}_{\mathbf{l},\mathbf{r}}$, further inputs $x_1, x_2, \ldots$ from $D$ to $\pi$ are simply forwarded to $\mathcal{S}_{\mathbf{l},\mathbf{r}}$, and the responses are given back to $D$. Moreover, $D$ can use the pub-interface of $\mathcal{S}_{\mathbf{l},\mathbf{r}}$ to input an algorithm $\mathsf{A}'$ and evaluate it.

The *ideal-world resource* also has two interfaces priv and pub. We consider only moderately hard functions with uniform outputs; therefore, the ideal-world resource $\mathcal{T}^{\mathrm{RRO}}$ we consider essentially implements a random function $D \to R$ and allows at both interfaces simply to query the random function. (In more detail, $\mathcal{T}^{\mathrm{RRO}}$ is defined as initially choosing a uniformly random function $f : D \to R$ and then, upon each input $x \in D$ at either priv or pub, respond with $f(x) \in R$ at the same interface.) We generally consider resources $\mathcal{T}^{\mathrm{RRO}}_{a,b}$ for $a, b \in \mathbb{N}$, which is the same as a resource $\mathcal{T}^{\mathrm{RRO}}$ allowing $a$ queries at the priv and $b$ queries at the pub-interface. All exceeding queries are answered with the special symbol $\perp$ (Fig. 4).

The resource is parametrized by bounds $a, b \in \mathbb{N}$. Initially, set $i, j \leftarrow 0$, and let $F : D \rightarrow R$ be empty.

On input $x \in D$ at priv:
If $i \geq a$ then return $\bot$
$i \leftarrow i + 1$
If $F[x] \neq \bot$ then $F[x] \leftarrow_\$ R$
Return $F[x]$

On input $x \in D$ at pub:
If $j \geq b$ then return $\bot$
$j \leftarrow j + 1$
If $F[x] \neq \bot$ then $F[x] \leftarrow_\$ R$
Return $F[x]$

**Fig. 4.** Lazy-sampling specification of the ideal-world resource $\mathcal{T}_{a,b}^{\mathrm{RRO}}$.

It is easy to see that the resource $\mathcal{T}_{a,b}^{\mathrm{RRO}}$ is one-way: it is a random oracle to which a bounded number of queries can be made.

Before we provide a more detailed general definitions, we complete the hash-chain example by instantiating an appropriate security notion.

*Example 4.* We extend Example 3 where the algorithm $\mathbf{A}^{\mathrm{HC}}$ evaluates a hash-chain of length $c$ on its input by defining the natural security notion such an algorithm achieves. The real-world resource $\mathcal{S}_{a,b}^{2\mathrm{OA}}$, with $a, b \in \mathbb{N}$, behaves as a resource $\mathcal{S}_a^{\mathrm{OA}}$ at the priv- and as a resource $\mathcal{S}_b^{\mathrm{OA}}$ at the pub-interface. That is $\mathcal{S}_{a,b}^{2\mathrm{OA}}$ first samples a random function $h \in \mathbb{H}$ uniformly, and then uses this for the evaluation of algorithms input at both interfaces priv and pub analogously to $\mathcal{S}_a^{\mathrm{OA}}$ and $\mathcal{S}_B^{\mathrm{OA}}$, respectively.

The converter system $\pi_{\mathrm{HC}}$ initially inputs $\mathbf{A}^{\mathrm{HC}}$ into $\mathcal{S}_{a,b}^{2\mathrm{OA}}$; which is a resource that allows for evaluating such algorithms at both interfaces priv and pub. As $\mathcal{S}_{a,b}^{2\mathrm{OA}}$ allows for $a$ oracle queries for $\mathbf{A}^{\mathrm{HC}}$, the system $\pi_{\mathrm{HC}}{}^{\mathrm{priv}}\mathcal{S}_{a,b}^{2\mathrm{OA}}$ allows for $\lfloor a/c \rfloor$ complete evaluations of $\mathbf{A}^{\mathrm{HC}}$ at the priv-interface. The resource $\mathcal{T}_{a',b'}^{\mathrm{RRO}}$ is a random oracle that can be queried at both interfaces priv and pub (and indeed the outside interface provided by $\pi$ is of that type). The simulator $\sigma$, therefore, will initially accept an algorithm $\mathbf{A}'$ as input and then evaluate $\mathbf{A}'$ with simulating the queries to $h$ potentially using queries to $\mathcal{T}_{a',b'}^{\mathrm{RRO}}$. In particular, we can rephrase the statement about (prefixed) iteration of random oracles of Demay *et al.* [26] as follows[4]: with $\pi_{\mathrm{HC}}$ being the system that inputs the algorithm $\mathbf{A}^{\mathrm{HC}}$, and $\mathcal{S}_{a,b}^{2\mathrm{OA}}$ the resource that allows $a$ and $b$ evaluations of $h$ at the priv- and pub-interfaces, respectively, $\pi_{\mathrm{HC}}{}^{\mathrm{priv}}\mathcal{S}_{a,b}^{2\mathrm{OA}}$ is $(b \cdot 2^{-w})$-indifferentiable, where $w$ is the output width of the oracle, from $\mathcal{T}_{a',b'}^{\mathrm{RRO}}$ allowing $a' = \lfloor a/c \rfloor$ queries at the priv- and $b' = \lfloor b/c \rfloor$ queries at the pub-interface. $\diamond$

The security statement ensures both that the honest party is able to perform its tasks using the prescribed algorithm and resource, and that the adversary *cannot* to perform *more* computations than allowed by its resources. We emphasize that the *ideal* execution in Example 4 will allow both the honest party and the adversary to query a random oracle for some bounded number of times.

---

[4] Similar statements have been proven earlier by Yao and Yin [56] and Bellare et al. [14]; however, we use the result on prefixed iteration from [26].

The fact that in the *real* execution the honest party can answer the queries with its bounded resource corresponds to the efficient implementation of the MoHF. The fact that any adversarial algorithm that has a certain amount of resources available can be "satisfied" with a bounded number of queries to the ideal random oracle means that the adversarial algorithm cannot gain more knowledge than by evaluating the ideal function for that number of times. Therefore, Example 4 models the basic properties that we require from a MoHF.

The security statement for an MoHF with naïve algorithm **naïve** has the following form. Intuitively, for resource limits $(l, r)$, the real model with those limits and the ideal model with limits $(a(l), b(r))$ are $\varepsilon$-indistinguishable, for some $\varepsilon = \varepsilon(l, r)$. I.e., there is a simulator $\sigma$ such that no distinguisher $D$ can tell the two models apart with advantage $> \varepsilon$.

We recall that the role of $\sigma$ is to "fool" $D$ into thinking it is interacting with $A$ in the real model. We claim that this forces $\sigma$ to be aware of the concrete parameters $\mathbf{r}$ of the real world $D$ is supposedly interacting with. Indeed, one strategy $D$ may employ is to provide code A at the pub-interface which consumes all available computational resources. In particular, using this technique $D$ will obtain a view encoding $\mathbf{r}$. Thus it had better be that $\sigma$ is able to produce a similar encoding itself. Thus in the following definition we allow $\sigma$ to depend on the choice of $\mathbf{r}$. Conversely, no such dependency between $l$ and $\sigma$ is needed.[5]

For many applications, we also want to parametrize the function by a hardness parameter $\mathbf{n} \in \mathbb{N}$. In that case we consider a sequence of oracle functions $f_\mathbf{n}^{(\cdot)}$ and algorithms $\mathbf{naïve_n}$ (which we will often want to be uniform) and also the functions $\mathsf{a}, \mathsf{b}, \varepsilon$ must be defined separately for each $\mathbf{n} \in \mathbb{N}$. This leads us to the following definition.

**Definition 3 (MoHF security).** *For each* $\mathbf{n} \in \mathbb{N}$, *let* $f_\mathbf{n}^{(\cdot)}$ *be an oracle function and* $\mathbf{naïve_n}$ *be an algorithm for computing* $f^{(\cdot)}$, *let* $\mathbb{P}$ *be a parameter space and* $\mathsf{a}, \mathsf{b} : \mathbb{P} \times \mathbb{N} \to \mathbb{N}$, *and let* $\varepsilon : \mathbb{P} \times \mathbb{P} \times \mathbb{N} \to \mathbb{R}_{\geq 0}$. *Then, for a family of models* $\mathcal{S}_{l,r}$, $(f_\mathbf{n}^{(\cdot)}, \mathbf{naïve_n})_{\mathbf{n} \in \mathbb{N}}$ *is a* $(\mathsf{a}, \mathsf{b}, \varepsilon)$-*secure moderately hard function family in the* $\mathcal{S}_{l,r}$-*model if*

$$\forall \mathbf{n} \in \mathbb{N}, \mathbf{r} \in \mathbb{P} \; \exists \sigma \; \forall l \in \mathbb{P} : \quad \pi_{\mathbf{naïve_n}}^{\mathrm{priv}} \, \mathcal{S}_{l,r} \quad \approx_{\varepsilon(l,r,n)} \quad \sigma^{\mathrm{pub}} \, \mathcal{T}_{\mathsf{a}(l,n),\mathsf{b}(r,n)}^{\mathrm{RRO}},$$

*The function family is called* uniform *if* $(\mathbf{naïve_n})_{\mathbf{n} \in \mathbb{N}}$ *is a uniform algorithm. The function family is* asymptotically secure *if* $\varepsilon(l, r, \cdot)$ *is a negligible function in the third parameter for all values of* $\mathbf{r}, l \in \mathbb{P}$.

We sometimes use the definition with a fixed hardness parameter $\mathbf{n}$. Note also that the definition is fundamentally different from resource-restricted indifferentiability [25] in that there the simulator is restricted, as the idea is to *preserve* the same complexity (notion).

---

[5] We remark that in contrast to, say, non-black box simulators, we are unaware of any actual advantage of this independence between $\sigma$ and $l$.

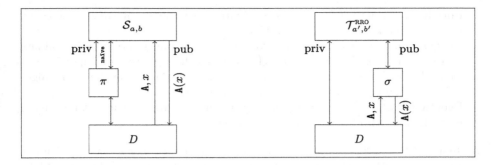

**Fig. 5.** Outline for the indifferentiability-based notion.

*Further Discussion on the Real Model.* In the real model, the resource described in Fig. 3 is available to the (honest) party at the priv-interface and the adversarial party at the pub-interface. Since our goal is to model different types of computational hardness of specific tasks, that is, describe the amount of resources needed to perform these tasks, the nature of the remaining resources will naturally vary depending on the particular type of hardness being modeled. For example, when modeling memory-hardness, the computation resource would limit the amount of memory available during the evaluation, and a bound on the computational power available to the party would correspond to defining computational hardness. Each resource is parametrized by two values $l$ and $r$ (from some arbitrary parameter space $\mathbb{P}$) denoting limits on the amount of the resources available to the parties at the priv- and pub-interfaces, respectively.[6] Beyond the local computation resources described above, oracle algorithms have access to an oracle that is chosen initially in the resource according to the prescribed distribution and *the same* instance is made available to the algorithms at all interfaces. In this work, the algorithms will always have access to a random oracle, i.e. a resource that behaves like a random function $h$.

We generally denote the real-world resource by the letter $\mathcal{S}$ and use the superscript to further specify the type of computational resource and the subscript for the resource bounds, as $\mathcal{S}_{a,b}^{2OA}$ in Example 4, where $\mathbb{P} = \mathbb{N}$, $l = a$ and $r = b$.

Both interfaces priv and pub of the real-world resource expect as an input a program that will be executed using the resources specified at the respective interface. Suppose we wish to make a security statement about the hardness of a particular MoHF with the naïve algorithm naïve. Besides the resources themselves, the real world contains a system $\pi$ that simply inputs naïve to be executed. Following the specification in Fig. 3, the execution in the real model can be described as follows:

---

[6] These parameters may specify bounds in terms of the cost function discussed above.

- Initially, $D$ is activated and can evaluate **naïve** on inputs of its choice by providing inputs at the priv-interface.[7]
- Next, $D$ can provide as input an algorithm **A** at the pub-interface, and evaluate **A** on one input $x$. The computation resource will evaluate **A** on input $x$.
- Next, $D$ can again provide queries at the priv-interface to evaluate the algorithms **naïve** (until the resources are exhausted).
- Eventually, $D$ outputs a bit (denoting its guess at whether it just interacted with the real world or not) and terminates.

At first sight, it might appear counter-intuitive that we allow the algorithm **A** input at pub to be evaluated only once, and not repeatedly, which would be stronger. The reason is that, for most complexity measures we are interested in, such as for memory-hard functions, continuous interaction with the environment $D$ would allow **A** to "outsource" relevant resource-use to $D$, and contradict our goal of precisely measuring **A**'s resource consumption (and thereby sometimes render non-trivial statements impossible). This restriction can be relaxed wherever possible, as in Example 4.

*Further Discussion on Ideal Model.* The (ideal-world) resource $\mathcal{T}$ also has a priv- and a pub-interface. In our definition of a MoHF, the ideal-world resource is always of the type $\mathcal{T}_{a,b}^{\mathrm{RRO}}$ with $a, b \in \mathbb{N}$, that is, a random oracle that allows $a$ queries at the priv- and $b$ queries at the pub-interface. The priv-interface can be used by the distinguisher to query the oracle, while the pub-interface is accessed by the *simulator* system $\sigma$ whose job it is to simulate the pub-interface of the real model consistently.

More precisely, for statements about parametrized real-world resources, we consider a class of ideal resources $\mathcal{T}_{a,b}^{\mathrm{RRO}}$ characterized by two functions $a$ and $b$ which map elements of $\mathbb{P}$ to $\mathbb{N}$. For any concrete real model given by parameters $(\mathbf{l}, \mathbf{r})$ we compare with the concrete ideal model with resource $\mathcal{T}_{a(\mathbf{l}),b(\mathbf{r})}^{\mathrm{RRO}}$ parametrized by $(a(\mathbf{l}), b(\mathbf{r}))$. These numbers denote an upper bound on the number of queries to the random oracle permitted on the priv- and pub-interfaces, respectively. In particular, after $a(\mathbf{l})$ queries on the priv-interface all future queries on that interface are responded to with $\bot$ (and similarly for the pub-interface with the limit $b(\mathbf{r})$).

To a distinguisher $D$, an execution with the ideal model looks as follows:

- Initially, $D$ is activated, and can make queries to $\mathcal{T}_{a(\mathbf{l}),b(\mathbf{r})}^{\mathrm{RRO}}$ at the priv-interface. (After $a(\mathbf{l})$ queries $\mathcal{T}_{a(\mathbf{l}),b(\mathbf{r})}^{\mathrm{RRO}}$ always responds with $\bot$.)
- Next, $D$ can provide as input an algorithm **A** at the pub-interface. Overall, the simulator $\sigma$ can make at most $b(\mathbf{r})$ queries to $\mathcal{T}_{a(\mathbf{l}),b(\mathbf{r})}^{\mathrm{RRO}}$.
- Next, $D$ can make further queries to $\mathcal{T}_{a(\mathbf{l}),b(\mathbf{r})}^{\mathrm{RRO}}$ on the priv-interface.
- Finally, $D$ outputs a bit (denoting its guess at whether it just interacted with the real world or not) and terminates.

---

[7] Once the resources at the priv-interface are exhausted, no further useful information is gained by $D$ in making additional evaluation calls for **naïve**.

An ideal model is outlined in Fig. 5 with priv and pub resource limits $a'$ and $b'$ respectively.

# 4    Memory-Hard Functions

Moving beyond the straightforward example of an MoHF based on computational hardness developed during the above examples, we describe more advanced types of MoHFs in this and the next section. Each one is based on a different complexity notion and computational model. For each one, we describe one (or more) constructions. Moreover, for the first two we provide a powerful tool for constructing provably secure MoHFs of those types. We begin, in this section, with memory-hard functions (MHF).

In the introduction, we discussed shortcomings of the existing definitions of MHFs. We address these concerns by instantiating MHFs within our general MoHF framework and providing a pebbling reduction with which we can "rescue" the MHF constructions [5,6,10] and security proofs [5,6] of several recent MHFs from the literature. More generally, the tool is likely to prove useful in the future as new, more practical graphs are developed [5] and/or new labeling functions are developed beyond an ideal compression function. (For more details what is meant by "rescue" we refer to discussion immediately after Theorem 1.)

## 4.1    The Parallel ROM

To define an MHF, we consider a resource-bounded computational device $\mathcal{S}$ with a priv- and a pub-interface capturing the pROM (adapted from [8]). Let $w \in \mathbb{N}$. Upon startup, $\mathcal{S}^{w\text{-PROM}}$ samples a fresh random oracle $h \leftarrow_{\$} \mathbb{H}_w$ with range $\{0,1\}^w$. Now, on both interfaces, $\mathcal{S}^{w\text{-PROM}}$ accepts as input a pROM algorithm $\mathsf{A}$ which is an oracle algorithm with the following behavior.

A *state* is a pair $(\tau, \mathbf{s})$ where *data* $\tau$ is a string and $\mathbf{s}$ is a tuple of strings. The output of step $i$ of algorithm $\mathsf{A}$ is an *output state* $\bar{\sigma}_i = (\tau_i, \mathbf{q}_i)$ where $\mathbf{q}_i = [q_i^1, \ldots, q_i^{z_i}]$ is a tuple of *queries* to $h$. As input to step $i+1$, algorithm $\mathsf{A}$ is given the corresponding *input state* $\sigma_i = (\tau_i, h(\mathbf{q}_i))$, where $h(\mathbf{q}_i) = [h(q_i^1), \ldots, h(q_i^{z_i})]$ is the tuple of *responses* from $h$ to the queries $\mathbf{q}_i$. In particular, for a given $h$ and random coins of $\mathsf{A}$, the input state $\sigma_{i+1}$ is a function of the input state $\sigma_i$. The initial state $\sigma_0$ is empty and the input $x_{\mathsf{in}}$ to the computation is given a special input in step 1.

For a given execution of a pROM, we are interested in the following complexity measure. We denote the bit-length of a string $s$ by $|s|$. The *length* of a state $\sigma = (\tau, \mathbf{s})$ with $\mathbf{s} = (s^1, s^2, \ldots, s^y)$ is $|\sigma| = |\tau| + \sum_{i \in [y]} |s^i|$. The *cumulative memory complexity* (CMC) of an execution is the sum of the lengths of the states in the execution. More precisely, let us consider an execution of algorithm $\mathsf{A}$ on input $x_{\mathsf{in}}$ using coins \$ with oracle $h$ resulting in $z \in \mathbb{Z}_{\geq 0}$ input states $\sigma_1, \ldots, \sigma_z$, where $\sigma_i = (\tau_i, \mathbf{s}_i)$ and $\mathbf{s}_i = (s_i^1, s_i^2, \ldots, s_i^{y_j})$. Then the *cumulative memory complexity* (CMC) of the execution is

$$\mathsf{cmc}(\mathsf{A}^h(x_{\mathsf{in}}; \$)) = \sum_{i \in [z]} |\sigma_i|,$$

while the *total number of RO calls* is $\sum_{i \in [z]} y_j$. More generally, the CMC (and total number of RO calls) of several executions is the sum of the CMC (and total RO calls) of the individual executions.

We now describe the resource constraints imposed by $\mathcal{S}^{w\text{-PROM}}$ on the pROM algorithms it executes. To quantify the constraints, $\mathcal{S}^{w\text{-PROM}}$ is parametrized by a left and a right tuple from the following parameter space $\mathbb{P}^{\text{PROM}} = (\mathbb{Z}_{\geq 0})^2$ describing the constraints for the priv and pub interfaces respectively. In particular, for parameters $(q, m) \in \mathbb{P}^{\text{PROM}}$, the corresponding pROM algorithm is allowed to make a total of $q$ RO calls and use CMC at most $m$ summed up across all of the algorithms executions.[8]

As usual for memory-hard functions, to ensure that the honest algorithm can be run on realistic devices, $\mathcal{S}^{w\text{-PROM}}$ restricts the algorithms on the priv-interface to be *sequential*. That is, the algorithms can make only a single call to $h$ per step. Technically, in any execution, for any step $j$ it must be that $y_j \leq 1$. No such restriction is placed on the adversarial algorithm reflecting the power (potentially) available to such a highly parallel device as an ASIC.

We conclude the section with the formal definition of a memory-hard function in the pROM. The definition is a particular instance of an MoHF defined in Definition 3 formulated in terms of exact security.

**Definition 4 ((Parallel) memory-hard function).** *For each* $\mathbf{n} \in \mathbb{N}$, *let* $f_{\mathbf{n}}^{(\cdot)}$ *be an oracle function and* **naïve$_{\mathbf{n}}$** *be a pROM algorithm for computing* $f^{(\cdot)}$. *Consider the function families:*

$$\mathsf{a} = \{\mathsf{a}_w : \mathbb{P}^{\text{PROM}} \times \mathbb{N} \to \mathbb{N}\}_{w \in \mathbb{N}}, \quad \mathsf{b} = \{\mathsf{b}_w : \mathbb{P}^{\text{PROM}} \times \mathbb{N} \to \mathbb{N}\}_{w \in \mathbb{N}},$$

$$\epsilon = \{\epsilon_w : \mathbb{P}^{\text{PROM}} \times \mathbb{P}^{\text{PROM}} \times \mathbb{N} \to \mathbb{R}_{\geq 0}\}_{w \in \mathbb{N}}.$$

*Then* $F = (f_{\mathbf{n}}^{(\cdot)}, \mathbf{naïve_n})_{\mathbf{n} \in \mathbb{N}}$ *is called an* $(\mathsf{a}, \mathsf{b}, \epsilon)$-*memory-hard function (MHF) if* $\forall w \in \mathbb{N}$ $F$ *is an* $(\mathsf{a}_w, \mathsf{b}_w, \epsilon_w)$-*secure moderately hard function family for* $\mathcal{S}^{w\text{-PROM}}$.

*Data-(In)dependent MHFs.* An important distinction in the literature of memory-hard functions concerns the memory-access pattern of **naïve**. In particular, if the pattern is independent of the input $x$ then we call this a *data-independent* MHF (iMHF) and otherwise we call it an *data-dependent* MHF (dMHF). The advantage of an iMHF is that the honest party running **naïve** is inherently more resistant to certain side-channel attacks (such as cache-timing attacks) which can lead to information leakage about the input $x$. When the MHF is used for, say, password hashing on a login server this can be a significant concern. Above, we have chosen to not make the addressing mechanism used to store a state $\sigma$ explicit in $\mathcal{S}^{w\text{-PROM}}$, as it would significantly complicate the exposition with little benefit. Yet, we remark that doing so would definitely be possible within the wider MoHF framework presented here if needed. Moreover the tools for constructing MHFs below actually construct iMHFs.

---

[8] In particular, for the algorithm input on the adversarial interface pub the single permitted execution can consume at most $r$ resources while for the honest algorithm input on priv the total consumed resources across all execution can be at most $l$.

## 4.2   Graph Functions

Now that we have a concrete definition in mind, we turn to constructions. We first define a large class of oracle functions (called graph functions) which have appeared in various guises in the literature [10,29,31] (although we differ slightly in some details which simplify later proofs). This allows us to prove the main result of this section; namely a "pebbling reduction" for graph functions. That is, for a graph function $F$ based on some graph $G$, we show function families $(a, b, \epsilon)$ depending on $G$, for which function $F$ is an MHF.

We start by formalizing (a slight refinement of) the usual notion of a graph function (as it appears in, say, [10,31]). For this, we use the following common notation and terminology. For a directed acyclic graph (DAG) $G = (V, E)$, we call a node with no incoming edges a *source* and a node with no outgoing edges a *sink*. The *in-degree* of a node is the number of its incoming edges and the in-degree of $G$ is the maximum in-degree of any of its nodes. The *parents* of a node $v$ are the set of nodes with outgoing edges leading to $v$. We also implicitly associate the elements of $V$ with unique strings.[9]

A graph function makes use of a oracle $h \in \mathbb{H}_w$ defined over bit strings. Technically, we assume an implicit prefix-free encoding such that $h$ is evaluated on unique strings. Inputs to $h$ are given as distinct tuples of strings (or even tuples of tuples of strings). For example, we assume that $h(0, 00)$, $h(00, 0)$, and $h((0, 0), 0)$ all denote distinct inputs to $h$.

**Definition 5 (Graph function).** *Let function $h : \{0, 1\}^* \to \{0, 1\}^w \in \mathbb{H}_w$ and DAG $G = (V, E)$ have source nodes $\{v_1^{in}, \ldots, v_a^{in}\}$ and sink nodes $(v_1^{out}, \ldots, v_z^{out})$. Then, for inputs $\mathbf{x} = (x_1, \ldots, x_a) \in (\{0, 1\}^*)^{\times a}$, the $(h, \mathbf{x})$-labeling of $G$ is a mapping* $\mathsf{lab} : V \to \{0, 1\}^w$ *defined recursively to be:*

$$\forall v \in V \quad \mathsf{lab}(v) := \begin{cases} h(\mathbf{x}, v, x_j)) & : v = v_j^{in} \\ h(\mathbf{x}, v, \mathsf{lab}(v_1), \ldots, \mathsf{lab}(v_d))) & : else \end{cases}$$

*where $\{v_1, \ldots, v_d\}$ are the parents of $v$ arranged in lexicographic order. The graph function (of $G$ and $\mathbb{H}_w$) is the oracle function*

$$f_G : (\{0, 1\}^*)^{\times a} \to (\{0, 1\}^w)^{\times z},$$

*which maps $\mathbf{x} \mapsto (\mathsf{lab}(v_1^{out}), \ldots, \mathsf{lab}(v_z^{out}))$ where $\mathsf{lab}$ is the $(h, \mathbf{x})$-labeling of $G$.*

The above definition differs from the one in [10] in two ways. First, it considers graphs with multiple source and sink nodes. Second it prefixes all calls to $h$ with the input $\mathbf{x}$. This ensures that, given any pair of distinct inputs $\mathbf{x}_1 \neq \mathbf{x}_2$, no call to $h$ made by $f_G(\mathbf{x}_1)$ is repeated by $f_G(\mathbf{x}_2)$. Intuitively, this ensures that finding collisions in $h$ can no longer help avoiding making a call to $h$ for each new label being computed. Technically, it simplifies proofs as we no longer need

---

[9] For example, we can associate $v \in V$ with the binary representation of its position in an arbitrary fixed topological ordering of $G$.

to compute and carry along the probability of such a collision. We remark that this is merely a technicality and if, as done in practice, the prefixing (of both $\mathbf{x}$ and the node $v$) is omitted, security will only degrade by a negligible amount.[10]

*The naïve Algorithm.* The naïve oracle algorithm $\mathbf{naïve}_G$ for $f_G$ computes one label of $G$ at a time in topological order appending the result to its state. If $G$ has $|V| = n$ nodes then $\mathbf{naïve}_G$ will terminate in $n$ steps making at 1 call to $h$ per step, for a total of $n$ calls, and will never store more than $w(i-1)$ bits in the data portion of its state in the $i$th round. In particular for all inputs $\mathbf{x}$, oracles $h$ (and coins $\$$) we have that $\mathsf{cmc}(\mathbf{naïve}_G^h(\mathbf{x}; \$)) = wn(n-1)/2$. Therefore, in the definition of an MHF we can set $\mathsf{a}_w(q, m) = \min(\lfloor q/n \rfloor, \lfloor 2m/wn(n-1) \rfloor)$. It remains to determine how to set $\mathsf{b}_w$ and $\epsilon_w$, which is the focus of the next section.

## 4.3  A Parallel Memory-Hard MoHF

In this section, we prove a pebbling reduction for memory hardness of a graph function $f_G$ in the pROM. To this end, we first recall the parallel pebbling game over DAGs and associated cumulative pebbling complexity (CPC).

**The Parallel Pebbling Game.** The sequential version of the following pebbling game first appeared in [24,38] and the parallel version in [10]. Put simply, the game is a variant of the standard black-pebbling game where pebbles can be placed according to the usual rules but in batches of moves performed in parallel rather than one at a time sequentially.

**Definition 6 (Pebbling a graph).** *Let $G = (V, E)$ be a DAG and $T, S \subseteq V$ be node sets. Then a (legal) pebbling of $G$ (with starting configuration $S$ and target $T$) is a sequence $P = (P_0, \ldots, P_t)$ of subsets of $V$ such that:*

*1. $P_0 \subseteq S$.*
*2. Pebbles are added only when their predecessors already have a pebble at the end of the previous step.*

$$\forall i \in [t] \quad \forall(x, y) \in E \quad \forall y \in P_i \setminus P_{i-1} \qquad x \in P_{i-1}.$$

*3. At some point every target node is pebbled (though not necessarily simultaneously).*

$$\forall x \in T \quad \exists z \leq t \qquad x \in P_z.$$

---

[10] Prefixing ensures domain separation; that is random oracle calls in a labeling are unique to that input. However, if inputs are chosen independently of the RO then finding two inputs that share an oracle call requires finding a collision in the RO. To concentrate on the more fundamental and novel aspects of the proofs below, we have chosen to instead assume full prefixing. A formal analysis with less prefixing can be found in [10].

*We call a pebbling of $G$ complete if $S = \emptyset$ and $T$ is the set of sink nodes of $G$. We call a pebbling sequential if no more than one new pebble is placed per step,*

$$\forall i \in [t] \quad |P_i \setminus P_{i-1}| \leq 1.$$

In this simple model of computation we are interested in the following complexity notion for DAGs taken from [10].

**Definition 7 (Cumulative pebbling complexity).** *Let $G$ be a DAG, $P = (P_0, \ldots, P_t)$ be an arbitrary pebbling of $G$, and $\Pi$ be the set of all complete pebblings of $G$. Then the (pebbling) cost of $P$ and the cumulative pebbling complexity (CPC) of $G$ are defined respectively to be:*

$$\mathsf{cpc}(P) := \sum_{i=0}^{t} |P_i|, \qquad \mathsf{cpc}(G) := \min\left\{\mathsf{cpc}(P) : P \in \Pi\right\}.$$

**A Pebbling Reduction for Memory-Hard Functions.** We are now ready to formally state and prove the main technical result: a security statement showing a graph function to be an MHF for parameters $(\mathsf{a}, \mathsf{b}, \epsilon)$ expressed in terms of the CPC of the graph and the number of bits in the output of $h$.

**Theorem 1 (Pebbling reduction).** *Let $G_n = (V_n, E_n)$ be a DAG of size $|V_n| = n$. Let $F = (f_{G,n}, \mathsf{na\ddot{\imath}ve}_{G,n})_{n \in \mathbb{N}}$ be the graph functions for $G_n$ and their naïve oracle algorithms. Then, for any $\lambda \geq 0$, $F$ is an $(\mathsf{a}, \mathsf{b}, \epsilon)$-memory-hard function where*

$$\mathsf{a} = \left\{\mathsf{a}_w(q, m) = \min(\lfloor q/n \rfloor, \lfloor 2m/wn(n-1) \rfloor)\right\}_{w \in \mathbb{N}},$$

$$\mathsf{b} = \left\{\mathsf{b}_w(q, m) = \frac{m(1 + \lambda)}{\mathsf{cpc}(G)(w - \log q)}\right\}_{w \in \mathbb{N}}, \quad \epsilon = \left\{\epsilon_w(q, m) \leq \frac{q}{2^w} + 2^{-\lambda}\right\}_{w \in \mathbb{N}}.$$

We note that $\mathsf{cpc}$ charges for keeping pebbles on $G$ which, intuitively, models storing the label of a node in the data component of an input state. However the complexity notion $\mathsf{cmc}$ for the pROM also charges for the responses to RO queries included in input states. We discuss three options to address this discrepancy.

1. Modify our definition of the pROM to that used in [10]. There, the $i^{th}$ batch of queries $\mathbf{q}_i$ to $h$ is made *during* step $i$. So the state stored between steps only contains the data component $\tau_i$. Thus $\mathsf{cmc}$ in that model is more closely modeled by $\mathsf{cpc}$. While the techniques used below to prove Theorem 1 carry over essentially unchanged to that model, we have opted to not go with that approach as we believe the version of the pROM used here (and in [7]) more closely captures computation for an ASIC. That is, it better models the constraint that during an evaluation of the hash function(s) a circuit must store

any remaining state it intends to make use of later in separate registers. Moreover, given the depth of the circuit of hash functions used to realize $h$, at least one register per output bit of $h$ will be needed.[11]

2. Modify the notion of cpc to obtain cpc′, which also charges for new pebbles being placed on the graph. That is use $\mathsf{cpc}' = \mathsf{cpc} + \sum_i |P_i \setminus P_{i-1}|$ as the pebbling cost.[12] Such a notion would more closely reflect the way cmc is defined in this work. In particular, it would allow for a tighter lower bound in Theorem 1, since for any graph $\mathsf{cpc}' \geq \mathsf{cpc}$. Moreover, it would be easy to adapt the proof of Theorem 1 to accommodate cpc′. Indeed, (using the terminology from the proof of Theorem 1) in the ex-post-facto pebbling $P$ of an execution, a node $v \notin P_{i-1}^x$ is only added to $P_i^x$ if it becomes necessary for $x$ at time $i$. By definition, this can only happen if there is a correct call for $(x, v)$ in the input state $\sigma_i$. Thus, we are guaranteed that for each time step $i$ it holds that $\sum_i \sum_x |P_i^x \setminus P_{i-1}^x| \leq y_i$, where $y_i$ is the number of queries to $h$ in input state $\sigma_i$. So we can indeed modify the second claim in the proof to also add the quantity $\sum_x |P_i^x \setminus P_{i-1}^x|$ to the left side of the inequality. The downside of this approach is that using cpc′ in Theorem 1 would mean that it is no longer (immediately) clear if we can use any past results from the literature about cpc.

3. The third option, which we have opted for in this work, is to borrow from the more intuitive formulation of the pROM of [7] while sticking with the traditional pebbling complexity notion of cpc. We do this because, on the one hand, for any graph $\mathsf{cpc}' \leq 2\mathsf{cpc}$, so at most a factor of 2 is lost the tightness of Theorem 1 when using cpc instead of cpc′. Yet on the other hand, for cpc we already have constructions of graphs with asymptotically maximal cpc as well as a variety of techniques for analyzing the cpc of graphs. In particular we have upper and lower bounds for the cpc of arbitrary DAGs as well as for many specific graphs (and graph distributions) used in the literature as the basis for interesting graph functions [3,4,6,9,10]. Thus we have opted for this route so as to (A) strengthen the intuition underpinning the model of computation, (B) leave it clear that Theorem 1 can be used in conjunction with all of the past concerning cpc while (C) only paying a small price in the tightness of the bound we show in that theorem.

The remainder of this subsection is dedicated to proving the theorem. For simplicity we will restrict ourselves to DAGs with a single source $v_\in$ and sink $v_{\mathsf{out}}$ but this only simplifies notation. The more general case for any DAG is identical. The rough outline of the proof is as follows. We begin by describing a simulator $\sigma$ as in Definition 3, whose goal is to simulate the pub-interface of $\mathcal{S}^{w\text{-PROM}}$ to a distinguisher $D$ while actually being connected to the pub-interface of $\mathcal{T}^{\mathrm{RRO}}$. In a nutshell, $\sigma$ will emulate the algorithm A it is given by $D$ internally by emulating a

---

[11] Note that any signal entering a circuit at the beginning of a clock cycle that does not reach a memory cell before the end of a clock cycle is lost. Yet, hash functions so complex and clock cycles so short that it is unrealistic to assume an entire evaluation of $h$ can be performed within a single cycle.

[12] cpc′ is essentially the special case of "energy complexity" for $R = 1$ in [3].

copy of $\mathcal{S}^{w\text{-}\mathrm{PROM}}$ to it. $\sigma$ will keep track of the RO calls made by A and, whenever A has made all the calls corresponding to a complete and legal $(x, h)$-labeling of $G$, then $\sigma$ will query $\mathcal{T}^{\mathrm{RRO}}$ at point $x$ and return the result to A as the result of the final RO call for that labeling.

To prove that $\sigma$ achieves this goal (with high probability) we introduce a generalization of the pebbling game, called an $m$-color pebbling, and state a trivial lemma showing that the cumulative $m$-color pebbling complexity of a graph is $m$ times the CC of the graph. Next, we define a mapping between a sequence of RO calls made during an execution in the pROM (such as that of A being emulated by $\sigma$) and an $m$-coloring $P$ of $G$. We prove a lemma stating that, w.h.p., if $m$ distinct I/O pairs for $f_G$ were produced during the execution, then $P$ is legal and complete. We also prove a lemma upper-bounding the pebbling cost of $P$ in terms of the CMC (and number of calls made to the RO) of the execution. But since the pebbling cost of $G$ cannot be smaller than $m \cdot \mathsf{cpc}(G)$, this gives us a lower bound on the memory cost of any such execution, as desired. Indeed, any algorithm in the pROM that violates our bound on memory cost with too high probability implies the existence of a pebbling of $G$ with too low pebbling cost, contradicting the pebbling complexity of $G$. But this means that when $\sigma$ limits CMC (and number of RO calls) of the emulation of A accordingly, then w.h.p. we can upper-bound the number of calls $\sigma$ will need to $\mathcal{T}^{\mathrm{RRO}}$.

To complete the proof, we have to show that using the above statements about $\sigma$ imply that indifferentiability holds. Indeed, the simulation, conditioned on the events that no lucky queries occur and that the simulator does not need excessive queries, is perfect. Therefore, the distinguishing advantage can be bounded by the probability of provoking either of those events, which can be done by the above statements about $\sigma$. A detailed proof can be found in the full version [11].

# 5    Other Types of MoHFs

Besides MHFs, several other types of MoHFs have been considered in the literature. In this section, we briefly review weak memory-hard functions and memory-bound functions. A discussion of one-time computable functions and uncomputable functions is given in Sect. 5.3.

## 5.1    Weak Memory-Hard Functions

A class of MoHFs considered in the literature that are closely related to MoHFs are *weak* MoHFs. Intuitively, they differ from MoHFs only in that they also restrict adversaries to being sequential.[13] On the one hand, it may be easier to construct such functions compared to full blown MoHF. In fact, for the data-independent variant of MoHFs, [3] proves that a graph function based on a DAG of size $n$ always has $\mathsf{cmc}$ of $O(wn^2/\log(n))$ (ignoring $\log\log$ factors). Yet,

---

[13] If the adversary is restricted to using general-purpose CPUs and not ASICs or FPGAs with their massive parallelism, this restriction may be reasonable.

as discussed below, the results of [33,42] and those described below show that we can build W-MoHFs from similar DAGs with sequential cmc of $\mathcal{O}(2n^2)$. Put differently, W-MoHFs allow for strictly more memory consumption per call to the RO than is possible with MoHFs. This is valuable since the limiting factor for an adversary is often the memory consumption while the cost for honest parties to enforce high memory consumption is the number of calls they must perform to the RO.

We capture weak MoHFs in the MoHFframework by restricting the real world resource-bounded computational device $\mathcal{S}^{w\text{-SROM}}$ to the *sequential random oracle model* (sROM). Given this definition we can now easily adapt the pebbling reduction of Theorem 1 to obtain a tool for constructing W-MoHFs, which has some immediate implications. In [42], Lengaur and Tarjan prove that the DAGs underlying the two graph functions Catena Dragonfly and Butterfly [33] have scpc $= \mathcal{O}(n^2)$. In [33], the authors extend these results to analyze the scpc of stacks of these DAGs. By combining those results with the pebbling reduction for the sROM, we obtain parameters $(a, b, \epsilon)$ for which the Catena functions are provably W-MoHFs. Similar implications hold for the pebbling analysis done for the Balloon Hashing function in [18]. Weak memory hard functions are discussed in more detail in the full version [11].

## 5.2   Memory-Bound Functions

Another important notion of MoHF from the literature has been considered in [27,29]. These predate MHFs and are based on the observation that while computation speeds vary greatly across real-world computational devices, this is much less so for memory-access speeds. Under the assumption that time spent on a computation correlates with the monetary cost of the computation, this observation motivates measuring the cost of a given execution by the number of cache misses (i.e., memory accesses) made during the computation. A function that requires a large number of misses, regardless of the algorithm used to evaluate the function, is called a *memory-bound* function.

*Memory-Bound Functions as MoHFs.* We show how to formalize memory-bound functions in the MoHF framework. In particular, we describe the real-world resource-bounded computational device $\mathcal{S}^{w\text{-MB}}$. It makes use of RO with $w$-bits of output and is parametrized by 6 positive integers $\mathbb{P}^{\text{MB}} = \mathbb{N}^{\times 6}$. That is, following the model of [29], an algorithm A, executed by $\mathcal{S}^{w\text{-MB}}$ with parameters $(m, b, s, \omega, c, q)$, makes a sequence of calls to the RO and has access to a two tiered memory consisting of a cache of limited size and a working memory (as large as needed). The memory is partitioned into $m$ blocks of $b$ bits each, while cache is divided into $s$ words of $\omega$ bits each. When A requests a location in memory, if the location is already contained in cache, then A is given the value for free, otherwise the block of memory containing that location is fetched into cache. The algorithm is permitted a total of $q$ calls to the RO and $c$ fetches (i.e. cache misses) across all executions.

In [27,29] the authors describe such functions (with several parameters each) and prove that the hash-trail construction applied to these functions results in a PoE for a notion of "effort" captured by memory-boundedness. (See Sect. 6 for more on the hash-trail construction and PoEs). We conjecture that the proofs in those works carry over to the notion of memory-bound MoHFs described above (using some of the techniques at the end of the proof of Theorem 1). Yet, we believe that a more general pebbling reduction (similar to Theorem 1) is possible for the above definition. Such a theorem would allow us to construct new and improved memory-bound functions. (On the one hand, the function described in [27] has a large description—many megabytes—while the function in [29] is based on superconcentrators which can be somewhat difficult to implement in practice with optimal constants.) In any case, we believe investigating memory-bound functions as MoHFs to be an interesting and tractable line of future work.

### 5.3   One-Time Computable and Uncomputable Functions

Another—less widely used—notion of MoHFs appearing in the literature are *one-time computable* functions [31]. Intuitively, these are sets of $T$ pseudo-random functions (PRFs) $f_1, \ldots, f_T$ with long keys (where $T$ is an *a priori* fixed, arbitrary number). An honest party can evaluate each function $f_i$ exactly once, using a device with limited memory containing these keys. On such a device, evaluating the $i^{th}$ PRF provably requires deleting all of the first $i$ keys. Therefore, if an adversary (with arbitrary memory and computational power) can only learn a limited amount of information about the internal state of the device, then regardless of the computation performed on the device, the adversary will never learn more than one input/output pair per PRF. The authors describe the intuitive application of a password-storage device secure against dictionary attacks. An advantage of using the MoHF framework to capture one-time computable functions could be proving security for such an application (using the framework's composition theorem).

We describe a model for one-time computable functions and uncomputable functions in Sect. 5, where we also sketch a new (hypothetical) application for one-time computable functions in the context of anonymous digital payment systems. We discuss this notion in more detail in the full version [11].

## 6   Interactive Proofs of Effort

One important practical application of MoHFs are proofs of effort (PoE), where the effort may correspond to computation, memory, or other types of resources that the hardness of which can be used in higher-level protocols to require one party, the prover, to spend a certain amount of resources before the other party, the verifier, has checked this spending and allows the protocol to continue.

## 6.1   Definition

Our composable definition of PoE is based on the idea of constructing an "ideal" proof-of-effort functionality from the bounded assumed resources the parties have access to in the real setting. Our Definition 3 for MoHFs can already be seen in a similar sense: from the *assumed* (bounded) resources available to the parties, evaluating the MoHF constructs a shared random function that can be evaluated for some bounded number of times. In the following, we describe the assumed and constructed resources that characterize a PoE.

*The Goal of PoE Protocols.* The high-level guarantees provided by a PoE to higher-level protocols can be described as follows. Prover $P$ and verifier $V$ interact in some number $n \in \mathbb{N}$ of sessions, and in each of the sessions verifier $V$ expects to be "convinced" by prover $P$'s spending of effort. Prover $P$ can decide how to distribute the available resources toward convincing verifier $V$ over the individual sessions; if prover $P$ does not have sufficient resources to succeed in all sessions, then $P$ can distribute its effort over the sessions. Verifier $V$'s protocol provides as output a bit that is 1 in all sessions where the prover attributed sufficient resources, and 0 otherwise. We formalize these guarantees in the resource POE that we describe in more detail below.

---

**Proof-of-effort resource $\mathsf{POE}_{\phi,n}^a$**

The resource is parametrized by the numbers $n, a \in \mathbb{N}$ and a mapping $\phi : \mathbb{N} \to \mathbb{R}_{\geq 0}$. It contains state bits $e_i, \hat{e}_i \in \{0, 1\}$ and counters $c_i \in \mathbb{N}$ for $i \in \mathbb{N}$ which are initially set to $e_i, \hat{e}_i \leftarrow 0$ and $c_i \leftarrow 0$.

**Verifier $V$:** On input a session number $i \in \{1, \ldots, n\}$, output the state $e_i$ of that session.

**Prover $P$:**  – On input a session number $i \in \{1, \ldots, n\}$, set $c_i \leftarrow c_i + 1$. If $e_i \vee \hat{e}_i = 1$ or $\sum_{i=1}^n c_i > a$ then return 0. Otherwise, draw $e_i$ (if $P$ is honest, else $\hat{e}_i$) at random such that it is 1 with probability $\phi(c_i)$ and 0 otherwise. Output $e_i$ (resp. $\hat{e}_i$) at interface $P$.

  – If $P$ is dishonest, then accept a special input $\mathsf{copy}_i$ that sets $e_i \leftarrow \hat{e}_i$.

---

The resource POE that formalizes the guarantee achieved by the PoE in a given real-world setting is parametrized by values $\underline{a}, \overline{a}, n \in \mathbb{N}$ and $\phi : \mathbb{N} \to \mathbb{R}_{\geq 0}$, and is written as $\mathsf{POE}_{\phi,n}^{\overline{a},\underline{a}} = (\mathsf{POE}_{\phi,n}^{\underline{a}}, \mathsf{POE}_{\phi,n}^{\overline{a}})$. For an honest prover $P$, the parameter $\underline{a} \in \mathbb{N}$ describes the overall number of "attempts" that $P$ can take. For a dishonest prover $P$, the same is described by the parameter $\overline{a} \in \mathbb{N}$.[14] The success probability of a prover in each session depends on the computational resources spent in that session and can be computed as $\phi(a)$, where $a \in \mathbb{N}$ is the number of proof attempts in that session.

---

[14] For the numbers $\underline{a}, \overline{a} \in \mathbb{N}$ it may hold that $\overline{a} > \underline{a}$ because one may only know rough bounds on the available resources (at least $\underline{a}$, at most $\overline{a}$).

*The "real-world" Setting for PoE Protocols.* The PoE protocols we consider in this work are based on the evaluation of an MoHF, which, following Definition 3, can be abstracted as giving the prover and the verifier access to a shared uniform random function $\mathcal{T}^{\mathrm{RRO}}$ that they can evaluate for a certain number of times. We need to consider both the case where the prover is honest (to formalize that the PoE can be achieved with a certain amount of resources) and the case where the prover is dishonest (to formalize that not much more can be achieved by a dishonest prover). In addition to $\mathcal{T}^{\mathrm{RRO}}$, for $n$ protocol sessions, the prover and verifier can also access $n$ pairs of channels for bilateral communication, which we denote by $[\longrightarrow, \longleftarrow]^n$ in the following. (This insecure communication resource is implicit in some composable frameworks such as Canetti's UC [20].)

The resource specifies a bound $\underline{b} \in \mathbb{N}$ for the number of queries that the verifier can make to $\mathcal{T}^{\mathrm{RRO}}$, and bounds $\underline{a}, \overline{a} \in \mathbb{N}$ for the cases where the prover is honest and dishonest, respectively. Considering the case $\underline{a} \leq \overline{a}$ makes sense because only loose bounds on the prover's available resources may be known.

*The Security Definition.* Having described the real-world and ideal-world settings, we are now ready to state the security definition. This definition will consider the above-described cases where the prover is honest (this requires that the proof can be performed efficiently) and where the prover is dishonest (this requires that each proof need at least a certain effort), while we restrict our treatment to the case of honest verifiers. The security definition below follows the construction notion introduced in [45] for this specific case. The protocol and definition can additionally be extended by a hardness parameter **n** analogously to Definition 3.

**Definition 8.** *A protocol $\pi = (\pi_1, \pi_2)$ is a $(\phi, n, \underline{b}, \varepsilon)$-proof of effort with respect to simulator $\sigma$ if for all $\underline{a}, \overline{a} \in \mathbb{N}$,*

$$\pi_1{}^P \pi_2{}^V \left[ \mathcal{T}^{\mathrm{RRO}}_{\underline{a}, \underline{b}}, [\longrightarrow, \longleftarrow]^n \right] \quad \approx_\varepsilon \quad \mathsf{POE}^{\underline{a}}_{\phi, n}$$

*and*

$$\pi_2{}^V \left[ \mathcal{T}^{\mathrm{RRO}}_{\overline{a}, \underline{b}}, [\longrightarrow, \longleftarrow]^n \right] \quad \approx_\varepsilon \quad \sigma^P \mathsf{POE}^{\overline{a}+n}_{\phi, n}.$$

The reason for the term $\overline{a} + n$ is that the dishonest prover can in each session decide to send a guess without verifying its correctness locally.

While the definition is phrased using the language of constructive cryptography [44,45], it can intuitively also be viewed as a statement in Canetti's UC framework [20].[15] For this, one would however have to additionally require the correctness formalized in the first equation of Definition 8, because UC-security would only correspond to the second equation.

---

[15] One main difference is that UC is tailored toward asymptotic statements. As UC *a priori* allows the environment to create arbitrarily many instances of all protocols and functionalities, making the precise concrete statements we aim for becomes difficult.

## 6.2   Protocols

The PoE protocols we discuss in this section are interactive and start by the verifier sending a challenge to the prover, who responds with a solution. The verifier then checks this solution; an output bit signifies acceptance or rejection. There are several ways to build a scheme for PoE from an MoHF; we describe two particular schemes in this section.

*Function Inversion.* A simple PoE can be built on the idea of having the prover invert the MoHF on a given output value. This output value is obtained by evaluating the function on a publicly known and efficiently sampleable distribution over the input space, such as the uniform distribution over a certain subset.

**Construction 1.** *The protocol is parametrized by a set $D \subseteq \{0,1\}^*$. For each session $1 \le i \le n$, it proceeds as follows:*

1. *The verifier samples $x_i \leftarrow\!\!\text{s}\ D$, queries $y_i \leftarrow T^{\text{RRO}}(i, x_i)$, and sends $y_i$ to the prover.*
2. *When activated in session $i$, the prover checks the next[16] possible input value $x' \in D$ for whether $T^{\text{RRO}}(i, x') = y_i$. If equality holds, send $x'$ to the verifier and output 1 locally. Otherwise, output 0 locally.*
3. *Receiving the value $x' \in D$ in session $i$, the verifier accepts iff $T^{\text{RRO}}(i, x') = y_i$. When activated in session $i$, output 1 if accepted, and 0 otherwise.*

Steps 1 and 3 comprise the verifier's protocol $\chi$, whereas step 2 describes the prover's protocol $\xi$. For this protocol, we show the following theorem. The proof is deferred to the full version [11].

**Theorem 2.** *Define $\zeta_j := (|D| - j + 1)^{-1}$. If $\underline{b} > 2n$, then the described protocol $(\xi, \chi)$ is a $(\phi, n, \underline{b}, 0)$-proof of effort, with $\phi : j \mapsto \zeta_j + \frac{1-\zeta_j}{|R|}$. The simulator is described in the proof.*

*Hash Trail.* The idea underlying PoEs based on a hash trail is that it is difficult to compute a value such that the output of a given hash function on input this value satisfies a certain condition; usually one asks for a preimage $x$ of a function $f_i$ such that the output string $f_i(x) : \{0,1\}^m \to \{0,1\}^k$ starts with some number $d$ of 0's, where $d \in \{1, \ldots, k\}$ can be chosen to adapt the (expected) effort necessary to provide a solution. For simplicity and to save on the number of parameters, we assume for the rest of the chapter that $d$, the hardness parameter of the moderately hard function, is also the bit-length of the output.

**Construction 2.** *The protocol is parametrized by sets $D, N \subseteq \{0,1\}^*$ and hardness parameter $d \in \mathbb{N}$. For each session $1 \le i \le n$, it proceeds as follows:*

1. *The verifier samples uniform $n_i \leftarrow\!\!\text{s}\ N$ and sends $n_i$ to the prover.*

---

[16] We assume that the elements in $D$ are ordered, e.g. lexicographically.

2. *When activated, the prover chooses one value $x' \in D$ uniformly at random (but without collisions), computes $y \leftarrow \mathcal{T}^{\mathrm{RRO}}(i, n_i, x_i)$, and checks whether $y[1, \ldots, d] = 0^d$. If equality holds, send $x'$ to the verifier and output 1 locally. Otherwise, output 0 locally.*
3. *Receiving the value $x' \in D$ from the prover, the verifier accepts iff $y' \leftarrow \mathcal{T}^{\mathrm{RRO}}(i, n_i, x')$ satisfies $y'[1, \ldots, d] = 0^d$. When activated, output 1 if the protocol has accepted and 0 otherwise.*

To capture the described scheme as a pair of algorithms $(\xi, \chi)$ as needed for our security definition, we view steps 1 and 3 as the algorithm $\chi$, whereas step 2 describes the algorithm $\xi$. For this protocol, we show the following theorem. The proof is deferred to the full version [11].

**Theorem 3.** *Let $d \in \mathbb{N}$ be the hardness parameter and $\underline{b} > n$. Then the described protocol $(\xi, \chi)$ is a $(2^{-d}, \underline{b}, n, 0)$-proof of effort. The simulator $\sigma$ is described in the proof.*

# 7 Non-interactive Proofs of Effort

The PoE protocols in Sect. 6.2 require the prover and the verifier to interact, because the verifier has to generate a fresh challenge for the prover in each session to prevent the prover from re-using (parts of) proofs in different sessions. This interaction is inappropriate in several settings, because it either imposes an additional round-trip on protocols (such as in key establishment) or because a setting may be inherently non-interactive, such as sending e-mail. In this section, we describe a non-interactive variant of PoE that can be used in such scenarios. Each proof is cryptographically bound to a certain value, and the higher-level protocol has to make sure that this value is bound to the application so that proofs cannot be re-used.

Although non-interactive PoE (niPoE) have appeared previously in certain applications, and have been suggested for fighting spam mail [1,27–29], to the best of our knowledge they have not been formalized as a tool of their own right.

## 7.1 Definition

Our formalization of non-interactive PoE (niPoE) follows along the same lines as the one for the interactive proofs. The main difference is that while for interactive proofs, it made sense to some notion of session to which the PoE is associated and in which the verifier sends the challenge, this is not the case for niPoE. Instead, we consider each niPoE as being bound to some particular *statement* $s \in \{0, 1\}^*$. This statement $s$ is useful for binding the PoE to a particular context: in the combatting-spam scenario this could be a hash of the message to be sent, in the DoS-protection for key exchange this could be the client's key share.

For consistency with Sect. 6, the treatment in this section is simplified to deal with either only honest or only dishonest provers. The case where both honest and dishonest provers occur simultaneously is deferred to full version [11].

*The Goal of niPoE Protocols.* The constructed resource is similar to the resource POE described in Sect. 6.1, with the main difference that each proof is not bound to a session $i \in \mathbb{N}$, but rather to a statement $s \in \mathcal{S} \subseteq \{0,1\}^*$. Consequently, the resource NIPOE takes as input at the $P$-interface statements $s \in \mathcal{S}$, and returns 1 if the proof succeeded and 0 otherwise. Upon an activation at the verifier's interface $V$, if for any statement $s \in \mathcal{S}$ a proof has been successful, the resource outputs this $s$, and it outputs $\bot$ otherwise. An output $s \neq \bot$ has the meaning that the party at the $P$-interface has spent enough effort for the particular statement $s$. Similarly to POE, the resource NIPOE is parametrized by a bound $a \in \mathbb{N}$ on the number of proof attempts and a performance function $\phi : \mathbb{N} \to \mathbb{R}_{\geq 0}$, but additionally the number of verification attempts $\underline{b} \in \mathbb{N}$ at the verifier is a parameter. The resource is denoted as $\mathsf{NIPOE}^a_{\phi,\underline{b}}$. The behavior of this resource is described in more formally below. There are two inputs for a dishonest prover $P$ that need further explanation:

- $(\mathsf{copy}, s)$: This corresponds to sending a proof to $V$. Prover $V$ is convinced if the proof was successful (i.e., $e_s = 1$), and has to spend one additional evaluation of $\mathcal{T}^{\mathrm{RRO}}$, so the corresponding counter is increased ($d \leftarrow d + 1$).
- $(\mathsf{spend})$: $E$ forces $V$ to spend one additional evaluation of $\mathcal{T}^{\mathrm{RRO}}$, for instance by sending an invalid proof. This decreases the number of verifications that $V$ can still do ($d \leftarrow d + 1$).

---

**Non-interactive proof-of-effort resource $\mathsf{NIPOE}^a_{\phi,\underline{b}}$**

The resource is parametrized by numbers $a, \underline{b} \in \mathbb{N}$ and a mapping $\phi : \mathbb{N} \to \mathbb{R}_{\geq 0}$. It contains as state bits $e_s \in \{0,1\}$ and counters $d, c_s \in \mathbb{N}$ for each $s \in \{0,1\}^*$ (all initially 0), and a list $\mathsf{S} \in (\{0,1\}^*)^*$ of strings that is initially empty.

**Verifier $V$:** On input a unary value, if $\mathsf{S}$ is empty then return $\bot$. Otherwise remove the first element of $\mathsf{S}$ and return it.

**Honest prover $P$:** On input a string $s \in \{0,1\}^*$, set $c_s \leftarrow c_s + 1$. If $e_s = 1$ or $\sum_{s \in \{0,1\}^*} c_s > a$, then return 0. Otherwise, draw $e_s$ at random such that it is 1 with probability $\phi(c_s)$ and 0 otherwise. If $e_s = 1$ and $d < \underline{b}$, then $d \leftarrow d + 1$ and then append $s$ to $\mathsf{S}$. Output $e_s$ at interface $P$.

**Dishonest prover $P$:**   – On input a string $s \in \{0,1\}^*$, set $c_s \leftarrow c_s + 1$. If $e_s = 1$ or $\sum_{s \in \{0,1\}^*} c_s > a$, then return 0. Otherwise, draw $e_s$ at random such that it is 1 with probability $\phi(c_s)$ and 0 otherwise. Output $e_s$ at interface $P$.
- Upon an input $(\mathsf{copy}, s)$, if $d < \underline{b}$ and $e_s = 1$, then $d \leftarrow d + 1$ append $s$ to $\mathsf{S}$.
- Upon an input $(\mathsf{spend})$, set $d \leftarrow d + 1$.

---

*The "real-world" Setting for niPoE Protocols.* The main difference between PoE and niPoE is that a PoE requires bidirectional communication, which in Sect. 6.1 we described by the channels $\longrightarrow$ and $\longleftarrow$ available in each session. A niPoE only requires communication from the prover to the verifier, which we denote by the channel $\longrightarrow$. Additionally, and as in the PoE case, the proof also requires computational resources, which are again formalized by the shared resource $\mathcal{T}^{\mathrm{RRO}}_{\underline{a},\underline{b}}$.

*The Security Definition.* The definition of niPoE security is analogous to the one for PoE.

**Definition 9.** *A protocol* $\pi = (\pi_1, \pi_2)$ *is a non-interactive* $(\phi, \underline{b}, \varepsilon)$-*proof-of-effort with respect to simulator* $\sigma$ *if for all* $\underline{a}, \overline{a} \in \mathbb{N}$,

$$\pi_1{}^P \pi_2{}^V \left[ \mathcal{T}_{\underline{a},\underline{b}}^{\mathrm{RRO}}, \longrightarrow \right] \quad \approx_\varepsilon \quad \mathsf{NIPOE}_{\phi,\underline{b}}^{\underline{a}+\underline{b}}$$

*and*

$$\pi_2{}^V \left[ \mathcal{T}_{\overline{a},\underline{b}}^{\mathrm{RRO}}, \longrightarrow \right] \quad \approx_\varepsilon \quad \sigma^P \mathsf{NIPOE}_{\phi,\underline{b}}^{\overline{a}+\underline{b}}.$$

### 7.2    Protocol

Our protocol for niPoE is similar to the one in Construction 2. Instead of binding the solution to a session identifier chosen by the server, however, the identifier is chosen by the client. This makes sense for instance in the setting of sending electronic mail where the PoE can be bound to a hash of the message, or in Denial-of-Service protection in the TLS setting, where the client can bind the proof to its ephemeral key share.

**Construction 3.** *The protocol is parametrized by sets* $D, \mathcal{S} \subseteq \{0,1\}^*$ *and a hardness parameter* $d \in \mathbb{N}$. *It proceeds as follows:*

1. *On input a statement* $s \in \mathcal{S}$, *the prover chooses* $x \in D$ *uniformly at random (but without collisions with previous attempts for the same* $s$), *computes* $y \leftarrow \mathcal{T}^{\mathrm{RRO}}(s,x)$, *and checks whether* $y[1, \ldots, d] = 0^d$. *If equality holds, send* $(s, x, y)$ *to the verifier and output 1 locally, otherwise output 0.*
2. *Upon receiving* $(s', x', y) \in \mathcal{S} \times D \times R$, *the verifier accepts* $s$ *iff* $y' \leftarrow \mathcal{T}^{\mathrm{RRO}}(s', x')$ *satisfies* $y = y'$ *and* $y'[1, \ldots, d] = 0^d$. *If the protocol is activated by the receiver and there is an accepted value* $s' \in \mathcal{S}$, *then output* $s'$.

To capture the described scheme as a pair of converters $(\xi, \chi)$ as needed for our security definition, we view step 2 as the converter $\chi$, whereas step 1 describes the converter $\xi$. For this protocol, we show the following theorem. The proof is deferred to the full version [11].

**Theorem 4.** *Let* $d \in \mathbb{N}$ *the hardness parameter. Then the described protocol* $(\xi, \chi)$ *is a non-interactive* $(2^{-d}, \underline{b}, 0)$-*proof-of-effort.*

## 8    Combining the Results

Before we can compose the MoHFs proven secure according to Definition 3 with the application protocols described in Sects. 6 and 7 using the respective composition theorem [44,45], we have to resolve one apparent incompatibility. The indifferentiability statement according to Definition 3 is not immediately applicable in the case with two honest parties, as required in the availability conditions of Definitions 8 and 9, where both the prover and verifier are honest.[17] We further explain how to resolve this issue in the full version [11]; the result is that for stateless algorithms, Definition 3 immediately implies the analogous statement for resources with more honest interfaces, written $\mathcal{S}_{l_1,l_2,r}$ and $\mathcal{T}^{\mathrm{RRO}}_{a_1,a_2,b}$, which have two "honest" interfaces $\mathrm{priv}_1$ and $\mathrm{priv}_2$.

We can then immediately conclude the following corollary from composition theorem [44,45] by instantiating it with the schemes of Definitions 3 and 8. In more detail, for an $(a, b, \varepsilon)$-MoHF in some model, and a proof of effort parametrized by $\phi$, the composition of the MoHF and the PoE construct the PoE resource described above with a attempts allowed to the prover $P$, and consequently $\alpha + n$ attempts for the dishonest prover and $n$ sessions. An analogous corollary holds for the niPoEs.

**Corollary 1.** *Let* $f^{(\cdot)}, \mathrm{na\ddot{i}ve}, \mathbb{P}, \pi, \mathsf{a}, \mathsf{b} : \mathbb{P} \to \mathbb{N}$, *and* $\varepsilon : \mathbb{P} \times \mathbb{P} \to \mathbb{R}_{\geq 0}$ *as in Definition 3, and let* $(\xi, \chi)$ *be a* $(\phi, n, \underline{b}, \varepsilon')$*-proof of effort. Then*

$$\xi^P \chi^V \left[ \pi^P \pi^V \perp^{\mathrm{pub}} \mathcal{S}_{l_1,l_2,r}, [\longrightarrow, \longleftarrow]^n \right] \quad \approx_\varepsilon \quad \mathsf{POE}^{\mathsf{a}(l_1)}_{\phi,n},$$

*with* $P = \mathrm{priv}_1$ *and* $V = \mathrm{priv}_2$, *for all* $l_1, l_2 \in \mathbb{P}$, *and where* $\perp^{\mathrm{pub}} \mathcal{S}_{l_1,l_2,r}$ *means that the pub-interface is not accessible to the distinguisher. Additionally,*

$$\chi^V \left[ \pi^V \perp^{\mathrm{priv}_1} \mathcal{S}_{l_1,l_2,r}, [\longrightarrow, \longleftarrow]^n \right] \quad \approx_\varepsilon \quad \tilde{\sigma}^P \mathsf{POE}^{\mathsf{b}(r)+n}_{\phi,n},$$

*with* $P = \mathrm{pub}$ *and* $V = \mathrm{priv}_2$, *for all* $r, l_2 \in \mathbb{P}$, *and where* $\tilde{\sigma}$ *is the composition of the two simulators guaranteed by Definitions 3 and 8.*

# 9    Open Questions

We discuss several interesting open questions raised by this work. The topic of moderately hard functions is an active topic of research both in terms of definitions and constructions and so many practically interesting (and used) moderately hard function constructions and proof-of-effort protocols could benefit from a more formal treatment (e.g. Equihash [16], CryptoNight, Ethash). Many of these will likely result in novel instantiates of the MoHF framework which we believe to be of independent interest as this requires formalizing new security goals motivated by practical considerations. In terms of new moderately hard functions, the recent work of Biryukov and Perrin [17] introduces several new constructions for use in hardening more conventional cryptographic primitives against brute-force attacks. For this type of application, a composable security notion of moderate hardness such as the one in this work would lend itself well to analyzing the effect on the cryptographic primitives being hardened. Other examples of recent proof-of-effort protocols designed to for particular higher-level applications in mind are the results in [13,23,32,35]. In each case, at most standalone security of the higher-level application can be reasoned about so

---

[17] The verifier is always considered honest in our work.

using the framework in this paper could help improve the understanding of the applications composition properties.

A natural question that arises from how the framework is currently formulated is whether the ideal-world resource could be relaxed. While modeling the ideal resource as a random oracle does make proving security for applications using the MoHF easier it seems to moot ever proving security for any candidate MoHF outside the random oracle model. However, it would be nice to show some form of moderate hardness based on other assumptions or, ideally, even unconditionally. Especially in the domain of client-puzzles several interesting constructions already exists based on various computational hardness assumptions [39,41,53,55].

# References

1. Abadi, M., Burrows, M., Manasse, M., Wobber, T.: Moderately hard, memory-bound functions. ACM Trans. Internet Technol. **5**(2), 299–327 (2005)
2. Back, A.: Hashcash - A Denial of Service Counter-Measure (2002)
3. Alwen, J., Blocki, J.: Efficiently computing data-independent memory-hard functions. In: Robshaw, M., Katz, J. (eds.) CRYPTO 2016. LNCS, vol. 9815, pp. 241–271. Springer, Heidelberg (2016). https://doi.org/10.1007/978-3-662-53008-5_9
4. Alwen, J., Blocki, J.: Towards practical attacks on Argon2i and balloon hashing. In: EuroS&P 2017 (2017)
5. Alwen, J., Blocki, J., Harsha, B.: Practical graphs for optimal side-channel resistant memory-hard functions. Cryptology ePrint Archive, Report 2017/443 (2017). http://eprint.iacr.org/2017/443
6. Alwen, J., Blocki, J., Pietrzak, K.: Depth-robust graphs and their cumulative memory complexity. In: Coron, J.-S., Nielsen, J.B. (eds.) EUROCRYPT 2017. LNCS, vol. 10212, pp. 3–32. Springer, Cham (2017). https://doi.org/10.1007/978-3-319-56617-7_1. https://eprint.iacr.org/
7. Alwen, J., Chen, B., Kamath, C., Kolmogorov, V., Pietrzak, K., Tessaro, S.: On the complexity of scrypt and proofs of space in the parallel random oracle model. In: Fischlin, M., Coron, J.-S. (eds.) EUROCRYPT 2016. LNCS, vol. 9666, pp. 358–387. Springer, Heidelberg (2016). https://doi.org/10.1007/978-3-662-49896-5_13
8. Alwen, J., Chen, B., Pietrzak, K., Reyzin, L., Tessaro, S.: Scrypt is maximally memory-hard. In: Coron, J.-S., Nielsen, J.B. (eds.) EUROCRYPT 2017. LNCS, vol. 10212, pp. 33–62. Springer, Cham (2017). https://doi.org/10.1007/978-3-319-56617-7_2
9. Alwen, J., Gaži, P., Kamath, C., Klein, K., Osang, G., Pietrzak, K., Reyzin, L., Rolínek, M., Rybár, M.: On the memory-hardness of data-independent password-hashing functions. Cryptology ePrint Archive, Report 2016/783 (2016)
10. Alwen, J., Serbinenko, V.: High parallel complexity graphs and memory-hard functions. In: STOC (2015)
11. Alwen, J., Tackmann, B.: Moderately hard functions: definition, instantiations, and applications moderately hard functions. Cryptology ePrint Archive, September 2017
12. Aura, T., Nikander, P., Leiwo, J.: DOS-resistant authentication with client puzzles. In: Christianson, B., Malcolm, J.A., Crispo, B., Roe, M. (eds.) Security Protocols 2000. LNCS, vol. 2133, pp. 170–177. Springer, Heidelberg (2001). https://doi.org/10.1007/3-540-44810-1_22

13. Ball, M., Rosen, A., Sabin, M., Vasudevan, P.N.: Proofs of useful work. Cryptology ePrint Archive, Report 2017/203 (2017). http://eprint.iacr.org/2017/203
14. Bellare, M., Ristenpart, T., Tessaro, S.: Multi-instance security and its application to password-based cryptography. In: Safavi-Naini, R., Canetti, R. (eds.) CRYPTO 2012. LNCS, vol. 7417, pp. 312–329. Springer, Heidelberg (2012). https://doi.org/10.1007/978-3-642-32009-5_19
15. Biryukov, A., Khovratovich, D.: Tradeoff cryptanalysis of memory-hard functions. In: Iwata, T., Cheon, J.H. (eds.) ASIACRYPT 2015. LNCS, vol. 9453, pp. 633–657. Springer, Heidelberg (2015). https://doi.org/10.1007/978-3-662-48800-3_26
16. Biryukov, A., Khovratovich, D.: Equihash: asymmetric proof-of-work based on the generalized birthday problem. Ledger J. **2**, 1–11 (2017)
17. Biryukov, A., Perrin, L.: Symmetrically and asymmetrically hard cryptography (full version). Cryptology ePrint Archive, Report 2017/414 (2017). http://eprint.iacr.org/2017/414
18. Boneh, D., Corrigan-Gibbs, H., Schechter, S.: Balloon hashing: a memory-hard function providing provable protection against sequential attacks. In: Cheon, J.H., Takagi, T. (eds.) ASIACRYPT 2016. LNCS, vol. 10031, pp. 220–248. Springer, Heidelberg (2016). https://doi.org/10.1007/978-3-662-53887-6_8
19. Buterin, V., Di Lorio, A., Hoskinson, C., Alisie, M.: Ethereum: a distributed cryptographic leger (2013). http://www.ethereum.org/
20. Canetti, R.: Universally composable security: a new paradigm for cryptographic protocols. In: Proceedings of the 42nd IEEE Symposium on Foundations of Computer Science, pp. 136–145. IEEE (2001)
21. Canetti, R., Halevi, S., Steiner, M.: Hardness amplification of weakly verifiable puzzles. In: Kilian, J. (ed.) TCC 2005. LNCS, vol. 3378, pp. 17–33. Springer, Heidelberg (2005). https://doi.org/10.1007/978-3-540-30576-7_2
22. Chen, L., Morrissey, P., Smart, N.P., Warinschi, B.: Security notions and generic constructions for client puzzles. In: Matsui, M. (ed.) ASIACRYPT 2009. LNCS, vol. 5912, pp. 505–523. Springer, Heidelberg (2009). https://doi.org/10.1007/978-3-642-10366-7_30
23. Chepurnoy, A., Duong, T., Fan, L., Zhou, H.S.: Twinscoin: a cryptocurrency via proof-of-work and proof-of-stake. Cryptology ePrint Archive, Report 2017/232 (2017). http://eprint.iacr.org/2017/232
24. Cook, S.A.: An observation on time-storage trade off. In: STOC, pp. 29–33 (1973)
25. Demay, G., Gaži, P., Hirt, M., Maurer, U.: Resource-restricted indifferentiability. In: Johansson, T., Nguyen, P.Q. (eds.) EUROCRYPT 2013. LNCS, vol. 7881, pp. 664–683. Springer, Heidelberg (2013). https://doi.org/10.1007/978-3-642-38348-9_39
26. Demay, G., Gaži, P., Maurer, U., Tackmann, B.: Query-complexity amplification for random oracles. In: Lehmann, A., Wolf, S. (eds.) ICITS 2015. LNCS, vol. 9063, pp. 159–180. Springer, Cham (2015). https://doi.org/10.1007/978-3-319-17470-9_10
27. Dwork, C., Goldberg, A., Naor, M.: On memory-bound functions for fighting spam. In: Boneh, D. (ed.) CRYPTO 2003. LNCS, vol. 2729, pp. 426–444. Springer, Heidelberg (2003). https://doi.org/10.1007/978-3-540-45146-4_25
28. Dwork, C., Naor, M.: Pricing via processing or combatting junk mail. In: Brickell, E.F. (ed.) CRYPTO 1992. LNCS, vol. 740, pp. 139–147. Springer, Heidelberg (1993). https://doi.org/10.1007/3-540-48071-4_10
29. Dwork, C., Naor, M., Wee, H.: Pebbling and proofs of work. In: Shoup, V. (ed.) CRYPTO 2005. LNCS, vol. 3621, pp. 37–54. Springer, Heidelberg (2005). https://doi.org/10.1007/11535218_3

30. Dziembowski, S., Faust, S., Kolmogorov, V., Pietrzak, K.: Proofs of space. In: Gennaro, R., Robshaw, M. (eds.) CRYPTO 2015. LNCS, vol. 9216, pp. 585–605. Springer, Heidelberg (2015). https://doi.org/10.1007/978-3-662-48000-7_29

31. Dziembowski, S., Kazana, T., Wichs, D.: One-time computable self-erasing functions. In: Ishai, Y. (ed.) TCC 2011. LNCS, vol. 6597, pp. 125–143. Springer, Heidelberg (2011). https://doi.org/10.1007/978-3-642-19571-6_9

32. Eckey, L., Faust, S., Loss, J.: Efficient algorithms for broadcast and consensus based on proofs of work. Cryptology ePrint Archive, Report 2017/915 (2017). http://eprint.iacr.org/2017/915

33. Forler, C., Lucks, S., Wenzel, J.: Catena: a memory-consuming password scrambler. Cryptology ePrint Archive, Report 2013/525 (2013)

34. Garay, J., Kiayias, A., Leonardos, N.: The bitcoin backbone protocol: analysis and applications. In: Oswald, E., Fischlin, M. (eds.) EUROCRYPT 2015. LNCS, vol. 9057, pp. 281–310. Springer, Heidelberg (2015). https://doi.org/10.1007/978-3-662-46803-6_10

35. Garay, J.A., Kiayias, A., Panagiotakos, G.: Proofs of work for blockchain protocols. Cryptology ePrint Archive, Report 2017/775 (2017). http://eprint.iacr.org/2017/775

36. Groza, B., Petrica, D.: On chained cryptographic puzzles. In: SACI, pp. 25–26 (2006)

37. Groza, B., Warinschi, B.: Cryptographic puzzles and DoS resilience, revisited. DCC 73(1), 177–207 (2014)

38. Hewitt, C.E., Paterson, M.S.: Record of the project MAC. In: Conference on Concurrent Systems and Parallel Computation, pp. 119–127. ACM, New York (1970)

39. Jerschow, Y.I., Mauve, M.: Non-parallelizable and non-interactive client puzzles from modular square roots. In: ARES, pp. 135–142. IEEE (2011)

40. Juels, A., Brainard, J.G.: Client puzzles: a cryptographic countermeasure against connection depletion attacks. In: NDSS (1999)

41. Karame, G.O., Čapkun, S.: Low-cost client puzzles based on modular exponentiation. In: Gritzalis, D., Preneel, B., Theoharidou, M. (eds.) ESORICS 2010. LNCS, vol. 6345, pp. 679–697. Springer, Heidelberg (2010). https://doi.org/10.1007/978-3-642-15497-3_41

42. Lengauer, T., Tarjan, R.E.: Asymptotically tight bounds on time-space trade-offs in a pebble game. J. ACM 29(4), 1087–1130 (1982)

43. Maurer, U.: Indistinguishability of random systems. In: Knudsen, L.R. (ed.) EUROCRYPT 2002. LNCS, vol. 2332, pp. 110–132. Springer, Heidelberg (2002). https://doi.org/10.1007/3-540-46035-7_8

44. Maurer, U.: Constructive cryptography – a new paradigm for security definitions and proofs. In: Mödersheim, S., Palamidessi, C. (eds.) TOSCA 2011. LNCS, vol. 6993, pp. 33–56. Springer, Heidelberg (2012). https://doi.org/10.1007/978-3-642-27375-9_3

45. Maurer, U., Renner, R.: Abstract cryptography. In: ICS (2011)

46. Maurer, U., Renner, R.: From indifferentiability to constructive cryptography (and back). In: Hirt, M., Smith, A. (eds.) TCC 2016. LNCS, vol. 9985, pp. 3–24. Springer, Heidelberg (2016). https://doi.org/10.1007/978-3-662-53641-4_1

47. Maurer, U., Renner, R., Holenstein, C.: Indifferentiability, impossibility results on reductions, and applications to the random oracle methodology. In: Naor, M. (ed.) TCC 2004. LNCS, vol. 2951, pp. 21–39. Springer, Heidelberg (2004). https://doi.org/10.1007/978-3-540-24638-1_2

48. Morris, R., Thompson, K.: Password security: a case history. Commun. ACM 22(11), 594–597 (1979)

49. Nakamoto, S.: Bitcoin: A Peer-to-Peer Electronic Cash System (2009)
50. Naor, M.: Moderately hard functions: from complexity to spam fighting. In: Pandya, P.K., Radhakrishnan, J. (eds.) FSTTCS 2003. LNCS, vol. 2914, pp. 434–442. Springer, Heidelberg (2003). https://doi.org/10.1007/978-3-540-24597-1_37
51. Percival, C.: Stronger key derivation via sequential memory-hard functions. In: BSDCan 2009 (2009)
52. Price, G.: A general attack model on hash-based client puzzles. In: Paterson, K.G. (ed.) Cryptography and Coding 2003. LNCS, vol. 2898, pp. 319–331. Springer, Heidelberg (2003). https://doi.org/10.1007/978-3-540-40974-8_26
53. Rivest, R.L., Shamir, A., Wagner, D.A.: Time-lock puzzles and timed-release Crypto. Technical report, Cambridge, MA, USA (1996)
54. Stebila, D., Kuppusamy, L., Rangasamy, J., Boyd, C., Gonzalez Nieto, J.: Stronger difficulty notions for client puzzles and denial-of-service-resistant protocols. In: Kiayias, A. (ed.) CT-RSA 2011. LNCS, vol. 6558, pp. 284–301. Springer, Heidelberg (2011). https://doi.org/10.1007/978-3-642-19074-2_19
55. Tritilanunt, S., Boyd, C., Foo, E., González Nieto, J.M.: Toward non-parallelizable client puzzles. In: Bao, F., Ling, S., Okamoto, T., Wang, H., Xing, C. (eds.) CANS 2007. LNCS, vol. 4856, pp. 247–264. Springer, Heidelberg (2007). https://doi.org/10.1007/978-3-540-76969-9_16
56. Yao, F.F., Yin, Y.L.: Design and analysis of password-based key derivation functions. In: Menezes, A. (ed.) CT-RSA 2005. LNCS, vol. 3376, pp. 245–261. Springer, Heidelberg (2005). https://doi.org/10.1007/978-3-540-30574-3_17

# Blockchains

# Overcoming Cryptographic Impossibility Results Using Blockchains

Rishab Goyal[1]($\boxtimes$) and Vipul Goyal[2]

[1] University of Texas at Austin, Austin, USA
goyal@utexas.edu
[2] Carnegie Mellon University, Pittsburgh, USA
vipul@cmu.edu

**Abstract.** Blockchain technology has the potential to disrupt how cryptography is done. In this work, we propose to view blockchains as an "enabler", much like indistinguishability obfuscation [5,23,46] or one-way functions, for building a variety of cryptographic systems. Our contributions in this work are as follows:

1. *A Framework for Proof-of-Stake based Blockchains:* We provide an abstract framework for formally analyzing and defining useful security properties for Proof-of-Stake (POS) based blockchain protocols. Interestingly, for some of our applications, POS based protocols are more suitable. We believe our framework and assumptions would be useful in building applications on top of POS based blockchain protocols even in the future.

2. *Blockchains as an Alternative to Trusted Setup Assumptions in Cryptography:* A trusted setup, such as a common reference string (CRS) has been used to realize numerous systems in cryptography. The paragon example of a primitive requiring trusted setup is a non-interactive zero-knowledge (NIZK) system. We show that already existing blockchains systems including Bitcoin, Ethereum etc. can be used as a foundation (instead of a CRS) to realize NIZK systems. The novel aspect of our work is that it allows for utilizing an already existing (and widely trusted) setup rather than proposing a new one. Our construction does not require any additional functionality from the miners over the already existing ones, nor do we need to modify the underlying blockchain protocol. If an adversary can violate the security of our NIZK, it could potentially also take over billions of dollars worth of coins in the Bitcoin, Ethereum or any such cryptocurrency!

   We believe that such a "trusted setup" represents significant progress over using CRS published by a central trusted party. Indeed, NIZKs could further serve as a foundation for a variety of other cryptographic applications such as round efficient secure computation [33,36].

3. *One-time programs and pay-per use programs:* Goldwasser et al. [29] introduced the notion of one time program and presented a construction using tamper-proof hardware. As noted by Goldwasser et al. [29], clearly a one-time program cannot be solely software

Y. Kalai and L. Reyzin (Eds.): TCC 2017, Part I, LNCS 10677, pp. 529–561, 2017.
https://doi.org/10.1007/978-3-319-70500-2_18

based, as software can always be copied and run again. While there have been a number of follow up works [4,6,30], there are indeed *no known constructions of one-time programs which do not rely on self destructing tamper-proof hardware (even if one uses trusted setup or random oracles)*. Somewhat surprisingly, we show that it is possible to base one-time programs on POS based blockchain systems without relying on trusted hardware. Our ideas do not seem to translate over to Proof-of-Work (POW) based blockchains.

We also introduce the notion of pay-per-use programs which is simply a contract between two parties — service provider and customer. A service provider supplies a program such that if the customer transfers a specific amount of coins to the provider, it can evaluate the program on any input of its choice once, even if the provider is *offline*. This is naturally useful in a subscription based model where your payment is based on your usage.

# 1    Introduction

The last few years have seen a dramatic rise of cryptocurrencies such as Bitcoin [42] and Ethereum [49]. Some of these cryptocurrencies have a market capitalization running into several billion dollars. This has fuelled a significant interest in the underlying blockchain technology. Blockchain technology has the potential to disrupt how cryptography is done. Much of cryptography can be seen as eliminating the need to trust (and allow for dealing with adversarial parties which can't be trusted). Indeed the purpose of blockchains is something similar: eliminate the central point of trust in cryptocurrencies and possibly other applications. Thus we believe that a sustained effort to bring together "traditional cryptography" with the blockchain technology has the potential to be truly rewarding.

*Blockchain Protocols.* In a blockchain protocol, the goal of all parties is to maintain a (consistent) global ordered set of records. The set of records is "append only", and publicly visible. Furthermore, records can only be added using a special mechanism to reach consensus on what must be added to the existing blockchain. A protocol can employ any arbitrary technique or mechanism for participants to converge on a uniform and reliable blockchain state.

In most cryptocurrencies instantiated in the blockchain model, the special mechanism to reach consensus is called a *mining* procedure. It is used by all parties to extend the blockchain (i.e., add new blocks) and in turn (potentially) receive rewards for successfully generating a new block consistent with respect to current blockchain state. The mining procedure is meant to simulate a puzzle-solving race between protocol participants and could be run by any party. The rewards mostly consist of freshly generated currency. Presently, the mining procedures employed by most cryptocurrencies could be classified into two broad categories — *Proof-of-Work (POW)* and *Proof-of-Stake (POS)* based puzzles. The basic difference being that in POW puzzles, the probability of successful mining is proportional to the amount of computational power; whereas in POS, it is proportional to the number of coins in possession of a miner. Therefore, POW miners have to spend significant portion of their computational resources (and in turn, monetary resources) to extend the blockchain and in turn get rewarded, whereas POS miners spend significantly less computational resources and just need to have a sufficient balance.

*Our Contributions.* In this work, we propose to view blockchains as an "enabler", much like indistinguishability obfuscation [5,23,46] or one-way functions, for building a variety of cryptographic systems. Basing cryptographic system on blockchains can provide very strong guarantees of the following form: *If an adversary could break the security of the cryptographic system, then it could also break the security of the underlying blockchain allowing it to potentially gain billions of dollars!* Indeed, this perspective is not new. Previous works [2,3,11,34,39,40] in this direction include using blockchains to construct fair secure multi-party computation, lottery systems, smart contracts and more. Our contributions in this work include the following:

- *A Framework for Proof-of-Stake based Blockchains:* We provide an abstract framework for formally analyzing and defining useful security properties and hardness relations for POS based blockchain protocols. Interestingly, we observe that for some of our applications, POS based protocols are more suitable than their POW counterparts. Furthermore, we also show how our framework can be instantiated based on existing POS based protocols [13,38]. Previously, various works [12,13,19–21,37,38,43–45] have analyzed the blockchain consensus protocols (of existing systems like Bitcoin) proving some fundamental properties as well as proposed new blockchain protocols. It is important to note that most of these works consider blockchain protocols with provable security guarantees as an end goal. However, as mentioned before, we consider blockchains as an "enabler". Therefore, we believe our framework and assumptions would be useful in building applications on top of POS based blockchain protocols even in the future.

  Recently, it was suggested that blockchains could potentially be used to obtain a common random string as they can be used as a source of public randomness, thereby allowing to generate trusted random parameters [10,14]. However, the results presented were limited in the sense that either adversaries with bounded budget were assumed or no security analysis was provided. We, on the other hand, proceed in an orthogonal direction by suggesting methods to directly extract cryptographic hardness from blockchains and developing hard-to-compute trapdoors with respect to blockchains.

- *Blockchains as an Alternative to Trusted Setup Assumptions in Cryptography:* A trusted setup, such as a common reference string (CRS) has been used to realize numerous systems in cryptography. Indeed, several of these systems have been shown to be impossible to realize without a trusted setup. In this work, we explore using blockchains as an alternative to a trusted setup (typically performed by a central trusted authority). The paragon example of a primitive requiring trusted setup is a non-interactive zero-knowledge (NIZK) system. Most well-known NIZK constructions are in the so called common reference string (CRS) model where there is a trusted third party which publishes some public parameters. However if the setup is done dishonestly, all security guarantees are lost.

We show that already existing blockchains systems including Bitcoin, Ethereum etc. could potentially be used as a foundation (instead of a CRS) to realize NIZK systems. Thus, the complex blockchain system consisting of various miners and users can be seen as a "trusted setup". The idea of a decentralized setup for realizing NIZKs is not entirely new: Groth and Ostrovsky [32] propose NIZKs with $n$ authorities where a majority of them must be honest. Goyal and Katz [31] propose a generalized model which allows for placing "differing levels of trust" in different authorities. However the novel aspect of our work is that it allows for utilizing an already existing (and widely trusted) setup rather than proposing a new one. Our construction does not require any additional functionality from the miners over the already existing ones, nor do we need to modify the underlying blockchain protocol.[1] If an adversary can violate the security of our NIZK, it could potentially also take over billions of dollars worth of coins in the Bitcoin, Ethereum or any such cryptocurrency!

We believe that such a "trusted setup" represents significant progress over using CRS published by a central trusted party. Indeed, NIZKs could further serve as a foundation for a variety of other cryptographic applications such as round efficient secure computation [33, 36].

- *One-time programs and pay-per use programs:* Say Alice wants to send a program to Bob. The program should run only once and then "self destruct". Is it possible to realize such "one-time programs"? Goldwasser et al. [29] introduced the notion of one time program and presented a construction using tamper-proof hardware. A one-time program can be executed on a single input, whose value can be specified at run time. Other than the result of the computation on this input, nothing else about the program is leaked. One-time programs, for example, lead naturally to electronic cash or token schemes: coins or tokens are generated by a program that can only be run once, and thus cannot be double spent. In the construction of Goldwasser et al. [29], a sender sends a set of very simple hardware tokens to a (potentially malicious) receiver. The hardware tokens allow the receiver to execute a program specified by the sender's tokens exactly once (or, more generally, up to a fixed $t$ times).

As noted by Goldwasser et al. [29], clearly a one-time program cannot be solely software based, as software can always be copied and run again. While there have been a number of follow up works [4, 6, 30], there are indeed *no known constructions of one-time programs which do not rely on self destructing*

---

[1] We would like to point out that (unlike other works like [2, 3, 11, 39]) *none* of our applications require the underlying blockchain protocol to provide a sufficiently expressive scripting language. This suggests that our applications could be based on top of almost all existing blockchain protocols.

*tamper-proof hardware (even if one uses trusted setup or random oracles)*. Somewhat surprisingly, we show that it is possible to base one-time programs on POS based blockchain systems without relying on trusted hardware. Our ideas do not seem to translate over to POW based blockchains. Our construction assumes the existence of extractable witness encryption (WE) [25,28] (which in turn requires strong knowledge assumptions related over multi-linear maps [15,22], see also [24]). However, we stress that our construction does not require WE for all **NP**-relations, instead we only need a WE scheme for very specific blockchain dependent relations. As noted by prior works [34,40], we, for example, already know efficient WE schemes for hash proof system compatible relations [1,9,16,35,48] with some works even achieving certain notions of extractability.[2]

We also introduce the notion of pay-per-use programs. Informally, a pay-per-use program is a contract between two parties which we call the service provider and customer. A service provider wants to supply a program (or service) such that if the customer transfers a specific amount of coins to the provider (over the blockchain), it can evaluate the program on any input of its choice once. Additionally, the service provider need not be executing the blockchain protocol after supplying the program, i.e. it could go *offline*. We could also generalize this notion to $k$-time pay-per-use programs. This is naturally useful in a subscription based model where your payment is based on your usage. The above construction of one-time programs can be easily extended to obtain pay-per-use $k$-time programs.

## 1.1  Technical Overview

First, we discuss an abstract model for blockchain protocols as well as the protocol execution model and describe various desirable security properties of blockchains. Next, we outline our NIZK construction based on blockchains and present the main ideas in the security proof. We also overview our construction for OTPs using blockchains and highlight the necessity of a POS based blockchain in the security proof. Finally, we briefly discuss how to extend our idea behind constructing OTPs to building pay-per-use programs.

---

[2] At first sight one might ask whether a strong assumption like extractable WE is necessary, or could it be relaxed. It turns out that, to construct one-time programs, it is *sufficient and necessary* to assume a slightly weaker primitive which we call *one-time extractable WE*. A one-time extractable WE is same as a standard extractable WE scheme, except the decryption algorithm could only be run once on each ciphertext. In other words, if we decrypt a one-time WE ciphertext with a bad witness the first time, then next time decryption (on that same ciphertext) will always fail even if we use a correct witness. Again this cannot be solely software based as then ciphertext could always be copied, and thus one-time decryption wouldn't make sense. It is straightforward to verify in our OTP construction that we could instead use such a one-time extractable WE scheme. Additionally, anologous to construction of extractable WE from VBB obfuscation, we could show that a OTP already implies a one-time extractable WE, therefore our assumption of one-time extractable WE for constructing OTPs is both necessary and sufficient.

**Proof-of-Stake Protocols: Abstraction and Properties.** Informally, a blockchain protocol is a distributed consensus protocol in which each participant (locally) stores an ordered sequence of blocks/records **B** (simply called blockchain). The goal of all (honest) parties is to maintain a globally consistent blockchain. Each party can try to include new blocks in their local blockchain as well as attempt to get it added in blockchains of other parties. Such new blocks are created using a special block generation procedure (simply called mining) that depends on the underlying consensus mechanism.

In POS based blockchains, each participant (apart from storing a local blockchain **B**) is also entitled with some *stake* in the system, which could be measured as a positive rational value.[3] The ideology behind mining in a POS based system is that the probability any party succeeds in generating the next block (i.e., gets to mine a new block) is proportional to its stake. Also, each party that generates a block must provide a *proof-of-stake* which could be used as a certificate by other parties to verify correctness. Such proofs-of-stake are usually provided in the form of signatures, as it prevents unforgeability and permits easy verification. An important aspect in such POS systems is that the stake distribution (among all parties) evolves over time, and is not necessarily static.

Recently, few works [19,37,43] initiated the study of formal analysis of blockchain protocols. They formalized and put forth some useful properties for blockchain protocols which were previously discussed only informally [41,42]. The most well-known properties analyzed are chain consistency and chain quality.[4] At a high level, these can be described as follows.

- $\ell$-**chain consistency:** blockchains of any two honest parties at any two (possibly different) rounds during protocol execution can differ only in the last $\ell$ blocks, with all but negligible probability.
- $(\mu, \ell)$-**chain quality:** fraction of blocks *mined by honest parties* in any sequence of $\ell$ or more consecutive blocks in an honest party's blockchain is at least $\mu$, with all but negligible probability.

Previous works demonstrated usefulness of the above properties by showing that any blockchain protocol (irrespective of it being POW or POS based) satisfying these properties could be used a public ledger and for byzantine agreement. While the above properties are interesting from the perspective of using blockchains as an *end-goal* or achieving consensus, it is not clear whether these could be used to extract some form of cryptographic hardness. In other words, it does not seem straightforward on how to use these properties if we want to use blockchains as a primitive/enabler. To this end, we introduce several new security properties that are aimed directly at extracting cryptographic hardness from POS blockchains. We exhibit their importance and usability by basing security of all our applications (NIZKs, OTPs and pay-per-use programs) on these properties. At a high level, the properties could be described as follows.

---

[3] In cryptocurrencies, stake of any party simply corresponds to the amount of coins it controls.

[4] Previous works also define chain growth as a desideratum, however in this work we will only focus on chain consistency and quality properties.

- $(\beta, \ell)$-**sufficient stake contribution:** the combined amount of stake whose proof was provided in any sequence of $\ell$ or more consecutive blocks in an honest party's blockchain is at least $\beta$ fraction of the total stake in the system, with all but negligible probability.
- $(\beta, \ell)$-**sufficient honest stake contribution:** the combined amount of *honestly held* stake whose proof was provided in any sequence of $\ell$ or more consecutive blocks in an honest party's blockchain is at least $\beta$ fraction of the total stake in the system, with all but negligible probability.
- $(\alpha, \ell_1, \ell_2)$-**bounded stake forking:** no adversary can create a *fork* of length $\ell_1 + \ell_2$ or more such that, in the last $\ell_2$ blocks of the fork, the amount of proof-of-stake provided is more than $\alpha$ fraction of the total stake in the system, with all but negligible probability.[5]
- $(\alpha, \beta, \ell_1, \ell_2)$-**distinguishable forking:** with all but negligible probability, any sequence of $\ell_1 + \ell_2$ or more consecutive blocks in an honest party's blockchain could always be *distinguished* from any adversarially generated fork of same length by measuring the amount of proof-of-stake proven in those sequences. The fraction of proof-of-stake proven in the (adversarial) fork will be at most $\alpha$, and in honest party's blockchain will be at least $\beta$. Hence, any fork which is created by the adversary on its own off-line is clearly distinguishable from a real blockchain.

Interestingly, we show that these properties with appropriate parameters are already implied (in an *almost black-box* way) by chain consistency and quality properties if we assume suitable stake distributions among honest parties. Since we already know of POS based blockchain protocols [13, 38] that fit our abstract framework and satisfy chain consistency and quality, this provides concrete instantiations of our framework and following applications.

We would like to point out that, in our analysis, we make certain simplifying assumptions about the blockchain execution model. First, we require that the number of honest miners who actively participate in mining (i.e., are online) as well as the amount of stake they jointly control does not fall below a certain threshold. In other words, we expect that (honest) miners which control a significant amount of stake do not remain *offline* for arbitrarily long periods. However, we stress that we do not assume that *all* honest parties are online, nor do we assume that *all* honest parties which control a significant fraction of stake are online. We only require that the number of such honest parties does not fall below a reasonable threshold. Second, we also expect each honest party to delete the signing keys after they lose significance, i.e. once the coins associated with a particular key are transferred, then the corresponding signing key must be deleted. More details about our proposed properties as well as their reductions to other desideratum is provided later in Sects. 4 and 5.

Now our applications give evidence that the above security properties as well as our POS framework are very useful in using POS based blockchains as a primitive, and we believe its scope is beyond this work as well. Also, we

---

[5] A *fork* is simply a *private* chain of blocks which significantly diverges from global blockchain in honest parties' view.

would like to point out that our reductions are not completely tight since we do not assume any special structure about underlying POS protocols, but instead work with an abstract model. We hope that future work on POS blockchains will consider these properties as desiderata, thereby proving these properties directly (possibly in a non-black-box way) with better parameters.

**Zero-Knowledge Systems Based on Blockchains.** For ease of exposition, assume that all parties executing the blockchain protocol have the same amount of stake (i.e., each new block contains a proof-of-stake of a fixed amount). Also, the adversary controls only a *minority stake* in the system (say $\alpha$). Below we describe a simplified construction. A formal treatment is given in the main body.

*Defining non-interactive zero-knowledge based on blockchains:* We would define the zero-knowledge property as follows. Very informally, we would require the existence of a simulator which should be able to simulate the view of the adversary without having access to the witness. In the real experiment, the adversary interacts with the honest parties: the honest prover, the honest miners and other honest blockchain participants. In the simulated experiment, the adversary interacts with the simulator alone. The simulator in turn emulates all the honest parties: including the honest prover, and the honest miners. We would require the view of the adversarial verifier to be computational indistinguishable in the two experiments. Note that in the simulated experiment, the simulator emulates (or controls) all the honest parties including even the honest blockchain miners. This can be seen as analogous to the simulator emulating the honest party publishing the CRS in the CRS model, or, the simulator controlling a majority of the parties in a secure multi-party computation protocol with honest majority [8], etc.

First, we define the notion of a *fork* with respect to blockchains. Let **B** be some blockchain. A fork w.r.t. **B** is a sequence of valid blocks that extends some prefix of blockchain **B** instead of extending **B** directly from its end. In other words, a fork is a sequence of valid blocks that starts extending the chain at some block which is not the most recently added block in **B**.

The starting point of our construction is the well-known FLS paradigm [17] for transforming proof of the statement $x \in L$ into a witness-indistinguishable proof for the statement — "$x \in L$ OR the common shared random string $\sigma$ is the output of a pseudorandom generator". Our idea is to use the already established blockchain **B** as the CRS $\sigma$, and instead of proving that $\sigma$ is the output of a pseudorandom generator, we will prove some trapdoor information (which is hard to compute) w.r.t. to the current blockchain **B**. A little more formally, we will generate a witness-indistinguishable proof for the statement — "$x \in L$ OR there exists a long valid fork $f$ w.r.t. blockchain **B**".

Suppose $\mathsf{Com}(\cdot)$ is a non-interactive statistically binding commitment scheme. Let **B** denote the current state of the blockchain and the adversary controls at most $\alpha$ fraction of total stake in the blockchain network. At a high level, the scheme works as follows. The prover constructs the NIZK as:

- Compute commitments $c_1 \leftarrow \mathsf{Com}(w)$ and $c_2 \leftarrow \mathsf{Com}(f)$ where $w$ is the witness for the given statement $x \in L$, and $f$ is simply an all zeros string of appropriate length.
- Compute a non-interactive witness indistinguishable (NIWI) argument using witness $w$ proving that either:
  1. $c_1$ is a commitment of a valid witness to $x \in L$, or
  2. $c_2$ is a commitment of a long *fork* w.r.t. blockchain **B** (i.e., a different sequence of valid blocks) such that the amount of proof-of-stake present in the fork is a clear majority (of total stake).

Completeness follows directly from the correctness of underlying primitives. To prove the zero-knowledge property, we would need to construct a simulator which would not have the witness $w$ but could still construct proofs which are indistinguishable from honestly generated proofs. Note that the simulator is permitted to control all honest parties, thus it can access their signing keys. Since honest parties are in (stake) majority, therefore the simulator could efficiently generate a fork of sufficient length that contains a combined proof of majority stake. Hence, it could alternatively compute $c_2$ as a commitment to the fork, and generate the NIWI using the witness for second condition.

Proving soundness of the above construction is not straightforward and turns out to be more complex. Suppose that an adversary manages to produce a NIZK for a false statement. How could we reduce it to an attack on some reasonable notion of security of the blockchain? For such a reduction, we would have to construct an adversary which controls only a *minority stake* in the system, but it could still generate a fork which contains a proof of majority stake. However, the above NIZK only contains a commitment to such a fork. This problem seems to suggest that some form of extraction (of the fork) would be required for the security reduction to go through. *And yet, we don't have any CRS!* To solve this problem we need to modify our construction such that extraction is possible without any CRS.

*Allowing Extraction of f.* To this end, we rely on the following idea. Note that each mined block also contains the public key of the corresponding party. At a very high level, our idea is to secret share the fork into $\ell$ shares, and encrypt $i^{th}$ share under public key of the party that mined $i^{th}$ most recent block (instead of generating a commitment of the fork). If a certain threshold of these $\ell$ parties are honest, then we could extract the appropriate secret shares and reconstruct the fork.

More formally, let the public keys of the parties who mined at least one block in the last $N$ blocks on blockchain **B** be $\mathsf{pk}_1, \ldots, \mathsf{pk}_\ell$ where $N$ is a sufficiently big number and $\ell$ could be smaller than $N$ (as some party could have mined multiple blocks). Note that in most blockchain protocols, each mined block contains the public (verification) key of its miner. We assume that these public keys could be used for encryption as well.[6] Also, recall that the fraction of total stake controlled

---

[6] For instance, most blockchain protocols (like Bitcoin, Ethereum etc.) already use ECDSA based signature schemes for which we could directly use ECIES-like integrated encryption schemes [47].

by adversary is at most $\alpha$, and for simplicity we assumed that all parties have the same amount of stake.

Now, the prover uses a $\beta\ell$-out-of-$\ell$ secret sharing scheme on $f$ to get shares $f_1, \ldots, f_\ell$. For all $i$, the share $f_i$ will be encrypted under $\mathsf{pk}_i$, where $\beta(<1)$ is a scheme parameter such that it is sufficiently higher than $\alpha$. The second condition (i.e., trapdoor condition) in the NIWI would now be that all these shares lead to a valid reconstruction of a string $f$ which represents a long fork such that it contains a proof of majority stake w.r.t. blockchain $\mathbf{B}$. With this modification, we observe the following:

- Given any $\beta\ell$ secret keys corresponding to these public keys, $f$ can be extracted. This is because the number of blocks a party mines is roughly proportional to its stake. Since we assume that all parties have same amount of stake, this implies that a set of miners controlling approximately $\beta$ fraction of total stake can now extract $f$.
- Suppose an adversary is able to prove a false statement. As noted above, a set of miners controlling $\beta$ fraction of total stake can perform the extraction. Also, these miners can emulate the adversary given more stake (as the adversary controls at most $\alpha$ of total stake), therefore for appropriate values of $\alpha$ and $\beta$, this would imply an algorithm using which a set of miners controlling only a minority amount of total stake could generate a sufficiently long fork containing a proof of majority stake. This would contradict the *bounded stake forking property* of the blockchain for suitable values of $\alpha, \beta$ and $N$.
- Further, this does not affect the zero-knowledge property since the amount of stake controlled by the adversary is significantly lower than $\beta$, therefore the adversary does not learn anything from the secret shares given to it. Also, the simulator, given signing keys of all honest parties (which control majority of stake), can still generate such a fork privately thereby using the fork instead of the actual witness to compute the NIWI.

The above construction could be naturally extended to be an *argument of knowledge* by additionally secret sharing the witness $w$ analogous to the fork $f$. Note that in the above exposition we made a few simplifying assumptions. Thus the current construction does not work as is, and there are a number of issues which must be resolved. For example, we assumed that the stake distribution was uniform (i.e., all parties had identical stake). Since this may be arbitrary and not necessarily uniform, the idea of a threshold secret sharing does not work in general for extraction. Instead we need to use a weighted threshold secret sharing scheme with the weights being proportional to the respective stakes. Also, it is likely that different honest parties may have a different view of the last few blocks w.r.t. their local blockchains so we need to define the notion of forks with respect to the consistent part of the blockchain. It is also possible that some honest parties might have mined a few blocks in the adversary's fork before converging with other honest participants. To overcome such difficulties due to *small* forks (and other ephemeral consensus problems) in honest parties local blockchains, we need to make some more modifications like only considering the amount of proof-of-stake proven in the last few blocks of the fork etc. Finally, we directly reduce the security of our NIZKAoK construction to chain consistency, sufficient honest stake contribution, and bounded stake forking properties of the underlying blockchain protocols in our framework. More details are provided in Sect. 6

*Using POW based blockchains.* We note that the above idea could potentially be ported to the POW based blockchains as well with the following caveat: the NIZK proof generated by the prover would be valid for a limited period of time. The main modification will be that now the prover simply proves that $c_2$ is a commitment to a very long fork instead. The rest of the construction would be mostly identical. However, the proof of security would now rely on the fact that any adversary which controls noticeably less than half of the computational resources can not compute a fork of length much longer than the honest parties blockchain. Intuitively, this can not happen because it would imply that any adversary with only minority voting power could fork the blockchain at any round. It is important to note that unlike the NIZKs based on POS blockchains, NIZKs based on POW blockchains will only be valid for atmost a bounded period of time as any verifier must reject such proofs once the length of its local blockchain is comparable to the length of the fork under $c_2$.

**One-Time Programs Using Blockchains.** There are two main ideas behind constructing one-time programs (OTPs) using blockchains — (1) the blockchain could be used as a public *immutable* bulletin board, and (2) any adversarially generated fork can be distinguished from the real blockchain state. Informally, the scheme works as follows. To compile a circuit $C$ over blockchain $\mathbf{B}$, the compilation algorithm first garbles the circuit to compute a garbled circuit and wire keys. Suppose we encrypt the wire keys using public key encryption and set the corresponding OTP as the garbled circuit and encrypted wire keys. This suggests that the evaluator must interact with the compiling party to be able to evaluate the program. Since OTPs are not defined in an interactive setting, we need to somehow allow conditional release/decryption of encrypted wire keys for evaluation. Additionally, we need to make sure that the evaluator only learns the wire keys corresponding to exactly *one* input as otherwise it will not satisfy the one-time secrecy condition. To this end, we encrypt the wire keys using witness encryption scheme. At a high level, an OTP for a circuit $C$ is generated as follows:

- First, the circuit $C$ is garbled to output a garbled circuit and corresponding input wire keys. Next, for each input wire, both wire keys are independently encrypted using a witness encryption (WE) scheme such that to decrypt the evaluator needs to produce a blockchain $\mathbf{B}'$ as a witness where $\mathbf{B}'$ must satisfy the following conditions — (1) there exists a block in $\mathbf{B}'$ which contains the input (on which evaluator wants to evaluate), and (2) $\mathbf{B}'$ contains a certain minimum number of blocks, say $n$, after the block containing input. The OTP for $C$ will simply be this garbled circuit and all the encrypted wire keys.

– To execute the OTP, the evaluator chooses an input $x$ and must commit it to the blockchain. Next, it must wait until its input $x$ is added to the blockchain and is extended by $n$ blocks. Let the resulting blockchain be $\widetilde{\mathbf{B}}$. The evaluator uses $\widetilde{\mathbf{B}}$ as the witness to decrypt the wire keys corresponding to the input $x$. In particular, for the $i^{th}$ input wire, $\widetilde{\mathbf{B}}$ would serve as the witness to decrypt exactly one of the two wire keys depending upon the $i^{th}$ bit of $x$. Finally, it could evaluate the garbled circuit using the decrypted wire keys.

There are various technical details we omit in the above sketch. For instance, the $n$ blocks added after the input block must contain a minimum amount of combined proof-of-stake, as otherwise any adversary could simply generate such $n$ blocks by itself. Also, the witness must be valid only if the user has committed to a *single* unique input $x$, as otherwise the user can commit to multiple inputs in the blockchain and be able to run the OTP on all of them. Mostly these could be dealt with by adding more checks on witness blockchain $\widetilde{\mathbf{B}}$ as part of the relation. Next, we briefly talk about the security.

Suppose that the adversarial user controls only minority stake. The security of this construction relies on the inability of the user to be able to extend the blockchain $\mathbf{B}$ by a sequence of $n$ or more valid blocks without the support of honest parties. To execute this idea, we additionally check that the sequence of $n$ blocks added after the input $x$ contain a minimum amount of combined proof-of-stake. For simplicity, consider that we check whether the sequence of $n$ blocks contain a proof of majority stake. Now the adversary will not be able to extend $\mathbf{B}$ on its own such that it satisfies this constraint. However, during honest execution, for sufficiently large values of $n$ this will always hold. Therefore, the adversary's inability to fork directly reduces the security of the OTP to security of garbling scheme. To formally prove one-time secrecy of above construction, we reduce security of the above scheme to chain consistency and distinguishable forking properties of the underlying blockchain protocols in our framework. More details are provided in Sect. 7.

We would like to point out that this idea fails in POW based systems. This is because after receiving the OTP, the user can simply go offline and compute multiple forks of the chain starting from $\mathbf{B}$ such that each fork has a different user input. The user can compute such a fork on its own (albeit at a much slower rate compared to the growth of the original blockchain). Thus, unlike NIZKs, we do not know how to port the above idea to POW based blockchains.

*Input Hiding.* We would also like to note that in the above scheme, the evaluator needs to publicly broadcast its input $x$. This might not be suitable for applications of one-time programs which want the evaluator's input to be hidden. To this end, the scheme could be modified as follows. The evaluator adds to the blockchain a statistically binding commitment to its input (instead of its actual input $x$). Now the witness to decrypt the wire keys would also includes opening for the commitment and the witness relation verifies opening as well. We discuss additional such improvements later in the full version.

*Pay-per-use Programs.* Lastly, the above construction of one-time programs can also be easily extended to obtain pay-per-use $k$-time programs. This can be done by requiring in the witness encryption relation that in the extension of the blockchain **B**, apart from $x$, there is also an evidence of cryptocurrency transfer of some pre-specified amount to the service provider. This is discussed in detail in the full version.

*Comparison with related work.* Recently it was shown that in [34, 40] that Bitcoin could be combined with extractable witness encryption to build time-lock encryptions. Their idea was to exploit the fact that it should be hard for an adversary to generate blocks (i.e., extend blockchain) faster than the rest of the network. Very briefly, to encrypt data in their schemes, they encrypted it using WE under the current blockchain such that after say $n$ more blocks have mined, those blocks could be used as a witness to decrypt the corresponding ciphertext. At a high level, they view mining of these $n$ blocks as a proof of time being elapsed. At first sight, it might seem that our OTP construction is a straightforward combination of such time-lock encryptions with garbled circuits, this is not the case. We briefly highlight the important differences. First, time-lock encryptions used blockchain only as a counter/clock. On the other hand, we exploit the fact that blockchains could be used as an immutable public bulletin board. Concretely, in our construction, the evaluator needs to commit its input on the blockchain. Second, in our construction, it is essential that the underlying blockchain protocol is POS based, whereas [34, 40] built schemes directy on top of Bitcoin. Lastly, we reduce the security of our construction to fundamental properties over blockchains and give examples of blockchain protocols for which those properties are satisfied, whereas [34, 40] only gave an ad hoc analysis arguing that Bitcoin could be used implement such reference clocks.

## 2    Background on Blockchain Protocols

In this section, we present an abstract model for blockchain protocols as well as the protocol execution model. Our model is an extension of the model used by Pass et al. [43], which in turn is an extension of [19].

### 2.1    Blockchain Protocols

A blockchain protocol $\Gamma$ consists of 3 polynomial-time algorithms (UpdateState, GetRecords, Broadcast) with the following syntax.

– UpdateState($1^\lambda$): It is a stateful algorithm that takes as input the security parameter $\lambda$, and maintains a local state st.[7]

---

[7] The local state should be considered as the entire blockchain (i.e., sequence of mined blocks along with metadata) in Bitcoin and other cryptocurrencies.

- GetRecords($1^\lambda$, st): It takes as input the security parameter $\lambda$ and state st. It outputs the longest *ordered* sequence of valid blocks **B** (or simply blockchain) contained in the state variable, where each block in the chain itself contains an *unordered* sequence of records/messages **m**.[8]
- Broadcast($1^\lambda$, $m$): It takes as input the security parameter $\lambda$ and a message $m$, and broadcasts the message over the network to all nodes executing the blockchain protocol. It does not give any output.

As in [19,43], the blockchain protocol is also parameterized by a validity predicate $V$ that captures semantics of any particular blockchain application. The validity predicate takes as input a sequence of blocks **B** and outputs a bit, where 1 certifies validity of blockchain **B** and 0 its invalidity.[9] Here we assume that the reader is familiar with the standard blockchain execution model. In the full version we will give a comprehensive overview.

# 3    Preliminaries

*Notations.* We will use bold letters for vectors (e.g., **v**). For any finite set $S$, $x \leftarrow S$ denotes a uniformly random element $x$ from the set $S$. Similarly, for any distribution $\mathcal{D}$, $x \leftarrow \mathcal{D}$ denotes an element $x$ drawn from distribution $\mathcal{D}$.

Let $\mathsf{EXEC}^{\Gamma^V}(\mathcal{A}(x), \mathcal{Z}, 1^\lambda)$ be the random variable denoting the joint view of all parties in the execution of protocol $\Gamma^V$ with adversary $\mathcal{A}$ and environment $\mathcal{Z}$ where $\mathcal{A}$ is given an additional private input $x$. This joint view fully determines the execution. Also, let $\mathsf{view}_{\mathcal{A}}(\mathsf{EXEC}^{\Gamma^V}(\mathcal{A}(x), \mathcal{Z}, 1^\lambda))$ denote the view of adversary $\mathcal{A}$ in the protocol execution.

Due to space constraints, we do not provide formal definitions of witness encryption [24,25], garbled circuits [7,50], (non-interactive) witness indistinguishable (WI) proofs [18], and weighted threshold secret sharing.

## 3.1    Public Key Integrated Encryption-Signature Scheme

First, we define an integrated scheme which works both as a public key encryption scheme as well as public key signature scheme. Let $\mathcal{M}_1$ and $\mathcal{M}_2$ be the message spaces for encryption and signature scheme respectively. A public key integrated encryption-signature scheme HS for message spaces $\mathcal{M}_1$ and $\mathcal{M}_2$ consists of following polynomial-time algorithms.

- Setup($1^\lambda$): The setup algorithm takes as input the security parameter $\lambda$, and outputs a master public-secret key pair (mpk, msk).

---

[8] The sequence **B** should be considered as the entire transaction history in Bitcoin and other cryptocurrencies, where the blocks are ordered in the sequence they were mined.

[9] The validity predicate could be used to capture various fundamental properties. E.g., In Bitcoin and other cryptocurrencies, it could be used to check for double spending, correct mining etc.

- Enc(mpk, $m \in \mathcal{M}_1$): The encryption algorithm takes as input master public key mpk and a message $m$, and outputs a ciphertext ct.
- Dec(msk, ct): The decryption algorithm takes as input master secret key msk and a ciphertext ct, and outputs a message $m$.
- Sign(msk, $m \in \mathcal{M}_2$): The signing algorithm takes as input master secret key msk and a message $m$, and outputs a signature $\sigma$.
- Verify(mpk, $m \in \mathcal{M}_2, \sigma$): The verification algorithm takes as input master public key mpk, a message $m$ and a signature $\sigma$, and outputs a bit.

*Correctness.* An integrated scheme HS for message spaces $\mathcal{M}_1, \mathcal{M}_2$ is said to be correct if for all $\lambda$, $m_1 \in \mathcal{M}_1$, $m_2 \in \mathcal{M}_2$ and (mpk, msk) $\leftarrow$ Setup($1^\lambda$), we have that Dec(msk, Enc(mpk, $m_1$)) = $m_1$ and Verify(mpk, $m_2$, Sign(msk, $m_2$)) = 1.

*Security.* Informally, an integrated encryption-signature scheme is said to be secure if it is both an unforgeable signature scheme as well as an IND-CPA secure public key encryption scheme. More formally,

**Definition 1.** *A public key integrated encryption-signature scheme* HS = (Setup, Enc, Dec, Sign, Verify) *is a secure integrated scheme if for every PPT adversary* $\mathcal{A} = (\mathcal{A}_0, \mathcal{A}_1, \mathcal{A}_2)$ *there exists a negligible functions* $negl_1(\cdot)$, $negl_2(\cdot)$, *such that for all* $\lambda \in \mathbb{N}$, *the following holds:*

$$\left| \Pr\left[ \mathcal{A}_1(\text{ct}, \text{st}) = b \,\middle|\, \begin{array}{l} (\text{mpk}, \text{msk}) \leftarrow \text{Setup}(1^\lambda); b \leftarrow \{0,1\} \\ (m_0, m_1, \text{st}) \leftarrow \mathcal{A}_0^{\text{Sign}(\text{msk}, \cdot)}(\text{mpk}); \text{ct} \leftarrow \text{Enc}(\text{mpk}, m_b) \end{array} \right] - \frac{1}{2} \right| \leq negl_1(\lambda),$$

*and*

$$\Pr\left[ \text{Verify}(\text{msk}, m^*, \sigma^*) = 1 \,\middle|\, \begin{array}{l} (\text{mpk}, \text{msk}) \leftarrow \text{Setup}(1^\lambda) \\ (m^*, \sigma^*) \leftarrow \mathcal{A}_2^{\text{Sign}(\text{msk}, \cdot)}(\text{mpk}) \end{array} \right] \leq negl_2(\lambda),$$

*where* $\mathcal{A}_2$ *must never have queried* $m^*$ *to signing oracle.*

While such an integrated scheme could always be generically constructed from any IND-CPA secure public key encryption scheme and any EUF-CMA secure public key signature scheme, we hope that the signature schemes used in current blockchain protocols could be used as integrated encryption-signature schemes as well. For instance, most blockchain protocols (like Bitcoin, Ethereum etc.) already use ECDSA based signature schemes for which we could directly use ECIES-like integrated encryption schemes [47]. However this will be a slightly stronger assumption.

### 3.2   Non-interactive Argument Systems

**Non-interactive Zero Knowledge Arguments.** The notion of Zero Knowledge for interactive protocols was introduced by Goldwasser, Micali and Rackoff [27]. A non-interactive zero knowledge argument system is a one-message ZK protocol. However, it is well known that NIZKs are impossible in the standard model [26]. They are usually defined with trusted setup.

In this work, we construct NIZKs over blockchain protocols without any additional setup assumption. Below we provide the formal definition.

**Definition 2** *(NIZK over Blockchains). A pair of PPT algorithms $(\mathcal{P}, \mathcal{V})$ over a blockchain protocol $\Gamma^V$ is a NIZK argument of knowledge for a language $\mathcal{L} \in \mathbf{NP}$ with witness relation $\mathcal{R}$ if it satisfies the following conditions:*

- *(Completeness) For all $(x, w)$ such that $\mathcal{R}(x, w) = 1$, all PPT adversaries $\mathcal{A}$ and players $i, j$ in environment $\mathcal{Z}$, there exists negligible functions $negl_1(\cdot), negl_2(\cdot)$ such that*

$$\Pr\left[\mathcal{V}(\widetilde{\mathbf{B}}, x, \pi) = 1 : \begin{array}{c} \mathsf{view} \leftarrow \mathsf{EXEC}^{\Gamma^V}\left(\mathcal{A}, \mathcal{Z}, 1^\lambda\right) \\ \mathbf{B} = \mathsf{GetRecords}(\mathsf{view}_i); \ \widetilde{\mathbf{B}} = \mathsf{GetRecords}(\mathsf{view}_j) \\ \pi \leftarrow \mathcal{P}(\mathbf{B}, x, w) \end{array}\right] \geq 1 - negl_1(|x|) - negl_2(\lambda),$$

*where $\mathsf{view}_i$ and $\mathsf{view}_j$ denote the view of players $i$ and $j$, and both $i, j$ are honest.*[10]

- *(Soundness) For every $x \notin \mathcal{L}$ and all stateful PPT adversaries $\mathcal{A}$ and each player $i$ in environment $\mathcal{Z}$, there exists negligible functions $negl_1(\cdot), negl_2(\cdot)$ such that*

$$\Pr\left[\mathcal{V}(\mathbf{B}, x, \pi) = 1 : \begin{array}{c} \mathsf{view} \leftarrow \mathsf{EXEC}^{\Gamma^V}\left(\mathcal{A}(x), \mathcal{Z}, 1^\lambda\right) \\ \mathbf{B} = \mathsf{GetRecords}(\mathsf{view}_i); \ \pi \leftarrow \mathcal{A} \end{array}\right] \leq negl_1(|x|) + negl_2(\lambda),$$

*where $\mathsf{view}_i$ denotes the view of player $i$, and $i$ is honest.*

- *(Knowledge Extractor) There is a stateful PPT algorithm $\mathcal{E}$, such that for all stateful PPT adversaries $\mathcal{A}$ and each player $i$ in environment $\mathcal{Z}$, there exists negligible functions $negl_1(\cdot), negl_2(\cdot)$ such that*

$$\left\{\mathsf{view}_\mathcal{A}\left(\mathsf{EXEC}^{\Gamma^V}\left(\mathcal{A}, \mathcal{Z}, 1^\lambda\right)\right)\right\} \approx_c \left\{\mathsf{view}_\mathcal{A}\left(\mathsf{EXEC}^{\Gamma^V}\left(\mathcal{A}, \mathcal{E}, \mathcal{Z}, 1^\lambda\right)\right)\right\}$$

*and*

$$\Pr\left[\begin{array}{c}\mathcal{V}(\mathbf{B}, x, \pi) = 0 \\ \vee \ \mathcal{R}(x, w) = 1\end{array} : \begin{array}{c} \mathsf{view} \leftarrow \mathsf{EXEC}^{\Gamma^V}\left(\mathcal{A}, \mathcal{E}, \mathcal{Z}, 1^\lambda\right); \ (x, \pi) \leftarrow \mathcal{A} \\ \mathbf{B} = \mathsf{GetRecords}(\mathsf{view}_i); \ w \leftarrow \mathcal{E}(x, \pi) \end{array}\right] \geq 1 - negl_1(|x|) - negl_2(\lambda),$$

*where $\mathsf{view}_i$ denotes the view of player $i$ and $i$ is honest, and $\mathsf{EXEC}^{\Gamma^V}\left(\mathcal{A}, \mathcal{E}, \mathcal{Z}, 1^\lambda\right)$ is the random variable denoting the joint view of all parties in the blockchain execution where adversary $\mathcal{A}$ controls all the corrupt parties, and $\mathcal{E}$ controls all the honest parties.*

- *(Zero Knowledge) There is a stateful PPT algorithm $\mathsf{Sim}$ for the argument system such that for all $(x, w)$ subject to $\mathcal{R}(x, w) = 1$ and all stateful PPT adversaries $\mathcal{A}$ and each player $i$ in environment $\mathcal{Z}$, the following holds*

$$\left\{(\pi, \mathsf{view}_\mathcal{A}) : \begin{array}{c} \mathsf{view} \leftarrow \mathsf{EXEC}^{\Gamma^V}\left(\mathcal{A}, \mathsf{Sim}, \mathcal{Z}, 1^\lambda\right) \\ \pi \leftarrow \mathsf{Sim}(x) \end{array}\right\}$$

$$\approx_c$$

$$\left\{(\pi, \mathsf{view}_\mathcal{A}) : \begin{array}{c} \mathsf{view} \leftarrow \mathsf{EXEC}^{\Gamma^V}\left(\mathcal{A}, \mathcal{Z}, 1^\lambda\right) \\ \mathbf{B} = \mathsf{GetRecords}(\mathsf{view}_i); \ \pi \leftarrow \mathcal{P}(\mathbf{B}, x, w) \end{array}\right\}$$

---

[10] We have overloaded the notation by using $\mathsf{GetRecords}$ algorithm to take as input the view of a party instead of its state. This is still well defined since the state of any party is part of its view.

*where* view$_i$ *denotes the view of player $i$ and $i$ is honest, and* $\mathsf{EXEC}^{\Gamma^V}\left(\mathcal{A}, \mathsf{Sim}, \mathcal{Z}, 1^\lambda\right)$ *is the random variable denoting the joint view of all parties in the blockchain execution where adversary $\mathcal{A}$ controls all the corrupt parties, and* $\mathsf{Sim}$ *controls all the honest parties.*

### 3.3 One-Time Programs and Compilers

The notion of one-time programs was introduced by Goldwasser et al. [29]. Let $\{\mathcal{C}_n\}_n$ be a family of circuits where each circuit in $\mathcal{C}_n$ takes $n$ bit inputs. A one-time compiler $\mathsf{OTC}$ for circuit family $\{\mathcal{C}_n\}_n$ consists of polynomial-time algorithms Compile and Eval with the following syntax.

- Compile($1^\lambda, C \in \mathcal{C}_n$): The compilation algorithm takes as input the security parameter $\lambda$ and a circuit $C \in \mathcal{C}_n$. It outputs a compiled circuit $CC$.
- Eval($CC, x \in \{0,1\}^n$): The evaluation algorithm takes as input a compiled circuit $CC$ and an $n$-bit input $x$, and outputs $y \in \{0,1\} \cup \perp$.

*Correctness.* A one-time compiler $\mathsf{OTC}$ for circuit family $\{\mathcal{C}_n\}_n$ is said to be correct if for all $\lambda$, $n$, $x \in \{0,1\}^n$ and $C \in \mathcal{C}_n$,

$$\Pr[\mathsf{Eval}(CC, x) = C(x) \mid CC \leftarrow \mathsf{Compile}(1^\lambda, C)] \geq 1 - \mathsf{negl}(\lambda),$$

where evaluation is run only once, and $\mathsf{negl}(\cdot)$ is a negligible function.

*One-Time Secrecy.* Traditionally, security for one-time compilers have been defined in presence of secure hardware or memory devices.

In this work we adapt the traditional definition of one-time compilers from a combination of *hardware-software* setting to only *software* setting, but in presence of a blockchain protocol.

**Definition 3.** *A one-time compiler* $\mathsf{OTC} = (\mathsf{Compile}, \mathsf{Eval})$ *for a class of circuits* $\mathcal{C} = \{\mathcal{C}_n\}_n$ *is said to be a* B/C-selectively-*secure one-time compiler if for every admissible PPT adversary $\mathcal{A}$, there exists a PPT simulator* $\mathsf{Sim}$ *such that for all* $\lambda$, $n$, $C \in \mathcal{C}_n$ *and* $x \in \{0,1\}^n$, *the following holds:*

$$\left\{ \mathsf{view}_{\mathsf{Sim}} \left( \mathsf{EXEC}^{\Gamma^V} \left( \mathsf{Sim} \left( 1^n, 1^{|C|}, x, C(x) \right), \mathcal{Z}, 1^\lambda \right) \right) \right\}$$

$$\approx_c$$

$$\left\{ \mathsf{view}_{\mathcal{A}} \left( \mathsf{EXEC}^{\Gamma^V} \left( \mathcal{A}\left( CC \right), \mathcal{Z}, 1^\lambda \right) \right) \; : \; CC \leftarrow \mathsf{Compile}(1^\lambda, C) \right\}$$

*where adversary $\mathcal{A}$ is* admissible *if it evaluates the one-time program $CC$ on $x$ before evaluating on any other input.*

# 4   Proof-of-Stake Protocols: Abstraction and Definitions

In this paper, we work in the execution model for proof-of-stake based protocols described in previous section. It is reasonable to assume that any adversary in this model would have full access to the blockchain as well as could possibly affect the protocol execution by adversarially mining for blocks or deviating from the protocol. It also seems reasonable to assume that no real-world adversary could run with a majority stake, or in other words majority voting power, as otherwise such an adversary could possibly affect the protocol execution arbitrarily, thereby destroying any guarantee that we could hope to get. All such restrictions could be captured by defining the adversary and environment to be sufficiently restrictive by considering appropriate compliant executions as discussed in previous section.

In this section, we define various security properties for proof-of-stake based blockchain protocols. We would like to point out that prior works [12,13,19–21,37,38,43–45] have mostly considered only chain consistency, chain quality and chain growth as desiderata for blockchain protocols. We, on the other hand, also introduce many new security properties inspired by the notions of stake contribution and adversarial forking in POS based protocols. Later we also show that existing POS based protocols [13,38] already satisfy these stronger security properties. We believe that these new properties will have wider applicability as already suggested by our NIZK, one-time program and pay-per-use program constructions.

We also extend the abstraction for blockchain protocols to introduce additional POS specific abstracts. Below we introduce some necessary notations and definitions.

*Notations.* We denote by $\mathbf{B}^{\lceil \ell}$ the chain resulting from the "pruning" last $\ell$ blocks in $\mathbf{B}$. Note that for $\ell \geq |\mathbf{B}|$, $\mathbf{B}^{\lceil \ell} = \epsilon$. Also, if $\mathbf{B}_1$ is a prefix of $\mathbf{B}_2$, then we write $\mathbf{B}_1 \preceq \mathbf{B}_2$. We also use $\mathbf{B}^{\ell \rceil}$ to denote the chain containing last $\ell$ blocks in $\mathbf{B}$, i.e. $\mathbf{B}^{\ell \rceil} = \mathbf{B} \setminus \mathbf{B}^{\lceil \ell}$. Note that for $\ell \geq |\mathbf{B}|$, $\mathbf{B}^{\ell \rceil} = \mathbf{B}$.

Let $\mathsf{EXEC}^{\Gamma}(\mathcal{A}, \mathcal{Z}, 1^{\lambda})$ be the random variable denoting the joint view of all parties in the protocol execution. This fully determines the execution. Recall that each blockchain protocol is also associated with a validity predicate, however we avoid explicitly mentioning it whenever possible.

For any POS based blockchain protocol $\Gamma$, there exists a polynomial time algorithm $\mathsf{stake} : \{0,1\}^* \times \{0,1\}^* \to \mathbb{Q}^+$ which takes as inputs the blockchain $\mathbf{B}$ and a public identity $\mathsf{id}$, and outputs a rational value. Concretely, consider a party $P$ with public identity $\mathsf{id}$, we use $\mathsf{stake}(\mathbf{B}, \mathsf{id})$ to denote the stake of party $P$ as per the blockchain $\mathbf{B}$. For an adversary $\mathcal{A}$ that controls all parties with public identities in the set $\mathcal{X}$, its total stake as per blockchain $\mathbf{B}$ can computed as $\sum_{\mathsf{id} \in \mathcal{X}} \mathsf{stake}(\mathbf{B}, \mathsf{id})$. We overload the notation and use $\mathsf{stake}(\mathbf{B}, \mathcal{A})$ to denote $\mathcal{A}$'s total stake, and $\mathsf{stake}_{\mathsf{total}}$ to denote the combined stake of all parties i.e. $\mathsf{stake}_{\mathsf{total}} = \sum_{\mathsf{id}} \mathsf{stake}(\mathbf{B}, \mathsf{id})$. Also, we will simply write $\mathsf{stake}_{\mathcal{A}}$ whenever $\mathbf{B}$ is clear from context.

For any PPT adversary $\mathcal{A}$, the adversarial stake ratio stake-ratio$_{\mathcal{A}}(\mathbf{B})$ w.r.t. blockchain $\mathbf{B}$ is defined as the ratio of $\mathcal{A}$'s total stake over combined stake of all parties. More formally,

$$\text{stake-ratio}_{\mathcal{A}}(\mathbf{B}) = \frac{\text{stake}_{\mathcal{A}}}{\text{stake}_{\text{total}}}.$$

We will drop dependence of stake-ratio$_{\mathcal{A}}$ on blockchain $\mathbf{B}$ whenever clear from context.

Also, let miner $: \{0,1\}^* \times \mathbb{N} \to \{0,1\}^*$ be a function that takes as input the blockchain $\mathbf{B}$ and an index $i$, and returns the public identity of the party that mined the $i^{th}$ block, where blocks are counted from the head of the blockchain.[11] We overload the notation and use miner$(\mathbf{B}, [\ell])$ to denote the *set* of public identities of all parties that mined at least one block in the last $\ell$ blocks of the blockchain $\mathbf{B}$.[12]

### 4.1 Chain Consistency

First, we define the chain consistency property for blockchain protocols $\Gamma$ with environment $\mathcal{Z}$ and adversary $\mathcal{A}$. At a very high level, it states that the blockchains of any two honest parties at any two (possibly different) rounds during protocol execution can differ only in the last $\ell$ blocks with all but negligible probability, where $\ell$ parameterizes strength of the property. In other words, this suggests that if any party is honestly executing the blockchain protocol, then it could always assert that any block which is at least $\ell$ blocks deep in its blockchain is immutable.

A more general definition appears in [43] which is an extension of the common prefix property by Garay et al. [19]. As in prior works, we first define the consistency predicate and then use it to define the chain consistency property for blockchain protocols.

**Predicate 1** *(Consistency).* *Let* consistent *be the predicate such that* consistent$^{\ell}$(view) $= 1$ *iff for all rounds* $r \leq \tilde{r}$, *and all players* $i, j$ *(potentially the same) in* view *such that* $i$ *is* honest *at round* $r$ *with blockchain* $\mathbf{B}$ *and* $j$ *is* honest *at round* $\tilde{r}$ *with blockchain* $\widetilde{\mathbf{B}}$, *we have that* $\mathbf{B}^{\lceil \ell} \preceq \widetilde{\mathbf{B}}$.

**Definition 4** *(Chain Consistency).* *A blockchain protocol* $\Gamma$ *satisfies* $\ell_0(\cdot)$-*consistency with adversary* $\mathcal{A}$ *in environment* $\mathcal{Z}$, *if there exists negligible function* negl$(\cdot)$ *such that for every* $\lambda \in \mathbb{N}$, $\ell > \ell_0(\lambda)$ *the following holds:*

$$\Pr\left[\text{consistent}^{\ell}(\text{view}) = 1 \mid \text{view} \leftarrow \mathsf{EXEC}^{\Gamma}\left(\mathcal{A}, \mathcal{Z}, 1^{\lambda}\right)\right] \geq 1 - negl(\lambda).$$

---

[11] The rightmost (i.e., most recently added) block is called the head of the blockchain.
[12] Note that a party could potentially mine more than one block in a sequence of $\ell$ blocks.

## 4.2 Defining Stake Fraction

For any POS based blockchain protocol, we could define special quantitative measures for a blockchain analogous to the *combined difficulty* or 'length' measure as in case of POW based protocols. For example, in Bitcoin 'length' of a chain of blocks is computed as the sum of *difficulty* of all individual blocks where difficulty is measured as the hardness of puzzle solved.

Note that in any POS based protocol, ideally the number of blocks mined by any party directly depends on its stake, or in other words, voting power is proportional to the amount of stake with a party. Also, each new block added to the blockchain contains an efficiently verifiable proof of stake provided by a miner in the form of digital signatures. So, for POS based protocols, we could measure difficulty in terms of the amount of stake proven per block. The analogy being that solving POW puzzles with high difficulty requires more work (higher voting power) from a miner, and since voting power in POS based protocols is measured in terms of stake ratio, so for such protocols difficulty is measured as the amount of stake proven. Below we formally define such a measure.

**Definition 5** *(Proof-of-Stake Fraction). The proof-of-stake fraction u-stakefrac($\mathbf{B}, \ell$) w.r.t. blockchain $\mathbf{B}$ is defined as the combined amount of unique stake whose proof is provided in last $\ell$ mined blocks. More formally, let $\mathcal{M} = \mathsf{miner}(\mathbf{B}, [\ell])$,*

$$u\text{-}stakefrac(\mathbf{B}, \ell) = \frac{\sum_{\mathsf{id} \in \mathcal{M}} \mathsf{stake}(\mathbf{B}, \mathsf{id})}{\mathsf{stake}_{\mathsf{total}}}.$$

In the above definition, it is important to note that we are only interested in the amount of *unique stake* proven. To understand this, first note that if some party added proof of its stake on the blockchain (i.e., mined a new block), then it would increase the probability of other parties mining on top of the newly mined block instead of mining on top of the previous block. However, if a certain single party with a low total stake is mining an unreasonably high proportion of blocks in a short span of rounds (or for simplicity all the blocks) on some chain, then other parties might not want to extend on top of such a blockchain as it could possibly correspond to an adversarial chain of blocks. So, by considering only unique stake we could use proof-of-stake fraction to (approximately) distinguish between (possibly) adversarial and honest blockchains as a higher proof-of-stake fraction increases confidence in that chain.

For some applications, we also need to consider only the amount of stake whose proof was provided by the honest parties in the blockchain. Below we define the proof-of-honest-stake fraction.

**Definition 6** *(Proof-of-Honest-Stake Fraction). The proof-of-honest-stake fraction u-honest-stakefrac($\mathbf{B}, \ell$) w.r.t. blockchain $\mathbf{B}$ is defined as the combined amount of unique stake held by the honest parties whose proof is provided in last $\ell$ mined blocks. More formally, let $\mathcal{M} = \mathsf{miner}(\mathbf{B}, [\ell])$ and $\mathcal{M}_{\mathsf{honest}}$ denote the honest parties in $\mathcal{M}$, then*

$$u\text{-}honest\text{-}stakefrac(\mathbf{B}, \ell) = \frac{\sum_{\mathsf{id} \in \mathcal{M}_{\mathsf{honest}}} \mathsf{stake}(\mathbf{B}, \mathsf{id})}{\mathsf{stake}_{\mathsf{total}}}.$$

### 4.3   Stake Contribution Properties

In the previous section, we defined the notion of proof-of-stake fraction and proof-of-honest-stake fraction. Now, we define some useful properties for POS based blockchain protocols inspired by the above stake abstraction. We know that in any POS based protocol each mined block contains a proof of stake. At a very high level, the sufficient stake contribution property says that in a sufficiently long sequence of valid blocks, a significant amount of stake has been proven.

In other words, it says that after sufficiently many rounds, the amount of proof-of-stake added in mining the $\ell$ most recent blocks is a fairly high fraction (at least $\beta$) of the total stake in the system, where $\ell$ and $\beta$ are property parameters denoting the length of chain and minimum amount of stake fraction in it (respectively). More formally, we define it as follows.

**Predicate 2** *(Sufficient Stake Contribution).* Let *suf-stake-contr* *be the predicate such that* *suf-stake-contr*$^\ell$*(view, $\beta$) = 1 iff for every round $r \geq \ell$, and each player $i$ in* view *such that $i$ is honest at round $r$ with blockchain $\mathbf{B}$, we have that last $\ell$ blocks in blockchain $\mathbf{B}$ contain a* combined *proof of stake of more than* $\beta \cdot \mathsf{stake}_{\mathsf{total}}$*, i.e.* *u-stakefrac*$(\mathbf{B}, \ell) > \beta$*.*

Below we define the sufficient stake contribution property for blockchain protocols.

**Definition 7** *(Sufficient Stake Contribution).* *A blockchain protocol $\Gamma$ satisfies* $(\beta(\cdot), \ell_0(\cdot))$*-sufficient stake contribution property with adversary $\mathcal{A}$ in environment $\mathcal{Z}$, if there exists a negligible function negl$(\cdot)$ such that for every $\lambda \in \mathbb{N}$, $\ell \geq \ell_0(\lambda)$ the following holds:*

$$\Pr\left[ \textit{suf-stake-contr}^\ell(\mathsf{view}, \beta(\lambda)) = 1 \mid \mathsf{view} \leftarrow \mathsf{EXEC}^\Gamma\left(\mathcal{A}, \mathcal{Z}, 1^\lambda\right)\right] \geq 1 - negl(\lambda).$$

Previously we defined the notion of proof-of-honest-stake fraction along the lines of proof-of-stake fraction in which only the amount of honestly held stake was measured. Analogously, we could define the sufficient honest stake contribution property which says that in a sufficiently long sequence of valid blocks, a significant amount of *honestly held* stake has been proven.

**Predicate 3** *(Sufficient Honest Stake Contribution).* *Let* *honest-suf-stake-contr* *be the predicate such that* *honest-suf-stake-contr*$^\ell$*(view, $\beta$) = 1 iff for every round $r \geq \ell$, and each player $i$ in* view *such that $i$ is honest at round $r$ with blockchain $\mathbf{B}$, we have that last $\ell$ blocks in blockchain $\mathbf{B}$ contain a* combined *proof of honest stake of more than* $\beta \cdot \mathsf{stake}_{\mathsf{total}}$*, i.e.* *u-honest-stakefrac*$(\mathbf{B}, \ell) > \beta$*.*

**Definition 8** *(Sufficient* Honest *Stake Contribution). A blockchain protocol* $\Gamma$ *satisfies* $(\beta(\cdot), \ell_0(\cdot))$*-sufficient honest stake contribution property with adversary* $\mathcal{A}$ *in environment* $\mathcal{Z}$, *if there exists a negligible function* $negl(\cdot)$ *such that for every* $\lambda \in \mathbb{N}$, $\ell \geq \ell_0(\lambda)$ *the following holds:*

$$\Pr\left[\textsf{honest-suf-stake-contr}^\ell(\textsf{view}, \beta(\lambda)) = 1 \mid \textsf{view} \leftarrow \textsf{EXEC}^\Gamma\left(\mathcal{A}, \mathcal{Z}, 1^\lambda\right)\right] \geq 1 - negl(\lambda).$$

## 4.4 Bounded Forking Properties

Note that during protocol execution, any adversary could possibly generate a *private* chain of blocks which may or may not satisfy blockchain validity predicate, and may significantly diverge from the local blockchain in the view of honest parties. We call such a private chain of blocks, created by the adversary, a *fork*. In this work, we consider the following bounded forking properties which (at a very high level) require that no polytime adversary can create a sufficiently long fork containing valid blocks such that the combined amount of proof of stake proven in that fork is higher than certain threshold.

We start by defining the bounded stake forking property which says that if an adversary creates a fork of length at least $\ell_1 + \ell_2$ then the proof-of-stake fraction in the last $\ell_2$ blocks of the fork is not more than $\alpha$, where $\alpha, \ell_1, \ell_2$ are property parameters with $\alpha$ being the threshold and $\ell_1 + \ell$ denoting the fork length. More formally, we first define the bounded stake fork predicate and then use it to define the bounded stake forking property.

**Predicate 4** *(Bounded Stake Fork). Let* $\textsf{bd-stake-fork}$ *be the predicate such that* $\textsf{bd-stake-fork}^{(\ell_1, \ell_2)}(\textsf{view}, \alpha) = 1$ *iff for all rounds* $r \geq \tilde{r}$, *for each pair of players* $i, j$ *in* $\textsf{view}$ *such that* $i$ *is honest at round* $r$ *with blockchain* $\mathbf{B}$ *and* $j$ *is corrupt in round* $\tilde{r}$ *with blockchain* $\tilde{\mathbf{B}}$, *if there exists* $\ell' \geq \ell_1 + \ell_2$ *such that* $\tilde{\mathbf{B}}^{\lceil \ell'} \preceq \mathbf{B}$ *and for all* $\tilde{\ell} < \ell'$, $\tilde{\mathbf{B}}^{\lceil \tilde{\ell}} \npreceq \mathbf{B}$, *then* $\textsf{u-stakefrac}(\tilde{\mathbf{B}}, \ell' - \ell_1) \leq \alpha$.

**Definition 9** *(Bounded Stake Forking). A blockchain protocol* $\Gamma$ *satisfies* $(\alpha(\cdot), \ell_1(\cdot), \ell_2(\cdot))$*-bounded stake forking property with adversary* $\mathcal{A}$ *in environment* $\mathcal{Z}$, *if there exists a negligible functions* $negl(\cdot), \delta(\cdot)$ *such that for every* $\lambda \in \mathbb{N}$, $\ell \geq \ell_1(\lambda)$, $\tilde{\ell} \geq \ell_2(\lambda)$ *the following holds:*

$$\Pr\left[\textsf{bd-stake-fork}^{(\ell, \tilde{\ell})}(\textsf{view}, \alpha(\lambda) + \delta(\lambda)) = 1 \mid \textsf{view} \leftarrow \textsf{EXEC}^\Gamma\left(\mathcal{A}, \mathcal{Z}, 1^\lambda\right)\right] \geq 1 - negl(\lambda).$$

The above property only stipulates that the proof-of-stake fraction of any adversarially generated fork is bounded. However, we additionally might expect a POS based blockchain protocol to satisfy the sufficient stake contribution property which states that any honest party's blockchain will have sufficiently high proof-of-stake fraction. Therefore, combining both these properties, we could define a stronger property for blockchain protocols which states that a sufficiently long chain of blocks generated during an honest protocol execution could always be *distinguished* from any adversarially generated fork. Also, the combined amount of stake proven in those sequences (i.e., its proof-of-stake fraction), which could be computed in polynomial time, could be used to distinguish such sequences. Formally, we could define it as follows.

**Definition 10** *(Distinguishable Forking). A blockchain protocol $\Gamma$ satisfies $(\alpha(\cdot), \beta(\cdot), \ell_1(\cdot), \ell_2(\cdot))$-distinguishable forking property with adversary $\mathcal{A}$ in environment $\mathcal{Z}$, if there exists a negligible functions $negl(\cdot), \delta(\cdot)$ such that for every $\lambda \in \mathbb{N}$, $\ell \geq \ell_1(\lambda)$, $\tilde{\ell} \geq \ell_2(\lambda)$ the following holds:*

$$\Pr\left[\begin{array}{l} \alpha(\lambda) + \delta(\lambda) < \beta(\lambda) \,\wedge\, \textit{suf-stake-contr}^{\tilde{\ell}}(\mathsf{view}, \beta(\lambda)) = 1 \\ \wedge\ \textit{bd-stake-fork}^{(\ell,\tilde{\ell})}(\mathsf{view}, \alpha(\lambda) + \delta(\lambda)) = 1 \end{array} \,\middle|\, \mathsf{view} \leftarrow \mathsf{EXEC}^{\Gamma}\left(\mathcal{A}, \mathcal{Z}, 1^{\lambda}\right)\right] \geq 1 - negl(\lambda).$$

# 5 Instantiating Our Framework

In this section, we show that the proposed proof-of-stake based blockchain protocols of [13,38] satisfy all the properties described in Sect. 4 for suitable parameters. We start by defining some additional properties for POS based blockchain protocols and then discuss relations among all these.

## 5.1 Chain Quality and Bounded Length Forking

*Chain Quality.* Another important property defined in prior works is of chain quality which was initially informally discussed on the Bitcoin forum [41], and formally defined by [19]. At a high level, it says that the number of blocks contributed by the adversary should not be very large, or in other words its contribution must be proportional to its voting power. Alternatively, this could be interpreted as a measure of fairness in the protocol and used to define a lower bound on the number of blocks contributed by honest parties. To be consistent with prior works, we define chain quality predicate with respect to the fraction of honest blocks.

**Predicate 5** *(Quality). Let* quality *be the predicate such that* $\mathsf{quality}^{\ell}_{\mathcal{A}}(\mathsf{view}, \mu) = 1$ *iff for every round $r \geq \ell$, and each player $i$ in* view *such that $i$ is* honest *at round $r$ with blockchain $\mathbf{B}$, we have that out of $\ell$ blocks in $\mathbf{B}^{\lceil \ell \rceil}$ at least $\mu$ fraction of blocks are "honest".*

Note that a block is said to be *honest* iff it is mined by an honest party. Below we recall the chain quality property for blockchain protocols as it appears in prior works.

**Definition 11** *(Chain Quality). A blockchain protocol $\Gamma$ satisfies $(\mu(\cdot), \ell_0(\cdot))$-chain quality with adversary $\mathcal{A}$ in environment $\mathcal{Z}$, if there exists a negligible function $negl(\cdot)$ such that for every $\lambda \in \mathbb{N}$, $\ell \geq \ell_0(\lambda)$ the following holds:*

$$\Pr\left[\mathsf{quality}^{\ell}_{\mathcal{A}}(\mathsf{view}, \mu(\lambda)) = 1 \,\middle|\, \mathsf{view} \leftarrow \mathsf{EXEC}^{\Gamma}\left(\mathcal{A}, \mathcal{Z}, 1^{\lambda}\right)\right] \geq 1 - negl(\lambda).$$

*Bounded Length Forking.* Additionally, we would expect a POS based blockchain protocol to satisfy the property that — no PPT adversary should be able to generate (with non-negligible probability) a sufficiently long *fork* that satisfies all validity conditions and *the last block in that fork was mined by an honest party.* The intuition behind this is that if the adversary can generate such a sufficiently long chain, then it would mean that it could prevent consensus between honest parties for a sufficiently long time. To formally capture this, we define the bounded length forking property over blockchain protocols as follows.

**Predicate 6** *(Bounded Length Fork).* Let bd-length-fork *be the predicate such that* bd-length-fork$^\ell$(view) $= 1$ *iff there exists rounds* $r, \widetilde{r}$, *players* $i, j$ *in* view *such that* $i$ *is honest at round* $r$ *with blockchain* $\mathbf{B}$ *and* $j$ *is corrupt at round* $\widetilde{r}$ *with blockchain* $\widetilde{\mathbf{B}}$, *and there exists* $\ell' \geq \ell$ *such that* $\widetilde{\mathbf{B}}^{\lceil \ell'} \preceq \mathbf{B}$ *and for all* $\widetilde{\ell} < \ell'$, $\widetilde{\mathbf{B}}^{\lceil \widetilde{\ell}} \npreceq \mathbf{B}$, *and the last block in chain vvB is honest (i.e., not mined by the adversary).*

**Definition 12** *(Bounded Length Forking).* *A blockchain protocol* $\Gamma$ *satisfies* $\ell_0(\cdot)$-*bounded length forking property with adversary* $\mathcal{A}$ *in environment* $\mathcal{Z}$, *if there exists a negligible function* negl$(\cdot)$ *such that for every* $\lambda \in \mathbb{N}$, $\ell \geq \ell_0(\lambda)$ *the following holds:*

$$\Pr\left[\text{bd-length-fork}^\ell(\text{view}) = 1 \mid \text{view} \leftarrow \text{EXEC}^\Gamma\left(\mathcal{A}, \mathcal{Z}, 1^\lambda\right)\right] \leq negl(\lambda).$$

In the full version, we prove the following theorem.

**Theorem 1.** *Let* $n$ *be the number of nodes executing the blockchain protocol* $\Gamma_{\text{snowwhite}}$, $p$ *be the probability that a node is elected leader in a given round, and* $\delta_h, \delta_c$ *be the respective probabilities of the elected node being honest or corrupt, and* $\delta_d$ *be the discounted version of* $\delta_h$ *in presence of adversarial network delays. If the stake is distributed as a* $(m, \beta, \gamma)$-*stake distribution and the adversary is* $\alpha$-*stake bounded and proof of stake is unforgeable, then for any constant* $\epsilon_1, \epsilon_2 > 0$, *any* $\ell_1 \geq \epsilon_1 \lambda, \ell_2 \geq \dfrac{\log(m) + \omega(\log(\lambda))}{\mu \gamma}$ *where* $\mu = (1 - \epsilon_2)(1 - \delta_c/\delta_h)$, $\Gamma_{\text{snowwhite}}$ *satisfies:*

1. $\ell_1$-*consistency,*
2. $((1 - \epsilon_2)(1 - \delta_c/\delta_h), \ell_1)$-*chain quality,*
3. $((1 - \epsilon_2)\delta_d, (1 - \epsilon_2)np, \ell_1)$-*chain growth,*
4. $(\beta, \ell_2)$-*sufficient stake contribution,*
5. $(\beta, \ell_2)$-*sufficient honest stake contribution,*
6. $\ell_1$-*bounded length forking,*
7. $(\alpha, \ell_1, \ell_2)$-*bounded stake forking,*
8. $(\alpha, \beta, \ell_1, \ell_2)$-*distinguishable forking*

*against any* $\Gamma_{\text{snowwhite}}$-*compliant adversary-environment pair* $(\mathcal{A}, \mathcal{Z})$.

A similar theorem could also be stated for $\Gamma_{\text{ouroboros}}$.

# 6    NIZKs over Blockchain

In this section, we provide our construction for NIZKs from NIWIs and weighted threshold secret sharing scheme over any POS based blockchain protocol under an additional assumption that each miner's signing-verification key pair could be used as an decryption-encryption key pair. In other words, we assume that the blockchain protocol uses a public key integrated encryption-signature scheme.[13] Below we describe the main ideas.

*Outline.* Suppose the blockchain protocol satisfies $\ell_1$-chain consistency, $(\beta, \ell_2)$-sufficient honest stake contribution and $(1 - \alpha, \ell_3, \ell_4)$-bounded stake forking properties. By chain consistency property, we know that all honest parties agree on all but last $\ell_1$ (or less) blocks of blockchain **B**. Also, bounded stake forking property suggests that no PPT adversary can generate a fork of length $\geq \ell_3 + \ell_4$ such that the proof-of-stake fraction after the first $\ell_3$ blocks of the fork is more than $1 - \alpha$.

At a high level, the scheme works as follows. An honest prover takes as input an instance-witness pair $(x, w)$ and a blockchain **B**. It starts by extracting, from its blockchain, the public identities (thereby public keys) of all the parties who mined a block in last $\ell_2$ blocks of blockchain $\mathbf{B}^{\lceil \ell_1}$. In other words, it selects a *committee* of miners from the most recent part of its blockchain which has become globally persistent. Now, the NIZK proof of the statement $x \in \mathcal{L}$ consists of — (1) a set of ciphertexts $\{\mathsf{ct_{id}}\}$ (one for each miner selected as part of the *committee*), and (2) a witness-indistinguishable proof for the statement "$x \in \mathcal{L}$ *OR the ciphertexts* $\{\mathsf{ct_{id}}\}$ *together encrypt a fork of length more than* $\ell_3 + \ell_4$ *such that the proof-of-stake fraction after the first* $\ell_3$ *blocks of the fork is more than* $1 - \alpha$". In short, the witness-indistinguishable proof proves that either $x \in \mathcal{L}$ or the prover can break the bounded stake forking property. Since the above language is in **NP**, an honest prover simply encrypts random values in ciphertexts $\{\mathsf{ct_{id}}\}$ and uses witness $w$ for the witness-indistinguishable proof. The prover outputs its blockchain **B**, ciphertexts $\{\mathsf{ct_{id}}\}$, witness-indistinguishable proof and all the blockchain property parameters.

The verifier on input an instance $x$, proof $\pi$ and blockchain **B** performs two checks — (1) the prover's blockchain is consistent with its local blockchain, and (2) the witness-indistinguishable proof gets verified. The completeness follows directly from the correctness properties of underlying primitives. Intuitively, the soundness is guaranteed by the fact that the blockchain protocol satisfies the $(1 - \alpha, \ell_3, \ell_4)$-bounded stake forking property, and the system is zero-knowledge because a simulator can generate a witness for the trapdoor part of the statement (i.e., it could generate a long fork satisfying the minimum proof-of-stake constraint) as it controls all the honest parties executing the blockchain, therefore it could use their signing keys to compute such a fork privately. For making

---

[13] As we mentioned before, most blockchain protocols (like Bitcoin, Ethereum etc.) use ECDSA based signature schemes for which we could directly use ECIES-like integrated encryption schemes [47]. Thus, our NIZKs are instantiable over existing blockchain protocols.

the system an argument of knowledge as well, we could additionally make the prover secret share the witness and encrypt a share to each member of the committee it selected. It will be crucial that the secret sharing scheme be a weighted threshold scheme as will become clearer later in this section.

Below we start by describing the valid-fork predicate which will be used later while defining the trapdoor part of the statement.

**Predicate 7.** *Let* valid-fork *be the predicate such that it is satisfied iff the blockchain* $\widetilde{\mathbf{B}}$ *contains a fork of length at least* $\ell_1 + \ell_2$ *such that the fork satisfies the blockchain validity predicate as well as the the proof-of-stake fraction in the last* $\ell_2$ *blocks of the fork is at least* $\gamma$. *More formally,* valid-fork$^V(\mathbf{B}, \widetilde{\mathbf{B}}, \ell_1, \ell_2, \gamma) = 1$ *iff there exists* $\ell' \geq \ell_1 + \ell_2$ *such that* $\widetilde{\mathbf{B}}^{\lceil \ell'} \preceq \mathbf{B}$ *and for all* $\widetilde{\ell} < \ell'$, $\widetilde{\mathbf{B}}^{\lceil \widetilde{\ell}} \npreceq \mathbf{B}$, *and* u-stakefrac$(\widetilde{\mathbf{B}}, \ell' - \ell_1) \geq \gamma$.

## 6.1 Construction

Let $\Gamma^V = (\mathsf{UpdateState}^V, \mathsf{GetRecords}, \mathsf{Broadcast})$ be a blockchain protocol, and $(\mathcal{P}_{\mathsf{NIWI}}, \mathcal{V}_{\mathsf{NIWI}})$ is a NIWI argument system for **NP**, and SS = (Share, Rec) be a weighted threshold secret sharing scheme, and HS = (Setup, Enc, Dec, Sign, Verify) be a public key integrated encryption-signature scheme. Below we describe our NIZK construction for an **NP** language $\mathcal{L}$ over blockchains.

- $\mathcal{P}\left(\mathsf{params} = (1^{\ell_1}, 1^{\ell_2}, 1^{\ell_3}, 1^{\ell_4}, \alpha, \beta), \mathbf{B}, x, w\right)$ : The prover algorithm takes as input the length parameters $\ell_1, \ell_2, \ell_3, \ell_4$, stake fraction parameters $\alpha, \beta$, a blockchain $\mathbf{B}$, an instance $x$ and a witness $w$ such that $\mathcal{R}(x, w) = 1$ where $\mathcal{R}$ is the instance-witness relation for language $\mathcal{L}$.

  Let $\mathbf{B}'$ correspond to the blockchain $\mathbf{B}$ with last $\ell_1$ blocks pruned, i.e. $\mathbf{B}' = \mathbf{B}^{\lceil \ell_1}$. Let $\mathcal{M}$ denote the set of miners who mined at least one block in the last $\ell_2$ blocks of the blockchain $\mathbf{B}'$, i.e. $\mathcal{M} = \mathsf{miner}(\mathbf{B}', [\ell_2])$. Also, let $\mathsf{stake}_{\mathsf{id}} = \mathsf{stake}(\mathbf{B}', \mathsf{id})$ and $\mathsf{pk}_{\mathsf{id}}$ be the stake and public key of party id, respectively.[14] First, it secret shares the witness $w$ and an all zeros string (separately) into $|\mathcal{M}|$ shares with weights $\{\mathsf{stake}_{\mathsf{id}}\}_{\mathsf{id} \in \mathcal{M}}$ and threshold $\beta \cdot \mathsf{stake}_{\mathsf{total}}$ as follows

  $$\{\mathsf{sh}_{\mathsf{id},1}\}_{\mathsf{id}} = \mathsf{Share}(w, \{\mathsf{stake}_{\mathsf{id}}\}_{\mathsf{id}}, \beta \cdot \mathsf{stake}_{\mathsf{total}}; s_1), \quad \{\mathsf{sh}_{\mathsf{id},2}\}_{\mathsf{id}} = \mathsf{Share}(0, \{\mathsf{stake}_{\mathsf{id}}\}_{\mathsf{id}}, \beta \cdot \mathsf{stake}_{\mathsf{total}}; s_2).$$

  Next, it encrypts all these shares as follows

  $$\forall \, \mathsf{id} \in \mathcal{M}, \quad \mathsf{ct}_{\mathsf{id},1} = \mathsf{Enc}(\mathsf{pk}_{\mathsf{id}}, \mathsf{sh}_{\mathsf{id},1}; r_{\mathsf{id},1}), \quad \mathsf{ct}_{\mathsf{id},2} = \mathsf{Enc}(\mathsf{pk}_{\mathsf{id}}, \mathsf{sh}_{\mathsf{id},2}; r_{\mathsf{id},2}).$$

  Finally, it computes a NIWI proof $\pi'$ for the following statement

  $$\exists \{\mathsf{sh}_i, r_i\}_{i \in \mathcal{M}}, s \text{ such that } \begin{pmatrix} \{\mathsf{sh}_i\}_i = \mathsf{Share}(w, \{\mathsf{stake}_{\mathsf{id}}\}_{\mathsf{id}}, \beta \cdot \mathsf{stake}_{\mathsf{total}}; s) \wedge \\ \forall \, i, \; \mathsf{ct}_{i,1} = \mathsf{Enc}(\mathsf{pk}_i, \mathsf{sh}_i; r_i) \wedge \mathcal{R}(x, w) = 1 \end{pmatrix}$$
  $$\vee \begin{pmatrix} \{\mathsf{sh}_i\}_i = \mathsf{Share}(\widetilde{\mathbf{B}}, \{\mathsf{stake}_{\mathsf{id}}\}_{\mathsf{id}}, \beta \cdot \mathsf{stake}_{\mathsf{total}}; s) \wedge \\ \forall \, i, \; \mathsf{ct}_{i,2} = \mathsf{Enc}(\mathsf{pk}_i, \mathsf{sh}_i; r_i) \wedge \mathsf{valid\text{-}fork}^V(\mathbf{B}', \widetilde{\mathbf{B}}, \ell_3, \ell_4, 1 - \alpha) \end{pmatrix}$$

---

[14] Observe that since HS is an integrated encryption-signature scheme, therefore the public verification keys of all parties executing the blockchain protocol could be used for encryption as well.

using the NIWI prover algorithm $\mathcal{P}_{\text{NIWI}}$ with $\left(\{\text{sh}_{\text{id},1}, r_{\text{id},1}\}_{\text{id}}, s_1\right)$ as the witness. Finally, it sets the proof $\pi$ as

$$\pi = \left(\pi', \mathbf{B}, \{\text{ct}_{\text{id},1}, \text{ct}_{\text{id},2}\}_{\text{id}}, \text{params} = (1^{\ell_1}, 1^{\ell_2}, 1^{\ell_3}, 1^{\ell_4}, \alpha, \beta)\right).$$

- $\mathcal{V}(\mathbf{B}, x, \pi)$ : Let $\pi = \left(\pi', \overline{\mathbf{B}}, \{\text{ct}_{i,1}, \text{ct}_{i,2}\}_i, \text{params} = (1^{\ell_1}, 1^{\ell_2}, 1^{\ell_3}, 1^{\ell_4}, \alpha, \beta)\right)$. The verifier starts by checking that blockchains $\overline{\mathbf{B}}$ and $\mathbf{B}$ are $\ell_1$-consistent, i.e. $\overline{\mathbf{B}}^{\lceil \ell_1} \preceq \mathbf{B}$, as well as verifier's blockchain $\mathbf{B}$ is at least as long as prover's blockchain $\overline{\mathbf{B}}$, i.e. $|\overline{\mathbf{B}}| \leq |\mathbf{B}|$. If these check fail, then verifier rejects the proof and outputs 0. Otherwise, it runs the NIWI verifier algorithm $\mathcal{V}_{\text{NIWI}}$ to verify proof $\pi'$ and outputs same as the NIWI verifier.

## 6.2   Security Proof

We will now show that the NIZKs described in Sect. 6.1 is NIZK argument of knowledge as per Definition 2. More formally, we prove the following theorem where all the parameters are polynomials in the security parameter $\lambda$.

**Theorem 2.** *If $(\mathcal{P}_{\text{NIWI}}, \mathcal{V}_{\text{NIWI}})$ is a NIWI argument system for* **NP***, SS is a weighted threshold secret sharing scheme, HS is a secure integrated public key encryption-signature scheme (Definition 1), and blockchain protocol $\Gamma^V$ satisfies $\ell_1$-chain consistency, $(\beta, \ell_2)$-sufficient honest stake contribution properties against all PPT adversaries with at most $\alpha$ stake ratio, and $(1-\alpha, \ell_3, \ell_4)$-bounded stake forking property against all PPT adversaries with at most $\alpha + \beta$ stake ratio, then $(\mathcal{P}, \mathcal{V})$ with parameters $\alpha, \beta, \ell_1, \ell_2, \ell_3, \ell_4$ is a NIZK argument of knowledge for any* **NP** *language $\mathcal{L}$ over blockchain protocol $\Gamma^V$ against all PPT adversaries with at most $\alpha$ stake ratio.*

We provide the proofs of completeness, soundness, zero-knowledge and argument of knowledge in the full version.

# 7   One-Time Programs over Blockchain

In this section, we provide our construction for one-time compilers from garbled circuits and extractable witness encryption over any POS based blockchain protocol. Below we describe the main ideas.

*Outline.* Suppose the blockchain protocol satisfies $(\alpha, \beta, \ell_1, \ell_2)$-distinguishable forking property. We know that distinguishable forking property suggests that no PPT adversary can generate a fork of length $\geq \ell_1 + \ell_2$ such that the proof-of-stake fraction after the first $\ell_1$ blocks of the fork is more than $\alpha$. Additionally, it also implies that the proof-of-stake fraction in any $\ell_2$ consecutive blocks in an honest party's blockchain will be at least $\beta$, with $\beta$ being non-negligibly higher than $\alpha$.

At a high level, the scheme works as follows. To compile a circuit $C$ over blockchain $\mathbf{B}$, the compilation algorithm first garbles the circuit to compute a garbled circuit and wire keys. Suppose we encrypt the wire keys using public key encryption and set the corresponding one-time program as the garbled circuit and encrypted wire keys. This suggests that the evaluator must interact with the compiling party to be able to evaluate the program. However, one-time programs are not defined in an interactive setting. Therefore, we need to somehow allow conditional release/conditional decryption of encrypted wire keys for evaluation. Additionally, we need to make sure that the evaluator only learns the wire keys corresponding to exactly *one* input as otherwise it will not satisfy the one-time secrecy condition. To this end, we encrypt the wire keys using witness encryption scheme such that, to decrypt the wire keys, the evaluator needs to produce a blockchain $\mathbf{B}'$ as a witness where $\mathbf{B}'$ must satisfy the following conditions — (1) there exists a block in $\mathbf{B}'$ which contains the input (on which evaluator wants to evaluate the circuit), (2) there are at least $\ell_1 + \ell_2$ more blocks after the input block such that the proof-of-stake fraction in the last $\ell_2$ blocks of $\mathbf{B}'$ is more than $\beta$, and (3) there does not exists any other block which posts a different input.

To evaluate such a compiled program, the evaluator needs to post its input on the blockchain, and then wait for it to get added to blockchain and get extended by $\ell_1 + \ell_2$ blocks. Afterwards, it could simply use its blockchain as a witness to decrypt appropriate wire keys and then evaluate the garbled circuit using those keys. Intuitively, this would satisfy the one-time secrecy property because in order to evaluate the program on a second input the adversary needs to fork the blockchain before the input block. Now, since the distinguishable forking property guarantees that no PPT adversary can generate such a fork (of length more than $\ell_1 + \ell_2$) with non-negligible probability, therefore one-time secrecy follows.

We start by describing the **NP** language for which we assume existence of a secure extractable witness encryption scheme. Next we develop our one-time compilers on top of a blockchain protocol, and finally show our construction satisfies one-time secrecy property.

## 7.1   NP Relation on Blockchain Protocols

Let $\Gamma = (\mathsf{UpdateState}, \mathsf{GetRecords}, \mathsf{Broadcast})$ be a blockchain protocol with validity $V$. Consider the following relation.

**Definition 13.** *Let $\mathcal{R}_{\Gamma^V}$ be a relation on the blockchain protocol $\Gamma^V$. The instances and witnesses satisfying the relation are of the form*

$$x = (1^\lambda, \mathsf{st}, 1^{\ell_1}, 1^{\ell_2}, 1^n, \beta, i, b, \mathsf{uid}), \quad w = \widetilde{\mathsf{st}}.$$

*Let $\mathbf{B} = \mathsf{GetRecords}(1^\lambda, \mathsf{st})$ and $\widetilde{\mathbf{B}} = \mathsf{GetRecords}(1^\lambda, \widetilde{\mathsf{st}})$. The instance-witness pair satisfies the relation $((x, w) \in \mathcal{R}_{\Gamma^V})$ if and only if all the following properties are satisfied:*

- *Blockchains $\mathbf{B}$ and $\widetilde{\mathbf{B}}$ are valid, i.e. $V(\mathbf{B}) = V(\widetilde{\mathbf{B}}) = 1$*

- $\mathbf{B}$ *is a prefix of* $\widetilde{\mathbf{B}}$, *i.e. they are consistent*[15]
- *There exists a* unique *block* $B^* \in \widetilde{\mathbf{B}} \setminus \mathbf{B}$ *such that the following are satisfied*
  - *There exists a* unique *record* $m^*$ *in* $B^*$ *such that* $m^* = (\mathsf{uid}, y)$, $y$ *is an n-bit string and* $y_i = b$
  - *Let* $\ell'$ *be the number of blocks in blockchain* $\widetilde{\mathbf{B}}$ *after block* $B^*$, *i.e.* $B^* \in$ $\widetilde{\mathbf{B}}^{\lceil \ell'}$. *It should hold that* $\ell' \geq \ell_1 + \ell_2$ *and* u-stakefrac$(\widetilde{\mathbf{B}}, \ell' - \ell_1) > \beta$

*Remark 1.* The *uniqueness* of block $B^*$ and record $m^*$ is defined in the following way. There must not exist any other block (i.e., apart from $B^*$) in the entire witness blockchain $\widetilde{\mathbf{B}}$ such that it contains a record $m$ of the form $(\mathsf{uid}, z)$ where $z$ is any $n$-bit string. Similarly, there must not exist any record $m$ other than $m^*$ in block $B^*$ that satisfies the same property.

Let $\mathcal{L}_{\Gamma^V}$ be the language specified by the relation $\mathcal{R}_{\Gamma^V}$. This language is in **NP** because verifying validity of blockchains take only polynomial time and all the properties in Definition 13 could also be verified simultaneously.

### 7.2   One-Time Compilers

Let $\Gamma^V = (\mathsf{UpdateState}^V, \mathsf{GetRecords}, \mathsf{Broadcast})$ be a blockchain protocol, and $\mathsf{GC} = (\mathsf{GC.Garble}, \mathsf{GC.Eval})$ be a garbling scheme for circuit family $\mathcal{C} = \{\mathcal{C}_n\}_n$, and $\mathsf{WE} = (\mathsf{Enc}, \mathsf{Dec})$ be a witness encryption scheme for language $\mathcal{L}_{\Gamma^V}$. Below we describe our one-time compilers $\mathsf{OTC} = (\mathsf{Compile}, \mathsf{Eval})$ for circuit family $\mathcal{C} = \{\mathcal{C}_n\}_n$ in the blockchain model.

- $\mathsf{Compile}(1^\lambda, 1^{\ell_1}, 1^{\ell_2}, \beta, C \in \mathcal{C}_n)$: The compilation algorithm first garbles the circuit $C$ by computing $(G, \{w_{i,b}\}_{i \leq n, b \in \{0,1\}}) \leftarrow \mathsf{GC.Garble}(1^\lambda, C)$. Next, it encrypts each of the wire keys $w_{i,b}$ separately under instances $x_{i,b}$ as follows:

  $$\forall i \leq n, b \in \{0,1\}, \quad x_{i,b} = (1^\lambda, \mathsf{st}, 1^{\ell_1}, 1^{\ell_2}, 1^n, \beta, i, b, \mathsf{uid} = G), \quad \mathsf{ct}_{i,b} \leftarrow \mathsf{Enc}(1^\lambda, x_{i,b}, w_{i,b}),$$

  where $\mathsf{st}$ is its local blockchain state. Finally, it sets the compiled circuit as $CC = \left(1^\lambda, 1^{\ell_1}, 1^{\ell_2}, G, \{\mathsf{ct}_{i,b}\}_{i \leq n, b \in \{0,1\}}\right)$.
- $\mathsf{Eval}(CC, y \in \{0,1\}^n)$: Let $CC = \left(1^\lambda, 1^{\ell_1}, 1^{\ell_2}, G, \{\mathsf{ct}_{i,b}\}_{i \leq n, b \in \{0,1\}}\right)$. It first posts input $y$ on the blockchain by running $\mathsf{Broadcast}$ algorithm as $\mathsf{Broadcast}(1^\lambda, (G, y))$.

  It runs the $\mathsf{UpdateState}$ algorithm, and waits for message $(G, y)$ to be posted on the blockchain and further the chain to be extended by $\ell_1 + \ell_2$ blocks. After the blockchain gets extended, it uses its own local state $\mathsf{st}$ as a witness to decrypt the wire keys corresponding to input $y$ as

  $$\forall i \leq n, \quad w_i = \mathsf{Dec}(\mathsf{ct}_{i,y_i}, \mathsf{st}).$$

  It then uses these $n$ wire keys to evaluate the garbled circuit, and outputs $\mathsf{GC.Eval}(G, \{w_i\}_{i \leq n})$. If the witnes decryption fails (outputs $\bot$), then it also outputs $\bot$.

---

[15] Formally, the consistency should be checked as $\mathbf{B}^{\lceil \kappa} \preceq \widetilde{\mathbf{B}}$ for an appropriate value of parameter $\kappa$ (Definition 4), however for ease of exposition we avoid it.

*Correctness.* Fix any $\lambda$, $n$, $\ell_1$, $\ell_2$, $\beta$, and circuit $C \in \mathcal{C}_n$. Let $(G, \{w_{i,b}\}) \leftarrow \mathsf{GC.Garble}(1^\lambda, C)$, $x_{i,b} = (1^\lambda, \mathsf{st}, 1^{\ell_1}, 1^{\ell_2}, 1^n, \beta, i, b, G)$, and $\mathsf{ct}_{i,b} \leftarrow \mathsf{Enc}(1^\lambda, x_{i,b}, w_{i,b})$.

For any input $y \in \{0,1\}^n$, consider that an evaluator runs Broadcast algorithm to post $(G, y)$ on the blockchain. Let $\widetilde{\mathsf{st}}$ be the local state of the evaluator after message $(G, y)$ is posted on blockchain and it is extended by $\ell_1 + \ell_2$ blocks. Assuming that evaluator and compiler's blockchain are consistent (Definition 4), then with all but negligible probability for all $i \leq n$, $\widetilde{\mathsf{st}}$ could be used as the witness to decrypt ciphertexts $\mathsf{ct}_{i,y_i}$ as $(x_{i,y_i}, \widetilde{\mathsf{st}}) \in \mathcal{R}_{\Gamma V}$. This is true because consistency property guarantees that, with all but negligible probability, the blockchains $\mathbf{B}$ and $\widetilde{\mathbf{B}}$ will be consistent. Additionally, the stake quantity property (Definition 7) guarantees that (with all but negligible probability) the condition $\mathsf{u\text{-}stakefrac}(\widetilde{\mathbf{B}}, \ell' - \ell_1) > \beta$ will be satisfied. Therefore, $\mathsf{Dec}(\mathsf{ct}_{i,y_i}, \mathsf{st}) = w_{i,y_i}$ which follows from correctness of the witness encryption scheme. Finally, $\mathsf{GC.Eval}(G, \{w_{i,y_i}\}_{i \leq n}) = C(y)$ as it follows from correctness of the garbling scheme. Therefore, OTC satisfies the one-time compiler correctness condition.

*Remark 2.* Our one-time compiler takes additional parameters $\ell_1, \ell_2$ and $\beta$ as inputs, which we refer to as the *hardness parameters*. The primary purpose of $\ell_1, \ell_2$ and $\beta$ is to connect the efficiency of our compiled circuit to an appropriate hardness assumption on the blockchain protocol. Informally, increasing value of $\ell_1$ and $\ell_2$ reduces efficiency of our compiled circuit as the evaluator needs to wait for longer time (more blocks) in order to evaluate the circuit. At the same time, reducing $\ell_1$ and $\ell_2$ increases the strength of the assumption on the blockchain. The latter will get highlighted in the security proof. The effect of choice of $\beta$ has an indirect impact on efficiency, although it affects the same way as $\ell_1, \ell_2$.

The security proof will be provided in the full version.

**Acknowledgements.** We thank Krzysztof Pietrzak and anonymous TCC reviewers for their useful feedback. The second author is supported in part by NSF CNS-1228599 and CNS-1414082, DARPA SafeWare.

# References

1. Abdalla, M., Benhamouda, F., Pointcheval, D.: Disjunctions for hash proof systems: new constructions and applications. In: Oswald, E., Fischlin, M. (eds.) EUROCRYPT 2015. LNCS, vol. 9057, pp. 69–100. Springer, Heidelberg (2015). doi:10.1007/978-3-662-46803-6_3
2. Andrychowicz, M., Dziembowski, S., Malinowski, D., Mazurek, Ł.: Fair two-party computations via bitcoin deposits. In: Böhme, R., Brenner, M., Moore, T., Smith, M. (eds.) FC 2014. LNCS, vol. 8438, pp. 105–121. Springer, Heidelberg (2014). doi:10.1007/978-3-662-44774-1_8
3. Andrychowicz, M., Dziembowski, S., Malinowski, D., Mazurek, L.: Secure multiparty computations on bitcoin. In: 2014 IEEE Symposium on Security and Privacy, SP 2014, Berkeley, CA, USA, 18–21 May 2014

4. Applebaum, B., Ishai, Y., Kushilevitz, E., Waters, B.: Encoding functions with constant online rate, or how to compress garbled circuit keys. SIAM J. Comput. **44**(2), 433–466 (2015)
5. Barak, B., Goldreich, O., Impagliazzo, R., Rudich, S., Sahai, A., Vadhan, S.P., Yang, K.: On the (im)possibility of obfuscating programs. J. ACM **59**(2), 6 (2012)
6. Bellare, M., Hoang, V.T., Rogaway, P.: Adaptively secure garbling with applications to one-time programs and secure outsourcing. In: Wang, X., Sako, K. (eds.) ASIACRYPT 2012. LNCS, vol. 7658, pp. 134–153. Springer, Heidelberg (2012). doi:10.1007/978-3-642-34961-4_10
7. Bellare, M., Hoang, V.T., Rogaway, P.: Foundations of garbled circuits. In: CCS 2012 (2012)
8. Ben-Or, M., Goldwasser, S., Wigderson, A.: Completeness theorems for non-cryptographic fault-tolerant distributed computation (extended abstract). In: Proceedings of the 20th Annual ACM Symposium on Theory of Computing, Chicago, Illinois, USA, 2–4 May 1988
9. Benhamouda, F., Blazy, O., Chevalier, C., Pointcheval, D., Vergnaud, D.: New techniques for SPHFs and efficient one-round PAKE protocols. In: Canetti, R., Garay, J.A. (eds.) CRYPTO 2013. LNCS, vol. 8042, pp. 449–475. Springer, Heidelberg (2013). doi:10.1007/978-3-642-40041-4_25
10. Bentov, I., Gabizon, A., Zuckerman, D.: Bitcoin beacon. arXiv preprint arxiv:1605.04559 (2016)
11. Bentov, I., Kumaresan, R.: How to use bitcoin to design fair protocols. In: Garay, J.A., Gennaro, R. (eds.) CRYPTO 2014. LNCS, vol. 8617, pp. 421–439. Springer, Heidelberg (2014). doi:10.1007/978-3-662-44381-1_24
12. Bentov, I., Pass, R., Shi, E.: The sleepy model of consensus. Cryptology ePrint Archive, Report 2016/918 (2016). http://eprint.iacr.org/2016/918
13. Bentov, I., Pass, R., Shi, E.: Snow white: provably secure proofs of stake. Cryptology ePrint Archive, Report 2016/919 (2016). http://eprint.iacr.org/2016/919
14. Bonneau, J., Clark, J., Goldfeder, S.: On bitcoin as a public randomness source. Cryptology ePrint Archive, Report 2015/1015 (2015)
15. Coron, J.-S., Lepoint, T., Tibouchi, M.: Practical multilinear maps over the integers. In: Canetti, R., Garay, J.A. (eds.) CRYPTO 2013. LNCS, vol. 8042, pp. 476–493. Springer, Heidelberg (2013). doi:10.1007/978-3-642-40041-4_26
16. Cramer, R., Shoup, V.: Universal hash proofs and a paradigm for adaptive chosen ciphertext secure public-key encryption. In: Knudsen, L.R. (ed.) EUROCRYPT 2002. LNCS, vol. 2332, pp. 45–64. Springer, Heidelberg (2002). doi:10.1007/3-540-46035-7_4
17. Feige, U., Lapidot, D., Shamir, A.: Multiple non-interactive zero knowledge proofs under general assumptions. SIAM J. Comput. **29**(1), 1–28 (1999)
18. Feige, U., Shamir, A.: Witness indistinguishable and witness hiding protocols. In: STOC, pp. 416–426 (1990)
19. Garay, J., Kiayias, A., Leonardos, N.: The bitcoin backbone protocol: analysis and applications. In: Oswald, E., Fischlin, M. (eds.) EUROCRYPT 2015. LNCS, vol. 9057, pp. 281–310. Springer, Heidelberg (2015). doi:10.1007/978-3-662-46803-6_10
20. Garay, J.A., Kiayias, A., Leonardos, N.: The bitcoin backbone protocol with chains of variable difficulty. Cryptology ePrint Archive, Report 2016/1048 (2016)
21. Garay, J.A., Kiayias, A., Leonardos, N., Panagiotakos, G.: Bootstrapping the blockchain – directly. Cryptology ePrint Archive, Report 2016/991 (2016). http://eprint.iacr.org/2016/991

22. Garg, S., Gentry, C., Halevi, S.: Candidate multilinear maps from ideal lattices. In: Johansson, T., Nguyen, P.Q. (eds.) EUROCRYPT 2013. LNCS, vol. 7881, pp. 1–17. Springer, Heidelberg (2013). doi:10.1007/978-3-642-38348-9_1

23. Garg, S., Gentry, C., Halevi, S., Raykova, M., Sahai, A., Waters, B.: Candidate indistinguishability obfuscation and functional encryption for all circuits. In: FOCS (2013)

24. Garg, S., Gentry, C., Halevi, S., Wichs, D.: On the implausibility of differing-inputs obfuscation and extractable witness encryption with auxiliary input. In: Garay, J.A., Gennaro, R. (eds.) CRYPTO 2014. LNCS, vol. 8616, pp. 518–535. Springer, Heidelberg (2014). doi:10.1007/978-3-662-44371-2_29

25. Garg, S., Gentry, C., Sahai, A., Waters, B.: Witness encryption and its applications. In: STOC (2013)

26. Goldreich, O., Oren, Y.: Definitions and properties of zero-knowledge proof systems. J. Cryptology (1994)

27. Goldwasser, S., Micali, S., Rackoff, C.: The knowledge complexity of interactive proof systems. SIAM J. Comput. 18(1), 186–208 (1989). http://dx.doi.org/10.1137/0218012

28. Goldwasser, S., Kalai, Y.T., Popa, R.A., Vaikuntanathan, V., Zeldovich, N.: How to run turing machines on encrypted data. In: Canetti, R., Garay, J.A. (eds.) CRYPTO 2013. LNCS, vol. 8043, pp. 536–553. Springer, Heidelberg (2013). doi:10.1007/978-3-642-40084-1_30

29. Goldwasser, S., Kalai, Y.T., Rothblum, G.N.: One-time programs. In: Wagner, D. (ed.) CRYPTO 2008. LNCS, vol. 5157, pp. 39–56. Springer, Heidelberg (2008). doi:10.1007/978-3-540-85174-5_3

30. Goyal, V., Ishai, Y., Sahai, A., Venkatesan, R., Wadia, A.: Founding cryptography on tamper-proof hardware tokens. In: Micciancio, D. (ed.) TCC 2010. LNCS, vol. 5978, pp. 308–326. Springer, Heidelberg (2010). doi:10.1007/978-3-642-11799-2_19

31. Goyal, V., Katz, J.: Universally composable multi-party computation with an unreliable common reference string. In: Canetti, R. (ed.) TCC 2008. LNCS, vol. 4948, pp. 142–154. Springer, Heidelberg (2008). doi:10.1007/978-3-540-78524-8_9

32. Groth, J., Ostrovsky, R.: Cryptography in the multi-string model. In: Menezes, A. (ed.) CRYPTO 2007. LNCS, vol. 4622, pp. 323–341. Springer, Heidelberg (2007). doi:10.1007/978-3-540-74143-5_18

33. Horvitz, O., Katz, J.: Universally-composable two-party computation in two rounds. In: Menezes, A. (ed.) CRYPTO 2007. LNCS, vol. 4622, pp. 111–129. Springer, Heidelberg (2007). doi:10.1007/978-3-540-74143-5_7

34. Jager, T.: How to build time-lock encryption. Cryptology ePrint Archive, Report 2015/478 (2015). http://eprint.iacr.org/2015/478

35. Jutla, C.S., Roy, A.: Shorter quasi-adaptive NIZK proofs for linear subspaces. In: Sako, K., Sarkar, P. (eds.) ASIACRYPT 2013. LNCS, vol. 8269, pp. 1–20. Springer, Heidelberg (2013). doi:10.1007/978-3-642-42033-7_1

36. Katz, J., Ostrovsky, R.: Round-optimal secure two-party computation. In: Franklin, M. (ed.) CRYPTO 2004. LNCS, vol. 3152, pp. 335–354. Springer, Heidelberg (2004). doi:10.1007/978-3-540-28628-8_21

37. Kiayias, A., Panagiotakos, G.: Speed-security tradeoffs in blockchain protocols. Cryptology ePrint Archive, Report 2015/1019 (2015). http://eprint.iacr.org/2015/1019

38. Kiayias, A., Russell, A., David, B., Oliynykov, R.: Ouroboros: a provably secure proof-of-stake blockchain protocol. Cryptology ePrint Archive, Report 2016/889 (2016). http://eprint.iacr.org/2016/889

39. Kumaresan, R., Bentov, I.: How to use bitcoin to incentivize correct computations. In: Proceedings of the 2014 ACM SIGSAC Conference on Computer and Communications Security, Scottsdale, AZ, USA, 3–7 November 2014
40. Liu, J., Kakvi, S.A., Warinschi, B.: Extractable witness encryption and timed-release encryption from bitcoin. Cryptology ePrint Archive, Report 2015/482 (2015). http://eprint.iacr.org/2015/482
41. mtgox        (2010).        https://bitcointalk.org/index.php?topic=2227.msg29606# msg29606
42. Nakamoto, S.: Bitcoin: a peer-to-peer electronic cash system (2008)
43. Pass, R., Seeman, L., Shelat, A.: Analysis of the blockchain protocol in asynchronous networks. IACR Cryptology ePrint Archive (2016). http://eprint.iacr.org/2016/454
44. Pass, R., Shi, E.: Fruitchains: a fair blockchain. Cryptology ePrint Archive, Report 2016/916 (2016). http://eprint.iacr.org/2016/916
45. Pass, R., Shi, E.: Hybrid consensus: efficient consensus in the permissionless model. Cryptology ePrint Archive, Report 2016/917 (2016). http://eprint.iacr.org/2016/917
46. Sahai, A., Waters, B.: How to use indistinguishability obfuscation: deniable encryption, and more. In: Symposium on Theory of Computing, STOC 2014, New York, NY, USA, 31 May–03 June 2014, pp. 475–484 (2014)
47. Shoup, V.: A proposal for an ISO standard for public key encryption (version 2.1) (2001)
48. Wee, H.: Efficient chosen-ciphertext security via extractable hash proofs. In: Rabin, T. (ed.) CRYPTO 2010. LNCS, vol. 6223, pp. 314–332. Springer, Heidelberg (2010). doi:10.1007/978-3-642-14623-7_17
49. Wood, G.: Ethereum: a secure decentralised generalised transaction ledger (2014)
50. Yao, A.: How to generate and exchange secrets. In: FOCS, pp. 162–167 (1986)

# Multiparty Computation

# Secure Two-Party Computation with Fairness - A Necessary Design Principle

Yehuda Lindell[1]([✉]) and Tal Rabin[2]

[1] Deptartment of Computer Science, Bar-Ilan University, Ramat Gan, Israel
`lindell@biu.ac.il`
[2] IBM T.J. Watson Research Center, New York, USA
`talr@us.ibm.com`

**Abstract.** Protocols for secure two-party computation enable a pair of mutually distrustful parties to carry out a joint computation of their private inputs without revealing anything but the output. One important security property that has been considered is that of *fairness* which guarantees that if one party learns the output then so does the other. In the case of two-party computation, fairness is not always possible, and in particular two parties cannot fairly toss a coin (Cleve, 1986). Despite this, it is actually possible to securely compute many two-party functions with fairness (Gordon et al., 2008 and follow-up work). However, *all* known two-party protocols that achieve fairness have the unique property that the effective input of the corrupted party is determined at an arbitrary point in the protocol. This is in stark contrast to almost all other known protocols that have an explicit fixed round at which the inputs are *committed*.

In this paper, we ask whether or not the property of not having an input committal round is *inherent* for achieving fairness for two parties. In order to do so, we revisit the definition of security of Micali and Rogaway (Technical report, 1992), that explicitly requires the existence of such a committal round. We adapt the definition of Canetti in the two-party setting to incorporate the spirit of a committal round, and show that under such a definition, it is *impossible* to achieve fairness for any non-constant two-party function. This result deepens our understanding as to the type of protocol construction that is needed for achieving fairness. In addition, our result discovers a fundamental difference between the definition of security of Micali and Rogaway and that of Canetti (Journal of Cryptology, 2000) which has become the standard today. Specifically, many functions can be securely computed with fairness under the definition of Canetti but no non-constant function can be securely computed with fairness under the definition of Micali and Rogaway.

**Keywords:** Secure two-party computation · Fairness · Definitions of security

© International Association for Cryptologic Research 2017
Y. Kalai and L. Reyzin (Eds.): TCC 2017, Part I, LNCS 10677, pp. 565–580, 2017.
https://doi.org/10.1007/978-3-319-70500-2_19

# 1    Introduction

In the setting of secure two-party computation, a pair of parties $P_1$ and $P_2$ wish to compute a joint function of their private inputs in a secure manner. The standard requirements for security are *privacy* (meaning that nothing but the output is revealed), *correctness* (meaning that the output is correctly computed) and *independence of inputs* (meaning that a corrupted party cannot make its input dependent on the honest party's input). An additional property that is highly desired in many applications is that of *fairness*, which guarantees that corrupted parties cannot receive output without the honest parties also receiving output. The fundamental question regarding the feasibility of achieving fairness has been studied since the late 1980 s starting with the seminal work of Cleve [14] who showed that it is *impossible* for two parties to securely toss an unbiased coin. Following this work, a folklore arose that assumed that essentially no interesting function can be securely computed with fairness. Intuitively, this makes sense since in order for two parties to compute the function by exchanging messages in turn, one must at some stage know more information than the other. As a result, *partial* notions of fairness were introduced, including gradual release [7] and the optimistic model that utilizes a trusted third party [2,22] (these models are not relevant to our work here that focuses on achieving full fairness).

However, over two decades later, it was shown by Gordon et al. [20] that it is in fact possible to securely compute some specific functions with (full) fairness. Later, it was shown that it is actually possible to compute *many* finite-domain Boolean functions securely with fairness in the presence of malicious adversaries [3–5,21]. These positive results demonstrate a specific methodology for protocol construction that achieves fair secure two-party computation. In contrast to these positive constructions, there has been very little work regarding *necessary conditions* for achieving fair secure two-party computation. In particular, there is no proof whether this methodology is in fact needed. In this paper, we prove that the central design principle used in all of [3–5,20,21] is in fact *necessary*.

*Background.* As we have mentioned, the classic definition of security for two-party computation guarantees central properties like privacy, correctness and independence of inputs. The actual security definition formalizes these security properties by comparing a real protocol execution to an ideal world in which an incorruptible trusted party computes the function for the parties [6,9,18,19,23]. In more detail, a protocol is proven secure by presenting an ideal-world simulator machine that interacts with a trusted party, sending the corrupted parties' inputs and receiving back their outputs. The requirement is then that for every real adversary attacking the protocol, the outputs of the adversary and honest parties in a real protocol execution is computationally indistinguishable from the output of the simulator and honest parties in the ideal model. Note that in the ideal model, the honest parties simply send their prescribed inputs to the trusted party and output whatever they receive back. This guarantees all the aforementioned security properties since the only thing that the simulator can do in the ideal model is modify the corrupted parties' inputs. Since the outputs in the real and ideal executions are indistinguishable, the same holds also for the real secure protocol. Definitions of this type are said to follow the ideal-real model paradigm.

Classically, the literature considers two types of adversaries; semi-honest adversaries who follow the protocol specification but try to learn more than allowed by inspecting the transcript, and malicious adversaries who may follow any arbitrary polynomial-time attack strategy. In this paper, we consider the setting of malicious adversaries.

In the case of secure multiparty computation with an honest majority, the additional property of *fairness* is typically also required. This property guarantees that if the corrupted party receives an output then so does the honest party. However, in the case of two-party computation – where there is no honest majority and malicious adversaries – fairness is usually not required, since it has been shown that fairness cannot always be achieved. In particular, it was shown in [14] that it is *impossible* for two parties to securely toss an unbiased coin.

*The protocol of Gordon et al.* [20]. The protocol of [20] and its extensions in [3,4,21] have a very unique property that there is no specific round at which the parties' inputs are "determined". In order to explain this, let us consider for a moment the GMW protocol [17,18]. The GMW protocol begins with the parties running an "input commitment" phase, and then forcing the parties to use these inputs using zero-knowledge proofs. This paradigm of construction is not unique to [18], but rather is the norm in all known protocols.[1] In contrast, in the protocols of [3,4,20,21] which are the *only* protocols that achieve fairness without an honest majority, the corrupted parties' input is essentially determined by the point at which they halt, if they halt before the end. As a result, there is no input-commitment phase, and indeed no point whereby the input of a corrupted party is explicitly fixed. A very interesting question that arises from this is whether or not protocols that achieve fairness *must* work in this way, or if this is just one possible approach.

*The Micali-Rogaway (MR) definition of security.* The definition of security for multiparty computation, formulated by Micali and Rogaway in [23], is based on the same ideal/real paradigm described above. One of the central differences between the definition of MR and Canetti [9] is the requirement that there exist an explicit committal round, which defines all parties' inputs. In order to understand why this requirement was included, we look back at the motivation provided by Micali and Rogaway for their definition. Micali and Rogaway articulate a number of key ideas for their notion of security (called "key choices" in [23, Sect. 1.6]). The three key choices are *blending privacy and correctness*, *adversarial awareness* and *tight mimicry*. The first two choices are common with the definition of Canetti (that also follows the ideal-real model paradigm), which has today become the standard for secure computation in the stand-alone

---

[1] In some cases, it is more subtle and the inputs are more implicitly committed; e.g., via oblivious transfer. However, this is still input commitment.

model. The requirement of *blending privacy and correctness* is important since there are examples showing that they cannot actually be separated (an attack on correctness can result in a breach of privacy), and the requirement of *adversarial awareness* means that the adversary's input is explicitly known (formulated by the simulator explicitly providing this input to the trusted party).

In contrast, the requirement of *tight mimicry* was not adopted by others to the same extent. This requirement is that the ideal-model simulation tightly mimics a real protocol execution. Micali-Rogaway observed that in all existing secure protocols, at the time, there was an explicit round whereby the parties commit to their inputs. This was true of the protocols of [8,13,18,24] and almost all protocols known today (with the exception of the fair protocols of [3,4,20,21] and the protocol of [1]), and they mimicked that. As a result they stated that it should be possible to know **what inputs** the adversary is using for the corrupted parties, **when these inputs are determined**, and **what output** is received by the corrupted parties. The first and third of these requirements of "tight mimicry" do appear in [9,17], but the second does not. The second requirement is formalized in [23] by requiring the existence of a committal round so that the corrupted parties' inputs are *fully determined* by this round.

In order to understand the committal round requirement in more depth, we informally describe how it is formulated. The MR definition formalizes two different phases of simulation. In the first phase, the simulator simulates up to the committal round and then outputs the inputs of the corrupted parties, supposedly as would be used by the corrupted parties in a real execution. Next, the function is computed on the corrupted parties' inputs as output by the simulator and the honest parties' prescribed inputs. The simulator receives this function's output and continues in the simulation to the end. Note that the simulator interacts with the real adversary as one interacts with an external real party; in particular, this means that the simulator has only black-box access to the adversary and also cannot rewind it. Observe that the aforementioned phases are distinct since the simulation is "straight line".[2] We refer the reader to [23] for more details, and to [15] for a more concise version of the definition.

Importantly, Dodis and Micali [15] inherently utilize the existence of a committal round in order to prove their concurrent composition theorem. Thus, beyond accurately mimicking the way protocols work, this feature of the definition also has technical advantages in the context of composition.

*Our results – fairness and committal rounds.* Interestingly, the requirement of a committal round rules out the fair protocols of [3,4,20,21], and these protocols cannot be proven secure under any definition with such a requirement, like the MR definition. As we have stated, these are the only protocols that achieve

---

[2] This makes some aspects of the definition reminiscent of the much-later UC framework [10]; in particular, in [10] the adversarial environment is external to the simulator and the simulator can interact with it as with a real party (meaning, black box and no rewinding). Indeed, in [15] it was shown that protocols proven secure under the MR definition are secure under concurrent composition.

fairness and they all do not have a committal round. A very natural question that arises is therefore whether fair protocols must be designed so that there is no fixed point at which inputs are committed. In particular, we ask:

*Is it possible to construct two-party protocols with fairness, with the property that the parties' inputs are committed at a fixed committal round?*

Answering this question will also shed light on whether the definition of Canetti is fundamentally different to the MR definition with respect to fairness.

In this paper, we show that the existence of a *committal round* does indeed result in a qualitatively different notion of security. In particular, it is impossible to securely compute any non-constant function in the two-party setting with fairness when there is a committal round. We prove the following theorem:

**Theorem 1 (Main theorem – informally stated).** *If $f$ is a non-constant function, then it cannot be securely computed in the two-party setting with fairness using a definition that requires a committal round.*

In order to prove the theorem, we adapt the definition of Canetti in a seemingly *minimal way*, to include a committal round conceptually similar to that of MR (with two distinct phases of simulation). Our definition enables rewinding the adversary like Canetti, since otherwise security is not possible without an honest majority (or some secure setup).[3] Our definition suffices for defining security without fairness, and as evidence, *all* non-fair protocols that we know of can be securely computed under our adapted definition.

Our proof of the theorem demonstrates that the effective input of a corrupted party must depend on when it halts. In addition, we show that in a definition with a committal round, the simulator must determine the corrupted party's input at some point before the end of the protocol. This implies that the simulator must determine the corrupted party's input before knowing when it will halt, preventing it from correctly determining the effective input. Thus, simulation is not possible.

*Conclusions.* Our result deepens our understanding of the type of protocol design needed in order to obtain fairness. Specifically, it is essential that in any fair protocol the input of the corrupted party not be determined at any fixed point. Thus, any protocol that achieves fairness in secure two-party computation must follow the same construction paradigm as [20], at least with respect to the fact that a party's input is not committed at any fixed point.

In addition, our results show that the existence or non-existence of a *required* committal round is not at all inconsequential, and has actual ramifications on the feasibility of achieving security, particularly fairness. This in turn implies that there is actually a fundamental difference between the definitions of Micali-Rogaway and Canetti.

---

[3] The fact that no rewinding results in impossibility was shown in the framework of universal composability [10] which does not allow rewinding; see [11,12].

## 2  Defining Secure Two-Party Computation with a Committal Round

In this section, we present a version of the definition of Canetti [9,17] for the two-party case that is minimally adapted to include a committal round like that of MR. As in MR, we formalize the committal round by mandating two distinct phases for the simulation, but we allow rewinding in each phase (as needed for proving the security of two-party protocols). The first phase until the simulator provides the input of the corrupted party, and the second phase from the point that the simulator receives the output to the end of the protocol. As will become clear in the definition below, the simulator may rewind the adversary within each phase but not beyond it, in order to ensure that the phases are indeed distinct.

Our definition below requires fairness, since we aim to show impossibility of fairness when a committal round is included. However, as we will explain at the end of this section, an analogous definition which includes a committal round but *not* fairness is satisfied by almost all protocols that we are aware of; see Theorem 2. Thus, the existence of a committal round alone is not a barrier to achieving security (without fairness).

*Preliminaries.* We denote the security parameter by $n$. A function $\mu(\cdot)$ is **negligible** in $n$, or just **negligible**, if for every positive polynomial $p(\cdot)$ and all sufficiently large $n$'s it holds that $\mu(n) < \frac{1}{p(n)}$. We say that two distribution ensembles $X = \{X(a,n)\}_{a\in\{0,1\}^*;n\in\mathbb{N}}$ and $Y = \{Y(a,n)\}_{a\in\{0,1\}^*;n\in\mathbb{N}}$ are **computationally indistinguishable** if for every non-uniform probabilistic polynomial-time distinguisher $D$ there exists a negligible function $\mu(\cdot)$ such that for every $a \in \{0,1\}^*$ and every $n \in \mathbb{N}$,

$$\big|\Pr[D(X(a,n)=1)] - \Pr[D(Y(a,n)=1)]\big| \le \mu(n).$$

*The real model.* In the real model, the two parties $P_1$ and $P_2$ interact directly running protocol $\pi$, exchanging messages with each other. To be concrete, we assume that in each round of the protocol, one party sends a message to the other party who waits to receive the message (this is the least restrictive and most general model). Each party $P_i$ is given its input $x_i$ and the security parameter $n$ in unary form. We consider a malicious static adversary, $\mathcal{A}$, that controls one of the parties. We denote the corrupted party by $P_i$ ($i \in \{1,2\}$) and denote the honest party by $P_j$ ($j \in \{1,2\}$ with $j \ne i$). The adversary $\mathcal{A}$ is given the corrupted party's input $x_i$, an auxiliary input $z$, and the value $1^n$ (the security parameter in unary) and interacts directly with the honest party $P_j$. The honest party outputs whatever is prescribed by the protocol, and the corrupted party outputs its *view* in the execution. We denote by $\text{REAL}_{\pi,i,\mathcal{A}}(x_1,x_2,z,n)$ the output of the honest party and the view of the adversary in a real execution, where $P_1$ has input $x_1$, $P_2$ has input $x_2$, the security parameter is $n$, and the adversary is given auxiliary input $z$ and controls party $P_i$.

*The ideal model.* In the ideal model, the parties do not interact with each other at all. Rather, they just send their input to an incorruptible trusted party who computes the output for them. We consider fairness and therefore the trusted party always sends output to both parties (if the corrupted party does not provide an input, then a default input is taken by the trusted party).[4] The honest party $P_j$ always sends its prescribed input to the trusted party, whereas the corrupted party can send any input it desires or none at all. We denote the ideal-model adversary by $\mathcal{S}$.

Following the MR definition, we define a committal round, which we view as a "break point" in the simulation. Let $CR$ be an integer that denotes the committal round. Our definition is *black-box*, and so the simulator $\mathcal{S}$ is given black-box (oracle) access to the real adversary $\mathcal{A}$ with its input $x_i$, auxiliary input $z$ and uniformly-distributed random tape $r$. As formalized in [16, Sec. 4.5], such black-box access is modeled by $\mathcal{S}$ sending oracle queries of the form $q = (m_1, \ldots, m_\ell)$ and receiving back $\mathcal{A}(x_i, z, r; m_1, \ldots, m_\ell)$, where $x_i, z, r$ are as stated and $m_1, \ldots, m_\ell$ is a series of incoming messages (we assume unique delimiters between each item in the query and so it is unambiguous). The response from $\mathcal{A}$ is its outgoing message (or output) when invoked on this input, random-tape and series of messages. We say that an oracle query $q$ is of length $\ell$ if it contains $\ell$ incoming messages.

In our definition, $\mathcal{A}$ controls party $P_i$ ($i \in \{1, 2\}$) and works in two distinct phases:

1. *Phase 1 – up to and including the committal round:* In this phase, $\mathcal{S}$ is allowed to send oracle queries of length at most $CR$ only. At the end of this phase, $\mathcal{S}$ outputs a partial view of $\mathcal{A}$ up to and including $CR$ – denoted by $\text{VIEW}^1_{\mathcal{S}\mathcal{A}}(x_i, z, n)$ – and also $\mathcal{A}$'s input $x'_i$ to be sent to the trusted party. The trusted party computes the function output from $x'_i$ and the input received from the honest party, and sends the honest party its specified output.

2. *Phase 2 – post-committal round:* In this phase, $\mathcal{S}$ receives the corrupted party's output from the trusted party, and generates a partial view of $\mathcal{A}$ from the round after $CR$ to the end of the protocol, denoted $\text{VIEW}^2_{\mathcal{S}\mathcal{A}}(x_i, z, n)$.

Note that the "break point" of the simulation is the point *between* the committal round and the round following it. As we have mentioned, the definition of security is black-box (as is the original definition of MR); this seems inherent when formalizing a committal round and break-point.

The output of the ideal execution is the concatenation of $\text{VIEW}^1_{\mathcal{S}\mathcal{A}}(x_i, z, n)$ with $\text{VIEW}^2_{\mathcal{S}\mathcal{A}}(x_i, z, n)$, and the honest party's output. We stress that

---

[4] Our definition requires guaranteed output delivery (meaning that both parties always receive output), and not just fairness (meaning that if one receives an output then so does the other but it's possible that neither receive). In the setting of two-party computation, these properties are equivalent, since in the case of abort the honest party can compute the function on its own input and on a default input for the other party. We therefore arbitrarily chose the definition where parties always receive output.

$\text{VIEW}^1_{\mathcal{SA}}(x_i, z, n)$ must contain exactly $CR$ incoming messages; otherwise the output of the ideal execution will be $\perp$. We denote this output by $\text{IDEAL}^{CR}_{f,i,\mathcal{SA}}(x_1, x_2, z, n)$.

We are now ready to define security:

**Definition 1.** *Let $f : \{0,1\}^* \times \{0,1\}^* \rightarrow \{0,1\}^* \times \{0,1\}^*$ be a two-party functionality. A protocol $\pi$ securely computes $f$ with a committal round and fairness if there exists a specific round $CR$ and a probabilistic non-uniform polynomial-time simulator $S$ for the ideal model such that for every probabilistic non-uniform polynomial-time real adversary $\mathcal{A}$ controlling party $P_i$ with $i \in \{1,2\}$:*

$$\Big\{ \text{IDEAL}^{CR}_{f,i,\mathcal{SA}}(x_1, x_2, z, n) \Big\}_{x_1,x_2,z\in\{0,1\}^*;n\in\mathbb{N}} \stackrel{\text{c}}{\equiv} \Big\{ \text{REAL}_{\pi,i,\mathcal{A}}(x_1, x_2, z, n) \Big\}_{x_1,x_2,z\in\{0,1\}^*;n\in\mathbb{N}}$$

*Feasibility of achieving an analogous definition without fairness.* We conclude this section by showing that a committal round in itself is not a barrier to achieving security, even for the case of no honest majority, as long as fairness is not also required. In order to see this, consider a modified version of Definition 1 which is exactly the same except that fairness is not guaranteed. In particular, the only difference is that in phase 2, $S$ receives the corrupted party's output first. Then, if $S$ sends abort to the trusted party, then the honest party does not receive the output (but rather $\perp$). In contrast, if $S$ sends continue to the trusted party, then the honest party does receive the actual output. We say that a protocol that achieves this definition is secure with a committal round but without fairness.

By observation of the simulator of the GMW two-party protocol [18] as described in [17, Chap. 7], we have that the simulator indeed can be separated into working in these two different phases. The first simulator works in the "input commitment" phase which essentially consists of each party committing to its input and proving a zero-knowledge proof of knowledge of the committed value. The simulator in this phase extracts the corrupted party's input from the proof of knowledge. Then, the second simulator simulates the rest of the protocol. We therefore have:

**Theorem 2.** *For every probabilistic polynomial-time two-party functionality $f$, there exists a protocol $\pi$ that securely computes $f$ with a committal round but without fairness. In particular, $\pi$ can be taken as the protocol of [17, 18].*

We remark that the protocol of [17, 18] is the rule and not the exception. Indeed, we do not know of *any* protocol that is not secure under this analogous definition that requires a committal round but does not require fairness (with the exception of the *fair* protocols of [20] and its extensions in [3, 4, 21] since they do not meet the committal round requirement).

## 3    Proof of Impossibility of Fairness

**Theorem 3.** *Let $f$ be a non-constant two-party function with a finite domain. Then there does not exist a protocol that securely computes $f$ with a committal round and fairness, as in Definition 1.*

*Proof.* We will use the notion of a protocol being "honest-correct" in the proof. We stress that this definition of correctness is very different to – and much weaker than – the standard notion. Specifically, when we say that a protocol is honest-correct, we mean that two *honest* parties running the protocol receive the correct output (the function computed on their prescribed inputs), and this does not say anything about the output of the honest party when one of the parties is malicious or halts before the end of the protocol.

**Definition 2.** *A protocol $\pi$ for computing a function $f$ is* honest-correct *if for every two inputs $x_1, x_2$ written on the input tapes of $P_1$ and $P_2$, respectively, the output of honest $P_1$ and honest $P_2$ running $\pi$ is $f(x_1, x_2)$, except with negligible probability.*

The proof of the theorem follows immediately from the following two lemmas. The first lemma states that in order to correctly compute the function, then there must be at least one round of communication after the committal round (formally, if there is no round after the committal round, then the protocol cannot be honest-correct). In contrast, the second lemma states that any protocol that is secure with a committal round and fairness can be truncated to the committal round and will still maintain honest-correctness. We therefore derive a contradiction.

**Lemma 1.** *Let $f$ be a non-constant two-party function, let $\pi$ be a protocol that securely computes $f$ with a committal round and fairness, and let $CR$ be the index of the committal round. Then, the protocol obtained by truncating $\pi$ to exactly $CR$ rounds is not honest-correct.*

*Proof.* This lemma relies on the assumption that $f$ is non-constant, since a constant function can be securely computed without any interaction. We prove the lemma by showing that since the simulator $\mathcal{S}$ receives the output only in the post-committal round phase, and after it outputs the view of $\mathcal{A}$ up to round $CR$, the view of the adversary in all rounds up to and including the $CR$ is independent of the output. Thus, there must be at least one additional round in the protocol beyond the $CR$ in order to obtain the correct output. Since the function being computed is non-constant, this implies either that the simulation is distinguishable from a real execution (which contradicts the assumed security) or that the protocol is not honest-correct (does not always provide even honest parties with the correct output based on their input). We now prove this formally.

Let $\pi'$ be the protocol $\pi$ truncated to round $CR$ (and including round $CR$). Assume, by contradiction, that $\pi'$ is honest-correct, as in Definition 2. If $f$ is non-constant then either there exist inputs $x_1, x_2, \tilde{x}_2$ such that $f(x_1, x_2) \neq f(x_1, \tilde{x}_2)$, or there exist inputs $x_1, \tilde{x}_1, x_2$ such that $f(x_1, x_2) \neq f(\tilde{x}_1, x_2)$. This holds since if $f$ is non-constant then there must be either a "row" or "column" in its function matrix with different values. Without loss of generality, assume that there exist $x_1, x_2, \tilde{x}_2$ such that $f(x_1, x_2) \neq f(x_1, \tilde{x}_2)$. Let $\mathcal{A}$ be an adversary attacking the non-truncated protocol $\pi$, who controls $P_1$ and runs $P_1$ honestly on input $x_1$, with the exception that it halts at round $CR$ and outputs whatever the protocol specifies it to output (as if the other party halted). By the contradicting assumption, $\mathcal{A}$ receives correct output by this round (where correct is defined by the honest party's input and by $\mathcal{A}$'s input; this is well defined since $\mathcal{A}$ behaves like an honest party in the truncated protocol $\pi'$).

Consider a real execution between $\mathcal{A}$ and $P_2$, where $P_2$ has input $x_2$. By the security of the non-truncated protocol $\pi$, we have

$$\left\{ \text{IDEAL}_{f,1,\mathcal{S}^{\mathcal{A}}}^{CR}(x_1, x_2, z, n) \right\}_{n \in \mathbb{N}} \overset{c}{\equiv} \left\{ \text{REAL}_{\pi,1,\mathcal{A}}(x_1, x_2, z, n) \right\}_{n \in \mathbb{N}}.$$

Likewise, in a real execution where $P_2$ has input $\tilde{x}_2$, the security of the protocol guarantees that

$$\left\{ \text{IDEAL}_{f,1,\mathcal{S}^{\mathcal{A}}}^{CR}(x_1, \tilde{x}_2, z, n) \right\}_{n \in \mathbb{N}} \overset{c}{\equiv} \left\{ \text{REAL}_{\pi,1,\mathcal{A}}(x_1, \tilde{x}_2, z, n) \right\}_{n \in \mathbb{N}}.$$

Consider now the truncation of the above distributions to include only the view of the adversary up until and including round $CR$. The truncation of these *ideal* distributions yields $\text{VIEW}_{\mathcal{S}^{\mathcal{A}}}^{1}(x_1, z, n)$ in both cases, and so are identical. This is due to the fact that $\mathcal{S}$'s view is identical in both cases because the output is received only after this part of the view is fixed. Denote by $\text{VIEW}_{\mathcal{A},\pi}(x_1, x_2, z, n)$ the view of $\mathcal{A}$ alone in the execution. Since $\mathcal{A}$ halts at round $CR$, we have

$$\left\{ \text{VIEW}_{\mathcal{S}^{\mathcal{A}}}^{1}(x_1, z, n) \right\}_{n \in \mathbb{N}} \overset{c}{\equiv} \left\{ \text{VIEW}_{\mathcal{A},\pi}(x_1, x_2, z, n) \right\}_{n \in \mathbb{N}}$$

and

$$\left\{ \text{VIEW}_{\mathcal{S}^{\mathcal{A}}}^{1}(x_1, z, n) \right\}_{n \in \mathbb{N}} \overset{c}{\equiv} \left\{ \text{VIEW}_{\mathcal{A},\pi}(x_1, \tilde{x}_2, z, n) \right\}_{n \in \mathbb{N}}.$$

Combining the above, we have

$$\left\{ \text{VIEW}_{\mathcal{A},\pi}(x_1, x_2, z, n) \right\}_{n \in \mathbb{N}} \overset{c}{\equiv} \left\{ \text{VIEW}_{\mathcal{A},\pi}(x_1, \tilde{x}_2, z, n) \right\}_{n \in \mathbb{N}}.$$

However, by the contradicting assumption, $\mathcal{A}$ receives correct output by round $CR$, and its view defines its output. Thus, the view with input $x_1, x_2$ defines the output $f(x_1, x_2)$ for $\mathcal{A}$, while the view with input $x_1, \tilde{x}_2$ defines the output $f(x_1, \tilde{x}_2)$ for $\mathcal{A}$. Since $f(x_1, x_2) \neq f(x_1, \tilde{x}_2)$, the distributions are easily distinguishable, in contradiction. This completes the proof.

We now proceed to prove the second lemma that states that a protocol that is secure with a committal round and fairness can actually be truncated to the committal round and remain honest-correct. Intuitively, this holds since in the ideal model the simulator must provide the input used by the corrupted party by the committal round. Now, since the output is determined at this point and cannot change, this implies that the honest party must always output the function computed on its own input and the input provided by the simulator (it can also never abort since the corrupted party already learned the output at the committal round). This in turn implies that the honest party must always output the same correct output in a real protocol execution, irrespective of where the corrupted party halts. In particular, it must hold even if the corrupted party halts immediately after the committal round. Formally, we prove this by showing that if correctness does not hold at the committal round, then there exists a specific round where it transitions from not holding to holding (clearly correctness holds for the full protocol $\pi$). Then, we show that a distinguisher can distinguish the real and ideal executions with an adversary that halts either at the round before the transition or at the transition. Note that the lemma does not hold for the case of multiparty computation with an honest majority; this is explained after the proof of the lemma.

**Lemma 2.** *Let $f$ be a two-party function with a finite domain, let $\pi$ be a protocol that securely computes $f$ with a committal round and fairness, and let $CR$ be the index of the committal round. Then, the protocol obtained by truncating $\pi$ to exactly $CR$ rounds is honest-correct.*

*Proof.* Denote by $\pi_0$ the protocol $\pi$ truncated to round $CR$, and denote by $\pi_\ell$ the protocol $\pi$ truncated to $\ell$ rounds *after* round $CR$. Let $m$ be the number of rounds in $\pi$ *after* the committal round and so $\pi_m = \pi$ (note that the total number of rounds in the protocol equals $CR + m$); clearly, $m$ is polynomial in the security parameter $n$. Recall that by our definition of the real model, in each round of interaction, exactly one party sends a message and the other waits to receive it. Without loss of generality, we assume that the first message after round $CR$ is from $P_1$ to $P_2$ (likewise all odd messages), and the second message after round $CR$ is from $P_2$ to $P_1$ (likewise all even messages). In addition, we assume that $m$ is even (if this is not true then just add a dummy message to $\pi$). In more detail, in protocol $\pi_\ell$, the parties output what $\pi$ specifies them to output in the event that the other party halts at this point. For example, if $P_1$ sends the last message in $\pi_\ell$, then $P_2$'s output in $\pi_\ell$ is the same as it would in $\pi$ in the case of an adversarial $P_1$ who halts after sending the $\ell$th message after $CR$. Observe that in this example, $P_1$'s output is the same in $\pi_\ell$ and $\pi_{\ell-1}$ since in both cases its last message received is from $P_2$ in the $(\ell - 1)$th round after $CR$. In contrast, $P_2$'s output *may* be different in these cases since its view is different.

Recall that by Definition 2, a protocol is honest-correct, if for *every* pair of inputs $x_1, x_2$ written on the parties' input tapes, their output when honestly running the protocol is $f(x_1, x_2)$, except with negligible probability. Observe that protocols $\pi_0, \ldots, \pi_m$ are fully specified and that we only consider executions of pairs of honest parties in these protocols. Thus, the notion of honest-correctness is well defined with respect to each $\pi_\ell$ (meaning that each of these protocols is either honest-correct or not honest-correct, and this is a property of the protocol alone).

We prove that $\pi_0$ is honest-correct. In order to see this, observe that $\pi_m$ is honest-correct since $\pi_m = \pi$ and $\pi$ is a secure protocol (since we consider here the case that both parties behave honestly, security in Definition 1 implies honest-correctness as in Definition 2). By contradiction, assume that $\pi_0$ is not honest-correct, meaning that there exist inputs so that at least one of the parties outputs an incorrect output in $\pi_0$ with non-negligible probability. Then, there exists a *maximal* index $\ell$ ($1 \leq \ell \leq m$) such that $\pi_\ell$ is honest-correct, but $\pi_{\ell-1}$ is not honest-correct.

Without loss of generality, let $P_1$ be the party who sends the message in the $\ell$th round. This implies that $P_1$'s view in $\pi_\ell$ and $\pi_{\ell-1}$ is identical, and thus its output is identical. However, since the protocol $\pi_{\ell-1}$ is not honest-correct, this in turn implies that $P_2$'s output is *correct* in $\pi_\ell$ (except with negligible probability) but *incorrect* in $\pi_{\ell-1}$ with non-negligible probability. By definition, $\pi_{\ell-1}$ being incorrect means that there exist some inputs $x_1, x_2$ such that in an execution of $\pi_{\ell-1}$ on these inputs, $P_2$ receives some output value $y' \neq f(x_1, x_2)$ with non-negligible probability. Recall that honest-correctness applies to *all* inputs, and thus its negation may apply only to a specific pair of inputs. Let $x_1, x_2$ be inputs for which $\pi_{\ell-1}$ is not honest-correct; concretely, this means that with non-negligible probability $P_2$ outputs $y' \neq f(x_1, x_2)$.

We first prove that in $\pi_{\ell-1}$, except with negligible probability, the output received by $P_2$ must be $f(\tilde{x}_1, x_2)$ for some $\tilde{x}_1$, where $x_2$ is the input written on $P_2$'s input tape. Intuitively this follows from the standard correctness property of secure protocols. Formally, in order to see this, we construct an adversary $\mathcal{A}$ who controls $P_1$ and interacts with an honest $P_2$ running $\pi$. $\mathcal{A}$ runs the protocol honestly with the exception that it halts after the $(\ell - 1)$th round, and in particular, does not send its message in the $\ell$th round. By the security of $\pi$, simulator $\mathcal{S}_1$ when run on adversary $\mathcal{A}$ outputs some $\tilde{x}_1$ as $P_1$'s input and it holds that the honest party's output in a real execution is indistinguishable from $f(\tilde{x}_1, x_2)$. Thus, $P_2$ must output $f(\tilde{x}_1, x_2)$ for some $\tilde{x}_1$.[5] (If this does not hold then the distinguisher can always distinguish since the function has a finite domain and so it can try all possible inputs for $P_1$ and see if $P_2$'s output is $f(\tilde{x}_1, x_2)$ for some $\tilde{x}_1$.)

By what we have shown so far, when $P_1$ and $P_2$ run on inputs $x_1$ and $x_2$, respectively, we have that $P_2$ outputs $f(x_1, x_2)$ in $\pi_\ell$, but with non-negligible probability outputs $f(\tilde{x}_1, x_2) \neq f(x_1, x_2)$ for some $\tilde{x}_1 \neq x_1$ in $\pi_{\ell-1}$. In contrast, in both $\pi_\ell$ and $\pi_{\ell-1}$, party $P_1$ has an identical view and thus has the same output. Since we know that $\pi_\ell$ is honest-correct, this implies that $P_1$ outputs $f(x_1, x_2)$ in both $\pi_\ell$ and $\pi_{\ell-1}$. We now show that this yields a contradiction. Before proceeding, we claim that there exist *specific* $x_1^*, x_2^*, \tilde{x}_1^*$ for which the above holds for infinitely many $n$'s. That is, we claim that there exist $x_1^*, x_2^*, \tilde{x}_1^*$, an infinite set of integers $N \subseteq \mathbb{N}$ and a polynomial $p(\cdot)$, such that when given inputs $x_1^*, x_2^*$, respectively, $P_1$ and $P_2$ output $f(x_1^*, x_2^*)$ in $\pi_\ell$ except with negligible probability and in particular with probability greater than $1 - \frac{1}{2p(n)}$. In contrast, $P_2$ outputs $f(\tilde{x}_1^*, x_2^*) \neq f(x_1^*, x_2^*)$ in $\pi_{\ell-1}$ with probability at least $\frac{1}{p(n)}$. This holds since $f$

---

[5] Note that this actually implies that $f$ is non-constant, since $f(\tilde{x}_1, x_2) = y' \neq f(x_1, x_2)$. Nevertheless, we do not need to assume this to prove this lemma (unlike Lemma 1), since this follows from the contradicting assumption.

has a finite domain: if $f$ had an infinite domain then it would be possible that for every $n$ there would exist a different pair of inputs for which the claim holds.[6]

Let $\mathcal{A}'$ be an adversary who controls $P_1$ and interacts with an honest $P_2$ with input $x_2^*$ in a real protocol execution of (the untruncated) protocol $\pi$. $\mathcal{A}'$ runs the honest party's instructions with input $x_1^*$ until the $(\ell - 1)$th round after $CR$. Then, $\mathcal{A}'$ applies a pseudorandom function (with a randomly chosen key taken from its random tape) to its view up to round $CR$ to determine if it sends the $\ell$th message. If the pseudorandom function's output is 0, then $\mathcal{A}'$ sends the $(CR + \ell)$th message to $P_2$ and halts; if the pseudorandom function's output is 1 then $\mathcal{A}'$ halts immediately in round $CR + \ell - 1$ and before it sends the $(CR + \ell)$th message. We stress that $S$ has only black-box access to $\mathcal{A}'$, and so cannot influence its input, auxiliary input and random-tape.[7]

We claim that $S$ fails in the simulation of $\mathcal{A}'$. In order to see this, we first replace the pseudorandom function used by $\mathcal{A}'$ by a truly random function. By a straightforward reduction, the output of $S$ with $\mathcal{A}'$ using a truly random function is computationally indistinguishable from when $\mathcal{A}'$ uses a pseudorandom function.

Next, observe that $S$ must send the corrupted $P_1$'s input to the trusted party in round $CR$ and thus before it can see whether $\mathcal{A}'$ sends its message in the $(CR + \ell)$th round or not. However, this determines whether $P_2$ outputs $f(x_1^*, x_2^*)$ or $f(\tilde{x}_1^*, x_2^*)$ in the real model. Thus, $S$ cannot know whether it should send $x_1^*$ or $\tilde{x}_1^*$ to the trusted party. We now formally prove this argument.

Let $D$ be a distinguisher who receives the output (including $\mathcal{A}'$'s view and $P_2$'s output) and runs $\mathcal{A}'$ on its view to see if $\mathcal{A}'$ aborts at round $CR + \ell$ or $CR + \ell - 1$. If $\mathcal{A}'$ aborts at round $CR + \ell$ and $P_2$'s output is $f(x_1^*, x_2^*)$ or if $\mathcal{A}'$ aborts at round $CR + \ell - 1$ and $P_2$'s output is $f(\tilde{x}_1^*, x_2^*)$ then $D$ outputs 1. Else, $D$ outputs 0. We now analyze the probability that $D$ outputs 1 in the real and ideal executions. Fix $n \in N$, where $N$ is the infinite set of integers specified above.

- *Real execution:* Recall that if $\mathcal{A}'$ proceeds to round $CR + \ell$ then $P_2$ outputs $f(x_1^*, x_2^*)$ with probability greater than $1 - 1/2p(n)$, whereas if $\mathcal{A}'$ halts at round $CR + \ell - 1$ then $P_2$ outputs $f(\tilde{x}_1^*, x_2^*)$ with probability at least $1/p(n)$. Furthermore, $\mathcal{A}'$ proceeds with probability $1/2$. We therefore have that for every $n \in N$:

$$\Pr[D \text{ outputs } 1] \geq \frac{1}{2} \cdot \left(1 - \frac{1}{2p(n)}\right) + \frac{1}{2} \cdot \frac{1}{p(n)} = \frac{1}{2} + \frac{1}{4p(n)}.$$

---

[6] We believe that the proof would still hold for the case of infinite domain by providing the inputs for which the claim holds as non-uniform advice to the adversary and distinguisher. However, this would needlessly complicate things.

[7] One could define a weaker type of black-box access where the simulator can provide these values as part of its query. However, this would make no difference since we would then define $\mathcal{A}'$ to ignore the input, auxiliary input and randomness and use hardwired values only.

– *Ideal execution:* The main observation here is that the probability that $P_2$ outputs $f(x_1^*, x_2^*)$ or $f(\tilde{x}_1^*, x_2^*)$ is *independent* of whether or not $\mathcal{A}'$ proceeds to round $CR + \ell$ or halts at $CR + \ell - 1$. This holds because $P_2$'s output is defined by the input provided by $\mathcal{S}$ and this is provided before $\mathcal{S}$ can know if $\mathcal{A}'$ halts in round $CR + \ell$ or $CR + \ell - 1$ since $\mathcal{S}$ can only send queries of length $CR$ to $\mathcal{A}'$ before sending the input. (Note that if $P_2$ outputs anything else then $D$ will output 0 and so this is not included in the calculation below.) Thus:

$$
\begin{aligned}
\Pr[D \text{ outputs } 1] &= \Pr[\mathcal{A}' \text{ halts at } CR + \ell \text{ and } P_2 \text{ outputs } f(x_1^*, x_2^*)] \\
&\quad + \Pr[\mathcal{A}' \text{ halts at } CR + \ell - 1 \text{ and } P_2 \text{ outputs } f(\tilde{x}_1^*, x_2^*)] \\
&= \Pr[\mathcal{A}' \text{ halts at } CR + \ell] \cdot \Pr[P_2 \text{ outputs } f(x_1^*, x_2^*)] \\
&\quad + \Pr[\mathcal{A}' \text{ halts at } CR + \ell - 1] \cdot \Pr[P_2 \text{ outputs } f(\tilde{x}_1^*, x_2^*)] \\
&= \frac{1}{2} \cdot \Pr[P_2 \text{ outputs } f(x_1^*, x_2^*)] + \frac{1}{2} \cdot \Pr[P_2 \text{ outputs } f(\tilde{x}_1^*, x_2^*)] \\
&= \frac{1}{2} \cdot \Big( \Pr[P_2 \text{ outputs } f(x_1^*, x_2^*)] + \Pr[P_2 \text{ outputs } f(\tilde{x}_1^*, x_2^*)] \Big) \\
&\leq \frac{1}{2}
\end{aligned}
$$

where the second equality is by the *independence* of probabilities explained above. We remark that in the last step, it is not equality since $P_2$ may output something else.

We have shown that for infinitely many $n$'s (for every $n \in N$), distinguisher $D$ distinguishes between the real and ideal executions with probability at least $1/4p(n)$. Thus, $D$ distinguishes with non-negligible probability, in contradiction to the assumed security of the protocol.

Lemmas 1 and 2 contradict each other therefore completing the proof of Theorem 3.

*The case of an honest majority.* In the setting of multiparty computation with an honest majority, our proof does not hold. This is due to the fact that our proof relies inherently on the fact that when the adversary halts, the honest party can receive no more information towards obtaining its output. Rather, its view until that halting point is all that it receives. (Formally, this can be seen in the proof of Lemma 2 where we say that $P_2$'s output changes if $\mathcal{A}$ halts in round $CR + \ell - 1$ or halts in round $CR + \ell$.) In contrast, when there is an honest majority, the honest parties may continue to exchange messages even if all corrupted parties halt.

*Semi-trivial functions.* Our proof holds for *all* non-constant functions, including functions $f$ that can be singlehandedly determined by one of the parties. In particular, consider a function $f$ such that for every $x_1$ and all $x_2, \tilde{x}_2$ it holds that $f(x_1, x_2) = f(x_1, \tilde{x}_2)$, meaning that $P_2$'s input is meaningless. Such a function *cannot* be securely computed with fairness under our definition with a committal round. However, observe that *all* such functions (with a polynomial-size domain) can be securely computed with fairness under Canetti's definition using a *trivial protocol* (in particular, the protocol of [20] is not required). Specifically, party $P_1$ can simply compute the output itself and send it to $P_2$. This protocol is fair since if $P_1$ does not send the output then $P_2$ can compute the function on its real input and a default input for $P_1$. (Note that $P_2$ must also check that the output is valid in that there exists such a value in the domain of $f$, and otherwise should also compute a default output. Since we consider finite-domain functions only here, $P_2$ can always do this.) More formally, a simulator under the definition of Canetti can obtain the value sent by a corrupted $P_1$ and simply find an input that leads to such an output (this is possible since the domain is polynomial-size). Furthermore, when $P_2$ is corrupted, the simulator just receives the output and simulates $P_1$ sending that value. Note that this protocol is not secure under our definition with a committal round: if the committal round is before $P_1$ sends the message then the simulator in the case that $P_1$ is corrupted cannot send the input to the trusted party, and if the committal round is after $P_1$ sends the message then the simulator in the case that $P_2$ is corrupted cannot simulate the first phase.

# References

1. Aggarwal, G., Mishra, N., Pinkas, B.: Secure computation of the $k^{th}$-ranked element. In: Cachin, C., Camenisch, J.L. (eds.) EUROCRYPT 2004. LNCS, vol. 3027, pp. 40–55. Springer, Heidelberg (2004). doi:10.1007/978-3-540-24676-3_3
2. Asokan, N., Schunter, M., Waidner, M.: Optimistic protocols for fair exchange. In: The 4th ACM Conference on Computer and Communications Security, pp. 8–17 (1997)
3. Asharov, G.: Towards characterizing complete fairness in secure two-party computation. In: Lindell, Y. (ed.) TCC 2014. LNCS, vol. 8349, pp. 291–316. Springer, Heidelberg (2014). doi:10.1007/978-3-642-54242-8_13
4. Asharov, G., Beimel, A., Makriyannis, N., Omri, E.: Complete characterization of fairness in secure two-party computation of boolean functions. In: Dodis, Y., Nielsen, J.B. (eds.) TCC 2015. LNCS, vol. 9014, pp. 199–228. Springer, Heidelberg (2015). doi:10.1007/978-3-662-46494-6_10
5. Asharov, G., Lindell, Y., Rabin, T.: A full characterization of functions that imply fair coin tossing and ramifications to fairness. In: Sahai, A. (ed.) TCC 2013. LNCS, vol. 7785, pp. 243–262. Springer, Heidelberg (2013). doi:10.1007/978-3-642-36594-2_14
6. Beaver, D.: Foundations of Secure Interactive Computing. In: Feigenbaum, J. (ed.) CRYPTO 1991. LNCS, vol. 576, pp. 377–391. Springer, Heidelberg (1992). doi:10.1007/3-540-46766-1_31
7. Beaver, D., Goldwasser, S.: Multiparty computation with faulty majority. In: 30th FOCS, pp. 468–473 (1989)
8. Ben-Or, M., Goldwasser, S., Wigderson, A.: Completeness theorems for non-cryptographic fault-tolerant distributed computation. In: 20th STOC, pp. 1–10 (1988)
9. Canetti, R.: Security and composition of multiparty cryptographic protocols. J. Cryptol. **13**(1), 143–202 (2000)

10. Canetti, R.: Universally Composable Security: A new paradigm for cryptographic protocols. In: 42nd FOCS, pp. 136–145 (2001). Full version http://eprint.iacr.org/2000/067

11. Canetti, R., Fischlin, M.: Universally composable commitments. In: Kilian, J. (ed.) CRYPTO 2001. LNCS, vol. 2139, pp. 19–40. Springer, Heidelberg (2001). doi:10.1007/3-540-44647-8_2

12. Canetti, R., Kushilevitz, E., Lindell, Y.: On the limitations of universal composable two-party computation without set-up assumptions. J. Crypt. 19(2), 135–167 (2006)

13. Chaum, D., Crépeau, C., Damgård, I.: Multi-party unconditionally secure protocols. In: 20th STOC, pp. 11–19 (1988)

14. Cleve, R.: Limits on the security of coin flips when half the processors are faulty. In: 18th STOC, pp. 364–369 (1986)

15. Dodis, Y., Micali, S.: Parallel reducibility for information-theoretically secure computation. In: Bellare, M. (ed.) CRYPTO 2000. LNCS, vol. 1880, pp. 74–92. Springer, Heidelberg (2000). doi:10.1007/3-540-44598-6_5

16. Goldreich, O.: Foundations of Cryptography: Basic Tools, vol. 1. Cambridge University Press, Cambridge (2001)

17. Goldreich, O.: Foundations of Cryptography: Basic Applications, vol. 2. Cambridge University Press, Cambridge (2004)

18. Goldreich, O., Micali, S., Wigderson, A.: How to play any mental game - a completeness theorem for protocols with honest majority. In: 19th STOC, pp. 218–229 (1987) For details see [17, Chap. 7]

19. Goldwasser, S., Levin, L.: Fair computation of general functions in presence of immoral majority. In: Menezes, A.J., Vanstone, S.A. (eds.) CRYPTO 1990. LNCS, vol. 537, pp. 77–93. Springer, Heidelberg (1991). doi:10.1007/3-540-38424-3_6

20. Gordon, S.D., Hazay, C., Katz, J., Lindell, Y.: Complete fairness in secure two-party computation. J. ACM 58(6), 24 (2011). An extended abstract appeared at the 40th STOC, pp. 413–422 (2008)

21. Gordon, S.D., Katz, J.: Complete fairness in multi-party computation without an honest majority. In: Reingold, O. (ed.) TCC 2009. LNCS, vol. 5444, pp. 19–35. Springer, Heidelberg (2009). doi:10.1007/978-3-642-00457-5_2

22. Micali, S.: Simple and fast optimistic protocols for fair electronic exchange. In: The 22nd PODC, pp. 12–19 (2003)

23. Micali, S., Rogaway, P.: Secure computation. In: Feigenbaum, J. (ed.) CRYPTO 1991. LNCS, vol. 576, pp. 392–404. Springer, Heidelberg (1992). doi:10.1007/3-540-46766-1_32

24. Rabin, T., Ben-Or, M.: Verifiable secret sharing and multiparty protocols with honest majority. In: The 21st STOC, pp. 73–85 (1989)

# Designing Fully Secure Protocols for Secure Two-Party Computation of Constant-Domain Functions

Vanesa Daza[1] and Nikolaos Makriyannis[2(✉)]

[1] Universitat Pompeu Fabra, Barcelona, Spain
vanesa.daza@upf.edu
[2] Tel Aviv University, Tel Aviv, Israel
n.makriyannis@gmail.com

**Abstract.** In a sense, a two-party protocol achieves fairness if the output from the computation is obtained simultaneously by both parties. A seminal result by Cleve (STOC 1986) states that fairness is impossible, in general. Surprisingly, Gordon et al. (JACM 2011) showed that there exist interesting functions that are computable with fairness. The two results give rise to a distinction between *fair* functions and *unfair* ones. The question of characterizing these functions has been studied in a sequence of works leading to the complete characterization of (symmetric) Boolean functions by Asharov et al. (TCC 2015). In this paper, we design new fully secure protocols for functions that were previously unknown to be fair. To this end, our main technical contribution is a generic construction of a fully secure (fair) protocol, starting with a constant-round protocol satisfying limited security requirements. Our construction introduces new conceptual tools for the analysis of fairness that apply to arbitrary (constant-domain) functions. While the characterization remains open, we believe that our results lay the foundation for a deeper understanding of fairness.

**Keywords:** Fairness · Secure two-party computation · Malicious adversaries · Cryptographic protocols

## 1 Introduction

A popular definition of two-party computation is that it enables two mutually distrusting parties to compute a joint function of their inputs while only revealing what the output suggests. However, the popular definition does not capture all the security requirements one may expect from such a computation. Among these requirements is *fairness*, which states that either both parties receive output or none of them do. It is a natural security requirement for many real-world tasks.

V. Daza—Research supported by Project TEC2015-66228-P (MINECO/FEDER, UE).
N. Makriyannis—Research supported by ERC starting grant 638121.

For example, when two parties are signing a contract, the contents of which may be legally binding, it is imperative that one party signs the contract if and only if the second party signs as well.

The study of two-party computation started with the work of Yao [14] in 1982. Secure computation was expanded to the multiparty case by Goldreich, Micali, and Wigderson [10] in 1987. Flagship results from the theory of secure computation state that, when an absolute majority of honest parties can be guaranteed, every task can be realized with full security, i.e. the relevant protocols provide correctness, privacy, independence of inputs, as well as fairness. However, when the honest parties are in the minority, as it happens in the important two-party case, classic protocols satisfy a weaker notion of security known as security-with-abort, which captures all the aforementioned security requirements, except for fairness. This relaxation is often attributed to an inherent limitation that was shown by Cleve [7].

Cleve showed that fairness is impossible to achieve in general when one of the parties behaves dishonestly. Specifically, Cleve proved that the coin-tossing functionality, i.e the inputless functionality that returns the same uniform random bit to the parties, is not computable with fairness. His proof exploits the fact that interactive computation involves exchanging messages back and forth, and thus at some point one party may break fairness by aborting prematurely. It goes without saying that any function that implies coin-tossing is not computable with fairness either, as is the case with the XOR function.

Amazingly, for more than two decades, Cleve's result led to the mistaken conclusion that interesting functions are not computable with fairness in the two-party setting, or the multi-party setting with dishonest majority. Only in 2008 was this interpretation proven false by Gordon, Hazay, Katz and Lindell [11], who showed that Cleve's impossibility does not apply to *all* non-trivial functions, and there are many interesting functions that are inherently *fair*. The remarkable work of Gordon et al. begins by making a distinction between XOR-embedded[1] and non XOR-embedded functions. Functions of the latter type, which includes OR and the greater-than function, are shown to be fair. Yet XOR-embedded functions are not necessarily excluded from fully secure computation. Gordon et al. propose a specific protocol, referred to as GHKL throughout the present paper, that computes many XOR-embedded functions with full security. The authors also show that fair computation of XOR-embedded functions requires super-logarithmic round complexity.

In this paper, we focus on the fundamental question raised by Gordon, Hazay, Katz and Lindell; the characterization of functions with respect to fairness. In particular, we propose a methodology for designing fully secure protocols.

## 1.1   Previous Works

The problem of characterizing fairness is equivalent to identifying a necessary and sufficient condition for a given two-party function to be fair. There are thus

---

[1] A function is XOR-embedded if restricting the function to a subset of inputs yields the XOR function.

two complementary ways to engage with the problem. The first one attempts to identify necessary conditions for fairness by means of impossibility results [1,4,7,13]. The second one attempts to identify sufficient conditions by means of feasibility results, i.e. by proving fairness for explicit protocols [2,3,11,13]. We mention that most of these works focus on fair computation of Boolean functions that are symmetric – the function returns the same output to both parties, deterministic – the output is fully determined by the inputs, and constant-domain – the function is independent of the security parameter. By abusing terminology, we refer to such functions simply as Boolean functions.

Necessary conditions can be traced back to Cleve's seminal work [7]. In [1], Agrawal and Prabhakaran generalized the impossibility of coin-tossing to nontrivial sampling functionalities, that is, inputless functionalities that return statistically correlated outputs are not computable with fairness. Asharov, Lindell, and Rabin [4] investigated the problem of characterizing Boolean functions that imply coin-tossing, and are thus inherently unfair. They showed that certain functions, dubbed *balanced*, can be used to toss a uniform random coin. Conversely, they found that coin-tossing is not reducible to any balanced function in the information theoretic-sense. Boolean functions that imply non-trivial sampling where identified by Makriyannis [13], who expanded the class of Boolean functions that are known to be unfair.

Regarding sufficient criteria, Gordon, Hazay, Katz and Lindell laid the foundation with [11], and all subsequent papers [2,3,13] on the topic are based on the GHKL protocol. By digging deep into the security analysis of the GHKL protocol, Asharov [2] deduced sufficient conditions for the protocol to compute functions with full security. Furthermore, the author showed that almost all Boolean functions with unequal-size domains satisfy these conditions, and thus a surprisingly large amount of functions are fair. Sufficient conditions for GHKL were also deduced independently by Makriyannis in [13].

Recently, Asharov, Beimel, Makriyannis and Omri [3] showed that a counter-intuitive modification of GHKL allows for the complete characterization of all Boolean functions. The characterization states that a Boolean function is computable with full security if and only if the all-one vector or the all-zero vector belong to the affine span of either the rows or the columns of the matrix describing the function. Remarkably, the characterization extends to randomized Boolean functions as well as multiparty Boolean functions when exactly half of the parties are corrupted.

Finally, we mention that Gordon and Katz [12] constructed a fully secure three-party protocol for the majority function and a $n$-party protocol for the AND of $n$ bits.

**Limits of the GHKL Approach.** While significant progress has been made towards characterizing fairness in secure computation, we argue that the methods that appear in the literature have reached their limits in terms of usefulness. Specifically, regarding the design of fully secure protocols for arbitrary functions, the "standard" approach of generalizing and modifying GHKL to extract sufficient conditions seems to offer few gains. Even for the limited case of Boolean functions that are not symmetric, straightforward generalizations of GHKL are either function-specific i.e. the resulting protocol is tailored to a specific function, or, the protocol computes a family of functions whose description is rather mysterious and artificial. Arguably, the present state of affairs calls for a systematic analysis of fair protocols.

## 1.2   Our Contributions

In this paper, we propose a framework for designing fully secure protocols. To this end, we introduce two new conceptual tools, refered to as *locking strategies* and *sampling attacks*, which are inspired by the impossibility results of [1, 4, 7, 13]. Our investigation naturally leads to a new security notion that we call *security against sampling attacks*; a strictly weaker notion than fairness and therefore a necessary requirement for fair protocols. An appealing feature of the proposed security notion is that it bypasses lower-bounds on fairness. Specifically, as was shown by Gordon et al. [11], fair functions may require computation in super-logarithmic round-complexity. In contrast, security against sampling attacks seems to be achievable in a constant number of rounds for the same functions. What's more, security against sampling attacks can be efficiently tested via a collection of linear algebraic properties. The appeal of our approach is further strengthened by our main result, stated next.

We propose a generic construction that transforms any protocol that is – constant-round – passively secure – secure against sampling attacks, into a fully-secure protocol. In the spirit of GHKL, this is achieved by introducing a special threshold round $i^*$. Our main result may be viewed as a framework for designing fair protocols, and we believe that it demystifies the "standard" approach that appears in the literature. What's more, it applies to any constant-domain two-party function (i.e. randomized, asymmetric and non-Boolean). Our main result is stated informally below.

**Theorem 1.1 (informal).** *A two-party function is fair if and only if it admits a suitable protocol that is secure against sampling attacks.*

Our techniques show the existence of a fair non-Boolean function where both parties have the same number of inputs. We stress that previous results [2] on non-Boolean functions only applied to functions where one party has at least twice as many inputs as the other.

**Theorem 1.2 (informal).** *The non-Boolean function described by the matrix below is computable with full security.*

| $f(x,y)$ | $y_1$ $y_2$ $y_3$ $y_4$ |
|----------|-------------------------|
| $x_1$    | 1    1    2    2        |
| $x_2$    | 1    0    1    2        |
| $x_3$    | 1    1    0    2        |
| $x_4$    | 2    2    0    2        |

Next, we propose an algorithm for designing suitable protocols (constant-round, passively secure, secure against sampling attacks). Our algorithm takes an asymmetric Boolean function as input, and it either returns an appropriate protocol, or it returns that it failed to do so. The algorithm is accompanied with a proof of correctness. In Sect. 5.3, we show how our algorithm handles the asymmetric function that was suggested as an open problem in [3], and we prove that it is fair.

**Theorem 1.3 (informal).** *The function from [3] described by the matrices below is computable with full security.*

| $f_1(x,y)$ | $y_1$ | $y_2$ | $y_3$ | $y_4$ |
|:---:|:---:|:---:|:---:|:---:|
| $x_1$ | 0 | 1 | 1 | 0 |
| $x_2$ | 1 | 0 | 1 | 1 |
| $x_3$ | 1 | 0 | 0 | 0 |
| $x_4$ | 0 | 1 | 0 | 1 |

| $f_2(x,y)$ | $y_1$ | $y_2$ | $y_3$ | $y_4$ |
|:---:|:---:|:---:|:---:|:---:|
| $x_1$ | 1 | 1 | 1 | 0 |
| $x_2$ | 1 | 0 | 1 | 1 |
| $x_3$ | 0 | 1 | 0 | 1 |
| $x_4$ | 1 | 1 | 0 | 0 |

Unfortunately, our methods do not settle the characterization of constant-domain two-party functions, even for the asymmetric Boolean case. That being said, we believe that the questions that are left unanswered may be as interesting as the results themselves. Specifically, for a function that lies in the gap, we show that it is computable with fairness as long as privacy is relaxed.

**Theorem 1.4 (informal).** *The function described by the matrices below admits a protocol that is fair-but-not-private.*

| $f_1(x,y)$ | $y_1$ | $y_2$ | $y_3$ | $y_4$ | $y_5$ |
|:---:|:---:|:---:|:---:|:---:|:---:|
| $x_1$ | 1 | 1 | 1 | 1 | 0 |
| $x_2$ | 0 | 1 | 0 | 1 | 1 |
| $x_3$ | 1 | 1 | 1 | 1 | 1 |
| $x_4$ | 0 | 0 | 1 | 0 | 1 |
| $x_5$ | 1 | 0 | 0 | 0 | 1 |

| $f_2(x,y)$ | $y_1$ | $y_2$ | $y_3$ | $y_4$ | $y_5$ |
|:---:|:---:|:---:|:---:|:---:|:---:|
| $x_1$ | 1 | 1 | 0 | 0 | 0 |
| $x_2$ | 1 | 0 | 0 | 0 | 1 |
| $x_3$ | 1 | 0 | 0 | 1 | 0 |
| $x_4$ | 0 | 0 | 1 | 1 | 1 |
| $x_5$ | 0 | 1 | 0 | 1 | 0 |

We emphasize that the function in question may still be computable with full security. However, we believe that our present analysis together with the theorem above strongly indicate that there is an inherent trade-off between fairness and privacy. To the best of our knowledge, the literature does not entertain the idea that fairness and privacy may be attainable only at the expense of one another; the two notions might as well be incomparable.

**Organization of the Paper.** After recalling some preliminaries in Sect. 2, we introduce locking strategies and sampling attacks in Sect. 3. Section 4 is dedicated to our main result and its proof. In Sect. 5, we show how to obtain suitable protocols by means of the algorithm mentioned above. Finally, open problems and future directions are discussed in Sect. 6.

For clarity, and to alleviate notation, we have decided to restrict our analysis to the family of asymmetric (possibly randomized) Boolean functions.

We emphasize that, with the exception of Sect. 5, our results generalize to arbitrary non-Boolean functions. While the generalization is not straightforward, it is beyound the scope of the present abstract. We refer to the full version [8] for the general case.

## 2  Preliminaries

Throughout this paper, $n$ denotes the security parameter and $\mathbb{N}$ denotes the set of positive integers. All vectors are column vectors over the real field $\mathbb{R}$. Vectors are denoted using bold letters, e.g. $\mathbf{v}$, $\mathbf{1}$ (the all-one vector). The $i$-th entry of some vector $\mathbf{v}$ is denoted $\mathbf{v}(i)$. If $\mathbf{v}_1, \ldots, \mathbf{v}_s$ denotes a family of vectors, then $\langle \mathbf{v}_1, \ldots, \mathbf{v}_s \rangle$ denotes the vector space generated by those vectors, and let $\langle \mathbf{v}_i \mid \mathbf{v}_j \rangle = \mathbf{v}_i^T \mathbf{v}_j$. Matrices are denoted with capital letters, e.g. $M$, $P$. The $i$-th row and $j$-th column of some matrix $M$ are denoted $[M]_{i,*}$ and $[M]_{*,j}$, respectively. Furthermore, the element indexed by $(i, j)$ in $M$ is denoted $M(i, j)$.

**Definition 2.1.** Let $A$ and $B$ be arbitrary matrices. We write $C = A * B$ if $C$ is equal to the entry-wise (Hadamard) product of the two matrices, i.e. $C(i, j) = A(i, j) \cdot B(i, j)$.

Finally, if $\mathcal{X}$ and $\mathcal{Y}$ denote distribution ensembles, we write $\mathcal{X} = \mathcal{Y}$, $\mathcal{X} \overset{s}{\equiv} \mathcal{Y}$ and $\mathcal{X} \overset{c}{\equiv} \mathcal{Y}$, respectively, if the ensembles are perfectly, statistically or computationally indistinguishable.

### 2.1  Secure Two-Party Computation

Let $P_1$ and $P_2$ denote the parties. A *two-party function* $f = (f_1, f_2)$ is a random process that maps pair of inputs (one for each party), to pairs of random variables called outputs (again, one for each party). The domain of $f$ is denoted $X \times Y$. For our purposes, we assume that $X = \{1, \ldots, \ell\}$, $Y = \{1, \ldots, k\}$ and the parties' outputs are sampled from $\{0, 1\}^2$. To every function $f$, we associate four matrices $\{M^{(a,b)}\}_{a,b \in \{0,1\}}$ such that

$$M^{(a,b)}(x, y) = \Pr\left[f(x, y) = (a, b)\right].$$

In addition, define $M^{(1,*)}$ and $M^{(*,1)}$, associated with $f_1$ and $f_2$ respectively, such that $M^{(1,*)}(x, y) = \Pr\left[f_1(x, y) = 1\right]$ and $M^{(*,1)}(x, y) = \Pr\left[f_2(x, y) = 1\right]$. A two-party protocol $\Pi$ for computing $f$ is a polynomial-time protocol such that, on global input $1^n$ (the security parameter) and private inputs $x \in X$, $y \in Y$, the joint distribution of the outputs $\{\Pi(1^n, x, y)\}_n$ is statistically close $(f_1, f_2)(x, y)$, assuming both parties behave honestly. The parties run in polynomial-time in $n$.

**The Adversary.** We introduce an adversary $\mathcal{A}$ given auxiliary input $z \in \{0, 1\}^*$ corrupting one of the parties. We assume the adversary is computationally bounded and malicious, i.e. the adversary runs in polynomial-time in $n$ and she may instruct the corrupted party to deviate from the protocol arbitrarily.

---

**The Fully-Secure Model**

- **Inputs:** $P_1$ is holding $1^n$ and $x \in X$, $P_2$ is holding $1^n$ and $y \in Y$. The adversary is given auxiliary input $z \in \{0,1\}^*$. The trusted has no input.
- **Parties send inputs:** The honest party sends his input to the trusted party. The corrupted party sends a value of the adversary's choice. Write $(x', y')$ for the pair of values received by the trusted party.
- **Trusted party performs computation:** If either $x'$ or $y'$ is not in the appropriate domain, the trusted party reassigns the aberrant input to some default value. Write $(x', y')$ for the pair of inputs after (possible) reassignment. The trusted party chooses a random string $r \in \{0,1\}^*$ and computes $f(x, y; r)$.
- **Parties receive outputs:** $P_1$ receives $f_1(x, y; r)$, $P_2$ receives $f_2(x, y; r)$.
- **Outputs:** The honest party outputs whatever he received for the trusted party, the corrupted party outputs nothing, the adversary outputs a probabilistic polynomial-time function of its view.

---

**Fig. 1.** The ideal model with full-security for computing $f$.

Write $(\mathsf{out}, \mathsf{view})^{\mathsf{Real}}_{\mathcal{A}(z),\Pi}$ for the pair consisting of the honest party's output and the adversary's view in an execution of protocol $\Pi$. Next, we define security in terms of the ideal model.

Let $\mathcal{S}$ denote the ideal-world adversary. Write $(\mathsf{out}, \mathsf{view})^{\mathsf{Ideal}}_{\mathcal{S}(z),f}$ for the pair consisting of the honest party's output and the adversary's view in the ideal model (Fig. 1).

**Definition 2.2.** Let $\Pi$ be a protocol for computing $f$. We say that $\Pi$ is fully secure if for every non-uniform polynomial time adversary $\mathcal{A}$ in the real model, there exists a non-uniform polynomial time adversary $\mathcal{S}$ in the ideal model such that

$$\left\{ (\mathsf{out}, \mathsf{view})^{\mathsf{Real}}_{\mathcal{A}(z),\Pi}(1^n, x, y) \right\}_{n \in \mathbb{N}, (x,y) \in X \times Y, z \in \{0,1\}^*}$$
$$\stackrel{c}{\equiv} \left\{ (\mathsf{out}, \mathsf{view})^{\mathsf{Ideal}}_{\mathcal{S}(z),f}(1^n, x, y) \right\}_{n \in \mathbb{N}, (x,y) \in X \times Y, z \in \{0,1\}^*}.$$

It is important to note that the only way for the ideal-world adversary to affect the honest party's output is through the choice of input. Finally, we remark that the fully-secure model is the standard model for the honest-majority multi-party setting.

**The Hybrid Model.** The hybrid model with ideal access to $\mathcal{F}$ is a communication model where the parties have access to a trusted computing some functionality $\mathcal{F}$ with full security. In this model, the parties communicate as in the plain model and they are allowed to make a single call to the trusted party for computing $\mathcal{F}$. Protocols and security for this communication model are defined along the same lines as above. By [6], as long as $\mathcal{F}$ admits a secure real-world protocol, the existence of a secure hybrid protocol for $f$ implies the existence of a secure protocol for $f$ in the real model. By contraposition, if $f$ cannot be realized securely, then the existence of a secure protocol for $f$ in the hybrid model implies the impossibility of realizing $\mathcal{F}$ securely in the real model.

**The Dealer Model.** Throughout the paper, we define protocols by describing the number of rounds $r(n)$ and the *backup outputs* $\{a_i\}_{i=0}^r$ for $P_1$ and $\{b_i\}_{i=0}^r$ for $P_2$. When executing a protocol, the parties hand their inputs to an entity called the *dealer*. In turn, the dealer performs all the computations and hands the relevant backup outputs to $P_1$ and then $P_2$ in a sequence of $r(n)$ iterations. Either party may abort the execution at any time and the protocol terminates at that point. The remaining party is instructed to output the last backup output he received. This approach is known as the *online dealer model*, and it does not incur any loss of generality as there is a standard transformation from the online dealer model to the plain model [2,3,5]. The online dealer model is convenient in that it provides clarity to our presentation and it greatly simplifies the security analysis.

## 3    Locking Strategies and Sampling Attacks

In this section, we introduce the notions of locking strategies and sampling attacks. To motivate our discussion, we use specific functions from the literature as illustrative examples. Namely, the XOR function encoded by matrices

$$M^{(1,*)} = M^{(*,1)} = \begin{pmatrix} 0 & 1 \\ 1 & 0 \end{pmatrix},$$

the function $f^{nm}$ from [13] encoded by matrices

$$M^{(1,*)} = M^{(*,1)} = \begin{pmatrix} 0 & 1 & 0 & 1 \\ 1 & 1 & 1 & 0 \\ 0 & 0 & 1 & 0 \\ 1 & 0 & 0 & 0 \end{pmatrix},$$

the function $f^{sp}$ from [3] encoded by matrices

$$M^{(1,*)} = \begin{pmatrix} 1 & 1 & 1 & 0 \\ 0 & 0 & 0 & 1 \\ 1 & 0 & 0 & 1 \\ 0 & 1 & 0 & 1 \end{pmatrix}, \quad M^{(*,1)} = \begin{pmatrix} 1 & 0 & 1 & 0 \\ 1 & 0 & 0 & 1 \\ 1 & 0 & 0 & 0 \\ 0 & 1 & 1 & 1 \end{pmatrix}.$$

We remark that since the functions above are deterministic, the corresponding matrices fully describe these functions. In addition, we note that $f^{sp}$ is computable with fairness [3], while XOR and $f^{nm}$ are not [7,13]. Next, we briefly discuss why that is the case.

## 3.1   Warm-Up

It is not hard to see that a fully-secure realization of XOR yields a fully-secure coin-toss. Indeed, by instructing the parties to choose their inputs uniformly at random, the output from a fully-secure computation of XOR is uniformly distributed, even in the presence of malicious adversaries. A slightly more involved procedure allows the parties to sample correlated bit, using a fully-secure protocol for $f^{nm}$. Indeed, instruct $P_1$ to choose his input among $\{x_1, x_3, x_4\}$ with uniform probability, instruct $P_2$ to choose $y_4$ with probability $2/5$ or one of his other inputs with probability $1/5$. Let $c$ denote the the output from the computation of $f^{nm}$. Party $P_1$ outputs $c$, party $P_2$ outputs $1 - c$ if he chose $y_2$ and $c$ otherwise.

For us, it is important to note that the procedures described above are encoded by certain vectors. For XOR, these vectors are $(1/2, 1/2)$ for $P_1$ and $(1/2, 1/2)$ for $P_2$. For $f^{nm}$, they are $(1/3, 0, 1/3, 1/3)$ for $P_1$ and $(1/5, -1/5, 1/5, 2/5)$ for $P_2$. To elaborate further, each vector instructs the relevant party how to choose its input (by taking the absolute value) and whether to flip the output from the computation of the function (negative values indicate that the party must flip the output). Observe that

$$(1/2, 1/2) \cdot \begin{pmatrix} 0 & 1 \\ 1 & 0 \end{pmatrix} \in \langle \mathbf{1}_2^T \rangle, \qquad \begin{pmatrix} 0 & 1 \\ 1 & 0 \end{pmatrix} \begin{pmatrix} 1/2 \\ 1/2 \end{pmatrix} \in \langle \mathbf{1}_2 \rangle,$$

and

$$(1/3, 0, 1/3, 1/3) \begin{pmatrix} 0 & 1 & 0 & 1 \\ 1 & 1 & 1 & 0 \\ 0 & 0 & 1 & 0 \\ 1 & 0 & 0 & 0 \end{pmatrix} \in \langle \mathbf{1}_4^T \rangle, \qquad \begin{pmatrix} 0 & 1 & 0 & 1 \\ 1 & 1 & 1 & 0 \\ 0 & 0 & 1 & 0 \\ 1 & 0 & 0 & 0 \end{pmatrix} \cdot \begin{pmatrix} 1/5 \\ -1/5 \\ 1/5 \\ 2/5 \end{pmatrix} \in \langle \mathbf{1}_4 \rangle.$$

The relations above capture the fact that the procedure encoded by the vector yields an output whose distribution is independent of the opponent's input, i.e. $P_i$'s output resulting from the procedure is independent of $P_{3-i}$'s choice of input, assuming the underlying function is computed with full security. It is straightforward to check that the parties' outputs exhibit statistical correlation, and thus the functions in question are not computable with full-security, by [1, 7].

On the other hand, it is interesting to note that similar vectors and procedures can be defined for function $f^{sp}$. Specifically, observe that

$$(1/2, 1/2, 0, 0) \begin{pmatrix} 1 & 1 & 1 & 0 \\ 0 & 0 & 0 & 1 \\ 1 & 0 & 0 & 1 \\ 0 & 1 & 0 & 1 \end{pmatrix} \in \langle \mathbf{1}_4^T \rangle, \qquad \begin{pmatrix} 1 & 0 & 1 & 0 \\ 1 & 0 & 0 & 1 \\ 1 & 0 & 0 & 0 \\ 0 & 1 & 1 & 1 \end{pmatrix} \cdot \begin{pmatrix} 1/2 \\ 1/2 \\ 0 \\ 0 \end{pmatrix} \in \langle \mathbf{1}_4 \rangle.$$

In more detail, by choosing one of their first two inputs uniformly at random, the outputs from a fully-secure computation of $f^{sp}$ are uniformly random, even in the presence of malicious adversaries. However, contrary to the previous cases, the parties' outputs are independent as random variables.

## 3.2   Locking Strategies

For an arbitrary function $f$, let $\mathcal{L}_2$ denote a basis of the vector space consisting of all vectors $\mathbf{y}$ such that $M^{(*,1)} \cdot \mathbf{y} \in \langle \mathbf{1}_\ell \rangle$. Similarly, let $\mathcal{L}_1$ denote a basis of the vector space consisting of all vectors $\mathbf{x}$ such that $M^{(1,*)T} \cdot \mathbf{x} \in \langle \mathbf{1}_k \rangle$.

**Definition 3.1.** Elements of $\langle \mathcal{L}_1 \rangle$ and $\langle \mathcal{L}_2 \rangle$ are referred to as *locking strategies* for $P_1$ and $P_2$, respectively.

As discussed above, a locking strategy (after normalization) encodes a distribution over the inputs and a local transformation that depends on the chosen input. Since $M^{(*,1)} \cdot \mathbf{y} \in \langle \mathbf{1}_\ell \rangle$ and $M^{(1,*)T} \cdot \mathbf{x} \in \langle \mathbf{1}_k \rangle$, it follows that the parties' outputs resulting from the locking strategies are independent of each others' inputs, assuming ideal access to $f$. In loose terms, a party applying some locking strategy "locks" the distribution of its output.

For us, it is important to note that fully-secure protocols "preserve" locking strategies, even in the presence of malicious adversaries. Specifically, the distribution of the honest party's output resulting from some locking strategy is independent of the adversary's course of action (e.g. premature abort). We elaborate on this point next.

## 3.3   Sampling Attacks

Consider the following single-round protocol for $f^{\text{sp}} = (f_1, f_2)$ defined by means of the backup outputs $\{a_i, b_i\}_{i=0,1}$:

$$a_0 = f_1(x, \widetilde{y}) \text{ where } \widetilde{y} \in_U Y \qquad b_0 = f_2(\widetilde{x}, y) \text{ where } \widetilde{x} \in_U X$$
$$a_1 = f_1(x, y) \qquad\qquad b_1 = f_2(x, y)$$

Suppose that party $P_2$ applies locking strategy $\mathbf{y} = (1/2, 1/2, 0, 0)^T$. Notice that in an honest execution of $\Pi$, party $P_2$ outputs a uniform random bit. Now, suppose that an adversary corrupting $P_1$ uses $x_3$ for the computation, and aborts the computation prematurely if $a_1 = 0$ (In that case $P_2$ outputs $b_0$). Deduce that the honest party outputs 1 with probability 3/4 and thus the protocol is not fully-secure.

On the other hand, consider the following two-round protocol $\Pi^{\text{sp}}$ for $f^{\text{sp}}$ defined by means of the backup outputs $\{a_i, b_i\}_{i=0...2}$:

$$a_0 = f_1(x, \widetilde{y}) \text{ where } \widetilde{y} \in_U Y \qquad\qquad b_0 = f_2(\widetilde{x}, y) \text{ where } \widetilde{x} \in_U X$$
$$a_1 = \begin{cases} f_1(x, y) & \text{if } x \in \{x_1, x_2\} \\ f_1(x, \widetilde{y}') \text{ where } \widetilde{y}' \in_U Y & \text{if } x \in \{x_3, x_4\} \end{cases} \qquad b_1 = f_2(x, y)$$
$$a_2 = f_1(x, y) \qquad\qquad b_2 = f_2(x, y)$$

Already, we see that the attack described above will not work for this protocol. In fact, a straightforward analysis shows that it is impossible to alter the distribution of the honest party's output resulting from a locking strategy, both for $P_1$ and $P_2$. To see that, let $\widehat{b}_j$ (resp. $\widehat{a}_j$) denote the bit obtained from $b_j$

(resp. $a_j$) by applying some locking strategy, and observe that the random variables $\widehat{b}_{i-1}$ and $\widehat{b}_2$ (resp. $\widehat{a}_i$ and $\widehat{a}_2$) conditioned on the adversary's view at round $i$ are identically distributed. For similar attacks on arbitrary protocols and functions, security is captured by the definition below.

**Definition 3.2.** Let $\Pi$ be an arbitrary protocol defined by means of its backup outputs $\{a_i, b_i\}_{i \in \{0, \ldots, r\}}$. We say that $\Pi$ is secure against sampling attacks if

- for every $i \le r$, for every $x \in X$, for every $\mathbf{y} \in \langle \mathcal{L}_2 \rangle$, it holds that the random sequences $(a_0, \ldots, a_i, \widehat{b}_{i-1})$ and $(a_0, \ldots, a_i, \widehat{b}_r)$ are statistically close.
- for every $i \le r$, for every $y \in Y$, for every $\mathbf{x} \in \langle \mathcal{L}_1 \rangle$, it holds that the random sequences $(b_1, \ldots, b_i, \widehat{a}_i)$ and $(b_1, \ldots, b_i, \widehat{a}_r)$ are statistically close.

*Remark 3.3.* Rather awkwardly, we define security against sampling attacks without defining sampling attacks. For the purposes of the present abstract, sampling attacks are simply fail-stop attacks with the intent of altering the distribution of the honest party's output resulting from some locking strategy. Furthermore, we note that Definition 3.2 is information-theoretic. We remark that this is probably too strong. However, since the protocols we will consider are constant-round, it does not affect our analysis.

### 3.3.1  Sampling Attacks in Linear-Algebraic Terms

In this section, we show how security against sampling attacks can be expressed in linear-algebraic terms. First, we define closeness for vectors. Let $\{\mathbf{v}_n\}_{n \in \mathbb{N}}$ and $\{\mathbf{u}_n\}_{n \in \mathbb{N}}$ denote two families of vectors indexed by $\mathbb{N}$. We say that $\mathbf{v}_n$ is *close* to $\mathbf{u}_n$ if $\|\mathbf{u}_n - \mathbf{v}_n\| \le \mathsf{negl}(n)$. By abusing notation, we write $\mathbf{u}_n \stackrel{s}{\equiv} \mathbf{v}_n$ if the vectors are close.

**Definition 3.4.** For every $i \le r$, for every $\vec{\alpha}_i = (\alpha_1, \ldots, \alpha_i) \in \{0, 1\}^i$, and every $\beta \in \{0, 1\}$, define matrices $B_-^{(\vec{\alpha}_i, \beta)}$, $B_+^{(\vec{\alpha}_i, \beta)} \in \mathbb{R}^{\ell \times k}$ such that

$$B_-^{(\vec{\alpha}_i, \beta)}(x, y) = \Pr\left[(\vec{a}_i, b_{i-1})(x, y) = (\vec{\alpha}_i, \beta)\right]$$
$$B_+^{(\vec{\alpha}_i, \beta)}(x, y) = \Pr\left[(\vec{a}_i, b_r)(x, y) = (\vec{\alpha}_i, \beta)\right].$$

Similarly, for every $\vec{\beta}_i = (\beta_1, \ldots, \beta_i) \in \{0, 1\}^i$ and every $\alpha \in \{0, 1\}$ define matrices $A_-^{(\alpha, \vec{\beta}_i)}$, $A_+^{(\alpha, \vec{\beta}_i)} \in \mathbb{R}^{\ell \times k}$ such that

$$A_-^{(\alpha, \vec{\beta}_i)}(x, y) = \Pr\left[(a_i, \vec{b}_i)(x, y) = (\alpha, \vec{\beta}_i)\right]$$
$$A_+^{(\alpha, \vec{\beta}_i)}(x, y) = \Pr\left[(a_r, \vec{b}_i)(x, y) = (\alpha, \vec{\beta}_i)\right].$$

**Proposition 3.5.** *Protocol $\Pi$ is secure against sampling attacks if and only if*

- *for every* $\mathbf{y} \in \langle \mathcal{L}_2 \rangle$, *for every* $i \leq r$, *for every* $\vec{\alpha}_i \in \{0,1\}^i$, *the vector below is close to* $\mathbf{0}_\ell$.

$$\left( B_+^{(\vec{\alpha}_i, 1)} - B_-^{(\vec{\alpha}_i, 1)} \right) \cdot \mathbf{y}. \tag{1}$$

- *for every* $\mathbf{x} \in \langle \mathcal{L}_1 \rangle$, *for every* $i \leq r$, *for every* $\vec{\beta}_i \in \{0,1\}^i$, *the vector below is close to* $\mathbf{0}_k$.

$$\left( A_+^{(1, \vec{\beta}_i)T} - A_-^{(1, \vec{\beta}_i)T} \right) \cdot \mathbf{x}. \tag{2}$$

For example, for protocol $\Pi^{\mathsf{sp}}$, the distributions of $(a_1, b_0)$ and $(a_1, b_2)$ is given by the following matrices.

$$B_-^{(0,1)} = \begin{pmatrix} 0 & 0 & 0 & 1/2 \\ 3/4 & 1/4 & 1/2 & 0 \\ 3/8 & 1/8 & 1/4 & 1/4 \\ 3/8 & 1/8 & 1/4 & 1/4 \end{pmatrix}, \qquad B_+^{(0,1)} = \begin{pmatrix} 0 & 0 & 0 & 0 \\ 1 & 0 & 0 & 0 \\ 1/2 & 0 & 0 & 0 \\ 0 & 1/2 & 1/2 & 1/2 \end{pmatrix}$$

$$B_-^{(1,1)} = \begin{pmatrix} 3/4 & 1/4 & 1/2 & 0 \\ 0 & 0 & 0 & 1/2 \\ 3/8 & 1/8 & 1/4 & 1/4 \\ 3/8 & 1/8 & 1/4 & 1/4 \end{pmatrix}, \qquad B_+^{(1,1)} = \begin{pmatrix} 1 & 0 & 1 & 0 \\ 0 & 0 & 0 & 1 \\ 1/2 & 0 & 0 & 0 \\ 0 & 1/2 & 1/2 & 1/2 \end{pmatrix}.$$

Similarly, the distributions of $(a_1, b_1)$ and $(a_2, b_1)$ is given by the following matrices.

$$A_-^{(0,1)} = \begin{pmatrix} 0 & 1 & 0 & 0 \\ 0 & 0 & 0 & 0 \\ 0 & 1/2 & 1/2 & 1/2 \\ 1/2 & 0 & 0 & 0 \end{pmatrix}, \qquad A_+^{(0,1)} = \begin{pmatrix} 0 & 1 & 0 & 0 \\ 0 & 0 & 0 & 0 \\ 0 & 0 & 0 & 1 \\ 0 & 0 & 0 & 0 \end{pmatrix}$$

$$A_-^{(1,1)} = \begin{pmatrix} 1 & 0 & 1 & 0 \\ 0 & 0 & 0 & 1 \\ 1/2 & 0 & 0 & 0 \\ 0 & 1/2 & 1/2 & 1/2 \end{pmatrix}, \qquad A_+^{(1,1)} = \begin{pmatrix} 1 & 0 & 1 & 0 \\ 0 & 0 & 0 & 1 \\ 1 & 0 & 0 & 0 \\ 0 & 1 & 0 & 1 \end{pmatrix}.$$

Notice that the matrices above satisfy Proposition 3.5.

## 4   Towards Full Security

In this section, we show that constant-round protocols that satisfy passive security *and* security against sampling attacks are easily transformed into fully secure protocols. The present section is dedicated to the construction and its security proof. Let $\Pi$ be a protocol for computing $f$. We model the protocol in the usual way. The parties' backup outputs for $\Pi$ will be denoted $(c_0, \ldots, c_{r'})$ and $(d_0, \ldots, d_{r'})$, respectively, where $r'$ denotes the number of rounds.

**Assumption on the round-complexity.** We assume that $r'$ is *constant* in the security parameter. This assumption is desirable for for the proof of our main theorem, and it is good enough for our purposes. Nevertheless, the question of determining the optimal round complexity for protocols that are passively secure and secure against sampling attacks may be of independent interest.

We assume that the protocol is passively secure. Therefore, there exist simulators, denoted $\{S_i^p\}_{i \in \{1,2\}}$, that can recreate the backup sequences in the ideal model. In addition, since the protocol is constant-round, it follows that the ideal sequences are statistically close to the real ones. Formally,

$$(c_0, \ldots, c_{r'}, d_{r'})^{\mathsf{Real}} \stackrel{s}{\equiv} (c_0, \ldots, c_{r'}, f_2)^{\mathsf{Ideal}}$$
$$(d_0, \ldots, d_{r'}, c_{r'})^{\mathsf{Real}} \stackrel{s}{\equiv} (d_0, \ldots, d_{r'}, f_1)^{\mathsf{Ideal}}.$$

Finally, we assume that $\Pi$ is secure against sampling attacks. Theorem 3.5 applies to $\Pi$ in a very straightforward way. Using the notation from the previous section,

- For every $\mathbf{y} \in \langle \mathcal{L}_2 \rangle$, for every $i = 1, \ldots, r'$, for every $\vec{\alpha}_i \in \{0,1\}^{i+1}$, the vector below is close $\mathbf{0}_\ell$.

$$\left( B_+^{(\vec{\alpha}_i, 1)} - B_-^{(\vec{\alpha}_i, 1)} \right) \cdot \mathbf{y}. \tag{3}$$

- For every $\mathbf{x} \in \langle \mathcal{L}_1 \rangle$, for every $i = 0, \ldots, r'-1$, for every $\vec{\beta}_i \in \{0,1\}^{i+1}$, the vector below is close to $\mathbf{0}_k$.

$$\left( A_+^{(1, \vec{\beta}_i)T} - A_-^{(1, \vec{\beta}_i)T} \right) \cdot \mathbf{x}. \tag{4}$$

## 4.1   Protocol $\textsc{SecSamp2Fair}(\Pi)$

We are going to *combine* the main ingredient of the GHKL protocol – the threshold round $i^*$ – with the protocol above. Specifically, we are going to instruct the parties to run a protocol such that, at some point in the execution, unbeknownst to them, the parties begin running $\Pi$.

This is achieved by choosing a random threshold round according to a geometric distribution. Prior to that round, the parties exchange backup outputs that are independent of each other, and, once the threshold round has been reached, the parties exchange backups according to the specifications of $\Pi$. Formally, consider protocol $\textsc{SecSamp2Fair}(\Pi)$ from Fig. 2. For the new protocol, $i^* \geq r' + 1$ is chosen according to a geometric distribution with parameter $\gamma$. If $i < i^* - r'$, then $a_i$ and $b_i$ are independent of one another. If $i^* - r' \leq i < i^*$, then $a_i$ and $b_i$ are equal to $c_{i-i^*+r'}$ and $d_{i-i^*+r'}$, respectively. Finally, if $i \geq i^*$, then $(a_i, b_i) = (c_{r'}, d_{r'}) \stackrel{s}{\equiv} (f_1, f_2)$.

---

**Protocol** SecSamp2Fair($\Pi$)

1. The parties $P_1$ and $P_2$ hand their inputs, denoted $x$ and $y$ respectively, to the dealer.[a]
2. The dealer executes $\Pi$ locally on inputs $x$ and $y$ and security parameter $n$. Write $(c_0, \ldots, c_{r'})$ and $(d_0, \ldots, d_{r'})$ for the sequences of backup outputs computed by the dealer.
3. The dealer chooses $i^* \geq r' + 1$ according to the geometric distribution with parameter $\gamma$.
4. The dealer computes $(\mathsf{out}_1, \mathsf{out}_2) = (c_{r'}, d_{r'})$, and, for $0 \leq i \leq r$,

$$
a_i = \begin{cases}
f_1(x, \widetilde{y}^{(i)}) \text{ where } \widetilde{y}^{(i)} \in_U Y & \text{if } i < i^* - r \\
c_{i-(i^*-r')} & \text{if } i^* - r' \leq i < i^* \\
\mathsf{out}_1 & \text{otherwise}
\end{cases}
$$

and

$$
b_i = \begin{cases}
f_2(\widetilde{x}^{(i)}, y) \text{ where } \widetilde{x}^{(i)} \in_U X & \text{if } i < i^* - r \\
d_{i-(i^*-r')} & \text{if } i^* - r' \leq i < i^* \\
\mathsf{out}_2 & \text{otherwise.}
\end{cases}
$$

5. The dealer gives $b_0$ to $P_2$.
6. For $i = 1, \ldots, r$,
   (a) The dealer gives $a_i$ to $P_1$. If $P_1$ aborts, then $P_2$ outputs $b_{i-1}$ and halts.
   (b) The dealer gives $b_i$ to $P_2$. If $P_2$ aborts, then $P_1$ outputs $a_i$ and halts.

---

[a] If $x$ is not in the appropriate domain or $P_1$ does not hand an input, then the dealer sends $f(\hat{x}, y)$ (where $\hat{x}$ is a default value) to $P_2$, which outputs this value and the protocol is terminated. The case of an inappropriate $y$ is dealt analogously.

**Fig. 2.** Protocol SecSamp2Fair($\Pi$) for computing $f$.

**Theorem 4.1.** *Suppose that protocol $\Pi$ for $f$ is constant-round, passively secure, and secure against sampling attacks. There exists $\gamma_0 \in [0, 1]$ such that protocol* SecSamp2Fair($\Pi$) *is fully secure for $f$, for every $\gamma < \gamma_0$.*

As a corollary, we show the existence of fair non-Boolean function where both parties have roughly the same number of inputs. We stress that previous results [2] on non-Boolean functions only applied to functions where one party has at least twice as many inputs as the other.

**Corollary 4.2.** *The non-Boolean function described by the matrix below is computable with full security.*

| $f(x,y)$ | $y_1$ | $y_2$ | $y_3$ | $y_4$ |
|----------|-------|-------|-------|-------|
| $x_1$    | 1     | 1     | 2     | 2     |
| $x_2$    | 1     | 0     | 1     | 2     |
| $x_3$    | 1     | 1     | 0     | 2     |
| $x_4$    | 2     | 2     | 0     | 2     |

*Proof.* Consider the following 2-round protocol defined by means of the backup outputs $\{a_i, b_i\}_{i=1...2}$.

$$a_0 = f(x, \widetilde{y}) \text{ where } \widetilde{y} \in_U Y \qquad\qquad b_0 \quad = 2$$

$$a_1 = \begin{cases} a \in_U \{0,1\} & \text{if } x = x_2 \text{ and } f(x,y) \neq 2 \\ f(x,y) & \text{otherwise} \end{cases} \qquad b_1 \quad = f(x,y).$$

$$a_2 = f(x,y) \qquad\qquad b_2 \quad = f(x,y)$$

The protocol is constant-round, passively secure and secure against sampling attacks. By Theorem 4.1, the function is fair.

## 4.2    Security Analysis

We only deal with the case where $P_1$ is corrupted. The other case is virtually analogous. Write $\mathcal{A}$ for the adversary corrupting $P_1$. We begin with a high-level description of the simulator. The simulator $\mathcal{S}$ chooses $i^*$ according to the specifications of the protocol, and simulates the rounds of the protocol as follows. Prior to iteration/round $i^* - r'$, the simulator generates backup outputs in exactly the same way as the dealer does in the real model. If the adversary decides to abort, $\mathcal{S}$ sends $x_0 \in X$ to the trusted party, where $x_0$ is sampled according to probability vector $\mathbf{z}_x^{(\vec{\alpha}_{r'})} \in \mathbb{R}^\ell$. As the notation suggests, $\mathbf{z}_x^{(\vec{\alpha}_{r'})}$ depends on $x$ (the input handed by the adversary for the computation) and the last $r' + 1$ backup outputs computed by the simulator. At iteration $i^* - r'$, assuming the adversary is still active, the simulator hands $x$ to the trusted party, and receives output $a = f_1(x, y)$. In order to reconstruct the next values of the backup sequence, the simulator invokes $\mathcal{S}_2^p$, and hands one-by-one to $\mathcal{A}$ the values computed by $\mathcal{S}_2^p$. At every iteration following $i^*$, the simulator hands $a$ to $\mathcal{A}$. At any given point, if the adversary aborts, the simulator outputs the sequence of values he handed to $\mathcal{A}$, and halts.

**Intuition.** By definition, the simulator's output together with the honest party's output in the ideal model is required to be indistinguishable from the adversary's view and the honest party's output in the real model. In our case, the adversary's view corresponds to the sequence of backup outputs she observes. Notice that the backup up sequences of each world are statistically close, which follows from the way $i^*$ is chosen in both worlds, the passive security of $\Pi$, and the fact that prior to $i^* - r'$ the backup outputs in the real and ideal world are identically distributed. The hard part is to argue that there exists $\mathbf{z}_x^{(\vec{\alpha}_{r'})}$ from which the simulator can sample from. As we shall see, the existence of $\mathbf{z}_x^{(\vec{\alpha}_{r'})}$ follows from a corollary of the fundamental theorem of Linear Algebra, which comes into play because of the security against sampling attacks assumption (Fig. 3).

---

**The simulator $\mathcal{S}$ for Protocol SecSamp2Fair($\Pi$)**

- The adversary $\mathcal{A}$ gives its input $x$ to the simulator.[a]
- The simulator chooses $i^* \geq r' + 1$ according to the geometric distribution with parameter $\gamma$.
- For $i = 1, \ldots, i^* - r' - 1$:
  - The simulator gives $a_i = f(x, \widetilde{y}^{(i)})$ to the adversary $\mathcal{A}$, where $\widetilde{y}^{(i)}$ is chosen according to the uniform distribution.
  - If $\mathcal{A}$ aborts, then the simulator chooses an input $x_0$ according to a distribution $\mathbf{z}_x^{(a_{i-\rho}, \ldots, a_i)}$ (which depends on the input $x$ and the last sequence $\rho + 1$ values that the simulator generated, where $\rho = \min(r', i)$), gives $x_0$ to the trusted party, outputs the bits $a_1, \ldots, a_i$, and halts.
- At round $i = i^* - r'$, the simulator gives $x$ to the trusted party and gets the output $a = f_1(x, y)$.
  - The simulator constructs $(a_{i^*-r'}, \ldots, a_{i^*-1})$ such that $a_{i^*-r'+j} = \widehat{a}_j$ by invoking $\mathcal{S}_2^{\mathrm{p}}$ on input $x$, output $a = f_1(x, y)$ and security parameter $n$.
- For $i = i^* - r', \ldots, i^* - 1$: The simulator gives $a_i$ to the adversary $\mathcal{A}$, if $\mathcal{A}$ aborts, then the simulator outputs the bits $a_1, \ldots, a_i$ and halts.
- For $i = i^*, \ldots, r$: The simulator gives $a_i = a$ to the adversary $\mathcal{A}$, if $\mathcal{A}$ aborts, then the simulator outputs the bits $a_1, \ldots, a_i$ and halts.
- The simulator outputs the bits $a_1, \ldots, a_r$ and halts.

---

[a] If the adversary gives an inappropriate $x$ (or no $x$), then the simulator sends some default $\widehat{x} \in X$ to the trusted party, outputs the empty string, and halts.

**Fig. 3.** The simulator $\mathcal{S}$ for protocol SecSamp2Fair($\Pi$)

Recall that for $i = 1 \ldots r'$ matrices $B_-^{(\alpha_0, \ldots, \alpha_i, \beta)}$ and $B_+^{(\alpha_0, \ldots, \alpha_i, \beta)}$ denote

$$B_-^{(\alpha_0 \ldots \alpha_i, \beta)}(x, y) = \Pr\left[(c_0, \ldots, c_i, d_{i-1})(x, y) = (\alpha_0, \ldots, \alpha_i, \beta)\right]$$
$$B_+^{(\alpha_0 \ldots \alpha_i, \beta)}(x, y) = \Pr\left[(c_0, \ldots, c_i, d_{r'})(x, y) = (\alpha_0, \ldots, \alpha_i, \beta)\right]$$

Now, define $p_x^{(\alpha)} = \Pr\left[f_1(x, \widetilde{y}) = \alpha \mid \widetilde{y} \in_U Y\right]$. To alleviate notation, we will omit the security parameter. As mentioned earlier, the corrupted party's backup sequences in the real and ideal world are statistically close. Therefore, if the adversary quits in the real world, then the adversary quits in the ideal world as well, with all but negligible probability – and vice versa. The whole point of the simulation is to show that early aborts do not breach security. In particular, if the adversary quits *after* round $i^*$, then the relevant distributions in the real and ideal world are statistically close. Our analysis only deals with aborts that take place prior to round $i^*$.

We only focus on the last $r' + 1$ elements of the corrupted party's backup sequence. Having assumed that $i^*$ has not been surpassed, anything prior to the last $r' + 1$ elements is essentially noise, and it has no bearing on the security analysis. For every sequence of elements $\vec{\alpha}_{r'} \in \{0,1\}^{r'+1}$ and every $\beta \in \{0,1\}$, we compute the probability that the adversary's view and honest party's output in the real world is equal to $(\vec{\alpha}_{r'}, \beta)$, and we express the result in terms of the $B_-^{(\cdot,\cdot)}$-matrices. Similarly, for the ideal world, we compute the probability that the simulator's output and honest party's output is equal to $(\vec{\alpha}_{r'}, \beta)$, and we express the result in terms of the $B_+^{(\cdot,\cdot)}$-matrices and vector $\mathbf{z}_x^{(\vec{\alpha}_{r'})}$.

The point of the exercise is to obtain (linear) constraints for vector $\mathbf{z}_x^{(\vec{\alpha}_{r'})}$. Then, we ask if the constraints are satisfiable, and, if so, whether solutions can be found efficiently. The second question can be readily answered. If an appropriate solution exists, the simulator can compute it efficiently. Indeed, the simulator can approximate the probability of all possible sequences of size $r' + 1$, and, assuming it exists, the simulator computes $\mathbf{z}_x^{(\vec{\alpha}_{r'})}$ by solving a linear system of size $|X| \times |Y|$. Thus, it suffices to show that $\mathbf{z}_x^{(\vec{\alpha}_{r'})}$ exists. The security features of $\Pi$ come into play in this regard.

An early abort on the part of the adversary alters the conditional[2] probability distribution of the honest party's output. Security against sampling attacks guarantees that the output remains consistent with the function at hand. Thus, by introducing a threshold round and fine-tuning its parameter, we restrict the distribution of the output until it falls within the range of the function, and the simulator can match it with an appropriate input.

**Three Simplifying Assumptions.** The case where the adversary aborts before round $r'$ needs special consideration. However, the only difference is that $\mathbf{z}_x^{(\vec{\alpha}_i)}$ depends on fewer elements. The analysis is largely the same and we do not address this case any further. Furthermore, we assume that $p_x^{(\alpha)} \neq 0$, for every $\alpha \in \{0,1\}$ and $x \in X$. This assumption allows for a smoother exposition by disregarding degenerate cases. Finally, regarding $\Pi$, we will assume that security against sampling attacks holds perfectly, i.e. (3) and (4) are equal to $\mathbf{0}_\ell$ and $\mathbf{0}_k$ respectively. Again, the latest assumption is not necessary to prove the theorem. We do so in order to avoid introducing notions from Topology to deal with the convergent sequences.

### 4.3 Real vs Ideal

For every sequence $\vec{\alpha}_{r'} = (\alpha_0, \ldots, \alpha_{r'}) \in \{0,1\}^{r'+1}$ and every $\beta \in \{0,1\}$, we compute the probability that the adversary quitting at round $i \leq i^*$ observes $\vec{\alpha}_{r'}$ and the honest party outputs $\beta$. The adversary is assumed to use input $x \in X$ for the computation. To account for every possible input of the honest party, the relevant probabilities are expressed in terms of vectors.

---

[2] Conditioned on the adversary's view.

**Claim 4.3.** *In the real model, it holds that*

$$\Pr\left[\left(a_{i-r'}, \ldots, a_i, b_{i-1}\right)^{Real} = (\vec{\alpha}_{r'}, \beta) \,\Big|\, i \leq i^*\right]$$

$$= (1-\gamma)^{r'+1} \cdot p_x^{(\alpha_0)} \cdots p_x^{(\alpha_{r'})} \cdot \mathbf{q}^{(\beta)T} + \gamma(1-\gamma)^{r'} \cdot p_x^{(\alpha_0)} \cdots p_x^{(\alpha_{r'-1})} \cdot \left[B_-^{(\alpha_{r'},\beta)}\right]_{x,*}$$

$$+ \ldots + \gamma(1-\gamma) \cdot p_x^{(\alpha_0)} \cdot \left[B_-^{(\alpha_1 \cdots \alpha_{r'},\beta)}\right]_{x,*} + \gamma \cdot \left[B_-^{(\vec{\alpha}_{r'},\beta)}\right]_{x,*},$$

*where* $\mathbf{q}^{(\beta)} = M^{(*,\beta)T} \cdot \mathbf{1}_\ell / \ell.$

*Proof.* Simple expansion over possible values of $i^*$.

Define $\mathbf{c}_x^{(\vec{\alpha}_{r'},\beta)} \in \mathbb{R}^k$ such that $\mathbf{c}_x^{(\vec{\alpha}_{r'},\beta)}(y) = \Pr\left[f_2(x_0,y) = \beta \,\Big|\, x_0 \leftarrow \mathbf{z}_x^{(\vec{\alpha}_{r'})}\right].$

**Claim 4.4.** *In the ideal model, it holds that*

$$\Pr\left[\left(a_{i-r'}, \ldots, a_i, f_2\right)^{Ideal} = (\vec{\alpha}_{r'}, \beta) \,\Big|\, i \leq i^*\right]$$

$$= (1-\gamma)^{r'+1} \cdot p_x^{(\alpha_0)} \cdots p_x^{(\alpha_{r'})} \cdot \mathbf{c}_x^{(\vec{\alpha}_{r'},\beta)T} + \gamma(1-\gamma)^{r'} \cdot p_x^{(\alpha_0)} \cdots p_x^{(\alpha_{r'-1})} \cdot \left[B_+^{(\alpha_{r'},\beta)}\right]_{x,*}$$

$$+ \ldots + \gamma(1-\gamma) \cdot p_x^{(\alpha_0)} \cdot \left[B_+^{(\alpha_1 \cdots \alpha_{r'},\beta)}\right]_{x,*} + \gamma \cdot \left[B_+^{(\vec{\alpha}_{r'},\beta)}\right]_{x,*}.$$

Thus, for every $\beta \in \{0,1\}$, we require that $\mathbf{c}_x^{(\vec{\alpha}_{r'},\beta)T}$ is close to

$$\mathbf{q}^{(\beta)T} + \sum_{i=0}^{r'} \lambda_i(\gamma, \vec{\alpha}_{r'}) \cdot \left[B_-^{(\alpha_{r'-i}\cdots\alpha_{r'},\beta)} - B_+^{(\alpha_{r'-i}\cdots\alpha_{r'},\beta)}\right]_{x,*},$$

where

$$\lambda_i(\gamma, \vec{\alpha}_{r'}) = \frac{\gamma(1-\gamma)^{r'-i} \cdot p_x^{(\alpha_0)} \cdots p_x^{(\alpha_{r'-i-1})}}{(1-\gamma)^{r'+1} \cdot p_x^{(\alpha_0)} \cdots p_x^{(\alpha_{r'})}} = \frac{\gamma}{(1-\gamma)^{i+1}} \cdot \frac{1}{p_x^{(\alpha_{r'-i})} \cdots p_x^{(\alpha_{r'})}}.$$

Knowing that $\mathbf{c}_x^{(\vec{\alpha}_{r'},\beta)T} = \mathbf{z}_x^{(\vec{\alpha}_{r'})T} \cdot M^{(*,\beta)}$ and that $M^{(*,0)} = \mathbf{1}_{\ell \times k} - M^{(*,1)}$, the simulation is successful if there exists probability vector $\mathbf{z}_x^{(\vec{\alpha}_{r'})} \in \mathbb{R}^k$ such that

$$\mathbf{z}_x^{(\vec{\alpha}_{r'})T} \cdot M^{(*,1)}$$

$$\stackrel{s}{\equiv} \mathbf{q}^{(1)T} + \lambda_0 \cdot \left[B_+^{(\alpha_{r'},1)} - B_-^{(\alpha_{r'},1)}\right]_{x,*} + \ldots + \lambda_{r'} \cdot \left[B_+^{(\vec{\alpha}_{r'},1)} - B_-^{(\vec{\alpha}_{r'},1)}\right]_{x,*}.$$

$$(5)$$

Define $\mathbf{u}_x^{(\vec{\alpha}_{r'})} = \mathbf{z}_x^{(\vec{\alpha}_{r'})} - \mathbf{1}_\ell/\ell$ and notice that (5) is equivalent to

$$
\begin{aligned}
&\mathbf{u}_x^{(\vec{\alpha}_{r'})T} \cdot M^{(*,1)} \\
&\overset{s}{\equiv} \lambda_0 \cdot \left[ B_+^{(\alpha_{r'},1)} - B_-^{(\alpha_{r'},1)} \right]_{x,*} + \cdots + \lambda_{r'} \cdot \left[ B_+^{(\vec{\alpha}_{r'},1)} - B_-^{(\vec{\alpha}_{r'},1)} \right]_{x,*},
\end{aligned}
\tag{6}
$$

and

$$
\begin{cases}
\sum_{x_0} \mathbf{u}_x^{(\vec{\alpha}_{r'})}(x_0) = 0 \\
\forall x_0 \in X,\ \mathbf{u}_x^{(\vec{\alpha}_{r'})}(x_0) \in [-1/\ell, 1 - 1/\ell]
\end{cases}.
$$

**Lemma 4.5.** *Let $\mathbf{c}$ be an arbitrary vector and let $M$ be an arbitrary matrix. There exists $\mathbf{u}$ such that $\sum_z \mathbf{u}(z) = 0$ and $\mathbf{u}^T \cdot M = \mathbf{c}^T$ if and only if $\mathbf{c}^T \mathbf{v} = 0$, for every $\mathbf{v}$ such that $M\mathbf{v} \in \langle \mathbf{1} \rangle$.*

*Proof.* Define

$$
M' = \begin{pmatrix} -1 & 1 & \ldots & 0 \\ \vdots & \vdots & \ddots & \vdots \\ -1 & 0 & \ldots & 1 \end{pmatrix} \cdot M.
$$

Observe that the row-space of $M'$ is equal to the image of the hyperplane $\{\mathbf{u} \mid \sum_z \mathbf{u}(z) = 0\}$ by $M^T$ and that $\ker(M') = \{\mathbf{v} \mid M\mathbf{v} \in \langle \mathbf{1} \rangle\}$. Conclude by applying the fundamental theorem of linear algebra. □

**Proof of Theorem** 4.1. We show that there exist suitable vectors $\mathbf{u}_x^{(\vec{\alpha}_{r'})}$ satisfying (6), for every $x \in X$ and $\vec{\alpha}_{r'} \in \{0,1\}^{r'+1}$. By assumption, security against sampling attacks holds perfectly for $\Pi$. It follows that

$$
\left( B_+^{(\vec{\alpha}_i,1)} - B_-^{(\vec{\alpha}_i,1)} \right) \cdot \mathbf{y} = \mathbf{0}_\ell,
$$

for every $\mathbf{y} \in \langle \mathcal{L}_2 \rangle$. By Lemma 4.5, there exists $\mathbf{u}_{x,i}^{(\vec{\alpha}_{r'})}$ such that $\sum_{x_0} \mathbf{u}_{x,i}^{(\vec{\alpha}_{r'})T}(x_0) = 0$ and

$$
\mathbf{u}_{x,i}^{(\vec{\alpha}_{r'})T} \cdot M^{(*,1)} = \left[ B_+^{(\vec{\alpha}_i,1)} - B_-^{(\vec{\alpha}_i,1)} \right]_{x,*}.
$$

Thus, $\mathbf{u}_x^{(\vec{\alpha}_{r'})} \overset{\text{def}}{=} \sum_i \lambda_i \mathbf{u}_{x,i}^{(\vec{\alpha}_{r'})}$ satisfies (6). To conclude, we argue that there exists $\gamma_0$ such that $\mathbf{u}_x^{(\vec{\alpha}_{r'})}(x_0) \in [-1/\ell, 1 - 1/\ell]$, for every $\gamma < \gamma_0$. Recall that

$$
\lambda_i(\gamma, \vec{\alpha}_{r'}) = \frac{\gamma}{(1-\gamma)^{i+1}} \cdot \frac{1}{p_x^{(\alpha_{r'-i})} \cdots p_x^{(\alpha_{r'})}}.
$$

Observe that $\lambda_i$ tends to 0 as $\gamma$ tends to 0. □

# 5   The Asymmetric Case

Our analysis of locking strategies and sampling attacks culminates in Theorem 4.1 from the previous section. The theorem states that, in order to demonstrate that a given function is computable with full security, it suffices to design a constant-round, passively-secure protocol that is secure against sampling attacks. In this section, we look for relevant protocols for asymmetric Boolean functions. We propose an algorithm that takes a description of the function as input, and, depending on the termination step, either returns the description of an appropriate protocol, or it returns that it failed to do so.

We begin by visiting some mathematical tools and a few useful lemmas. Next, we define a game involving the parties computing $f$ and the dealer. The game simulates the last interaction in a correct protocol computing $f$, and whose purpose is for the dealer to hand a backup[3] output to the disadvantaged party *without* compromising any of the security requirements. Finally, largely as an extension of the game, we obtain an algorithm for designing constant-round protocols that are passively secure and secure against sampling attacks. Using the tools and the lemmas from Sect. 5.1, we demonstrate that our algorithm satisfies correctness.

**Speculative Remark.** For what it is worth, numerical results on small cases indicate that our algorithm accounts for the overwhelmingly majority of non semi-balanced functions. We also encountered a handful of non semi-balanced functions for which our algorithm fails to come up with a suitable protocol. These functions are noteworthy because we suspect that their unknown status cannot be attributed to potential shortcomings of our algorithm. We believe that our algorithm is as good at finding suitable protocols as can be expected.

## 5.1   Irreducible Locking Strategies

Let $f : X \times Y \to \{0,1\}^2$ denote some Boolean asymmetric (possibly randomized) finite function. Since $f$ is asymmetric, it has four associated matrices $M^{(0,0)}$, $M^{(0,1)}$, $M^{(1,0)}$, $M^{(1,1)} \in [0,1]^{\ell \times k}$. Recall that locking strategies for $P_1$ and $P_2$ correspond to elements of the vector spaces $\langle \mathcal{L}_1 \rangle = \{ \mathbf{x} \in \mathbb{R}^\ell \,|\, \mathbf{x}^T M^{(1,*)} \in \langle \mathbf{1}_k^T \rangle \}$ and $\langle \mathcal{L}_2 \rangle = \{ \mathbf{y} \in \mathbb{R}^k \,|\, M^{(*,1)} \mathbf{y} \in \langle \mathbf{1}_\ell \rangle \}$, where $\mathcal{L}_1$ and $\mathcal{L}_2$ denote arbitrary bases of each space. Without loss of generality, assume $|\mathcal{L}_1| = s_1$ and $|\mathcal{L}_2| = s_2$. Locking strategies endow a matrix with a matroid structure, in the same way that linear dependence does. We define the matroid by means of its *minimally dependent sets*, i.e. circuits.

**Definition 5.1.** We say that the columns of $M^{(*,1)}$ indexed by $Y' \subseteq Y$ are *minimally dependent* if

- $\left\{ M^{(*,1)} \mathbf{e}_y \right\}_{y \in Y'} \cup \{ \mathbf{1}_\ell \}$ are linearly dependent,

---

[3] Other than the actual output.

- for every $y_0 \in Y'$, it holds that $\left\{M^{(*,1)}\mathbf{e}_y\right\}_{y \in Y' \setminus \{y_0\}} \cup \{\mathbf{1}_\ell\}$ are linearly independent.

Similarly, we say that the rows of $M^{(1,*)}$ indexed by $X' \subseteq X$ are *minimally dependent* if

- $\left\{\mathbf{e}_x^T M^{(1,*)}\right\}_{x \in X'} \cup \{\mathbf{1}_k^T\}$ are linearly dependent,
- for every $x_0 \in X'$, it holds that $\left\{\mathbf{e}_x^T M^{(1,*)}\right\}_{x \in X' \setminus \{x_0\}} \cup \{\mathbf{1}_k^T\}$ are linearly independent.

**Proposition 5.2.** *Suppose that the columns of $M^{(*,1)}$ indexed by $Y' \subseteq Y$ are minimally dependent. Up to a multiplicative factor, there exists a unique $\mathbf{q} \in \mathbb{R}^k \setminus \{\mathbf{0}_k\}$ such that $M^{(*,1)}\mathbf{q} \in \langle \mathbf{1}_\ell \rangle$ and $\mathsf{supp}(\mathbf{q}) = Y'$.*

*Proof.* By definition, there exists $\mathbf{q} \in \mathbb{R}^k$ such that $M^{(*,1)}\mathbf{q} \in \langle \mathbf{1}_\ell \rangle$ and $\mathsf{supp}(\mathbf{q}) = Y'$. The non-trivial task is to show that this vector is unique, *up to a multiplicative factor*. Suppose there exists $\mathbf{q}'$ such that $\mathsf{supp}(\mathbf{q}') \subseteq Y'$ and $M^{(*,1)}\mathbf{q}' \in \langle \mathbf{1}_\ell \rangle$. In pursuit of a contradiction, assume that $\mathbf{q}' \neq \lambda \mathbf{q}$, for every $\lambda \in \mathbb{R}$. Equivalently, there exists $i, j \in Y'$ such that $\mathbf{q}(i) = \lambda_i \mathbf{q}'(i)$ and $\mathbf{q}(j) = \lambda_j \mathbf{q}'(j)$, with $\lambda_i \neq \lambda_j$. Without loss of generality, say that $\lambda_i \neq 0$ and define $\mathbf{q}'' = \lambda_i \cdot \mathbf{q}' - \mathbf{q}$. Deduce that $M^{(*,1)}\mathbf{q}'' \in \langle \mathbf{1}_\ell \rangle$ and $\mathsf{supp}(\mathbf{q}'') \subsetneq Y'$, in contradiction with the fact that the columns indexed by $Y'$ are minimally dependent. $\square$

**Definition 5.3.** *If $\mathbf{q} \in \mathbb{R}^k$ is as in Proposition 5.2, we say that $\mathbf{q}$ is irreducible.*

**Proposition 5.4.** *There exists a basis of $\langle \mathcal{L}_2 \rangle$ consisting of irreducible strategies.*

*Proof.* It is a well known that any generating set contains a basis. Thus, it suffices to show that irreducible locking strategies form a generating set. Let $\mathbf{y} \in \langle \mathcal{L}_2 \rangle$ and consider $\mathsf{supp}(\mathbf{y})$. Let $\mu_1, \ldots, \mu_{t_\mathbf{y}}$ denote all the subsets of $\mathsf{supp}(\mathbf{y})$ that index minimally dependent columns, and write $\mathbf{q}_1, \ldots, \mathbf{q}_{t_\mathbf{y}}$ for the associated unique *irreducible* locking strategies. We show that $\mathbf{y} \in \langle \mathbf{q}_1, \ldots, \mathbf{q}_{t_\mathbf{y}} \rangle$ by constructing a sequence of locking strategies $\mathbf{y}_0, \ldots, \mathbf{y}_{s_\mathbf{y}}$ such that

$$\begin{cases} \mathbf{y}_0 = \mathbf{y} \\ \mathbf{y}_{j+1} = \mathbf{y}_j - \alpha_j \cdot \mathbf{q}^{(j)} \\ \mathbf{y}_{s_\mathbf{y}} = \mathbf{0}_\ell \end{cases},$$

where $\alpha_j \in \mathbb{R}$ and $\mathbf{q}^{(j)} \in \{\mathbf{q}_1, \ldots, \mathbf{q}_{t_\mathbf{y}}\}$. Let $\mathbf{q}^{(0)}$ be an arbitrary element of $\{\mathbf{q}_1, \ldots, \mathbf{q}_{t_\mathbf{y}}\}$ and fix $j_0$ such that $\mathbf{q}^{(0)}(j_0) \neq 0$. Define $\mathbf{y}_1 = \mathbf{y} - \frac{\mathbf{y}(j_0)}{\mathbf{q}^{(0)}(j_0)} \cdot \mathbf{q}^{(0)}$. Notice that $\mathbf{y}_1$ is a locking strategy and that $\mathsf{supp}(\mathbf{y}_1) \subsetneq \mathsf{supp}(\mathbf{y})$. Since $\mathbf{y}_1$ is a locking strategy, it follows that $\mu^{(1)} \subset \mathsf{supp}(y_1)$, for some $\mu^{(1)} \in \{\mu_1, \ldots, \mu_{t_\mathbf{y}}\}$. Write $\mathbf{q}^{(1)}$ for the associated locking strategy. Similarly to what we just did, fix $j_1$ such that $\mathbf{q}^{(1)}(j_1) \neq 0$, define $\mathbf{y}_2 = \mathbf{y}_1 - \frac{\mathbf{y}_1(j_1)}{\mathbf{q}^{(1)}(j_1)} \cdot \mathbf{q}^{(1)}$, and notice that $\mathbf{y}_2$ is a locking strategy and that $\mathsf{supp}(\mathbf{y}_2) \subsetneq \mathsf{supp}(\mathbf{y}_1)$. Repeat the procedure and conclude that it terminates in at most $|\mathsf{supp}(\mathbf{y})|$ steps. $\square$

Define $Y_0, \ldots, Y_{k'}$ to be a partitioning of the input domain $Y$ that we construct as follows. First, $y \in Y_0$ if $\mathbf{e}_y$ is orthogonal to $\langle \mathcal{L}_2 \rangle$. Next, for $i \geq 1$, let $\mathbf{q}^{(i)}$ be an irreducible locking strategy such that $\mathsf{supp}(\mathbf{q}^{(i)}) \cap (Y_{i-1} \cup \ldots, \cup Y_0) = \emptyset$. Finally, $y \in Y_i$ if there exist irreducibles $\mathbf{q}_1^{(i)}, \ldots, \mathbf{q}_{t_y}^{(i)}$ such that

$$
\begin{cases}
\mathbf{q}^{(i)} = \mathbf{q}_1^{(i)} \\
\mathsf{supp}(\mathbf{q}_j^{(i)}) \cap \mathsf{supp}(\mathbf{q}_{j+1}^{(i)}) \neq \emptyset \\
y \in \mathsf{supp}(\mathbf{q}_{t_y}^{(i)})
\end{cases} .
$$

## 5.2   The Dealer Game

In this section, we present a game involving the parties computing $f$ and the dealer. The purpose of the game is to define a simplified variant of the security against sampling attacks requirement. Assume that the honest party, say $P_2$, applies some locking strategy $\mathbf{y}$ while executing a protocol for computing $f$. If the protocol is secure against sampling attacks, then the adversary cannot distinguish between the correct output and the backup output of the honest party. In the worst case, the adversary is handed the output of the corrupted party before the honest party's receives his. In such an event, we ask what the honest party's backup output ought to be, other than the correct output.

Write $a_i$ (resp. $b_i$) for $P_1$'s (resp. $P_2$'s) backup output at round $i$. Let $\widehat{b}_*$ denote the bit obtained from $b_*$ by applying[4] $\mathbf{y}$, and $r$ denotes the number of rounds. From an honest $P_2$'s perspective, we require that the pairs $(a_i, \widehat{b}_{i-1})$ and $(a_i, \widehat{b}_r)$ are statistically close, for every $x \in X$, $\mathbf{y} \in \langle \mathcal{L}_2 \rangle$ and $i \in \{1 \ldots r\}$. Consider the following process involving a dealer. The dealer receives inputs $x$ and $y$ from $P_1$ and $P_2$, respectively, and computes $f(x, y) = (f_1(x, y), f_2(x, y))$. Then, the dealer hands $f_1(x, y)$ to $P_1$ and a bit $b$ to $P_2$, where $b$ is a probabilistic function of $P_2$'s input and $f_2(x, y)$. We investigate how to construct $b$ with the following goals in mind.

1. *minimize* the information $b$ contains about $f_2(x, y)$
2. $(f_1, \widehat{f_2})$ is statistically close to $(f_1, \widehat{b})$, for every $x \in X$ and $\mathbf{q} \in \langle \mathcal{L}_2 \rangle$.

Let us introduce vectors $\mathbf{b}^{(0)}, \mathbf{b}^{(1)} \in \mathbb{R}^k$ such that

$$
\mathbf{b}^{(\beta)}(y_0) = \Pr\left[ b = 1 \,\middle|\, f_2(x, y) = \beta \wedge y = y_0 \right].
$$

Fix $y \in Y$, and notice that $b \equiv f_2$ on input $y$ if $\mathbf{b}^{(0)}(y) = 0$ and $\mathbf{b}^{(1)}(y) = 1$. On the other hand, $b$ contains no information about $f_2(x, y)$ if and only if $\mathbf{b}^{(0)}(y) = \mathbf{b}^{(1)}(y)$. Consequently, our aim is for $\mathbf{b}^{(0)}$ and $\mathbf{b}^{(1)}$ to be equal on as many indices as possible.

---

[4] Recall that $\mathbf{y}$ encodes an input distribution but also a certain transformation.

**Claim 5.5.** *Using the notation above, It holds that $(f_1, \widehat{f_2})$ is statistically close to $(f_1, \widehat{b})$ if and only if, for every $\mathbf{y} \in \langle \mathcal{L}_2 \rangle$,*

$$\begin{cases} M^{(0,0)} \left( \mathbf{b}^{(0)} * \mathbf{y} \right) + M^{(0,1)} \left( \mathbf{b}^{(1)} * \mathbf{y} \right) = M^{(0,1)} \mathbf{y} \\ M^{(1,0)} \left( \mathbf{b}^{(0)} * \mathbf{y} \right) + M^{(1,1)} \left( \mathbf{b}^{(1)} * \mathbf{y} \right) = M^{(1,1)} \mathbf{y} \end{cases} \quad . \tag{7}$$

*Proof.* Fix $x \in X$, $\mathbf{y} \in \langle \mathcal{L}_2 \rangle$, $\alpha \in \{0, 1\}$, and note that

$$\Pr\left[ (f_1, \widehat{f_2}) = (\alpha, 1) \right] = \mathbf{e}_x^T \left( \sum_{\mathbf{y}(y) \geq 0} \left[ M^{(\alpha, 1)} \right]_{*, y} \mathbf{y}(y) + \sum_{\mathbf{y}(y) < 0} \left[ M^{(\alpha, 0)} \right]_{*, y} |\mathbf{y}(y)| \right)$$

$$= \mathbf{e}_x^T \left( M^{(\alpha, 1)} \mathbf{y} + \sum_{\mathbf{y}(y) < 0} \left[ M^{(\alpha, *)} \right]_{*, y} |\mathbf{y}(y)| \right)$$

On the other hand, $\Pr\left[ (f_1, \widehat{b}) = (\alpha, 1) \right]$

$$= \sum_{\mathbf{y}(y) \geq 0} \mathbf{e}_x^T \left( \left[ M^{(\alpha, 1)} \right]_{*, y} \cdot \mathbf{b}^{(1)}(y) + \left[ M^{(\alpha, 0)} \right]_{*, y} \cdot \mathbf{b}^{(0)}(y) \right) \mathbf{y}(y)$$

$$+ \sum_{\mathbf{y}(y) < 0} \left( \left[ M^{(\alpha, 1)} \right]_{*, y} \cdot (1 - \mathbf{b}^{(1)}(y)) + \left[ M^{(\alpha, 0)} \right]_{*, y} \cdot (1 - \mathbf{b}^{(0)}(y)) \right) |\mathbf{y}(y)|,$$

and thus $\Pr\left[ (f_1, \widehat{b}) = (\alpha, 1) \right]$

$$= \mathbf{e}_x^T \left( M^{(\alpha, 0)} \left( \mathbf{b}^{(0)} * \mathbf{y} \right) + M^{(\alpha, 1)} \left( \mathbf{b}^{(1)} * \mathbf{y} \right) + \sum_{\mathbf{y}(y) < 0} \left[ M^{(\alpha, *)} \right]_{*, y} |\mathbf{y}(y)| \right).$$

To conclude, note that since $\mathbf{b}^{(0)}, \mathbf{b}^{(1)}$ are fixed vectors, it holds that $(f_1, \widehat{f_2})$ and $(f_1, \widehat{b})$ are statistically close if and only if they are *identically distributed.* $\square$

Moving on, fix $Y_i \in \{Y_0, \ldots, Y_{k'}\}$ and suppose there exist $\mathbf{b}^{(0)}, \mathbf{b}^{(1)}$ satisfying Eq. (7) such that $\mathbf{b}^{(0)}(y_0) \neq 0$ or $\mathbf{b}^{(1)}(y_0) \neq 1$, for some $y_0 \in Y_i$. We show that there exist $\mathbf{b}'^{(0)}, \mathbf{b}'^{(1)}$ satisfying Eq. (7) such that $\mathbf{b}'^{(0)}(y) = \mathbf{b}'^{(1)}(y)$, for every $y \in Y_i$. This is where the underlying matroid structure will come in handy.

**Proposition 5.6.** *It holds that $\mathbf{b}^{(1)}(y) - \mathbf{b}^{(0)}(y) = \mathbf{b}^{(1)}(y_0) - \mathbf{b}^{(0)}(y_0)$, for every $y \in Y_i$. In addition, vectors $\mathbf{b}'^{(1)}, \mathbf{b}'^{(0)}$ satisfy Eq. (7), where*

$$\mathbf{b}'^{(b)}(y) = \begin{cases} \mathbf{b}^{(b)}(y) & \text{if } y \notin Y_j \\ \dfrac{\mathbf{b}^{(0)}(y)}{\mathbf{b}^{(0)}(y_0) - \mathbf{b}^{(1)}(y_0) + 1} & \text{if } y \in Y_j \end{cases} \quad .$$

*Proof.* For the first part of the claim, we apply Proposition 5.2. The case $i = 0$ is left to the reader. Let $i \geq 1$ and fix irreducible $\mathbf{q}$ such that $y_0 \in \mathsf{supp}(\mathbf{q})$. We know that, for any $\mathbf{y} \in \langle \mathcal{L}_2 \rangle$,

$$M^{(0,0)} \left( \mathbf{b}^{(0)} * \mathbf{y} \right) + M^{(0,1)} \left( \mathbf{b}^{(1)} * \mathbf{y} \right) = M^{(0,1)} \mathbf{y}, \tag{8}$$

$$M^{(1,0)} \left( \mathbf{b}^{(0)} * \mathbf{y} \right) + M^{(1,1)} \left( \mathbf{b}^{(1)} * \mathbf{y} \right) = M^{(1,1)} \mathbf{y}. \tag{9}$$

Let $\mathbf{y} = \mathbf{q}$ and add the two expressions.

$$\left( \mathbf{1}_{\ell \times k} - M^{(*,1)} \right) \left( \mathbf{b}^{(0)} * \mathbf{q} \right) + M^{(*,1)} \left( \mathbf{b}^{(1)} * \mathbf{q} \right) = M^{(*,1)} \mathbf{q}.$$

By moving a few terms around, deduce that $M^{(*,1)} \left( (\mathbf{b}^{(1)} - \mathbf{b}^{(0)}) * \mathbf{q} \right) \in \langle \mathbf{1}_\ell \rangle$. Consequently, by Proposition 5.2, $\mathbf{b}^{(1)}(y) - \mathbf{b}^{(0)}(y) = \mathbf{b}^{(1)}(y_0) - \mathbf{b}^{(0)}(y_0)$, for every $y \in \mathsf{supp}(\mathbf{q})$. Moving on, fix an arbitrary $y \in Y_i$. We know there exists a sequence of irreducibles $\mathbf{q}_1^{(i)} \ldots \mathbf{q}_{t'_y}^{(i)}$ such that

$$\begin{cases} \mathbf{q} = \mathbf{q}_1^{(i)} \\ \mathsf{supp}(\mathbf{q}_j^{(i)}) \cap \mathsf{supp}(\mathbf{q}_{j+1}^{(i)}) \neq \emptyset \\ y \in \mathsf{supp}(\mathbf{q}_{t'_y}^{(i)}) \end{cases},$$

Apply the same argument as above and, by induction, deduce that $\mathbf{b}^{(1)}(y) - \mathbf{b}^{(0)}(y) = \mathbf{b}^{(1)}(y_0) - \mathbf{b}^{(0)}(y_0)$. For the second part of the claim, we rely on the following observations.

- Vectors $\mathbf{b}_0^{(0)}$ and $\mathbf{b}_0^{(1)}$ satisfy Eqs. (8) and (9), where

$$\mathbf{b}_0^{(0)} = \begin{cases} \mathbf{b}^{(0)}(y) & \text{if } y \notin Y_i \\ 0 & \text{if } y \in Y_i \end{cases}, \qquad \mathbf{b}_0^{(1)} = \begin{cases} \mathbf{b}^{(1)}(y) & \text{if } y \notin Y_i \\ 1 & \text{if } y \in Y_i \end{cases}.$$

- Solutions to Eqs. (8) and (9) can be combined linearly.

The second item is trivial. For the first item, we show that vectors $\mathbf{b}_0^{(0)}$ and $\mathbf{b}_0^{(1)}$ are solutions to the equations for a particular basis of $\langle \mathcal{L}_2 \rangle$. By Proposition 5.4, consider a basis of $\langle \mathcal{L}_2 \rangle$ that consists of irreducible strategies. Conclude by observing that $Y_i \cap \mathsf{supp}(\mathbf{q}') = \emptyset$, for every irreducible $\mathbf{q}'$ such that $\mathsf{supp}(\mathbf{q}) \not\subseteq Y_i$. Next, define

$$\mathbf{b}'^{(b)} = \frac{1}{\mathbf{b}^{(0)}(y_0) - \mathbf{b}^{(1)}(y_0) + 1} \cdot \mathbf{b}^{(b)} + \left( 1 - \frac{1}{\mathbf{b}^{(0)}(y_0) - \mathbf{b}^{(1)}(y_0) + 1} \right) \cdot \mathbf{b}_0^{(b)}.$$

We note that $\mathbf{b}'^{(0)}$, $\mathbf{b}'^{(1)}$ admit the right expression. It remains to show that $\mathbf{b}'^{(b)}(y) \in [0,1]$, for every $y$. Since $\mathbf{b}'^{(b)}(y) = \mathbf{b}^{(b)}(y)$ if $y \notin Y_j$, it suffices to show that

$$\frac{\mathbf{b}^{(0)}(y)}{\mathbf{b}^{(0)}(y) - \mathbf{b}^{(1)}(y) + 1} \in [0,1], \tag{10}$$

for $y \in Y_i$. We conclude by observing that (10) is equivalent to $0 \leq \mathbf{b}^{(0)}(y)$ and $\mathbf{b}^{(1)}(y) \leq 1$. $\qquad \square$

## 5.3 The Algorithm

Next, we show how to construct passively-secure protocols that are also secure against sampling attacks. The idea is to build the backup outputs from the bottom-up, i.e. start with $a_r \equiv f_1$ and $b_r \equiv f_2$, and construct $a_{r-1}$ and $b_{r-1}$ such that $a_{r-1}$ (resp. $b_{r-1}$) only depends on $x$ and $f_1(x, y)$ (resp. $y$ and $f_2(x, y)$) without compromising security against sampling attacks.

To this end, we employ a minimization algorithm in combination with Proposition 5.6. Without loss of generality, we begin by assuming that $P_1$ is corrupted, and that he observes $a_r \equiv f_1(x, y)$. To define $b_{r-1}$, we run an optimization algorithm that constructs vectors $\{\mathbf{b}^{(\beta)}\}_{\beta \in \{0,1\}}$, and we delete any input $y \in Y$ for which $\mathbf{b}^{(1)}(y) - \mathbf{b}^{(0)}(y) \neq 1$. Then, in order to define $a_{r-1}$, we run an optimization algorithm that constructs vectors $\{\mathbf{a}^{(\alpha)}\}_{\alpha \in \{0,1\}}$, assuming $P_2$ is corrupted, and the party is privy to the output *only if the input he used was not deleted in the previous step*. We proceed by deleting any input $x \in X$ for which $\mathbf{a}^{(1)}(y) - \mathbf{a}^{(0)}(y) \neq 1$. We carry on in this fashion until one party runs out of inputs, *or* the process does not allow for any further deletions.

Getting ahead of ourselves, we note that deleted inputs cannot be used by the adversary to mount a successful sampling attack. In light of Proposition 5.6, if an input was deleted at iteration $i$, then every backup output until round $r - i$ contains no information about the output.

**Additional Notation.** Before we describe the algorithm, let us introduce some notation. For every $\mathbf{q} \in \mathcal{L}_2$ and $X' \subseteq X$, define

$$A_{\mathbf{q}}(X') = \begin{pmatrix} \left[M^{(0,0)} * Q\right]_{X'} & \left[M_{X'}^{(0,1)} * Q\right]_{X'} \\ \left[M^{(1,0)} * Q\right]_{X'} & \left[M^{(1,1)} * Q\right]_{X'} \\ M^{(*,0)} * Q & M^{(*,1)} * Q \end{pmatrix}, \qquad \vec{b}_{\mathbf{q}} = \begin{pmatrix} \left[M^{(0,1)}\right]_{X'} \mathbf{q} \\ \left[M^{(1,1)}\right]_{X'} \mathbf{q} \\ M^{(*,1)} \mathbf{q} \end{pmatrix}$$

where $Q = \mathbf{1}_\ell \cdot \mathbf{q}^T$ and the notation $[\ \cdot\ ]_{X'}$ indicates that only the rows indexed by $X' \subseteq X$ appear. Write $\mathcal{L}_2 = \{\mathbf{q}_1, \dots, \mathbf{q}_{s_2}\}$ and consider the following linear system for unknown $(\mathbf{b}^{(0)T}, \mathbf{b}^{(1)T})$.

$$\begin{pmatrix} A_{\mathbf{q}_1}(X') \\ A_{\mathbf{q}_2}(X') \\ \vdots \\ A_{\mathbf{q}_{s_2}}(X') \end{pmatrix} \cdot \begin{pmatrix} \mathbf{b}^{(0)} \\ \mathbf{b}^{(1)} \end{pmatrix} = \begin{pmatrix} \vec{b}_{\mathbf{q}_1}(X') \\ \vec{b}_{\mathbf{q}_2}(X') \\ \vdots \\ \vec{b}_{\mathbf{q}_{s_2}}(X') \end{pmatrix} \tag{11}$$

$$\begin{pmatrix} \mathbf{0}_k \\ \mathbf{0}_k \end{pmatrix} \leq \begin{pmatrix} \mathbf{b}^{(0)} \\ \mathbf{b}^{(1)} \end{pmatrix} \leq \begin{pmatrix} \mathbf{1}_k \\ \mathbf{1}_k \end{pmatrix}$$

Similarly, for every $\mathbf{p} \in \mathcal{L}_1$ and $Y \subseteq Y'$, define

$$B_{\mathbf{p}}(Y') = \begin{pmatrix} \left[M^{(0,0)T} * P\right]_{Y'} & \left[M^{(1,0)T} * P\right]_{Y'} \\ \left[M^{(0,1)T} * P\right]_{Y'} & \left[M^{(1,1)T} * P\right]_{Y'} \\ M^{(0,*)T} * P & M^{(1,*)T} * P \end{pmatrix}, \qquad \vec{a}_{\mathbf{p}} = \begin{pmatrix} \left[M^{(1,0)T}\right]_{Y'} \mathbf{p} \\ \left[M^{(1,1)T}\right]_{Y'} \mathbf{p} \\ M^{(1,*)T} \mathbf{p} \end{pmatrix}$$

where $P = 1_k \cdot \mathbf{p}^T$ and the notation $[\ \cdot\ ]_{Y'}$ indicates that only the rows indexed by $Y' \subseteq Y$ appear. Write $\mathcal{L}_1 = \{\mathbf{p}_1, \ldots, \mathbf{p}_{s_1}\}$ and consider the following linear system for unknown $(\mathbf{a}^{(0)T}, \mathbf{a}^{(1)T})$.

$$\begin{pmatrix} B_{\mathbf{p}_1}(Y') \\ B_{\mathbf{p}_2}(Y') \\ \vdots \\ B_{\mathbf{p}_{s_1}}(Y') \end{pmatrix} \cdot \begin{pmatrix} \mathbf{a}^{(0)} \\ \mathbf{a}^{(1)} \end{pmatrix} = \begin{pmatrix} \vec{a}_{\mathbf{p}_1}(Y') \\ \vec{a}_{\mathbf{p}_2}(Y') \\ \vdots \\ \vec{a}_{\mathbf{p}_{s_1}}(Y') \end{pmatrix} \tag{12}$$

$$\begin{pmatrix} \mathbf{0}_\ell \\ \mathbf{0}_\ell \end{pmatrix} \leq \begin{pmatrix} \mathbf{a}^{(0)} \\ \mathbf{a}^{(1)} \end{pmatrix} \leq \begin{pmatrix} \mathbf{1}_\ell \\ \mathbf{1}_\ell \end{pmatrix}$$

As noted earlier, the idea is to delete inputs from the parties in a sequence of iterations. Namely, we begin by running a linear program that minimizes $-1_k^T \mathbf{b}^{(0)} + 1_k^T \mathbf{b}^{(1)}$ under the constraints of Eq. (11), with $X' = X$. At this point, we delete any input $y \in Y$ for which $\mathbf{b}^{(1)}(y) - \mathbf{b}^{(0)}(y) < 1$. Write $Y^- \subseteq Y$ for the remaining inputs. We proceed by running a linear program that minimizes $-1_\ell^T \mathbf{a}^{(0)} + 1_\ell^T \mathbf{a}^{(1)}$ under the constraints of Eq. (12), with $Y' = Y^-$. Again, we delete any input $x \in X$ for which $\mathbf{a}^{(1)}(x) - \mathbf{a}^{(0)}(x) < 1$. We repeat the procedure until either one of the parties runs out of inputs *or* no further deletions can be made, for either party. See Fig. 4 for a full description of the algorithm. Before we discuss the general ramifications of the terminating step, we illustrate the usefulness of our algorithm with an example.

**Example.** Consider the deterministic asymmetric Boolean function from [3] described by the following matrices.

$$M^{(1,*)} = \begin{pmatrix} 0 & 1 & 1 & 0 \\ 1 & 0 & 1 & 1 \\ 1 & 0 & 0 & 0 \\ 0 & 1 & 0 & 1 \end{pmatrix}, \qquad M^{(*,1)} = \begin{pmatrix} 1 & 1 & 1 & 0 \\ 1 & 0 & 1 & 1 \\ 0 & 1 & 0 & 1 \\ 1 & 1 & 0 & 0 \end{pmatrix}.$$

For this function, each party has a unique locking strategy. Namely, $\mathbf{p}^T = (1,1,1,1)$ and $\mathbf{q}^T = (1,1,0,1)$ respectively. Let us walk through each iteration of the algorithm. The first optimization returns $\mathbf{b}^{(0)T} = (0,0,1,0)$ and $\mathbf{b}^{(1)T} = (1,1,0,1)$. Notice that $Y^+ = \{y_1, y_2, y_4\}$. The algorithm assigns $Y^- = Y^+$ and moves on to the next step. The second optimization returns $\mathbf{a}^{(0)T} = (1/2, 0, 1, 1/2)$ and $\mathbf{a}^{(1)T} = (1/2, 0, 1, 1/2)$. Notice that $X^+ = \emptyset$, and the algorithm terminates. Now, we will use these vectors to define backup outputs for the parties. Consider the following two-round protocol described by means of the backup outputs $\{(a_i, b_i)\}_{i=0\ldots2}$. Assuming the parties use $x \in X$ and $y \in Y$ for the computation,

---

**Building the Backup Outputs**

1. **Inputs:** $f$, $\mathcal{L}_1$, $\mathcal{L}_2$.
2. Define $X^- = X$ and $Y^- = Y \cup \{k+1\}$.
3. Minimize $-\mathbf{1}_k^T \mathbf{b}^{(0)} + \mathbf{1}_k^T \mathbf{b}^{(1)}$ subject to

$$\begin{pmatrix} A_{\mathbf{q}_1}(X^-) \\ A_{\mathbf{q}_2}(X^-) \\ \vdots \\ A_{\mathbf{q}_{s_2}}(X^-) \end{pmatrix} \cdot \begin{pmatrix} \mathbf{b}^{(0)} \\ \mathbf{b}^{(1)} \end{pmatrix} = \begin{pmatrix} \vec{b}_{\mathbf{q}_1}(X^-) \\ \vec{b}_{\mathbf{q}_2}(X^-) \\ \vdots \\ \vec{b}_{\mathbf{q}_{s_2}}(X^-) \end{pmatrix}$$

$$\begin{pmatrix} \mathbf{0}_k \\ \mathbf{0}_k \end{pmatrix} \le \begin{pmatrix} \mathbf{b}^{(0)} \\ \mathbf{b}^{(1)} \end{pmatrix} \le \begin{pmatrix} \mathbf{1}_k \\ \mathbf{1}_k \end{pmatrix}$$

Define $Y^+$ consisting of all the $y$'s such that $\mathbf{b}^{(1)}(y) - \mathbf{b}^{(0)}(y) = 1$.
4. **If** $Y^+ = Y^-$ *or* $Y^+ = \emptyset$ stop, otherwise set $Y^- \stackrel{\text{def}}{=} Y^+$ and go to Step 5.
5. Minimize $-\mathbf{1}_\ell^T \mathbf{a}^{(0)} + \mathbf{1}_\ell^T \mathbf{a}^{(1)}$ subject to

$$\begin{pmatrix} B_{\mathbf{p}_1}(Y^-) \\ B_{\mathbf{p}_2}(Y^-) \\ \vdots \\ B_{\mathbf{p}_{s_1}}(Y^-) \end{pmatrix} \cdot \begin{pmatrix} \mathbf{a}^{(0)} \\ \mathbf{a}^{(1)} \end{pmatrix} = \begin{pmatrix} \vec{a}_{\mathbf{p}_1}(Y^-) \\ \vec{a}_{\mathbf{p}_2}(Y^-) \\ \vdots \\ \vec{a}_{\mathbf{p}_{s_1}}(Y^-) \end{pmatrix}$$

$$\begin{pmatrix} \mathbf{0}_\ell \\ \mathbf{0}_\ell \end{pmatrix} \le \begin{pmatrix} \mathbf{a}^{(0)} \\ \mathbf{a}^{(1)} \end{pmatrix} \le \begin{pmatrix} \mathbf{1}_\ell \\ \mathbf{1}_\ell \end{pmatrix}$$

Define $X^+$ consisting of all the $x$'s such that $\mathbf{a}^{(1)}(x) - \mathbf{a}^{(0)}(x) = 1$.
6. **If** $X^+ = X^-$ *or* $X^+ = \emptyset$ stop, otherwise set $X^- \stackrel{\text{def}}{=} X^+$ and go to Step 3.
7. **Output:** The transcript of the execution.

---

**Fig. 4.** An algorithm for designing fully-secure protocols.

$$a_0 = f_1(x, \widetilde{y}) \text{ where } \widetilde{y} \in_U Y \qquad\qquad b_0 = f_2(\widetilde{x}, y) \text{ where } \widetilde{x} \in_U X$$

$$a_1 = \begin{cases} a \in_U \{0,1\} & \text{if } x \in \{x_1, x_4\} \\ 1 & \text{if } x = x_2 \\ 0 & \text{if } x = x_3 \end{cases} \qquad b_1 = \begin{cases} b \in_U \{0,1\} & \text{if } y = y_3 \\ f_2(x,y) & \text{if } y \ne y_3 \end{cases}.$$

$$a_2 = f_1(x, y) \qquad\qquad b_2 = f_2(x, y)$$

Observe that $a_1$ and $b_1$ are constructed in accordance with $\mathbf{a}^{(0)}$, $\mathbf{a}^{(1)}$ and $\mathbf{b}^{(0)}$, $\mathbf{b}^{(1)}$, respectively. It is not hard to see that the resulting protocol is passively secure and secure against sampling attacks. In light of Theorem 4.1, function $f$ is computable with full security. Next, we discuss the general case.

**General Case.** Assume that the algorithm terminates because one of the parties ran out of inputs. Without loss of generality, say that $Y^+ = \emptyset$ and write

$$\begin{pmatrix} \mathbf{b}_0^{(0)} \\ \mathbf{b}_0^{(1)} \end{pmatrix} \cdots \begin{pmatrix} \mathbf{b}_t^{(0)} \\ \mathbf{b}_t^{(1)} \end{pmatrix}, \qquad \begin{pmatrix} \mathbf{a}_1^{(0)} \\ \mathbf{a}_1^{(1)} \end{pmatrix} \cdots \begin{pmatrix} \mathbf{a}_t^{(0)} \\ \mathbf{a}_t^{(1)} \end{pmatrix}$$

for the vectors computed in the execution of the algorithm – starting from the bottom-up – i.e. $\mathbf{b}_0^{(0)}, \mathbf{b}_0^{(1)}$ denote the *last* vectors computed for $P_2$ and $\mathbf{b}_t^{(0)}, \mathbf{b}_t^{(1)}$ denote the *first* vectors computed for $P_2$. Similarly, $\mathbf{a}_1^{(0)}, \mathbf{a}_1^{(1)}$ denote the *last* vectors computed for $P_1$ and $\mathbf{a}_t^{(0)}, \mathbf{a}_t^{(1)}$ denote the *first* vectors computed for $P_1$. Now, assume[5] that for every $i \in \{1, \ldots, t\}$, and every $j \in \{1, \ldots, \ell\}$, either $\mathbf{a}_i^{(1)}(j) - \mathbf{a}_i^{(0)}(j) = 1$ or $\mathbf{a}_i^{(1)}(j) = \mathbf{a}_i^{(0)}(j)$. Similarly, for every $i \in \{0, \ldots, t\}$, and every $j \in \{1, \ldots, k\}$, either $\mathbf{b}_i^{(1)}(j) - \mathbf{b}_i^{(0)}(j) = 1$ or $\mathbf{b}_i^{(1)}(j) = \mathbf{b}_i^{(0)}(j)$. Write $\mathcal{T}_f$ for the transcript of the algorithm and consider the protocol from Fig. 5.

**Theorem 5.7.** *Using the notation above, Protocol* $\mathrm{SecSamp}(\mathcal{T}_f)$ *is passively secure and secure against sampling attacks.*

---

**Protocol** $\mathrm{SecSamp}(\mathcal{T}_f)$

1. The parties $P_1$ and $P_2$ hand their inputs, denoted $x$ and $y$ respectively, to the dealer.[a]
2. The dealer computes $f(x,y) = (\alpha, \beta)$ and constructs $(a_0, \ldots, a_{t+1})$ and $(b_0, \ldots, b_{t+1})$ such that
   - $a_0 = f_1(x, \widetilde{y})$, where $\widetilde{y} \in_U Y$.
   - $b_0$ is sampled independently such that $\Pr[b_0 = 1] = \mathbf{b}_0^{(0)}(y) = \mathbf{b}_0^{(1)}(y)$.
   - For every $i \in \{1, \ldots, t\}$, $a_i$ and $b_i$ are bits satisfying
   
   $$\begin{cases} \Pr[a_i = 1] = \mathbf{a}_i^{(\alpha)}(x) \\ \Pr[b_i = 1] = \mathbf{b}_i^{(\beta)}(y) \end{cases}$$
   
   - $a_{t+1} = f_1(x, y)$ and $b_{t+1} = f_2(x, y)$.
3. The dealer hands $a_0$ to $P_1$ and $b_0$ to $P_2$.
4. For $i = 1, \ldots, t+1$,
   (a) The dealer gives $a_i$ to $P_1$. If $P_1$ aborts, then $P_2$ outputs $b_{i-1}$ and halts.
   (b) The dealer gives $b_i$ to $P_2$. If $P_2$ aborts, then $P_1$ outputs $a_i$ and halts.

---
[a] If $x$ is not in the appropriate domain or $P_1$ does not hand an input, then the dealer sends $f(\hat{x}, y)$ (where $\hat{x}$ is a default value) to $P_2$, which outputs this value and the protocol is terminated. The case of an inappropriate $y$ is dealt analogously.

---

**Fig. 5.** Protocol $\mathrm{SecSamp}(\mathcal{T}_f)$ for computing $f$.

---
[5] In light of Proposition 5.6, we can construct vectors admitting the required expression.

*Proof (Sketch).* The fact that the protocol is passively secure is trivial. Regarding security against sampling attacks, notice that, at any given round, the adversary either knows the output or knows nothing about it (other than what the corrupted party's input suggests). The adversary will not be able to mount a successful sampling attack in neither case. If the output has not been revealed to her, then her view is independent of the honest party's output resulting from some locking strategy (regardless of whether she quits at that round or at the end). If the output has been revealed to the adversary, then sampling attacks are foiled by design thanks to the algorithm.                                    □

**When the algorithm fails.** We turn our attention to functions for which the algorithm returns $Y^+ \neq \emptyset$ and $X^+ \neq \emptyset$. Semi-balanced functions fall under this category. By Cleve [7], protocols that satisfy both correctness *and* security against sampling attacks do not exist in the plain model. However, there are functions other than semi-balanced for which the algorithm fails. Unfortunately, we do not fully understand why that is the case and there appears to be a trade off between fairness and privacy. To illustrate, we show that a certain function that lies in the gap can be computed with fairness but not privacy.

We emphasize that the function in question may still be computable with full security. However, our previous analysis together with the theorem below strongly indicate that the trade-off may be inherent.

**Theorem 5.8.** *The function described by the matrices below admits a protocol that is fair-but-not-private.*

$$M^{(1,*)} = \begin{pmatrix} 1 & 1 & 1 & 1 & 0 \\ 0 & 1 & 0 & 1 & 1 \\ 1 & 1 & 1 & 1 & 1 \\ 0 & 0 & 1 & 0 & 1 \\ 1 & 0 & 0 & 0 & 1 \end{pmatrix}, \quad M^{(*,1)} = \begin{pmatrix} 1 & 1 & 0 & 0 & 0 \\ 1 & 0 & 0 & 0 & 1 \\ 1 & 0 & 0 & 1 & 0 \\ 0 & 0 & 1 & 1 & 1 \\ 0 & 1 & 0 & 1 & 0 \end{pmatrix}.$$

*Proof.* Consider the following 2-round protocol defined by means of the backup outputs $\{a_i, b_i\}_{i=1...2}$.

$a_0 = f_1(x, \tilde{y})$ where $\tilde{y} \in_U Y$                                                              $b_0 = b \in_U \{0,1\}$

If $y \in \{y_1, y_3, y_5\}$         $a_1 = \begin{cases} a \in_U \{0,1\} & \text{if } x = x_1 \\ 0 & \text{if } x = x_5 \\ 1 & \text{otherwise} \end{cases}$         $b_1 = f(x,y)$.

If $y \in \{y_2, y_4\}$              $a_1 = \begin{cases} 0 & \text{if } x \in \{x_4, x_5\} \\ 1 & \text{otherwise} \end{cases}$

$a_2 = f(x,y)$                                                                                      $b_2 = f(x,y)$

A straightforward computation shows that the protocol is secure against sampling attacks. However, the protocol is obviously not passively secure. Notice that the backup output $a_1$ leaks information about $P_2$'s input. Nevertheless, by plugging the protocol into our compiler, the resulting protocol satisfies fairness.

Formally, by having the trusted party leak the honest party's input to the simulator in the ideal model, one can show that the resulting protocol is secure with respect to the new model.                                                                    □

## 6    Conclusions and Open Problems

In this paper, we introduced a notion of security referred to as *security against sampling attacks*. The notion of security is useful because it is necessary for fairness and it appears easier to achieve compared to fairness. What is more, we showed how certain protocols satisfying security against sampling attacks can be transformed into fully-secure protocols. We emphasize that the route towards full-security we propose is not arbitrary; every known protocol based on GHKL can be viewed as a special case of our approach. Finally, for asymmetric functions, we showed how to design suitable protocols by means of an algorithm. Given an asymmetric (possibly randomized) Boolean function, our algorithm either returns an appropriate protocol or it returns that it failed to do so. Unfortunately, our algorithm fails for functions other than semi-balanced, and the status of these functions is still unknown. We provide a few conjectures as to why that may be the case.

First, we believe that a failure on the part of the algorithm is essentially a proof of impossibility. In other words, we believe that if our algorithm fails to come up with an suitable protocol for some function, then any realization of the function is susceptible to some attack. At the same time, we believe that the attack in question cannot rely solely on sampling attacks, but on some combination of passive and sampling attacks. The motivation behind this belief is that we suspect certain functions to be computable with fairness-but-privacy[6] but not with full security. A candidate for such a function is given at the end of the last section.

**The Multi-party Case.** We note that, like [3], our analysis extends to the multi-party case where the total number of parties is constant and exactly half of the parties are corrupted. Specifically, if $f = (f_1, \ldots, f_t) : Z_1 \times \ldots \times Z_t \to [m]^t$ denotes a (possibly randomized) $t$-party function, there are $\binom{t}{t/2}$ two-party functions that result from partitioning the set into two equal-sized subsets. These functions can be viewed as non-Boolean asymmetric functions in $X \times Y \to [m^{t/2}]^2$. Using the techniques from [3,5], functionality $f$ is fair if and only if all of the underlying two-party functions are fair as well. Thus, our framework is also useful in this regard.

Finally, our work says little about the multi-party case with absolute dishonest majorities as well as two-party and multi-party functionalities that depend on the security parameter $\mathcal{F} = \{f_n\}_{n \in \mathbb{N}}$. Of course, locking strategies and sampling attacks are still meaningful in these settings, and it would be interesting to see how they can be put to use.

---

[6] Of course, this notion needs to be formalized.

# References

1. Agrawal, S., Prabhakaran, M.: On fair exchange, fair coins and fair sampling. In: Canetti, R., Garay, J.A. (eds.) CRYPTO 2013. LNCS, vol. 8042, pp. 259–276. Springer, Heidelberg (2013). https://doi.org/10.1007/978-3-642-40041-4_15

2. Asharov, G.: Towards characterizing complete fairness in secure two-party computation. In: Lindell, Y. (ed.) TCC 2014. LNCS, vol. 8349, pp. 291–316. Springer, Heidelberg (2014). https://doi.org/10.1007/978-3-642-54242-8_13

3. Asharov, G., Beimel, A., Makriyannis, N., Omri, E.: Complete characterization of fairness in secure two-party computation of boolean functions. In: Dodis, Y., Nielsen, J.B. (eds.) TCC 2015. LNCS, vol. 9014, pp. 199–228. Springer, Heidelberg (2015). https://doi.org/10.1007/978-3-662-46494-6_10

4. Asharov, G., Lindell, Y., Rabin, T.: A full characterization of functions that imply fair coin tossing and ramifications to fairness. In: Sahai, A. (ed.) TCC 2013. LNCS, vol. 7785, pp. 243–262. Springer, Heidelberg (2013). https://doi.org/10.1007/978-3-642-36594-2_14

5. Beimel, A., Omri, E., Orlov, I.: Protocols for multiparty coin toss with a dishonest majority. J. Cryptol. **28**, 551–600 (2015)

6. Canetti, R.: Security and composition of multiparty cryptographic protocols. J. Cryptol. **13**(1), 143–202 (2000)

7. Cleve, R.: Limits on the security of coin flips when half the processors are faulty. In: STOC, pp. 364–369 (1986)

8. Daza, V., Makriyannis, N.: Designing Fully Secure Protocols for Secure Two-Party Computation of Constant-Domain Functions. Cryptology ePrint Archive, Report 2017/098 (2017)

9. Goldreich, O.: Foundations of Cryptography: Basic Applications, vol. II. Cambridge University Press, Cambridge (2004)

10. Goldreich, O., Micali, S., Wigderson, A.: How to play any mental game or a completeness theorem for protocols with honest majority. In: STOC, pp. 218–229 (1987)

11. Gordon, S.D., Hazay, C., Katz, J., Lindell, Y.: Complete fairness in secure two-party computation. J. ACM **58**, 24:1–24:37 (2011)

12. Gordon, S.D., Katz, J.: Complete fairness in multi-party computation without an honest majority. In: Reingold, O. (ed.) TCC 2009. LNCS, vol. 5444, pp. 19–35. Springer, Heidelberg (2009). https://doi.org/10.1007/978-3-642-00457-5_2

13. Makriyannis, N.: On the classification of finite boolean functions up to fairness. In: Proceeding of the Security and Cryptography for Networks Conference, pp. 135–154 (2014)

14. Yao, A.C.: Protocols for secure computations. In: FOCS, pp. 160–164 (1982)

# On Secure Two-Party Computation in Three Rounds

Prabhanjan Ananth[1($\boxtimes$)] and Abhishek Jain[2]

[1] University of California Los Angeles, Los Angeles, USA
prabhanjan@cs.ucla.edu
[2] Johns Hopkins University, Baltimore, USA
abhishek@cs.jhu.edu

**Abstract.** We revisit the exact round complexity of secure two-party computation. While four rounds are known to be sufficient for securely computing general functions that provide output to one party [Katz-Ostrovsky, CRYPTO'04], Goldreich-Krawczyk [SIAM J. Computing'96] proved that three rounds are insufficient for this task w.r.t. black-box simulation.

In this work, we study the feasibility of secure computation in three rounds using *non-black-box* simulation. Our main result is a three-round two-party computation protocol for general functions against adversaries with auxiliary inputs of a priori *bounded* size. This result relies on a new two round input-extraction protocol based on succinct randomized encodings.

We also provide a partial answer to the question of achieving security against non-uniform adversaries. Assuming sub-exponentially secure iO and one-way functions, we rule out three-round protocols that achieve polynomial simulation-based security against the output party and exponential indistinguishability-based security against the other party.

## 1 Introduction

The notion of secure computation [24,39] is fundamental in cryptography. Informally speaking, secure two-party computation allows two mutually distrusting parties to jointly compute a function over their private inputs in a manner such that no one learns anything beyond the function output.

An important measure of efficiency of secure computation protocols is *round complexity*. Clearly, the smaller the number of rounds, the lesser the impact of network latency on the communication between the parties. Indeed, ever since the introduction of secure computation, its round complexity has been the subject of intensive study, both in the two-party and multiparty setting.

In this work, we study the *exact* round complexity of secure two-party computation against malicious adversaries in the plain model (i.e., without any

P. Ananth—Supported in part by grant 360584 from the Simons Foundation.

A. Jain—Supported in part by a DARPA/ARL Safeware Grant W911NF-15-C-0213 and a sub-award from NSF CNS-1414023.

Y. Kalai and L. Reyzin (Eds.): TCC 2017, Part I, LNCS 10677, pp. 612–644, 2017.
https://doi.org/10.1007/978-3-319-70500-2_21

trusted setup assumptions). We focus on the classical unidirectional message model where a round of communication consists of a single message sent by one party to the other.

In this setting, constant round protocols can be readily obtained by compiling a two-round semi-honest protocol (e.g., using garbled circuits [39] and oblivious transfer [15,37]) with constant-round zero-knowledge proofs [16,21,26] following the GMW paradigm [24]. Katz and Ostrovsky [30] established an upper bound on the exact round complexity of secure two-party computation by showing that four rounds are sufficient for computing general functions that provide output to one party. On the negative side, Goldreich and Krawczyk [22] proved that two-party computation with black-box simulation cannot be realized in three rounds.

Ever since the introduction of non-black-box techniques in cryptography nearly two decades ago [3], the following important question has remained open:

*Can secure two-party computation be realized in three rounds using non-black-box simulation?*

In this work, we address this question and provide both positive and negative results.

## 1.1 Our Results

We investigate the feasibility of three-round secure two-party computation against malicious adversaries in the plain model. We consider functions where only one party (a.k.a *receiver*) learns the output. The other party is referred to as the *sender*.

**I. Positive Result.** Our main result is a three-round two-party computation protocol for general functions that achieves security against adversarial senders with auxiliary inputs of arbitrary polynomial size and adversarial receivers with auxiliary inputs of a priori *bounded* size.

In order to obtain our result, we devise a new non-black-box technique for extracting adversary's input in only two rounds based on succinct randomized encodings [9,12,32] and two-round oblivious transfer (OT) with indistinguishability-based security [36]. To prove security of our three-round protocol, we additionally require two-message witness indistinguishable proofs (a.k.a. Zaps) [14] and Learning with Errors (LWE) assumption.

**Theorem 1.** *Assuming the existence of succinct randomized encodings, two-round OT, Zaps and LWE, there exists a three-round two-party computation protocol $(P_1, P_2)$ for computing general functions that achieves security against adversarial $P_1$ with auxiliary inputs of arbitrary polynomial size and adversarial $P_2$ with auxiliary inputs of bounded size.*

*On Succinct Randomized Encodings.* A succinct randomized encoding (SRE) scheme allows one to encode the computation of a Turing machine $M$ on an input $x$ such that the encoding time is independent of the time it takes to compute $M(x)$. The security of SRE is defined in a similar manner as standard (non-succinct) randomized encodings [28]. Presently, all known constructions of SRE are based on indistinguishability obfuscation (iO) [4,17]. We note, however, that SRE is *not* known to imply iO and may likely be a weaker assumption.[1]

*On Bounded Auxiliary Inputs.* Our positive result is motivated by the recent beautiful works of [7,8] on three-round zero-knowledge proofs that achieve security against adversaries with auxiliary inputs of a priori bounded size. Specifically, [8] considers malicious verifiers with bounded-size auxiliary inputs while [7] consider malicious provers with bounded-size auxiliary inputs.

Our positive result can be viewed as a generalization of [8] to general-purpose secure computation.

*Outputs for Both Parties.* Theorem 1 only considers functions that provide output to one party. As observed in [30], a protocol for this setting can be easily transformed into one where both parties receive the output by computing a modified functionality that outputs signed values. Now the output recipient can forward the output to the other party who accepts it only if the signature verifies.

**II. Negative Result.** We also explore the possibility of achieving security in the case where each adversarial party may receive auxiliary inputs of arbitrary polynomial size.

We provide a partial answer to this question. We show that three-round secure two-party computation for general functions is impossible if we require simulation-based security against PPT adversarial receivers and exponential indistinguishability security against adversarial senders. Our result relies on the existence of sub-exponentially secure iO and one-way functions.

**Theorem 2.** *Suppose that sub-exponentially secure iO and one-way functions exist. Then there exists a two-party functionality $f$ such that no three-round protocol $\Pi$ for computing $f$ can achieve the following two properties:*

- *Simulation-based security against PPT adversarial receivers.*
- *$2^{O(L)}$-indistinguishability security against adversarial senders, where $L$ denotes the length of the first message in $\Pi$.*

Here, $2^k$-indistinguishability security means that for any pair of inputs $(y, y')$ for the receiver, an adversarial sender can distinguish which input was used in a protocol execution with probability at most $\frac{1}{2^k}$.

We stress that Theorem 2 even rules out non-black-box simulation techniques.

*Discussion.* Our negative result can be viewed as a first step towards disproving the existence of three-round two-party computation against non-uniform adversaries. We remark that ruling out non-black-box techniques in three-rounds is

---

[1] If SRE satisfies an additional "output compactness" property where the size of an encoding of $(M, x)$ is also independent of the size of the machine's output, i.e., $|M(x)|$, then sub-exponentially secure SRE is known to imply iO [2]. We do not require such output compactness property for our result.

highly non-trivial even when we require exponential (indistinguishability) security for one party. Indeed, a somewhat analogous question regarding the existence of three-round zero-knowledge *proofs* was recently addressed by Kalai et al. in [29]. Specifically, [29] prove the impossibility of three-round (public-coin) zero-knowledge proofs with non-black-box simulators assuming sub-exponentially secure iO and one-way functions and exponentially secure input-hiding obfuscation for multi-bit point functions.[2]

A proof system achieves *statistical* security against adversarial provers. In a similar vein, Theorem 2 requires exponential indistinguishability-security against adversarial senders. As such, Theorem 2 can be viewed as providing a complementary result to [29].

Needless to say, it remains an intriguing open question to extend our lower bound to rule out protocols that achieve polynomial-security against adversarial senders.

### 1.2   Our Techniques

In this section, we describe the main ideas used in our positive and negative results.

**I. Positive Result.** We start by describing the main ideas in our positive result. We first describe the setting: we consider two parties $P_1$ and $P_2$ holding private inputs $x_1$ and $x_2$, respectively, for computing a function $f$. At the end of the protocol, $P_2$ gets $f(x_1, x_2)$ while $P_1$ gets no output. We want to achieve security against adversarial $P_1$ who may receive auxiliary inputs of unbounded (polynomial) size and adversarial $P_2$ who may receive auxiliary inputs of an a priori bounded size.

Recently, Bitansky et al. [8] constructed a three-round zero-knowledge argument of knowledge (ZKAOK) that achieves standard soundness guarantee and zero-knowledge guarantee against adversarial verifiers with bounded auxiliary inputs. Given their protocol, a natural starting idea to achieve our goal is to "compile" a two-round semi-honest two-party computation protocol into a maliciously secure one (a la [24]) with their ZKAOK system. Note, however, that while we have enough in the protocol to enforce semi-honest behavior on $P_1$ using ZKAOK, we cannot use the same approach for $P_2$. Nevertheless, as a first step, let us fix a three-round protocol that guarantees security against adversarial $P_1$. For concreteness, we instantiate the semi-honest two-party computation using garbled circuits and two-round oblivious transfer. We also use a delayed-input ZKAOK [33] where the instance is only used in the last round. This property is satisfied by argument system of [8].

- In the first round, $P_1$ sends the first message of a delayed-input ZKAOK.
- In the second round, $P_2$ sends the second message of ZKAOK together with the receiver message of a two-round oblivious transfer (OT) computed using its input for $f$.

---

[2] Their result, in fact, extends to constant-round protocols.

– In the third round, $P_1$ sends garbled circuit for $f$ with its input hardwired, together with the OT sender message (computed using the inputs labels for the garbled circuit) and the third message of ZKAOK to prove that the garbled circuit and the OT sender message are computed "honestly".

*Main Challenge #1.* Note that in the above protocol, it is already guaranteed that $P_2$'s input is independent of $P_1$'s input. Nevertheless, this is not enough and in order to achieve security against malicious $P_2$, we need to construct a polynomial-time simulator that can *extract* $P_2$'s input by the end of the second round, and then simulate the third round of the protocol to "force" the correct output on $P_2$. In light of our lower bound, we need to devise a two-round input extraction procedure that works against adversaries with bounded auxiliary inputs. At first, it is not at all clear how such an input-extraction protocol can be constructed. In particular, black-box techniques do not suffice for this purpose [22]. Instead, we must use non-black-box techniques.

The problem of extraction in two-rounds or less was recently considered by Bitansky et al. [8]. They study extractable one-way functions and then use them to construct three-round ZKAOK against verifiers with bounded non-uniformity. We note, however, that their notion of extractable one-way functions is unsuitable for our goal of extracting adversary's input. In particular, in their notion, the extracted value can be from a completely different distribution than the actual value $x$ used to compute the one-way function. In contrast, we want to extract a "committed" input of the adversary.

*Main Challenge #2.* To make matters worse, we cannot hope to extract the input of a malicious adversary in two rounds with guarantee of correct extraction. Indeed, two-round zero-knowledge proofs (with polynomial-time simulation) are known to be impossible against non-uniform verifiers even w.r.t. non-black-box simulation [25].[3]

In light of the above, we settle on a "weak extraction" guarantee, namely, where correctness of extraction is only guaranteed if the adversary behaves honestly. Note that this means that our simulator may fail to extract the input of $P_2$ if it behaves maliciously. In this case, it may not be able to produce an indistinguishable third message of the protocol.

For now, we ignore this important issue and proceed to describe a two-round protocol that enables weak input-extraction. Later, we describe how we construct our scheme using only this weak extraction property.

*(Weak) Input-Extraction in Two Rounds.* We want to construct a two-round protocol that allows a simulator (that has access to the Turing machine description and bounded auxiliary input of adversarial $P_2$) to extract $P_2$'s input for $f$

---

[3] Bitansky et al. [8] construct a two-round zero-knowledge argument against verifiers with bounded non-uniformity. Using their system, however, would necessarily require even $P_1$ (who will play the role of the verifier) to have bounded non-uniformity. Our goal instead is to limit the bounded non-uniformity assumption to $P_2$ and allow $P_1$ to be fully non-uniform.

as long as $P_2$ behaves semi-honestly in this protocol. However, an adversarial $P_1$ should not be able to learn any information about an honest $P_2$'s input. For simplicity of exposition, below, we restrict ourselves to the case where $P_2$ is a uniform Turing machine. It is easy to verify that our protocol also works when $P_2$ has an auxiliary input of bounded length.

We first note that the problem of constructing an input-extraction protocol can be reduced to the problem of constructing a "trapdoor" extraction protocol where the trapdoor is a random string. This is because the trapdoor can be set to the randomness $r$ used by $P_2$ for computing its OT receiver message in our three-round protocol described earlier. If we use an OT protocol where the receiver's message is perfectly binding (e.g., [36]), then once the simulator has extracted $P_2$'s randomness in OT, it can also recover its input.

In order to construct a trapdoor extraction protocol, we build on ideas from Barak's non-black-box technique [3]. Consider the following two-party functionality $g$: it takes as input a string TM from $P_1$ and a tuple $(\beta, \text{trap}, m)$ from $P_2$. It treats TM as a valid Turing machine and computes $\beta' = \text{TM}(m)$. If $\beta' = \beta$, it outputs trap, else it outputs $\bot$.[4] Let $\Pi$ be a two-round two-party computation protocol for computing $g$.

Now, consider the following candidate two-round protocol for extracting a trapdoor from $P_2$: $P_1$ sends the first message of $\Pi$ computed using input $\text{TM} = 0$. Let $\text{msg}_1$ denote this message. Upon receiving $\text{msg}_1$, $P_2$ first prepares an input tuple $(\beta, \text{trap}, m)$ for $g$ as follows: it samples a random string $\beta$ of length $\ell$ s.t. $\ell \gg |\text{msg}_1|$ and sets trap to be a random string and $m = \text{msg}_1$. Finally, $P_2$ sends the second message of $\Pi$ computed using $(\beta, \text{trap}, m)$ together with $\beta$.

A non-black-box simulator that knows the Turing machine description $\text{TM}_2$ of adversarial $P_2$ can set its input $\text{TM} = \text{TM}_2$ in the above protocol. If $P_2$ behaves semi-honestly, then at the end of the protocol, the simulator should obtain trap. Security against a malicious $P_1$ can be argued using the fact that $\beta \gg |\text{msg}_1|$ in the same manner as the proof of soundness in Barak's protocol.

A reader familiar with [3] may notice a major problem with the above extraction protocol. Note that since $\Pi$ is a secure computation protocol, its running time must be strictly greater than the size of the circuit representation of $g$. Now, since the functionality $g$ internally computes the next-step function of $P_2$, the running time of $\Pi$ is strictly greater than the running time of $P_2$!

Our key idea to solve this problem is to *delegate* the "expensive" computation inside $g$ to $P_1$ (or more accurately, the simulator when $P_2$ is corrupted).[5] Let $M$ be an "input-less" Turing machine that has hardwired in its description a tuple $(\text{TM}, \beta, \text{trap}, m)$. Upon execution, it performs the same computation as $g$. Now, instead of using the two-party computation protocol to compute the function $g$, we use it to compute a "secure encoding" of $M$. We want the encoding scheme

---

[4] Note that $g$ internally transforms TM into a circuit and uses it to perform the rest of the computation.

[5] Indeed, an honest $P_1$ is never required the functionality $g$. However, when $P_2$ is corrupted, then the simulator acting on behalf of $P_1$ does compute $g$ to learn the trapdoor.

to be such that the time to encode $M$ is *independent* of the running time of $M$. Note that in this case, the running time of the protocol is also independent of the running time of $M$. The honest $P_1$ ignores the encoding it obtains at the end of the two-party computation protocol. However, the simulator can simply "decode" the secure encoding to learn its output.

An encoding scheme with the above efficiency property is referred to as a succinct randomized encoding (SRE) [9,12,32]. By using an SRE scheme, we are able to resolve the running-time problem.

*Using Weak Extraction Guarantee.* Finally, we explain how we obtain our construction by only relying on the weak extraction property of our input extraction protocol. Note that if an adversarial $P_2$ cheats in the input extraction protocol, then due to the weak extraction guarantee, the simulator may extract an incorrect input (or no input at all). In this case, the simulated garbled circuit computed by the simulator would be easily distinguishable from the garbled circuit in the real execution. Therefore, we need a mechanism that "hides" $P_1$'s third round message from $P_2$ if $P_2$ cheated in the input-extraction protocol. On the other hand, if $P_2$ did behave honestly, then the mechanism should "reveal" the third round message to $P_2$.

We solve this problem by using conditional disclosure of secrets [1,19]. Recall that a CDS scheme consists of two players: a sender $S$ and a receiver $R$. The parties share a common instance $x$ of an NP language. Using this instance, the sender $S$ can "encrypt" a secret message $m$ s.t. a receiver $R$ can only "decrypt" it using a witness $w$ for $x$.

Using a CDS scheme for NP, we modify our protocol as follows. Now, $P_1$ will send a CDS encryption of the garbled circuit for $f$ and its OT sender message. The instance for this encryption is simply the transcript of the input extraction protocol. In order to decrypt, $P_2$ must use a witness that establishes honest behavior during the input extraction protocol. The input and randomness of $P_2$ in the input-extraction protocol constitutes such a witness. In other words, if $P_2$ cheated in the input-extraction protocol, then it cannot recover the third round message of $P_1$.

A subtle point here is that a CDS scheme only promises security against adversarial receivers when the instance used for encryption is *false*. Therefore, in order to use the security of CDS, we must ensure that there does *not exist* a valid witness if $P_2$ cheats in the input extraction protocol. We achieve this property by ensuring that the input-extraction protocol is perfectly binding for $P_2$.

We implement a CDS scheme using a two-round two-party computation protocol that achieves indistinguishability security against malicious receivers and semi-honest senders. Such a scheme can be implemented using garbled circuits and two-round oblivious transfer of [36]. Finally, to prevent an adversarial $P_1$ from created "malformed" CDS encryptions, we require $P_1$ to prove its well-formedness using delayed-input ZKAOK.

**II. Negative Result.** We now provide an overview of our lower bound. Due to space constraints, we describe the lower bound in the full version.

Recall that simulation-based security for any two-party computation protocol is argued by constructing a polynomial-time simulator who can simulate the view of the adversary in an indistinguishable manner without any knowledge of the honest party input. One of the main tasks of such a simulator is to *extract* the input of the adversary. We establish our negative result by ruling out the possibility of extracting the input of adversarial receiver in a three-round secure computation protocol.

More concretely, we consider three round protocols $(P_1, P_2)$ where $P_2$ receives the output. We describe a two-party functionality $f$ and an adversary $P_2$ such that no polynomial-time simulator can extract $P_2$'s input from any three-round protocol $\Pi$ for computing $f$, if $\Pi$ achieves $2^{O(L)}$-indistinguishability security against $P_1$. Here, $L$ is the length of the first message of $\Pi$.

Note that in a three-round protocol, $P_2$ only sends a single message. Clearly, black-box techniques are insufficient for extracting $P_2$'s input in this setting. The main challenge here is to rule out extraction via *non-black-box* techniques.

In order to "hide" the input of an adversarial $P_2$ from a non-black-box simulator who has access to $P_2$'s code, we make use of program obfuscation [4]. Namely, we construct a "dummy" adversary $P_2$, who receives as *auxiliary input*, an obfuscated program that has an input hardwired in its description and uses it to compute the adversary's message in the two-party computation protocol. During the protocol execution, the adversary simply uses the obfuscated program to compute its protocol message. Our goal is to then argue that having access to the code of this dummy adversary as well as his obfuscated auxiliary input gives no advantage to a polynomial-time simulator. We note that a similar strategy was recently used by Bitansky et al. [8] in order to prove the impossibility of extractable one-way functions.

Below, we first describe our proof strategy using the strong notion of virtual black-box obfuscation [4]. Most of the main challenges that we address already arise in this case. Later, we explain how we can derive our negative result using the weaker notion of indistinguishability obfuscation.

*Function $f$.* Recall that the main reason why the simulator needs to extract the adversary's input is to learn the function output from the ideal functionality. In order to ensure that the simulator cannot "bypass" input extraction, we choose a function with unpredictable outputs. Furthermore, we also want that the input of the honest party cannot be trivially determined from the function.

We choose $f$ to be a pseudorandom function PRF that takes as input a PRF key $x_1$ from $P_1$ and an input $x_2$ from $P_2$ and outputs the evaluation of the PRF on $x_2$ using key $x_1$. It is easy to see that $f$ satisfies the above desired properties.

*Adversary $P_2$ and Auxiliary Input $Z$.* Towards a contradiction, let $\Pi$ be any three-round two-party protocol for securely computing $f$ with the security properties stated in Theorem 2.

The auxiliary input $Z$ consists of an obfuscated program that has an input $x_2$ and a key $K$ hardwired in its description:

1. Upon receiving a message $\mathsf{msg}_1$ from $P_1$ as input, the program honestly computes the protocol message $\mathsf{msg}_2$ of $P_2$ (as per protocol $\Pi$) using input $x_2$ and randomness $r = F(K, \mathsf{msg})$, where $F$ is another PRF.
2. Upon receiving a protocol transcript $(\mathsf{msg}_1, \mathsf{msg}_2, \mathsf{msg}_3)$, it re-computes the randomness $r$ used to compute $\mathsf{msg}_2$. Using the transcript, randomness $r$ and input $x_2$, it computes the output honestly.

The adversary $P_2$ does not perform any computation on its own. Upon receiving a message $\mathsf{msg}_1$ from $P_1$, it runs the obfuscated program on $\mathsf{msg}_1$ to obtain $\mathsf{msg}_2$ and then forwards it to $P_1$. Finally, upon receiving $\mathsf{msg}_3$ from $P_1$, it submits the protocol transcript $(\mathsf{msg}_1, \mathsf{msg}_2, \mathsf{msg}_3)$ to the obfuscated program to obtain an output $y$.

*Proof Strategy: Attempt #1.* For any simulator $S$ for $\Pi$, let $\mathsf{Q}$ denote the possible set of queries made by $S$ to the ideal function. The core argument in our proof is that the query set $\mathsf{Q}$ *cannot* contain $P_2$'s input $x_2$. At a high-level, our strategy for proving this is as follows: first, we want to switch the auxiliary input $Z$ to a different auxiliary input $Z'$ that has some other input $x_2'$ hardwired inside it. We want to rely upon the security of $\Pi$ against adversarial $P_1$ in order to make this switch. Once we have made this switch, then we can easily argue that the $\mathsf{Q}$ cannot contain $x_2$ since the view of $S$ is independent of $x_2$.

*Problem: Rewinding Attacks.* The above proof strategy runs into the following issue: since the adversary $P_2$ includes the protocol output in its view, a simulator $S$ may fix the first two messages of the protocol and then try to observe the output of $P_2$ on many different third messages. Indeed, a simulator may be able to learn non-trivial information by simply observing whether the adversary accepts or aborts on different trials.

A naive approach to try to address this problem is to simply remove the output from adversary's view. That is, we simply delete the second instruction in the obfuscated program $Z$. Now, $P_2$ never processes the messages received from $P_1$. This approach, however, immediately fails because now a simulator can simply simulate a "rejecting" transcript. Since there is no way for the distinguisher to check the validity of the transcript (since $P_2$'s output is not part of its view), the simulator can easily fool the distinguisher.

*Non-uniform Distinguishers.* We address this problem by using non-uniform distinguishers, in a manner similar to [25]. Specifically, we modify $P_2$ to be such that it simply outputs the protocol transcript at the end of the protocol. The PRF key $K$ hardwired inside $Z$ (and used to compute $P_2$'s protocol message) is given as non-uniform advice to the distinguisher. Note that this information is not available to the simulator.

Now, given $K$ and the protocol transcript, the distinguisher can easily compute $P_2$'s output. Therefore, a simulator can no longer fool the distinguisher via a rejecting transcript. Furthermore, now, the protocol output is not part of $P_2$'s view, and therefore, rewinding attacks are also ruled out.

*Revised Proof Strategy.* Let us now return to our proof strategy. Recall that we want to switch the auxiliary input $Z$ to a different auxiliary input $Z'$ that has some other input $x_2'$ hardwired inside it. Once we have made this switch, then we can easily argue that the $Q$ cannot contain $x_2$ since the view of $S$ is independent of $x_2$.

We make the switch from auxiliary input $Z$ to $Z'$ via a sequence of hybrids. In particular, we go through $2^L$ number of hybrids, one for every possible first message $\mathsf{msg}_1$ of $P_1$. In the $i^{\text{th}}$ hybrid, we use an auxiliary input $Z_i$ that has both $x_2$ and $x_2'$ hardwired inside it. On input first messages $\mathsf{msg}_1 < i$, it uses $x_2$ to compute the second message, and otherwise, it uses $x_2'$. In order to argue indistinguishability of hybrids $i$ and $i + 1$, we use the security of protocol $\Pi$ against malicious $P_1$. Indeed, this is why we require $2^{O(L)}$-indistinguishability security against adversarial $P_1$.

In order to perform the above proof strategy using indistinguishability obfuscation (as opposed to virtual black-box obfuscation), we make use of puncturable PRFs and use the "punctured programming" techniques [38] that have been used in a large body of works over the last few years. We refer the reader to the technical sections for further details.

### 1.3 Related Works

Katz and Ostrovsky [30] constructed a four-round two-party computation protocol for general functions where one of the parties receives the output. Recently, Garg et al. [18] extended their work to the simultaneous-message model.

Three round zero-knowledge proofs were first constructed in [6,27] using "knowledge assumptions." More recently, [7,8] construct three-round zero-knowledge proofs adversaries that receive auxiliary inputs of a priori bounded size. Our positive result is directly inspired by these works.

A recent work of Döttling et al. [13] constructs a two-round two-party computation protocol for oblivious computation of cryptographic functionalities. They consider semi-honest senders and malicious receivers, and prove game-based security against the latter. In contrast, in this work, we consider polynomial-time simulation-based security.

## 2    Preliminaries

We denote the security parameter by $\lambda$. We assume familiarity with standard cryptographic primitives.

*General Notation.* If $A$ is a probabilistic polynomial time algorithm, then we write $y \leftarrow A(x)$ to denote that one execution of $A$ on $x$ yields $y$. Furthermore, we denote $y \leftarrow A(x; r)$ to denote that $A$ on input $x$ and randomness $r$, outputs $y$. If $\mathcal{D}$ is a distribution, we mean $x \xleftarrow{\$} \mathcal{D}$ to mean that $x$ is sampled from $\mathcal{D}$.

Two distributions $\mathcal{D}_1$ and $\mathcal{D}_2$, defined on the same sample space, are said to be computationally distinguishable, denoted by $\mathcal{D}_1 \cong_{c,\varepsilon} \mathcal{D}_2$ if the following holds: for any PPT adversary $\mathcal{A}$ and sufficiently large security parameter $\lambda \in \mathbb{N}$ it holds that,

$$|\Pr[1 \leftarrow \mathcal{A}(1^\lambda, s_1) \; : \; s_1 \xleftarrow{\$} \mathcal{D}_1(1^\lambda)] - \Pr[1 \leftarrow \mathcal{A}(1^\lambda, s_2) \; : \; s_2 \xleftarrow{\$} \mathcal{D}_2(1^\lambda)]| \leq \varepsilon,$$

If $\varepsilon$ is some negligible function then we denote this by $\mathcal{D}_1 \cong_c \mathcal{D}_2$.

*Languages and Relations.* A language $L$ is a subset of $\{0,1\}^*$. A relation $\mathcal{R}$ is a subset of $\{0,1\}^* \times \{0,1\}^*$. We use the following notation:

- Suppose $\mathcal{R}$ is a relation. We define $\mathcal{R}$ to be *efficiently decidable* if there exists an algorithm $A$ and fixed polynomial $p$ such that $(x, w) \in \mathcal{R}$ if and only if $A(x, w) = 1$ and the running time of $A$ is upper bounded by $p(|x|, |w|)$.
- Suppose $\mathcal{R}$ is an efficiently decidable relation. We say that $\mathcal{R}$ is a NP relation if $L(\mathcal{R})$ is a NP language, where $L(\mathcal{R})$ is defined as follows: $x \in L(R)$ if and only if there exists $w$ such that $(x, w) \in \mathcal{R}$ and $|w| \leq p(|x|)$ for some fixed polynomial $p$.

*Modeling Real World Adversaries: Uniform versus Non Uniform.* One way to model real world adversaries $\mathcal{A}$ is by representing them as a class of non uniform circuits $\mathcal{C}$, one circuit per input length. This is the standard definition of adversaries considered in the literature. We call such adversaries *non uniform* adversaries.

Yet another type of adversaries are $\mu$-*bounded uniform* adversaries: in this case, the real world $\mathcal{A}$ is represented by a probabilistic Turing machine $M$ and can additionally receive as input auxiliary information of length at most $\mu(\lambda)$. The description size of $\mathcal{A}$ is the sum total of the description size of $M$ and $\mu(\lambda)$. We say that $\mathcal{A}$ is uniform if it does not receive any additional auxiliary information. In this case, the description size of $\mathcal{A}$ is nothing but the description size of the Turing machine representing $\mathcal{A}$.

*Notation for Protocols.* Consider a two party protocol $\Pi$ between parties $P_1$ and $P_2$. We define the notation $P_1.\mathsf{MsgGen}[\Pi]$ (resp., $P_2.\mathsf{MsgGen}[\Pi]$) to denote the algorithm that generates the next message of $P_1$ (resp., $P_2$). The notation $\beta \leftarrow P_1.\mathsf{MsgGen}[\Pi](\alpha, \mathsf{st}; r)$ indicates that the output of next message algorithm of party $P_1$ on input $\alpha$, current state $\mathsf{st}$ and randomness $r$ is the string $\beta$. Initially, $\mathsf{st}$ is set to $\perp$. For convenience of notation, we assume that the $\mathsf{MsgGen}[\cdot]$ is a stateful algorithm and hence, we avoid describing the parameter $\mathsf{st}$ explicitly.

We denote the view of a party in a secure protocol to consist of its input, randomness and the transcript of messages exchanged by the party. For a party $P$ with input $y$ (that includes randomness), we denote its view by $\mathsf{View}_{P,y}$.

## 2.1   Secure Two-Party Computation

A secure two-party computation protocol is carried out between two parties $P_1$ and $P_2$ (modeled as interactive Turing machines) and is associated with a deterministic functionality $f$. Party $P_1$ has input $x_1$ and $P_2$ has input $x_2$. At the end of the protocol, $P_2$ gets the output.

*Simulation-based Security.* We follow the real/ideal world paradigm to formalize the security of a two party computation protocol $\Pi_{2PC}$ secure against malicious adversaries.[6] We follow the description presented in Lindell-Pinkas [34]. First, we begin with the ideal process.

IDEAL PROCESS: The ideal world is associated with a trusted party and parties $P_1, P_2$. At most one of $P_1, P_2$ is controlled by an adversary[7]. The process proceeds in the following steps:

1. **Input Distribution:** The environment distributes the inputs $x_1$ and $x_2$ to parties $P_1$ and $P_2$ respectively.
2. **Inputs to Trusted Party:** The parties now send their inputs to the trusted party. The honest party sends the same input it received from the environment to the trusted party. The adversary, however, can send a different input to the trusted party.
3. **Aborting Adversaries:** An adversarial party can then send a message to the trusted party to abort the execution. Upon receiving this, the trusted party terminates the ideal world execution. Otherwise, the following steps are executed.
4. **Trusted party answers party $P_2$:** Suppose the trusted party receives inputs $x_1'$ and $x_2'$ from $P_1$ and $P_2$ respectively. It sends the output $\mathsf{out} = f(x_1', x_2')$ to $P_2$.
5. **Output:** If the party $P_2$ is honest, then it outputs $\mathsf{out}$. The adversarial party ($P_1$ or $P_2$) outputs its entire view.

We denote the adversary participating in the above protocol to be $\mathcal{B}$ and the auxiliary input to $\mathcal{B}$ is denoted by $\mathbf{z}$. We define $\mathsf{Ideal}_{f,\mathcal{B}}^{\Pi_{2PC}}(x_1, x_2, \mathbf{z})$ to be the joint distribution over the outputs of the adversary and the honest party[8].

REAL PROCESS: In the real process, both the parties execute the protocol $\Pi_{2PC}$. At most one of $P_1, P_2$ is controlled by an adversary. We denote the adversarial party to be $\mathcal{A}$. As in the ideal process, they receive inputs from the environment. We define $\mathsf{Real}_{f,\vec{P}}^{\Pi_{2PC}}(x_1, x_2, \mathbf{z})$ to be the joint distribution over the outputs of the adversary and the honest party, where $\mathbf{z}$ denotes the auxiliary information.

We define the security of two party computation as follows:

**Definition 1 (Security).** *Consider a two party functionality $f$ as defined above. Let $\Pi_{2PC}$ be a two party protocol implementing $f$. We say that $\Pi_{2PC}$*

---

[6] Malicious adversaries can arbitrarily deviate from the protocol. The other type of adversaries commonly considered are semi-honest adversaries, where the adversaries follow the protocol but try to gain information by observing the conversation with the honest party. Both type of adversaries are allowed to substitute the inputs they receive from the external environment with inputs of their choice.

[7] This means that at most one of the parties could deviate from the rules prescribed by the ideal process.

[8] If $P_1$ is honest, it does not have any output.

**securely computes** $f$ *if for every PPT malicious adversary* $\mathcal{A}$ *in the real world, there exists a PPT adversary* $\mathcal{B}$ *in the ideal world such that: for every auxiliary information* $\mathbf{z} \in \{0,1\}^{\text{poly}(\lambda)}$,

$$\text{Ideal}_{f,\mathcal{B}}^{\Pi_{2\text{PC}}}(x_1, x_2, \mathbf{z}) \cong_c \text{Real}_{f,\mathcal{A}}^{\Pi_{2\text{PC}}}(x_1, x_2, \mathbf{z})$$

In this work, we are interested in the setting when the adversary corrupting $P_2$ (who receives the output) in the above protocol is $\mu$-uniform. We allow for adversarial $P_1$ to be non-uniform. We formally define this below.

**Definition 2 (Security Against $\mu$-Bounded Uniform $P_2$).** *Consider a two party functionality* $f$ *as defined above. Let* $\Pi_{2\text{PC}}$ *be a two party protocol computing* $f$. *We say that* $\Pi_{2\text{PC}}$ **securely computes** $f$ *if the following holds:*

- *For every $\mu$-bounded uniform malicious adversary* $\mathcal{A}$ *in the real world corrupting party* $P_2$, *there exists a PPT adversary* $\mathcal{B}$ *in the ideal world such that: for every auxiliary information* $\mathbf{z} \in \{0,1\}^{\mu(\lambda)}$,

$$\text{Ideal}_{f,\mathcal{B}}^{\Pi_{2\text{PC}}}(x_1, x_2, \mathbf{z}) \cong_c \text{Real}_{f,\mathcal{A}}^{\Pi_{2\text{PC}}}(x_1, x_2, \mathbf{z})$$

- *For every PPT non-uniform malicious adversary* $\mathcal{A}$ *in the real world corrupting* $P_1$, *there exists a PPT adversary* $\mathcal{B}$ *in the ideal world such that: for every auxiliary information* $\mathbf{z} \in \{0,1\}^{\text{poly}(\lambda)}$,

$$\text{Ideal}_{f,\mathcal{B}}^{\Pi_{2\text{PC}}}(x_1, x_2, \mathbf{z}) \cong_c \text{Real}_{f,\mathcal{A}}^{\Pi_{2\text{PC}}}(x_1, x_2, \mathbf{z})$$

## 3    Building Blocks

We describe the building blocks used in our results.

### 3.1    Garbling Schemes

We recall the definition of garbling schemes [5,39].

**Definition 3 (Garbling Schemes).** *A garbling scheme* $\text{GC} = (\text{Gen}, \text{GrbC}, \text{Grbl}, \text{EvalGC})$ *defined for a class of circuits* $\mathcal{C}$ *consists of the following polynomial time algorithms:*

- **Setup, $\text{Gen}(1^\lambda)$:** *On input security parameter* $\lambda$, *it generates the secret parameters* gcsk.
- **Garbled Circuit Generation, $\text{GrbC}(\text{gcsk}, C)$:** *On input secret parameters* gcsk *and circuit* $C \in \mathcal{C}$, *it generates the garbled circuit* $\widehat{C}$.
- **Generation of Garbling Keys, $\text{Grbl}(\text{gcsk})$:** *On input secret parameters* gcsk, *it generates the wire keys* $\langle \mathbf{k} \rangle = (\mathbf{k}_1, \ldots, \mathbf{k}_\ell)$, *where* $\mathbf{k}_i = (k_i^0, k_i^1)$.
- **Evaluation, $\text{EvalGC}(\widehat{C}, (k_1^{x_1}, \ldots, k_\ell^{x_\ell}))$:** *On input garbled circuit* $\widehat{C}$, *wire keys* $(k_1^{x_1}, \ldots, k_\ell^{x_\ell})$, *it generates the output* out.

*It satisfies the following properties:*

– *Correctness: For every circuit $C \in \mathcal{C}$ of input length $\ell$, $x \in \{0,1\}^\ell$, for every security parameter $\lambda \in \mathbb{N}$, it should hold that:*

$$\Pr\left[ C(x) \leftarrow \mathsf{EvalGC}(\widehat{C}, (k_1^{x_1}, \ldots, k_\ell^{x_\ell})) \; : \; \begin{array}{c} \mathsf{gcsk} \leftarrow \mathsf{Gen}(1^\lambda), \\ \widehat{C} \leftarrow \mathsf{GrbC}(\mathsf{gcsk}, C), \\ ((k_1^0, k_1^1), \ldots, (k_\ell^0, k_\ell^1)) \leftarrow \mathsf{Grbl}(\mathsf{gcsk}) \end{array} \right] = 1$$

– *Security: There exists a PPT simulator $\mathsf{Sim}$ such that the following holds for every circuit $C \in \mathcal{C}$ of input length $\ell$, $x \in \{0,1\}^\ell$,*

$$\left\{ \left( \widehat{C}, k_1^{x_1}, \ldots, k_\ell^{x_\ell} \right) \right\} \cong_c \left\{ \mathsf{Sim}(1^\lambda, \phi(C), C(x)) \right\},$$

*where:*
- $\mathsf{gcsk} \leftarrow \mathsf{Gen}(1^\lambda)$
- $\widehat{C} \leftarrow \mathsf{GrbC}(\mathsf{gcsk}, C)$
- $((k_1^0, k_1^1), \ldots, (k_\ell^0, k_\ell^1)) \leftarrow \mathsf{Grbl}(\mathsf{gcsk})$
- $\phi(C)$ *is the topology of* $C$.

**Theorem 3** ([39]). *Assuming one-way functions, there exists a secure garbling scheme.*

*Deterministic Garbling.* For our results, we need a garbling scheme where the circuit garbling algorithms and the garbling key generation algorithms are deterministic. Any garbling scheme can be transformed into one satisfying these properties by generating a PRF key as part of the setup algorithm. The randomness in the circuit garbling and the garbling key generation algorithms can be derived from the PRF key.

## 3.2 Oblivious Transfer

We recall the notion of oblivious transfer [15,37] below. We adopt the indistinguishability security notion. Against malicious senders, indistinguishability security says that a malicious sender should not be able to distinguish the receiver's input. Defining security against malicious receivers is more tricky, we require that if $c$ is the choice bit committed to by the receiver then the receiver should get no information about the bit $b_{\bar{c}}$ in the pair $(b_0, b_1)$, where $(b_0, b_1)$ is the pair of bits used by the honest sender. This is formalized by using unbounded extraction.

**Definition 4 (Oblivious Transfer).** *A 1-out-2 oblivious transfer (OT) protocol $\mathsf{OT}$ is a two party protocol between a sender and a receiver. A sender has two input bits $(b_0, b_1)$ and the receiver has a choice bit $c$. At the end of the protocol, the receiver receives an output bit $b'$. We denote this process by $b' \leftarrow \langle \mathsf{Sen}(b_0, b_1), \mathsf{Rec}(c) \rangle$.*

*We require that an OT protocol satisfies the following properties:*

– **Correctness**: *For every $b_0, b_1, c \in \{0,1\}$, we have:*

$$\Pr[b_c \leftarrow \langle \mathsf{Sen}(b_0, b_1), \mathsf{Rec}(c) \rangle] = 1$$

- **Indistinguishability security against malicious senders**: *For all PPT senders* $\mathsf{Sen}^*$, *for all auxiliary information* $\mathbf{z} \in \{0,1\}^*$ *we have,*

$$|\Pr[1 \leftarrow \langle \mathsf{Sen}^*(\mathbf{z}),\ \mathsf{Rec}(0)\rangle] - \Pr[1 \leftarrow \langle \mathsf{Sen}^*(\mathbf{z}),\ \mathsf{Rec}(1)\rangle]| \leq \frac{1}{2} + \mathsf{negl}(\lambda).$$

- **Indistinguishability Security against malicious receivers**: *For all PPT receivers* $\mathsf{Rec}^*$, *we require that the following holds. There exists an extractor* $\mathsf{Ext}$ *(not necessarily efficient) that extracts a bit from the view of* $\mathsf{Rec}^*$ *such that the following holds: For any auxiliary information* $\mathbf{z} \in \{0,1\}^*$,

$$|\Pr[1 \leftarrow \langle \mathsf{Sen}(\{b_c, b_{\overline{c}}\}_{c \in \{0,1\}}),\ \mathsf{Rec}^*(\mathbf{z})\rangle \mid c \leftarrow \mathsf{Ext}(\mathsf{View}_{\mathsf{Rec}^*, \mathbf{z}})]$$
$$-\ \Pr[1 \leftarrow \langle \mathsf{Sen}(\{b_c, \overline{b_{\overline{c}}}\}_{c \in \{0,1\}}),\ \mathsf{Rec}^*(\mathbf{z})\rangle \mid c \leftarrow \mathsf{Ext}(\mathsf{View}_{\mathsf{Rec}^*, \mathbf{z}})]| \leq \frac{1}{2} + \mathsf{negl}(\lambda).$$

*We define $\ell$-parallel 1-out-2 OT to be a protocol that is composed of $\ell$ parallel executions of 1-ou-2 OT protocol.*

For our main result, we require an oblivious transfer protocol that satisfies the following additional property.

**Definition 5 (Uniqueness of Transcript).** *Consider an 1-out-2 oblivious transfer protocol* $\mathsf{OT}$ *between two parties $P_1$ (sender) and $P_2$ (receiver). We say that* $\mathsf{OT}$ *satisfies* **uniqueness of transcript** *property if the following holds: Consider an execution of $P_1(b_0, b_1; r_1)$ and $P_2(c; r_2)$ and let the transcript of the execution be denoted by* $\mathsf{Transcript} = (OT_1, \ldots, OT_k)$. *Suppose there exists $c' \in \{0,1\}$ and string $r'_2$ such that the execution of $P_1(b_0, b_1; r_1)$ and $P_2(c'; r'_2)$ leads to the same transcript* $\mathsf{Transcript}$ *then it should hold that $c' = c$ and $r_2 = r'_2$. Also it follows that, given $r_2$, we can recover $c$ in polynomial time.*

*Remark 1.* The above property can also be defined for the $n$-parallel 1-out-2 oblivious transfer protocol. If a $n$-parallel 1-out-2 oblivious transfer protocol, denoted by $\mathsf{OT}_n$, is composed of $n$ parallel copies of $\mathsf{OT}$ and if $\mathsf{OT}$ satisfies uniqueness of transcript property then so does $\mathsf{OT}_n$. In particular, given the randomness of the receiver of $\mathsf{OT}_n$, it is possible to recover the $n$ bit length string of the receiver efficiently.

*Instantiation: Naor-Pinkas Protocol* [35]. Naor-Pinkas proposed a two message oblivious transfer protocol whose security is based on the Decisional Diffie-Hellman (DDH) assumption.

We claim that their protocol satisfies uniqueness of transcript property. In order to do that, we recall the first message (sent by receiver to sender) in their protocol: Let $\mathsf{bit}$ be the input of receiver. Consider a group $\mathbb{G}$ where DDH is hard. Let $g$ be a generator of $\mathbb{G}$. The receiver generates $g^a, g^b$ and $c_{\mathsf{bit}} = ab$. It generates $c_{1-\mathsf{bit}}$ at random such that $c_{\mathsf{bit}} \neq c_{1-\mathsf{bit}}$. It sends $v_1 = g^a, v_2 = g^b, v_3 = g^{c_0}, v_4 = g^{c_1}$ to the sender.

The elements $v_1$ and $v_2$ uniquely determine $a$ and $b$. Furthermore, exactly one of $v_3$ or $v_4$ corresponds to $g^{ab}$ and this uniquely determines the bit. Furthermore, note that this also uniquely determines the randomness used.

While we only deal with 1-out-2 OT protocol above, we can generalize the above proof to also work for $n$-parallel 1-out-2 OT protocol.

**Theorem 4** ([35]). *Assuming DDH, there exists an oblivious transfer protocol satisfying Definition 5 as well as the uniqueness of transcript property.*

### 3.3 Two Message Secure Function Evaluation

As a building block in our construction, we consider a two message secure function evaluation protocol. Since we are restricted to just two messages, we can only expect one of the parties to get the output.

We designate $P_1$ to be the party receiving the output and the other party to be $P_2$. That is, the protocol proceeds by $P_1$ sending the first message to $P_2$ and the second message is the response by $P_2$.

*Indistinguishability Security.* We require malicious (indistinguishability) security against $P_1$ and malicious (indistinguishability) security against $P_2$. We define both of them below.

First, we define an indistinguishability security notion against malicious $P_1$. To do that, we employ an extraction mechanism to extract $P_1$'s input $x_1^*$. We then argue that $P_1$ should not be able to distinguish whether $P_2$ uses $x_2^0$ or $x_2^1$ in the protocol as long as $f(x_1^*, x_2^0) = f(x_1^*, x_2^1)$. We don't place any requirements on the computational complexity of the extraction mechanism.

**Definition 6 (Indistinguishability Security: Malicious $P_1$).** *Consider a two message secure function evaluation protocol for a functionality $f$ between parties $P_1$ and $P_2$ such that $P_1$ is getting the output. We say that the two party secure computation protocol satisfies* **indistinguishability security against malicious $P_1$** *if for every adversarial $P_1^*$, there is an extractor* Ext *(not necessarily efficient) such the following holds. Consider the following experiment:* $\mathsf{Expt}(1^\lambda, b)$:

- $P_1^*$ *outputs the first message* $\mathsf{msg}_1$.
- *Extractor* Ext *on input* $\mathsf{msg}_1$ *outputs* $x_1^*$.
- *Let* $x_2^0, x_2^1$ *be two inputs such that* $f(x_1^*, x_2^0) = f(x_1^*, x_2^1)$. *Party $P_2$ on input* $\mathsf{msg}_1$ *and* $x_2^b$, *outputs the second message* $\mathsf{msg}_2$.
- $P_1^*$ *upon receiving the second message outputs a bit* out.
- *Output* out.

*We require that,*

$$\left| \Pr[1 \leftarrow \mathsf{Expt}(1^\lambda, 0)] - \Pr[1 \leftarrow \mathsf{Expt}(1^\lambda, 1)] \right| \leq \mathsf{negl}(\lambda),$$

*for some negligible function* negl.

We now define security against malicious $P_2$. We insist that $P_2$ should not be able to distinguish which input $P_1$ used to compute its messages.

**Definition 7 (Indistinguishability Security: Malicious $P_2$).** *Consider a two message secure function evaluation protocol for a functionality $f$ between parties $P_1$ and $P_2$ where $P_1$ gets the output. We say that the two party secure* *computation protocol satisfies* **indistinguishability security against malicious** $P_2$ *if for every adversarial* $P_2^*$, *the following holds: Consider two strings* $x_1^0$ *and* $x_2^1$. *Denote by* $\mathcal{D}_b$ *the distribution of the first message (sent to* $P_2$) *generated using* $x_1^b$ *as* $P_1$ *'s input. The distributions* $\mathcal{D}_0$ *and* $\mathcal{D}_1$ *are computationally indistinguishable.*

*Instantiation.* We can instantiate such a two message secure evaluation protocol using garbled circuits and $\ell_1$-parallel 1-out-2 two message oblivious transfer protocol OT by Naor-Pinkas [35]. Recall that this protocol satisfies uniqueness of transcript property (Definition 5). We denote the garbling schemes by GC.

We describe this protocol below. The input of $P_1$ is $x_1$ and the input of $P_2$ is $x_2$. Recall that $P_1$ is designated to receive the output.

- $P_1 \to P_2$: $P_1$ computes the first message of OT as a function of its input $x_1$ of input length $\ell_1$. Denote this message by $OT_1$. It sends $OT_1$ to $P_2$.
- $P_2 \to P_1$: $P_2$ computes the following:
  - It generates $\mathsf{Gen}(1^\lambda)$ to get gcsk.
  - It then computes $\mathsf{GrbC}(\mathsf{gcsk}, C)$ to obtain $\widehat{C}$. $C$ is a circuit with $x_2$ hardwired in it; it takes as input $x_1$ and computes $f(x_1, x_2)$.
  - It computes $\mathsf{Grbl}(\mathsf{gcsk})$ to obtain the wire keys $(\mathbf{k}_1, \ldots, \mathbf{k}_{\ell_1})$, where every $\mathbf{k}_i$ is composed of two keys $(k_i^0, k_i^1)$.
  - It computes the second message of OT, denoted by $OT_2$, as a function of $(\mathbf{k}_1, \ldots, \mathbf{k}_{\ell_1})$.
  It sends $(\widehat{C}, OT_2)$ to $P_1$.
- $P_1$: Upon receiving $(\widehat{C}, OT_2)$, it recovers the wire keys $(k_1, \ldots, k_{\ell_1})$. It then executes $\mathsf{EvalGC}(\widehat{C}, (k_1, \ldots, k_{\ell_1}))$ to obtain out. It outputs out.

The correctness of the above protocol immediately follows from the correctness of garbling schemes and oblivious transfer protocol. We now focus on security.

**Theorem 5.** *Assuming the security of* GC *and* OT *and assuming that* OT *satisfies uniqueness of transcript property (Definition 5), the above protocol is secure against malicious* $P_1$ *(Definition 6).*

*Proof.* We first describe the inefficient extractor Ext that extracts $P_1$'s input from its first message. From the uniqueness of transcript property of OT, it follows that given $P_1$'s first message $OT_1$, there exists a unique input $x_1^*$ and randomness $r$ that was used to compute the message of $P_1$. Thus, Ext can find this input $x_1^*$ by performing a brute force search on all possible inputs and randomness.

We prove the theorem with respect to the extractor described above. In the first hybrid described below, challenge bit $b$ is used to determine which of the two inputs of $P_2$ needs to be picked. In the final hybrid, $P_2$ always picks the first of the two inputs.

$\underline{\mathsf{Hyb}_{1.b}}$ for $b \xleftarrow{\$} \{0, 1\}$: Let $x_1^*$ be the input extracted by the extractor. Let $x_2^0$ and $x_2^1$ be two inputs such that $f(x_1^*, x_2^0) = f(x_1^*, x_2^1)$. Party $P_2$ uses $x_2^b$ to compute the second message.

$\mathsf{Hyb}_{2.b}$ for $b \xleftarrow{\$} \{0,1\}$: Let $x_1^*$ be the input extracted by the extractor. We denote the $i^{th}$ bit of $x_1^*$ to be $x_{1,i}^*$. As part of the second message, the wire keys $(\mathbf{k}_1, \ldots, \mathbf{k}_{\ell_1})$, where every $\mathbf{k}_i$ is composed of two keys $(k_i^0, k_i^1)$. Instead of generating $OT_2$ as a function of $(\mathbf{k}_1, \ldots, \mathbf{k}_{\ell_1})$, it generates $OT_2$ as a function of $(\mathbf{k}_1', \ldots, \mathbf{k}_{\ell_1}')$. $\mathbf{k}_i'$ contains $\left(0, k_i^{x_{1,i}^*}\right)$ if $x_{1,i}^* = 1$, otherwise it contains $\left(k_i^{x_{1,i}^*}, 0\right)$.

Hybrids $\mathsf{Hyb}_{1.b}$ and $\mathsf{Hyb}_{2.b}$ are computationally distinguishable from the indistinguishability security against malicious receivers property of the oblivious transfer protocol.

$\mathsf{Hyb}_{3.0}$: Let $x_1^*$ be the input extracted by the extractor. Let $x_2^0$ and $x_2^1$ be two inputs such that $f(x_1^*, x_2^0) = f(x_1^*, x_2^1)$. $P_2$ computes the second message as in the previous hybrid. Instead of using $x_2^b$ in the computation of the garbled circuit, it instead uses the input $x_2^0$.

Hybrids $\mathsf{Hyb}_{2.b}$ and $\mathsf{Hyb}_{3.0}$ are computationally indistinguishable from the security of the garbling schemes[9].

The final hybrid does not contain any information about the challenge bit. This completes the proof.

**Theorem 6.** *Assuming the security of* OT, *the above protocol is secure against malicious* $P_2$ *(Definition 7).*

*Proof.* The proof of this theorem directly follows from the security against malicious senders property of the oblivious transfer protocol.

### 3.4  Conditional Disclosure of Secrets (CDS) Protocols

We require another key primitive, conditional disclosure of secrets (CDS) [1,19] protocol. A CDS protocol consists of two parties $P_1$ and $P_2$. Both these parties share a common instance $\mathbf{X}$ belonging to a NP language. Further, $P_2$ has a secret $s$ and $P_1$ additionally has a private input $w$. If $w$ is a valid witness for $\mathbf{X}$ then we require that $P_1$ should be able to recover the secret $s$ at the end of the protocol. However, if $\mathbf{X}$ does not belong to the language then we require that $P_1$ does not get any information about the secret.

We give the formal definition below.

**Definition 8 (CDS Protocols).** *Conditional Disclosure of Secret protocol, associated with a NP relation* $\mathcal{R}$, *is an interactive protocol between two parties* $P_1$ *(receiver) and* $P_2$ *(sender). Both* $P_1$ *and* $P_2$ *hold the same instance* $\mathbf{X}$. *Party* $P_2$ *holds the secret* $s \in \{0,1\}^\lambda$ *and* $P_1$ *holds a string* $w \in \{0,1\}^*$. *At the end of the protocol* $P_1$ *outputs* $s'$. *We denote this by* $s' \leftarrow \langle P_1(\mathbf{X}, w),\ P_2(\mathbf{X}, s) \rangle$.

*We require that the CDS protocol satisfies the following properties:*

- **Correctness**: *If* $(\mathbf{X}, w) \in \mathcal{R}$ *then it holds with probability 1 that* $s \leftarrow \langle P_1(\mathbf{X}, w),\ P_2(\mathbf{X}, s) \rangle$.

---

[9] Formally this is argued by first simulating the garbled circuit and then switching the input.

- **Soundness**: If $\mathbf{X} \notin L(\mathcal{R})$ then, for any boolean distinguisher $P_1^*$, for any $s_0, s_1 \in \{0,1\}^\lambda$ and for any auxiliary information $\mathbf{z} \in \{0,1\}^*$, it holds that,

$$|\Pr[1 \leftarrow \langle P_1^*(\mathbf{X}, s_0, s_1, \mathbf{z}), \ P_2(\mathbf{X}, s_0) \rangle] - \Pr[1 \leftarrow \langle P_1^*(\mathbf{X}, s_0, s_1, \mathbf{z}), \ P_2^*(\mathbf{X}, s_1) \rangle] \ |$$
$$\leq \mathsf{negl}(\lambda)$$

for some negligible function $\mathsf{negl}$.

*Construction of Two Message CDS Protocol.* Since a CDS protocol is a special case of two party secure computation, we show how a two message secure function evaluation protocol (Sect. 3.3) implies a two message CDS protocol.

**Theorem 7.** *Consider a NP relation $\mathcal{R}$. Consider the following two party functionality $f$ that takes as input $((\mathbf{X}', w); (\mathbf{X}, s))$ and outputs $s$ if and only if $((\mathbf{X}, w) \in \mathcal{R}) \wedge \mathbf{X} = \mathbf{X}'$, otherwise it outputs 0. A two message secure function evaluation protocol for $f$ is a CDS protocol associated with the relation $\mathcal{R}$.*

*Proof.* The correctness of the CDS protocol immediately follows from the correctness of the two message secure function evaluation protocol. We now argue soundness.

Consider an instance $\mathbf{X} \notin \mathcal{L}(\mathcal{R})$. We now invoke the security of two message SFE (specifically, Definition 6). There exists an extractor Ext that extracts $x_1^*$ from $P_1^*$'s first message. We claim that for every $x_2$ of the form $(\mathbf{X}, s')$, it holds that $f(x_1^*, x_2)$ outputs 0. This follows from the fact that $\mathbf{X} \notin \mathcal{L}(\mathcal{R})$. Using this fact, it follows that $P_1^*$ cannot distinguish whether $P_2$ used the input $(\mathbf{X}, s_0)$ or $(\mathbf{X}, s_1)$ to compute its message. The theorem thus follows.

### 3.5    Zero Knowledge Proof Systems

We now recall the notion of zero knowledge [23]. In the definition below, we consider computationally bounded provers.

**Definition 9 (Zero Knowledge Argument of Knowledge).** *A Zero Knowledge Argument of Knowledge (ZKAoK) system (Prover, Verifier) for a relation $\mathcal{R}$, associated with a NP language $\mathcal{L}(\mathcal{R})$, is an interactive protocol between Prover and Verifier. Prover takes as input $(\mathbf{y}, \mathbf{w})$ and verifier Verifier takes as input $\mathbf{y}$. At the end of the protocol, verifier outputs accept/reject. This process is denoted by $\langle \mathsf{Prover}(\mathbf{y}, \mathbf{w}), \ \mathsf{Verifier}(\mathbf{y}) \rangle$. It consists of the following properties:*

- **Completeness**: *For every $(\mathbf{y}, \mathbf{w}) \in \mathcal{R}$, we have:*

$$\Pr[\text{accept} \leftarrow \langle \mathsf{Prover}(\mathbf{y}, \mathbf{w}), \ \mathsf{Verifier}(\mathbf{y}) \rangle] = 1$$

- **Extractability**: *For every PPT Prover\*, there exists an extractor Ext (that could use the code of Prover\* in a non black box manner) such that the following holds: for every auxiliary information $z \in \{0,1\}^*$,*

$$\Big| \Pr[\text{accept} \leftarrow \langle \mathsf{Prover}^*(\mathbf{y}, z), \ \mathsf{Verifier}(\mathbf{y}) \rangle] - \Pr[\mathbf{w}^* \leftarrow \mathsf{Ext}(1^\lambda, z) \ : \ (\mathbf{y}, \mathbf{w}^*) \in \mathcal{R}] \Big|$$
$$\leq \mathsf{negl}(\lambda)$$

- **Zero Knowledge**: *For every* $(\mathbf{y}, \mathbf{w}) \in \mathcal{R}$, *for every PPT* Verifier*, *there exists a PPT simulator* Sim *(that could use the code of* Verifier* *in a non black box manner) such that the following holds:*

$$\{\langle \mathsf{Prover}(\mathbf{y}, \mathbf{w}), \ \mathsf{Verifier}^*(\mathbf{y}) \rangle\} \approx_c \left\{ \mathsf{Sim}(1^\lambda, \mathbf{y}) \right\}$$

*We define a ZKAoK system to be $k$-message if the number of messages between* Prover *and* Verifier *is $k$.*

We require zero knowledge systems satisfying additional properties. We consider them one by one.

*Bounded Uniform Zero Knowledge.* In the zero knowledge property considered in the definition above, we require that the malicious verifier is uniform.

**Definition 10 ($\mu$-Bounded Uniform Zero Knowledge).** *A proof system* (Prover, Verifier) *for a relation $\mathcal{R}$ is said to be $\mu$-bounded uniform ZKAoK if the following holds:*

- *It satisfies correctness and extractability properties as in Definition 9.*
- *$\mu$-Bounded Uniform Zero Knowledge*: *For every* $(\mathbf{y}, \mathbf{w}) \in \mathcal{R}$, *for every PPT* Verifier* *(represented as a Turing machine), there exists a PPT simulator* Sim *(that could use the code of* Verifier* *in a non black box manner) such that the following holds: for any auxiliary information* $\mathbf{z} \in \{0,1\}^{\mu(|\mathbf{y}|)}$.

$$\{\langle \mathsf{Prover}(\mathbf{y}, \mathbf{w}), \ \mathsf{Verifier}^*(\mathbf{y}, \mathbf{z}) \rangle\} \approx_c \left\{ \mathsf{Sim}(1^\lambda, \mathbf{y}, \mathbf{z}) \right\}$$

*Remark 2.* The special case of 0-bounded uniform zero knowledge (interpreted as a constant function that always outputs 0) reduces to having the malicious verifiers as uniform algorithms (in particular, they receive no external advice).

*Delayed Statement-Witness.* Another useful property we require is to be able to choose the statement and the witness in the last message of the protocol. We call this, delayed statement-witness property.

**Definition 11 (Delayed Statement-Witness).** *A Zero Knowledge (proof or argument) system is said to satisfy delayed statement-witness property if both the statement and the witness are fixed only in the last message of the protocol. In particular, all the messages except the last message depend only on the length of the instance and the witness.*

*Instantiation.* In this work, we require a ZKAoK system that is both bounded uniform zero knowledge and satisfies delayed statement-witness property. The protocol of Bitansky et al. [8] satisfies both these properties. Their protocol can be instantiated from Zaps [14], DDH and the Learning with Errors (LWE) assumption.

**Theorem 8 ([8]).** *Assuming Zaps, DDH and LWE, there exists a ZKAoK system that satisfies both $\mu$-bounded uniform zero knowledge for some function $\mu$, and delayed statement-witness property.*

## 3.6    Succinct Randomized Encodings

We recall the notion of succinct randomized encodings [9,12,32] next.

**Definition 12.** *A succinct randomized encodings scheme* SRE $=$ $(E, D)$ *for a class of Turing machines* $\mathcal{M}$ *consists of the following probabilistic polynomial time algorithms:*

- **Encoding,** $E(1^\lambda, M, x)$: *On input security parameter* $\lambda$, *Turing machine* $M \in$ $\mathcal{M}$ *and input* $x$, *it outputs the randomized encoding* $\langle M, x \rangle$.
- **Decoding,** $D(\langle M, x \rangle)$: *On input randomized encoding of* $M$ *and* $x$, *it outputs* out.

*We require that the above algorithms satisfies the following properties:*

- **Correctness**: *We require that the following holds for every* $M \in \mathcal{M}, x \in$ $\{0,1\}^*$,
$$\Pr\left[D(\langle M, x \rangle) = M(x) \ : \ \langle M, x \rangle \leftarrow E(1^\lambda, M, x)\right] = 1$$

- **Security**: *For every PPT adversary* $\mathcal{A}$, *there exists a PPT simulator* Sim *such that the following holds:*

$$\{\langle M, x \rangle\} \approx_c \left\{ \mathsf{Sim}(1^\lambda, 1^{|M|}, 1^{|x|}, M(x)) \right\},$$

*where:*
  - $\langle M, x \rangle \leftarrow E(1^\lambda, M, x)$

*Input-less Turing machines.* In this work, we consider input-less Turing machines. These are Turing machines which on input $\perp$, executes some computation and outputs out. We denote the randomized encoding of an input-less TM to be $\langle M \rangle \leftarrow E(1^\lambda, M, \perp)$.

## 3.7    Indistinguishability Obfuscation for Circuits

We define the notion of indistinguishability obfuscation (iO) for circuits [4,17] below.

**Definition 13 (Indistinguishability Obfuscator (iO) for Circuits).** *A uniform PPT algorithm* iO *is called an* $\varepsilon$-*secure indistinguishability obfuscator for a circuit family* $\{\mathcal{C}_\lambda\}_{\lambda \in \mathbb{N}}$, *where* $\mathcal{C}_\lambda$ *consists of circuits* $C$ *of the form* $C :$ $\{0,1\}^\ell \to \{0,1\}$, *if the following holds:*

- **Completeness:** *For every* $\lambda \in \mathbb{N}$, *every* $C \in \mathcal{C}_\lambda$, *every input* $x \in \{0,1\}^\ell$, *where* $\ell = \ell(\lambda)$ *is the input length of* $C$, *we have that*

$$\Pr\left[C'(x) = C(x) \ : \ C' \leftarrow iO(\lambda, C)\right] = 1$$

- **$\varepsilon$-Indistinguishability:** *For any PPT distinguisher $D$, there exists a negligible function $\mathsf{negl}(\cdot)$ such that the following holds: for all sufficiently large $\lambda \in \mathbb{N}$, for all pairs of circuits $C_0, C_1 \in \mathcal{C}_\lambda$ such that $C_0(x) = C_1(x)$ for all inputs $x \in \{0,1\}^\ell$, where $\ell = \ell(\lambda)$ is the input length of $C_0, C_1$, we have:*

$$\Big| \Pr\left[D(\lambda, i\mathsf{O}(\lambda, C_0)) = 1\right] - \Pr[D(\lambda, i\mathsf{O}(\lambda, C_1)) = 1] \Big| \leq \varepsilon$$

*If $\varepsilon$ is negligible in $\lambda$ then we refer to $i\mathsf{O}$ as a secure indistinguishability obfuscator.*

*Remark 3.* In our work, we require indistinguishability obfuscators where the indistinguishability property holds against adversaries running in subexponential time (rather than polynomial time). We refer to such indistinguishability obfuscators as sub-exponentially secure indistinguishability obfuscators. Currently, the existence of several cryptographic primitives are based only on the assumption of sub-exponential iO.

### 3.8 Puncturable Pseudorandom Functions

We define the notion of puncturable pseudorandom functions below.

**Definition 14.** *A pseudorandom function of the form $\mathsf{PRF}_{punc}(K, \cdot)$ is said to be a $\mu$-secure puncturable PRF if there exists a PPT algorithm Puncture that satisfies the following properties:*

- ***Functionality preserved under puncturing.*** *Puncture takes as input a PRF key $K$ and an input $x$ and outputs $K \backslash \{x\}$ such that for all $x' \neq x$, $\mathsf{PRF}_{punc}(K \backslash \{x\}, x') = \mathsf{PRF}_{punc}(K, x')$.*
- **Pseudorandom at punctured points.** *For every PPT adversary $(\mathcal{A}_1, \mathcal{A}_2)$ such that $\mathcal{A}_1(1^\lambda)$ outputs an input $x$, consider an experiment where $K \xleftarrow{\$} \{0,1\}^\lambda$ and $K \backslash \{x\} \leftarrow \mathsf{Puncture}(K, x)$. Then for all sufficiently large $\lambda \in \mathbb{N}$,*

$$\Big| \Pr[\mathcal{A}_2(K \backslash \{x\}, x, \mathsf{PRF}_{punc}(K, x)) = 1] - \Pr[\mathcal{A}_2(K \backslash \{x\}, x, U_{\chi(\lambda)}) = 1] \Big| \leq \mu(\lambda)$$

*where $U_{\chi(\lambda)}$ is a string drawn uniformly at random from $\{0,1\}^{\chi(\lambda)}$.*

*If $\mu$ is negligible, we refer to $\mathsf{PRF}_{punc}$ as a secure puncturable PRF.*

As observed by [10,11,31], the GGM construction [20] of PRFs from one-way functions yields puncturable PRFs.

**Theorem 9** ([10,11,20,31]). *If $\frac{\mu}{\mathsf{poly}}$-secure one-way functions exist, for some fixed polynomial $\mathsf{poly}$, then there exists $\mu$-secure puncturable pseudorandom functions.*

# 4    Generation Protocols

A crucial ingredient in our two party secure computation protocol is a protocol that enables extraction of the input of $P_2$ during the simulation phase. To achieve this, we introduce the notion of generation protocols[10] below.

This is a two party protocol between a sender and a receiver. The sender has a trapdoor and in the end of the protocol, the receiver outputs a string. It consists of two properties: (i) *soundness*: any adversarial receiver having black-box access to the code of the sender will not be able to recover the trapdoor of the sender, (ii) *extractability*: an extractor can successfully recover the trapdoor of the sender. In the extractability property, we only consider the case when the sender is semi-honest (i.e., it behaves according to the description of the protocol).

To make sure that both soundness and extractability don't contradict each other, we make sure that the extractor has more capabilities than an adversarial receiver – for instance, an extractor could rewind the receiver or it could have non black box access to the code of the receiver.

The formal definition of generation protocols is provided below.

**Definition 15 (Generation Protocols).** *A generation protocol is an interactive protocol between two parties $P_1$ (also termed receiver) and $P_2$ (also termed sender). The input to both parties is auxiliary information $\mathbf{z}$. Party $P_2$, in addition, gets as input trapdoor $K \in \{0,1\}^{\text{poly}(\lambda)}$. At the end of the protocol, $P_1$ outputs $K'$. We denote this process by $K' = \langle P_1(\mathbf{z}),\ P_2(\mathbf{z}, K) \rangle$.*

*The following properties are associated with a generation protocol:*

- **Soundness:** *For any PPT non-uniform boolean distinguisher $P_1^*$, for any large enough security parameter $\lambda \in \mathbb{N}$: for every two strings $K_0, K_1 \in \{0,1\}^{\text{poly}(\lambda)}$ and auxiliary information $\mathbf{z} \in \{0,1\}^{\text{poly}'(\lambda)}$,*

$$|\Pr\left[1 \leftarrow \langle P_1^*(\mathbf{z}, K_0, K_1),\ P_2(\mathbf{z}, K_0) \rangle\right] - \Pr\left[1 \leftarrow \langle P_1^*(\mathbf{z}, K_0, K_1),\ P_2(\mathbf{z}, K_1) \rangle\right]|$$
$$\leq \frac{1}{2} + \mathsf{negl}(\lambda)$$

*for some negligible function $\mathsf{negl}$. That is, any distinguisher $P_1^*$ having black box access to $P_2$ cannot distinguish whether which of $K_0$ and $K_1$ was used in the protocol.*
- **Extractability:** *For every semi-honest PPT $P_2^*$, there exists a PPT extractor $\mathsf{ExtGP}$ (that could possibly use code of $P_2^*$ in a non black box manner) such that the following holds: for any auxiliary information $\mathbf{z} \in \{0,1\}^{\text{poly}'(\lambda)}$,*
  - *The view of $P_2^*(\mathbf{z}, K)$ when it is interacting with $P_1(\mathbf{z}, K)$ is computationally indistinguishable from the view of $P_2^*(\mathbf{z}, K)$ when it is interacting with $\mathsf{ExtGP}(1^\lambda, \mathbf{z})$.*
  - *$\Pr\left[K' \leftarrow \langle \mathsf{ExtGP}(1^\lambda, \mathbf{z}),\ P_2^*(\mathbf{z}, K) \rangle \text{ and } K' = K\right] \geq 1 - \mathsf{negl}(\lambda)$*

---

[10] The name "generation protocol" is taken from the work of [3]. The definition in their work is slightly different, however they too use the notion of generation protocols to achieve trapdoor extraction.

*Extractability Against $\mu$-Bounded Uniform Senders.* We consider generation protocols where the extractability property needs to hold against senders modeled as $\mu$-bounded uniform algorithms. We formally define this below.

**Definition 16.** *A protocol* GenProt *between sender $P_1$ and receiver $P_2$ is said to be $\mu$-bounded uniform generation protocol if the following holds:*

- *It satisfies the soundness property in Definition 16.*
- **Extractability against $\mu$-bounded uniform senders***: For every semi-honest PPT $P_2$ (modeled as a Turing machine), there exists a PPT extractor* ExtGP *(that could possibly use code of $P_2$ in a non black box manner) such that the following holds: for any bounded auxiliary information $\mathbf{z} \in \{0,1\}^{\mu(\lambda)}$,*

$$\Pr\left[K' \leftarrow \langle \mathsf{ExtGP}(1^\lambda, \mathbf{z}), \ P_2(\mathbf{z}, K) \rangle \ and \ K' = K\right] \geq 1 - \mathsf{negl}(\lambda)$$

*Remark 4.* If $\mu$ in the above definition is a constant function that always outputs 0 then this boils down to the case when the sender is a uniform algorithm (hence, no external advice). In this case, we refer to the above generation protocol as uniform generation protocol.

### 4.1 Two-Message GP from Succinct RE

We present a two-message generation protocol starting from a succinct randomized encoding scheme and a two party secure function evaluation protocol. The security of this scheme will be against $\mu$-bounded uniform senders.

*Tools.* The first tool we use is succinct randomized encodings for Turing machines, denoted by $\mathsf{SRE} = (\mathsf{E}, \mathsf{D})$. Another tool we use is a two message secure function evaluation protocol $\Pi_{\mathsf{2PC}}$. In particular, we use the two message secure function evaluation protocol defined in Sect. 3.3. We denote $\mathcal{P}_1$ and $\mathcal{P}_2$ to be the parties involved in this protocol. Only $\mathcal{P}_1$ outputs in the protocol. Recall that this protocol satisfies indistinguishability security (Definitions 6 and 7).

FUNCTIONALITY OF $\Pi_{\mathsf{2PC}}$: The functionality $f$ associated with $\Pi_{\mathsf{2PC}}$ is the following: $f$ on input $x_2 = (\beta, K, m, R_2, \mathsf{md}, \theta)$ from $\mathcal{P}_2$ and $x_1 = (M, R_1)$ (here, $|M| \leq \mathcal{O}(\mu(\lambda) + \lambda)$) from $\mathcal{P}_1$, it computes the following:

- If $\mathsf{md} = 1$ then compute the succinct randomized encoding $\langle N \rangle \leftarrow \mathsf{E}(1^\lambda, N[\beta, K, m, M], \bot; R)$ (i.e., $R$ is the randomness used in $\mathsf{E}$), where $R$ is set to $R_1 \oplus R_2$. The Turing machine $N$ is an input-less Turing machine (refer Sect. 3.6) that does the following: hardwired inside it are the values $(\beta, K, m, M)$.
  1. It first computes $M(m)$ to get as output out.
  2. It interprets the first $|\beta|$ number of bits of out to be the string $\beta'$.
  3. It checks if $\beta' = \beta$. If so, it outputs $K$. Otherwise, it outputs $\bot$.
  It outputs $\langle N \rangle$.
- If $\mathsf{md} = 2$ then:
  1. It outputs $\theta$.

*Construction.* We describe the protocol below. Denote the receiver to be $P_1$ and the sender to be $P_2$. Call this protocol GenProt.

- Upon input $\mathbf{z}$, $P_1$ (receiver) prepares an input $x_1$ for $\Pi_{2PC}$ as a $\mu(\lambda)$-length string of all zeroes. It takes the role of the party $\mathcal{P}_1$ in the protocol $\Pi_{2PC}$. It computes the first message $\mathbf{msg}_1$ of $\Pi_{2PC}$ using the input $x_1$. That is, $\mathbf{msg}_1 \leftarrow \mathcal{P}_1.\mathsf{MsgGen}[\Pi_{2PC}](1^\lambda, x_1)$. It sends $\mathbf{msg}_1$ to $P_2$ (sender).
- Upon input $\mathbf{z}$ and trapdoor $K$, $P_2$ (sender) first picks a string $\beta$ of length $\ell_\beta = \mathrm{poly}(\lambda)$ such that $\ell_\beta \gg |\mathbf{msg}_1|$. In particular, we require that $2^{-(\ell_\beta - \mu(\lambda) - \lambda)}$ to be negligible. It sets $m = \mathbf{msg}_1$. It samples a string $R$ uniformly at random. It takes the role of $\mathcal{P}_2$ in the protocol $\Pi_{2PC}$. It then sets its input to $\Pi_{2PC}$ to be $x_2 = (\beta, K, \mathbf{msg}_1, R, \mathsf{md}, \theta)$, where $\mathsf{md} = 1$ and $\theta = 0$. Using $x_2$ and $\mathbf{msg}_1$, it computes the second message $\mathbf{msg}_2$ of $\Pi_{2PC}$ using the input $x_2$. That is, $\mathbf{msg}_2 \leftarrow \mathcal{P}_2.\mathsf{MsgGen}[\Pi_{2PC}](1^\lambda, x_2, \mathbf{msg}_1)$. It sends $(\beta, \mathbf{msg}_2)$ to $P_1$.

Finally, $P_1$ computes the output of $\Pi_{2PC}$ and recovers the randomized encoding $\langle N \rangle$. It then evaluates the decoding algorithm $\mathsf{D}(\langle N \rangle)$ to get the output $K'$. It outputs $K'$.

This concludes the construction. We argue that the above protocol satisfies the properties of the generation protocol.

**Theorem 10.** *Assuming the security of $\Pi_{2PC}$ (Definition 7) and* SRE, GenProt *satisfies soundness.*

*Proof.* Suppose $P_1^*$ receives as input two trapdoors $K_0$ and $K_1$. In this case we need to argue that a malicious $P_1^*$ having just black box access to (honest) $P_2$ will be unable to distinguish whether $P_2$ is using $K_0$ or $K_1$. In fact, we argue a stronger property: we argue that the behavior of $P_1^*$ can be simulated by a PPT simulator even without the knowledge of $K$. That is, for every adversarial receiver $P_1^*$, there exists a PPT simulator Sim, for every $K \in \{0,1\}^{\mathrm{poly}(\lambda)}$ and auxiliary information $\mathbf{z} \in \{0,1\}^{\mathrm{poly}'(\lambda)}$,

$$|\Pr[1 \leftarrow \langle P_1^*(\mathbf{z}),\ P_2(\mathbf{z}, K)\rangle] - \Pr[1 \leftarrow \langle P_1^*(\mathbf{z}),\ \mathsf{Sim}(\mathbf{z})\rangle]| \leq \frac{1}{2} + \mathsf{negl}(\lambda)$$

Note that the above property implies soundness property.

*Description of* Sim($\mathbf{z}$). It receives as input $\mathsf{msg}_1$ from $P_1$. It generates $\mathsf{msg}_2$ as follows:

- Let $\mathsf{Sim}_{\mathsf{SRE}}$ be the simulator of the succinct randomized encodings scheme. It then executes $\mathsf{Sim}_{\mathsf{SRE}}(1^\lambda, 1^{\ell_1}, 1^{\ell_2}, v)$, where $\ell_1$ is the size of $M$, $\ell_2$ is the size of $m$ as defined in the description of functionality for $\Pi_{2PC}$ and $v$ is set to be $\perp$. The output of $\mathsf{Sim}_{\mathsf{SRE}}(1^\lambda, 1^{\ell_1}, 1^{\ell_2}, v)$ is denoted by $\langle N \rangle$.
- It sets $x_2 = (0, 0, 0, 0, 2, \langle N \rangle)$. It then computes $\mathsf{msg}_2$ as a function of $x_2$ and $\mathsf{msg}_1$. The generation of $\mathsf{msg}_2$ is performed by running the algorithm of (honest) $\mathcal{P}_2$ in $\Pi_{2PC}$. That is, $\mathsf{msg}_2 \leftarrow \mathcal{P}_2.\mathsf{MsgGen}[\Pi_{2PC}](1^\lambda, x_2, \mathsf{msg}_1)$.
- Finally, it samples a string $\beta$ of length $\ell_\beta$.

Sim then sends $(\beta, \mathsf{msg}_2)$ to $P_2$. This ends the description of Sim.

We focus on proving the above stronger property. In the following hybrids, we use extractor Ext associated with $\Pi_{\mathsf{2PC}}$ (see Definition 6). Recall that Ext need not necessarily be efficient.

$\mathsf{Hyb}_1$: This corresponds to the real experiment where $P_1^*(\mathbf{z})$ is interacting with $P_2(\mathbf{z}, K)$. The output of this hybrid is the output of $P_1^*$.

$\mathsf{Hyb}_2$: In this hybrid, party $P_2$ deviates from the description of the protocol. It uses the extractor Ext to extract $x_1^* = (M, R_1)$. It then sets $x_2' = (0, 0, 0, 0, 2, \theta)$ and uses this input to generate the second message of the protocol $\Pi_{\mathsf{2PC}}$. That is, $\mathsf{msg}_2 \leftarrow \mathcal{P}_2.\mathsf{MsgGen}[\Pi_{\mathsf{2PC}}](1^\lambda, x_2', \mathsf{msg}_1)$, where $\mathsf{msg}_1$ is the message sent by $P_1^*$. Here, $\theta$ is set to be the output $f(x_1^*, (\beta, K, \mathsf{msg}_1, R_2, 1, 0))$, where $R_2$ is sampled uniformly at random. $P_2$ sends $(\beta, \mathsf{msg}_2)$ to $P_1^*$, where $\beta$ is a string of length $\ell_\beta$ sampled uniformly at random. The output of this hybrid is the output of $P_1^*$.

Since Ext need not be efficient, $P_2$ is not necessarily efficient.

*Claim.* Assuming the security of $\Pi_{\mathsf{2PC}}$, hybrids $\mathsf{Hyb}_1$ and $\mathsf{Hyb}_2$ are computationally indistinguishable.

*Proof.* Suppose $x_1^* = (M, R_1)$, interpreted as the description of a Turing machine $M$ (with the bounded auxiliary information part of this) along with randomness $R_1$, is the input extracted by the extractor Ext from the first message of the generation protocol. Let $x_2'$ be the input used by $\mathcal{P}_2$ in $\mathsf{Hyb}_1$ and let $x_2''$ be the input used by $\mathcal{P}_2$ in $\mathsf{Hyb}_2$. We have that $f(x_1, x_2') = f(x_1, x_2'')$. And thus, from the security of $\Pi_{\mathsf{2PC}}$ (Definition 6), we have that $P_1^*$ cannot distinguish whether $P_2$ used $x_2'$ or $x_2''$. The claim thus follows.

$\mathsf{Hyb}_3$: In this hybrid, $P_2$ essentially executes the simulator Sim described above.

*Claim.* Assuming the security of SRE, hybrids $\mathsf{Hyb}_2$ and $\mathsf{Hyb}_3$ are computationally indistinguishable.

*Proof.* Suppose $x_1^* = (M, R_1)$, interpreted as a Turing machine $M$ (with the auxiliary information hardcoded in it) along with randomness $R_1$, is the input extracted by the extractor Ext from the first message $\mathsf{msg}_1$ of $\Pi_{\mathsf{2PC}}$. Sample string $\beta$ of length $\ell_\beta$ uniformly at random. We first make the following observation. The probability that for any $\gamma$, $M(\gamma)$ outputs the random string $\beta$ is at most $2^{-\mathcal{O}(\ell_\beta - \mu(\lambda) - \lambda)}$, which is negligible. Thus with overwhelming probability we have that $N[\beta, K, \mathsf{msg}_1, M]$ outputs $\bot$.

The only difference between $\mathsf{Hyb}_2$ and $\mathsf{Hyb}_3$ is that in $\mathsf{Hyb}_2$, $\theta$ is set to $\langle N \rangle$ whereas in $\mathsf{Hyb}_3$, $\theta$ is set to be the simulated randomized encoding corresponding to the output $\bot$. As observed above, $N$ outputs $\bot$ except with negligible probability. Thus, we can invoke the security of randomized encodings to argue that $\mathsf{Hyb}_2$ and $\mathsf{Hyb}_3$ are computationally indistinguishable.

From the indistinguishability of $\mathsf{Hyb}_1$ and $\mathsf{Hyb}_3$, we have that $P_1^*$ cannot distinguish whether it is interacting with $P_2$ versus interacting with $\mathsf{Sim}$. This completes the proof.

**Theorem 11.** *Assuming the correctness, security properties of $\Pi_{\mathsf{2PC}}$ (Definition 6) and $\mathsf{SRE}$, $\mathsf{GenProt}$ satisfies extractability against $\mu$-uniform senders.*

*Proof.* We design an extractor $\mathsf{ExtGP}$ that extracts the trapdoor from the semi-honest sender $P_2^*$. The extractor has the knowledge of the code used by $P_2^*$. Call the Turing machine executed by $P_2^*$ to be $M$ (which has auxiliary information hardcoded in it). Since we are assuming that $P_2^*$ is $\mu$-bounded uniform, we have $|M| \le \mathcal{O}(\mu(\lambda) + \lambda)$: this is to account for the auxiliary information whose length is at most $\mu(\lambda)$ and representing the Turing machine requires size at most $\lambda$.

Now, the extractor proceeds as follows: it sets the input to $\Pi_{\mathsf{2PC}}$ to be $M$. It then computes the first message $\mathbf{msg}_1$ of $\Pi_{\mathsf{2PC}}$ and sends it to $P_2^*$. Then, $P_2^*$ computes $(\beta, \mathbf{msg}_2)$ and sends it to the extractor.

- From the security of $\Pi_{\mathsf{2PC}}$ (Definition 6), the view of $P_2^*$ when interacting with $P_1$ is computationally indistinguishable from the view of $P_2$ when interacting with $\mathsf{ExtGP}$. Recall that $P_1$ uses the input 0 in the first message and $\mathsf{ExtGP}$ uses the input $M$ in the first message.
- Since $P_2^*$ is semi-honest, it computes the second message of $\Pi_{\mathsf{2PC}}$ honestly. From the correctness of $\Pi_{\mathsf{2PC}}$, it follows that the extractor can recover the randomized encoding $\langle N \rangle$ from $\Pi_{\mathsf{2PC}}$. From the correctness of $\mathsf{SRE}$, it further follows that the decoding of $\langle N \rangle$ yields $K$ if and only if the first $\ell_\beta$ bits of $M(\mathbf{msg}_1)$ yields $\beta$. Since $M$ was chosen to be the code of $P_2^*$, it follows that the decoding of $\langle N \rangle$ does yield $K$.

From the above two bullets, we have that $\mathsf{GenProt}$ satisfies extractability property.

## 5    Three-Round Secure Computation

Consider any boolean functionality $f : \{0, 1\}^{\ell_1} \times \{0, 1\}^{\ell_2} \to \{0, 1\}$, where the output is delivered to the second party. We construct a three-round secure two-party computation protocol $\Pi_{\mathsf{2PC}}$ that securely computes $f$ against bounded non-uniform adversaries. We denote the two parties involved in the protocol as $P_1$ and $P_2$.

*Building Blocks.* We describe the building blocks used in our protocol.

1. GARBLING SCHEME FOR CIRCUITS (Definition 3), denoted by $\mathsf{GC} = (\mathsf{Gen}, \mathsf{GrbC}, \mathsf{Grbl}, \mathsf{EvalGC})$. Without loss of generality we can assume that $\mathsf{GrbC}$ and $\mathsf{Grbl}$ are deterministic algorithms.

2. TWO MESSAGE $\ell_2$-PARALLEL 1-OUT-2 OBLIVIOUS TRANSFER PROTOCOL (Definition 4), denoted by $\mathsf{OT}$. We require security against malicious receivers.

We additionally require that the OT protocol satisfies uniqueness of transcript property (Definition 5).

3. THREE MESSAGE ZERO KNOWLEDGE ARGUMENT OF KNOWLEDGE (ZKAoK) SYSTEM (Definition 9) for NP. We require that the 3-message ZKAoK system ZK = (Prover, Verifier) satisfies the delayed statement-witness property (Definition 11).

We denote the relation associated with the above system to be $\mathcal{R}_{zk}$. And let $\mathcal{L}(\mathcal{R}_{zk})$ be the associated language. The relation $\mathcal{R}_{zk}$ is described in Fig. 2.

4. TWO MESSAGE GENERATION PROTOCOL (Definition 16) denoted by GenProt. In particular, we are interested in generation protocols satisfying *special extraction* property. We consider a two message generation protocol. The role of the sender of GenProt is played by $P_2$ and the role of the receiver of GenProt is played by $P_1$.

5. TWO MESSAGE CONDITIONAL DISCLOSE OF SECRET (CDS) PROTOCOL (Definition 8), denoted by CDSProt. The associated relation $\mathcal{R}_{cds}$ is described in Fig. 1.

6. OTHER TOOLS. We additionally use pseudorandom functions, denoted by PRF, in this construction.

---

**Relation $\mathcal{R}_{cds}$ for CDS Protocol**

**Input:** $\mathbf{y} = (OT_1, s, GP_1, GP_2)$
**Witness:** $w = (x_2, R_{ot}^{rec}, K, R_{gp}^{sen})$

$(\mathbf{y}, w)$ is in relation $\mathcal{R}_{cds}$ if and only if the following conditions are satisfied:

1. $OT_1$ is generated as a function of $x_2$ and $R_{ot}^{rec}$. That is, $OT_1 \leftarrow$ Rec.MsgGen[OT]$(x_2; R_{ot}^{rec})$.

2. The trapdoor $K$ was used honestly to generate the message $GP_1$ using GenProt. The randomness used by the sender in this protocol is $R_{gp}^{sen}$. That is, $GP_1 \leftarrow$ Sen.MsgGen[GenProt]$(K; R_{gp}^{sen})$.

3. $R_{ot}^{rec} \leftarrow$ PRF$(K, 1)$.

4. $s \leftarrow$ PRF$(K, 2) \oplus x_2$.

---

**Fig. 1.** Relation $\mathcal{R}_{cds}$ associated with CDS

---

**Relation $\mathcal{R}_{zk}$ for ZKAoK Protocol**

**Input** : $\mathbf{y} = (CDS_1, CDS_2, OT_1, OT_2)$
**Witness** : $w = (R_{gc}, R_{ot}^{sen}, R_{cds}^{sen}, \widehat{C})$

$(\mathbf{y}, w)$ is in relation $\mathcal{R}_{zk}$ if and only if the following conditions are satisfied:

1. Garbling key is generated as follows; $\mathsf{gcsk} \leftarrow \mathsf{Gen}(1^\lambda; R_{gc})$. Garbled circuit $\widehat{C}$ is generated as $\widehat{C} \leftarrow \mathsf{GrbC}(\mathsf{gcsk}, C)$. Wire keys are generated as $\langle \mathbf{k} \rangle \leftarrow \mathsf{Grbl}(\mathsf{gcsk})$.

2. The second message of OT is generated as $OT_2 \leftarrow$ $\mathsf{Sen.MsgGen[OT]}(\langle \mathbf{k} \rangle, OT_1; R_{ot}^{sen})$.

3. $CDS_2$ is computed as a function of $CDS_1$ and randomness $R_{cds}^{sen}$. That is, $CDS_2 \leftarrow \mathsf{Sen.MsgGen[CDSProt]}(CDS_1; R_{cds}^{sen})$.

---

**Fig. 2.** Relation $\mathcal{R}_{zk}$ associated with ZKAoK

---

**Output Computation:**

$P_2$ computes the following:

- Checks if the verifier of ZK accepts on input the transcript of ZK. If the check fails, abort.
- From the transcript of OT protocol, recover the value $\langle \mathbf{k} \rangle_{x_2} = (k_1^{b_1}, \ldots, k_{\ell_2}^{b_{\ell_2}})$.
- Recover the garbled circuit $\widehat{C}$ from the transcript of the CDS protocol.
- Finally, execute the evaluation algorithm $\mathsf{EvalGC}(\widehat{C}, \langle \mathbf{k} \rangle_{x_2})$ to obtain the value out.

Output out.

---

**Fig. 3.** Computation of output

*Protocol* $\Pi_{2PC}$. We now proceed to describe protocol $\Pi_{2PC}$.

1. $P_1 \rightarrow P_2$: On input $x_1$ of length $\ell_1$, party $P_1$ does the following:
   - Compute the prover's message of ZK, denoted by $ZK_1$.
   - It computes the first message of the generation protocol using randomness $R_{gp}^{rec}$. That is, $GP_1 \leftarrow \mathsf{Rec.MsgGen[GenProt]}(R_{gp}^{rec})$.
   It sends $(ZK_1, GP_1)$ to $P_2$.
2. $P_2 \rightarrow P_1$: Party $P_2$ computes the third message as follows:
   - Compute the verifier's message of ZK. Denote this by $ZK_2$.
   - It computes $R_{ot}^{rec} = \mathsf{PRF}(K, 1)$, randomness used in OT.
   - It computes the first message of OT, denoted by $OT_1$, as a function of its input $x_2$ and randomness $R_{ot}^{rec}$. That is, $OT_1 \leftarrow \mathsf{Rec.MsgGen[OT]}(x_2; R_{ot}^{rec})$, where Rec is the receiver algorithm of OT.

Here, $x_2$ is interpreted as a vector with the $i^{th}$ entry being the $i^{th}$ bit of $x_2$.

- Generate the second message of GenProt, i.e., $GP_2$, as a function of $GP_1$, and freshly sampled randomness $R_{gp}^{sen}$. That is, $GP_2 \leftarrow$ Sen.MsgGen[GenProt]$(K, GP_1; R_{gp}^{sen})$.
- Compute $s = \mathsf{PRF}(K, 2) \oplus x_2$.
- Generate the first message of CDS protocol, denoted by $CDS_1$, as a function of instance $\mathbf{y} = (OT_1, s, GP_1, GP_2)$, witness $w = (x_2, R_{ot})$ and randomness $R_{cds}^{rec}$. That is, $CDS_1 \leftarrow$ Rec.MsgGen$(\mathbf{y}, w; R_{cds}^{rec})$.

It sends $(ZK_2, OT_1, GP_2, CDS_1, s)$ to $P_1$.

3. $P_1 \to P_2$: $P_1$ computes the final message as follows:
   - Execute gcsk $\leftarrow$ GC.Gen$(1^\lambda; R_{gc})$, where $R_{gc}$ is the randomness used in the algorithm. Execute $\langle \mathbf{k} \rangle = (\mathbf{k}_1, \dots, \mathbf{k}_{\ell_2}) \leftarrow$ GC.Grbl(gcsk), where $\ell_2$ is the input length of party $P_2$. For every $i \in [\ell_2]$, we have $\mathbf{k}_i = (k_i^0, k_i^1)$.
   - It computes the garbled circuit $\widehat{C} \leftarrow$ GrbC(gcsk, $C$), where $C$ is a boolean circuit defined as $C(y) = f(x_1, y)$, where $y$ is of length $\ell_2$.
   - It computes the second message of OT as a function of first message and randomness $R_{ot}^{sen}$. That is, $OT_2 \leftarrow$ Sen.MsgGen[OT]$(\langle \mathbf{k} \rangle, OT_1; R_{ot}^{sen})$.
   - It computes the second message of CDSProt as a function of first message $CDS_1$, instance $\mathbf{y}$ (its computed the same way as $P_2$ does), secret $s = \widehat{C}$ and randomness $R_{cds}^{sen}$. That is, $CDS_2 \leftarrow$ Sen.MsgGen[CDSProt]$(CDS_1, \mathbf{y}, s; R_{cds}^{sen})$.
   - It computes the final message of ZK, namely $ZK_3$. This is computed as a function of instance $(CDS_1, CDS_2, OT_1, OT_2)$ and witness $(R_{gc}, R_{ot}^{sen}, R_{cds}^{sen}, \widehat{C})$.

Finally, $P_2$ recovers out from its view using the algorithm in Fig. 3.

**Theorem 12.** *Assuming the security of the following primitives: garbling scheme* GC, *oblivious transfer protocol* OT, *ZKAoK system* ZK, *generation protocol* GenProt, *conditional disclosure of secrets protocol* CDSProt *and pseudorandom functions* PRF, *we have that* $\Pi_{\mathsf{2PC}}$ *is secure against malicious adversaries (Definition 1).*

The proof of the above theorem can be found in the full version.

Instantiating the building blocks (see Sect. 3), we obtain the following corollary.

**Corollary 1.** *Assuming DDH, LWE, Zaps and succinct randomized encodings, protocol* $\Pi_{\mathsf{2PC}}$ *is a secure* $\mu$-*bounded uniform two party computation protocol satisfying Definition 2.*

# References

1. Aiello, B., Ishai, Y., Reingold, O.: Priced oblivious transfer: how to sell digital goods. In: Pfitzmann, B. (ed.) EUROCRYPT 2001. LNCS, vol. 2045, pp. 119–135. Springer, Heidelberg (2001). doi:10.1007/3-540-44987-6_8

2. Ananth, P., Jain, A.: Indistinguishability obfuscation from compact functional encryption. In: Gennaro, R., Robshaw, M. (eds.) CRYPTO 2015. LNCS, vol. 9215, pp. 308–326. Springer, Heidelberg (2015). doi:10.1007/978-3-662-47989-6_15

3. Barak, B.: How to go beyond the black-box simulation barrier. In: Proceedings of the 42nd IEEE Symposium on Foundations of Computer Science, pp. 106–115. IEEE (2001)

4. Barak, B., Goldreich, O., Impagliazzo, R., Rudich, S., Sahai, A., Vadhan, S., Yang, K.: On the (im)possibility of obfuscating programs. In: Kilian, J. (ed.) CRYPTO 2001. LNCS, vol. 2139, pp. 1–18. Springer, Heidelberg (2001). doi:10.1007/3-540-44647-8_1

5. Bellare, M., Hoang, V.T., Rogaway, P.: Foundations of garbled circuits. In: Proceedings of the 2012 ACM Conference on Computer and Communications Security, CCS 2012, New York, NY, USA, pp. 784–796. ACM (2012)

6. Bellare, M., Palacio, A.: The knowledge-of-exponent assumptions and 3-round zero-knowledge protocols. In: Franklin, M. (ed.) CRYPTO 2004. LNCS, vol. 3152, pp. 273–289. Springer, Heidelberg (2004). doi:10.1007/978-3-540-28628-8_17

7. Bitansky, N., Brakerski, Z., Kalai, Y., Paneth, O., Vaikuntanathan, V.: 3-message zero knowledge against human ignorance. In: Hirt, M., Smith, A. (eds.) TCC 2016. LNCS, vol. 9985, pp. 57–83. Springer, Heidelberg (2016). doi:10.1007/978-3-662-53641-4_3

8. Bitansky, N., Canetti, R., Paneth, O., Rosen, A.: On the existence of extractable one-way functions. SIAM J. Comput. **45**(5), 1910–1952 (2016)

9. Bitansky, N., Garg, S., Lin, H., Pass, R., Telang, S.: Succinct randomized encodings and their applications. In: STOC (2015)

10. Boneh, D., Waters, B.: Constrained pseudorandom functions and their applications. In: Sako, K., Sarkar, P. (eds.) ASIACRYPT 2013. LNCS, vol. 8270, pp. 280–300. Springer, Heidelberg (2013). doi:10.1007/978-3-642-42045-0_15

11. Boyle, E., Goldwasser, S., Ivan, I.: Functional signatures and pseudorandom functions. In: Krawczyk, H. (ed.) PKC 2014. LNCS, vol. 8383, pp. 501–519. Springer, Heidelberg (2014). doi:10.1007/978-3-642-54631-0_29

12. Canetti, R., Holmgren, J., Jain, A., Vaikuntanathan, V.: Indistinguishability obfuscation of iterated circuits and RAM programs. In: STOC (2015)

13. Döttling, N., Fleischhacker, N., Krupp, J., Schröder, D.: Two-message, oblivious evaluation of cryptographic functionalities. In: Robshaw, M., Katz, J. (eds.) CRYPTO 2016. LNCS, vol. 9816, pp. 619–648. Springer, Heidelberg (2016). doi:10.1007/978-3-662-53015-3_22

14. Dwork, C., Naor, M.: Zaps and their applications. In: 41st Annual Symposium on Foundations of Computer Science, FOCS 2000, 12–14 November 2000, Redondo Beach, California, USA, pp. 283–293 (2000)

15. Even, S., Goldreich, O., Lempel, A.: A randomized protocol for signing contracts. In: Chaum, D., Rivest, R.L., Sherman, A.T. (eds.) CRYPTO 1982, pp. 205–210. Springer, Boston (1982). doi:10.1007/978-1-4757-0602-4_19

16. Feige, U., Shamir, A.: Witness indistinguishable and witness hiding protocols. In: Proceedings of the 22nd Annual ACM Symposium on Theory of Computing, 13–17 May 1990, Baltimore, Maryland, USA, pp. 416–426 (1990)

17. Garg, S., Gentry, C., Halevi, S., Raykova, M., Sahai, A., Waters, B.: Candidate indistinguishability obfuscation and functional encryption for all circuits. In: 54th Annual IEEE Symposium on Foundations of Computer Science, FOCS 2013, 26–29 October 2013, Berkeley, CA, USA, pp. 40–49. IEEE Computer Society (2013)

18. Garg, S., Mukherjee, P., Pandey, O., Polychroniadou, A.: The exact round complexity of secure computation. In: Fischlin, M., Coron, J.-S. (eds.) EUROCRYPT 2016. LNCS, vol. 9666, pp. 448–476. Springer, Heidelberg (2016). doi:10.1007/978-3-662-49896-5_16

19. Gertner, Y., Ishai, Y., Kushilevitz, E., Malkin, T.: Protecting data privacy in private information retrieval schemes. J. Comput. Syst. Sci. **60**(3), 592–629 (2000)

20. Goldreich, O., Goldwasser, S., Micali, S.: How to construct random functions. J. ACM (JACM) **33**(4), 792–807 (1986)

21. Goldreich, O., Kahan, A.: How to construct constant-round zero-knowledge proof systems for NP. J. Cryptol. **9**(3), 167–190 (1996)

22. Goldreich, O., Krawczyk, H.: On the composition of zero-knowledge proof systems. SIAM J. Comput. **25**(1), 169–192 (1996)

23. Goldreich, O., Micali, S., Wigderson, A.: Proofs that yield nothing but their validity and a methodology of cryptographic protocol design. In: 27th Annual Symposium on Foundations of Computer Science, pp. 174–187. IEEE (1986)

24. Goldreich, O., Micali, S., Wigderson, A.: How to play any mental game. In: STOC (1987)

25. Goldreich, O., Oren, Y.: Definitions and properties of zero-knowledge proof systems. J. Cryptol. **7**(1), 1–32 (1994)

26. Goldwasser, S., Micali, S., Rackoff, C.: The knowledge complexity of interactive proof-systems. In: STOC, pp. 291–304 (1985)

27. Hada, S., Tanaka, T.: On the existence of 3-round zero-knowledge protocols. In: Krawczyk, H. (ed.) CRYPTO 1998. LNCS, vol. 1462, pp. 408–423. Springer, Heidelberg (1998). doi:10.1007/BFb0055744

28. Ishai, Y., Kushilevitz, E.: Randomizing polynomials: a new representation with applications to round-efficient secure computation. In: Proceedings of the 41st Annual Symposium on Foundations of Computer Science, pp. 294–304. IEEE (2000)

29. Kalai, Y.T., Rothblum, G.N., Rothblum, R.D.: From obfuscation to the security of Fiat-Shamir for proofs. In: Katz, J., Shacham, H. (eds.) CRYPTO 2017. LNCS, vol. 10402, pp. 224–251. Springer, Cham (2017). doi:10.1007/978-3-319-63715-0_8

30. Katz, J., Ostrovsky, R.: Round-optimal secure two-party computation. In: Franklin, M. (ed.) CRYPTO 2004. LNCS, vol. 3152, pp. 335–354. Springer, Heidelberg (2004). doi:10.1007/978-3-540-28628-8_21

31. Kiayias, A., Papadopoulos, S., Triandopoulos, N., Zacharias, T.: Delegatable pseudorandom functions and applications. In: Proceedings of the 2013 ACM SIGSAC Conference on Computer & Communications Security, pp. 669–684. ACM (2013)

32. Koppula, V., Lewko, A.B., Waters, B.: Indistinguishability obfuscation for turing machines with unbounded memory. In: STOC (2015)

33. Lapidot, D., Shamir, A.: Publicly verifiable non-interactive zero-knowledge proofs. In: Menezes, A.J., Vanstone, S.A. (eds.) CRYPTO 1990. LNCS, vol. 537, pp. 353–365. Springer, Heidelberg (1991). doi:10.1007/3-540-38424-3_26

34. Lindell, Y., Pinkas, B.: An efficient protocol for secure two-party computation in the presence of malicious adversaries. In: Naor, M. (ed.) EUROCRYPT 2007. LNCS, vol. 4515, pp. 52–78. Springer, Heidelberg (2007). doi:10.1007/978-3-540-72540-4_4

35. Naor, M., Pinkas, B.: Oblivious transfer and polynomial evaluation. In: Proceedings of the Thirty-First Annual ACM Symposium on Theory of Computing, pp. 245–254. ACM (1999)

36. Naor, M., Pinkas, B.: Efficient oblivious transfer protocols. In: Proceedings of the Twelfth Annual Symposium on Discrete Algorithms, 7–9 January 2001, Washington, D.C., USA., pp. 448–457 (2001)
37. Rabin, M.O.: How to exchange secrets with oblivious transfer. IACR Cryptology ePrint Archive, 2005:187 (2005)
38. Sahai, A., Waters, B.: How to use indistinguishability obfuscation: deniable encryption, and more. In: Shmoys, D.B. (ed.) Symposium on Theory of Computing, STOC 2014, New York, NY, USA, 31 May–03 June 2014, pp. 475–484. ACM (2014)
39. Yao, A.C.-C.: How to generate and exchange secrets (extended abstract). In: FOCS, pp. 162–167 (1986)

# Four Round Secure Computation Without Setup

Zvika Brakerski[1], Shai Halevi[2], and Antigoni Polychroniadou[3]([✉])

[1] Weizmann Institute of Science, Rehovot, Israel
zvika.brakerski@weizmann.ac.il
[2] IBM, Yorktown Heights, USA
shaih@alum.mit.edu
[3] Cornell Tech, New York, USA
antigoni@cornell.edu

**Abstract.** We construct a 4-round multi-party computation protocol in the plain model for any functionality, secure against a malicious adversary. Our protocol relies on the sub-exponential hardness of the Learning with Errors (LWE) problem with slightly super-polynomial noise ratio, and on the existence of adaptively secure commitments based on standard assumptions. Our round complexity matches a lower bound of Garg et al. (EUROCRYPT '16), and outperforms the state of the art of 6 rounds based on similar assumptions to ours, and 5 rounds relying on indistinguishability obfuscation and other strong assumptions.

To do this, we construct an LWE based multi-key FHE scheme with a very simple one-round *distributed setup procedure* (vs. the trusted setup required in previous LWE based constructions). This lets us construct the first 3-round semi-malicious MPC protocol without setup from standard LWE using the approach of Mukherjee and Wichs (EUROCRYPT '16). Finally, subexponential hardness and adaptive commitments are used to "compile" the protocol into the fully malicious setting.

## 1 Introduction

Secure Multi-party Computation (MPC) allows mutually suspicious parties to evaluate a function on their joint private inputs without revealing these inputs to each other. One fruitful line of investigation is concerned with the *round*

Z. Brakerski—Supported by the Israel Science Foundation (Grant No. 468/14) and Binational Science Foundation (Grants No. 2016726, 2014276) and ERC Project 756482 REACT.

S. Halevi—Supported by the Defense Advanced Research Projects Agency (DARPA) and Army Research Office (ARO) under Contract No. W911NF-15-C-0236.

A. Polychroniadou—Supported by the National Science Foundation under Grant No. 1617676, IBM under Agreement 4915013672, the Packard Foundation under Grant 2015-63124, and the Danish National Research Foundation and the National Science Foundation of China (under the grant 61361136003) for the Sino-Danish Center for the Theory of Interactive Computation. Any opinions, findings, and conclusions or recommendations expressed in this material are those of the author(s) and do not necessarily reflect the views of the sponsors.

© International Association for Cryptologic Research 2017
Y. Kalai and L. Reyzin (Eds.): TCC 2017, Part I, LNCS 10677, pp. 645–677, 2017.
https://doi.org/10.1007/978-3-319-70500-2_22

*complexity* of these protocols. More specifically, we consider a model where at each round, each party is allowed to broadcast a message to everyone else. We allow the adversary to be malicious and corrupt any fraction of the parties.

If a Common Random String (CRS) is allowed, then two rounds are necessary and sufficient for secure multi-party protocols under plausible cryptographic assumptions [GGHR14, MW16].

Without relying on trusted setup, it was still known that constant round protocols are possible [BMR90], but the exact round complexity remained open. A lower bound in the simultaneous message model was established in the recent work of Garg et al. [GMPP16], who proved that four rounds are necessary. They also showed how to perform multi-party coin flipping in four rounds, which can then be used to generate a CRS and execute the aforementioned protocols in the CRS model. That technique implied a five-round protocol based on 3-round 3-robust non-malleable commitments[1] and indistinguishability obfuscation, and a 6-round protocol based on 3-round 3-robust non-malleable commitments and LWE.

For the important special case of only two parties, it is known that two message protocols with sequential rounds, i.e. each party talks in turn, are necessary and sufficient in the CRS model [JS07, HK07] and five message protocols are necessary and sufficient without setup [KO04, ORS15].

**Our Results.** Our work addresses the following fundamental question:

*Can we obtain round-optimal multi-party computation protocols without setup?*

We answer this question in the affirmative, obtaining a round-optimal multi-party computation protocol in the plain model for general functionalities in the presence of a malicious adversary. Informally, we prove the following:

**Theorem 1** *(Informal). Assuming the existence of adaptive commitments, as well as the sub-exponential hardness of Learning-with-Errors, there exists a four-round protocol that securely realizes any multi-party functionality against a malicious adversary in the plain model without setup.*

In particular, we use a two-round *adaptively secure* commitment scheme (e.g., as constructed by Pandey et al. [PPV08], using Naor's protocol [Nao91] with adaptive PRGs - a non-standard assumption). However, the recent two-round non-malleable commitment scheme [LPS17] from "Time-Lock Puzzles" can be made adaptively secure.

To establish our result, we depart from the coin flipping approach of [GMPP16] and instead rely on a new generalized notion of multi-key fully homomorphic encryption [LTV12] which we show how to construct based on the hardness of LWE. In a nutshell, whereas prior LWE based constructions required trusted setup (essentially a CRS) [CM15, MW16, BP16, PS16], we show that the

---

[1] Such commitments can be instantiated from one-way permutations secure w.r.t. sub-exponential time adversaries [COSV16].

setup procedure can be distributed. Each party only needs to broadcast a random string[2], and generate its public key based on the collection of strings by all other parties. We show that the resulting scheme is secure even when some of the broadcast strings are adversarial (and even when the adversary is *rushing*). Similarly to Mukherjee and Wichs [MW16], we can transform our multi-key FHE into an MPC protocol in the *semi-malicious* model (where the adversary is only allowed to corrupt parties in a way that is consistent with *some* random tape). Our protocol requires 3 rounds without setup (vs. 2 rounds in the CRS model), and only requires *polynomial* hardness of LWE with slightly super polynomial noise ratio. Informally, we establish the following theorem:

**Theorem 2** *(Informal).* *Assuming hardness of Learning-with-Errors with super-polynomial noise ratio, there exists a three-round protocol that securely realizes any multi-party functionality against a rushing semi-malicious adversary in the plain model without setup.*

**Concurrent work.** In a concurrent and independent work, Ananth, Choudhuri, and Jain construct a maliciously-secure 4-round MPC protocol based on one-way permutations and sub-exponential hardness of DDH [ACJ17]. Their approach is very different from ours, they construct and use a "robust semi-honest" MPC protocol from DDH, while our main building block is an LWE-based 3-round protocol secure against semi-malicious adversaries.

**Related work on LWE-based MPC protocols.** Asharov et al. [AJL+12] first show a three-round *multi-party* computation protocol in the CRS model and a two-round multi-party computation protocol in the reusable public-key infrastructure setup model based on LWE. The work of Mukherjee and Wichs [MW16], and its extensions [BP16,PS16], based on multi-key FHE [LTV12,CM15], shows how to obtain optimal two-round constructions based on LWE and NIZKs in the CRS model. See Chap. 3 of [Pol16] for related work of MPC protocols based on different assumptions both in the CRS and plain model.

## 2    Overview of Our Protocol

Our starting point is the multi-key FHE approach to MPC, first introduced by [LTV12]. As explained above, it was shown in [MW16] that the Clear-McGoldrick scheme [CM15] implies a two-round protocol in the semi-malicious setting in the CRS model under LWE. Furthermore, using NIZK it is possible to also achieve fully malicious security. Constructing a multi-key FHE without setup and with the necessary properties for compiling it into an MPC protocol is still an open problem, but we show that the trusted setup can be replaced by a distributed process which only adds a single round to the MPC protocol. While our final solution is quite simple, it relies on a number of insights as to the construction and use of multi-key FHE.

---

[2] Essentially its public matrix for a dual-Regev encryption scheme [Reg09,GPV08].

1. While the schemes in [GSW13, CM15, MW16] rely on *primal* Regev-style LWE-based encryption as a basis for their FHE scheme, it is also possible to instantiate them based on the *dual*-Regev scheme [GPV08] (with asymptotically similar performance). However, the same form of CRS is required for this instantiation as well, so at first glance it does not seem to offer any advantages.

2. The multi-key FHE schemes of [CM15, MW16] are presented as requiring trusted setup, but a deeper look reveals that this trusted setup is only needed to ensure a single property, related to the functionality: In LWE based encryption (Regev or dual-Regev) the public key contains a matrix $A$ and a vector $t \cdot A$ (possibly with some additional noise, depending on the flavour of the scheme) where $t$ is the secret key. In order to allow multi-key homomorphism between parties that each have their own $A_i, t_i$, it is only required that the values $b_{i,j} = t_i A_j$ for all $i, j$, are known to all participating parties (up to small noise). The use of CRS in previous works comes in setting all $A_i$ to be the same matrix $A$, which is taken from the CRS, and thus the public key $b_i \approx t_i A_i = t_i A$ is the only required information.

3. Lastly, we notice that dual-Regev with the appropriate parameters is *leakage resilient* [DGK+10]. This means that so long as a party honestly generates its $t_i$ and $A_i$, it can expose *arbitrary* (length-bounded) information on $t_i$ without compromising the security of its own ciphertexts. Combining this with the above, we can afford to expose all $b_{i,j} = t_i A_j$ without creating a security concern (for appropriate setting of the parameters).

Putting the above observations together, we present a multi-key FHE scheme with a *distributed setup*, in which each party generates a piece of the common setup, namely the matrix $A_i$. After this step, each party can generate a public key $\mathsf{pk}_i$ containing all vectors $b_{i,j}$, the respective secret key is the vector $t_i$. Given all $\mathsf{pk}_i$ and the matrices $A_i$, it is possible to perform multi-key homomorphism in a very similar manner to [CM15, MW16]. The 3-round semi-malicious protocol is therefore as follows.

**Round 1: Distributed Setup.** Every player $P_i$ broadcasts a random matrix $A_i$ of the appropriate dimension.

**Round 2: Encryption.** Each party generates a public/secret key-pair for the multi-key FHE, encrypts its input under these keys, and broadcasts the public key and ciphertext.

**Round 3: Partial Decryption.** Each party separately evaluates the function on the encrypted inputs, then use its secret key to compute a decryption share of the resulting evaluated ciphertext and broadcasts that share to everyone.

**Epilogue: Output.** Once all the decryption shares are received, each party can combine them to get the function value, which is the output of the protocol.

This skeleton protocol can be shown to be secure in the semi-malicious adversary model, but it is clearly *insecure* in the presence of a malicious adversary. Although the protocol can tolerate adversarial choice of the first-round matrices $A_i$, the adversary can still violate privacy by sending invalid ciphertexts in

Round 2 and observing the partial decryption that the honest players send in the next round. It can also violate correctness by sending the wrong decryption shares in the last round.

These two attacks can be countered by having the parties prove that they behaved correctly, namely that the public keys and ciphertexts in Round 2 were generated honestly, and that the decryption shares in Round 3 were obtained by faithful decryption. To be effective we need the proof of correct encryption to complete before the parties send their decryption shares (and of course the proof of correct decryption must be completed before the output can be produced). Hence, if we have a $k$-round input-delayed proof of correct encryption (and a $(k+1)$-round input-delayed proof of correct decryption) then we get a $(k+1)$-round protocol overall. Much of the technical difficulties to achieve malicious security in the current work are related to using 3-round proofs of correct encryptions, resulting in a 4-round protocol.

## 2.1 The Maliciously-Secure Protocol

Our maliciously-secure protocol builds on the above 3-round semi-malicious protocol, and in addition it uses a two-round adaptive commitment protocol $\mathsf{aCom} = (\mathsf{acom}_1, \mathsf{acom}_2)$, a three-round delayed-input proof of correct encryption $\varPi_{\mathrm{WIPOK}} = (\mathsf{p}_1, \mathsf{p}_2, \mathsf{p}_3)$, and a four-round delayed-input proof of correct decryption $\varPi_{\mathrm{FS}} = (\mathsf{fs}_1, \mathsf{fs}_2, \mathsf{fs}_3, \mathsf{fs}_4)$. (The names $\varPi_{\mathrm{WIPOK}}$ and $\varPi_{\mathrm{FS}}$ are meant to hint on the implementation of these proofs, see more discussion in the next subsection.)

**Round 1: Distributed Setup, commitment & proof.** Every party $i$ broadcasts its setup matrix $A_i$. It also broadcasts the first message $\mathsf{acom}_1$ of the adaptive commitment for its randomness and input, the first message $\mathsf{p}_1$ of the proof of correct encryption, and the first message $\mathsf{fs}_1$ of the proof of correct decryption (both proofs with respect to the committed values).

**Round 2: Continued commitment & proofs.** Each party broadcasts $\mathsf{acom}_2, \mathsf{p}_2, \mathsf{fs}_2$.

**Round 3: Encryption & proofs.** The parties collect all the first round matrices $A_i$ and run the key-generation and encryption procedures of the multi-key FHE. Then, each party broadcasts its public key and encrypted input. In the same round, each party also broadcasts messages $\mathsf{p}_3, \mathsf{fs}_3$.

**Round 4: Verification & decryption.** Each party runs the verifier algorithm for the $\varPi_{\mathrm{WIPOK}}$ proof of correct encryption, verifying all the instances. If all of them passed then it evaluates the function on the encrypted inputs, then uses its secret key to compute a decryption share of the resulting evaluated ciphertext, and broadcasts that share to everyone. It also broadcasts the message $\mathsf{fs}_4$ of the proof of correct decryption.

**Epilogue: Verification & output.** Once all the decryption shares and proofs are received, each party runs the verifier algorithm for the $\varPi_{\mathrm{FS}}$ proof of correct decryption, again verifying all the instances. If all of them passed then it combines all the decryption shares to get the function value, which is the output of the protocol.

If any of the messages is missing or mal-formed, or if any of the verification algorithms fail, then the parties are instructed to immediately abort with no output.

As explained in the next section, subtle technicalities arise in the security proof that lead to an extended version of the above protocol description.

## 2.2   A Tale of Malleability and Extraction

To prove security of our protocol, we must exhibit a simulator that can somehow extract the inputs of the adversary, so that it can send these inputs to the trusted party in order to get the function output. To that end we make the three-round proof of correct encryption a *Proof of Knowledge* (POK), and let the simulator use the knowledge extractor to get these adversarial inputs.

At the same time, we must ensure that this proof of knowledge is non-malleable, so that the extracted adversarial inputs do not change between the real protocol (in which the honest parties prove knowledge of their true input) and the simulated protocol (in which the simulator generates proofs for the honest players without knowing their true inputs). A few subtle technicalities are discussed below.

**Two-round commitment with straight-line extraction.** The main technical tool that we use in our proofs is two-round adaptive commitments, that the parties use to commit to their inputs and randomness. Commitments in this scheme are marked by *tags*, and the scheme has the remarkable property of *adaptive security*: Namely, commitments with one tag are secure *even in the presence of an oracle that breaks commitments for all other tags*.

Some hybrid games in our proof of security are therefore staged in a mental-experiment game where such a breaking oracle exists, providing us with straight-line (rewinding-free) extraction of the values that the adversary commits to, while keeping the honest-party commitments secret. Looking ahead, straight-line extraction is used in some of our hybrids to fake the (WIPOK) zero knowledge proofs.

However, we also need our other primitives (MFHE, POK, etc.) to remain secure in the presence of a breaking oracle, and we use complexity leveraging for that purpose: We assume that these primitives are sub-exponentially secure, and set their parameters much larger that those of the commitment scheme. This way, all these primitives remain secure even against sub-exponential time adversaries that can break the commitment by brute force. When arguing the indistinguishability of two hybrids, we reduce to the sub-exponential security of these primitives and use brute force to implement the breaking oracle in those hybrids.[3]

**Delayed-input proofs.** In the three-round proofs for correct encryption and in the four-round proofs for correct decryption, the statement to be proved is not defined until just before the last round of the protocols. We therefore need to

---

[3] Technically we "only" need to assume standard security in a world with such a breaking oracle, which is a weaker assumption than full sub-exponential security.

use delayed-input proofs that can handle this case and squeeze rounds in order to achieve a four round protocol.

**Fake proofs via Feige-Shamir.** The simulator needs to fake the four-round proof of correct decryption on behalf of the correct parties, as it derives their decryption shares from the function output that it gets from the trusted party. For this purpose we use a Feige-Shamir-type four-round proof [FS90], which has a trapdoor that we extract and can be used to fake these proofs.

**WI-POK with a trapdoor.** Some steps in our proof have hybrid games in which the commitment contains the honest parties' true inputs while the encryption contains zeros. In such hybrids, the statement that the values committed to are consistent with the encryption is not true, so we need to fake that three-round proof as well.

For that purpose we use another Feige-Shamir-type trapdoor as follows: Each party chooses a random string $R$, encloses $\hat{R} = OWF(R)$ with its first-flow message, encloses $R$ inside the commitment aCom (together with its input and randomness) and adds the statement $\hat{R} = OWF(R)$ to the list of things that it proves in the 3-round POK protocol.

In addition, the parties execute *a second commitment protocol* bCom (which is normally used to commit to zero in the real protocol), and we modify the POK statement to say that EITHER the original statement is true, OR the value committed in that second commitment bCom is a pre-image of the $\hat{R}$ value sent by the *verifier* in the first round. Letting the POK protocol be witness-indistinguishable (WI-POK), we then extract the $R$ value from the adversary (in some hybrids), let the challenger commit to that value in the second commitment bCom, and use it as a trapdoor to fake the proof in the POK protocol.

We note that the second commitment bCom need not be non-malleable or adaptive, but it does need to remain secure in the presence of a breaking oracle for the first commitment. Since we already assume a 2-round adaptive commitment aCom, then we use the same scheme also for this second commitment, and appeal to its adaptive security to argue that the second commitment remains secure in the presence of a breaking oracle for the first commitment.

**Public-coin proofs.** In the multi-party setting, the adversary may choose to fail the proofs with some honest parties and succeed with others. We thus need to specify what honest parties do in case one of the proofs fail. The easiest solution is to use public-coin proofs with perfect completeness, and have the parties broadcast their proofs and verify them all (not only the ones where they chose the challenge). This way we ensure that if one honest party fails the proof, then all of them do.

## 2.3 Roadmap

In Part I we provide our 3-round semi-malicious protocol based on multi-key FHE. In Part II we "compile" our 3-round semi-malicious protocol to a 4-round fully maliciously-secure protocol. We conclude in Sect. 7 with open problems.

# 3    Part I: 3-Round Semi-malicious Protocols

## 3.1    LWE-Based Multi-key FHE with Distributed Setup

**Notations.** Throughout the text we denote the security parameter by $\kappa$. A function $\mu : \mathbb{N} \to \mathbb{N}$ is *negligible* if for every positive polynomial $p(\cdot)$ and all sufficiently large $\kappa$'s it holds that $\mu(\kappa) < \frac{1}{p(\kappa)}$. We often use $[n]$ to denote the set $\{1, ..., n\}$.

Let $d \leftarrow \mathcal{D}$ denote the process of sampling $d$ from the distribution $\mathcal{D}$ or, if $\mathcal{D}$ is a set, a uniform choice from it. For two distributions $\mathcal{D}_1$ and $\mathcal{D}_2$, we use $\mathcal{D}_1 \approx_s \mathcal{D}_2$ to denote that they are statistically close (up to negligible distance), $\mathcal{D}_1 \approx_c \mathcal{D}_2$ denotes computational indistinguishability, and $\mathcal{D}_1 \equiv \mathcal{D}_2$ denotes identical distributions.

## 3.2    Definitions

An encryption scheme is *multi-key homomorphic* if it can evaluate circuits on ciphertexts that are encrypted under different keys. Decrypting an evaluated ciphertext requires the secret keys of all the ciphertexts that were included in the computation. In more detail, a multi-key homomorphic encryption scheme (with trusted setup) consists of five procedures, MFHE = (MFHE.Setup, MFHE.Keygen, MFHE.Encrypt, MFHE.Decrypt, MFHE.Eval):

- **Setup** params $\leftarrow$ MFHE.Setup($1^\kappa$): On input the security parameter $\kappa$ the setup algorithm outputs the system parameters params.
- **Key Generation** (pk, sk) $\leftarrow$ MFHE.Keygen(params): On input params the key generation algorithm outputs a public/secret key pair (pk, sk).
- **Encryption** $c \leftarrow$ MFHE.Encrypt(pk, $x$): On input pk and a plaintext message $x \in \{0,1\}^*$ output a "fresh ciphertext" $c$. (We assume for convenience that the ciphertext includes also the respective public key.)
- **Evaluation** $\hat{c} :=$ MFHE.Eval(params; $\mathcal{C}$; $(c_1, \ldots, c_\ell)$): On input a (description of a) Boolean circuit $\mathcal{C}$ and a sequence of $\ell$ fresh ciphertexts $(c_1, \ldots, c_\ell)$, output an "evaluated ciphertext" $\hat{c}$. (Here we assume that the evaluated ciphertext includes also all the public keys from the $c_i$'s.)
- **Decryption** $x :=$ MFHE.Decrypt($(\mathsf{sk}_1, \ldots, \mathsf{sk}_N), \hat{c}$): On input an evaluated ciphertext $c$ (with $N$ public keys) and the corresponding $N$ secret keys $(\mathsf{sk}_1, \ldots, \mathsf{sk}_N)$, output the message $x \in \{0,1\}^*$.

The scheme is correct if for every circuit $\mathcal{C}$ on $N$ inputs and any input sequence $x_1, \ldots, x_N$ for $\mathcal{C}$, we set params $\leftarrow$ MFHE.Setup($1^\kappa$) and then generate $N$ key-pairs and $N$ ciphertexts $(\mathsf{pk}_i, \mathsf{sk}_i) \leftarrow$ MFHE.Keygen(params) and $c_i \leftarrow$ MFHE.Encrypt($pk_i, x_i$), then we get

$$\mathsf{MFHE.Decrypt}\big((\mathsf{sk}_1, \ldots, \mathsf{sk}_N), \mathsf{MFHE.Eval}(\mathsf{params}; \mathcal{C}; (c_1, \ldots, c_N))\big) = \mathcal{C}(x_1, \ldots, x_N)]$$

except with negligible probability (in $\kappa$) taken over the randomness of all these algorithms.[4]

---

[4] We often consider a slightly weaker notion of homomorphism, where the **Setup** algorithm gets also a depth-bound $d$ and correctness is then defined only relative to circuits of depth upto $d$.

**Local decryption and simulated shares.** A special property that we need of the multi-key FHE schemes from [CM15,MW16], is that the decryption procedure consists of a "local" partial-decryption procedure $ev_i \leftarrow$ MFHE.PartDec$(\hat{c}, \mathsf{sk}_i)$ that only takes one of the secret keys and outputs a partial decryption share, and a public combination procedure that takes these partial shares and outputs the plaintext, $x \leftarrow$ MFHE.FinDec$(ev_1, \ldots, ev_N, \hat{c})$.

Another property of these schemes that we need is the ability to simulate the decryption shares. Specifically, there exists a $PPT$ simulator $\mathcal{S}^T$, that gets for input:

- the evaluated ciphertext $\hat{c}$,
- the output plaintext $x := $ MFHE.Decrypt$((\mathsf{sk}_1, \ldots, \mathsf{sk}_N), \hat{c})$,
- a subset $I \subset [N]$, and all secret keys *except the one for* $I$, $\{\mathsf{sk}_j\}_{j \in [N] \setminus I}$.

The simulator produces as output simulated partial evaluation decryption shares: $\{\widetilde{ev_i}\}_{i \in I} \leftarrow \mathcal{S}^T(x, \hat{c}, I, \{\mathsf{sk}_j\}_{j \in [N] \setminus I})$. We want the simulated shares to be statistically close to the shares produced by the local partial decryption procedures using the keys $\{sk_i\}_{i \in I}$, even conditioned on all the inputs of $\mathcal{S}^T$.

We say that a scheme is *simulatable* if it has local decryption and a simulator as described here. As in [MW16], in our case too we only achieve simulatability of the basic scheme when all parties but one are corrupted (i.e., when the set $I$ is a singleton).

## Distributed Setup

The variant that we need for our protocol does not require the setup procedure to be run by a trusted entity, but rather it is run in a distributed manner by all parties in the protocol. In our definition we allow the setup to depend on the maximum number of users $N$. This restriction does not pose a problem for our application.

- **Distributed Setup** params$_i \leftarrow$ MFHE.DistSetup$(1^\kappa, 1^N, i)$: On input the security parameter $\kappa$ and number of users $N$, outputs the system parameters for the $i$-th player params$_i$.

The remaining functions have the same functionality as above, where params $= \{$params$_i\}_{i \in [N]}$, the key generation takes $i$ as an additional parameter in order to specify which entry in params it refers to.

## Semantic Security and Simulatability

Semantic security for multi-key FHE is defined as the usual notion of semantic security. For the distributed setup variant, we require that semantic security for the $i$-th party holds even when all $\{$params$_j\}_{j \in [N] \setminus \{i\}}$ are generated adversarially and possibly depending on params$_i$.

Namely, we consider a *rushing adversary* that chooses $N$ and $i \in [N]$, then it sees params$_i$ and produces params$_j$ for all $j \in [N] \setminus \{i\}$. After this setup, the adversary is engaged in the usual semantic-security game, where it is given the public key, chooses two messages and is given the encryption of one of them, and it needs to guess which one was encrypted.

Simulatability of the decryption shares is defined as before, but now the evaluated ciphertext is produced by the honest party interacting with the same rushing adversary (and statistical closeness holds even conditioned on everything that the adversary sees).

### 3.3  A "Dual" LWE-Based Multi-key FHE with Distributed Setup

For our protocol we use an adaptation of the "dual" of the multi-key FHE scheme from [CM15, MW16]. Just like the "primal" version, our scheme uses the GSW FHE scheme [GSW13], and its security is based on the hardness of LWE.

Recall that the LWE problem is parametrized by integers $n, m, q$ (with $m > n \log q$) and a distribution $\chi$ over $\mathbb{Z}$ that produces whp integers much smaller than $q$. The LWE assumption says that given a random matrix $A \in \mathbb{Z}_q^{n \times m}$, the distribution $sA + e$ with random $s \in \mathbb{Z}_q^n$ and $e \leftarrow \chi^m$ is indistinguishable from uniform in $\mathbb{Z}_q^m$.

For the "dual" GSW scheme below, we use parameters $n < m < w < q$ with $m > n \log q$ and $w > m \log q$, and two error distributions $\chi, \chi'$ with $\chi'$ producing much larger errors than $\chi$ (but still much smaller than $q$). Specifically, consider the distribution

$$\chi'' = \{a \leftarrow \{0,1\}^m, b \leftarrow \chi^m, c \leftarrow \chi', \text{ output } c - \langle a, b \rangle\}. \tag{1}$$

We need the condition that the statistical distance between $\chi'$ and $\chi''$ is negligible (in the security parameter $n$). This condition holds, for example, if $\chi, \chi'$ are discrete Gaussian distributions around zero with parameters $p, p'$, respectively, such that $p'/p$ is super-polynomial (in $n$).

- **Distributed Setup** $\mathsf{params}_i \leftarrow \mathsf{MFHE.DistSetup}(1^\kappa, 1^N, i)$: Set the parameters $q = \mathrm{poly}(N) n^{\omega(1)}$ (as needed for FHE correctness), $m > (Nn+1) \log q + 2\kappa$, and $w = m \log q$.[5] Sample and output a random matrix $A_i \in \mathbb{Z}_q^{(m-1) \times n}$.
- **Key Generation** $(\mathsf{pk}_i, \mathsf{sk}_i) \leftarrow \mathsf{MFHE.Keygen}(\mathsf{params}, i)$: Recall that $\mathsf{params} = \{\mathsf{params}_i\}_{i \in [N]} = \{A_i\}_{i \in [N]}$. The public key of party $i$ is a sequence of vectors $\mathsf{pk}_i = \{b_{i,j}\}_{j \in [N]}$ to be formally defined below. The corresponding secret key is a *low-norm vector* $t_i \in \mathbb{Z}_q^m$.

  We will define $b_{i,j}, t_i$ such that for $B_{i,j} = \begin{pmatrix} A_j \\ -b_{i,j} \end{pmatrix}$ it holds that $t_i B_{i,j} = b_{i,i} - b_{i,j} \pmod{q}$ for all $j$.

  In more detail, sample a random binary vector $s_i \leftarrow \{0,1\}^{m-1}$, we set $b_{i,j} = s_i A_j \bmod q$. Denoting $t_i = (s_i, 1)$, we indeed have $t_i B_{i,j} = b_{i,i} - b_{i,j} \pmod{q}$.

---

[5] Parmeters $q, n, w$ are global and fixed once at the onset of the protocol.

- **Encryption** $C \leftarrow \mathsf{MFHE.Encrypt}(\mathsf{pk}_i, \mu)$: To encrypt a bit $\mu$ under the public key $\mathsf{pk}_i$, choose a random matrix $R \in \mathbb{Z}_q^{n \times w}$ and a low-norm error matrix $E \in \mathbb{Z}_q^{m \times w}$, and set

$$C := B_{i,i} R + E + \mu G \mod q, \tag{2}$$

where $G$ is a fixed $m$-by-$w$ "gadget matrix" (whose structure is not important for us here, cf. [MP12]). Furthermore, as in [CM15, MW16], encrypt all bits of $R$ in a similar manner. For our protocol, we use more error for the last row of the error matrix $E$ than for the top $m - 1$ rows. Namely, we choose $\hat{E} \leftarrow \chi^{(m-1) \times w}$ and $e' \leftarrow \chi'^w$ and set $E = \begin{pmatrix} \hat{E} \\ e' \end{pmatrix}$.

- **Decryption** $\mu := \mathsf{MFHE.Decrypt}((\mathsf{sk}_1, \ldots, \mathsf{sk}_N), C)$: The invariant satisfied by ciphertexts in this scheme, similarly to GSW, is that an encryption of a bit $\mu$ relative to secret key $t$ is a matrix $C$ that satisfies

$$tC = \mu \cdot tG + e \pmod{q} \tag{3}$$

for a low-norm error vector $e$, where $G$ is the same "gadget matrix". The vector $t$ is the concatenation of all $\mathsf{sk}_i = t_i$ for all parties $i$ participating in the evaluation.

This invariant holds for freshly encrypted ciphertexts since $t_i B_{i,i} = 0$ $\pmod{q}$, and so $t_i(B_{i,i} R + E + \mu G) = \mu \cdot t_i G + t_i E \pmod{q}$, where $e = t_i E$ has low norm (as both $t_i$ and $E$ have low norm).

To decrypt, the secret-key holders compute $u = t \cdot C \mod q$, outputting 1 if the result is closer to $tG$ or 0 if the result is closer to 0.

- **Evaluation** $C := \mathsf{MFHE.Eval}(\mathsf{params}; \mathcal{C}; (c_1, \ldots, c_\ell))$: Since ciphertexts satisfy the same invariant as in the original GSW scheme, then the homomorphic operations in GSW work just as well for this "dual" variant. Similarly the ciphertext-extension technique from [CM15, MW16] works also for this variant exactly as it does for the "primal" scheme (see below). Hence we get a multi-key FHE scheme.

## Security

Security with distributed setup follows from LWE so long as $(m - 1) > (Nn + 1) \log q + 2\kappa$. The basis for security is the following lemma, which is essentially the same argument from [DGK+10] showing that dual Regev is leakage resilient for bounded leakage.

**Lemma 1.** *Let $A_i \in \mathbb{Z}_q^{(m-1) \times n}$ be uniform, and let $A_j$ for all $j \neq i$ be chosen by a rushing adversary after seeing $A_i$. Let $s_i \leftarrow \{0, 1\}^{m-1}$ and $b_{i,j} = s_i A_j$. Let $r \in \mathbb{Z}_q^n$ be uniform, $e \leftarrow \chi^{m-1}$, $e' \leftarrow \chi'$. Then, under the LWE assumption, the vector $c = A_i r + e$ and number $c' = b_{i,i} r + e'$ are (jointly) pseudorandom, even given the $b_{i,j}$'s for all $j \in [N]$ and the view of the adversary that generated the $A_j$'s.*

**Proof:** Consider the distribution of $c, c'$ as in the lemma statement. We notice that $c' = b_{i,i}r + e' = s_i A_i r + e' = s_i c - s_i e + e'$. The proof proceeds by a sequence of hybrids. Our first hybrid changes the distribution of $c'$ to $c' = s_i c + e'$. Noting that $c' - s_i c$ is drawn from $\chi''$ before the change and from $\chi'$ after the change (cf. Eq. (1)), we get that the statistical distance between the hybrids is negligible.

In the next hybrid, we use LWE to replace $c$ with a uniform vector. Since $c$ could have been sampled before $s_i$ or any of the $A_j$ with $j \neq i$, LWE implies indistinguishability with the previous hybrid.

Finally, we apply the leftover hash lemma, noting that all the $b_{i,j}$'s only leak at most $Nn \log q$ bits of information on $s_i$ and therefore the average min-entropy of $s_i$ is at least $(m-1) - Nn \log q > \log q + 2\kappa$. Using the leftover hash lemma with $c$ as seed and $s_i$ as source, we have that $(c, s_i c)$ are jointly statistically indistinguishable from uniform. This implies that $(c, c')$ are jointly statistically indistinguishable from uniform, even given all $A_j, b_{i,j}$ for all $j \in [N]$. The lemma follows. $\qquad\square$

Applying this lemma repeatedly for every column via a hybrid argument shows that the ciphertext components $c = A_i R + \hat{E}$ and $c' = b_{i,i}R + e'$ are also jointly pseudorandom, even given the view of the adversary, and semantic security of the scheme follows.

### Multi-key Homomorphism and Simulatability

The other components of the multi-key FHE scheme from [CM15, MW16] work for our variant as well, simply because the encryption and decryption formulas are identical (except with slightly different parameter setting), namely Eqs. (2) and (3). Below we briefly sketch these components for the sake of self-containment.

**The ciphertext-expansion procedure.** The "gadget matrix" $G$ used for these schemes has the property that there exists a low-norm vector $u$ such that $Gu = (0, 0, \ldots, 0, 1)$. Therefore, for every secret key $t = (s|1)$ we have $tGu = 1$ (mod $q$). It follows that if $C$ is an encryption of $\mu$ wrt secret key $t = (s|1)$, then the vector $v = Cu$ satisfies

$$\langle t, v \rangle = tCu = (\mu tG + e)u = \mu tGu + \langle e, u \rangle = \mu + \epsilon \pmod{q}$$

where $\epsilon$ is a small integer. In other words, given an encryption of $\mu$ wrt $t$ we can construct a vector $v$ such that $\langle t, v \rangle \approx \mu \pmod{q}$. Let $A_1, A_2$ be public parameters for two users with secret keys $t_1 = (s_1|1)$, $t_2 = (s_2|1)$, and recall that we denote $b_{i,j} = s_i A_j$ and $B_{i,i} = \begin{pmatrix} A_i \\ -s_i A_i \end{pmatrix} = \begin{pmatrix} A_i \\ -b_{i,i} \end{pmatrix}$.

Let $C = B_{1,1}R + E + \mu G$ be fresh encryption of $\mu$ w.r.t $B_{1,1}$, and suppose that we also have an encryption under $t_1$ of the matrix $R$. We note that given any vector $\delta$, we can apply homomorphic operations to the encryption of $R$ to get an encryption of the entries of the vector $\rho = \rho(\delta) = \delta R$. Then, using the technique above, we can compute for every entry $\rho_i$ a vector $x_i$ such that $\langle t_1, x_i \rangle \approx \rho_i$

(mod $q$). Concatenating all these vectors we get a matrix $X = X(\delta)$ such that $t_1 X \approx \rho = \delta R \pmod{q}$.

We consider the matrix $C' = \begin{pmatrix} C & X \\ 0 & C \end{pmatrix}$, where $X = X(\delta)$ for a $\delta$ to be determined later. We claim that for an appropriate $\delta$ this is an encryption of the same plaintext $\mu$ under the concatenated secret key $t' = (t_1|t_2)$. To see this, notice that

$$t_2 C = (s_2|1)\left(\begin{pmatrix} A_1 \\ -s_1 A_1 \end{pmatrix} R + E + \mu G\right) \approx (b_{2,1} - b_{1,1})R + \mu t_2 G \pmod{q},$$

and therefore setting $\delta = b_{1,1} - b_{2,1}$, which is a value that can be computed from $\mathsf{pk}_1, \mathsf{pk}_2$ we get

$$t'C' = (t_1 C \mid t_1 X + t_2 C) \approx (\mu t_1 G \mid (b_{1,1} - b_{2,1})R + (b_{2,1} - b_{1,1})R + \mu t_2 G)$$

$$= \mu(t_1 G \mid t_2 G) = \mu(t_1|t_2)\begin{pmatrix} G \\ & G \end{pmatrix},$$

as needed. As in the schemes from [CM15, MW16], this technique can be generalized to extend the ciphertext $C$ into an encryption of the same plaintext $\mu$ under the concatenation of any number of keys.

**Partial decryption and Simulatability.** This aspect works exactly as in [MW16, Theorem 5.6]. Let $\mathbf{v}$ be a fixed low-norm vector satisfying $G\mathbf{v} = (0, 0, \ldots, 0, \lceil q/2 \rceil) \pmod{q}$ (such a vector exists). Let $C$ be an encryption of a bit $\mu$ relative to the concatenated secret key $t = (t_1|t_2|\ldots|t_N)$ (whose last entry is 1). Then on one hand $C$ satisfies Eq. (3) so we have

$$tC\mathbf{v} = \mu \underbrace{tG\mathbf{v}}_{=\lceil q/2 \rceil} + \underbrace{\langle e, \mathbf{v} \rangle}_{=\epsilon, |\epsilon| \ll q} \approx \mu \cdot \lceil q/2 \rceil \pmod{q}.$$

On the other hand, breaking $C$ into $N$ bands of $m$ rows each (i.e., $C = (C_1^T|C_2^T|\ldots|C_N^T)^T$ with each $C_i \in \mathbb{Z}_q^{m \times mN}$), we have $tC\mathbf{v} = \sum_{i=1}^N t_i C_i \mathbf{v}$. Hence in principle we could set the partial decryption procedure as $ev_i = \mathsf{MFHE.PartDec}(C, t_i) := t_i C_i \mathbf{v} \bmod q$, and the combination procedure will just add all these $ev_i$'s and output 0 if it is smaller than $q/4$ in magnitude and 1 otherwise.

To be able to simulate (when there are $N - 1$ corruptions), we need the partial decryption to add its own noise, large enough to "drown" the noise in $tC\mathbf{v}$ (but small enough so decryption still works). Given the ciphertext $C$, $N - 1$ keys $t_j$ for all $j \in [N] \setminus \{i\}$, and the plaintext bit $\mu$, the simulator will sample its own noise $e$ and output the share $ev_i = \mu \cdot \lceil q/2 \rceil + e - \sum_j t_j C_j \mathbf{v} \bmod q$.

## 4   A Semi-malicious Protocol Without Setup

The semi-malicious adversary model [AJL+12] is a useful mid-point between the semi-honest and fully-malicious models. Somewhat similarly to a semi-honest adversary, a semi-malicious adversary is restricted to run the prescribed protocol, but differently than the semi-honest model it can choose the randomness that this protocol expects arbitrarily and adaptively (as opposed to just choosing it at random). Namely, at any point in the protocol, there must exists a choice of inputs and randomness that completely explain the messages sent by the adversary, but these inputs and randomness can be arbitrarily chosen by the adversary itself. A somewhat subtle point is that the adversary must always know the inputs and randomness that explain its actions (i.e., the model requires the adversary to explicitly output these before any messages that it sends).

We still assume a rushing adversary that can choose its messages after seeing the messages of the honest parties (subject to the constraint above). Similarly to the malicious model, an adversarial party can abort the computation at any point. Security is defined in the usual way, by requiring that a real-model execution is simulatable by an adversary/simulator in the ideal model, cf. Definition 7 in Sect. 5.4.

### 4.1 A Semi-malicious Protocol from Multi-key FHE With Distributed Setup

Our construction of 3-round semi-malicious protocol without setup is nearly identical to the Mukherjee-Wichs construction with a common reference string [MW16, Sect. 6], except that we use multi-Key FHE with distributed setup, instead of their multi-Key FHE with trusted setup. We briefly describe this construction here for the sake of self-containment.

- To compute an $N$-party function $\mathcal{F} : (\{0,1\}^*)^N \to \{0,1\}^*$ on input vector $\mathbf{w}$, the parties first run the setup round and broadcast their local parameters $\mathsf{params}_i$.
- Setting $\mathsf{params} = (\mathsf{params}_1, \ldots, \mathsf{params}_N)$, each party runs the key generation to get $(\mathsf{pk}_i, \mathsf{sk}_i) \leftarrow \mathsf{MFHE.Keygen}(\mathsf{params}, i)$ and then the encryption algorithm $c_i \leftarrow \mathsf{MFHE.Encrypt}(pk_i, w_i)$, and broadcasts $(\mathsf{pk}_i, c_i)$.
- Once the parties have all the public keys and ciphertexts, they each evaluate homomorphically the function $\mathcal{F}$ and all get the same evaluated ciphertext $\hat{c}$. Each party applies its partial decryption procedure to get $ev_i \leftarrow \mathsf{MFHE.PartDec}(\hat{c}, \mathsf{sk}_i)$ and broadcasts its decryption share $ev_i$ to everyone.
- Finally, given all the shares $ev_i$, every party runs the combination procedure and outputs $\mu \leftarrow \mathsf{MFHE.FinDec}(ev_1, \ldots, ev_N, \hat{c})$.

**Security.** Security is argued exactly as in [MW16, Theorem 6.1]: First we use the simulatability property to replace the partial decryption by the honest parties by a simulated partial decryption (cf. [MW16, Lemma 6.2]), and once the keys of the honest parties are no longer needed we can appeal to the semantic security of the FHE scheme (cf. [MW16, Lemma 6.3]).

Exactly as in the Mukherjee-Wichs construction, here too the underlying multi-key scheme only satisfies simulatability when all but one of the parties are corrupted, and as a result also the protocol above is only secure against adversaries that corrupt all but one of the parties. Mukherjee and Wichs described in [MW16, Sect. 6.2] a transformation from a protocol secure against exactly

$N - 1$ corruptions to one which is secure against any number of corruptions. Their transformation is generic and can be applied also in our context, resulting in a semi-malicious-secure protocol.

# 5  Part II: 4-Round Malicious Protocols

## 5.1  Tools and Definitions

We use tools of commitment and proofs to "compile" our semi-malicious protocol to a protocol secure in the malicious model. Below we define these tools and review the properties that we rely on.

## 5.2  Commitment Schemes

Commitment schemes allow a *committer* $C$ to commit itself to a value while keeping it (temporarily) secret from the *receiver* $R$. Later the commitment can be "opened", allowing the receiver to see the committed value and check that it is consistent with the earlier commitment. In this work, we consider commitment schemes that are *statistically binding*. This means that even an unbounded cheating committer cannot create a commitment that can be opened in two different ways. We also use *tag-based* commitment, which means that in addition to the secret committed value there is also a public tag associated with the commitment. The notion of hiding that we use is *adaptive-security* (due to Pandey et al. [PPV08]): it roughly means that the committed value relative to some tag is hidden, even in a world that the receiver has access to an oracle that breaks the commitment relative to any other tag.

**Definition 1 (Adaptively-secure Commitment [PPV08]).** *A tag-based commitment scheme* $(C, R)$ *is statistically binding and adaptively hiding if it satisfies the following properties:*

**Statistical binding:** *For any (computationally unbounded) cheating committer* $C^*$ *and auxiliary input* $z$, *it holds that the probability, after the commitment stage, that there exist two executions of the opening stage in which the receiver outputs two different values (other than $\bot$), is negligible.*

**Adaptive hiding:** *For every cheating* PPT *receiver* $R^*$ *and every tag value* tag, *it holds that the following ensembles computationally indistinguishable.*

- $\{\mathsf{view}_{\mathsf{aCom}}^{R^*(\mathsf{tag}),\mathcal{B}_{\mathsf{tag}}}(m_1, z)\}_{\kappa \in N, m_1, m_2 \in \{0,1\}^\kappa, z \in \{0,1\}^*}$
- $\{\mathsf{view}_{\mathsf{aCom}}^{R^*(\mathsf{tag}),\mathcal{B}_{\mathsf{tag}}}(m_2, z)\}_{\kappa \in N, m_1, m_2 \in \{0,1\}^\kappa, z \in \{0,1\}^*}$

*where* $\mathsf{view}_{\mathsf{aCom}}^{R^*(\mathsf{tag}),\mathcal{B}_{\mathsf{tag}}}(m, z)$ *denotes the random variable describing the output of* $R^*(\mathsf{tag})$ *after receiving a commitment to* $m$ *relative to* tag *using* aCom, *while interacting with a commitment-breaking oracle* $\mathcal{B}_{\mathsf{tag}}$.

*The oracle* $\mathcal{B}_{\mathsf{tag}}$ *gets as input an alleged view* $v'$ *and tag* $\mathsf{tag}'$. *If* $\mathsf{tag}' \neq \mathsf{tag}$ *and* $v'$ *is a valid transcript of a commitment to some value* $m'$ *relative to* $\mathsf{tag}'$, *then* $\mathcal{B}_{\mathsf{tag}}$ *returns that value* $m'$. *(If there is no such value, or if* $\mathsf{tag} = \mathsf{tag}'$, *then* $\mathcal{B}'_{\mathsf{tag}}$ *returns* $\bot$. *If there is more than one possible value* $m'$ *then* $\mathcal{B}_{\mathsf{tag}'}$ *returns an arbitrary one.)*

To set up some notations, for a two-message commitment we let $\mathsf{aCom}_1 = \mathsf{aCom}_{\mathsf{tag}}(r)$ and $\mathsf{aCom}_2 = \mathsf{aCom}_{\mathsf{tag}}(m; \mathsf{aCom}_1; r')$ denote the two messages of the protocol, the first depending only on the randomness of the receiver and the second depending on the message to be committed, the first-round message from the receiver, and the randomness of the sender.

## 5.3   Proof Systems

Given a pair of interactive Turing machines, $P$ and $V$, we denote by $\langle P(w), V \rangle(x)$ the random variable representing the (local) output of $V$, on common input $x$, when interacting with machine $P$ with private input $w$, when the random input to each machine is uniformly and independently chosen.

**Definition 2 (Interactive Proof System).** *A pair of interactive machines* $\langle P, V \rangle$ *is called an* interactive proof *system for a language $L$ if there is a negligible function $\mu(\cdot)$ such that the following two conditions hold:*

- *Completeness: For every $x \in L$, and every $w \in R_L(x)$, $\Pr[\langle P(w), V \rangle(x) = 1] = 1$.*
- *Soundness: For every $x \notin L$, and every $P^*$, $\Pr[\langle P^*, V \rangle(x) = 1] \leq \mu(\kappa)$*

*In case the soundness condition is required to hold only with respect to a computationally bounded prover, the pair $\langle P, V \rangle$ is called an* interactive argument *system.*

**Definition 3 (ZK).** *Let $L$ be a language in $\mathcal{NP}$, $R_L$ a witness relation for $L$, $(P, V)$ an interactive proof (argument) system for $L$. We say that $(P, V)$ is statistical/computational ZK, if for every probabilistic polynomial-time interactive machine $V$ there exists a probabilistic algorithm $\mathcal{S}$ whose expected running-time is polynomial in the length of its first input, such that the following ensembles are statistically close/computationally indistinguishable over $L$.*

- $\{\langle P(y), V(z) \rangle(x)\}_{\kappa \in \mathbb{N}\, x \in \{0,1\}^\kappa \cap L, y \in R_L(x), z \in \{0,1\}^*}$
- $\{\mathcal{S}(x, z)\}_{\kappa \in \mathbb{N}\, x \in \{0,1\}^\kappa \cap L, y \in R_L(x), z \in \{0,1\}^*}$

*where $\langle P(y), V(z) \rangle(x)$ denotes the view of $V$ in interaction with $P$ on common input $x$ and private inputs $y$ and $z$, respectively.*

**Definition 4 (Witness-indistinguishability).** *Let $\langle P, V \rangle$ be an interactive proof (or argument) system for a language $L \in \mathcal{NP}$. We say that $\langle P, V \rangle$ is* witness-indistinguishable *for $R_L$, if for every probabilistic polynomial-time interactive machine $V^*$ and for every two sequences $\{w^1_{\kappa,x}\}_{\kappa \in \mathbb{N}, x \in L}$ and $\{w^2_{\kappa,x}\}_{\kappa \in \mathbb{N}, x \in L}$, such that $w^1_{\kappa,x}, w^2_{\kappa,x} \in R_L(x)$ for every $x \in L \cap \{0,1\}^\kappa$, the following probability ensembles are computationally indistinguishable over $\kappa \in \mathbb{N}$.*

- $\{\langle P(w^1_{\kappa,x}), V^*(z) \rangle(x)\}_{\kappa \in \mathbb{N}\, x \in \{0,1\}^\kappa \cap L, z \in \{0,1\}^*}$
- $\{\langle P(w^2_{\kappa,x}), V^*(z) \rangle(x)\}_{\kappa \in \mathbb{N}\, x \in \{0,1\}^\kappa \cap L, z \in \{0,1\}^*}$

**Definition 5 (Proof of knowledge).** *Let $(P, V)$ be an interactive proof system for the language $L$. We say that $(P, V)$ is a proof of knowledge for the witness relation $R_L$ for the language $L$ it there exists an probabilistic expected polynomial-time machine $E$, called the extractor, and a negligible function $\mu(\cdot)$ such that for every machine $P^*$, every statement $x \in \{0, 1\}^\kappa$, every random tape $x \in \{0, 1\}^*$, and every auxiliary input $z \in \{0, 1\}^*$,*

$$Pr[\langle P_r^*(z), V \rangle(x) = 1] \leq Pr[E^{P_r^*(x,z)}(x) \in R_L(x)] + \mu(\kappa)$$

An interactive argument system $\langle P, V \rangle$ is an argument of knowledge if the above condition holds w.r.t. probabilistic polynomial-time provers.

**Delayed-Input Witness Indistinguishability.** The notion of delayed-input Witness Indistinguishability formalizes security of the prover with respect to an adversarial verifier that adaptively chooses the input statement to the proof system in the last round. Once we consider such adaptive instance selection, we also need to specify where the witnesses come from; to make the definition as general as possible, we consider an arbitrary (potentially unbounded) *witness selecting machine* that receives as input the views of all parties and outputs a witness $w$ for any statement $x$ requested by the adversary. In particular, this machine is a (randomized) Turing machine that runs in exponential time, and on input a statement $x$ and the current view of all parties, picks a witness $w \in R_L(x)$ as the private input of the prover.

Let $\langle P, V \rangle$ be a 3-round Witness Indistinguishable proof system for a language $L \in \mathcal{NP}$ with witness relation $R_L$. Denote the messages exchanged by $(\mathsf{p}_1, \mathsf{p}_2, \mathsf{p}_3)$ where $\mathsf{p}_i$ denotes the message in the $i$-th round. For a delayed-input 3-round Witness Indistinguishable proof system, we consider the game ExpAWI between a challenger $\mathcal{C}$ and an adversary $\mathcal{A}$ in which the instance $x$ is chosen by $\mathcal{A}$ after seeing the first message of the protocol played by the challenger. Then, the challenger receives as local input two witnesses $w_0$ and $w_1$ for $x$ chosen adaptively by a witness-selecting machine. The challenger then continues the game by randomly selecting one of the two witnesses and by computing the third message by running the prover's algorithm on input the instance $x$, the selected witness $w_b$ and the challenge received from the adversary in the second round. The adversary wins the game if he can guess which of the two witnesses was used by the challenger.

**Definition 6 (Delayed-Input   Witness   Indistinguishability).** *Let $\mathsf{ExpAWI}_{\langle P, V \rangle}^{\mathcal{A}}$ be a delayed-input WI experiment parametrized by a PPT adversary $\mathcal{A}$ and an delayed-input 3-round Witness Indistinguishable proof system $\langle P, V \rangle$ for a language $L \in \mathcal{NP}$ with witness relation $R_L$. The experiment has as input the security parameter $\kappa$ and auxiliary information $aux$ for $\mathcal{A}$. The experiment $\mathsf{ExpAWI}$ proceeds as follows:*

$\mathsf{ExpAWI}^{\mathcal{A}}_{\langle P,V \rangle}(\kappa, aux)$:

**Round-1:** *The challenger $\mathcal{C}$ randomly selects coin tosses $r$ and runs $P$ on input $(1^{\kappa}; r)$ to obtain the first message $\mathsf{p}_1$;*

**Round-2:** $\mathcal{A}$ *on input $\mathsf{p}_1$ and $aux$ chooses an instance $x$ and a challenge $\mathsf{p}_2$. The witness-selecting machine on inputs the statement $x$ and the current view of all parties outputs witnesses $w_0$ and $w_1$ such that $(x, w_0), (x, w_1) \in R_L$. $\mathcal{A}$ outputs $x, w_0, w_1, \mathsf{p}_2$ and internal state* state;

**Round-3:** $\mathcal{C}$ *randomly selects $b \leftarrow \{0,1\}$ and runs $P$ on input $(x, w_b, \mathsf{p}_2)$ to obtain $\mathsf{p}_3$;*

$b' \leftarrow \mathcal{A}((\mathsf{p}_1, \mathsf{p}_2, \mathsf{p}_3), aux, \mathsf{state})$;

*If $b = b'$ then output 1 else output 0.*

*A 3-round Witness Indistinguishable proof system for a language $L \in \mathcal{NP}$ with witness relation $R_L$ is* delayed-input *if for any PPT adversary $\mathcal{A}$ there exists a negligible function $\mu(\cdot)$ such that for any $aux \in \{0,1\}^*$ it holds that*

$$|Pr[\mathsf{ExpAWI}^{\mathcal{A}}_{\langle P,V \rangle}(\kappa, aux) = 1] - 1/2| \leq \mu(\kappa)$$

The most recent 3 round delayed input delayed input WI proof system appeared in [COSV16].

**Feige-Shamir ZK Proof Systems.** For our construction we use the 3-round, public-coin, input-delayed witness-indistinguishable proof-of-knowledge $\Pi_{\mathrm{WIPOK}}$ based on the work of Feige et al. [FLS99], and the 4-round zero-knowledge argument-of-knowledge protocol of Feige and Shamir $\Pi_{\mathrm{FS}}$ [FS90].

Recall that the Feige-Shamir protocol consists of two executions of a WIPOK protocol in reverse directions. The first execution has the verifier prove something about a secret that it chooses, and the second execution has the prover proving that either the input statement is true or the prover knows the verifier's secret. The zero-knowledge simulator then uses the knowledge extraction to extract the secret of the verifier, making it possible to complete the proof.

## 5.4 Secure Computation

The security of a protocol is analyzed by comparing what an adversary can do in the protocol to what it can do in an "ideal model". A protocol is secure if any adversary interacting in the real protocol can do no more harm than if it was involved in this "ideal" computation.

**Execution in the ideal model.** In the "ideal model" we have an incorruptible trusted party to whom the parties send their inputs. The trusted party computes the functionality on the inputs and returns to each party its respective output. Even this model is not completely "ideal", however, since some malicious behavior that cannot be prevented (such as early aborting) is permitted here too. An ideal execution proceeds as follows:

**Inputs:** Each party obtains an input, denoted by $w$.

**Send inputs to trusted party:** An honest party always sends $w$ to the trusted party. A malicious party may, depending on $w$, either abort or send some $w' \in \{0,1\}^{|w|}$ to the trusted party.

**Trusted party answers malicious parties:** The trusted party realizing the functionality $\mathcal{F} = (\mathcal{F}_M, \mathcal{F}_H)$ is informed of the set of malicious parties $M$, and let us denote the complementing set of honest parties by $H$.

Once it received all the inputs, the trusted party first replies to the malicious parties with $\mathcal{F}_M(\mathbf{w})$.

**Trusted party answers second party:** The malicious parties reply to the trusted party by either "proceed" or "abort". If they all reply "proceed" then the trusted party sends $\mathcal{F}_H(\mathbf{w})$ to the honest parties. If any of them reply "abort" then the trusted party sends $\bot$ to the honest parties.

**Outputs:** An honest party always outputs the message it received from the trusted party. A malicious party may output an arbitrary (probabilistic polynomial-time computable) function of its initial input and the message received from the trusted party.

The random variable containing the joint outputs of the honest and malicious parties in this execution (including an identification of the set $M$ of malicious parties) is denoted by $\mathrm{IDEAL}_{\mathcal{F},\mathcal{S}}(\kappa, \mathbf{w})$, where $\kappa$ is the security parameter, $\mathcal{S}$ is representing parties in the ideal model and $\mathbf{w}$ are the inputs.

**Execution in the real model.** In the real model, where there is no trusted party, a malicious party may follow an arbitrary feasible strategy; that is, any strategy implementable by (non-uniform) probabilistic polynomial-time machines. In particular, the malicious party may abort the execution at any point in time (and when this happens prematurely, the other party is left with no output). The (static) adversary chooses the set $M$ of malicious parties before it receives any inputs to the protocol, and it can be *rushing*, in that in every communication round it first sees the messages from the honest parties and only then chooses the messages on behalf of the malicious parties.

Let $\mathcal{F} : (\{0,1\}^*)^N \to (\{0,1\}^*)^N$ be an $N$-party function, let $\Pi$ be an $N$-party protocol for computing $\mathcal{F}$, and let $\mathcal{A}$ be an adversary. The *joint execution of $\Pi$ with adversary $\mathcal{A}$ in the real model*, denoted $\mathrm{REAL}_{\Pi,\mathcal{A}}(\kappa, \mathbf{w})$ (with $\kappa$ the security parameter and $\mathbf{w}$ the inputs), is defined as the output of the honest and malicious parties (and an identification of the set $M$ of malicious parties), resulting from the protocol interaction.

**Definition 7 (secure MPC).** *Let $\mathcal{F}$ and $\Pi$ be as above. Protocol $\Pi$ is said to securely compute $\mathcal{F}$ (in the malicious model) if for every (non-uniform) probabilistic polynomial-time adversary $\mathcal{A}$ for the real model, there exists a (non-uniform) probabilistic expected polynomial-time adversary $\mathcal{S}$ for the ideal model, such that:*

$$\{\mathrm{IDEAL}_{\mathcal{F},\mathcal{S}}(\kappa, \mathbf{w})\}_{\kappa \in \mathbb{N}, \mathbf{w} \in (\{0,1\}^*)^N} \overset{c}{\approx} \{\mathrm{REAL}_{\Pi,\mathcal{A}}(\kappa, \mathbf{w})\}_{\kappa \in \mathbb{N}, \mathbf{w} \in (\{0,1\}^*)^N}.$$

**Notations.** For a sub-protocol $\pi$ between two parties $P_i$ and $P_j$, denote by $(\mathsf{p_1}^{i,j}, \ldots, \mathsf{p_t}^{i,j})$ the view of the messages in all $t$ rounds where the subscripts

$(i, j)$ denote that the *first* message of the sub-protocol is sent by $P_i$ to $P_j$. Likewise, subscripts $(j, i)$ denote that the *first* message of the sub-protocol is sent by $P_j$ to $P_i$.

# 6   A Malicious Protocol Without Setup

Our 4-round protocol for the malicious case is obtained by "compiling" the 3-round semi-malicious protocol from Sect. 4, adding round-efficient proofs of correct behavior. The components of this protocol are:

- The 3-round semi-malicious protocol from Sect. 4, based on the "dual"-GSW-based multi-key FHE scheme with distributed setup. We denote this multi-key FHE scheme by MFHE = (MFHE.DistSetup, MFHE.Keygen, MFHE.Encrypt, MFHE.Eval, MFHE.PartDec, MFHE.FinDec).
- Two instances of a two-round adaptively secure commitment scheme, supporting tags/identities of length $\kappa$. We denote the first instance by aCom = (acom$_1$, acom$_2$) and the second by bCom = (bcom$_1$, bcom$_2$).
- A one-way function $OWF$.
- A three-round public coin witness-indistinguishable proof of knowledge with delayed input, $\Pi_{\mathrm{WIPOK}} = (\mathsf{p}_1, \mathsf{p}_2, \mathsf{p}_3)$, for the $\mathcal{NP}$-Language $\mathcal{L}_P^{\mathrm{WIPOK}}$ from Fig. 2. We often refer to this protocol as "proof of correct encryption", but what it really proves is that EITHER the encryption is consistent with the values committed in aCom, OR the value committed in bCom is a pre-image under $OWF$ of values sent by the other parties.
- A four-round zero-knowledge argument of knowledge with delayed input, $\Pi_{\mathrm{FS}} = (\mathsf{fs}_1, \mathsf{fs}_2, \mathsf{fs}_3, \mathsf{fs}_4)$, for the $\mathcal{NP}$-Language $\mathcal{L}_P^{\mathrm{FS}}$ from Fig. 2. We often refer to this protocol as "proof of correct decryption".

The parameters for the MFHE scheme, the $OWF$, and the two proof systems, are chosen polynomially larger than those for the commitment schemes. Hence (assuming sub-exponential security), all these constructions remain secure even against an adversary that can break aCom, bCom by exhaustive search.

**The protocol.** Let $F : (\{0, 1\}^*)^N \to \{0, 1\}^*$ be a deterministic $N$-party function to be computed. Each party $P_i$ holds input $x_i \in \{0, 1\}^\kappa$ and identity id$_i$.[6] The protocol consists of four broadcast rounds, where messages $(m_t^1, \ldots, m_t^N)$ are exchanged simultaneously in the $t$-th round for $t \in [4]$. The message flow is detailed in Fig. 1, and Fig. 3 depicts the exchanged messages between two parties $P_i$ and $P_j$. Blue messages are sub-protocols where party $P_i$ is the prover/committer and party $P_j$ is the verifier/receiver, red messages denote the opposite.

---

[6] Known transformations yield also protocols for randomized functionalities without increasing the rounds, see [Gol04, Sect. 7.3].

---

**Protocol $\Pi_{\mathrm{MPC}}$**

**Private Inputs:** For $i \in [N]$, party $P_i$ has input $x_i$.

**Round 1:** For $i \in [N]$ each party $P_i$ proceeds as follows:

1. Choose randomness $r_i = (r_i^{gen}, r_i^{enc})$ for the MFHE scheme.
2. Choose an unrelated $\kappa$-bit randomness value $R_i$, and set $\hat{R}_i = OWF(R_i)$.
3. For every $j$, engage in a two-round commitment protocol with $P_j$ for the values $(x_i, r_i, R_i)$, using an instance of aCom with tag $\mathsf{id}_i$. Note that the first message in this protocol is sent by $P_j$ (so $P_i$ sends the first message to all the $P_j$'s for their respective commitments). Denote the messages initiated in each sub-protocol by $P_i$ to $P_j$ by $\mathsf{acom}_1^{i,j}$.
4. For every $j$, prepare the first message $\mathsf{p}_1^{i,j}$ of $\Pi_{\mathrm{WIPOK}}$ (acting as the Prover) for the $\mathcal{NP}$-Language $\mathcal{L}_{P_i}^{\mathrm{WIPOK}} = \mathcal{L}_{i,j,1} \vee \mathcal{L}_{i,j,2}$ for $j \in [N] \setminus \{i\}$ and the first message $\mathsf{fs}_1^{i,j}$ of $\Pi_{\mathrm{FS}}$ (acting as the Verifier) for $\mathcal{L}_{P_j}^{\mathrm{FS}} = (\mathcal{L}_{j,i,1} \wedge \mathcal{L}_{j,i,3})$ where the $\mathcal{NP}$-Languages $\mathcal{L}_{j,i,1}, \mathcal{L}_{i,j,2}, \mathcal{L}_{i,j,3}$ are defined in Figure 6.
5. Run the distributed setup of MFHE to get $\mathsf{params}_i = \mathsf{MFHE.DistSetup}(1^{\kappa}, 1^N, i)$.
6. For all $j(\neq i)$ broadcast the message $m_1^{i,j} := \left( \mathsf{acom}_1^{i,j}, \mathsf{p}_1^{i,j}, \mathsf{fs}_1^{i,j}, \hat{R}_i, \mathsf{params}_i \right)$ to party $P_j$.

**Round 2:** For $i \in [N]$ each party $P_i$ proceeds as follows:

1. Generate the second commitment messages $\mathsf{acom}_2^{j,i}$ for $\mathsf{aCom}_{\mathsf{id}_i}(x_i, r_i, R_i)$, the second message $\mathsf{p}_2^{j,i}$ of the $\Pi_{\mathrm{WIPOK}}$ proof system, and the second message $\mathsf{fs}_2^{j,i}$ of the $\Pi_{\mathrm{FS}}$ proof system.
2. For every $j$, engage in a two-round commitment protocol with $P_j$ for the value $\mathbf{0}$, using an instance of bCom with tag $\mathsf{id}_i$. As before, $P_i$ sends the first message to all the $P_j$'s for their respective commitments, and we denote the message sent from $P_i$ to $P_j$ by $\mathsf{bcom}_1^{i,j}$.
3. For all $j$ broadcast the messages $m_2^{i,j} := (\mathsf{acom}_2^{j,i}, \mathsf{p}_2^{j,i}, \mathsf{fs}_2^{j,i}, \mathsf{bcom}_1^{i,j})$.

**Round 3:** For $i \in [N]$ each party $P_i$ proceeds as follows:

1. Generate the second messages $\mathsf{bcom}_2^{j,i}$ corresponding to all $\mathsf{bCom}_{\mathsf{id}_i}(\mathbf{0})$, the final message $\mathsf{p}_3^{i,j}$ of the $\Pi_{\mathrm{WIPOK}}$ protocol, and the third message $\mathsf{fs}_3^{i,j}$ of $\Pi_{\mathrm{FS}}$.
2. Set $\mathsf{params} = \{\mathsf{params}_i\}_{i \in [N]}$. Use randomness $r_i^{gen}, r_i^{enc}$ to generate a key pair for MFHE, $(\mathsf{pk}_i, \mathsf{sk}_i) \leftarrow \mathsf{MFHE.Keygen}(\mathsf{params}, i)$, and an encryption of the private input $c_i = \mathsf{MFHE.Encrypt}(\mathsf{pk}_i, x_i)$.
3. For all $j$ broadcast the message $m_3^{i,j} := (\mathsf{pk}_i, c_i, \mathsf{p}_3^{i,j}, \mathsf{fs}_3^{i,j}, \mathsf{bcom}_2^{j,i})$.

**Round 4:** If any $\mathsf{p}^{j,i}$ does not pass verification then abort. Otherwise each party $P_i$ proceeds as follows:

1. Compute the evaluated ciphertext $\hat{c} := \mathsf{MFHE.Eval}(\mathsf{params}; F; (c_1, \ldots, c_N))$, and the decryption shares $ev_i \leftarrow \mathsf{MFHE.PartDec}(\hat{c}, (\mathsf{pk}_1, \ldots, \mathsf{pk}_N), i, \mathsf{sk}_i)$.
2. Prepare the final message $\mathsf{fs}_4^{j,i}$ of $\Pi_{\mathrm{FS}}$ protocol.
3. For all $j$, broadcast the message $m_4^{i,j} := (ev_i, \mathsf{fs}_4^{j,i})$.

**Output phase:** If any $\mathsf{fs}^{i,j}$ does not pass verification then abort. Else run the combining algorithm on the decryption shares, and output $y \leftarrow \mathsf{MFHE.FinDec}(ev_1, \ldots, ev_N, \hat{c})$.

---

**Fig. 1.** Protocol $\Pi_{\mathrm{MPC}}$ with respect to party $P_i$.

## 6.1 Proof of Security

**Theorem 3.** *Assuming sub-exponential hardness of LWE, and the existence of an adaptively-secure commitment scheme, there exists a four-broadcast-round protocol for securely realizing any functionality against a malicious adversary in the plain model with no setup.*

$\mathcal{NP}$-Language $\mathcal{L}_{P_i}^{\text{WIPOK}}$ and $\mathcal{L}_{P_i}^{\text{FS}}$ for $\Pi_{\text{FS}}$ and $\Pi_{\text{WIPOK}}$ proof systems where $P_i$ acts as the prover:

Fix the identities $\text{id}_i$, and then for all $i, j$ define:

$$\mathcal{L}_{i,j,1} = \left\{ \begin{pmatrix} \hat{R}_i, \hat{R}_j, \text{acom}_1^{j,i}, \text{bcom}_1^{j,i} \\ \text{params},, \text{pk}_i, c_i, \hat{c}, \\ \text{acom}_2^{j,i}, \text{bcom}_2^{j,i} \end{pmatrix} \middle| \begin{array}{l} \exists (x_i, r_i^{gen}, r_i^{enc}, \text{sk}_i, R_i, \omega_i) : \\ \text{acom}_2^{j,i} = \text{aCom}_{\text{id}_i}(x_i, r_i^{gen}, r_i^{enc}, R_i; \text{acom}_1^{j,i}; \omega_i) \\ \wedge \ \hat{R}_i = OWF(R_i) \\ \wedge \ (\text{sk}_i, \text{pk}_i) = \text{MFHE.Keygen}(\text{params}, i; r_i^{gen}) \\ \wedge \ c_i = \text{MFHE.Encrypt}(\text{pk}_i, x_i; r_i^{enc}) \end{array} \right\}$$

$$\mathcal{L}_{i,j,2} = \left\{ \begin{pmatrix} \hat{R}_i, \hat{R}_j, \text{acom}_1^{j,i}, \text{bcom}_1^{j,i} \\ \text{params}, \text{pk}_i, c_i, \hat{c}, \text{acom}_2^{j,i}, \text{bcom}_2^{j,i} \end{pmatrix} \middle| \begin{array}{l} \exists \ (R', \zeta_i) : \ \hat{R}_j = OWF(R') \\ \wedge \ \text{bcom}_2^{j,i} = \text{bCom}_{\text{id}_i}(R'; \text{bcom}_2^{j,i}; \zeta_i) \end{array} \right\}$$

$$\mathcal{L}_{i,j,3} = \left\{ \begin{pmatrix} \hat{R}_i, \hat{R}_j, \text{acom}_1^{j,i}, \text{bcom}_1^{j,i} \\ \text{params}, \text{pk}_i, c_i, \hat{c}, \\ \text{acom}_2^{j,i}, \text{bcom}_2^{j,i} \end{pmatrix} \middle| \begin{array}{l} \exists (x_i, r_i^{gen}, r_i^{enc}, \text{sk}_i, R_i, \omega_i) : \\ \text{acom}_2^{j,i} = \text{aCom}_{\text{id}_i}(x_i, r_i^{gen}, r_i^{enc}, R_i; \text{acom}_1^{j,i}; \omega_i) \\ \wedge \ (\text{sk}_i, \text{pk}_i) = \text{MFHE.Keygen}(\text{params}; r_i^{gen}) \\ \wedge \ ev_i = \text{MFHE.PartDec}(\hat{c}, i, \text{sk}_i) \end{array} \right\}$$

We define $\mathcal{L}_{P_i}^{\text{WIPOK}} = \{\mathcal{L}_{i,j,1} \vee \mathcal{L}_{i,j,2}\}_j$ and $\mathcal{L}_{P_i}^{\text{FS}} = \{\mathcal{L}_{i,j,3}\}_j$.

**Fig. 2.** $\mathcal{NP}$-Language $\mathcal{L}_{i,j,1}, \mathcal{L}_{i,j,2}, \mathcal{L}_{i,j,3}$ for $\Pi_{\text{FS}}$ and $\Pi_{\text{WIPOK}}$ proof systems.

To prove Theorem 3, we note that the two assumptions listed suffice for instantiating all the components of our protocol $\Pi_{\text{MPC}}$: the commitment is used directly for aCom and bCom, and sub-exponential LWE suffices for everything else. We also note that while we think of the protocol from Fig. 1 as a "compilation" of the 3-round protocol from Sect. 4 using zero-knowledge proofs, it is not a generic compiler, as it relies on the specifics of our semi-malicious protocol. See more discussion in Sect. 7 below.

In the following, we prove security of $\Pi_{\text{MPC}}$ by describing a simulator and proving that the simulated view is indistinguishable from the real one.

### Description of the Simulator

Let $\mathcal{P} = \{P_1, \ldots, P_N\}$ be the set of parties, let $\mathcal{A}$ be a malicious, static adversary in the plain model, and let $\mathcal{P}^* \subseteq \mathcal{P}$ be the set of parties corrupted by $\mathcal{A}$. We construct a simulator $\mathcal{S}$ (the ideal world adversary) with access to the ideal functionality $\mathcal{F}$, such that the ideal world experiment with $\mathcal{S}$ and $\mathcal{F}$ is indistinguishable from a real execution of $\Pi_{\text{MPC}}$ with $\mathcal{A}$. The simulator $\mathcal{S}$ only generates messages on behalf of parties $\mathcal{P} \backslash \mathcal{P}^*$, as follows:

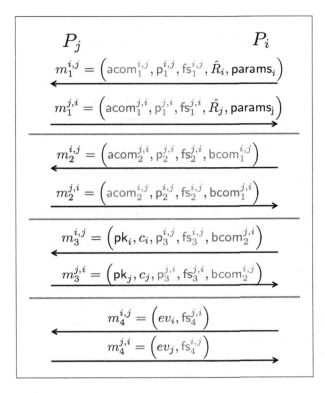

**Fig. 3.** Messages exchanged between party $P_i$ and $P_j$ in $\Pi_{\text{MPC}}$. $(\text{acom}_1, \text{acom}_2)$ and $(\text{bcom}_1, \text{bcom}_2)$ are commitments, $(\text{p}_1, \text{p}_2, \text{p}_3)$ belong to the 3-round $\Pi_{\text{WIPOK}}$, $(\text{fs}_1, \text{fs}_2, \text{fs}_3, \text{fs}_4)$ belong to the 4-round $\Pi_{\text{FS}}$, and $(\text{params}, \text{pk}, c, ev)$ denote the MFHE messages. Blue messages are sub-protocols where party $P_i$ is the prover/committer and party $P_j$ is the verifier/receiver, red messages donete the opposite. (Color figure online)

**Round 1 Messages $\mathcal{S} \to \mathcal{A}$:** In the first round, $\mathcal{S}$ generates messages on behalf of each honest party $P_h \notin \mathcal{P}^*$, as follows:

1. Choose randomness $r_h = (r_h^{gen}, r_h^{enc})$ for the MFHE scheme and an unrelated $\kappa$-bit randomness value $R_h$, and set $\hat{R}_h = OWF(R_h)$.
2. For every $j$ engage in a two-round commitment protocol with $P_j$. To this end, prepare the first message $\text{acom}_1^{h,j}$ corresponding to the execution of $\text{aCom}_{\text{id}_j}(x_j, r_j^{gen}, r_j^{enc}, R_j; \omega_j)$ on behalf of $P_h$, acting as the receiver of the commitment. Since the commitment $\text{aCom}$ is a two-round protocol, the message of the committer $P_j$ is only sent in the second round.
3. Prepare the first message $\text{p}_1^{h,j}$ of $\Pi_{\text{WIPOK}}$ (with $P_h$ as Prover) for the $\mathcal{NP}$-Language $\mathcal{L}_{P_h}^{\text{WIPOK}}$, and the first message $\text{fs}_1^{h,j}$ of $\Pi_{\text{FS}}$ (with $P_h$ as Verifier) for $\mathcal{L}_{P_j}^{\text{FS}}$.
4. Run $\text{params}_h \leftarrow \text{MFHE.DistSetup}(1^\kappa, 1^N, h)$.
5. Send the message $m_1^{h,j} = \left( \text{acom}_1^{h,j}, \text{p}_1^{h,j}, \text{fs}_1^{h,j}, \hat{R}_h, \text{params}_h \right)$ to $\mathcal{A}$.

**Round 1 Messages $\mathcal{A} \to \mathcal{S}$:** Also in the first round the adversary $\mathcal{A}$ generates the messages $m_1^{j,h} = \left(\mathsf{acom}_1^{j,h}, \mathsf{p}_1^{j,h}, \mathsf{fs}_1^{j,h}, \hat{R}_j, \mathsf{params}_j\right)$ on behalf of corrupted parties $j \in \mathcal{P}^*$ to honest parties $h \notin \mathcal{P}^*$. Messages $\{\mathsf{acom}_1^{j,h}\}$ correspond to an execution of $\mathsf{aCom}_{\mathsf{id}_h}(\mathbf{0}; \omega_h)$.

**Round 2 Messages $\mathcal{S} \to \mathcal{A}$:** In the second round $\mathcal{S}$ generates messages on behalf of each honest party $P_h \in \mathcal{P}^*$ as follows:

1. Complete the commitment to the zero string generating the second messages $\mathsf{acom}_2^{j,h}$ corresponding to all executions of $\mathsf{aCom}_{\mathsf{id}_h}(\mathbf{0}; \omega_h)$.
2. Honestly prepare the second message $\mathsf{p}_2^{j,h}$ ($\mathsf{fs}_2^{j,h}$) of $\Pi_{\mathrm{WIPOK}}(\Pi_{\mathrm{FS}})$ initiated by $P_j$ acting as the prover (verifier) in the first round.
3. Generate the second commitment messages $\mathsf{bcom}_1^{h,j}$ for $\mathsf{bCom}_{\mathsf{id}_j}(\mathbf{0}; \zeta_j)$ where party $P_h$ acts as the Receiver.
4. Send the message $m_2^{h,j} = (\mathsf{acom}_2^{j,h}, \mathsf{p}_2^{j,h}, \mathsf{fs}_2^{j,h}, \mathsf{bcom}_1^{h,j})$ to $\mathcal{A}$.

**Round 2 Messages $\mathcal{A} \to \mathcal{S}$:** In the second round the adversary $\mathcal{A}$ generates the messages $m_2^{j,h} := (\mathsf{acom}_2^{h,j}, \mathsf{p}_2^{h,j}, \mathsf{fs}_2^{h,j}, \mathsf{bcom}_1^{j,h})$ on behalf of corrupted parties $j \in \mathcal{P}^*$ to honest parties $h \notin \mathcal{P}^*$. Messages $\{\mathsf{acom}_2^{h,j}\}$ correspond to an execution of $\mathsf{aCom}_{\mathsf{id}_j}(x_j, r_j^{gen}, r_j^{enc}, R_j; \omega_j)$ and messages $\{\mathsf{bcom}_1^{h,j}\}$ correspond to an execution of $\mathsf{bCom}_{\mathsf{id}_h}(\mathbf{0}; \zeta_h)$.

**Round 3 Messages $\mathcal{S} \to \mathcal{A}$:** In the third round $\mathcal{S}$ generates messages on behalf of each honest party $P_h \notin \mathcal{P}^*$ as follows:

1. Generate the second messages $\mathsf{bcom}_2^{j,h}$ corresponding to all $\mathsf{bCom}_{\mathsf{id}_h}(\mathbf{0}; \zeta_h)$.
2. Set $\mathsf{params} = (\mathsf{params}_1, \ldots, \mathsf{params}_N)$ for the MFHE scheme and generate the keys $(\mathsf{pk}_h, \mathsf{sk}_h) = \mathsf{MFHE.Keygen}(\mathsf{params}, h; r_h^{gen})$. Generate an encryption of zero using randomness $r_h^{enc}$, $c_h = \mathsf{MFHE.Encrypt}(\mathsf{pk}_h, \mathbf{0}; r_h^{enc})$.
3. Honestly prepare the final message $\mathsf{p}_3^{h,j}$ ($\mathsf{fs}_3^{h,j}$) of $\Pi_{\mathrm{WIPOK}}(\Pi_{\mathrm{FS}})$ initiated by $P_h$ acting as the prover (verifier) in the first round.
4. Send the message $m_3^{h,j} = (\mathsf{pk}_h, c_h, \mathsf{p}_3^{h,j}, \mathsf{fs}_3^{h,j}, \mathsf{bcom}_2^{j,h})$ to $\mathcal{A}$.

**Round 3 Messages $\mathcal{A} \to \mathcal{S}$:** $\mathcal{S}$ receives $m_3^{j,h} = (\mathsf{pk}_j, c_j, \mathsf{p}_3^{j,h}, \mathsf{fs}_3^{j,h}, \mathsf{bcom}_2^{h,j})$ from $\mathcal{A}$, where messages $\{\mathsf{bcom}_2^{h,j}\}$ correspond to an execution of $\mathsf{bCom}_{\mathsf{id}_j}(\mathbf{0}; \zeta_j)$.

Then, $\mathcal{S}$ proceeds to extract the witness corresponding to each proof-of-knowledge $(\mathsf{p}_1^{j,h}, \mathsf{p}_2^{j,h}, \mathsf{p}_3^{j,h})$ completed in the first three rounds, using rewinding.

To this end, $\mathcal{S}$ applies the knowledge extractor of $\Pi_{WIPOK}$ to obtain the "witnesses" which consist of the inputs and secret keys of the corrupted parties $(x_j, r_j)$[7]. $\mathcal{S}$ also uses the zero-knowledge simulator of $\Pi_{FS}$ to obtain the "trapdoors" associated with that protocol. (Note that here we rely on the specific structure of Feige-Shamir proofs, where the zero-knowledge simulator extracts a "verifier secret" after the 3rd round, that makes it possible to simulate the last round.)

---

[7] For simplicity of exposition, we omit the rest of the witness values.

Next $S$ sends $\{x_j\}_{j \in [N] \setminus \{h\}}$ to the ideal functionality $\mathcal{F}$ which responds by sending back $y$ such that $y = F(\{x_j\}_{j \in [N]})$.

**Round 4 Messages $\mathcal{S} \to \mathcal{A}$:** In the fourth round $S$ generates messages on behalf of each honest party $P_h \notin \mathcal{P}^*$ as follows:

1. Generate the evaluated ciphertext $\hat{c} := \mathsf{MFHE.Eval}(\mathsf{params}; F; (c_1, \ldots, c_N))$.
2. $S$ reconstructs all the secret keys $\{\mathsf{sk}_j\}_{j \in \mathcal{P}^*}$ from the witnesses $\{r_j^{gen}\}_{j \in \mathcal{P}^*}$, and computes the simulated decryption shares $\{ev_h\}_{h \notin \mathcal{P}^*} \leftarrow S^T(y, \hat{c}, h, \{\mathsf{sk}_j\}_{j \in \mathcal{P}^*})$. (The simulator $S^T$ is the one provided by [MW16, Sect. 6.2].[8])
3. Simulate the final message $\mathsf{fs}_4^{j,h}$ of $\Pi_{\mathsf{FS}}$ protocol using the extracted trapdoor. $S$ sends the message $m_4^{h,j} = (ev_h, \mathsf{fs}_4^{j,h})$ on behalf of $P_h$.

**Round 4 Messages $\mathcal{A} \to \mathcal{S}$:** In the last round the adversary $\mathcal{A}$ generates the messages on behalf of corrupted parties in $\mathcal{P}^*$. For each party $j \in \mathcal{P}^*$ our simulator receives messages $m_4^{j,h} = (ev_j, \mathsf{fs}_4^{h,j})$ from $\mathcal{A}$.

This completes the description of the simulator.

**Proof of Indistinguishability**

**Overview.** We need to prove that for any malicious (static) adversary $\mathcal{A}$, the view generated by the simulator $S$ above is indistinguishable from the real view, namely:

$$\{\mathrm{IDEAL}_{\mathcal{F},\mathcal{S}}(\kappa, \cdot)\}_\kappa \overset{c}{\approx} \{\mathrm{REAL}_{\Pi,\mathcal{A}}(\kappa, \cdot)\}_\kappa$$

To prove indistinguishability, we consider a sequence of hybrid experiments. Let $H_0$ be the hybrid describing the real-world execution of the protocol, and we modify it in steps:

$H_1$ Use the zero-knowledge simulator to generate the proof in the 4-round $\Pi_{\mathsf{FS}}$, indistinguishability follows by the ZK property of $\Pi_{\mathsf{FS}}$.

$H_2$ Starting in this hybrid, the challenger is given access to a breaking oracle $\mathcal{B}_{\mathsf{tag}}$ (with $\mathsf{tag} = (\mathsf{id}_h, \star)$ where $h$ is one of the honest parties). Here the challenger uses the breaking oracle to extract the values committed to by the adversary in $\mathsf{acom}_2^{h,\mathcal{A}}$ (in the second round), then commits to these same values in $\mathsf{bcom}_2^{\mathcal{A},h}$ on behalf of the honest party (in the third round). Indistinguishability follows by the adaptive-hiding of bCom.

$H_3$ Change the proof in $\Pi_{\mathsf{WIPOK}}$ to use the "OR branch". Indistinguishability follows by the WI property of $\Pi_{\mathsf{WIPOK}}$ (which must hold even in the presence of the breaking-oracle $\mathcal{B}_{\mathsf{tag}}$).

---

[8] To use $S^T$ from [MW16, Sect. 6.2] we need to evaluate the protocol on a different function $\mathcal{F}'$ rather than $\mathcal{F}$, we ignore this detail in the rest of the presentation here.

$H_4$ Here the challenger also has access to the ideal-world functionality that gives it the output of the function. Having extracted the secret keys using $\mathcal{B}_{\mathsf{tag}}$, the challenger *simulates the decryption shares* of the honest parties rather than using the decryption procedure. Indistinguishability follows since the FHE scheme is simulatable.

$H_5$ Encrypt $\mathbf{0}$'s rather than the true inputs. Indistinguishability follows due to the semantic security of the encryption scheme.

$H_6$ Commit to 0's in $\mathsf{acom}_2^{\mathcal{A},h}$, rather than to the real inputs. Indistinguishable due to the adaptive-hiding of $\mathsf{aCom}$.

$H_7$ Revert the change in $H_3$, make the proof in $\Pi_{\mathrm{WIPOK}}$ use the normal branch rather than the "OR branch". Indistinguishability follows by the WI property of $\Pi_{\mathrm{WIPOK}}$.

$H_8$ Revert the change in $H_2$ and thus commit to zero in $\mathsf{bcom}_2^{\mathcal{A},h}$ (instead of committing to the extracted values). Indistinguishability follows by the adaptive-hiding of $\mathsf{bCom}$.

$H_9$ Here the challenger no longer has access to a breaking oracle, and instead it uses the POK extractor to get the randomness and inputs (witnesses) from $\Pi_{\mathrm{WIPOK}}$. Indistinguishability follows from the extraction property of $\Pi_{\mathrm{WIPOK}}$, combined with the one-wayness of $OWF$.

As $H_9$ no longer uses the inputs of the honest parties, the view of this hybrid can be simulated. (We also note that the simulator *does not use a breaking oracle*, rather it is a traditional rewinding simulator.)

**Security in the presence of a breaking oracle:** Note that some of our indistinguishability arguments must holds in worlds with a breaking oracle $\mathcal{B}_{\mathsf{tag}}$. In particular, we require that $\mathsf{aCom}$ is still hiding, that LWE still holds, and that $\Pi_{\mathrm{WIPOK}}$ is still witness-indistinguishable in the presence of the oracle. The hiding property of $\mathsf{aCom}$ follows directly from its adaptive-hiding property. As for LWE and $\Pi_{\mathrm{WIPOK}}$, security in the presence of $\mathcal{B}_{\mathsf{tag}}$ follows from sub-exponential hardness and complexity leveraging. Namely, in the relevant reductions we can implement $\mathcal{B}_{\mathsf{tag}}$ ourselves in subexponential time, while still relying on the hardness of LWE or $\Pi_{\mathrm{WIPOK}}$.

Another point to note is that using the zero-knowledge simulator (in hybrids $H_2$–$H_9$) requires rewinding, which may be problematic when doing other reductions. As we explain below, we are able to handle rewinding by introducing many sub-hybrids, essentially cutting the distinguishing advantage by a factor equal to the number of rewinding operations. We now proceed to give more details.

**$H_0$:** This hybrid is the real execution. In particular, $H_0$ starts the execution of $\mathcal{A}$ providing it fresh randomness and input $\{x_j\}_{P_j \in \mathcal{P}^*}$, and interacts with it honestly by performing all actions of the honest parties with uniform randomness and input. The output consists of $\mathcal{A}$'s view.

**$H_1$:** In this hybrid the challenger uses the zero-knowledge simulator of $\Pi_{\mathrm{FS}}$ to generate the proofs on behalf of each honest party $P_h$, rather than the honest prover strategy as is done in **$H_0$**. We note that the challenger in this hybrid needs to rewind the adversary $\mathcal{A}$ (up to the second round) as needed for the Feige-Shamir ZK simulator. Since in these two hybrids the protocol $\Pi_{\text{FS}}$ is used to prove the same true statement, then the simulated proofs are indistinguishable from the real ones, so we get:

**Lemma 61.** $H_0 \approx_s H_1$.

**$H_2$:** In this "mental-experiment hybrid" the challenger is given access to a breaking oracle $\mathcal{B}_{\text{id}_h}$, with the tag being the identity of an arbitrary honest parties $(h \notin \mathcal{P}^*)$. The challenger begins as in the real execution for the first two rounds, but then it uses $\mathcal{B}_{\text{tag}}$ to extract the values $(x_j, r_j, R_j)$ of all the adversarial players $j \in \mathcal{P}^*$ from $\text{acom}_2^{h,j}$.

Then the challenger changes the commitments $\text{bcom}_2^{j,h}$ on behalf of the honest party $P_h$, committing to the values $R_j$ that were extracted from $\text{acom}_2^{h,j}$ (and thus making the language $\mathcal{L}_{h,j,2}$ –the "OR branch"– in $\Pi_{\text{WIPOK}}$ a true statement).[9]

**Lemma 62.** $H_1 \approx_c H_2$.

**Proof:** Since the only differences between these hybrids are the values committed to in $\text{bcom}^{j,h}$, then indistinguishability should follow from the adaptive-hiding of the commitment scheme bCom (as the challenger never queries its breaking oracle with any tag containing the identity $\text{id}_h$ of the honest party).

One subtle point here, is that in both $H_1$ and $H_2$ we use the rewinding Feige-Shamir ZK simulator, so we need to explain how the single value $\text{bcom}_2^{j,h}$ provided by the committer in the reduction (which is a commitment to either 0 or $R_j$) is used in all these transcripts. To that end let $M$ be some polynomial upper bound on the number of rewinding operations needed by the zero-knowledge simulator. The reduction to the security of bCom will choose at random $t \in [1, M]$ and will only use the bCom committer that it interacts with to commit to a value in the $t$'th rewinding, committing to 0 in all the rewindings $i < t$ and to the value $R_j$ (that it has from the breaking oracle) in all the rewindings $i > t$.

By a standard argument, if we can distinguish between $H_1 \approx_c H_2$ with probability $\epsilon$ then the reduction algorithm can distinguish commitments to 0 and $R_j$ with probability $\epsilon/M$.    $\square$

**$H_3$:** In this hybrid, we change the witness used in $\Pi_{\text{WIPOK}}$ on behalf of each honest party $P_h$. In particular, all $\Pi_{\text{WIPOK}}$ executions use the "OR branch" $\mathcal{L}_{h,j,2}$.

**Lemma 63.** $H_2 \approx_c H_3$.

**Proof:** We make sub-hybrids that change one honest party at a time, and show that a distinguisher $D$ that distinguishes two such sub-hybrids can be used by

---

[9] The commitment bCom starts in the second round, but this is a two-round commitment so the committed value only affects the second message in the commitment, which happens in the third round of the larger protocol.

another distinguisher $D'$ to distinguish between the two witnesses of $\Pi_{WIPOK}$ (as per Definition 6).

**Description of $D'$:** $D'$ plays the role of both the challenger and the adversary in the two hybrids, except that the prover messages of $\Pi_{\text{WIPOK}}$ (on behalf of $P_h$) are obtained from the external prover that the WI-distinguisher $D'$ has access to.

At the third round of the protocol, $D'$ has the statement that $P_h$ needs to prove, and it gets the two witnesses for that statement from the witness-selecting machine in Definition 6. Sending the statement and witnesses to its external prover, $D'$ obtains the relevant $\Pi_{\text{WIPOK}}$ message (for one of them). $D'$ also uses these witnesses to complete the other flows of the protocol (e.g., the commitments $\text{bcom}_2^{j,h}$ that include some of these witnesses). Once the protocol run is finished, it gives the transcript to $D$ and outputs whatever $D$ outputs.

As above, we still need to support rewinding by the Feige-Shamir ZK simulator, while having access to only a single interaction with the external prover, and we do it by sub-sub-hybrids where we embed this interaction in a random rewinding $t$, producing all the other proofs by the $H_2$ challenger (for $i < t$) or the $H_3$ challenger (for $i > t$). It is clear that the advantage of $D'$ is a $1/M$ fraction of the advantage of $D$.    □

We note that $D'$ above still uses the breaking oracle $\mathcal{B}_{\text{tag}}$ (to extract the $\Pi_{\text{FS}}$ secrets), so we need to assume that delayed-input-WI holds even in a world with the breaking oracle. As explained above, we rely on complexity leveraging for that purpose. That is, we let $D'$ run in subexponential time (so it can implement $\mathcal{B}_{\text{tag}}$ itself), and set the parameters of $\Pi_{\text{WIPOK}}$ large enough so we can assume witness-indistinguishability even for such a strong $D'$. (We can implement subexponential WI protocol from subexponential LWE.)

**$H_4$:** The difference from $H_3$ is that in $H_4$ we simulate the decryption shares of the honest parties. More specifically, the challenger in $H_4$ has access also to the ideal functionality, and it proceeds as follows:

1. It completes the first three broadcast rounds exactly as in $H_3$.
2. Having extracted the input of all the corrupted parties, the challenger sends all these inputs to the ideal functionality $\mathcal{F}$ and receives back the output $y = F(\{x_j\}_{j \in [N]})$.
3. Having extracted also all the secret keys of the corrupted parties, the challenger has everything that it needs to compute the simulated decryption shares of the honest parties, $\{ev_h\}_{h \notin \mathcal{P}^*} \leftarrow \mathcal{S}^T(y, \hat{c}, h, \{\text{sk}_j\}_{j \in \mathcal{P}^*})$.
4. The challenger computes also the last message of $\Pi_{\text{FS}}$ (using the simulator as before), and sends it together with decryption shares $\{ev_h\}_h$ in the last round.

**Lemma 64.** $H_3 \approx_s H_4$.

**Proof:** The only change between these two experiments is that the partial decryption shares of the honest parties are not generated by partial decryption. Instead they are generated via the threshold simulator $\mathcal{S}^T$ of the MFHE scheme. By the simulatability of threshold decryption, the partial decryptions shares are statistically indistinguishable.    □

**H<sub>5</sub>:** We change $H_4$ by making $\mathcal{S}$ broadcast encryptions of **0** on behalf of the honest parties in the third round, instead of encrypting the real inputs.

**Lemma 65.** $H_4 \approx_c H_5$.

**Proof:** The proof follows directly from semantic security, which in our case follows from LWE. As in the previous hybrid, here too we need this assumption to hold even in the presence of a breaking oracle, and we lose a factor of $M$ in the distinguishing probability due to rewinding. □

**H<sub>6</sub>:** In this hybrid, we get rid of the honest parties' inputs $\{(x_h, r_h)\}_h$ (that are present in the values of $\mathsf{acom}_2^{j,h}$). Formally, $H_6$ is identical to $H_5$ except that in the first round it sets $x_h = \mathbf{0}$ for all $h \notin \mathcal{P}^*$.

**Lemma 66.** $H_5 \approx_c H_6$.

**Proof:** This proof is very similar to the proof of $H_1 \approx_c H_2$, and indistinguishability follows from adaptive-hiding of $\mathsf{aCom}$. Since the challenger never asks its breaking oracle $\mathcal{B}_{\mathsf{tag}}$ to break commitments relative to the honest party's tags (and since these committed values are no longer used by the challenger for anything else), then having the honest parties commit to $x_h$ is indistinguishable from having it commit to **0**. □

**H<sub>7</sub>:** In this hybrid we essentially reverse the change that was made in going from $H_2$ to $H_3$. Namely, since now both the encryption and the commitment at each honest party are for the value **0** then there is no need to use the "OR branch" in $\Pi_{\mathsf{WIPOK}}$. Hence we return in using the honest prover strategy there, relative to the input $x_h = \mathbf{0}$. As in Lemma 63 indistinguishability follows by the WI property of $\Pi_{\mathsf{WIPOK}}$.

**H<sub>8</sub>:** Revert the change that was made in going from $H_1$ to $H_2$ and thus commit to a random value $s_h$ in $\mathsf{bcom}_2^{j,h}$. Indistinguishability follows by the computational hiding of $\mathsf{bCom}$, just like in Lemma 62.

**H<sub>9</sub>:** In this hybrid the challenger no longer has access to the breaking oracle $\mathcal{B}_{\mathsf{tag}}$. Instead, it uses the knowledge extractor of $\Pi_{\mathsf{WIPOK}}$ to get the input and secret keys of the corrupted parties, and the "standard" zero-knowledge simulator to get the proof in $\Pi_{\mathsf{FS}}$.

**Lemma 67.** $H_8 \approx_s H_9$.

**Proof:** The only difference between these hybrids is the method used by the challenger to extract the adversary secrets. Two technical points needs to be addressed here:

- This hybrid requires rewinding by *both* the FS ZK simulator and the FLS knowledge extractor, so we need to argue that after polynomially many trials they will *both succeed* on the same transcript. This is a rather standard argument (which essentially boils down to looking at the knowledge-extractor inside $\Pi_{\mathsf{FS}}$ and the one used explicitly in $\Pi_{\mathsf{WIPOK}}$ as extracting knowledge for and AND language.)

- We also need to argue that the value extracted from the adversary by the $\Pi_{\text{WIPOK}}$ extractor in $H_9$ is a witness for $\mathcal{L}_{i,j,1}$ and not for $\mathcal{L}_{i,j,2}$. This is done by appealing to the one-wayness of $OWF$, if there is a noticeable probability to extract an $\mathcal{L}_{i,j,2}$ witness in $H_9$ then we get an inverter for this one-way function.

We conclude that in both $H_8$ and $H_9$ we succeed in extraction with about the same probability, and moreover extract the very same thing, and (statistical) indistinguishability follows.                                                                                   $\square$

Observing that the hybrid $H_9$ is identical to the ideal-world game with the simulator completes the proof of security.                                                                       $\square$

## 7    Discussion and Open Problems

**Compiling semi-malicious to malicious protocols.** Our protocol and its proof can be viewed as starting from a 3-round semi-malicious protocol and "compiling" it into a 4-round malicious protocol using commitments and zero-knowledge proofs. However our construction *is not* a generic compiler of semi-malicious to malicious protocols, rather it relies on the specifics of our 3-round semi-malicious protocol from Sect. 4. At the very least, our construction needs the following two properties of the underlying semi-malicious protocol:

**Public-coin 1st round.** In our protocol we must send the second-round messages of the underlying protocol no later than the 3rd round of the compiled protocol. We thus have at most two rounds to prove that the first-round messages are valid, before we must send the second-round messages, severely limiting the type of proofs that we can use.

This is not a problem in our case, since the first round of the semi-malicious protocol is *public coin*, i.e., the parties just send to each other random bits. Hence, there is nothing to prove about them and the semi-malicious protocol can withstand any messages sent by the adversary.

**Committing 2nd round.** We also use the fact that the second round of the semi-malicious protocol is fully committing to the input, since our simulator extracts the inputs after these rounds.

We remark that in some sense every 3-round semi-malicious protocol with a public-coin first round and fully-committing second round can be thought of as a multi-key homomorphic encryption with distributed setup, by viewing the random coins send in the first round as the params, and the second-round messages as encryptions of the inputs.

**Adaptive commitments.** Although the intuitive property that we need from the commitment component of our protocol is non malleability, our actual proof relies heavily on the stronger notion of *adaptive security*, that lets us use straight-line extraction from the adversary's commitment. Oversimplifying here, the use of adaptive commitments with straight-line extraction together with the WI proofs let us construct a 3-round non-malleable zero-knowledge proof of knowledge system.

While it is plausible that our 3-round semi-malicious protocol can be "compiled" using only non-malleable commitments and avoid complexity leveraging, we were not able to do it, this question remains open.[10]

# A    The Need for Dual GSW

For the interested reader, we explain below why we need to use the "dual" rather than "primal" GSW scheme for our multi-key FHE. The main difference is that in the scheme from [CM15, MW16], the common matrix $A$ has dimension $(n-1)$-by-$m$ (with $m > n$), while in our scheme the dimensions are flipped and the matrix $A = (A_1 | \ldots | A_n)$ is of dimension $(m-1)$-by-$Nn$ with $m > Nn$. While it is possible that a secure one-round distributed setup procedure exists also for the "primal" scheme, we were not able to find one that we can prove secure under any standard assumption. Below we detail some specific failed attempts.

**Failed attempt #1, parties choose different columns.** Consider a protocol in which each party $P_i$ is choosing a random $n \times m'$ matrix $A_i$ ($n < m'$), and then using the column-concatenation of all the $A_i$'s, $A = (A_1 | A_2 | \ldots | A_N)$.

Since $n < m'$, an adversary (who controls $P_N$ without loss of generality), can just set its matrix as $A_N = G$ where $G$ is the GSW "gadget matrix". That gadget matrix has the property that given any vector $v \approx sG$ it is easy to find $s$, making it possible for the adversary to recover the secret keys of the honest parties. (This is exactly where the "dual" scheme helps: the adversary still sees some "leakage" $v \approx sA_N$, but it cannot recover $s$ since $s$ still has a lot of min-entropy even given that leakage.)

**Failed attempt #2, parties choose different rows.** One way to avoid attacks as above is to let each party choose a random $n' \times m$ matrix $A_i$ and set $A \in \mathbb{Z}_q^{Nn' \times m}$ as the row-concatenation of the $A_i$'s, $A^T = (A_1^T | \ldots | A_N^T)$. It is now easy to prove that $sA + e$ is pseudorandom (under LWE), no matter what the adversary does. But this arrangement opens another avenue of attack: The adversary (still controlling $P_N$) set $A_N = A_1$, so the bottom few rows in $A$ are equal to the top few rows. Hence, also the bottom few rows in $AR$ are equal to the top few rows, which lets the adversary distinguish $AR$ from a uniform random $U$.

At this point one may hope that if we let the parties choose different diagonals then neither of the attacks above would apply, but this is not the case. For example, an adversary controlling all but one party can force the matrix $A$ to have many identical rows, which would mean that so does the matrix $AR$. More generally, it seems that any arrangement where each party chooses a subset of the entries in $A$ will let the adversary force $A$ to be low rank, and hence also $AR$ will be of low rank. (Here too the "dual" scheme works better, since the attacker sees $AR + E$ rather than $AR$ itself.)

---

[10] The concurrent work of [ACJ17] achieves a "compilation" of their robust semi-honest protocol to the malicious setting based on non-malleable commitments but still requires complexity leveraging.

# References

ACJ17. Ananth, P., Choudhuri, A.R., Jain, A.: A new approach to round-optimal secure multiparty computation. Cryptology ePrint Archive, Report 2017/402 (2017). http://eprint.iacr.org/2017/402

AJL+12. Asharov, G., Jain, A., López-Alt, A., Tromer, E., Vaikuntanathan, V., Wichs, D.: Multiparty computation with low communication, computation and interaction via threshold FHE. In: Pointcheval, D., Johansson, T. (eds.) EUROCRYPT 2012. LNCS, vol. 7237, pp. 483–501. Springer, Heidelberg (2012). doi:10.1007/978-3-642-29011-4_29

BMR90. Beaver, D., Micali, S., Rogaway, P.: The round complexity of secure protocols (extended abstract). In: 22nd ACM STOC, pp. 503–513. ACM Press, May 1990

BP16. Brakerski, Z., Perlman, R.: Lattice-based fully dynamic multi-key FHE with short ciphertexts. In: Robshaw, M., Katz, J. (eds.) CRYPTO 2016. LNCS, vol. 9814, pp. 190–213. Springer, Heidelberg (2016). doi:10.1007/978-3-662-53018-4_8

CM15. Clear, M., McGoldrick, C.: Multi-identity and multi-key leveled FHE from learning with errors. In: Gennaro, R., Robshaw, M. (eds.) CRYPTO 2015. LNCS, vol. 9216, pp. 630–656. Springer, Heidelberg (2015). doi:10.1007/978-3-662-48000-7_31

COSV16. Ciampi, M., Ostrovsky, R., Siniscalchi, L., Visconti, I.: Concurrent non-malleable commitments (and more) in 3 rounds. In: Robshaw, M., Katz, J. (eds.) CRYPTO 2016. LNCS, vol. 9816, pp. 270–299. Springer, Heidelberg (2016). doi:10.1007/978-3-662-53015-3_10

DGK+10. Dodis, Y., Goldwasser, S., Tauman Kalai, Y., Peikert, C., Vaikuntanathan, V.: Public-key encryption schemes with auxiliary inputs. In: Micciancio, D. (ed.) TCC 2010. LNCS, vol. 5978, pp. 361–381. Springer, Heidelberg (2010). doi:10.1007/978-3-642-11799-2_22

FLS99. Feige, U., Lapidot, D., Shamir, A.: Multiple noninteractive zero knowledge proofs under general assumptions. SIAM J. Comput. **29**(1), 1–28 (1999)

FS90. Feige, U., Shamir, A.: Witness indistinguishable and witness hiding protocols. In: 22nd ACM STOC, pp. 416–426. ACM Press, May 1990

GGHR14. Garg, S., Gentry, C., Halevi, S., Raykova, M.: Two-round secure MPC from indistinguishability obfuscation. In: Lindell, Y. (ed.) TCC 2014. LNCS, vol. 8349, pp. 74–94. Springer, Heidelberg (2014). doi:10.1007/978-3-642-54242-8_4

GMPP16. Garg, S., Mukherjee, P., Pandey, O., Polychroniadou, A.: The exact round complexity of secure computation. In: Fischlin, M., Coron, J.-S. (eds.) EUROCRYPT 2016. LNCS, vol. 9666, pp. 448–476. Springer, Heidelberg (2016). doi:10.1007/978-3-662-49896-5_16

Gol04. Goldreich, O.: Foundations of Cryptography: Basic Applications, vol. 2. Cambridge University Press, Cambridge (2004)

GPV08. Gentry, C., Peikert, C., Vaikuntanathan, V.: Trapdoors for hard lattices and new cryptographic constructions. In: STOC, pp. 197–206. ACM (2008)

GSW13. Gentry, C., Sahai, A., Waters, B.: Homomorphic encryption from learning with errors: conceptually-simpler, asymptotically-faster, attribute-based. In: Canetti, R., Garay, J.A. (eds.) CRYPTO 2013. LNCS, vol. 8042, pp. 75–92. Springer, Heidelberg (2013). doi:10.1007/978-3-642-40041-4_5

HK07.   Horvitz, O., Katz, J.: Universally-composable two-party computation in two rounds. In: Menezes, A. (ed.) CRYPTO 2007. LNCS, vol. 4622, pp. 111–129. Springer, Heidelberg (2007). doi:10.1007/978-3-540-74143-5_7

JS07.   Jarecki, S., Shmatikov, V.: Efficient two-party secure computation on committed inputs. In: Naor, M. (ed.) EUROCRYPT 2007. LNCS, vol. 4515, pp. 97–114. Springer, Heidelberg (2007). doi:10.1007/978-3-540-72540-4_6

KO04.   Katz, J., Ostrovsky, R.: Round-optimal secure two-party computation. In: Franklin, M. (ed.) CRYPTO 2004. LNCS, vol. 3152, pp. 335–354. Springer, Heidelberg (2004). doi:10.1007/978-3-540-28628-8_21

LPS17.  Lin, H., Pass, R., Soni, P.: Two-round concurrent non-malleable commitment from time-lock puzzles. IACR Cryptology ePrint Archive, 2017:273 (2017)

LTV12.  López-Alt, A., Tromer, E., Vaikuntanathan, V.: On-the-fly multiparty computation on the cloud via multikey fully homomorphic encryption. In: Karloff, H.J., Pitassi, T. (eds.) 44th ACM STOC, pp. 1219–1234. ACM Press, May 2012

MP12.   Micciancio, D., Peikert, C.: Trapdoors for lattices: simpler, tighter, faster, smaller. In: Pointcheval, D., Johansson, T. (eds.) EUROCRYPT 2012. LNCS, vol. 7237, pp. 700–718. Springer, Heidelberg (2012). doi:10.1007/978-3-642-29011-4_41

MW16.   Mukherjee, P., Wichs, D.: Two round multiparty computation via multikey FHE. In: Fischlin, M., Coron, J.-S. (eds.) EUROCRYPT 2016. LNCS, vol. 9666, pp. 735–763. Springer, Heidelberg (2016). doi:10.1007/978-3-662-49896-5_26

Nao91.  Naor, M.: Bit commitment using pseudorandomness. J. Cryptology 4(2), 151–158 (1991)

ORS15.  Ostrovsky, R., Richelson, S., Scafuro, A.: Round-optimal black-box two-party computation. In: Gennaro, R., Robshaw, M. (eds.) CRYPTO 2015. LNCS, vol. 9216, pp. 339–358. Springer, Heidelberg (2015). doi:10.1007/978-3-662-48000-7_17

Pol16.  Polychroniadou, A.: On the Communication and Round Complexity of Secure Computation. Ph.D. thesis, Aarhus University, December 2016

PPV08.  Pandey, O., Pass, R., Vaikuntanathan, V.: Adaptive one-way functions and applications. In: Wagner, D. (ed.) CRYPTO 2008. LNCS, vol. 5157, pp. 57–74. Springer, Heidelberg (2008). doi:10.1007/978-3-540-85174-5_4

PS16.   Peikert, C., Shiehian, S.: Multi-key FHE from LWE, revisited. In: Hirt, M., Smith, A. (eds.) TCC 2016. LNCS, vol. 9986, pp. 217–238. Springer, Heidelberg (2016). doi:10.1007/978-3-662-53644-5_9

Reg09.  Regev, O.: On lattices, learning with errors, random linear codes, and cryptography. J. ACM 56(6), 1–40 (2009)

# Round-Optimal Secure Two-Party Computation from Trapdoor Permutations

Michele Ciampi[1]([✉]), Rafail Ostrovsky[2], Luisa Siniscalchi[1], and Ivan Visconti[1]

[1] DIEM, University of Salerno, Fisciano, Italy
{mciampi,lsiniscalchi,visconti}@unisa.it
[2] UCLA, Los Angeles, USA
rafail@cs.ucla.edu

**Abstract.** In this work we continue the study on the round complexity of secure two-party computation with black-box simulation.

Katz and Ostrovsky in CRYPTO 2004 showed a 5 (optimal) round construction assuming trapdoor permutations for the general case where both players receive the output. They also proved that their result is round optimal. This lower bound has been recently revisited by Garg et al. in Eurocrypt 2016 where a 4 (optimal) round protocol is showed assuming a simultaneous message exchange channel. Unfortunately there is no instantiation of the protocol of Garg et al. under standard polynomial-time hardness assumptions.

In this work we close the above gap by showing a 4 (optimal) round construction for secure two-party computation in the simultaneous message channel model with black-box simulation, assuming trapdoor permutations against polynomial-time adversaries.

Our construction for secure two-party computation relies on a special 4-round protocol for oblivious transfer that nicely composes with other protocols in parallel. We define and construct such special oblivious transfer protocol from trapdoor permutations. This building block is clearly interesting on its own. Our construction also makes use of a recent advance on non-malleability: a delayed-input 4-round non-malleable zero knowledge argument.

## 1 Introduction

Obtaining round-optimal secure computation [14,19] has been a long standing open problem. For the two-party case the work of Katz and Ostrovsky [15] demonstrated that 5 rounds are both necessary and sufficient, with black-box simulation, when both parties need to obtain the output. Their construction relies on the use of trapdoor permutations[1]. A more recent work of Ostrovsky et al. [16] showed that a black-box use of trapdoor permutations is sufficient for obtaining the above round-optimal construction.

---

[1] The actual assumption is *enhanced* trapdoor permutations, but for simplicity in this paper we will omit the word *enhanced* assuming it implicitly.

© International Association for Cryptologic Research 2017
Y. Kalai and L. Reyzin (Eds.): TCC 2017, Part I, LNCS 10677, pp. 678–710, 2017.
https://doi.org/10.1007/978-3-319-70500-2_23

A very recent work of Garg et al. [12] revisited the lower bound of [15] when the communication channel allows both players to send messages in the same round, a setting that has been widely used when studying the round complexity of multi-party computation. Focusing on the simultaneous message exchange model, Garg et al. showed that 4 rounds are necessary to build a secure two-party computation (2PC) protocol for every functionality with black-box simulation. In the same work they also designed a 4-round secure 2PC protocol for every functionality. However their construction compared to the one of [15] relies on much stronger complexity assumptions. Indeed the security of their protocol crucially relies on the existence of a 3-round 3-robust [11,18] parallel non-malleable commitment scheme. According to [11,18] such commitment scheme can be constructed either through non-falsifiable assumptions (i.e., using the construction of [17]) or through sub-exponentially-strong assumptions (i.e., using the construction of [3]). A recent work of Ananth et al. [1] studies the multi-party case in the simultaneous message exchange channel. More precisely the authors of [1] provide a 5-round protocol to securely compute every functionality for the multi-party case under the Decisional Diffie-Hellman (DDH) assumption and a 4-round protocol assuming one-way permutations and sub-exponentially secure DDH. The above gap in the state of affairs leaves open the following interesting open question:

**Open Question:** *is there a 4-round construction for secure 2PC for any functionality in the simultaneous message exchange model assuming (standard) trapdoor permutations?*

## 1.1   Our Contribution

In this work we solve the above open question. Moreover our construction only requires black-box simulation and is therefore round optimal. We now describe our approach.

As discussed before, the construction of [12] needs a 3-round 3-robust parallel non-malleable commitment, and constructing this primitive from standard polynomial-time assumptions is still an open problem. We circumvent the use of this primitive through a different approach. As done in [12], we start considering the 4-round 2PC protocol of [15] (KO protocol) that works only for those functionalities where only one player receives the output (we recall that the KO protocols do not assume the existence of a simultaneous message exchange channel). Then as in [12] we consider two simultaneous executions of the KO protocol in order to make both parties able to obtain the output *assuming the existence of a simultaneous message exchange channel*. We describe now the KO protocol and then we explain how we manage to avoid 3-round 3-robust parallel non-malleable commitments.

**The 4-round KO protocol.** Following Fig. 1, at a very high level the KO protocol between the players $P_1$ and $P_2$, where only $P_1$ gets the output, works as follows. Let $f$ be the function that $P_1$ and $P_2$ want to compute. In the second round $P_2$ generates, using his input, a Yao's garbled circuit $C$ for the function

$f$ with the associated labels $L$. Then $P_2$ commits to $C$ using a commitment scheme that is binding if $P_2$ runs the honest committer procedure. This commitment scheme however admits also an indistinguishable equivocal commitment procedure that allows later to open the equivocal commitment as any message. Let $com_0$ be such commitment. In addition $P_2$ commits to $L$ using a statistically binding commitment scheme. Let $com_1$ be such commitment. In the last round $P_2$ sends the opening of the equivocal commitment to the message $C$. Furthermore, using $L$ as input, $P_2$ in the 2nd and in the 4th round runs as a sender of a specific 4-round oblivious transfer protocol KOOT that is secure against a malicious receiver and secure against a semi-honest sender. Finally, in parallel with KOOT, $P_2$ computes a specific delayed-input zero-knowledge argument of knowledge (ZKAoK) to prove that the labels $L$ committed in $com_1$ correspond to the ones used in KOOT, and that $com_0$ is binding since it has been computed running the honest committer on input some randomness and some message. $P_1$ plays as a receiver of KOOT in order to obtain the labels associated to his input and computes the output of the two-party computation by running $C$ on input the received labels. Moreover $P_1$ acts as a verifier for the ZKAoK where $P_2$ acts as a prover.

**The 4-round protocol of Garg et al.** In order to allow both parties to get the output in 4 rounds using a simultaneous message exchange channel, [12] first considers two simultaneous execution of the KO protocol (Fig. 2). Such natural approach yields to the following two problems (as stated in [12]): (1) nothing prevents an adversary from using two different inputs in the two executions of the KO protocol; (2) an adversary could adapt his input based on the input of the other party, for instance the adversary could simply forward the messages that he receives from the honest party. To address the first problem the authors of [12] add another statement to the ZKAoK where the player $P_j$ (with $j = 1, 2$) proves that both executions of the KO protocol use the same input. The second problem is solved in [12] by using a 3-round 3-robust non-malleable commitment to construct KOOT and the ZKAoK in such a way that the input used by the honest party in KOOT cannot be mauled by the malicious party. The 3-robustness is required to avoid rewinding issues in the security proof. Indeed, in parallel with the 3-round 3-robust non-malleable commitment a WIPoK is executed in KOOT. At some point the security proof of [12] needs to rely on the witness-indistinguishability property of the WIPoK while the simulator of the ZKAoK is run. The simulator for the ZKAoK rewinds the adversary from the third to the second round, therefore rewinding also the challenger of the WIPoK of the reduction. To solve this problem [12,18] rely on the stronger security of a 3-round 3-robust parallel non-malleable commitment scheme. Unfortunately, constructing this tool with standard polynomial-time assumptions is still an open question.

**Our 4-round protocol.** In our approach (that is summarized in Fig. 3), in order to solve problems 1 and 2 listed above using standard polynomial-time assumption (trapdoor permutations), we replace the ZKAoK and KOOT (that uses the 3-round 3-robust parallel commitment scheme) with the following four tools.

(1) A 4-round delayed-input non-malleable zero-knowledge (NMZK) argument of knowledge (AoK) NMZK from one-way functions (OWFs) recently constructed in [4] (the theorem proved by NMZK is roughly the same as the theorem proved ZKAoK of [12]). (2) A new special OT protocol $\Pi_{\overrightarrow{OT}}^{\gamma}$ that is *one-sided* simulatable [16]. In this security notion for OT it is not required the existence of a simulator against a malicious sender, but only that a malicious sender cannot distinguish whether the honest receiver uses his real input or a fixed input (e.g., a string of 0s). Moreover some security against a malicious sender still holds even if the adversary can perform a mild form of "rewinds" against the receiver, and the security against a malicious receiver holds even when an interactive primitive (like a WIPoK) is run in parallel (more details about the security provided by $\Pi_{\overrightarrow{OT}}^{\gamma}$ will be provided later). (3) An interactive commitment scheme PBCOM that allows each party to commit to his input. In more details, in our 2PC protocol each party commits two times to his input and then proves using NMZK that (a) the two values committed are equal and (b) this committed value corresponds to the input used in the 2 simultaneous executions of our (modified KO) protocol[2]. (4) A combination of two instantiations of Special Honest Verifier Zero-Knowledge (Special HVZK) PoK thus obtaining a WIPoK $\Pi_{OR}$. The idea behind the use of a combination of Special HVZK PoKs was introduced recently in [4]. The aim of this technique is to replace a WIPoK by non-interactive primitives (like Special HVZK) in such a way that rewinding issues, due to the other subprotocols, can be avoided. We use $\Pi_{OR}$ in our protocol to force each party to prove knowledge of one of the values committed using PBCOM. In the security proof we will use the PoK property of $\Pi_{OR}$ to extract the input from the malicious party.

**Our security proof.** In our security proof we exploit immediately the major differences with [12]. Indeed we start the security proof with an hybrid experiment where the simulator of NMZK is used, and we are guaranteed that the malicious party is behaving honestly by the non-malleability/extractability of NMZK. Another major difference with the KO security proof is that in our 2PC protocol the simulator extracts the input from the malicious party through $\Pi_{OR}$ whereas in the KO protocol's security proof the extraction is made from KOOT (that is used in a non-black box way).

We remark that, in all the steps of our security proof the simulator-extractor of NMZK is used to check every time that the adversary is using the same input in both the executions of the KO protocol even though the adversary is receiving a simulated NMZK of a false statement. More precisely, every time that we change something obtaining a new hybrid experiment, we prove that: (1) the output distributions of the experiments are indistinguishable; (2) the malicious party is behaving honestly (the statement proved by the NMZK given

---

[2] Only one execution of NMZK is run by each party, in order to allow a party to prove that the committed values using PBCOM are the same. We just "expand" the statement proved by NMZK.

by the adversary is true). We will show that if one of these two invariants does not hold then we can make a reduction that breaks a cryptographic primitive.

**The need of a special 4-round OT protocol.** Interestingly, the security proof has to address a major issue. After we switch to the simulator of the NMZK, we have that in some hybrid experiment $H_i$, we change the input of the receiver of $\Pi_{\overrightarrow{OT}}^{\gamma}$ (following the approach used in the security proof of the KO protocol). To demonstrate the indistinguishability between $H_i$ and $H_{i-1}$ we want to rely on the security of $\Pi_{\overrightarrow{OT}}^{\gamma}$ against a malicious sender. Therefore we construct an adversarial sender $\mathcal{A}_{OT}$ of $\Pi_{\overrightarrow{OT}}^{\gamma}$. $\mathcal{A}_{OT}$ acts as a proxy for the messages of $\Pi_{\overrightarrow{OT}}^{\gamma}$ and internally computes the other messages of our protocol. In particular, the 1st and the 3rd rounds of $\Pi_{\overrightarrow{OT}}^{\gamma}$ are given by the challenger (that acts as a receiver of $\Pi_{\overrightarrow{OT}}^{\gamma}$), and the 2nd and the 4th messages of $\Pi_{\overrightarrow{OT}}^{\gamma}$ are given by the malicious party. Furthermore, in order to compute the other messages of our 2PC protocol $\mathcal{A}_{OT}$ needs to run the simulator-extractor of NMZK, and this requires to rewind from the 3rd to 2nd round. This means that $\mathcal{A}_{OT}$ needs to complete a 3rd round of $\Pi_{\overrightarrow{OT}}^{\gamma}$, for every different 2nd round that he receives (this is due to the rewinds made by the simulator of NMZK that are emulated by $\mathcal{A}_{OT}$). We observe that since the challenger cannot be rewound, $\mathcal{A}_{OT}$ needs a strategy to answer to these multiple queries w.r.t. $\Pi_{\overrightarrow{OT}}^{\gamma}$ without knowing the randomness and the input used by the challenger so far. For these reasons we need $\Pi_{\overrightarrow{OT}}^{\gamma}$ to enjoy an additional property: the *replayability* of the 3rd round. More precisely, given the messages computed by an honest receiver, the third round can be indistinguishability used to answer to any second round of $\Pi_{\overrightarrow{OT}}^{\gamma}$ sent by a malicious sender. Another issue is that the idea of the security proof explained so far relies on the simulator-extractor of NMZK and this simulator rewinds also from the 4th to the 3rd round. The rewinds made by the simulator-extractor allow a malicious receiver to ask for different 3rd rounds of $\Pi_{\overrightarrow{OT}}^{\gamma}$. Therefore we need our $\Pi_{\overrightarrow{OT}}^{\gamma}$ to be also secure against a more powerful malicious receiver that can send multiple (up to a polynomial $\gamma$) third rounds to the honest sender. As far as we know the literature does not provide an OT with the properties that we require, so in this work we also provide an OT protocol with these additional features. This clearly is of independent interest.

**Input extraction.** One drawback of $\Pi_{\overrightarrow{OT}}^{\gamma}$ is that the simulator against a malicious receiver $R_{OT}^{\star}$ is not able to extract the input of $R_{OT}^{\star}$. This feature is crucial in the security proof of KO, therefore we need another way to allow the extraction of the input from the malicious party. In order to do that, as described before, each party commits two times using PBCOM; let $c_0, c_1$ be the commitments computed by $P_2$. $P_2$ proves, using $\Pi_{OR}$, knowledge of either the message committed in $c_0$ or the message committed in $c_1$. Additionally, using NMZK, $P_2$ proves that $c_0$ and $c_1$ are commitments of the same value and that this value corresponds to the input used in the two executions of the modified KO protocol. This combination of commitments, $\Pi_{OR}$ and NMZK allow the correct extraction through the PoK-extractor of $\Pi_{OR}$.

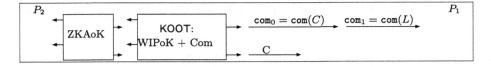

**Fig. 1.** The 4-round KO protocol from trapdoor permutations for functionalities where only one player receives the output.

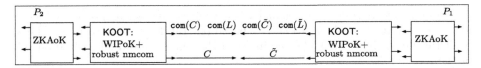

**Fig. 2.** The 4-round protocol of [12] for any functionality assuming 3-round 3-robust parallel non-malleable commitments in the simultaneous message exchange model.

### 1.2 Special One-Sided Simulatable OT

One of the main building blocks of our 2PC protocol is an OT protocol $\Pi_{\mathcal{OT}}^{\gamma} = (S_{\mathcal{OT}}, R_{\mathcal{OT}})$ one-sided simulatable[3]. Our $\Pi_{\mathcal{OT}}^{\gamma}$ has four rounds where the first ($\mathsf{ot}_1$) and the third ($\mathsf{ot}_3$) rounds are played by the receiver, and the remaining rounds ($\mathsf{ot}_2$ and $\mathsf{ot}_4$) are played by the sender. In addition $\Pi_{\mathcal{OT}}^{\gamma}$ enjoys the following two additional properties.

1. *Replayable third round.* Let $(\mathsf{ot}_1, \mathsf{ot}_2, \mathsf{ot}_3, \mathsf{ot}_4)$ be the messages exchanged by an honest receiver and a malicious sender during an execution of $\Pi_{\mathcal{OT}}^{\gamma}$. For any honestly computed $\mathsf{ot}_2'$, we have that $(\mathsf{ot}_1, \mathsf{ot}_2, \mathsf{ot}_3)$ and $(\mathsf{ot}_1, \mathsf{ot}_2', \mathsf{ot}_3)$ are identically distributed. Roughly, we are requiring that the third round can be reused in order to answer to any second round $\mathsf{ot}_2'$ sent by a malicious sender.
2. *Repeatability.* We require $\Pi_{\mathcal{OT}}^{\gamma}$ to be secure against a malicious receiver $R^{\star}$ even when the last two rounds of $\Pi_{\mathcal{OT}}^{\gamma}$ can be repeated multiple times. More precisely a 4-round OT protocol that is secure in this setting can be seen as an OT protocol of $2 + 2\gamma$ rounds, with $\gamma \in \{1, \ldots, \mathsf{poly}(\lambda)\}$ where $\lambda$ represents the security parameter. In this protocol $R^{\star}$, upon receiving the 4th round,

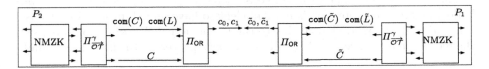

**Fig. 3.** Our 4-round protocol for any functionality assuming trapdoor permutations in the simultaneous message exchange model. $c_0$ and $c_1$ ($\tilde{c}_0$ and $\tilde{c}_1$) are commitments of $P_2$'s ($P_1$'s) input.

---

[3] In the 2PC protocol we will actually use $\Pi_{\overrightarrow{\mathcal{OT}}}^{\gamma}$ that roughly corresponds to parallel executions of $\Pi_{\mathcal{OT}}^{\gamma}$. More details will be provided later.

can continue the execution with $S_{\mathcal{OT}}$ by sending a freshly generated third round of $\Pi_{\mathcal{OT}}^\gamma$ up to total of $\gamma$ 3rd rounds.

Roughly, we require that the output of such $R^\star$ that runs $\Pi_{\mathcal{OT}}^\gamma$ against an honest sender can be simulated by an efficient simulator $\mathsf{Sim}$ that has only access to the ideal world functionality $F_{\mathcal{OT}}$ and oracle access to $R^\star$.

The security of $\Pi_{\mathcal{OT}}^\gamma$ is based on the existence of trapdoor permutations[4].

*Our techniques.* In order to construct $\Pi_{\mathcal{OT}}^\gamma$ we use as a starting point the following basic 3-round semi-honest OT $\Pi_{\mathsf{sh}}$ based on trapdoor permutations (TDPs) of [9,15]. Let $l_0, l_1 \in \{0,1\}^\lambda$ be the input of the sender $S$ and $b$ be the input bit of the receiver $R$.

1. The sender $S$ chooses a trapdoor permutation $(f, f^{-1}) \leftarrow \mathsf{Gen}(1^\lambda)$ and sends $f$ to the receiver $R$.
2. $R$ chooses $x \leftarrow \{0,1\}^\lambda$ and $z_{1-b} \leftarrow \{0,1\}^\lambda$, computes $z_b = f(x)$ and sends $(z_0, z_1)$.
3. For $c = 0, 1$ $S$ computes and sends $w_c = l_c \oplus \mathsf{hc}(f^{-1}(z_c))$

where $\mathsf{hc}(\cdot)$ is a hardcore bit of $f$. If the parties follow the protocol (i.e. in the semi-honest setting) then $S$ cannot learn the receiver's input (the bit $b$) as both $z_0$ and $z_1$ are random strings. Also, due to the security of the TDP $f$, $R$ cannot distinguish $w_{1-b}$ from random as long as $z_{1-b}$ is randomly chosen. If we consider a fully malicious receiver $R^\star$ then this protocol is not secure anymore. Indeed $R^\star$ could just compute $z_{1-b} = f(y)$ picking a random $y \leftarrow \{0,1\}^\lambda$. In this way $R^\star$ can retrieve both the inputs of the sender $l_0$ and $l_1$. In [15] the authors solve this problem by having the parties engaging a coin-flipping protocol such that the receiver is forced to set at least one between $z_0$ and $z_1$ to a random string. This is done by forcing the receiver to commit to two strings $(r_0, r_1)$ in the first round (for the coin-flipping) and providing a witness-indistinguishable proof of knowledge (WIPoK) that either $z_0 = r_0 \oplus r_0'$ or $z_1 = r_1 \oplus r_1'$ where $r_0'$ and $r_1'$ are random strings sent by the sender in the second round. The resulting protocol, as observed in [16], leaks no information to $S$ about $R$'s input. Moreover the soundness of the WIPoK forces a malicious $R^\star$ to behave honestly, and the PoK allows to extract the input from the adversary in the simulation. Therefore the protocol constructed in [15] is one-sided simulatable. Unfortunately this approach is not sufficient to have an OT protocol that has a *replayable* third round. This is due to the to the added WIPoK. More precisely, the receiver has to execute a WIPoK (acting as a prover) in the first three rounds.

---

[4] As suggested by Ivan Damgård and Claudio Orlandi in a personal communication, following the approach of [13], $\Pi_{\mathcal{OT}}^\gamma$ can be also constructed by relying on public key encryption schemes with special properties. More precisely the public key encryption scheme has to be such that either the ciphertexts can be sampled without knowing the plaintext, or the public key can be sampled without knowing the corresponding secret key. In this paper we give a formal construction and proof only for trapdoor permutations.

Clearly, there is no 3-round WIPoK such that given an accepting transcript $(a, c, z)$ one can efficiently compute multiple accepting transcripts w.r.t. different second rounds without knowing the randomness used to compute $a$. This is the reason why we need to use a different approach in order to construct an OT protocol simulation-based secure against a malicious receiver that also has a replayable 3rd round.

*Our construction: $\Pi^\gamma_{OT}$.* We start by considering a trick proposed in [16]. In [16] the authors construct a 4-round black-box OT starting from $\Pi_{sh}$. In order to force the receiver to compute a random $z_{b-1}$, in the first round $R$ sends two commitments $c_0$ and $c_1$ such that $c_b = \mathsf{Eqcom}(\cdot), c_{1-b} = \mathsf{Eqcom}(r_{1-b})$. $\mathsf{Eqcom}$ is a commitment scheme that is binding if the committer runs the honest committer procedure; however this commitment scheme admits also an indistinguishable equivocal commitment procedure that allows later to open the equivocal commitment as any message. $R$ then proves using a special WIPoK that either $c_0$ or $c_1$ is computed using the honest procedure (i.e., at least one of these commitments is binding). Then $S$ in the second round computes $r'_0 \leftarrow \{0,1\}^\lambda$, $r'_1 \leftarrow \{0,1\}^\lambda$ and two TDPs $f_0, f_1$ with the respective trapdoor and sends $(r'_0, r'_1, f_0, f_1)$ to $R$. $R$, upon receiving $(r'_0, r'_1, f_0, f_1)$, picks $x \leftarrow \{0,1\}^\lambda$, computes $r_b = f_b(x) \oplus r'_b$ and sends the opening of $c_{1-b}$ to the message $r_{1-b}$ and the opening of $c_b$ to the message $r_b$. At this point the sender computes and sends $w_0 = l_0 \oplus \mathsf{hc}(f_0^{-1}(r_0 \oplus r'_0))$, $w_1 = l_1 \oplus \mathsf{hc}(f_1^{-1}(r_1 \oplus r'_1))$. Since at least one between $c_0$ and $c_1$ is binding (due to the WIPoK), a malicious receiver can retrieve only one of the sender's input $l_b$. We observe that this OT protocol is still not sufficient for our propose due to the WIPoK used by the receiver (i.e., the 3rd round is not *replayable*). Moreover we cannot remove the WIPoK otherwise a malicious receiver could compute both $c_0$ and $c_1$ using the equivocal procedure thus obtaining $l_0$ and $l_1$. Our solution is to replace the WIPoK with some primitives that make replayable the 3rd round, still allowing the receiver to prove that at least one of the commitments sent in the first round is binding. Our key-idea is two use a combination of instance-dependent trapdoor commitment (IDTCom) and non-interactive commitment schemes. An IDTCom is defined over an instance $x$ that could belong to the $\mathcal{NP}$-language $L$ or not. If $x \notin L$ then the IDTCom is perfectly binding, otherwise it is equivocal and the trapdoor information is represented by the witness $w$ for $x$. Our protocol is described as follows. $R$ sends an IDTCom $\mathsf{tcom}_0$ of $r_0$ and an IDTCom $\mathsf{tcom}_1$ of $r_1$. In both cases the instance used is $\mathsf{com}$, a perfectly binding commitment of the bit $b$. The $\mathcal{NP}$-language used to compute $\mathsf{tcom}_0$ consists of all valid perfectly binding commitments of the message 0, while the $\mathcal{NP}$-language used to compute $\mathsf{tcom}_1$ consists of all valid perfectly binding commitments of the message 1.

This means that $\mathsf{tcom}_b$ can be opened to any value[5] and $\mathsf{tcom}_{1-b}$ is perfectly binding (we recall that $b$ is the input of the receiver). It is important to observe that due to the binding property of $\mathsf{com}$ it could be that both $\mathsf{tcom}_0$ and $\mathsf{tcom}_1$

---

[5] The decommitment information of $\mathsf{com}$ represents the trapdoor of the IDTCom $\mathsf{tcom}_b$.

are binding, but it can never happen that they are both equivocal. Now we can replace the two commitments and the WIPoK used in [16] with $\mathsf{tcom}_0, \mathsf{tcom}_1$ and $\mathsf{com}(b)$ that are sent in the first round. The rest of the protocol stay the same as in [16] with the difference that in the third round the openings to the messages $r_0$ and $r_1$ are w.r.t. $\mathsf{tcom}_0$ and $\mathsf{tcom}_1$. What remains to observe is that when a receiver provides a valid third round of this protocol then the same message can be used to answer all second rounds. Indeed, a well formed third round is accepting if and only if the opening w.r.t. $\mathsf{tcom}_0$ and $\mathsf{tcom}_1$ are well computed. Therefore whether the third round is accepting or not does not depend on the second round sent by the sender.

Intuitively this protocol is also already secure when we consider a malicious receiver that can send multiple third rounds up to a total of $\gamma$ 3rd rounds, thus obtaining an OT protocol of $2 + 2\gamma$ rounds (repeatability). This is because, even though a malicious receiver obtains multiple fourth rounds in response to multiple third rounds sent by $R^\star$, no information about the input of the sender is leaked. Indeed, in our $\Pi_{\mathcal{OT}}^\gamma$, the input of the receiver is fixed in the first round (only one between $\mathsf{tcom}_0$ and $\mathsf{tcom}_1$ can be equivocal). Therefore the security of the TDP ensures that only $l_b$ can be obtained by $R^\star$ independently of what he does in the third round. In the formal part of the paper we will show that the security of the TDP is enough to deal with such scenario.

We finally point out that the OT protocol that we need has to allow parties to use strings instead of bits as input. More precisely the sender's input is represented by $(l_0^1, l_1^1, \ldots, l_0^m, l_1^m)$ where each $l_b^i$ is an $\lambda$-bit length string (for $i = 1, \ldots, m$ and $b = 0, 1$), while the input of the receiver is $\lambda$-bit length string.

This is achieved in two steps. First we construct an OT protocol where the sender's input is represented by just two $m$-bit strings $l_0$ and $l_1$ and the receiver's input is still a bit. We obtain this protocol by just using in $\Pi_{\mathcal{OT}}^\gamma$ a vector of $m$ hard-core bits instead of just a single hard core bit following the approach of [12,15]. Then we consider $m$ parallel execution of this modified $\Pi_{\mathcal{OT}}^\gamma$ (where the sender uses a pair of strings as input) thus obtaining $\Pi_{\overrightarrow{\mathcal{OT}}}^\gamma$.

## 2  Definitions and Tools

### 2.1  Preliminaries

We denote the security parameter by $\lambda$ and use "$||$" as concatenation operator (i.e., if $a$ and $b$ are two strings then by $a|b$ we denote the concatenation of $a$ and $b$). For a finite set $Q$, $x \leftarrow Q$ sampling of $x$ from $Q$ with uniform distribution. We use the abbreviation PPT that stays for probabilistic polynomial time. We use $\mathsf{poly}(\cdot)$ to indicate a generic polynomial function.

A *polynomial-time relation* Rel (or *polynomial relation*, in short) is a subset of $\{0, 1\}^* \times \{0, 1\}^*$ such that membership of $(x, w)$ in Rel can be decided in time polynomial in $|x|$. For $(x, w) \in$ Rel, we call $x$ the *instance* and $w$ a *witness* for $x$. For a polynomial-time relation Rel, we define the $\mathcal{NP}$-language $L_{\mathsf{Rel}}$ as $L_{\mathsf{Rel}} = \{x | \exists w : (x, w) \in \mathsf{Rel}\}$. Analogously, unless otherwise specified, for an $\mathcal{NP}$-language $L$ we denote by $\mathsf{Rel}_L$ the corresponding polynomial-time relation (that is, $\mathsf{Rel}_L$ is such that $L = L_{\mathsf{Rel}_L}$). We denote by $\hat{L}$ the language that includes both $L$ and all well formed instances that do not have a witness. Moreover we require that membership in $\hat{L}$ can be tested in polynomial time. We implicitly assume that a PPT algorithm that is supposed to receive an instance in $\hat{L}$ will abort immediately if the instance does not belong to $\hat{L}$.

Let $A$ and $B$ be two interactive probabilistic algorithms. We denote by $\langle A(\alpha), B(\beta) \rangle(\gamma)$ the distribution of $B$'s output after running on private input $\beta$ with $A$ using private input $\alpha$, both running on common input $\gamma$. Typically, one of the two algorithms receives $1^\lambda$ as input. A *transcript* of $\langle A(\alpha), B(\beta) \rangle(\gamma)$ consists of the messages exchanged during an execution where $A$ receives a private input $\alpha$, $B$ receives a private input $\beta$ and both $A$ and $B$ receive a common input $\gamma$. Moreover, we will refer to the *view* of $A$ (resp. $B$) as the messages it received during the execution of $\langle A(\alpha), B(\beta) \rangle(\gamma)$, along with its randomness and its input. We say that a protocol $(A, B)$ is public coin if $B$ sends to $A$ random bits only. When it is necessary to refer to the randomness $r$ used by and algorithm $A$ we use the following notation: $A(\cdot; r)$.

## 2.2 Standard Definitions

**Definition 1 (Trapdoor permutation).** *Let $\mathcal{F}$ be a triple of* PPT *algorithms* (Gen, Eval, Invert) *such that if* $\mathsf{Gen}(1^\lambda)$ *outputs a pair* $(f, \mathsf{td})$*, then* $\mathsf{Eval}(f, \cdot)$ *is a permutation over* $\{0,1\}^\lambda$ *and* $\mathsf{Invert}(f, \mathsf{td}, \cdot)$ *is its inverse.* $\mathcal{F}$ *is a trapdoor permutation such that for all* PPT *adversaries* $\mathcal{A}$:

$$\mathrm{Prob}\left[ (f, \mathsf{td}) \leftarrow \mathsf{Gen}(1^\lambda); y \leftarrow \{0,1\}^\lambda, x \leftarrow \mathcal{A}(f, y) : \mathsf{Eval}(f, x) = y \right] \leq \nu(\lambda).$$

For convenience, we drop $(f, \mathsf{td})$ from the notation, and write $f(\cdot)$, $f^{-1}(\cdot)$ to denote algorithms $\mathsf{Eval}(f, \cdot)$, $\mathsf{Invert}(f, \mathsf{td}, \cdot)$ respectively, when $f$, $\mathsf{td}$ are clear from the context. Following [12,15] we assume that $\mathcal{F}$ satisfies (a weak variant of) "certifiability": namely, given some $f$ it is possible to decide in polynomial time whether $\mathsf{Eval}(f, \cdot)$ is a permutation over $\{0,1\}^\lambda$. Let hc be the hardcore bit function for $\lambda$ bits for the family $\mathcal{F}$. $\lambda$ hardcore bits are obtained from a single-bit hardcore function $h$ and $f \in \mathcal{F}$ as follows: $\mathsf{hc}(z) = h(z)||h(f(z))|| \ldots ||h(f^{\lambda-1}(z))$. Informally, $\mathsf{hc}(z)$ looks pseudorandom given $f^\lambda(z)$[6].

In this paper we also use the notions of $\Sigma$-protocol, zero-knowledge (ZK) argument of knowledge (AoK), non-malleable zero-knowledge, commitment, instance-dependent commitment and garbled circuit. Because of the space constraint we give only an informal descriptions of those notions when is needed in the paper. We refer the reader to the full version [5] for the formal definitions. We also use the adaptive-input version of WI and AoK. The only difference is that in the adaptive version of ZK and AoK, the adversary can chose the statement to be proved (and the corresponding witness in the case of ZK) before that the last round of the protocol is played. For a more thorough treatment of these concepts, see [6,7].

---

[6] $f^\lambda(z)$ means the $\lambda$-th iteration of applying $f$ on $z$.

### 2.3 OR Composition of $\Sigma$-Protocols

In our paper we use the trick for composing two $\Sigma$-protocols to compute the OR of two statements [8,10]. In more details, let $\Pi = (\mathcal{P}, \mathcal{V})$ be a $\Sigma$-protocol for the relation $\mathsf{Rel}_L$ with SHVZK simulator Sim. Then it is possible to use $\Pi$ to construct $\Pi_{OR} = (\mathcal{P}_{OR}, \mathcal{V}_{OR})$ for relation $\mathsf{Rel}_{L_{OR}} = \{((x_0, x_1), w) : ((x_0, w) \in \mathsf{Rel}_L)$ OR $((x_1, w) \in \mathsf{Rel}_L)\}$ that works as follows.

**Protocol $\Pi_{OR} = (\mathcal{P}_{OR}, \mathcal{V}_{OR})$:** $\mathcal{P}_{OR}$ and $\mathcal{V}_{OR}$ on common input $x_0, x_1$ and private input $w$ of $\mathcal{P}_{OR}$ s.t. $((x_0, x_1), w) \in \mathsf{Rel}_{L_{OR}}$ compute the following steps.

- $\mathcal{P}_{OR}$ computes $a_0 \leftarrow \mathcal{P}(1^\lambda, x_0, w)$. Furthermore he picks $c_1 \leftarrow \{0,1\}^\lambda$ and computes $(a_1, z_1) \leftarrow \mathsf{Sim}(1^\lambda, x_1, c_1)$. $\mathcal{P}_{OR}$ sends $a_0, a_1$ to $\mathcal{V}_{OR}$.
- $\mathcal{V}_{OR}$ picks $c \leftarrow \{0,1\}^\lambda$ and sends $c$ to $\mathcal{P}_{OR}$.
- $\mathcal{P}_{OR}$ computes $c_0 = c_1 \oplus c$ and computes $z_0 \leftarrow \mathcal{P}(c_0)$. $\mathcal{P}_{OR}$ sends $c_0, c_1, z_0$ $z_1$ to $\mathcal{V}_{OR}$.
- $\mathcal{V}_{OR}$ checks that $c = c_0 \oplus c_1$ and if $\mathcal{V}(x_0, a_0, c_0, z_0) = 1$ and $\mathcal{V}(x_1, a_1, c_1, z_1) = 1$. If all checks succeed then he outputs 1, otherwise he outputs 0.

**Theorem 1** ([8,10]). $\Pi_{OR} = (\mathcal{P}_{OR}, \mathcal{V}_{OR})$ *is a $\Sigma$-protocol for* $\mathsf{Rel}_{L_{OR}}$, *moreover* $\Pi_{OR}$ *is WI for the relation* $\mathsf{Rel}_{\hat{L}_{OR}} = \{((x_0, x_1), w) : ((x_0, w) \in \mathsf{Rel}_L$ *AND* $x_1 \in L)$ *OR* $((x_1, w) \in \mathsf{Rel}_L$ *AND* $x_0 \in L)\}$.

In our work we use as $\Pi = (\mathcal{P}, \mathcal{V})$ Blum's protocol [2] for the $\mathcal{NP}$-complete language Hamiltonicity (that also is a $\Sigma$-Protocol). We will use the PoK of $\Pi_{OR}$ in a black-box way, but we will rely on the Special HVZK of the underlying $\Pi$ following the approach proposed in [4]. Note that since Hamiltonicity is an $\mathcal{NP}$-complete language, the above construction of $\Pi_{OR}$ works for any $\mathcal{NP}$-language through $\mathcal{NP}$ reductions. For simplicity in the rest of the paper we will omit the $\mathcal{NP}$-reduction therefore assuming that the above scheme works directly on a given $\mathcal{NP}$-language $L$.

### 2.4 Oblivious Transfer

Here we follow [16]. Oblivious Transfer (OT) is a two-party functionality $F_{\mathcal{OT}}$, in which a sender $S$ holds a pair of strings $(l_0, l_1)$, and a receiver $R$ holds a bit $b$, and wants to obtain the string $l_b$. The security requirement for the $F_{\mathcal{OT}}$ functionality is that any malicious receiver does not learn anything about the string $l_{1-b}$ and any malicious sender does not learn which string has been transferred. This security requirement is formalized via the ideal/real world paradigm. In the ideal world, the functionality is implemented by a trusted party that takes the inputs from $S$ and $R$ and provides the output to $R$ and is therefore secure by definition. A real world protocol $\Pi$ securely realizes the ideal $F_{\mathcal{OT}}$ functionalities, if the following two conditions hold. (a) Security against a malicious receiver: the output of any malicious receiver $R^\star$ running one execution of $\Pi$ with an honest sender $S$ can be simulated by a PPT simulator Sim that has only access to the ideal world functionality $F_{\mathcal{OT}}$ and oracle access to $R^\star$. (b) Security against a malicious sender. The joint view of the output of any malicious sender $S^\star$

running one execution of $\Pi$ with $R$ and the output of $R$ can be simulated by a PPT simulator Sim that has only access to the ideal world functionality $F_{OT}$ and oracle access to $S^\star$. In this paper we consider a weaker definition of $F_{OT}$ that is called one-sided simulatable $F_{OT}$, in which we do not demand the existence of a simulator against a malicious sender, but we only require that a malicious sender cannot distinguish whether the honest receiver is playing with bit 0 or 1. A bit more formally, we require that for any PPT malicious sender $S^\star$ the view of $S^\star$ executing $\Pi$ with the $R$ playing with bit 0 is computationally indistinguishable from the view of $S^\star$ where $R$ is playing with bit 1. Finally, we consider the $F_{OT}^m$ functionality where the sender $S$ and the receiver $R$ run $m$ executions of OT in parallel. The formal definitions of one-sided secure $F_{OT}$ and one-sided secure $F_{OT}^m$ follow.

---

### Functionality $F_{OT}$

$F_{OT}$ running with a sender $S$ a receiver $R$ and an adversary Sim proceeds as follows:

- Upon receiving a message (send, $l_0, l_1, S, R$) from $S$ where each $l_0, l_1 \in \{0,1\}^\lambda$, record the tuple $(l_0, l_1)$ and send send to $R$ and Sim. Ignore any subsequent send messages.
- Upon receiving a message (receive, $b$) from R, where $b \in \{0,1\}$ send $l_b$ to $R$ and receive to $S$ and Sim and halt. (If no (send, $\cdot$) message was previously sent, do nothing).

---

**Fig. 4.** The Oblivious Transfer Functionality $F_{OT}$.

**Definition 2** ([16]). *Let $F_{OT}$ be the Oblivious Transfer functionality as shown in Fig. 4. We say that a protocol $\Pi$ securely computes $F_{OT}$ with one-sided simulation if the following holds:*

1. *For every non-uniform PPT adversary $R^\star$ controlling the receiver in the real model, there exists a non-uniform PPT adversary Sim for the ideal model such that $\{\mathsf{REAL}_{\Pi,R^\star(z)}(1^\lambda)\}_{z\in\{0,1\}^\lambda} \approx \{\mathsf{IDEAL}_{f,\mathsf{Sim}(z)}(1^\lambda)\}_{z\in\{0,1\}^\lambda}$, where $\mathsf{REAL}_{\Pi,R^\star(z)}(1^\lambda)$ denotes the distribution of the output of the adversary $R^\star$ (controlling the receiver) after a real execution of protocol $\Pi$, where the sender $S$ has inputs $l_0, l_1$ and the receiver has input $b$. $\mathsf{IDEAL}_{f,\mathsf{Sim}(z)}(1^\lambda)$ denotes the analogous distribution in an ideal execution with a trusted party that computes $F_{OT}$ for the parties and hands the output to the receiver.*
2. *For every non-uniform PPT adversary $S^\star$ controlling the sender it holds that: $\{\mathsf{View}_{\Pi,S^\star(z)}^R(l_0,l_1,0)\}_{z\in\{0,1\}^\star} \approx \{\mathsf{View}_{\Pi,S^\star(z)}^R(l_0,l_1,1)\}_{z\in\{0,1\}^\star}$, where $\mathsf{View}_{\Pi,S^\star(z)}^R$ denotes the view of adversary $S^\star$ after a real execution of protocol $\Pi$ with the honest receiver $R$.*

**Definition 3 (Parallel oblivious transfer functionality $F_{\mathcal{OT}}^m$ [16]).** *The parallel Oblivious Transfer Functionality $F_{\mathcal{OT}}^m$ is identical to the functionality $F_{\mathcal{OT}}$, with the difference that takes in input $m$ pairs of string from S $(l_0^1, l_1^1, \ldots, l_0^m, l_1^m)$ (whereas $F_{\mathcal{OT}}$ takes just one pair of strings from S) and $m$ bits from R, $b_1, \ldots, b_m$ (whereas $F_{\mathcal{OT}}$ takes one bit from R) and outputs to the receiver values $(l_{b_1}^1, \ldots, l_{b_m}^m)$ while the sender receives nothing.*

**Definition 4 ([16]).** *Let $F_{\mathcal{OT}}^m$ be the Oblivious Transfer functionality as described in Definition 3. We say that a protocol $\Pi$ securely computes $F_{\mathcal{OT}}^m$ with one-sided simulation if the following holds[7]:*

1. *For every non-uniform PPT adversary $R^\star$ controlling the receiver in the real model, there exists a non-uniform PPT adversary Sim for the ideal model such that for every $x_1 \in \{0,1\}, \ldots, x_m \in \{0,1\}$ it holds that*
   $\{\mathsf{REAL}_{\Pi, R^\star(z)}(1^\lambda, (l_0^1, l_1^1, \ldots, l_0^m, l_1^m), (x_1, \ldots, x_m))\}_{z \in \{0,1\}^\lambda} \approx$
   $\mathsf{IDEAL}_{f, \mathsf{Sim}(z)}(1^\lambda), (l_0^1, l_1^1, \ldots, l_0^m, l_1^m), (x_1, \ldots, x_m))\}_{z \in \{0,1\}^\lambda}$
   *where $\mathsf{REAL}_{\Pi, R^\star(z)}(1^\lambda)$ denotes the distribution of the output of the adversary $R^\star$ (controlling the receiver) after a real execution of protocol $\Pi$, where the sender S has inputs $(l_0^1, l_1^1, \ldots, l_0^m, l_1^m)$ and the receiver has input $(x_1, \ldots, x_m)$. $\mathsf{IDEAL}_{f, \mathsf{Sim}(z)}(1^\lambda)$ denotes the analogous distribution in an ideal execution with a trusted party that computes $F_{\mathcal{OT}}^m$ for the parties and hands the output to the receiver.*

2. *For every non-uniform PPT adversary $S^\star$ controlling the sender it holds that for every $x_1 \in \{0,1\}, \ldots, x_m \in \{0,1\}$ and for every $y_1 \in \{0,1\}, \ldots, y_m \in \{0,1\}$: $\{\mathsf{View}_{\Pi, S^\star(z)}^R((l_0^1, l_1^1, \ldots, l_0^m, l_1^m), (x_1, \ldots, x_m))\}_{z \in \{0,1\}^\star} \approx \{\mathsf{View}_{\Pi, S^\star(z)}^R ((l_0^1, l_1^1, \ldots, l_0^m, l_1^m), (y_1, \ldots, y_m))\}_{z \in \{0,1\}^\star}$, where $\mathsf{View}_{\Pi, S^\star(z)}^R$ denotes the view of adversary $S^\star$ after a real execution of protocol $\Pi$ with the honest receiver R.*

# 3  Our OT Protocol $\Pi_{\mathcal{OT}}^\gamma = (S_{\mathcal{OT}}, R_{\mathcal{OT}})$

We use the following tools.

1. A non-interactive perfectly binding, computationally hiding commitment scheme $\mathsf{PBCOM} = (\mathsf{Com}, \mathsf{Dec})$.
2. A trapdoor permutation $\mathcal{F} = (\mathsf{Gen}, \mathsf{Eval}, \mathsf{Invert})$[8] with the hardcore bit function for $\lambda$ bits $\mathsf{hc}(\cdot)$ (see Definition 1).
3. A non-interactive IDTC scheme $\mathsf{TC}_0 = (\mathsf{Sen}_0, \mathsf{Rec}_0, \mathsf{TFake}_0)$[9] for the $\mathcal{NP}$-language $L_0 = \{\mathsf{com} : \exists\, \mathsf{dec}\ \text{s.t.}\ \mathsf{Dec}(\mathsf{com}, \mathsf{dec}, 0) = 1\}$.

---

[7] We remark that in this notions of OT we do not suppose the existence of a simultaneous message exchange channel.

[8] We recall that for convenience, we drop $(f, \mathsf{td})$ from the notation, and write $f(\cdot)$, $f^{-1}(\cdot)$ to denote algorithms $\mathsf{Eval}(f, \cdot)$, $\mathsf{Invert}(f, \mathsf{td}, \cdot)$ respectively, when $f$, $\mathsf{td}$ are clear from the context. Also we omit the generalization to a family of TDPs.

[9] For the IDTCom we use following notation. (1) Commitment phase: $(\mathsf{com}, \mathsf{dec}) \leftarrow \mathsf{Sen}(m, 1^\lambda, x)$ denotes that $\mathsf{com}$ is the commitment of the message $m$ and $\mathsf{dec}$ represents the corresponding decommitment information. (2) Decommitment phase: $1 \leftarrow \mathsf{Rec}(m, x, \mathsf{com}, \mathsf{dec})$. (3) Trapdoor algorithms: $(\mathsf{com}, \mathsf{aux}) \leftarrow \mathsf{TFake}(1^\lambda, x)$, $\mathsf{dec} \leftarrow \mathsf{TFake}(\mathsf{tk}, x, \mathsf{com}, \mathsf{aux}, m)$ with $(x, \mathsf{tk}) \in \mathsf{Rel}_L$.

4. A non-interactive IDTC scheme $\mathsf{TC}_1 = (\mathsf{Sen}_1, \mathsf{Rec}_1, \mathsf{TFake}_1)$ for the $\mathcal{NP}$-language $L_1 = \{\mathsf{com} : \exists\ \mathsf{dec}\ \text{s.t.}\ \mathsf{Dec}(\mathsf{com}, \mathsf{dec}, 1) = 1\}$.

Let $b \in \{0, 1\}$ be the input of $R_{\mathcal{OT}}$ and $l_0, l_1 \in \{0, 1\}^\lambda$ be the input of $S_{\mathcal{OT}}$, we now give the description of our protocol following Fig. 5.

In the **first round** $R_{\mathcal{OT}}$ runs $\mathsf{Com}$ on input the message to be committed $b$ in order to obtain the pair $(\mathsf{com}, \mathsf{dec})$. On input the instance $\mathsf{com}$ and a random string $r_{b-1}^1$, $R_{\mathcal{OT}}$ runs $\mathsf{Sen}_{1-b}$ in order to compute the pair $(\mathsf{tcom}_{1-b}, \mathsf{tdec}_{1-b})$. We observe that the *Instance-Dependent Binding* property of the IDTCs, the escription of the $\mathcal{NP}$-language $L_{1-b}$ and the fact that in $\mathsf{com}$ the bit $b$ has been committed, ensure that $\mathsf{tcom}_{1-b}$ can be opened only to the value $r_{b-1}^1$.[10] $R_{\mathcal{OT}}$ runs the trapdoor procedure of the IDTC scheme $\mathsf{TC}_b$. More precisely $R_{\mathcal{OT}}$ runs $\mathsf{TFake}_b$ on input the instance $\mathsf{com}$ to compute the pair $(\mathsf{tcom}_b, \mathsf{aux})$. In this case $\mathsf{tcom}_b$ can be equivocated to any message using the trapdoor (the opening information of $\mathsf{com}$), due to the trapdoorness of the IDTC, the description of the $\mathcal{NP}$-language $L_b$ and the message committed in $\mathsf{com}$ (that is represented by the bit $b$). $R_{\mathcal{OT}}$ sends $\mathsf{tcom}_0$, $\mathsf{tcom}_1$ and $\mathsf{com}$ to $S_{\mathcal{OT}}$.

In the **second round** $S_{\mathcal{OT}}$ picks two random strings $R_0$, $R_1$ and two trapdoor permutations $(f_{0,1}, f_{1,1})$ along with their trapdoors $(f_{0,1}^{-1}, f_{1,1}^{-1})$. Then $S_{\mathcal{OT}}$ sends $R_0$, $R_1$, $f_{0,1}$ and $f_{1,1}$ to $R_{\mathcal{OT}}$.

In the **third round** $R_{\mathcal{OT}}$ checks whether or not $f_{0,1}$ and $f_{1,1}$ are valid trapdoor permutations. In the negative case $R_{\mathcal{OT}}$ aborts, otherwise $R_{\mathcal{OT}}$ continues with the following steps. $R_{\mathcal{OT}}$ picks a random string $z_1'$ and computes $z_1 = f(z_1')$. $R_{\mathcal{OT}}$ now computes $r_b^1 = z_1 \oplus R_b$ and runs $\mathsf{TFake}_b$ on input $\mathsf{dec}$, $\mathsf{com}$, $\mathsf{tcom}_b$, $\mathsf{aux}$ and $r_b^1$ in order to obtain the equivocal opening $\mathsf{tdec}_b$ of the commitment $\mathsf{tcom}_b$ to the message $r_b^1$. $R_{\mathcal{OT}}$ renames $r_b$ to $r_b^1$ and $\mathsf{tdec}_b$ to $\mathsf{tdec}_b^1$ and sends to $S_{\mathcal{OT}}$ $(\mathsf{tdec}_0^1, r_0^1)$ and $(\mathsf{tdec}_1^1, r_1^1)$.

In the **fourth round** $S_{\mathcal{OT}}$ checks whether or not $(\mathsf{tdec}_0^1, r_0^1)$ and $(\mathsf{tdec}_1^1, r_1^1)$ are valid openings w.r.t. $\mathsf{tcom}_0$ and $\mathsf{tcom}_1$. In the negative case $S_{\mathcal{OT}}$ aborts, otherwise $S_{\mathcal{OT}}$ computes $W_0^1 = l_0 \oplus \mathsf{hc}(f_{0,1}^{-\lambda}(r_0^1 \oplus R_0))$ and $W_1^1 = l_1 \oplus \mathsf{hc}(f_{1,1}^{-\lambda}(r_1^1 \oplus R_1))$. Informally $S_{\mathcal{OT}}$ encrypts his inputs $l_0$ and $l_1$ through a one-time pad using as a secret key the pre-image of $r_0^1 \oplus R_0$ for $l_0$ and the pre-image of $r_1^1 \oplus R_1$ for $l_1$. $S_{\mathcal{OT}}$ also computes two trapdoor permutations $(f_{0,2}, f_{1,2})$ along with their trapdoors $(f_{0,2}^{-1}, f_{1,2}^{-1})$ and sends $(W_0^1, W_1^1, f_{0,2}, f_{1,2})$ to $R_{\mathcal{OT}}$. At this point the third and the fourth rounds are repeated up to $\gamma - 1$ times using fresh randomness as showed in Fig. 5. In the last round no trapdoor permutation is needed/sent.

In the **output phase**, $R_{\mathcal{OT}}$ computes and outputs $l_b = W_b^1 \oplus \mathsf{hc}(z_1')$. That is, $R_{\mathcal{OT}}$ just uses the information gained in the first four rounds to compute the output. It is important to observe that $R_{\mathcal{OT}}$ can correctly and efficiently compute the output because $z' = r_b^1 \oplus R_b$. Moreover $R_{\mathcal{OT}}$ cannot compute $l_{1-b}$ because he has no way to change the value committed in $\mathsf{tcom}_{1-b}$ and invert the TDP is suppose to be hard without having the trapdoor.

In order to construct our protocol for two-party computation in the simultaneous message exchange model we need to consider an extended version of $\Pi_{\mathcal{OT}}^\gamma$,

---

[10] $\mathsf{com}$ does not belong to the $\mathcal{NP}$-language $L_{b-1}$, therefore $\mathsf{tcom}_{1-b}$ is perfectly binding.

$R_{\mathcal{OT}}(b)$                                                                           $S_{\mathcal{OT}}(l_0, l_1)$

$(\mathsf{com}, \mathsf{dec}) \leftarrow \mathsf{Com}(1^\lambda, b);$
$(\mathsf{tcom}_b, \mathsf{aux}) \leftarrow \mathsf{TFake}_b(1^\lambda, \mathsf{com});$
$r_{1-b} \leftarrow \{0,1\}^\lambda;$
$(\mathsf{tcom}_{1-b}, \mathsf{tdec}_{1-b}) \leftarrow \mathsf{Sen}_{1-b}(1^\lambda, r_{1-b}, \mathsf{com}).$

$\xrightarrow{\mathsf{com}, \mathsf{tcom}_0, \mathsf{tcom}_1}$

$R_0 \leftarrow \{0,1\}^\lambda;$
$R_1 \leftarrow \{0,1\}^\lambda;$
$(f_{0,1}, f_{0,1}^{-1}) \leftarrow \mathsf{Gen}(1^\lambda);$
$(f_{1,1}, f_{1,1}^{-1}) \leftarrow \mathsf{Gen}(1^\lambda).$

$\xleftarrow{R_0, R_1, f_{0,1}, f_{1,1}}$

$z_1' \leftarrow \{0,1\}^\lambda;$
$z_1 = f_b^\lambda(z_1');$
$r_b^1 = z_1 \oplus R_b;$
$\mathsf{tdec}_b^1 \leftarrow \mathsf{TFake}_b(\mathsf{dec}, \mathsf{com}, \mathsf{tcom}_b, \mathsf{aux}, r_b^1);$
$\mathsf{tdec}_{1-b}^1 = \mathsf{tdec}_{1-b}, r_{1-b}^1 = r_{1-b}.$

$\xrightarrow{(\mathsf{tdec}_0^1, r_0^1), (\mathsf{tdec}_1^1, r_1^1)}$

$(f_{0,2}, f_{0,2}^{-1}) \leftarrow \mathsf{Gen}(1^\lambda);$
$(f_{1,2}, f_{1,2}^{-1}) \leftarrow \mathsf{Gen}(1^\lambda);$
$W_0^1 = l_0 \oplus \mathsf{hc}(f_{0,1}^{-\lambda}(r_0^1 \oplus R_0));$
$W_1^1 = l_1 \oplus \mathsf{hc}(f_{1,1}^{-\lambda}(r_1^1 \oplus R_1)).$

$\xleftarrow{W_0^1, W_1^1, f_{0,2}, f_{1,2}}$

$z_2' \leftarrow \{0,1\}^\lambda;$
$z_2 = f_b^\lambda(z_2');$
$r_b^2 = z_2 \oplus R_b;$
$\mathsf{tdec}_b^2 \leftarrow \mathsf{TFake}_b(\mathsf{dec}, \mathsf{com}, \mathsf{tcom}_b, \mathsf{aux}, r_b^2);$
$\mathsf{tdec}_{1-b}^2 = \mathsf{tdec}_{1-b}, r_{1-b}^2 = r_{1-b}.$

$\xrightarrow{(\mathsf{tdec}_0^2, r_0^2), (\mathsf{tdec}_1^2, r_1^2)}$

$(f_{0,3}, f_{0,3}^{-1}) \leftarrow \mathsf{Gen}(1^\lambda);$
$(f_{1,3}, f_{1,3}^{-1}) \leftarrow \mathsf{Gen}(1^\lambda);$
$W_0^2 = l_0 \oplus \mathsf{hc}(f_{0,2}^{-\lambda}(r_0^2 \oplus R_0));$
$W_1^2 = l_1 \oplus \mathsf{hc}(f_{1,2}^{-\lambda}(r_1^2 \oplus R_1)).$

$\xleftarrow{W_0^2, W_1^2, f_{0,3}, f_{1,3}}$

.
.
.

$\xrightarrow{(\mathsf{tdec}_0^\gamma, r_0^\gamma), (\mathsf{tdec}_1^\gamma, r_1^\gamma)}$

$\xleftarrow{W_0^\gamma, W_1^\gamma}$

Output $l_b = W_b^1 \oplus \mathsf{hc}(z_1').$

**Fig. 5.** Description of $\Pi_{\mathcal{OT}}^\gamma$.

that we denote by $\Pi_{\overrightarrow{\mathcal{OT}}}^\gamma = (S_{\overrightarrow{\mathcal{OT}}}, R_{\overrightarrow{\mathcal{OT}}})$. In $\Pi_{\overrightarrow{\mathcal{OT}}}^\gamma$ the $S_{\overrightarrow{\mathcal{OT}}}$'s input is represented by $m$ pairs $(l_0^1, l_1^1, \ldots, l_0^m, l_1^m)$ and the $R_{\overrightarrow{\mathcal{OT}}}$'s input is represented by the sequence $b_1, \ldots, b_m$ with $b_i \in \{0,1\}$ for all $i = 1, \ldots, m$. In this case the output of $R_{\overrightarrow{\mathcal{OT}}}$ is $(l_{b_1}, \ldots, l_{b_m})$. We construct $\Pi_{\overrightarrow{\mathcal{OT}}}^\gamma = (S_{\overrightarrow{\mathcal{OT}}}, R_{\overrightarrow{\mathcal{OT}}})$ by simply considering $m$ parallel iterations of $\Pi_{\mathcal{OT}}^\gamma$ and then we prove that it securely computes $F_{\mathcal{OT}}^m$ with one-sided simulation (see Definition 4).

*Proof sketch.* The security proof of $\Pi_{\mathcal{OT}}^{\gamma}$ is divided in two parts. In the former we prove the security against a malicious sender and in the latter we prove the security of $\Pi_{\mathcal{OT}}^{\gamma}$ against a malicious receiver. In order to prove the security against malicious sender we recall that for the definition of one-sided simulation it is just needed the no information about $R$'s input is leaked to $S^\star$. We consider the experiment $H_0$ where $R$'s input is 0 and the experiment $H_1$ where $R$'s input is 1 and we prove that $S^\star$ cannot distinguish between $H_0$ and $H_1$. More precisely we consider the experiment $H^a$ where $\mathsf{tcom}_0$ and the corresponding opening is computed without using the trapdoor (the randomness of $\mathsf{com}$) and relying on the trapdoorness of the IDTCom $\mathsf{TC}_0$ we prove that $H_0 \approx H^a$. Then we consider the experiment $H^b$ where the value committed in $\mathsf{com}$ goes from 0 to 1 and prove that $H^a \approx H^b$ due to the hiding of $\mathsf{com}$. We observe that this reduction can be made because to compute both $H^a$ and $H^b$ the opening informations of $\mathsf{com}$ are not required anymore. The proof ends with the observation the $H^b \approx H_1$ due to the trapdoorness of the IDTCom $\mathsf{TC}_1$. To prove the security against a malicious receiver $R^\star$ we need to show a simulator $\mathsf{Sim}$. $\mathsf{Sim}$ rewinds $R^\star$ from the third to the second round by sending every time freshly generated $R_0$ and $R_1$. $\mathsf{Sim}$ then checks whether the values $r_0^1$ and $r_1^1$ change during the rewinds. We recall that $\mathsf{com}$ is a perfectly binging commitment, therefore only one between $\mathsf{tcom}_0$ and $\mathsf{tcom}_1$ can be opened to multiple values using the trapdoor procedure ($\mathsf{com}$ can belong only to one of the $\mathcal{NP}$-languages $L_0$ and $L_1$). Moreover, intuitively, the only way that $R^\star$ can compute the output is by equivocating one between $\mathsf{tcom}_0$ and $\mathsf{tcom}_1$ based on the values $R_0, R_1$ received in the second round. This means that if during the rewinds the value opened w.r.t. $\mathsf{tcom}_b$ changes, then the input that $R^\star$ is using is $b$. Therefore the simulator can call the ideal functionality thus obtaining $l_b$. At this point $\mathsf{Sim}$ uses $l_b$ to compute $W_b^1$ according to the description of $\Pi_{\mathcal{OT}}^{\gamma}$ and sets $W_{1-b}^1$ to a random string. Moreover $\mathsf{Sim}$ will use the same strategy used to compute $W_b^1$ and $W_{1-b}^1$ to compute, respectively $W_b^i$ and $W_{1-b}^i$ for $i = 2, \ldots, \gamma$. In case during the rewinds the value $r_0^1, r_1^1$ stay the same, then $\mathsf{Sim}$ sets both $W_0^1$ and $W_1^1$ to random strings. We observe that $R^\star$ could detect that now $W_0^1$ and $W_1^1$ are computed in a different way, but this would violate the security of the TDPs.

**Theorem 2.** *Assuming TDPs, for any $\gamma > 0$ $\Pi_{\mathcal{OT}}^{\gamma}$ securely computes $F_{\mathcal{OT}}$ with one-sided simulation. Moreover the third round is* replayable.

*Proof.* We first observe that in third round of $\Pi_{\mathcal{OT}}^{\gamma}$ only the opening information for the IDTCs $\mathsf{tcom}_0$ and $\mathsf{tcom}_1$ are sent. Therefore once that a valid third round is received, it is possible to replay it in order to answer to many second rounds sent by a malicious sender. Roughly, whether the third round of $\Pi_{\mathcal{OT}}^{\gamma}$ is accepting or not is independent of what a malicious sender sends in the second round. Therefore we have proved that $\Pi_{\mathcal{OT}}^{\gamma}$ has a *replayable* third round. In order to prove that $\Pi_{\mathcal{OT}}^{\gamma}$ is one-sided simulatable secure for $F_{\mathcal{OT}}$ (see Definition 2) we divide the security proof in two parts; the former proves the security against a malicious sender, and the latter proves the security against a malicious receiver. More precisely we prove that $\Pi_{\mathcal{OT}}^{\gamma}$ is secure against a malicious receiver for an arbitrary chosen $\gamma = \mathsf{poly}(\lambda)$, and is secure against malicious sender for $\gamma = 1$ (i.e. when just the first four rounds of the protocol are executed).

*Security against a malicious sender.* In this case we just need to prove that the output of $S^\star_{\mathcal{OT}}$ of the execution of $\varPi^\gamma_{\mathcal{OT}}$ when $R_{\mathcal{OT}}$ interacts with $S^\star_{\mathcal{OT}}$ using $b = 0$ as input is computationally indistinguishable from when $R_{\mathcal{OT}}$ uses $b = 1$ as input. The differences between these two hybrid experiments consist of the message committed in com and the way in which the IDTCs are computed. More precisely, in the first experiment, when $b = 0$ is used as input, $\mathsf{tcom}_0$ and the corresponding opening $(\mathsf{tdec}^1_0, r^1_0)$ are computed using the trapdoor procedure (in this case the message committed in com is 0), while $\mathsf{tcom}_1$ and $(\mathsf{tdec}^1_1, r^1_1)$ are computed using the *honest* procedure. In the second experiment, $\mathsf{tcom}_0$ and the respective opening $(\mathsf{tdec}^1_0, r^1_0)$ are computed using the honest procedure, while $\mathsf{tcom}_1$ and $(\mathsf{tdec}^1_1, r^1_1)$ are computed using the trapdoor procedure of the IDTC scheme. In order to prove the indistinguishability between these two experiments we proceed via hybrid arguments. The first hybrid experiment $\mathcal{H}_1$ is equal to when $R_{\mathcal{OT}}$ interacts with against $S^\star_{\mathcal{OT}}$ according $\varPi^\gamma_{\mathcal{OT}}$ when $b = 0$ is used as input. In $\mathcal{H}_2$ the honest procedure of IDTC is used instead of the trapdoor one in order to compute $\mathsf{tcom}_0$ and the opening $(\mathsf{tdec}^1_0, r^1_0)$. We observe that in $\mathcal{H}_2$ both the IDTCs are computed using the honest procedure, therefore no trapdoor information (i.e. the randomness used to compute com) is required. The computational-indistinguishability between $\mathcal{H}_1$ and $\mathcal{H}_2$ comes from the trapdoorness of the IDTC $\mathsf{TC}_0$. In $\mathcal{H}_3$ the value committed in com goes from 0 to 1. $\mathcal{H}_2$ and $\mathcal{H}_3$ are indistinguishable due to the hiding of PBCOM. It is important to observe that a reduction to the hiding of PBCOM is possible because the randomness used to compute com is no longer used in the protocol execution to run one of the IDTCs. In the last hybrid experiment $\mathcal{H}_4$ the trapdoor procedure is used in order to compute $\mathsf{tcom}_1$ and the opening $(\mathsf{tdec}^1_1, r^1_1)$. We observe that it is possible to run the trapdoor procedure for $\mathsf{TC}_1$ because the message committed in com is 1. The indistinguishability between $\mathcal{H}_3$ and $\mathcal{H}_4$ comes from the trapdoorness of the IDTC. The observation that $\mathcal{H}_4$ corresponds to the experiment where the honest receiver executes $\varPi^\gamma_{\mathcal{OT}}$ using $b = 1$ as input concludes the security proof.

*Security against a malicious receiver.* In order to prove that $\varPi^\gamma_{\mathcal{OT}}$ is simulation-based secure against malicious receiver $R^\star_{\mathcal{OT}}$ we need to show a PPT simulator Sim that, having only access to the ideal world functionality $\mathcal{F}_{\mathcal{OT}}$, can simulate the output of any malicious $R^\star_{\mathcal{OT}}$ running one execution of $\varPi^\gamma_{\mathcal{OT}}$ with an honest sender $S_{\mathcal{OT}}$. The simulator Sim works as follows. Having oracle access to $R^\star_{\mathcal{OT}}$, Sim runs as a sender in $\varPi^\gamma_{\mathcal{OT}}$ by sending two random strings $R_0$ and $R_1$ and the pair of TDPs $f_{0,1}$ and $f_{1,1}$ in the second round. Let $(\mathsf{tdec}^1_0, r^1_0), (\mathsf{tdec}^1_1, r^1_1)$ be the messages sent in the third round by $R^\star_{\mathcal{OT}}$. Now Sim rewinds $R^\star_{\mathcal{OT}}$ by sending two fresh random strings $\overline{R}_0$ and $\overline{R}_1$ such that $\overline{R}_0 \neq R_0$ and $\overline{R}_1 \neq R_1$.

Let $(\overline{\mathtt{tdec}}_0^1, \overline{r}_0^1), (\overline{\mathtt{tdec}}_1^1, \overline{r}_1^1)$ be the messages sent in the third round by $R^\star_{\mathcal{OT}}$ after this rewind, then there are only two things that can happen[11]:

1. $r_{b^\star}^1 \neq \overline{r}_{b^\star}^1$ and $r_{1-b^\star}^1 = \overline{r}_{1-b^\star}^1$ for some $b^\star \in \{0,1\}$ or
2. $r_0^1 = \overline{r}_0^1$ and $r_1^1 = \overline{r}_1^1$.

More precisely, due to the perfect binding of PBCOM at most one between $\mathtt{tcom}_0$ and $\mathtt{tcom}_1$ can be opened to a different message. Therefore $R^\star_{\mathcal{OT}}$ can either open both $\mathtt{tcom}_0$ and $\mathtt{tcom}_1$ to the same messages $r_0^1$ and $r_1^1$, or change in the opening at most one of them. This yields to the following important observation. If one among $r_0^1$ and $r_1^1$ changes during the rewind, let us say $r_{b^\star}$ for $b^\star \in \{0,1\}$ (case 1), then the input bit used by $R^\star_{\mathcal{OT}}$ has to be $b^\star$. Indeed we recall that the only efficient way (i.e. without inverting the TDP) for a receiver to get the output is to equivocate one of the IDTCs in order to compute the inverse of one between $R_0 \oplus r_0^1$ and $R_1 \oplus r_1^1$. Therefore the simulator invokes the ideal world functionality $F_{\mathcal{OT}}$ using $b^\star$ as input, and upon receiving $l_{b^\star}$ computes $W_{b^\star}^1 = l_{b^\star} \oplus \mathsf{hc}(f_{b^\star,1}^{-\lambda}(r_{b^\star}^1 \oplus R_{b^\star}))$ and sets $W_{1-b^\star}^1$ to a random string. Then sends $W_0^1$ and $W_1^1$ with two freshly generated TDPs $f_{0,2}, f_{1,2}$ (according to the description of $\Pi^\gamma_{\mathcal{OT}}$ given in Fig. 5) to $R^\star_{\mathcal{OT}}$. Let us now consider the case where the opening of $\mathtt{tcom}_0$ and $\mathtt{tcom}_1$ stay the same after the rewinding procedure (case two). In this case, Sim comes back to the main thread and sets both $W_0^1$ and $W_1^1$ to a random string. Intuitively if $R^\star_{\mathcal{OT}}$ does not change neither $r_0^1$ nor $r_1^1$ after the rewind, then his behavior is not adaptive on the second round sent by Sim. Therefore, he will be able to compute the inverse of neither $R_0 \oplus r_0^1$ nor $R_1 \oplus r_1^1$. That is, both $R_0 \oplus r_0^1$ and $R_1 \oplus r_1^1$ would be the results of the execution of two coin-flipping protocols, therefore both of them are difficult to invert without knowing the trapdoors of the TDPs. This implies that $R^\star_{\mathcal{OT}}$ has no efficient way to tells apart whether $W_0^1$ and $W_1^1$ are random strings or not.

Completed the fourth round, for $i = 2, \ldots, \gamma$, Sim continues the interaction with $R^\star_{\mathcal{OT}}$ by always setting both $W_0^i$ and $W_1^i$ to a random string when $r_0^1 = r_0^i$ and $r_1^1 = r_1^i$, and using the following strategy when $r_{b^\star}^1 \neq r_{b^\star}^i$ and $r_{1-b^\star}^1 = r_{1-b^\star}^i$ for some $b^\star \in \{0,1\}$. Sim invokes the ideal world functionality $F_{\mathcal{OT}}$ using $b^\star$ as input, and upon receiving $l_{b^\star}$ computes $W_{b^\star}^i = l_{b^\star} \oplus \mathsf{hc}(f_{b^\star,i}^{-\lambda}(r_{b^\star}^i \oplus R_{b^\star}))$, sets $W_{1-b^\star}^i$ to a random string and sends with them two freshly generated TDPs $f_{0,i+1}, f_{1,i+1}$ to $R^\star_{\mathcal{OT}}$. When the interaction against $R^\star_{\mathcal{OT}}$ is over, Sim stops and outputs what $R^\star_{\mathcal{OT}}$ outputs. We observe that the simulator needs to invoke the ideal world functionality just once. Indeed, we recall that only one of the IDTCs can be equivocated, therefore once that the bit $b^\star$ is decided (using the strategy described before) it cannot change during the simulation. The last thing that remains to observe is that it could happen that Sim never needs to invoke the ideal world functionality in the case that: (1) during the rewind the values $(r_0^1, r_1^1)$ stay the same; (2) $r_b^i = r_b^j$ for all $i, j \in \{1, \ldots, \gamma\}$ and $b = \{0,1\}$. In this case Sim never outputs the bit $b^\star$ that corresponds to the $R^\star_{\mathcal{OT}}$'s input. That

---

[11] $R^\star_{\mathcal{OT}}$ could also abort after the rewind. In this case we use the following standard argument. If $p$ is the probability of $R^\star_{\mathcal{OT}}$ of giving an accepting third round, $\lambda/p$ rewinds are made until $R^\star_{\mathcal{OT}}$ gives another answer.

is, even though Sim is sufficient to prove that $\Pi_{\mathcal{OT}}^\gamma$ is simulation-based secure against malicious receiver, it is insufficient to extract the input from $R_{\mathcal{OT}}^\star$. We formally prove that the output of Sim is computationally indistinguishable from the output of $R_{\mathcal{OT}}^\star$ in the real world execution for every $\gamma = \mathsf{poly}(\lambda)$. The proof goes trough hybrid arguments starting from the real world execution. We gradually modify the real world execution until the input of the honest party is not needed anymore such that the final hybrid would represent the simulator for the ideal world. We denote by $\mathsf{OUT}_{\mathcal{H}_i, R_{\mathcal{OT}}^\star(z)}(1^\lambda)$ the output distribution of $R_{\mathcal{OT}}^\star$ in the hybrid experiment $\mathcal{H}_i$.

-$\mathcal{H}_0$ is identical to the real execution. More precisely $\mathcal{H}_0$ runs $R_{\mathcal{OT}}^\star$ using fresh randomness and interacts with him as the honest sender would do on input $(l_0, l_1)$.

-$\mathcal{H}_0^{\mathsf{rew}}$ proceeds according to $\mathcal{H}_0$ with the difference that $R_{\mathcal{OT}}^\star$ is rewound up to the second round by receiving two fresh random strings $\overline{R}_0$ and $\overline{R}_1$. This process is repeated until $R_{\mathcal{OT}}^\star$ completes the third round again (every time using different randomness). More precisely, if $R_{\mathcal{OT}}^\star$ aborts after the rewind then a fresh second round is sent up to $\lambda/p$ times, where $p$ is the probability of $R_{\mathcal{OT}}^\star$ of completing the third round in $\mathcal{H}_0$. If $p = \mathsf{poly}(\lambda)$ then the expected running time of $\mathcal{H}^{\mathsf{rew}}$ is $\mathsf{poly}(\lambda)$ and its output is statistically close to the output of $\mathcal{H}_0$. When the third round is completed the hybrid experiment comes back to the main thread and continues according to $\mathcal{H}_0$

-$\mathcal{H}_1$ proceeds according to $\mathcal{H}_0^{\mathsf{rew}}$ with the difference that after the rewinds executes the following steps. Let $r_0^1$ and $r_1^1$ be the messages opened by $R_{\mathcal{OT}}^\star$ in the third round of the main thread and $\overline{r}_0^1$ and $\overline{r}_1^1$ be the messages opened during the rewind. We distinguish two cases that could happen:

1. $r_0^1 = \overline{r}_0^1$ and $r_1^1 = \overline{r}_1^1$ or
2. $r_{b^\star}^1 \neq \overline{r}_{b^\star}^1$ and $\overline{r}_{1-b^\star}^1 = r_{1-b^\star}^1$ for some $b^\star \in \{0,1\}$.

In this hybrid we assume that the first case happen with non-negligible probability. After the rewind $\mathcal{H}_1$ goes back to the main thread, and in order to compute the fourth round, picks $W_0^1 \leftarrow \{0,1\}^\lambda$ computes $W_1^1 = l_1 \oplus \mathsf{hc}(f_{1,1}^{-\lambda}(r_1^1 \oplus R_1))$, $(f_{0,2}, f_{0,2}^{-1}) \leftarrow \mathsf{Gen}(1^\lambda)$, $(f_{1,2}, f_{1,2}^{-1}) \leftarrow \mathsf{Gen}(1^\lambda)$ and sends $(W_0^1, W_1^1, f_{0,2}, f_{1,2})$ to $R_{\mathcal{OT}}^\star$. Then the experiment continues according to $\mathcal{H}_0$. Roughly, the difference between $\mathcal{H}_0$ and $\mathcal{H}_1$ is that in the latter hybrid experiment $W_0^1$ is a random string whereas in $\mathcal{H}_1$ $W_0^1 = l_0 \oplus \mathsf{hc}(f_{0,1}^{-\lambda}(r_0^1 \oplus R_0))$. We now prove that the indistinguishability between $\mathcal{H}_0$ and $\mathcal{H}_1$ comes from the security of the hardcore bit function for $\lambda$ bits $\mathsf{hc}$ for the TDP $\mathcal{F}$. More precisely, assuming by contradiction that the outputs of $\mathcal{H}_0$ and $\mathcal{H}_1$ are distinguishable we construct and adversary $\mathcal{A}^\mathcal{F}$ that distinguishes between the output of $\mathsf{hc}(x)$ and a random string of $\lambda$ bits having as input $f^\lambda(x)$. Consider an execution where $R_{\mathcal{OT}}^\star$ has non-negligible advantage in distinguishing $\mathcal{H}_0$ from $\mathcal{H}_1$ and consider the randomness $\rho$ used by $R_{\mathcal{OT}}^\star$ and the first round computed by $R_{\mathcal{OT}}^\star$ in this execution, let us say $\mathsf{com}, \mathsf{tcom}_0, \mathsf{tcom}_1$. $\mathcal{A}^\mathcal{F}$, on input the randomness $\rho$, the messages $r_0^1$ and $r_1^1$ executes the following steps.

1. Start $R^\star_{\mathcal{OT}}$ with randomness $\rho$.
2. Let $(f, H, f^\lambda(x))$ be the challenge. Upon receiving the first round $(\mathsf{com}, \mathsf{tcom}_0, \mathsf{tcom}_1)$ by $R^\star_{\mathcal{OT}}$, compute $R_0 = r^1_0 \oplus f^\lambda(x)$, pick a random string $R_1$, compute $(f_{1,1}, f^{-1}_{1,1}) \leftarrow \mathsf{Gen}(1^\lambda)$, set $f_{0,1} = f$ and sends $R_0, R_1, f_{0,1}, f_{1,1}$ to $R^\star_{\mathcal{OT}}$.
3. Upon receiving $(\mathsf{tdec}^1_0, r^1_0), (\mathsf{tdec}^1_1, r^1_1)$ compute $W^1_0 = l_0 \oplus H$, $W^1_1 = l_1 \oplus \mathsf{hc}(f^{-\lambda}_{1,1}(r^1_1 \oplus R_1))$, $(f_{0,2}, f^{-1}_{0,2}) \leftarrow \mathsf{Gen}(1^\lambda)$, $(f_{1,2}, f^{-1}_{1,2}) \leftarrow \mathsf{Gen}(1^\lambda)$ and send $(W^1_0, W^1_1, f_{0,2}, f_{1,2})$.[12]
4. Continue the interaction with $R^\star_{\mathcal{OT}}$ according to $\mathcal{H}_1$ (and $\mathcal{H}_0$) and output what $R^\star_{\mathcal{OT}}$ outputs.

This part of the security proof ends with the observation that if $H = \mathsf{hc}(x)$ then $R^\star_{\mathcal{OT}}$ acts as in $\mathcal{H}_0$, otherwise $R^\star_{\mathcal{OT}}$ acts as in $\mathcal{H}_1$.

- $\mathcal{H}_2$ proceeds according to $\mathcal{H}_1$ with the difference that both $W_0$ and $W_1$ are set to random strings. Also in this case the indistinguishability between $\mathcal{H}_1$ and $\mathcal{H}_2$ comes from the security of the hardcore bit function for $\lambda$ bits $\mathsf{hc}$ for the family $\mathcal{F}$ (the same arguments of the previous security proof can be used to prove the indistinguishability between $\mathcal{H}_2$ and $\mathcal{H}_1$).

- $\mathcal{H}_3$ In this hybrid experiment we consider the case where after the rewind, with non-negligible probability, $r^1_{b^\star} \neq \overline{r}^1_{b^\star}$ and $\overline{r}^1_{1-b^\star} = r^1_{1-b^\star}$ for some $b^\star \in \{0, 1\}$.

In this case, in the main thread the hybrid experiment computes $W^1_{b^\star} = l_{b^\star} \oplus \mathsf{hc}(f^{-\lambda}_{b^\star,1}(r^1_{b^\star} \oplus R_{b^\star}))$, picks $W^1_{1-b^\star} \leftarrow \{0, 1\}^\star$ sends $W^1_0, W^1_1$ with two freshly generated TDPs $f_{0,2}, f_{1,2}$. $\mathcal{H}_3$ now continues the interaction with $R^\star_{\mathcal{OT}}$ according to $\mathcal{H}_2$. The indistinguishability between $\mathcal{H}_2$ and $\mathcal{H}_3$ comes from the security of the hardcore bit function for $\lambda$ bits $\mathsf{hc}$ for the TDP $\mathcal{F}$. More precisely, assuming by contradiction that $\mathcal{H}_2$ and $\mathcal{H}_3$ are distinguishable, we construct and adversary $\mathcal{A}^\mathcal{F}$ that distinguishes between the output of $\mathsf{hc}(x)$ and a random string of $\lambda$ bits having as input $f^\lambda(x)$. Consider an execution where $R^\star_{\mathcal{OT}}$ has non-negligible advantage in distinguish $\mathcal{H}_2$ from $\mathcal{H}_3$ and consider the randomness $\rho$ used by $R^\star_{\mathcal{OT}}$ and the first round computed in this execution, let us say $\mathsf{com}, \mathsf{tcom}_0, \mathsf{tcom}_1$. $\mathcal{A}^\mathcal{F}$, on input the randomness $\rho$, the message $b^\star$ committed in $\mathsf{com}$ and the message $r^1_{1-b^\star}$ committed $\mathsf{tcom}_{1-b^\star}$, $\mathcal{A}^\mathcal{F}$ executes the following steps.

1. Start $R^\star_{\mathcal{OT}}$ with randomness $\rho$.
2. Let $(f, H, f^\lambda(x))$ be the challenge. Upon receiving the first round $(\mathsf{com}, \mathsf{tcom}_0, \mathsf{tcom}_1)$ by $R^\star_{\mathcal{OT}}$, compute $R_{1-b^\star} = r^1_{1-b^\star} \oplus f^\lambda(x)$, pick a random string $R_{b^\star}$, computes $(f_{b^\star,1}, f^{-1}_{b^\star,1}) \leftarrow \mathsf{Gen}(1^\lambda)$, sets $f_{1-b^\star,1} = f$ and send $(R_0, R_1, f_{0,1}, f_{1,1})$ to $R^\star_{\mathcal{OT}}$.

---

[12] Observe that $R^\star_{\mathcal{OT}}$ could send values different from $r^1_0$ and $r^1_1$ in the third round. In this case $\mathcal{A}^\mathcal{F}$ just recomputes the second round using fresh randomness and asking another challenge $\overline{f}, \overline{H}, \overline{f}^\lambda(x)$ to the challenger until in the third round the messages $r^1_0$ and $r^1_1$ are received again. This allows $\mathcal{A}^\mathcal{F}$ to break the security of $\overline{f}$ because we are assuming that in this experiment $R^\star_{\mathcal{OT}}$ opens, with non-negligible probability, $\mathsf{tcom}_0$ to $r^1_0$ and $\mathsf{tcom}_1$ to $r^1_1$.

3. Upon receiving $(\mathsf{tdec}_0^1, r_0^1), (\mathsf{tdec}_1^1, r_1^1)$ compute $W_{1-b^\star}^1 = l_{1-b^\star} \oplus H$, $W_{b^\star}^1 = l_{b^\star} \oplus \mathsf{hc}(f_{b^\star,1}^{-\lambda}(r_{b^\star}^1 \oplus R_{b^\star}))$, $(f_{0,2}, f_{0,2}^{-1}) \leftarrow \mathsf{Gen}(1^\lambda)$, $(f_{1,2}, f_{1,2}^{-1}) \leftarrow \mathsf{Gen}(1^\lambda)$ and send $(W_0^1, W_1^1, f_{0,2}, f_{1,2})$.
4. Continue the interaction with $R_{\mathcal{OT}}^\star$ according to $\mathcal{H}_2$ (and $\mathcal{H}_3$) and output what $R_{\mathcal{OT}}^\star$ outputs.

This part of the security proof ends with the observation that if $H = \mathsf{hc}(x)$ then $R_{\mathcal{OT}}^\star$ acts as in $\mathcal{H}_2$, otherwise he acts as in $\mathcal{H}_3$.

- $\mathcal{H}_3^j$ proceeds according to $\mathcal{H}_3$ with the differences that for $i = 2, \dots, j$

1. if $r_{b^\star}^i \neq r_{b^\star}^1$ for some $b^\star \in \{0,1\}$ then $\mathcal{H}_3^j$ picks $W_{1-b^\star}^i \leftarrow \{0,1\}^\lambda$, computes $W_{b^\star}^i = l_{b^\star} \oplus \mathsf{hc}(f_{b^\star,i}^{-\lambda}(r_{b^\star}^i \oplus R_{b^\star}))$ and sends $W_0^i, W_1^i$ with two freshly generated TDPs $f_{0,i+1}, f_{1,i+1}$ to $R_{\mathcal{OT}}^\star$ otherwise
2. $\mathcal{H}_3^j$ picks $W_0^i \leftarrow \{0,1\}^\lambda$ and $W_1^i \leftarrow \{0,1\}^\lambda$ and sends $W_0^i, W_1^i$ with two freshly generated TDPs $f_{0,i+1}, f_{1,i+1}$ to $R_{\mathcal{OT}}^\star$.

Roughly speaking, if $R_{\mathcal{OT}}^\star$ changes the opened message w.r.t. $\mathsf{tcom}_{b^\star}$, then $W_{b^\star}^i$ is correctly computed and $W_{1-b^\star}^i$ is sets to a random string. Otherwise, if the opening of $\mathsf{tcom}_0$ and $\mathsf{tcom}_1$ stay the same as in the third round, then both $W_0^i$ and $W_1^i$ are random strings (for $i = 2, \dots, j$). We show that $\mathsf{OUT}_{\mathcal{H}_3^{j-1}, R_{\mathcal{OT}}^\star(z)}(1^\lambda) \approx \mathsf{OUT}_{\mathcal{H}_3^j, R_{\mathcal{OT}}^\star(z)}(1^\lambda)$ in two steps. In the first step we show that the indistinguishability between these two hybrid experiments holds for the first case (when $r_{b^\star}^i \neq r_{b^\star}^1$ for some bit $b^\star$), and in the second step we show that the same holds when $r_0^i = r_0^1$ and $r_1^i = r_1^1$. We first recall that if $r_{b^\star}^i \neq r_{b^\star}^1$, then $\mathsf{tcom}_{1-b^\star}$ is perfectly binding, therefore we have that $r_{1-b^\star}^i = r_{1-b^\star}^1$. Assuming by contradiction that $\mathcal{H}_3^{j-1}$ and $\mathcal{H}_3^j$ are distinguishable then we construct and adversary $\mathcal{A}^{\mathcal{F}}$ that distinguishes between the output of $\mathsf{hc}(x)$ and a random string of $\lambda$ bits having as input $f^\lambda(x)$. Consider an execution where $R_{\mathcal{OT}}^\star$ has non-negligible advantage in distinguishing $\mathcal{H}_3^{j-1}$ from $\mathcal{H}_3^j$ and consider the randomness $\rho$ used by $R_{\mathcal{OT}}^\star$ and the first round computed by $R_{\mathcal{OT}}^\star$ in this execution, let us say $\mathsf{com}, \mathsf{tcom}_0, \mathsf{tcom}_1$. $\mathcal{A}^{\mathcal{F}}$, on input the randomness $\rho$, the message $b^\star$ committed in $\mathsf{com}$ and the message $r_{1-b^\star}^1$ committed $\mathsf{tcom}_{1-b^\star}$, executes the following steps.

1. Start $R_{\mathcal{OT}}^\star$ with randomness $\rho$.
2. Let $f, H, f^\lambda(x)$ be the challenge. Upon receiving the first round $(\mathsf{com}, \mathsf{tcom}_0, \mathsf{tcom}_1)$ by $R_{\mathcal{OT}}^\star$, $\mathcal{A}^{\mathcal{F}}$ compute $R_{1-b^\star} = r_{1-b^\star}^1 \oplus f^\lambda(x)$, pick a random string $R_{b^\star}$, compute $(f_{0,1}, f_{0,1}^{-1}) \leftarrow \mathsf{Gen}(1^\lambda)$ and $(f_{1,1}, f_{1,1}^{-1}) \leftarrow \mathsf{Gen}(1^\lambda)$ send $R_0, R_1, f_{0,1}, f_{1,1}$ to $R_{\mathcal{OT}}^\star$.
3. Continue the interaction with $R_{\mathcal{OT}}^\star$ according to $\mathcal{H}_3^{j-1}$ using $f_{1-b^\star,j} = f$ instead of using the generation function $\mathsf{Gen}(\cdot)$ when it is required.
4. Upon receiving $(\mathsf{tdec}_0^j, r_0^j), (\mathsf{tdec}_1^1, r_1^j)$ compute $W_{1-b^\star}^j = l_{1-b^\star} \oplus H$,[13] $W_{b^\star}^j = l_{b^\star} \oplus \mathsf{hc}(f_{b^\star,j}^{-\lambda}(r_{b^\star}^j \oplus R_{b^\star}))$, $(f_{0,j+1}, f_{0,j+1}^{-1}) \leftarrow \mathsf{Gen}(1^\lambda)$, $(f_{1,j+1}, f_{1,j+1}^{-1}) \leftarrow \mathsf{Gen}(1^\lambda)$ and sends $(W_0^{j+1}, W_1^{j+1}, f_{0,j+1}, f_{1,j+1})$.

---

[13] It is important to observe that $r_{b^\star}^1 = r_{b^\star}^j$.

5. Continue the interaction with $R^\star_{\mathcal{OT}}$ according to $\mathcal{H}_3^{j-1}$ (and $\mathcal{H}_3^j$) and output what $R^\star_{\mathcal{OT}}$ outputs.

This step of the security proof ends with the observation that if $H = \mathsf{hc}(x)$ then $R^\star_{\mathcal{OT}}$ acts as in $\mathcal{H}_3^{j-1}$, otherwise he acts as in $\mathcal{H}_3^j$.

The second step of the security proof is almost identical to the proof used to prove the indistinguishability between $\mathcal{H}_0$ and $\mathcal{H}_2$.

The entire security proof is almost over, indeed the output of $\mathcal{H}_3^\gamma$ corresponds to the output of the simulator Sim and $\mathsf{OUT}_{\mathcal{H}_3, R^\star_{\mathcal{OT}}(z)}(1^\lambda) = \mathsf{OUT}_{\mathcal{H}_3^1, R^\star_{\mathcal{OT}}(z)}(1^\lambda) \approx \mathsf{OUT}_{\mathcal{H}_3^2, R^\star_{\mathcal{OT}}(z)}(1^\lambda) \approx \cdots \approx \mathsf{OUT}_{\mathcal{H}_3^\gamma, R^\star_{\mathcal{OT}}(z)}(1^\lambda)$. Therefore we can claim that the output of $\mathcal{H}_0$ is indistinguishable from the output of Sim when at most one between $l_0$ and $l_1$ is used.

**Theorem 3.** *Assuming TDPs, for any $\gamma > 0$ $\Pi^\gamma_{\overrightarrow{\mathcal{OT}}}$ securely computes $F^m_{\mathcal{OT}}$ with one-sided simulation. Moreover the third round is* replayable.

*Proof.* The third round of $\Pi^\gamma_{\overrightarrow{\mathcal{OT}}}$ is *replayable* due to the same arguments used in the security proof of Theorem 2. We now prove that $\Pi^\gamma_{\overrightarrow{\mathcal{OT}}}$ securely computes $F^m_{\mathcal{OT}}$ with one-sided simulation according to Definition 4. More precisely to prove the security against the malicious sender $S^\star_{\overrightarrow{\mathcal{OT}}}$ we start by consider the execution $\mathcal{H}_0$ that correspond to the real execution where the input $b_1, \ldots, b_m$ is used by the receiver and then we consider the experiment $\mathcal{H}_i$ where the input used by the receiver is $1 - b_1, \ldots, 1 - b_i, b_{i+1}, \ldots, b_m$. Suppose now by contradiction that the output distributions of $\mathcal{H}_i$ and $\mathcal{H}_{i+1}$ (for some $i \in \{1, m-1\}$) are distinguishable, then we can construct a malicious sender $S^\star_{\mathcal{OT}}$ that breaks the security of $\Pi^\gamma_{\mathcal{OT}}$ against malicious sender. This allow us to claim that the output distribution of $\mathcal{H}_0$ is indistinguishable from the output distribution of $\mathcal{H}_m$. A similar proof can be made when the malicious party is the receiver, but this time we need to consider how the the security proof for $\Pi^\gamma_{\mathcal{OT}}$ works. More precisely, we start by consider the execution $\mathcal{H}_0$ that correspond to the real execution where the input $((l_0^1, l_1^1) \ldots, (l_0^m, l_1^m))$ is used by the sender and then we consider the experiment $\mathcal{H}_i$ where the simulator instead of the honest sender procedure is used in the first $i$ parallel executions of $\Pi^\gamma_{\mathcal{OT}}$. Supposing by contradiction that the output distributions of $\mathcal{H}_i$ and $\mathcal{H}_{i+1}$ (for some $i \in \{1, m-1\}$) are distinguishable, then we can construct a malicious receiver $R^\star_{\mathcal{OT}}$ that breaks the security of $\Pi^\gamma_{\mathcal{OT}}$ against malicious sender. We observe that in $\mathcal{H}_i$ in the first $i$ parallel executions of $\Pi^\gamma_{\mathcal{OT}}$ the simulator Sim is used and this could disturb the reduction to the security of $\Pi^\gamma_{\mathcal{OT}}$ when proving that the output distribution of $\mathcal{H}_i$ is indistinguishable from the output distribution of $\mathcal{H}_{i+1}$. In order to conclude the security proof we need just to show that Sim's behaviour does not disturb the reduction. As described in the security proof of $\Pi^\gamma_{\mathcal{OT}}$, the simulation made by Sim roughly works by rewinding from the third to the second round while from the fourth round onwards Sim works straight line. An important feature enjoyed by Sim is that he maintains the main thread. Let $\mathcal{C}^{\mathcal{OT}}$ be the challenger of $\Pi^\gamma_{\mathcal{OT}}$ against malicious receiver, our adversary $R^\star_{\mathcal{OT}}$ works as following.

1. Upon receiving the first round of $\Pi^\gamma_{\overrightarrow{OT}}$ from $R^\star_{\overrightarrow{OT}}$, forward the $(i+1)$-th component $ot_1$ to $\mathcal{C}^{OT}$ [14].
2. Upon receiving $ot_2$ from $\mathcal{C}^{OT}$ interacts against $R^\star_{\overrightarrow{OT}}$ by computing the second round of $\Pi^\gamma_{\overrightarrow{OT}}$ according to $\mathcal{H}_i$ ($\mathcal{H}_{i+1}$) with the difference that in the $(i+1)$-th position the value $ot_2$ is used.
3. Upon receiving the third round of $\Pi^\gamma_{\overrightarrow{OT}}$ from $R^\star_{\overrightarrow{OT}}$, forward the $(i+1)$-th component $ot_3$ to $\mathcal{C}^{OT}$.
4. Upon receiving $ot_4$ from $\mathcal{C}^{OT}$ interacts against $R^\star_{\overrightarrow{OT}}$ by computing the fourth round of $\Pi^\gamma_{\overrightarrow{OT}}$ according to $\mathcal{H}_i$ ($\mathcal{H}_{i+1}$) with the difference that in the $(i+1)$-th position the value $ot_4$ is used.
5. for $i = 2, \ldots, \gamma$ follow the strategy described in step 3 and 4 and output what $R^\star_{\overrightarrow{OT}}$ outputs.

We recall that in $\mathcal{H}_i$ (as well as in $\mathcal{H}_{i+1}$) in the first $i$ execution of $\Pi^\gamma_{\overrightarrow{OT}}$ the simulator is used, therefore a rewind is made from the third to the second round. During the rewinds $R^\star_{OT}$ can forward to $R^\star_{\overrightarrow{OT}}$ the same second round $ot_2$. Moreover, due to the main thread property enjoyed by Sim, after the rewind $R^\star_{OT}$ can continue the interaction against $R^\star_{\overrightarrow{OT}}$ without rewind $\mathcal{C}^\star$. Indeed if Sim does not maintains the main thread then, even though the same $ot_2$ is used during the rewind, $R^\star_{\overrightarrow{OT}}$ could send a different $ot_3$ making impossible to efficiently continue the reduction.

## 4 Secure 2PC in the Simultaneous Message Exchange Model

In this section we give an high-level overview of our 4-round 2PC protocol $\Pi_{2PC} = (P_1, P_2)$ for every functionality $F = (F_1, F_2)$ in the simultaneous message exchange model. $\Pi_{2PC}$ consists of two simultaneous symmetric executions of the same subprotocol in which only one party learns the output. In the rest of the paper we indicate as left execution the execution of the protocol where $P_1$ learns the output and as right execution the execution of the protocol where $P_2$ learns the output. In Fig. 6 we provide the high level description of the left execution of $\Pi_{2PC}$. We denoted by $(m_1, m_2, m_3, m_4)$ the messages played in the left execution where $(m_1, m_3)$ are sent by $P_1$ and $(m_2, m_4)$ are sent by $P_2$. Likewise, in the right execution of the protocol the messages are denoted by $(\tilde{m}_1, \tilde{m}_2, \tilde{m}_3, \tilde{m}_4)$ where $(\tilde{m}_1, \tilde{m}_3)$ are sent by $P_2$ and $(\tilde{m}_2, \tilde{m}_4)$ are sent by $P_1$. Therefore, messages $(m_j, \tilde{m}_j)$ are exchanged simultaneously in the j-th round, for $j \in \{1, \ldots, 4\}$. Our construction uses the following tools.

---

[14] We recall that $\Pi^\gamma_{\overrightarrow{OT}}$ is constructed by executing in parallel $m$ instantiations of $\Pi_{\overrightarrow{OT}}$, therefore in this reduction we are just replacing the $(i+1)$-th component of every rounds sent to $R^\star_{\overrightarrow{OT}}$ with the value received by $\mathcal{C}^{OT}$. Vice versa, we forward to $\mathcal{C}^\star$ the $(i+1)$-th component of the rounds received from $R^\star_{\overrightarrow{OT}}$.

- A non-interactive perfectly binding computationally hiding commitment scheme PBCOM = (Com, Dec).
- A Yao's garbled circuit scheme (GenGC, EvalGC) with simulator SimGC.
- A protocol $\Pi_{\overrightarrow{\mathcal{OT}}}^{\gamma} = (S_{\overrightarrow{\mathcal{OT}}}, R_{\overrightarrow{\mathcal{OT}}})$ that securely computes $F_{\mathcal{OT}}^m$ with one-sided simulation.
- A $\Sigma$-protocol $\mathsf{BL}_L = (\mathcal{P}_L, \mathcal{V}_L)$ for the $\mathcal{NP}$-language $L = \{\mathsf{com} : \exists\ (\mathsf{dec}, m)\ \text{s.t.}\ \mathsf{Dec}(\mathsf{com}, \mathsf{dec}, m) = 1\}$ with Special HVZK simulator $\mathsf{Sim}_L$. We uses two instantiations of $\mathsf{BL}_L$ in order to construct the protocol for the OR of two statements $\Pi_{\mathsf{OR}}$ as described in Sect. 2.3. $\Pi_{\mathsf{OR}}$ is a proof system for the $\mathcal{NP}$-language $L_{\mathsf{OR}} = \{(\mathsf{com}_0, \mathsf{com}_1) : \exists\ (\mathsf{dec}, m)\ \text{s.t.}\ \mathsf{Dec}(\mathsf{com}_0, \mathsf{dec}, m) = 1\ \text{OR}\ \mathsf{Dec}(\mathsf{com}_1, \mathsf{dec}, m) = 1\}^{15}$.
- A 4-round delayed-input NMZK AoK NMZK = $(\mathcal{P}_{\mathsf{NMZK}}, \mathcal{V}_{\mathsf{NMZK}})$ for the $\mathcal{NP}$-language $L_{\mathsf{NMZK}}$ that will be specified later (see Sect. 4.1 for the formal definition of $L_{\mathsf{NMZK}}$).

In Fig. 6 we propose the high-level description of the left execution of $\Pi_{2\mathcal{PC}}$ where $P_1$ runs on input $x \in \{0,1\}^{\lambda}$ and $P_2$ on input $y \in \{0,1\}^{\lambda}$.

## 4.1   Formal Description of Our $\Pi_{2\mathcal{PC}} = (P_1, P_2)$

We first start by defining the following $\mathcal{NP}$-language

$$L_{\mathsf{NMZK}} = \big\{ \big(\mathsf{com}_{\mathsf{GC}}, \mathsf{com}_L, \mathsf{com}_0, \mathsf{com}_1, \mathsf{GC}, (\mathsf{ot}^1, \mathsf{ot}^2, \mathsf{ot}^3, \mathsf{ot}^4)\big) :$$

$$\exists(\mathsf{dec}_{\mathsf{GC}}, \mathsf{dec}_L, \mathsf{dec}_0, \mathsf{dec}_1, \mathsf{input}, \alpha, \beta, \omega)\ \text{s.t.}$$

$$\big((Z_{1,0}, Z_{1,1}, \ldots, Z_{\lambda,0}, Z_{\lambda,1}, \mathsf{GC}) \leftarrow \mathsf{GenGC}(1^{\lambda}, F_1, \mathsf{input}; \omega)\big)\ \text{AND}$$

$$\big(\mathsf{Dec}(\mathsf{com}_0, \mathsf{dec}_0, \mathsf{input}) = 1\big)\ \text{AND}\ \big(\mathsf{Dec}(\mathsf{com}_1, \mathsf{dec}_1, \mathsf{input}) = 1\big)\ \text{AND}$$

$$\big(\mathsf{Dec}(\mathsf{com}_L, \mathsf{dec}_L, Z_{1,0}||Z_{1,1}||, \ldots, ||Z_{\lambda,0}||Z_{\lambda,1}) = 1\big)\ \text{AND}$$

$$\big(\mathsf{ot}^1\ \text{and}\ \mathsf{ot}^3 \text{are obtained by running}\ R_{\overrightarrow{\mathcal{OT}}}\ \text{on input}\ 1^{\lambda}, \mathsf{input}, \alpha\big)\ \text{AND}$$

$$\big(\tilde{\mathsf{ot}}^2\ \text{and}\ \tilde{\mathsf{ot}}^4\ \text{are obtained by running}\ S_{\overrightarrow{\mathcal{OT}}}\ \text{on input}$$

$$(1^{\lambda}, Z_{1,0}, Z_{1,1}, \ldots, Z_{\lambda,0}, Z_{\lambda,1}, \beta)\big)\big\}.$$

The NMZK AoK NMZK used in our protocol is for the $\mathcal{NP}$-language $L_{\mathsf{NMZK}}$ described above. Now we are ready to describe our protocol $\Pi_{2\mathcal{PC}} = (P_1, P_2)$ in a formal way.

**Protocol $\Pi_{2\mathcal{PC}} = (P_1, P_2)$.**
  *Common input:* security parameter $\lambda$ and instance length $\ell_{\mathsf{NMZK}}$ of the statement of the NMZK.
  $P_1$'s input: $x \in \{0,1\}^{\lambda}$, $P_2$'s input: $y \in \{0,1\}^{\lambda}$.

**Round 1.** In this round $P_1$ sends the message $m_1$ and $P_2$ the message $\tilde{m}_1$. The steps computed by $P_1$ to construct $m_1$ are the following.

---

[15] We use $\Pi_{\mathsf{OR}}$ in a non-black box way, but for ease of exposition sometimes we will refer to the entire protocol $\Pi_{\mathsf{OR}}$ in order to invoke its proof of knowledge property.

$$P_1(x) \hspace{6cm} P_2(y)$$

Run $R_{\overline{OT}}$ on input $1^\lambda, x$ and randomness $\alpha$
to get $\mathsf{ot}^1$;
Run $\mathcal{V}_{\mathsf{NMZK}}$ on input $1^\lambda$ to get $\mathsf{nmzk}^1$;
$(\mathsf{com}_0, \mathsf{dec}_0) \leftarrow \mathsf{Com}(x)$;
$(\mathsf{com}_1, \mathsf{dec}_1) \leftarrow \mathsf{Com}(x)$;
$\mathsf{a}_0 \leftarrow \mathcal{P}_L(1^\lambda, \mathsf{com}_0, \mathsf{dec}_0, x)$;
Pick $\mathsf{c}_1 \leftarrow \{0,1\}^\lambda$;
$(\mathsf{a}_1, \mathsf{z}_1) \leftarrow \mathsf{Sim}_L(1^\lambda, \mathsf{com}_1, \mathsf{c}_1)$.

$$m_1 = $$
$$(\mathsf{com}_0, \mathsf{com}_1, \mathsf{a}_0, \mathsf{a}_1, \mathsf{ot}^1, \mathsf{nmzk}^1)$$
$$\xrightarrow{\hspace{3cm}}$$

$(Z_{1,0}, Z_{1,1}, \ldots, Z_{\lambda,0}, Z_{\lambda,1}, \mathsf{GC}_y)$
$\leftarrow \mathsf{GenGC}(1^\lambda, F_1, y; \omega)$;
$(\mathsf{com}_L, \mathsf{dec}_L)$
$\leftarrow \mathsf{Com}(Z_{1,0}||Z_{1,1}||, \ldots, ||Z_{\lambda,1})$;
$(\mathsf{com}_{\mathsf{GC}_y}, \mathsf{dec}_{\mathsf{GC}_y}) \leftarrow \mathsf{Com}(\mathsf{GC}_y)$;
Run $S_{\overline{OT}}$ on input $1^\lambda, \mathsf{ot}^1, (Z_{1,0},$
$Z_{1,1}, \ldots, Z_{\lambda,0}, Z_{\lambda,1})$
and randomness $\beta$ to get $\mathsf{ot}^2$;
Run $\mathcal{P}_{\mathsf{NMZK}}$ on input $1^\lambda$ and $\mathsf{nmzk}^1$
to get $\mathsf{nmzk}^2$;
Pick $\mathsf{c} \leftarrow \{0,1\}^\lambda$.

$$m_2 = $$
$$(\mathsf{com}_L, \mathsf{ot}^2, \mathsf{com}_{\mathsf{GC}_y}, \mathsf{nmzk}^2, \mathsf{c})$$
$$\xleftarrow{\hspace{3cm}}$$

Run $R_{\overline{OT}}$ on input $\mathsf{ot}^2$ to get $\mathsf{ot}^3$;
Run $\mathcal{V}_{\mathsf{NMZK}}$ on input $\mathsf{nmzk}^2$ to get
$\mathsf{nmzk}^3$;
$\mathsf{c}_0 = \mathsf{c} \oplus \mathsf{c}_1$, $\mathsf{z}_0 \leftarrow \mathcal{P}_L(\mathsf{c}_0)$.

$$m_3 = $$
$$(\mathsf{c}_0, \mathsf{z}_0, \mathsf{c}_1, \mathsf{z}_1, \mathsf{ot}^3, \mathsf{nmzk}^3)$$
$$\xrightarrow{\hspace{3cm}}$$

If $\mathsf{c}$ is equal to $\mathsf{c}_0 \oplus \mathsf{c}_1$
and $\mathcal{V}_L(\mathsf{a}_0, \mathsf{c}_0, \mathsf{z}_0, \mathsf{com}_0) = 1$
and $\mathcal{V}_L(\mathsf{a}_1, \mathsf{c}_1, \mathsf{z}_1, \mathsf{com}_1) = 1$
    continue the execution;
otherwise output $\perp$;
Run $S_{\overline{OT}}$ on input $\mathsf{ot}^3$ to get $\mathsf{ot}^4$;
Run $\mathcal{P}_{\mathsf{NMZK}}$ on input $\mathsf{nmzk}^3$,
$\mathsf{stm}^a$ and $w_{\mathsf{stm}}{}^b$ to get $\mathsf{nmzk}^4$.

$$m_4 = $$
$$(\mathsf{ot}^4, \mathsf{GC}_y, \mathsf{nmzk}^4)$$
$$\xleftarrow{\hspace{3cm}}$$

Run $R_{\overline{OT}}$ in input $\mathsf{ot}^4$ thus
obtaining $Z_{1,x_1}, \ldots, Z_{\lambda,x_\lambda}$;
If $\mathcal{V}_{\mathsf{NMZK}}$ on input $\mathsf{nmzk}^4$ and $\mathsf{stm}$ outputs 1
    output $v = \mathsf{EvalGC}(\mathsf{GC}_y, Z_{1,x_1}, \ldots, Z_{\lambda,x_\lambda})$;
otherwise output $\perp$.

---

[a] Informally, NMZK proves that: 1) $P_2$ has performed both oblivious transfers correctly using the same input $y$; 2) the value $y$ is committed in both $\tilde{\mathsf{com}}_0, \tilde{\mathsf{com}}_1$ (that $P_2$ computes in the first round) and 3) the Yao's gabled circuit $\mathsf{GC}_y$ sent in the last round represents the message committed in $\mathsf{com}_{\mathsf{GC}_y}$.

[b] $w_{\mathsf{stm}}$ is s.t. $(\mathsf{stm}, w_{\mathsf{stm}}) \in \mathsf{Rel}_{\mathsf{L}_{\mathsf{NMZK}}}$.

**Fig. 6.** High-level description of the left execution of $\Pi_{2\mathcal{PC}}$.

1. Run $\mathcal{V}_{\mathsf{NMZK}}$ on input the security parameter $1^\lambda$ and $\ell_{\mathsf{NMZK}}$ thus obtaining the first round $\mathsf{nmzk}^1$ of NMZK.
2. Run $R_{\overrightarrow{\mathcal{OT}}}$ on input $1^\lambda$, $x$ and the randomness $\alpha$ thus obtaining the first round $\mathsf{ot}^1$ of $\Pi^\gamma_{\overrightarrow{\mathcal{OT}}}$.
3. Compute $(\mathsf{com}_0, \mathsf{dec}_0) \leftarrow \mathsf{Com}(x)$ and $(\mathsf{com}_1, \mathsf{dec}_1) \leftarrow \mathsf{Com}(x)$.
4. Compute $a_0 \leftarrow \mathcal{P}_L(1^\lambda, \mathsf{com}_0, (\mathsf{dec}_0, x))$.
5. Pick $c_1 \leftarrow \{0,1\}^\lambda$ and compute $(a_1, z_1) \leftarrow \mathsf{Sim}_L(1^\lambda, \mathsf{com}_1, c_1)$.
6. Set $m_1 = (\mathsf{nmzk}^1, \mathsf{ot}^1, \mathsf{com}_0, \mathsf{com}_1, a_0, a_1)$ and send $m_1$ to $P_2$.

Likewise, $P_2$ performs the same actions of $P_1$ constructing message $\tilde{m}_1 = (\tilde{\mathsf{nmzk}}^1, \tilde{\mathsf{ot}}^1, \tilde{\mathsf{com}}_0, \tilde{\mathsf{com}}_1, \tilde{a}_0, \tilde{a}_1)$.

**Round 2.** In this round $P_2$ sends the message $m_2$ and $P_1$ the message $\tilde{m}_2$. The steps computed by $P_2$ to construct $m_2$ are the following.

1. Compute $(Z_{1,0}, Z_{1,1}, \ldots, Z_{\lambda,0}, Z_{\lambda,1}, \mathsf{GC}_y) \leftarrow \mathsf{GenGC}(1^\lambda, F_2, y; \omega)$.
2. Compute $(\mathsf{com}_{\mathsf{GC}_y}, \mathsf{dec}_{\mathsf{GC}_y}) \leftarrow \mathsf{Com}(\mathsf{GC}_y)$ and $(\mathsf{com}_L, \mathsf{dec}_L) \leftarrow \mathsf{Com}(Z_{1,0}|| Z_{1,1}||, \ldots, ||Z_{\lambda,0}||Z_{\lambda,1})$.
3. Run $\mathcal{P}_{\mathsf{NMZK}}$ on input $1^\lambda$ and $\mathsf{nmzk}^1$ thus obtaining the second round $\mathsf{nmzk}^2$ of NMZK.
4. Run $S_{\overrightarrow{\mathcal{OT}}}$ on input $1^\lambda, Z_{1,0}, Z_{1,1}, \ldots, Z_{\lambda,0}, Z_{\lambda,1}, \mathsf{ot}^1$ and the randomness $\beta$ thus obtaining the second round $\mathsf{ot}^2$ of $\Pi^\gamma_{\overrightarrow{\mathcal{OT}}}$.
5. Pick $c \leftarrow \{0,1\}^\lambda$.
6. Set $m_2 = (\mathsf{ot}^2, \mathsf{com}_L, \mathsf{com}_{\mathsf{GC}_y}, \mathsf{nmzk}^2, c)$ and send $m_2$ to $P_1$.

Likewise, $P_2$ performs the same actions of $P_1$ constructing message $\tilde{m}_2 = (\tilde{\mathsf{ot}}^2, \tilde{\mathsf{com}}_L, \tilde{\mathsf{com}}_{\mathsf{GC}_x}, \tilde{\mathsf{nmzk}}^2, \tilde{c})$.

**Round 3.** In this round $P_1$ sends the message $m_3$ and $P_2$ the message $\tilde{m}_3$. The steps computed by $P_1$ to construct $m_3$ are the following.

1. Run $\mathcal{V}_{\mathsf{NMZK}}$ on input $\mathsf{nmzk}^2$ thus obtaining the third round $\mathsf{nmzk}^3$ of NMZK.
2. Run $R_{\overrightarrow{\mathcal{OT}}}$ on input $\mathsf{ot}^2$ thus obtaining the third round $\mathsf{ot}^3$ of $\Pi^\gamma_{\overrightarrow{\mathcal{OT}}}$.
3. Compute $c_0 = c \oplus c_1$ and $z_0 \leftarrow \mathcal{P}_L(c_0)$.
4. Set $m_3 = (\mathsf{nmzk}^3, \mathsf{ot}^3, c_0, c_1, z_0, z_1)$ and send $m_3$ to $P_2$.

Likewise, $P_2$ performs the same actions of $P_1$ constructing message $\tilde{m}_3 = (\tilde{\mathsf{nmzk}}^3, \tilde{\mathsf{ot}}^3, \tilde{c}_0, \tilde{c}_1, \tilde{z}_0, \tilde{z}_1)$.

**Round 4.** In this round $P_2$ sends the message $m_4$ and $P_1$ the message $\tilde{m}_4$. The steps computed by $P_2$ to construct $m_4$ are the following.

1. Check if: $c = c_0 \oplus c_1$, the transcript $a_0, c_0, z_0$ is accepting w.r.t. the instance $\mathsf{com}_0$ and the transcript $a_1, c_1, z_1$ is accepting w.r.t. the instance $\mathsf{com}_1$. If one of the checks fails then output $\bot$, otherwise continue with the following steps.
2. Run $S_{\overrightarrow{\mathcal{OT}}}$ on input $\mathsf{ot}^3$, thus obtaining the fourth round $\mathsf{ot}^4$ of $\Pi^\gamma_{\overrightarrow{\mathcal{OT}}}$.

3. Set $\mathsf{stm} = (\mathsf{com_{GC_y}}, \mathsf{com_L}, \mathsf{c\tilde{o}m_0}, \mathsf{c\tilde{o}m_1}, \mathsf{GC_y}, \tilde{\mathsf{ot}}_1, \mathsf{ot}_2, \tilde{\mathsf{ot}}_3, \mathsf{ot}_4)^{16}$ and $w_{\mathsf{stm}} = (\mathsf{dec_{GC_y}}, \mathsf{dec_L}, \tilde{\mathsf{dec}}_0, \tilde{\mathsf{dec}}_1, y, \alpha, \tilde{\beta}, \omega)$.

4. Run $\mathcal{P}_{\mathsf{NMZK}}$ on input $\mathsf{nmzk}^3$, $\mathsf{stm}$ and $w_{\mathsf{stm}}$ thus obtaining the fourth round $\mathsf{nmzk}^4$ of NMZK.

5. Set $m_4 = (\mathsf{nmzk}^4, \mathsf{ot}^4, \mathsf{GC_y})$ and send $m_4$ to $P_1$.

Likewise, $P_1$ performs the same actions of $P_2$ constructing message $\tilde{m}_4 = (\tilde{\mathsf{nmzk}}^4, \tilde{\mathsf{ot}}^4, \tilde{\mathsf{GC}}_x)$.

**Output computation.** $P_1$'s output: $P_1$ checks if the transcript $(\mathsf{nmzk}^1, \mathsf{nmzk}^2, \mathsf{nmzk}^3, \mathsf{nmzk}^4)$ is accepting w.r.t. $\mathsf{stm}$. In the negative case $P_1$ outputs $\bot$, otherwise $P_1$ runs $R_{\overrightarrow{\mathcal{OT}}}$ on input $\mathsf{ot}^4$ thus obtaining $Z_{1,x_1}, \ldots, Z_{\lambda,x_\lambda}$ and computes the output $v_1 = \mathsf{EvalGC}(\mathsf{GC_y}, Z_{1,x_1}, \ldots, Z_{\lambda,x_\lambda})$.

$P_2$'s output: $P_2$ checks if the transcript $\tilde{\mathsf{nmzk}}^1, \tilde{\mathsf{nmzk}}^2, \tilde{\mathsf{nmzk}}^3, \tilde{\mathsf{nmzk}}^4$ is accepting w.r.t. $\tilde{\mathsf{stm}}$. In the negative case $P_2$ outputs $\bot$, otherwise $P_2$ runs $R_{\overrightarrow{\mathcal{OT}}}$ on input $\tilde{\mathsf{ot}}^4$ thus obtaining $\tilde{Z}_{1,y_1}, \ldots, \tilde{Z}_{\lambda,y_\lambda}$ and computes the output $v_2 = \mathsf{EvalGC}(\tilde{\mathsf{GC}}_x, \tilde{Z}_{1,y_1}, \ldots, \tilde{Z}_{\lambda,y_\lambda})$.

**High-level overview of the security proof.** Due to the symmetrical nature of the protocol, it is sufficient to prove the security against one party (let this party be $P_2$). We start with the description of the simulator Sim. Sim uses the PoK extractor $\mathsf{E_{OR}}$ for $\Pi_{\mathsf{OR}}$ to extract the input $y^\star$ from the malicious party. Sim sends $y^\star$ to the ideal functionality $F$ and receives back $v_2 = F_2(x, y^\star)$. Then, Sim computes $(\tilde{\mathsf{GC}}_\star, (\tilde{Z}_1, \ldots, \tilde{Z}_\lambda)) \leftarrow \mathsf{SimGC}(1^\lambda, F_2, y^\star, v_2)$ and sends $\tilde{\mathsf{GC}}_\star$ in the last round. Moreover instead of committing to the labels of Yao's garbled circuit and $P_1$'s inputs in $\mathsf{com_0}$ and $\mathsf{com_1}$, Sim commits to 0. Sim runs the simulator $\mathsf{Sim_{NMZK}}$ of NMZK and the simulator $\mathsf{Sim}_{\mathcal{OT}}$ of $\Pi^\gamma_{\overrightarrow{\mathcal{OT}}}$ where $P_1$ acts as $S_{\overrightarrow{\mathcal{OT}}}$ using $(\tilde{Z}_1, \ldots, \tilde{Z}_\lambda)$ as input. For the messages of $\Pi_{\mathcal{OT}}$ where $P_1$ acts as the receiver, Sim runs $R_{\overrightarrow{\mathcal{OT}}}$ on input $0^\lambda$ instead of using $x$. In our security proof we proceed through a sequence of hybrid experiments, where the first one corresponds to the real-world execution and the final represents the execution of Sim in the ideal world. The core idea of our approach is to run the simulator of NMZK, while extracting the input from $P_2^\star$. By running the simulator of NMZK we are able to guarantee that the value extracted from $\Pi_{\mathsf{OR}}$ is correct, even though $P_2^\star$ is receiving proofs for a false statement (e.g. the value committed in $\mathsf{com_0}$ differs form $\mathsf{com_1}$). Indeed in each intermediate hybrid experiment that we will consider, also the extractor of NMZK is run in order to extract the witness for the theorem proved by $P_2^\star$. In this way we can prove that the value extracted from $\Pi_{\mathsf{OR}}$ is consistent with the input that $P_2$ is using. For what we have discussed, the

---

[16] Informally, NMZK is used to prove that $P_2$ in both executions of OT (one in which he acts as a receiver, and one in which he acts as a sender) behaves correctly and he uses the same input committed in $\mathsf{c\tilde{o}m_0}$ and $\mathsf{com_1}$. Furthermore NMZK is used to prove that Yao's gabled circuit $\mathsf{GC_y}$ sent in the last round is consistent with the message committed in $\mathsf{com_{GC_y}}$.

simulator of NMZK rewinds first from the third to the second round (to extract the trapdoor), and then from the fourth to the third round (to extract the witness for the statement proved by $P_2^\star$). We need to show that these rewinding procedures do not disturb the security proof when we rely on the security of $\Pi_{\overrightarrow{OT}}^\gamma$ and $\Pi_{OR}$. This is roughly the reason why we require the third round of $\Pi_{\overrightarrow{OT}}^\gamma$ to be reusable and rely on the security of Special HVZK of the underlying $\mathsf{BL}_L$ instead of relying directly on the WI of $\Pi_{OR}$.

**Theorem 4.** *Assuming TDPs, $\Pi_{2\mathcal{PC}}$ securely computes every two-party functionality $F = (F_1, F_2)$ with black-box simulation.*

*Proof.* In order to prove that $\Pi_{2\mathcal{PC}}$ securely computes $F = (F_1, F_2)$, we first observe that, due to the symmetrical nature of the protocol, it is sufficient to prove the security against one party (let this party be $P_2$). We now show that for every adversary $P_2^\star$, there exists an ideal-world adversary (simulator) Sim such that for all inputs $x$, $y$ of equal length and security parameter $\lambda$: $\{\mathsf{REAL}_{\Pi_{2\mathcal{PC}}, P_2^\star(z)}(1^\lambda, x, y)\} \approx \{\mathsf{IDEAL}_{F, \mathsf{Sim}(z)}(1^\lambda, x, y)\}$. Our simulator Sim is the one showed in Sect. 4.1. In our security proof we proceed through a series of hybrid experiments, where the first one corresponds to the execution of $\Pi_{2\mathcal{PC}}$ between $P_1$ and $P_2^\star$ (real-world execution). Then, we gradually modify this hybrid experiment until the input of the honest party is not needed anymore, such that the final hybrid would represent the simulator (simulated execution). We now give the descriptions of the hybrid experiments and of the corresponding security reductions. We denote the output of $P_2^\star$ and the output of the procedure that interacts against $P_2^\star$ on the behalf of $P_1$ in the hybrid experiment $\mathcal{H}_i$ with $\{\mathsf{OUT}_{\mathcal{H}_i, P_2^\star(z)}(1^\lambda, x, y)\}_{x \in \{0,1\}^\lambda, y \in \{0,1\}^\lambda}$.

-$\mathcal{H}_0$ corresponds to the real executions. More in details, $\mathcal{H}_0$ runs $P_2^\star$ with a fresh randomness, and interacts with it as the honest player $P_1$ does using $x$ as input. The output of the experiment is $P_2^\star$'s view and the output of $P_1$. Note that we are guarantee from the soundness of NMZK that $\mathsf{stm} \in L_{\mathsf{NMZK}}$, that is: (1) $P_2^\star$ uses the same input $y^\star$ in both the OT executions; (2) the garbled circuit committed in $\mathsf{com}_{\mathsf{GC}_y}$ and the corresponding labels committed in $\mathsf{com}_L$, are computed using the input $y^\star$; (3) $y^\star$ is committed in both $\tilde{\mathsf{com}}_0$ and $\tilde{\mathsf{com}}_1$ and that the garbled circuit sent in the last round is actually the one committed in $\mathsf{com}_{\mathsf{GC}_y}$.

-$\mathcal{H}_1$ proceeds in the same way of $\mathcal{H}_0$ except that the input $y^\star$ of the malicious party $P_2^\star$ is extracted. In order to obtain $y^\star$, $\mathcal{H}_1$ runs the extractor $\mathsf{E}_{\mathsf{OR}}$ of $\Pi_{\mathsf{OR}}$ (that exists from the property of PoK) of $\Pi_{\mathsf{OR}}$. If the extractor fail, then $\mathcal{H}_1$ aborts. The PoK property of $\Pi_{\mathsf{OR}}$ ensures that with all but negligible probability the value $y^\star$ is extracted, therefore $\{\mathsf{OUT}_{\mathcal{H}_0, P_2^\star(z)}(1^\lambda, x, y)\}$ and $\{\mathsf{OUT}_{\mathcal{H}_1, P_2^\star(z)}(1^\lambda, x, y)\}$ are statistically close[17].

-$\mathcal{H}_2$ proceeds in the same way of $\mathcal{H}_1$ except that the simulator $\mathsf{Sim}_{\mathsf{NMZK}}$ of NMZK is used in order to compute the messages of NMZK played by $P_1$. Note that

---

[17] To simplify the notation here, and in the rest of the proof, we will omit that the indistinguishability between two distributions must hold for every $x \in \{0,1\}^\lambda$, $y \in \{0,1\}^\lambda$.

$Sim_{NMZK}$ rewinds $P_2^*$ from the 3rd to the 2nd round in oder to extract the trapdoor. The same is done by $E_{OR}$. Following [1,12] we let $E_{OR}$ and the extraction procedure of $Sim_{NMZK}$ work in parallel. Indeed they just rewind from the third to the second round by sending a freshly generated second round. The indistinguishability between the output distribution of these two hybrids experiments holds from the property 1 of NMZK (see the full version of this paper). In this, and also in the next hybrids, we prove that $Prob[\,stm \notin L_{NMZK}\,] \leq \nu(\lambda)$. That is, we prove that $P_2^*$ behaves honestly across the hybrid experiments even though he is receiving a simulated proof w.r.t. NMZK and st̃m does not belong to $L_{NMZK}$. In this hybrid experiment we can prove that if by contradiction this probability is non-negligible, then we can construct a reduction that breaks the property 2 of NMZK (see the full version of this paper for a formal definition). Indeed, in this hybrid experiment, the theorem that $P_2^*$ receives belongs to $L_{NMZK}$ and the simulator of $Sim_{NMZK}$ is used in order to compute and accepting transcript w.r.t. NMZK. Therefore, relying on property 2 of the definition of NMZK, we know that there exists a simulator that extracts the witness for the statement stm proved by $P_2^*$ with all but negligible probability.

-$\mathcal{H}_3$ proceeds exactly as $\mathcal{H}_2$ except for the message committed in $com_1$. More precisely in this hybrid experiment $com_1$ is a commitment of 0 instead of $x$. The indistinguishability between the output of the experiments $\mathcal{H}_2$ and $\mathcal{H}_3$ follows from the hiding property of PBCOM. Indeed we observe that the rewind made by $Sim_{NMZK}$ does not involve $com_1$ that is sent in the first round, moreover the decommitment information of $com_1$ is not used neither in $\Pi_{OR}$ nor in NMZK. To argue that $Prob[\,stm \notin L_{NMZK}\,] \leq \nu(\lambda)$ also in this hybrid experiment we still use the simulator-extractor $Sim_{NMZK}$ in order to check whether the theorem proved by $P_2^*$ is still true. If it is not the case then we can construct a reduction to the hiding of PBCOM. Note that $Sim_{NMZK}$ rewinds from the 4th to the 3rd round in order to extract the witness $w_{stm}$ for the statement stm proved by $P_2^*$, and the rewinds do not effect the reduction.

-$\mathcal{H}_4$ proceeds exactly as $\mathcal{H}_3$ except that the honest prover procedure ($\mathcal{P}_L$), instead of the special HVZK simulator ($Sim_L$), is used to compute the messages $a_1, z_1$ of the transcript $\tau_1 = (a_1, c_1, z_1)$ w.r.t. the instance $com_1$. Suppose now by contradiction that the output distributions of the hybrid experiments are distinguishable, then we can show a malicious verifier $\mathcal{V}^*$ that distinguishes between the transcript $\tau_1 = (a_1, c_1, z_1)$ computed using $Sim_L$ from a transcript computed using the honest prover procedure. In more details, let $\mathcal{C}_{SHVZK}$ be the challenger of the Special HVZK. $\mathcal{V}^*$ picks $c_1 \leftarrow \{0,1\}^\lambda$ and sends $c_1$ to $\mathcal{C}_{SHVZK}$. Upon receiving $a_1, z_1$ from $\mathcal{C}_{SHVZK}$ $\mathcal{V}^*$ plays all the messages of $\Pi_{2PC}$ as in $\mathcal{H}_3$ ($\mathcal{H}_4$) except for the messages of $\tau_1$. For these messages $\mathcal{V}^*$ acts as a proxy between $\mathcal{C}_{SHVZK}$ and $R_{\overrightarrow{OT}}^*$. At the end of the execution $\mathcal{V}^*$ runs the distinguisher $D$ that distinguishes $\{OUT_{\mathcal{H}_3, P_2^*(z)}(1^\lambda, x, y)\}$ from $\{OUT_{\mathcal{H}_4, P_2^*(z)}(1^\lambda, x, y)\}$ and outputs what $D$ outputs. We observe that if $\mathcal{C}_{SHVZK}$ sends a simulated transcript then $P_2^*$ acts as in $\mathcal{H}_3$ otherwise he acts as in $\mathcal{H}_4$. There is a subtlety in the reduction. $\mathcal{V}^*$ runs $Sim_{NMZK}$ that rewinds from the third to the second round. This means that $\mathcal{V}^*$ has to be able to complete every time the third round even though he is receiving different challenges $c^1, \ldots, c^{\mathsf{poly}(\lambda)}$ w.r.t to $\Pi_{\mathsf{OR}}$. Since we are splitting the challenge $c$, $V^\star$ can just keep fixed the value $c_1$ reusing the same $z_1$ (sent by $C_{\mathsf{SHVZK}}$) and can compute an answer to a different $c'_0 = c^i \oplus c_1$ using the knowledge of the decommitment information of $\mathsf{com}_0$. To argue that $\mathrm{Prob}\,[\,\mathsf{stm} \notin L_{\mathsf{NMZK}}\,] \leq \nu(\lambda)$, also in this hybrid experiment we can use the simulator-extractor $\mathsf{Sim}_{\mathsf{NMZK}}$ to check whether the theorem proved by $P^\star_2$ is still true. If it is not the case we can construct a reduction to the special HVZK property of $\mathsf{BL}_L$. Note that the rewinds of $\mathsf{Sim}_{\mathsf{NMZK}}$ from the fourth to the third round do not affect the reduction.

-$\mathcal{H}_5$ proceeds exactly as $\mathcal{H}_4$ except that the special HVZK simulator ($\mathsf{Sim}_L$), instead of honest prover procedure, is used to compute the prover's messages $a_0, z_0$ for the transcript $\tau_0 = (a_0, c_0, z_0)$ w.r.t. the instance $\mathsf{com}_0$. The indistinguishability between the outputs of $\mathcal{H}_4$ and $\mathcal{H}_5$ comes from the same arguments used to prove that $\{\mathsf{OUT}_{\mathcal{H}_3, P^\star_2(z)}(1^\lambda, x, y)\} \approx \{\mathsf{OUT}_{\mathcal{H}_4, P^\star_2(z)}(1^\lambda, x, y)\}$. Moreover the same arguments of before can be used to prove that $\mathrm{Prob}\,[\,\mathsf{stm} \notin L_{\mathsf{NMZK}}\,] \leq \nu(\lambda)$.

-$\mathcal{H}_6$ proceeds exactly as $\mathcal{H}_5$ except for the message committed in $\mathsf{com}_0$. More precisely in this hybrid experiment $\mathsf{com}_0$ is a commitment of $0$ instead of $x$. The indistinguishability between the outputs of $\mathcal{H}_5$ and $\mathcal{H}_6$ comes from the same arguments used to prove that $\{\mathsf{OUT}_{\mathcal{H}_2, P^\star_2(z)}(1^\lambda, x, y)\} \approx \{\mathsf{OUT}_{\mathcal{H}_3, P^\star_2(z)}(1^\lambda, x, y)\}$. Moreover the same arguments as before can be used to prove that $\mathrm{Prob}\,[\,\mathsf{stm} \notin L_{\mathsf{NMZK}}\,] \leq \nu(\lambda)$.

-$\mathcal{H}_7$ proceeds in the same way of $\mathcal{H}_6$ except that the simulator of $\Pi^\gamma_{\overrightarrow{\mathcal{OT}}}$, $\mathsf{Sim}_{\mathcal{OT}}$, is used instead of the sender algorithm $S_{\overrightarrow{\mathcal{OT}}}$. From the simulatable security against malicious receiver of $\Pi^\gamma_{\overrightarrow{\mathcal{OT}}}$ for every $\gamma = \mathsf{poly}(\lambda)$ follows that the output distributions of $\mathcal{H}_7$ and $\mathcal{H}_6$ are indistinguishable. Suppose by contradiction this claim does not hold, then we can show a malicious receiver $R^\star_{\overrightarrow{\mathcal{OT}}}$ that breaks the simulatable security of $\Pi^\gamma_{\overrightarrow{\mathcal{OT}}}$ against a malicious receiver. In more details, let $\mathcal{C}_{\mathcal{OT}}$ be the challenger of $\Pi^\gamma_{\overrightarrow{\mathcal{OT}}}$. $R^\star_{\overrightarrow{\mathcal{OT}}}$ plays all the messages of $\Pi_{2\mathcal{PC}}$ as in $\mathcal{H}_6$ ($\mathcal{H}_7$) except for the messages of $\Pi^\gamma_{\overrightarrow{\mathcal{OT}}}$. For these messages $R^\star_{\overrightarrow{\mathcal{OT}}}$ acts as a proxy between $\mathcal{C}_{\mathcal{OT}}$ and $P^\star_2$. In the end of the execution $R^\star_{\overrightarrow{\mathcal{OT}}}$ runs the distinguisher $D$ that distinguishes $\{\mathsf{OUT}_{\mathcal{H}_6, P^\star_2(z)}(1^\lambda, x, y)\}$ from $\{\mathsf{OUT}_{\mathcal{H}_7, P^\star_2(z)}(1^\lambda, x, y)\}$ and outputs what $D$ outputs. We observe that if $\mathcal{C}_{\mathcal{OT}}$ acts as the simulator then $P^\star_2$ acts as in $\mathcal{H}_7$ otherwise he acts as in $\mathcal{H}_6$. To prove that $\mathrm{Prob}\,[\,\mathsf{stm} \notin L_{\mathsf{NMZK}}\,]$ is still negligible we use the same arguments as before with this additional important observation. The simulator-extractor $\mathsf{Sim}_{\mathsf{NMZK}}$ rewinds also from the 4th to the 3rd round. These rewinds could cause $P^\star_2$ to ask multiple third rounds of OT $\tilde{\mathsf{ot}}^3_i$ ($i = 1, \ldots, \mathsf{poly}(\lambda)$). In this case $R^\star_{\overrightarrow{\mathcal{OT}}}$ can simply forward $\tilde{\mathsf{ot}}^3_i$ to $\mathcal{C}_{\mathcal{OT}}$ and obtains from $\mathcal{C}_{\mathcal{OT}}$ an additional $\tilde{\mathsf{ot}}^4_i$. This behavior of $R^\star_{\overrightarrow{\mathcal{OT}}}$ is allowed because $\Pi^\gamma_{\overrightarrow{\mathcal{OT}}}$ is simulatable secure against a malicious receiver even when the last two rounds of $\Pi^\gamma_{\overrightarrow{\mathcal{OT}}}$ are executed $\gamma$ times (as stated in Theorem 2). Therefore the reduction still works if we set $\gamma$ equals to the expected number of rewinds that

$\mathsf{Sim}_{\mathsf{NMZK}}$ could do. We observe that since we have proved that $\mathsf{stm} \in L_{\mathsf{NMZK}}$, then the value extracted $y^\star$ is compatible with the query that $\mathsf{Sim}_{\mathcal{OT}}$ could do. That is, $\mathsf{Sim}_{\mathcal{OT}}$ will ask only the value $(\tilde{Z}_{1,y_1}, \ldots, \tilde{Z}_{\lambda,y_\lambda})$.

-$\mathcal{H}_8$ differs from $\mathcal{H}_7$ in the way the rounds of $\Pi_{\overrightarrow{\mathcal{OT}}}^\gamma$, where $P_2^\star$ acts as sender, are computed. More precisely instead of using $x$ as input, $0^\lambda$ is used. Note that from this hybrid onward it is not possible anymore to compute the output by running $\mathsf{EvalGC}$ as in the previous hybrid experiments. This is because we are not able to recover the correct labels to evaluate the garbled circuit. Therefore $\mathcal{H}_8$ computes the output by directly evaluating $v_1 = F_1(x, y^\star)$, where $y^\star$ is the input of $P_2^\star$ obtained by using $\mathsf{E}_{\mathsf{OR}}$. The indistinguishability between the output distributions of $\mathcal{H}_7$ and $\mathcal{H}_8$ comes from the security of $\Pi_{\overrightarrow{\mathcal{OT}}}^\gamma$ against malicious sender. Indeed, suppose by contradiction that it is not the case, then we can show a malicious sender $S_{\overrightarrow{\mathcal{OT}}}^\star$ that breaks the indistinguishability security of $\Pi_{\overrightarrow{\mathcal{OT}}}^\gamma$ against a malicious sender. In more details, let $\mathcal{C}_{\mathcal{OT}}$ be the challenger. $S_{\overrightarrow{\mathcal{OT}}}^\star$ plays all the messages of $\Pi_{2\mathcal{PC}}$ as in $\mathcal{H}_7$ ($\mathcal{H}_8$) except for the messages of OT where he acts as a receiver. For these messages $S_{\overrightarrow{\mathcal{OT}}}^\star$ plays as a proxy between $\mathcal{C}_{\mathcal{OT}}$ and $P_2^\star$. At the end of the execution $S_{\overrightarrow{\mathcal{OT}}}^\star$ runs the distinguisher $D$ that distinguishes the output of $\mathcal{H}_7$ from $\mathcal{H}_8$ and outputs what $D$ outputs. We observe that if $\mathcal{C}_{\mathcal{OT}}$ computes the messages of $\Pi_{\overrightarrow{\mathcal{OT}}}^\gamma$ using the input $0^\lambda$ then $P_2^\star$ acts as in $\mathcal{H}_8$ otherwise he acts as in $\mathcal{H}_7$. In this security proof there is another subtlety. During the reduction $S_{\overrightarrow{\mathcal{OT}}}^\star$ runs $\mathsf{Sim}_{\mathsf{NMZK}}$ that rewinds from the third to the second round. This means that $P_2^\star$ could send multiple different second round $\mathsf{ot}_i^2$ of OT (with $i = 1, \ldots, \mathsf{poly}(\lambda)$). $S_{\overrightarrow{\mathcal{OT}}}^\star$ cannot forward these other messages to $\mathcal{C}_{\mathcal{OT}}$ (he cannot rewind the challenger). This is not a problem because the third round of $\Pi_{\overrightarrow{\mathcal{OT}}}^\gamma$ is replayable (as proved in Theorem 2). That is the round $\mathsf{ot}^3$ received from the challenger can be used to answer to any $\mathsf{ot}^2$. To prove that $\mathrm{Prob}[\,\mathsf{stm} \notin L_{\mathsf{NMZK}}\,] \leq \nu(\lambda)$ we use the same arguments as before by observing the rewinds made by the simulator-extractor from the fourth round to the third one do not affect the reduction.

-$\mathcal{H}_9$ proceeds in the same way of $\mathcal{H}_8$ except for the message committed in $\tilde{\mathsf{com}}_{lab}$. More precisely, instead of computing a commitment of the labels $(\tilde{Z}_{1,0}, \tilde{Z}_{1,1}, \ldots, \tilde{Z}_{\lambda,0}, \tilde{Z}_{\lambda,1})$, a commitment of $0^\lambda || \ldots || 0^\lambda$ is computed. The indistinguishability between the output distributions of $\mathcal{H}_8$ and $\mathcal{H}_9$ follows from the hiding of PBCOM. Moreover, $\mathrm{Prob}[\,\mathsf{stm} \notin L_{\mathsf{NMZK}}\,] \leq \nu(\lambda)$ in this hybrid experiment due to the same arguments used previously.

-$\mathcal{H}_{10}$ proceeds in the same way of $\mathcal{H}_9$ except for the message committed in $\tilde{\mathsf{com}}_{\mathsf{GC}_y}$: instead of computing a commitment of the Yao's garbled circuit $\tilde{\mathsf{GC}}_x$, a commitment of 0 is computed. The indistinguishability between the output distributions of $\mathcal{H}_9$ and $\mathcal{H}_{10}$ follow from the hiding of PBCOM. $\mathrm{Prob}[\,\mathsf{stm} \notin L_{\mathsf{NMZK}}\,] \leq \nu(\lambda)$ in this hybrid experiment due to the same arguments used previously.

-$\mathcal{H}_{11}$ proceeds in the same way of $\mathcal{H}_{10}$ except that the simulator $\mathsf{SimGC}$ it is run (instead of $\mathsf{GenGC}$) in order to obtain the Yao's garbled circuit and the corresponding labels. In more details, once $y^\star$ is obtained by $\mathsf{E}_{\mathsf{OR}}$ (in the third round), the ideal functionality $F$ is invoked on input $y^\star$. Upon receiving $v_2 = F_2(x, y^\star)$ the hybrid experiment compute $(\tilde{\mathsf{GC}}_\star, \tilde{Z}_1, \ldots, \tilde{Z}_\lambda) \leftarrow \mathsf{SimGC}(1^\lambda, F_2, y^\star, v_2)$ and replies to the query made by $\mathsf{Sim}_{\mathcal{OT}}$ with $(\tilde{Z}_1, \ldots, \tilde{Z}_\lambda)$. Furthermore, in the 4th round the simulated Yao's garbled circuit $\tilde{\mathsf{GC}}_\star$ is sent, instead of the one generated using $\mathsf{GenGC}$. The indistinguishability between the output distributions of $\mathcal{H}_{10}$ and $\mathcal{H}_{11}$ follows from the security of the Yao's garbled circuit. To prove that $\mathrm{Prob}\,[\,\mathsf{stm} \notin L_{\mathsf{NMZK}}\,] \leq \nu(\lambda)$ we use the same arguments as before by observing the rewinds made by the simulator-extractor from the fourth round to the third one do not affect the reduction. The proof ends with the observation that $\mathcal{H}_{11}$ corresponds to the simulated execution with the simulator $\mathsf{Sim}$.

**Acknowledgments.** We thank Ivan Damgård and Claudio Orlandi for remarkable discussions on two-party computations and the suggestion of using public key encryption schemes with special properties instead of trapdoor permutations to construct our oblivious transfer protocol. Research supported in part by "GNCS - INdAM", EU COST Action IC1306, NSF grant 1619348, DARPA, US-Israel BSF grant 2012366, OKAWA Foundation Research Award, IBM Faculty Research Award, Xerox Faculty Research Award, B. John Garrick Foundation Award, Teradata Research Award, and Lockheed-Martin Corporation Research Award. The views expressed are those of the authors and do not reflect position of the Department of Defense or the U.S. Government.

# References

1. Ananth, P., Choudhuri, A.R., Jain, A.: A new approach to round-optimal secure multiparty computation. In: Katz, J., Shacham, H. (eds.) CRYPTO 2017. LNCS, vol. 10401, pp. 468–499. Springer, Cham (2017). https://doi.org/10.1007/978-3-319-63688-7_16

2. Blum, M.: How to prove a theorem so no one else can claim it. In: Proceedings of the International Congress of Mathematicians, pp. 1444–1454 (1986)

3. Ciampi, M., Ostrovsky, R., Siniscalchi, L., Visconti, I.: Concurrent non-malleable commitments (and more) in 3 rounds. In: Robshaw, M., Katz, J. (eds.) CRYPTO 2016. LNCS, vol. 9816, pp. 270–299. Springer, Heidelberg (2016). https://doi.org/10.1007/978-3-662-53015-3_10

4. Ciampi, M., Ostrovsky, R., Siniscalchi, L., Visconti, I.: Delayed-input non-malleable zero knowledge and multi-party coin tossing in four rounds. In: Kalai, Y., Reyzin, L. (eds.) TCC 2017, Part I. LNCS, vol. 10677, pp. 711–742. Springer, Cham (2017). Full version. https://eprint.iacr.org/2017/931

5. Ciampi, M., Ostrovsky, R., Siniscalchi, L., Visconti, I.: Round-optimal secure two-party computation from trapdoor permutations. Cryptology ePrint Archive, Report 2017/920 (2017). http://eprint.iacr.org/2017/920

6. Ciampi, M., Persiano, G., Scafuro, A., Siniscalchi, L., Visconti, I.: Improved or-composition of sigma-protocols. In: Kushilevitz, E., Malkin, T. (eds.) TCC 2016. LNCS, vol. 9563, pp. 112–141. Springer, Heidelberg (2016). https://doi.org/10.1007/978-3-662-49099-0_5

7. Ciampi, M., Persiano, G., Scafuro, A., Siniscalchi, L., Visconti, I.: Online/Offline or composition of sigma protocols. In: Fischlin, M., Coron, J.-S. (eds.) EUROCRYPT 2016. LNCS, vol. 9666, pp. 63–92. Springer, Heidelberg (2016). https://doi.org/10.1007/978-3-662-49896-5_3

8. Cramer, R., Damgård, I., Schoenmakers, B.: Proofs of partial knowledge and simplified design of witness hiding protocols. In: Desmedt, Y.G. (ed.) CRYPTO 1994. LNCS, vol. 839, pp. 174–187. Springer, Heidelberg (1994). https://doi.org/10.1007/3-540-48658-5_19

9. Even, S., Goldreich, O., Lempel, A.: A randomized protocol for signing contracts. In: Advances in Cryptology: Proceedings of CRYPTO 06982, 1982. pp. 205–210. Plenum Press, New York (1982)

10. Garay, J.A., MacKenzie, P., Yang, K.: Strengthening zero-knowledge protocols using signatures. J. Cryptol. **19**(2), 169–209 (2006)

11. Garg, S., Mukherjee, P., Pandey, O., Polychroniadou, A.: Personal communication, August 2016

12. Garg, S., Mukherjee, P., Pandey, O., Polychroniadou, A.: The Exact Round Complexity of Secure Computation. In: Fischlin, M., Coron, J.-S. (eds.) EUROCRYPT 2016. LNCS, vol. 9666, pp. 448–476. Springer, Heidelberg (2016). https://doi.org/10.1007/978-3-662-49896-5_16

13. Gertner, Y., Kannan, S., Malkin, T., Reingold, O., Viswanathan, M.: The relationship between public key encryption and oblivious transfer. In: 41st Annual Symposium on Foundations of Computer Science, FOCS 2000, pp. 325–335 (2000)

14. Goldreich, O., Micali, S., Wigderson, A.: How to play any mental game or A completeness theorem for protocols with honest majority. In: Proceedings of the 19th Annual ACMSymposium on Theory of Computing (1987)

15. Katz, J., Ostrovsky, R.: Round-Optimal Secure Two-Party Computation. In: Franklin, M. (ed.) CRYPTO 2004. LNCS, vol. 3152, pp. 335–354. Springer, Heidelberg (2004). https://doi.org/10.1007/978-3-540-28628-8_21

16. Ostrovsky, R., Richelson, S., Scafuro, A.: Round-Optimal Black-Box Two-Party Computation. In: Gennaro, R., Robshaw, M. (eds.) CRYPTO 2015. LNCS, vol. 9216, pp. 339–358. Springer, Heidelberg (2015). https://doi.org/10.1007/978-3-662-48000-7_17

17. Pandey, O., Pass, R., Vaikuntanathan, V.: Adaptive One-Way Functions and Applications. In: Wagner, D. (ed.) CRYPTO 2008. LNCS, vol. 5157, pp. 57–74. Springer, Heidelberg (2008). https://doi.org/10.1007/978-3-540-85174-5_4

18. Polychroniadou, A.: On the Communication and Round Complexity of Secure Computation. Ph.D. thesis, Aarhus University (2016)

19. Yao, A.C.: Protocols for secure computations (extended abstract). In: 23rd Annual Symposium on Foundations of Computer Science, 1982. pp. 160–164. IEEE Computer Society (1982)

# Delayed-Input Non-Malleable Zero Knowledge and Multi-Party Coin Tossing in Four Rounds

Michele Ciampi[1], Rafail Ostrovsky[2], Luisa Siniscalchi[1(✉)], and Ivan Visconti[1]

[1] DIEM, University of Salerno, Fisciano, Italy
{mciampi,lsiniscalchi,visconti}@unisa.it
[2] UCLA, Los Angeles, USA
rafail@cs.ucla.edu

**Abstract.** In this work we start from the following two results in the state-of-the art:

1. 4-round non-malleable zero knowledge (NMZK): Goyal et al. in FOCS 2014 showed the first 4-round one-one NMZK argument from one-way functions (OWFs). Their construction requires the prover to know the instance and the witness already at the 2nd round.
2. 4-round multi-party coin tossing (MPCT): Garg et al. in Eurocrypt 2016 showed the first 4-round protocol for MPCT. Their result crucially relies on 3-round 3-robust parallel non-malleable commitments. So far there is no candidate construction for such a commitment scheme under standard polynomial-time hardness assumptions.

We improve the state-of-the art on NMZK and MPCT by presenting the following two results:

1. a *delayed-input* 4-round one-*many* NMZK argument $\Pi_{\mathsf{NMZK}}$ from OWFs; moreover $\Pi_{\mathsf{NMZK}}$ is also a *delayed-input* many-many *synchronous* NMZK argument.
2. a 4-round MPCT protocol $\Pi_{\mathsf{MPCT}}$ from one-to-one OWFs; $\Pi_{\mathsf{MPCT}}$ uses $\Pi_{\mathsf{NMZK}}$ as subprotocol and exploits the special properties (e.g., delayed input, many-many synchronous) of $\Pi_{\mathsf{NMZK}}$.

Both $\Pi_{\mathsf{NMZK}}$ and $\Pi_{\mathsf{MPCT}}$ make use of a special proof of knowledge that offers additional security guarantees when played in parallel with other protocols. The new technique behind such a proof of knowledge is an additional contribution of this work and is of independent interest.

## 1 Introduction

Non-malleable zero-knowledge (NMZK) and secure multi-party computation (MPC) are fundamental primitives in Cryptography. In this work we will study these two primitives and for the case of MPC we will focus on the coin-tossing functionality that is among the most studied functionalities.

© International Association for Cryptologic Research 2017
Y. Kalai and L. Reyzin (Eds.): TCC 2017, Part I, LNCS 10677, pp. 711–742, 2017.
https://doi.org/10.1007/978-3-319-70500-2_24

**NMZK.** The first construction of NMZK was given by Dolev et al. in [15]. Later on, Barak in [2] showed the first constant-round construction. An improved construction was then given by Pass and Rosen in [35,36]. The work of Goyal et al. [23] obtained the first round-optimal construction requiring only 4 rounds and one-way functions (OWFs). Their construction requires the instance and the witness to be known already when the prover plays his first round. Their definition is the standard one-one definition where the adversary opens two sessions, one with a prover and one with a verifier.

The fact that the instance and the witness need to be known already at the second round is an important limitation when NMZK is used as subprotocol to prove statements about another subprotocol played in parallel. Moreover the one-one security is an important limitation when NMZK is used in a multi-party scenario where several of such argument systems are played in parallel.

The above two limitations clearly raise the following natural and interesting open questions:

*Open Question 1:* is there a 4-round delayed-input NMZK argument system?

*Open Question 2:* is there a 4-round many-many synchronous NMZK argument system?

**Multi-party coin-flipping (MPCT).** In [24], Katz et al. obtained a constant-round secure MPC protocol using sub-exponential hardness assumptions. This results was then improved by Pass in [34] that showed how to get bounded-concurrent secure MPC for any functionality with standard assumptions. Further results of Goyal [19] and Goyal et al. [21] relied on better assumptions but with a round complexity still far from optimal.

A very recent work of Garg et al. [18] makes a long jump ahead towards fully understanding the round complexity of secure MPCT. They show that the existence of a 3-round 3-robust parallel non-malleable commitment scheme implies a 4-round protocol for secure MPCT for polynomially many coins with black-box simulation. Some candidate instantiations of such special commitment scheme [17,38] are the one of Pass et al. [33] based on non-falsifiable assumptions, or the one of Ciampi et al. [6] based on sub-exponentially strong one-to-one one-way functions. The achieved round complexity (i.e., 4 rounds) is proven optimal in [18] when simulation is black box and the number of bits in the output of the functionality is superlogarithmic.

A very recent result of Ananth et al. [1] constructs a 4-round MPC protocol for any functionality assuming DDH w.r.t. superpolynomial-time adversaries. The above state-of-the art leaves open the following question.

*Open Question 3:* is there a 4-round secure MPCT protocol under standard assumptions?

## 1.1   Our Contribution

In this paper we solve the above 3 open problems. More precisely we present the following results:

1. a *delayed-input* 4-round one-*many* NMZK argument $\Pi_{\mathsf{NMZK}}$ from OWFs, therefore solving Open Question 1; moreover $\Pi_{\mathsf{NMZK}}$ is also a *delayed-input* many-many *synchronous* NMZK argument, therefore solving Open Question 2;
2. a 4-round MPCT protocol $\Pi_{\mathsf{MPCT}}$ from one-to-one OWFs, therefore solving Open Question 3[1].

The two constructions are not uncorrelated. Indeed $\Pi_{\mathsf{MPCT}}$ uses $\Pi_{\mathsf{NMZK}}$ as subprotocol and exploits the special properties (e.g., delayed input, many-many synchronous) of $\Pi_{\mathsf{NMZK}}$. Moreover both $\Pi_{\mathsf{NMZK}}$ and $\Pi_{\mathsf{MPCT}}$ make use of a special proof of knowledge that offers additional security guarantees when played in parallel with other protocols. Designing such a proof of knowledge is an additional contribution of this work and is of independent interest.

Interestingly, several years after the 4-round zero knowledge argument system from OWFs of [3], the same optimal round complexity and optimal complexity assumptions have been shown sufficient in this work for delayed-input NMZK and in [5] for resettably sound zero knowledge.

More details on our two new constructions follow below.

**MPCT from NMZK.** A first main idea that allows us to bypass the strong requirements of the construction of [18] is that we avoid robust/non-malleable commitments and instead focus on non-malleable zero knowledge. Since we want a 4-round MPCT protocol, we need to rely on 4-round NMZK. The only known construction is the one of [23]. Unfortunately their NMZK argument system seems to be problematic to use in our design of a 4-round MPCT protocol. There are two main reasons. The first reason is that the construction of [23] uses the technique of secure computation in the head and therefore requires the instance already in the second round. This is often a problem when the NMZK argument is played in parallel with other subprotocols as in our construction. Indeed these additional subprotocols end in the 3rd or 4th round and typically[2] need to be strengthened by a zero-knowledge proof of correctness. The second reason is that in the setting of 4-round MPCT the adversary can play as a many-many synchronous man-in-the-middle (MiM), while the construction of [23] is proved one-one non-malleable only.

We therefore improve the state-of-the-art on NMZK constructing a delayed-input NMZK argument system. Our construction only needs one-way functions and is secure even when (a) there are polynomially many verifiers (i.e., it is a one-many NMZK argument), and (b) there are polynomially many provers and they are in parallel. We will crucially use both the delayed-input property and security with parallelized many provers and verifiers in our secure MPCT construction. Moreover our NMZK is also crucially used in [8].

---

[1] An unpublished prior work of Goyal et al. [20] achieves the same result on MPCT using completely different techniques.

[2] Indeed, even the construction of [18] that makes use of a special non-malleable commitments requires also a delayed-input zero-knowledge argument.

## 1.2   Technical Overview on Our NMZK

**Issues in natural constructions of NMZK.** A natural construction of a NMZK argument from OWFs consists of having: (1) a 3-round sub-protocol useful to extract a trapdoor from the verifier of NMZK; (2) a 4-round non-malleable commitment of the witness for the statement to be proved; (3) a 4-round witness-indistinguishable proof of knowledge (WIPoK) to prove that either the committed message is a witness or the trapdoor is known. By combining instantiations from OWFs of the above 3 tools in parallel we could obtain 4-round NMZK from OWFs. The simulator-extractor for such a scheme would (1) extract the trapdoor from the verifier; (2) commit to 0 in the non-malleable commitment; (3) use the trapdoor as witness in the WIPoK; (4) extract the witness from the arguments given by the MiM by extracting from the WIPoK or from the non-malleable commitment.

Unfortunately it is not clear how to prove the security of this scheme when all sub-protocols are squeezed into 4 rounds. The problem arises from the interactive nature of the involved primitives. Indeed notice that the 4-round non-malleable commitment is executed in parallel with the 4-round WIPoK. When in a hybrid of the security proof the trapdoor is used as witness in the 4-round WIPoK played on the left, the MiM could do the same and also commits to the message 0 in the non-malleable commitment. To detect this behavior, in order to break the WI, the reduction should extract the message committed in the non-malleable commitment by rewinding the MiM. This implies that also the 4-round WIPoK involved in the reduction must be rewound (we recall that these two sub-protocols are executed in parallel). It is important to observe that if in some hybrid we allow the MiM to commit to the message 0 when the witness of the WIPoK given on the left is switched to the trapdoor, then the simulator-extractor (that corresponds to the final hybrid) will have no way to extract a witness from the MiM (and this is required by the definition of NMZK). Indeed from a successful MiM that commits to 0 the extraction from the WIPoK can only give in output the trapdoor. Therefore the simulator-extractor would fail.

**A special delayed-input WIPoK $\Pi^{\mathsf{OR}}$.** In order to overcome the above problem we follow a recent idea proposed in [7] where non-interactive primitives instead of 3-rounds WIPoKs are used in order to construct a concurrent non-malleable commitment in four rounds. In this way, in every security reduction to such primitives, it will be always possible to extract the message committed in the non-malleable commitment without interfering with the challenger involved in the reduction.

In [7] the authors propose an ad-hoc technique that avoids such a *rewinding issue* by using a combination of instance-dependent trapdoor commitments (IDTCom) and special honest-verifier zero knowledge (Special HVZK) proofs of knowledge. In this paper we propose a generic approach to construct a special delayed-input WIPoK $\Pi^{\mathsf{OR}}$ that can be nicely composed with other protocols in parallel. We construct $\Pi^{\mathsf{OR}}$ in two steps.

In 1st step we consider the construction of 3-round WIPoK for $\mathcal{NP}$ of Lapidot and Shamir (LS) [25][3] that enjoys adaptive-input Special HVZK[4] and observe that LS does not enjoy adaptive-input special soundness. That is, given and accepting transcript $(a, 0, z_0)$ for the statement $x_0$ and an accepting transcript $(a, 1, z_1)$ for the statement $x_1$, then only the witness $x_1$ can be efficiently extracted. More precisely, only the witness for the statement where the challenge-bit was equal to $1$[5] (see Definition 5 for a formal definition of adaptive-input special soundness) can be extracted. Therefore we propose a compiler that using $\mathsf{LS} = (\mathcal{P}, \mathcal{V})$ in a black-box way outputs a 3-round protocol $\mathsf{LS}' = (\mathcal{P}', \mathcal{V}')$ that maintains the adaptive-input Special HVZK and moreover enjoys adaptive-input special soundness.

In the second step we show how to combine the OR composition of statements proposed in [12] with $\mathsf{LS}'$ in oder to obtain a WIPoK $\varPi^{\mathsf{OR}}$ such that: (a) a reduction can be successfully completed even when there are rewinds due to another protocol played in parallel; (b) the statement (and the corresponding witness) are required to be known only in the last round. Both properties are extremely helpful when a WIPoK is played with other protocols in parallel.

We now give more details about the two steps mentioned above.

– *First step:* $\mathsf{LS}' = (\mathcal{P}', \mathcal{V}')$. Our construction of $\mathsf{LS}'$ works as follows. The prover $\mathcal{P}'$ runs two times $\mathcal{P}$ using different randomnesses thus obtaining two first rounds of LS $a_0$ and $a_1$. Upon receiving the challenge-bit $b$ from the verifier $\mathcal{V}$, the statement $x$ to be proved and the corresponding witness $w$, $\mathcal{P}'$ runs $\mathcal{P}$ in order to compute the answer $z_0$ with respect to the challenge $b$ for $a_0$ and the answer $z_1$ with respect to the challenge $1 - b$ for $a_1$. $\mathcal{V}'$ accepts if both $(a_0, b, z_0, x)$ and $(a_1, 1 - b, z_1, x)$ are accepting for $\mathcal{V}$. We now observe that every accepting transcript for $\mathsf{LS}'$ contains a sub-transcript that is accepting for $\mathcal{V}$ where the bit $1$ has been used as a challenge. From what we have discussed above, it is easy to see that $\mathsf{LS}'$ enjoys adaptive-input special soundness.

– *Second step: adaptive-input PoK for the OR of compound statements.* We combine together two executions of $\mathsf{LS}'$ by using the trick for composing two $\varSigma$-protocols $\varSigma_0, \varSigma_1$ to construct a $\varSigma$-protocol for the $\mathcal{NP}$-language $L_0$ OR $L_1$ [12]. Let the compound statement to be proved be $(x_0, x_1)$, with $x_0 \in L_0$ and $x_1 \in L_1$, and let $w_b$ be the witness for $x_b$. The protocol $\varPi^{\mathsf{OR}}$ proposed in [12] considers two $\varSigma$-protocols $\varSigma_0$ and $\varSigma_1$ (respectively for $L_0$ and $L_1$) executed in parallel, but after receiving the challenge $c$ form the verifier, the prover can use as challenges for $\varSigma_0$ and $\varSigma_1$ every pair $(c_0, c_1)$ s.t. $c_0 \oplus c_1 = c$. Therefore the prover could choose in advance one of the challenge to be used, (e.g., $c_{1-b}$), and compute the other one by setting $c_b = c \oplus c_{1-b}$. In this way the transcript for $\varSigma_{1-b}$ can be computed using the Special HVZK simulator while the transcript for $\varSigma_b$ is computed using the witness $w_b$. Thus the prover has the "freedom" of picking

---

[3] See Appendix B.1 for a detailed description of [25].

[4] By *adaptive-input* we mean that the security of the cryptographic primitive holds even when the statement to be proved is adversarially chosen in the last round.

[5] For ease of exposition be consider LS with one-bit challenge, but our result hold for an arbitrarily chosen challenge length.

one out of two of the challenge before seeing $c$, but still being able to complete the execution of both $\Sigma_0$ and $\Sigma_1$ for every $c$. We will show that this "freedom" is sufficient to switch between using $w_0$ and $w_1$ (in order to prove WI) even when it is required to answer to additional (and different) challenges $c^1, \ldots, c^{\mathsf{poly}(\lambda)}$ (i.e., when some rewinds occur). Indeed it is possible to change the witness used (from $w_0$ to $w_1$) in two steps relying first on the Special HVZK of $\Sigma_1$, and then on the Special HVZK of $\Sigma_0$. More precisely we consider the hybrid experiment $H^{w_0}$ as the experiment where in $\Pi^{\mathsf{OR}}$ the witness $w_0$ is used (analogously we define $H^{w_1}$). We now consider $H^{w_0, w_1}$ that differs from $H^{w_0}$ because both the witnesses $w_0$ and $w_1$ are used. We prove that $H^{w_0}$ and $H^{w_0, w_1}$ are indistinguishable due to the Special HVZK of $\Sigma_1$ even tough $\Pi^{\mathsf{OR}}$ is rewound polynomially many times. The reduction works as follows. A challenge $c_1$ is chosen before the protocol $\Pi^{\mathsf{OR}}$ starts and the Special HVZK challenger is invoked thus obtaining $(a_1, z_1)$. The transcript for $\Sigma_0$ is computed by the reduction using the witness $w_0$ in order to answer to the challenge $c_0^i = c^i \oplus c_1$ for $i = 1, \ldots, \mathsf{poly}(\lambda)$. We recall the we are in a setting where $\Pi^{\mathsf{OR}}$ could be rewound, and therefore the reduction needs to answer to multiple challenges. We observe that the reduction to the Special HVZK is not disturbed by these rewinds because $c_1$ can be kept fixed. The same arguments can be used to prove that $H^{w_0, w_1}$ is computationally indistinguishable from $H^{w_1}$.

We then show that as $\Pi^{\mathsf{OR}}$ preserves the special-soundness of the input $\Sigma$-protocols, as well as preserves the adaptive-input special soundness when two instantiations of $\mathsf{LS}'$ are used. Moreover the above reductions to Special HVZK can be done relying on adaptive-input Special HVZK. Finally $\Pi^{\mathsf{OR}}$ can be upgrade from adaptive-input special soundness to adaptive-input PoK using a theorem of [11].

**Our NMZK argument system NMZK.** We run $\Pi^{\mathsf{OR}}$ in parallel with a 4-round public-coin one-one honest-extractable synchronous non-malleable commitment scheme $\Pi_{\mathsf{nm}}$[6]. A construction for such a scheme in 4 rounds was given by [22]. The prover of the NMZK argument runs $\Pi^{\mathsf{OR}}$ in order to prove either the validity of some $\mathcal{NP}$-statement, or that the non-malleable commitment computed using $\Pi_{\mathsf{nm}}$ contains a trapdoor. The simulator for NMZK works by extracting the trapdoor, committing to it using the non-malleable commitment, and using knowledge of both the trapdoor and the opening information used to compute the non-malleable commitment as a witness for $\Pi^{\mathsf{OR}}$. The 3-round subprotocol from OWFs for the trapdoor extraction follows the one of [7]. More precisely the trapdoor is represented by the knowledge of two signatures under a verification key sent by the verifier in the 1st round. In order to allow the extraction of the trapdoor, the verifier of NMZK sends a signature of a message randomly chosen in the 3rd round by the prover.

---

[6] All such properties are pretty standard except honest extractability. Informally, this property means that there is a successful extractor that gives in output the committed message having black-box access to an honest sender.

**The security proof of one-many NMZK.** The simulator of NMZK extracts the trapdoor[7], and commits to it using $\Pi_{\mathsf{nm}}$. Following the proof approach provided in [6], we need to prove that the MiM adversary does not do the same. More precisely we want to guarantee that there is no right session where the MiM commits to two signatures of two different messages. The reduction to the non-malleability of the underlying commitment scheme isolates one right session guessing that the MiM has committed there to the trapdoor. The distinguisher for the non-malleable commitment takes as input the committed message an checks if it corresponds to two signatures of two different messages for a given signature key. The above proof approach works only with synchronous sessions (i.e., for synchronous one-many NMZK). Indeed $\Pi_{\mathsf{nm}}$ is secure only in the synchronous case. In order to deal with the asynchronous case we rely on the *honest-extractability* of $\Pi_{\mathsf{nm}}$.

We recall that $\Pi^{\mathsf{OR}}$ is run in parallel with $\Pi_{\mathsf{nm}}$ in order to ensure that either the witness for an $\mathcal{NP}$-statement $x$ is known or the trapdoor has been *correctly* committed using $\Pi_{\mathsf{nm}}$. For our propose we only need to ensure that the MiM never commits to the trapdoor. If this is not the case than there exists a right session where the MiM is committing correctly to the trapdoor using $\Pi_{\mathsf{nm}}$ with non-negligible probability. This means that we can extract the message committed by the MiM by just relying on the honest-extractability of $\Pi_{\mathsf{nm}}$. Therefore we can make a reduction to the hiding of $\Pi_{\mathsf{nm}}$[8].

In order to prove that also in the reductions to adaptive-input Special HVZK the MiM still does not commit to the trapdoor we can uses the same approach explained above. Note that in these reductions it is crucial that the rewinds needed to extract the committed message in $\Pi_{\mathsf{nm}}$ do not disturb the challengers involved in the reductions.

**From one-many NMZK to synchronous many-many NMZK.** Our one-many NMZK is also synchronous many-many NMZK. Indeed, the simulator can extract (simultaneously) the trapdoor from the right sessions, playing as described above. The only substantial difference is that we need to use a many-one non-malleable commitment with all the properties listed above. Following the approach proposed in the security proof of Proposition 1 provided in [28], it is possible to claim that a synchronous (one-one) non-malleable commitment is also synchronous many-one non-malleable.

### 1.3    4-Round Secure Multi-Party Coin Tossing

Our MPCT protocol will critically make use of our delayed-input synchronous many-many NMZK from OWFs, and of an instantiation of $\Pi^{\mathsf{OR}}$. However, similarly to [18] our protocol consists of each party committing to a random string

---

[7] The trapdoor for our protocol is represented by two signatures for a verification key chosen by the verifier.

[8] A rewind made in an asynchronous session does not interfere with (i.e., does not rewind) the challenger of the hiding of $\Pi_{\mathsf{nm}}$.

$r$, that is then sent in the clear in the last round. Moreover there will be a simulatable proof of correctness of the above commitment w.r.t. $r$, that is given to all parties independently. The output consists of the $\bigoplus$ of all opened strings. We now discuss in more details the messages exchanged by a pair of parties $P_1$ and $P_2$ in our multi-party coin tossing protocol $\Pi_{\mathsf{MPCT}}$. The generalization to $n$ players is straight-forward and discussed in Sect. 4.1.

**Informal description of the protocol.** $P_1$, using a perfectly binding computationally hiding commitment scheme, commits in the first round to a random string $r_1$ two times thus obtaining $\mathsf{com}_0, \mathsf{com}_1$. Moreover $P_1$ runs $\Pi^{\mathsf{OR}}$ in order to prove knowledge of either the message committed in $\mathsf{com}_0$ or the message committed in $\mathsf{com}_1$. In the last (fourth) round $P_1$ sends $r_1$. In parallel, an execution of a NMZK ensures that both $\mathsf{com}_0$ and $\mathsf{com}_1$ contain the same message $r_1$ (that is sent in the fourth round)[9]. When $P_1$ receives the last round that contains $r_2$, $P_1$ computes and outputs $r_1 \oplus r_2$. $P_2$ symmetrically executes the same steps using as input $r_2$.

The simulator for $\Pi_{\mathsf{MPCT}}$ runs the simulator of NMZK and extracts the input $r^\star$ from the malicious party using the PoK extractor of $\Pi^{\mathsf{OR}}$. At this point the simulator invokes the functionality thus obtaining $r$ and plays in the last round $r_s = r \oplus r^\star$. Note that the values that the simulator commits in $\mathsf{com}_0$ and $\mathsf{com}_1$ are unrelated to $r_s$ and this is possible because the NMZK is simulated. The extraction of the input from the adversary made by the simulator needs more attention. Indeed the security of NMZK will ensure that, even though the simulator cheats (he commits to a random string in both $\mathsf{com}_0$ and $\mathsf{com}_1$) the adversary can not do the same. Therefore the only way he can complete an execution of $\Pi_{\mathsf{MPCT}}$ consists of committing two times to $r^\star$ in the first round, and send the same value in the fourth round. This means that the value extracted (in the third round) from the PoK extractor of $\Pi^{\mathsf{OR}}$ is the input of the malicious party.

Our security proof consists of showing the indistinguishability of the following hybrid experiments. The first hybrid experiment differs from the real game by using the simulator of NMZK. The simulator, in order to extract the trapdoor from the adversary, rewinds from the third to the second round, thus rewinding also $\Pi^{\mathsf{OR}}$. Indeed the adversary, for every different second round of the NMZK could sent a different second round for $\Pi^{\mathsf{OR}}$. This becomes a problem when we consider the hybrid experiment $H_i$ where the witness for $\Pi^{\mathsf{OR}}$ changes. Due to the rewinds made by the simulator of the NMZK it is not clear how to rely on the security of the WI property of $\Pi^{\mathsf{OR}}$ (the challenger of WI would be rewound). This is the reason why, also in this case, we need to consider an intermediate hybrid experiment $H^{w_0,w_1}$ where both witnesses of $\Pi^{\mathsf{OR}}$ can be used. Then we can prove the indistinguishability between $H^{w_0,w_1}$ and $H_i$ still relying on the Special HVZK of the sub-protocol used in $\Pi^{\mathsf{OR}}$ (Blum's protocol suffices in this case).

---

[9] Notice here how crucial is to delayed-input have synchronous many-many NMZK.

## 2    Definitions and Tools

**Preliminaries.** We denote the security parameter by $\lambda$ and use "$||$" as concatenation operator (i.e., if $a$ and $b$ are two strings then by $a||b$ we denote the concatenation of $a$ and $b$). For a finite set $Q$, $x \leftarrow Q$ sampling of $x$ from $Q$ with uniform distribution. We use the abbreviation PPT that stays for probabilistic polynomial time. We use $\mathsf{poly}(\cdot)$ to indicate a generic polynomial function. A *polynomial-time relation* Rel (or *polynomial relation*, in short) is a subset of $\{0,1\}^* \times \{0,1\}^*$ such that membership of $(x, w)$ in Rel can be decided in time polynomial in $|x|$. For $(x, w) \in$ Rel, we call $x$ the *instance* and $w$ a *witness* for $x$. For a polynomial-time relation Rel, we define the $\mathcal{NP}$-language $L_{\mathsf{Rel}}$ as $L_{\mathsf{Rel}} = \{x | \exists\, w : (x, w) \in \mathsf{Rel}\}$. Analogously, unless otherwise specified, for an $\mathcal{NP}$-language $L$ we denote by $\mathsf{Rel}_L$ the corresponding polynomial-time relation (that is, $\mathsf{Rel}_L$ is such that $L = L_{\mathsf{Rel}_L}$). We also use $\hat{L}$ to denotes the language that includes $L$ and all well formed instances that are not in $L$. Let $A$ and $B$ be two interactive probabilistic algorithms. We denote by $\langle A(\alpha), B(\beta)\rangle(\gamma)$ the distribution of $B$'s output after running on private input $\beta$ with $A$ using private input $\alpha$, both running on common input $\gamma$. A *transcript* of $\langle A(\alpha), B(\beta)\rangle(\gamma)$ consists of the messages exchanged during an execution where $A$ receives a private input $\alpha$, $B$ receives a private input $\beta$ and both $A$ and $B$ receive a common input $\gamma$. Moreover, we will refer to the *view* of $A$ (resp. $B$) as the messages it received during the execution of $\langle A(\alpha), B(\beta)\rangle(\gamma)$, along with its randomness and its input. We denote by $A_r$ an algorithm $A$ that receives as randomness $r$. In Appendix A we recall some useful definitions. We assume familiarity with the well-known formal definitions for secure multi-party computation.

## 3    4-Round Delayed-Input NMZK from OWFs

**Delayed-Input non-malleable zero knowledge.** Following [26] we use a definition that gives to the adversary the power of adaptive-input selection. More precisely, in [26] the adversary selects the instance and then a Turing machine outputs the witness in exponential time. Here we slightly deviate (similarly to [14]) by (1) requiring the adversary to output also the witness and (2) allowing the adversary to make this choice at the last round. This choice is due to our application where delayed-input non-malleable zero knowledge is used. Indeed we will show that this definition is enough for our propose. More precisely our definition (similarly to [7]) we will allow the adversary to explicitly select the statement, and as such the adversary will provide also the witness for the prover. The simulated game however will filter out the witness so that the simulator will receive only the instance. This approach strictly follows the one of [14] where adaptive-input selection is explicitly allowed and managed in a similar way. As final remark, our definition will require the existence of a black-box simulator since a non-black-box simulator could retrieve from the code of the adversary the witness for the adaptively generated statement. The non-black-box simulator could then run the honest prover procedure, therefore canceling completely the security flavor of the simulation paradigm.

Let $\Pi = (\mathcal{P}, \mathcal{V})$ be a delayed-input interactive argument system for a $\mathcal{NP}$-language $L$ with witness relation $\mathsf{Rel}_L$. Consider a PPT MiM adversary $\mathcal{A}$ that is simultaneously participating in one left session and $\mathsf{poly}(\lambda)$ right sessions. Before the execution starts, $\mathcal{P}, \mathcal{V}$ and $\mathcal{A}$ receive as a common input the security parameter in unary $1^\lambda$. Additionally $\mathcal{A}$ receives as auxiliary input $z \in \{0,1\}^\star$. In the left session $\mathcal{A}$ verifies the validity of a statement $x$ (chosen adaptively in the last round of $\Pi$) by interacting with $\mathcal{P}$ using identity $\mathsf{id}$ of $\mathcal{A}$'s choice. In the right sessions $\mathcal{A}$ proves the validity of the statements $\tilde{x}_1 \ldots, \tilde{x}_{\mathsf{poly}(\lambda)}$[10] (chosen adaptively in the last round of $\Pi$) to the honest verifiers $\mathcal{V}_1, \ldots, \mathcal{V}_{\mathsf{poly}(\lambda)}$, using identities $\tilde{\mathsf{id}}_1, \ldots, \tilde{\mathsf{id}}_{\mathsf{poly}(\lambda)}$ of $\mathcal{A}$'s choice.

More precisely in the left session $\mathcal{A}$, before the last round of $\Pi$ is executed, adaptively selects the statement $x$ to be proved and the witness $w$, s.t. $(x, w) \in \mathsf{Rel}_L$, and sends them to $\mathcal{P}$[11].

Let $\mathsf{View}^{\mathcal{A}}(1^\lambda, z)$ denote a random variable that describes the view of $\mathcal{A}$ in the above experiment.

**Definition 1 (Delayed-input NMZK).** *A delayed-input argument system* $\Pi = (\mathcal{P}, \mathcal{V})$ *for an $\mathcal{NP}$-language $L$ with witness relation $\mathsf{Rel}_L$ is delayed-input non-malleable zero knowledge (NMZK) if for any MiM adversary $\mathcal{A}$ that participates in one left session and $\mathsf{poly}(\lambda)$ right sessions, there exists a expected PPT machine $S(1^\lambda, z)$ such that:*

1. *The probability ensembles $\{S^1(1^\lambda, z)\}_{\lambda \in \mathbb{N}, z \in \{0,1\}^\star}$ and $\{\mathsf{View}^{\mathcal{A}}(1^\lambda, z)\}_{\lambda \in \mathbb{N}, z \in \{0,1\}^\star}$ are computationally indistinguishable over $\lambda$, where $S^1(1^\lambda, z)$ denotes the first output of $S(1^\lambda, z)$.*
2. *Let $(\mathsf{View}, w_1, \ldots, w_{\mathsf{poly}(\lambda)})$ denote the output of $S(1^\lambda, z)$, for some $z \in \{0,1\}^\star$. Let $\tilde{x}_1, \ldots, \tilde{x}_{\mathsf{poly}(\lambda)}$ be the right-session statements appearing in $\mathsf{View}$ and let $\mathsf{id}$ and $\tilde{\mathsf{id}}_1, \ldots, \tilde{\mathsf{id}}_{\mathsf{poly}(\lambda)}$ be respectively the identities used in the left and right sessions appearing in $\mathsf{View}$. Then for every $i \in \{1, \ldots, \mathsf{poly}(\lambda)\}$, if the $i$-th right session is accepting and $\mathsf{id} \neq \tilde{\mathsf{id}}_i$, then $\tilde{w}_i$ is s.t. $(\tilde{x}_i, \tilde{w}_i) \in \mathsf{Rel}_L$.*

The above definition of NMZK allows the adversary to select statements adaptively in the last round both in left and in the right sessions. Therefore any argument system that is NMZK according to the above definition enjoys also adaptive-input argument of knowledge. Following [27] we say that a MiM is *synchronous* if it "aligns" the left and the right sessions; that is, whenever it receives message $i$ on the left, it directly sends message $i$ on the right, and vice versa. In our paper we also consider the notion of *delayed-input many-many synchronous NMZK*, that is equal to the notion of delayed-input NMZK except that polynomially many left and right sessions are played in synchronously.

In the rest of the paper, following [23], we assume that identities are known before the protocol begins, though strictly speaking this is not necessary, as the identities do not appear in the protocol until after the first prover message.

---

[10] We denote (here and in the rest of the paper) by $\tilde{\delta}$ a value associated with the right session where $\delta$ is the corresponding value in the left session.

[11] The witness $w$ sent by $\mathcal{A}$ will be just ignored by the simulator.

The MiM can choose his identity adversarially as long as it differs from the identities used by honest senders. As already observed in previous works, when the identity is selected by the sender the id-based definitions guarantee non-malleability as long as the MiM does not behave like a proxy (an unavoidable attack). Indeed the sender can pick as id the public key of a signature scheme signing the transcript. The MiM will have to use a different id or to break the signature scheme.

### 3.1 Our Protocol: NMZK

For our construction of a 4-round delayed-input non-malleable zero knowledge $\mathsf{NMZK} = (\mathcal{P}_{\mathsf{NMZK}}, \mathcal{V}_{\mathsf{NMZK}})$ for the $\mathcal{NP}$-language $L$ we use the following tools.

1. A signature scheme $\Sigma = (\mathsf{Gen}, \mathsf{Sign}, \mathsf{Ver})$.
2. A 4-round public-coin synchronous honest-extractable non-malleable commitment scheme $\mathsf{NM} = (\mathcal{S}, \mathcal{R})$ (See Appendix A.3 for a formal definition).
3. Two instantiations of the adaptive-input special sound LS protocol described in Appendix B in order to construct a 4-round delayed-input public-coin proof system for the OR of compound statement $\Pi_{\mathsf{OR}} = (\mathcal{P}_{\mathsf{OR}}, \mathcal{V}_{\mathsf{OR}})$ as described in Appendix B.2. More in details we use the following proof systems.
   3.1 A 4-round delayed-input public coin $\mathsf{LS}_L = (\mathcal{P}_L, \mathcal{V}_L)$ for the $\mathcal{NP}$-language $L$ with adaptive-input Special HVZK simulator $S_L$. $\mathsf{LS}_L = (\mathcal{P}_L, \mathcal{V}_L)$ is adaptive-input special sound for the corresponding relation $\mathsf{Rel}_L$ with instance length $\ell_L$.
   3.2 A 4-round delayed-input public coin $\mathsf{LS}_{\mathsf{nm}} = (\mathcal{P}_{\mathsf{nm}}, \mathcal{V}_{\mathsf{nm}})$ with adaptive-input Special HVZK simulator $S_{\mathsf{nm}}$. $\mathsf{LS}_{\mathsf{nm}} = (\mathcal{P}_{\mathsf{nm}}, \mathcal{V}_{\mathsf{nm}})$ is adaptive-input special sound for the $\mathcal{NP}$-relation $\mathsf{Rel}_{L_{\mathsf{nm}}}$ where

   $$L_{\mathsf{nm}} = \{(\mathsf{vk}, \tau = (\mathsf{id}, \mathsf{nm}_1, \mathsf{nm}_2, \mathsf{nm}_3, \mathsf{nm}_4), s_1 : \exists (\mathsf{dec}_{\mathsf{nm}}, s_0, \sigma_1, \mathsf{msg}_1, \sigma_2, \mathsf{msg}_2)$$
   $$\text{s.t. } \mathsf{Ver}(\mathsf{vk}, \mathsf{msg}_1, \sigma_1) = 1 \text{ AND } \mathsf{Ver}(\mathsf{vk}, \mathsf{msg}_2, \sigma_2) = 1 \text{ AND } \mathsf{msg}_1 \neq \mathsf{msg}_2 \text{ AND}$$
   $$\mathcal{R} \text{ accepts } (\mathsf{id}, s_1, \mathsf{dec}_{\mathsf{nm}}) \text{ as a valid decommitment of } \tau \text{ AND } s_0 \oplus s_1 = \sigma_1 || \sigma_2 \}.$$

   We denote with $\ell_{\mathsf{nm}}$ the dimension of the instances belonging to $L_{\mathsf{nm}}$. Informally by running $\mathsf{LS}_{\mathsf{nm}}$ one can prove that the message committed using a non-malleable commitment XORed with the value $s_1$ represents two signatures for two different messages w.r.t. the verification key $\mathsf{vk}$. Moreover $\Pi^{\mathsf{OR}}$ is also adaptive-input PoK for the relation $\mathsf{Rel}_{L_{\mathsf{OR}}} = \{((x_L, x_{\mathsf{nm}}), w) : ((x_L, w) \in \mathsf{Rel}_L) \text{ OR } ((x_{\mathsf{nm}}, w) \in \mathsf{Rel}_{L_{\mathsf{nm}}})\}$ (see Theorem 10 in Appendix B.2 for more details).

**Overview of our protocol.** We now give an high-level description of our delayed-input NMZK of Fig. 1. For a formal description see Fig. 2.

   In the **first round** $\mathcal{V}_{\mathsf{NMZK}}$ computes a pair of signature-verification keys $(\mathsf{sk}, \mathsf{vk})$ sending $\mathsf{vk}$ to $\mathcal{P}_{\mathsf{NMZK}}$. Also $\mathcal{V}_{\mathsf{NMZK}}$ computes the (public coin) first rounds $\mathsf{nm}_1$ of $\mathsf{NM}$, $\mathsf{ls}_L^1 \leftarrow \mathcal{V}_L(1^\lambda, \ell_L)$ and $\mathsf{ls}_{\mathsf{nm}}^1 \leftarrow \mathcal{V}_L(1^\lambda, \ell_{\mathsf{nm}})$. $\mathcal{V}_{\mathsf{NMZK}}$ completes the first round by sending $(\mathsf{vk}, \mathsf{ls}_L^1, \mathsf{ls}_{\mathsf{nm}}^1, \mathsf{nm}^1)$ to $\mathcal{P}_{\mathsf{NMZK}}$.

In the **second round** $\mathcal{P}_{\text{NMZK}}$ computes $\text{ls}_L^2 \leftarrow \mathcal{P}_L(1^\lambda, \text{ls}_L^1, \ell_L)$ and sends $\text{ls}_L^2$. Furthermore picks $\text{ls}_{\text{nm}}^3 \leftarrow \{0,1\}^\lambda$ and runs $\text{ls}_{\text{nm}}^2 \leftarrow S_{\text{nm}}(1^\lambda, \text{ls}_{\text{nm}}^1, \text{ls}_{\text{nm}}^3, \ell_{\text{nm}})$ in order to send $\text{ls}_{\text{nm}}^2$. $\mathcal{P}_{\text{NMZK}}$ now commits to a random message $s_0$ using the nonmalleable commitment NM by running $\mathcal{S}$ on input $1^\lambda, s_0, \text{nm}_1$ and the identity id thus obtaining and sending $\text{nm}_2$. Also $\mathcal{P}_{\text{NMZK}}$ sends a random message msg.

In the **third round** of the protocol, upon receiving msg, $\mathcal{V}_{\text{NMZK}}$ computes and sends a signature $\sigma$ of msg by running $\text{Sign}(\text{sk}, \text{msg})$. $\mathcal{V}_{\text{NMZK}}$ picks and sends $\text{c} \leftarrow \{0,1\}^\lambda$. Also he computes and sends the (public coin) third rounds $\text{nm}_3$ of NM.

In the **fourth round** $\mathcal{P}_{\text{NMZK}}$ checks whether or not $\sigma$ is a valid signature for msg w.r.t. the verification key vk. In the negative case $\mathcal{P}_{\text{NMZK}}$ aborts, otherwise he continues with the following steps. $\mathcal{P}_{\text{NMZK}}$ computes $\text{ls}_L^3 = \text{ls}_{\text{nm}}^3 \oplus \text{c}$. Upon receiving the instance $x$ to be proved and the witness $w$ s.t. $(x,w) \in \text{Rel}_L$, $\mathcal{P}_{\text{NMZK}}$ completes the transcript for $\text{LS}_L$ running $\text{ls}_L^4 \leftarrow \mathcal{P}_L(x, w, \text{ls}_L^3)$. At this point $\mathcal{P}_{\text{NMZK}}$ completes the commitment of $s_0$ by running $\mathcal{S}$ on input $\text{nm}_3$ thus obtaining $(\text{nm}_4, \text{dec}_{\text{nm}})$. $\mathcal{P}_{\text{NMZK}}$ picks a random string $s_1$, sets $x_{\text{nm}} = (\text{vk}, \text{id}, \text{nm}_1, \text{nm}_2, \text{nm}_3, \text{nm}_4, s_1)$ and runs $\text{ls}_{\text{nm}}^4 \leftarrow S_{\text{nm}}(x_{\text{nm}})$. $\mathcal{P}_{\text{NMZK}}$ completes the fourth round by sending $(\text{ls}_L^3, \text{ls}_L^4, \text{nm}_4, s_1, \text{ls}_{\text{nm}}^3, \text{ls}_{\text{nm}}^4, x, x_{\text{nm}})$.

The verifier $\mathcal{V}_{\text{NMZK}}$ accepts $x$ iff the following conditions are satisfied: (1) $\text{c}$ is equal to $\text{ls}_L^3 \oplus \text{ls}_{\text{nm}}^3$; (2) $\mathcal{V}_L(x, \text{ls}_L^1, \text{ls}_L^2, \text{ls}_L^3, \text{ls}_L^4) = 1$; (3) $\mathcal{V}_{\text{nm}}(x_{\text{nm}}, \text{ls}_{\text{nm}}^1, \text{ls}_{\text{nm}}^2, \text{ls}_{\text{nm}}^3, \text{ls}_{\text{nm}}^4) = 1$.

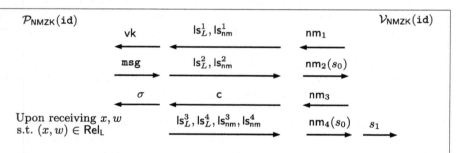

- vk is a a verification key of a signature scheme and $\sigma$ is a valid signature of the message msg.
- $s_0$ and $s_1$ are two random strings.
- $\tau = (\text{id}, \text{nm}_1, \text{nm}_2, \text{nm}_3, \text{nm}_4)$ represents the transcript of $\langle \mathcal{S}(s_0), \mathcal{R} \rangle(\text{id})$ that is, a commitment of the message $s_0$ computed using the synchronous honest-extractable non-malleable commitment scheme NM.
- $((\text{ls}_L^1, \text{ls}_{\text{nm}}^1), (\text{ls}_L^2, \text{ls}_{\text{nm}}^2), \text{c}, (\text{ls}_L^3, \text{ls}_L^4, \text{ls}_{\text{nm}}^3, \text{ls}_{\text{nm}}^4))$ is the transcript generated from an execution of $\Pi_{\text{OR}}$, in more details:
    - $\text{c}$ is equal to $\text{ls}_{\text{nm}}^3 \oplus \text{ls}_L^3$.
    - $(\text{ls}_L^1, \text{ls}_L^2, \text{ls}_L^3, \text{ls}_L^4)$ is the transcript output from the honest prover procedure of $\text{LS}_L$ proving the knowledge of the witness for $x \in L$.
    - $(\text{ls}_{\text{nm}}^1, \text{ls}_{\text{nm}}^2, \text{ls}_{\text{nm}}^3, \text{ls}_{\text{nm}}^4)$ is the transcript output of a adaptive-input Special HVZK simulator of $\text{LS}_{\text{nm}}$ proving knowledge of a decommitment of $\tau$ to the message $s_0$ s.t. $s_0 \oplus s_1 = \sigma_1 \| \sigma_2$ where $\sigma_1, \sigma_2$ are two signatures of two different messages w.r.t vk.

**Fig. 1.** Our 4-round delayed-input NMZK

---

**Protocol NMZK** $= (\mathcal{P}_{\mathsf{NMZK}}, \mathcal{V}_{\mathsf{NMZK}})$
**Common input:** security parameter $\lambda$, identity $\mathtt{id} \in \{0,1\}^\lambda$ instances length: $\ell_L$, $\ell_{\mathsf{nm}}$.
**Input to** $\mathcal{P}_{\mathsf{NMZK}}$: $(x,w)$ s.t. $(x,w) \in \mathsf{Rel}_L$, with $(x,w)$ available only in the 4th round.

1. $\mathcal{V}_{\mathsf{NMZK}} \to \mathcal{P}_{\mathsf{NMZK}}$
    1.1. Run $(\mathsf{sk}, \mathsf{vk}) \leftarrow \mathsf{Gen}(1^\lambda)$.
    1.2. Run $\mathsf{ls}_L^1 \leftarrow \mathcal{V}_L(1^\lambda, \ell_L)$.
    1.3. Run $\mathsf{ls}_{\mathsf{nm}}^1 \leftarrow \mathcal{V}_{\mathsf{nm}}(1^\lambda, \ell_{\mathsf{nm}})$.
    1.4. Run $\mathcal{R}$ on input $1^\lambda$ and $\mathtt{id}$ thus obtaining $\mathsf{nm}_1$.
    1.5. Send $(\mathsf{vk}, \mathsf{ls}_L^1, \mathsf{ls}_{\mathsf{nm}}^1, \mathsf{nm}_1)$ to $\mathcal{P}_{\mathsf{NMZK}}$.
2. $\mathcal{P}_{\mathsf{NMZK}} \to \mathcal{V}_{\mathsf{NMZK}}$
    2.1. Run $\mathsf{ls}_L^2 \leftarrow \mathcal{P}_L(1^\lambda, \ell_L)$.
    2.2. Pick $\mathsf{ls}_{\mathsf{nm}}^3 \leftarrow \{0,1\}^\lambda$ run $\mathsf{ls}_{\mathsf{nm}}^2 \leftarrow \mathcal{S}_{\mathsf{nm}}(1^\lambda, \mathsf{ls}_{\mathsf{nm}}^1, \mathsf{ls}_{\mathsf{nm}}^3, \ell_{\mathsf{nm}})$.
    2.3. Pick $s_0 \leftarrow \{0,1\}^\lambda$ and run $\mathcal{S}$ on input $1^\lambda$, $\mathtt{id}$, $\mathsf{nm}_1$, $s_0$ (in order to commit to the message $s_0$) thus obtaining $\mathsf{nm}_2$.
    2.4. Pick a message $\mathbf{msg} \leftarrow \{0,1\}^\lambda$.
    2.5. Send $(\mathsf{ls}_L^2, \mathsf{ls}_{\mathsf{nm}}^2, \mathbf{msg}, \mathsf{nm}_2)$ to $\mathcal{V}_{\mathsf{NMZK}}$.
3. $\mathcal{V}_{\mathsf{NMZK}} \to \mathcal{P}_{\mathsf{NMZK}}$
    3.1. Pick $\mathsf{c} \leftarrow \{0,1\}^\lambda$.
    3.2. Run $\mathcal{R}$ on input $\mathsf{nm}_2$ thus obtaining $\mathsf{nm}_3$.
    3.3. Run $\mathsf{Sign}(\mathsf{sk}, \mathbf{msg})$ to obtain a signature $\sigma$ of $\mathbf{msg}$.
    3.4. Send $(\mathsf{c}, \mathsf{nm}_3, \sigma)$ to $\mathcal{P}_{\mathsf{NMZK}}$.
4. $\mathcal{P}_{\mathsf{NMZK}} \to \mathcal{V}_{\mathsf{NMZK}}$
    4.1. If $\mathsf{Ver}(\mathsf{vk}, \mathbf{msg}, \sigma) \neq 1$ then abort, continue as follows otherwise.
    4.2. Compute $\mathsf{ls}_L^3 = \mathsf{c} \oplus \mathsf{ls}_{\mathsf{nm}}^3$.
    4.3. Run $\mathsf{ls}_L^4 \leftarrow \mathcal{P}_L(x, w, \mathsf{ls}_L^3)$.
    4.4. Run $\mathcal{S}$ on input $\mathsf{nm}_3$ thus obtaining $(\mathsf{nm}_4, \mathbf{dec}_{\mathsf{nm}})$.
    4.5. Pick $s_1 \leftarrow \{0,1\}^\lambda$, set $x_{\mathsf{nm}} = (\mathsf{vk}, \mathsf{nm}_1, \mathsf{nm}_2, \mathsf{nm}_3, \mathsf{nm}_4, s_1)$ and run $\mathsf{ls}_{\mathsf{nm}}^4 \leftarrow \mathcal{S}_{\mathsf{nm}}(x_{\mathsf{nm}})$.
    4.6. Send $(\mathsf{ls}_L^3, \mathsf{ls}_L^4, \mathsf{nm}_4, s_1, \mathsf{ls}_{\mathsf{nm}}^3, \mathsf{ls}_{\mathsf{nm}}^4, x, x_{\mathsf{nm}})$ to $\mathcal{V}_{\mathsf{NMZK}}$.
5. $\mathcal{V}_{\mathsf{NMZK}}$: output 1 iff the following conditions are satisfied.
    5.1. $\mathsf{c}$ is equal to $\mathsf{ls}_L^3 \oplus \mathsf{ls}_{\mathsf{nm}}^3$.
    5.2. $\mathcal{V}_L(x, \mathsf{ls}_L^1, \mathsf{ls}_L^2, \mathsf{ls}_L^3, \mathsf{ls}_L^4) = 1$.
    5.3. $\mathcal{V}_{\mathsf{nm}}(x_{\mathsf{nm}}, \mathsf{ls}_{\mathsf{nm}}^1, \mathsf{ls}_{\mathsf{nm}}^2, \mathsf{ls}_{\mathsf{nm}}^3, \mathsf{ls}_{\mathsf{nm}}^4) = 1$.
    5.4. The transcript $\tau_{\mathsf{nm}} = (\mathtt{id}, \mathsf{nm}_1, \mathsf{nm}_2, \mathsf{nm}_3, \mathsf{nm}_4)$ is accepting.

---

**Fig. 2.** Formal construction of our delayed-input NMZK.

**The simulator extractor.** Informally, the simulator $\mathsf{Sim}_{\mathsf{NMZK}}$ of our protocol interacts with the adversary $\mathcal{A}_{\mathsf{NMZK}}$ emulating both the prover in the left session and polynomially many verifiers in the right sessions. In the right sessions $\mathsf{Sim}_{\mathsf{NMZK}}$ interacts with $\mathcal{A}_{\mathsf{NMZK}}$ as the honest verifiers do. While, in the left session for an instance $x \in L$ chosen adaptively by $\mathcal{A}_{\mathsf{NMZK}}$, $\mathsf{Sim}_{\mathsf{NMZK}}$ proves, using $\Pi_{\mathsf{OR}}$, that the message committed in NM contains two signatures of two different messages w.r.t. the verification key $\mathsf{vk}$. In more details $\mathsf{Sim}_{\mathsf{NMZK}}$ runs the adaptive-input Special HVZK simulator of $\mathsf{LS}_L$ to complete the transcript for $\mathsf{LS}_L$ w.r.t. the instance $x$. In order to use the honest prover procedure to compute the transcript of $\mathsf{LS}_{nm}$, $\mathsf{Sim}_{NMZK}$ extracts two signatures for two different messages by rewinding $\mathcal{A}_{NMZK}$ from the third to the second round and by committing to them using $\mathsf{NM}^{12}$. More precisely the simulator commits to a random string $s_0$, but computes $s_1$ s.t. $s_1 = (\sigma_1 \| \sigma_2) \oplus s_0^{13}$. Therefore the execution of $\Pi_{OR}$ can be completed by using the knowledge of the two signatures committed using $\mathsf{NM}$. We use the xor trick originally provided in [6] in order to avoid any additional requirement w.r.t. the underlying non-malleable commitment scheme $\mathsf{NM}$. Indeed if the sender of $\mathsf{NM}$ could decide the message to commit in the last round, then $\mathsf{Sim}_{NMZK}$ can simply compute the first round of $\mathsf{NM}$, extract the signature, and compute the last round of $\mathsf{NM}$ by committing to $\sigma_1 \| \sigma_2$. It is important to observe that even though the non-malleable commitment scheme of [22] fixes the message to be committed in the third round, there is in general no guarantee that such a scheme is secure against an adversary that adaptively chooses the challenge messages in the last round of the non-malleability security game. Therefore, even though the completeness of our scheme would work without using the trick of [6], it would be unclear, in general, how to prove the security of our final scheme. A formal description of $\mathsf{Sim}_{NMZK}$ can be found in the proof of Theorem 1.

The formal construction of our delayed-input NMZK $\mathsf{NMZK} = (\mathcal{P}_{NMZK}, \mathcal{V}_{NMZK})$ for the $\mathcal{NP}$-language $L$ can be found in Fig. 2.

**Theorem 1.** *If OWFs exist, then* NMZK *is a 4-round delayed-input NMZK AoK for* $\mathcal{NP}$.

*Proof.* We divide the security proof in two parts, proving that NMZK enjoys delayed-input completeness and NMZK. The proof of NMZK is divided also in two lemmas, one for each of the two properties of Definition 1. Before that, we recall that $\mathsf{LS}_{nm}$ and $\mathsf{LS}_L$ can be constructed from OWFs (see Appendix A) as well as $\Sigma$ (using [39]) and the 4-round public-coin synchronous honest-extractable non-malleable commitment scheme $\mathsf{NM}$ (see Appendix A.3).

**(Delayed-Input) Completeness.** The completeness follows directly from the delayed-input completeness of $\mathsf{LS}_{nm}$ and $\mathsf{LS}_L$, the correctness of $\mathsf{NM}$ and the validity of $\Sigma$. We observe that, due to the delayed-input property of $\mathsf{LS}_L$, the statement $x$ (and the respective witness $w$) are used by $\mathcal{P}_{NMZK}$ only to compute the last round. Therefore also NMZK enjoys delayed-input completeness.

**(Delayed-Input) NMZK.** Following Definition 1 we start by describing how the simulator $\mathsf{Sim}_{NMZK}$ for NMZK works. In the left session $\mathsf{Sim}_{NMZK}$ interacts with the MiM adversary $\mathcal{A}_{NMZK}$ in the following way. Upon receiving the first round, $\mathsf{vk}$, $\mathsf{ls}_L^1$, $\mathsf{ls}_{nm}^1$, $\mathsf{nm}_1$, from $\mathcal{A}_{NMZK}$, $\mathsf{Sim}_{NMZK}$ on input $\mathsf{ls}_{nm}^1$ computes $\mathsf{ls}_{nm}^2$ by running $\mathcal{P}_{nm}$. $\mathsf{Sim}_{NMZK}$ picks $\mathsf{ls}_L^3 \leftarrow \{0,1\}^\lambda$ and runs $S_L$ on input $1^\lambda$, $\ell_L$, $\mathsf{ls}_L^1$,

---

[12] W.l.o.g. we assume that the signatures $\sigma_1, \sigma_2$ include the signed messages.

[13] For ease of exposition we will simply say that $\mathcal{A}_{NMZK}$ commits to two signatures using $\mathsf{NM}$.

$\mathsf{ls}_L^3$ thus obtaining $\mathsf{ls}_L^2$. $\mathsf{Sim}_{\mathsf{NMZK}}$, in order to commit to a random message $s_0$ runs $\mathcal{S}$ on input $\mathsf{nm}_1$, the identity $\mathsf{id}$ and $s_0$ thus obtaining $\mathsf{nm}_2$. $\mathsf{Sim}_{\mathsf{NMZK}}$ sends $\mathsf{ls}_L^2, \mathsf{ls}_{\mathsf{nm}}^2, \mathsf{nm}_2$ and a random message $\mathsf{msg}_1$ to $\mathcal{A}_{\mathsf{NMZK}}$. Upon receiving the third round, $\mathsf{c}, \mathsf{nm}_3, \sigma_1$, and instance $x$ to be proved from $\mathcal{A}_{\mathsf{NMZK}}$, the simulator checks whether or not $\sigma_1$ is a valid signature for $\mathsf{msg}_1$ w.r.t. the verification key $\mathsf{vk}$. In the negative case $\mathsf{Sim}_{\mathsf{NMZK}}$ aborts, otherwise $\mathsf{Sim}_{\mathsf{NMZK}}$ rewinds $\mathcal{A}_{\mathsf{NMZK}}$ from the third to the second round in order to obtain a second signature $\sigma_2$ for a different message $\mathsf{msg}_2$. After the extraction of the signatures $\mathsf{Sim}_{\mathsf{NMZK}}$ returns to the main thread and computes the fourth round as follows[14].

$\mathsf{Sim}_{\mathsf{NMZK}}$ completes the commitment of $s_0$ by running $\mathcal{S}$ on input $\mathsf{nm}_3$ thus obtaining $(\mathsf{nm}_4, \mathsf{dec}_{\mathsf{nm}})$ and sending $\mathsf{nm}_4$. Furthermore $\mathsf{Sim}_{\mathsf{NMZK}}$ sets $s_1$ s.t. $s_1 = (\sigma_1 \| \sigma_2) \oplus s_0$, $x_{\mathsf{nm}} = (\mathsf{vk}, \mathsf{id}, \mathsf{nm}_1, \mathsf{nm}_2, \mathsf{nm}_3, \mathsf{nm}_4, s_1)$, $w_{\mathsf{nm}} = (\mathsf{dec}_{\mathsf{nm}}, s_0, \sigma_1, \mathsf{msg}_1, \sigma_2, \mathsf{msg}_2)$ and completes the transcript for $\mathsf{LS}_{\mathsf{nm}}$ obtaining $\mathsf{ls}_{\mathsf{nm}}^4$ by running the prover procedure $\mathcal{P}_{\mathsf{nm}}$ on input $x_{\mathsf{nm}}, w_{\mathsf{nm}}$ and $\mathsf{ls}_L^3 \oplus \mathsf{c}$. At this point $\mathsf{Sim}_{\mathsf{NMZK}}$ runs the adaptive-input Special HVZK simulator $S_L$ on input $x$ thus obtaining $\mathsf{ls}_L^4$. Then the values $(\mathsf{ls}_L^3, \mathsf{ls}_L^4, \mathsf{nm}_4, s_1, \mathsf{ls}_{\mathsf{nm}}^3, \mathsf{ls}_{\mathsf{nm}}^4, x, x_{\mathsf{nm}})$ are sent to $\mathcal{A}_{\mathsf{NMZK}}$. At the end of the execution $\mathsf{Sim}_{\mathsf{NMZK}}$ outputs $\mathcal{A}_{\mathsf{NMZK}}$'s view in the main thread. Furthermore, he uses the extractor of $\mathsf{LS}_L$ to extract and output, from the $\mathsf{poly}(\lambda)$ right sessions, the witnesses $\tilde{w}_1, \ldots, \tilde{w}_{\mathsf{poly}(\lambda)}$ used by $\mathcal{A}_{\mathsf{NMZK}}$ to compute the transcript of $\Pi^{\mathsf{OR}}$ (the witnesses correspond to statements $\tilde{x}_i$ proved by $\mathcal{A}_{\mathsf{NMZK}}$ in the $i$-th right session, for $i = 1, \ldots, \mathsf{poly}(\lambda)$).

**Lemma 1.** $\{\mathsf{Sim}_{\mathsf{NMZK}}^1(1^\lambda, z)\}_{\lambda \in \mathbb{N}, z \in \{0,1\}^*} \approx \{\mathsf{View}^{\mathcal{A}_{\mathsf{NMZK}}}(1^\lambda, z)\}_{\lambda \in \mathbb{N}, z \in \{0,1\}^*}$, where $\mathsf{Sim}_{\mathsf{NMZK}}^1(1^\lambda, z)$ denotes the 1st output of $\mathsf{Sim}_{\mathsf{NMZK}}$.

In order to prove the above lemma we consider the series of hybrid experiments described below. In the proof we denote with $\{\mathsf{View}_{\mathcal{H}_i}^{\mathcal{A}_{\mathsf{NMZK}}}(1^\lambda, z)\}_{\lambda \in \mathbb{N}, z \in \{0,1\}^*}$ the random variable that describes the view of $\mathcal{A}_{\mathsf{NMZK}}$ in the hybrid $\mathcal{H}_i(1^\lambda, z)$. Let $p$ the probability that in the real execution $\mathcal{A}_{\mathsf{NMZK}}$ completes the left session.

- We start considering the hybrid experiment $\mathcal{H}_0(1^\lambda, z)$ in which in the left session $\mathcal{P}_{\mathsf{NMZK}}$ interacts with $\mathcal{A}_{\mathsf{NMZK}}$ and in the $i$-th right session $\mathcal{V}_{\mathsf{NMZK}i}$ interacts with $\mathcal{A}_{\mathsf{NMZK}}$, for $i = 1, \ldots, \mathsf{poly}(\lambda)$. Note that $\{\mathsf{View}_{\mathcal{H}_0}^{\mathcal{A}_{\mathsf{NMZK}}}(1^\lambda, z)\}_{\lambda \in \mathbb{N}, z \in \{0,1\}^*} = \{\mathsf{View}_{\mathsf{NMZK}}^{\mathcal{A}}(1^\lambda, z)\}_{\lambda \in \mathbb{N}, z \in \{0,1\}^*}$.
  The hybrid experiment $\mathcal{H}_1(1^\lambda, z)$ differs from $\mathcal{H}_0(1^\lambda, z)$ only in the fact that in the left session of $\mathcal{H}_1(1^\lambda, z)$ $\mathcal{A}_{\mathsf{NMZK}}$ is rewound from the third to the second round, in order to extract two signatures $\sigma_1, \sigma_2$ for two distinct messages $(\mathsf{msg}_1, \mathsf{msg}_2)$ w.r.t. a verification key $\mathsf{vk}$. Note that after $p$ rewinds the probability of not obtaining a valid new signature is less than $1/2$. Therefore the probability that $\mathcal{A}_{\mathsf{NMZK}}$ does not give a second valid signature for a randomly chosen message after $\lambda/p$ rewinds is negligible in $\lambda$. For the above reason

---

[14] Note that it is possible to complete the main thread, due to the delayed-input completeness of $\mathsf{LS}_{\mathsf{nm}}$, and to the fact that we do not need to change the second round of NM (that is, we do not need to change the committed message $s_0$) in order to have $x_{\mathsf{nm}} \in L_{\mathsf{nm}}$.

the procedure of extraction of signatures for different messages in $\mathcal{H}_1(1^\lambda, z)$ succeeds except with negligible probability. Observe that the above deviation increases the abort probability of the experiment only by a negligible amount, therefore $\{\text{View}_{\mathcal{H}_0}^{\mathcal{A}_{\text{NMZK}}}(1^\lambda, z)\}_{\lambda \in \mathbb{N}, z \in \{0,1\}^*} \equiv_s \{\text{View}_{\mathcal{H}_1}^{\mathcal{A}_{\text{NMZK}}}(1^\lambda, z)\}_{\lambda \in \mathbb{N}, z \in \{0,1\}^*}$.

- The hybrid experiment $\mathcal{H}_2(1^\lambda, z)$ differs from $\mathcal{H}_1(1^\lambda, z)$ only in the message committed using NM. Indeed $\mathcal{P}_{\text{NMZK}}$ commits using NM to two signatures $\sigma_1, \sigma_2$ of two distinct messages $(\text{msg}_1, \text{msg}_2)$ instead of a random message. In more details, $\mathcal{P}_{\text{NMZK}}$ commits to a random string $s_0$ using NM and in 4th round sets and sends $s_1 = (\sigma_1 || \sigma_2) \oplus s_0$, instead of sending $s_1$ as a random string. Observe that the procedure of extraction of the signatures succeeds in $\mathcal{H}_2(1^\lambda, z)$ with non-negligible probability, because the first three rounds are played exactly as in $\mathcal{H}_1(1^\lambda, z)$. Now we can claim that $\{\text{View}_{\mathcal{H}_2}^{\mathcal{A}_{\text{NMZK}}}(1^\lambda, z)\}_{\lambda \in \mathbb{N}, z \in \{0,1\}^*}$ and $\{\text{View}_{\mathcal{H}_1}^{\mathcal{A}_{\text{NMZK}}}(1^\lambda, z)\}_{\lambda \in \mathbb{N}, z \in \{0,1\}^*}$ are computationally indistinguishable by using the computationally-hiding property of NM. Suppose by contradiction that there exist an adversary $\mathcal{A}_{\text{NMZK}}$ and a distinguisher $\mathcal{D}_{\text{NMZK}}$ such that $\mathcal{D}_{\text{NMZK}}$ distinguishes $\{\text{View}_{\mathcal{H}_1}^{\mathcal{A}_{\text{NMZK}}}(1^\lambda, z)\}_{\lambda \in \mathbb{N}, z \in \{0,1\}^*}$ from $\{\text{View}_{\mathcal{H}_2}^{\mathcal{A}_{\text{NMZK}}}(1^\lambda, z)\}_{\lambda \in \mathbb{N}, z \in \{0,1\}^*}$. Then we can construct an adversary $\mathcal{A}_{\text{Hiding}}$ that breaks the computationally hiding of NM in the following way. $\mathcal{A}_{\text{Hiding}}$ sends to the challenger of the hiding game $\mathcal{C}_{\text{Hiding}}$ two random messages $(m_0, m_1)$. Then, in the left session $\mathcal{A}_{\text{Hiding}}$ acts as $\mathcal{P}_{\text{NMZK}}$ except for messages of NM for which he acts as proxy between $\mathcal{C}_{\text{Hiding}}$ and $\mathcal{A}_{\text{NMZK}}$. When $\mathcal{A}_{\text{Hiding}}$ computes the last round of the left session $\mathcal{A}_{\text{Hiding}}$ sets and sends $s_1 = \sigma_1 || \sigma_2 \oplus m_0$. In the right sessions $\mathcal{A}_{\text{Hiding}}$ interacts with $\mathcal{A}_{\text{ZK}}$ acting as $\mathcal{V}_{\text{NMZK}}$ does. At the end of the execution $\mathcal{A}_{\text{Hiding}}$ runs $\mathcal{D}_{\text{NMZK}}$ and outputs what $\mathcal{D}_{\text{NMZK}}$ outputs. It is easy to see that if $\mathcal{C}_{\text{Hiding}}$ commits to $m_1$ then, $\mathcal{A}_{\text{ZK}}$ acts as in $\mathcal{H}_1(1^\lambda, z)$, otherwise he acts as in $\mathcal{H}_2(1^\lambda, z)$. Note that the reduction to the hiding property of NM is possible because the rewinds to extract a second signature do not affect the execution with the challenger of NM that remains straight-line.

- The hybrid experiment $\mathcal{H}_3(1^\lambda, z)$ differs from $\mathcal{H}_2(1^\lambda, z)$ in the way the transcript of $\text{LS}_{\text{nm}}$ is computed. More precisely, the prover $\mathcal{P}_{\text{nm}}$ of $\text{LS}_{\text{nm}}$ is used to compute the messages $\text{ls}_{\text{nm}}^2$ and $\text{ls}_{\text{nm}}^4$ instead of using the adaptive-input Special HVZK simulator. Note that due to the delayed-input property of $\text{LS}_{\text{nm}}$ the statement $x_{\text{nm}} = (\text{vk}, \text{nm}_1, \text{nm}_2, \text{nm}_3, \text{nm}_4, s_1)$ and the witness $w_{\text{nm}} = (\text{dec}_{\text{nm}}, s_0, \sigma_1, \text{msg}_1, \sigma_2, \text{msg}_2)$ are required by $\mathcal{P}_{\text{nm}}$ only to compute $\text{ls}_{\text{nm}}^4$ and are not needed to compute $\text{ls}_{\text{nm}}^2$. Observe that the procedure of extraction of the signatures succeeds in $\mathcal{H}_3(1^\lambda, z)$ with non-negligible probability due to the adaptive-input Special HVZK of $\text{LS}_{\text{nm}}$. From the adaptive-input Special HVZK of $\text{LS}_{\text{nm}}$ it follows that $\{\text{View}_{\mathcal{H}_2}^{\mathcal{A}_{\text{NMZK}}}(1^\lambda, z)\}_{\lambda \in \mathbb{N}, z \in \{0,1\}^*}$ and $\{\text{View}_{\mathcal{H}_3}^{\mathcal{A}_{\text{NMZK}}}(1^\lambda, z)\}_{\lambda \in \mathbb{N}, z \in \{0,1\}^*}$ are computationally indistinguishable.

- The hybrid $\mathcal{H}_4(1^\lambda, z)$ differs from $\mathcal{H}_3(1^\lambda, z)$ in the way the transcript of $\text{LS}_L$ is computed. More precisely, the adaptive-input Special HVZK simulator of $\text{LS}_L$ is used to compute the messages $\text{ls}_L^2$ and $\text{ls}_L^4$ using as input $\text{ls}_L^1$ received by $\mathcal{A}_{\text{NMZK}}$, the statement $x$ and a random string $\text{ls}_L^3$ chosen by the hybrid experiment. We observe that in order to complete the execution of $\Pi_{\text{OR}}$ the honest prover procedure $\mathcal{P}_{nm}$ can be used on input $x_{nm}$, $w_{nm}$ and $\mathsf{ls}^3_{nm} = \mathsf{ls}^3_L \oplus c$. Moreover adaptive-input Special HVZK of $\mathsf{LS}_L$ ensures that the extraction procedure of the signatures succeeds in $\mathcal{H}_4(1^\lambda, z)$ with non-negligible probability and that $\{\mathsf{View}^{\mathcal{A}_{NMZK}}_{\mathcal{H}_4}(1^\lambda, z)\}_{\lambda \in \mathbb{N}, z \in \{0,1\}^*} \approx \{\mathsf{View}^{\mathcal{A}_{NMZK}}_{\mathcal{H}_3}(1^\lambda, z)\}_{\lambda \in \mathbb{N}, z \in \{0,1\}^*}$. Note that $\mathcal{H}_4(1^\lambda, z)$ corresponds to the simulated experiment, that is the experiment where $\mathsf{Sim}_{NMZK}$ interacts with the adversary $\mathcal{A}_{NMZK}$ emulating both a prover in the left session and polynomially many verifiers in the right sessions. This implies that $\{\mathsf{View}^{\mathcal{A}_{NMZK}}_{\mathcal{H}_4}(1^\lambda, z)\}_{\lambda \in \mathbb{N}, z \in \{0,1\}^*} = \{S^1(1^\lambda, z)\}_{\lambda \in \mathbb{N}, z \in \{0,1\}^*}$.

The proof ends with the observation that for all $\lambda \in \mathbb{N}, z \in \{0,1\}^*$ it holds that: $\{\mathsf{View}^{\mathcal{A}}_{NMZK}(1^\lambda, z)\}_{\lambda, z} = \{\mathsf{View}^{\mathcal{A}_{NMZK}}_{\mathcal{H}_0}(1^\lambda, z)\}_{\lambda, z} \approx \cdots \approx \{\mathsf{View}^{\mathcal{A}_{NMZK}}_{\mathcal{H}_4}(1^\lambda, z)\}_{\lambda, z} = \{S^1(1^\lambda, z)\}_{\lambda, z}$

**Lemma 2.** *Let $\tilde{x}_1, \ldots, \tilde{x}_{\mathsf{poly}(\lambda)}$ be the right-session statements appearing in* $\mathsf{View} = \mathsf{Sim}_{NMZK}^1(1^\lambda, z)$ *and let* $\mathsf{id}$ *be the identity of the left session and* $\tilde{\mathsf{id}}_1, \ldots, \tilde{\mathsf{id}}_{\mathsf{poly}(\lambda)}$ *be the identities of right sessions appearing in* $\mathsf{View}$*. If the i-th right session is accepting and* $\mathsf{id} \neq \tilde{\mathsf{id}}_i$ *for* $i = 1, \ldots, \mathsf{poly}(\lambda)$*, then except with negligible probability, the second output of* $\mathsf{Sim}_{NMZK}(1^\lambda, z)$ *is* $\tilde{w}_i$ *such that* $(\tilde{x}_i, \tilde{w}_i) \in \mathsf{Rel}_L$ *for* $i = 1, \ldots, \mathsf{poly}(\lambda)$*.*

We now reconsider the hybrid experiments $\mathcal{H}_k$ for $k = 0, \ldots, 4$ described in the security proof of Lemma 1, and prove that they all enjoys an additional property. That is, in the right sessions $\mathcal{A}_{NMZK}$ never commits, using NM, to a message $\tilde{s}_0$ and sends a value $\tilde{s}_1$ s.t. $\tilde{s}_0 \oplus \tilde{s}_1 = \tilde{\sigma}_1 || \tilde{\sigma}_2$ where $\tilde{\sigma}_1, \tilde{\sigma}_2$ are two signatures for to different messages. Since $\mathcal{A}_{NMZK}$ does not commit to the signatures then the transcript computed using $\mathsf{LS}_{nm}$ correspond to a false instance, therefore for the adaptive-input PoK property of $\Pi_{OR}$, $\mathcal{A}_{NMZK}$ in the $i$-th right session chooses a statement $\tilde{x}_i$ and essentially completes the corresponding transcript of $\mathsf{LS}_L$ using the witness $\tilde{w}_i$ s.t. $(\tilde{x}_i, \tilde{w}_i) \in \mathsf{Rel}_L$ for $i \in \{1, \ldots, \mathsf{poly}(\lambda)\}$. For the above chain of implications we are ensured that in all hybrids $\mathcal{A}_{NMZK}$ uses the witnesses to complete the transcripts of $\Pi^{OR}$ in the right sessions. Therefore also in the simulated experiment, that corresponds to the last hybrid experiment, the $\mathcal{A}_{NMZK}$ behavior allows $\mathsf{Sim}_{NMZK}$ to extract the witness used by $\mathcal{A}_{NMZK}$ (that is internally executed by $\mathsf{Sim}_{NMZK}$) using the extractor of $\Pi^{OR}$ (that exists from the adaptive-PoK property enjoyed by $\Pi^{OR}$).

In order to prove that in $\mathcal{H}_0, \ldots, \mathcal{H}_4$ $\mathcal{A}_{NMZK}$ does not commit to two signatures in any of the right sessions we rely on the "mild" non-malleability and the honest-extraction property enjoyed by NM. More precisely, in each hybrid experiment, we use the honest-extraction[15] property to extract the signatures from the right sessions (that by contradiction are committed using NM). During the proof we need to show that the rewinds made by the honest-extractor do not interfere with the various reductions. Roughly speaking our security proof works

---

[15] Observe that in our case is sufficient that the extraction holds against honest sender, because for our security proof we only need to be sure that the commitment computed using NM is not a commitment of signatures.

because only non-interactive primitives are used, therefore the rewinds made by the extractor of NM do not rewind the challenger involved in the reduction. In particular, consider the hybrid $\mathcal{H}_3$ where we switch from the adaptive-input Special HVZK simulator of $\mathsf{LS}_{nm}$ to the honest prover procedure and $\mathcal{H}_4$ where we start to use adaptive-input Special HVZK simulator of $\mathsf{LS}_L$. In this two hybrid experiments in order to prove that $\mathcal{A}_{NMZK}$ does not commit to the signatures we rely on the adaptive-input Special HVZK and the rewinds do not affect the reduction. Indeed when we rely on adaptive-input Special HVZK of $\mathsf{LS}_L$ ($\mathsf{LS}_{nm}$) the honest prover procedure of $\mathsf{LS}_{nm}$ ($\mathsf{LS}_L$) can be used in order to complete the execution of $\Pi_{\mathsf{OR}}$. In this way the third round $\mathsf{ls}_L^3$ ($\mathsf{ls}_{nm}^3$) can be kept fixed thus computing $\mathsf{ls}_{nm}^3 = c^i \oplus \mathsf{ls}_L^3$ ($\mathsf{ls}_L^3 = c^i \oplus \mathsf{ls}_{nm}^3$) for every $c^i$ that could be sent by $\mathcal{A}_{NMZK}$ during the rewinds. It is not clear how to do such a security proof by directly relying on the WI property of $\Pi_{\mathsf{OR}}$. The formal proof for this lemma can be found in the full version (see [9]).

**Theorem 2.** *If OWFs exists, then* NMZK *is a delayed-input synchronous many-many NMZK AoK for* $\mathcal{NP}$.

*Proof.* The proof proceeds very similarly to the one showed for Theorem 1. The main difference between these two proofs is that we now have to consider also polynomially many synchronous left sessions played in parallel. Therefore the only difference between this proof and the one of Theorem 1 is that in the reductions we need to rely on the security of a many-one non-malleable commitment scheme and on the adaptive-input SHVZK (that is closed under parallel composition). Therefore, when we make a reduction on the adaptive-input SHVZK, we can simply use the parallel version of the primitives. Regarding a many-one non-malleable commitment, we notice that using the same arguments of the security proof of Proposition 1 provided in [28], it is possible to claim that a synchronous (one-one) non-malleable commitment is also synchronous many-one non-malleable. Therefore no additional assumptions are required in order to prove that NMZK is also delayed-input synchronous many-many NMZK. Note also that, the simulator needs to extract the trapdoor (the signatures of two different messages) in all the left (synchronous) sessions completed in the main thread. We can show that the extraction succeeds except with negligible probability using the same arguments used in the security proof of Theorem 1.

# 4    Multi-Party Coin-Tossing Protocol

## 4.1    4-Round Secure Multi-Party Coin Tossing: $\Pi_{\mathsf{MPCT}}$

The high-level idea of our protocol $\Pi_{\mathsf{MPCT}}$ significantly differs from the one of [18] (e.g., we use our 4-round delayed-input synchronous many-many NMZK instead of 3-round 3-robust parallel non-malleable commitment scheme). However, similarly to [18] our protocol simply consists of each party committing to a random string $r$, which is opened in the last round along with a simulatable proof of correct opening given to all parties independently. The output consists of the

$\oplus$ of all opened strings. Let's see in more details how our $\Pi_{\mathsf{MPCT}}$ works. For our construction we use the following tools.

1. A non-interactive perfectly binding computationally hiding commitment scheme $\mathsf{PBCOM} = (\mathsf{Com}, \mathsf{Dec})$.
2. A $\Sigma$-protocol $\mathsf{BL}_L = (\mathcal{P}_L, \mathcal{V}_L)$ for the $\mathcal{NP}$-language $L = \{\mathsf{com} : \exists\ (\mathsf{dec}, m)$ s.t. $\mathsf{Dec}(\mathsf{com}, \mathsf{dec}, m) = 1\}$ with Special HVZK simulator $\mathsf{Sim}_L$. We uses two instantiations of $\mathsf{BL}_L$ in order to construct the protocol for the OR of two statements $\Pi_{\mathsf{OR}}$ as described earlier (Appendix B.2 for more details). $\Pi_{\mathsf{OR}}$ is a proof system for the $\mathcal{NP}$-language $L_{\mathsf{com}} = \{(\mathsf{com}_0, \mathsf{com}_1) : \exists\ (\mathsf{dec}, m)$s.t. $\mathsf{Dec}(\mathsf{com}_0, \mathsf{dec}, m) = 1$ OR $\mathsf{Dec}(\mathsf{com}_1, \mathsf{dec}, m) = 1\}$[16]. Informally, by running $\Pi_{\mathsf{OR}}$, one can prove the knowledge of the message committed in $\mathsf{com}_0$ or in $\mathsf{com}_1$.
4. A 4-round delayed-input synchronous many-many NMZK $\mathsf{NMZK} = (\mathcal{P}_{\mathsf{NMZK}}, \mathcal{V}_{\mathsf{NMZK}})$ for the following $\mathcal{NP}$-language

$$L_{\mathsf{NMZK}} = \{((\mathsf{com}_0, \mathsf{com}_1), m) : \forall i \in \{0, 1\}\ \exists\ \mathsf{dec}_i \text{ s.t. } \mathsf{Dec}(\mathsf{com}_i, \mathsf{dec}_i, m) = 1\}.$$

Informally, by running $\mathsf{NMZK}$, one can prove that 2 commitments contain the same message $m$.

### 4.2  $\Pi_{\mathsf{MPCT}}$: Informal Description and Security Intuition

The high level description of our protocol between just two parties $(A_1, A_2)$ is given in Fig. 3. For a formal description of $\Pi_{\mathsf{MPCT}}$ we refer the reader to Sect. 4.3. In Fig. 3 we consider an execution of $\Pi_{\mathsf{MPCT}}$ that goes from $A_1$ to $A_2$ (the execution from $A_2$ to $A_1$ is symmetric). We recall that the protocol is executed simultaneously by both $A_1$ and $A_2$. The main idea is the following. Each party commits to his input using two instantiations of a non-interactive commitment. More precisely we have that $A_1$ computes two non-interactive commitments $\mathsf{com}_0$ and $\mathsf{com}_1$ (along with their decommitment information $\mathsf{dec}_0$ and $\mathsf{dec}_1$) of the message $r_1$. Each party also runs $\Pi_{\mathsf{OR}}$ for the $\mathcal{NP}$-language $L_{\mathsf{com}}$, from the first to the third round, in order to prove knowledge of the message committed in $\mathsf{com}_0$ or in $\mathsf{com}_1$. In the last round each party sends his own input (i.e. $r_1$ for $A_1$ and $r_2$ for $A_2$) and proves, using a delayed-input synchronous many-many non-malleable ZK for the $\mathcal{NP}$-language $L_{\mathsf{NMZK}}$, that messages committed using $\mathsf{PBCOM}$ were actually equal to that input (i.e. $r_1$ for $A_1$ and $r_2$ for $A_2$). That is, $A_1$ sends $r_1$ and proves that $\mathsf{com}_0$ and $\mathsf{com}_1$ are valid commitments of the message $r_1$.

**Intuition about the security of $\Pi_{\mathsf{MPCT}}$.** Let $A_1^*$ be the corrupted party. Informally the simulator Sim works as follows. Sim starts an interaction against $A_1^*$ using as input a random string $y$ until the third round of $\Pi_{\mathsf{MPCT}}$ is received by $A_1^*$. More precisely, in the first round he computes two commitments $\mathsf{com}_0$

---

[16] We use $\Pi_{\mathsf{OR}}$ in a non-black box way, but for ease of exposition sometimes we will refer to entire protocol $\Pi_{\mathsf{OR}}$ in order to invoke the proof of knowledge property enjoyed by $\Pi_{\mathsf{OR}}$.

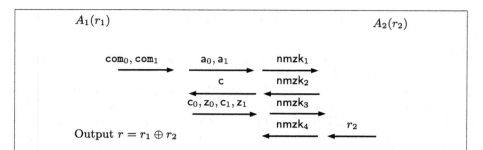

- $com_0$ and $com_1$ are two non-interactive commitments of the message $r_1$ computed using PBCOM.
- $(a_0, a_1, c_0, c_1, z_0, z_1)$ is the transcript generated from an execution of the WIPoK $\Pi_{OR}$ in which $\mathcal{P}_{OR}$ proves the knowledge of either the message committed in $com_0$ or in $com_1$.
- $(nmzk_1, nmzk_2, nmzk_3, nmzk_4)$ in the transcript generated from an execution of the delayed-input synchronous many-many NMZK NMZK in which $\mathcal{P}_{NMZK}$ proves that both $com_0$ and $com_1$ are valid commitments of the message $r_1$.

**Fig. 3.** $\Pi_{MPCT}$: Informal description of the execution from $A_1$ to $A_2$. The execution from $A_2$ to $A_1$ is symmetric.

and $com_1$ (along with their decommitment information $dec_0$ and $dec_1$) of $y$, and runs $\mathcal{P}_{OR}$ using as a witness $(dec_1, y)$. After the 3rd round Sim extracts the input $r_1^*$ of the corrupted party $A_1^*$ using the extractor $E_{OR}$ of $\Pi_{OR}$ (that exists from the PoK property of $\Pi_{OR}$) and sends $r_1^*$ to the ideal world functionality. At this point Sim receives $r$ from the ideal-world functionality, and completes the execution of the 4th round by sending $r_2 = r \oplus r_1^*$. We observe that Sim, in order to send a string $r_2$ that differs from $y$ in the 4th round, has to cheat in NMZK. This is done by simply running the simulator of NMZK. To prove the security of our scheme we will go through a sequence of hybrid experiments in order to show that the output view of the adversary in the real world can be simulated in the ideal world by Sim. The security proof strongly relies on the non-malleable zero knowledge property of NMZK. Indeed the aim of NMZK is to ensure that the adversary does not maul the messages received from Sim. That is, the behavior of $A_1^*$ allows to extract, in every hybrid experiments that we will consider, the correct input of $A_1^*$. This holds even in case the commitments sent by Sim to $A_1^*$ are commitments of a random string $y$, and the value sent in the 4th round is inconsistent with the value committed in the first round.

## 4.3   Formal Description

Let $P = \{P_1, \ldots, P_n\}$ be the set of parties. Furthermore, denote by $(id_1, \ldots, id_n)$[17] the unique identities of parties $\{P_1, \ldots, P_n\}$, respectively. Let us

---

[17] As discuss in the Definition 1 the use of the identifiers can be avoid, we use them, to uniformity of notation.

denote by $F_{MPCT} : (1^\lambda)^n \rightarrow \{0,1\}^\lambda$ the function $F_{MPCT}(r_1, \ldots, r_n) = r_1 \oplus \cdots \oplus r_n$. The protocol starts with each party $P_i$ choosing a random string $r_i$ for $i = 1, \ldots, n$. It consists of four rounds, i.e., all parties send messages in each round and the messages of all executions are seen by every party. Following [18] we describe the protocol between two parties $(A_1, A_2)$ observing that the real protocol actually consists of $n$ simultaneous executions of a two-party coin-tossing protocol $\Pi_{MPCT} = (A_1, A_2)$ between parties $(P_i, P_j)$ where $P_i$ acts as $A_1$ with input $r_i$ and $P_j$ acts as $A_2$ with input $r_j$ (both are symmetric). Let the input of $A_1$ be $r_1$, and the input of $A_2$ be $r_2$. The set of messages enabling $A_1$ to learn the output are denoted by $(m_1, m_2, m_3, m_4)$ where $(m_1, m_3)$ are sent by $A_1$ and $(m_2, m_4)$ are sent by $A_2$. Likewise, the set of messages enabling $A_2$ to learn the output are denoted by $(\tilde{m}_1, \tilde{m}_2, \tilde{m}_3, \tilde{m}_4)$ where $(\tilde{m}_1, \tilde{m}_3)$ are sent by $A_2$ and $(\tilde{m}_2, \tilde{m}_4)$ are sent by $A_1$. Therefore, messages $(m_l, \tilde{m}_l)$ are simultaneously exchanged in the $l$-th round for $l = 1, \ldots, 4$.

**Protocol $\Pi_{MPCT}$.** *Common input:* security parameter $\lambda$, instances length: $\ell_{NMZK}$, $\ell_{com}$.

**Round 1.** We first describe how $A_1$ constructs $m_1$.

1. Compute $(com_0, dec_0) \leftarrow Com(r_1)$ and $(com_1, dec_1) \leftarrow Com(r_1)$.
2. Compute $a_0 \leftarrow \mathcal{P}_L(1^\lambda, com_0, (dec_0, r_1))$.
3. Pick $c_1 \leftarrow \{0,1\}^\lambda$ and compute $(a_1, z_1) \leftarrow Sim_L(1^\lambda, com_1, c_1)$.
4. Run $\mathcal{V}_{NMZK}$ on input $1^\lambda$ and $\ell_{NMZK}$ thus obtaining the 1st round $nmzk_1$ of NMZK.
5. Message $m_1$ is defined to be $(com_0, com_1, a_0, a_1, nmzk_1)$.

Likewise, $A_2$ performs the same action as $A_1$ in order to construct $\tilde{m}_1 = (\tilde{com}_0, \tilde{com}_1, \tilde{a}_0, \tilde{a}_1, \tilde{nmzk}_1)$.

**Round 2.** In this round $A_2$ sends message $m_2$ and $A_1$ sends $\tilde{m}_2$. We first describe how $A_2$ constructs $m_2$.

1. Run $\mathcal{P}_{NMZK}$ on input $1^\lambda$, $id_2$, $\ell_{NMZK}$ and $nmzk_1$ thus obtaining the 2nd round $nmzk_2$ of NMZK.
2. Pick $c \leftarrow \{0,1\}^\lambda$.
3. Define message $m_2 = (c, nmzk_2)$.

Likewise, $A_1$ performs the same actions as $A_2$ in the previous step to construct the message $\tilde{m}_2 = (\tilde{c}, \tilde{nmzk}_2)$.

**Round 3.** In this round $A_1$ sends message $m_3$ and $A_2$ sends $\tilde{m}_3$. $A_1$ prepares $m_3$ as follows.

1. Compute $c_0 = c \oplus c_1$ and $z_0 \leftarrow \mathcal{P}_L(c_0)$.
2. Run $\mathcal{V}_{NMZK}$ on input $nmzk_2$ thus obtaining the 3rd round $nmzk_3$ of NMZK.
3. Define $m_3 = (nmzk_3, c_0, c_1, z_0, z_1)$.

Likewise, $A_2$ performs the same actions as $A_1$ in the previous step to construct the message $\tilde{m}_3 = (\tilde{nmzk}_3, \tilde{c}_0, \tilde{c}_1, \tilde{z}_0, \tilde{z}_1)$.

**Round 4.** In this round $A_2$ sends message $m_4$ and $A_1$ sends $\tilde{m}_4$. $A_2$ prepares $m_4$ as follows.

1. Check that the following conditions are satisfied: (a) $c = c_0 \oplus c_1$; (b) the transcript $a_0, c_0, z_0$ is accepting w.r.t. the instance $com_0$; (c) the transcript $a_1, c_1, z_1$ is accepting w.r.t. the instance $com_1$. If one of the check fails then output $\perp$, otherwise continue with the following steps.

2. Set $x_{\mathsf{NMZK}} = (\tilde{\mathsf{com}}_0, \tilde{\mathsf{com}}_1, r_2)$ and $w_{\mathsf{NMZK}} = (\tilde{\mathsf{dec}}_0, \tilde{\mathsf{dec}}_1)$.
3. Run $\mathcal{P}_{\mathsf{NMZK}}$ on input $\mathsf{nmzk}_3$, the statement to be proved $x_{\mathsf{NMZK}}$ and the witness $w_{\mathsf{NMZK}}$ s.t. $(x_{\mathsf{NMZK}}, w_{\mathsf{NMZK}}) \in \mathsf{Rel}_{L_{\mathsf{NMZK}}}$, thus obtaining the 4th round $\mathsf{nmzk}_4$ of NMZK.
4. Define $m_4 = (r_2, x_{\mathsf{NMZK}}, \mathsf{nmzk}_4)$.

Likewise, $A_1$ performs the same actions as $A_2$ in the previous step to construct the message $\tilde{m}_4 = (r_1, \tilde{x}_{\mathsf{NMZK}}, \tilde{\mathsf{nmzk}}_4)$.

**Output computation of $\Pi_{\mathsf{MPCT}}$.** Check, for each party, if $(\mathsf{nmzk}_1^i, \mathsf{nmzk}_2^i, \mathsf{nmzk}_3^i, \mathsf{nmzk}_4^i)$ is accepting for $\mathcal{V}_{\mathsf{NMZK}}$ with respect to the instance $x_{\mathsf{NMZK}}^i$ $(i = 1, \ldots, n)$ and that all pairs of parties used the same inputs $(r_1, \ldots, r_n)$. If so, output $r = r_1 \oplus \cdots \oplus r_n$.

**Theorem 3.** *If one-to-one OWFs exist, then the multi-party protocol $\Pi_{\mathsf{MPCT}}$ securely computes the multi-party coin-tossing functionality with black-box simulation.*

The formal security proof can be found in the full version (see [9]).

**Acknowledgments.** We thank Giuseppe Persiano and Alessandra Scafuro for several discussions on delayed-input protocols. Research supported in part by "GNCS - INdAM", EU COST Action IC1306, NSF grant 1619348, DARPA, US-Israel BSF grant 2012366, OKAWA Foundation Research Award, IBM Faculty Research Award, Xerox Faculty Research Award, B. John Garrick Foundation Award, Teradata Research Award, and Lockheed-Martin Corporation Research Award. The views expressed are those of the authors and do not reflect position of the Department of Defense or the U.S. Government. The work of 1st, 3rd and 4th authors has been done in part while visiting UCLA.

## A    Standard Definitions

**Definition 2 (Proof/argument system).** *A pair of PPT interactive algorithms $\Pi = (\mathcal{P}, \mathcal{V})$ constitute a proof system (resp., an argument system) for an $\mathcal{NP}$-language $L$, if the following conditions hold:*

**Completeness:** *For every $x \in L$ and $w$ such that $(x, w) \in \mathsf{Rel}_L$, it holds that:* $\mathrm{Prob}\left[\langle \mathcal{P}(w), \mathcal{V}\rangle(x) = 1\right] = 1$.
**Soundness:** *For every interactive (resp., PPT interactive) algorithm $\mathcal{P}^\star$, there exists a negligible function $\nu$ such that for every $x \notin L$ and every $z$:* $\mathrm{Prob}\left[\langle \mathcal{P}^\star(z), \mathcal{V}\rangle(x) = 1\right] < \nu(|x|)$.

A proof/argument system $\Pi = (\mathcal{P}, \mathcal{V})$ for an $\mathcal{NP}$-language $L$, enjoys *delayed-input* completeness if $\mathcal{P}$ needs $x$ and $w$ only to compute the last round and $\mathcal{V}$ needs $x$ only to compute the output. Before that, $\mathcal{P}$ and $\mathcal{V}$ run having as input only the size of $x$. The notion of delayed-input completeness was defined in [10]. An interactive protocol $\Pi = (\mathcal{P}, \mathcal{V})$ is *public coin* if, at every round, $\mathcal{V}$ simply tosses a predetermined number of coins (i.e. a random challenge) and sends the outcome to the prover. Moreover we say that the transcript $\tau$ of an execution $b = \langle \mathcal{P}(z), \mathcal{V}\rangle(x)$ is *accepting* if $b = 1$.

**Definition 3 (Proof of Knowledge [27]).** *A protocol* $\Pi = (\mathcal{P}, \mathcal{V})$ *that enjoys completeness is a* proof of knowledge *(PoK) for the relation* $\mathsf{Rel}_\mathsf{L}$ *if there exists a probabilistic expected polynomial-time machine* $\mathsf{E}$, *called the extractor, such that for every algorithm* $\mathcal{P}^\star$, *there exists a negligible function* $\nu$, *every statement* $x \in \{0,1\}^\lambda$, *every randomness* $r \in \{0,1\}^\star$ *and every auxiliary input* $z \in \{0,1\}^\star$,
$$\mathrm{Prob}\left[\langle \mathcal{P}_r^\star(z), \mathcal{V}\rangle(x) = 1\right] \leq \mathrm{Prob}\left[w \leftarrow \mathsf{E}^{\mathcal{P}_r^\star(z)}(x) : (x,w) \in \mathsf{Rel}_\mathsf{L}\right] + \nu(\lambda).$$
*We also say that an argument system* $\Pi$ *is a* argument of knowledge *(AoK) if the above condition holds w.r.t. any* PPT $\mathcal{P}^\star$.

In our security proofs we make use of the following observation. An interactive protocol $\Pi$ that enjoys the property of completeness and PoK (AoK) is a proof (an argument) system. Indeed suppose by contradiction that is not. By the definition of PoK (AoK) it is possible to extract the witness for every theorem $x \in \{0,1\}^\lambda$ proved by $\mathcal{P}_r^\star$ with probability greater than $\mathrm{Prob}\left[\langle \mathcal{P}_r^\star(z), \mathcal{V}\rangle(x) = 1\right]$; contradiction. In this paper we also consider the *adaptive-input* PoK/AoK property for all the protocols that enjoy delayed-input completeness. Adaptive-input PoK/AoK ensures that the PoK/AoK property still holds when a malicious prover can choose the statement adaptively at the last round.

A *3-round protocol* $\Pi = (\mathcal{P}, \mathcal{V})$ for a relation $\mathsf{Rel}_\mathsf{L}$ is an interactive protocol played between a prover $\mathcal{P}$ and a verifier $\mathcal{V}$ on common input $x$ and private input $w$ of $\mathcal{P}$ s.t. $(x,w) \in \mathsf{Rel}_\mathsf{L}$. In a 3-round protocol the first message $\mathsf{a}$ and the third message $\mathsf{z}$ are sent by $\mathcal{P}$ and the second messages $\mathsf{c}$ is played by $\mathcal{V}$. At the end of the protocol $\mathcal{V}$ decides to accept or reject based on the data that he has seen, i.e. $x, \mathsf{a}, \mathsf{c}, \mathsf{z}$. We usually denote the message $\mathsf{c}$ sent by $\mathcal{V}$ as a *challenge*, and as *challenge length* the number of bit of $\mathsf{c}$.

**Definition 4 ($\Sigma$-Protocol).** *A 3-round public-coin protocol* $\Pi = (\mathcal{P}, \mathcal{V})$ *for a relation* $\mathsf{Rel}_\mathsf{L}$ *is a $\Sigma$-Protocol if the following properties hold:*

- *Completeness: if* $(\mathcal{P}, \mathcal{V})$ *follow the protocol on input* $x$ *and private input* $w$ *to* $\mathcal{P}$ *s.t.* $(x,w) \in \mathsf{Rel}_\mathsf{L}$, $\mathcal{V}$ *always accepts.*
- *Special soundness: if there exists a polynomial time algorithm such that, for any pair of accepting transcripts on input* $x$, $(\mathsf{a}, \mathsf{c}_1, \mathsf{z}_1), (\mathsf{a}, \mathsf{c}_2, \mathsf{z}_2)$ *where* $\mathsf{c}_1 \neq \mathsf{c}_2$, *outputs witness* $w$ *such that* $(x,w) \in \mathsf{Rel}_\mathsf{L}$.
- *Special Honest Verifier Zero-knowledge (Special HVZK): there exists a* PPT *simulator algorithm* $\mathsf{Sim}$ *that for any* $x \in L$, *security parameter* $\lambda$ *and any challenge* $\mathsf{c}$ *works as follow:* $(\mathsf{a}, \mathsf{z}) \leftarrow \mathsf{Sim}(1^\lambda, x, \mathsf{c})$. *Furthermore, the distribution of the output of* $\mathsf{Sim}$ *is computationally indistinguishable from the distribution of a transcript obtained when* $\mathcal{V}$ *sends* $\mathsf{c}$ *as challenge and* $\mathcal{P}$ *runs on common input* $x$ *and any* $w$ *such that* $(x,w) \in \mathsf{Rel}_\mathsf{L}$ [18].

**Definition 5.** *A delayed-input 3-round protocol* $\Pi = (\mathcal{P}, \mathcal{V})$ *for relation* $\mathsf{Rel}_\mathsf{L}$ *enjoys* adaptive-input special soundness *if there exists a polynomial time algorithm such that, for any pair of accepting transcripts* $(\mathsf{a}, \mathsf{c}_1, \mathsf{z}_1)$ *for input* $x_1$ *and*

---

[18] Note that we require that the two transcripts are computationally indistinguishable as in [16], instead of following [12] that requires the perfect indistinguishability between the two transcripts.

$(a, c_2, z_2)$ *for input* $x_2$ *with* $c_1 \neq c_2$, *outputs witnesses* $w_1$ *and* $w_2$ *such that* $(x_1, w_1) \in \mathsf{Rel_L}$ *and* $(x_2, w_2) \in \mathsf{Rel_L}$.

**Definition 6.** *A delayed-input 3-round protocol* $\Pi = (\mathcal{P}, \mathcal{V})$ *for relation* $\mathsf{Rel_L}$ *enjoys* adaptive-input Special Honest Verifier Zero-knowledge (adaptive-input Special HVZK) *if there exists a two phases* PPT *simulator algorithm* Sim *that works as follow:*

1. $a \leftarrow \mathsf{Sim}(1^\lambda, c, \kappa; \rho)$, *where* $1^\lambda$ *is the security parameter,* $c$ *is the challenge* $\kappa$ *is the size of the instance to be proved and the randomness* $\rho$;
2. $z \leftarrow \mathsf{Sim}(x, \rho)^{19}$, *where* $x$ *is the instance to be proved.*

$\Pi$ *is adaptive-input Special HVZK if any* $x \in L$ *and for any* $c \in \{0,1\}^\lambda$, *the distribution of the transcripts* $(a, c, z)$, *computed by* Sim, *is computationally indistinguishable from the distribution of a transcript obtained when* $\mathcal{V}$ *sends* $c$ *as challenge and* $\mathcal{P}$ *runs on common input* $x$ *and any* $w$ *(available only in the third round) such that* $(x, w) \in \mathsf{Rel_L}$.

## A.1   Commitment Schemes

**Definition 7 (Commitment Scheme).** *Given a security parameter* $1^\lambda$, *a commitment scheme* CS $=$ (Sen, Rec) *is a two-phase protocol between two* PPT *interactive algorithms, a sender* Sen *and a receiver* Rec. *In the commitment phase* Sen *on input a message* m *interacts with* Rec *to produce a commitment* com, *and the private output* d *of* Sen.

*In the decommitment phase,* Sen *sends to* Rec *a decommitment information* $(m, d)$ *such that* Rec *accepts* m *as the decommitment of* com.

*We consider the classic notions of correctness, perfect and statistical binding, computation and statistical hiding.*

## A.2   3-Round Honest-Extractable Commitment Schemes

Informally, a 3-round commitment scheme is honest-extractable if there exists an efficient extractor that having black-box access to any efficient honest sender that successfully performs the commitment phase, outputs the only committed string that can be successfully decommitted. We give now a definition that follows the one of [37].

**Definition 8 (Honest-Extractable Commitment Scheme).** *A perfectly (resp. statistically) binding commitment scheme* ExCS $=$ (ExSen, ExRec) *is an* honest-extractable commitment scheme *if there exists an expected* PPT *extractor* ExtCom *that given oracle access to any honest sender* ExSen, *outputs a pair* $(\tau, m)$ *such that the following two properties hold:*

---

[19] To not overburden the notation we omit the randomness when we use the adaptive-input Special HVZK simulator.

- **Simulatability:** $\tau$ *is identically distributed to the view of* ExSen *(when interacting with an honest* ExRec*) in the commitment phase.*
- **Extractability:** *The probability that there exists a decommitment of* $\tau$ *to a message* $m'$, *where* $m' \neq m$ *is 0 (resp. negligible).*

### A.3 Non-malleable Commitments

In order to define a non-malleable commitment we follow [28,29]. Let $\Pi = $ (Sen, Rec) be a statistically binding commitment scheme. And let $\lambda$ be the security parameter. Consider a MiM adversary $\mathcal{A}$ that, on auxiliary input $z$ participates in a left and a right session. In the left sessions the MiM adversary $\mathcal{A}$ interacts with Sen receiving commitment to value $m$ using an identity id of its choice. In the right session $\mathcal{A}$ interacts with Rec attempting to commit to a related value $\tilde{m}$ again using identity of its choice $\tilde{\text{id}}$. If the right commitment is invalid, or undefined, its value is set to $\bot$. Furthermore, if $\tilde{\text{id}} = \text{id}$ then $\tilde{m}$ is also set to $\bot$ (i.e., a commitment where the adversary uses the same identity of the honest senders is considered invalid). Let $\text{mim}_\Pi^{\mathcal{A},m}(z)$ denote a random variable that describes the values $\tilde{m}$ and the view of $\mathcal{A}$ in the above experiment.

**Definition 9. (Non-malleable commitment scheme [28,29]).** *A commitment scheme is* non-malleable *with respect to commitment if, for every* PPT *MiM adversary* $\mathcal{A}$, *for every* $m_0 \in \{0,1\}^{\text{poly}(\lambda)}$ *and* $m_1 \in \{0,1\}^{\text{poly}(\lambda)}$ *the following holds*

$$\{\text{mim}_\Pi^{\mathcal{A},m_0}(z)\}_{z\in\{0,1\}^*} \approx \{\text{mim}_\Pi^{\mathcal{A},m_1}(z)\}_{z\in\{0,1\}^*}.$$

We say that a commitment is valid or well formed if it admits a decommitment to a message $m \neq \bot$.

For our propose we use a 4-round synchronous honest-extractable non-malleable commitment. That is, a commitment scheme that enjoys (1) non-malleability only against synchronous adversaries, (2) is extractable w.r.t. honest sender (honest-extractable) and (3) is public-coin. The non-malleable commitment $\Pi$ provided in Fig. 2 of [22] enjoys non-malleability against synchronous adversary (as proved in Theorem 1 of [22]), is public coin and can be instantiated in 4 rounds relying on OWFs (the protocol can be squeezed to 3 rounds using one-to-one OWFs).

Also, as stated in Sect. 5 of [22], given a commitment computed by the sender of $\Pi$ one can rewind the sender in order to obtain a new accepting transcript with the same first round (resp., first two rounds if we consider the instantiation that relies on OWFs) in order to extract a message $m$. Moreover, if the sender is honest, then it is possible to claim that $m$ is the actual message committed by the sender. We remark that we do not require any form of extractability against malicious senders.

## B    Special WIPoK

### B.1    Improving the Soundness of LS

In this section we consider the 3-round WIPoK for the $\mathcal{NP}$-complete language of graph Hamiltonicity (HC), provided in [25], and we will refer to this construction as the *LS protocol*. An interesting property of this WIPoK is that only the size of the statement need to be known before the last round by both the prover and the verifier. We show that the LS protocol does not enjoys special soundness when the statement to be proved is adaptively chosen by the prover in the last round. That is, if two accepting transcripts (that share the first round) are provided w.r.t. to two different instances $x_0$ and $x_1$, then only the witness $w$ for $x_b$ is extracted (with $b \in \{0,1\}$). More precisely, given the accepting transcript $(\mathsf{ls}^1, \mathsf{ls}_0^2, \mathsf{ls}_0^3)$ for the statement $x_0$ and $(\mathsf{ls}^1, \mathsf{ls}_1^2, \mathsf{ls}_1^3)$ for the statement $x_1$ (with $\mathsf{ls}_0^2 \neq \mathsf{ls}_1^2$) then it could be that only $w_b$ can be extracted. We provide a construction that overcomes this issue, allowing the extraction of the witnesses for both $x_0$ and $x_1$ thus obtaining a $\Sigma$-protocol where the special soundness holds even when the two accepting transcripts refer to different theorems adaptively chosen in the last round. Following [11] we refer to this property as adaptive-input special soundness (see Definition 5).

Before showing why LS is not already adaptive-input special sound and how our construction works, we briefly describe the LS protocol with one-bit challenge following [32]. Let $\mathcal{P}$ be prover and $\mathcal{V}$ the verifier. The common input of $\mathcal{P}$ and $\mathcal{V}$ is $\kappa$, that represents the number of vertexes of the instance $G$ to be proved. The graph $G$ is represented by a $\kappa \times \kappa$ adjacency matrix $\mathsf{MG}$ where $\mathsf{MG}[i][j] = 1$ if there exists an edge between vertexes $i$ and $j$ in $G$. A non-edge position $i, j$ is a pair of vertexes that are not connected in $G$ and for which $\mathsf{MG}[i][j] = 0$.

- $\mathcal{P}$ picks a random $\kappa$-vertex cycle graph $C$ and commits bit-by-bit to the corresponding adjacency matrix using a statistically binding commitment scheme.
- $\mathcal{V}$ responds with a randomly chosen bit b.
- $\mathcal{P}$ on input the graph $G$ and the Hamiltonian cycle $w$ executes the following steps. If $b = 0$, $\mathcal{P}$ opens all the commitments, showing that the matrix committed in the first round is actually an $\kappa$-vertex cycle. If $b = 1$, $\mathcal{P}$ sends a permutation $\pi$ mapping the vertex of $C$ in $G$. Then it opens the commitment of the adjacency matrix of $C$ corresponding to the non-edges of $G$.
- $\mathcal{V}$ accepts (outputs 1) if what he receives in the third round is consistent with the bit $b$ that he was sent in the second round.

Getting the answer for both $b = 0$ and $b = 1$ (w.r.t. to the same graph $G$) allows the extraction of the cycle for $G$. The reason is the following. For $b = 0$ one gets the random cycle $C$. Then for $b = 1$ one gets the permutation mapping the random cycle in the actual cycle that is given to $\mathcal{P}$ before the last message of the protocol.

We now observe that a malicious prover $\mathcal{P}^\star$ could gives the answer for $b = 0$ w.r.t. to the graph $G_0$ and the answer for $b = 1$ w.r.t. the graph $G_1$ (due to the delayed-input nature of LS). This means that even knowing two accepting transcripts that share the first round, the permutation that maps the vertexes of $C$ in $G_0$ it is not known. Therefore an efficient algorithm can only compute the cycle $w_1$ of $G_1$ and gets no information about the Hamiltonian cycle of $G_0$. Summing up, given the accepting transcripts $(\mathsf{ls}^1, 0, \mathsf{ls}_0^3)$ for the graph $G_0$ and $(\mathsf{ls}^1, 1, \mathsf{ls}_1^3)$ for the graph $G_1$, only the Hamiltonian cycle for $G_1$ can be computed. That is, only the cycle for the graph proved by $\mathcal{P}^\star$ to be Hamiltonian using as a second round the challenge 1 can be efficiently computed. Starting from this observation, in order to allow an efficient algorithm to compute cycles for both $G_0$ and $G_1$, we construct an improved version of LS that we denoted with $\mathsf{LS}^{\mathsf{imp}} = (\mathcal{P}^{\mathsf{imp}}, \mathcal{V}^{\mathsf{imp}})$. $\mathsf{LS}^{\mathsf{imp}}$ uses LS in a black-box way. For ease of exposition we use the following notation. $\mathsf{ls}^1 \leftarrow \mathcal{P}(1^\lambda, \kappa; \rho)$ denotes that $\mathcal{P}$ is executed on input the security parameter (in unary) $1^\lambda$, $\kappa$ and the randomness $\rho$ and gives in output the first round of LS $\mathsf{ls}^1$. $\mathsf{ls}^3 \leftarrow \mathcal{P}(G, w, \mathsf{ls}^2, \rho)$ denotes that $\mathcal{P}$ has computed the third round of LS by running on input the graph $G$, the cycle $w$ for the graph $G$, the bit $\mathsf{ls}^2$ and the randomness used to compute $\mathsf{ls}^1$. $\mathcal{V}(\mathsf{ls}^1, \mathsf{ls}^2, \mathsf{ls}^3, G)$ denotes the output of $\mathcal{V}$ on input $\mathsf{ls}^1, \mathsf{ls}^2, \mathsf{ls}^3$ and the graph $G$. Let $\kappa$ be the number of vertexes of the graph $G$ to be proved, our $\mathsf{LS}^{\mathsf{imp}} = (\mathcal{P}^{\mathsf{imp}}, \mathcal{V}^{\mathsf{imp}})$ works as follows.

1. $\mathcal{P}^{\mathsf{imp}}$ on input the security parameter $\lambda$, $\kappa$ and the randomness $\rho_0 || \rho_1$ computes and sends $\mathsf{ls}_0^1 \leftarrow \mathcal{P}(1^\lambda, \kappa; \rho_0)$, $\mathsf{ls}_1^1 \leftarrow \mathcal{P}(1^\lambda, \kappa; \rho_1)$.
2. $\mathcal{V}^{\mathsf{imp}}$ picks and sends a random bit $b$.
3. $\mathcal{P}^{\mathsf{imp}}$, upon receiving $b$, on input the graph $G$ and the Hamiltonian cycle $w$ for $G$ computes and sends $\mathsf{ls}_0^3 \leftarrow \mathcal{P}(G, w, b, \rho_0)$, $\mathsf{ls}_1^3 \leftarrow \mathcal{P}(G, w, 1 - b, \rho_1)$.
4. $\mathcal{V}^{\mathsf{imp}}$ accepts iff $\mathcal{V}(G, \mathsf{ls}_0^1, b, \mathsf{ls}_0^3) = 1$ and $\mathcal{V}(G, \mathsf{ls}_1^1, 1 - b, \mathsf{ls}_1^3) = 1$.

**Theorem 4.** *Assuming one-to-one OWFs, $\mathsf{LS}^{\mathsf{imp}}$ is a $\Sigma$-protocol with adaptive-input Special HVZK and adaptive-input special soundness. Moreover $\mathsf{LS}^{\mathsf{imp}}$ is Zero Knowledge.*

*Proof.* **(Delayed-input) Completeness.** The (delayed-input) completeness of $\mathsf{LS}^{\mathsf{imp}}$ comes from the (delayed-input) completeness of LS.

**Adaptive-input special soundness.** Let us consider two accepting transcripts that share the first round for $\mathsf{LS}^{\mathsf{imp}}$: $((\mathsf{ls}_0, \mathsf{ls}_1), 0, (\mathsf{ls}_0^3, \mathsf{ls}_1^3))$ for the statement $G$ and $((\mathsf{ls}_0, \mathsf{ls}_1), 1, (\mathsf{ls}_1^{3'}, \mathsf{ls}_1^{3'}))$ for the statement $G'$. We can isolate the sub-transcripts $(\mathsf{ls}_0, 0, \mathsf{ls}_0^3)$ and $(\mathsf{ls}_0, 1, \mathsf{ls}_0^{3'})$ and observe that $\mathcal{V}(G, \mathsf{ls}_0^1, 0, \mathsf{ls}_0^3) = 1 = \mathcal{V}(G'|\mathsf{ls}_0^1, 1, \mathsf{ls}_0^{3'})$. From what we discuss before about LS we know that in this case the witness $w$ for $G'$ can be extracted. Also let us now consider the two sub-transcripts $(\mathsf{ls}_1, 1, \mathsf{ls}_1^3)$ and $(\mathsf{ls}_1, 0, \mathsf{ls}_1^{3'})$. Also in this case, by observing that $\mathcal{V}(G, \mathsf{ls}_1, 1, \mathsf{ls}_1^3) = 1 = \mathcal{V}(G', \mathsf{ls}_1, 0, \mathsf{ls}_1^{3'})$, the cycle for $G$ can be efficiently computed.

**Adaptive-input Special HVZK.** Following [30], we consider an adaptive-input Special HVZK simulator $S$ associated to the LS's protocol. This is equal to a Special HVZK simulator with the additional property that the first round can be simulated without knowing the instance to be proved (see Definition 6). In more details $S$ works in two phases. In the first phase just $1^\lambda$, the challenge $\mathsf{ls}^2$, the number of vertexes $\kappa$ is used to output the first round $\mathsf{ls}^1$. We denote this phase using: $\mathsf{ls}^1 \leftarrow S(1^\lambda, \mathsf{ls}^2, \kappa)$. In the second phase $S$ takes as input the instance and output the third round $\mathsf{ls}^3$. We denote this phase using $\mathsf{ls}^3 \leftarrow S(G)$. The adaptive-input Special HVZK simulator $S^{\mathsf{imp}}$ for $\mathsf{LS}^{\mathsf{imp}}$ just internally runs $S$ two times, once using $b$ and once using $1 - b$ as a challenge. In more details the two phase of $S^{\mathsf{imp}}$ are the following.

1. $S^{\mathsf{imp}}$, on input $1^\lambda$, the challenge $b$, $\kappa$ and the randomness $\rho_b || \rho_{1-b}$, computes $\mathsf{ls}_b^1 \leftarrow S(1^\lambda, b, \kappa; \rho_b)$, $\mathsf{ls}_{1-b}^1 \leftarrow S(1^\lambda, 1 - b, \kappa; \rho_{1-b})$ and outputs $(\mathsf{ls}_b^1, \mathsf{ls}_{1-b}^1)$.

2. $S^{imp}$, on input the graph $G$, $\rho_0$ and $\rho_1$ computes $ls_b^3 \leftarrow S(G, \rho_b)$, $ls_{1-b}^3 \leftarrow S(G, \rho_{1-b})$ and outputs $(ls_b^3, ls_{1-b}^3)$.

The transcript $\left((ls_b^1, ls_{1-b}^1), b, (ls_b^3, ls_{1-b}^3)\right)$ output by $S^{imp}$ is computationally indistinguishable from a transcript computed by $\mathcal{P}^{imp}$ (that uses as input an Hamiltonian cycle $w$ of $G$) due to the security of the underlying adaptive-input Special HVZK simulator $S$.

**Zero-Knowledge.** The ZK simulator of $LS^{imp}$ just needs to guess the bit $b$ chosen by the adversarial verifier and runs the adaptive-input Special HVZK simulator.

It is easy to see that (as for LS) if we consider $\lambda$ parallel executions of $LS^{imp}$ then we obtain a protocol $LS^\lambda$ that still enjoys adaptive-input completeness, adaptive-input special soundness, adaptive-input Special HVZK. Moreover $LS^\lambda$ is WI. Formally, we can claim the following theorems.

**Theorem 5.** *Assuming one-to-one OWFs, $LS^\lambda$ is a $\Sigma$-protocol with adaptive-input Special HVZK, and adaptive-input special soundness. Moreover $LS^\lambda$ is witness indistinguishable (WI).*

*Proof.* Completeness, adaptive-input special soundness and adaptive-input Special HVZK come immediately from the adaptive-input special soundness and adaptive-input Special HVZK of $LS^{imp}$. The WI comes from the observation that $LS^{imp}$ is WI (due to the zero knowledge property), and that WI is preserved under parallel (and concurrent) composition.

**Theorem 6.** *Assuming OWFs, $LS^\lambda$ is a 4-round public-coin proof system with adaptive-input Special HVZK, adaptive-input special soundness and WI.*

*Proof.* The proof of this theorem just relies on the observation that in order to instantiate a statistically binding commitment scheme using OWFs an additional round is required to compute the first round of Naor's commitment scheme [31].

Observe that since Hamiltonicity is an $\mathcal{NP}$-complete language, the above constructions work for any $\mathcal{NP}$ language through $\mathcal{NP}$ reductions. For simplicity in the rest of the paper we will omit the $\mathcal{NP}$ reduction therefore assuming that the above scheme works directly on a given $\mathcal{NP}$-language $L$.

## B.2   Combining (Adaptive-Input) Special HVZK PoK Through [12]

In our paper we use the well known technique for composing two $\Sigma$-protocols to compute the OR for compound statement [12,16]. In more details, let $\Pi_0 = (\mathcal{P}_0, \mathcal{V}_0)$ and $\Pi_1 = (\mathcal{P}_1, \mathcal{V}_1)$ be $\Sigma$-protocols for the respective $\mathcal{NP}$-relation $Rel_{L_0}$ (with Special HVZK simulator $Sim_0$) and $Rel_{L_1}$ (with Special HVZK simulator $Sim_1$). Then it is possible to use $\Pi_0$ and $\Pi_1$ to construct $\Pi^{OR} = (\mathcal{P}_{OR}, \mathcal{V}_{OR})$ for relation $Rel_{OR} = \{((x_0, x_1), w) : ((x_0, w) \in Rel_{L_0}) \text{ OR } ((x_1, w) \in Rel_{L_1})\}$ that works as follows.

**Protocol** $\Pi^{OR} = (\mathcal{P}_{OR}, \mathcal{V}_{OR})$: Let $w_b$ with $b \in \{0,1\}$ be s.t. $(x_b, w_b) \in \mathsf{Rel}_{L_b}$. $\mathcal{P}_{OR}$ and $\mathcal{V}_{OR}$ on common input $(x_0, x_1)$ and private input $w_b$ compute the following steps.

- $\mathcal{P}_{OR}$ computes $a_b \leftarrow \mathcal{P}_b(1^\lambda, x_b, w_b)$. Furthermore he picks $c_{1-b} \leftarrow \{0,1\}^\lambda$ and computes $(a_{1-b}, z_{1-b}) \leftarrow \mathsf{Sim}_{1-b}(1^\lambda, x_{1-b}, c_{1-b})$. $\mathcal{P}_{OR}$ sends $a_0, a_1$ to $\mathcal{V}_{OR}$.
- $\mathcal{V}_{OR}$, upon receiving $a_0, a_1$ picks $c \leftarrow \{0,1\}^\lambda$ and sends $c$ to $\mathcal{P}_{OR}$.
- $\mathcal{P}_{OR}$, upon receiving $c$ computes $c_b = c_{1-b} \oplus c$ and computes $z_b \leftarrow \mathcal{P}_b(c_b)$. $\mathcal{P}_{OR}$ sends $c_0, c_1, z_0\ z_1$ to $\mathcal{V}_{OR}$.
- $\mathcal{V}_{OR}$ checks that the following conditions holds: $c = c_0 \oplus c_1$, $\mathcal{V}_0(x_0, a_0, c_0, z_0) = 1$ and $\mathcal{V}_1(x_1, a_1, c_1, z_1) = 1$. If all the checks succeed then outputs 1, otherwise outputs 0.

**Theorem 7** *([12]). Let $\Sigma_0$ and $\Sigma_1$ be two $\Sigma$-protocols, then $\Pi^{OR} = (\mathcal{P}_{OR}, \mathcal{V}_{OR})$ is a $\Sigma$-protocol for $\mathsf{Rel}_{L_{OR}}$.*

**Theorem 8** *([13]). Let $\Pi = (\mathcal{P}, \mathcal{V})$ be a $\Sigma$-protocol for relation $\mathsf{Rel}_L$ with negligible soundness error[20], then $\Pi$ is a proof of knowledge for $\mathsf{Rel}_L$.*

In our work we instantiate $\Pi^{OR}$ using as $\Pi_0$ and $\Pi_1$ the Blum's protocol [4] for the $\mathcal{NP}$-complete language for graph Hamiltonicity (that also is a $\Sigma$-Protocol). Therefore Theorem 7 (and Theorem 8) can be applied.

We also consider an instantiation of $\Pi^{OR}$ using as $\Pi = (\mathcal{P}, \mathcal{V})$ our $\mathsf{LS}^\lambda$. If we instantiate $\Pi^{OR}$ using $\mathsf{LS}^\lambda$ and the corresponding adaptive-input Special HVZK simulator $\mathsf{LS}^\lambda$, then $\Pi^{OR}$ is adaptive-input special soundness. More formally we can claim the following theorem.

**Theorem 9.** *If $\Pi^{OR}$ is instantiated using $\mathsf{LS}^\lambda$ (and the corresponding adaptive-input Special HVZK simulator $S^\lambda$), then $\Pi^{OR}$ enjoys the delayed-input completeness and adaptive-input special soundness for the $\mathcal{NP}$-relation $\mathsf{Rel}_{L_{OR}}$.*

*Proof.* The delayed-input completeness follows from the delayed-input completeness of $\mathsf{LS}^\lambda$.

**Adaptive-input special soundness.** Let us consider two accepting transcripts that share the first round for $\Pi^{OR}$: $((\pi_0, \pi_1), \pi^2, (\pi_0^2, \pi_0^3, \pi_1^2, \pi_1^3))$ for the statement $(x_0, x_1)$ and $((\pi_0, \pi_1), \pi^{2'}, (\pi_0^{2'}, \pi_0^{3'}, \pi_1^{2'}\pi_1^{3'}))$ for the statement $(x_0', x_1')$, where $\pi^2 \neq \pi^{2'}$. We observe that since $\pi^2 \neq \pi^{2'}$, $\pi^2 = \pi_0^2 \oplus \pi_1^2$ and $\pi^{2'} = \pi_0^{2'} \oplus \pi_1^{2'}$ it holds that either $\pi_0^2 \neq \pi_0^{2'}$ or $\pi_1^2 \neq \pi_1^{2'}$. Suppose w.l.o.g. that $\pi_0^2 \neq \pi_0^{2'}$. Then we are guaranteed from the adaptive-input special soundness of $\mathsf{LS}^\lambda$ that using the transcripts $(\pi_0, \pi_0^2, \pi_0^3)$ and $(\pi_0, \pi_0^{2'}, \pi_0^{3'})$ the values $(w_a, w_b)$ s.t. $(x_0, w_a) \in \mathsf{Rel}_{L_0}$ and $(x_0', w_b) \in \mathsf{Rel}_{L_0}$ can be extracted in polynomial-time. The same arguments can be used when $\pi_1^2 \neq \pi_1^{2'}$.

Using a result of [11] we can claim the following theorem.

**Theorem 10.** *$\Pi^{OR}$ instantiated using $\mathsf{LS}^\lambda$ is an adaptive-input PoK for the $\mathcal{NP}$-relation $\mathsf{Rel}_{L_{OR}}$.*

---

[20] The soundness error represents the probability of a malicious prover to convince the verifier of a false statement.

It would be easy to prove that $\Pi^{OR}$ is also WI, however in this paper we are not going to rely directly on the WI property of $\Pi^{OR}$, in order to deal with the rewinding issue that we have described earlier. More precisely, in the two main contributions of this paper we will use $\Pi^{OR}$ (the one instantiated from Blum's protocol and the one instantiated using $LS^{\lambda}$) in a non-black box way in order to prove the security of our protocols. It will be crucial for our reduction to rely on the (adaptive-input) Special HVZK of $\Pi_0$ and $\Pi_1$ instead of using directly the WI property of $\Pi^{OR}$. The intuitively reason is that it is often easier in a reduction to rely on the security of a non-interactive primitive (like Special HVZK is) instead of an interactive primitive (like WI). This is the reason why we use the OR composition of [12,16] combined with the Blum's protocol (or the LS protocol) instead of relying on the (adaptive-input) WI provided by a Blum's protocol (LS protocol). In the rest of the paper, in order to rely on OWFs only, we sometimes use a four round version of Blum's and LS protocols. In this case there is an additional initial round that goes from the verifier to the prover and corresponds to the first round of Naor's commitment scheme [31].

# References

1. Ananth, P., Choudhuri, A.R., Jain, A.: A new approach to round-optimal secure multiparty computation. In: Katz, J., Shacham, H. (eds.) CRYPTO 2017. LNCS, vol. 10401, pp. 468–499. Springer, Cham (2017). https://doi.org/10.1007/978-3-319-63688-7_16

2. Barak, B.: Constant-round coin-tossing with a man in the middle or realizing the shared random string model. In: Proceedings of the 43rd Symposium on Foundations of Computer Science (FOCS 2002), Vancouver, BC, Canada, pp. 345–355, 16–19 November 2002

3. Bellare, M., Jakobsson, M., Yung, M.: Round-optimal zero-knowledge arguments based on any one-way function. In: Fumy, W. (ed.) EUROCRYPT 1997. LNCS, vol. 1233, pp. 280–305. Springer, Heidelberg (1997). https://doi.org/10.1007/3-540-69053-0_20

4. Blum, M.: How to prove a theorem so no one else can claim it. In: Proceedings of the International Congress of Mathematicians, pp. 1444–1454 (1986)

5. Chung, K.-M., Ostrovsky, R., Pass, R., Venkitasubramaniam, M., Visconti, I.: 4-round resettably-sound zero knowledge. In: Lindell, Y. (ed.) TCC 2014. LNCS, vol. 8349, pp. 192–216. Springer, Heidelberg (2014). https://doi.org/10.1007/978-3-642-54242-8_9

6. Ciampi, M., Ostrovsky, R., Siniscalchi, L., Visconti, I.: Concurrent non-malleable commitments (and more) in 3 rounds. In: Robshaw, M., Katz, J. (eds.) CRYPTO 2016. LNCS, vol. 9816, pp. 270–299. Springer, Heidelberg (2016). https://doi.org/10.1007/978-3-662-53015-3_10. Full version https://eprint.iacr.org/2016/566

7. Ciampi, M., Ostrovsky, R., Siniscalchi, L., Visconti, I.: Four-round concurrent non-malleable commitments from one-way functions. In: Katz, J., Shacham, H. (eds.) CRYPTO 2017. LNCS, vol. 10402, pp. 127–157. Springer, Cham (2017). https://doi.org/10.1007/978-3-319-63715-0_5. Full version https://eprint.iacr.org/2016/621

8. Ciampi, M., Ostrovsky, R., Siniscalchi, L., Visconti, I.: Round-optimal secure two-party computation from trapdoor permutations. In: Kalai, Y., Reyzin, L. (eds.) TCC 2017. LNCS, vol. 10677, pp. 678–710. Springer, Cham (2017). Full version https://eprint.iacr.org/2017/920

9. Ciampi, M., Ostrovsky, R., Siniscalchi, L., Visconti, I.: Delayed-input non-malleable zero knowledge and multi-party coin tossing in four rounds. Cryptology ePrint Archive, Report 2017/931 (2017). https://eprint.iacr.org/2017/931

10. Ciampi, M., Persiano, G., Scafuro, A., Siniscalchi, L., Visconti, I.: Improved OR-composition of sigma-protocols. In: Kushilevitz, E., Malkin, T. (eds.) TCC 2016. LNCS, vol. 9563, pp. 112–141. Springer, Heidelberg (2016). https://doi.org/10.1007/978-3-662-49099-0_5. Full version http://eprint.iacr.org/2015/810

11. Ciampi, M., Persiano, G., Scafuro, A., Siniscalchi, L., Visconti, I.: Online/offline OR composition of sigma protocols. In: Fischlin, M., Coron, J.-S. (eds.) EUROCRYPT 2016. LNCS, vol. 9666, pp. 63–92. Springer, Heidelberg (2016). https://doi.org/10.1007/978-3-662-49896-5_3. Full version https://eprint.iacr.org/2016/175

12. Cramer, R., Damgård, I., Schoenmakers, B.: Proofs of partial knowledge and simplified design of witness hiding protocols. In: Desmedt, Y.G. (ed.) CRYPTO 1994. LNCS, vol. 839, pp. 174–187. Springer, Heidelberg (1994). https://doi.org/10.1007/3-540-48658-5_19

13. Damgård, I.: On $\Sigma$-protocol (2010). http://www.cs.au.dk/~ivan/Sigma.pdf

14. Santis, A., Crescenzo, G., Ostrovsky, R., Persiano, G., Sahai, A.: Robust non-interactive zero knowledge. In: Kilian, J. (ed.) CRYPTO 2001. LNCS, vol. 2139, pp. 566–598. Springer, Heidelberg (2001). https://doi.org/10.1007/3-540-44647-8_33

15. Dolev, D., Dwork, C., Naor, M.: Non-malleable cryptography (extended abstract). In: Proceedings of the 23rd Annual ACM Symposium on Theory of Computing, New Orleans, Louisiana, USA, pp. 542–552, 5–8 May 1991

16. Garay, J.A., MacKenzie, P., Yang, K.: Strengthening zero-knowledge protocols using signatures. J. Crypt. **19**(2), 169–209 (2006)

17. Garg, S., Mukherjee, P., Pandey, O., Polychroniadou, A.: Personal communication, August 2016

18. Garg, S., Mukherjee, P., Pandey, O., Polychroniadou, A.: The exact round complexity of secure computation. In: Fischlin, M., Coron, J.-S. (eds.) EUROCRYPT 2016. LNCS, vol. 9666, pp. 448–476. Springer, Heidelberg (2016). https://doi.org/10.1007/978-3-662-49896-5_16

19. Goyal, V.: Constant round non-malleable protocols using one way functions. In: Proceedings of the 43rd ACM Symposium on Theory of Computing, STOC 2011, San Jose, CA, USA, pp. 695–704, 6–8 June 2011

20. Goyal, V., Kumar, A., Park, S., Richelson, S., Srinivasan, A.: New constructions of non-malleable commitments and applications. In: Private Communication (2017)

21. Goyal, V., Lee, C., Ostrovsky, R., Visconti, I.: Constructing non-malleable commitments: a black-box approach. In: 53rd Annual IEEE Symposium on Foundations of Computer Science, FOCS 2012, New Brunswick, NJ, USA, pp. 51–60 (2012)

22. Goyal, V., Pandey, O., Richelson, S.: Textbook non-malleable commitments. In: Proceedings of the 48th Annual ACM SIGACT Symposium on Theory of Computing, STOC 2016, Cambridge, MA, USA, pp. 1128–1141, 18–21 June 2016. Full version: Cryptology ePrint Archive, Report 2015/1178

23. Goyal, V., Richelson, S., Rosen, A., Vald, M.: An algebraic approach to non-malleability. In: 55th IEEE Annual Symposium on Foundations of Computer Science, FOCS 2014, Philadelphia, PA, USA, pp. 41–50, 18–21 October 2014. An updated full version http://eprint.iacr.org/2014/586

24. Katz, J., Ostrovsky, R., Smith, A.: Round efficiency of multi-party computation with a dishonest majority. In: Biham, E. (ed.) EUROCRYPT 2003. LNCS, vol. 2656, pp. 578–595. Springer, Heidelberg (2003). https://doi.org/10.1007/3-540-39200-9_36

25. Lapidot, D., Shamir, A.: Publicly verifiable non-interactive zero-knowledge proofs. In: Menezes, A.J., Vanstone, S.A. (eds.) CRYPTO 1990. LNCS, vol. 537, pp. 353–365. Springer, Heidelberg (1991). https://doi.org/10.1007/3-540-38424-3_26

26. Lin, H., Pass, R.: Concurrent non-malleable zero knowledge with adaptive inputs. In: Ishai, Y. (ed.) TCC 2011. LNCS, vol. 6597, pp. 274–292. Springer, Heidelberg (2011). https://doi.org/10.1007/978-3-642-19571-6_17

27. Lin, H., Pass, R.: Constant-round non-malleable commitments from any one-way function. In: Proceedings of the 43rd ACM Symposium on Theory of Computing, STOC 2011, San Jose, CA, USA, pp. 705–714. ACM, 6–8 June 2011

28. Lin, H., Pass, R., Venkitasubramaniam, M.: Concurrent non-malleable commitments from any one-way function. In: Canetti, R. (ed.) TCC 2008. LNCS, vol. 4948, pp. 571–588. Springer, Heidelberg (2008). https://doi.org/10.1007/978-3-540-78524-8_31

29. Lin, H., Pass, R., Venkitasubramaniam, M.: A unified framework for concurrent security: universal composability from stand-alone non-malleability. In: Proceedings of the 41st Annual ACM Symposium on Theory of Computing, STOC 2009, Bethesda, MD, USA, pp. 179–188, 31 May–2 June 2009

30. Mittelbach, A., Venturi, D.: Fiat–Shamir for highly sound protocols is instantiable. In: Zikas, V., De Prisco, R. (eds.) SCN 2016. LNCS, vol. 9841, pp. 198–215. Springer, Cham (2016). https://doi.org/10.1007/978-3-319-44618-9_11

31. Naor, M.: Bit commitment using pseudorandomness. J. Crypt. 4(2), 151–158 (1991)

32. Ostrovsky, R., Visconti, I.: Simultaneous resettability from collision resistance. In: Electronic Colloquium on Computational Complexity (ECCC), vol. 19, p. 164 (2012)

33. Pandey, O., Pass, R., Vaikuntanathan, V.: Adaptive one-way functions and applications. In: Wagner, D. (ed.) CRYPTO 2008. LNCS, vol. 5157, pp. 57–74. Springer, Heidelberg (2008). https://doi.org/10.1007/978-3-540-85174-5_4

34. Pass, R.: Bounded-concurrent secure multi-party computation with a dishonest majority. In: Proceedings of the 36th Annual ACM Symposium on Theory of Computing, Chicago, IL, USA, pp. 232–241. ACM, 13–16 June 2004

35. Pass, R., Rosen, A.: New and improved constructions of non-malleable cryptographic protocols. In: Proceedings of the 37th Annual ACM Symposium on Theory of Computing, Baltimore, MD, USA, pp. 533–542, 22–24 May 2005

36. Pass, R., Rosen, A.: New and improved constructions of nonmalleable cryptographic protocols. SIAM J. Comput. 38(2), 702–752 (2008)

37. Pass, R., Wee, H.: Black-box constructions of two-party protocols from one-way functions. In: Reingold, O. (ed.) TCC 2009. LNCS, vol. 5444, pp. 403–418. Springer, Heidelberg (2009). https://doi.org/10.1007/978-3-642-00457-5_24

38. Polychroniadou, A.: On the communication and round complexity of secure computation. Ph.D. thesis, Aarhus University, December 2016

39. Rompel, J.: One-way functions are necessary and sufficient for secure signatures. In: Proceedings of the 22nd Annual ACM Symposium on Theory of Computing, Baltimore, Maryland, USA, pp. 387–394, 13–17 May 1990

# Round Optimal Concurrent MPC
# via Strong Simulation

Saikrishna Badrinarayanan[1], Vipul Goyal[2], Abhishek Jain[3],
Dakshita Khurana[1(✉)], and Amit Sahai[1]

[1] UCLA, Los Angeles, USA
{saikrishna,dakshita,sahai}@cs.ucla.edu
[2] Carnegie Mellon University, Pittsburgh, USA
goyal@cs.cmu.edu
[3] Johns Hopkins University, Baltimore, USA
abhishek@cs.jhu.edu

**Abstract.** In this paper, we study the round complexity of concurrently secure multi-party computation (MPC) with super-polynomial simulation (SPS) in the plain model. In the plain model, there are known explicit attacks that show that concurrently secure MPC with polynomial simulation is impossible to achieve; SPS security is the most widely studied model for concurrently secure MPC in the plain model. We obtain the following results:

- Three-round concurrent MPC with SPS security against Byzantine adversaries, assuming sub-exponentially secure DDH and LWE.
- Two-round concurrent MPC with SPS security against Byzantine adversaries for input-less randomized functionalities, assuming sub-exponentially secure indistinguishability obfuscation and DDH. In particular, this class includes sampling functionalities that allow parties to jointly sample a secure common reference string for cryptographic applications.

Prior to our work, to the best of our knowledge, concurrent MPC with SPS security required roughly 20 rounds, although we are not aware of any work that even gave an approximation of the constant round complexity sufficient for the multi-party setting. We also improve over the previous best round complexity for the two-party setting, where 5 rounds

S. Badrinarayanan, D. Khurana and A. Sahai—Research supported in part from a DARPA/ARL SAFEWARE award, NSF Frontier Award 1413955, NSF grants 1619348, 1228984, 1136174, and 1065276, BSF grant 2012378, a Xerox Faculty Research Award, a Google Faculty Research Award, an equipment grant from Intel, and an Okawa Foundation Research Grant. This material is based upon work supported by the Defense Advanced Research Projects Agency through the ARL under Contract W911NF-15-C-0205. The views expressed are those of the authors and do not reflect the official policy or position of the Department of Defense, the National Science Foundation, or the U.S. Government.

A. Jain—Research supported in part by a DARPA/ARL Safeware Grant W911NF-15-C-0213 and a sub-award from NSF CNS-1414023.

D. Khurana—Research supported in part by the UCLA Dissertation Year Fellowship.

Y. Kalai and L. Reyzin (Eds.): TCC 2017, Part I, LNCS 10677, pp. 743–775, 2017.
https://doi.org/10.1007/978-3-319-70500-2_25

were needed (Garg, Kiyoshima, and Pandey, Eurocrypt 2017).

To obtain our results, we compile protocols that already achieve security against "semi-malicious" adversaries, to protocols secure against fully malicious adversaries, additionally assuming sub-exponential DDH. Our protocols develop new techniques to use two-round zero-knowledge with super-polynomial *strong* simulation, defined by Pass (Eurocrypt 2003) and very recently realized by Khurana and Sahai (FOCS 2017). These remain zero-knowledge against adversaries running in time larger than the running time of the simulator.

# 1    Introduction

The round complexity of secure multi-party computation (MPC) [19,39,40] has been a problem of fundamental interest in cryptography. The last few years have seen major advances in improving the round complexity of secure computation with dishonest majority [1,6,7,9,10,16,20,22,24,27,32,34,38], culminating eventually in four round protocols for secure multi-party computation from general assumptions such as DDH and LWE [1,7,16].

Intriguingly, however, when we only require security against (semi-malicious) adversaries that follow protocol specifications, recent research has also constructed MPC protocols that require even less that four rounds of simultaneous message exchange in the plain model. For instance, [11] give a two-round protocol based on indistinguishability obfuscation, while [7] very recently gave a three round protocol from the hardness of the learning with errors assumption.

However, these protocols do not offer any privacy guarantees at all against Byzantine adversaries that may deviate from protocol specifications. Can we achieve meaningful security against Byzantine adversaries in two or three rounds? This question is even more interesting in the setting where parties participate in multiple executions of the MPC protocol concurrently. Indeed, as our world becomes increasingly interconnected, it is hard to imagine that future cryptographic protocols will be carried out in a standalone setting, where participants interact in only a single instance of the protocol. Thus, we ask:

*"Can we achieve concurrently secure MPC in two or three rounds?"*

**Super-polynomial security.** Indeed, even defining security against concurrent adversaries in the plain model requires care. Barak, Prabhakaran and Sahai [4] give an explicit "chosen protocol attack" that rules out concurrently secure MPC with polynomial simulation in *any number of rounds* in the plain model. In fact, even in the stand-alone setting, three round secure computation with polynomial simulation and black-box reductions turns out to be impossible to achieve [16].

However, it has been known for a long time that for MPC, a powerful security notion in the plain model is security with super-polynomial time simulation (SPS) [3,5,8,13,15,25,30,33,36]. SPS security circumvents the impossibility results above including the chosen protocol attack in the concurrent setting, and is the most widely studied security model for concurrent MPC in the plain model.

To understand the intuition behind SPS security, it is instructive to view SPS security through the lens of the security loss inherent in all security reductions. In ordinary polynomial-time simulation, the security reduction has a polynomial security loss with respect to the ideal world. That is, an adversary in the real world has as much power as another adversary that runs in polynomially more time in the ideal world. In SPS security, the security reduction has a fixed super-polynomial security loss, for example $2^{n^{\epsilon}}$, where $n$ is the security parameter, with respect to the ideal world. Just as in other applications in cryptography using super-polynomial assumptions, this situation still guarantees security as long as the ideal model is itself super-polynomially secure. For instance, if the ideal model hides honest party inputs *information-theoretically*, then security is maintained even with SPS. For example, this is true for applications like online auctions, where no information is leaked in the ideal world about honest party inputs beyond what can be easily computed from the output. But SPS also guarantees security for ideal worlds with cryptographic outputs, like blind signatures, as long as the security of the cryptographic output is guaranteed against super-polynomial adversaries. Indeed, SPS security was explicitly considered for blind signatures in [14,17] with practically relevant security parameters computed in [14]. Additional discussion on the meaningfulness of SPS security can be found in the original works of [33,36] that introduced SPS security in the protocol context.

Prior to our work, the best round complexity even for concurrent two-party computation with SPS security was 5 rounds [15] from standard sub-exponential assumptions. For concurrent MPC with SPS security from standard sub-exponential assumptions, the previous best round complexity was perhaps approximately 20 rounds in the simultaneous message exchange model [13,26], although to the best of our knowledge, no previous work even gave an approximation of the constant round complexity that is sufficient for the multi-party setting.

## 1.1 Our Results

We obtain several results on concurrently secure MPC in 2 or 3 rounds:

1. We obtain the following results for multi-party secure computation with SPS in *three rounds* in the simultaneous message model, against rushing adversaries.
   - A compiler that converts a large class of three round protocols secure against semi-malicious adversaries, into protocols secure against malicious adversaries, additionally assuming the sub-exponential hardness of DDH or QR or $N^{th}$ residuosity.
   - A compiler that converts a large class of three round protocols secure against semi-malicious adversaries, into protocols secure against malicious *concurrent* adversaries, additionally assuming the sub-exponential hardness of DDH or QR or $N^{th}$ residuosity.

On instantiating these compilers with the three-round semi-malicious protocol in the recent work of Brakerski et al. [7], we obtain the following main result.

**Informal Theorem 1.** *Assuming sub-exponentially secure LWE and DDH, there exists a three-round protocol in the simultaneous message exchange model with rushing adversaries, that achieves sub-exponential concurrent SPS security for secure multi-party computation for any efficiently computable function, in which all parties can receive output.*

*The same result holds if the sub-exponential DDH assumption above is replaced with the sub-exponential QR or $N^{th}$ residuosity assumptions.*

2. We also obtain the following results for multi-party secure computation with SPS in *two rounds* in the simultaneous message model, against rushing adversaries.
   - A compiler that converts a large class of two round protocols secure against semi-malicious adversaries, into protocols secure against malicious adversaries computing input-less *randomized* functionalities, assuming assuming sub-exponential hardness of DDH and indistinguishability obfuscation.
   - A compiler that converts a large class of two round protocols secure against semi-malicious adversaries, into protocols secure against *concurrent* malicious adversaries computing input-less *randomized* functionalities, assuming assuming sub-exponential hardness of DDH and indistinguishability obfuscation.

On instantiating these compilers with the two-round semi-malicious protocol in [11], we obtain the following main result.

**Informal Theorem 2.** *Assuming sub-exponentially secure indistinguishability obfuscation and DDH, there exists a two-round protocol in the simultaneous message exchange model with rushing adversaries, that achieves sub-exponential concurrent SPS security for secure multi-party computation for any efficiently computable randomized input-less function, in which all parties can receive output.*

In particular, our protocols can be used to generate samples from any efficiently sampleable distribution. For example, they can be used to concurrently securely sample common reference strings from arbitrary distributions for cryptographic applications, such that the randomness used for sampling remains hidden as long as at least one of the participants is honest. Applications include generating a common reference string sufficient for building universal samplers [23]. Before our work, only the special case of multi-party coin-flipping with SPS was known to be achievable in two rounds [25].

## 2   Technical Overview

We will now give an overview of the techniques used in our work.

## 2.1  Three Round MPC Without Setup

A well established approach to constructing secure computation protocols against malicious adversaries in the standalone setting is to use the GMW compiler [19]: "compile" a semi-honest protocol with zero-knowledge arguments to enforce correct behavior. Normally, such compilers involve an initial 'coin-tossing' phase, which determines the randomness that will be used by all parties in the rest of the protocol. Unfortunately, in two or three rounds, there is no scope at all to carry out an initial coin-tossing.

However, as observed by [2,7,31], certain two and three round protocols satisfy semi-malicious security: that is, the protocol remains secure even when the adversary is allowed to chose malicious randomness, as long as the adversary behaves according to protocol specifications. When compiling semi-malicious protocols, the coin-tossing phase is no longer necessary: at a very high level, it seems like it should suffice to have all parties give proofs of correct behavior. Several difficulties arise when trying to implement such compilers in extremely few rounds. Specifically, in many parts of our protocols, we will have *only* two rounds to complete the proof of correct behavior. However, attempts to use two-round zero-knowledge with super-polynomial simulation [33] run into a few key difficulties, that we now discuss.

A key concern in MPC is that malicious parties may be arbitrarily mauling the messages sent by other parties. In order to prevent this, we will use two-round non-malleable commitments, that were recently constructed in [21,25,28]. In particular, we will rely on a construction of two-round concurrent non-malleable commitments with simultaneous messages, that were constructed by [25] assuming sub-exponential DDH.

The very first difficulty arises as soon as we try to compose non-malleable commitments with SPS-ZK.

**Difficulty of using two-round SPS-ZK in few rounds with Simultaneous Messages.** Standard constructions of two-round SPS zero-knowledge can be described as follows: the verifier generates a challenge that is hard to invert by adversaries running in time $T$, then the prover proves (via WI) that either the statement being proven is in the language, or that he knows the inverse of the challenge used by the verifier. This WI argument is such that the witness used by the prover can be extracted (via brute-force) in time $T' \ll T$. Naturally, this restricts the argument to be zero-knowledge against verifiers that run in time $T_{\mathsf{zk}} \ll T' \ll T$.

Thus, if a prover generates an accepting proof for a false statement, the WI argument can be broken in time $T'$ to invert the challenge, leading to a contradiction. On the other hand, there exists a simulator that runs in time $T_{\mathsf{Sim}} \gg T$ to invert the receiver's challenge and simulate the proof (alternatively, such a simulator can non-uniformly obtain the inverse of the receiver's challenge). Thus, we have $T_{\mathsf{Sim}} \gg T_{\mathsf{zk}}$.

Let us now consider an SPS-ZK protocol, run simultaneously with a non-malleable commitment, as illustrated in Fig. 1. The two-round concurrent non-malleable commitment scheme from [25] requires the committer and receiver to

$$P \xleftarrow{\text{SPS-ZK}_{\text{challenge}}, \ \text{NMC}_{\text{challenge}}} \xrightarrow{\text{NMC}(M;r)} V$$
$$\xrightarrow{\text{SPS-ZK}_{\text{response}}, \ \text{NMC}_{\text{response}}}$$

**Fig. 1.** Composing SPS-ZK with Non-malleable commitments

send simultaneous messages in the first round of the execution, followed by a single message from the committer in the second round.

Let us also imagine that multiple parties running such a protocol are sending non-malleable commitments to their inputs, together with messages of the underlying semi-malicious protocol, and SPS-ZK proofs of correct behavior.

In order to begin a reduction between the real and ideal worlds, we would have to begin by simulating the proofs sent by honest parties, and then argue that adversarial parties cannot maul honest parties' inputs. However, while arguing non-malleability, *we cannot simulate proofs non-uniformly*, since that would end up also non-uniformly fixing the messages of the non-malleable commitments. Thus, we would want non-malleability of NMCom to hold even while we are sending simulated proofs in time $T_{\text{Sim}}$.

On the other hand, when we switch a real SPS ZK proof to being simulated, we must argue that the values within the non-malleable commitments provided by the adversary did not suddenly change. To achieve this, it must be true that the quality of the SPS ZK simulation is sufficiently high to guarantee that the messages inside the non-malleable commitments did not change. Specifically, we must be able to break the non-malleable commitments and extract from them in time that is less than $T_{\text{zk}}$. Putting together all these constraints, we have that non-malleable commitments should be breakable in time that is less than the time against which they remain non-malleable: this is a direct contradiction.

In order to solve this problem, we must rely on ZK argument systems where the quality of the SPS ZK simulation *exceeds* the running time of the SPS simulator, namely where $T_{\text{Sim}} \ll T_{\text{zk}}$. Zero-knowledge with strong simulation ([33]), is roughly a primitive that satisfies exactly this constraint. We call such a ZK protocol an SPSS-ZK argument. Such a primitive was recently realized by [25], by constructing a new form of two-round extractable commitments. Note that if one uses SPSS-ZK instead of SPS-ZK, the contradiction described above no longer holds. This is a key insight that allows us to have significantly simpler arguments of SPS security, especially in the concurrent security setting.

However, as we already mentioned, in arguing security against malicious adversaries, we must be particularly wary of malleability attacks. In particular, we would like to ensure that while the simulator provides simulated proofs, the adversary continues to behave honestly – thereby allowing such a simulator to correctly extract the adversary's input and force the right output. This is the notion of simulation soundness [37]. However, it is unknown how to build a two-round concurrently simulation-sound SPSS ZK argument. We address this by providing a mechanism to emulates two-round and three-round simulation-soundness via strong simulation, in a simultaneous message setting. This mechanism allows us to compile a semi-malicious protocol with a type of non-malleable proofs of honest behavior.

Roughly speaking, the idea behind our strategy for enforcing simulation soundness is to have each party commit not only to its input, but also all the randomness that it will use in the underlying semi-malicious secure protocol. Then, the high quality of the SPSS ZK simulation will ensure that even the joint distribution of the input, the randomness, and the protocol transcript cannot change when we move to SPS simulation. Since honest behavior can be checked by computing the correct messages using the input and randomness, the quality of the SPSS ZK simulation guarantees that adversarial behavior must remain correct. Counter-intuitively, we enforce a situation where we cannot rule out that the adversary isn't "cheating" on his ZK arguments, but nevertheless the adversary's behavior in the underlying semi-malicious MPC protocol cannot have deviated from honest behavior.

We note that our simulation strategy is uniform and straight-line. The only non-trivial use of rewinding in our protocol is in arguing non-malleability, and this is abstracted away into the underlying non-malleable commitment scheme that we invoke. This leads to a significantly simpler proof of concurrent security.

Several additional subtleties arise in the proofs of security. Please refer to Sect. 4 for additional details on our protocol and complete proofs.

**Barriers to Two Round Secure Computation of General Functionalities.** We also note that barriers exist to constructing two-round two-party SPS-secure computation of general functionalities with super-polynomial simulation, where both parties receive the output. Let us focus on protocols for the secure computation of a specific functionality $\mathcal{F}(x, y) = (x + y)$, which computes the sum of the inputs of both parties, when interpreted as natural numbers. However, our arguments also extend to all functionalities that are sensitive to the private inputs of individual parties. We will also restrict ourselves to two-round protocols where both parties send an encoding of their message in the first round while the next round is used to compute the output. It is not difficult to see that any protocol for two-round two-party secure computation of general functionalities, must satisfy this property, as long as security must hold against non-uniform adversaries. If the first message wasn't committing, then a non-uniform adversary could obtain a first message that is consistent with two inputs, and then by aborting in the second round, it could obtain two outputs of the function with two different inputs, violating security.

Let $\Pi$ denote a two-round secure computation protocol between two parties $A$ and $B$, where both parties receive the output. We will also consider a "mauling" rushing adversary that corrupts $B$, let us denote this corrupted party by $\widetilde{B}$. At the beginning of the protocol $A$ sends an honest encoding of its input $X$. After obtaining the first round message from party $A$, suppose that $\widetilde{B}$ "mauls" the encoding sent by $A$ and generates another encoding of the same input $X$. Because the encodings must necessarily hide the inputs of parties, the honest PPT party $A$ cannot detect if such a mauling occurred, and sends the second message of the protocol. At this point, $\widetilde{B}$ generates its second round message on its own, *but does not send this message.* Instead, $\widetilde{B}$ computes the output of the protocol (which is guaranteed by correctness). The adversary $\widetilde{B}$ learns $2X$, and blatantly breaks security of the SPS-secure protocol. Similarly, a rushing adversary could choose to corrupt party $A$ and launch the same attack. Getting over this barrier would clearly require constructing non-interactive non-malleable commitments.

## 2.2   Two Round MPC Without Setup for Input-Less Randomized Functionalities

We begin by noting that the discussion above on the hardness of two-round MPC with super-polynomial simulation does not rule out functionalities that are *not* sensitive to the private inputs of parties. In particular, let us consider input-less randomized functionalities. Even though the functionality is input-less, still each party must contribute to selecting the secret randomness on which the function is to be evaluated. At first glance, it may appear that we still have the same problem: in only two rounds, perhaps this "implied input" can be compromised. However, note that for input-less functionalities, if the adversary aborts, then even if the adversary learns the "implied inputs" of the honest parties, this does not violate security because the honest parties will not accept the output of the protocol. Thus, the honest parties' contributions to the randomness is discarded since the protocol execution is aborted. As such, we only need to guarantee security of the honest party inputs *if* the protocol terminates correctly – that is, if the adversary is able to send second-round messages that do not cause the protocol to abort.

More technically, the only actual requirement is that a super-polynomial simulator must be able to correctly and indistinguishably, force the output of the computation to an externally generated value. The security of each honest party's contribution to the randomness is implied by this forcing.

We show that this is indeed possible using only two rounds of interaction in the simultaneous message model, under suitable cryptographic assumptions. We describe a compiler that compiles a large class of two-round secure computation protocols for input-less randomized functionalities from semi-malicious to full malicious (and even concurrent) security. We consider functionalities where each party contributes some randomness, and the joint randomness of all parties is used to sample an output from some efficiently sampleable distribution.

Our protocol follows a similar template to the protocol described for the 3-round case: parties first commit to all the input and randomness that they will use throughout the execution via a non-malleable commitment. Simultaneously, parties run an underlying two-round semi-malicious protocol and by the end of the second round, provide SPSS-ZK proofs that they correctly computed all messages. We stress again that it is *only* if the adversary successfully completes both rounds of the protocol without causing an abort, that we actually need to care about hiding the shares of randomness contributed by honest parties – in order to argue overall security.

At the same time, in order to enforce correctness, the simulator would still need to extract the randomness used by the adversary at the end of the first round of the computation. Unlike our three round protocol, here, the simulator will try to extract randomness at the end of the first round anyway. This is because the simulator can afford to be optimistic: Either its extraction is correct, and it can make use of this in forcing the output. Or its extraction is incorrect, but in this case we will guarantee that the adversary will cause the protocol to abort in the second round because of the SPSS ZK argument that the adversary must give proving that it behaved honestly in the first round.

We need to take additional care when defining the simulation strategy when the simulator extracts incorrect randomness: this causes other subtleties in our proof of security. The complete constructions and proofs of standalone as well as concurrent security, can be found in Sect. 5.

## 3   Preliminaries

Here, we recall some preliminaries that will be useful in the rest of the paper. We will typically use $n$ to denote the security parameter. We will say that $T_1(n) \gg T_2(n)$ if $T_1(n) > T_2(n) \cdot n^c$ for all constants $c$.

We define a $T$-time machine as a non-uniform Turing Machine that runs in time at most $T$. All honest parties in definitions below are by default uniform interactive Turing Machines, unless otherwise specified.

### 3.1   ZK with Superpolynomial Simulation

We will use two message ZK arguments with strong superpolynomial simulation (SPS) and with super-polynomial strong simulation (SPSS) [34].

**Definition 1 (Two Message $(T_{\mathsf{Sim}}, T_{\mathsf{zk}}, \delta_{\mathsf{zk}})$-ZK Arguments With Superpolynomial Simulation).** *[34] We say that an interactive proof (or argument) $\langle P, V \rangle$ for the language $L \in \mathsf{NP}$, with the witness relation $R_L$, is $(T_{\mathsf{Sim}}, T_{\mathsf{zk}}, \delta_{\mathsf{zk}})$-simulatable if for every $T_{\mathsf{zk}}$-time machine $V^*$ exists a probabilistic simulator $\mathcal{S}$ with running time bounded by $T_{\mathsf{Sim}}$ such that the following two ensembles are $T_{\mathsf{zk}}, \delta_{\mathsf{zk}})$-computationally indistinguishable (when the distinguishing gap is a function in $n = |x|$):*

- *$\{(\langle P(y), V^*(z) \rangle(x))\}_{z \in \{0,1\}^*, x \in L}$ for arbitrary $y \in R_L(x)$*
- *$\{\mathcal{S}(x, z)\}_{z \in \{0,1\}^*, x \in L}$*

*That is, for every probabilistic algorithm $D$ running in time polynomial in the length of its first input, every polynomial $p$, all sufficiently long $x \in L$, all $y \in R_L(x)$ and all auxiliary inputs $z \in \{0,1\}^*$ it holds that*

$$\Pr[D(x, z, (\langle P(y), V^*(z) \rangle(x))) = 1] - \Pr[D(x, z, S(x, z)) = 1] < \delta_{\mathsf{zk}}(\lambda)$$

**Definition 2.** *We say that a two-message $(T_{\mathsf{Sim}}, T_{\mathsf{zk}}, \delta_{\mathsf{zk}})$-SPS ZK argument satisfies non-uniform simulation (for delayed statements) if we can write the simulator $\mathcal{S} = (\mathcal{S}_1, \mathcal{S}_2)$ where $\mathcal{S}_1(V^*(z))$, which outputs $\sigma$, runs in $T_{\mathsf{Sim}}$-time, but where $\mathcal{S}_2(x, z, \sigma)$, which outputs the simulated view of the verifier $V^*$, runs in only polynomial time.*

### 3.2 ZK with Super-Polynomial Strong Simulation

We now define zero-knowledge with strong simulation. We use the definition in [25].

**Definition 3** $((T_\Pi, T_{\mathsf{Sim}}, T_{\mathsf{zk}}, T_L, \delta_{\mathsf{zk}})$-**SPSS Zero Knowledge Arguments**).
*We call an interactive protocol between a PPT prover $P$ with input $(x, w) \in R_L$ for some language $L$, and PPT verifier $V$ with input $x$, denoted by $\langle P, V \rangle(x, w)$, a super-polynomial strong simulation (SPSS) zero-knowledge argument if it satisfies the following properties and $T_\Pi \ll T_{\mathsf{Sim}} \ll T_{\mathsf{zk}} \ll T_L$:*

- **Completeness.** *For every $(x, w) \in R_L$, $\Pr[V \text{ outputs } 1 | \langle P, V \rangle(x, w)] \geq 1 - \mathsf{negl}(\lambda)$, where the probability is over the random coins of $P$ and $V$.*
- $T_\Pi$-**Adaptive-Soundness.** *For any language $L$ that can be decided in time at most $T_L$, every $x$, every $z \in \{0, 1\}^*$, and every poly-non-uniform prover $P^*$ running in time at most $T_\Pi$ that chooses $x$ adaptively after observing verifier message, $\Pr[\langle P^*(z), V \rangle(x) = 1 \ \wedge \ x \notin L] \leq \mathsf{negl}(\lambda)$, where the probability is over the random coins of $\mathcal{V}$.*
- $T_{\mathsf{Sim}}, T_{\mathsf{zk}}, \delta_{\mathsf{zk}}$-**Zero Knowledge.** *There exists a (uniform) simulator $\mathcal{S}$ that runs in time $T_{\mathsf{Sim}}$, such that for every $x$, every non-uniform $T_{\mathsf{zk}}$-verifier $V^*$ with advice $z$, and every $T_{\mathsf{zk}}$-distinguisher $\mathcal{D}$: $\big|\Pr[\mathcal{D}(x, z, \mathsf{view}_{V^*}[\langle P, V^*(z) \rangle(x, w)]) = 1]$ $- \Pr[\mathcal{D}(x, z, \mathcal{S}^{V^*}(x, z)) = 1]\big| \leq \delta_{\mathsf{zk}}(\lambda)$*

### 3.3 Non-Malleability w.r.t. Commitment

Throughout this paper, we will use $\lambda$ to denote the security parameter, and $\mathsf{negl}(\lambda)$ to denote any function that is asymptotically smaller than $\frac{1}{\mathsf{poly}(\lambda)}$ for any polynomial $\mathsf{poly}(\cdot)$. We will use PPT to describe a probabilistic polynomial time machine. We will also use the words "rounds" and "messages" interchangeably.

We follow the definition of non-malleable commitments introduced by Pass and Rosen [35] and further refined by Lin et al. [29] and Goyal [20] (which in turn build on the original definition of [12]). In the real interaction, there is a man-in-the-middle adversary MIM interacting with a committer $\mathcal{C}$ (where $\mathcal{C}$ commits to value $v$) in the left session, and interacting with receiver $\mathcal{R}$ in the right session. Prior to the interaction, the value $v$ is given to $C$ as local input. MIM receives an auxiliary input $z$, which might contain a-priori information about $v$. Then the commit phase is executed. Let $\mathsf{MIM}_{\langle C, R \rangle}(\mathsf{val}, z)$ denote a random variable that describes the value $\widetilde{\mathsf{val}}$ committed by the MIM in the right session, jointly with the view of the MIM in the full experiment. In the simulated experiment, a PPT simulator $\mathcal{S}$ directly interacts with the MIM. Let $\mathsf{Sim}_{\langle C, R \rangle}(1^\lambda, z)$ denote the random variable describing the value $\widetilde{\mathsf{val}}$ committed to by $\mathcal{S}$ and the output view of $\mathcal{S}$. If the tags in the left and right interaction are equal, the value $\widetilde{\mathsf{val}}$ committed in the right interaction, is defined to be $\perp$ in both experiments.

Concurrent non-malleable commitment schemes consider a setting where the MIM interacts with committers in polynomially many (a-priori unbounded) left sessions, and interacts with receiver(s) in upto $\ell(n)$ right sessions. If any of the tags (in any right session) are equal to any of the tags in any left session, we set the value committed by the MIM to $\perp$ for that session. The we let $\mathsf{MIM}_{\langle C,R \rangle}(\mathsf{val}, z)^{\mathsf{many}}$ denote the joint distribution of all the values committed by the MIM in all right sessions, together with the view of the MIM in the full experiment, and $\mathsf{Sim}_{\langle C,R \rangle}(1^\lambda, z)^{\mathsf{many}}$ denotes the joint distribution of all the values committed by the simulator $\mathcal{S}$ (with access to the MIM) in all right sessions together with the view.

**Definition 4 (Non-malleable Commitments w.r.t. Commitment).** *A commitment scheme $\langle C, R \rangle$ is said to be non-malleable if for every PPT MIM, there exists a PPT simulator $\mathcal{S}$ such that the following ensembles are computationally indistinguishable:*

$$\{\mathsf{MIM}_{\langle C,R \rangle}(\mathsf{val}, z)\}_{n \in \mathbb{N}, v \in \{0,1\}^\lambda, z \in \{0,1\}^*} \ and \ \{\mathsf{Sim}_{\langle C,R \rangle}(1^\lambda, z)\}_{n \in \mathbb{N}, v \in \{0,1\}^\lambda, z \in \{0,1\}^*}$$

**Definition 5 ($\ell(n)$-Concurrent Non-malleable Commitments w.r.t. Commitment).** *A commitment scheme $\langle C, R \rangle$ is said to be $\ell(n)$-concurrent non-malleable if for every PPT MIM, there exists a PPT simulator $\mathcal{S}$ such that the following ensembles are computationally indistinguishable:*

$$\{\mathsf{MIM}_{\langle C,R \rangle}(\mathsf{val}, z)^{\mathsf{many}}\}_{n \in \mathbb{N}, v \in \{0,1\}^\lambda, z \in \{0,1\}^*} \ and \ \{\mathsf{Sim}_{\langle C,R \rangle}(1^\lambda, z)^{\mathsf{many}}\}_{n \in \mathbb{N}, v \in \{0,1\}^\lambda, z \in \{0,1\}^*}$$

We say that a commitment scheme is fully concurrent, with respect to commitment, if it is concurrent for any a-priori unbounded polynomial $\ell(n)$.

## 3.4 Secure Multiparty Computation

As in [18], we follow the real-ideal paradigm for defining secure multi-party computation. The only difference is that our simulator can run in super-polynomial time. A formal definition can be found in the full version.

*Semi-malicious adversary:* An adversary is said to be semi-malicious if it follows the protocol correctly, but with potentially maliciously chosen randomness. We refer the reader to the full version for more details.

*Concurrent security:* The definition of concurrent secure multi-party computation considers an extension of the real-ideal model where the adversary participates simultaneously in many executions, corrupting subsets of parties in each execution. We refer the reader to [8,13] for a detailed definition of concurrent security.

# 4    Three Round Malicious Secure MPC

Let $f$ be any functionality. Consider $n$ parties $\mathsf{P}_1, \ldots, \mathsf{P}_n$ with inputs $\mathsf{x}_1, \ldots, \mathsf{x}_n$ respectively who wish to compute $f$ on their joint inputs by running a secure multiparty computation (MPC) protocol. Let $\pi^{SM}$ be any 3 round protocol that runs without any setup for the above task and is secure against adversaries that can be completely malicious in the first round, semi-malicious in the next two rounds and can corrupt upto $(n-1)$ parties. In this section, we show how to generically transform $\pi^{SM}$ into a 3 round protocol $\pi$ without setup with super-polynomial simulation and secure against malicious adversaries that can corrupt upto $(n-1)$ parties. Formally, we prove the following theorem:

**Theorem 1.** *Assuming sub-exponentially secure:*

- *$A$, where $A \in \{DDH,\ Quadratic\ Residuosity,\ N^{th}\ Residuosity\}$ AND*
- *3 round MPC protocol for any functionality $f$ that is secure against malicious adversaries in the first round and semi-malicious adversaries in the next two rounds,*

*the protocol presented in Fig. 2 is a 3 round MPC protocol for any functionality $f$, in the plain model with super-polynomial simulation.*

We can instantiate the underlying MPC protocol with the construction of Brakerski et al. [7], which satisfies our requirements. That is:

**Imported Lemma 1** ([7]): *There exists a 3 round MPC protocol for any functionality $f$ based on the LWE assumption that is secure against malicious adversaries in the first round and semi-malicious adversaries in the next 2 rounds.*

Additionally, Dodis et al. [11] give a 2 round construction based on indistinguishability obfuscation that is secure against semi-malicious adversaries. Of course, this can be interpreted as a 3 round construction where the first round has no message and is trivially secure against malicious adversaries in the first round.

Formally, we obtain the following corollary on instantiating the MPC protocol with the sub-exponentially secure variants of the above:

**Corollary 1.** *Assuming sub-exponentially secure:*

- *$A$, where $A \in \{DDH,\ Quadratic\ Residuosity,\ N^{th}\ Residuosity\}$ AND*
- *$B$, where $B \in \{LWE,\ Indistinguishability\ Obfuscation\}$*

*the protocol presented in Fig. 2 is a 3 round MPC protocol for any functionality $f$, in the plain model with super-polynomial simulation.*

Note that though the two underlying MPC protocols can be based on the security of polynomially hard LWE and polynomially hard iO respectively, we require sub-exponentially secure variants of the MPC protocol and hence we use sub-exponentially secure LWE and iO in our constructions.

*Remark 1 (On the Semi-Malicious security of* [11]*).* We note that the protocol in [11] works in two rounds: In the first round, each party provides a suitably "spooky" homomorphic encryption of its input, under public keys chosen by each party independently. After the first round, each party carries out a deterministic homomorphic evaluation procedure that results in an encryption of $f(\mathbf{x})$, where $\mathbf{x}$ is a vector that combines inputs of all parties. In the second round, each party computes a partial decryption of this ciphertext. The result is guaranteed to be the sum of these partial decryptions in a suitable cyclic group.

Furthermore, their protocol satisfies the invariant that given the (possibly maliciously chosen) randomness of the corrupted parties for the first round, and given the vector of ciphertexts that are fixed after the first round, it is possible to efficiently compute, at the end of the first round, the decryption shares for all corrupted parties. Thus, if there is one honest party and the other parties are corrupted, given the final output value $f(\mathbf{x})$, the first round ciphertexts and the randomness of the corrupted semi-malicious parties, it is possible to compute the unique decryption share of the honest party that would force the desired output value. This property shows that their protocol satisfies semi-malicious security, since the first round message of the simulated honest party can simply be the honest first round message corresponding to the input 0, and the second round message can be computed from $f(\mathbf{x})$, the first round ciphertexts and the randomness of the corrupted semi-malicious parties. The work of [31] further showed how to transform such a 2-round semi-malicious MPC protocol that handles exactly all-but-one corruptions into a 2-round semi-malicious MPC protocol that handles any number of corruptions.

### 4.1 High-Level Overview

Before describing our protocol formally, to help the exposition, we first give a brief overview of the construction in this subsection.

Consider $n$ parties $P_1, \ldots, P_n$ with inputs $x_1, \ldots, x_n$ respectively who wish to run a secure MPC to compute a function $f$ on their joint inputs. Initially, each party $P_i$ picks some randomness $r_i$ that it will use to run the semi-malicious protocol $\pi^{\mathsf{SM}}$.

In the first round, each party $P_i$ sends the first round message of the protocol $\pi^{\mathsf{SM}}$. Then, with every other party $P_j$, $P_i$ initiates two executions of the SPSS.ZK argument system playing the verifier's role. Additionally, $P_i$ and $P_j$ also initiate two executions of a non-malleable commitment scheme - each acting as the committer in one of them. $P_i$ commits to the pair $(x_i, r_i)$ - that is, the input and randomness used in the protocol $\pi^{\mathsf{SM}}$. Recall that the first round messages of $\pi^{\mathsf{SM}}$ are already secure against malicious adversaries, so intuitively, the protocol doesn't require any proofs in the first round.

In the second round, each party $P_i$ sends the second round message of the protocol $\pi^{\mathsf{SM}}$ using input $x_i$ and randomness $r_i$. Then, $P_i$ finishes executing the non-malleable commitments (playing the committer's role) with every other party $P_j$, committing to $(x_i, r_i)$. Finally, with every other party $P_j$, $P_i$ completes the execution of the SPSS.ZK argument by sending its second message - $P_i$ proves that the two messages sent so far using the protocol $\pi^{SM}$ were correctly generated using the pair $(x_i, r_i)$ committed to using the non-malleable commitment.

In the third round, each party $P_i$ first verifies all the proofs it received in the last round and sends a global abort (asking all the parties to abort) if any proof does not verify. Then, $P_i$ sends the third round message of the protocol $\pi^{SM}$ using input $x_i$ and randomness $r_i$. Finally, as before, with every other party $P_j$, $P_i$ completes the execution of the SPSS.ZK argument by sending its second message - $P_i$ proves that the two messages sent so far using the protocol $\pi^{SM}$ were correctly generated using the pair $(x_i, r_i)$ committed to using the non-malleable commitment.

Each party $P_i$ now computes its final output as follows. $P_i$ first verifies all the proofs it received in the previous round and sends a global abort (asking all the parties to abort) if any proof does not verify. Then, $P_i$ computes the output using the output computation algorithm of the semi-malicious protocol $\pi^{SM}$. This completes the protocol description.

**Security Proof:** We now briefly describe how the security proof works. Let's consider an adversary $\mathcal{A}$ who corrupts a set of parties. Recall that the goal is to move from the real world to the ideal world such that the outputs of the honest parties along with the view of the adversary is indistinguishable. We do this via a sequence of computationally indistinguishable hybrids.

The first hybrid $\mathsf{Hyb}_1$, refers to the real world. In $\mathsf{Hyb}_2$, the simulator extracts the adversary's input and randomness (used in protocol $\pi^{SM}$) by a brute force break of the non-malleable commitment. The simulator aborts if the extracted values don't reconstruct the protocol messages for the underlying semi-malicious protocol correctly. These two hybrids are indistinguishable because from the soundness of the proof system, except with negligible probability, the values extracted by the simulator correctly reconstruct to protocol messages.

Then, in $\mathsf{Hyb}_3$, we switch the SPSS.ZK arguments used by all honest parties in rounds 2 and 3 to simulated ones. This hybrid is computationally indistinguishable from the previous hybrid by the security of the SPSS.ZK system. Notice that when we switch from real to simulated arguments, we can no longer rely on the adversary's zero knowledge arguments to argue the correctness of the values extracted by breaking the non-malleable commitment. That is, the adversary's arguments may not be simulation sound. However, recall that to check the validity of the extracted values, we only rely on the correct reconstruction of the semi-malicious protocol messages, and hence this is not a problem. Also, the running time of the simulator in these two hybrids is the time taken to break the non-malleable commitment $T_{Com}^{Brk}$ - which must be lesser than the time against which the zero knowledge property holds - $T_{ZK}$.

In $\mathsf{Hyb}_4$, we switch all the non-malleable commitments sent by honest parties to be commitments of 0 instead of the actual input and randomness. Recall that since the arguments of the honest parties are simulated, this doesn't violate correctness. Also, this hybrid is computationally indistinguishable from the previous hybrid by the security of the non-malleable commitment scheme. One issue that arises here is whether the simulator continues to extract the adversary's inputs correctly. Recall that to extract, the simulator has to break the non-malleable commitment for which it has to run in time $T_{Com}^{Brk}$. However, then the reduction to the security of the non-malleable commitment only makes sense if the simulator runs in time lesser than that needed to break the non-malleable commitment. We overcome this issue by a sequence of sub-hybrids where we first switch the simulator to not extract the adversary's inputs, then switch the non-malleable commitments and then finally go back to the simulator extracting the adversary's inputs. We elaborate on this in the formal proof.

Then, in $Hyb_5$ we run the simulator of $\pi^{SM}$ using the extracted values to generate the protocol messages. This hybrid is indistinguishable from the previous one by the security of $\pi^{SM}$. Once again, in order to ensure correctness of the extracted values, we require the running time of the simulator - which is $T_{Com}^{Brk}$ to be lesser than the time against which the semi-malicious protocol $\pi^{SM}$ is secure. This is because, then, the simulator can continue to extract the adversary's message and randomness used for the protocol $\pi^{SM}$ by breaking the semi-malicious protocol. This hybrid ($Hyb_5$) now corresponds to the ideal world. Notice that our simulation is in fact straight-line. There are other minor technicalities that arise and we elaborate on this in the formal proof.

### 4.2   Construction

We first list some notation and the primitives used before describing the construction.

*Notation:*

- $\lambda$ denotes the security parameter.
- SPSS.ZK = $(ZK_1, ZK_2, ZK_3)$ is a two message zero knowledge argument with super polynomial strong simulation (SPSS-ZK). The zero knowledge property holds against all adversaries running in time $T_{ZK}$. Let $Sim^{ZK}$ denote the simulator that produces simulated ZK proofs and let $T_{ZK}^{Sim}$ denote its running time. [25] give a construction of an SPSS.ZK scheme satisfying these properties that can be based on one of the following sub-exponential assumptions: (1) DDH; (2) Quadratic Residuosity; (3) $N^{th}$ Residuosity.
- NMCom = $(NMCom_1^R, NMCom_1^S, NMCom_2^S)$ is a two message concurrent non-malleable commitment scheme with respect to commitment in the simultaneous message model. Here, $NMCom_1^R, NMCom_1^S$ denote the first message of the receiver and sender respectively while $NMCom_2^S$ denotes the second message of the sender. It is secure against all adversaries running in time $T_{Com}^{Sec}$, but can be broken by adversaries running in time $T_{Com}^{Brk}$. Let Ext.Com denote a brute force algorithm running in time $T_{Com}^{Brk}$ that can break the commitment scheme. [25] give a construction of an NMCom scheme satisfying these properties that can be based on one of the following sub-exponential assumptions: (1) DDH; (2) Quadratic Residuosity; (3) $N^{th}$ Residuosity.

The NMCom we use is tagged. In the authenticated channels setting, the tag of each user performing a non-malleable commitment can just be its identity. In the general setting, in the first round, each party can choose a strong digital signature verification key VK and signing key, and then sign all its messages using this signature scheme for every message sent in the protocol. This VK is then used as the tag for all non-malleable commitments. This ensures that every adversarial party must choose a tag that is different than any tags chosen by honest parties, otherwise the adversary will not be able to sign any of its messages by the existential unforgeability property of the signature scheme. This is precisely the property that is assumed when applying NMCom. For ease of notation, we suppress writing the tags explicitly in our protocols below.

- $\pi^{SM}$ is a sub-exponentially secure 3 round MPC protocol that is secure against malicious adversaries in the first round and semi-malicious adversaries in the next two rounds. This protocol is secure against all adversaries running in time $T_{SM}$. Let $(MSG_1, MSG_2, MSG_3)$ denote the algorithms used by any party to compute the messages in each of the three rounds and OUT denotes the algorithm to compute the final output. Further, let's assume that this protocol $\pi^{SM}$ runs over a broadcast channel. Let $\mathcal{S} = (\mathcal{S}_1, \mathcal{S}_2, \mathcal{S}_3)$ denote the straight line simulator for this protocol - that is, $\mathcal{S}_i$ is the simulator's algorithm to compute the $i^{th}$ round messages. Also, we make the following assumptions about the protocol structure, that is satisfied by the instantiations:

  1. $\mathcal{S}_1$ and $\mathcal{S}_2$ run without any input other than the protocol transcript so far - in particular, they don't need the input, randomness and output of the malicious parties. For $\mathcal{S}_1$, this must necessarily be true since the first round of $\pi^{SM}$ is secure against malicious adversaries. We make the assumption only on $\mathcal{S}_2$.[1]

  2. The algorithm $MSG_3$ doesn't require any new input or randomness that was not already used in the algorithms $MSG_1, MSG_2$. Looking ahead, this is used in our security proof when we want to invoke the simulator of this protocol $\pi^{SM}$, we need to be sure that we have fed the correct input and randomness to the simulator. This is true for all instantiantions we consider, where the semi-malicious simulator requires only the secret keys of corrupted parties (that are fixed in the second round) apart from the protocol transcript.

In order to realize our protocol, we require that $\mathsf{poly}(\lambda) < T_{ZK}^{Sim} < T_{Com}^{Sec} < T_{Com}^{Brk} < T_{ZK}, T_{SM}$.

The construction of the protocol is described in Fig. 2. We assume broadcast channels. In our construction, we use proofs for a some NP languages that we elaborate on below.

NP language $L$ is characterized by the following relation $R$.
Statement : $\mathsf{st} = (c_1, \hat{c}_1, c_2, \mathsf{msg}_1, \mathsf{msg}_2, \tau)$
Witness : $\mathsf{w} = (\mathsf{inp}, r, r_c)$
$R(\mathsf{st}, \mathsf{w}) = 1$ if and only if :

- $\hat{c}_1 = \mathsf{NMCom}_1^{S}(\mathsf{inp}, r; r_c)$ AND

---

[1] This assumption can be removed by running the commitment extractor on the first round messages itself. This idea is used in Sect. 5.

- $c_2 = \mathsf{NMCom}_2^S(\mathsf{inp}, r, c_1; r_c)$ AND
- $\mathsf{msg}_1 = \mathsf{MSG}_1(\mathsf{inp}; r)$ AND
- $\mathsf{msg}_2 = \mathsf{MSG}_2(\mathsf{inp}, \tau; r)$

That is, the messages $(c_1, \hat{c}_1, c_2)$ form a non-malleable commitment of $(\mathsf{inp}, r)$ such that $\mathsf{msg}_2$ is the second round message using input $\mathsf{inp}$, randomness $r$ by running the protocol $\pi^{\mathsf{SM}}$, where the protocol transcript so far is $\tau$.

NP language $L_1$ is characterized by the following relation $R_1$.
Statement : $\mathsf{st} = (c_1, \hat{c}_1, c_2, \mathsf{msg}_3, \tau)$
Witness : $w = (\mathsf{inp}, r, r_c)$
$R(\mathsf{st}, w) = 1$ if and only if :

- $\hat{c}_1 = \mathsf{NMCom}_1^S(\mathsf{inp}, r; r_c)$ AND
- $c_2 = \mathsf{NMCom}_2^S(\mathsf{inp}, r, c_1; r_c)$ AND
- $\mathsf{msg}_3 = \mathsf{MSG}_3(\mathsf{inp}, \tau; r)$

That is, the messages $(c_1, \hat{c}_1, c_2)$ form a non-malleable commitment of $(\mathsf{inp}, r)$ such that $\mathsf{msg}_3$ is the third round message using input $\mathsf{inp}$, randomness $r$ by running the protocol $\pi^{\mathsf{SM}}$, where the protocol transcript so far is $\tau$.

In the protocol, let's assume that every party has an associated identity $\mathsf{id}$. For any session $\mathsf{sid}$, each parties generates its non-malleable commitment using the tag $(\mathsf{id}\|\mathsf{sid})$.

The correctness of the protocol follows from the correctness of the protocol $\pi^{\mathsf{SM}}$, the non-malleable commitment scheme $\mathsf{NMCom}$ and the zero knowledge proof system $\mathsf{SPSS.ZK}$.

### 4.3   Security Proof

In this section, we formally prove Theorem 1.

Consider an adversary $\mathcal{A}$ who corrupts $t$ parties where $t < n$. For each party $P_i$, let's say that the size of input and randomness used in the protocol $\pi^{\mathsf{SM}}$ is $p(\lambda)$ for some polynomial $p$. That is, $|(x_i, r_i)| = p(\lambda)$. The strategy of the simulator $\mathsf{Sim}$ against a malicious adversary $\mathcal{A}$ is described in Fig. 3.

Here, in the simulation, we crucially use the two assumptions about the protocol structure. The first one is easy to notice since the simulator $\mathsf{Sim}$ has to run the semi-malicious to produce the first and second messages before it has extracted the adversary's input and randomness. For the second assumption, observe that in order to run the simulator algorithm $\mathcal{S}_3$, $\mathsf{Sim}$ has to feed it the entire input and randomness of the adversary and so these have to be bound to by the end of the second round.

We now show that the simulation strategy described in Fig. 3 is successful against all malicious PPT adversaries. That is, the view of the adversary along with the output of the honest parties is computationally indistinguishable in the real and ideal worlds. We will show this via a series of computationally indistinguishable hybrids where the first hybrid $\mathsf{Hyb}_1$ corresponds to the real world and the last hybrid $\mathsf{Hyb}_6$ corresponds to the ideal world.

**Inputs:** Each party $P_i$ has input $x_i$ and uses randomness $r_i$ to compute the message in each round of the protocol $\pi^{SM}$. We now describe the messages sent by party $P_i$. We will use superscripts to denote the intended recipient of the message if it is not meant to be used by all parties.

1. **Round 1:**
   $P_i$ does the following:
   - Compute $msg_{1,i} \leftarrow MSG_1(x_i; r_i)$.
   - For each $j \in [n]$ with $j \neq i$, compute:
     - $\hat{c}^j_{1,i} \leftarrow NMCom^S_1(x_i, r_i; r^j_{c,i})$ using a random string $r^j_{c,i}$ and $c^j_{1,i} \leftarrow NMCom^R_1(1^\lambda)$.
     - $(ver^j_{1,i}, zkst^j_{1,i}) \leftarrow ZK_1(1^\lambda)$ and $(ver^j_{2,i}, zkst^j_{2,i}) \leftarrow ZK_1(1^\lambda)$.
   - Send $(msg_{1,i}, \hat{c}^j_{1,i}, c^j_{1,i}, ver^j_{1,i}, ver^j_{2,i})$ for all $j$.

2. **Round 2:**
   Let $\tau_1$ denote the protocol transcript after round 1. $P_i$ does the following:
   - Compute $msg_{2,i} \leftarrow MSG_2(x_i, \tau_1; r_i)$.
   - For each $j \in [n]$ with $j \neq i$, compute:
     - $c^j_{2,i} \leftarrow NMCom^S_2(x_i, r_i, c^i_{1,j}; r^j_{c,i})$ using the same random string $r^j_{c,i}$.
     - $prove^j_{2,i} \leftarrow ZK_2(ver^i_{1,j}, st^j_{2,i}, w^j_{2,i})$ for the statement $st^j_{2,i} = (c^i_{1,j}, \hat{c}^j_{1,i}, c^j_{2,i}, msg_{1,i},$
       $msg_{2,i}, \tau_1) \in L$ using witness $w^j_{2,i} = (x_i, r_i, r^j_{c,i})$.
   - Send $(msg_{2,i}, c^j_{2,i}, prove^j_{2,i})$ for all $j$.

3. **Round 3:**
   Let $\tau_2$ denote the protocol transcript after round 2. $P_i$ does the following:
   - Compute $msg_{3,i} \leftarrow MSG_3(x_i, \tau_2; r_i)$.
   - For each $j \in [n]$ with $j \neq i$, do:
     - Abort if $ZK_3(zkst^j_{1,i}, st^i_{2,j}) \neq 1$ where $st^i_{2,j} = (c^j_{1,i}, \hat{c}^i_{1,j}, c^i_{2,j}, msg_{1,j}, msg_{2,j}, \tau_1)$. In particular, send a global abort signal to all parties so that everyone aborts.
     - $prove^j_{3,i} \leftarrow ZK_2(ver^i_{2,j}, st^j_{3,i}, w^j_{3,i})$ for the statement $st^j_{3,i} = (c^i_{1,j}, \hat{c}^j_{1,i}, c^j_{2,i}, msg_{3,i}, \tau_2) \in L_1$ using witness $w^j_{3,i} = (x_i, r_i, r^j_{c,i})$.
   - Send $(msg_{3,i}, prove^j_{3,i})$ for all $j$.

4. **Output Computation:**
   Let $\tau_3$ denote the protocol transcript after round 3. $P_i$ does the following:
   - For each $j \in [n]$ with $j \neq i$, do:
     - Abort if $ZK_3(zkst^j_{2,i}, st^i_{3,j}) \neq 1$ where $st^i_{3,j} = (c^j_{1,i}, \hat{c}^i_{1,j}, c^i_{2,j}, msg_{3,j}, \tau_2)$. In particular, send a global abort signal to all parties so that everyone aborts.
   - Compute output $y_i \leftarrow OUT(x_i, \tau_3; r_i)$.

**Fig. 2.** 3 round MPC Protocol $\pi$ for functionality $f$.

1. $Hyb_1$: In this hybrid, consider a simulator $Sim_{Hyb}$ that plays the role of the honest parties. $Sim_{Hyb}$ runs in polynomial time.
2. $Hyb_2$: In this hybrid, the simulator $Sim_{Hyb}$ also runs the "Input Extraction" phase and the "Special Abort" phase in step3 and 5 in Fig. 3. $Sim_{Hyb}$ runs in time $T^{Brk}_{Com}$.

1. **Round 1:** For each honest party $P_i$, Sim does the following:
   - Compute $\mathsf{msg}_{1,i} \leftarrow \mathcal{S}_1(1^\lambda, i)$. For each $j \in [n]$ with $j \neq i$, compute:
     - $\hat{c}_{1,i}^j \leftarrow \mathsf{NMCom}_1^S(0^{p(\lambda)})$, $c_{1,i}^j \leftarrow \mathsf{NMCom}_1^R(1^\lambda)$.
     - $(\mathsf{ver}_{1,i}^j, \mathsf{zkst}_{1,i}^j) \leftarrow \mathsf{ZK}_1(1^\lambda)$ and $(\mathsf{ver}_{2,i}^j, \mathsf{zkst}_{2,i}^j) \leftarrow \mathsf{ZK}_1(1^\lambda)$.
   - Send $(\mathsf{msg}_{1,i}, \hat{c}_{1,i}^j, c_{1,i}^j, \mathsf{ver}_{1,i}^j, \mathsf{ver}_{2,i}^j)$ for all $j \in [n]$.
2. **Round 2:** Let $\tau_1$ denote the protocol transcript after round 1. For each honest party $P_i$,
   - Compute $\mathsf{msg}_{2,i} \leftarrow \mathcal{S}_2(\tau_1, i)$. For each $j \in [n]$ with $j \neq i$, compute:
     - $c_{2,i}^j \leftarrow \mathsf{NMCom}_2^S(0^{p(\lambda)}, c_{1,j}^i; r_{c,i}^j)$ using a random string $r_{c,i}^j$.
     - $\mathsf{prove}_{2,i}^j \leftarrow \mathsf{Sim}^{\mathsf{ZK}}(\mathsf{ver}_{1,j}^i, \mathsf{st}_{2,i}^j)$ for $\mathsf{st}_{2,i}^j = (c_{1,j}^i, \hat{c}_{1,i}^j, c_{2,i}^j, \mathsf{msg}_{1,i}, \mathsf{msg}_{2,i}, \tau_1)$ $\in L$. Observe that this takes time $T_{\mathsf{ZK}}^{\mathsf{Sim}}$.
   - Send $(\mathsf{msg}_{2,i}, c_{2,i}^j, \mathsf{prove}_{2,i}^j)$ for all $j \in [n]$.
3. **Input Extraction:** Sim does the following:
   - For each honest party $P_i$ and for each $j \in [n]$ with $j \neq i$, do:
     - Abort if $\mathsf{ZK}_3(\mathsf{zkst}_{1,i}^j, \mathsf{st}_{2,j}^i) \neq 1$ where $\tau_1$ is the protocol transcript after round 1 such that $\mathsf{st}_{2,j}^i = (c_{1,i}^j, \hat{c}_{1,j}^i, c_{2,j}^i, \mathsf{msg}_{1,j}, \mathsf{msg}_{2,j}, \tau_1)$
     - Compute $(x_j^i, r_j^i) = \mathsf{Ext}.\mathsf{Com}(c_{1,i}^j, \hat{c}_{1,j}^i, c_{2,j}^i)$. That is, this is the input and randomness of party $P_j$ seen by party $P_i$. This step takes time $T_{\mathsf{Com}}^{\mathsf{Brk}}$.
   - For each malicious party $P_j$, do:
     - Output "Special Abort" if the set of values $\{(x_j^i, r_j^i)\}$ computed in the last step, for all $i$ corresponding to honest parties $P_i$ is not equal. Set $(x_j, r_j) = (x_j^1, r_j^1)$. Output "Special Abort" if $\mathsf{msg}_{1,j} \neq \mathsf{MSG}_1(x_j, r_j)$ and $\mathsf{msg}_{2,j} \neq \mathsf{MSG}_2(x_j, r_j, \tau_1)$.
     - Send all extracted $x_j$ to the trusted functionality and receive output $y$.
     - Let $R$ denote the set of all $\{x_j, r_j\}$.
4. **Round 3:** Let $\tau_2$ denote the protocol transcript after round 2. For each honest party $P_i$, compute and send $\mathsf{msg}_{3,i} \leftarrow \mathcal{S}_3(y, R, \tau_2, i)$ together with $\mathsf{prove}_{3,i}^j$ for $j \in [n], j \neq i$ where $\mathsf{prove}_{3,i}^j \leftarrow \mathsf{Sim}^{\mathsf{ZK}}(\mathsf{ver}_{2,j}^i, \mathsf{st}_{3,i}^j)$ for the statement $\mathsf{st}_{3,i}^j = (c_{1,j}^i, \hat{c}_{1,i}^j, c_{2,i}^j, \mathsf{msg}_{3,i}, \tau_2) \in L_1$. Observe that this takes time $T_{\mathsf{ZK}}^{\mathsf{Sim}}$.
5. **Special Abort Phase:** Sim does the following:
   - Output "Special Abort" if for each malicious party $P_j$, $\mathsf{msg}_{3,j} \neq \mathsf{MSG}_3(x_j, r_j, \tau_2)$.
6. **Output Computation:** Sim does the following:
   - For each honest party $P_i$ and for each $j \in [n]$ with $j \neq i$, abort if $\mathsf{ZK}_3(\mathsf{zkst}_{2,i}^j, \mathsf{st}_{3,j}^i) \neq 1$ where $\mathsf{st}_{3,j}^i = (c_{1,i}^j, \hat{c}_{1,j}^i, c_{2,j}^i, \mathsf{msg}_{3,j}, \tau_2)$.
   - Else instruct the ideal functionality to deliver output to the honest parties.

**Fig. 3.** Simulation strategy in the 3 round protocol

3. $\mathsf{Hyb}_3$: This hybrid is identical to the previous hybrid except that in Rounds 2 and 3, $\mathsf{Sim}_{\mathsf{Hyb}}$ now computes simulated SPSSZK proofs as done in Round 2 in Fig. 3. Once again, $\mathsf{Sim}_{\mathsf{Hyb}}$ runs in time $T_{\mathsf{Com}}^{\mathsf{Brk}}$.
4. $\mathsf{Hyb}_4$: This hybrid is identical to the previous hybrid except that $\mathsf{Sim}_{\mathsf{Hyb}}$ now computes all the $(\hat{c}_{1,i}^j, c_{2,i}^j)$ as non-malleable commitments of $0^{p(\lambda)}$ as done in Round 2 in Fig. 3. Once again, $\mathsf{Sim}_{\mathsf{Hyb}}$ runs in time $T_{\mathsf{Com}}^{\mathsf{Brk}}$.

5. $\text{Hyb}_5$: This hybrid is identical to the previous hybrid except that in Round 3, $\text{Sim}_{\text{Hyb}}$ now computes the messages of the protocol $\pi^{\text{SM}}$ using the simulator algorithms $\mathcal{S} = (\mathcal{S}_1, \mathcal{S}_2, \mathcal{S}_3)$ as done by $\text{Sim}$ in the ideal world. $\text{Sim}_{\text{Hyb}}$ also instructs the ideal functionality to deliver outputs to the honest parties as done by $\text{Sim}$. This hybrid is now same as the ideal world. Once again, $\text{Sim}_{\text{Hyb}}$ runs in time $\text{T}_{\text{Com}}^{\text{Brk}}$.

We now show that every pair of successive hybrids is computationally indistinguishable.

**Lemma 1.** *Assuming soundness of the* SPSS.ZK *argument system, binding of the non-malleable commitment scheme and correctness of the protocol* $\pi^{\text{SM}}$, $\text{Hyb}_1$ *is computationally indistinguishable from* $\text{Hyb}_2$.

*Proof.* The only difference between the two hybrids is that in $\text{Hyb}_2$, $\text{Sim}_{\text{Hyb}}$ may output "Special Abort" which doesn't happen in $\text{Hyb}_1$. More specifically, in $\text{Hyb}_2$, "Special Abort" occurs if event E described below is true.

**Event E:** Is true if : For any malicious party $P_j$

- All the SPSS.ZK proofs sent by $P_j$ in round 2 and 3 verify correctly. (AND)
- Either of the following occur:
  - The set of values $\{(x_j^i, r_j^i)\}$ that are committed to using the non-malleable commitment is not same for every $i$ where $P_i$ is honest. (OR)
  - $\text{msg}_{1,j} \neq \text{MSG}_1(x_j, r_j)$ (OR)
  - $\text{msg}_{2,j} \neq \text{MSG}_2(x_j, r_j, \tau_1)$ where $\tau_1$ is the protocol transcript after round 1. (OR)
  - $\text{msg}_{3,j} \neq \text{MSG}_3(x_j, r_j, \tau_2)$ where $\tau_2$ is the protocol transcript after round 2.

That is, in simpler terms, the event E occurs if for any malicious party, it gives valid ZK proofs in round 2 and 3 but its protocol transcript is not consistent with the values it committed to.

Therefore, in order to prove the indistinguishability of the two hybrids, it is enough to prove the lemma below.

**Sub-Lemma 1.** $\Pr[\text{Event E is true in } \text{Hyb}_2] = \text{negl}(\lambda)$.

*Proof.* We now prove the sub-lemma. Suppose the event E does occur. From the binding property of the commitment scheme and the correctness of the protocol $\pi^{\text{SM}}$, observe that if any of the above conditions are true, it means there exists $i, j$ such that the statement $\text{st}_{2,j}^i = (c_{1,i}^j, c_{2,j}^i, \text{msg}_{1,j}, \text{msg}_{2,j}, \tau_1) \notin L$, where $P_i$ is honest and $P_j$ is malicious. However, the proof for the statement verified correctly which means that the adversary has produced a valid proof for a false statement. This violates the soundness property of the SPSSZK argument system which is a contradiction.

**Lemma 2.** *Assuming the zero knowledge property of the* SPSS.ZK *argument system,* $\text{Hyb}_2$ *is computationally indistinguishable from* $\text{Hyb}_3$.

*Proof.* The only difference between the two hybrids is that in $\mathsf{Hyb}_2$, $\mathsf{Sim}_{\mathsf{Hyb}}$ computes the proofs in Rounds 2 and 3 honestly, by running the algorithm $\mathsf{ZK}_2$ of the $\mathsf{SPSS.ZK}$ argument system, whereas in $\mathsf{Hyb}_3$, a simulated proof is used. If the adversary $\mathcal{A}$ can distinguish between the two hybrids, we can use $\mathcal{A}$ to design an algorithm $\mathcal{A}_{\mathsf{ZK}}$ that breaks the zero knowledge property of the argument system.

Suppose the adversary can distinguish between the two hybrids with non-negligible probability $p$. Then, by a simple hybrid argument, there exists hybrids $\mathsf{Hyb}_{2,k}$ and $\mathsf{Hyb}_{2,k+1}$ that the adversary can distinguish with non-negligible probability $p' < p$ such that: the only difference between the two hybrids is in the proof sent by an honest party $\mathsf{P}_i$ to a (malicious) party $\mathsf{P}_j$ in one of the rounds. Let's say it is the proof in round 2.

$\mathcal{A}_{\mathsf{ZK}}$ performs the role of $\mathsf{Sim}_{\mathsf{Hyb}}$ in its interaction with $\mathcal{A}$ and performs all the steps exactly as in $\mathsf{Hyb}_{2,k}$ except the proof in Round 2 sent by $\mathsf{P}_i$ to $\mathsf{P}_j$. It interacts with a challenger $\mathcal{C}$ of the $\mathsf{SPSS.ZK}$ argument system and sends the first round message $\mathsf{ver}^i_{1,j}$ it received from the adversary. $\mathcal{A}_{\mathsf{ZK}}$ receives from $\mathcal{C}$ a proof that is either honestly computed or simulated. $\mathcal{A}_{\mathsf{ZK}}$ sets this received proof as its message $\mathsf{prove}^j_{i,2}$ in Round 2 of its interaction with $\mathcal{A}$. In the first case, this exactly corresponds to $\mathsf{Hyb}_{2,k}$ while the latter exactly corresponds to $\mathsf{Hyb}_{2,k+1}$. Therefore, if $\mathcal{A}$ can distinguish between the two hybrids, $\mathcal{A}_{\mathsf{ZK}}$ can use the same distinguishing guess to distinguish the proofs: i.e., decide whether the proofs received from $\mathcal{C}$ were honest or simulated. Now, notice that $\mathcal{A}_{\mathsf{ZK}}$ runs only in time $\mathsf{T}^{\mathsf{Brk}}_{\mathsf{Com}}$ (during the input extraction phase), while the $\mathsf{SPSS.ZK}$ system is secure against adversaries running in time $\mathsf{T}_{\mathsf{ZK}}$. Since $\mathsf{T}^{\mathsf{Brk}}_{\mathsf{Com}} < \mathsf{T}_{\mathsf{ZK}}$, this is a contradiction and hence proves the lemma.

In particular, this also means the following: $\Pr[\text{Event } \mathsf{E} \text{ is true in } \mathsf{Hyb}_3] = \mathsf{negl}(\lambda)$.

**Lemma 3.** *Assuming the non-malleability property of the non-malleable commitment scheme* $\mathsf{NMCom}$, $\mathsf{Hyb}_3$ *is computationally indistinguishable from* $\mathsf{Hyb}_4$.

*Proof.* We will prove this using a series of computationally indistinguishable intermediate hybrids as follows.

- $\mathsf{Hyb}_{3,1}$: This is same as $\mathsf{Hyb}_3$ except that the simulator $\mathsf{Sim}_{\mathsf{Hyb}}$ does not run the input extraction phase apart from verifying the $\mathsf{SPSS.ZK}$ proofs. Also, $\mathsf{Sim}_{\mathsf{Hyb}}$ does not run the special abort phase. In particular, the $\mathsf{Ext.Com}$ algorithm is not run and there is no "Special Abort". In this hybrid, $\mathsf{Sim}_{\mathsf{Hyb}}$ runs in time $\mathsf{T}^{\mathsf{Sim}}_{\mathsf{ZK}}$ which is lesser than $\mathsf{T}^{\mathsf{Brk}}_{\mathsf{Com}}$.
- $\mathsf{Hyb}_{3,2}$: This hybrid is identical to the previous hybrid except that in Round 2, $\mathsf{Sim}_{\mathsf{Hyb}}$ now computes all the messages $(\hat{\mathsf{c}}^j_{1,i}, \mathsf{c}^j_{2,i})$ as non-malleable commitments of $0^{p(\lambda)}$ as done by $\mathsf{Sim}$ in the ideal world. In this hybrid too, $\mathsf{Sim}_{\mathsf{Hyb}}$ runs in time $\mathsf{T}^{\mathsf{Sim}}_{\mathsf{ZK}}$.
- $\mathsf{Hyb}_{3,3}$: This is same as $\mathsf{Hyb}_3$ except that the simulator does run the input extraction phase and the special abort phase. It is easy to see that $\mathsf{Hyb}_{3,3}$ is the same as $\mathsf{Hyb}_4$. In this hybrid, $\mathsf{Sim}_{\mathsf{Hyb}}$ runs in time $\mathsf{T}^{\mathsf{Brk}}_{\mathsf{Com}}$ which is greater than $\mathsf{T}^{\mathsf{Sim}}_{\mathsf{ZK}}$.

We now prove the indistinguishability of these intermediate hybrids and this completes the proof of the lemma.

**Sub-Lemma 2.** $\mathsf{Hyb}_3$ *is statistically indistinguishable from* $\mathsf{Hyb}_{3,1}$.

*Proof.* The only difference between the two hybrids is that in $\mathsf{Hyb}_3$, the simulator might output "Special Abort" which doesn't happen in $\mathsf{Hyb}_{3,1}$. As shown in the proof of Lemma 2, the probability that Event E occurs in $\mathsf{Hyb}_3$ is negligible. This means that the probability that the simulator outputs "Special Abort" in $\mathsf{Hyb}_3$ is negligible and this completes the proof.

**Sub-Lemma 3.** *Assuming the non-malleability property of the non-malleable commitment scheme* NMCom, $\mathsf{Hyb}_{3,1}$ *is computationally indistinguishable from* $\mathsf{Hyb}_{3,2}$.

*Proof.* The only difference between the two hybrids is that in $\mathsf{Hyb}_{3,1}$, for every honest party $\mathsf{P}_i$, $\mathsf{Sim}_{\mathsf{Hyb}}$ computes the commitment messages $(\hat{\mathsf{c}}^j_{1,i}, \mathsf{c}^j_{2,i})$ as a commitment of $(x_i, r_i)$, whereas in $\mathsf{Hyb}_{3,2}$, they are computed as a commitment of $(0^{p(\lambda)})$. If the adversary $\mathcal{A}$ can distinguish between the two hybrids), we can use $\mathcal{A}$ to design an algorithm $\mathcal{A}_{\mathsf{NMC}}$ that breaks the security of the non-malleable commitment scheme NMCom. We defer the details about the reduction to the full version.

**Sub-Lemma 4.** $\mathsf{Hyb}_{3,2}$ *is statistically indistinguishable from* $\mathsf{Hyb}_{3,3}$.

*Proof.* The only difference between the two hybrids is that in $\mathsf{Hyb}_{3,3}$, the simulator might output "Special Abort" which doesn't happen in $\mathsf{Hyb}_{3,2}$. As shown in the proof of Sub-Lemma 3, the probability that Event E occurs in $\mathsf{Hyb}_{3,2}$ is negligible. This means that the probability that the simulator outputs "Special Abort" in $\mathsf{Hyb}_{3,3}$ is negligible and this completes the proof.

**Lemma 4.** *Assuming the security of the protocol* $\pi^{\mathsf{SM}}$, $\mathsf{Hyb}_4$ *is computationally indistinguishable from* $\mathsf{Hyb}_5$.

*Proof.* The only difference between the two hybrids is that in $\mathsf{Hyb}_4$, $\mathsf{Sim}_{\mathsf{Hyb}}$ computes the messages of protocol $\pi^{\mathsf{SM}}$ correctly using the honest parties' inputs, whereas in $\mathsf{Hyb}_5$, they are computed by running the simulator $\mathcal{S}$ for protocol $\pi^{\mathsf{SM}}$. If the adversary $\mathcal{A}$ can distinguish between the two hybrids, we can use $\mathcal{A}$ to design an algorithm $\mathcal{A}_{\mathsf{SM}}$ that breaks the security of protocol $\pi^{\mathsf{SM}}$. We defer the details about the reduction to the full version.

## 5    Two Round Malicious Secure MPC for Input-Less Functionalities

Let $f$ be any input-less functionality randomized functionalities. Consider $n$ parties $\mathsf{P}_1, \ldots, \mathsf{P}_n$ who wish to compute $f$ by running a secure multiparty computation(MPC) protocol. Let $\pi^{SM}$ be any 2 round MPC protocol for $f$ in the plain model, that is secure against semi-malicious adversaries corrupting upto $(n-1)$ parties (such a protocol for general functionalities was described in [7]). In this section, we show how to generically transform $\pi^{SM}$ into a 2 round protocol $\pi_1$ without setup with super-polynomial simulation and secure against malicious adversaries that can corrupt upto $(n-1)$ parties. Formally, we prove the following theorem:

**Theorem 2.** *Assuming sub-exponentially secure:*

- *A, where $A \in \{DDH,\ Quadratic\ Residuosity,\ N^{th}\ Residuosity\}$ AND*
- *2 round MPC protocol for any functionality $f$ that is secure against semi-malicious adversaries,*

*the protocol presented in Fig. 4 is a 2 round MPC protocol for any input-less randomized functionality $f$, in the plain model with super-polynomial simulation.*

We can instantiate the underlying MPC protocol with the 2 round construction of [11] to get the following corollary:

**Corollary 2.** *Assuming sub-exponentially secure:*

- *A, where $A \in \{DDH,\ Quadratic\ Residuosity,\ N^{th}\ Residuosity\}$ AND*
- *Indistinguishability Obfuscation,*

*the protocol presented in Fig. 4 is a 2 round MPC protocol for any input-less randomized functionality $f$ in the plain model with super-polynomial simulation.*

### 5.1   High-Level Overview

Before describing our protocol formally, to help the exposition, we first give a brief overview of the construction in this subsection.

Consider $n$ parties $P_1, \ldots, P_n$ with no inputs who wish to run a secure MPC to compute an input-less randomized function $f$. Initially, each party $P_i$ picks some randomness $r_i$ that it will use to run the semi-malicious protocol $\pi^{SM}$ for the same functionality $f$.

In the first round, each party $P_i$ sends the first round message of the protocol $\pi^{SM}$. Then, with every other party $P_j$, $P_i$ initiates an execution of the SPSS.ZK argument system playing the verifier's role. Additionally, $P_i$ and $P_j$ also initiate two executions of a non-malleable commitment scheme - each acting as the committer in one of them. $P_i$ commits to the randomness $r_i$ used in the protocol $\pi^{SM}$.

In the second round, each party $P_i$ sends the second round message of the protocol $\pi^{SM}$ using randomness $r_i$. Then, $P_i$ finishes executing the non-malleable commitments (playing the committer's role) with every other party $P_j$, committing to $rr_i$. Finally, with every other party $P_j$, $P_i$ completes the execution of the SPSS.ZK argument by sending its second message - $P_i$ proves that the two messages sent so far using the protocol $\pi^{SM}$ were correctly generated using the randomness $r_i$ committed to using the non-malleable commitment.

Each party $P_i$ now computes its final output as follows. $P_i$ first verifies all the proofs it received in the last round and sends a global abort (asking all the parties to abort) if any proof does not verify. Then, $P_i$ computes the output using the output computation algorithm of the semi-malicious protocol $\pi^{SM}$. This completes the protocol description.

**Security Proof:** We now briefly describe how the security proof works. Let's consider an adversary $\mathcal{A}$ who corrupts a set of parties. Recall that the goal is to move from the real world to the ideal world such that the outputs of the honest parties along with the view of the adversary is indistinguishable. We do this via a sequence of computationally indistinguishable hybrids.

In the first hybrid $\mathsf{Hyb}_1$, we start with the real world.

Then, in $\mathsf{Hyb}_2$, we switch the SPSS.ZK proofs used by all honest parties in round 2 to simulated proofs. This hybrid is computationally indistinguishable from the previous hybrid by the security of the SPSS.ZK system.

In $\mathsf{Hyb}_3$, we switch all the non-malleable commitments sent by honest parties to be commitments of 0 rather than the randomness. Recall that since the proofs were simulated, this doesn't violate correctness. Also, this hybrid is computationally indistinguishable from the previous hybrid by the security of the non-malleable commitment scheme.

Then, in $\mathsf{Hyb}_4$, the simulator extracts the adversary's randomness (used in protocol $\pi^{SM}$) by a brute force break of the non-malleable commitment. The simulator aborts if the extracted values don't reconstruct the protocol messages correctly. These two hybrids are indistinguishable because from the soundness of the proof system, the extraction works correctly except with negligible probability. One technicality here is that since we are giving simulated proofs at this point, we cannot rely on soundness anymore. To get around this, from the very first hybrid, we maintain the invariant that in every hybrid, the value committed by the adversary using the non-malleable commitments can be used to reconstruct the messages used in the semi-malicious protocol. Therefore, at this point, as in Sect. 4, we need the time taken to break the non-malleable commitment scheme $T_{\mathsf{Com}}^{\mathsf{Brk}}$ to be lesser than the time against which the zero knowledge property holds - $T_{\mathsf{ZK}}$. We elaborate on this in the formal proof.

Then, in $\mathsf{Hyb}_5$ we run the simulator of $\pi^{SM}$ using the extracted values to generate the protocol messages. This hybrid is indistinguishable from the previous one by the security of $\pi^{SM}$. Once again, in order to ensure correctness of the extracted values, we require the running time of the simulator - which is $T_{\mathsf{Com}}^{\mathsf{Brk}}$ to be lesser than the time against which the semi-malicious protocol $\pi^{SM}$ is secure. This is because, then, the simulator can continue to extract the adversary's message and randomness used for the protocol $\pi^{SM}$ by breaking the semi-malicious protocol.

Finally, $\mathsf{Hyb}_5$ corresponds to the ideal world. Notice that our simulation is in fact straight-line. There are some slight technicalities that arise and we elaborate on this in the formal proof. We now refer the reader to the formal protocol construction.

## 5.2   Construction

As in Sect. 4, we first list some notation and the primitives used before describing the construction.

*Notation:*

- $\lambda$ denotes the security parameter.
- SPSS.ZK = $(\mathsf{ZK}_1, \mathsf{ZK}_2, \mathsf{ZK}_3)$ is a two message zero knowledge argument with super polynomial strong simulation (SPSS-ZK). The zero knowledge property holds against all adversaries running in time $\mathsf{T}_{\mathsf{ZK}}$. Let $\mathsf{Sim}^{\mathsf{ZK}}$ denote the simulator that produces simulated ZK proofs and let $\mathsf{T}_{\mathsf{ZK}}^{\mathsf{Sim}}$ denote its running time. [25] give a construction of an SPSS.ZK scheme satisfying these properties that can be based on one of the following sub-exponential assumptions: (1) DDH; (2) Quadratic Residuosity; (3) $N^{th}$ Residuosity.
- NMCom = $(\mathsf{NMCom}_1^R, \mathsf{NMCom}_1^S, \mathsf{NMCom}_2^S)$ is a two message concurrent non-malleable commitment scheme with respect to commitment in the simultaneous message model. Here, $\mathsf{NMCom}_1^R, \mathsf{NMCom}_1^S$ denote the first message of the receiver and sender respectively while $\mathsf{NMCom}_2^S$ denotes the second message of the sender. It is secure against all adversaries running in time $\mathsf{T}_{\mathsf{Com}}^{\mathsf{Sec}}$, but can be broken by adversaries running in time $\mathsf{T}_{\mathsf{Com}}^{\mathsf{Brk}}$. Let Ext.Com denote a brute force algorithm running in time $\mathsf{T}_{\mathsf{Com}}^{\mathsf{Brk}}$ that can break the commitment scheme just using the first round messages. [25] give a construction of an NMCom scheme satisfying these properties that can be based on one of the following sub-exponential assumptions: (1) DDH; (2) Quadratic Residuosity; (3) $N^{th}$ Residuosity.
- $\pi^{\mathsf{SM}}$ is a sub-exponentially secure 2 round MPC protocol that is secure against semi-malicious adversaries. This protocol is secure against all adversaries running in time $\mathsf{T}_{\mathsf{SM}}$. Let $(\mathsf{MSG}_1, \mathsf{MSG}_2)$ denote the algorithms used by any party to compute the messages in each of the two rounds and OUT denotes the algorithm to compute the final output. Further, let's assume that this protocol $\pi^{\mathsf{SM}}$ runs over a broadcast channel. Let $\mathcal{S} = (\mathcal{S}_1, \mathcal{S}_2)$ denote the simulator for the protocol $\pi^{\mathsf{SM}}$ - that is, $\mathcal{S}_i$ is the simulator's algorithm to compute the $i^{th}$ round messages. Also, we make the following assumptions about the protocol structure that is satisfied by the instantiations:
  1. Since the protocol is for input-less functionalities, we assume that $\mathcal{S}_1$ is identical to the algorithm $\mathsf{MSG}_1$ used by honest parties to generate their first message.
  2. The algorithm $\mathsf{MSG}_2$ doesn't use any new randomness that was not already used in the algorithm $\mathsf{MSG}_1$. This is similar to the assumption used in Sect. 4.

In order to realize our protocol, we require that $\mathsf{poly}(\lambda) < \mathsf{T}_{\mathsf{ZK}}^{\mathsf{Sim}} < \mathsf{T}_{\mathsf{Com}}^{\mathsf{Sec}} < \mathsf{T}_{\mathsf{Com}}^{\mathsf{Brk}} < \mathsf{T}_{\mathsf{ZK}}, \mathsf{T}_{\mathsf{SM}}$.

The construction of the protocol is described in Fig. 4. We assume broadcast channels. In our construction, we use proofs for a some NP languages that we elaborate on below.

NP language $L$ is characterized by the following relation $R$.

Statement : $\mathsf{st} = (c_1, \hat{c}_1, c_2, \mathsf{msg}_1, \mathsf{msg}_2, \tau)$

Witness : $\mathsf{w} = (\mathsf{r}, \mathsf{r}_c)$

$R(\mathsf{st}, \mathsf{w}) = 1$ if and only if :

- $\hat{c}_1 = \mathsf{NMCom}_1^{\mathsf{S}}(\mathsf{r}; \mathsf{r}_c)$ AND
- $c_2 = \mathsf{NMCom}_2^{\mathsf{S}}(\mathsf{r}, c_1; \mathsf{r}_c)$ AND
- $\mathsf{msg}_1 = \mathsf{MSG}_1(\bot; \mathsf{r})$ AND
- $\mathsf{msg}_2 = \mathsf{MSG}_2(\bot, \tau; \mathsf{r})$

That is, the messages $(c_1, \hat{c}_1, c_2)$ form a non-malleable commitment of $(\mathsf{inp}, \mathsf{r})$ such that $\mathsf{msg}_2$ is the second round message using input $\mathsf{inp}$, randomness $\mathsf{r}$ by running the protocol $\pi^{\mathsf{SM}}$, where the protocol transcript so far is $\tau$.

In the protocol, let's assume that every party has an associated identity id. For any session sid, each parties generates its non-malleable commitment using the tag $(\mathsf{id}||\mathsf{sid})$.

The correctness of the protocol follows from the correctness of the protocol $\pi^{\mathsf{SM}}$, the non-malleable commitment scheme NMCom and the zero knowledge proof system SPSS.ZK.

### 5.3 Security Proof

In this section, we formally prove Theorem 2.

Consider an adversary $\mathcal{A}$ who corrupts $t$ parties where $t < n$. For each party $P_i$, let's say that the size of randomness used in the protocol $\pi^{\mathsf{SM}}$ is $p(\lambda)$ for some polynomial $p$. That is, $|r_i| = p(\lambda)$. The strategy of the simulator Sim against a malicious adversary $\mathcal{A}$ is described in Fig. 5.

Here, notice that since there is no input, the simulator gets the output from the ideal functionality - y right at the beginning. It still has to instruct the functionality to deliver output to the honest party.

We now show that the simulation strategy described in Fig. 5 is successful against all malicious PPT adversaries. That is, the view of the adversary along with the output of the honest parties is computationally indistinguishable in the real and ideal worlds. We will show this via a series of computationally indistinguishable hybrids where the first hybrid $\mathsf{Hyb}_1$ corresponds to the real world and the last hybrid $\mathsf{Hyb}_6$ corresponds to the ideal world.

We prove indistinguishability of these hybrids via similar reductions as those in Sect. 4. Please refer to the full version for these reductions.

1. $\mathsf{Hyb}_1$: In this hybrid, consider a simulator $\mathsf{Sim}_{\mathsf{Hyb}}$ that plays the role of the honest parties. $\mathsf{Sim}_{\mathsf{Hyb}}$ runs in polynomial time.
2. $\mathsf{Hyb}_2$: This hybrid is identical to the previous hybrid except that in Round 2, $\mathsf{Sim}_{\mathsf{Hyb}}$ now computes simulated SPSSZK proofs as done in Round 2 in Fig. 5. Here, $\mathsf{Sim}_{\mathsf{Hyb}}$ runs in time $\mathsf{T}_{\mathsf{ZK}}^{\mathsf{Sim}}$.
3. $\mathsf{Hyb}_3$: This hybrid is identical to the previous hybrid except that $\mathsf{Sim}_{\mathsf{Hyb}}$ now computes all the $(\hat{c}_{1,i}^j, c_{2,i}^j)$ as non-malleable commitments of $0^{p(\lambda)}$ as done in Round 2 in Fig. 5. Once again, $\mathsf{Sim}_{\mathsf{Hyb}}$ runs in time $\mathsf{T}_{\mathsf{ZK}}^{\mathsf{Sim}}$.

---

**Inputs:** Each party $P_i$ uses randomness $r_i$ to compute the message in each round of the protocol $\pi^{\mathsf{SM}}$. To make the exposition easier, we think of each party's input as being $\perp$. We now describe the messages sent by party $P_i$. We will use superscripts to denote the intended recipient of the message if it isn't meant to be used by all parties.

1. **Round 1:**
   $P_i$ does the following:
   - Compute $\mathsf{msg}_{1,i} \leftarrow \mathsf{MSG}_1(\perp; r_i)$.
   - For each $j \in [n]$ with $j \neq i$, compute:
     - $\hat{c}_{1,i}^j \leftarrow \mathsf{NMCom}_1^S(r_i; r_{c,i}^j)$ using a random string $r_{c,i}^j$. $c_{1,i}^j \leftarrow \mathsf{NMCom}_1^R(1^\lambda)$.
     - $(\mathsf{ver}_{1,i}^j, \mathsf{zkst}_{1,i}^j) \leftarrow \mathsf{ZK}_1(1^\lambda)$.
   - Send $(\mathsf{msg}_{1,i}, \hat{c}_{1,i}^j, c_{1,i}^j, \mathsf{ver}_{1,i}^j)$ for all $j$.

2. **Round 2:**
   Let $\tau_1$ denote the protocol transcript after round 1. $P_i$ does the following:
   - Compute $\mathsf{msg}_{2,i} \leftarrow \mathsf{MSG}_2(\perp, \tau_1; r_i)$.
   - For each $j \in [n]$ with $j \neq i$, compute:
     - $c_{2,i}^j \leftarrow \mathsf{NMCom}_2^S(r_i, c_{1,j}^i; r_{c,i}^j)$ using the same random string $r_{c,i}^j$.
     - $\mathsf{prove}_{2,i}^j \leftarrow \mathsf{ZK}_2(\mathsf{ver}_{1,j}^i, \mathsf{st}_{2,i}^j, \mathsf{w}_{2,i}^j)$ for the statement $\mathsf{st}_{2,i}^j = (c_{1,j}^i, \hat{c}_{1,i}^j, c_{2,i}^j, \mathsf{msg}_{1,i},$
       $\mathsf{msg}_{2,i}, \tau_1) \in L$ using witness $\mathsf{w}_{2,i}^j = (r_i, r_{c,i}^j)$.
   - Send $(\mathsf{msg}_{2,i}, c_{2,i}^j, \mathsf{prove}_{2,i}^j)$ for all $j$.

3. **Output Computation:**
   Let $\tau_2$ denote the protocol transcript after round 2. $P_i$ does the following:
   - For each $j \in [n]$ with $j \neq i$, do:
     - Abort if $\mathsf{ZK}_3(\mathsf{zkst}_{1,i}^j, \mathsf{st}_{2,j}^i) \neq 1$ where $\mathsf{st}_{2,j}^i = (c_{1,i}^j, \hat{c}_{1,j}^i, c_{2,j}^i, \mathsf{msg}_{1,j}, \mathsf{msg}_{2,j}, \tau_1)$. In particular, send a global abort signal to all parties so that everyone aborts.
   - Compute output $y_i \leftarrow \mathsf{OUT}(\perp, \tau_2; r_i)$.

**Fig. 4.** 2 Round MPC protocol $\pi_1$ for input-less randomized functionality $f$.

4. $\mathsf{Hyb}_4$: In this hybrid, the simulator $\mathsf{Sim}_{\mathsf{Hyb}}$ also runs the "Randomness Extraction" phase and the "Special Abort" phase in steps 2 and 4 in Fig. 5. Now, $\mathsf{Sim}_{\mathsf{Hyb}}$ runs in time $\mathsf{T}_{\mathsf{Com}}^{\mathsf{Brk}}$.
5. $\mathsf{Hyb}_5$: In this hybrid, if the value of the variable $\mathsf{correct} = 1$, $\mathsf{Sim}_{\mathsf{Hyb}}$ now computes the second round message of the protocol $\pi^{\mathsf{SM}}$ using the simulator algorithms $\mathcal{S}_2$ as done by $\mathsf{Sim}$ in the ideal world. $\mathsf{Sim}_{\mathsf{Hyb}}$ also instructs the ideal functionality to deliver outputs to the honest parties as done by $\mathsf{Sim}$. This hybrid is now same as the ideal world. Once again, $\mathsf{Sim}_{\mathsf{Hyb}}$ runs in time $\mathsf{T}_{\mathsf{Com}}^{\mathsf{Brk}}$.

## 6  Three Round Concurrently Secure MPC

Let $f$ be any functionality. Consider $n$ parties $P_1, \ldots, P_n$ with inputs $x_1, \ldots, x_n$ respectively who wish to compute $f$ on their joint inputs by running a concurrently secure multiparty computation(MPC) protocol. Let $\pi^{SM}$ be any 3 round

1. **Round 1:** For each honest party $P_i$, Sim does the following:
   - Compute $\mathsf{msg}_{1,i} \leftarrow \mathsf{MSG}_1(\bot; r_i)$ using some random string $r_i$. Recall that this is identical to running the simulator $\mathcal{S}_1(1^\lambda, i)$. For each $j \in [n]$ with $j \neq i$, compute $\hat{c}^j_{1,i} \leftarrow \mathsf{NMCom}^S_1(0^{p(\lambda)})$, $c^j_{1,i} \leftarrow \mathsf{NMCom}^R_1(1^\lambda)$ and $(\mathsf{ver}^j_{1,i}, \mathsf{zkst}^j_{1,i}) \leftarrow \mathsf{ZK}_1(1^\lambda)$.
   - Send $(\mathsf{msg}_{1,i}, \hat{c}^j_{1,i}, c^j_{1,i}, \mathsf{ver}^j_{1,i})$ for all $j \in [n]$.
2. **Randomness Extraction:** Sim does the following:
   - For each honest party $P_i$ and for each $j \in [n]$ with $j \neq i$, do:
     - Compute $(r^i_j) = \mathsf{Ext.Com}(c^j_{1,i}, \hat{c}^i_{1,j})$. That is, this is the randomness of party $P_j$ seen by party $P_i$. This step takes time $\mathsf{T}^{\mathsf{Brk}}_{\mathsf{Com}}$.
   - Initialize a variable $\mathsf{correct} = 1$. Then, for each malicious party $P_j$, do:
     - Set $\mathsf{correct} = 0$ if the set of values $\{r^i_j\}$, for all $i$ corresponding to honest parties $P_i$ is not equal. Set $r_j = r^1_j$ and let R denote the set of all $\{r_j\}$.
     - Set $\mathsf{correct} = 0$ if $\mathsf{msg}_{1,j} \neq \mathsf{MSG}_1(\bot, r_j)$.
3. **Round 2:** Let $\tau_1$ denote the protocol transcript after round 1. Sim does the following:
   - For each honest party $P_i$:
     - If $\mathsf{correct} = 1$, compute $\mathsf{msg}_{2,i} \leftarrow \mathcal{S}_2(\tau_1, \mathsf{R}, i)$.
     - Else, compute $\mathsf{msg}_{2,i} \leftarrow \mathsf{MSG}_2(\bot, \tau_1; r_i)$ where $r_i$ was used in round 1.
   - For each honest party $P_i$ and for each $j \in [n]$ with $j \neq i$, compute:
     - $c^j_{2,i} \leftarrow \mathsf{NMCom}^S_2(0^{p(\lambda)}, c^i_{1,j}; r^j_{c,i})$ using a random string $r^j_{c,i}$.
     - $\mathsf{prove}^j_{2,i} \leftarrow \mathsf{Sim}^{\mathsf{ZK}}(\mathsf{ver}^i_{1,j}, \mathsf{st}^j_{2,i})$ for $\mathsf{st}^j_{2,i} = (c^i_{1,j}, \hat{c}^j_{1,i}, c^j_{2,i}, \mathsf{msg}_{1,i}, \mathsf{msg}_{2,i}, \tau_1) \in L$. Observe that this takes time $\mathsf{T}^{\mathsf{Sim}}_{\mathsf{ZK}}$.
   - Send $(\mathsf{msg}_{2,i}, c^j_{2,i}, \mathsf{prove}^j_{2,i})$ for all $j \in [n]$.
4. **Special Abort Phase:** For each malicious party $P_j$:
   - Output "Special Abort" if $\mathsf{correct} = 0$.
   - Also, output "Special Abort" if $\mathsf{msg}_{2,j} \neq \mathsf{MSG}_2(\bot, r_j, \tau_1)$.
5. **Output Computation:** Sim does the following:
   - For each honest party $P_i$ and for each $j \in [n]$ with $j \neq i$, abort if $\mathsf{ZK}_3(\mathsf{zkst}^j_{1,i}, \mathsf{st}^i_{2,j}) \neq 1$ where $\mathsf{st}^i_{2,j} = (c^j_{1,i}, \hat{c}^i_{1,j}, c^i_{2,j}, \mathsf{msg}_{1,j}, \mathsf{msg}_{2,j}, \tau_1)$.
   - Else, instruct the ideal functionality to deliver output to the honest parties.

**Fig. 5.** Simulation strategy in the 2 round protocol

protocol that runs without any setup for the above task and is secure against adversaries that can be completely malicious in the first round, semi-malicious in the next two rounds and can corrupt upto $(n-1)$ parties. In this section, we show how to generically transform $\pi^{SM}$ into a 3 round concurrently secure protocol $\pi^{\mathsf{Conc}}$ without setup with super-polynomial simulation that is secure against malicious adversaries which can corrupt upto $(n-1)$ parties. Formally, we prove the following theorem:

**Theorem 3.** *Assuming sub-exponentially secure:*

- *A, where $A \in \{DDH,\ Quadratic\ Residuosity,\ N^{th}\ Residuosity\}$ AND*
- *3 round MPC protocol for any functionality f that is stand-alone secure against malicious adversaries in the first round and semi-malicious adversaries in the next two rounds,*

*the protocol presented in Fig. 2 is a 3 round concurrently secure MPC protocol without any setup with super-polynomial simulation for any functionality $f$, secure against malicious adversaries.*

We can instantiate the underlying MPC protocol with the constructions of [7,11] to get the following corollary:

**Corollary 3.** *Assuming sub-exponentially secure:*

- *A, where $A \in \{DDH, Quadratic\ Residuosity,\ N^{th}\ Residuosity\}$ AND*
- *B, where $B \in \{LWE,\ Indistinguishability\ Obfuscation\}$*

*the protocol presented in Fig. 2 is a 3 round concurrently secure MPC protocol without any setup with super-polynomial simulation for any functionality $f$, secure against malicious adversaries.*

We essentially prove that the same protocol from Sect. 4 is also concurrently secure. The proof is fairly simple and not too different from the proof of stand-alone security, because the simulation strategy as well as all reductions are straight-line. The only use of rewinding occurs (implicitly) within the proof of non-malleability, which we carefully combine with identities to ensure that the protocol remains concurrently secure. For the sake of completeness, we write out the protocol and the proof in their entirety in the full version.

## 7    Two Round Concurrently Secure MPC for Input-Less Functionalities

Let $f$ be any input-less functionality randomized functionalities. Consider $n$ parties $P_1, \ldots, P_n$ who wish to compute $f$ by running a concurrently secure multiparty computation(MPC) protocol. Let $\pi^{SM}$ be any 2 round protocol that runs without any setup for the above task and is secure against semi-malicious adversaries that can corrupt upto $(n-1)$ parties. In this section, we show how to generically transform $\pi^{SM}$ into a 2 round concurrently secure protocol $\pi_1^{Conc}$ without setup with super-polynomial simulation and secure against malicious adversaries that can corrupt upto $(n-1)$ parties. Formally, we prove the following theorem:

**Theorem 4.** *Assuming sub-exponentially secure:*

- *A, where $A \in \{DDH,\ Quadratic\ Residuosity,\ N^{th}\ Residuosity\}$ AND*
- *2 round MPC protocol for any functionality $f$ that is stand-alone secure against semi-malicious adversaries,*

*the protocol presented in Fig. 4 is a 2 round concurrently secure MPC protocol without any setup with super-polynomial simulation for any input-less randomized functionality $f$, secure against malicious adversaries.*

We can instantiate the underlying MPC protocol with the 2 round construction of [11] to get the following corollary:

**Corollary 4.** *Assuming sub-exponentially secure:*

- *A, where $A \in \{DDH,$ Quadratic Residuosity, $N^{th}$ Residuosity$\}$ AND*
- *Indistinguishability Obfuscation,*

*the protocol presented in Fig. 4 is a 2 round concurrently secure MPC protocol without any setup with super-polynomial simulation for any input-less randomized functionality $f$.*

We essentially prove that the same protocol from Sect. 5 is also concurrently secure. The proof is fairly simple and not too different from the proof of stand-alone security, because the simulation strategy as well as all reductions are straight-line. The only use of rewinding occurs (implicitly) within the proof of non-malleability, which we carefully combine with identities to ensure that the protocol remains concurrently secure. For the sake of completeness, we write out the protocol and the proof in their entirety in the full version.

**Acknowledgements.** We thank Ron Rothblum for useful discussions.

# References

1. Ananth, P., Choudhuri, A.R., Jain, A.: A new approach to round-optimal secure multiparty computation. In: Katz, J., Shacham, H. (eds.) CRYPTO 2017. LNCS, vol. 10401, pp. 468–499. Springer, Cham (2017). doi:10.1007/978-3-319-63688-7_16
2. Asharov, G., Jain, A., López-Alt, A., Tromer, E., Vaikuntanathan, V., Wichs, D.: Multiparty computation with low communication, computation and interaction via threshold FHE. In: Pointcheval, D., Johansson, T. (eds.) EUROCRYPT 2012. LNCS, vol. 7237, pp. 483–501. Springer, Heidelberg (2012). doi:10.1007/978-3-642-29011-4_29
3. Badrinarayanan, S., Garg, S., Ishai, Y., Sahai, A., Wadia, A.: Two-message witness indistinguishability and secure computation in the plain model from new assumptions. IACR Cryptology ePrint Archive 2017, 433 (2017). http://eprint.iacr.org/2017/433
4. Barak, B., Prabhakaran, M., Sahai, A.: Concurrent non-malleable zero knowledge. In: 47th Annual IEEE Symposium on Foundations of Computer Science (FOCS 2006), Berkeley, California, USA, Proceedings, pp. 345–354, 21–24 October 2006. https://doi.org/10.1109/FOCS.2006.21
5. Barak, B., Sahai, A.: How to play almost any mental game over the net - concurrent composition via super-polynomial simulation. In: 46th Annual IEEE Symposium on Foundations of Computer Science (FOCS 2005), Pittsburgh, PA, USA, Proceedings, pp. 543–552, 23–25 October 2005. https://doi.org/10.1109/SFCS.2005.43
6. Beaver, D., Micali, S., Rogaway, P.: The round complexity of secure protocols (extended abstract). In: Proceedings of the 22nd Annual ACM Symposium on Theory of Computing, Baltimore, Maryland, USA, pp. 503–513, 13–17 May 1990. http://doi.acm.org/10.1145/100216.100287
7. Brakerski, Z., Halevi, S., Polychroniadou, A.: Four round secure computation without setup. IACR Cryptology ePrint Archive 2017, 386 (2017). http://eprint.iacr.org/2017/386

8. Canetti, R., Lin, H., Pass, R.: Adaptive hardness and composable security in the plain model from standard assumptions. In: 51th Annual IEEE Symposium on Foundations of Computer Science, FOCS 2010, Las Vegas, Nevada, USA, pp. 541–550, 23–26 October 2010. https://doi.org/10.1109/FOCS.2010.86
9. Damgård, I., Ishai, Y.: Constant-round multiparty computation using a black-box pseudorandom generator. In: Shoup, V. (ed.) CRYPTO 2005. LNCS, vol. 3621, pp. 378–394. Springer, Heidelberg (2005). doi:10.1007/11535218_23
10. Damgård, I., Ishai, Y.: Scalable secure multiparty computation. In: Dwork, C. (ed.) CRYPTO 2006. LNCS, vol. 4117, pp. 501–520. Springer, Heidelberg (2006). doi:10.1007/11818175_30
11. Dodis, Y., Halevi, S., Rothblum, R.D., Wichs, D.: Spooky encryption and its applications. In: Robshaw, M., Katz, J. (eds.) CRYPTO 2016. LNCS, vol. 9816, pp. 93–122. Springer, Heidelberg (2016). doi:10.1007/978-3-662-53015-3_4
12. Dolev, D., Dwork, C., Naor, M.: Non-malleable cryptography (extended abstract). In: Proceedings of the 23rd Annual ACM Symposium on Theory of Computing, New Orleans, Louisiana, USA, pp. 542–552, 5–8 May 1991. http://doi.acm.org/10.1145/103418.103474
13. Garg, S., Goyal, V., Jain, A., Sahai, A.: Concurrently secure computation in constant rounds. In: Pointcheval, D., Johansson, T. (eds.) EUROCRYPT 2012. LNCS, vol. 7237, pp. 99–116. Springer, Heidelberg (2012). doi:10.1007/978-3-642-29011-4_8
14. Garg, S., Gupta, D.: Efficient round optimal blind signatures. In: Nguyen, P.Q., Oswald, E. (eds.) EUROCRYPT 2014. LNCS, vol. 8441, pp. 477–495. Springer, Heidelberg (2014). doi:10.1007/978-3-642-55220-5_27
15. Garg, S., Kiyoshima, S., Pandey, O.: On the exact round complexity of self-composable two-party computation. In: Coron, J.-S., Nielsen, J.B. (eds.) EUROCRYPT 2017. LNCS, vol. 10211, pp. 194–224. Springer, Cham (2017). doi:10.1007/978-3-319-56614-6_7
16. Garg, S., Mukherjee, P., Pandey, O., Polychroniadou, A.: The exact round complexity of secure computation. In: Fischlin, M., Coron, J.-S. (eds.) EUROCRYPT 2016. LNCS, vol. 9666, pp. 448–476. Springer, Heidelberg (2016). doi:10.1007/978-3-662-49896-5_16
17. Garg, S., Rao, V., Sahai, A., Schröder, D., Unruh, D.: Round optimal blind signatures. In: Rogaway, P. (ed.) CRYPTO 2011. LNCS, vol. 6841, pp. 630–648. Springer, Heidelberg (2011). doi:10.1007/978-3-642-22792-9_36
18. Goldreich, O.: The Foundations of Cryptography - Volume 2, Basic Applications. Cambridge University Press, Cambridge (2004)
19. Goldreich, O., Micali, S., Wigderson, A.: How to play any mental game or A completeness theorem for protocols with honest majority. In: Proceedings of the 19th Annual ACM Symposium on Theory of Computing 1987, New York, NY, USA, pp. 218–229 (1987). http://doi.acm.org/10.1145/28395.28420
20. Goyal, V.: Constant round non-malleable protocols using one way functions. In: Proceedings of the 43rd ACM Symposium on Theory of Computing, STOC 2011, San Jose, CA, USA, pp. 695–704, 6–8 June 2011. http://doi.acm.org/10.1145/1993636.1993729
21. Goyal, V., Khurana, D., Sahai, A.: Breaking the three round barrier for non-malleable commitments. In: FOCS (2016)
22. Goyal, V., Lee, C., Ostrovsky, R., Visconti, I.: Constructing non-malleable commitments: a black-box approach. In: 53rd Annual IEEE Symposium on Foundations of Computer Science, FOCS 2012, New Brunswick, NJ, USA, pp. 51–60, 20–23 October 2012 . https://doi.org/10.1109/FOCS.2012.47

23. Hofheinz, D., Jager, T., Khurana, D., Sahai, A., Waters, B., Zhandry, M.: How to generate and use universal samplers. In: Cheon, J.H., Takagi, T. (eds.) ASIACRYPT 2016. LNCS, vol. 10032, pp. 715–744. Springer, Heidelberg (2016). doi:10.1007/978-3-662-53890-6_24

24. Katz, J., Ostrovsky, R., Smith, A.: Round efficiency of multi-party computation with a dishonest majority. In: Biham, E. (ed.) EUROCRYPT 2003. LNCS, vol. 2656, pp. 578–595. Springer, Heidelberg (2003). doi:10.1007/3-540-39200-9_36

25. Khurana, D., Sahai, A.: Two-message non-malleable commitments from standard sub-exponential assumptions. IACR Cryptology ePrint Archive 2017, 291 (2017). http://eprint.iacr.org/2017/291

26. Kiyoshima, S., Manabe, Y., Okamoto, T.: Constant-round black-box construction of composable multi-party computation protocol. In: Lindell, Y. (ed.) TCC 2014. LNCS, vol. 8349, pp. 343–367. Springer, Heidelberg (2014). doi:10.1007/978-3-642-54242-8_15

27. Lin, H., Pass, R.: Constant-round non-malleable commitments from any one-way function. In: Proceedings of the 43rd ACM Symposium on Theory of Computing, STOC 2011, San Jose, CA, USA, pp. 705–714, 6–8 June 2011. http://doi.acm.org/10.1145/1993636.1993730

28. Lin, H., Pass, R., Soni, P.: Two-round concurrent non-malleable commitment from time-lock puzzles. IACR Cryptology ePrint Archive 2017, 273 (2017). http://eprint.iacr.org/2017/273

29. Lin, H., Pass, R., Venkitasubramaniam, M.: Concurrent non-malleable commitments from any one-way function. In: Canetti, R. (ed.) TCC 2008. LNCS, vol. 4948, pp. 571–588. Springer, Heidelberg (2008). doi:10.1007/978-3-540-78524-8_31

30. Malkin, T., Moriarty, R., Yakovenko, N.: Generalized environmental security from number theoretic assumptions. In: Halevi, S., Rabin, T. (eds.) TCC 2006. LNCS, vol. 3876, pp. 343–359. Springer, Heidelberg (2006). doi:10.1007/11681878_18

31. Mukherjee, P., Wichs, D.: Two round multiparty computation via multi-key FHE. In: Advances in Cryptology - EUROCRYPT 2016 - 35th Annual International Conference on the Theory and Applications of Cryptographic Techniques, Vienna, Austria, Proceedings, Part II, pp. 735–763, 8–12 May 2016. https://doi.org/10.1007/978-3-662-49896-5_26

32. Pandey, O., Pass, R., Vaikuntanathan, V.: Adaptive one-way functions and applications. In: Advances in Cryptology - CRYPTO 2008, 28th Annual International Cryptology Conference, Santa Barbara, CA, USA, Proceedings, pp. 57–74, 17–21 August 2008. http://dx.doi.org/10.1007/978-3-540-85174-5_4

33. Pass, R.: Simulation in quasi-polynomial time, and its application to protocol composition. In: Biham, E. (ed.) EUROCRYPT 2003. LNCS, vol. 2656, pp. 160–176. Springer, Heidelberg (2003). doi:10.1007/3-540-39200-9_10

34. Pass, R.: Bounded-concurrent secure multi-party computation with a dishonest majority. In: Proceedings of the 36th Annual ACM Symposium on Theory of Computing, Chicago, IL, USA, pp. 232–241, 13–16 June 2004. http://doi.acm.org/10.1145/1007352.1007393

35. Pass, R., Rosen, A.: Concurrent non-malleable commitments. In: 46th Annual IEEE Symposium on Foundations of Computer Science (FOCS 2005), Pittsburgh, PA, USA, Proceedings, pp. 563–572, 23–25 October 2005. https://doi.org/10.1109/SFCS.2005.27

36. Prabhakaran, M., Sahai, A.: New notions of security: achieving universal composability without trusted setup. In: Proceedings of the 36th Annual ACM Symposium on Theory of Computing, Chicago, IL, USA, pp. 242–251, 13–16 June 2004. http://doi.acm.org/10.1145/1007352.1007394

37. Sahai, A.: Non-malleable non-interactive zero knowledge and adaptive chosen-ciphertext security. In: 40th Annual Symposium on Foundations of Computer Science, FOCS 1999, New York, NY, USA, pp. 543–553, 17–18 October 1999. https://doi.org/10.1109/SFFCS.1999.814628

38. Wee, H.: Black-box, round-efficient secure computation via non-malleability amplification. In: FOCS 2010, pp. 531–540 (2010). https://doi.org/10.1109/FOCS.2010.87

39. Yao, A.C.: Protocols for secure computations (extended abstract). In: FOCS (1982)

40. Yao, A.C.: How to generate and exchange secrets (extended abstract). In: FOCS (1986)

# A Unified Approach to Constructing Black-Box UC Protocols in Trusted Setup Models

Susumu Kiyoshima[1(✉)], Huijia Lin[2],
and Muthuramakrishnan Venkitasubramaniam[3]

[1] NTT Secure Platform Laboratories, Tokyo, Japan
kiyoshima.susumu@lab.ntt.co.jp
[2] University of California, Santa Barbara, CA, USA
rachel.lin@cs.ucsb.edu
[3] University of Rochester, Rochester, NY, USA
muthuv@cs.rochester.edu

**Abstract.** We present a unified framework for obtaining *black-box* constructions of *Universal Composable* (UC) protocol in trusted setup models. Our result is analogous to the unified framework of Lin, Pass, and Venkitasubramaniam [STOC'09, Asiacrypt'12] that, however, only yields *non-black-box* constructions of UC protocols. Our unified framework shows that to obtain black-box constructions of UC protocols, it suffices to implement a special purpose commitment scheme that is, in particular, concurrently extractable using a given trusted setup. Using our framework, we improve black-box constructions in the common reference string and tamper-proof hardware token models by weakening the underlying computational and setup assumptions.

## 1 Introduction

Secure multi-party computation (MPC) protocols enable a set of $m$ mutually distrustful parties with private inputs $x_1, \cdots, x_m$ to jointly compute a function $f$, learn the output $f(x_1, \cdots, x_m)$ and nothing else. In the classical *stand-alone* setting, security of MPC protocols is analyzed where a single instance of a protocol runs in isolation. However, such analysis falls short of guaranteeing security in more realistic, *concurrent*, settings, where multiple instances of different protocols co-exist and are subject to coordinated attacks. To address this, Canetti formulated the *Universally Composable* (UC) framework [1] for reasoning about the security of protocols in arbitrary execution environments that dynamically interact with the analyzed protocol. The UC framework formulates, so far, the most stringent and realistic model of protocol execution, and provides a strong composability property —known as the *universal composition theorem*— that protocols shown secure in the UC framework remain secure when executed concurrently within arbitrary larger complex system.

Unfortunately, these strong properties come at a price: Many natural functionalities cannot be realized with UC security in the *plain model*, where the

© International Association for Cryptologic Research 2017
Y. Kalai and L. Reyzin (Eds.): TCC 2017, Part I, LNCS 10677, pp. 776–809, 2017.
https://doi.org/10.1007/978-3-319-70500-2_26

only setup provided is authenticated communication channels; some additional *trusted setup* is necessary [2,3]. Following Canetti and Fischlin [2], Canetti et al. [4] demonstrated the feasibility of UC-secure protocols realizing general functionalities, in the *Common Reference String* (CRS) Model, where a trusted entity samples a single CRS from a prescribed distribution that can be referenced to by all executions of the designed protocol. Since its conception, a long line of work have focused on designing UC secure protocols under various *trusted setups*, from CRS, to public key infrastructure, to tamper-proof hardware tokens, and many others (see for example [5–11]), and led to a comprehensive understanding on *what are the minimal trusted setups and computational assumptions needed for achieving UC security.*

**Black-box vs Non-black-box Construction:** A basic distinction between cryptographic constructions is whether they make only black-box use of the underlying primitives or not. *Black-box constructions* only call the designated input/output interface of the underlying primitives, whereas *non-black-box constructions* depend on specifics of the code implementing the primitives. Typically, non-black-box constructions are more versatile for demonstrating feasibility of cryptographic tasks and minimizing underlying primitives. However, black-box constructions are more modular and tend to be more efficient. A natural theoretical direction seeks to narrow the gap between what is achieved via non-black-box and black-box constructions for important cryptographic tasks, under minimal assumptions (as done in, for example [12–22]), which leads to new constructions, techniques, and understanding.

For the task of achieving UC security with trusted setups, there still remain significant gaps between what is achievable via non-black-box and black-box constructions. First, generic approaches for achieving UC-security have been developed using non-black-box techniques. Lin et al. [11,23] presented a unified framework for developing UC-secure protocols in general trusted setup models. In particular, they identified a (simple) "minimal primitive" called *UC-puzzles* that give non-black-box constructions of UC-secure protocols for general functionalities. At a high-level this primitive facilitates *concurrent simulation*, which is a necessary condition to achieve UC-security. Moreover, an important consequence of the unified framework was the weakening of trusted infrastructure and other assumptions in many models. It also significantly reduced the complexity of designing UC-secure protocols, as UC puzzles are often easy (if not trivial) to attain using trusted setups. Thus a natural question we ask in this work is,

*Can we have a unified framework for developing*
*black-box constructions of UC-secure protocols, under general setup?*

Thus far, no generic approach using black-box techniques exist, and, in fact, to the best of our knowledge, there are only a few black-box constructions [21,22,24] of UC-secure protocols for specific trusted-setup, namely the CRS and tamper-proof hardware tokens models, which fall short in the following ways:

**In the CRS model,** the state-of-the-art non-black-box constructions assume only the existence of semi-honest secure Oblivious Transfer (OT) protocols, whereas black-box constructions are based on either the existence of enhanced trapdoor permutations [4], or specific assumptions, such as, Strong RSA, DDH, DLIN [25–27]. All these assumption imply CCA encryption and semi-honest OT. This raises the question:

> *Can we have black-box constructions of UC-secure protocols in the CRS model, from weaker assumptions?*

Hazay and Venkitasubramaniam [21] gave partial answer to this question in the stronger "local CRS model". They gave black-box construction of UC-protocols from public-key encryption and semi-honest OT; however, every execution of their protocols needs to rely on an independently sampled *local* CRS. In contrast, the CRS model as defined originally [4] considers a *single* CRS that is shared by all concurrent executions. Clearly, having a trusted entity sampling a single CRS once and for all is a much more realistic setup than sampling a CRS for every protocol execution.

**In the tamper-proof hardware token model,**[1] unconditionally UC-secure protocols exist using *stateful* tokens [28,29]. When relying on much weaker (and more realistic) *stateless* tokens, computational assumptions are necessary [28]. Following a body of works [28,30–34], Hazay et al. [22] showed that the minimal assumption of one-way functions suffices. However, all UC-protocols using stateless tokens require each instance of protocol execution to create a token that has specific information of the instance (namely, the session id) hardwired inside. This means parties must have the capability to create customized tokens. In this work, we consider a even weaker model of tokens, namely stateless and *instance-independent* tokens, which runs codes sampled from a universal distribution, independent of protocol instances. We believe that this model is more realistic as tokens with instance-independent codes may be obtained and distributed ahead of protocol execution, and can potentially be reused across different execution instances. We ask,

> *Can we have UC-secure protocols using stateless and* instance-independent *tokens?*

## 1.1 Our Result

In this work, we present a unified framework for obtaining black-box construction of UC-secure protocols under general trusted setup, assuming semi-honest OT. At a high-level, our framework reduces the task of achieving UC-security to that of constructing a *UC-special-purpose commitment scheme* CECom with the following properties.

---

[1] In the tamper-proof hardware model, parties are assumed to have tamper-proof hardware tokens that only provide input/output (i.e. black-box) access to the token holder.

- CECom is *straight-line concurrently extractable w.r.t. opening*, that is, there is a straight-line extraction strategy $E$ that can extract values from any concurrent committer $C^*$ with the guarantee that $C^*$ cannot successfully open to any values different from what $E$ extracts.
- CECom is *hiding against resetting receivers*.

We observe that comparing with UC commitments, UC-special-purpose commitments are weaker in the sense that it does not guarantee simulation-extractability nor equivocation, but stronger in the sense that they are resettably hiding.

Given such a commitment scheme CECom under trusted setup $\mathcal{T}$, our unified framework shows how to construct general UC-secure protocols that make use of 4 independent instances of $\mathcal{T}$ and black-box use of CECom. We model the 4 independent instances of $\mathcal{T}$ as a single trusted-setup:

- The quadruple-$\mathcal{T}$ trusted setup $4\mathcal{T}$ simply runs 4 independent instances of $\mathcal{T}$ internally, and make them available to all parties.

In fact, for many specific trusted setups, 4 independent instances can be emulated using just a single instance. For example, in the CRS model, 4 reference strings can be concatenated into one. In the tamper proof token model, operations related to tokens are captured by an ideal functionality that allows parties to create an arbitrary number of tokens, transfer them, and execute them. One single such ideal functionality provides the same functionality as 4 of them. In these cases, our unified framework shows that to obtain black-box UC-secure protocols, it suffices to focus on constructing *UC-special-purpose commitment schemes*.

**Theorem 1 (Main Theorem, Informal).** *Let $\mathcal{T}$ be any trusted-setup. Assume the existence of a UC-special-purpose commitment scheme CECom under $\mathcal{T}$, and a constant-round semi-honest oblivious transfer protocol. Then, for every well-formed functionality $\mathcal{F}$, there is a black-box construction of a protocol $\pi$ that UC-realizes $\mathcal{F}$ in the $4\mathcal{T}$-trusted setup model. Moreover, if CECom has $r_{\mathrm{CEC}}$ rounds, then $\pi$ has $O(r_{\mathrm{CEC}})$ rounds.*

We remark that we rely on our setup in an "instance independent" way. In particular, in the CRS model, four references strings are sampled at the beginning and all instances rely on the same reference strings. Whereas in the token model, our result implies that we require tokens with "instance-independent" code. Technically, we follow the Joint Universal Composition (JUC) paradigm [1] and show that our protocol $\pi$ when executed concurrently implement directly the multi-session extension $\hat{F}$ of the functionality $\mathcal{F}$, using a single instance of $4\mathcal{T}$.

COMPARISON WITH THE LPV FRAMEWORK. The unified framework (dubbed as the LPV framework) of [11,23] formulated the notion of *UC puzzles* and showed how to use them to obtain non-black-box constructions of UC-protocols. Roughly speaking, UC puzzle is a protocol between a sender and a receiver with two properties: (i) soundness guarantees that the puzzle is hard to solve for an honest receiver, yet (ii) *concurrent simulation* guarantees that the view of a concurrent sender can be simulated while obtaining all puzzle solutions. From there, the LPV framework shows how to use the UC puzzles to construct protocols that can be concurrently simulated by following the Feige-Shamir paradigm with the puzzle solutions as trapdoors.

In comparison, our unified framework requires constructing UC-special purpose commitment, which captures the capability of *concurrent extraction*. While it is known that using non-black-box techniques concurrent extraction can be achieved through concurrent simulation, as done implicitly in the LPV framework, these techniques often require the use of zero-knowledge or witness indistinguishable proofs, and are not suitable for black-box constructions. This is why in our framework, we directly require a concurrently extractable commitment scheme to start with.

Next, using the generic framework, we improve black-box construction of UC secure protocols in the CRS and tamper-proof hardware token model.

COMPARISON WITH THE GUC FRAMEWORK. In this work, we follow the JUC framework [1] for modeling concurrent security of protocols. In particular, we show that for every functionality $\mathcal{F}$, the concurrent execution of our protocol $\pi_{\mathcal{F}}$ that implements $\mathcal{F}$ securely computes the multi-session extension of $\mathcal{F}$. This means that all instances of execution of $\pi_{\mathcal{F}}$ refer to the same trusted setup, for example, the same CRS. This model should be compared with the Global UC (GUC) framework of [7], where a trusted setup is not only available to all protocol instances, but also to the environment. This means the trusted setup can be shared between arbitrary, even potentially unknown, protocols. Therefore, protocols secure in the GUC framework provide stronger composition guarantees. However, this comes at a price, in particular, it is known that general GUC protocols in the CRS model is infeasible. In the tamper-proof hardware model, the protocols by [22] are secure in the GUC framework, but their tokens are instance-dependent.

**Black-box UC Protocols in the CRS Model.** In the CRS model, UC-special purpose commitment scheme is trivial to construct, simply use any public key encryption scheme. (In fact, even public key encryption with an *interactive* encryption phase suffices.) Thus, plugging into our unified framework, we immediately obtain black-box UC-protocols in the CRS model, from public key encryption and semi-honest OT.

**Theorem 2.** *Assuming the existence of a public-key encryption scheme and a semi-honest oblivious-transfer protocol, there exists a fully black-box construction of UC-secure protocols for general functionalities in the CRS model. Moreover, if both underlying primitives have constant rounds, then the UC-secure protocols also have constant rounds.*

Previous black-box constructions in the CRS model either relies on the existence of a trapdoor permutation [4], or specific algebraic or number theoretic assumptions, such as, DDH [27], Strong RSA [26], and DLin [26]. Note that all these assumptions imply CCA encryption, which is used in all previous constructions.

In comparison, our construction only relies on a public key encryption scheme and a semi-honest OT protocol, which are not known to imply CCA encryption. Instead, in our construction, we use the public key encryption scheme to implement an *interactive* CCA encryption scheme, where the encryption phase is interactive (while the key generation and decryption procedures remain the same). Our notion of interactive CCA encryption should be compared with that of Dodis and Fiore [35]. Our notion is stronger in the sense that the receiver in the interactive encryption phase does not need to know the secret key, whereas in the notion by [35], only receivers knowing the secret key can "receive" the encryption. In particular, their notion is insufficient for constructing UC-secure protocols in the CRS model.

On the other hand, comparing with non-black-box constructions, the best non-black-box construction assumes only the existence of semi-honest OT [11]. We thus narrow the gap in assumptions between non-black-box and black-box constructions, and leaving open the question whether public key encryption can be eliminated for black-box constructions.

Since the common reference string used in our protocols is simply the public keys of the encryption scheme, we obtain as a corollary UC secure protocols in the Uniform Reference String (URS) model assuming public key encryptions with pseudorandom public key (also referred to as dense public-key cryptosystems [36]), which also implies semi-honest OT [37].

**Corollary 1.** *Assuming the existence of an public-key encryption scheme with pseudorandom public keys, there exists a fully black-box construction of UC-secure protocols for general functionalities in the URS model. Moreover, if both underlying primitives have constant rounds, then the UC-secure protocols also have constant rounds.*

Using the same techniques, we believe we can also obtain black-box UC-secure protocols in the public key infrastructure model.

**Black-box UC Protocols in the Tamper Proof Hardware Token Model.** Extending the work of [22], we show how to construct a UC-special purpose commitment scheme using tamper-proof hardware tokens, with black-box use of a one-way function. The tokens used in our protocols are stateless and instance independent, in the sense, every token implements a stateless function that is sampled from a predefined distribution. Thus, plugging this commitment scheme into our unified framework, we immediately obtain black-box UC-protocols in the token model from semi-honest OT.

**Theorem 3.** *Assuming the existence of semi-honest oblivious-transfer. Then, there is black-box construction of UC-secure protocols for general functionalities in the tamper-proof hardware token model, using stateless and instance-independent hardware tokens.*

In contrast, previous works [22, 28, 34] either rely on *stateful* or *instance-dependent* tokens.

We believe that our framework will yield analogous improvements in other setups such as, PUF [38], global random oracle models [39], etc., and we leave it as future work to explore these instantiations.

## 1.2   Our Techniques

We now give an overview of our techniques. Recall that our main theorem states that for a given trusted setup $\mathcal{T}$, we can obtain black-box UC protocols in the $4\mathcal{T}$ model from semi-honest OT and UC-special-purpose commitment schemes in the $\mathcal{T}$ model, where UC-special-purpose commitment schemes are concurrently extractable commitment schemes that are also resettably hiding. We prove this theorem in two steps. For simplicity of this overview, our discussion below will only use the concurrently extractability property of the commitments, and not the resettable hiding property. For the use of resettable hiding property, see Remark 2 at the bottom of this overview.

**From CCA Commitment to Black-box UC Protocols in Trusted Setup Models.** We first show that a black-box construction of UC-secure protocols in $4\mathcal{T}$-model can be obtained from semi-honest OT and *CCA-secure commitment schemes* [40] in $4\mathcal{T}$-model. We recall here that CCA-secure commitment schemes are a stronger variant of non-malleable commitment schemes that additionally require the hiding property to hold even against adversaries that have access to the *committed-value oracle*, which can break arbitrary commitments sent by the adversary using brute force.

CCA-secure commitments were originally proposed for the purpose of constructing concurrent secure protocol in the *plain* model (without any trusted setups) that satisfy a weaker security notion called angel-based security [41] or UC with super-polynomial time helpers [40]. In these models, to circumvent the aforementioned impossibility results of UC security [2,3], the security definition is modified by allowing the adversary/simulator to have access to a *super-polynomial time* helper $H$ or angel. Since the helper can be implemented in super-polynomial time, these models imply super-polynomial-time simulation security [42]. The security in these models can be realized in the plain model [19,20,40,41,43,44], and in particular black-box constructions of protocols satisfying UC-security with super-polynomial time helpers in the plain model can be obtained from CCA-secure commitment schemes and semi-honest OT protocol [19,20].

Our starting point is the work of [19] which builds upon techniques in [13, 14,45], and show how to obtain UC-secure protocols with a super-polynomial time helper starting from semi-honest OT and CCA-secure commitments in a black-box way. We show that a direct extension of this yields an analogous result where we rely on CCA-secure commitments in $4\mathcal{T}$-model as opposed to CCA-commitments in the plain model. Moreover, the helper $H$ is a super-polynomial machine that breaks CCACom commitments in $4\mathcal{T}$-model.

In our next step, we eliminate access to super-polynomial helpers to guarantee standard UC-security. Suppose that the CCACom is also straight-line concurrently extractable, i.e., there exists a (polynomial-time) extractor $E$ that by simulating the $4\mathcal{T}$-setup for the concurrent committer can extract the committed values in a straight-line way, then we can simply remove the super-polynomial time helper $H$ by simulating the trusted setup (in polynomial time), achieving UC-security. Then, we will be able to emulate $H$ with standard UC-simulation in $4\mathcal{T}$-model.

**From Concurrently Extractable Commitments to CCA-secure Commitments in Trusted Setup Models.** We next show that a black-box CCA-secure commitment scheme (with straight-line concurrent extractability as required in the above step) in $4\mathcal{T}$-model can be obtained from a straight-line concurrent extractable commitment scheme in $\mathcal{T}$-model.

Our high-level approach is to use the well-known Naor-Yung paradigm [46] that has been used to construct many CCA-secure encryption schemes. Recall that in the Naor-Yung technique, the sender encrypts a single message twice and proves "consistency" (i.e., the plaintext encrypted in both ciphertexts are equal) using a simulation-sound (non-interactive) zero-knowledge proof. Similarly, we consider a commitment scheme where, at a very high-level, the committer commits to a single message twice using a concurrently extractable commitment scheme and proves consistency. However, since our goal is to obtain black-box constructions, the committer of our protocol cannot use generic zero-knowledge proofs for proving consistency. We address this problem using the elegant technique of Choi et al. [45], developed in the context of constructing black-box non-malleable encryption from just public key encryption, and later extended to the context of constructing black-box non-malleable commitments by Wee [17]. Their techniques combine the cut-and-choose technique with Shamir's secret sharing scheme.

In more detail, we consider the following scheme as the starting point. Let $\mathsf{CECom}$ be a straight-line concurrently extractable commitment scheme in $\mathcal{T}$-model, and $\mathsf{ECom}$ be a straight-line (stand-alone) extractable commitment scheme in $\mathcal{T}$-model ($\mathsf{ECom}$ can be obtained from $\mathsf{CECom}$ trivially). Let $v$ be the message to be committed, and $\mathcal{T}_0, \mathcal{T}_1, \mathcal{T}_2$ be three independent instances of $\mathcal{T}$.

**Stage 1.** The receiver $R$ commits to a random subset $\Gamma \subset [10\lambda]$ of size $\lambda$ using $\mathsf{ECom}$ and trusted setup $\mathcal{T}_0$.

**Stage 2.** The committer $C$ computes a $(\lambda+1)$-out-of-$10\lambda$ Shamir's secret sharing $\boldsymbol{s} = (s_1, \ldots, s_{10\lambda})$ of value $v$. Next, for each $j \in [10\lambda]$, $C$ commits to $s_j$ in parallel, using $\mathsf{CECom}$ and the setup $\mathcal{T}_1$. We will refer to commitments made in this stage as "commitments in the first row".

**Stage 3.** For each $j \in [10\lambda]$, $C$ commits to $s_j$ in parallel, using $\mathsf{CECom}$ and the setups $\mathcal{T}_2$. We will refer to commitments made in this stage as "commitments in the second row".

**Stage 4 (Cut and Choose).** $R$ decommits the Stage 1 commitment to $\Gamma$. For each $j \in \Gamma$, $C$ decommits both the $j^{th}$ commitment in the first row and the $j^{th}$ one in the second row, and $R$ checks whether the two commitments are correctly decommitted to the same value $s_j$.

**Decommitment.** To decommit, simply decommit all commitments in the first row. If the shares $\boldsymbol{s} = (s_1, \ldots, s_{10\lambda})$ committed in the first row is 0.9-close to a valid codeword of $v$, then the committed value is $v$, otherwise, it is set to $\perp$.

Note that this scheme works in $3\mathcal{T}$-model since it uses three instances of $\mathcal{T}$. We remark that, similar to the scheme by Naor and Yung, this scheme satisfies the following two properties.

1. The committer is required to commit to the same value in the two rows of the commitments. Specifically, it is guaranteed by the values revealed in the cut-and-choose stage (i.e., Stage 4) and the hiding of ECom, that the shares that are committed in the two rows are very "close" (that is, agree in most coordinates). This "closeness" ensures that there is a way of reconstructing the committed value from the shares committed in the second row. (We remark that this reconstruction works differently from that in the actual decommitment.)

2. The commitments made in the two rows are "independent" since they are generated using two independent instances of $\mathcal{T}$. When considering man-in-the-middle adversaries playing the roles of receiver and sender in the different executions, this independence will allow us to extract commitments made by the adversary from one row "correctly" while maintaining the "hiding" property of the commitments received by the adversary made in the other row.

Now, we rely on the following hybrid experiments to prove the CCA security.

$H_0$ The real experiment, where an adversary tries to break the hiding property of the above scheme in the "left" interaction while interacting with the committed-value oracle in the "right" interaction.

$H_1$ Follows the experiment as in $H_0$ with the following exceptions:
  1. In the left interaction, the committed subset $\Gamma$ is extracted from the adversary in Stage 1 using the extractability of ECom, and then $0^{|s_j|}$ is committed in the $j^{th}$ commitment of the *second row* for every $j \notin \Gamma$
  2. In the right interaction, the committed-value oracle is emulated in polynomial time as follows. All shares committed to in the *first row* are extracted relying on the extractability of the underlying CECom scheme and then the committed value is reconstructed from those extracted shares.
  Notice that in this experiment, the setups $\mathcal{T}_0$ and $\mathcal{T}_1$ are simulated for extraction.

$H_2$ Follows experiment $H_1$ with the following exceptions:
  1. In the left interaction, $0^{|s_j|}$ is committed in the $j^{th}$ commitment of the *first row* for every $j \notin \Gamma$.
  2. In the right interaction, the committed-value oracle is emulated in polynomial time by extracting shares from the *second row* and reconstructing the committed value.
  In this experiment, the setups $\mathcal{T}_0$ and $\mathcal{T}_2$ are simulated for extraction. We notice that in this experiment, only $|\Gamma| = \lambda$ shares are set and revealed in the left execution for both rows. Hence from the perfect privacy of the underlying Shamir secret sharing scheme, the committed value in the left interaction is hidden.

Intuitively, $H_0$ and $H_1$ are indistinguishable because *(i)* in $H_1$ the committed value oracle is emulated correctly using the shares extracted from the first rows, which defines the committed values, and thus *(ii)* the only difference in the adversary's view are the values committed to in the second row on the left (which are committed using the setup $T_2$), and the setup $T_2$ is not simulated in these hybrids. Additionally, at first sight, $H_1$ and $H_2$ also seem indistinguishable because *(i)* in $H_2$ the committed-value oracle seems to be emulated correctly using values extracted from the second row thanks of the closeness, and thus *(ii)* the only difference in the adversary's view is the values committed in the first row on the left (which are committed using the setup $T_1$) and the setup $T_1$ is not simulated in $H_2$.

Unfortunately, we cannot show the indistinguishability between the above hybrids since the above scheme does not guarantee *simulation soundness*. The problem is that if we simulate $T_0$ on the left (as in $H_1, H_2$), we can no longer rely on the hiding property of ECom on the right, so we cannot show the closeness of the two rows on the right directly. This is problematic because when showing the indistinguishability between $H_1$ and $H_2$, we need to use the closeness of the two rows to argue that the committed-value oracle can be emulated correctly even from the second row.

To address this problem, we add a non-malleable commitment scheme into the above scheme. Specifically, we modify the scheme so that the second row is generated by using a commitment scheme that is both non-malleable and straight-line concurrently extractable, and additionally require the committer to commit to the decommitment of the first rows when generating the second row (i.e., we require the committer to commit to $(s_j, d_j)$ in the second row, where $d_j$ is the decommitment of the $j^{th}$ commitment in the first row). With these modifications, we can prove the closeness of the two rows in $H_1$ as follows.

1. First, we observe that, since the decommitments of the first row are committed in the second row, the closeness of the two rows can be verified by seeing only the committed values of the second row. In particular, the closeness holds between the two rows if the second row is "consistent", meaning that a correct decommitment of the first row is committed in most coordinates.
2. Based on this observation, we show the closeness in $H_1$ as follows. First, we show the consistency of the second row in $H_0$ using the hiding property of ECom. (Recall that we do not break ECom in $H_0$ and can use its hiding property in $H_0$.) Next, when we move to $H_1$ from $H_0$, we use the non-malleability of the second row to argue that the committed values of the second row on the right does not change non-negligibly, which implies that the second row on the right remains consistent in $H_1$. (Here we use the ability to efficiently verify the consistency condition given the committed values of the second row). Now, since the consistency condition implies the closeness, we conclude that the closeness holds in $H_1$ as desired.

Given the closeness in $H_1$, we can show the indistinguishability between $H_1$ and $H_2$ as follows. Consider an intermediate hybrid where the left interaction is generated as in $H_1$ but the committed-value oracle is emulated using the second row as in $H_2$. Then, we first use the closeness in $H_1$ to argue that this intermediate hybrid is indistinguishable from $H_1$. Next, observing that the setup $T_1$ is not simulated in this intermediate hybrid and $H_2$, we show that this intermediate hybrid is also indistinguishable from $H_2$ by using the hiding property of the second row on the left.

Finally, to complete the proof, we argue that the non-malleable commitment scheme that we use above (i.e., a commitment scheme that is both non-malleable and straight-line concurrently extractable) can be obtained without any additional assumptions. We know that constant-round black-box non-malleable commitments in the plain model can be obtained from one-way functions in a black-box way [18], which in turn can be obtained from semi-honest OT (which we assume to exist in the main theorem). Then, our idea is to combine this non-malleable commitments and CECom in $T$-model in a similar manner as in the protocol above (i.e., by using secret sharing and cut-and-choose technique). Now, non-malleability follows analogous to the plain-model non-malleability of the underlying scheme and straight-line concurrent extractability follows from the properties of the latter. The resulting non-malleable commitment is proven secure in the $2T$-model; thus, if this scheme is plugged into our first protocol (as the commitment used in the second row), the final protocol will be in the $4T$-model.

*Remark 1.* We remark that several issues arise when making the preceding high-level argument formal. For example, one subtlety that we ignore is the case that the concurrently extractable commitment scheme that we use is only computationally binding (which is the case in our instantiation for the token model.) This subtlety makes the above argument complicated because the closeness of the two rows is hard to define if the shares that are committed in the rows are not uniquely determined. In our formal proof, we address this subtlety by defining the closeness property only w.r.t. the shares that are *extracted* from the rows.

*Remark 2.* As noted at the beginning of this overview, we actually assume the existence of concurrently extractable commitment scheme that is also resettably hiding. We use this requirement when constructing straight-line concurrently extractable non-malleable commitment schemes. Moreover, we obtain such schemes by combining a non-malleable commitment in the plain model and concurrently extractable commitment in $T$-model. In the actual argument, we additionally use plain-model extractable commitments, and rely on its plain-model (i.e. rewinding based) extractability in the analysis. However relying on a rewinding analysis in the presence of trusted setups is subtle. Specifically, since the adversary might have an arbitrary unbounded-round interaction with the setups, the interaction with the setups can be rewound when the extractor rewinds the adversary. To circumvent this, we simply assume that the schemes in the setup models remain secure even when they are rewound (i.e., reset). In the two concrete setup models we consider, CRS and tamper-proof hardware model, we show that achieving resettable hiding is not hard.

# 2 Definitions of Commitments in Trusted-Setup Models

In this work, we consider commitment protocols that use trusted setups, meaning that the honest committer and receiver communicate with the setup $\mathcal{T}$ for committing and decommitting, and the security of the commitment scheme relies on that $\mathcal{T}$ is never controlled by the adversary — we say such a protocol is in the trusted setup $\mathcal{T}$-model, or simply in $\mathcal{T}$-model.

For clarity, we indicate the parts related to trusted-setup models in red in the definitions we give below; removing them gives the definitions in the plain model.

## 2.1 Trusted Setups

We model a trusted-setup $\mathcal{T}$ as an *ideal functionality* in the UC model, which is simply given by an Interactive Turning Machine (ITM) $\mathcal{M}$. Different from UC, which models the execution of arbitrary protocol in arbitrary environment, for commitments, we only need to consider the execution of security games that define different properties, such as, hiding, binding, and CCA security. Therefore, below we describe a much simpler model of execution.

In a security game with setup $\mathcal{T}$, a set of $m$ (honest or corrupted) parties $\{P_i\}_{i \in [m]}$, and an adversary $A$, the setup $\mathcal{T}$ can concurrently communicate with all entities following the rules described below:

- Whenever a party $P_i$, or a subroutine invoked by $P_i$, sends a message $m$ to $\mathcal{T}$, $\mathcal{T}$ receives input $(\mathsf{ID}, m)$, where $\mathsf{ID}$ is the identifier of $P_i$ or its subroutine. The identifiers of all parties and their subroutines are adaptively chosen by the adversary $A$ at the beginning of their invocation.
- The adversary can communicate with $\mathcal{T}$ either directly according to the code of $\mathcal{T}$, or indirectly by acting as a party with identifier $\mathsf{ID}$.
- All identifiers (of all parties and their subroutines and of parties acted by $A$) must be distinct.

## 2.2 Commitments in $\mathcal{T}$-Model

First we define the structure of a commitment scheme.

**Definition 1 (Commitment Schemes).** *A commitment scheme in $\mathcal{T}$-model is a pair of PPT ITMs $\langle C, R \rangle$ with the following properties:*

1. *The commitment scheme has two stages, a commit stage and a reveal stage, where $C$ and $R$ receive as common input a security parameter $1^n$ and $C$ receives a private input $v \in \{0,1\}^n$ that is the string to be committed.*
2. *The commit stage results in a joint output $c$, called the commitment, a private output for $C$, $d$, called the decommitment string. In the commit stage, both $C$ and $R$ can access $\mathcal{T}$ using their respective identities $\mathsf{ID}_C \neq \mathsf{ID}_R$.*

3. *In the reveal stage, upon receiving pair $(v, d)$, the receiver $R$ decides to accept or reject deterministically, depending only on $(c, v, d)$.*
   *We let* open *denote the function that verifies the validity of $(v, d)$; the receiver accepts $(v, d)$ if* open$(c, v, d) = 1$, *and rejects otherwise,*

*If $C$ and $R$ do not deviate from the protocol, then $R$ should accept with probability 1 during the reveal stage.*

We define the binding and hiding property of a commitment scheme in trusted setup models naturally as in the plain model.[2] (We provide their formal definition in the full version.) We say that a commitment $c$ is *accepting* if $R$ does not abort at the end of commit stage, and is *valid* if there exists an accepting decommitment.

Next we define the resettably hiding property of a commitment scheme. Roughly speaking, a commitment scheme in $\mathcal{T}$-setup model is resettably hiding if its hiding property holds even against any cheating receiver that can "reset" an honest committer and $\mathcal{T}$ and restart the interaction with them from an arbitrary point of the interaction.

**Definition 2 (Resettably Hiding).** *A commitment scheme $\langle C, R \rangle$ in $\mathcal{T}$-model is computationally (resp. statistically) resettably hiding if for every non-uniform PPT machine (resp. for every machine) $R^*$, the view of $R^*$ in the following two games, Game 0 and Game 1, are computationally indistinguishable over $\lambda \in N$ (resp. statistically indistinguishable over $\lambda \in N$).*

- *Game $b$ ($b \in \{0, 1\}$): Let $C(b)$ be a committer that upon receiving $(v_0, v_1)$ gives a commitment to $v_b$ by using $\langle C, R \rangle$. Let $F$ denote the forest of execution threads, initialized as empty. Then, in Game $b$, $R^*$ can interact with $C(b)$ and $\mathcal{T}$ in an arbitrary number of interactions as below: $R^*$ specifies a prefix $\rho$ of execution in $F$, and starts interacting with $C(b)$ and $\mathcal{T}$ from $\rho$, where $R^*$, $C$ and and $\mathcal{T}$ use fresh randomness after $\rho$.*

In the rest of the paper, by default we refer to commitment schemes as ones that are statistically binding and computationally hiding, and will specify explicitly when considering commitment schemes that are computationally binding. In addition, we consider tag-based commitment schemes.

**Definition 3 (Tag-based Commitment Schemes).** *A commitment scheme $\langle C, R \rangle$ is tag-based w.r.t. $l(\lambda)$-bit identities if, in addition to the security parameter $1^\lambda$, the committer and the receiver also receive a "tag" — a.k.a. identity— id of length $l(\lambda)$ as common input. In $\mathcal{T}$-model, the tag*

---

[2] As described in Sect. 2.1, in the binding game with $\mathcal{T}$, $R$, and $C^*$, $R$ can interact with the trusted setup $\mathcal{T}$ using an identity $\mathsf{ID}_R$ chosen by $C^*$, and $C^*$ can interact with $\mathcal{T}$ directly according to $\mathcal{T}$'s code, or indirectly as any parties with identities different from $\mathsf{ID}_R$. Similarly, in the hiding game with $\mathcal{T}$, $C$, and $R^*$, $C$ can interact with the trusted setup $\mathcal{T}$ using an identity $\mathsf{ID}_C$ chosen by $R^*$, and $R^*$ can interact with $\mathcal{T}$ directly according to $\mathcal{T}$'s code, or indirectly as any parties with identities different from $\mathsf{ID}_C$.

*is set to the identity of the committer input. In $\mathcal{T}$-model, the tag is set to the identity of the committer* id $=$ ID$_C$.

## 2.3    Concurrent Non-malleable Commitments in $\mathcal{T}$-Model

Next we define the concurrent non-malleability of a commitment scheme. Roughly speaking, a commitment scheme is non-malleable if a man-in-the-middle adversary, who receives a commitment in the left interaction, cannot commit to a value that is related to the values committed in the left interaction. A commitment scheme is concurrent non-malleable if it is non-malleable even when the man-in-the-middle adversary can give multiple commitments concurrently.

Formally, the concurrent non-malleability of a commitment scheme is defined as follows. Let $\langle C, R \rangle$ be a tag-based commitment scheme; recall that in $\mathcal{T}$-model, the tag of a commitment is set to the identity of the committer id $=$ ID$_C$. Let $M^*$ be a man-in-the-middle adversary and consider the following experiment. On input security parameter $\lambda \in \mathbb{N}$ and auxiliary input $z \in \{0,1\}^*$, $M^*$ participates in one left and $m$ right interactions simultaneously. In the left interaction, $M^*$ interacts with the committer of $\langle C, R \rangle$ and receives a commitment to value $v$ using identity $id \in \{0,1\}^\lambda$ of its choice, where both have access to $\mathcal{T}$. In the right interaction, $M^*$ interacts with the receiver of $\langle C, R \rangle$ and gives commitments using identity $\widetilde{\mathsf{id}}_0, \ldots, \widetilde{\mathsf{id}}_m$ of its choice, where the commitments can be scheduled arbitrarily by $M^*$, and both $M^*$ and the receiver have access to $\mathcal{T}$. Let $\widetilde{v}_1, \ldots, \widetilde{v}_m$ be the values that $M^*$ commits to on the right. If any of the right commitments is invalid or undefined, its committed value is defined to be $\bot$. For any $i$, if id $= \widetilde{\mathsf{id}}_i$, set $\widetilde{v}_i = \bot$. Let c-mim$(\langle C, R \rangle, M^*, v, z)$ denote a random variable that describes $\widetilde{v}_1, \ldots, \widetilde{v}_m$ and the view of $M^*$ in the above experiment.

**Definition 4.** *A commitment scheme $\langle C, R \rangle$ in $\mathcal{T}$-model is* **concurrent non-malleable** *if for any* PPT *man-in-the-middle adversary $M^*$, the following are computationally indistinguishable.*

- $\{\text{c-mim}(\langle C, R \rangle, M^*, v_0, z)\}_{\lambda \in \mathbb{N}, v_0 \in \{0,1\}^\lambda, v_1 \in \{0,1\}^\lambda, z \in \{0,1\}^*}$
- $\{\text{c-mim}(\langle C, R \rangle, M^*, v_1, z)\}_{\lambda \in \mathbb{N}, v_0 \in \{0,1\}^\lambda, v_1 \in \{0,1\}^\lambda, z \in \{0,1\}^*}$

We remark that the above definition captures "one-many" setting, where the adversary participates in one left and $m$ right interactions simultaneously. We can easily generalize the definition so that it captures "many-many" setting, where the adversary participates in $m$ left and $m$ right interactions simultaneously. It is known that the "one-many" version of the definition implies the "many-many" one [47].

## 2.4    CCA Commitments in Trusted-Setup Models

The notion of CCA security for *statistically-binding and computationally hiding* tag-based commitment schemes was introduced in [40]. We here adapt the definition of CCA security in the plain model of [19] to trusted setup models.

Roughly speaking, a (statistically binding) commitment scheme is CCA secure if the commitment scheme retains its hiding property even if the receiver has access to a *committed-value oracle*. Let CCACom be a tag-based commitment scheme with $l(\lambda)$-bit identities; recall that in $\mathcal{T}$-model, the tag of a commitment is set to the identity of the committer $\mathsf{id} = \mathsf{ID}_C$. A committed-value oracle $\mathcal{O}_{\mathsf{CCACom}}$ of CCACom acts as follows in interaction with an adversary $A$, both with access to $\mathcal{T}$: It participates with $A$ in many sessions of the commit phase of CCACom as an honest receiver, using identities chosen adaptively by $A$. At the end of each session, if the session is *accepting and valid*, it returns to $A$ the unique committed value in that session (by the statistical binding property of the commitment scheme, there exists such a unique value when the commitment is valid except with negligible probability; if not output $\bot$); otherwise, it sends $\bot$.

More precisely, let $\mathsf{IND}_b(\mathsf{CCACom}, A, \lambda, z)$, where $b \in \{0, 1\}$, denote the output of the following probabilistic experiment: on common input $1^\lambda$ and auxiliary input $z$, $A^{\mathcal{O}_{\mathsf{CCACom}}}$ (adaptively) chooses a pair of challenge values $(v_0, v_1) \in \{0, 1\}^\lambda$ —the values to be committed to— and an identity $\mathsf{id}$, and receives a commitment to $v_b$ using identity $\mathsf{id}$, where $C$ and $A^{\mathcal{O}_{\mathsf{CCACom}}}$ all have access to $\mathcal{T}$. Finally, the experiment outputs the output $y$ of $A^{\mathcal{O}_{\mathsf{CCACom}}}$; the output $y$ is replaced by $\bot$ if the identity of the commitment that $A$ receives is the same as the identity of any of the commitments that $A$ sends to $\mathcal{O}_{\mathsf{CCACom}}$ (that is, any execution where the adversary queries the decommitment oracle on a commitment using the same identity as the commitment it receives, is considered invalid).

**Definition 5 (CCA-security).** *Let* CCACom *be a tag-based statistically binding commitment scheme in* $\mathcal{T}$*-model. We say that* CCACom *is* CCA*-secure, if for every* PPT *ITM* $A$*, the following ensembles are computationally indistinguishable:*

- *$\{\mathsf{IND}_0(\mathsf{CCACom}, A, \lambda, z)\}_{\lambda \in N, z \in \{0,1\}^*}$*
- *$\{\mathsf{IND}_1(\mathsf{CCACom}, A, \lambda, z)\}_{\lambda \in N, z \in \{0,1\}^*}$*

$k$**-Robustness.** Roughly speaking, $k$-robustness states the committed-value oracle can be simulated efficiently for an attacker, without "disturbing" any $k$-round interaction that the attacker participates in.

Consider a man-in-the-middle adversary $A$ that participates in an *arbitrary* left interaction with $B$ of a *limited number of rounds*, while having access to a committed-value oracle $\mathcal{O}_{\mathsf{CCACom}}$; $A^{\mathcal{O}_{\mathsf{CCACom}}}$ has access to $\mathcal{T}$, but importantly $B$ does not. CCACom is $k$-robust if the (joint) output of every $k$-round interaction, with an adversary having access to the oracle $\mathcal{O}_{\mathsf{CCACom}}$, can be simulated without the oracle. In other words, having access to the oracle does not help the adversary in participating in any $k$-round protocols that does not access $\mathcal{T}$.

**Definition 6 ($k$-Robustness).** *Let* CCACom *be a statistically binding commitment scheme in* $\mathcal{T}$*-model. We say that* CCACom *is* $k$*-robust, if for every* PPT *adversary* $A$*, there exists a* PPT *simulator* $S$*, such that, the following holds.*

*Simulation: For every* PPT $k$*-round ITM* $B$ *that interacts only with* $A$*, the following two ensembles are computationally indistinguishable.*

- $\left\{ \mathsf{output}_{B,A}[\langle B(1^{\lambda}, x), A^{\mathcal{O}_{\mathsf{CCACom}}, \mathcal{T}}(1^{\lambda}, z)\rangle] \right\}_{\lambda \in N, x, z \in \{0,1\}^{\mathrm{poly}(\lambda)}}$
- $\left\{ \mathsf{output}_{B,S}[\langle B(1^{\lambda}, x), S(1^{\lambda}, z)\rangle] \right\}_{\lambda \in N, x, z \in \{0,1\}^{\mathrm{poly}(\lambda)}}$

where $\mathsf{output}_{X,Y}[\langle X(x), Y(y)\rangle]$ denote the joint output of an interaction between ITMs $X$ and $Y$ on private input $x$ and $y$ respectively, and with uniformly and independently chosen random inputs to each machine.

We say that CCACom is poly-robust if it is k-robust against arbitrary polynomial $k(\lambda)$.

## 2.5   Concurrent Extractability w.r.t. Commitment in $\mathcal{T}$-Model

We now define concurrent extractability w.r.t. commitment. Extraction w.r.t. commitment is defined only for statistically binding commitments and guarantees to extract from (malicious) committers the statistically defined committed values.

**Definition 7 (Concurrent Extractability w.r.t. Commitment).** *Let* CCACom *be a statistically binding commitment scheme in $\mathcal{T}$-model. We say that* CCACom *is* straight-line concurrently extractable w.r.t. commitment, *if there exists a universal* PPT *simulator $S$, such that,*

*Simulation of Committed-value Oracle: for every* PPT *adversary $A$, the following two ensembles are computationally indistinguishable.*
- $\left\{ \langle (\mathcal{O}_{\mathsf{CCACom}}, \mathcal{T}),\ A(1^{\lambda}, z)\rangle \right\}_{\lambda \in N, z \in \{0,1\}^{\mathrm{poly}(\lambda)}}$
- $\left\{ \langle S(1^{\lambda}),\ A(1^{\lambda}, z)\rangle \right\}_{\lambda \in N, z \in \{0,1\}^{\mathrm{poly}(\lambda)}}$

We say that CCACom is straight-line extractable w.r.t. commitment if the above condition holds for attackers that sends only a single commitment to $\mathcal{O}_{\mathsf{CCACom}}$.

**Claim 1.** *If a statistically binding commitment scheme* CCACom *in $\mathcal{T}$-model is straight-line concurrently extractable w.r.t. commitment, then it is also k-robust for any polynomial $k(\lambda)$.*

Due to space restrictions, we defer the proof of claim to the full version. At a very high level, straight-line concurrent extractability w.r.t. commitment implies poly-robustness as it essentially guarantees that $\mathcal{O}_{\mathsf{CCACom}}$ can be simulated in a straight-line, and straight-line simulation does not "disturb" the concurrent interaction with $B$, no matter how many rounds the interaction has.

## 2.6   Concurrent Extractability w.r.t. Opening in $\mathcal{T}$-Model

We now introduce the new notion of *straight-line concurrent extractability w.r.t. opening*. This notion is defined for any *computationally binding and computationally hiding* commitment scheme. Roughly speaking, it requires the commitment scheme to have an efficient extractor $E$ satisfying the following two properties:

(1) when interacting with any efficient attacker $A$ acting as a concurrent committer, the value $v$ that $E$ extracts for each commitment that $A$ sends is guaranteed to be consistent with the value $v'$ that $A$ opens to (i.e., $v' = \bot$ or $v = v'$), even if $A$ receives the extracted values $v$'s. (2) The messages that $E$ send statistically emulate that of honest receivers, for even computationally unbounded attackers.

**Definition 8.** *Let* CECom *be any computationally hiding and computationally binding commitment scheme in a trusted-setup $\mathcal{T}$-model. We say that* CECom *is straight-line concurrently extractable w.r.t. opening if there exists a universal* PPT *extractor $E$ with the following properties:*

**Syntax and Statistical Emulation:** *For any (potentially unbounded) adversary $A$, it holds that the view of $A$ in the following real and simulated games are statistically close.*

    *− In the real game, $A$ (acting as a concurrent committer) interacts with honest receivers $R$ in multiple sessions of* CECom. *At the end of each session, if $A$ sends a decommitment, $R$ replies with the decision of whether the decommitment is accepted. All parties have access to $\mathcal{T}$.*

    *− In the simulated game, $E$ emulates the honest receivers and trusted-setup for $A$ in a straight-line.*

*At the end of the commit stage of each session $j$, $E$ outputs a value $v_j$ on its special output tape.*

**Concurrent Extractability w.r.t. Opening:** *For any PPT adversary $A$, consider another simulated game where $A$ interacts with $E$ as described above, and at the end of the commit stage of each session j, it receives the value $v_j$ that E outputs on its special output tape. The probability that in any session $j$, $A$ successfully decommits to a value $v'_j \neq \bot$ that is different from the value $v_j$ that $E$ outputs is negligible, that is, if* $\mathsf{open}(c_j, v'_j, d_j) = 1$ *then* $v_j = v'_j$ *with overwhelming probability.*

## 3  Robust CCACom from CECom w.r.t Opening

In this section, given a commitment scheme CECom that is straight-line concurrently extractable w.r.t. opening in $\mathcal{T}$-model, we construct a robust CCA-secure commitment scheme CCACom that uses a related trusted-setup $4\mathcal{T}$, called the quadruple-$\mathcal{T}$ trusted-setup, which runs four independent copies of $\mathcal{T}$ internally.

**The $\mathsf{x}\mathcal{T}$ Trusted Setup:** $\mathsf{x}\mathcal{T}$, parameterized by an integer $x$, is an ITM that upon invocation invokes internally $x$ instances of $\mathcal{T}$—denoted as $\mathcal{T}_0, \mathcal{T}_1, \cdots, \mathcal{T}_{x-1}$. In an experiment with $\mathsf{x}\mathcal{T}$, all parties and adversaries can interact with any instance, by pre-pending to every message to/from copy $\mathcal{T}_i$ with the index $i \in \{0, \cdots, x-1\}$. That is, upon receiving input $i \| v$ from party $P$, $\mathsf{x}\mathcal{T}$ activates internally the copy $\mathcal{T}_i$ with input $v$ from party $P$, and upon receiving output $o$ from $\mathcal{T}_i$, returns $i \| o$ to $P$. Additionally, each copy $\mathcal{T}_i$ can interact with the adversary as its code specifies, with all messages exchanged of form $i \| \mathsf{mesg}$.

**Theorem 4.** *Let $T$ be any trusted setup, and $4T$ the corresponding quadruple-$T$ trusted setup. There is a* fully black-box *construction of a poly-robust CCA-secure commitment scheme* CCACom *in the $4T$-trusted setup model from any one-way function and any commitment scheme* CECom *in the $T$-trusted setup model that is straight-line concurrently extractable w.r.t. opening and resettably hiding. Moreover, if* CECom *has $r_{\mathrm{CEC}}$ rounds, then* CCACom *has $O(r_{\mathrm{CEC}})$ rounds.*

**Proof.** In our protocol CCACom, we use the following building blocks:

- A standard constant-round statistically-binding commitment scheme com in the plain model, which is known from one-way functions [48].
- A $r_{\mathrm{CEC}}$-round commitment scheme CECom that is (straight-line) concurrently extractable w.r.t. opening in the $T$-trusted setup model.
- A commitment scheme ECom that is straight-line extractable w.r.t. opening in the $T$-model, which is implied by CECom in $T$-model.
- A $O(r_{\mathrm{CEC}})$-round concurrent non-malleable commitment scheme NMCom in the double-$T$, $2T$, trusted-setup model that is also straight-line concurrently extractable w.r.t. commitment.

  Such a commitment scheme can be constructed from any concurrent non-malleable commitment scheme in the plain model, and any commitment scheme in $T$-model that is straight-line concurrently extractable w.r.t. opening and resettably hiding. (Note that the CCACom protocol itself does not directly rely on the resettable hiding property of CECom.) Due to space limitations, we provide our construction in the full version.

Next, we present our protocol CCACom formally.

**Commit Phase of CCACom.** On common inputs $1^\lambda$ and identities $\mathsf{ID}_C, \mathsf{ID}_R$, and private input $v \in \{0,1\}^\lambda$ to $C$, the committer $C$ and receiver $R$ interact with each other as follows:

**Stage 1.** $R$ commits to a random subset $\Gamma \subset [10\lambda]$ of size $\lambda$ using ECom and trusted setup $T_0$. We will refer to $T_0$ as the ECom-setup.

**Stage 2 (The Com Row).** $C$ computes a $(\lambda + 1)$-out-of-$10\lambda$ Shamir's secret sharing $s = (s_1, \ldots, s_{10\lambda})$ of value $v$. Next, for each $j \in [10\lambda]$, $C$ commit to $s_j$ in parallel, using com. We will refer to commitments made in this stage as "commitments in the com row".

Let $\phi_j$ and $d_j$ be the commitment and decommitment for share $s_j$.

**Stage 3 (The CECom Row).** For each $j \in [10\lambda]$, $C$ commits to $(s_j, d_j)$ in parallel, using the protocol CECom and the setup $T_1$. We will refer to commitments made in this stage as "commitments in the CECom row", and $T_1$ as the CECom-setup.

Let $\psi_j$ and $e_j$ be the commitment and decommitment for $(s_j, d_j)$.

**Stage 4 (The NMCom Row).** For each $j \in [10\lambda]$, $C$ commits to $(s_j, d_j, e_j)$ in parallel, using the protocol NMCom and the setups $T_2$ and $T_3$ to emulate the double-$T$ setup $2T$. We will refer to commitments made in this stage as "commitments in the NMCom row", and $T_2, T_3$ as the NMCom-setup.

**Stage 5 (Cut and Choose).** $R$ decommits the Stage 1 commitment to $\Gamma$. For each $j \in \Gamma$, $C$ decommits the $j^{th}$ commitment in the NMCom row to $(s_j, d_j, e_j)$. $R$ accepts if for every $j \in \Gamma$, the decommitment to the $j^{th}$ NMCom commitment is accepting, and $(s_j, d_j)$ is a valid decommitment to commitment $\phi_j$ in the Stage 2, and $((s_j, d_j), e_j)$ is a valid decommitment to $\psi_j$ in Stage 3.

**Decommit Phase.** $C$ sends $v$ and the decommitments $(s_1, d_1), \cdots, (s_{10\lambda}, d_{10\lambda})$ to all com commitments $\phi_1, \cdots, \phi_{10\lambda}$. $R$ checks all decommitments and does the following. If for any $i \in [10\lambda]$, the decommitment $(s_i, d_i)$ is invalid w.r.t. $\phi_i$, set $s_i$ to $\perp$. $R$ accepts the decommitments if and only if $\mathsf{Value}(s) = v$, where $\mathsf{Value}(s)$ for $s = \{s_1, \cdots, s_{10\lambda}\}$ is defined as follows:

$$\mathsf{Value}(s) = \begin{cases} v & \begin{array}{l} s \text{ is 0.9-close to a valid codeword } w = (w_1, \ldots, w_{10\lambda}), \\ \text{for each } j \in \Gamma, w_j \text{ equals the value revealed in Stage 5, and} \\ w \text{ decodes to } v \end{array} \\ \perp & \text{otherwise} \end{cases} \quad (1)$$

Clearly, The round complexity of the above protocol is $O(r_{\mathrm{CEC}})$. The statistical binding property of CCACom follows directly from that of com in Stage 2. Thus, it remains to show that CCACom is CCA secure and poly-robust; for the latter property, we show the stronger property of straight-line concurrently extractability w.r.t. commitment, which implies poly-robustness by Claim 1.

**Proposition 1.** CCACom *in the $4\mathcal{T}$-trusted setup model is CCA secure and straight-line concurrently extractable w.r.t. commitment.*

Due to space restrictions, we prove only CCA security below, and defer the proof of straight-line concurrently extractable w.r.t. commitment in the full version.

**Proof of CCA Security.** For any PPT adversary $A$, we need to show that the outputs of the games $\mathsf{IND}_0$ and $\mathsf{IND}_1$ are indistinguishable (cf. Definition 5).

- $\{\mathsf{IND}_0(\mathsf{CCACom}, A, \lambda, z)\}_{\lambda \in N, z \in \{0,1\}^*}$
- $\{\mathsf{IND}_1(\mathsf{CCACom}, A, \lambda, z)\}_{\lambda \in N, z \in \{0,1\}^*}$

Towards showing the indistinguishability, for each $b \in \{0, 1\}$, we consider the following hybrid experiments $H_0^b \cdots H_7^b$; we use $\mathsf{H}_k^b(\lambda, z)$ to denote the random variable representing the view of $A$ in the execution of $H_k^b(\lambda, z)$. Throughout the hybrids, we will keep the invariant that certain bad events do not happen except with negligible probabilities. Roughly speaking, we would like to maintain that in all hybrids, in every right session, the shares that $A$ commits to in the com, CECom, and/or NMCom rows are "consistent", so that, we can efficiently emulate the $\mathcal{O}_{\mathsf{CCACom}}$ oracle by extracting from either the CECom rows or from the NMCom rows. Below, we first define these bad events.

INCONSISTENCY CONDITION: We say that a vector of shares $\tilde{s}$ is inconsistent w.r.t. a transcript Trans of protocol CCACom, if

– Either, more than 0.1 fraction of $\tilde{s}$ are $\perp$, that is, $|A_1 = \{j|\tilde{s}_j = \perp\}| > \lambda$.
– or, $\tilde{s}$ is 0.8-close to a valid codeword $w$, yet 0.1-far from it, that is, $|A_2 = \{j|\tilde{s}_j \neq w_j\}| > \lambda$, and additionally $w$ agrees with the shares $\{s_j\}_{j \in \Gamma}$ opened to in Stage 5 in transcript Trans.

EVENT $\mathrm{Bad_{CEC}}$ is defined for hybrids below where the extractor $\mathcal{S}_{\mathsf{CECom}}$ of CECom is used to extract values from the CECom rows (i.e., $H_1^b, H_2^b, H_3^b$). Let $\{(\tilde{s}_j^k, d_j^k)\}_{j \in [10\lambda]}$ denote the values extracted by $\mathcal{S}_{\mathsf{CECom}}$ from the CECom commitment in right session $k$. Set

$$\tilde{s}_j^k = \widetilde{\mathsf{Extract}}(\tilde{s}_j^k, d_j^k) := \begin{cases} \tilde{s}_j^k & \text{if } (\tilde{s}_j^k, d_j^k) \text{ is a valid decommitment for } \phi_j^k \\ \perp & \text{otherwise} \end{cases} \quad (2)$$

Event $\mathrm{Bad}_{CEC}$ occurs if there is an *accepting* right session $k$ in which the shares $\{\tilde{s}_j^k\}_{10\lambda}$ extracted from the CECom row is *inconsistent* w.r.t. the transcript of this session.

EVENT $\mathrm{Bad_{NM}}$ is defined for all hybrids below and concerns the values committed to in the NMCom commitments on the right. Let $\{((\hat{s}_j^k, d_j^k), e_j^k)\}_{j \in [10\lambda]}$ denote the values committed to in the NMCom row in right session $k$. (Since NMCom is statistically binding, the committed values are well-defined.) Set

$$\hat{s}_j^k = \widetilde{\mathsf{Extract}}((\hat{s}_j^k, d_j^k), e_j^k)$$
$$:= \begin{cases} \hat{s}_j^k & \begin{array}{l} \text{if } ((\hat{s}_j^k, d_j^k), e_j^k) \text{ is a valid decommitment for } \psi_j^k, \\ \text{and } (\hat{s}_j^k, d_j^k) \text{ is a valid decommitment for } \phi_j^k \end{array} \\ \perp & \text{otherwise} \end{cases} \quad (3)$$

where $\psi_j^k$ and $\phi_j^k$ are respectively the $j^{th}$ commitment in the CECom row and in the com row in the $k^{th}$ right session. Event $\mathrm{Bad_{NM}}$ occurs if there is an *accepting* right session $k$, in which the shares $\{\hat{s}_j^k\}_{10\lambda}$ extracted from the values committed in the NMCom row are *inconsistent* w.r.t. the transcript of this session.

**Hybrid** $H_0^b(\lambda, z)$ is the same as experiment $\mathsf{IND}_b(\mathsf{CCACom}, A, \lambda, z)$.
**Hybrid** $H_1^b(\lambda, z)$ is the same as $H_0^b(\lambda, z)$ except that on the right the $\mathcal{O}_{\mathsf{CCACom}}$ oracle is emulated efficiently using the extractor $\mathcal{S}_{\mathsf{CECom}}$ of CECom as follows:
  1. Generate the receiver messages of CCACom honestly, except for messages in the CECom-rows.
  2. Use $\mathcal{S}_{\mathsf{CECom}}$ to emulate (i) the CECom receivers in the CECom-rows and in Stage 5 when $A$ open some of the CECom commitments, and (ii) the CECom-setup $\mathcal{T}_1$. By definition, at the end of each CECom-row, say in the right session $k$, $\mathcal{S}_{\mathsf{CECom}}$ outputs a vector of values $\{(\tilde{s}_j^k, d_j^k)\}_{j \in [10\lambda]}$ on its special output tape. Set $\tilde{s}_j^k = \widetilde{\mathsf{Extract}}(\tilde{s}_j^k, d_j^k)$, where $\widetilde{\mathsf{Extract}}$ is described in Eq. (2).

3. At the end of each right session $k$, emulate the committed value that $\mathcal{O}_{\mathsf{CCACom}}$ returns, by returning the value $\tilde{v}^k = \widetilde{\mathsf{Value}}(\tilde{\boldsymbol{s}}^k)$ reconstructed from the shares $\tilde{\boldsymbol{s}}^k = \{\tilde{s}_j^k\}_{j \in [10\lambda]}$ where $\widetilde{\mathsf{Value}}$ is defined as

$$\widetilde{\mathsf{Value}}(\tilde{\boldsymbol{s}}) = \begin{cases} & \tilde{\boldsymbol{s}} \text{ is } \textit{0.8-close to a valid codeword } \boldsymbol{w} = (w_1, \ldots, w_{10\lambda}), \\ \tilde{v} & \forall\, j \in \Gamma,\, w_j \text{ equals the value revealed in Stage 5,} \\ & \text{and } \boldsymbol{w} \text{ decodes to } \tilde{v} \\ \bot & \text{otherwise} \end{cases} \tag{4}$$

We first show that bad events $\mathrm{Bad}_{\mathrm{NM}}$ and $\mathrm{Bad}_{CEC}$ occur in $H_1^b$ with negligible probability.

**Lemma 1.** *For every $b \in \{0, 1\}$, it holds that, the probabilities that event $\mathrm{Bad}_{\mathrm{NM}}$ and $\mathrm{Bad}_{CEC}$ occur are negligible in $H_1^b$.*

*Proof.* We first bound the probability of $\mathrm{Bad}_{CEC}$ occurring. Suppose for contradiction that there is an *accepting* right session $k$ in which the shares $\{\tilde{s}_j^k = \mathsf{Extract}(\tilde{s}_j^k, d_j^k)\}_{10\lambda}$ extracted from the CECom row is *inconsistent*. The inconsistency condition states that

- Either, $\tilde{\boldsymbol{s}}^k$ contains more than $\lambda \perp$, i.e., $|\Lambda_1 = \{j \mid \tilde{s}_j^k = \perp\}| \geq \lambda$.
- Or, $\tilde{\boldsymbol{s}}^k$ is 0.8-close to $\boldsymbol{w}^k$, yet 0.1-far from it, i.e., $|\Lambda_2 = \{j \mid \tilde{s}_j^k \neq w_j^k\}| > \lambda$, and $\boldsymbol{w}^k$ agree with the shares opened in Stage 5 of right session $k$.

In case 1, for this session to be accepting, it must happen that none of the locations in $\Lambda_1$ was opened in Stage 5, that is, $\Lambda_1 \cap \Gamma^k = \emptyset$, where $\Gamma^k$ is the subset opened in Stage 5 of right session $k$; otherwise, the attacker must manage to open to a non-$\perp$ share for some $j \in \Lambda_1$, which contradicts with the concurrent extractability w.r.t. opening property of CECom. Similarly, in case 2, it must be that $\Lambda_2 \cap \Gamma^k = \emptyset$, as otherwise, the attacker must manage to open to a share $\tilde{s}_j^k = w_j^k$ for some $j \in \Lambda_2$. In both cases, $A$ manage to form a set, $\Lambda_1$ or $\Lambda_2$, of size $\lambda$ that does not intersect with $\Gamma^k$ also of size $\lambda$, which violates hiding of the ECom commitment to $\Gamma^k$. (See the full version for a formal argument).

We next bound the probability of $\mathrm{Bad}_{\mathrm{NM}}$ occurring in $H_1^b$ by using the following hybrid $G_1^b, G_2^b$.

**Hybrids $G_1^b, G_2^b$** are identical to $H_1^b$ except that on the right the values committed to in the NMCom commitments are extracted using the committed-value oracle $\mathcal{O}_{\mathsf{NMCom}}$ in $G_1^b$ and using the extractor $\mathcal{S}_{\mathsf{NMCom}}$ in $G_2^b$. That is,
- On the right, $G_1^b$ (resp. $G_2^b$) forwards all NMCom commitments to $\mathcal{O}_{\mathsf{NMCom}}$ (resp. $\mathcal{S}_{\mathsf{NMCom}}$). By definition, $\mathcal{O}_{\mathsf{NMCom}}$ (resp. $\mathcal{S}_{\mathsf{NMCom}}$) returns after every NMCom row the values committed to in this row. $G_1^b$ (resp. $G_2^b$) ignores these values.

Since $G_2^b$ is completely efficient, it follows from the same argument as above that event $\mathrm{Bad}_{\mathrm{NM}}$ does not occur w.r.t. the values extracted by $\mathcal{S}_{\mathsf{NMCom}}$ except for negligible probability. Then, by the concurrent extractability w.r.t. commitment of NMCom, $G_1^b$ and $G_2^b$ are indistinguishable and hence $\mathsf{Bad}_{\mathsf{NM}}$ does not occur w.r.t. the values returned by $\mathcal{O}_{\mathsf{NMCom}}$, except for negligible probability in $G_1^b$. Finally, since $\mathcal{O}_{\mathsf{NMCom}}$ emulates the receivers of NMCom perfectly for $A$, the views of $A$ in $H_1^b$ and $G_1^b$ are identical. Thus, event $\mathsf{Bad}_{\mathsf{NM}}$ (w.r.t. the values committed to in the NMCom commitments) occurs with only negligible probability in $H_1^b$. ∎

Now, we are ready to show the indistinguishability between $H_0^b$ and $H_1^b$.

**Lemma 2.** *For every $b \in \{0,1\}$, it holds that,*

$$\left\{ H_0^b(\lambda, z) \right\}_{\lambda \in \mathbb{N}, z \in \{0,1\}^{\mathrm{poly}(\lambda)}} \approx \left\{ H_1^b(\lambda, z) \right\}_{\lambda \in \mathbb{N}, z \in \{0,1\}^{\mathrm{poly}(\lambda)}}$$

*Proof.* We show that both $H_0^b$ and $H_1^b$ are indistinguishable from the following simulated hybrid $G^b$.

**Hybrid $G^b$** is the same as $H_1^b(\lambda, z)$ except for the following:
  – On the right, it emulates the right receiver messages as $H_1^b$ does (i.e., the CECom receivers of commitments in CECom-rows and the CECom-setup are simulated using $\mathcal{S}_{\mathsf{CECom}}$, and other receiver messages are generated honestly). However, at the end of each right session $k$, committed value that $\mathcal{O}_{\mathsf{CCACom}}$ returns is emulated differently: It extracts the shares $s = (s_1, \ldots, s_{10\lambda})$ committed to in the com row by brute force, and reply $\mathsf{Value}(s)$, where $\mathsf{Value}$ is defined in Eq. (1). (That is, $G^b$ returns to $A$ the actual committed value in each right session.)

**Claim 2.** *For every $b \in \{0,1\}$, it holds that,*

$$\left\{ H_1^b(\lambda, z) \right\}_{\lambda \in \mathbb{N}, z \in \{0,1\}^{\mathrm{poly}(\lambda)}} \approx \left\{ G^b(\lambda, z) \right\}_{\lambda \in \mathbb{N}, z \in \{0,1\}^{\mathrm{poly}(\lambda)}}$$

*Proof.* The only difference between these two hybrids lies in how the committed values of the right sessions are extracted: in $H_1^b$, they are reconstructed from the shares extracted from the CECom-rows, whereas in $G^b$, the actually committed value is extracted by brute-force. Thus it suffices to show that in $H_1^b$ the values $\{\tilde{v}^k\}$ reconstructed from the shares extracted from the CECom-rows are the actual committed values $\{v^k\}$ with overwhelming probability. Since Lemma 1 gives that event $\mathsf{Bad}_{CEC}$ occurs with negligible probability in $H_1^b$, it suffices to argue that when $\mathsf{Bad}_{CEC}$ does not occur, $\tilde{v}^k = v^k$ for every right session $k$. Recall that if $\mathsf{Bad}_{CEC}$ does not occur, in any accepting right session $k$ the shares $\{\tilde{s}_j^k = \widetilde{\mathsf{Extract}}(\tilde{s}_j^k, d_j^k)\}_{10\lambda}$ extracted from the CECom row is consistent, so they satisfy the following condition.

1. $|\Lambda_1| \le \lambda$, where $\Lambda_1 := \{j \mid \tilde{s}_j^k = \bot\}$, and
2. if $\tilde{s}^k$ is 0.8-close to a valid codeword $w = (w_1, \ldots, w_{10\lambda})$ such that $w_j$ equals the value revealed in Stage 5 for each $j \in \Gamma^k$, then $|\Lambda_2| \le \lambda$, where $\Lambda_2 := \{j \mid \tilde{s}_j^k \ne w_j\}$.

Let $s^k = s_{j\,10\lambda}^k$ be the share that are committed to in the com row in the right session $k$. We consider two cases.

**Case 1.** $s^k$ **is 0.9-close to a valid codeword** $w = (w_1, \ldots, w_{10\lambda})$.

Since $|\Lambda_1| \leq \lambda$, $s^k$ and $\tilde{s}^k$ are 0.9-close (this follows from Eq. (2)), so $\tilde{s}^k$ is 0.8-close to $w$. Hence, $\mathsf{Value}(s^k) = \widetilde{\mathsf{Value}}(\tilde{s}^k) = \mathsf{Decode}(w)$ if $w_j$ equals to the value revealed in Stage 5 for every $j \in \Gamma$, and $\mathsf{Value}(s^k) = \widetilde{\mathsf{Value}}(\tilde{s}^k) = \bot$ otherwise.

**Case 2.** $s^k$ **is 0.1-far from any valid codeword.**

We have $\mathsf{Value}(s^k) = \widetilde{\mathsf{Value}}(\tilde{s}^k) = \bot$ if $\tilde{s}^k$ is 0.2-far from any valid codeword, or is 0.8-close to a valid codeword $w = (w_1, \ldots, w_{10\lambda})$ but $w_j$ does not equal the value revealed in Stage 5 for some $j \in \Gamma^k$. Now, we argue that $\tilde{s}^k$ cannot be 0.8-close to a valid codeword $w = (w_1, \ldots, w_{10\lambda})$ such that $w_j$ equals the value that is revealed in Stage 5 for every $j \in \Gamma^k$. Assume for contradiction that $\tilde{s}^k$ is 0.8-close to such $w = (w_1, \ldots, w_{10\lambda})$. Then, since $|\Lambda_2| \leq \lambda$, it follows that $\tilde{s}^k$ is actually 0.9-close to $w$. However, since we have $\tilde{s}_j^k = s_j^k$ for every $j \in \{j | \tilde{s}_j^k \neq \bot\}$ (this follows from Eq. (2)), and we have $\tilde{s}_j^k \neq \bot$ for every $j \in \{j | \tilde{s}_j^k = w_j\}$ (this is because $w$ is a valid codeword), 0.9-closeness between $\tilde{s}^k$ and $w$ implies that $s^k$ is also 0.9-close to $w$. This is contradiction because we assume that $s^k$ is 0.1-far from any valid codeword.

Hence, we have $\mathsf{Value}(s^k) = \widetilde{\mathsf{Value}}(\tilde{s}^k)$, i.e., $v^k = \tilde{v}^k$, in both cases. ∎

**Claim 3.** *For every* $b \in \{0, 1\}$, *it holds that,*

$$\left\{ \mathsf{H}_0^b(\lambda, z) \right\}_{\lambda \in \mathbb{N}, z \in \{0,1\}^{\mathrm{poly}(\lambda)}} \approx \left\{ \mathsf{G}^b(\lambda, z) \right\}_{\lambda \in \mathbb{N}, z \in \{0,1\}^{\mathrm{poly}(\lambda)}}$$

*Proof.* Note that the only difference between $G^b$ and $H_0^b$ is that in the former the CECom receivers and the CECom-setup are simulated by $\mathcal{S}_{\mathsf{CECom}}$, whereas in the latter, they are emulated honestly. It follows directly from the statistical emulation property of $\mathcal{S}_{\mathsf{CECom}}$ that these two hybrids are statistically close. (Note that the statistical emulation property of $\mathcal{S}_{\mathsf{CECom}}$ applies to even computationally unbound committers, which is the case here as hybrid $H_0^b$ and $G^b$ are not efficient.) ∎

It follows from the above claims and a standard hybrid argument that hybrids $H_0^b$ and $H_1^b$ are indistinguishable. This concludes the proof of Lemma 2. ∎

**Hybrid** $H_2^b(\lambda, z)$ is the same as $H_1^b(\lambda, z)$ except that on the left it uses the extractor $\mathcal{S}_{\mathsf{ECom}}$ of ECom to extract a subset $\Gamma'$ from Stage 1 of the left session. More precisely,

- Use the extractor $\mathcal{S}_{\mathsf{ECom}}$ of ECom to emulate (i) the receiver of ECom in Stage 1 of the left session and in Stage 5 when $A$ opens this ECom commitment, as well as (ii) the ECom-setup.

  By definition, at the end of Stage 1 in the left session, $\mathcal{S}_{\mathsf{ECom}}$ outputs a value $\Gamma'$, interpreted as a subset, on its special output tape.

- Furthermore, in Stage 5, if $A$ opens successfully to a set $\Gamma$ and $\Gamma \neq \Gamma'$, abort and output ERR.

**Lemma 3.** *For every $b \in \{0,1\}$, it holds that,*

$$\left\{ \mathsf{H}_1^b(\lambda, z) \right\}_{\lambda \in \mathbb{N}, z \in \{0,1\}^{\text{poly}(\lambda)}} \stackrel{s}{\approx} \left\{ \mathsf{H}_2^b(\lambda, z) \right\}_{\lambda \in \mathbb{N}, z \in \{0,1\}^{\text{poly}(\lambda)}}$$

*Proof.* The only difference between these two hybrids lies in that in $H_2^b$, the receiver of ECom in the left session and the ECom-setup are emulated, and the hybrid aborts if the extracted subset $\Gamma'$ disagree with the subset that $A$ opens to. Since $H_2^b$ is completely efficient, it follows from the extractability w.r.t. opening property of $\mathcal{S}_{\mathsf{ECom}}$ that the subset $\Gamma$ that $A$ opens to must agree with the extracted subset $\Gamma'$ except for negligible probability. Moreover, conditioned on not aborting, since the extracted subset $\Gamma'$ is never used otherwise, it follows from the statistical emulation property of $\mathcal{S}_{\mathsf{ECom}}$ that $\mathcal{S}_{\mathsf{ECom}}$ statistically emulates the receiver of ECom and the ECom-setup. Therefore, $H_1^b$ and $H_2^b$ are statistically close. $\blacksquare$

Then, since the two hybrids $H_1^b$ and $H_2^b$ are statistically close, and by Lemma 1, bad events $\mathrm{Bad}_{\mathrm{NM}}, \mathrm{Bad}_{\mathrm{CEC}}$ do not happen in $H_1^b$, they do not happen in $H_2^b$ either.

**Lemma 4.** *For every $b \in \{0,1\}$, it holds that, the probabilities that event $\mathrm{Bad}_{\mathrm{NM}}$ and $\mathrm{Bad}_{\mathrm{CEC}}$ occur are negligible in $H_2^b$.*

**Hybrid** $H_3^b(\lambda, z)$ is the same as $H_2^b(\lambda, z)$ except that in the NMCom-row on the left, the left committer commits to 0 instead of $((s_j, d_j), e_j)$ for every $j \notin \Gamma$. Note that both $H_2^b$ and $H_3^b$ are completely efficient. Thus, it follows directly from the hiding property of the left NMCom commitments that $H_2^b$ and $H_3^b$ are indistinguishable.

**Lemma 5.** *For every $b \in \{0,1\}$, it holds that,*

$$\left\{ \mathsf{H}_2^b(\lambda, z) \right\}_{\lambda \in \mathbb{N}, z \in \{0,1\}^{\text{poly}(\lambda)}} \approx \left\{ \mathsf{H}_3^b(\lambda, z) \right\}_{\lambda \in \mathbb{N}, z \in \{0,1\}^{\text{poly}(\lambda)}}$$

Moreover, we argue that the bad events $\mathrm{Bad}_{\mathrm{NM}}$ and $\mathrm{Bad}_{\mathrm{CEC}}$ do not occur in $H_3^b$ either.

**Lemma 6.** *For every $b \in \{0,1\}$, it holds that, the probabilities that event $\mathrm{Bad}_{\mathrm{NM}}$ and $\mathrm{Bad}_{\mathrm{CEC}}$ occur are negligible in $H_3^b$.*

It follows from the hiding property of the left NMCom commitments that if event $\mathrm{Bad}_{CEC}$ does not occur in $H_2^b$, then it does not occur in $H_3^b$ either. Furthermore, it follows from the concurrent non-malleability property of NMCom that the values committed to in the NMCom commitments are indistinguishable in $H_2^b$ and $H_3^b$. Therefore, it follows from Lemma 4 that $\mathrm{Bad}_{\mathrm{NM}}$ almost never occurs in $H_3^b$.

**Hybrid** $H_4^b(\lambda, z)$ is the same as $H_3^b(\lambda, z)$ except that on the right $A$ interacts with the $\mathcal{O}_{\mathsf{CCACom}}$ oracle.

The only difference between $H_4^b$ and $H_3^b$ lies in that in the former $A$ interacts with $\mathcal{O}_{\mathsf{CCACom}}$ on the right, whereas in the latter $\mathcal{O}_{\mathsf{CCACom}}$ is emulated using the extractor $\mathcal{S}_{\mathsf{CECom}}$ of $\mathsf{CECom}$. This difference is the same as that between $H_0^b$ and $H_1^b$. Furthermore, as in $H_1^b$, event $\mathrm{Bad}_{CEC}$ does not occur in hybrid $H_3^b$ by Lemma 6. Thus, it follows from the same proof that $H_3^b$ and $H_4^b$ are statistically close.

**Lemma 7.** *For every $b \in \{0,1\}$, it holds that,*

$$\left\{H_3^b(\lambda, z)\right\}_{\lambda \in \mathbb{N}, z \in \{0,1\}^{\mathrm{poly}(\lambda)}} \stackrel{s}{\approx} \left\{H_4^b(\lambda, z)\right\}_{\lambda \in \mathbb{N}, z \in \{0,1\}^{\mathrm{poly}(\lambda)}}$$

Given that $H_3^b$ and $H_4^b$ are statistically close, it follows from Lemma 6 that event $\mathrm{Bad}_{\mathrm{NM}}$ occurs with only negligible probability in $H_4^b$.

**Lemma 8.** *For every $b \in \{0,1\}$, it holds that, the probability that event $\mathrm{Bad}_{\mathrm{NM}}$ occur is negligible in $H_4^b$.*

**Hybrid** $H_5^b(\lambda, z)$ is the same as $H_4^b(\lambda, z)$ except that on the right, it uses the committed-value oracle $\mathcal{O}_{\mathsf{NMCom}}$ of $\mathsf{NMCom}$ to emulate $\mathcal{O}_{\mathsf{CCACom}}$ as follows:

1. Emulate the receivers of $\mathsf{CCACom}$ honestly for $A$, except that all $\mathsf{NMCom}$ commitments are forwarded to $\mathcal{O}_{\mathsf{NMCom}}$, which emulates the receivers of $\mathsf{NMCom}$ perfectly. By definition of $\mathcal{O}_{\mathsf{NMCom}}$, at the end of each $\mathsf{NMCom}$-row, say in the right session $k$, $\mathcal{O}_{\mathsf{NMCom}}$ returns the vector of committed values, parsed as $\{(\hat{s}_j^k, d_j^k), e_j^k\}_{j \in [10\lambda]}$. Set $\hat{s}_j^k = \widehat{\mathsf{Extract}}(\hat{s}_j^k, d_j^k)$, where $\widehat{\mathsf{Extract}}$ is described in Eq. (3).

2. At the end of each right session $k$, emulate the committed value that $\mathcal{O}_{\mathsf{CCACom}}$ returns, by returning the value $\hat{v}^k = \widehat{\mathsf{Value}}(\hat{s}^k)$, where $\widehat{\mathsf{Value}}$ is defined in Eq. (4).

**Lemma 9.** *For every $b \in \{0,1\}$, it holds that,*

$$\left\{H_4^b(\lambda, z)\right\}_{\lambda \in \mathbb{N}, z \in \{0,1\}^{\mathrm{poly}(\lambda)}} \stackrel{s}{\approx} \left\{H_5^b(\lambda, z)\right\}_{\lambda \in \mathbb{N}, z \in \{0,1\}^{\mathrm{poly}(\lambda)}}$$

*Proof.* Note that in $H_5^b$, the receivers of $\mathsf{CCACom}$ are emulated perfectly for $A$. Therefore, the only difference between $H_5^b$ and $H_4^b$ lies in how the committed values of the right sessions are extracted: in $H_5^b$ they are reconstructed from the values committed to in the $\mathsf{NMCom}$-rows, whereas in $H_4^b$, the actually committed values are extracted by brute-force by $\mathcal{O}_{\mathsf{CCACom}}$. Thus it suffices to show that in $H_5^b$ the values $\{\hat{v}^k\}$ reconstructed from the values committed to in the $\mathsf{NMCom}$-rows are the actual committed values $\{v^k\}$ with overwhelming probability. By Lemma 8, event $\mathrm{Bad}_{\mathrm{NM}}$ does not occur in $H_4^b$, except for negligible probability. Then, it follows from the same argument as in the proof of Claim 2 that when $\mathrm{Bad}_{\mathrm{NM}}$ does not occur, $\hat{v}^k = v^k$ for every right session $k$. ∎

Given that $H_5^b$ and $H_4^b$ are statistically close, it follows from Lemma 8 that event $\mathrm{Bad}_{\mathrm{NM}}$ occurs with negligible probability in $H_5^b$.

**Lemma 10.** *For every $b \in \{0,1\}$, it holds that, the probability that event $\mathrm{Bad}_{NM}$ occur is negligible in $H_5^b$.*

**Hybrid** $H_6^b(\lambda, z)$ is the same as $H_5^b(\lambda, z)$ except that on the right, it uses the universal simulator $\mathcal{S}_{\mathsf{NMCom}}$ of $\mathsf{NMCom}$ to emulate $\mathcal{O}_{\mathsf{NMCom}}$.

It follows directly from the concurrent extractability w.r.t. commitment property of $\mathsf{NMCom}$ that $H_6^b$ and $H_5^b$ are indistinguishable.

**Lemma 11.** *For every $b \in \{0,1\}$, it holds that,*

$$\left\{H_5^b(\lambda, z)\right\}_{\lambda \in \mathbb{N}, z \in \{0,1\}^{\mathrm{poly}(\lambda)}} \approx \left\{H_6^b(\lambda, z)\right\}_{\lambda \in \mathbb{N}, z \in \{0,1\}^{\mathrm{poly}(\lambda)}}$$

**Hybrid** $H_7^b(\lambda, z)$ is the same as $H_6^b(\lambda, z)$ except that on the left, the left committer (i) commits to 0 instead of $s_j$ for every $j \notin \Gamma$ in the com-row, and (ii) commits to 0 instead of $(s_j, d_j)$ for every $j \notin \Gamma$ in the CECom-row.

Note that both $H_6^b$ and $H_7^b$ are completely efficient. Thus, it follows directly from the hiding property of the left com commitments and CECom commitments that $H_7^b$ and $H_6^b$ are indistinguishable.

**Lemma 12.** *For every $b \in \{0,1\}$, it holds that,*

$$\left\{H_6^b(\lambda, z)\right\}_{\lambda \in \mathbb{N}, z \in \{0,1\}^{\mathrm{poly}(\lambda)}} \approx \left\{H_7^b(\lambda, z)\right\}_{\lambda \in \mathbb{N}, z \in \{0,1\}^{\mathrm{poly}(\lambda)}}$$

Finally, notice that in hybrid $H_7^b$, in the left session, the committer commits to 0 in all of the com, CECom, and NMCom rows. This means $A$ receives no information about whether $v_0$ or $v_1$ is committed in $H_7^b(\lambda, z)$. Thus, the views of $A$ in $H_7^0(\lambda, z)$ and $H_7^1(\lambda, z)$ are identically distributed.

**Lemma 13.** *It holds that,*

$$\left\{H_7^0(\lambda, z)\right\}_{\lambda \in \mathbb{N}, z \in \{0,1\}^{\mathrm{poly}(\lambda)}} = \left\{H_7^1(\lambda, z)\right\}_{\lambda \in \mathbb{N}, z \in \{0,1\}^{\mathrm{poly}(\lambda)}}$$

Given the lemmas, it follows from a hybrid argument that for every $b$, $\{H_0^b(\lambda, z)\} \approx \{H_7^b(\lambda, z)\}$. Furthermore, given that $H_7^0(\lambda, z)$ and $H_7^1(\lambda, z)$ are identically distributed, we conclude that $\{H_0^0(\lambda, z)\} \approx \{H_0^1(\lambda, z)\}$ and thus the CCACom protocol is CCA-secure.

## 4    From CCA Commitments to UC Secure Protocols

We assume familiarity with the models of UC, Externalized UC (EUC), and Angel-based security/UC with super-polynomial helpers. See the full version for more details on these models.

## 4.1   The General Transformation

In this session, we show that given any commitment scheme CECom in $\mathcal{T}$-model that is straight-line concurrently extractable w.r.t. opening, we can UC-realize every functionality in the $4\mathcal{T}$-trusted-setup model. Formally,

**Theorem 5 (UC-secure Protocols in $4\mathcal{T}$-trusted-setup model from CECom in $\mathcal{T}$-model).** *Let $\mathcal{T}$ be any trusted-setup, and $4\mathcal{T}$ the corresponding quadruple-$\mathcal{T}$ setup. Then, for every well-formed functionality $\mathcal{F}$, there is a fully black-box construction of a protocol $\pi$ that UC-realizes $\mathcal{F}$ in the $4\mathcal{T}$-trusted setup model, from the following primitives:*

- *a $O(1)$-round semi-honest secure oblivious transfer protocol, and*
- *a commitment scheme CECom in $\mathcal{T}$-model that is straight-line concurrently extractable w.r.t. opening and resettably hiding.*

*Moreover, if CECom has $r_{\text{CEC}}$ rounds, $\pi$ has $O(r_{\text{CEC}})$ rounds.*

We achieve the theorem in three steps.

**Step 1:** Starting from a $r_{\text{CEC}}$-round commitment scheme CECom that is straight-line concurrently extractable w.r.t. opening and resettably hiding in the $\mathcal{T}$-model, by Theorem 4, there is fully black-box construction of a CCA-secure commitment scheme CCACom in $4\mathcal{T}$-model that is also straight-line concurrently extractable w.r.t. commitment, and the scheme has $r_{\text{CCA}} = O(r_{\text{CEC}})$ rounds. Recall that by Claim 1, such a scheme is also poly-robust.

**Step 2:** Given a poly-robust CCA-secure commitment scheme CCACom, it follows from the work of Lin and Pass [19] that every well-formed functionality $\mathcal{F}$ can be EUC-realized w.r.t. the shared functionality $\bar{\mathcal{H}}_{\text{CCACom}}$ defined by CCACom. Roughly speaking, $\bar{\mathcal{H}}_{\text{CCACom}}$ runs the committed-value oracle of

---

**Shared Functionality $\bar{\mathcal{H}}_{\text{CCACom}}$**

**Initialize a session with $\mathcal{O}_{\text{CCACom}}$:** Upon receiving an input (Init, $P_i, sid, k$) from party $P_i$ in the protocol instance $sid$, if there is a previously recorded session $(P_i, sid, k)$, ignore this message; otherwise, initialize a session of CCACom with $\mathcal{O}_{\text{CCACom}}$ using identity $(P_i, sid)$, and record session $(P_i, sid, k)$.

**Access $\mathcal{O}_{\text{CCACom}}$:** Upon receiving an input (Mesg, $P_i, sid, k, m$) from party $P_i$ in the protocol instance $sid$, if there is no previously recorded session $(P_i, sid, k)$, ignore the message; otherwise, forward $m$ to $\mathcal{O}_{\text{CCACom}}$ in the $k^{\text{th}}$ session that uses identity $(P_i, sid)$, obtain a reply $m'$, and return (Mesg, $P_i, sid, k, m'$) to $P_i$.

**Accessing $4\mathcal{T}$:** Upon receiving an input (setup, $P_i, sid, m$) from party $P_i$ in the protocol instance $sid$, forward $((P_i, sid), m)$ to $\mathcal{T}$, obtain a reply $m'$, and return (setup, $P_i, sid, m'$) to $P_i$.

**Fig. 1.** The ideal shared functionality $\bar{\mathcal{H}}_{\text{CCACom}}$

CCACom for every party with the restriction that when invoked by a party with identity $\mathsf{ID} = (P_i, sid)$ (consisting of party ID $P_i$ and session ID $sid$), it only breaks CCACom commitments with exactly the same identity $\mathsf{ID}$. Since we here consider robust CCA-secure CCACom in $4\mathcal{T}$-model, all parties also have access to $4\mathcal{T}$. Thus, we let $\bar{\mathcal{H}}_{\mathsf{CCACom}}$ run also the setup $4\mathcal{T}$. A formal description of the functionality is in Fig. 1.

Therefore, honest parties interact with $\bar{\mathcal{H}}_{\mathsf{CCACom}}$ to access $4\mathcal{T}$, while corrupted parties, adversaries $A/S$, and environment $Z$ can interact with $\bar{\mathcal{H}}_{\mathsf{CCACom}}$ to access both $4\mathcal{T}$ and the committed-value oracles $\mathcal{O}_{\mathsf{CCACom}}$. We note that since the work of [19] considers CCA secure commitment schemes in the plain model, their helper functionalities only run the committed-value oracle, and the honest parties never access the helper functionality. Their construction and security proof extends directly to our case where the honest parties access the helper functionality for $4\mathcal{T}$ only, but not $\mathcal{O}_{\mathsf{CCACom}}$.

**Theorem 6** ([19]). *Assume the existence of a $r_{\mathrm{CCA}}$-round poly-robust CCA-secure commitment scheme CCACom in the $4\mathcal{T}$-trusted-setup model, and a constant-round semi-honest secure oblivious transfer protocol. Then, for every well-formed functionality $\mathcal{F}$, there is a fully black-box construction of a $O(r_{\mathrm{CEC}})$-round protocol $\pi$ that $\bar{\mathcal{H}}_{\mathsf{CCACom}}$-EUC-realizes $\mathcal{F}$.*

**Step 3:** Finally, we move from EUC-security w.r.t. shared functionality $\bar{\mathcal{H}}_{\mathsf{CCACom}}$ back to UC-security w.r.t. $4\mathcal{T}$-trusted-setup, by crucially relying on the fact that CCACom is straight-line concurrently extractable w.r.t. commitment.

**Theorem 7.** *Let CCACom be any commitment scheme that is CCA-secure and straight-line concurrently extractable w.r.t. commitment in the $4\mathcal{T}$-trusted-setup model. For every well-formed functionality $\mathcal{F}$, if protocol $\pi$ $\bar{\mathcal{H}}_{\mathsf{CCACom}}$-EUC-realizes $\mathcal{F}$, then $\pi$ UC-realizes $\mathcal{F}$ in the $4\mathcal{T}$-trusted-setup model.*

To show that $\pi$ UC-realizes $\mathcal{F}$ in the $4\mathcal{T}$-trusted-setup model, we need to show that its multi-session extension $\hat{\pi}$ UC-realizes the multi-session extension $\hat{\mathcal{F}}$ of $\mathcal{F}$ in the $4\mathcal{T}$-hybrid model. This follows from the following two simple observations.

First, combining the universal composition theorem of EUC with Theorem 6 gives that $\hat{\pi}$ $\bar{\mathcal{H}}_{\mathsf{CCACom}}$-EUC-realizes $\hat{\mathcal{F}}$. That is, for any PPT adversary $\mathcal{A}$, there exists a PPT simulator $S$, such that, for every PPT environment $Z$, it holds that

$$\mathrm{EXEC}^{\bar{\mathcal{H}}}_{\hat{\pi}, \mathcal{A}, Z} \approx \mathrm{EXEC}^{\bar{\mathcal{H}}}_{\mathcal{I}_{\hat{\mathcal{F}}}, S, Z},$$

where $\bar{\mathcal{H}}$ is a short hand for $\bar{\mathcal{H}}_{\mathsf{CCACom}}$.

By definition of EUC, the above indistinguishability holds for arbitrary $A$ and $Z$ that may or may not access the shared functionality $\bar{\mathcal{H}}$. Consider the special case where $\mathcal{A}$ never accesses $\mathcal{O}_{\mathsf{CCACom}}$ in $\bar{\mathcal{H}}$ (but may access $4\mathcal{T}$ in $\bar{\mathcal{H}}$), and $Z$ never accesses $\bar{\mathcal{H}}$ at all. In this case, in the real execution, honest parties of $\hat{\pi}$ and $\mathcal{A}$ may access $4\mathcal{T}$ in $\bar{\mathcal{H}}$, and no party accesses $\mathcal{O}_{\mathsf{CCACom}}$ in $\bar{\mathcal{H}}$. Note that this is simply an execution $\mathrm{EXEC}_{\hat{\pi}, \mathcal{A}, Z}(\lambda, z)$ of $\hat{\pi}$ with adversary $\mathcal{A}$ and environment $Z$

$Z$ in the $4\mathcal{T}$-hybrid-model. On the other hand, in the ideal execution, only the simulator $S$ interacts with $\bar{\mathcal{H}}$ and no other party interacts with $\bar{\mathcal{H}}$ at all.

Next, to show that $\pi$ UC-realizes $\mathcal{F}$ in $4\mathcal{T}$ trusted-setup model, we need to show that $\hat{\pi}$ UC-emulates the ideal protocol $\mathcal{I}_{\hat{F}}$ of $\hat{F}$ in the $4\mathcal{T}$-hybrid model. That is, for any PPT adversary $\mathcal{A}$, there exists a PPT simulator $S'$, such that, for any PPT environment $Z$, it holds that

$$\mathrm{EXEC}_{\hat{\pi},\mathcal{A},Z} \approx \mathrm{EXEC}_{\mathcal{I}_{\hat{F}},S',Z}.$$

As discussed above, for any $\mathcal{A}$, $Z$, $\lambda$ and $z$, the experiments $\mathrm{EXEC}_{\hat{\pi},\mathcal{A},Z}(\lambda, z)$ and $\mathrm{EXEC}^{\bar{\mathcal{H}}}_{\hat{\pi},\mathcal{A},Z}(\lambda, z)$ are identically distributed. We now use the simulator $S$ for $\mathcal{A}$ in the EUC model to construct the a simulator $S'$ for $\mathcal{A}$ in the UC model satisfying that

$$\mathrm{EXEC}_{\mathcal{I}_{\hat{F}},S',Z} \approx \mathrm{EXEC}^{\bar{\mathcal{H}}}_{\mathcal{I}_{\hat{F}},S,Z}$$

The only difference between these two ideal executions is that in the former $Z$ interacts with $S'$ and in the latter $Z$ interacts with $S$ who interacts with $\bar{\mathcal{H}}$ (no other party accesses $\bar{\mathcal{H}}$). Construct $S'$ as follows: It internally runs $S$ and emulates (the committed-value oracle of CCACom and the setup $4\mathcal{T}$ in) $\bar{\mathcal{H}}$ for $S$, using the simulator $\mathcal{S}_{\mathsf{CCACom}}$ of CCACom. It follows directly from the concurrent extractability w.r.t. commitment property of CCACom that the simulation is indistinguishable and so are the above two experiments. It then follows from a hybrid argument that $S'$ is a valid simulator for $\mathcal{A}$ in the UC model. Therefore, we conclude that $\pi$ UC-realizes $\mathcal{F}$ in the $4\mathcal{T}$-trusted setup model.

Combining the above three steps gives a protocol $\pi$ that UC-realizes an arbitrary functionality $\mathcal{F}$ in the $4\mathcal{T}$-trusted setup model. In addition, it is easy to see that the protocol has $O(r_{\mathrm{CCA}}) = O(r_{\mathrm{CEC}})$ rounds. This concludes Theorem 5.

### 4.2   Instantiation of CECom in the CRS Model

In this section we present our CECom in the $\mathcal{F}_{\mathsf{CRS}}$-hybrid model.

**Protocol CECom$_{\mathsf{CRS}}$** We will require a *perfectly-correct* semantically-secure public-key encryption scheme (Gen, Enc, Dec) for this construction.

**Common Reference String.** The common reference string is set to pk where (pk, sk) is sampled according to $\mathsf{Gen}(1^\kappa)$.

**Input.** $C$ and $R$ have as common input $1^\lambda$ and identities sid, and $C$ has private input $v \in \{0,1\}^\lambda$.

**Commit Phase of CECom$_{\mathsf{CRS}}$.** Sen queries $\mathcal{F}_{\mathsf{CRS}}$ to obtain the $\mathsf{CRS} = \mathsf{pk}$. Then it samples randomness $r$ and sends $c = \mathsf{Enc}_{\mathsf{pk}}(v; r)$ to the receiver.

**Decommitment Phase.** The sender simply reveals $v, r$.

From semantic security and correctness of the underlying encryption scheme, CECom$_{\mathsf{CRS}}$ is statistically binding, computationally hiding, straight-line concurrently extractable w.r.t. commitment, and resettably-hiding in the $\mathcal{F}_{\mathsf{CRS}}$-model. Therefore we have the following lemma:

**Lemma 14.** *Assume the existence of public-key encryption scheme. Then, there exists a computationally-hiding statistically-binding commitment scheme that is (1) Straight-line concurrently extractable w.r.t commitment, and (2) Resettably-hiding in the Common Reference String Model.*

**Instantiation of CECom in the Uniform Reference String Model.** An immediate corollary to our instantiation in the CRS model is an instantiation in the uniform reference string (URS) model. Recall that in the URS model, the reference string is sampled as uniformly random. We can rely on the same construction as in the CRS model if the we rely on a dense public-key encryption scheme where additionally the distribution of the sampled public-keys are pseudorandom. More precisely we have the following corollary.

**Corollary 1.** *Assume the existence of a dense public-key encryption scheme. Then, there exists a computationally-hiding statistically-binding commitment scheme that is (1) Straight-line concurrently extractable w.r.t commitment, and (2) Resettably-hiding in the Uniform Reference String Model.*

### 4.3 Instantiation of CECom in the Tamper Proof Hardware Model

We assume familiarity of the global tamper proof model of [22], where operations related to tokens are captured by the ideal functionality $\mathcal{F}_{\mathsf{gwrap}}$.

A simple extractable commitment based on tokens can be achieved as follows: The receiver chooses a function $F$ from a pseudorandom function family that maps $\{0,1\}^m$ to $\{0,1\}^n$ bits where $m \gg n$, and incorporates it into a token that it sends to the sender. Next, the sender commits to its input $b$ by first sampling a random string $u \in \{0,1\}^m$ and querying the PRF token on $u$ to receive the value $v$. It sends as its commitment the string $\mathsf{com}_b = (\mathsf{Ext}(u;r) \oplus b, r, v)$ where $\mathsf{Ext}(\cdot, \cdot)$ is a strong randomness extractor. Hiding follows from the fact that the PRF is highly compressing, while binding follows from the pseudorandomness of the underlying PRF. Extraction on the other hand can be achieved by allowing the simulator to observe the queries made by the sender to the token and waiting for a query to give the answer $v$. First, we remark that this commitment only achieves commitment w.r.t opening as the extraction procedure does not know when the commitment is correct. This is however not an issue as our general framework can rely on CECom that has straight-line extractability w.r.t opening. A larger issue however is to handle resettability of tokens. A resetting receiver can leak information by creating a stateful token and rewinding the committer. We tackle this problem by observing that resettable hiding of our protocol can be solved by using a commitment scheme with "reusable" tokens. Such a scheme was presented in [22] and we here rely on a milder variant of this protocol.

#### Protocol CECom$_{\mathsf{TK}}$

**Input.** $C$ and $R$ receive as common inputs $1^\lambda$ and identity $(\mathsf{sid}, \mathsf{ssid})$, and individual inputs $\mathsf{pid}_C$ and $\mathsf{pid}_R$ respectively. $C$ also receives as private input $v \in \{0,1\}^\lambda$.

**Commit Phase of CECom$_{\mathsf{TK}}$**

**Round 1.** The Receiver creates the following tokens and sends it to the sender.
- For every $l \in [2\kappa]$, Receiver chooses a random PRF keys $\gamma_{b,l}$ ($l \in [\kappa], b \in \{0,1\}$) from a PRF family $\mathcal{F}$ from $5\kappa$ bits to $\kappa$. Then, for every $(b,l)$, the Receiver creates the tokens $\mathsf{TK}^{\mathsf{PRF},l}$ by sending the message $\{\mathsf{create}, \mathsf{sid}, \mathsf{ssid}, \mathsf{Rec}, \mathsf{Sen}, \mathsf{tid}_{b,l}, M_{b,l}\}$, that on input $x$, outputs $\mathsf{PRF}_{\gamma_{b,l}}(x)$, where $M_{b,l}$ is the functionality.

**Round 2.** Sen $\rightarrow$ Rec: Sen picks $\kappa$ random bits $h_1, \ldots, h_k$. For every $i \in [\kappa]$, run $\mathsf{TK}_{i,h_i}$ on input $u$ and check if all token output the same value $v$. It they don't output the receiver halts. Otherwise, it commits by transmitting $(\mathsf{Ext}(u) \oplus m, v)$ to the sender, where $\mathsf{Ext} : \{0,1\}^{5\kappa} \times \{0,1\}^d \rightarrow \{0,1\}$ is a $(2\kappa + 1, 2^{-\kappa})$ randomness extractor and the seed has length $d$ (for simpler exposition we drop the seed in the expression above).

**Decommitment Phase.** The sender simply reveals $u$ and $m$.

The following properties follow directly from the pseudorandomness of the underlying PRF and the fact that the function is highly compressing. We provide formal proofs in the full version.

**Proposition 1.** $\mathsf{CECom}_{\mathsf{TK}} = \langle C, R \rangle$ *presented above is a computationally binding commitment scheme in the* $\mathcal{F}_{\mathsf{gwrap}}$*-model.*

**Proposition 2.** $\mathsf{CECom}_{\mathsf{TK}}$ *is statistically hiding commitment scheme in the* $\mathcal{F}_{\mathsf{gwrap}}$*-model.*

We can further show a stronger hiding property.

**Proposition 3.** $\mathsf{CECom}_{\mathsf{TK}}$ *is straight-line concurrently extractable w.r.t. opening in* $\mathcal{F}_{\mathsf{gwrap}}$*-model.*

**Proposition 4.** $\mathsf{CECom}_{\mathsf{TK}}$ *is resettably-hiding in* $\mathcal{F}_{\mathsf{gwrap}}$*-model.*

**Acknowledgments.** We sincerely thank the anonymous reviewers for their incredibly helpful and insightful comments and suggestions.

Huijia Lin was supported by NSF grants CNS-1528178, CNS-1514526, CNS-1652849 (CAREER), a Hellman Fellowship, the Defense Advanced Research Projects Agency (DARPA) and Army Research Office (ARO) under a subcontract No. 2017-002 through Galois. Muthuramakrishnan Venkitasubramaniam is supported by a Google Faculty Research Grant and NSF Awards CNS-1526377 and CNS-1618884. The views expressed are those of the authors and do not reflect the official policy or position of the Department of Defense, the National Science Foundation, the U.S. Government or Google.

# References

1. Canetti, R.: Universally composable security: a new paradigm for cryptographic protocols. In: FOCS, pp. 136–145 (2001)
2. Canetti, R., Fischlin, M.: Universally composable commitments. In: Kilian, J. (ed.) CRYPTO 2001. LNCS, vol. 2139, pp. 19–40. Springer, Heidelberg (2001). doi:10.1007/3-540-44647-8_2

3. Canetti, R., Kushilevitz, E., Lindell, Y.: On the limitations of universally composable two-party computation without set-up assumptions. In: Biham, E. (ed.) EUROCRYPT 2003. LNCS, vol. 2656, pp. 68–86. Springer, Heidelberg (2003). doi:10.1007/3-540-39200-9_5

4. Canetti, R., Lindell, Y., Ostrovsky, R., Sahai, A.: Universally composable two-party and multi-party secure computation. In: STOC (2002)

5. Groth, J., Ostrovsky, R.: Cryptography in the multi-string model. In: Menezes, A. (ed.) CRYPTO 2007. LNCS, vol. 4622, pp. 323–341. Springer, Heidelberg (2007). doi:10.1007/978-3-540-74143-5_18

6. Barak, B., Canetti, R., Nielsen, J.B., Pass, R.: Universally composable protocols with relaxed set-up assumptions. In: FOCS, pp. 186–195 (2004)

7. Canetti, R., Dodis, Y., Pass, R., Walfish, S.: Universally composable security with global setup. IACR Cryptology ePrint Archive 2006/432 (2006)

8. Kalai, Y.T., Lindell, Y., Prabhakaran, M.: Concurrent composition of secure protocols in the timing model. J. Cryptol. **20**(4), 431–492 (2007)

9. Katz, J.: Universally composable multi-party computation using tamper-proof hardware. In: Naor, M. (ed.) EUROCRYPT 2007. LNCS, vol. 4515, pp. 115–128. Springer, Heidelberg (2007). doi:10.1007/978-3-540-72540-4_7

10. Canetti, R., Pass, R., Shelat, A.: Cryptography from sunspots: how to use an imperfect reference string. In: FOCS, pp. 249–259 (2007)

11. Lin, H., Pass, R., Venkitasubramaniam, M.: A unified framework for concurrent security: universal composability from stand-alone non-malleability. In: STOC, pp. 179–188 (2009)

12. Kilian, J.: Founding cryptography on oblivious transfer. In: 20th ACM STOC, pp. 20–31. ACM Press, May 2008

13. Ishai, Y., Kushilevitz, E., Lindell, Y., Petrank, E.: Black-box constructions for secure computation. In: STOC, pp. 99–108 (2006)

14. Haitner, I.: Semi-honest to malicious oblivious transfer—the black-box way. In: Canetti, R. (ed.) TCC 2008. LNCS, vol. 4948, pp. 412–426. Springer, Heidelberg (2008). doi:10.1007/978-3-540-78524-8_23

15. Ishai, Y., Prabhakaran, M., Sahai, A.: Founding cryptography on oblivious transfer – efficiently. In: Wagner, D. (ed.) CRYPTO 2008. LNCS, vol. 5157, pp. 572–591. Springer, Heidelberg (2008). doi:10.1007/978-3-540-85174-5_32

16. Pass, R., Wee, H.: Black-box constructions of two-party protocols from one-way functions. In: Reingold, O. (ed.) TCC 2009. LNCS, vol. 5444, pp. 403–418. Springer, Heidelberg (2009). doi:10.1007/978-3-642-00457-5_24

17. Wee, H.: Black-box, round-efficient secure computation via non-malleability amplification. In: 51st FOCS, pp. 531–540. IEEE Computer Society Press, October 2010

18. Goyal, V., Lee, C., Ostrovsky, R., Visconti, I.: Constructing non-malleable commitments: a black-box approach. In: FOCS, pp. 51–60 (2012)

19. Lin, H., Pass, R.: Black-box constructions of composable protocols without setup. In: Safavi-Naini, R., Canetti, R. (eds.) CRYPTO 2012. LNCS, vol. 7417, pp. 461–478. Springer, Heidelberg (2012). doi:10.1007/978-3-642-32009-5_27

20. Kiyoshima, S.: Round-efficient black-box construction of composable multi-party computation. In: Garay, J.A., Gennaro, R. (eds.) CRYPTO 2014. LNCS, vol. 8617, pp. 351–368. Springer, Heidelberg (2014). doi:10.1007/978-3-662-44381-1_20

21. Hazay, C., Venkitasubramaniam, M.: On black-box complexity of universally composable security in the CRS model. In: Iwata, T., Cheon, J.H. (eds.) ASIACRYPT 2015. LNCS, vol. 9453, pp. 183–209. Springer, Heidelberg (2015). doi:10.1007/978-3-662-48800-3_8

22. Hazay, C., Polychroniadou, A., Venkitasubramaniam, M.: Composable security in the tamper-proof hardware model under minimal complexity. In: Hirt, M., Smith, A. (eds.) TCC 2016. LNCS, vol. 9985, pp. 367–399. Springer, Heidelberg (2016). doi:10.1007/978-3-662-53641-4_15

23. Pass, R., Lin, H., Venkitasubramaniam, M.: A unified framework for UC from only OT. In: Wang, X., Sako, K. (eds.) ASIACRYPT 2012. LNCS, vol. 7658, pp. 699–717. Springer, Heidelberg (2012). doi:10.1007/978-3-642-34961-4_42

24. Damgård, I., Nielsen, J.B.: Improved non-committing encryption schemes based on a general complexity assumption. In: Bellare, M. (ed.) CRYPTO 2000. LNCS, vol. 1880, pp. 432–450. Springer, Heidelberg (2000). doi:10.1007/3-540-44598-6_27

25. Damgård, I., Groth, J.: Non-interactive and reusable non-malleable commitment schemes. In: STOC, pp. 426–437 (2003)

26. Choi, S.G., Katz, J., Wee, H., Zhou, H.-S.: Efficient, adaptively secure, and composable oblivious transfer with a single, global CRS. In: Kurosawa, K., Hanaoka, G. (eds.) PKC 2013. LNCS, vol. 7778, pp. 73–88. Springer, Heidelberg (2013). doi:10.1007/978-3-642-36362-7_6

27. Lindell, Y.: Highly-efficient universally-composable commitments based on the DDH assumption. In: Paterson, K.G. (ed.) EUROCRYPT 2011. LNCS, vol. 6632, pp. 446–466. Springer, Heidelberg (2011). doi:10.1007/978-3-642-20465-4_25

28. Goyal, V., Ishai, Y., Sahai, A., Venkatesan, R., Wadia, A.: Founding cryptography on tamper-proof hardware tokens. In: Micciancio, D. (ed.) TCC 2010. LNCS, vol. 5978, pp. 308–326. Springer, Heidelberg (2010). doi:10.1007/978-3-642-11799-2_19

29. Moran, T., Segev, G.: David and Goliath commitments: UC computation for asymmetric parties using tamper-proof hardware. In: Smart, N. (ed.) EUROCRYPT 2008. LNCS, vol. 4965, pp. 527–544. Springer, Heidelberg (2008). doi:10.1007/978-3-540-78967-3_30

30. Chandran, N., Goyal, V., Sahai, A.: New constructions for UC secure computation using tamper-proof hardware. In: Smart, N. (ed.) EUROCRYPT 2008. LNCS, vol. 4965, pp. 545–562. Springer, Heidelberg (2008). doi:10.1007/978-3-540-78967-3_31

31. Döttling, N., Kraschewski, D., Müller-Quade, J.: Unconditional and composable security using a single stateful tamper-proof hardware token. In: Ishai, Y. (ed.) TCC 2011. LNCS, vol. 6597, pp. 164–181. Springer, Heidelberg (2011). doi:10.1007/978-3-642-19571-6_11

32. Döttling, N., Mie, T., Müller-Quade, J., Nilges, T.: Implementing resettable UC-functionalities with untrusted tamper-proof hardware-tokens. In: Sahai, A. (ed.) TCC 2013. LNCS, vol. 7785, pp. 642–661. Springer, Heidelberg (2013). doi:10.1007/978-3-642-36594-2_36

33. Döttling, N., Kraschewski, D., Müller-Quade, J., Nilges, T.: General statistically secure computation with bounded-resettable hardware tokens. In: Dodis, Y., Nielsen, J.B. (eds.) TCC 2015. LNCS, vol. 9014, pp. 319–344. Springer, Heidelberg (2015). doi:10.1007/978-3-662-46494-6_14

34. Choi, S.G., Katz, J., Schröder, D., Yerukhimovich, A., Zhou, H.-S.: (Efficient) Universally composable oblivious transfer using a minimal number of stateless tokens. In: Lindell, Y. (ed.) TCC 2014. LNCS, vol. 8349, pp. 638–662. Springer, Heidelberg (2014). doi:10.1007/978-3-642-54242-8_27

35. Dodis, Y., Fiore, D.: Interactive encryption and message authentication. In: Abdalla, M., De Prisco, R. (eds.) SCN 2014. LNCS, vol. 8642, pp. 494–513. Springer, Cham (2014). doi:10.1007/978-3-319-10879-7_28

36. De Santis, A., Persiano, G.: Zero-knowledge proofs of knowledge without interaction (extended abstract). In: 33rd FOCS, pp. 427–436. IEEE Computer Society Press, October 1992

37. Gertner, Y., Kannan, S., Malkin, T., Reingold, O., Viswanathan, M.: The relationship between public key encryption and oblivious transfer. In: 41st FOCS, pp. 325–335. IEEE Computer Society Press, November 2000

38. van Dijk, M., Rührmair, U.: Physical unclonable functions in cryptographic protocols: security proofs and impossibility results. IACR Cryptology ePrint Archive 2012/228 (2012)

39. Canetti, R., Jain, A., Scafuro, A.: Practical UC security with a global random oracle. In: CCS, pp. 597–608 (2014)

40. Canetti, R., Lin, H., Pass, R.: Adaptive hardness and composable security in the plain model from standard assumptions. In: FOCS, pp. 541–550 (2010)

41. Prabhakaran, M., Sahai, A.: New notions of security: achieving universal composability without trusted setup. In: STOC, pp. 242–251 (2004)

42. Pass, R.: Simulation in quasi-polynomial time, and its application to protocol composition. In: Biham, E. (ed.) EUROCRYPT 2003. LNCS, vol. 2656, pp. 160–176. Springer, Heidelberg (2003). doi:10.1007/3-540-39200-9_10

43. Malkin, T., Moriarty, R., Yakovenko, N.: Generalized environmental security from number theoretic assumptions. In: Halevi, S., Rabin, T. (eds.) TCC 2006. LNCS, vol. 3876, pp. 343–359. Springer, Heidelberg (2006). doi:10.1007/11681878_18

44. Goyal, V., Lin, H., Pandey, O., Pass, R., Sahai, A.: Round-efficient concurrently composable secure computation via a robust extraction lemma. In: Dodis, Y., Nielsen, J.B. (eds.) TCC 2015. LNCS, vol. 9014, pp. 260–289. Springer, Heidelberg (2015). doi:10.1007/978-3-662-46494-6_12

45. Choi, S.G., Dachman-Soled, D., Malkin, T., Wee, H.: Black-box construction of a non-malleable encryption scheme from any semantically secure one. In: Canetti, R. (ed.) TCC 2008. LNCS, vol. 4948, pp. 427–444. Springer, Heidelberg (2008). doi:10.1007/978-3-540-78524-8_24

46. Naor, M., Yung, M.: Public-key cryptosystems provably secure against chosen ciphertext attacks. In: 22nd ACM STOC, pp. 427–437. ACM Press, May 1990

47. Lin, H., Pass, R., Venkitasubramaniam, M.: Concurrent non-malleable commitments from any one-way function. In: Canetti, R. (ed.) TCC 2008. LNCS, vol. 4948, pp. 571–588. Springer, Heidelberg (2008). doi:10.1007/978-3-540-78524-8_31

48. Naor, M.: Bit commitment using pseudorandomness. J. Cryptol. 4, 151–158 (1991)

# Author Index

Printed in the United States
By Bookmasters